CW01456042

Insurance Claims

4th Edition

For Andy
and in memory of
Philip and Pauline Padfield

Insurance Claims

4th Edition

By
Alison Padfield
BA (Oxon), Lic Spéc Dr Eur (Brussels), BCL (Oxon), of Lincoln's Inn, Barrister

Bloomsbury Professional

Bloomsbury Professional Ltd, Maxwelton House, 41–43 Boltro Road, Haywards Heath, West Sussex, RH16 1BJ

© Alison Padfield 2016

Bloomsbury Professional is an imprint of Bloomsbury Publishing plc

A CIP Catalogue record for this book is available from the British Library.

ISBN: 978 1 78043 896 2

Typeset by Compuscript Ltd, Shannon
Printed and bound in Great Britain by CPI Group (UK) Ltd, Croydon, CR0 4YY

FOREWORD TO THE FIRST EDITION

Alison Padfield has produced a wonderfully clear and concise summary of the law in relation to insurance claims which, as she says, means largely, although not exclusively, claims against insurers and insurance brokers.

The propositions of law are supported by detailed but easy to follow references to authority. She has deliberately not overloaded those references with citation of more ancient authority where modern authority will suffice. The headings and general layout of the book make it easy to find the right place for assistance. Its style makes it readily comprehensible to lawyer and layman alike. It is a book which those in the insurance industry and legal practitioners will welcome.

I am honoured to have been asked to write this foreword, and wish the book the success which it seems to me that it deserves.

Mark Waller

Lord Justice of Appeal

PREFACE

The aim of this book is to give an accurate summary of the law as it relates to insurance claims, which means largely, but not exclusively, claims against insurers and insurance brokers. This is a work for those involved in the application of the law on a daily basis, whether as solicitors, barristers or insurance claims handlers. Where the law is clear, I have tried to set it out concisely; only where it is unclear, or there is (or appears to be) a gap in the law, have I suggested what I think the law should be. Discussion of the development of the law has been included only where necessary to understand the current position. Old authorities, particularly those which pre-date the publication of the official law reports in 1865, are referred to only where they are still relied on as authoritative statements of fundamental principles.

In order to facilitate a quick sifting of authorities, the following principles have been adopted: where a case is cited as support for a proposition, references are given to specific pages or paragraphs, along with the name of the judge, unless the whole or a large part of the judgment is relevant; and appellate decisions are always identified in the case citations. Source materials including case law and legislation are increasingly becoming available free of charge on the internet, and I continue to find one website in particular to be invaluable: www.bailii.org, which is maintained by the British and Irish Legal Information Institute.

I would like to thank the following for, variously, their assistance, support and encouragement: Sophie Belgrove; Veronica Berry; Janet Bignell QC; Marian Boyle; Sir Nicolas Bratza; Hannah Brown; Andrew Burns QC; Jonathan Butters; Lorna Claridge; Melissa Collett; Jesse Crozier; Nicholas Davidson QC; Christine Deacon; Anh Doan; Colin Edelman QC; Ben Elkington QC; Fiona Garvey; Susan Ghaiwal; Katie Gollop QC; Jubriel Hanid; Lucinda Harris; Richard Harrison; Andy Hill; Lexa Hilliard QC; Oliver Hyams; Will Jackman; Lisa Jensen; Natasha Joffe; Andrew Mansell; Sam McDowall; Professor Rob Merkin QC; Samuel Nicholls; April Peacham; Nikki Singla; Mary-Emma Smith; Robert Sowersby; Robert Weir QC; Charles Wynn-Evans; and Colin Wynter QC.

The book states the law as at 31 March 2016, with one or two subsequent additions at proof stage, and considers prospectively the effect of the Insurance Act 2015, including the late payment provisions inserted by way of amendment by the Enterprise Act 2016. The Third Parties (Rights Against Insurers) Act 2010, as amended, is also considered; this will come into force, very belatedly, on 1 August 2016.

Alison Padfield
May 2016

CONTENTS

Foreword to the First Edition	*v*
Preface	*vii*
Table of Statutes	*xv*
Table of Statutory Instruments	*xxi*
Table of Cases	*xxiii*
Table of European Legislation	*lxv*

Chapter 1: The basics	**1**
Scope of this book	1
Foreign law	1
Indemnity and contingency insurance	2
Terminology: 'assurance' and 'insurance'	2
The London insurance market	2
Insurance documentation	5

Chapter 2: The claimant	**7**
Introduction	7
Insurable interest	9
Subrogated claims	15
Assignment	15
Claims by insurers	17
Claims by third parties	17

Chapter 3: The contract of insurance	**31**
Cover notes	31
Time of binding contract and of inception of risk	32
Classification of policy terms	33
Construction	45
Rectification	71

Chapter 4: Causation of loss	**79**
General principles of causation	79
Identifying the proximate cause in a sequence of events	79
Concurrent causes	82
Wordings denoting proximate cause	84
'Directly or indirectly'	85
'Independent', 'exclusive' or 'sole' cause	86
'In respect of'	87
'On account of'	87

Contents

Latin terminology   87
Opportunity to avert loss   88
Negligence by the insured   89
Attempts to avoid a peril   89

Chapter 5:   Proof of loss   **91**
Burden of proof   91
Standard of proof   96
Proof 'satisfactory to' insurer   97

Chapter 6:   Measurement of loss   **99**
Indemnity and contingency insurance   99
Total loss   99
Valued and unvalued policies   99
Consequential loss   104
Betterment and giving credit for collateral benefits   106
Excess clauses and deductibles   106
Aggregation   107
Average and under-insurance   113
Salvage   113
Limited interest in property   114
Mitigation of loss   114

Chapter 7:   Presentation of claims   **117**
ICOBS   117
Burden of proof   118
Construction of procedural conditions including notification clauses   118
Innominate or intermediate terms   121
Damages for breach of a procedural condition   121
What must be notified   122
Who must give notice   126
The party who must be given notice   127
Meaning of 'notice' or 'notification'   127
Expressions as to time   129
Specific periods   130
Scope of notification of circumstances   131
No notification requirement   132
Delivery of particulars of loss and damage or of claim   133
Status of procedural conditions following repudiation of liability   134
Waiver and estoppel   135
Double insurance   136

Chapter 8:   Claims handling   **137**
Introduction   137
Regulatory obligations (ICOBS and COBS)   137
Speed and efficiency in handling claims and damages for late payment   138
Reservation of rights by insurer   141
Human Rights Act 1998   142

Costs of investigating fraudulent claims 143
Rejection of a claim 143
Interim payments 143
Requirement for insurer's consent 144
Claims co-operation and claims control clauses 145
Costs of defending claims 145
Indemnity under liability policy following judgment, award or
    settlement between insured and third party 146
Privilege 148
Agreements with third parties for repair or reinstatement 148
Recovery of payments made to settle claims 150

Chapter 9:   Insurance litigation **153**
The pre-action protocols 153
Identifying the appropriate court 154
Representative actions 155
After the event (ATE) legal expenses insurance and security for costs 155
Human Rights Act 1998 156
Claims co-operation and claims control clauses 159
Disclosure 164
Legal professional privilege 171
'Without prejudice' communications 179
Evidence for trial 182
Remedies 183
Interest 186
Costs against non-parties 188
Joinder of insurer or broker to proceedings involving insured 193

Chapter 10:   Alternatives to litigation **195**
Alternative dispute resolution 195
Financial Ombudsman Service 202

Chapter 11:   Insurers' defences **209**
Introduction 209
Breach of condition precedent as to liability 209
Breach of warranty 210
Duty of utmost good faith 210
Duty of utmost good faith in the presentation of the risk: non-disclosure
    and misrepresentation: pre-Consumer Insurance (Disclosure
    and Representations) Act 2012 and pre-Insurance Act 2015 213
Duty of fair presentation: Insurance Act 2015 251
Consumer Insurance (Disclosure and Representations) Act 2012 259
Fraudulent claims and fraudulent devices 264
Lack of insurable interest 273
Supervening illegality 274
Limitation of actions 274
Waiver, affirmation and estoppel 279

Chapter 12: Subrogation **287**
Introduction 287
Nature of the doctrine 287
Entitlement to exercise subrogated rights 288
Exercise of rights of subrogation 293
Subrogation and contribution 301
Subrogation and s 14A of the Limitation Act 1980 301

Chapter 13: Double insurance and contribution **303**
Double insurance 303
Interest and insured must be same under each policy 303
Non-contribution and excess insurance clauses 305
Contribution where one insurer entitled to repudiate liability 306
Rateable proportion clauses 308
Calculation of contribution 309
Clauses requiring disclosure of 'other insurance' 310
Prohibition of other insurances 310
Voluntary payments 311
Civil Liability (Contribution) Act 1978 311
Contribution and average 312
Parties to a claim for contribution 312
Contribution and subrogation 312
Employer's liability insurance and the 'Fairchild enclave' 313

Chapter 14: Reinsurance **315**
'Follow the settlements' clauses 315
Claims co-operation and claims control clauses 318
Policies containing both 'follow the settlements' and claims
      co-operation and control clauses 320
Limitation of actions 323
Construction of policy of insurance in light of reinsurance 324

Chapter 15: Conflict of laws **325**
Applicable law 325
Jurisdiction under Regulation 1215/2012 (the 'Brussels I' Regulation) 335
Jurisdiction where Brussels I Regulation does not apply 340

Chapter 16: Claims against insurance brokers **343**
Introduction 343
Identifying the principal 343
The importance of identifying the principal 346
Duties to client 348
Duties to insurer 351
Duties to other third parties 352
Standard of skill and care required 353
Breach of duty 354
Specific defences 369
Damages 375

Interest   387
Whether to join the broker to an action against the insurer   387
Costs of civil proceedings brought against broker and insurer   388

Chapter 17:   Specific types of insurance   **389**
Introduction   389
Accident insurance   389
Business interruption insurance   392
Contractor's all risks insurance   394
Legal expenses insurance   394
Permanent health insurance   397
Product liability insurance   399
Professional indemnity insurance   403
Public liability insurance   405

Index   407

Table of Statutes

	PARA
Arbitration Act 1996	10.3, 10.10, 10.12, 10.13
s 2	10.3
4	10.7
6(1), (2)	10.5
7	10.5, 10.12; 11.31
9	10.6
(1), (2), (4)	10.6
(5)	3.5; 10.6
30(1)	10.5
32	10.5
33(1), (2)	10.7
34(1), (2)	10.7
36, 43	10.7
44	10.8
(1)	10.8
(2)(e)	10.8
(3)–(5)	10.8
45(1), (2)	10.9
66	10.10
(3)	10.10
67	9.9; 10.10
(4)	10.11
69	9.9; 10.11
(1), (2)	10.11
(3)	10.11
(c)(i), (ii)	9.9; 10.11
(6)	9.9; 10.11
(8)	10.11
73	10.10
85(2)	10.6
86	10.6
87(1)(a)	10.9
(b)	10.11
89	3.20
(1)	3.20
90	3.20
91(1)	3.20
(2)–(4)	10.14
Pt III (ss 99–104)	10.10
s 105	9.9; 10.11
Sch 1	10.7
Banking Act 2009	
Pt 2 (ss 90–135)	2.29

	PARA
Civil Jurisdiction and Judgments Act 1982	
s 16, 17	15.7
Sch 4	15.7
Civil Liability (Contribution) Act 1978	13.10
s 1(1)	13.10
Companies Act 2006	
s 1029	2.24
Company Directors Disqualification Act 1986	9.6
Consumer Insurance (Disclosure and Representations) Act 2012	3.7, 3.8; 8.7; 11.5, 11.16, 11.20, 11.31, 11.32, 11.35, 11.40, 11.41, 11.42, 11.43, 11.44, 11.45, 11.46, 11.47; 16.6
s 1	3.8; 11.35
2(1)–(4)	11.42
(5)(a), (b)	11.42
3(2)	11.46
4	11.33
(2)	11.44
(3)	11.45
5(1)(a), (b)11.44	
(2)–(5)	11.44
9	11.46
10(1)–(3)	11.47
12(4)	11.5, 11.33
Sch 1	11.33
para 4–8	11.45
9(2), (5)–(9)	11.45
11, 12	11.45
17	11.33
Sch 2	
para 2	11.46
3(1)–(4)	11.46
Consumer Rights Act 2015	3.20; 11.49
s 2(2)–(4)	3.20
Pt 2 (ss 61–76)	3.19, 3.20; 7.5; 11.49
s 61(1), (3), (4)	3.20
62(4), (5)	3.20
63(1)	3.20

PARA

Consumer Rights Act 2015 – *contd*
s 64(1), (2)................................... 3.20
   (3) 3.19, 3.20
   (4)–(6)................................. 3.20
  68(1) 3.19, 3.20
  69(1) 3.19, 3.20
   (2) 3.19
  71(1)–(3)............................... 3.20
  73(1) 3.20
  74(1) 3.20
  76(1), (2)............................... 3.20
  Sch 4................................. 3.20
Contracts (Applicable Law) Act
  1990.................................. 15.4, 15.5
s 2(1), (2)............................... 15.5
   (1A) 15.4
  3(3)(a)............................... 15.4, 15.5
  4................................. 9.46
  7................................. 15.5
Contracts (Rights of Third Parties)
  Act 1999................ 2.10, 2.18; 17.14
s 1............................... 2.18
  7(1) 2.10, 2.18
  8................................. 2.18
  10(2) 2.10, 2.18
Counter-Terrorism Act 2008 .... 11.56
County Courts Act 1984
s 52................................. 9.22
  53................................. 9.16, 9.23
  69................................. 9.45
Courts and Legal Services Act 1990
s 4................................. 9.46
  (1), (3)............................... 9.46
Enterprise Act 2016
s 28(1), (2)............................... 8.3
  29................................. 8.3
   (1) 8.3
  30................................. 8.3
  44................................. 8.3
   (3) 8.3
Financial Services Act 1986............. 3.16
Financial Services and Markets
  Act 2000...... 1.6, 1.8; 3.8; 8.2; 10.17,
      10.18; 11.35, 11.41; 16.1, 16.7
s 22................................. 16.7
  (1) 8.2; 10.18
  31................................. 8.2; 10.18
  39(3), (4)............................... 16.8
Pt IV (ss 40–55) 8.2; 10.18
s 138................................. 8.2; 10.17
  150................................. 8.2
  153................................. 8.2; 10.17
  157, 225................................. 10.17

PARA

Financial Services and Markets
  Act 2000 – *contd*
s 226, 227................................. 10.18
  228(2) 10.17
  (4)(a)–(c) 10.19
  (5), (6)............................... 10.19
  229................................. 10.17
  (5) 10.17
  (9)(a)............................... 10.17
  315................................. 1.6
  417................................. 8.2
  424(3) 15.4
  Sch 2................................. 8.2; 10.18; 16.7
  Sch 17................................. 10.17
  para 13................................. 8.2
  14, 18................................. 10.17
Fires Prevention (Metropolis) Act
  1774................................. 2.11
s 83................................. 2.11
Gambling Act 1774 *see* Life
  Assurance Act 1774
Gambling Act 2005
s 18, 356................................. 2.4
  Sch 2................................. 2.4
Gaming Act 1845
s 18................................. 2.4, 2.6
Human Rights Act 1998................. 9.6
s 6(3)(a)............................... 8.5
Insolvency Act 1986
Pt I (ss 1–7)............................. 2.19
Pt II (ss 8–27)............................ 2.29
Insurance Act 2015 .... 3.4, 3.8, 3.10;
      8.3; 11.4, 11.5, 11.34,
      11.37, 11.38, 11.49, 11.54
s 1................................. 3.8; 11.35
Pt 2 (ss 2–8) 11.35
s 2................... 11.4, 11.5, 11.33, 11.35
  (1), (2)............................... 11.36
  3................... 11.4, 11.5, 11.33, 11.35
  (1) 11.36
  (3)(a)–(c) 11.36
  (4)(a)............................... 11.36, 11.37
  (b)................................. 11.36
  (5)(a)–(e) 11.36, 11.38
  4................... 11.4, 11.5, 11.33, 11.35
  (1) 11.37
  (2) 11.37
  (b)................................. 11.37
  (3) 11.37
  (4)–(7)............................... 11.37
  5................... 11.4, 11.5, 11.33, 11.35
  (1), (2)............................... 11.38
  (3)(a), (b) 11.38

PARA

Insurance Act 2015 – *contd*

s 5A(1), (2)	8.3
6	11.4, 11.5, 11.33, 11.35
(1)	11.37, 11.38
(2)	11.37, 11.38
7	11.4, 11.5, 11.33, 11.35
(1)–(3)	11.36
(4)(a)–(c)	11.36
(5), (6)	11.36
8	11.4, 11.5, 11.33, 11.35
(1)	11.39
(a)	11.37
(b)	11.37, 11.39
(c)	11.37
(3)	11.39
(4)(a), (b)	11.39
(5), (6)	11.39
9	3.8; 11.3, 11.16
10	3.6, 3.7, 3.8
(1)–(4)	3.8
(5)(a), (b)	3.8
(6)	3.7
11	3.6, 3.7, 3.8, 3.10, 3.18
(1)	3.10; 11.42
(2), (3)	3.10
(4)	3.8, 3.10
12	3.8; 11.48, 11.49, 11.54
(1)–(4)	11.54
13	11.54
(1)–(3)	11.54
13A(1)–(5)	8.3
Pt 5 (ss 14–18)	11.54
s 14(1)	11.4
(2)	11.4, 11.42
(3)	11.4, 11.42
(4)	11.42
15(1) (3)	3.8
16(1)	11.16
(2), (3)	3.8; 11.35
(4)	3.8
16A(1)–(6)	8.3
17(1)–(5)	3.8; 11.35
18(1)–(6)	11.54
20	2.28, 2.29
21(2), (3), (6)	11.42
22(1)	3.6, 3.7, 3.8, 3.10, 3.18; 11.5, 11.33, 11.35, 11.42, 11.48, 11.49, 11.54
(2)	11.3, 11.16, 11.35
(3)	3.6, 3.7, 3.8, 3.10, 3.18; 11.3, 11.5, 11.16, 11.33, 11.35, 11.42, 11.48, 11.49, 11.54
(4)	3.8; 11.35, 11.36

Insurance Act 2015 – *contd*

s 23(2)	3.6, 3.8, 3.10; 8.3; 11.5, 11.42
(3A)	8.3
Sch 1	11.33
para 2–5	11.39
6	11.39
(1), (2)	11.39
Pt 2 (paras 7–11)	11.39
para 12	11.33
Sch 2	2.28, 2.29

Insurance Companies Act 1982

s 94B	15.4
Sch 3A	15.4

Judgments Act 1838	9.45

Latent Damage Act 1986

s 1	16.31

Law of Property Act 1925

s 136	2.13

Law Reform (Contributory Negligence) Act 1945 ..... 16.38, 16.43

s 1(1)	16.28, 16.38

Life Assurance Act 1774	2.4, 2.5
s 1, 2	2.5, 2.6
3	2.5
4	2.6

Limitation Act 1939

s 2(1)	11.61; 16.32

Limitation Act 1980	8.3
s 2	16.29, 16.31
5	11.59; 16.29
5A(1), (2)	8.3
11	16.31
14A	12.15; 16.31
(1)	16.31
(5)	12.15; 16.31
(6)–(10)	16.31
32	11.59; 16.31
(1)(a)–(c)	16.31
(2), (5)	16.31

Lloyd's Act 1871	1.6
Lloyd's Act 1911	1.6
Lloyd's Act 1951	1.6
Lloyd's Act 1982	1.6

Marine Insurance Act 1906 .... 1.1; 11.27

s 4(2)(b)	16.34
5	2.8
6	2.6
7	2.9
17	1.1; 9.14; 11.4, 11.5, 11.37, 11.49
18	1.1; 11.4, 11.5, 11.11, 11.12, 11.13, 11.19, 11.37, 11.39, 11.42

PARA

Marine Insurance Act 1906 – *contd*
s 18(1) 11.6, 11.9, 11.13
   (2) 11.6, 11.7, 11.36
   (3) 11.6
    (a) 11.8
    (b) 11.8, 11.38
    (c) 11.8, 11.14
    (d) 11.8, 11.21
   (4) 11.6, 11.7, 11.19
   (5) 11.19, 11.36
19 .... 1.1; 11.4, 11.5, 11.9,
             11.11, 11.13, 11.37,
             11.42; 16.6, 16.19
   (a), (b) 11.13
20 .... 1.1; 11.4, 11.5, 11.18,
             11.20, 11.21, 11.22,
             11.37, 11.39, 11.42
   (1) 11.13, 11.20, 11.21
   (2) 11.6, 11.36
   (3) 11.22
   (4) 11.21
   (5) 8.15; 11.16, 11.21,
             11.22, 11.25
   (6) 11.18
   (7) 11.6, 11.7
21 .... 3.3
26(3) 2.10
27(2) 6.3
28 .... 6.3
33 .... 1.1; 3.7
34 .... 3.7; 11.63
   (3) 3.7
39 .... 3.8
   (5) 11.38
40, 41 .... 3.8
50 .... 2.13
56–61 .... 6.2
77(1) 6.9
78(4) 4.10
81 .... 6.10
84 .... 11.33
   (3)(a) 11.33
    (c) 11.55
Merchant Shipping Act 1995
s 165 .... 2.40
   (5) 2.40
Misrepresentation Act 1967
s 2(1) 11.23
   (2) 11.32
Race Relations Act 1976
s 1, 3, 20 .... 11.17
Rehabilitation of Offenders Act
  1974 .... 11.17, 11.19

PARA

Rehabilitation of Offenders Act
  1974 – *contd*
s 1 .... 11.17
4 .... 11.17
   (1), (2) 11.17
5(1) 11.17
   (2)(a), (b) 11.17
7(3) 11.17
Road Traffic Act 1934
s 10(5) 11.6
Road Traffic Act 1988
s 151 .... 2.40; 13.9
152 .... 2.40
Senior Courts Act 1981
s 33 .... 9.22
   (2) 9.22
34 .... 9.16, 9.23
35A 9.45
37 .... 10.8
51 .... 9.13, 9.46; 17.10
   (3) 2.24; 9.46
Solicitors Act 1974
s 37 .... 2.24
Supply of Goods and Services
  Act 1982
s 13 .... 16.7
Supreme Court Act 1981 *see* Senior
  Courts Act 1981
Supreme Court of Judicature Act 1890
s 5 .... 9.46
Theft Act 1968 .... 3.22
Third Parties (Rights against
  Insurers) Act 1930 .... 2.1, 2.17,
             2.19, 2.21, 2.23,
             2.24, 2.28, 2.40;
             9.46, 9.47; 11.60;
             13.4, 13.14
s 1(1) 2.19, 2.25, 2.28; 13.14
   (a), (b) 2.19
   (2) 2.19
   (3) 2.22
   (4)(b) 2.26
   (5) 2.21
   (6) 2.19
2 .... 2.28
   (1) 2.23
3 .... 2.22
3A(1), (2) 2.19
Third Parties (Rights against
  Insurers) Act 2010 ...... 2.1, 2.28, 2.29,
         2.28, 2.29, 2.40, 2.39, 2.40, 2.40,
             2.39, 2.40; 13.14
s 1 .... 2.28

PARA

Third Parties (Rights against Insurers) Act 2010 – *contd*

	PARA
s 1(1)	2.28
2	2.28
(4)	2.40
(7), (9), (10)	2.28
4	2.29
5	2.29
(2)	2.40
6	2.29
(2)(b)	2.29
6A	2.29
8	2.40
9(1)–(8)	2.40
10	2.39
11	2.39
12(1)–(3)	2.40
(4)(a)	2.40
13(1)–(3)	2.39
14(1), (6)	2.39
15, 16	2.29

PARA

Third Parties (Rights against Insurers) Act 2010 – *contd*

	PARA
s 17	2.40
(1)(b)	2.40
18	2.39
20	2.28
Sch A1	2.29
Sch 1	
para 1(1)–(4)	2.39
2(1)–(3)	2.39
Sch 3	
para 1	2.28
1A	2.28, 2.29
(2)	2.29
(4)	2.28, 2.29
2, 3, 5	2.28
Sch 4	2.28
Unfair Contract Terms Act 1977	3.20
Workmen's Compensation Act 1897	11.62

Table of Statutory Instruments

PARA

Civil Procedure Rules 1998, SI
  1998/3132 .... 9.1, 9.2, 9.7, 9.16,
                    9.40; 12.8; 16.47
  r 3.1(2)(m)................................. 9.15
  6.36 .... 15.13
  Pt 8 (rr 8.1–8.6)....................... 10.12
  Pt 18 (rr 18.1, 18.2).................... 9.15
  Pt 19 (rr 19.1–19.17).................. 9.46
  r 19.2(2)............................ 9.13, 9.47
  19.7(1), (4).............................. 9.4
  27.1 .... 10.14
  Pt 31 (rr 31.1–31.23).... 9.14, 9.15; 12.8
  r 31.1(1)................................ 9.14
  31.2A 9.14
  31.3(2).................................... 9.14
  31.6 .... 9.14, 9.33
  31.7...................................... 9.14
    (1)...................................... 9.14
  31.8 .... 9.14
  31.9(1), (2)............................. 9.17
  31.10 .... 9.17
    (6), (9)............................... 9.17
  31.11 .... 9.18
  31.12(2).................................. 9.19
  31.14 .... 9.33
    (1), (2)............................... 9.20
  31.15(a)–(c) 9.20
  31.16 .... 2.23; 9.22
    (1)...................................... 9.22
    (3)(a), (b), (d).................... 9.22
  31.17 .... 2.23; 9.16, 9.23; 12.8
  31.19(1), (3), (4) 9.21
    (5), (6)............................... 9.30
  31.20 .... 9.21, 9.33
  31.21 .... 9.17
  31.22(1).................................. 9.24
    (a)–(c)........................... 9.24
  32.6(2)–(5)............................ 9.39
  Pt 34 (rr 34.1–34.24).................. 10.7
  Pt 35 (rr 35.1–35.15)................. 9.40
  r 40.20 .... 9.42
  Pt 43 (rr 43.1–43.4).................... 9.46
  Pt 44 (rr 44.1–44.20).......... 9.46; 10.15
  r 44.3 .... 16.47
    (5)(a) 9.2

PARA

Civil Procedure Rules 1998, SI
  1998/3132 – contd
  Pt 45 (rr 45.1–45.47).................... 9.46
  Pt 46 (rr 46.1–46.4)..................... 9.46
  Pt 47 (rr 47.1–47.26)................... 9.46
  Pt 48 (rr 48.1–48.7)..................... 17.8
  r 48.2(1)(a), (b) 9.46
  Pt 58 (rr 58.1–58.12)................... 9.1
  r 58.1(2)(e) 9.3
    58.4(1)................................... 9.3
  Pt 59 (rr 59.1–59.13)................... 9.1
  r 59.1(2)(a), (b) 9.3
  Pt 62 (rr 62.1–62.23)................... 10.12
  r 62.4(1), (2)............................. 10.12
Consumer Insurance (Disclosure
  and Representations) Act 2012
  (Commencement) Order 2013,
  SI 2013/450...................... 11.41
Consumer Protection from Unfair
  Trading Regulations 2008,
  SI 2008/1277
  Sch 1
    para 27.................................... 8.3
European Communities (Rights
  against Insurers) Regulations
  2002, SI 2002/3061 .... 2.40
Financial Services and Markets
  Act 2000 (Law Applicable
  to Contracts of Insurance)
  Regulations 2001,
  SI 2001/2635 .... 15.3, 15.4
  reg 2(1)................................... 15.3
    (3), (4)................................ 15.4
    3(1), (1A), (2)..................... 15.4
    4(1)–(9)............................. 15.4
    5 .... 15.4
    6(1), (2)............................. 15.4
    7(1)–(3)............................. 15.4
    8(1)–(3) 15.4
    9 .... 15.4
    10(1), (2)............................ 15.4
Financial Services and Markets Act
  2000 (Regulated Activities)
  Order 2001, SI 2001/544......... 8.2;
                        10.18; 16.7

PARA

Financial Services and Markets Act
2000 (Regulated Activities)
Order 2001, SI 2001/544 – *contd*
reg 25 .... 1.6, 1.8
56–58 .... 1.6
Financial Services and Markets
Act 2000 (Rights of Action)
Regulations 2001, SI 2001/2256
reg 3(1)... 8.2
High Court and County Courts
(Allocation of Arbitration
Proceedings) Order 1996,
SI 1996/3215
art 3, 4 .... 10.12
5(4)... 10.12
6 .... 10.12
High Court and County Courts
Jurisdiction Order 1991, SI
1991/724 .... 9.3
Insurance Companies (Legal
Expenses Insurance)
Regulations 1990,
SI 1990/1159........................... 17.8
reg 3(3).................................. 17.8, 17.9
6 .... 17.8
(1)–(3) 17.8
7 .... 17.8
8(1), (2) 17.8
Rules of the Supreme Court 1965, SI
1965/1776 Order 15
r 12... 9.4
16....................................... 9.42
Third Parties (Rights against Insurers)
Act 2010 (Commencement)
Order 2016, SI 2016/550.......... 2.28

PARA

Third Parties (Rights Against
Insurers) Regulations 2016
reg 1 .... 2.28, 2.29
5 .... 2.34
Unfair Arbitration Agreements
(Specified Amount) Order 1999,
SI 1999/2167.................... 3.20; 10.14
Unfair Terms in Consumer Contracts
Regulations 1994, SI 1994/3159
.... 3.20; 11.49
reg 2–7 .... 10.14
Unfair Terms in Consumer
Contracts Regulations 1999,
SI 1999/2083.......... 3.13, 3.19, 3.20;
7.5, 7.19; 10.14; 11.49
reg 3 .... 3.20; 10.14
(1)... 3.20
4 .... 3.20; 10.14
(2)... 3.20
5 .... 3.20; 10.14
(1)................................ 3.20; 10.14
(2), (3) 3.20
6 .... 3.20; 10.14
(1), (2) 3.20
7 .... 3.20; 10.14
(1), (2) 3.20
8 .... 3.20; 10.14
9 .... 3.20; 10.14
Sch 1
para 1(a) 3.20
Sch 2........................... 3.20; 10.14
para 1(i)........................... 3.20; 7.19
(p)......................... 3.20; 10.14

Table of Cases

A

PARA

A & J Inglis v John Buttery & Co (1877-78) 3 App Cas 552, (1878) 5 R (HL) 87...   3.16

A-G v Adelaide Steamship Co Ltd (No 1) [1923] AC 292, (1923) 14 Ll L Rep 549 ....   4.11

A-G of Belize v Belize Telecom Ltd [2009] UKPC 10, [2009] 1 WLR 1988, [2009] Bus LR 1316 ....   3.27; 12.4

AIG Europe Ltd v OC320301 LLP [2015] EWHC 2398 (Comm), [2016] Lloyd's Rep IR 147 ....   3.16; 6.9

AIC Ltd v ITS Testing Services (UK) Ltd (The Kriti Palm) [2006] EWCA Civ 1601, [2007] 1 All ER (Comm) 667, [2007] 1 Lloyd's Rep 555 ....   11.50

AJ Building & Plastering Ltd v Turner [2013] EWHC 484 (QB), [2015] TCLR 3, [2013] Lloyd's Rep IR 629 ....   3.19, 3.20; 8.14

AMT Futures Ltd v Marziller, Dr Meier & Dr Guntner Rechtsanwaltsgesellschaft mbH [2014] EWHC 1085 (Comm), [2015] 2 WLR 187, [2014] 2 Lloyd's Rep 349 ....   3.20

ARC Capital Partners Ltd v Brit Syndicates Ltd [2016] EWHC 141 (Comm), [2016] 4 WLR 18...   4.4

AS Screenprinting Ltd v British Reserve Insurance Co Ltd [1996] CLC 1470, [1999] Lloyd's Rep IR 430...   17.17

Aaron's Reefs Ltd v Twiss [1896] AC 273 ....   11.28

Abbey National plc v Frost [1999] 1 WLR 1080, [1999] 2 All ER 206, [1999] Lloyd's Rep PN 301 ....   2.24

Absalom v TCRU Ltd (formerly Monument Insurance Brokers Ltd) [2005] EWCA Civ 1586, [2006] 1 All ER (Comm) 375, [2006] 2 Lloyd's Rep 129 ....   3.4, 3.14, 3.15, 3.16, 3.23; 16.6

AceGroup Ltd v Chartis Insurance UK Ltd (formerly AIG (UK) Ltd & AIG Europe (UK) Ltd [2013] EWCA Civ 224, [2013] Lloyd's Rep IR 485 ....   5.1; 6.9

Ace European Group v Standard Life Assurance Ltd see Standard Life Assurance Ltd v Ace European Group

Adams v London Improved Motor Coach Buiders Ltd [1921] 1 KB 495, [1920] All ER Rep 340...   8.14

Adamson (TH) & Sons v Liverpool & London & Globe Insurance Co Ltd [1953] 2 Lloyd's Rep 355 ....   7.17

Adcock v Cooperative Insurance Society Ltd [2000] Lloyd's Rep IR 657 ....   8.9; 9.45

Aegon, The. See Agapitos v Agnew

Agapitos v Agnew (The Aegeon) (No 1) [2002] EWCA Civ 247, [2003] QB 556, [2002] 2 Lloyd's Rep 42 ....   9.14; 11.27, 11.49, 11.51

Agip SpA v Navigazione Alta Italia SpA (The Nai Genova & Nai Superba) [1984] 1 Lloyd's Rep 353..   3.29, 3.35

Agnew v Johnson [1980] AC 367, [1979] 1 All ER 883 ....   6.4

Agnew v Länsforsäkringsbolagens AB [2001] 1 AC 223, [2000] 1 All ER 737 ....   14.5; 15.7

Aiden Shipping Co Ltd v Interbulk Ltd (The Vimeira) (No 2) [1986] AC 965, [1986] 2 WLR 1051, [1986] 2 All ER 409...   9.46

Aiken v Stewart Wrightson Members Agency Ltd [1995] 1 WLR 1281, [1995] 3 All ER 449, [1995] 2 Lloyd's Rep 618 ....   11.14

PARA

Aioi Nissay Insurance Co Ltd (formerly Chiyoda Fire & Marine Insurance Co Ltd)
    v Heraldglen Ltd [2013] EWHC 154 (Comm), [2013] 2 All ER (Comm) 231,
    [2013] Lloyd's Rep IR 281 .... 6.9
Air Canada v United Kingdom (application no 18465/91) (1995) 20 EHRR 150 .... 9.6
Albacruz v Albazero, The Albazero... 2.10
Alcoa Minerals of Jamaica Inc v Broderick [2002] 1 AC 371, [2000] BLR 279 ...... 16.34
Alexander Forbes Europe Ltd (formerly Nelson Hurst UK Ltd) v SBJ Ltd [2002]
    EWHC 3121 (Comm), [2003] Lloyd's Rep IR 432, [2003] Lloyd's Rep
    PN 137 .... 16.18, 16.23, 16.34, 16.35, 16.43
Alexandros T, The *see* Starlight Shipping Co v Allianz Marine & Aviation
    Versicherungs AG
Alexion Hope, The. *See* Schiffshypothenkenbank Zu Luebeck AG
Alfred McAlpine plc v BAI (Run-Off) Ltd [2000] 1 All ER (Comm) 545, [2000]
    1 Lloyd's Rep 437, [2000] CLC 812 .... 3.5, 3.9; 7.6
Alizia Glacial, The. *See* Handelsbanken Norwegian Branch of Svenska
    Handelsbanked AB (Publ)
Al-Koronky v Time-Life Entertainment Group Ltd [2006] EWCA Civ 1123, [2006]
    CP Rep 47, [2007] 1 Costs LR 57 .... 9.5
Allen v London Guarantee & Accident Co Ltd (1912) 28 TLR 254 .... 6.9
Allen v Robles [1969] 1 WLR 1193, [1969] 3 All ER 154, [1969] 2 Lloyd's
    Rep 61 .... 7.22; 11.63
Allen v Universal Automobile Insurance Co Ltd (1933) 45 Ll L Rep 55 .... 11.13, 11.16
Alliance Aeroplane Co Ltd v Union Insurance Society of Canton Ltd (1920) 5 Ll L
    Rep 406 .... 3.32, 3.34
Allianz Insurance Co Egypt v Aigaion Insurance Co SA (No 2) The Ocean Dirk
    [2008] EWCA Civ 1455, [2009] 2 All ER (Comm) 745, [2009] Lloyd's Rep
    IR 533.. 3.3
Allied Maples Group Ltd v Simmons & Simmons [1995] 1 WLR 1602, [1995] 4 All
    ER 907, [1996] CLC 153 .... 16.35, 16.40
Allied Marine Transport Ltd v Vale do Rio Doce Navegacao SA (The Leonidas D)
    [1985] 1 WLR 925, [1985] 2 All ER 796, [1985] 2 Lloyd's Rep 18 .... 11.63
All Leisure Holidays Ltd v Europaische Reiseversicherung AG [2011] EWHC 2629
    (Comm), [2012] Lloyd's Rep IR 193.. 2.13; 5.1, 5.4; 7.20
Amalgamated Investment & Property Co Ltd (in liquidation) v Texas Commerce
    International Bank Ltd [1982] QB 84, [1981] 3 All ER 577 .... 11.63
American Airlines Inc v Hope [1974] 2 Lloyd's Rep 301 .... 3.15, 3.16, 3.31
American Centennial Insurance Co v Insco Ltd [1996] LRLR 407, [1997] 6 Re
    LR 138 .... 6.9
American Home Products Corpn v Novartis Pharmaceuticals UK Ltd (application
    for disclosure) [2001] EWCA Civ 165, [2001] FSR 41, (2001) 24 (4)
    IPD 24021 .... 9.23
American Motorists Insurance Co (AMICO) v Cellstar Corpn [2003] EWCA Civ
    206, [2003] 2 CLC 599, [2003] Lloyd's Rep IR 295............................ 15.3, 15.4, 15.5
American Surety Co of New York v Wrightson (1910) 16 Com Cas 37 .... 13.6
Amey Properties Ltd v Cornhill Insurance plc [1996] LRLR 259, [1996]
    CLC 401... 5.2
Amlin Corporate Member Ltd v Oriental Assurance Corpn (The Princess of the
    Stars) [2014] EWCA Civ 1135, [2014] 2 Lloyd's Rep 561, [2014] 2 CLC
    436... 3.6, 3.14
Anders & Kern UK Ltd (t/a Anders & Kern Presentation Systems) v CGU Insurance
    plc (t/a Norwich Union Insurance) [2007] EWCA Civ 1481, [2008] 2 All ER
    (Comm) 1185, [2008] Lloyd's Rep IR 460.. 3.27
Anderson v The Commercial Union Assurance Co (1775) 55 LJQB 146................ 6.5

PARA

Anderson v Commercial Union Assurance Co plc (No 1) 1998 SC 197, 1998 SLT 826, 1997 GWD 29-1486... 8.8

Anderson v Fitzgerald (1853) 4 HL Cas 484, 10 ER 551.................................. 11.15, 11.16

Anderson v Morice (1875-76) 1 App Cas 713... 2.6, 2.8

Anderson v Pacific Fire & Marine Insurance Co (1871-72) LR 7 CP 65.................. 11.13

Aneco Reinsurance Underwriting Ltd (in liquidation) v Johnson & Higgins Ltd [2001] UKHL 51, [2001] 2 All ER (Comm) 929, [2002] 1 Lloyd's Rep 157... 16.21, 16.33, 16.34, 16.36, 16.37, 16.40, 16.46

Anglo-African Merchants Ltd v Bayley [1970] 1 QB 311, [1969] 2 All ER 421 .... 11.6, 11.14; 16.4

Anonima Petroli Italiana SpA & Neste Oy v Marlucidez Armadora SA (The Filiatra Legacy) [1991] 2 Lloyd's Rep 337 .... 5.3

Ansari v New India Assurance Ltd [2009] EWCA Civ 93, [2009] 2 All ER (Comm) 926, [2009] Lloyd's Rep IR 562 .... 11.18

Antaios, The. *See* Antaios Compania Naviera SA v Salen Rederierna AB

Antaios Compania Naviera SA v Salen Rederierna AB (The Antaios) [1985] AC 191, [1984] 3 All ER 229 .... 3.15

Arab Bank plc v John D Wood (Commercial) Ltd [2000] 1 WLR 857, [2000] Lloyd's Rep IR 471, [2000] Lloyd's Rep PN 173.. 12.1

Arab Bank plc v Zurich Insurance Co [1999] 1 Lloyd's Rep 262, [1998] CLC 1351... 11.11, 11.30

Arash Shipping Enterprises Co Ltd v Groupama Transport [2011] EWCA Civ 620, [2012] Lloyd's Rep IR 40, [2011] 1 CLC 984... 9.4, 9.40

Arbory Group Ltd v West Craven Insurance Services [2007] Lloyd's Rep IR 491, [2007] PNLR 23.. 16.21

Arbitration between Wiliams & Thomas & The Lancashire & Yorkshire Accident Insurance Co, Re (1902) 19 TLR 82.. 3.5

Arbory Group Ltd v West Craven Insurance Services [2007] Lloyd's Rep IR 491, [2007] PNLR 23.. 16.38

Arbuthnott v Fagan [1996] LRLR 135, [1995] CLC 1396........................... 3.14, 3.16

Argo Systems FZE v Liberty Insurance (Pte), The Copa Casino [2011] EWHC 301 (Comm), [2011] 1 All ER (Comm) 1111, [2011] 2 Lloyd's Rep 61; [2011] EWCA Civ 1572, [2012] 1 Lloyd's Rep 129... 11.23

Arkin v Borchard Lines Ltd [2005] EWCA Civ 655, [2005] 1 WLR 3055, [2005] 3 All ER 613 .... 9.46

Arnold v Britton [2015] UKSC 36, [2015] AC 1619, [2015] 2 WLR 1593 .... 3.15

Arnott v United Kingdom (unreported, 3 October 2000) 8.5

Arts & Antiques Ltd v Richards [2013] EWHC 3361 (Comm), [2014] Lloyd's Rep IR 219, [2014] PNLR 10... 16.46

Asfar & Co v Blundell [1896] 1 QB 123... 11.14

Ashburton (Lord) v Pape [1913] 2 Ch 469 .... 9.32

Ashmore v Corpn of Lloyd's (No 2) [1992] 2 Lloyd's Rep 620............................. 3.27

Aspen Insurance UK Ltd v Adana Construction Ltd [2015] EWCA Civ 176, [2015] 1 CLC 270, [2015] Lloyd's Rep IR 522 .... 9.42; 17.15, 17.18

Assicurazioni Generali de Trieste v Empress Assurance Co Ltd [1907] 2 KB 814.. 12.8

Assicurazioni Generali SpA v Arab Insurance Group (BSC) [2002] EWCA Civ 1642, [2003] 1 WLR 577, [2003] Lloyd's Rep IR 131...................................... 11.6, 11.7

Assicurazioni Generali SpA v CGU International Insurance plc [2004] EWCA Civ 429, [2004] 2 All ER (Comm) 114, [2004] Lloyd's Rep IR 457....................... 14.2

AstraZeneca Insurance Co Ltd v XL Insurance Ltd [2013] EWCA Civ 1660, [2014] 2 All ER (Comm) 55, [2014] Lloyd's Rep IR 509............................... 8.11, 8.12; 14.2

PARA

Athel Line Ltd v Liverpool & London War Risks Insurance Association (No 2)
[1946] KB 117, (1946) 79 Ll L Rep 18 .... 4.2
Athenian Harmony, The. *See* Derby Resources AG v Blue Corinth Marine Co Ltd
(No 2)
Athletic Union of Constantinople (AEK) v National Basketball Association (No 2)
[2002] EWCA Civ 830, [2002] 1 WLR 2863, [2002] 3 All ER 897 .... 9.9; 10.11
Attaleia Marine Co Ltd v Bimeh Iran (Iran Insurance Co) (The Zeus) [1993]
2 Lloyd's Rep 497 .... 8.8, 8.15; 11.33
Austin v Zurich General Accident & Liability Insurance Co Ltd [1945] KB 250,
(1945) 78 Ll L Rep 185 .... 7.19; 11.15, 11.29; 13.3, 13.4, 13.12
Australia & New Zealand Bank Ltd v Colonial & Eagle Wharves Ltd [1960]
2 Lloyd's Rep 241 .... 7.8
Australian Agricultural Co v Saunders (1874-75) LR 10 CP 668 ....3.14; 13.1, 13.7
Australian Widows' Fund Life Assurance Society Ltd v National Mutual Life
Association of Australisia Ltd [1914] AC 634..3.24
Aviva Insurance Ltd v Brown [2011] EWHC 362 (QB), [2012] Lloyd's Rep
IR 211.. 11.50, 11.51
Avon Insurance plc v Swire Fraser Ltd [2000] 1 All ER (Comm) 573, [2000]
CLC 665, [2000] Lloyd's Rep IR 535 .... 11.6, 11.18, 11.20, 11.21, 11.22
Avondale Blouse Co Ltd v Williamson & Geo Town (1948) 81 Ll L
Rep 504 .... 16.21, 16.34
Axa Corporate Solutions SA v National Westminster Bank plc [2010] EWHC 1915
(Comm), [2010] 2 CLC 149, [2011] Lloyd's Rep IR 438 .... 3.3
Axa General Insurance Co Ltd v Gottlieb [2005] EWCA Civ 112, [2005] 1 All ER
(Comm) 445, [2005] Lloyd's Rep IR 359... 11.49
Axa Reinsurance (UK) Ltd v Field [1996] 1 WLR 1026, [1996] 3 All ER 517, [1996]
2 Lloyd's Rep 233 .... 6.9; 14.6
Axa Seguros SA de CV v Allianz Insurance plc [2011] EWHC 268 (Comm), [2011]
Lloyd's Rep IR 544 .... 8.13; 9.25
Axa Versicherung AG v Arab Insurance Group (BSC) [2015] EWHC 1939, [2016]
Lloyd's Rep IR 1 .... 11.7
Ayrey v British Legal & Provident Assurance Co Ltd [1918] 1 KB 136............... 11.63
Aziz v Caixa d'Estalvis de Catalunya, Tarragona i Manresa (Case C-415/11) [2013]
3 CMLR 5, [2013] All ER (EC) 770.. 3.20

B
B (children) (sexual abuse: standard of proof), Re [2008] UKHL 35, [2009]
1 AC 11 .... 5.3
BP Exploration (Libya) Ltd v Hunt (No 2) [1979] 1 WLR 783, (1979) 123
SJ 455.. 9.45
Bache v Zurich Insurance plc [2014] EWHC 2430 (TCC), [2014] Lloyd's Rep IR
663, [2014] CILL 3545 .... 3.19, 3.20
Bailey v Barclays Bank plc [2014] EWHC 2882 (QB) 8.2
Baker v Black Sea & Baltic General Insurance Co Ltd [1998] 1 WLR 974, [1998]
2 All ER 833, [1998] CLC 820...................................... 3.27; 9.45; 14.4, 14.5
Balabel v Air India [1988] Ch 317, [1988] 2 All ER 246.. 9.25
Balfour v Beaumont [1984] 1 Lloyd's Rep 272, (1984) 81 LSG 197 .... 3.16, 3.19
Baltic Insurance Association of London Ltd v Cambrian Coaching & Goods
Transport Ltd (1926) 25 Ll L Rep 195 .... 7.3, 7.14
Baltic Universal, The. *See* Structural Polymer Systems v Brown
Ballast plc, Re; St Paul Travelers Insurance Co Ltd v Dargan [2006] EWHC 3189
(Ch), [2007] BCC 620, [2007] Lloyd's Rep IR 742 .... 12.3, 12.6, 12.8

PARA

Banco Espanol de Credito SA v Camino [2012] 3 CMLR 25, [2013] CEC 182 ...... 3.20
Banfield v Leeds Building Society (unreported, 19 December 2007) 12.4
Bankers Insurance Co Ltd v South [2003] EWHC 380 (QB), [2004] Lloyd's Rep IR
  1, [2003] PIQR P28.. 3.14, 3.20; 7.5
Bank Leumi le Israel BM v British National Insurance Co Ltd [1988] 1 Lloyd's
  Rep 71 .... 11.22
Bank of America National Trust & Savings Association v Chrismas (The Kyriaki)
  [1994] 1 All ER 401, [1993] 1 Lloyd's Rep 137.. 9.4; 11.60
Bank of Credit & Commerce International SA (in liquidation) v Ali (No 1) [2001]
  UKHL 8, [2002] 1 AC 251.. 8.15
Bank of New Zealand v Simpson [1900] AC 182... 3.16
Bank of Nova Scotia v Hellenic Mutual War Risks Association (Bermuda) Ltd (The
  Good Luck) [1992] 1 AC 233, [1991] 3 All ER 1............................. 3.4, 3.6, 3.7; 9.27
Banque Financière de la Cité v Parc (Battersea) Ltd [1999] 1 AC 221, [1998] 2 WLR
  475, [1998] 1 All ER 737 .... 12.2, 12.3
Banque Financière de la Cité SA (formerly Banque Keyser Ullmann) SA v Westgate
  Insurance Co Ltd (formerly Hodge General & Mercantile Co Ltd) [1991]
  2 AC 249, [1990] 3 WLR 364, [1990] 2 All ER 947 .... 11.30, 11.49
Barber v Imperio Reinsurance Co (UK) Ltd (unreported, 15 July 1993)................. 11.63
Barclays Bank plc v Fairclough Building Ltd (No 1) [1995] QB 214, [1995] 1 All
  ER 289 .... 16.38
Barr v Biffa Waste Servces Ltd [2009] EWHC 1033 (TCC), [2010] 3 Costs LR 291,
  [2010] Lloyd's Rep IR 428 .... 9.15, 9.20
Barrett Bros (Taxis) Ltd v Davies [1966] 1 WLR 1334, [1966] 2 All ER 972, [1966]
  2 Lloyd's Rep 1 .... 7.4, 7.5, 7.11, 7.22; 11.63
Bartlett & Partners Ltd v Meller [1961] 1 Lloyd's Rep 487..................................... 3.19
Bastick v Yamaichi International Europe Ltd (unreported, 15 January 1993).......... 17.14
Bate v Aviva Insurance UK Ltd [2014] EWCA Civ 334, [2014] Lloyd's Rep
  IR 527.. 11.49
Bates v Hewitt (1866-67) LR 2 QB 595 .... 11.8
Baumvoll Manufactur von Carl Scheibler v Gilchrest & Co [1892] 1 QB 253......... 3.16
Beacon Insurance Co Ltd v Langdale [1939] 4 All ER 204, (1939) 65 Ll L
  Rep 57 .... 9.13
Beazley Horizon Offshore Contractors Inc [2044] EWHC 2555 (Comm), [2005] IL
  Pr 11, [2005] Lloyd's Rep IR 231... 15.13
Beazley Underwriting Ltd v Al Ahleia Insurance Co [2013] EWHC 677 (Comm),
  [2013] Lloyd's Rep IR 561 .... 3.5; 5.1; 9.13
Beazley Underwriting Ltd v The Travelers Companies Inc [2011] EWHC 1520
  (Comm), [2012] Lloyd's Rep IR 78, (2011) 108 (27) LSG 25................ 3.2, 3.3; 16.25
Becker Gray & Co v London Assurance Corpn [1918] AC 101.....3.17; 4.1, 4.2, 4.9, 4.12; 5.2
Bedfordshire Police Authority v Constable [2009] EWCA Civ 64, [2009] 2 All ER
  (Comm) 200, [2009] Lloyd's Rep IR 607.. 3.17; 17.24
Bee v Jenson (No 2) [2007] EWCA Civ 923, [2008] Lloyd's Rep
  IR 221.. 8.14; 12.6, 12.12
Belco Trading Co v Kondo [2008] EWCA Civ 205 .... 9.5
Bell v Peter Browne & Co [1990] 2 QB 495, [1990] 3 All ER 124 .... 16.29
Benincasa v Dentalkit Srl (Case C-269/95) [1997] ECR I-3767, [1998] All ER (EC)
  135, [1997] ETMR 447.. 3.20
Bennett v Axa Insurance Ltd [1999] Lloyd's Rep IR 542 .... 3.6
Beresford v Royal Insurance Co Ltd [1938] AC 586... 5.2
Berger & Light Diffusers Pty Ltd v Pollock [1973] 2 Lloyd's Rep 442...... 9.45; 11.6, 11.19

PARA

Berry Trade Ltd v Moussavi (No 3) [2003] EWCA Civ 715, (2003) 100 (29) LSG
    36, (2003) 147 SJLB 625 .... 9.38
Beursgracht, The. *See* Glencore International AG v Ryan
Biggar v Rock Life Assurance Co [1902] 1 KB 516 .... 11.15; 16.6
Birkett v Hayes [1982] 1 WLR 816, [1982] 2 All ER 70, (1982) 126 SJ 399 .... 9.45
Birrell v Dryer (1883-84) 9 App Cas 345, (1884) 11 R (HL) 41 .... 3.15, 3.16, 3.18,
    3.19, 3.23
Bisset v Wilkinson [1927] AC 177 .... 11.22
Black v Sumitomo Corpn [2001] EWCA Civ 1819, [2001] 1 WLR 1562 .... 9.22
Blackburn, Low & Co v Haslam (1888) 21 QBD 144 .... 11.13; 16.6
Blackburn, Low & Co v Vigors (1887) 12 App Cas 531 .... 11.13
Blackburn Rovers Football & Athletic Club plc v Avon Insurance plc [2005] EWCA
    Civ 423, [2005] 1 CLC 554, [2005] Lloyd's Rep IR 447 .... 4.6
Black King Shipping Corpn v Massie (The Litsion Pride) [1985] 1 Lloyd's Rep 437,
    (1984) 134 NLJ 887 .... 2.3; 3.16; 8.4; 11.4, 11.18,
    11.30, 11.52, 11.63
Boag v Standard Marine Insurance Co Ltd [1937] 2 KB 113, (1937) 57 Ll L
    Rep 83 .... 12.3, 12.6
Board of Trade v Hain Steamship Co Ltd [1929] AC 534, (1929) 34 Ll L
    Rep 197 .... 4.3, 4.11
Boggan v Motor Union Insurance Co (1923) 16 Ll L Rep 64 .... 5.1
Boiler Inspection & Insurance Co of Canada v Sherwin-Williams Co of Canada Ltd
    [1951] AC 319, [1951] 1 Lloyd's Rep 91, [1951] 1 TLR 497 .... 4.2
Bollom (JW) & Co Ltd v Byas Moseley & Co Ltd [2000] Lloyd's Rep IR 136,
    [1999] Lloyd's Rep PN 598 .... 16.20, 16.21, 16.33, 16.34,
    16.35, 16.38, 16.44
Bolton Metropolitan Borough Council v Municipal Mutual Insurance Ltd [2006]
    EWCA Civ 50, [2006] 1 WLR 1492, [2006] 1 CLC 242 .... 7.21; 11.63; 13.4
Bond Air Services Ltd v Hill [1955] 2 QB 417, [1955] 2 All ER 476 .... 3.5; 5.1
Bonner v Cox [2005] EWCA Civ 1512, [2006] 1 All ER (Comm) 565, [2006]
    Lloyd's Rep 152 .... 3.2; 11.7
Boss v Kingston [1963] 1 WLR 99, [1963] 1 All ER 177, [1962] 2 Lloyd's
    Rep 431 .... 2.15
Bovis Construction Ltd v Commercial Union Assurance Co plc [2001] 1 Lloyd's
    Rep 416, [2002] TCLR 11, [2001] Lloyd's Rep IR 321 .... 13.1, 13.9, 13.10
Bradburn v Great Western Railway Co (1874) LR 10 Ex Ch 1 .... 12.1
Bradford & Bingley plc v Rashid [2006] UKHL 37, [2006] 1 WLR 2066, [2006]
    4 All ER 705 .... 9.38
Bradley v Eagle Star Insurance Co Ltd [1989] AC 957, [1989] 1 All ER 961 ...... 8.11, 8.12;
    9.40; 11.60
Bradley & Essex & Suffolk Accident Indemnity Society, Re [1912] 1 KB 415 .... 3.5, 3.19;
    7.1, 7.4
Braganza v BP Shipping Ltd [2015] UKSC 17, [2015] 1 WLR 1661, [2015] 4 All
    ER 639 .... 5.4; 8.9; 14.4; 17.12
Brennan v Bolt Burdon [2004] EWCA Civ 1017, [2005] QB 303 .... 8.15
Brice v JH Wackerbarth (Australasia) Pty Ltd [1974] 2 Lloyd's Rep 274 .... 2.24; 9.40
Brimnes, The [1975] QB 929 .... 7.13
Bristol & West plc v Bhadresa (No 2) [1999] CPLR 209, [1999] 1 Lloyd's Rep
    IR 138, [1999] Lloyd's Rep PN 11 .... 9.46
Bristol & West Building Society plc v Mothew (t/a Stapley & Co) [1998] 9 Ch 1,
    [1996] 4 All RR 698 .... 16.10
Bristol Alliance Ltd Partnership v Williams [2011] EWHC 1657 (QB), [2011] 2 All
    ER (Comm) 1113, [2012] RTR 9 .... 5.2

PARA

Britain Steamship Co Ltd v R [1921] 1 AC 99, (1920) 4 Ll L Rep 245 .... 4.12
British & Foreign Marine Insurance Co Ltd v Sanday [1916] 1 AC 650 .... 4.2
British & Foreign Marine Insurance Co Ltd v Wilson Shipping Co Ltd [1921] 1 AC
   188, (1920) 4 Ll L Rep 371 .... 6.10
British Citizens Assurance Co v L Woolland & Co (1921) 8 Ll L Rep 89 .... 16.38
British Equitable Assurance Co Ltd v Baily [1906] AC 35 .... 3.12, 3.32
British Waterways v Royal & Sun Alliance Insurance plc [2012] EWHC 460
   (Comm), [2012] Lloyd's Rep IR 562 .... 4.4
Brit Syndicates Ltd v Italaudit SpA (in liquidation) (formerly Grant Thornton
   International SpA) [2006] EWCA Civ 1661, [2007] 1 All ER (Comm) 785,
   [2007] 1 Lloyd's Rep 329 .... 2.2
Brit Syndicates Ltd v Italaudit SpA (formally Grant Thornton SpA) [2008] UKHL
   18, [2008] 2 All ER 1140, [2008] Lloyd's Rep IR 601 .... 3.4, 3.7; 11.16
Brit UW Ltd v F & B Trenchless Solutions Ltd [2015] EWHC 2237 (Comm), [2016]
   Lloyd's Rep IR 69 .... 8.4; 11.7
Broad & Montague Ltd v South East Lancashire Insurance Co Ltd (1931) 40 Ll
   L Rep 328 .... 11.13; 16.6
Brocklesby v Armitage & Guest [2002] 1 WLR 598, [2001] 1 All ER 172, [1999]
   Lloyd's Rep PN 888 .... 16.31
Brook v Trafalgar Insurance Co Ltd (1946) 79 Ll L Rep 365 .... 7.12; 11.63; 16.4
Brotherton v Aseguradora Colseguros SA [2003] EWCA Civ 705, [2003] 2 All ER
   (Comm) 298, [2003] Lloyd's Rep IR 746 .... 11.6, 11.30
Brown & Davis Ltd v Galbraith [1972] 1 WLR 997, CA [1972] 3 All ER 31, CA
   [1972] 2 Loyd's Rep 1 .... 8.14
Brown v GIO Insurance Ltd [1998] CLC 650, [1998] Lloyd's Rep IR 201, (1998) 95
   (9) LSG 29 .... 4.1; 5.4; 6.9; 17.12
Brown v Guardian Royal Exchange Assurance plc [1994] 2 Lloyd's Rep 325,
   (1994) 91 (9) LSG 40, (1994) 138 SJLB 35 .... 9.33
Brown v Raphael [1958] Ch 636, [1958] 2 All ER 79 .... 11.22
Brown-Quinn v Equity Syndicate Management Ltd [2011] EWHC 2661 (Comm),
   [2012] 1 All ER 778, [2013] 1 WLR 1740 .... 17.8
Bunga Melati Dua, The. *See* Masefield AG v Amlin Corporate Member Ltd
Bunney v Burns Anderson plc [2007] EWHC 1240 (Ch), [2008] Bus LR 22, [2008]
   Lloyd's Rep IR 198 .... 10.17
Burnand v Rodocanachi (1881-82) 7 App Cas 333 .... 12.13
Burnell v British Transport Commission [1956] 1 QB 187, [1955] 3 All ER 822 .... 9.33
Buttes Gas & Oil Co v Hammer (No 3) [1981] QB 223, [1980] 3 All ER 475 ..... 9.25, 9.31,
   9.32, 9.34

C

CGU International plc v AstraZeneca Insurance Co Ltd [2006] EWCA Civ 1340,
   [2007] Bus LR 162, [2007] 1 Lloyd's Rep 142 .... 9.9; 10.11
CVG Siderurgicia de Orinoco SA v London Steamship Owners' Mutual Insurance
   Assocation Ltd (The Vainqueur José) [1979] 1 Lloyd's Rep 557 .... 2.21; 5.4;
   7.5, 7.11, 7.11, 7.12
Caffin v Aldridge [1895] 2 QB 648 .... 3.16
Caird v Moss (1886) LR 33 Ch D 22 .... 3.34
Calcraft v Gest [1898] 1 QB 759 .... 9.32, 9.33
Caledonia North Sea Ltd v British Telcommunications plc [2002] UKHL 4, [2002]
   1 All ER (Comm) 321, [2002] 1 Lloyd's Rep 553 .... 12.14; 13.13
Calf, Re [1920] 2 KB 366, (1920) 2 Ll L Rep 304 .... 3.17

PARA

Callaghan (t/a Stage 3 Discotheque) v Thompson [2000] CLC 360, [2000] Lloyd's
Rep IR 125 .... 9.16; 11.58, 11.60, 11.63; 16.3,
16.4, 16.5, 16.10, 16.40
Camerata Property Inc v Credit Suisse Securities (Europe) Ltd [2012] EWHC 7
(Comm), [2012] PNLR 15 .... 8.2
Campbell & Fell v United Kingdom (Series A/80) (1984) 7 EHRR 165 .... 9.12
Canada Rice Mills Ltd v Union Marine & General Insurance Co Ltd [1941] AC 55,
[1940] 4 All ER 169, (1940) 67 Ll L Rep 549.. 4.11
Canelhas Comercio Importacao e Exportacao Ltd v Wooldridge [2004] EWCA Civ
984, [2005] 1 All ER (Comm) 43, [2004] 1 Lloyd's Rep IR 915 .... 3.18, 3.22
Canning v Farquhar (1885-86) LR 16 QBD 727 .... 3.3; 11.18
Caparo Industries plc v Dickman [1990] 2 AC 605, [1990] 1 All ER 568 .... 16.12, 16.33
Capel Cure Myers Capital Management Ltd v McCarthy [1995] LRLR 498 ... 4.3; 8.9, 8.11
Capricom, The. *See* Cepheus Shipping Corpn v Guardian Royal Exchange Assurance plc
Carpenter v Ebblewhite [1939] 1 KB 347, (1938) 62 Ll L Rep 1 .... 2.24; 9.40
Carr & Sun Fire Insurance Co, Re (1897) 13 TLR 186.................................... 2.13; 11.52
Carreras Ltd v Cunard Steamship Co Ltd [1918] 1 KB 118.................................... 6.10
Carter v Boehm (1766) 3 Burr 1905, 97 ER 1162... 11.4, 11.5, 11.6
Cartledge v E Jopling & Sons Ltd [1963] AC 758, [1963] 1 All ER 341 .... 11.59
Cartwright v MacCormack [1963] 1 WLR 18, [1963] 1 All ER 11, [1962] 2 Lloyd's
Rep 328 .... 3.2
Carvill America Inc v Camperdown UK Ltd [2005] EWCA Civ 645, [2005] 2
Lloyd's Rep 457, [2005] 1 CLC 845 .... 16.3
Castellain v Preston (1882–83) LR 11 QBD 380 .... 2.8; 6.3; 12.1, 12.3, 12.6, 12.13
Castle Insurance Co Ltd v Hong Kong Islands Shipping Co Ltd (The Potoi Chau)
[1984] AC 226, [1983] 3 WLR 524, [1983] 3 All ER 706.............................. 11.60
Catalyst Investment Group Ltd v Lewinsohn [2009] EWHC 1964 (Ch), [2010] Ch
218, [2010] 2 WLR 839 .... 15.9
Cathay Pacific Airways Ltd v Nation Life & General Assurance Co Ltd [1966]
2 Lloyd's Rep 179, (1966) 110 SJ 583 .... 17.3, 17.14
Caudle v Sharp [1995] LRLR 433, [1995] CLC 642, [1995] 4 Re LR 389 .... 6.9
Cave v Robinson Jarvis & Rolf [2002] UKHL 18, [2003] 1 AC 384.............. 11.57; 16.31
Cavendish Square Holding BV v El Makdessi [2015] UKSC 67, [2015] 3 WLR
1373, [2016] 1 Lloyd's Rep 55 .... 3.20
Cawley v National Employers' Accident & General Assurance Association (1885)
1 TLR 255 .... 7.16
Cendor Mopu, The. *See* Global Process Systems
Central Trading & Exports Ltd v Fioralba Shipping Co (The Kalisti) [2014] EWHC
2397 (Comm), [2014] 2 Lloyd's Rep 449... 10.10
Centre Reinsurance International Co v Freakley [2006] UKHL 45, [2007] Lloyd's
Rep IR 32, [2005] EWCA Civ 115, [2005] 2 All ER (Comm) 65, [2005]
1 Lloyd's Rep IR 303 .... 2.25, 2.26
Cepheus Shipping Corpn v Guardian Royal Exchange Assurance plc (The Capricorn)
[1995] 1 Lloyd's Rep 622 .... 11.55
Cetelem SA v Roust Holdings Ltd [2005] EWCA Civ 618, [2005] 1 WLR 3555,
[2005] 4 All ER 52.. 10.8
Challinor v Juliet Bellis & Co [2013] EWHC 620 (Ch).. 9.45
Chandris v Argo Insurance Co Ltd [1963] 2 Lloyd's Rep 65, (1963)
107 SJ 575... 9.41; 11.58, 11.59, 11.60
Chandris v Isbrandtsen-Moller Co Inc [1951] 1 KB 240, [1950] 2 All ER 618,
(1950) 84 Ll L Rep 347 .... 3.21
Chapman (TGA) Ltd v Christopher [1998] 1 WLR 12, [1998] 2 All ER 873, [1997]
CLC 1306.. 9.46

PARA

Chapman, Assignees of Richardson, a Bankrupt v Walton (1833) 10 Bing 57, 131
ER 826 .... 16.16, 16.17, 16.21
Chappell v United Kingdom (Series A/152-A) (1989) 12 EHRR 1, [1989]
1 FSR 617 .... 9.7
Chartbrook Ltd v Persimmon Homes Ltd [2009] UKHL 38, [2009] 1
AC 1101 .... 3.15, 3.16, 3.29, 3.30, 3.31
Churchill Car Insurance v Kelly [2006] EWHC 18 (QB), [2007] RTR 26 .... 11.49
Charlton v Fisher [2001] EWCA Civ 112, [2002] QB 578, [2001] 3 WLR 1435..... 2.25; 5.2
Charman v Guardian Royal Exchange Assurance plc [1992] 2 Lloyd's Rep 607..... 14.2, 14.3
Charnock v Liverpool Corpn [1968] 1 WLR 1498, [1968] 3 All ER 473, [1968]
2 Lloyd's Rep 113 .... 8.14
Charter Reinsurance Co Ltd (in liquidation) v Fagan [1997] AC 313, [1996] 3 All
ER 46 .... 3.14, 3.15, 3.16; 14.2, 14.5
Cherry Ltd v Allied Insurance Brokers Ltd [1978] 1 Lloyd's Rep 274 .... 16.20, 16.34
Chubb Insurance Co of Europe SA v Davies [2004] EWHC 2138 (Comm), [2004]
2 All ER (Comm) 827, [2005] Lloyd's Rep IR 1 .... 9.47
Citibank NA v Excess Insurance Co Ltd (t/a ITT London & Edinburgh) [1999] CLC
120, [1999] Lloyd's Rep IR 122 .... 6.9; 9.46
City & Westminster Properties (1934) Ltd v Mudd [1959] Ch 129, [1958] 2 All
ER 733 .... 3.16
Clark v In Focus Asset Management & Tax Solutions Ltd [2014] EWCA Civ 118,
[2014] 1 WLR 2502, [2014] 3 All ER 313 .... 10.17
Cleland v London General Insurance Co Ltd (1935) 51 Ll L Rep 156 .... 11.15
Clothing Management Technology Ltd v Beazley Solutions Ltd [2012] EWHC 727
(QB), [2012] Lloyd's Rep IR 571, [2012] Lloyd's Rep IR 329 .... 4.10; 6.3
Coburn v Colledge [1897] 1 QB 702 .... 11.58
Cock, Russell & Co v Bray, Gibb & Co Ltd (1920) 3 Ll L Rep 71 .... 16.18
Coleman's Depositories Ltd & Health Assurance Association's Arbitration, Re
[1907] 2 KB 798 .... 3.15; 7.1, 7.14, 7.15, 7.19, 7.21
Coles v Hetherton [2013] EWCA Civ 1704,[2015] 1 WLR 160, [2014] Lloyd's Rep
IR 367 .... 12.6
Collingridge v Royal Exchange Assurance Corpn (1877-78) 3 QBD 173 .... 12.1
Colonial Fire & General Insurance Co Ltd v Chung (unreported, 13 December
2000) 7.20
Colonia Versicherung AG v Amoco Oil Co (The Wind Star) [1997] 1 Lloyd's Rep
261, [19997] CLC 454, [1997] 6 Re LR 86 .... 12.13
Comninos v United Kingdom (1996) 23 EHRR CD 165 .... 9.9
Commission for the New Towns v Cooper (GB) Ltd [1995] Ch 259, [1995] 2 All
ER 929 .... 3.35
Compania Merabella San Nicholas SA, Re [1973] Ch 75, [1972] 3 All ER 448 ...... 2.19
Connelly v RTZ Corpn plc (No 2) [1998] AC 854, [1997] 4 All ER 335 .... 15.13
Co-operative Retail Services Ltd v Taylor Young Partnership Ltd [2002] UKHL 17,
[2002] QB 1419, [2002] 1 All ER (Comm) 918 .... 12.4
Cooter & Green Ltd v Tyrell [1962] 2 Lloyd's Rep 377 .... 8.14
Commercial Union Assurance Co v Lister (1873-74) LR 9 Ch App 483 .... 12.3, 12.8
Commercial Union Assurance Co Ltd v Hayden [1977] QB 804, [1977] 1 Lloyd's
Rep 1 .... 13.5, 13.6
Commercial Union Insurance Co plc v Mander [1996] 2 Lloyd's Rep 640, [1997]
CLC 32 .... 9.31
Commonwealth Insurance Co of Vancouver v Groupe Sprinks SA [1983] 1 Lloyd's
Rep 67 .... 16.19
Commonwealth of Australia v Verwayen (1990) 170 CLR 394 .... 11.62

PARA

Comptoir Commercial Anversois & Power, Son & Co, Arbitration between,
Re [1920] 1 KB 868, (1919) 1 Ll L Rep 266 .... 3.27
Condogianis v Guardian Assurance Co Ltd [1921] 2 AC 125, (1921) 7 Ll L
Rep 155 .... 11.15, 11.16, 11.28
Connecticut Mutual Life Insurance Co of Hertford v Moore (1881) LR 6
HL 644 .... 11.15, 11.16
Cook v Financial Insurance Co Ltd [1998] 1 WLR 1765, [1999] Lloyd's Rep IR 1,
(1999) 46 BMLR 1 .... 17.13
Container Transport International Inc v Oceanus Mutual Underwriting Association
(Bermuda) Ltd (No 1) [1984] 1 Lloyd's Rep 476 .... 11.6, 11.8, 11.14,
11.15, 11.63
Corcos v De Rougemont (1925) 23 Ll L Rep 164 .... 11.7, 11.15
Cormack v Excess Insurance Co Ltd [2000] CPLR 358, [2000] CLC 1039, [2002]
Lloyd's Rep IR 398 .... 2.24; 9.46
Cornhill Insurance Co Ltd v Assenheim (1937) 58 Ll L Rep 27 .... 11.30, 11.33
Cornish v Accident Insurance Co (1889) LR 23 QBD 453 .... 3.14, 3.19
Coromin Ltd v AXA Re [2007] EWHC 2818 (Comm), [2008] Lloyd's
Rep IR 467 .... 17.5
Countrywise Assured Group plc v Marshall [2002] EWHC 2082 (Comm), [2003]
1 All ER (Comm) 237, [2003] Lloyd's Rep IR 195 .... 6.9
County Personnel (Employment Agency) Ltd v Alan R Pulver & Co [1987] 1 WLR
916, [1987] 1 All ER 289, [1986] 2 EGLR 246 .... 16.33
Cousins (H) & Co Ltd v D & C Carriers Ltd [1971] 2 QB 230, [1971] 1 All ER 55
.... 9.45; 12.10
Coven SpA v Hong Kong Chinese Insurance Co [1999] Lloyd's Rep IR 565 .... 3.14
Cox v Bankside Members Agency Ltd [1995] 2 Lloyd's Rep 437, [1995]
CLC 671 .... 2.3, 2.20, 2.22, 2.24, 2.25;
6.9; 9.13, 9.15; 12.3
Cox v Orion Insurance Co Ltd [1982] RTR 1 .... 7.20
Coxe v Employers' Liability Assurance Corpn Ltd [1916] 2 KB 629 .... 4.1, 4.2, 4.4, 4.5
Crane v Hegeman-Harris Co Inc [1971] 1 WLR 1390, [1939] 1 All ER 662 .... 3.30, 3.31,
3.33, 3.34
Crédit Lyonnais v New Hampshire Insurance Co [1997] 2 Lloyd's Rep 1, [1997]
CLC 909, [1997] 2 CMLR 610 .... 15.4, 15.5
Crema v Cenkos Securities plc [2010] EWCA Civ 1444, [2011] 1 WLR 2066,
[2011] 2 All ER (Comm) 676 .... 3.16
Crocker, Re [1936] Ch 696 .... 9.16
Cutts v Head [1984] Ch 290, [1984] 1 All ER 597 .... 9.35, 9.36

D

D (a child) (care proceedings: legal privilege), Re [2011] EWCA Civ 684, [2011] 4
All ER 434, [2011] 2 FLR 1183 .... 9.33
DC, HS & AD v United Kingdom (application 39031/97) [2000] BCC 710 .... 9.6
Daintrey, Re, ex p Holt [1893] 2 QB 116 .... 9.38
Dalby v India & London Life Assurance Co (1854) 15 CB 365, 139 ER 465 .... 2.5
Dallah Real Estate & Tourism Holding Co v Ministry of Religious Affairs of
the Government of Pakistan [2010] UKSC 46, [2011] 1 AC 763, [2010]
3 WLR 1472 .... 10.10
Dane v Mortgage Insurance Corpn Ltd [1894] 1 QB 54 .... 6.11
Danepoint Ltd v Underwriting Insurance Ltd [2005] EWHC 2318 (TCC), [2006]
Lloyd's Rep IR 429 .... 11.49
Davies v National Fire & Marine Insurance Co of New Zealand [1891]
AC 485 .... 7.11; 11.29

PARA

Dawsons Ltd v Bonnin [1922] 2 AC 413, (1922) 12 Ll L Rep 237, 1922 SC
(HL) 156.. 11.16, 11.24

Daylam, The. *See* Roar Marine Ltd v Bimeh Iran Insurance Co

Decorum Investments Ltd v Atkin (The Elena G) [2001] 2 Lloyd's Rep 378, [2002]
Lloyd's Rep IR 450.. 11.6, 11.14

De Laselle v Guildford [1901] 2 KB 215 .... 3.16

Deeny v Gooda Walker Ltd (No 4) [1996] LRLR 168, [1995] STC 696 .... 9.45

Deepak Fertilisers & Petrochemicals Corpn v ICI Chemicals & Polymers Ltd [1999]
1 All ER (Comm) 69, [1999] 1 Lloyd's Rep 387, [1999] BLR 41 .... 2.10

De Maurier (Jewels) Ltd v Bastion Insurance Co Ltd [1967] 2 Lloyd's Rep 550,
(1967) 117 NLJ 1112... 3.19; 11.21, 11.63

Demetra K, The. *See* Kiriacoulis Lines SA

Denby v English & Scottish Maritime Insurance Co Ltd [1998] CLC 760, [1998]
Lloyd's Rep IR 343.. 3.3, 3.19

Dent v Blackmore (1927-28) 29 Ll L Rep 9............................ 11.15, 11.19, 11.33

Derby Resources AG v Blue Corinth Marine Co Ltd (No 2) (The Athenian Harmony)
(No 2) [1998] 2 Lloyd's Rep 425... 9.45

Derry v Peek (1889) 14 App Cas 337, (1889) 5 TLR 625 .... 11.27, 11.50, 11.54

De Souza v Home & Overseas Insurance Co Ltd [1995] LRLR 453....................... 17.2

Deutsche Genossenschaftsbank v Burnhope [1995] 1 WLR 1580, [1995] 4 All ER
717, [1996] 1 Lloyd's Rep 113 .... 3.16, 3.22

Deutsche Morgan Grenfell Group plc v IRC [2006] UKHL 49, [2007] 1 AC 558 ... 8.15

Devco Holder Ltd v Legal & General Assurance Society Ltd [1993] 2 Lloyd's Rep
567.. 4.11; 5.2

Dhak v Insurance Co of North America (UK) Ltd [1996] 1 WLR 936, [1996] 2 All
ER 609, [1996] 1 Lloyd's Rep 632 .... 17.2

Diab v Regent Insurance Co Ltd [2006] UKPC 29, [2007] Bus LR 915, [2006]
Lloyd's Rep IR 779.. 3.5; 7.16, 7.21; 11.4

Digital Satellite Warranty Cover Ltd v Financial Services Authority [2013] UKSC 7,
[2013] 1 WLR 605, [2013] Lloyd's Rep IR 236... 1.1

Direct Line Insurance v Khan [2001] EWCA Civ 1794, [2002] Lloyd's
Rep IR 364 .... 11.49, 11.52

Director General of Fair Trading v First National Bank plc [2001] UKHL 52, [2002]
1 AC 481, [2001] 3 WLR 1297... 3.20

Director General of Fair Trading v Proprietary Association of Great Britain [2001] 1
WLR 700, [2001] UKCLR 550, [2001] ICR 564 .... 9.12

Distillers Co Bio Chemicals (Australia) Pty Ltd v Ajax (Insurance) Co Ltd (1974)
130 CLR 1... 6.9

Dobson v General Accident Fire & Life Assurance Corpn plc [1990] 1 QB 274,
[1989] 3 WLR 1066, [1989] 3 All ER 927 .... 3.22

Dodd Properties (Kent) Ltd v Canterbury City Council [1980] 1 WLR 433, [1980] 1
All ER 928, 13 BLR 45... 16.33

Dodson v Peter H Dodson Insurance Services [2001] 1 WLR 1012, [2001] 3 All ER
75, [2001] 1 All ER (Comm) 300 .... 2.15; 3.13, 3.16, 3.17, 3.19; 16.16, 16.21

Doheny v New India Assurance Co Ltd [2004] EWCA Civ 1705, [2005] 1 All ER
(Comm) 382, [2005] Lloyd's Rep IR 251... 11.15

Dominator, The. *See* Dreyfus (Louis) & Cie v Parnaso Cie Naviera SA

Dora, The. *See* Inversiones Manria SA

Dornoch Ltd v Mauritius Union Assurance Co Ltd (No 2) [2007] EWHC 155
(Comm), [2007] Lloyd's Rep IR 350.. 6.9

Dornoch Ltd v Westminster International BV [2009] EWHC 1782 (Admlty), [2009]
2 Lloyd's Rep 420, [2009] 2 CLC 226 .... 6.11; 11.63

PARA

Drake Insurance plc (in provisional liquidation) v Provident Insurance plc [2003]
  EWCA Civ 1834, [2004] QB 601, [2004] 1 Lloyd's Rep 268............. 11.4, 11.6, 11.7,
                                                                    11.15; 13.1, 13.5, 13.9; 16.4
Dreyfus (Louis) & Cie v Parnaso Cia Naviera SA (The Dominator) [1959] 1 QB
  498, [1959] 1 All ER 502.. 3.16
Dubai Bank Ltd v Galadari [1990] Ch 98, [1989] 3 WLR 1044, [1989] 3 All
  ER 769 .... 9.32
Duchess of Argyll v Beuselinck [1972] 2 Lloyd's Rep 172 .... 16.13
Dudgeon v Pembroke (1876-77) LR 2 App Cas 284.. 3.24; 4.1, 4.2
Dufourcet & Co v Bishop (1886) LR 18 QBD 373 .... 12.6, 12.8
Dunbar (Alfred James) v A & B Painters Ltd & Economic Insurance Co Ltd &
  Whitehouse & Co [1985] 2 Lloyd's Rep 616, [1986] 2 Lloyd's Rep 38 .... 16.19,
                                                                    16.34, 16.35
Dunlop Haywards (DHL) Ltd (formerly Dunlop Heywood Lorenz Ltd) (in
  liquidation) v Barbon Insurance Group Ltd (formerly Erinaceous Insurance
  Services Ltd (formerly Hanover Park Commercial Ltd)) [2009] EWHC 2900
  (Comm), [2010] Lloyd's Rep IR 149... 16.9, 16.13
Dunlop Haywards (DHL) Ltd (formerly Dunlop Heywod Lorenz Ltd) (in liquidation)
  v Barbon Insurance Group Ltd (formerly Erinaceous Insurance Services Ltd
  (formerly Hanover Park Commercial Ltd)) [2009] EWCA Civ 354, [2009]
  Lloyd's Rep IR 464... 3.29, 3.30; 9.47
Dunn (T) v WC Campbell (1920) 4 Ll L Rep 36.. 3.19
Dunn v Ocean Accident & Guarantee Corpn Ltd (1933) 47 Ll L Rep 129 .... 16.6
Duus Brown & Co v Binning (1906) 11 Com Cas 190 .... 12.8
Dymocks Franchise Systems (NSW) Pty Ltd v Todd [2004] UKPC 39, [2004] 1
  WLR 2807, [2005] 4 All ER 195 .... 9.46

E

E I Du Pont de Nemours & Co v Agnew [1987] 2 Lloyd's Rep 585, [1987] 2 FTLR
  487, [1987] FSR 376... 9.40
Eagle Star Insurance Co Ltd v Cresswell [2004] EWCA Civ 602, [2004] 2 All ER
  (Comm) 244, [2004] 1 Lloyd's Rep IR 537.................................... 3.5, 3.24; 14.3, 14.4
Eagle Star Insurance Co Ltd v Games Video Co (GVC) SA (The Game Boy)
  [2004] EWHC 15 (Comm), [2004] 1 All ER (Comm) 560, [2004] 1 Lloyd's
  Rep 238 .... 11.49
Eagle Star Insurance Co Ltd v National Westminster Finance Australia Ltd (1985)
  58 ALR 165... 11.7, 11.19, 11.33; 16.3, 16.15,
                                                                    16.17, 16.19, 16.34
Eagle Star Insurance Co Ltd v Provincial Insurance plc [1994] 1 AC 130, [1993]
  3 All ER 1 .... 13.4, 13.9
Eagle, Star & British Dominions Insurance Co Ltd v AV Reiner (1927) 27 Ll L Rep
  173... 3.32, 3.34
Earl v Cantor Fitzgerald International [2000] EWHC 555 (QB)............................... 17.3
Earl v Hector Whaling Ltd [1961] 1 Lloyd's Rep 459, (1961) 105 SJ 321 .... 3.30, 3.33
Ebsworth v Alliance Marine Insurance Co (1873) LR & CP 596 .... 2.10
Economides v Commercial Assurance Co plc [1998] QB 587, [1997] 3 All
  ER 636 .... 11.10, 11.16, 11.22, 11.23
Eddystone Marine Insurance Co, ex p Western Insurance Co, Re [1892]
  2 Ch 423.. 14.2
Edgington v Fitzmaurice (1885) 29 Ch D 459.. 11.6, 11.24
Edney v De Rougemont (1927) 28 Ll L Rep 215... 6.4
Edward Wong Finance Co Ltd v Johnson Stokes & Master [1984] AC 296, (1983)
  80 LSG 3163 .... 16.13

PARA

El Ajou v Dollar Land Holdings plc (No 1) [1994] 2 All ER 685, [1994] BCC 143,
[1994] 1 BCLC 464 .... 11.13
Elcock v Thomson [1949] 2 KB 755, [1949] 2 All ER 381, (1948-49) 82 Ll L
Rep 892 .... 6.3
Emmott v Michael Wilson & Partners Ltd [2008] EWCA Civ 184, [2008] Bus LR
1361, [2008] 1 Lloyd's Rep 616 .... 10.4
Encia Remediation Ltd v Canopius Managing Agents Ltd [2007] EWHC 916
(Comm), [2007] 2 All ER (Comm) 947, [2008] Lloyd's Rep IR 79 .... 3.16, 3.29
Engel v Lancashire & General Assurance Co Ltd (1925) 21 Ll L R 327 .... 2.10
England v Guardian Insurance Ltd [1999] 2 All ER (Comm) 481, [2000] Lloyd's
Rep IR 404 .... 6.6; 12.8
English Scottish Mercantile Investment Co Ltd v Brunton [1892] 2 QB 700 .... 2.13
Enterprise Oil Ltd v Strand Insurance Co Ltd [2006] EWHC 58 (Comm), [2006]
1 Lloyd's Rep 500, [2006] 1 CLC 33 .... 8.12
Equitable Fire & Accident Office Ltd v Ching Wo Hong [1907] AC 96 .... 13.7
Equitable Trust Co of New York v Whittaker (1923-24) 17 Ll L Rep 153 .... 6.9
Equitas Ltd v Walsham Bros & Co Ltd [2013] EWHC 3264 (Comm), [2014] Lloyd's
Rep IR 398, [2014] PNLR 8 .... 2.13; 9.45
Equity Synidcate Management Ltd v GlaxoSmithKline plc [2015] EWHC 2163
(Comm), [2016] Lloyd's Rep IR 155 .... 3.29, 3.31
Eschig v UNIQA Sachversicherung AG (Case C-199/08) [2010] Bus LR 1404,
[2010] 1 All ER (Comm) 576, [2010] Lloyd's Rep IR 552 .... 17.8
Esso Burnica, The. *See* Esso Petroleum Co Ltd
Esso Petroleum Co Ltd v Hall Russell & Co Ltd (The Esso Bernicia) [1989] AC 643,
[1989] 1 All ER 37 .... 12.8
Etablissements Levy v Adderley Navigation Co Panama SA (The Olympic Pride)
[1980] 2 Lloyd's Rep 67 .... 3.31, 3.33, 3.35
Etherington & Lancashire & Yorkshire Accident Insurance Co's Arbitration, Re
[1909] 1 KB 591 .... 3.19; 4.2, 4.11, 4.12
Eurodale Manufacturing Ltd (t/a Connekt Cellular Communications) v Ecclesiastical
Insurance Office plc [2002] EWHC 697 (QB) 3.24
Euro-Diam Ltd v Bathurst [1990] 1 QB 1, [1988] 2 All ER 23 .... 3.27
Eurokey Recycling Ltd v Giles Insurance Brokers Ltd [2014] EWHC 2989 (Comm),
[2015] Lloyd's Rep IR 225 .... 16.21, 16.23, 16.38
European International Reinsurance Co Ltd v Curzon Insurance Ltd [2003] EWCA
Civ 1074, [2003] Lloyd's Rep IR 793, (2003) 100 (36) LSG 43 .... 16.5, 16.8
Evans v Employers' Mutual Insurance Association Ltd [1936] 1 KB 505, [1935] All
ER Rep 659, (1935) 52 Ll L Rep 51 .... 11.63
Everett v Hogg, Robinson & Gardner Mountain (Insurance) Ltd [1973] 2 Lloyd's
Rep 217 .... 16.19, 16.35
Ewing v United Kingdom (No 14720/89) (Comm Dec 6.5.89) 9.7
Exchange Theatre Ltd v Iron Trade Mutual Insurance Co Ltd [1984] 1 Lloyd's
Rep 149 .... 11.18
Expandable Ltd v Rubin [2008] EWCA Civ 59, [2008] 1 WLR 1099, [2008] CP
Rep 22 .... 9.20

F

FBTO Schadeberzeringen NV v Odenbreit (Case C-463/06) [2008] Lloyd's Rep
IR 354 .... 15.9
FNCB Ltd (formerly First International Commercial Bank plc) v Barnet Devanney
(Harrow) Ltd (formerly Barnet Devanney & Co Ltd) [1999] 2 All ER (Comm)
233, [1999] Lloyd's Rep IR 459, [1999] Lloyd's Rep PN 908 .... 16.16, 16.21

PARA

Fairchild v Glenhaven Funeral Services Ltd [2002] UKHL 22, [2003] 1 AC 32,
[2002] 3 WLR 89 .... 13.14

Family Housing Association (Manchester) Ltd v Michael Hyde & Partners [1993]
1 WLR 354, [1993] 2 All ER 567, [1993] 2 EGLR 239 .... 9.38

Fanti, The. *See* Firma C-Trade SA

Faraday Capital Ltd v Copenhagen Reinsurance Co Ltd [2006] EWHC 1474
(Comm), [2007] Lloyd's Rep IR 23 .... 14.2

Faraday Rensurance Co Ltd v Howden North America Inc [2011] EWHC
2837 (Comm) 15.13

Farmers' Co-operative Ltd v National Benefit Assurance Co Ltd (1922) 13 Ll L
Rep 417 .... 3.24

Farrell v Federated Employers Insurance Association Ltd [1970] 1 WLR 1400,
[1970] 3 All ER 632, [1970] 2 Lloyd's Rep 170 .... 2.25; 7.5, 7.14

Feasey v Sun Life Assurance Corpn of Canada [2003] EWCA Civ 885, [2003] 2 All
ER (Comm) 587, [2003] 1 Lloyd's Rep IR 637 .... 2.4, 2.5, 2.6, 2.7,
2.10; 11.55

Federal-Mogul Asbestos Personal Injury Trust v Federal-Mogul Ltd (formerly T &
N plc) [2014] EWHC 2002 (Comm), [2014] Lloyd's Rep IR 671 .... 9.42

Ferexpo AG v Gilson Investments Ltd [2012] EWHC 721 (Comm), [2012] 1 Lloyd's
Rep 588, [2012] 1 CLC 645 .... 15.9

Fidelity & Casualty Co of New York v Mitchell [1917] AC 592 .... 4.2, 4.6

Filiatra Legacy, The. *See* Anonima Petroli Italiana SpA & Neste Oy v Marlucidez
Armadora SpA

Financial Services Compensation Scheme Ltd v Lamell (Insurances) Ltd (in
liquidation) [2005] EWCA Civ 1408, [2006] QB 808, [2006] 2 WLR 751 ...... 2.24, 2.27

Firma C-Trade SA v Newcastle P & I Association (The Fanti) [1991] 2 AC 1, [1990]
2 All ER 705 .... 2.25; 7.16; 9.41, 9.42; 11.60

Fir Shipping Co Ltd v Kawasaki Kisen Kaisha Ltd (The Hongkong Fir) [1962] 2 QB
26, [1962] 1 All ER 474 .... 3.4

First Gulf Bank v Wachovia Bank National Association (formerly First Union
National Bank) [2005] EWHC 2827 (Comm) 9.22

First National Commercial Bank plc v Humberts [1995] 2 All ER 673, [1996] 5
Bank LR 177, 73 BLR 90 .... 16.29

First National Reinsurance Co v Greenfield [1921] 2 KB 260, (1920) 5 Ll L
Rep 402 .... 11.33

Fisk v Brian Thornhill & Son (a firm) [2007] EWCA Civ 152, [2007] Lloyd's Rep
IR 699, [2007] PNLR 21 .... 16.5, 16.19, 16.20

Flexsys America LP v XL Insurance Co Ltd [2009] EWHC 1115 (Comm), [2009] 1
CLC 754, [2010] Lloyd's Rep IR 132 .... 3.23

Flora v Wakom (Heathrow) Ltd (formerly Abela Airline Catering Ltd) [2006]
EWCA Civ 1103, [2007] 1 WLR 482, [2006] 4 All ER 982 .... 3.8, 3.10; 8.3;
11.4, 11.37, 11.38, 11.39, 11.54

Formica Ltd v Export Credits Guarantee Department [1995] 1 Lloyd's Rep 692,
[1994] CLC 1078 .... 9.13, 9.16, 9.31

Forney v Dominion Insurance Co Ltd [1969] 1 WLR 928, [1969] 3 All ER 831,
[1969] 1 Lloyd's Rep 502 .... 6.9; 8.11; 9.13

Forsikringsaktieselskapet Vesta v Butcher [1986] 2 All ER 488, [1986] 2 Lloyd's
Rep 179 .... 16.4, 16.14, 16.18, 16.26, 16.38

Forsikringsaktieselskapet Vesta v Butcher [1989] AC 852, [1989] 2 WLR 290,
[1989] 1 All ER 402 .... 14.6

Forster v Outred & Co [1982] 1 WLR 86, [1982] 2 All ER 753, (1981) 125
SJ 309 .... 16.29

PARA

Fortisbank SA v Trenwick International Ltd [2005] EWHC 399 (Comm), [2005]
    Lloyd's Rep IR 464.. 9.38; 11.63
Fortress Value Recovery Fund I LLC v Blue Skye Special Opportunities Fund LP
    [2013] EWCA Civ 367, [2013] 1 WLR 3466, [2013] 1 Lloyd's Rep 606........   2.18
Fowler v Scottish Equitable Life Insurance Society (1858) 28 LJ Ch 225............... 3.34, 3.33
Fraser v BN Furman (Productions) Ltd [1967] 1 WLR 898, [1967] 3 All ER 57,
    [1967] 2 Lloyd's Rep 1 .... 4.11; 5.2; 16.35
Frederick E Rose (London) Ltd v William H Pim Junior & Co Ltd [1953] 2 QB 450,
    [1953] 2 All ER 739.. 3.30, 3.31
Friends Provident Life & Pensions Ltd v Sirius International Insurance [2005]
    EWCA Civ 601, [2005] 2 All ER (Comm) 145, [2005] 2 Lloyd's Rep 517......   3.5, 3.9;
                                                                                                        7.6, 7.7, 7.13

G

GE Capital Corporate Finance Group Ltd v Bankers Trust Co [1995] 1 WLR 172,
    [1995] 2 All ER 993, (1994) 91 (37) LSG 50...   9.21
GE Frankona Reinsurance Ltd v CMM Trust No 1400 (The Newfoundland Explorer)
    [2006] EWHC (Admiralty) 429, [2006] 1 All ER (Comm) 665, [2006] Lloyd's
    Rep IR 704 ....   3.6, 3.13
GE Reinsurance Corpn v New Hampshire Insurance Co [2003] EWHC 302, [2004]
    1 Lloyd's Rep IR 404...   3.16
Gagnière (A) & Co Ltd v Eastern Co of Warehouses Insurance & Transport of
    Goods with Advances Ltd (1921) 8 Ll L Rep 365.......................   3.31, 3.32, 3.33, 3.34
Gale v Motor Union Insurance Co [1928] 1 KB 359, (1926) 26 Ll L Rep 65 ....   3.26; 13.3
Game Boy, The. *See* Eagle Star Insurance Co Ltd v Games Video Co (GVC) SA
Galloway v Guardian Royal Exchange (UK) Ltd [1999] Lloyd's Rep IR 209..........   11.51
Gan v Tai Ping (Nos 2 & 3) [2001] EWCA Civ 1047, [2001] 2 All ER (Comm) 299,
    [2001] Lloyd's Rep IR 667 ....   3.5, 3.6, 3.17, 3.19; 5.4; 9.13; 14.3, 14.4, 14.5
Gard Marine & Energy Ltd v China National Chartering Ltd (The Ocean Victory)
    [2015] EWCA Civ 16, [2015] 2 All ER (Comm) 894, , [2015] 1 Lloyd's
    Rep 381 ....   12.4
Garnat Trading & Shipping (Singapore) Pte Ltd v Baominh Insurance Corpn
    [2010] EWHC 2578 (Comm), [2011] 1 All ER (Comm) 573, [2011] 1 Lloyd's
    Rep 589 ....   11.8
Gaunt v British & Foreign Insurance Co Ltd (No 3) [1920] 1 KB 903, (1920) 5 Ll L
    Rep 202 ....   5.1, 5.2
General Accident Fire & Life Assurance Corpn Ltd v JH Minet & Co Ltd (1942) 74
    Ll L Rep 1 ....   16.26
General Accident Fire & Life Assurance Corpn Ltd v Midland Bank Ltd [1940] 2
    KB 388, (1940) 67 Ll L Rep 218.............................   2.3, 2.15; 3.24; 11.30, 11.52; 13.5
General Accident Fire & Life Assurance Corpn Ltd v Tanter (The Zephyr) [1984] 1
    WLR 100, [1984] 1 All ER 35, [1984] 1 Lloyd's Rep 58............................   16.3, 16.11
General Accident Fire & Life Assurance Corpn Ltd v Tanter (The Zephyr) [1985]
    2 Lloyd's Rep 529...   11.6
General Insurance Co of Trieste Ltd (Assicurazioni Generali) v Cory [1897]
    1 QB 335..   13.8
General Motors Ltd v Crowder (1931) 40 Ll L Rep 87...   7.8
General Reinsurance Corpn v Fenna Patria [1983] QB 856, [1983] 2 Lloyd's
    Rep 287 ....   3.3, 3.27
Genesis Housing Association Ltd v Liberty Syndicate Management Ltd
    [2013] EWCA Civ 1173, [2013] Bus LR 1399, [2014] Lloyd's Rep
    IR 318..   1.10; 3.14; 11.16

PARA

Geophysical Service Centre Co v Dowell Schumberger (ME) Inc [2013] EWHC 147
(TCC), 147 Con LR 240 .... 9.5
George Barkes (London) Ltd v LFC (1988) Ltd (t/a LFC Insurance Group) [2000]
PNLR 21 .... 16.34, 16.45
George Hunt Cranes Ltd v Scottish Boiler & General Insurance Co Ltd [2001]
EWCA Civ 1964, [2002] 1 All ER (Comm) 366, [2002] Lloyd's Rep
IR 178... 3.5, 3.17; 7.1, 7.4
Glasgow Assurance Corpn Ltd v Symondson & Co (1911) 16 Comm Cas 109 .... 11.19
Glencore International AG v Alpina Insurance Co Ltd [2003] EWHC 2792, [2004]
1 All ER (Comm) 766, [2004] 1 Lloyd's Rep 111.. 11.21
Glencore International AG v Ryan (The Beursgracht) [2001] EWCA Civ 2051,
[2002] 1 Lloyd's Rep 574, [2002] Lloyd's Rep IR 335 .... 3.9; 6.9
Glengate-KG Properties Ltd v Norwich Union Fire Insurance Society Ltd [1996] 2
All ER 487, [1996] 1 Lloyd's Rep 614, [1996] CLC 676................................ 17.5
Glen Line v Attorney General (1930) 36 Com Cas 1 .... 12.11
Glicksman v Lancashire & General Assurance Co Ltd [1927] AC 139, (1926) 26 Ll
L Rep 69.. 11.7, 11.15, 11.16, 11.19
Global Process Systems Inc v Syarikat Takaful Malaysia Berhad (The
Cendor Mopu) [2011] UKSC 5, [2011] Bus LR 537, [2011] 1 Lloyd's
Rep 560 .... 3.7; 4.1, 4.2, 4.3
Global Tankers Inc v Amercoat Europa NV [1977] 1 Lloyd's Rep 61 .... 4.11
Globe Equities Ltd v Globe Legal Services Ltd [2000] CPLR 233, [1999]
BLR 232.. 9.46
Gloucestershire Health Authority v MA Torpy & Partners Ltd (t/a Torpy & Partners)
(No 2) [1999] Lloyd's Rep IR 203.. 9.46
Glynn v Margetson & Co [1893] AC 351 .... 3.24
Godfrey Davis Ltd v Cullling [1962] 2 Lloyd's Rep 349, (1962) 106 SJ 918.......... 8.14
Golder v United Kingdom (Series A/18) (1979-80) 1 EHRR 524............................ 9.8; 10.13
Goldstein v Salvation Army Assurance Society [1917] 2 KB 291 .... 11.29
Good Luck, The. *See* Bank of Nova Scotia v Hellenic Mutual War Risks Associaton
(Bermuda) Ltd
Goodwood Recoveries Ltd v Breen [2005] EWCA Civ 414, [2006] 1 WLR 2723,
[2006] 2 All ER 533.. 9.46
Gorely (Charles Benjamin), ex p (1864) 4 De GJ & Sm 477, 46 ER 1003 .... 2.11
Gorham v British Telecommunications plc [2000] 1 WLR 2129, [2000] 4 All ER
867, [2001] Lloyd's Rep IR 531 .... 16.12
Goshawk Ltd v Tyser & Co Ltd [2006] EWCA Civ 54, [2006] 1 All ER (Comm)
501, [2006] 1 Lloyd's Rep 566 .... 9.16
Grace v Leslie & Godwin Financial Services Ltd [1995] LRLR 472, [1995] CLC
801.. 16.24, 16.30, 16.38
Graham v Entec Europe Ltd (t/a Exploration Associates) [2003] EWCA Civ 1177,
[2004] Lloyd's Rep IR 660, [2003] 4 All ER 1345.. 12.15
Grant v Royal Exchange Assurance Co (1816) 5 M & S 438, 105 ER 1111 .... 9.41; 11.60
Gray v Barr [1971] 2 QB 554, [1971] 2 All ER 949.. 5.2
Great Atlantic Insurance Co v Home Insurance Co [1981] 1 WLR 529, [1981] 2 All
ER 485, [1981] 2 Lloyd's Rep 138 .... 9.28, 9.33
Great North Eastern Railway Ltd v JLT Corporate Risks Ltd [2006] EWHC 1478
(Comm). [2007] Lloyd's Rep IR 38, [2006] PNLR 34.............................. 16.23, 16.30
Great Peace Shipping Ltd v Tsavliris Salvage (International) Ltd [2002] EWCA Civ
1407, [2003] QB 679 .... 8.15
Great Western Insurance Co v Cunliffe (1873-74) LR 9 Ch App 525 .... 16.6
Greaves v Drydale [1936] 2 All ER 470, (1936) 55 Ll L Rep 95............................. 5.1

PARA

Grecia Express, The. *See* Strive Shipping Corpn
Green v Royal Bank of Scotland plc [2013] EWCA Civ 1197, [2014] Bus LR 168,
  [2014] PNLR 6... 8.2; 16.9, 16.13
Greenhill v Federal Insurance Co Ltd [1927] 1 KB 65, (1926) 24 Ll L
  Rep 383 .... 11.5, 11.14, 11.29
Griffiths v Fleming [1909] 1 KB 805.. 3.12, 3.32
Griparion, The. *See* Tharros Shipping Co Ltd
Groom v Crocker [1939] 1 KB 194, (1938) 60 Ll L Rep 393 .... 9.13, 9.16
Ground Gilbey Ltd v Jardine Lloyd Thompson UK Ltd [2011] EWHC 124 (Comm),
  [2012] Lloyd's Rep IR 12, [2011] PNLR 15 .... 16.16, 16.19, 16.20,
                                                                       16.23, 16.35, 16.43
Groupama Insurance Co Ltd v Overseas Partners Re Ltd [2003] EWCA Civ 1846,
  [2004] 1 All ER (Comm) 893, [2004] CP Rep 18 .... 16.47
Groupama Navigation et Transports v Catatumbo CA Seguros [2000] 2 All ER
  (Comm) 193, [2000] 2 Lloyd's Rep 350, [2000] CLC 1534 .... 3.23; 14.6
Group Josi Reinsurance v Walbrook Insurance Co Ltd [1996] 1 WLR 1152, [1996]
  1 All ER 791, [1996] 1 Lloyd's Rep 345 .... 11.11, 11.143
Group Josi Reinsurance Co SA v Universal General Insurance Co [2001] QB 68,
  [2000] All ER (EC) 653 .... 15.9
Groupement d'Intérêt Economique (GIE) Réunion Européenne v Zurich España
  (Case C-77/04) [2006] 1 All ER (Comm) 488, [2005] ECR I-4509, [2006]
  Lloyd's Rep IR 215... 15.9
Guinness Peat Properties Ltd v Fitzroy Robinson Partnership [1987] 1 WLR 1027,
  [1987] 2 All ER 716, 38 BLR 57 .... 9.26, 9.29, 9.33
Gunns v Par Insurance Brokers [1997] 1 Lloyd's Rep 173 .... 16.19, 16.35

H

H (minors) (sexual abuse: standard of proof), Re [1996] AC 563, [1996] 1 All
  ER 1 .... 5.3
HIH Casualty and General Insurance Ltd v Axa Corporate Solutions [2003] EWCA
  Civ 1253, [2003] Lloyd's Rep IR 1.. 11.63
HIH Casualty & General Insurance Ltd v Chase Manhattan Bank [2003] UKHL 6,
  [2003] 1 All ER (Comm) 349, [2003] Lloyd's Rep IR 230 .... 1.1; 3.6, 3.12,
                                                               3.16, 3.26; 11.4, 11.5, 11.13, 11.23,
                                                               11.30, 11.33, 11.34, 11.63; 16.6,
                                                               16.10, 16.23, 16.30, 16.43, 16.46
HLB Kidsons (a firm) v Lloyd's Underwriters [2008] EWCA Civ 1206, [2009] Bus
  LR 759, [2009] 1 Lloyd's Rep 8 .... 7.4, 7.9, 7.13
HMV UK v Propinvest Friar Ltd Partnership [2011] EWCA Civ 1708, [2012]
  1 Lloyd's Rep 416, [2013] Bus LR D5 .... 10.11
HSBC Rail (UK) Ltd v Network Rail Infrastructure Ltd (formerly Railtrack plc)
  [2005] EWCA Civ 1437, [2006] 1 WLR 643, [2006] 1 Lloyd's Rep 358......... 2.10; 12.4
Hackney Empire Ltd v Aviva Insurance UK Ltd (No 2) (formerly t/a Norwich Union
  Insurance Ltd) [2013] EWHC 2212 (TCC), 149 Con LR 213 .... 9.45
Hadenfayre Ltd v British National Insurance Society Ltd [1984] 2 Lloyd's Rep 393,
  (1984) 134 NLJ 1017... 3.3; 7.19; 8.4; 11.18, 11.63
Hagen v ICI Chemicals & Polymers Ltd [2002] IRLR 31, [2002] Emp LR 160,
  [2002] Lloyd's Rep PN 288 .... 16.33
Hair v Prudential Assurance Co Ltd [1983] 2 Lloyd's Rep 667, (1983)
  133 NLJ 282... 2.15; 11.15
Hales v Reliance Fire & Accident Insurance Corpn Ltd [1960] 2 Lloyd's
  Rep 391 .... 11.8, 11.15

PARA

Halki Shipping Corpn v Sopex Oils Ltd [1998] 1 WLR 726, [1998] 2 All ER 23,
[1998] 1 Lloyd's Rep 465 .... 10.6
Hallam-Eames v Merrett Syndicates Ltd (No 1) [1995] CLC 173, [1996] 5 Re LR
110, [2001] Lloyd's Rep PN 178 .... 16.31
Halsey v Milton Keynes General NHS Trust [2004] EWCA Civ 576, [2004] 1 WLR
3002, [2004] 4 All ER 920 .... 10.15
Halvanon Insurance Co Ltd v Companhia de Sueguros do Estado de Sao Paulo
[1995] Lloyd's Rep IR 303, CA 14.5
Hamlyn v Crown Accidental Insurance Co Ltd [1893] 1 QB 750 .... 3.14
Hampshire Land Co (No 2), Re [1896] 2 Ch 743 .... 11.11; 16.6
Handelsbanken Norwegian Branch of Svenska Handelsbanked AB (Publ) v
Dandridge (The Alizia Glacial) [2002] EWCA Civ 577, [2002] 2 All ER
(Comm) 39, [2002] Lloyd's Rep 421 .... 3.18; 4.3, 4.10
Harbutt's Plasticine Ltd v Wayne Tank & Pump Co Ltd [1970] 1 QB 447 .... 9.45; 12.10
Harcourt v FEF Griffin [2007] EWHC 1500 (QB), [2008] Lloyd's Rep IR 386,
[2007] PIQR Q9 .... 9.15
Harman v Crilly [1943] KB 168, (1942) 74 Ll L Rep 141 .... 2.24
Harris v Poland [1941] 1 KB 462, (1941) 69 Ll L Rep 35 .... 4.11
Harrison v Bloom Camillin (No 2) [2000] Lloyd's Rep PN 89, [2001] PNLR 7,
(1999) 96 (45) LSG 32 .... 16.35
Harrods (Buenos Aires) Ltd (No 2), Re [1992] Ch 72, [1991] 4 All ER 348 .... 15.9
Hart v Standard Marine Insurance Co Ltd (1889) LR 22 QBD 499 .... 3.16, 3.22
Harvest Trucking Co Ltd v PB Davis Insurance Services (t/a PB Davis Insurance
Services) [1991] 2 Lloyd's Rep 638, (1991) 135 SJLB 443 .... 16.20, 16.21
Hassett v Legal & General Assurance Society Ltd (1939) 63 Ll L Rep 278 .... 7.4; 9.13
Haward v Fawcetts (a firm) [2006] UKHL 9, [2006] 1 WLR 682, [2006] 3 All
ER 497 .... 16.31
Hawley v Luminar Leisure Ltd [2006] EWCA Civ 18, [2006] IRLR 817, [2006]
Lloyd's Rep IR 307 .... 5.2
Haviland v Long [1952] 2 QB 80, [1952] 1 All ER 463, [1952] 1 TLR 576 .... 2.13
Haydon v Lo & Lo [1997] 1 WLR 198, [1997] 1 Lloyd's Rep 336, [1997]
CLC 626 .... 6.9; 7.8
Hayes v Dodd (a firm) [1990] 2 All ER 815, [1988] EG 107 (CS), (1988) 138 NLJ
Rep 259 .... 16.39
Hayward v Norwich Union Insurance Ltd [2001] EWCA Civ 243, [2001] 1 All ER
(Comm) 545, [2001] Lloyd's Rep IR 410 .... 4.11; 5.2
Hayward v Zurich Insurance Co plc [2015] EWCA Civ 327, [2015] CP Rep 30,
[2015] Lloyd's Rep IR 585 .... 8.15
Hazel (for Lloyd's Syndicate 260) v Whitlam [2004] EWCA Civ 1600, [2005] 1
Lloyd's Rep IR 168 .... 11.7
Heesens Yacht Builders BV v Cox Syndicate Management Ltd (The Red Sapphire)
[2006] EWCA Civ 384, [2006] 2 All ER (Comm) 173, [2006] 2 Lloyd's
Rep 35 .... 3.16
Hellenic Mutual War Risks Association (Bermuda) Ltd v Harrison (The Sagheera)
[1997] 1 Lloyd's Rep 160 .... 9.25, 9.27, 9.33
Hemmings v Sceptre Life Association Ltd [1905] 1 Ch 365 .... 11.16, 11.63
Henderson v Henderson [1843–60] All ER Rep 378, 67 ER 313, (1843)
3 Hare 100 .... 10.17
Henderson v Merrett Syndicates Ltd (No 1) [1995] 2 AC 145, [1994] 3 All
ER 506 .... 16.7, 16.10, 16.11
Henry Boot Construction (UK) Ltd v Malmaison Hotel (Manchester) Ltd [2001] QB
388, [2001] 1 All ER 257 .... 9.9; 10.11

PARA

Hepburn v A Tomlinson (Hauliers) Ltd [1966] AC 451, [1966] 2 WLR 453, [1966]
　1 All ER 418... 2.8, 2.10; 11.55
Herridge v Parker [2014] Lloyd's Rep IR 177... 9.46
Hiddle v National Fire & Marine Insurance Co of New Zealand [1896] AC 372..... 7.20
Highgrade Traders Ltd, Re [1984] BCLC 151.. 8.13
Highland Insruance Co v Continental Insurance [1987] 1 Lloyd's Rep
　109 (Note)... 11.22, 11.32
Hill v Citadel Insurance Co (UK) Ltd [1995] LRLR 218, [1995] CLC 69 .... 11.14
Hill v Mercantile & General Reinsurance Co plc [1996] 1 WLR 1239, [1996] 3 All
　ER 865, [1996] LRLR 341.. 14.2
Hillingdon Borough Council v ARC Ltd (No 2) [2001] CP Rep 33, [2000] 3 EGLR
　97, [2000] RVR 283... 11.62
Hilton v Barker Booth & Eastwood [2005] UKHL 8, [2005] 1 WLR 567, [2005]
　1 All ER 651 .... 16.40
Hiscox v Outhwaite (No 3) [1991] 2 Lloyd's Rep 524.................................... 11.63; 14.2
Hiscox Underwriting Ltd v Dickson Manchester & Co Ltd [2004] EWHC 479
　(Comm), [2004] 1 All ER (Comm) 753, [2004] 2 Lloyd's Rep 438 .... 10.8
Hobbs v Marlowe [1978] AC 16, [1977] 2 All ER 241 .... 12.2, 12.8
Hodgson v Imperial Tobacco Ltd (No 1) [1998] 1 WLR 1056, [1998] 2 All ER 673,
　[1998] 1 Costs LR 14.. 9.10
Holt's Motors Ltd v South-East Lancashire Insurance Co Ltd (1930)
　37 Ll L Rep 1 .... 11.15, 11.19
Holmes v Payne [1930] 2 KB 301, (1930) 37 Ll L Rep 41 .... 5.2; 8.15
Holwell Securities v Hughes [1974] 1 WLR 155, [1974] 1 All ER 161, (1973) 26 P
　& CR 544 .... 7.13
Hongkong Fir, The. *See* Fir Shipping Co Ltd v Kawasaki Kisen Kaisha Ltd
Hornal v Neuberger Products Ltd [1957] 1 QB 247, [1956] 3 All ER 970.............. 5.3
Horne v Poland [1922] 2 KB 364, (1922) 10 Ll L Rep 275 .... 11.6, 11.10, 11.17
Home Insurance Co of New York v Victoria-Montreal Fire Insurance Co [1907]
　AC 59 .... 3.15, 3.24; 7.17
Hood v West End Motor Car Packing Co [1917] 2 KB 38............................. 16.14, 16.15
Hooley Hill Rubber & Chemical Co Ltd, Re [1920] 1 KB 257, (1919) 1 Ll L
　Rep 25 .... 3.17; 4.3
Hooper v Accidental Death Insurance Co (1860) 5 Hurl & N 546, 157 ER 1297..... 17.3
Hopewell Project Management Ltd v Ewbank Preece Ltd [1998] 1 Lloyd's
　Rep 448 .... 12.4
Hopkins v UNUM Ltd [2005] EWHC 1758 (QB)... 17.3
Horbury Building Systems Ltd v Hampden Insurance NV [2004] EWCA Civ 418,
　[2004] 2 CLC 453, [2004] BLR 431............... 3.14, 3.16, 3.22; 4.7; 9.40; 17.17, 17.25
Horner (t/a F & H Contractors) v Commercial Union Assurance Co plc (unreported,
　18 May 1993)... 17.16, 17.24
Horwood v Land of Leather Ltd [2010] EWHC 546 (Comm), [2010] 1 CLC 423,
　[2010] Lloyd's Rep IR 453 .... 9.13; 12.6
Houghton v Trafalgar Insurance Co Ltd [1953] 2 Lloyd's Rep 18........................... 3.2
Huddersfield Banking Co Ltd v Henry Lister & Son Ltd (No 2) [1895] 2 Ch 273... 8.15
Hulton (E) & Co v Mountain (1921) 8 Ll Rep 249 .... 3.15; 8.9
Humber Work Boats Ltd v Owners of the Selby Paradigm [2004] EWHC 1804
　(Admlty), [2004] 2 Lloyd's Rep 714 .... 9.47
Hurst v Evans [1917] 1 KB 352.. 5.1
Hussain v Brown [1996] 1 Lloyd's Rep 627.. 3.6; 11.15, 11.16
Hutton v Watling [1948] Ch 398, [1948] 1 All ER 803, 64 TLR 326...................... 3.16
Hydarnes Steamship Co v Indemnity Mutual Marine Insurance Co [1895]
　1 QB 500.. 3.15, 3.24

I

PARA

IF P & C Insurance Ltd (Publ) v Silversea Cruises Ltd [2004] EWCA Civ 769,
[2004] 1 Lloyd's Rep IR 696 .... 3.22, 3.30; 4.3
IM Properties plc v Cape & Dalgleish [1999] QB 297, [1998] 3 All ER 203 .... 9.41, 9.45
Ide v ATB Sales Ltd [2008] EWCA Civ 424, [2009] RTR 8, [2008] PIQR P13 ...... 5.1
Ikarian Reefer, The. *See* National Justice Compania Naviera SA
Ikerigi Compania Naviera SA v Palmer (The Wondrous) [1991] 1 Lloyd's
Rep 400 .... 5.2
Impact Funding Solutions Ltd v Barrington Support Services Ltd (formerly Lawyers
At Work Ltd) [2015] EWCA Civ 31, [2015] 4 All ER 319, [2015] Lloyd's Rep
IR 371 .... 17.19
Infields Ltd v P Rosen & Son [1938] 3 All ER 591 .... 9.33
Insurance Co of Africa v Scor (UK) Reinsurance Co Ltd [1985] 1 Lloyd's
Rep 312 .... 14.2, 14.3, 14.4
Insurance Corpn of the Channel Islands Ltd v McHugh [1997] LRLR 94 ..... 6.6; 8.3; 11.63
Insurance Corpn of the Channel Islands Ltd v Royal Hotel Ltd [1998] Lloyd's
Rep IR 151 .... 8.8; 11.19, 11.63
Insurance Co of the State of Pennsylvania v Equitas Insurance Ltd [2013] EWHC
3713 (Comm), [2013] Lloyd's Rep IR 195 .... 15.13
International Business Machines Corpn v Phoenix International (Computers) Ltd
[1995] 1 All ER 413, [1995] FSR 184 .... 9.28, 9.33
International Energy Group Ltd v Zurich Insurance plc [2015] UKSC 33, [2016]
AC 509, [2015] 4 All ER 813 .... 1.2; 2.25; 4.3; 8.11;
13.10, 13.14
International Management Group (UK) Ltd v Simmonds [2003] EWHC 177
(Comm), [2004] Lloyd's Rep iR 247 .... 11.8
Inversiones Manria SA v Sphere Drake Insurance Co plc, Malvern Insurance Co &
Niagara Fire Insurance Co (The Dora) [1989] 1 Lloyd's Rep 69 .... 11.6, 11.8, 11.14
Investors Compensation Scheme Ltd v West Bromwich Building Society (No 1)
[1998] 1 WLR 896, [1998] 1 All ER 98, [1998] 1 BCLC 531 .... 3.14, 3.16
Involnert Management Inc v Aprilgrange Ltd [2015] EWHC 2225 (Comm), [2015]
2 Lloyd's Rep 289, [2015] Lloyd's Rep IR 661 .... 1.9; 3.5; 8.4; 9.45;
11.7, 11.15, 11.19, 11.63;
16.5, 16.13, 16.19, 16.23
Ionides v Pender (1873–74) LR 9 QB 531 .... 11.6, 11.19, 11.22
Irish National Insurance Co Ltd & Sedgwick v Oman Insurance Co Ltd [1983] 2
Lloyd's Rep 453 .... 11.22
Irish Rowan, The. *See* Irish Shipping Ltd v Commercial Union Assurance Co Ltd
Irish Shipping Ltd v Commercial Union Assurance Co Ltd (The Irish Rowan) [1991]
2 QB 206, [1989] 3 All ER 853 .... 2.19
Iron Trades Mutual Insurance Co Ltd v Companhia de Seguros Imperio (1992) 1
Rep LR 213 .... 11.63
Iron Trades Mutual Insurance Co Ltd v JK Buckenham Ltd [1990] 1 All ER 808,
[1989] 2 Lloyd's Rep 85 .... 16.29
Irving v Manning (1847) 1 HL Cas 287, 9 ER 766 .... 6.3; 9.41; 11.60
Islander Trucking Ltd (in liquidation) v Robinson & Gardner Mountain (Marine)
Ltd [1990] 1 All ER 826 .... 16.29
Islamic Republic of Iran Shipping Lines v Steamship Mutual Underwriting
Association (Bermuda) Ltd [2010] EWHC 2661 (Comm), [2011] 2 All ER
(Comm) 609, [2011] 1 Lloyd's Rep 195 .... 11.56

J

JEB Fasteners Ltd v Marks Bloom & Co [1983] 1 All ER 583 .... 11.6

PARA

Jabbour (F & K) v Custodian of Israeli Absentee Property [1954] 1 WLR 139,
[1954] 1 All ER 145, [1953] 2 Lloyd's Rep 760.. 11.60
Jacobs v Coster (t/a Newington Commercials Service Station) [2000] Lloyd's
Rep IR 506 .... 7.9
Jaglom v Excess Insurance Co Ltd [1972] 2 QB 250, [1971] 3 WLR 594, [1972] 1
All ER 267 .... 3.3, 3.19
James v CGU Insurance plc [2002] Lloyd's Rep IR 206... 11.30
James Budgett Sugars Ltd v Norwich Union Insurance [2002] EWHC 968 (Comm),
[2003] Lloyd's Rep IR 110 .... 3.15; 17.17
James Miller & Partners Ltd v Whitworth Street Estates (Manchester) Ltd [1970]
AC 583, [1970] 1 All ER 796 .... 3.16
James Nelson & Sons Ltd v Nelson Line (Liverpool) Ltd (No 1) [1906]
2 KB 217 .... 12.7
James Vale & Co v Van Oppen & Co Ltd (1921) 6 Ll L Rep 167 .... 16.17, 16.21
Jan de Nul (UK) Ltd v Axa Royale Belge (formerly NV Royale Belge) [2006]
EWHC 48 (QB), [2001] 1 Lloyd's Rep IR 327 .... 2.13
Jascon 5, The. *See* Talbot Underwriting Ltd v Nausch
Jason v British Traders' Insurance Co Ltd [1969] 1 Lloyd's Rep 281, (1969) 119
NLJ 697.. 3.14; 4.6
Jaura v Ahmed [2002] EWCA Civ 210 .... 9.45
Jenkins v Deane (1933) 47 Ll L Rep 342 .... 13.4
Joel v Law Union & Crown Insurance Co [1908] 2 KB 863.................... 11.6, 11.10, 11.11,
11.15, 11.16, 11.29
John Edwards & Co v Motor Union Insurance Co Ltd [1922] 2 KB 249, (1922) 11
Ll L Rep 170 .... 12.3
Johnson v Gore Wood & Co (No 1) [2002] 2 AC 1, [2001] 1 All ER 481 .... 2.8; 11.63
Jones v Environcom Ltd [2009] EWHC 16 (Comm), [2010] 1 BCLC 150, [2010]
Lloyd's Rep IR 190.. 9.40
Jones v Environcom Ltd [2009] EWHC 759 (Comm), [2010] Lloyd's Rep IR 676;
on appeal [2011] EWCA Civ 1152, [2012] Lloyd's Rep IR 277 .... 16.19, 16.21,
16.33
Jones v Environcom Ltd [2011] EWCA Civ 1152, [2012] Lloyd's
Rep IR 277 .... 16.21, 16.33
Jones v University of Warwick [2003] EWCA Civ 151, [2003] 1 WLR 954, [2003]
3 All ER 760.. 8.5
Jordan Grand Prix Ltd v Baltic Insurance Group [1999] 2 AC 127, [1999]
1 WLR 134... 15.7, 15.8, 15.9
Joscelyne v Nissen [1970] 2 QB 86, [1970] 1 All ER 1213 .... 3.30, 3.33
Joseph Fielding Properties (Blackpool) Ltd v Aviva Insurance Ltd [2010] EWHC
2192 (QB), [2011] Lloyd's Rep IR 238 .... 11.7, 11.17
Jowitt v Pioneer Technology (UK) Ltd [2003] EWCA Civ 411, [2003] ICR 1120,
[2003] IRLR 356.. 17.3, 17.14
Joyce v Realm Marine Insurance Co (1871–72) LR 7 QB 580................................ 3.24
Jureidini v National British & Irish Millers Insurance Co Ltd [1915] AC 499 ....7.21; 11.63

K

KR v Royal & Sun Alliance plc [2006] EWCA Civ 1454, [2007] Bus LR 139, [2007]
1 All ER (Comm) 161 .... 5.2
K/S Merc-Scandia XXXXII v Certain Lloyd's Underwriters (The Mercandian
Continent) [2001] EWCA Civ 1275, [2001] 2 Lloyd's Rep 563, [2001] CLC
1836.. 3.7, 3.9; 7.6; 9.13, 9.14;
11.18, 11.30, 11.49

PARA

Kacianoff v China Traders Insurance Co Ltd [1914] 3 KB 1121 .... 4.12
Kajima UK Engineering Ltd v Underwriter Insurance Co Ltd [2008] EWHC 83
   (TCC), [2008] 1 All ER (Comm) 855, [2008] Lloyd's Rep IR 391................... 7.19
Kamidian v Wareham Holt [2008] EWHC 1483 (Comm), [2009] Lloyd's
   Rep IR 242 .... 11.22
Kanchenjunga, The. *See* Motor Oil Hellas (Corinth) Refineries SA
Kapur v JW Francis & Co (No 2) [2000] Lloyd's Rep IR 361, [1999] Lloyd's
   Rep PN 834.. 16.19
Kaufmann v British Surety Insurance Co Ltd (1929) 33 Ll L Rep 315 .... 3.26
Kaur (Pritam) v S Russel & Sons Ltd [1973] QB 336, [1973]
   1 All ER 617... 11.61; 16.32
Kausar v Eagle Star Insurance Co Ltd [1997] CLC 129, [2000] Lloyds Rep IR 154,
   [1996] 5 Re LR 191 .... 11.7, 11.17, 11.18
Kelly v Cooper [1993] AC 205, [1994] 1 BCLC 395 .... 9.16; 16.3, 16.10, 16.40
Kennecott Utah Copper Corpn v Minet Ltd [2003] EWCA Civ 905, [2004] 1 All ER
   (Comm) 60, [2003] Lloyd's Rep IR 503... 16.46
King v Victoria Insurance Co Ltd [1896] AC 250 .... 12.3
King, Re *see* Robinson v Gray
Kingscroft Insurance Co Ltd v Nissan Fire & Marine Insurance Co Ltd [1999]
   Lloyd's Rep IR 371.. 11.11
Kirkcaldy & Sons Ltd v Walker [1999] 1 All ER (Comm) 334, [1999] CLC 722,
   [1999] Lloyd's Rep IR 410 .... 11.8
Kiriacoulis Lines SA v Compagnie d'Assurances Maritime Aeriennes et Terrestres
   (CAMAT) (The Demetra K) [2002] EWCA Civ 1070, [2002] 2 Lloyd's Rep
   581, [2003] 1 CLC 579 .... 3.29, 3.30, 3.33; 4.3
Kitchen v RAF Association [1958] 1 WLR 563, [1958] 2 All ER 241, [1955–95]
   PNLR 18 .... 16.35
Kitchen Design & Advice Ltd v Lea Valley Water Co [1989] 2 Lloyd's
   Rep 221 .... 9.13
Kleinwort Benson Ltd v Lincoln City Council [1999] 2 AC 349, [1998] 4 All
   ER 513 .... 8.15
Kleovoulos of Rhodes, The. *See* Sunport Shipping Ltd
Knapp v Ecclesiastical Insurance Group plc [1998] Lloyd's Rep IR 390, [1998]
   PNLR 172 .... 16.29
Knight of St Michael, The [1898] P 30.. 4.12
Koskas (D & J) v Standard Marine Insurance Co Ltd (1927) 27 Ll L Rep 59 .... 3.25
Kosmar Villa Holidays plc v Trustees of Syndicate 1243 [2008] EWCA Civ 147,
   [2008] Bus LR 931, [2008] Lloyd's Rep IR 489 .... 7.22; 8.4; 11.63
Krantz v Allan (1921) 9 Ll L Rep 410.. 11.5, 11.16, 11.28
Kumar v AGF Insurance Ltd [1999] 1 WLR 1747, [1998] 4 All ER 788, [1999]
   Lloyd's Rep IR 147.. 3.14, 3.16
Kuwait Airways Corpn v Iraqi Airways Co (No 6) [2005] EWCA Civ 286, [2005] 1
   WLR 2734, [2005] CP Rep 32.. 9.34
Kuwait Airways Corpn SAK v Kuwait Insurance Co SA [2005] EWCA Civ 286,
   [2005] 1 WLR 2734, [1999] 1 Lloyd's Rep 803.............................. 4.3; 6.9
Kyle Bay Ltd (t/a Astons Nightclub) v Underwriters [2007] EWCA Civ 57, [2007]
   1 CLC 164, [2007] Lloyd's Rep IR 460 .... 8.15; 11.25; 17.5
Kyriaki, The. *See* Bank of America National Trusts & Savings Association v Chrismas
Kyzuna Investments Ltd v Ocean Marine Insurance Association (Europe) [2000]
   1 All ER (Comm) 557, [2000] 1 Lloyd's Rep 505, [2000] CLC 925............... 6.3

L   PARA

Lagden v O'Connor [2003] UKHL 64, [2004] 1 AC 1067 .... 16.34
Lake v Simmons [1927] AC 487, (1927) 27 Ll L Rep 377 .... 3.22
Lambert v Cooperative Insurance Society Ltd [1975] 2 Lloyd's Rep 485 .... 11.6
Lancaster City Council v Unique Group Ltd (unreported, 15 December 1995) 11.23
Laurence v Davies [1972] 2 Lloyd's Rep 231 .... 3.16
Law Guarantee Trust & Accident Society v Munich Reinsurance Co [1912]
    1 Ch 138 .... 11.18
Law Society v Sephton & Co [2006] UKHL 22, [2006] 2 AC 543 .... 16.29
Law Society v Shah [2007] EWHC 2841 (Ch), [2009] Ch 223 .... 2.24
Lawrence v Accidental Insurance Co (1880–81) LR 7 QBD 216 .... 3.17; 4.2
Layher Ltd v Lowe [2000] Lloyd's Rep IR 510, 58 Con LR 42, (1997)
    73 P & CR D37 .... 7.9
Lefevre v White [1990] 1 Lloyd's Rep 569 .... 2.27
Legal & General Assurance Society Ltd v Drake Insurance Co Ltd [1992] QB 887,
    [1992] 1 All ER 283 .... 13.3, 13.4, 13.9
Lek v Matthews (1927–28) 29 Ll L Rep 141 .... 11.50, 11.51
Leonidas D, The. *See* Allied Marine Transport Ltd
Leppard v Excess Insurance Co Ltd [1979] 1 WLR 512, [1979] 2 All ER 668, [1979]
    2 Lloyd's Rep 91 .... 6.3, 6.4
Les Affréteurs Réunis SA v Walford (London) Ltd [1919] AC 801 .... 3.27; 17.14
Letang v Cooper [1965] 1 QB 232, [1964] 2 All ER 929 .... 11.59
Levy v Assicurazioni Generali [1940] AC 791, (1940) 67 Ll L Rep 174 .... 5.1
Lexington Insurance Co v Multinacional de Seguros SA [2008] EWHC 1170
    (Comm), [2009] 1 All ER (Comm) 35, [2009] Loyd's Rep IR 1 .... 7.21
Leyland Shipping Co Ltd v Norwich Union Fire Insurance Society Ltd [1918]
    AC 350 .... 4.2
Liberty Insurance Pte Ltd v Argo Systems FZE (The Copa Casino) [2011] EWCA
    Civ 1572, [2012] Lloyd's Rep IR 67 .... 11.23, 11.63
Liesboch, The [1933] AC 449, [1933] All ER Rep 144, (1933) 45 Ll L Rep 123 ..... 16.34
Limit No 2 Ltd v Axa Versicherung AG (formerly Albingia Versicherung AG)
    [2008] EWCA Civ 1231, [2008] 2 CLC 673, [2009] Lloyd's
    Rep IR 396 .... 11.21, 11.24, 11.30
Linden Gardens Trust Ltd v Lenesta Sludge Disposals Ltd [1994] 1 AC 85, [1993] 3
    WLR 408, [1993] 3 All ER 417 .... 2.14
Lindenau v Desborough (1828) 8 B & C 586, 108 ER 1160 .... 11.6, 11.15
Linelevel Ltd v Powszechny Zakla Ubezpieczen SA (The Nore Challenger) [2005]
    EWHC 421 (Comm), [2005] 2 Lloyd's Rep 534 .... 4.10, 4.12
Lion Mutual Marine Insurance Association Ltd v Tucker (1883–84) LR 12 QBD
    176, (1883) 32 WR 546 .... 3.15
Lipkin Gorman v Karpnale [1991] 2 AC 548, [1992] 4 All ER 512 .... 8.15
Litsion Pride, The. *See* Black King Shipping Corpn v Massie
Litster v Forth Dry Dock & Engineering Co Ltd [1990] 1 AC 546, [1989]
    1 All ER 1134 .... 15.4
Liverpool City Council v Irwin [1977] AC 239, [1976] 2 All ER 39 .... 3.27
Liverpool Roman Catholic Archdiocese Trustees Inc v Goldberg (No 1) [2001] 1 All
    ER 182, [2000] Lloyd's Rep PN 836, [2001] PNLR 19 .... 16.31
Livingstone v Raywards Coal Co (1879-80) 5 App Cas 25, (1880) 7 R (HL) 1 .... 16.33
Lloyd (JJ) Instruments Ltd v Northern Star Insurance Co Ltd (The Miss Jay Jay)
    [1987] 1 Lloyd's Rep 32, [1987] FTLR 14, [1987] Fin LR 120 .... 4.3; 5.2
Lloyds TSB General Insurance Holdings v Lloyds Bank Group Insurance Co Ltd
    [2001] EWCA Civ 1643, [2002] 1 All ER (Comm) 42, [2002] Lloyd's Rep
    IR 113 .... 4.1, 4.4

PARA

Lloyds TSB General Insurance Holdings v Lloyds Bank Group Insurance Co [2003]
UKHL 48, [2003] 4 All ER 43, [2003] Lloyd's Rep IR 623 .... 3.16; 6.9
London & Lancashire Fire Insurance Co Ltd v Bolands Ltd [1924] AC 836, (1924)
19 Ll L Rep 1 .... 3.19, 3.22
London Assurance v Clare (1937) 57 Ll L Rep 254 .... 8.6; 11.53
London Assurance v Mansell (1879) LR 11 Ch D 363 .... 11.16, 11.19, 11.28
London Borough of Bromley v Ellis (Luff & Sons, Third Party) [1971] 1 Lloyd's
Rep 97, (1970) 114 SJ 906 .... 16.4
London Borough of Redbridge v Municipal Insurance Ltd [2001] Lloyd's Rep IR
545, [2001] OPLR 101 .... 8.12
London County Commercial Reinsurance Office Ltd [1922] Ch 67 .... 14.2
London General Insurance Co v General Marine Underwriters' Association [1921]
1 KB 104, (1920) 4 Ll L Rep 382 .... 11.11
London Guarantie Co v Fearnley (1879-80) LR 5 App Cas 911 .... 3.5, 3.15; 7.1
London & Provincial Leather Processes Ltd v Hudson [1939] 2 KB 724, (1939) 64
Ll L Rep 352 .... 5.2
London Transport Co Ltd v Trechmann Bros [1904] 1 KB 635 .... 3.16
Lonrho Exports Ltd v Export Credit Guarantee Department [1999] Ch 158, [1996]
2 Lloyd's Rep 649 .... 12.11
Lonsdale & Thompson Ltd v Black Arrow Group plc [1993] Ch 361, [1993] 3 All
ER 648 .... 2.8, 2.10
Looker v Law Union & Rock Insurance Co Ltd [1928] 1 KB 554 .... 11.18
Lord Napier & Ettrick v Hunter [1993] AC 713, [1993] 1 All ER 385 ..... 12.2, 12.8, 12.11, 12.12
Louden v British Merchants Insurance Co Ltd [1961] 1 WLR 798, [1961] 1 All ER
705, [1961] 1 Lloyd's Rep 154 .... 3.17
Low v Bouverie [1891] 3 Ch 82 .... 11.63
Loyaltrend Ltd v Creechurch Dedicated Ltd [2010] EWHC 425 (Comm), [2010]
Lloyd's Rep IR 466 .... 17.5
Lubbe v Cape plc [2000] 1 WLR 1545, [2000] 4 All ER 268, [2000]
2 Lloyd's Rep 383 .... 15.13
Lucena v Craufurd (1806) 2 Bos & PNR 269, 127 ER 630 .... 2.4, 2.8; 6.3
Luckie v Bushby (1853) 13 CB 864, 138 ER 1443 .... 9.41; 11.60
Lumberman's Mutual Casualty Co v Bovis Lend Lease Ltd [2004] EWHC 2197
(Comm), [2005] 2 All ER (Comm) 669, [2005] 1 Lloyd's Rep 494 .... 8.12
Lyell v Kennedy (No 3) (1884) LR 27 Ch D 1 .... 9.32
Lyons v JW Bentley Ltd (1944) 77 Ll L Rep 335 .... 11.19; 16.19

M

MDIS Ltd (formerly McDonnell Information Systems Ltd) v Swinbank [1999]
Lloyd's Rep IR 98 .... 3.17; 8.12
MSC Mediterranean Shipping Co SA v Polish Ocean Lines (The Tychy) [2001]
EWCA Civ 1198, [2001] 2 Lloyd's Rep 403 .... 3.16
McClean Enterprises Ltd v Ecclesiastical Insurance Office plc [1986] 2 Lloyd's
Rep 416 .... 6.4, 6.5, 6.6
McCormick v National Motor & Accident Insurance Union Ltd (1934) 49 Ll L
Rep 361 .... 7.22; 11.19, 11.63
McGeown v Direct Travel Insurance [2003] EWCA Civ 1606, [2004] 1 All ER
(Comm) 609, [2004] Lloyd's Rep IR 599 .... 3.15, 3.16, 3.19; 17.3
Mackender, Hill & White v Feldia AG [1967] 2 QB 590, [1966] 2 Lloyd's
Rep 449 .... 11.30
MacKenzie v Coulson (1869) LR 8 Eq 368 .... 3.30, 3.31
MacLeay v Tait [1906] AC 24 .... 11.27

PARA

McNealy v The Pennine Insurance Co Ltd [1978] 2 Lloyd's Rep 18, [1978] RTR 285, (1978) 122 SJ 229 .... 16.4, 16.19, 16.34

Mabey & Johnson Ltd v Ecclesiastical Insurance Office plc [2000] CLC 1570, [2001] Lloyd's Rep IR 369 .... 6.9

Macaura v Northern Assurance Co Ltd [1925] AC 619................................. 2.4, 2.8; 11.55

Maccaferri Ltd v Zurich Insurance plc [2015] EWHC 1708 (Comm), [2015] Lloyd's Rep IR 594 .... 7.15

Macmillan v A W Knott Becker Scott Ltd [1990] 1 Lloyd's Rep 98 .... 16.12

Magee v Pennine Insurance Co Ltd [1969] 2 QB 507, [1969] 2 All ER 891 .... 8.15; 11.15

Maggs (t/a BM Builders) v Marsh [2006] EWCA Civ 1058, [2006] BLR 395, [2006] CILL 2369.. 3.16

Maher v Groupama Grand Est [2009] EWCA Civ 1191, [2010] 1 WLR 1564, [2010] 2 All ER 455.. 15.9

Mainstream Properties Ltd v Young [2005] EWCA Civ 861, [2005] IRLR 964, (2005) 102 (30) LSG 31... 8.15

Malhi v Abbey Life Assurance Co Ltd [1996] LRLR 237, [1994] CLC 615, [1995] 4 Re LR 305.. 11.63

Mallett v McMonagle [1921] 1 KB 104, (1920) 4 Ll L Rep 382 .... 16.35

Mammoth Pine, The. *See* Netherlands Insurance Co Ltd v Karl Ljungberg & Co AB

Mandarin, The. *See* Nishina Trading Co Ltd

Mander v Commercial Union Assurance Co plc [1998] Lloyd's Rep IR 93 .... 16.15, 16.34, 16.43

Mandrake Holdings Ltd v Countrywide Assured Group plc [2005] EWCA Civ 840.. 6.6

Manifest Shipping Co Ltd v Uni-Polaris Insurance Co Ltd (The Star Sea) [2001] UKHL 1, [2003] AC 469........................ 9.14; 11.18, 11.30, 11.37, 11.38, 11.49, 11.50

Mann v Lexington Insurance Co [2001] 1 All ER (Comm) 28, [2001] 1 Lloyd's Rep 1, [2000] CLC 1409... 6.9

Mannai Investment Co Ltd v Eagle Star Life Assurance Co Ltd [1997] AC 749, [1997] 3 All ER 352.. 3.15, 3.16

Maher v Groupama Grand Est [2009] EWCA Civ 1191, [2010] 1 WLR 1564, [2010] 2 All ER 455.. 15.9

Mapfre Mutualidad Compania de Seguros y Reaseguros SA v Keefe; Hotees Pinero Canarias SL v Keefe [2015] EWCA Civ 598, [2016] Lloyd's Rep IR 94 .... 15.9

Maple Leaf Macro Volatility Master Fund v Rouvroy [2009] EWHC 257 (Comm), [2009] 2 All ER (Comm) 287, [2009] 1 Lloyd's Rep 475 .... 3.20

Marc Rich & Co AG v Portman [1996] 1 Lloyd's Rep 430...................... 11.7, 11.14, 11.33

March Cabaret Club & Casino Ltd v London Assurance Ltd [1975] 1 Lloyd's Rep 169 .... 11.15, 11.63

Mardorf v Accident Insurance Co [1881] 1 KB 584.. 4.2

Marks and Spencer plc v BNP Paribas Securities Service Trust Co (Jersey) Ltd [2015] UKSC 72, [2015] 3 WLR 1843, 163 Con LR 1 .... 3.27; 12.4

Marine Insurance Co Ltd v Grimmer (1944) 77 Ll L Rep 224 .... 3.16

Mark Rowlands Ltd v Berni Inns Ltd [1986] QB 211, [1985] 3 All ER 4773 .... 2.4, 2.5, 2.6, 2.8; 12.6

Marren v Dawson Bentley & Co Ltd [1961] 2 QB 135, [1961] 2 All ER 270 .... 11.61; 16.32

Marsden v City & County Assurance Co (1865-66) LR 1 CP 232, (1865) 12 Jur NS 76, (1865) 14 WR 106 .... 4.1, 4.2, 4.4

Masefield AG v Amlin Corporate Member Ltd (The Bunga Melati Dua) [2011] EWCA Civ 24, [2011] 1 WLR 2012, [2011] 1 Lloyd's Rep 630 .... 3.18; 4.10; 6.2

Mason v Harvey (1853) 8 Ex Ch 819 .... 7.1

Matadeen v Caribbean Insurance Co Ltd [2002] UKPC 69, [2003] 1 WLR 670...... 2.27

	PARA
Mathie v Argonaut Marine Insurance Co Ltd (1925) 21 Ll L Rep 145	11.19
Maurice v Goldsbrough Mort & Co Ltd [1939] AC 452, (1939) 64 Ll L Rep 1	6.3, 6.6
Meadows Indemnity Co Ltd v The Insurance Corpn of Ireland plc [1989] 2 Lloyd's Rep 298	9.42
Melik (Victor) & Co Ltd v Norwich Union Fire Insurance Society Ltd [1980] 1 Lloyd's Rep 523	8.4, 8.13; 16.21
Mercandian Continent, The. *See* K/S Merc Scandia XXXXII	
Mercantile Bank of Sydney v Taylor [1893] AC 317	3.16
Merrett v Babb [2001] EWCA Civ 214, [2001] QB 1174	16.8
Merrett v Capitol Indemnity Corpn [1991] 1 Lloyd's Rep 169	12.13
Meridian Global Funds Management Asia Ltd v Securities Commission [1995] 2 AC 500, [1995] 3 All ER 918	11.12, 11.37
Metal Box Co Ltd v Currys Ltd [1988] 1 WLR 175, [1988] 1 All ER 341, (1987) 84 LSG 3657	9.45
Michael Phillips Associates Ltd v Riklin [2010] EWHC 834 (TCC), [2010] BLR 569, [2010] Lloyd's Rep IR 479	9.5
Midland Bank Trust Co Ltd v Hett, Stubbs & Kemp [1979] Ch 384, [1978] 3 All ER 571	16.7, 16.13, 16.30
Midland Mainline Ltd v Eagle Star Insurance Co Ltd [2004] EWCA Civ 1042, [2004] 2 Lloyd's Rep 604, [2004] 2 CLC 480	4.3
Miller, Gibb & Co Ltd, Re [1957] 1 WLR 703, [1957] 2 All ER 266, [1957] 1 Lloyd's Rep 258	12.1, 12.2
Milton Furniture Ltd v Brit Insurance Ltd [2015] EWCA Civ 671, [2016] Lloyd's Rep IR 192	3.14, 3.15, 3.24
Milton Keynes Borough Council v Nulty [2011] EWHC 2847 (TCC), [2012] Lloyd's Rep IR 453	7.7, 7.20
Mint Security Ltd v Blair, Miller (Thomas R) & Son (Home) & Darwin Clayton (EC) & Co [1982] 1 Lloyd's Rep 188	16.34, 16.38
Minter v Priest [1930] AC 558	9.25
Miss Jay Jay, The. *See* Lloyd (JJ) Instruments Ltd v Northern Star Insurance Co Ltd	
Mitsubishi Electric UK Ltd v Royal London Insurance (UK) Ltd [1994] 2 Lloyd's Rep 249, [1994] CLC 367, 74 BLR 87	6.9
Mitsui Sumitomo Insurance Co (Europe) Ltd v The Mayor's Office for Policing and Crime [2013] EWHC 2734, [2014] 1 All ER 422, [2014] Lloyd's Rep IR 20	6.6
Monksfield v Vehicle & General Insurance Co Ltd [1971] 1 Lloyd's Rep 139	13.4
Monkton Court Ltd (t/a CATS) v Perry Prowse (Insurance Services) Ltd [2000] 1 All ER (Comm) 566, [2002] Lloyd's Rep IR 408	2.24; 9.46
Moorcock, The (1889) LR 14 PD 64, [1886–90] All ER Rep 530	3.27
Moore (DW) & Co Ltd v Ferrier [1988] 1 WLR 267, [1988] 1 All ER 400, (1988) 132 SJ 227	16.29
Moore Large & Co Ltd v Hermes Credit & Guarantee plc [2003] EWHC 26 (Comm), [2003] 1 Lloyds' Rep 163, [2003] Lloyd's Rep IR 315	11.63
Mopani Copper Mines plc v Millenium Underwriting Ltd [2008] EWHC 1331 (Comm), [2008] 2 All ER (Comm) 976, [2009] Lloyd's Rep R 158	3.14, 3.16
Moran, Galloway & Co v Uzielli [1905] 2 KB 555	2.4
Morley v Moore [1936] 2 KB 359, (1936) 55 Ll L Rep 10	12.8
Morley v United Friendly Insurance plc [1993] 1 WLR 996, [1993] 2 All ER 47, [1993] 1 Lloyd's Rep 490	3.17, 3.18
Morris v Ford Motor Co Ltd [1973] QB 792, [1973] 2 All ER 1084	12.2, 12.3, 12.4
Morrison v Universal Marine Insurance Co (1872) LR 8 Exch 40	11.8, 11.63
Morser v Eagle, Star & British Dominions Insurance Co Ltd (1931) 40 Ll L Rep 254	11.19

PARA

Moss v Norwich & London Accident Insurance Association (1922) 10 Ll L
Rep 396 .... 3.16

Motor & General Insurance Co Ltd v Pavy [1994] 1 WLR 462, [1994] 1 Lloyd's
Rep 607 .... 7.5

Motor Oil Hellas (Corinth) Refineries SA v Shippping Corpn of India (The
Kanchenjunga) [1990] 1 Lloyd's Rep 391 .... 11.63

Mount I, The. *See* Raiffeisen Zentralbank Österreich AG

Mousaka Inc v Golden Seagull Maritime Inc [2002] 1 WLR 395, [2002] 1 All ER
726, [2001] 2 Lloyd's Rep 657 .... 9.6

Mozart, The [1985] 1 Lloyd's Rep 239.. 7.5

Mulchrone v Swiss Life (UK) plc [2005] EWHC 1808 (Comm), [2006] Lloyd's Rep
IR 339.. 17.14

Muller v Linsley & Mortimer [1996] PNLR 74, (1995) 92 (3) LSG 38, (1995) 139
SJLB 43.. 9.38

Mundi v Lincoln Assurance Ltd [2005] EWHC 2678 (Ch), [2006] Lloyd's Rep
IR 353.. 11.7

Municipal Mutual Insurance Ltd v Sea Insurance Co Ltd [1998] CLC 957, [1998]
Lloyd's Rep IR 421 .... 6.9

Munro, Brice & Co v War Risks Association Ltd [1918] 2 KB 78 .... 5.1

Murphy v Young & Co's Brewery [1997] 1 WLR 1591, [1997] 1 All ER 518, [1997]
1 Lloyd's Rep 236.. 2.24; 9.46

Murray v Legal & General Assurance Society Ltd [1970] 2 QB 495, [1970] 2 WLR
465, [1969] 3 All ER 794.. 2.25; 13.14

Mutual Life Ins Co of New York v Ontario Metal Products Co Ltd [1925]
AC 344 .... 11.6, 11.7, 11.15

Mylcrist Builders Ltd v Buck [2008] EWHC 2172 (TCC), [2009] 2 All ER (Comm)
259, [2008] BLR 611 .... 3.20; 10.14

N

NLA Group Ltd v Bowers [1999] 1 Lloyd's Rep 109 .... 3.16, 3.22

Nai Geneva and Nai Superba, The. *See* Agip SpA v Navigazione Alta Italia SpA

Napier & Ettrick v Hunter [1993] AC 713, [1993] 1 All ER 385 .... 12.2, 12.8,
12.11, 12.12

Napier v UNUM Ltd [1996] 2 Lloyd's Rep 550, [1996] 7 Med LR 349 .... 5.4; 17.12

Nasser v United Bank of Kuwait [2001] EWCA Civ 556, [2002] 1 WLR 1868,
[2002] 1 All ER 401 .... 9.5

National Bank of Sharjah v Dellborg (unreported, 9 July 1997)............................ 3.16

National Employers Mutual General Insurance Association Ltd v Haydon [1980]
2 Lloyd's Rep 149.. 7.9; 13.5, 13.7

National Farmers Union Mutual Insurance Society Ltd v HSBC Insurance
(UK) Ltd [2010] EWHC 773 (Comm), [2010] 1 CLC 557, [2011] Lloyd's
Rep IR 86 .... 2.8; 3.26; 5.1; 13.2, 13.3

National Insurance & Guarantee Corpn v Imperio Reinsurance Co (UK) Ltd [1999]
Lloyd's Rep IR 249... 16.17, 16.26, 16.27, 16.28

National Justice Compania Naviera SA v Prudential Assurance Co Ltd (The Ikarian
Reefer) (No 1) [1995] 1 Lloyd's Rep 455... 5.3

National Justice Compania Naviera SA v Prudential Assurance Co Ltd (The Ikarian
Reefer) (No 2) [2000] 1 WLR 603, [2000] 1 All ER 37, [1999] 2 All ER
(Comm) 672 .... 9.46

National Oilwell (UK) Ltd v Davy Offshore Co [1994] CLY 4086 .... 2.10; 4.10;
6.14; 12.4

National Protector Fire Insurance Co Ltd v Nivert [1913] AC 507 .... 3.15, 3.19, 13.7

PARA

Netherlands Insurance Co Est 1845 Ltd v Karl Ljungberg & Co AB (The Mammoth
    Pine) [1986] 3 All ER 767, [1986] 2 Lloyd's Rep 19 .... 6.13; 12.3
Netherlands v Youell [1997] 2 Lloyd's Rep 440, [1997] CLC 938 .... 1.1; 2.3; 11.52; 12.4
Netherlands v Youell [1998] 1 Lloyd's Rep 236, [1998] CLC 44 .... 4.10
Newcastle Fire Insurance Co v Macmorran & Co (1815) 3 Dow 255, 3 ER 1057 ... 11.16
New England Reinsurance Corpn v Messoghios Insurance Co SA [1992] 2 Lloyd's
    Rep 251 .... 15.7
Newbury International Ltd v Reliance National Insurance Co (UK) Ltd [1994] 1
    Lloyd's Rep 82 .... 2.5; 11.8, 11.14, 11.18
Newfoundland Explorer, The. *See* GE Fran kena Reinsurance Ltd v CMM Trust No 1400
New Hampshire Insurance Co v MGN Ltd [1997] LRLR 24, [1996]
    CLC 1728 .... 2.3, 3.12, 3.14, 3.19; 11.4,
                                           11.18, 11.30, 11.37, 11.52
New Hampshire Insurance Co v Oil Refineries Ltd [2002] 2 Lloyd's Rep 462, [2003]
    Lloyd's Rep IR 386 .... 11.7
New Hampshire Insurance Co v Strabag Bau AG [1992] 1 Lloyd's Rep 361, [1992]
    IL Pr 478 .... 15.9, 15.13
Newsholme Brothers v Road Transport & General Insurance Co Ltd [1929] 2 KB
    356, (1929) 34 Ll L Rep 247 .... 3.2; 11.11, 11.15; 16.3, 16.4, 16.6
New Zealand Forest Products Ltd v New Zealand Insurance Co Ltd [1997]
    1 WLR 1237 .... 8.11
Niemietz v Germany (Series A/251-B) (1992) 16 EHRR 97 .... 8.5
Nigel Upchurch Associates v Aldridge Estates Investment Co Ltd [1993] 1 Lloyd's
    Rep 535 .... 2.23
Nishina Trading Co Ltd v Chiyoda Fire & Marine Insurance Co Ltd (The Mandarin
    Star) [1969] 2 QB 449, [1969] 2 All ER 776 .... 3.22
Nissan Fire & Marine v Malaysia British (unreported, 8 July 1996) 14.5
Nisshin Shipping Co Ltd v Cleaves & Co Ltd [2003] EWHC 2602 (Comm), [2004]
    1 All ER (Comm) 481, [2004] 1 Lloyd's Rep 38 ....2.18; 17.14
Nobahar-Cookson v The Hut Group Ltd [2016] EWCA Civ 128 .... 3.19
Nordström-Janzon v Netherlands (No 28101/95) (Comm Dec 27.11.1996) 9.8; 10.13
Nore Challenger, The. *See* Linelevel Ltd
Normid Housing Association Ltd v Ralphs (No 2) [1989] 1 Lloyd's Rep 274, CA 2.22
Normid Housing Association Ltd v Ralphs & Mansell (Third Party Rights: Mareva
    Injunction) [1989] 1 Lloyd's Rep 265, 21 Con LR 98, [1988] EG 108 .... 2.22
North & South Trust Co v Berkeley [1971] 1 WLR 470, [1971] 1 All ER 980, [1970]
    2 Lloyd's Rep 467 .... 9.16; 16.3, 16.4, 16.10, 16.40
North Atlantic Insurance Co Ltd v Bishopgate Insurance Ltd [1998] 1 Lloyd's
    Rep 462 .... 14.5
North British & Mercantile Insurance Co v London, Liverpool & Globe Insurance
    Co (1877) LR 5 Ch D 675 .... 3.15; 12.14; 13.2, 13.5, 13.13
North British & Mercantile Insurance Co v Moffatt (1871-72) LR 7 CP 25 .... 2.10
North Range Shipping Ltd v Seatrans Shipping Corpn (The Western Triumph)
    [2002] EWCA Civ 405, [2002] 1 WLR 2397, [2001] UKHHR 610 .... 9.9; 10.11
North Star Shipping Ltd v Sphere Drake Insurance plc [2006] EWCA Civ 378,
    [2006] 2 All ER (Comm) 65, [2006] 2 Lloyd's Rep 183 .... 11.6, 11.7, 11.19
Norwegian American Cruises A/S v Paul Mundy Ltd (The Vistafjord) [1988] 2
    Lloyd's Rep 343 .... 11.63
Norwich Union Fire Insurance Society Ltd v William H Price Ltd [1934] AC 455,
    (1934) 49 Ll L Rep 55 .... 8.15
Norwich Union Insurance Ltd v Meisels [2006] EWHC 2811 (QB), [2007] 1 All ER
    (Comm) 1138, [2007] 1 Lloyd's Rep IR 69 .... 11.6

PARA

Noten (TM) BV v Harding [1990] 2 Lloyd's Rep 283 .... 4.2
Nykredit Mortgage Bank plc v Edward Erdman Group Ltd (No 2) [1997] 1 WLR
    1627, [1998] 1 All ER 305, [1998] Lloyd's Rep Bank 39 .... 16.29

O

O & R Jewellers Ltd v Terry [1999] Lloyd's Rep IR 436................................... 16.19, 16.35
OT Africa Line Ltd v Hijazy (The Kribi) (No 1) [2001] 1 Lloyd's Rep 76, [2001]
    CLC 148, [2002] IL Pr 18.. 9.8
OT Computers Ltd (in administration), Re [2004] EWCA Civ 653, [2004]
    Ch 317.. 2.20, 2.21, 2.23, 2.25; 3.15, 3.18
O'Brien v Hughes-Gibb & Co Ltd [1995] LRLR 80, [1994]
    CLC 216.. 16.13, 16.14, 16.16
Ocean A/S v Black Sea & Baltic General Insurance Co Ltd (1935) 51 Ll L
    Rep 305 .... 3.19
Ocean Dirk, The. *See* Allianz Insurance Co Egypt v Aigaion Insurance Co SA (No 2)
Oceanbulk Shipping & Trading SA v TMT Asia Ltd [2010] UKSC 44, [2011]
    1 AC 662 .... 9.38
Oceano Grupo Editorial SA v Murciano Quintero (Case C-240/98-C-244/98) [2000]
    ECR I-4941, [2002] 1 CMLR 43 .... 3.20
O'Connor v BDB Kirby & Co [1972] 1 QB 90, [1971] 2 All ER 1415 .... 16.19
O'Donoghue (T) Ltd v Harding [1988] 2 Lloyd's Rep 281..................................... 16.21
Oei v Foster (formerly Crawford) & Eagle Star Insurance Co Ltd [1982] 2 Lloyd's
    Rep 170.. 4.5
O'Kane v Jones (The Martin P) [2003] EWHC 3470 (Comm), [2004] 1 Lloyd's Rep
    389, [2005] Lloyd's Rep IR 174 .... 11.8
Olympic Pride, The. *See* Etablissements Levy
Omega Proteins Ltd v Aspen Insurance UK Ltd [2010] EWHC 2280 (Comm),
    [2011] 1 All ER (Comm) 313, [2011] Lloyd's Rep IR 183 .... 8.12
Orakpo v Manson Investments Ltd [1977] 1 WLR 347, [1977] 1 All ER 666, (1977)
    121 SJ 256... 11.49, 11.51; 12.2
Orient Express Hotels Ltd v Assicurazioni Generali SA (UK) (t/a Generali Global
    Risk) [2010] EWHC 1186 (Comm), [2010] 1 CLC 847, [2010] Lloyd's
    Rep IR 531 .... 17.5
O'Rourke v Darbishire [1920] AC 581 .... 9.34
Osman v J Ralph Moss Ltd [1970] 1 Lloyd's Rep 313.......................... 16.21, 16.41, 16.42
Outokumpu Stainless Steel Ltd v Axa Global Risks (UK) Ltd [2007] EWHC 2555
    (Comm), [2008] Lloyd's Rep IR 147.. 3.14
Overseas Commodities Ltd v Style [1958] 1 Lloyd's Rep 546 .... 3.6
Overseas Union Insurance Ltd v New Hampshire Insurance Co (Case C-351/89)
    [1992] QB 434, [1992] 2 All ER 138.. 15.11
Owners and/or Demise Charterers of the Dredger 'Kamal XXVI' & the Barge 'Kamal
    XXIV' v The Owners of the Ship 'Ariela' [2009] EWHC 3256 (Comm), [2010]
    2 Lloyd's Rep 274.. 8.6; 9.46; 11.53
Owners and/or Demise Charterers of the Dredger 'Kamal XXVI' & the Barge 'Kamal
    XXIV' v The Owners of the Ship 'Ariela' [2010] EWHC 2531 (Comm), [2011]
    1 Lloyd's Rep 291 .... 9.34
Owusu v Jackson (t/a Villa Holidays Bal Inn Villas) (Case C-281/02) [2005] QB
    801, [2005] 2 WLR 942, [2005] 2 All ER (Comm) 577.................................. 15.9

P

PCW Syndicates v PCW Reinsurers [1996] 1 WLR 1136, [1996] 1 All ER 774,
    [1996] 1 Lloyd's Rep 241 .... 1.1; 11.4, 11.10, 11.11,
                                           11.12, 11.13, 11.19

PARA

PM Law Ltd v Motorplus Ltd [2016] EWHC 193 (QB), [2016] 1 Costs LR 143 .....2.1, 2.18; 17.7
PT Buana Pratama v Marine Mutual Association (NZ) Ltd (The Buana Dua)
    [2011] EWHC 2413 (Comm), [2012] 1 All ER (Comm) 581, [2012] Lloyd's
    Rep IR 52 .... 11.49
Page v Scottish Union Insurance Corpn Ltd (1929) 33 Ll L Rep 134, (1929) 140
    LTR 571 .... 12.3, 12.8
Paine v Catlins [2004] EWHC 3054 (TCC), 98 Con LR 107, [2005] Lloyd's
    Rep IR 665 .... 5.2
Palmer v Palmer [2008] EWCA Civ 46, [2008] CP Rep 21, [2008] Lloyd's Rep
    IR 535 .... 9.46
Pan Atlantic Insurance Co Ltd v Pine Top Insurance Co Ltd [1995] 1 AC 501, [1994]
    2 Lloyd's Rep 427 .... 1.1; 11.4, 11.5, 11.6, 11.7, 11.19, 11.27, 11.39
Pangood Ltd v Barclay Brown & Co Ltd [1999] 1 All ER (Comm) 460, [1999]
    Lloyd's Rep IR 405 .... 16.5
Pankhania v London Borough of Hackney [2002] EWHC 2441 (Ch), [2002]
    NPC 123 .... 8.15
Parker v National Farmers Union Mutual Insurance Society Ltd [2012] EWHC 2156
    (Comm), [2013] Lloyd's Rep IR 253 .... 3.5, 3.20; 9.13; 11.52; 12.3
Parry v Cleaver [1970] AC 1, [1969] 1 All ER 555 .... 12.1
Partenreederei M/S Karen Oltmann v Scarsdale Shipping Co Ltd (The Karen
    Oltmann) [1976] 2 Lloyd's Rep 708 .... 3.16
Pasquali & Co v Traders' & General Insurance Association (1921) 9 Ll
    L Rep 514 .... 3.31
Passmore v Vulcan Boiler & General Insurance Co Ltd (1936) 54 Ll L Rep 92 .... 3.19
Patel v Windsor Life Assurance Co Ltd [2008] EWHC 76 (Comm), [2008] Lloyd's
    Rep IR 359 .... 2.13; 11.53
Patrick v Royal London Mutual Insurance Society Ltd [2006] EWCA Civ 421,
    [2006] 2 All ER (Comm) 344 , [2006] 1 CLC 576 .... 3.21; 5.2
Pattni v First Leicester Buses Ltd [2011] EWCA Civ 1384, [2012] RTR 17, [2012]
    Lloyd's Rep IR 577 .... 12.10
Pearl Life Assurance Co v Johnson [1909] 2 KB 288 .... 11.15
Pendennis Shipyard Ltd v Magrathea (Pendennis) Ltd [1998] 1 Lloyd's Rep 315,
    (1997) 94 (35) LSG 35, (1997) 141 SJLB 185 .... 9.46
Peninsular & Oriental Steam Navigation Co v Youell [1997] 2 Lloyd's Rep 136 ..... 8.12
Pennsylvania Co for Insurances on Lives & Granting Annuities v Mumford [1920]
    2 KB 537, (1920) 2 Ll L Rep 444 .... 6.9
Persimmon Homes Ltd v Great Lakes Reinsurance (UK) Ltd [2010] EWHC 1705,
    [2011] Lloyd's Rep IR 101 .... 9.5
Persimmon Homes (South Coast) Ltd v Hall Aggregates (South Coast) Ltd [2012]
    EWHC 2429 (TCC), [2012] CILL 3265 .... 9.45
Peters v General Accident & Life Assurance Corpn Ltd [1937] 4 All ER 628, (1937)
    59 Ll L Rep 148 .... 2.15
Petrofina (UK) Ltd v Magnaload Ltd [1984] QB 127, [1983] 3 All ER 35 .... 2.10; 12.4
Peyman v Lanjani [1985] Ch 457, [1984] 3 All ER 703 .... 11.63
Philadelphia National Bank v Price (1938) 60 Ll L Rep 257 .... 6.9
Phoenix Assurance Co v Spooner [1905] 2 KB 753 .... 12.6
Phoenix General Insurance Co of Greece SA v Halvanon Insurance Co Ltd [1988]
    QB 216, [1987] 2 All ER 152 .... 3.9
Pike (John A) (Butchers) Ltd v Independent Insurance Co Ltd [1998] Lloyd's Rep
    IR 410 .... 3.19
Pilkington UK Ltd v CGU Insurance plc [2004] EWCA Civ 23, [2005] 1 All ER
    (Comm) 283, [2004] Lloyd's Rep IR 891 .... 3.5; 17.15, 17.16

PARA

Pilkington United Kingdom Ltd v Commercial Union Assurance Co plc [1999]
Lloyd's Rep 495 .... 17.15
Pindos Shipping Corpn v Raven (The Mata Hari) [1983] 2 Lloyd's Rep 449 .... 3.32, 3.33
Pine v DAS Legal Expenses Insurance Co Ltd [2011] EWHC 658 (QB), [2012]
Lloyd's Rep IR 346 .... 6.6; 17.8
Pioneer Concrete (UK) Ltd v National Employers Mutual General Insurance
Association Ltd [1985] 2 All ER 395, [1985] 1 Lloyd's Rep 274, [1985] Fin
LR 251 .... 2.25; 7.1, 7.3, 7.5, 7.8
Piper v Royal Exchange Assurance (1932) 44 Ll L Rep 103 .... 8.15
Pirelli General Cable Works Ltd v Oscar Faber & Partners [1983] 2 AC 1, [1983]
1 All ER 65 .... 11.59
Pizzey v Ford Motor Co Ltd [1994] PIQR P15 .... 9.33
Plaza BV v Law Debenture Trust Corpn plc [2015] EWHC 43 (Ch) 15.9
Pleasurama Ltd v Sun Alliance & London Insurance Ltd [1979]
1 Lloyd's Rep 389 .... 6.4, 6.5, 6.7
Plymouth & South West Co-operative Society v Architecture, Structure &
Management Ltd [2006] EWHC 3252 (TCC), 111 Con LR 189, [2007] Lloyd's
Rep IR 596 .... 9.46
Pocock v Century Insurance Co Ltd [1960] 2 Lloyd's Rep 150 .... 17.3
Popi M, The. *See* Rhesa Shipping Co SA v Edmunds
Portavon Cinema Co Ltd v Price (1939) 65 Ll L Rep 161 .... 13.1
Porter v Magill [2001] UKHL 67, [2002] 2 AC 357 .... 9.12
Porter v Zurich Insurance Co [2009] EWHC 376 (QB), [2009] 2 All ER (Comm)
658, [2010] Lloyd's Rep IR 373 .... 5.2; 7.7
Portsmouth City Football Club Ltd v Sellar Properties (Portsmouth) Ltd [2004]
EWCA Civ 760, (2004) 148 SJLB 790 .... 3.16
Post Office v Norwich Union Fire Insurance Society Ltd [1967] 2 QB 363, [1967]
1 All ER 577 .... 2.24; 8.12; 9.40; 11.60
Potoi Chau, The. *See* Castle Insurance Co Ltd v Hong Kong Islands Shipping Co Ltd
Pratt v Aigaion Insurance Co SA (The Resolute) [2008] EWCA Civ 1314, [2009] 2
All ER (Comm) 387, [2009] 1 Lloyd's Rep 225 .... 3.6, 3.19
Prenn v Simmonds [1971] 1 WLR 1381, [1971] 3 All ER 237, (1971)
115 SJ 654 .... 3.15, 3.16, 3.30, 3.35
Prentis Donegan & Partners Ltd v Leeds & Leeds Co Inc [1998] 2 Lloyd's Rep 326,
[1998] CLC 1132 .... 16.5
Pride Valley Foods Ltd v Independent Insurance Co Ltd [1999] Lloyd's Rep
IR 120 .... 6.6
Printpak v AGF Insurance Ltd [1999] 1 All ER (Comm) 466 .... 1.1; 3.6, 3.7
Proudfoot v Montefiore (1866-67) LR 2 QB 511 .... 11.37
Provincial Insurance Co Ltd v Morgan & Foxon [1933] AC 240, (1932) 44 Ll
L Rep 275 .... 3.7, 3.16, 3.17; 11.16
Provincial Insurance Co of Canada v Leduc (1874-75) LR 6 PC 224 .... 2.8
Prudential Insurance Co v IRC [1904] 2 KB 658 .... 1.1
Prudential Staff Union v Hall [1947] KB 685, (1947) 80 Ll L Rep 410, 63
TLR 392 .... 2.10
Pryke (John W) v Gibbs Hartley Cooper Ltd [1991] 1 Lloyd's Rep 602 .... 11.5; 16.3,
16.11, 16.35
Pullar v United Kingdom (application 22399/93) 1996 SCCR 755, (1996)
22 EHRR 391 .... 9.12
Punjab National Bank v De Boinville [1992] 1 WLR 1138, [1992] 3 All ER 104,
[1992] 1 Lloyd's Rep 7 .... 3.16; 16.8, 16.12

Q

PARA

Quorum A/S v Schramm (costs) [2002] 2 All ER (Comm) 179, [2002] 2 Lloyd's Rep
72, [2002] CLC 77 .... 9.45; 11.60
Quorum A/S v Schramm (damage) [2002] 2 All ER (Comm) 147, [2002] 1 Lloyd's
Rep 249, [2002] CLC 77... 6.3, 6.4

R

R v Bow Street Metropolitan Stipendiary Magistrate, ex p Pinochet Ugarte (No 2)
[2000] 1 AC 119, [1999] 1 All ER 577 .... 9.12
R v Cox & Railton (1884-85) 14 QBD 153, [1881-85] All ER Rep 68 .... 9.34
R v Gough [1993] AC 646, [1993] 2 All ER 724 .... 9.12
R v Personal Investment Authority Ombudsman Bureau, ex p Royal & Sun Alliance
Life & Pensions Ltd [2002] Lloyd's Rep IR 41................................. 3.15, 3.19
R v Tymen [1980] 3 CMLR 101 .... 3.20
R & R Developments Ltd v AXA Insurance UK plc [2009] EWHC 2429 (Ch),
[2010] 2 All ER (Comm) 527, [2010] Lloyd's Rep IR 521 .... 11.15
R (on the application of Bluefin Insurance Services Ltd) v Financial Ombudsman
Service Ltd [2014] EWHC 3413 (Admin), [2015] Bus LR 656, [2015] Lloyd's
Rep IR 457 .... 10.18
R (on the application of Chancery (UK) LLP) v Financial Ombudsman Service Ltd
& Sir Ian Robinson [2015] EWHC 407 (Admin), [2015] BTC 13................... 10.18
R (on the application of Heather Moor & Edgecomb Ltd) v Financial Ombudsman
Service [2008] EWCA Civ 642, [2008] Bus LR 1486, (2008) 158
NLJ 897.. 10.17, 10.19
R (on the application of IFG Financial Services Ltd) v Financial Ombudsman Ltd
[2005] EWHC 1153 (Admin), [2006] 1 BCLC 534 .... 10.17
R (on the application of Shields) v Liverpool Crown Court [2001] EWHC Admin
90, [2001] UKHHR 610, [2001] ACD 60... 9.9
Raiffeisen Zentralbank Österreich AG v Five Star Trading LLC (The Mount I)
[2001] EWCA Civ 68, [2001] QB 825 .... 2.13; 9.42
Rainy Sky SA v Kookmin Bank [2011] UKSC 50, [2011] 1 WLR 2900, [2012] Bus
LR 313 .... 3.15
Rall v Hume [2001] EWCA Civ 146, [2001] 3 All ER 248, [2001] CP Rep 58 .... 8.5
Ramco (UK) Ltd v International Insurance Co of Hannover Ltd [2004] EWCA Civ
675, [2004] 2 All ER (Comm) 866, [2004] 2 Lloyd's Rep 595 .... 2.10; 3.17
Ramwade Ltd v WJ Emson & Co Ltd [1987] RTR 72, (1986) 83 LSG 2996, (186)
130 SJ 804... 6.6; 16.34
Randall v Cockran (1748) 1 Ves Sen 98, 27 ER 916 .... 12.13
Rankin v Potter (1873) LR 6 HL 83 .... 6.11
Rathbone Bros plc v Novae Corporate Underwriting Ltd [2014] EWCA Civ 1464,
[2014] 2 CLC 818, [2015] Lloyd's Rep IR 95.................................. 8.11; 12.4; 13.13;
                                                                                 17.22, 17.23
Rawlinson & Hunter Trustees SA v Director of the Seirous Fraud Office (No 2) *see*
Tchenguiz v Director of the Serious Fraud Office
Rayner v Preston (1881) 18 Ch D 1.. 2.15
Reardon Smith Line Ltd v Yngvar Hansen-Tangen [1976] 1 WLR 989, [1976] 3 All
ER 570, [1976] 2 Lloyd's Rep 621 .... 3.16
Red Sapphire, The. *See* Heesons Yacht Builders
Reed Executive plc v Reed Business Information Ltd [2004] EWCA Civ 887, [2004]
1 WLR 3026, [2004] 4 All ER 942 .... 9.35; 10.15
Rees v Mabco (102) Ltd (1999) 96(4) LSG 40, (1999) 143 SJLB 22...................... 9.47
Regina Fur Co Ltd v Bossom [1958] 2 Lloyd's Rep 425 .... 5.2

PARA

Reilly v National Insurance & Guarantee Corpn Ltd [2008] EWCA Civ 1460, [2009]
1 All ER (Comm) 1166, [2009] Lloyd's Rep IR 488 .... 3.19
Reinhard v Ondra LLP [2015] EWHC 2943 (Ch) 9.45
Reischer v Borwick [1894] 2 QB 548 .... 4.1, 4.3
Reliance Marine Insurance Co v Duder [1913] 1 KB 265 .... 3.16
Rendall v Combined Insurance Co of America [2005] EWHC 678 (Comm), [2005]
1 CLC 565, [2006] Lloyd's Rep IR 732 .... 11.22
Republic of India v India Steamship Co (No 2) [1998] AC 878, [1997] 4 All ER 380
.... 11.62, 11.63
Republic of Kazakhstan v Istil Group Inc [2007] EWCA Civ 471, [2008] Bus LR
878, [2007] 2 Lloyd's Rep 548 .... 9.9; 10.11
Revell v London General Insurance Co Ltd (1934) 50 Ll L Rep 114 .... 11.15
Reynolds v Phoenix Assurance Co Ltd [1978] 2 Lloyd's Rep 440 .... 2.11; 6.4, 6.5,
6.7; 9.45; 11.17
Rhesa Shipping Co SA v Edmunds (The Popi M) [1985] 1 WLR 948, [1985] 2 All
ER 712, [1985] 2 Lloyd's Rep 5.1, 5.2
Richard Aubrey Film Productions Ltd v Graham [1960] 2 Lloyd's Rep 101 .... 6.4
Ridehalgh v Horsefield [1994] Ch 205, [1994] 3 All ER 848 .... 9.33
Rivaz v Gerussi Bros & Co (1880-81) LR 6 QBD 222 .... 11.33
Riverlate Properties Ltd v Paul [1975] Ch 133, [1974] 2 All ER 656 .... 3.35
Roar Marine Ltd v Bimeh Iran Insurance Co (The Daylam) [1998] 1 Lloyd's
Rep 423 .... 3.22
Roberts v Anglo-Saxon Insurance Association Ltd (1927) 27 Ll L Rep 313 .... 3.7
Roberts v Avon Insurance Co Ltd [1956] 2 Lloyd's Rep 240 .... 11.15, 11.19
Roberts v Plaisted [1989] 2 Lloyd's Rep 341 .... 11.15
Roberts (A) & Co Ltd v Leicestershire County Council [1961] Ch 555, [1961] 2 All
ER 545 .... 3.33, 3.35
Robertson v French (1803) 4 East 130, 102 ER 779 .... 3.22, 3.24
Robinson v Gray [1963] Ch 459, [1963] 1 All ER 781 .... 2.6
Robinson Gold Mining Co v Alliance Insurance Co [1902] 2 KB 489 .... 3.15
Roche v Roberts (1921) 9 Ll L Rep 59 .... 7.16
Rodan International Ltd v Commercial Union Assurance Co plc [1999] Lloyd's Rep
IR 495 .... 3.14; 17.15, 17.17
Rogers v Whittaker [1917] 1 KB 942 .... 3.32
Rogerson v Scottish Automobile & General Insurance Co Ltd (1931) 41 Ll L
Rep 1 .... 2.15
Roselodge Ltd (formerly Rose Diamond Products Ltd) v Castle [1966] 2 Lloyd's
Rep 113, 116 NLJ 1378 .... 11.6, 11.7
Rothschild (J) Assurance plc v Collyear [1998] CLC 1697, [1999] Lloyd's Rep IR
6, [1999] Pens LR 77 .... 3.16; 7.9, 7.10
Rowett, Leakey & Co v Scottish Provident Institution [1927] 1 Ch 55 .... 3.19; 5.1
Royal & Sun Alliance Insurance plc v Dornoch [2005] EWCA Civ 238, [2005] 1 All
ER (Comm) 590, [2005] Lloyd's Rep IR 544 .... 3.5, 3.15, 3.18; 5.1; 7.8; 9.13
Royal Brompton Hospital NHS Trust v Hammond (No 3) [2002] UKHL 14, [2002]
1 WLR 1397, [2002] 2 All ER 801 .... 13.10
Rozanes v Bowen (1928) 32 Ll L Rep 98 .... 11.19; 16.3, 16.4
Rubenstein v HSBC Bank plc [2012] EWCA Civ 1184, [2013] 1 All ER (Comm)
915, [2013] PNLR 9 .... 8.2
Rush & Tompkins Ltd v Greater London Council [1989] AC 1280, [1988] 3 All ER
737 .... 9.35, 9.36, 9.37
Rust v Abbey Life Assurance Co Ltd [1979] 2 Lloyd's Rep 334 .... 3.3, 3.12

S   PARA

St Paul Fire & Marine Insurance Co (UK) Ltd v McConnell Dowell Constructors
    Ltd [1996] 1 All ER 96, [1995] 2 Lloyd's Rep 116, [1995] CLC 818 ....   11.6
St Paul Travelers Insurance Co Ltd v Dargan & Edwards [2006] EWHC 3189 (Ch)
    see Ballast plc, Re
Sagheera, The. *See* Hellenic Mutual War Risks Association (Bermuda) Ltd v Harrison
Sahib Foods Ltd (in liquidation) v Paskin Kyriakides Sands (a firm) [2003] EWCA
    Civ 1832, 93 Con LR 1, [2004] PNLR 22 ....   16.38
Samuel (P) & Co v Dumas [1924] AC 431, (1924) 18 Ll L Rep 211 ....2.3, 2.8, 2.13;
    4.2, 4.3; 11.52
Sargent v GRE (UK) Ltd [2000] Lloyd's Rep IR 77, [1997] 6 Re LR 281, [1997]
    PIQR Q128 ....   17.3
Sarginson Bros v Keith Moulton & Co Ltd (1942) 73 Ll L Rep 104 ....   16.21
Sarwar v Alam [2001] EWCA Civ 1401, [2002] 1 WLR 125, [2001] 4 All
    ER 541 ....   17.8
Sassoon (MA) & Sons Ltd v International Banking Corpn [1927] AC 711 ....   3.16
Savings & Investment Bank Ltd (in liquidation) v Fincken [2003] EWCA Civ 1630,
    [2004] 1 WLR 667, [2004] 1 All ER 1125 ....   9.38
Schiffshypothenkenbank Zu Luebeck AG v Compton (The Alexion Hope) [1988] 1
    Lloyd's Rep 311, [1988] FTLR 270, [1988] Fin LR 131 ....3.15; 5.2
Schoolman v Hall [1951] 1 Lloyd's Rep 139 ....11.15, 11.16
Schuler (L) AG v Wickman Machine Tool Sales Ltd [1974] AC 235, [1973] 2 All
    ER 39 ....   3.4, 3.14, 3.15, 3.16, 3.17
Scott v Copenhagen Reinsurance Co (UK) Ltd [2003] EWCA Civ 688, [2003] 2 All
    ER (Comm) 190, [2003] Lloyd's Rep IR 696 ....   6.9
Scottish Coal Co Ltd v Royal & Sun Alliance Insurance plc [2008] EWHC 880
    (Comm), [2008] Lloyd's Rep IR 718 ....   11.63
Scottish Power v Britoil Exploration Ltd (unreported, 18 November 1997) 3.16
Scottish Union & National Insurance Co v Davis [1970] 1 Lloyd's Rep 1 ....   12.3
Scragg v United Kingdom Temperance & General Provident Institution [1976] 2
    Lloyd's Rep 227 ....   3.22
Sea Glory Maritime Co v Al Sagr National Insurance Co (The MV Nancy) [2013]
    EWHC 2116 (Comm), [2013] 2 All ER (Comm) 913, [2014] 1 Lloyd's
    Rep 14 ....   3.6, 3.15; 11.7, 11.8, 11.11, 11.63
Sealion Shipping Ltd v Valiant Insurance Co (The Toisa Pisces) [2012] EWCA Civ
    1625, [2013] 1 All ER (Comm) 1179, [2013] 1 Lloyd's Rep 108 ....   6.7
Searle v AR Hales & Co Ltd [1996] LRLR 68, [1995] CLC 738 ....   3.2; 16.4
Seashell of Lisson Grove Ltd v Aviva Insurance Ltd [2011] EWHC 1761 (Comm),
    [2012] Lloyd's Rep IR 356 ....   3.4
Seaton v Heath [1899] 1 QB 782 ....   1.3
Seavision Investment SA v Evennett (The Tiburon) [1990] 2 Lloyd's
    Rep 418 ....   16.15, 16.47
Seechurn v Ace Insurance SA NV [2002] EWCA Civ 67, [2002] 2 Lloyd's Rep 390,
    [2002] Lloyd's Rep IR 489 ....   11.62, 11.63
Sempra Metals Ltd (formerly Metallgesellschaft Ltd) v IRC [2007] UKHL 34,
    [2008] 1 AC 561, [2008] Bus LR 49 ....   6.6; 9.45; 16.23
Sharon's Bakery (Europe) Ltd v Axa Insurance UK plc [2011] EWHC 210
    (Comm) 11.49
Sharp v Sphere Drake Insurance plc (The Moonacre) [1992] 2 Lloyd's
    Rep 501 ....   11.13, 11.15; 16.13, 16.14, 16.17, 16.21, 16.34, 16.38
Shearson Lehman Hutton Inc v Maclaine Watson & Co Ltd (damages & interest)
    [1990] 3 All ER 723, [1990] 1 Lloyd's Rep 441 ....   9.45

PARA

Shearson Lehman Hutton Inc v TVB Treithandgesellschaft fur Vermogensverwaltung und Beteiligungen mBH (Case C-89/91) [1993] ECR I-139, [1993] ILPr 199 .... 15.9
Sheffield Nickel & Silver Plating Co Ltd v Unwin (1876-77) LR 2 QBD 214 .... 11.33
Shelbourne & Co v Law Investment & Insurance Corpn Ltd [1898] 2 QB 626 .... 6.6
Sheldon v RHM Outhwaite (Underwriting Agencies) Ltd [1996] AC 102, [1995] 2 All ER 558 .... 16.31
Shell International Petroleum Co Ltd v Gibbs [1983] 2 AC 375, [1983] 1 Lloyd's Rep 342 .... 4.1
Sherdley v Nordea Life & Pension SA [2012] EWCA Civ 88, [2012] Lloyd's Rep IR 437 .... 15.9
Shinedean Ltd v Alldown Demolition (London) Ltd (in liquidation) [2006] EWCA Civ 939, [2006] 1 WLR 2696, [2006] 2 All ER (Comm) 982 .... 7.5
Shipley Urban DC v Bradford Corpn [1936] Ch 375 .... 3.30, 3.35
Shirlaw v Southern Foundries (1926) Ltd [1939] 2 KB 206, [1939] 2 All ER 113... 3.27
Simpson v Thomson (1877-78) LR 3 App Cas 279, (1877) 5 R (HL) 40 .... 12.3, 12.4
Simner v New India Assurance Co Ltd [1995] LRLR 240 .... 11.14, 11.63
Sirius International Insurance Corpn v Oriental Assurance Corpn [1999] 1 All ER (Comm) 699, [1999] Lloyd's Rep IR 343 .... 11.22
Sirius International Insurance Co (Publ) v FAI General Insurance Ltd [2004] UKHL 54, [2004] 1 WLR 3251, [2005] 1 All ER 191 .... 3.15, 3.16; 11.7
Sir William Garthwaite (Insurance) Ltd v Port of Manchester Insurance Co Ltd (1930) 37 Ll L Rep 194 .... 14.2
Siu Yin Kwan v Eastern Insurance Co Ltd [1994] 2 AC 199, [1994] 1 Lloyd's Rep 616 .... 2.6
Slattery v Mance [1962] 1 QB 676, [1962] 1 All ER 525 .... 5.2
Smith v Accident Insurance Co (1869-70) LR 5 Ex 302 .... 3.14, 3.19
Smith v Land & House Property Corpn (1884) LR 28 Ch D 7 .... 11.22
Smith (MH) (Plant Hire) Ltd v D L Mainwaring (t/a Inshore) [1986] 2 Lloyd's Rep 244, (1986) 2 BCC 99262 .... 12.6
Sneller v DAS Nederlandse Rechtsbijstand Verzekeringsmaatschappij NV (Case C-442/12) [2014] Bus LR 180, [2014] Lloyd's Rep IR 238 .... 17.8
Société Anonyme d'Intermédiaires Luxembourgeois (SAIL) v Farex Gie [1995] LRLR 116, [1994] CLC 1094 .... 3.3; 11.4, 11.11, 11.13; 16.6
Société Commerciale de Réassurances v ERAS (International) Ltd (formerly Eras (UK)) [1992] 2 All ER 82 (Note), [1992] 1 Lloyd's Rep 570 .... 16.31
Sofi v Prudential Assurance Co Ltd [1993] 2 Lloyd's Rep 559 .... 4.11; 5.1, 5.2
Solle v Butcher [1950] 1 KB 671, [1949] 2 All ER 1107, 66 TLR (Pt 1) 448 .... 8.15
Somatra Ltd v Sinclair Roche & Temperley (No 1) [2000] 1 WLR 2453, [2000] 2 Lloyd's Rep 673, [2000] CPLR 601 .... 9.38
Soole v Royal Insurance Co Ltd [1971] 2 Lloyd's Rep 332 .... 7.22; 11.25, 11.63
Sousa v Waltham Forest London Borough Council [2011] EWCA Civ 194, [2011] 1 WLR 2197, [2011] 4 Costs LR 584 .... 12.6
South Australia Asset Management Corpn v York Montague Ltd [1997] AC 191, [1996] 3 WLR 87, [1996] 3 All ER 365 .... 16.33, 16.37
South British Fire & Marine Insurance Co of New Zealand v Da Costa [1906] 1 KB 456 .... 3.15, 3.24
South Shropshire District Council v Amos [1986] 1 WLR 1271, [1987] 1 All ER 340, [1986] 2 EGLR 194 .... 9.35
South Staffordshire Tramways Co Ltd v Sickness & Accident Assurance Association Ltd [1891] 1 QB 402 .... 3.15; 6.9
Southwark & Vauxhall Water Co, The v Quick (1877-78) LR 3 QBD 315 .... 9.25

PARA

Spiliada Maritime Corpn v Cansulex Ltd (The Spiliada) [1987] AC 460, [1986] 3 All
ER 843 .... 15.13
Spinney's (1948) Ltd v Royal Insurance Co Ltd [1980] 1 Lloyd's Rep 406 .... 4.5; 5.1
Spriggs v Wessington Court School Ltd [2004] EWHC 1432 (QB), [2005] Lloyd's
Rep IR 474 .... 11.63
Sprung v Royal Insurance (UK) Ltd [1997] CLC 70, [1999] Lloyd's Rep
IR 111 .... 6.6; 8.9
Standard Bank London Ltd v Apostolakis [2002] CLC 933, [2000] IL Pr 766 .... 3.20
Standard Life Assureance Ltd v ACE European Group [2012] EWHC 104
(Comm) 6.9
Standard Life Assurance Ltd v Ace European Group [2012] EWCA Civ 1713,
[2013] Lloyd's Rep IR 415 .... 6.10, 6.13; 8.11
Standard Life Assurance Ltd v Oak Dedicated Ltd [2008] EWHC 222 (Comm),
[2008] 2 All ER (Comm) 916, [2008] Lloyd's Rep IR 552 .... 3.12; 6.9;
16.14, 16.16, 16.43
Stanley v Western Insurance Co (1867-68) LR 3 Exch 71 .... 3.14; 4.3, 4.12
Stanton & Stanton Ltd v Starr (1920) 3 Ll L Rep 259 .... 3.32, 3.33
Starfire Diamond Rings Ltd v Angel [1962] 2 Lloyd's Rep 217, (1962)
106 SJ 854 .... 3.14
Starlight Shipping Co v Allianz Marine & Aviation Versicherungs AG [2013]
UKSC 70, [2014] 1 Lloyd's Rep 223 .... 6.6; 15.11
Stark v DAS Osterreichishe Allgemeine Rechtsschutzversicherung AG (Case
C-293/10) (judgment 26 May 2011) 17.8
Star Sea, The. *See* Manifest Shipping Co Ltd v Uni-Polans Insurance Co Ltd
State Trading Corpn of India Ltd v M Golodetz Ltd [1989] 2 Lloyd's Rep 277 .... 3.7
Stemson v AMP General Insurance (NZ) Ltd [2006] UKPC 30, [2006] Lloyd's Rep
IR 852 .... 11.49
Stephen (AP) v Scottish Boatowners Mutual Insurance Association (The Talisman)
[1989] 1 Lloyd's Rep 535, 1989 SC (HL) 24, 1989 SLT 283 .... 4.10
Stirling (Sir Walter) v Vaughan (1809) 11 East 619, 103 ER 1145 .... 2.9
Stock v Inglis (1883-84) LR 12 QBD 564 .... 11.55
Stockton v Mason [1978] 2 Lloyd's Rep 430, [1979] RTR 130 .... 3.2; 16.4
Stocznia Gdanska SA v Latreefers Inc [2000] CPLR 65, [2001 BCC 174, [2001]
2 BCLC 116 .... 2.19
Stoneham v Ocean Railway & General Accident Insurance Co (1887) LR 19 QBD
237 .... 3.5; 7.4
Stretford v Football Association Ltd [2007] EWCA Civ 238, [2007] Bus LR 1052,
[2007] 2 Lloyd's Rep 31 .... 10.13
Strive Shipping Corpn v Hellenic Mutual War Risks Association (The Grecia
Express) [2002] EWHC 203 (Comm), [2002] 2 All ER (Comm) 213, [2002] 2
Lloyd's Rep 88 .... 3.17; 4.10; 5.3; 11.29, 11.30, 11.63
Strong & Pearl v S Allison & Co Ltd (1926) 25 Ll L Rep 504 .... 3.23; 16.21, 16.47
Structural Polymer Systems v Brown (The Baltic Universal) [1999] CLC 268,
[2000] Lloyd's Rep IR 64 .... 8.12; 13.3
Sugar Hut Group Ltd v Great Lakes Reinsurance (UK) plc [2010] EWHC 2636
(Comm), [2011] Lloyd's Rep IR 198 .... 3.6; 11.7
Sumitomo Bank Ltd v Banque Bruxelles Lambert SA [1997] 1 Lloyd's Rep 487,
[1996] EG 150 (CS) .... 11.23 , 11.34
Sun Life Assurance Co of Canada v Jervis [1944] AC 111 .... 3.12, 3.32
Sunport Shipping Ltd v Tryg-Baltica International (UK) Ltd (The Kleovoulos of
Rhodes) [2003] EWCA Civ 12, [2003] 1 All ER (Comm) 586, [2003] 1 Lloyd's
Rep 138 .... 3.17

PARA

Super Chem Products Ltd v American Life & General Insurance Co Ltd [2004]
UKPC 2, [2004] 2 All ER 358, [2004] Lloyd's Rep IR 446 .... 3.3; 7.21; 11.62, 11.63
Surf City, The [1995] 2 Lloyd's Rep 242.. 12.5
Sutherland Professional Funding Ltd v Bakewells [2011] EWHC 2658 (QB), [2013]
Lloyd's Re IR 93 ....17.19, 17.22
Sutro (L) & Heilbut Symons & Co, arbitration between, Re [1917] 2 KB 348 .... 3.27
Svenska Handelsbanken v Sun Alliance & London Insurance plc (No 2) [1996]
1 Lloyd's Rep 519, [1996] CLC 833 .... 9.31, 9.33; 11.63
Swingcastle Ltd v Alastair Gibson (a firm) [1991] 2 AC 223, [1991] 2 All
ER 353 .... 16.33
Swan v North British Australiasian Co (1863) 2 H & C 175.................................... 16.38
Swiss Reinsurance Co v United India Insurance Co Ltd [2005] EWHC 237 (Comm),
[2005] 2 All ER (Comm) 367, [2005] Lloyd's Rep IR 341 .... 11.18
Symington & Co v Union Insurance Society of Canton Ltd (1928) 31 Ll L
Rep 179 .... 4.12
Symphony Group plc v Hodgson [1994] QB 179, [1993] 4 All ER 143................. 9.46
Synergy Health (UK) Ltd v CGU Insurance plc (t/a Norwich Union) [2010] EWHC
2583 (Comm), [2011] Lloyd's Rep IR 500..................... 9.45; 11.7, 11.8, 11.15, 11.21,
11.22, 11.24; 16.19, 16.21,
16.25, 16.38; 17.5

T

T & N Ltd (in administration) v Royal & Sun Alliance plc [2003] EWHC 1016 (Ch),
[2003] 2 All ER (Comm) 939, [2004] 1 Lloyd's Rep IR 106............................ 2.21
TSB Bank Ltd v Robert Irving & Burns [2000] 2 All ER 826, [1999] Lloyd's Rep
PN 956, [2000] PNLR 384.. 8.13; 9.13, 9.33
Talbot Underwriting Ltd v Nausch, Hogan & Murray Inc (The Jascon 5)
[2006] EWCA Civ 889, [2006] 2 All ER (Comm) 751, [2006] 2 Lloyd's
Rep 195 .... 2.2, 2.10; 12.4, 12.13; 16.16, 16.36
Talisman, The. *See* Stephen (AP) v Scottish Boatowners
Tarbuck v Avon Insurance plc [2002] QB 571, [2001] 2 All ER 503 .... 2.21
Tate & Sons v Hyslop (1884-85) LR 15 QBD 368.. 12.6
Tate Gallery, Board of Trustees v Duffy Construction Ltd [2007] EWHC 912 (TCC),
[2008] Lloyd's Rep IR 159 .... 5.2
Tattersall v Drysdale [1935] 2 KB 174, (1935) 52 Ll L Rep 21 .... 2.15
Taylor v Allon [1966] 1 QB 304, [1965] 2 WLR 598, [1965] 1 Lloyd's Rep 155 .... 3.2
Taylor v Dunbar (1868-69) LR 4 CP 206 .... 4.2
Taylor v Eagle Star Insurance Co Ltd (1940) 67 Ll L Rep 136................................11.7, 11.15
Tchenguiz v Director of the Serious Fraud Office [2014] EWCA Civ 1129, [2015] 1
WLR 797... 9.33
Teal Assurance Co Ltd v WR Berkley Insurance (Europe) Ltd [2011] EWCA Civ
1570, [2012] Lloyd's Rep IR 315 .... 2.25; 3.14, 3.15; 6.13; 11.58, 11.59, 11.60
Ted Baker plc v AXA Insurance UK plc [2012] EWHC 1406 (Comm), [2013] 1 All
ER (Comm) 129, [2013] Lloyd's Rep IR 174.................................. 3.16; 5.1, 5.2; 6.3;
9.13; 11.4, 11.14
Tektrol Ltd v International Insurance Co of Hanover Ltd [2005] EWCA Civ 845,
[2006] 1 All ER (Comm) 780, [2005] 2 Lloyd's Rep 701 .... 3.18, 3.21
Temple Legal Protection Ltd v QBE Insurance (Europe) Ltd [2009] EWCA Civ 453,
[2010] 1 All ER (Comm) 703, [2009] Lloyd's Rep IR 544............................. 2.1
Tesco Stores Ltd v Constable [2008] EWCA Civ 362, [2008] 1 CLC 727, [2008]
Lloyd's Rep IR 636...3.14; 4.7; 17.17, 17.24, 17.25

PARA

Thai Airways International Public Co Ltd v KI Holdings Co Ltd (formerly Koito
   Industries Ltd) [2015] EWHC 1476 (Comm), [2015] 3 Costs LR 545 ....9.45
Thames & Mersey Marine Insurance Co Ltd v Gunford Ship Co Ltd [1911] AC 529,
   1911 SC (HL) 84, 1911 2 SLT 185.. 11.13, 11.19
Tharros Shipping Co Ltd v Bias Shipping Ltd (The Griparion) (No 3) [1995] 1
   Lloyd's Rep 541.. 2.24; 9.46
Thomas Bates & Son Ltd v Wyndham's (Lingerie) Ltd [1981] 1 WLR 505, [1981] 1
   All ER 1077, (1981) 41 P & CR 345 .... 3.33, 3.35
Thomas Cheshire & Co v Vaughan Bros & Co [1920] 3 KB 240, (1920) 3 Ll L Rep 213 16.34
Thomson v Weems (1883-84) LR 9 App Cas 671, (1884) 11 R (HL) 48 .... 3.4, 3.7;
                                                                         11.16, 11.23, 11.29
Thorman v New Hampshire Insurance Co (UK) Ltd [1988] 1 Lloyd's Rep 7, 39 BLR
   41, [1988] 1 FTLR 30 .... 6.9; 7.9
Thornbridge Ltd v Barclays Bank plc [2015] EWHC 3430 (QB)............................ 8.2
Thornton Springer v NEM Insurance Co Ltd [2000] 2 All ER 489, [2000] 1 All ER
   (Comm) 486, [2000] Lloyd's Rep IR 590... 8.9, 8.11
Three Rivers District Council v Bank of England (disclosure) (No 1) [2002] EWCA
   Civ 1182, [2003] 1 WLR 210, [2002] 4 All ER 881 .... 9.22, 9.23, 9.25
Tilley & Noad v Dominion Insurance Co Ltd (1987) 284 EG 1056 .... 7.9; 11.30
Tioxide Europe Ltd v CGU International Insurance plc [2004] EWHC 2116
   (Comm), [2005] Lloyd's Rep IR 114.. 4.8; 7.11; 17.17
Titan Steel Wheels Ltd v Royal Bank of Scotland plc [2010] EWHC 211 (Comm),
   [2010] 2 Lloyd's Rep 92, [2012] 1 CLC 191 .... 8.2
Tokio Marine Europe Insurance Ltd v Novae Corporate Underwriting Ltd (No 2)
   [2014] EWHC 2105 (Comm), [2014] Lloyd's Rep IR 638 .... 14.2
Tolstoy Miloslavsky v United Kingdom (Series A/323) [1996] EMLR 52, (1995) 20
   EHRR 442.. 9.9
Tonkin v UK Insurance Ltd [2006] EWHC 1120 (TCC), [2006] 2 All ER (Comm)
   550, 107 Con LR 107.. 6.4, 6.5, 6.6
Toomey v Banco Vitalicio de Espana SA de Seguros y Reasseguros [2004] EWCA
   Civ 622, [2004] 1 CLC 965, [2005] Lloyd's Rep IR 423 .... 3.6
Toomey v Eagle Star Insurance Co Ltd (No 1) [1994] 1 Lloyd's
   Rep 516.. 3.16, 3.17; 14.2
Toropdar v D [2009] EWHC 567 (QB), [2010] Lloyd's Rep IR 358 .... 9.40
Total Gas Marketing Ltd v Arco British Ltd [1998] 2 Lloyd's Rep 209, [1998]
   CLC 1275.. 3.14
Touche Ross & Co v Baker [1992] 2 Lloyd's Rep 207, (1992) 89 (28) LSG 31,
   (1992) 136 SJLB 190.. 3.14
Travelers Casualty & Surety Co of Canada v Sun Life Assurance Co of Canada
   (UK) Ltd [2006] EWHC 2716, [2007] Lloyd's Rep IR 619 .... 15.3, 15.4,
                                                                             15.5, 15.13
Trinder, Anderson & Co v Thames & Mersey Marine Insurance Co [1898]
   2 QB 114.. 4.11
Turner (CF) v Manx Line Ltd [1990] 1 Lloyd's Rep 137.............................. 3.14, 3.15
Tychy, The. *See* MSC Mediterranean Shipping Co SA
Tyco Fire & Integrated Solutions (UK) Ltd (formerly Wormald Ansul (UK) Ltd) v
   Rolls-Royce Motor Cars Ltd (formerly Hireus Ltd) [2008] EWCA Civ 286,
   [2008] 2 All ER (Comm) 584, [2008] Lloyd's Rep IR 617 .... 12.4

U

Unilever plc v Proctor & Gamble Co [2000] 1 WLR 2436, [2001] 1 All ER 783,
   [2000] FSR 344.. 9.36, 9.38

PARA

United London & Scottish Insurance Co Ltd, Re [1915] 2 Ch 167............................ 3.15, 3.19
United Mills Agencies Ltd v Harvey, Bray & Co [1952] 1 All ER 225 (Note), [1951]
    2 Lloyd's Rep 631, [1952] 1 TLR 149... 16.13, 16.21
United States of America v Motor Trucks Ltd [1924] AC 196................................. 3.30
United States of America v Phillip Morris Inc (No 1) [2004] EWCA Civ 330, [2004]
    1 CLC 811, (2004) 148 SJLB 388 .... 9.25
Universal Non-Tariff Fire Insurance Co, Re (1874-75) LR 19 Eq 485 .... 11.7, 11.13; 16.6
Universities Superannuation Scheme Ltd v Royal Insurance (UK) Ltd [2000] 1 All
    ER (Comm) 266, [2000] Lloyd's Rep IR 524.. 11.58

V

Vainqueur José, The. *See* CVG Siderurgicia de Orinoco SA
Van Hove v CNP Assurances SA (Case C-96/14) [2015] 3 CMLR 31, [2015] CEC
    1172, [2016] Lloyd's Rep IR 61 .... 3.20
Venables v News Group Newspaper Ltd [2001] Fam 430, [2001] 1 All ER 908 ...... 8.5
Ventouris v Mountain (The Italia Express) (No 3) [1992] 2 Lloyd's
    Rep 281 .... 6.6; 9.32; 11.60
Verderame v Commercial Union Assurance Co plc [1992] BCLC 793, [2000]
    Lloyd's Rep PN 557, [1955-95] PNLR 612.................................... 16.12, 16.39
Verelst's Administratrix v Motor Union Insurance Co Ltd [1925] 2 KB 137, (1925)
    21 Ll L Rep 227 .... 7.15, 7.17
Versloot Dredging BV v HDI Gerling Industrie Versicherung AG [2013] EWHC 658
    (Comm)... 9.5
Versloot Dredging BV v HDI Gerling Industrie Versicherung AG [2014] EWCA Civ
    1349, [2015] QB 608, [2015] 2 WLR 1063...................................... 11.49
Vesta v Butcher [1986] 2 All ER 488, [1986] 2 Lloyd's Rep 179 16.4, 16.14, 16.18,
    16.26, 16.38
Vesta v Butcher [1989] AC 852, [1989] 2 WLR 290, [1989] 1 All ER 402 .... 14.6
Vimeira, The. *See* Aiden Shipping Co v Interbulk Ltd
Virk v Gan Life Holdings plc [2000] Lloyd's Rep IR 159, (2000)
    52 BMLR 207 .... 3.5; 7.3, 7.5; 9.13; 11.58, 11.60
Vistafjord, The. *See* Norwegian American Cruises A/S v Paul Makundy Ltd

W

W & J Lane v Spratt [1970] 2 QB 480, [1970] 1 All ER 162........................... 4.2, 4.11; 5.2
WD Fairway (No 3), Re *see* Dornoch Ltd v Westminster International BV [2009]
    EWHC 1782 (Admlty), [2009] 2 Lloyd's Rep 420, [2009] 2 CLC 226
Wakefield v Outhwaite [1990] 2 Lloyd's Rep 157.. 9.23
Walker v Pennine Insurance Ltd [1980] 2 Lloyd's Rep 156............................ 11.58, 11.60
Walker v Wilsher (1889) 23 QBD 335... 9.35
Walton v Airtours plc [2002] EWCA Civ 1659, [2003] IRLR 161, [2002] Lloyd's
    Rep IR 69 .... 17.3
Ward (AC) & Son Ltd v Catlin (Five) Ltd (No 2) [2009] EWHC 3122 (Comm),
    [2010] 2 All ER (Comm) 683, [2010] Lloyd's Rep IR 695 .... 3.6; 11.7
Warren v Henry Sutton & Co [1976] 2 Lloyd's Rep 276 .... 16.19
Wasa International Insurance Co v Lexington Insurance Co [2009] UKHL 40,
    [2010] 1 AC 180.. 14.2, 14.6
Waterkeyn v Eagle, Star & British Dominions Insurance Co Ltd (1920) 5 Ll
    L Rep 42.. 16.15, 16.17
Waters v Monarch Fire & Life Assurance Co [1846-60] All ER Rep 654, 119 ER
    705, (1856) 5 E & B 870.. 2.10
Watts v Morrow [1991] 1 WLR 1421, [1991] 4 All ER 937, 54 BLR 86........... 16.33, 16.39

PARA

Watson (Joseph) & Son Ltd v Firemen's Fund Insurance Co of San Francisco [1922]
2 KB 355, (1922) 12 Ll L Rep 133 .... 4.12
Waugh v British Railways Board [1980] AC 521, [1979] 2 All ER 1169 .... 9.25, 9.29
Wayne Tank & Pump Co Ltd v Employers' Liability Assurance Corpn [1974] QB
57, [1973] 3 WLR 483, [1973] 3 All ER 825 .... 3.14; 4.3; 17.24
Webb v United Kingdom (1997) 24 EHRR CD 73 .... 9.9
Webster v General Accident Fire & Life Assurance Corpn Ltd [1953] 1 QB 520,
[1953] 1 All ER 663 .... 4.10; 5.2; 7.22; 11.63
Weddell v Road Transport & General Insurance Co Ltd [1932] 2 KB 563, (1931)
41 Ll L Rep 69 .... 13.3, 13.4
Welch v Royal Exchange Assurance [1939] 1 KB 294, (1938) 62 Ll L Rep 83 .... 3.5,
3.17, 3.19; 7.4
Wellesley Partners LLP v Withers LLP [2015] EWCA Civ 1146, 163 Con R 53,
[2016] PNLR 19... 16.34
Westdeutsche Landesbank Girozentrale v Islington London Borough Council
[1996] AC 669, [1996] 2 All ER 961 .... 9.45
Western Assurance Co of Toronto v Poole [1903] 1 KB 376 .... 3.24; 14.2
Western Trading Ltd v Great Lakes Reinsurance (UK) Ltd [2015] EWHC 103 (QB),
[2015] Lloyd's Rep IR 561 .... 6.5
West v Ian Finlay & Associates [2014] EWCA Civ 316, [2014] BLR 324, 153 Con
LR 1 .... 9.45
West London Commercial Bank Ltd v Kitson (1883-84) LR 13
QBD 360.. 8.15; 11.25, 11.26
West London Pipeline & Storage Ltd v Total UK Ltd [2008] EWHC 1296 (Comm),
[2008] CP Rep 35, [2008] Lloyd's Rep IR 688 .... 9.15
Westminster Fire Office v Glasgow Provident Investment Society (1888) LR 13 App
Cas 699, (1888) 15 R (HL) 89 .... 2.8, 2.11
Westminster International BV v Dornoch [2009] EWCA Civ 1323......................... 9.25
West of England Fire Insurance Co v Isaacs [1897] 1 QB 226 .... 12.6
West of England Shipowners Mutual Insurance Association (Luxembourg) v Cristal
Ltd (The Glacier Bay) [1996] 1 Lloyd's Rep 370, [1996] CLC 240................. 5.4
West Tankers Inc v Allianz SpA (The Front Comor) [2012] EWCA Civ 27, [2012] 2
All ER (Comm) 113, [2012] Lloyd's Rep 398 .... 10.10
West Wake Price & Co v Ching [1957] 1 WLR 45, [1956] 3 All ER 821, [1956] 2
Lloyd's Rep 618.................................... 4.3; 5.2; 6.9; 7.8; 8.11, 8.12; 9.40
White v Jones [1995] 2 AC 207, [1995] 1 All ER 691 .... 16.11, 16.12
Widefree Ltd (t/a Abrahams & Ballard) v Brit Insurance Ltd [2009] EWHC 3671
(QB), [2010] 2 All ER (Comm) 477, [2011] Lloyd's Rep IR 63...................... 7.7
William McIlroy (Swindon) Ltd v Quinn Insurance Ltd [2011] EWCA Civ 825,
[2012] 1 All ER (Comm) 241, [2011] BLR 570............................. 9.40; 11.58, 11.60
William Pickersgill & Sons Ltd v London & Provincial Marine & General Insurance
Co Ltd [1912] 3 KB 614 .... 11.60
Williams v Natural Life Health Foods Ltd [1998] 1 WLR 830, [1998] 2 All ER 477,
[1998] BCC 428... 16.8
Williams Bros v Agius Ltd [1914] AC 510... 3.26
Williams, Re (1902) 19 TLR 82 .... 7.14
Wilsher v Essex Area Health Authority [1988] AC 1074, [1988] 1 All ER 871........ 16.33
Wilson & Scottish Insurance Corpn Ltd, Re [1920] 2 Ch 28 .... 6.4
Wilson v Raffalovich (1880-81) LR 7 QBD 553..................................... 12.7
Wimpey Construction (UK) Ltd v DV Poole [1984] 2 Lloyd's Rep 499, 27 BLR 58,
(1984) 128 SJ 969... 3.12
Wind Star, The. *See* Colonia Versicherung AG v Amoco Oil Co

PARA

Winspear v Accident Insurance Co (1880-81) LR 6 QBD 42 .... 4.2
Winter v Irish Life Assurance plc [1995] 2 Lloyd's Rep 274, [1995]
    CLC 722.. 11.8, 11.15, 11.16; 16.4
Winterthur Swiss Insurance Co v AG (Manchester) Ltd [2006] EWHC 839
    (Comm).. 9.33
Wise (Underwriting Agency) Ltd v Grupo Nacional Provincial SA [2004] EWCA
    Civ 962, [2004] 2 All ER (Comm) 613, [2004] Lloyd's Rep 483 .... 11.14
Wondrous, The. *See* Ikerigi Compania Naviera SA v Palmer
Wood v Perfection Travel Ltd [1996] LRLR 233, [1996] CLC 1121 .... 9.47
Woodhouse AC Israel Cocoa Ltd SA v Nigerian Produce Marketing Co Ltd [1972]
    AC 741, [1972] 2 All ER 271 .... 11.63
Woolcott v Excess Insurance Co Ltd & Miles, Smith Anderson & Game Ltd (No 2)
    [1979] 2 Lloyd's Rep 210 .... 11.13, 11.15, 11.19, 11.52; 16.4, 16.6
Woolcott v Sun Alliance & London Insurance Ltd [1978] 1 WLR 493, [1978] 1 All
    ER 1253, [1978] 1 Lloyd's Rep 629 .... 2.3; 11.30
Woolwich Building Society v Brown [1996] CLC 625 .... 12.4
Woolwich Building Society v Taylor [1995] 1 BCLC 132, [1994] CLC 516 .... 2.23
Worsley v Tambrands Ltd [2002] Lloyd's Rep IR 382... 9.46
Wright v John Bagnall & Sons Ltd [1900] 2 QB 240.. 11.62
Wyeth (John) & Brothers Ltd v Cigna Insurance Co of Europe SA NV (No 1) [2001]
    EWCA Civ 175, [2001] CLC 970, [2001] Lloyd's Rep IR 420 .... 8.11

X

X v United Kingdom (1970) 30 EHRR CD 70.. 9.10
XL London Market Ltd v Zenith Syndicate Management Ltd [2004] EWHC 1182
    (Comm).. 9.22
XYZ v Various Companies (The PIP Breast Implant Litigation) [2013] EWHC 3643
    (QB), [2014] 2 Costs LO 197, [2014] Lloyd's Rep IR 431 .... 9.15
XYZ v Various Companies [2014] EWHC 4056 (QB)... 9.47

Y

Yager & Guardian Assurance Co, Re (1912) 108 LT 38 .... 11.6, 11.18
Yasin, The [1979] 2 Lloyd's Rep 45 .... 12.4
Yona International Ltd v La Réunion Française SA D'Assurances et de Reassurances
    [1996] 2 Lloyd's Rep 84 .... 3.3, 3.12
Yorke v Yorkshire Insurance Co [1918] 1 KB 662 .... 11.7, 11.23
Yorkshire Dale Steamship Co Ltd v Minister of War Transport [1942] AC 691,
    (1942) 73 Ll L Rep 1, 1942 AMC 1000... 4.2, 4.11
Yorkshire Insurance Co Ltd v Campbell [1917] AC 218.................. 3.19, 3.24, 3.25; 11.16
Yorkshire Insurance Co Ltd v Craine [1922] 2 AC 541, (1922) 12 Ll L Rep 399..... 7.22
Yorkshire Insurance Co Ltd v Nisbet Shipping Co Ltd [1962] 2 QB 330, [1961] 2 All
    ER 487 .... 3.27; 12.2, 12.8, 12.11, 12.12
Yorkshire Water Services Ltd v Sun Alliance & London Insurance plc (No 1) [1997]
    2 Lloyd's Rep 21, [1997] CLC 213, (1996) 93 (34) LSG 34................. 1.2; 3.15, 3.19;
    4.10; 6.14
Youell v Bland Welch & Co Ltd (No 1) [1992] 2 Lloyd's Rep 127 .... 3.3, 3.12, 3.16,
    3.19, 3.23, 3.32
Youell v Bland Welch & Co Ltd (No 2) [1990] 2 Lloyd's Rep 431 .... 16.7, 16.14,
    16.16, 16.17, 16.20, 16.22, 16.26,
    16.27, 16.28, 16.38, 16.43
Youell v La Réunion Aerienne [2009] EWCA Civ 175, [2009] Bus LR 1504, [2009]
    1 Lloyd's Rep 586.. 15.9

PARA

Young v Sun Alliance & London Insurance Ltd [1977] 1 WLR 104, [1976] 3 All ER
 561, [1976] 2 Lloyd's Rep 189 .... 3.14, 3.21

Z

Zaki v Credit Suisse (UK) Ltd [2011] EWHC 2422 (Comm), [2011] 2 CLC 523....   8.2
Zanussi v Anglo Venezuelan Real Estate & Agricultural Development Ltd (The
 Times, 17 April 1996) 9.46
Zealander v Laing Homes Ltd (2000) 2 TCLR 724................................... 3.20; 10.14
Zeller v British Caymanian Insurance Co Ltd [2008] UKPC 4, [2008] Lloyd's Rep
 IR 545...   11.22
Zephyr, The. *See* General Accident Fire & Life Assurance Corpn Ltd
Zeus, The. *See* Attaleia Marine Co Ltd v Bimeh Iran
Zeus Tradition Marine Ltd v Bell (The Zeus V) [2000] 2 All ER (Comm) 769,
 [2000] 2 Lloyd's Rep 587, [2000] CLC 1705...   3.19
Zurich General Accident & Liability Insurance Co Ltd v Morrison [1942] 2 KB 253,
 (1942) 72 Ll L Rep 167 .... 11.6, 11.15
Zurich Insurance Co plc v Hayward [2011] EWCA Civ 641, [2011] CP Rep 39 .....   8.15

Table of European Legislation

PARA

TREATIES AND CONVENTIONS

Convention for the Protection of Human Rights and Fundamental Freedoms
(Rome, 4 November 1950)... 8.5; 10.19
  art 6 .... 8.5; 9.6, 9.8, 9.9, 9.10; 10.17
    (1)... 9.6
    8 .... 8.5
    (1), (2)... 8.5
Convention on Jurisdiction and the Enforcement of Judgments in Civil and Commercial
Matters (Brussels, 27 September 1968)... 15.7
Convention on Jurisdiction and the Enforcement of Judgments in Civil and Commercial
Matters (Lugano, 16 September 1988) 15.7
Convention on the Law Applicable to Contractual Obligations (Rome, 19 June
1980)... 15.3, 15.4, 15.5
  art 1(1)... 15.4
    (2)(d) 15.5
    (3)... 15.4, 15.5
    (4)... 15.5
    2 .... 15.5
    3(1)–(3) 15.5
    4 .... 15.5
    (1), (2), (5) 15.5
    7(1)... 15.5
    8 .... 15.4, 15.5
    (1)... 15.4
    9 .... 15.4, 15.5
    10(1)(e) 15.5
    11 .... 15.4, 15.5
    12, 13 .... 15.5

REGULATIONS

Reg 44/2001/EC... 15.7
  Art 76 .... 15.7
Reg 593/2008/EC.. 3.20; 15.6
  art 3(1).. 15.6
    4 .... 15.6
    (a), (b) 15.6
    7(2)... 15.6
    (3)... 15.6
    (a)–(e).. 15.6
    (6)... 15.6

PARA

Reg 1215/2012/EC.. 15.7, 15.9, 15.10, 15.12, 15.13
  art 4 .... 15.8
   (1).. 15.13
   5(1)... 15.8
   10 .... 15.7, 15.8
   11 .... 15.7, 15.8
    (1), (2).. 15.9
   12 .... 15.7, 15.8, 159
   13 .... 15.7, 15.8
    (1)... 15.9
    (2), (3)... 15.8, 15.9
   14 .... 15.7, 15.8
    (1), (2).. 15.8
   15 .... 15.7, 15.8, 15.9
    (1)–(5).. 15.9
   16 .... 15.7, 15.8, 15.9
   22, 23 .... 15.13
   24 .... 15.10, 15.13
   25 .... 15.9, 15.11
   26 .... 15.10, 15.11
   29(1), (3)... 15.11
   30(1)–(3)... 15.11
   31 .... 15.12
    (1), (2).. 15.11
   32 .... 15.11
   62(1), (2)... 15.8
   63(1), (2)... 15.8
   66(1), (2)... 15.7
   80 .... 15.7

DIRECTIVES

Dir 73/239/EEC 15.4, 15.6, 15.9
Dir 78/473/EEC 15.4
Dir 79/267/EEC 15.4
Dir 87/334/EC..17.8, 17.9
Dir 88/357/EC..15.3, 15.4, 15.6
Dir 90/619/EC 15.4
Dir 92/49/EC.. 15.4
Dir 92/96/EC.. 15.4
Dir 93/13/EC.. 3.20
Dir 2002/83/EC... 15.6
Dir 2009/138/EC... 17.8

Chapter 1

The basics

SCOPE OF THIS BOOK

1.1   A contract of insurance is 'a contract for the payment of a sum of money, or for some corresponding benefit such as the rebuilding of a house or the repairing of a ship, to become due on the happening of an event, which event must have some amount of uncertainty about it, and must be of a character more or less adverse to the interest of the person effecting the insurance.'[1]

This book is concerned with insurance claims, primarily against insurers and brokers, and in relation to non-marine insurance. The principles of marine insurance, including the Marine Insurance Act 1906, are considered only to the extent that they are applicable to non-marine insurance. The Act of 1906 was a partial codification of the common law, and although it applies directly only in relation to marine insurance, the courts have sometimes applied it, or derived relevant principles from it, in the context of non-marine insurance. The sections applied in this way include ss 17 to 20[2] and 33.[3] Although reference is commonly made without objection to the commentary on the 1906 Act published by its draftsman, Sir M D Chalmers,[4] the extent to which it is legitimate to consider the existing law at the time the Bill was drafted as an aid to interpretation of the 1906 Act is undecided.[5]

1 *Prudential Insurance Co v Commissioners of Inland Revenue* [1904] 2 KB 658, 664 (Channell J); approved: *Digital Satellite Warranty Cover Ltd v Financial Services Authority* [2013] UKSC 7, [2013] Lloyd's Rep IR 236, para 19.
2 See *Pan Atlantic Insurance Co Ltd v Pine Top Insurance Co Ltd* [1995] 1 AC 501, 518, 541, [1994] 2 Lloyd's Rep 427, 432, 447, HL (Lord Mustill); *PCW Syndicates v PCW Reinsurers* [1996] 1 WLR 1136, 1140, CA (Staughton LJ); *HIH Casualty and General Insurance Ltd v Chase Manhattan Bank* [2003] UKHL 6, [2003] Lloyd's Rep IR 230, 244, para 42 (Lord Hoffmann).
3 See *Printpak v AGF Insurance Ltd* [1999] Lloyd's Rep IR 542, 545, CA (Hirst LJ).
4 *The Marine Insurance Act 1906*, Sir M D Chalmers and Douglas Owen (1st edn, 1907).
5 See *State of the Netherlands v Youell* [1998] 1 Lloyd's Rep 236, CA, 240 (Phillips LJ – legitimate to do so) and 246 (Buxton LJ – would be an exception to the general rule; not argued and no pressing need to consider in the context of that appeal).

FOREIGN LAW

1.2   Case law from other jurisdictions may be of assistance if there is no English case in which a principle is decided. Generally, the closer the links with the English legal system, the more useful the case will be. Australian, New Zealand and Canadian cases are particularly likely to be of assistance; Scottish cases may also sometimes be useful. American cases should be approached with caution, as the underlying approach to contracts of insurance tends to favour the insured in a way in which English law does not.[1]

1 See eg *Yorkshire Water Services Ltd v Sun Alliance & London Insurance plc* [1997] 2 Lloyd's Rep 21, 28, CA (Stuart-Smith LJ); *International Energy Group Ltd v Zurich Insurance plc* [2015] UKSC 33, [2016] AC 509, para 164 (Lord Sumption).

INDEMNITY AND CONTINGENCY INSURANCE

1.3 Contracts of indemnity insurance are matters of speculation, where the insured has greater means of knowledge as to the risk than the insurer. The insured proposes the risk to the insurer as a business transaction; the insurer fixes a premium to remunerate him for the risk undertaken, and the insurer agrees to pay the loss suffered by the insured in the event of specified contingencies happening.[1] In non-indemnity insurance (also known as contingency insurance), which includes life, accident and permanent health insurance, the sum payable by the insurer is not defined by reference to the loss suffered by the insured, but is a benefit, the level of which is agreed when the contract is concluded. It would be possible to view certain contracts of contingency insurance as contracts of indemnity insurance written on a valued basis,[2] for example, where the level of the benefits under an accident policy is fixed by reference to the insured's annual income; but this is not the conventional analysis.

1 *Seaton v Heath* [1899] 1 QB 782, 793, CA (Romer LJ). For the distinction between contracts of insurance and contracts of guarantee, see *Seaton v Heath*, 792–793 (Romer LJ).
2 See **CHAPTER 6**, Measurement of loss.

TERMINOLOGY: 'ASSURANCE' AND 'INSURANCE'

1.4 Historically, the term 'assurance' tended to be used for life insurance, and 'insurance' for indemnity insurance such as fire or property insurance. The two terms (together with 'assure', 'insure', 'assured' and 'insured') are now used interchangeably, although 'insurance' (together with 'insure' and 'insured') is more common.

THE LONDON INSURANCE MARKET

1.5 There are two main elements to the London insurance market: Lloyd's; and the non-Lloyd's sector, which is known as the company market. In addition to disputes about the meaning of policy wording, it was until recently common in the London market, and particularly where policies were written on the basis of a slip, for the wording of the policy not to be agreed before inception of the risk (before the policy enters into force). The situation has improved significantly since the introduction of the concept of 'contract certainty', which requires 'the complete and final agreement of all terms (including signed down lines) between the insured and insurers before inception'; in addition, the full wording must be agreed before any insurer formally commits the contract, and an appropriate evidence of cover is to be issued within 30 days of inception.[1]

1 See the press release issued by the Financial Services Authority on 24 January 2007.

Lloyd's of London

1.6 Lloyd's of London[1] is an insurance market in which members form groups (known as 'syndicates') to accept insurance risks. The syndicates operate on an ongoing basis, although technically each is an annual venture. Each syndicate is run by a managing agent, which appoints the syndicate's underwriters (sometimes known as 'active underwriters') who are insurance professionals with responsibility for deciding on behalf of the syndicate whether to accept risks, and on what terms. Business at Lloyd's is still conducted face-to-face. Each underwriter operates from an area (known as a 'box') in the underwriting room at Lloyd's ('the Room'), and specialises in a particular type of risk.

In addition to making underwriting decisions, the underwriter is responsible for settling claims, and reinsuring the syndicate's risks. Risks are placed at Lloyd's by brokers acting on behalf of clients. Lloyd's brokers are the agent of the insured rather than the underwriter.[2] In order to transact business at Lloyd's, and use the title 'Lloyd's broker', a broker must be accredited by Lloyd's.

Lloyd's has legal personality and is run by its Council, the powers and functions of which are set out in the Lloyd's Act 1982.[3] Lloyd's does not itself underwrite risks.

Lloyd's is regulated by the Financial Conduct Authority ('FCA') under the Financial Services and Markets Act 2000.[4] The FCA also regulates Lloyd's members' agents[5] and managing agents[6] and Lloyd's brokers.[7] The FCA delegates to Lloyd's certain of its powers and duties in relation to supervision and enforcement in the Lloyd's market.

The interests of underwriting businesses (both managing and members' agents) in the Lloyd's market are represented by the Lloyd's Market Association ('LMA'), and those of Lloyd's brokers by the London & International Insurance Brokers' Association ('LIIBA').

1 For further information, see the Lloyd's of London website: www.lloyds.com.
2 See **PARA 16.3**.
3 Parts of the Lloyd's Acts 1871, 1911 and 1951 also remain in force.
4 Financial Services and Markets Act 2000, s 315 and Financial Services and Markets Act 2000 (Regulated Activities) Order 2001 (SI 2001/544), as amended, reg 58.
5 Financial Services and Markets Act 2000 (Regulated Activities) Order 2001 (SI 2001/544), as amended, reg 56.
6 Financial Services and Markets Act 2000 (Regulated Activities) Order 2001 (SI 2001/544), as amended, reg 57.
7 Financial Services and Markets Act 2000 (Regulated Activities) Order 2001 (SI 2001/544), as amended, reg 25.

The London company market

1.7 International insurance and reinsurance companies operating in or through London but outside the Lloyd's market are known as the London company market. The International Underwriting Association of London ('IUA') is a trade and market association which represents the interests of non-Lloyd's insurance and reinsurance companies in the London market.

Insurance brokers

1.8 Insurance brokers are specialist intermediaries who arrange insurance and offer advice to clients. They are involved in placing the risk, and in negotiating the settlement of claims, on behalf of their clients. An insurance broker is usually the agent of the insured, even if (as is common) its remuneration is by way of a commission from the insurers. Insurance brokers typically owe their clients duties in both contract and tort, and fiduciary duties. They are also subject to the provisions of the Financial Services and Markets Act 2000, and regulations made thereunder, and may be liable to a client in damages for breach of statutory duty. In certain limited circumstances they may owe duties to third parties, including insurers. Insurance brokers are also regulated by the Financial Conduct Authority ('FCA') under the Financial Services and Markets Act 2000.[1] The London & International Insurance Brokers' Association ('LIIBA') is the trade association representing the interests of insurance and reinsurance brokers in the London and international markets. Claims against insurance brokers are considered in **CHAPTER 16**.

1 Financial Services and Markets Act 2000 (Regulated Activities) Order 2001 (SI 2001/544), as amended, reg 25.

Placing the risk

1.9 The size of the risks underwritten in the London market means that a single risk is often shared between several underwriters, each subscribing to a proportion of the risk. The risk is proposed to the syndicates at Lloyd's, or the companies in the company market, on the basis of a 'slip', on which the details of the proposed risk are recorded. These details usually include:[1] the name of the insured; the perils or type of cover; the period of cover and the inception date; the sum insured or limit of liability; the excess; any special conditions; any form of wording which it is anticipated will be used; the anticipated level of premium; payment terms; brokerage and other deductions; taxes; signing provisions; a statement of several liability; and choice of law and jurisdiction or arbitration provisions. The broker then presents the risk to the underwriter in a meeting with the underwriter. Outside the London market, the risk is usually presented by means of a proposal form completed by the insured together with any additional relevant information, or, on renewal, by the presentation of updated information together with a declaration or statement of fact from the insured.[2]

At Lloyd's, the meeting usually takes place at the syndicate's box in the Room. Brokers queue to see the underwriter at the box. If the underwriter is prepared to accept the risk or, more usually, a proportion of it, he will indicate this on the slip, 'scratch' (initial) and stamp the slip to show his acceptance. The broker will usually take the slip first to a syndicate or company which specialises in the type of risk in question, which will quote the proportion and rate of premium which it is willing to accept, as the 'lead underwriter' for the risk. The broker then presents the slip to other underwriters, asking them whether they will accept the risk on the same terms as the lead underwriter. If they accept, they are known as the 'following market'. If the risk is oversubscribed (ie if all the acceptances together add up to more than 100 per cent) the line written by each underwriter is 'signed down' proportionately.

A broker may give a signing down indication to underwriters when taking the slip around the market if he anticipates that the risk may be oversubscribed.[3] The contract of insurance may provide that the following market agree to be bound by certain decisions of the leading underwriter during the policy year; any such decision will then be evidenced by an endorsement scratched by the leading underwriter. A facility whereby a number of insurers authorise one or more leading underwriters to accept on their behalf risks presented by a particular broker which fall within a pre-defined scope is known as a lineslip.[4]

Where a risk is underwritten partly at Lloyd's and partly in the company market, it is usual for the company market to issue a contract of insurance which includes a co-insurance clause incorporating the wording of the Lloyd's policy. Insurance in the London market is written on the basis of several, rather than joint, liability, and each policy contains a condition providing that each insurer is liable only for the proportion of the risk that it has undertaken. This means that if a company subscribing to the risk becomes insolvent, the insured cannot look to the other insurers to make up any shortfall and may not recover a full indemnity under the policy. Similarly, some insurers may decide to repudiate a claim and defend any legal proceedings which the insured may bring against them, while others may decide to pay their proportion in respect of the same claim.

In the case of a policy placed on the basis of a slip in the London market (whether Lloyd's or the company market), the contract becomes binding when the slip is signed.[5] In the case of a policy placed on the basis of a proposal form, which is accepted by the insurer, it is only when the premium is tendered by the insured that the contract becomes binding (unless the insurer has expressly agreed that the period of insurance should commence on a particular date in return for a promise by the insured to pay the premium).[6]

1 There is now a set of standard slip headings, known as the Market Reform Contract – Lineslip, which must be used for all insurance underwritten at Lloyd's.
2 See PARAS **3.12** and **11.15**.
3 See PARA **16.11**.
4 See *Involnert Management Inc v Aprilgrange Ltd* [2015] EWHC 2225 (Comm), [2015] 2 Lloyd's Rep 289, para 5 (Leggatt J).
5 See PARA **3.3**.
6 See PARA **3.3**.

INSURANCE DOCUMENTATION

1.10 Documents of each of the following types may come into existence in relation to a single risk: a proposal form; a quotation; a slip; a cover note; a policy summary; a policy of insurance (and schedule); and a certificate of insurance. The proposal form forms part of the contract of insurance only if it is incorporated by virtue of a clause, whether in the proposal form or in the policy, making it the basis of the contract (and therefore known as a 'basis clause'). In the absence of such a clause, the proposal form is not a contractual document, and its terms may not be considered in construing the policy. It is suggested that a quotation is typically not a contractual document in this sense.[1] Although a Lloyd's slip is a contractual document, it is generally superseded by the policy of insurance when the policy is issued. If, unusually, the court concludes that the parties did not intend the slip to be superseded, it will construe the slip and the policy together.[2] A cover note may be issued for the period before the risk attaches. The cover note is a contract of interim insurance, and ceases to have effect once the contract itself is concluded. Cover notes are often issued by brokers. In issuing a cover note, the broker is acting as the insurer's coverholder rather than as the insured's agent.[3]

The policy itself is typically made up of a series of standard terms and conditions, some clauses specific to the risk (usually known as 'endorsements' or, if they enlarge the risk, 'extensions'), and a schedule which summarises some important features of the risk, such as the name of the insured, the limit of liability, and the level of any excess. The schedule may include a list of numbers or letters indicating which of the standard sections or exclusions in the policy apply to the risk.

A certificate of insurance may be provided by the insurer as evidence of the existence and scope of the insurance cover. Insurers are required to issue certificates in relation to certain types of compulsory insurance, notably motor insurance and employers' liability insurance. Certificates are not commonly issued unless required by statute.

The insurer or broker may also be required to provide a statement of demands and needs or key features document.[4]

1 In *Genesis Housing Association Ltd v Liberty Syndicate Management Ltd* [2013] EWCA Civ 1173, [2014] Lloyd's Rep IR 318, Jackson LJ doubted (at para 44) Akenhead J's finding (at [2012] EWHC 3105 (TCC), [2013] BLR 28, para 44) that the quotation was a contractual document, but did not decide the point.
2 See **CHAPTER 3**, The contract of insurance.
3 This may have consequences in relation to the broker's duty to the insured: see **PARA 16.4**.
4 See ICOBS 5 and COBS 13. Breach of ICOBS may be actionable: see **PARA 8.2**.

Chapter 2

The claimant

INTRODUCTION

2.1   In a typical insurance case, the insured makes a claim against the insurer.[1] If the claim is not paid, the insured may bring proceedings against the insurer, or against his insurance broker, or perhaps both. Sometimes, usually in higher-value cases, the roles of claimant and defendant are reversed, and the insurer sues for a declaration that a policy has been validly avoided, or that there is no cover in respect of a particular claim. This chapter is concerned with the position of the insured and of those claiming under him, including by way of assignment and subrogation, and with proceedings brought by or against insurers including claims under the Third Parties (Rights Against Insurers) Acts 1930 and 2010.

1 The fact that an insurance agent administers policies and commonly pays claims does not make it personally and directly liable to make payments under policies: *Temple Legal Protection Ltd v QBE Insurance (Europe) Ltd* [2009] EWCA Civ 453, [2009] Lloyd's Rep IR 544, paras 30–31 (Moore-Bick LJ); applied: *PM Law Ltd v Motorplus Ltd* [2016] EWHC 193 (QB), para 58 (Picken J).

Identifying the insured

2.2   Policies of insurance may identify the insured by name or by description, and questions about whether a particular party is or is not insured are resolved by the application of normal principles of construction.[1] The doctrine of the undisclosed principal is unlikely to be relevant in this context. This is because the fact that the law generally recognises the right of an undisclosed principal to sue and be sued on a contract does not relieve the nominal insured from the duty to make full disclosure of all material circumstances in each case, including any which may relate to his undisclosed principal, in order to ensure a fair presentation of the risk to the insurer.[2]

1 See, eg, *Talbot Underwriting Ltd v Nausch, Hogan & Murray Inc (The Jascon 5)* [2006] EWCA Civ 889, [2006] 2 Lloyd's Rep 195, paras 14–22 (Moore-Bick LJ); *Brit Syndicates Ltd v Italaudit SpA* [2008] UKHL 18, [2008] Lloyd's Rep IR 601.
2 *Talbot Underwriting Ltd v Nausch, Hogan & Murray Inc (The Jascon 5)* [2006] EWCA Civ 889, [2006] 2 Lloyd's Rep 195, para 43 (Moore-Bick LJ).

Joint and composite insurance

2.3   The interests of more than one person may be insured under a single policy. Where those interests are joint, the insurance may itself be a joint insurance, entailing an obligation to indemnify them jointly in respect of a joint loss which they will suffer, if they suffer it at all, only jointly. An obvious example is joint owners of property. Where the insurance is truly joint, misrepresentation or non-disclosure by one of the insureds in the proposal for insurance, or fraud in the making of a claim by one of the insureds, will entitle the insurer to avoid or forfeit the policy as against the others. Often, however, although several parties are insured for convenience in a single policy, their interests are different. A common example is a contractors' all risks policy, which may provide property and liability cover not only in respect of the employer and main contractor, but also all of the sub-contractors. Such insurance is composite rather than joint, and misrepresentation or non-disclosure, or fraud, by one of the insureds will not entitle the insurer to avoid or forfeit the policy as against the others.[1] Conversely, affirmation of the policy in respect of one insured does not constitute affirmation of the policy in respect of another.[2] This is illustrated by *P Samuel & Co v Dumas*,[3] in which the interests of a shipowner and mortgagee were insured under a single policy. The mortgagee was held not to be affected by the owner's fraud in scuttling the ship and, although the language of the distinction between 'joint' and 'composite' interests had yet to be developed, the analysis is in fact that of joint and composite interests.[4] Viscount Cave described the relevant principle as follows:[5]

> 'It may well be that, when two persons are jointly insured and their interests are inseparably connected so that a loss or gain necessarily affects them both, the misconduct of one is sufficient to contaminate the whole insurance: Phillips on Marine Insurance, vol. I., § 235. But in this case there is no difficulty in separating the interest of the mortgagee from that of the owner; and if the mortgagee should recover on the policy, the owner will not be advantaged, as the insurers will be subrogated as against him to the rights of the mortgagee.'

Similarly, Lord Sumner distinguished between the interests of the owner and the mortgagee, saying:[6]

> 'Of course, it is true that [the insured] cannot take advantage of his own wrong ... This, however, seems to me to be obviously a case of personal disability, which cannot affect persons, who are neither parties to the dolus nor stand in the guilty person's shoes. Fraud is not something absolute, existing in vacuo; it is a fraud upon some one. A man who tries to cheat his underwriters fails if they find him out, but how does his wrong against them invest them with new rights against innocent strangers to it?'

In the special situation of a composite policy in which the interests of the co-insureds are pervasive, as in a contractors' all risks policy, fraud by one insured severs the unity of interest, so that the innocent insureds are not affected by the fraud.[7]

In many cases, there will be no need to embark on an analysis of the interests of the co-insureds, because an application of agency principles will provide a short answer to the question of whether fraud by one affects another.[8]

A policy of group errors and omissions cover is not a joint policy: it provides cover to each of the insured severally, and in contradistinction to the position of co-insurers, the co-insured are not exposed in relation to the same interest and the same perils; rights to claim under the cover will almost inevitably arise sequentially; and when co-insured enter into a contract of insurance that gives them several rights, subject to an overall limit, each simply takes the risk that cover may become exhausted, leaving all thereafter exposed to third party claims.[9]

1 *General Accident Fire and Life Assurance Corpn Ltd v Midland Bank Ltd* [1940] 2 KB 388, 404–406, CA (Sir Wilfred Greene MR); *Woolcott v Sun Alliance and London Insurance Ltd* [1978] 1 WLR 493, 496–497 (Caulfield J) (interests of mortgagor and mortgagee not joint; retrial ordered by Court of Appeal on other grounds: [1979] 1 Lloyd's Rep 231, CA); *New Hampshire Insurance Co v MGN Ltd* [1997] LRLR 24, 56–58, CA (Staughton LJ).
2 *Black King Shipping Corpn v Massie, The Litsion Pride* [1985] 1 Lloyd's Rep 437, 516–517 (Hirst J).
3 [1924] AC 431, HL.
4 *Netherlands v Youell* [1997] 2 Lloyd's Rep 440, 447 (Rix J).
5 At 445–446.
6 At 469.
7 *Netherlands v Youell* [1997] 2 Lloyd's Rep 440, 450–451 (Rix J).
8 See **PARA 11.52**.
9 *Cox v Bankside Members Agency Ltd* [1995] 2 Lloyd's Rep 437, 443 (Phillips J) (group errors and omissions (E&O) cover shared by members' and managing agents of Lloyd's syndicates).

INSURABLE INTEREST[1]

2.4   In order to be entitled to enforce a policy of insurance, the law has long been that a person must have an insurable interest in the subject matter of the insurance.[2] The repeal of s 18 of the Gambling Act 1845 has however introduced an element of uncertainty into this area, at least in relation to indemnity insurance, to which the Life Assurance Act 1774 does not apply. The principles that follow assume that the repeal of s 18 by the Gambling Act 2005, which does not expressly refer to contracts of insurance or the concept of insurable interest, has not removed the requirement of insurable interest in relation to indemnity insurance. The Law Commission consulted on insurable interest in the summer of 2015 and expects to report in 2016.

In property insurance, a legal or beneficial interest in the property is sufficient to constitute an insurable interest, but is not required: a person has an insurable interest if he will suffer any sort of detriment or prejudice if the property is damaged or destroyed. The classic definition of insurable interest was given by Lawrence J in *Lucena v Craufurd*:[3]

'A man is interested in a thing to whom advantage may arise or prejudice happen from the circumstances which may attend it ... And whom it importeth, that its condition as to safety or other quality should continue: interest does not necessarily imply a right to the whole, or a part of a thing, nor necessarily and exclusively that which may be the subject of privation, but the having some relation to, or concern in the subject of the insurance, which relation or concern by the happening of the perils insured against may be so affected as to produce a damage, detriment, or prejudice to the person insuring: and where a man is so circumstanced with respect to matters exposed to certain risks or dangers, as to have a moral certainty of advantage or benefit, but for those risks or dangers he may be said to be interested in the safety of the thing. To be interested in the preservation of a thing, is to be so circumstanced with respect to it as to have benefit from its existence, prejudice from its destruction.'

It is difficult to define insurable interest in words which will apply in all situations.[4] The context and the terms of a policy with which the court is concerned are all-important.[5] The words used to define insurable interest in, for example, a property context should not be slavishly followed in different contexts, and words used in a life insurance context where one identified life is the subject of the insurance may not be totally apposite where the subject is many lives and many events.[6] It is from the terms of the policy that the subject of the insurance must be ascertained and from all the surrounding circumstances that the nature of an insured's insurable interest must be discovered, and there is no hard and fast rule that because the nature of an insurable interest relates to a liability to compensate for loss, that insurable interest could only be covered by a liability policy rather than a policy insuring property or life or indeed properties or lives.[7]

1 See also **PARA 11.55**.
2 Life Assurance Act 1774; Gaming Act 1845, s 18 (repealed by the Gaming Act 2005, s 356 and Schedule 2 with effect from 21 May 2007); *Macaura v Northern Assurance Co Ltd* [1925] AC 619, HL.
3 (1806) 2 Bos & PNR 269, 302. Lawrence J's judgment has always been accepted as a correct statement of the law: *Moran, Galloway & Co v Uzielli* [1905] 2 KB 555, 561 (Walton J); more recently, a shorter quotation from this passage from Lawrence J's judgment was quoted, with approval, by Kerr LJ in *Mark Rowlands Ltd v Berni Inns Ltd* [1986] QB 211, CA (at 228).
4 *Feasey v Sun Life Assurance Corpn of Canada* [2003] EWCA Civ 885, [2003] 1 Lloyd's Rep IR 637, para 66 (Waller LJ).
5 *Feasey v Sun Life Assurance Corpn of Canada* [2003] EWCA Civ 885, [2003] 1 Lloyd's Rep IR 637, para 66 (Waller LJ).
6 *Feasey v Sun Life Assurance Corpn of Canada* [2003] EWCA Civ 885, [2003] 1 Lloyd's Rep IR 637, para 66 (Waller LJ); Ward LJ (dissenting) said that, for the sake of clarity and consistency, insurable interest should bear as nearly as possible the same meaning for all categories of insurance (para 178).
7 *Feasey v Sun Life Assurance Corpn of Canada* [2003] EWCA Civ 885, [2003] 1 Lloyd's Rep IR 637, paras 92 (Waller LJ) and 118 (Dyson LJ).

Life insurance

2.5   Section 1 of the Life Assurance Act 1774 requires the insured to have an insurable interest in the life insured, and s 2 provides that the names of any persons interested in a life insurance policy must be stated in the policy. If these requirements are not satisfied, the policy will be illegal and unenforceable. Section 3 provides that in all cases where the insured has an insurable interest, no greater sum shall be recoverable than the value of the interest of the insured in the life. Historically, the main reason for English law requiring an insurable interest in insurance policies was to avoid gambling; for this reason, the Life Assurance Act 1774 was also known as the Gambling Act 1774.[1] Although the question whether the contract of insurance can be correctly described as a gaming or wagering contract is a material factor, the critical question is, in accordance with s 1 of the 1774 Act, whether the contract is an insurance made 'on the life or lives of any person or persons, or on any other event or events whatsoever' in which the insured has no interest.[2] In life insurance, the claimant is required to have an insurable interest at the date the policy is effected,[3] which is also the date for valuing the insurable interest.[4]

1 See *Mark Rowlands Ltd v Berni Inns Ltd* [1986] QB 211, 227, CA (Kerr LJ). The preamble to s 1 of the Life Assurance Act 1774 provides:

> 'Whereas it hath been found by experience that the making of insurance on lives or other events wherein the assured shall have no interest hath introduced a mischievous kind of gambling'.

See also *Newbury International Ltd v Reliance National Insurance Co (UK) Ltd* [1994] 1 Lloyd's Rep 83, 92–93 (Hobhouse J): prize indemnity insurance policies held to be a device by means of which the insured placed a series of bets on the outcome of a Formula 3 racing championship.
2 *Feasey v Sun Life Assurance Corpn of Canada* [2003] EWCA Civ 885, [2003] 1 Lloyd's Rep IR 637, paras 51–54 (Waller LJ).
3 *Dalby v India and London Life-Assurance Co* (1854) 15 CB 365, 391–393 (judgment of the court, given by Parke B); *Feasey v Sun Life Assurance Corpn of Canada* [2003] EWCA Civ 885, [2003] 1 Lloyd's Rep IR 637, para 68 (Waller LJ).
4 *Dalby v India and London Life-Assurance Co* (1854) 15 CB 365, 391–393 (judgment of the court, given by Parke B); *Feasey v Sun Life Assurance Corpn of Canada* [2003] EWCA Civ 885, [2003] 1 Lloyd's Rep IR 637, para 68 (Waller LJ).

Indemnity insurance

2.6 Prior to the repeal of s 18 of the Gaming Act 1845, a claimant had to have an insurable interest at the date of loss in order to be able to enforce a policy of indemnity insurance.[1] Following the repeal of s 18, the position is less clear.[2]

Section 1 of the Life Assurance Act 1774 includes wording which appears to widen the scope of the Act from life insurance to most types of insurance other than marine.[3] This would have meant that the requirement of s 2 of the Act, that the names of any persons interested in an insurance policy be stated in the policy, would have applied to those types of insurance. The wording in question is as follows:

'... no insurance shall be made ... on the life or lives of any person or persons, or on any other event or events whatsoever ...'

The Court of Appeal decided in *Mark Rowlands Ltd v Berni Inns Ltd*[4] that the 1774 Act was not intended to apply, and did not apply, to indemnity insurance, but only to insurances which provide for the payment of a specified sum on the happening of an insured event.

1 *Anderson v Morice* (1876) 1 App Cas 713, HL; *Feasey v Sun Life Assurance Corpn of Canada* [2003] EWCA Civ 885, [2003] 1 Lloyd's Rep IR 637, para 67 (Waller LJ). Section 6 of the Marine Insurance Act 1906 provides that the insured must be interested in the subject matter insured at the time of the loss, although he need not be interested when the insurance is effected.
2 See **PARA 2.4**.
3 Section 4 provides that the Act does not extend to insurances made in good faith on 'ships, goods or merchandises'.
4 [1986] QB 211, CA; applied in *Siu Yin Kwan v Eastern Insurance Co Ltd* [1994] 2 AC 199, PC (in preference to an obiter dictum of Lord Denning MR in *Re King, Robinson v Gray* [1963] Ch 459, 485, CA).

Liability insurance

2.7 An insured has an insurable interest in protecting himself against liability he might incur to others.[1] If an insurable interest is required in relation to liability insurance, it is suggested that this is sufficient to constitute an insurable interest. In practice, as the right to an indemnity does not arise until a claim is made by a third party, there is no risk of liability insurance policies being used as a form of wagering. There are therefore no public policy considerations which require the courts to seek an insurable interest in order to justify upholding a policy of liability insurance, and issues concerning insurable interest do not usually arise in the context of liability insurance.

1 *Feasey v Sun Life Assurance Corpn of Canada* [2003] EWCA Civ 885, [2003] 1 Lloyd's Rep IR 637, para 89 (Waller LJ).

Limited interest in property

2.8 A limited interest in property is sufficient for there to be an insurable interest in the property. Ordinarily, the following will have an insurable interest, although, exceptionally, an agreement between the parties as to their rights and obligations in certain circumstances might mean that there is no such interest:[1] bailor and bailee;[2] landlord and tenant;[3] mortgagor and mortgagee;[4] trustee[5] and beneficiary. A vendor and purchaser may each have an insurable interest, depending on factors such as whether ownership has passed and any contractual stipulation regarding who is to bear the risk.[6] In the case of real property, the vendor has an insurable interest until the land is conveyed.[7] Since the decision of the House of Lords in *Macaura v Northern Assurance Co Ltd*[8] in 1925, it has been settled law that a shareholder or creditor of a company has no insurable interest in the assets of the company (even if he is the sole shareholder), although he may have an insurable interest in the success of a venture in which the company is involved. It is suggested that this distinction is supported by the decision of the House of Lords in another context in *Johnson v Gore Wood & Co*,[9] in which it was held that a majority shareholder had a cause of action, separate from the company's cause of action, against solicitors acting for the company in connection with a purchase of land, but only in respect of losses suffered by the shareholder which did not simply reflect the losses suffered by the company. Further, it is suggested that *Johnson v Gore Wood & Co* tends to support the taking of a more generous approach to the question of whether a majority or sole shareholder has an insurable interest in the success of his company (rather than in the assets of the company themselves).

1 This was argued, unsuccessfully, on behalf of the insurer (pursuing a subrogated claim on behalf of the landlord insured) in *Mark Rowlands Ltd v Berni Inns Ltd* [1986] QB 211, CA, on the basis that the stipulations in the lease relieved the tenant of basement business premises of all of its obligations following a fire.
2 *Hepburn v A Tomlinson (Hauliers) Ltd* [1966] AC 451, HL; *Macaura v Northern Assurance Co Ltd* [1925] AC 619, HL; *Mark Rowlands Ltd v Berni Inns Ltd* [1986] QB 211, CA.
3 *Mark Rowlands Ltd v Berni Inns Ltd* [1986] QB 211, CA; *Lonsdale & Thompson plc v Black Arrow Group plc* [1993] Ch 361.
4 *Westminster Fire Office v Glasgow Provident Investment Society* (1888) 13 App Cas 699, 708–709, HL (Lord Halsbury LC); *P Samuel & Co v Dumas* [1924] AC 431, HL (mortgagee of a ship 'interested in a marine adventure' within meaning of s 5, Marine Insurance Act 1906); *Provincial Insurance Co of Canada v Leduc* (1874) LR 6 PC 224, 244, PC (Sir Barnes Peacock); *Mark Rowlands Ltd v Berni Inns Ltd* [1986] QB 211, 226, CA (Kerr LJ).
5 *Lucena v Craufurd* (1806) 2 Bos & PNR 269.
6 *Anderson v Morice* (1876) 1 App Cas 713, HL (cargo).
7 *Castellain v Preston* (1883) 11 QBD 380, 385, CA (Brett LJ); *National Farmers Union Mutual Insurance Society Ltd v HSBC Insurance Ltd* [2010] EWHC 773 (Comm), [2011] Lloyd's Rep IR 86, para 18 (Gavin Kealey QC, sitting as a Deputy High Court Judge). These were both cases where a house which was insured against fire burnt down between contract and conveyance.
8 [1925] AC 619, HL.
9 [2002] 2 AC 1, HL.

Defeasible interest in property

2.9   A person with a defeasible interest in property has an insurable interest in that property.[1] Thus, a consignee of goods under a bill of lading has an insurable interest in the goods; and, even before probate is granted, an executor has an insurable interest in the testator's estate.[2]

1 *Stirling v Vaughan* (1809) 11 East 619, 628–629 (Lord Ellenborough). This is the position in marine insurance, pursuant to s 7 of the Marine Insurance Act 1906.
2 *Stirling v Vaughan* (1809) 11 East 619, 629 (Lord Ellenborough).

Mercantile or commercial 'trust'

2.10   In certain circumstances, defined by the courts in a series of decisions beginning in the nineteenth century,[1] a person with a limited interest in property is entitled to insure the whole of the property and recover in respect of the whole loss. He will then hold on 'trust' for others interested in the property the surplus over what he requires for his own indemnification.[2] This is known as the *Hepburn* principle. The principle applies to bailees (including wharfingers[3] and carriers of goods),[4] mortgagees, and others in analogous positions,[5] and allows a bailee to insure to the full extent of his insurable interest (which is the full value of the goods) even in circumstances where his personal loss is nil.[6] An obligation of a similar kind may also arise out of a relationship created between the parties by contract.[7] The principle grew out of commercial convenience and mercantile practice, and to subject it to rigorous legal analysis is probably futile.[8] When a bailee takes out an 'all risks' insurance policy covering goods in his possession and the policy expresses the cover to be on goods 'held by the insured in trust for which the insured is responsible', the addition of the words 'for which he is responsible' restricts insurers' liability to those goods damaged in a way which imposes liability on the bailee.[9] It is unclear whether, in those circumstances, the bailee is entitled to an indemnity from insurers in respect of the full value of those goods or only the amount of his legal liability to the owner of the goods.[10]

The *Hepburn* principle has been applied to allow a trade union to insure in its own name property for which its members were responsible to their employer, subject to an obligation on the part of the union to account to the member who suffered the loss, in respect of moneys claimed from the insurer.[11] In *Petrofina (UK) Ltd v Magnaload Ltd*,[12] the principle was extended, on the grounds of commercial convenience and by analogy to the position of bailees, to allow the contractors and sub-contractors on a construction contract to insure the whole of the contract works under a property policy. For a sub-contractor to have an insurable interest in the property in this context, it is sufficient for a sub-contractor to have a contract that relates to the property and a potential liability for damage to the property, and it is not a requirement that the sub-contractor must have a 'legal or equitable' interest in the property as those terms might normally be understood.[13] It appears that whether a sub-contractor has such an interest and, if so, its duration, is a question of construction of the policy,[14] although the authorities suggest that the sub-contractor's insurable interest in the property is likely to cease when construction comes to an end.[15]

13

The Contracts (Rights of Third Parties) Act 1999 gives a direct right of enforcement of the policy to the third party who is entitled to the indemnity or other benefit[16] in respect of contracts of insurance entered into from 11 May 2000.[17] The right of action given by the Act is in addition to any right or remedy of a third party that exists or is available apart from the Act,[18] and the *Hepburn* principle is therefore unaffected.

1 *Waters v Monarch Fire & Life Assurance Co* (1856) 5 E & B 870; *Ebsworth v Alliance Marine Insurance Co* (1873) LR 8 CP 596; *Hepburn v A Tomlinson (Hauliers) Ltd* [1966] AC 451, HL; *Albacruz v Albazero, The Albazero* [1977] AC 774, 846, HL (Lord Diplock). As regards marine insurance, the same principle applies: s 26(3) of the Marine Insurance Act 1906; *Albacruz v Albazero, The Albazero* [1977] AC 774, 846, HL (Lord Diplock).

2 *Hepburn v A Tomlinson (Hauliers) Ltd* [1966] AC 451, HL. It is not a true trust, but a pragmatic response to the needs of commerce: see *Hepburn v A Tomlinson (Hauliers) Ltd* at 467–468 (Lord Reid) and 477 (Lord Pearce). Lord Pearce said at 480 that a bailee has a right to sue for conversion, holding in trust for the owner such of the damages as represent the owner's interest, and may also sue in negligence, and that it would seem irrational if he could not also insure for their full value.

3 *Waters v Monarch Fire & Life Assurance Co* (1856) 5 E & B 870, approved by the House of Lords in *Hepburn v A Tomlinson (Hauliers) Ltd* [1966] AC 451.

4 *Hepburn v A Tomlinson (Hauliers) Ltd* [1966] AC 451, HL.

5 *Hepburn v A Tomlinson (Hauliers) Ltd* [1966] AC 451, 481, HL (Lord Pearce).

6 *Hepburn v A Tomlinson (Hauliers) Ltd* [1966] AC 451, HL; see also *HSBC Rail (UK) Ltd v Network Rail Infrastructure Ltd* [2005] EWCA Civ 1437, [2006] 1 Lloyd's Rep 358, paras 34–38 (Longmore LJ).

7 *Talbot Underwriting Ltd v Nausch, Hogan & Murray Inc (The Jascon 5)* [2006] EWCA Civ 889, [2006] 2 Lloyd's Rep 195, para 72 (Moore-Bick LJ) (shipyard and shipowner), approving *Lonsdale & Thompson Ltd v Black Arrow Group plc* [1993] Ch 361 (landlord and tenant).

8 See *Hepburn v A Tomlinson (Hauliers) Ltd* [1966] AC 451, HL, 467–468, 470–471 (Lord Reid), 477 (Lord Pearce).

9 *Ramco (UK) Ltd v International Insurance Co of Hannover Ltd* [2004] EWCA Civ 675, [2004] 2 Lloyd's Rep 595, para 32 (Waller LJ, applying, reluctantly, *North British and Mercantile Insurance Co v Moffatt* (1871) LR 7 CP 25 and *Engel v Lancashire & General Assurance Co Ltd* (1925) 21 Ll L R 327).

10 *Ramco (UK) Ltd v International Insurance Co of Hannover Ltd* [2004] EWCA Civ 675, [2004] 2 Lloyd's Rep 595, para 5 (Waller LJ), doubting *Ramco (UK) Ltd v International Insurance Co of Hannover Ltd* [2003] EWHC 2360 (Comm), paras 34–39 (Andrew Smith J) (there being no appeal on this issue).

11 *Prudential Staff Union v Hall* [1947] KB 685.

12 [1984] QB 127; see also **PARA 12.4**. See also *National Oilwell (UK) Ltd v Davy Offshore Co* [1993] 2 Lloyd's Rep 582, 611 (Colman J); *Deepak Fertilisers and Petrochemicals Corpn v ICI Chemicals and Polymers Ltd* [1999] 1 Lloyd's Rep 387, CA, para 64 (Stuart-Smith LJ).

13 *Feasey v Sun Life Assurance Corpn of Canada* [2003] EWCA Civ 885, [2003] 1 Lloyd's Rep IR 637, paras 89–92 (Waller LJ).

14 *Feasey v Sun Life Assurance Corpn of Canada* [2003] EWCA Civ 885, [2003] 1 Lloyd's Rep IR 637, para 90 (Waller LJ).

15 *Deepak Fertilisers and Petrochemicals Corpn v ICI Chemicals and Polymers Ltd* [1999] 1 Lloyd's Rep 387, CA, paras 64–66 (Stuart-Smith LJ); *Feasey v Sun Life Assurance Corpn of Canada* [2003] EWCA Civ 885, [2003] 1 Lloyd's Rep IR 637, paras 89–90 (Waller LJ).

16 Section 1. See also **PARA 2.17**.

17 Six months after the entry into force of the Act on 11 November 1999: s 10(2).

18 Section 7(1).

The Fires Prevention (Metropolis) Act 1774

2.11 Where an insured building has been damaged or destroyed by fire, s 83 of the Fires Prevention (Metropolis) Act 1774 requires the insurer to cause the insurance moneys to be used for the reinstatement of the building, if any person interested in the building[1] requests them to do so, or if the insurer has grounds to suspect that the person insuring the building has been guilty of fraud or has deliberately set fire to the building. The opening words of s 83 explain that it was enacted to protect families in multiple occupation of buildings which they did not own, and who were considered to be at risk from arson by the owners who wished to claim the insurance moneys. It does not oblige an insurer to reinstate a building where the only person interested in it is the insured, and does not therefore provide a means of recovering the cost of reinstatement where the entitlement under the policy is limited to replacement value.[2] The Act applies to the whole of England and Wales.[3]

1 A mortgagee is probably not a person interested in the building within the meaning of the section: *Westminster Fire Office v Glasgow Provident Investment Society* (1888) 13 App Cas 699, 713–714, HL.
2 *Reynolds v Phoenix Assurance Co Ltd* [1978] 2 Lloyd's Rep 440, 462 (Forbes J). See **PARA 6.5**.
3 *Re Barker, ex p Gorely* (1864) 4 De GJ & SM 477 (Lord Westbury LC).

SUBROGATED CLAIMS

2.12 'Subrogation' is the term applied to the legal doctrine which, in certain circumstances, allows one person to exercise the rights of another. In insurance law, the doctrine of subrogation allows an insurer, once he has indemnified his insured, to exercise all of the insured's rights in relation to the subject matter of the insurance, usually by bringing a recovery action against a third party. Although the insured has no financial interest in the action, it is brought in his name rather than that of the insurer. Subrogation is considered in **CHAPTER 12**.

ASSIGNMENT

2.13 Insurance policies, and rights of claim under them, are *choses* (things) *in action*, and are therefore capable of being assigned.[1] An assignment may be legal or equitable, a legal assignment having certain procedural advantages over an equitable assignment.[2] For there to be a legal assignment, the requirements of s 136 of the Law of Property Act 1925 must be complied with, otherwise the assignment will take place in equity only.[3] An equitable assignment may take effect without the consent of the insurer, but the assignee would be well advised to require that the assignor give the insurer notice of the assignment, as without it, they are not under any obligation to pay the assignee.

It is important to distinguish between assignment of the policy of insurance and assignment of the proceeds of any recovery under the policy. An assignee of the policy is entitled to be indemnified for losses in relation to his insured interest, whereas an assignee of the benefit of the policy is entitled to have paid to him the proceeds of any recovery by the assignor of the indemnity to which he is entitled for losses in relation to his insured interest.[4] An assignment of the proceeds may take place at any time before payment, whether before or after the loss.[5] Where an insured assigns a claim under a policy of insurance, any benefit obtained by the insured from the agreement with the assignee is *res inter alios acta* as far as the insurer is concerned (which means it is of no relevance to the insurer), and should not be regarded as eliminating the insured's loss which existed immediately prior to that agreement.[6] Where fraud has been committed by the assignor of a policy, the assignee can be on no better footing than the assignor and will therefore be affected by the fraud.[7] Where interest is claimed by an assignee by reference to loss of return on investments, the losses which an assignee is entitled to recover are the insured's losses, and are to be assessed by reference to the returns which the insured would have achieved if there had been no assignment.[8]

1 *Raiffeisen Zentralbank Österreich AG v Five Star Trading LLC* [2001] EWCA Civ 68, [2001] QB 825, para 74 (Mance LJ).
2 See *Chitty on Contracts* (32nd edition, 2015), Chapter 19.
3 *Raiffeisen Zentralbank Österreich AG v Five Star Trading LLC* [2001] EWCA Civ 68, [2001] QB 825. Assignment in marine insurance is also governed by s 50 of the Marine Insurance Act 1906.
4 *Jan de Nul (UK) Ltd v NV Royale Belge* [2001] Lloyd's Rep IR 327, 355–356 (Moore-Bick J) (this point was not considered on appeal: [2002] EWCA Civ 209, [2002] 1 Lloyd's Rep 583).
5 See *English Scottish Mercantile Investment Co Ltd v Brunton* [1892] 2 QB 700, CA; *Jan de Nul (UK) Ltd v NV Royale Belge* [2001] Lloyd's Rep IR 327, 355–356 (Moore-Bick J) (both examples of assignment after loss).
6 *All Leisure Holidays Ltd v Europaische Reiseversicherung AG* [2011] EWHC 2629 (Comm), [2012] Lloyd's Rep IR 193, para 25 (Teare J), applying *Haviland v Long* [1952] 2 QB 80, 83 (Somervell LJ) and 84 (Denning LJ) (which involved a landlord and tenant repairing covenant). In the *All Leisure Holidays* case, the benefits (a substitute holiday on the same cruise ship) would have eliminated the loss; the same principle must apply in relation to a payment which is less than the value of the claim and which would, if taken into account, reduce rather than eliminate the loss.
7 *Re Carr and Sun Fire Insurance Co* (1897) 13 TLR 186, CA; *P Samuel & Co v Dumas* [1924] AC 431, HL; *Patel v Windsor Life Assurance Co Ltd* [2008] EWHC 76 (Comm), [2008] Lloyd's Rep IR 359, para 94 (Teare J).
8 *Equitas Ltd v Walsham Brothers & Co Ltd* [2013] EWHC 3264 (Comm), [2014] Lloyd's Rep IR 398, paras 132–133 (Males J). See also PARA **9.45**.

Clause prohibiting assignment of policy or proceeds

2.14 As insurance is a personal contract, the insured's obligations under a policy of insurance cannot be assigned without the consent of the insurer, and a provision in a policy of insurance prohibiting assignment of the policy therefore adds nothing to the position at common law. A provision prohibiting assignment of the proceeds of recovery would be valid, and a provision simply prohibiting assignment might be construed as prohibiting assignment of the proceeds of recovery.[1]

1 In *Linden Gardens Trust Ltd v Lenesta Sludge Disposals Ltd* [1994] 1 AC 85, the House of Lords held that the prohibition on assignment of a building contract by the contractor was effective to prevent the assignment of any *chose in action* under the contract.

Effect of disposal of subject matter insured

2.15 Property insurance is regarded as a personal contract in English law, and is not automatically transferred on a disposal of the property insured.[1] Unless the policy of insurance, or the proceeds of the policy, is assigned when the insured disposes of the subject matter of property insurance, the subsequent occurrence of an insured event will cause him no loss and neither he nor the purchaser will have any claim under the policy.[2] If he disposes of the subject matter of the insurance after an insured event, he will be entitled to claim under the policy, and the subsequent disposal will not deprive him of his right to an indemnity.[3] If an insured event occurs after disposal, but the insured retains a limited interest in the subject matter of the insurance, for example, by virtue of an unpaid vendor's lien, it is suggested that he will be entitled to an indemnity in respect of whatever losses he in fact sustains, unless the policy provides otherwise. Difficult issues of construction have arisen in relation to the third-party liability element of motor vehicle policies, as to whether the cover lapses on or continues after the sale of the insured vehicle.[4]

1 *Rayner v Preston* (1881) 18 Ch D 1, 6 (Cotton LJ), 11 (Brett LJ), CA.
2 *Rayner v Preston* (1881) 18 Ch D 1, 7, CA (Cotton LJ).
3 See *Hair v Prudential Assurance Co Ltd* [1983] 2 Lloyd's Rep 667. The policy may provide that the purchaser is entitled to the proceeds, as was the case in *General Accident Fire and Life Assurance Corpn Ltd v Midland Bank Ltd* [1940] 2 KB 388, 410, CA.
4 *Rogerson v Scottish Automobile and General Insurance Co Ltd* (1931) 41 Ll L Rep 1, HL; *Tattersall v Drysdale* [1935] 2 KB 174; *Peters v General Accident and Life Assurance Corpn Ltd* [1937] 4 All ER 628 (affirmed: [1938] 2 All ER 267, CA); *Dodson v Peter H Dodson Insurance Services* [2001] 1 WLR 1012, CA (doubting *Boss v Kingston* [1963] 1 WLR 99, [1962] 2 Lloyd's Rep 431, DC).

CLAIMS BY INSURERS

2.16   Insurers may bring proceedings against an insured seeking a declaration that they are not liable in respect of a claim or that a policy has been validly avoided or discharged for breach of warranty.[1] Where more than one insurer has the same interest in a claim, one may sue or be sued as a representative of the others.[2]

1 See **PARA 9.42**.
2 See **PARA 9.4**.

CLAIMS BY THIRD PARTIES

2.17   This section considers the situations in which a third party may wish to enforce a policy of insurance. This may arise in the context of a contract of insurance which provides benefits for individuals who are not parties to it. It may also arise in the context of liability insurance. In the absence of statute, a third party who establishes liability against a defendant who is insured has no direct right of action against the insurer for the moneys which the insured is entitled to be paid by the insurer by reason of the third party's claim. Where the insured is solvent, this is of no significance to the third party, for whom the right to recover against the insured will result in the payment of its claim. Where the insured is insolvent, however, the lack of a direct right of action against the insurer means that the payment by the insurer to the insured becomes part of the insured's assets, available to the general body of creditors when the insured is wound up or made bankrupt. It was to reverse this result that the Third Parties (Rights Against Insurers) Act 1930 was passed. Criticisms of the 1930 Act led to a report by the Law Commission[1] and, eventually, the Third Parties (Rights Against Insurers) Act 2010. The 2010 Act will come into force on 1 August 2016.[2] The 1930 and 2010 Acts are considered below.

1 Law Commission Report on Third Parties – Rights Against Insurers, Law Com No 272, Cm 5217, published in July 2001.
2 See further **PARA 2.28**, note 1.

Contract of insurance for the benefit of third parties

2.18   A contract of insurance may provide benefits for individuals who are not parties to it. A common example is a group contract of medical or accident insurance obtained by an employer on behalf of its employees. Unless its application is excluded by the policy wording, the Contracts (Rights of Third Parties) Act 1999 gives a direct right of enforcement of the policy to the third party who is entitled to the indemnity or other benefit[1] in respect of contracts of insurance entered into from 11 May 2000.[2] This may be significant if the employer is unable or unwilling to enforce the contract on behalf of the employee.[3] In enforcing the policy against the insurer, the third party is bound by any arbitration agreement within the contract of insurance.[4] The right of action given by the Act is in addition to any right or remedy of a third party that exists or is available apart from the Act.[5] These include rights under a mercantile or commercial 'trust'.[6]

A contract of liability insurance does not purport to confer a benefit on a third party with a claim against the insured, and the third party therefore has no right to enforce the contract under the Contracts (Rights of Third Parties) Act 1999.[7]

1 Section 1.
2 Section 10(2) provides that the Act does not apply in relation to contracts entered into before the end of the period of six months beginning with the day on which the Act was passed. The Act was passed on 11 November 1999.
3 See **PARA 17.14**.
4 Section 8; *Mulchrone v Swiss Life (UK) plc* [2005] EWHC 1808 (Comm), [2006] Lloyd's Rep IR 339, para 14 (Gavin Kealey QC, sitting as a Deputy Judge of the High Court); see also *Fortress Value Recovery Fund I LLC v Blue Skye Special Opportunities Fund LP* [2013] EWCA Civ 367, [2013] 1 Lloyd's Rep 606, approving *Nisshin Shipping Co Ltd v Cleaves & Co Ltd* [2003] EWHC 2602 (Comm), [2004] 1 Lloyd's Rep 38.
5 Section 7(1).
6 See also **PARA 2.10**.
7 *PM Law Ltd v Motorplus Ltd* [2016] EWHC 193 (QB), paras 28–31 (Picken J).

The Third Parties (Rights Against Insurers) Act 1930

Events triggering transfer to third party of rights against insurer

2.19   Where the insured has insurance in respect of a liability which he has incurred to a third party, s 1(1) of the Third Parties (Rights Against Insurers) Act 1930 sets out the events which trigger a transfer to the third party of the insured's rights against the insurer. Where the insured is a natural person, these events are the insured becoming bankrupt, or making a composition or arrangement with his creditors.[1] Where the insured is a company or limited liability partnership,[2] the events are the making of a winding-up order; a resolution for a winding-up being passed; the company entering administration; a receiver or manager being appointed; possession being taken by, or on behalf of, the holders of debentures secured by a floating charge, of any property subject to the charge; or a voluntary arrangement being approved under Part I of the Insolvency Act 1986.[3]

It is unclear whether, assuming the English courts have jurisdiction, a third party is entitled to bring proceedings in England against insurers by virtue of the 1930 Act where the proper law of the contract of insurance is not English law.[4]

1 Section 1(1)(a) of the 1930 Act. A transfer may also be effected where the insured has died and his estate is insolvent: s 1(2) of the 1930 Act.
2 Section 3A(1) of the 1930 Act. Where the insured is a limited liability partnership, references to a resolution for a voluntary winding-up being passed are references to a determination for a voluntary winding-up being made: s 3A(2). A foreign company which has a claim for an indemnity under a contract of liability insurance issued by an English insurer has assets within the jurisdiction for the purposes of winding it up under the Companies Act 1948 (see now the Insolvency Act 1986) even though any benefit which the assets may provide for the petitioning creditor may accrue not through the winding up but through the 1930 Act: *Re Compania Merabella San Nicholas SA* [1973] Ch 75, 90–92 (Megarry J); considered: *Stocznia Gdanska SA v Latreefers Inc (No 2)* [2001] 2 BCLC 116, CA.
3 Section 1(1)(b) of the 1930 Act. The Act does not apply where a company is wound up voluntarily merely for the purposes of reconstruction or of amalgamation with another company: s 1(6).
4 *Irish Shipping Ltd v Commercial Union Assurance Co Ltd* [1991] 2 QB 206, CA, 219–221 (Staughton LJ), 232 (Sir John Megaw), 246 and 248 (Purchas LJ).

Timing of transfer of rights to third party

2.20 The transfer of the insured's rights to the third party takes place on the occurrence of one of the triggering events.[1] At that stage, the rights transferred are inchoate or contingent[2] and may be rendered nugatory if, before the third party establishes a quantified claim, other quantified claims are established which exhaust the cover.[3]

1 *Re OT Computers Ltd (in administration)* [2004] EWCA Civ 653, [2004] Ch 317, paras 44–46 (Longmore LJ).
2 *Re OT Computers Ltd (in administration)* [2004] EWCA Civ 653, [2004] Ch 317, paras 44–46 (Longmore LJ).
3 *Re OT Computers Ltd (in administration)* [2004] EWCA Civ 653, [2004] Ch 317, paras 44–46 (Longmore LJ); approving: *Cox v Bankside Members Agency Ltd* [1995] 2 Lloyd's Rep 437, 443 (Phillips J).

Types of insurance to which the 1930 Act applies

2.21 The 1930 Act applies to all types of liability insurance including tortious liability and liability for breach of contract.[1] The 1930 Act does not apply to contracts of reinsurance[2] or in relation to provisions in a contract of insurance which allow for payments to be made at the insurer's discretion.[3]

1 *Re OT Computers Ltd (in administration)* [2004] EWCA Civ 653, [2004] Ch 317, paras 14–22 and 53 (Longmore LJ), disapproving *Tarbuck v Avon Insurance plc* [2002] QB 571 and *T&N Ltd v Royal and Sun Alliance plc (No 2)* [2003] EWHC 1016 (Ch), [2004] 1 Lloyd's Rep IR 106.
2 Section 1(5) of the 1930 Act.
3 *CVG Siderurgicia del Orinoco SA v London Steamship Owners' Mutual Insurance Association Ltd (The Vainqueur José)* [1979] 1 Lloyd's Rep 557, 580 (Mocatta J): rules of P & I club excluded liability for costs of forwarding cargo unless the Committee in its sole discretion determined otherwise.

Avoidance provisions are of no effect

2.22 Provisions in a contract of insurance which purport, directly or indirectly, to avoid the contract or to alter the rights of the parties on the happening of any of the triggering events are of no effect.[1] Similarly, agreements between the insured and the insurer entered into after any such event are of no effect.[2] However, the 1930 Act does not prevent a solvent insured, even if it is in financial difficulties, from entering into an agreement with the insurer in full and final settlement of the insurer's liability under the policy.[3] The position may be different if the proposed settlement would be entered into in bad faith or collusively, with the intention of injuring the third party claimant, or if the insured had been under a contractual or professional (regulatory) obligation to effect the policy: in these circumstances, it may be open to the court to restrain a proposed surrender or repudiation by the insured of the liability insurance.[4]

1 Section 1(3) of the 1930 Act.
2 Section 3 of the 1930 Act.
3 *Normid Housing Association v Ralphs* [1989] 1 Lloyd's Rep 265, CA.
4 *Normid Housing Association v Ralphs* [1989] 1 Lloyd's Rep 265, 273, CA (Slade LJ); *Cox v Bankside Members Agency Ltd* [1995] 2 Lloyd's Rep 437, CA, 458 (Sir Thomas Bingham MR), 464–465 (Peter Gibson LJ). In *Normid Housing Association v Ralphs* (No 2) [1989] 1 Lloyd's Rep 274, the Court of Appeal extended an earlier injunction in order to allow the third party claimants an opportunity to apply for a *Mareva* (freezing) injunction. For the position where the insurer brings proceedings against the (still solvent) insured for a declaration that it is not liable under the contract of insurance and the third party claimant wishes to be joined to those proceedings, see **PARA 9.47**.

Third party's entitlement to information

2.23   The third party is entitled to information under the 1930 Act from the insured, or from those who have assumed responsibility for his (or its) affairs following a triggering event, such as a trustee in bankruptcy or liquidator.[1] The information to which the third party is entitled is such information as may reasonably be required by him for the purpose of ascertaining whether any rights have been transferred to and vested in him by the 1930 Act, and for the purpose of enforcing such rights.[2] As the transfer of the insured's rights to the third party takes place on the occurrence of one of the triggering events, the third party is entitled to obtain information about the insurance policy from that date onwards without first establishing the liability of the insured.[3] If the information is not forthcoming, it may be possible for the third party to obtain it by making an application for disclosure against the insured or those who have assumed responsibility for his or its affairs or against the insurer.[4]

1 Section 2(1) of the 1930 Act.
2 Section 2(1) of the 1930 Act.
3 *Re OT Computers Ltd (in administration)* [2004] EWCA Civ 653, [2004] Ch 317, para 46 (Longmore LJ) (disapproving *Nigel Upchurch Associates v Aldridge Estates Investment Co Ltd* [1993] 1 Lloyd's Rep 535 and *Woolwich Building Society v Taylor* [1995] 1 BCLC 132). If a triggering event has not yet occurred, the court has no jurisdiction pursuant to Part 18 or 31 to order disclosure of a party's insurance position: see **PARA 9.14**.
4 Depending on the identity of the party from whom the information is sought and on whether or not proceedings have begun, an application might be made under s 2(1) of the 1930 Act and/or CPR r 31.16 (disclosure before proceedings start) and/or CPR r 31.17 (orders for disclosure against a person not a party).

Transfer of insured's rights to third party

2.24   The third party is entitled to issue proceedings seeking an indemnity against the insurer under the 1930 Act only once he has established liability on the part of the insured and the amount of that liability has been ascertained.[1] This is because the insured's right is to be indemnified against his legal liability to third parties, and until that liability has been established, no right to an indemnity arises, whether in the insured or in the third party following a transfer of the insured's rights under the 1930 Act.[2] In an appropriate case, the third party might seek a declaration against the insurer before establishing the insured's liability, as a solvent insured would itself be entitled to do,[3] or the insurer may be joined to the liability proceedings.[4] If the insured is a company which has been dissolved, it is necessary to take proceedings to restore it to the register[5] in order to bring proceedings against it, so that its liability may be established. Where insurers who have funded litigation are subject to a contractual obligation to the insured to indemnify him against his liability to pay the costs of the successful party, the court is likely to make an order under s 51(3) of the Senior Courts Act 1981[6] that the insurer pay those costs directly to the unsuccessful party.[7] This may save time and costs in short-circuiting the 1930 Act,[8] although where the applicant's only right is under the 1930 Act and the right is not clear, a summary process under s 51(3) is not appropriate.[9]

1 *Post Office v Norwich Union Fire Insurance Society Ltd* [1967] 2 QB 363, CA. In *Abbey National plc v Frost* [1999] 1 WLR 1080, the Court of Appeal granted the third party claimant permission to effect substituted service on the insurer of proceedings against the insured, who could not be traced, on the grounds that otherwise the purpose of the scheme of compulsory insurance for solicitors pursuant to s 37 of the Solicitors Act 1974 would be frustrated (Nourse LJ at 1090). Proof of the debt in the bankruptcy or insolvency is adequate to establish it for the purposes of a claim against insurers: *Financial Services Compensation Scheme Ltd v Larnell (Insurances) Ltd (in liquidation)* [2006] QB 808, CA, paras 11 (Lloyd LJ) and 63 (Moore-Bick LJ); *Law Society v Shah* [2007] EWHC 2841 (Ch), [2009] Ch 223, para 47 (Floyd J); in the case of bankruptcy, this applies both before and after discharge: *Law Society v Shah* [2007] EWHC 2841 (Ch), [2009] Ch 223, para 53 (Floyd J).
2 *Cox v Bankside Members Agency Ltd* [1995] 2 Lloyd's Rep 437, 467, CA (Saville LJ).
3 See **PARA 9.42**.
4 *Carpenter v Ebblewhite* [1939] 1 KB 347, CA, 357–358 (Greer LJ) and 363 (MacKinnon LJ) (third party claimant joined insurer as co-defendant in action against insured; claim for a declaration premature because no dispute had yet arisen between third party claimant and insurer); *Harman v Crilly* [1943] 1 KB 168, CA (approving joinder of insurer as third party); *Brice v J H Wackerbarth (Australasia) Pty Ltd* [1974] 2 Lloyd's Rep 274, CA (Lord Denning MR at 276: there is no objection in principle to the bringing in of insurers as third parties; the sole question is whether it is just and convenient; Roskill LJ at 277: the test is whether the court can conveniently decide all issues between all parties involved without having underwriters present as third parties).
5 Pursuant to s 1029 of the Companies Act 2006.
6 See **PARA 9.46**.
7 *Murphy v Young & Co's Brewery* [1997] 1 WLR 1591, 1601, CA (Phillips LJ).
8 *Murphy v Young & Co's Brewery* [1997] 1 WLR 1591, 1601, CA (Phillips LJ).
9 See *Tharros Shipping Co Ltd v Bias Shipping Ltd* (No 3) [1995] 1 Lloyd's Rep 541, 555–556 (Rix J), [1997] 1 Lloyd's Rep 246, 251, CA (Phillips LJ); *Monkton Court Ltd v Perry Prowse (Insurance Services) Ltd* [2002] Lloyd's Rep IR 408, 412 (His Honour Judge Raymond Jack QC). Where the policy limits are not exhausted, an order under s 51(3) will usually be unnecessary because the insurer will simply satisfy the costs order made against the insured: *Cormack v Excess Insurance Co Ltd* [2002] Lloyd's Rep IR 398, 400, CA (Auld LJ).

Extent of third party's rights against insurer

2.25 The rights transferred to the third party pursuant to s 1(1) of the 1930 Act are those of the insured.[1] It follows from this that the third party can be in no better position, in claiming under the policy, than the insured would have been, and the third party's claim will be defeated if the insurer would have had a valid defence to the insured's claim, for example, because the insured failed to comply with a condition precedent such as a notification clause[2] or because the insured's liability to the third party arose out of his own deliberate wrongful act.[3] Similarly, if the contract of insurance contains an arbitration agreement, the agreement to arbitrate must be treated as transferred to the third party as part of, or inseparably connected with, the insured's right against the insurer under the contract of insurance.[4] The third party is entitled to succeed against the insurer only to the extent that its claim against the insured is within the scope of the policy, and any elements of the claim which fall outside the policy are not recoverable against the insurer even if the third party has obtained judgment against the insured for the whole amount.[5] Similarly, the third party is not entitled to recover from the insurer any part of the claim which is within a policy excess.[6] There is conflicting authority as to whether, where an insurer has a right of set-off, the right is excluded by the 1930 Act.[7] The ascertainment, by agreement, judgment or award, of the insured's liability gives rise to the claim under the insurance, which exhausts the insurance either entirely or pro tanto;[8] the policy thus serves the purpose of meeting each ascertained loss when and in the order in which it occurs,[9] and the insurer is obliged to make payments to third parties on a 'first past the post' basis.[10] Consequently, if the limit of indemnity is reached, later claimants may find that they are unable to recover from the insurer;[11] conversely, if there is a large policy excess to which an aggregation clause applies, earlier claimants may find that their claim is entirely within the policy excess and that they are able to recover nothing from the insurer, whereas later claimants may be able to recover.[12] In *Firma C-Trade SA v Newcastle P & I Association*,[13] the House of Lords decided that rights transferred to a third party by the 1930 Act remain subject to a 'pay first' clause. The effect of this is that the rights transferred to the third party cannot be exercised, as the third party is only seeking to exercise its rights because the insured has not paid it.

1 Section 1(1) of the 1930 Act; *Farrell v Federated Employers Insurance Association Ltd* [1970] 1 WLR 1400, CA. The third party 'stands in the shoes of the insured person': Lord Denning MR (at 1405).
2 See, eg, *Farrell v Federated Employers Insurance Association Ltd* [1970] 1 WLR 1400, CA.
3 *Charlton v Fisher* [2001] EWCA Civ 112, [2002] QB 578, CA, 589–91, paras 23 and 25 (Kennedy LJ), paras 31 and 38 (Laws LJ) and paras 91–97 (Rix LJ). See further **PARA 5.2**.
4 *Firma C-Trade SA v Newcastle P & I Association, The Fanti and the Padre Island (No 2)* [1991] 2 AC 1, 33, HL (Lord Goff).
5 See, eg, *Pioneer Concrete (UK) Ltd v National Employers Mutual General Insurance Association Ltd* [1985] 1 Lloyd's Rep 274, 277–278 (Bingham J): judgment against insured included sum for additional work which was held to constitute making good of faulty workmanship and to fall within policy exclusion.
6 See *Re OT Computers Ltd (in administration)* [2004] EWCA Civ 653, [2004] Ch 317, para 46 (Longmore LJ) and *Centre Reinsurance International Co v Freakley* [2005] EWCA Civ 115, [2005] Lloyd's Rep IR 303, para 36 (Chadwick LJ) (point not considered in House of Lords: [2006] UKHL 45, [2007] Lloyd's Rep IR 32) (discussing the position where the whole of the third party's claim is within the excess).
7 *International Energy Group Ltd v Zurich Insurance plc* [2015] UKSC 33, [2016] AC 509, para 92 (Lord Mance, with whom Lords Clarke, Carnwath and Hodge agreed), referring to *Murray v Legal and General Assurance Society Ltd* [1970] 2 QB 495, 503 (Cumming-Bruce J: insurer's right to recovery of unpaid premiums not set off against claim for indemnity by third party claimant) and *Cox v Bankside Members Agency Ltd* [1995] 2 Lloyd's Rep 437, 451 (Phillips J: obligation of insured to reimburse defence costs funded by underwriters within the excess subject to set off against claim for indemnity (point not considered on appeal: *Cox v Bankside Members Agency Ltd* [1995] 2 Lloyd's Rep 437, CA)). For the application of the 1930 Act and the special right of contribution in employer's liability insurance in cases falling within the '*Fairchild* enclave', see **PARA 13.13**.
8 *Teal Assurance Co Ltd v W R Berkley Insurance (Europe) Ltd* [2013] UKSC 57, [2014] Lloyd's Rep IR 56, para 17 (Lord Mance).
9 *Teal Assurance Co Ltd v W R Berkley Insurance (Europe) Ltd* [2013] UKSC 57, [2014] Lloyd's Rep IR 56, para 19 (Lord Mance).

10 *Cox v Bankside Members Agency Ltd* [1995] 2 Lloyd's Rep 437, 467, CA (Saville LJ).
11 *Centre Reinsurance International Co v Freakley* [2005] EWCA Civ 115, [2005] Lloyd's Rep IR 303, para 34 (Chadwick LJ) (point not considered in House of Lords: [2006] UKHL 45, [2007] Lloyd's Rep IR 32).
12 *Re OT Computers Ltd (in administration)* [2004] EWCA Civ 653, [2004] Ch 317, para 46 (Longmore LJ); *Centre Reinsurance International Co v Freakley* [2005] EWCA Civ 115, [2005] Lloyd's Rep IR 303, para 36 (Chadwick LJ) (point not considered in House of Lords: [2006] UKHL 45, [2007] Lloyd's Rep IR 32). This might happen if, for example, there were a large number of claimants whose claims arose out of the same occurrence, and an aggregation clause which provided that the claims were to be aggregated for the purposes of the application of the excess. If (as is often the case) the aggregation clause applied to the excess and to the limit of indemnity under the policy, both earlier and later claimants might find that they were unable to recover.
13 *The Fanti and the Padre Island (No 2)* [1991] 2 AC 1, HL.

Third party may retain rights against insured

2.26 Where the insurer's liability to the insured is less than the liability of the insured to the third party, the third party's rights against the insured in respect of the balance are unaffected by the transfer.[1]

1 Section 1(4)(b) of the 1930 Act. In *Centre Reinsurance International Co v Freakley* [2005] EWCA Civ 115, [2005] Lloyd's Rep IR 303, para 39, Chadwick LJ said that although it was clear from s 1(4)(b) that the third party's cause of action against the insured was not extinguished, it appeared to be implicit that following a transfer of the insured's rights to the third party the third party must look first to the insurer for payment (to the extent of the rights transferred) rather than to the insured, although this would have practical significance only if the insurer were also insolvent (point not considered in House of Lords: [2006] UKHL 45, [2007] Lloyd's Rep IR 32).

Limitation periods

2.27 The third party's claim against the insurer must be brought within the limitation period which applied to the insured's claim against the insurer from the outset,[1] save that if the claim is not time-barred when the insured is made bankrupt or wound up, it does not become time-barred by the passage of further time thereafter.[2]

1 *Lefevre v White* [1990] 1 Lloyd's Rep 569; *Matadeen v Caribbean Insurance Co Ltd* [2002] UKPC 69, [2003] 1 WLR 670. See also PARAS **11.57–11.62**.
2 *Financial Services Compensation Scheme Ltd v Larnell (Insurances) Ltd (in liquidation)* [2006] QB 808, CA.

The Third Parties (Rights Against Insurers) Act 2010

Main changes and transitional provisions

2.28 The Third Parties (Rights Against Insurers) Act 2010 will come into force on 1 August 2016.[1]

The main changes introduced by the Third Parties (Rights Against Insurers) Act 2010 are that the third party is entitled to a remedy directly against the insurer and is not required to sue the insured; that if the third party wishes to sue both insured and insurer, he may do so in a single set of proceedings; and that the third party has improved rights to information about the insurance position.

The effect of the transitional provisions in the 2010 Act is that, despite its repeal by the 2010 Act,[2] the 1930 Act will continue to apply in those cases where, before the date when 2010 Act comes into force, one of the triggering events in the 1930 Act has occurred and the insured has incurred liability to the third party, or, in the case of debts provable in bankruptcy, the insured has died.[3] In all other cases, the 2010 Act will apply.[4]

1 Third Parties (Rights against Insurers) Act 2010 (Commencement) Order 2016, para 2. The 2010 Act received Royal Assent on 25 March 2010. The Ministry of Justice confirmed in March 2012 that the 2010 Act required amendment to cover all forms of administration and that it was unlikely to come into force until 2013: Report on the implementation of Law Commission Proposals (HC 1900). The necessary amendments were made in part by the Insurance Act 2015, s 20 and Sch 2; further amendments were made by the Third Parties (Rights Against Insurers) Regulations 2016, which come into force with the 2010 Act on 1 August 2016: see reg 1. Both sets of amendments are referred to below where relevant.
2 By Sch 4 to the 2010 Act.
3 Sections 1(1) and 2 of the 1930 Act and s 20 of and paras 3 and 5 of Sch 3 to the 2010 Act. Paragraph 1A of Sch 3 to the 2010 Act (inserted by s 20 and Sch 2 of the Insurance Act 2015) provides that individuals, companies or limited liability companies not 'relevant persons' pursuant to ss 4 to 6 (see **PARA 2.29**) are to be treated as 'relevant persons' for the purposes of the 2010 Act if the relevant insolvency event occurred before commencement day and the insolvency remains in force (eg the individual has not been discharged from bankruptcy: para 1A(2); or the company or partnership is still wound up: para 1A(4)). If paragraph 1A of Sch 3 had not been inserted, there would have been a gap between the application of the two Acts: if the triggering event in the 1930 Act had occurred before the 2010 Act came into force, and the insured had incurred the liability afterwards, the effect of the unamended transitional provisions in the 2010 Act would have been that the 1930 Act did not apply, and the effect of ss 1(1) and 2 of the 2010 Act would have been that the insured was not a 'relevant person', meaning that the 2010 Act would not have applied either.
4 Section 20 of and paras 1, 3 and 5 of Sch 3 to the 2010 Act.

Events triggering transfer of third parties rights against insurer

2.29 The 2010 Act applies to 'relevant persons' and defines these by reference to specified insolvency regimes.[1] A body corporate or unincorporated body is a relevant person if the body has been dissolved unless, since it was dissolved (or, if it has been dissolved more than once, since it was last dissolved), something has happened which has the effect that the body is treated as not having been dissolved or as no longer being dissolved.[2] For these purposes, 'dissolved' means dissolved under the law of England and Wales, whether or not by a process referred to as dissolution.[3]

1 Sections 4 to 5 (individuals) and 6 (bodies corporate and unincorporated bodies). Paragraph 1A of Sch 3 to the 2010 Act (inserted by s 20 and Sch 2 of the Insurance Act 2015) provides that individuals, companies or limited liability companies not 'relevant persons' pursuant to ss 4 to 6 are to be treated as relevant persons for the purposes of the 2010 Act if the relevant insolvency event occurred before commencement day and the insolvency remains in force (eg the individual has not been discharged from bankruptcy: para 1A(2); or the company or partnership is still wound up: para 1A(4)). Section 6(2)(b) of the 2010 Act as originally enacted referred only to administration pursuant to an administration order made under Part 2 of the Insolvency Act 1986. Following amendment by the Insurance Act 2015, s 6(2)(b) of the 2010 Act now applies to bodies 'in administration' under Sch B1 to the Insolvency Act 1986. Further amendments were made by the Third Parties (Rights Against Insurers) Regulations 2016, which come into force with the 2010 Act on 1 August 2016: see reg 1 and see **PARA 2.28**, note 1. The 2016 Regulations provide that bodies in insolvency under Part 2 of the Banking Act 2009 and in administration under relevant sectoral legislation as defined in Sch A1 of the 2009 Act are relevant persons. The sectors listed in Sch A1 are aviation, energy, financial services, postal services, railways and water and sewerage.
2 Section 6A of the 2010 Act, as inserted by reg 4 of the Third Parties (Rights Against Insurers) Regulations 2016, which come into force with the 2010 Act on 1 August 2016: see reg 1 and see **PARA 2.28**, note 1. Section 6A applies to a partnership only if it is a body corporate: s 6A(3).
3 Section 6A(4) of the 2010 Act, as inserted by reg 4 of the Third Parties (Rights Against Insurers) Regulations 2016, which come into force with the 2010 Act on 1 August 2016: see reg 1 and see **PARA 2.28**, note 1.

Proceedings against the insurer or against the insured and the insurer

2.30 The 2010 Act gives third parties a right to issue proceedings against the insurer without first establishing the liability of the insured, and to establish and quantify that liability in those proceedings.[1] The third party may also join the insured as a defendant in proceedings against the insurer, and only if he does so will the judgment be binding on the insured as well as on the insurer.[2] As it will not be necessary for the third party to bring proceedings against the insured, it will no longer be necessary, where the insured is a company which has been dissolved, to restore it to the register. The 2010 Act does not affect the operation of any arbitration agreement which requires the parties to a contract of insurance refer their disputes to arbitration, save that it provides that where a third party claimant applying for a declaration as to the insured's liability is entitled or required, by virtue of the contract of insurance, to do so in arbitral proceedings, the third party claimant may also apply in the same proceedings for a declaration as to the insured's liability to him.[3]

1 Sections 1 and 2 of the 2010 Act.
2 Section 2(9)–(10) of the 2010 Act.
3 Section 2(7) of the 2010 Act.

Types of insurance to which the 2010 Act applies

2.31 The 2010 Act does not apply to contracts of reinsurance.[1]

It is irrelevant for the purposes of the transfer of rights under the 2010 Act whether or not the liability of the insured is or was incurred voluntarily.[2]

1 Section 15 of the 2010 Act.
2 Section 16 of the 2010 Act.

Avoidance provisions are of no effect

2.32 A contract of insurance under which the insured's rights are capable of being transferred under the 2010 Act is of no effect in so far as it purports, whether directly or indirectly, to terminate the contract or alter the rights of the parties under it in the event of the insured becoming a relevant person (which means a person in relation to whom one of the insolvency events has occurred) or dying insolvent.[1]

1 Section 17 of the 2010 Act. For the meaning of 'dying insolvent' for these purposes, see s 5(2) of the 2010 Act: s 17(1)(b).

Third party's entitlement to information

2.33 If a person (A) reasonably believes that another person (B) has incurred a liability to A, and that B is a relevant person (which means a person in relation to whom one of the insolvency events has occurred), the 2010 Act entitles A, by notice in writing, to request from B information specified in the notice.[1] The information which A is entitled to request is specified in the 2010 Act, and is as follows: whether there is a contract of insurance which covers the supposed liability or might reasonably be regarded as covering it and, if there is such a contract, who the insurer is; what the terms of the contract are; whether the insured has been informed that the insured has claimed not to be liable under the contract in respect of the supposed liability; whether there are or have been any proceedings between the insurer and the insured in respect of the supposed liability and, if so, relevant details of those proceedings; in a case where the contract sets a limit on the fund available to meet claims in respect of the supposed liability and other liabilities, how much of it (if any) has been paid out in respect of other liabilities; and whether there is a fixed charge to which any sums paid out under the contract in respect of the supposed liability would be subject.[2]

If A reasonably believes that a liability has been incurred to A, that the person who incurred the liability is insured against it under a contract of insurance, that the rights of that person under the contract of insurance have been transferred to A by the 2010 Act, and that there is another person (C) who is able to provide the information set out above, the 2010 Act entitles A, by notice in writing, to request from C such of that information as the notice specifies.[3] The 2010 Act requires the provision of the information, or of an explanation of why the information cannot be provided, within the period of 28 days beginning with the day of receipt of the notice.[4] Compliance with the duty to provide information may be enforced by court order.[5]

1 Section 11 of and Sch 1, para 1(1) to the 2010 Act.
2 Section 11 of and Sch 1, para 1(3) to the 2010 Act. The relevant details of proceedings for these purposes are, in the case of court proceedings, the name of the court, the case number and the contents of all documents served in the proceedings in accordance with rules of court or orders made in the proceedings, and the contents of any such orders; and in the case of arbitral proceedings, the name of the arbitrator and equivalent information to that required in relation to court proceedings: s 11 and Sch 1, para 1(4) of the 2010 Act.
3 Section 11 of and Sch 1, para 1(2)–(3) to the 2010 Act.
4 Section 11 of and Sch 1, para 2(1) to the 2010 Act. If the recipient of a notice is unable to provide information because a document containing the information is no longer in his control but he knows or believes it to be in another person's control, he must provide the party serving the notice with whatever particulars he can as to the nature of the information and the identity of that other person: s 11 and Sch 1, para 2(2).
5 Section 11 of and Sch 1, para 2(3) to the 2010 Act.

Extent of third party's rights against insurer

2.34   The 2010 Act gives the insurer the right to rely on any defence on which the insured could have relied had the proceedings been brought against him by the third party.[1] The 2010 Act preserves the insurer's right to rely, as against the third party, on any defences which would have been available to him as against the insured,[2] with certain limited but important exceptions. First, if the insured's rights under a policy of insurance are subject to a condition which the insured has to fulfil, anything done by the third party in fulfilment of the condition is to be treated as having been done by the insured.[3] This is likely to be of particular significance in relation to procedural conditions. Secondly, the transferred rights are not subject to a condition requiring the insured to provide information or assistance to the insurer if that condition cannot be fulfilled because the insured is an individual who has died, a body corporate or unincorporated body (other than a partnership) that has been dissolved.[4] However, a condition requiring the insured to provide information or assistance to the insurer does not include a condition requiring the insured to notify the insurer of the existence of a claim under the contract of insurance.[5] Thirdly, the third party's claim under the 2010 Act is not adversely affected by a 'pay first' clause, except in relation to marine insurance, and then only in cases other than liability for death or personal injury.[6] Where insurers are relying on defences in relation to their liability under the policy, it may be appropriate for those defences to be tried as preliminary issues, in order to avoid unnecessarily incurring the costs of a trial in relation to the insured's liability to the third party should the insurer's defences succeed.

1 Section 2(4) of the 2010 Act. For the application of the 2010 Act and the special right of contribution in employer's liability insurance in cases falling within the '*Fairchild* enclave', see **PARA 13.13**.
2 Section 2(4) of the 2010 Act.
3 Section 9(1)–(2) of the 2010 Act.
4 Section 9(3) of the 2010 Act, as amended by reg 5 of the Third Parties (Rights Against Insurers) Regulations 2016. For these purposes, 'dissolved' means dissolved under the law of England and Wales, whether or not by a process referred to as dissolution and a body has been dissolved even if, since it was dissolved, something has happened which has the effect that (but for this provision) the body is treated as not having been dissolved or as no longer being dissolved: s 9(8), as inserted by reg 5 of the 2016 Regulations.
5 Section 9(4) of the 2010 Act.
6 Section 9(5)–(7).

Third party may retain rights against insured

2.35   Where rights in respect of an insured's liability to a third party are transferred under the 2010 Act, the third party may enforce that liability against the insured only to the extent (if any) that it exceeds the amount recoverable from the insurer by virtue of the transfer.[1]

1 Section 14(1) of the 2010 Act. For these purposes, the amount recoverable from the insurer does not include any amount that the third party is unable to recover as a result of either a shortage of assets on the insurer's part, in a case where the insurer is a relevant person (which means a person in relation to whom one of the insolvency events has occurred), or a limit set by the contract of insurance on the fund available to meet claims in respect of a particular description of liability of the insured: s 14(6).

Insured may retain rights against insurer

2.36   Where the liability of an insured to a third party is less than the liability of the insurer to the insured, ignoring any transferred rights, no rights are transferred under the 2010 Act in respect of the difference.[1]

1 Section 8 of the 2010 Act.

Insurer may exercise right of set off against third party

2.37   Where the insured is under a liability to the insurer under the contract, and if there had been no transfer, the insurer would have been entitled to set off the amount of the insured's liability against the amount of the insurer's own liability to the insured, the insurer is entitled to set off the amount of the insured's liability against the amount of the insurer's own liability to the third party in relation to the transferred rights.[1]

1 Section 10 of the 2010 Act. See also PARA **13.14**.

Limitation periods

2.38 Where a third party brings proceedings against the insurer for a declaration as to the insured's liability and the proceedings are started after the expiry of a period of limitation applicable to an action against the insured to enforce the insured's liability, but while such an action is in progress, the insurer may not rely on the expiry of that limitation period as a defence unless the insured is able to rely on it in the action against the insured.[1] Where a third party who has already established an insured's liability brings proceedings under the 2010 Act against the insurer, nothing in the 2010 Act is to be read as meaning that, for the purposes of the law of limitation in England and Wales, the third party's cause of action against the insurer arose otherwise than at the time when that person established the liability of the insured.[2]

1 Section 12(1)–(2) of the 2010 Act. For these purposes, an action is to be treated as no longer in progress if it has been concluded by a judgment, or by an award, even if there is an appeal or right of appeal: s 12(3) of the 2010 Act.
2 Section 12(4)(a) of the 2010 Act.

Territorial scope and jurisdiction

2.39 Except as expressly provided, the application of the 2010 Act does not depend on whether there is a connection with a part of the United Kingdom; and in particular it does not depend on whether or not the liability (or the alleged liability) of the insured to the third party was incurred in or under the law of England and Wales, Scotland or Northern Ireland; or on the place of residence or domicile of any of the parties; or on whether or not the contract of insurance (or part of it) is governed by the law of England and Wales, Scotland or Northern Ireland; or on the place where sums due under the contract of insurance are payable.[1] Where a person domiciled in part of the United Kingdom is entitled to bring proceedings under the 2010 Act against an insurer domiciled in another part, that person may do so in the part where he is domiciled or in the part where the insurer is domiciled (whatever the contract of insurance may stipulate as to where proceedings are to be brought).[2]

1 Section 18 of the 2010 Act.
2 Section 13(1) of the 2010 Act. For these purposes, domicile is determined in accordance with specified sections of the Civil Jurisdiction and Judgments Act 1982: s 13(2) of the 2010 Act; and the 2010 Act is excluded from the general provisions of the 1982 Act as to allocation of jurisdiction within the United Kingdom: s 13(3) of the 2010 Act.

Other statutory schemes giving third parties rights against insurers

2.40 There are statutory provisions giving third parties rights against insurers in other contexts, including road traffic accidents[1] and oil pollution by ships.[2] The application of these schemes is not dependent upon the insured being declared insolvent.

1 Sections 151–152 of the Road Traffic Act 1988; European Communities (Rights against Insurers) Regulations 2002.
2 Section 165 of the Merchant Shipping Act 1995, which also excludes the application of the Third Parties (Rights Against Insurers) Act 1930 and the Third Parties (Rights Against Insurers) Act 2010 (see s 165(5)).

Chapter 3

The contract of insurance

3.1 This chapter considers the following: cover notes; the date when the contract becomes binding; the classification of policy terms and the effect of breach; principles of construction applicable to contracts of insurance; and the circumstances in which rectification of insurance contracts may be granted.

COVER NOTES

3.2 Where insurance cover is required as a matter of urgency, or while an insurer is considering a proposal, insurers may grant cover on a 'held covered' basis.[1] This is a contract which is ancillary to the proposed contract of insurance.[2] This type of cover is a feature of the motor insurance market and is also prevalent in fire, burglary and accident insurance.[3] Initially, the contract of interim insurance may be oral (for example, as a result of the insured phoning the broker).[4] When reduced to writing, such a contract is commonly known as a 'cover note'. Unless otherwise agreed, a cover note is a temporary contract, generally for a maximum period of about 30 days,[5] and terminable by notice by the insurer at any time during that period.[6] The consideration for a cover note is an implied promise to pay the appropriate premium.[7] Where a cover note is issued by a broker, the broker is acting as agent for the insurer rather than the insured.[8] The broker may be expressly authorised by the insurer to issue a cover note on its behalf; in the absence of express authority, the broker has implied authority to issue a cover note.[9] If a contract of insurance is subsequently issued, it replaces the temporary cover provided pursuant to the cover note.[10]

1 *Beazley Underwriting Ltd v The Travelers Companies Inc* [2011] EWHC 1520 (Comm), [2012] Lloyd's Rep IR 78, para 188 (Christopher Clarke J).
2 *Beazley Underwriting Ltd v The Travelers Companies Inc* [2011] EWHC 1520 (Comm), [2012] Lloyd's Rep IR 78, para 188 (Christopher Clarke J).
3 *Beazley Underwriting Ltd v The Travelers Companies Inc* [2011] EWHC 1520 (Comm), [2012] Lloyd's Rep IR 78, para 188 (Christopher Clarke J).
4 See, eg, *Stockton v Mason* [1978] 2 Lloyd's Rep 430, 432, CA (Lord Diplock).
5 Cover stated to be '15 days from commencement date of risk' is cover for 15 days starting from the day after the cover note was issued and expiring at midnight, so a cover note issued at 11.45 am on 2 December provides immediate cover which expires at midnight on 17 December: *Cartwright v MacCormack* [1962] 2 Lloyd's Rep 328, CA. Cover stated to be '15 days from commencement of risk' or '15 days from time of commencement of risk' is cover for 15 consecutive periods of 24 hours and expires at 11.45 am on 17 December: *Cartwright v MacCormack* [1962] 2 Lloyd's Rep 328, CA.
6 *Stockton v Mason* [1978] 2 Lloyd's Rep 430, 431, CA (Lord Diplock). In *Houghton v Trafalgar Insurance Co Ltd* [1953] 2 Lloyd's Rep 18, the insured completed a proposal form before the cover note was issued; the cover note was held to constitute not temporary cover but a provisional contract of insurance and to be subject therefore to an exclusion in the policy which was expressly stated in the proposal form.

7 *Taylor v Allon* [1965] 1 Lloyd's Rep 155, 158, DC (Lord Parker CJ). The appropriate premium is either the premium for the policy of insurance or, if no policy is subsequently issued, a premium for the period of temporary cover provided pursuant to the cover note: *Taylor v Allon* [1965] 1 Lloyd's Rep 155, 158, DC (Lord Parker CJ).

8 *Stockton v Mason* [1978] 2 Lloyd's Rep 430, 431, CA (Lord Diplock); *Searle v A R Hales & Co Ltd* [1996] LRLR 68, 71 (Mr Adrian Whitfield QC).

9 *Stockton v Mason* [1978] 2 Lloyd's Rep 430, 431, CA (Lord Diplock). It seems that the position has changed: in *Newsholme Brothers v Road Transport and General Insurance Co Ltd* [1929] 2 KB 356, 377, CA, Greer LJ stated that, in the absence of express authority, an agent to procure signed proposal forms was not authorised to give cover notes or enter into any policy of insurance.

10 *Stockton v Mason* [1978] 2 Lloyd's Rep 430, 431, CA (Lord Diplock). In *Houghton v Trafalgar Insurance Co Ltd* [1953] 2 Lloyd's Rep 18 (see note 6 above), the cover note was a provisional contract of insurance and would therefore have been confirmed rather than replaced by the issue of the contract of insurance.

TIME OF BINDING CONTRACT AND OF INCEPTION OF RISK

3.3   In the case of a policy placed on the basis of a slip in the London market (whether Lloyd's or the company market), a draft slip is an offer to contract and each unconditional subscription to it by an underwriter constitutes an acceptance for the line accepted, so that the contract becomes binding when the slip is signed.[1] If the underwriter qualifies his acceptance by putting a subjectivity next to his scratch there has been no acceptance of the offer,[2] and the scratched slip is a counter offer which may be revoked at any time prior to its acceptance.[3] It is a matter of construction whether a subjectivity is a qualification of acceptance in this way or purely an administrative formality.[4]

It is a common feature of the London market that parties contemplate a fuller wording to follow the slip or short-form statement of their agreed terms; those terms are binding nonetheless.[5] When the policy is issued, it is the policy and not the slip that constitutes the agreement between the parties.[6]

In the case of a policy placed on the basis of a proposal form which is accepted by the insurer, it is a matter of construction whether it is only when the premium is tendered by the insured that the contract becomes binding[7] or whether the period of insurance begins on a particular date in return for a promise by the insured to pay the premium). The contract becomes binding at this stage even where the insured has not seen or expressly agreed to the detailed terms of the policy, provided that those terms are the insurers' usual terms.[8] The contract may become binding before inception or attachment of the risk (the point at which the policy begins to respond to insured perils).

1 *General Reinsurance Corpn v Fenna Patria* [1983] QB 856, CA (disapproving in part *Jaglom v Excess Insurance Co Ltd* [1972] 2 QB 250); *Hadenfayre Ltd v British National Insurance Society Ltd* [1984] 2 Lloyd's Rep 393, 398 (Lloyd J); *Beazley Underwriting Ltd v The Travelers Companies Inc* [2011] EWHC 1520 (Comm), [2012] Lloyd's Rep IR 78, paras 169–173 (Christopher Clarke J). The underwriter's 'scratch' is simply his initial or signature on the slip. Placing the syndicate's stamp on the slip is a step preparatory to the writing of a line; it is only the underwriter's signature or initial which is binding: *Denby v English & Scottish Maritime Insurance Co Ltd* [1998] Lloyd's Rep IR 343, CA, (Hobhouse LJ); and the underwriter's stamp is not required in order for a contract to be formed: *Beazley Underwriting Ltd v The Travelers Companies Inc* [2011] EWHC 1520 (Comm), [2012] Lloyd's Rep

IR 78, para 176 (Christopher Clarke J); see also *Allianz Insurance Co Egypt v Aigaion Insurance Co SA (No 2), The Ocean Dirk* [2008] EWCA Civ 1455, [2009] Lloyd's Rep IR 533, paras 33–36 (Rix LJ) (parties in separate countries unable to act by face-to-face presentation and signature (or initialling or stamping) of the slip; email construed as acceptance of terms in proffered slip rather than counter-offer). A contract of marine insurance is deemed to be concluded when the proposal is accepted by the insurer: s 21 of the Marine Insurance Act 1906.

2 *Société Anonyme d'Intermédiares Luxembourgeois v Farex Gie* [1995] 1 LRLR 116, 121 (Evans J) ('subject to reinsurance and security'; issue not considered on appeal: [1995] 1 LRLR 116, CA); *Beazley Underwriting Ltd v The Travelers Companies Inc* [2011] EWHC 1520 (Comm), [2012] Lloyd's Rep IR 78, paras 169–173 (Christopher Clarke J) (scratch made subject to reinsurance, satisfactory proposal form and Y2K questionnaire).

3 *Beazley Underwriting Ltd v The Travelers Companies Inc* [2011] EWHC 1520 (Comm), [2012] Lloyd's Rep IR 78, para 184 (Christopher Clarke J).

4 *Bonner v Cox Dedicated Corporate Member Ltd* [2004] EWHC 2963 (Comm), [2005] Lloyd's Rep IR 569, 589 (Morison J) ('subject re-referencing and new stamp with effect from 1 January 1999'; stamping and referencing for new syndicate as from 1 January 1999 were purely administrative acts which did not need to be completed before the risks attached; issue not considered on appeal: [2005] EWCA Civ 1512, [2006] 2 Lloyd's Rep 152); *Beazley Underwriting Ltd v The Travelers Companies Inc* [2011] EWHC 1520 (Comm), [2012] Lloyd's Rep IR 78, para 176 (Christopher Clarke J).

5 *Axa Corporate Solutions SA v National Westminster Bank plc* [2010] EWHC 1915 (Comm), [2011] Lloyd's Rep IR 438, para 124 (Hamblen J) (terms on which cover renewed included: 'Terrorism exclusion (wording to be agreed)'; fact that parties contemplated fuller expression of same exclusion in wording subsequently to be agreed did not undermine fact that exclusion was cast in words which were capable of both interpretation and application).

6 *Youell v Bland Welch & Co Ltd* [1992] 2 Lloyd's Rep 127, 141, CA (Beldam LJ). See also **PARA 3.12**.

7 *Canning v Farquhar* (1886) 16 QBD 727, CA.

8 *Rust v Abbey Life Assurance Co Ltd* [1979] 2 Lloyd's Rep 334, 339, CA (Brandon LJ); *Super Chem Products Ltd v American Life and General Insurance Co Ltd* [2004] UKPC 2, [2004] Lloyd's Rep IR 446, 451, para 9 (Lord Steyn) (whatever they may have known about the terms of the policy, the brokers, with the insured's authority, committed the insured to a contract on all the standard form terms of the policy, and the insured was therefore bound by those terms). In *Yona International Ltd v La Réunion Française SA* [1996] 2 Lloyd's Rep 84, Moore-Bick J considered that the insured in *Rust* would have been entitled to reject the policy within a reasonable time of receipt (at 110). ICOBS imposes obligations in relation to the provision of information, including a policy summary, before conclusion of a contract of insurance: see ICOBS 6 (Product information).

CLASSIFICATION OF POLICY TERMS

3.4 Policy terms fall into various categories, and breach of a policy term has radically different consequences according to the type of term which is breached. A term may be a condition precedent to the insurer's liability to make any payment to the insured. Policy terms which are not conditions precedent[1] are traditionally divided into the following categories:[2]

(1) 'warranties': the consequences of breach of a warranty depend on whether the contract was entered into before, or on or after, 12 August 2016;[3]

(2) 'innominate' or 'intermediate' terms[4]; and

(3) all other terms: these 'ordinary' terms are, confusingly, called 'warranties' in ordinary contract law; they have no special name in insurance law.

In insurance law, 'condition' is frequently used in a neutral sense to mean any clause in a policy. In this sense, it is interchangeable with a variety of other neutral labels such as 'clause', 'term', 'provision' or 'stipulation'. 'Warranty' also has other meanings, which are considered below.[5]

The Insurance Act 2015 has added a further type of term: 'terms not relevant to the actual loss'.[6]

In construing a policy, the court is attempting to gauge the intentions of the parties,[7] and where the court is construing a term and assigning it to one of the categories, it does so by attempting to ascertain what the parties intended the consequences of breach to be. If the policy indicates what the consequences of breach are to be, this is fairly straightforward, as clear indications are usually respected by the courts, unless they lead to absurd or wholly unreasonable results. Typically, however, instead of stating expressly what the consequences of breach are to be, the parties rely on labels, sometimes applied indiscriminately to all or a large number of the terms in the policy, as a shorthand for what they intend the consequences of breach to be. In this situation, the court must construe the policy in order to ascertain the parties' intentions. The consequences of breach of each type of term, and how the courts approach the construction exercise, are considered below.

1 See **PARA 3.5**. Warranties are conditions precedent to the attachment of the risk: *Thomson v Weems* (1884) 9 App Cas 671, 684, HL (Lord Blackburn); *Bank of Nova Scotia v Hellenic Mutual War Risks Association (Bermuda) Ltd, The Good Luck* [1992] 1 AC 233, 262–263, HL (Lord Goff); *Brit Syndicates Ltd v Italaudit SpA* [2008] UKHL 18, [2008] Lloyd's Rep IR 601, para 24 (Lord Mance); (this is not the sense in which the label or shorthand expression 'condition precedent' is usually used in insurance law: see **PARA 3.5**). On this analysis, it would appear that a continuing warranty is a condition precedent to the continuation of the risk.
2 See the authoritative statement of the law in *Fir Shipping Co Ltd v Kawasaki Kisen Kaisha Ltd* [1962] 2 QB 26, CA (approved: *L Schuler AG v Wickman Machine Tool Sales Ltd* [1974] AC 235, HL); and *K/S Merc-Scandia XXXXII v Certain Lloyd's Underwriters, The Mercandian Continent* [2001] EWCA Civ 1275, [2001] 2 Lloyd's Rep 563, para 13, CA (Longmore LJ). The parties may also agree to modify the consequences of breach of a term: see eg *The Seashell of Lisson Grove Ltd v Aviva Insurance Ltd* [2011] EWHC 1761 (Comm), [2012] Lloyd's Rep IR 356, paras 3–12 (Teare J) (modification of consequences of breach of warranty).
3 See **PARA 3.7**.
4 See **PARA 3.9**.
5 See **PARA 3.7**.
6 See **PARA 3.10**.
7 The court is not concerned with the parties' subjective intentions, but is seeking to ascertain what the language which the parties used in the contract would signify to hypothetical reasonable persons in their position: see, eg, *Absalom v TCRU Ltd* [2005] EWCA Civ 1586, [2006] 2 Lloyd's Rep 129, para 7 (Longmore LJ). See **PARAS 3.13–3.16**.

Conditions precedent[1]

3.5 In insurance law, a condition precedent is an obligation imposed on the insured which must be strictly complied with if insurers are to be liable in respect of a particular claim.[2] For this reason, the question of whether compliance with a particular term in an insurance policy is a condition precedent to the liability of the insurer typically arises in the context of clauses governing the form and time within which notice of loss must be given, the particulars and mode of proof of loss required, the provision of assistance or co-operation by the insured, and arbitration clauses.[3] In determining whether a clause is a condition precedent, the court will construe the policy as a whole,[4] and will consider the wider context and commercial purpose of the condition, however it is labelled.[5] The heart of the matter lies in ascertaining from the terms of the particular contract the event or events upon which the right to claim indemnity is conditioned[6]: if the parties intended that the insurer's obligations under the policy were to be dependent on the prior fulfilment by the insured of the specified condition, the clause is a condition precedent. Breach of a condition precedent entitles the insurer to refuse payment even though he may have suffered no prejudice from the breach.[7]

Provisions in a policy which are stated to be conditions precedent should not be treated as a mere formality which is to be evaded at the cost of a forced and unnatural construction of the words used in the policy; they should be construed fairly to give effect to the object for which they were inserted, but at the same time so as to protect the assured from being trapped by obscure or ambiguous phraseology.[8] If a policy states that a condition is a 'condition precedent', that is influential but not decisive as to its status, particularly where the label 'condition precedent' is attached on an indiscriminate basis to a number of terms of different nature and varying importance in the policy, or even to every term in the policy.[9] Such provisions will be given only limited weight by the court, which will examine the term to see whether it is in fact capable of amounting to a condition precedent.[10] Where, in construing a clause labelled 'condition precedent', the policy contains other clauses not so labelled, the court will be more likely to respect the label.[11] Where, however, one or more clauses are labelled 'condition precedent' and a question arises as to the status of a clause not so labelled, the lack of the label is not determinative if, after considering the wording of the clause against the background of the policy as a whole, the court concludes that the parties intended it to operate as a condition precedent.[12] However, clear and unambiguous wording is required before the court will reach this conclusion.[13] Where the question is left at large, it is for the court to determine, looking at all the terms of the policy, what the true meaning of the contract is, and whether a particular term is a condition precedent to insurers' liability.[14] It is not essential that the very words 'condition precedent' be used to achieve the result that insurers will not be liable unless a certain event happens; other words can be used, if they are clear,[15] and this may be so even if the words 'condition precedent' are used elsewhere in the same policy.[16] A term relating to things to be done after payment by insurers cannot be a condition precedent to liability.[17] The fact that there may be major or minor failures to comply with a procedural condition may be relevant to its scope rather than to whether or not, properly construed, it is a condition precedent.[18] A condition precedent is an exemption from the insurer's liability under the policy of insurance and will relieve the insurer from liability only if on a fair construction of the clause the meaning is clear.[19]

The burden of proving that the insured is in breach of a condition precedent is on the insurer.[20] Compliance by the insured with a condition precedent may be waived by the insurer either before or after the insured is in breach of the obligation.[21]

ICOBS provides that an insurer must not unreasonably reject a claim (including by terminating or avoiding a policy),[22] and that a rejection of a consumer policyholder's claim is unreasonable, except where there is evidence of fraud, except in certain circumstances including breach of condition where the circumstances of the claim are connected with the breach.[23] If a failure to comply with a condition precedent has not caused prejudice to the insurer, ICOBS requires the insurer not to reject a consumer policyholder's claim on the basis of breach of the condition precedent, as the circumstances of the claim would not be connected with the breach.[24] Breach of ICOBS is actionable at the suit of a 'private person',[25] and the loss caused by the breach of statutory duty in these circumstances would normally be the value of the claim.

1 *See also* **CHAPTER 7**.
2 For other types of condition precedent, see **PARA 3.4**, note 1.
3 See eg *Virk v Gan Life Holdings plc* [2000] Lloyd's Rep IR 159, para 12, CA (Potter LJ). See also **PARA 7.5**. If an application for a stay of legal proceedings under the Arbitration Act 1996 is refused, any provision that an award is a condition precedent to the bringing of legal proceedings in respect of any matter is of no effect in relation to those proceedings: Arbitration Act 1996, s 9(5).
4 *George Hunt Cranes Ltd v Scottish Boiler and General Insurance Co Ltd* [2001] EWCA Civ 1964, [2002] Lloyd's Rep IR 178, para 11 (Potter LJ).
5 *Virk v Gan Life Holdings plc* [2000] Lloyd's Rep IR 159, para 15, CA (Potter LJ).
6 *Virk v Gan Life Holdings plc* [2000] Lloyd's Rep IR 159, para 15, CA (Potter LJ). In *Friends Provident Life & Pensions Ltd v Sirius International Insurance* [2005] EWCA Civ 601, [2005] 2 Lloyd's Rep 517, at para 31, Mance LJ described the issue as whether 'some conditional link can, as a matter of construction, be found between performance of the two obligations' (ie between the insured's obligation in question, and the insurer's obligation to indemnify the insured in respect of the claim); applied: *Aspen Insurance UK Ltd v Pectel Ltd* [2008] EWHC 2804, [2009] Lloyd's Rep IR, para 62 (Teare J).
7 *Virk v Gan Life Holdings plc* [2000] Lloyd's Rep IR 159, para 13, CA (Potter LJ). See also **PARA 7.5**.
8 *Pilkington United Kingdom Ltd v CGU Insurance plc* [2004] EWCA Civ 23, [2004] Lloyd's Rep IR 891, para 65 (Potter LJ).
9 *London Guarantie Co v Fearnley* (1880) 5 App Cas 911, HL; *Re Bradley and Essex and Suffolk Accident Indemnity Society* [1912] 1 KB 415, CA; *Virk v Gan Life Holdings plc* [2000] Lloyd's Rep IR 159, paras 14–15, CA (Potter LJ); *George Hunt Cranes Ltd v Scottish Boiler and General Insurance Co Ltd* [2001] EWCA Civ 1964, [2002] Lloyd's Rep IR 178, para 11 (Potter LJ).
10 *Re Bradley and Essex and Suffolk Accident Indemnity Society* [1912] 1 KB 415, CA; *Welch v Royal Exchange Assurance* [1939] 1 KB 294, CA, 312 (MacKinnon LJ), 314 (Finlay LJ, concurring) (provision that the policy conditions 'so far as the nature of them respectively will permit, shall be deemed to be conditions precedent to the right of the insured to recover hereunder' permitted a clause requiring insured to provide proofs and information to insurers to operate as a condition precedent); *George Hunt Cranes Ltd v Scottish Boiler and General Insurance Co Ltd* [2001] EWCA Civ 1964, [2002] Lloyd's Rep IR 178, para 11 (Potter LJ).
11 *Stoneham v Ocean Railway and General Accident Insurance Co* (1887) 19 QBD 237, CA, 240 (Mathew J), 241 (Cave J); *George Hunt Cranes Ltd v Scottish Boiler and General Insurance Co Ltd* [2001] EWCA Civ 1964, [2002] Lloyd's Rep IR 178, para 11 (Potter LJ).
12 *George Hunt Cranes Ltd v Scottish Boiler and General Insurance Co Ltd* [2001] EWCA Civ 1964, [2002] Lloyd's Rep IR 178, para 11 (Potter LJ).
13 *George Hunt Cranes Ltd v Scottish Boiler and General Insurance Co Ltd* [2001] EWCA Civ 1964, [2002] Lloyd's Rep IR 178, paras 11–12 (Potter LJ).
14 *Stoneham v Ocean Railway and General Accident Insurance Co* (1887) 19 QBD 237, CA, 239 (Mathew J); applied: *Virk v Gan Life Holdings plc* [2000] Lloyd's Rep IR 159, para 15, CA (Potter LJ).
15 *Eagle Star Insurance Co Ltd v Cresswell* [2004] EWCA Civ 602, [2004] 1 Lloyd's Rep IR 537, paras 20 (Longmore LJ), 41 and 53 (Rix LJ) (the wording was 'will not be liable to pay any claim'). In *Re an Arbitration between Williams and Thomas and The Lancashire and Yorkshire Accident Insurance Co* (1902) 19 TLR 82, Bigham J construed as a condition precedent a clause requiring 'immediate' notification which stipulated that 'Time shall be deemed to be of the essence of this condition'; and in *Involnert Management Inc v Aprilgrange Ltd* [2015] EWHC 2225 (Comm), [2015] 2 Lloyd's Rep 289, Leggatt J construed as a condition precedent policy wording which stated that 'No suit or action on this Policy for the recovery of any claim shall be sustainable in any court of law or equity unless the Assured shall have fully complied with all the requirements of this Policy', so that breach by the insured of an obligation to file with insurers a detailed sworn proof of loss within 90 days of date of loss barred the insured from bringing proceedings for recovery of its claim (see paras 228, 243 and 248).
16 *George Hunt Cranes Ltd v Scottish Boiler and General Insurance Co Ltd* [2001] EWCA Civ 1964, [2002] Lloyd's Rep IR 178, para 11 (Potter LJ).
17 *London Guarantie Co v Fearnley* (1880) 5 App Cas 911, HL.
18 See *Gan v Tai Ping (Nos 2 and 3)* [2001] EWCA Civ 1047, [2001] Lloyd's Rep IR 667, para 26 (Mance LJ) (claims co-operation clause).

19 *Royal & Sun Alliance Insurance plc v Dornoch* [2005] EWCA Civ 238, [2005] Lloyd's Rep IR 544, para 19 (Longmore LJ).
20 *Bond Air Services Ltd v Hill* [1955] 2 QB 417, 427–428 (Lord Goddard CJ); *Sofi v Prudential Assurance Co Ltd* [1993] 2 Lloyd's Rep 559, 564, CA (Lloyd LJ); *Royal & Sun Alliance Insurance plc v Dornoch* [2005] EWCA Civ 238, [2005] Lloyd's Rep IR 544, para 19 (Longmore LJ); applied: *Beazley Underwriting Ltd v Al Ahleia Insurance Co* [2013] EWHC, 677 (Comm), [2013] Lloyd's Rep IR 561, para 90 (Eder J). See further **PARA 5.1**. Potter LJ's remark in *Virk v Gan Life Holdings plc* [2000] Lloyd's Rep IR 159, CA (at para 12) that if a procedural condition is a condition precedent, the onus of proving breach is on the insured, does not represent the law.
21 *Diab v Regent Insurance Co Ltd* [2006] UKPC 29, [2007] 1 WLR 797, para 25 (Lord Scott). See further **PARAS 7.22** and **11.63**.
22 ICOBS 8.1.1R.
23 ICOBS 8.1.2R.
24 *Parker v National Farmers Union Mutual Insurance Society Ltd* [2012] EWHC 2156 (Comm), [2013] Lloyd's Rep IR 253, paras 193–201 (Teare J) (condition precedent requiring insured to provide documents requested by insurer).
25 See **PARA 8.2**.

Warranties

3.6 Where the court is construing a term and assigning it to one of the categories, it does so by attempting to ascertain what the parties intended the consequences of breach to be. If the court considers that the parties intended the consequence of any breach of the term, however trivial and whether or not it was causally connected with any loss covered by the policy, to be to discharge the innocent party from further performance, it will conclude that the term is a warranty. One way to achieve this result is to state expressly that this is to be the consequence of breach of the term. This is unusual, however, and use of the shorthand label 'warranty' as a means of achieving this result is more common. In determining whether a term is a warranty, the court will consider the contract as a whole in order to determine the intentions of the parties and will have regard to the draconian effect of a breach of warranty in that it discharges the insurer even if it is not causative of the loss.[1] If a term is important to the insurer, he can seek to make the term an express warranty, and where he has not done so, this is a consideration which the court will take into account in construing the policy.[2] However, the presence or absence of the word 'warranty' or 'warranted' is not conclusive.[3] In *HIH Casualty and General Insurance Ltd v New Hampshire Insurance Co*,[4] Rix LJ set out three tests for determining whether a term is a warranty:[5]

(1)   whether it is a term which goes to the root of the transaction;
(2)   whether it is descriptive of or bears materially on the risk of loss;
(3)   whether damages would be an unsatisfactory or inadequate remedy.

Where a term is descriptive of the risk, the fact that a misdescription is not material to the risk may mean that the term is not a warranty;[6] alternatively, the lack of materiality of the misdescription might be relevant not to whether the term is properly to be characterised as a warranty but to its scope.[7] A *de minimis* approach to compliance with a warranty would have the same effect.[8]

Policies of insurance covering commercial risks are sometimes composite in nature, covering a number of types of loss which might otherwise have been insured separately under individual policies. It is a matter of construction whether a warranty applies to the policy as a whole, or applies only to one or more sections of the policy. If the warranty applies to the policy as a whole, breach of warranty discharges the insurers in respect of their obligations under the entire policy. Breach of a warranty which applies only to one or more sections of the policy discharges the insurers in respect of those sections only.[9]

It is a matter of construction whether a warranty gives rise to a continuing obligation, or relates only to the state of affairs at the time the contract was entered into. A continuing warranty is a draconian term, and particularly clear language is required before a court will construe a clause as a continuing warranty.[10] Similarly, the court may construe a warranty as to maintenance obligations as applying only to protections which were in place at the time of inception of the insurance, and not to future protections which the insured may put in place after inception of the insurance, as that would be potentially open-ended and onerous and would require clear words to that effect.[11]

One reason why the word 'warranty' or 'warranted' is not determinative of whether a term is a warranty in the sense discussed in this paragraph is that the word is sometimes used in a different sense, to mean a stipulation in a policy which is descriptive of the subject matter or of the risk in the sense that the insurer is only on risk at times when the stipulation is fulfilled.[12] This type of warranty is sometimes called a delimiting warranty.[13] For example, in *Roberts v Anglo-Saxon Insurance Association Ltd*,[14] a clause in the schedule to a policy of motor vehicle insurance stated: 'Warranted used only for the following purposes: commercial travelling'. The clause, despite being described as a 'warranty', was held to be descriptive of the risk, so that its effect was simply that when the vehicle was not being used for the purposes of commercial travelling, it was not covered. Similarly, in *GE Frankona Reinsurance Ltd v CMM Trust No 1400, The Newfoundland Explorer*,[15] a clause in a policy of marine insurance in relation to a yacht stated: 'Warranted fully crewed at all times'. Gross J indicated that his inclination (a decision on the issue not being necessary) would be to hold that on the proper construction of the clause, the insurer would be off-risk in the event that a casualty occurred at a time of non-compliance with the warranty, as there was no good commercial reason why, if a breach of the warranty were remedied, the insurer should not be liable for a subsequent casualty.[16] In *Pratt v Aigaion Insurance Co SA, The Resolute*,[17] it was common ground that an endorsement which provided 'Warranted Owner and/or Owner's experienced Skipper on board and in charge at all times and one experienced crew member' was a delimiting warranty.[18]

In construing a warranty, whether delimiting or otherwise, the court will pay close attention to the context. In *Pratt v Aigaion Insurance Co SA, The Resolute*,[19] the warranty was construed by reference to its primary purpose, which Sir Anthony Clarke MR said was to protect the vessel from risks which a skipper and experienced crew member could be expected to guard against, which in his view meant to protect the vessel against navigational hazards; this was not the case when the crew left the vessel to go ashore, because in such circumstances, the parties could not have contemplated that a skipper might be required or that more than one crew member might be required, say to put out a fire.[20] In *Amlin Corporate Member Ltd v Oriental Assurance Corpn, The Princess of the Stars*,[21] Gloster LJ said that the relevant background knowledge against which a typhoon warranty fell to be interpreted included the prevalence of typhoons in the Philippines from the end of May to October, the grave danger typhoons posed to shipping, and the routine issuance of storm warnings, and guidelines issued from time to time on movements of vessels when there were warnings of storms and typhoons,[22] and rejected a construction of a typhoon warranty which involved an after-the-event assessment of whether it would have been reasonable for the vessel to have left port, holding instead that reinsurers were entitled to have the certainty of knowing that, on the happening of the stipulated event, namely the existence of a relevant typhoon or storm warning at the port of departure, a scheduled vessel was not going to leave port.[23]

The consequences of breach of a warranty depend on whether the contract was entered into before, or on or after, 12 August 2016.[24]

1 *Toomey v Banco Vitalicio de Espana SA de Seguros y Reasseguros* [2004] EWCA Civ 622, [2005] Lloyd's Rep IR 423, para 42 (Thomas LJ).
2 *Toomey v Banco Vitalicio de Espana SA de Seguros y Reasseguros* [2004] EWCA Civ 622, [2005] Lloyd's Rep IR 423, para 42 (Thomas LJ).
3 *HIH Casualty and General Insurance Ltd v New Hampshire Insurance Co* [2001] EWCA Civ 735, [2001] 2 Lloyd's Rep 161, para 101 (Rix LJ).
4 [2001] EWCA Civ 735, [2001] 2 Lloyd's Rep 161.
5 [2001] EWCA Civ 735, [2001] 2 Lloyd's Rep 161, para 101 (Rix LJ).
6 *Toomey v Banco Vitalicio de Espana SA de Seguros y Reasseguros* [2004] EWCA Civ 622, [2005] Lloyd's Rep IR 423, paras 44–46 (Thomas LJ).
7 This was the approach taken by the Court of Appeal in relation to the construction of a claims co-operation clause where there might be major or minor failures to comply, and which was nonetheless held to be a condition precedent: *Gan v Tai Ping (Nos 2 and 3)* [2001] EWCA Civ 1047, [2001] Lloyd's Rep IR 667, para 26 (Mance LJ).
8 See the following references to the concept of de minimis in the context of breach of warranty: *Overseas Commodities Ltd v Style* [1958] 1 Lloyd's Rep 546, 557 (McNair J); *Bennett v Axa Insurance plc* [2003] EWHC 86 (Comm), [2004] Lloyd's Rep IR 615, para 20 (Tomlinson J); *Sugar Hut Group Ltd v Great Lakes Reinsurance (UK) plc* [2010] EWHC 2636 (Comm), [2011] Lloyd's Rep IR 198, para 44 (Burton J).
9 *Printpak v AGF Insurance Ltd* [1999] Lloyd's Rep IR 542, CA.
10 *Hussain v Brown* [1996] 1 Lloyd's Rep 627, CA; applied: *Printpak v AGF Insurance Ltd* [1999] Lloyd's Rep IR 542, 545–546, CA (Hirst LJ). See also the discussion of *Hussain v Brown*, **PARA 11.15**.
11 *A C Ward & Son Ltd v Catlin (Five) Ltd (No 2)* [2009] EWHC 3122 (Comm), para 168 (Flaux J).
12 *Bank of Nova Scotia v Hellenic Mutual War Risks Association (Bermuda) Ltd, The Good Luck* [1992] 1 AC 233, 261–262, HL (Lord Goff); *GE Frankona Reinsurance Ltd v CMM Trust No 1400, The Newfoundland Explorer* [2006] EWHC (Admiralty) 429, [2006] Lloyd's Rep IR 704, para 23 (Gross J).
13 See *Pratt v Aigaion Insurance Co SA, The Resolute* [2008] EWCA Civ 1314, [2009] 1 Lloyd's Rep 225, para 13 (Sir Anthony Clarke MR).
14 (1927) 27 Ll L Rep 313, CA.
15 [2006] EWHC (Admiralty) 429, [2006] Lloyd's Rep IR 704; approved: *Pratt v Aigaion Insurance Co SA, The Resolute* [2008] EWCA Civ 1314, [2009] 1 Lloyd's Rep 225.
16 *GE Frankona Reinsurance Ltd v CMM Trust No 1400, The Newfoundland Explorer* [2006] EWHC (Admiralty) 429, [2006] Lloyd's Rep IR 704, para 23 (Gross J).
17 [2008] EWCA Civ 1314, [2009] 1 Lloyd's Rep 225.
18 See para 13 (Sir Anthony Clarke MR).
19 [2008] EWCA Civ 1314, [2009] 1 Lloyd's Rep 225.
20 At paras 20 and 23 to 27.
21 [2014] EWCA Civ 1135, [2014] 2 Lloyd's Rep 561.
22 At para 43.
23 At para 54. See also *Sea Glory Maritime Co v Al Sagr National Insurance Co, The MV Nancy* [2013] EWHC 2116 (Comm), [2014] 1 Lloyd's Rep 14, in which (at para 219) Blair J construed a warranty which provided 'Vessels ISM Compliant' as requiring documentary compliance with the International Safety Management (ISM) Code, on the basis that, if the warranty related to compliance with the Code as a matter of fact, even if limited to major non-conformities, that would be difficult to apply, difficult

to evaluate, and would give rise to commercial uncertainty, and that that would not be what the parties intended.
24 Insurance Act 2015, ss 10, 11, 22(1) and (3), and 23(2) (the 2015 Act was passed on 12 February 2015). See PARAS **3.7** and **3.8**.

Warranties: consequences of breach: pre-Insurance Act 2015

3.7   This paragraph sets out the law as it applies to contracts of insurance entered into before 12 August 2016, and variations to such contracts.[1]

The consequences of breach of a warranty are set out in s 33 of the Marine Insurance Act 1906.[2] The section provides that a warranty, whether material to the risk or not, must be exactly complied with, and that if it is not so complied with, then, subject to any express provision in the policy, the insurer is discharged from liability as from the date of the breach of warranty, but without prejudice to any liability incurred by him before that date. It is immaterial whether the breach of warranty has caused any loss in respect of which the policy would otherwise respond. Strictly, breach of warranty does not call for any action by insurers.[3] A breach of warranty produces an automatic discharge of a contract of insurance from the moment of breach, unless the insurer subsequently affirms the contract.[4] In *Bank of Nova Scotia v Hellenic Mutual War Risks Association (Bermuda) Ltd, The Good Luck*,[5] Lord Goff analysed fulfilment of a warranty as a condition precedent to the liability of the insurer, on the basis that the insurer only accepted the risk provided that the warranty was fulfilled.[6] The remedy for breach of warranty therefore differs in important respects from the remedy for non-disclosure or misrepresentation. A breach of warranty gives rise to an automatic discharge; non-disclosure or misrepresentation has no effect, unless the insurer elects to avoid the contract, in which case the contract is not discharged for the future, but is rescinded *ab initio* (which means that it is unravelled with retrospective effect, as though the contract had not been entered into).[7] Breach of warranty does not have the effect of bringing the contract to an end, as there may be obligations of the insured which survive the discharge of the insurer from liability, such as a continuing liability to pay a premium.[8] Where a basis of the contract clause makes the correctness or completeness of the insured's disclosure into a warranty, a breach of that warranty has the effect that the insurance cover never attaches under the contract.[9] The Consumer Insurance (Disclosure and Representations) Act 2012 provides that representations made by a consumer in connection with a proposed consumer insurance contract, or in connection with a proposed variation to a consumer insurance contract, are not capable of being converted into a warranty by means of any provision of the consumer insurance contract (or of the terms of the variation), or of any other contract (and whether by declaring the representation to form the basis of the contract or otherwise).[10]

The effect of a breach of warranty may be modified by ICOBS.[11]

1 Insurance Act 2015, ss 10, 11, 22(1) and (3), and 23(2) (the Insurance Act 2015 was passed on 12 February 2015). This is different from the position in relation to the duty of fair presentation, which applies to contracts of insurance entered into before 12 August 2016, and variations agreed after 12 August 2016 to contracts entered into at any time: see PARA **11.35**.
2 Section 33 is a codification of the existing common law principles in the field of marine insurance, which are applicable in relation to both marine and non-marine insurance: *Printpak v AGF Insurance Ltd* [1999] Lloyd's Rep IR 542, 545, CA (Hirst LJ). Section 33 is a codification of the existing common

law principles in the field of marine insurance, which are applicable in relation to both marine and non-marine insurance: *Printpak v AGF Insurance Ltd* [1999] Lloyd's Rep IR 542, 545, CA (Hirst LJ). Warranties are called 'conditions' in ordinary contract law: *Provincial Insurance Co Ltd v Morgan* [1933] AC 240, 253–254, HL (Lord Wright); *W & J Lane v Spratt* [1970] 2 QB 480, 486–487 (Roskill J); *K/S Merc-Scandia XXXXII v Certain Lloyd's Underwriters, The Mercandian Continent* [2001] EWCA Civ 1275, [2001] 2 Lloyd's Rep 563, para 13, CA (Longmore LJ). Warranties were the product of the Victorian 'last in time' view of causation (see **PARA 4.2**): if the only relevant cause is the last cause in time, then a prior breach of a contractual condition regarding fitness of the goods and the carrying vessel could have been regarded as irrelevant; hence, the development of the concept of a warranty which, if broken, automatically discharged from liability for loss or damage, irrespective of how such loss or damage was in law to be regarded as caused: *Global Process Systems Inc v Syarikat Takaful Malaysia Berhad, The Cendor Mopu* [2011] UKSC 5, [2011] 1 Lloyd's Rep 560, para 56 (Lord Mance).

3 *Brit Syndicates Ltd v Italaudit SpA* [2008] UKHL 18, [2008] Lloyd's Rep IR 601, para 24 (Lord Mance).
4 *Bank of Nova Scotia v Hellenic Mutual War Risks Association (Bermuda) Ltd, The Good Luck* [1992] 1 AC 233, 262–263, HL (Lord Goff), approving *State Trading Corpn of India Ltd v M Golodetz Ltd* [1989] 2 Lloyd's Rep 277, 287, CA (Kerr LJ); applied: *HIH Casualty and General Insurance Ltd v New Hampshire Insurance Co* [2001] EWCA Civ 735, [2001] 2 Lloyd's Rep 161, paras 122–124 (Rix LJ). Affirmation in these circumstances is also referred to as waiver of breach: see *Bank of Nova Scotia v Hellenic Mutual War Risks Association (Bermuda) Ltd, The Good Luck* [1992] 1 AC 233, 263–264, HL (Lord Goff); and see s 34(3) of the Marine Insurance Act 1906, which provides that a breach of warranty may be waived by the insurer.
5 [1992] 1 AC 233, HL.
6 At 262–263; applied: *HIH Casualty and General Insurance Ltd v Axa Corporate Solutions* [2002] EWCA Civ 1253, [2003] Lloyd's Rep IR 1, para 2 (Tuckey LJ). On this analysis, it would appear that a continuing warranty is a condition precedent to the continuation of the risk. In *HIH Casualty and General Insurance Ltd v New Hampshire Insurance Co* [2001] EWCA Civ 735, [2001] 2 Lloyd's Rep 161, Rix LJ said (at para 124) that a warranty is akin to a statement of the cover provided by the insurer, because the insurer only agrees to cover the risk provided that the warranty is performed.
7 *Bank of Nova Scotia v Hellenic Mutual War Risks Association (Bermuda) Ltd, The Good Luck* [1992] 1 AC 233, 263–264, HL (Lord Goff); *HIH Casualty and General Insurance Ltd v New Hampshire Insurance Co* [2001] EWCA Civ 735, [2001] 2 Lloyd's Rep 161, para 124 (Rix LJ). See **PARA 11.31**.
8 *Bank of Nova Scotia v Hellenic Mutual War Risks Association (Bermuda) Ltd, The Good Luck* [1992] 1 AC 233, 263, HL (Lord Goff).
9 *Brit Syndicates Ltd v Italaudit SpA* [2008] UKHL 18, [2008] Lloyd's Rep IR 601, para 24 (Lord Mance, referring to *Thomson v Weems* (1884) 9 App Cas 671, HL); see **PARA 11.16**.
10 Section 6.
11 See **PARAS 8.2** and **11.4**.

Warranties: consequence of breach: Insurance Act 2015

3.8 The consequences of breach of a warranty in a contract entered into on or after 12 August 2016 are as set out in this paragraph.[1] Any rule of law that breach of a warranty (express or implied) in a contract of insurance results in the discharge of the insurer's liability under the contract is abolished.[2] An insurer has no liability under a contract of insurance in respect of any loss occurring, or attributable to something happening,[3] after a warranty (express or implied) in the contract has been breached but before the breach has been remedied.[4] This does not affect the liability of the insurer in respect of losses occurring, or attributable to something happening,[5] before the breach of warranty, or, if the breach can be remedied, after it has been remedied;[6] and it does not apply if, because of a change in circumstances, the warranty ceases to be applicable to the circumstances of the contract, if compliance with the warranty is rendered unlawful by any subsequent law, or if the insurer waives the breach of warranty.[7] If the warranty in question requires that by an ascertainable time something is to be done (or not done), or a condition is to be fulfilled, or something is (or is not) to be the case, and that requirement is not complied with, a breach of warranty is to be taken as remedied if the risk to which the warranty relates later becomes essentially the same as that originally contemplated by the parties.[8] In any other case, the breach of warranty is to be taken as remedied if the insured ceases to be in breach of the warranty.[9]

In addition, the provisions of the Insurance Act 2015 in relation to terms 'not relevant to the actual loss' may apply in relation to a breach of warranty.[10]

Unless the contrary intention appears, where the provisions of the Insurance Act 2015 in relation to breach of warranty or terms 'not relevant to the actual loss'[11] refer to something done by or in relation to the insurer or the insured, those references include it being done by or in relation to that person's agent.[12]

There are restrictions on the parties' ability to contract out of these provisions, and these vary according to whether the contract is consumer or non-consumer insurance. A term of a consumer insurance contract,[13] or of any other contract, which would put the consumer in a worse position than the consumer would be in by virtue of the provisions of the Insurance Act 2015 in relation to breach of warranty and terms 'not relevant to the actual loss', so far as relating to consumer insurance contracts, is to that extent of no effect,[14] but this does not apply in relation to a contract for the settlement of a claim.[15]

A term of a non-consumer insurance contract,[16] or of any other contract, which would put the insured in a worse position than the insured would be in by virtue of the provisions of the Insurance Act 2015 in relation to breach of warranty and terms 'not relevant to the actual loss', so far as relating to consumer insurance contracts, is known as a 'disadvantageous term' and is of no effect unless the transparency requirements in the 2015 Act are complied with.[17] This means that the insurer must take sufficient steps to draw the disadvantageous term to the insured's attention before the contract is entered into or variation agreed (unless the insured or its agent had actual knowledge of the disadvantageous term at that stage),[18] and that the disadvantageous term must be clear and unambiguous as to its effect.[19] In determining whether these requirements have been met, the characteristics of insured persons of the kind in question, and the circumstances of the transaction, are to be taken into account.[20] These provisions do not apply in relation to a contract for the settlement of a claim.[21]

1 Insurance Act 2015, ss 10, 11, 22(1) and (3), and 23(2) (the 2015 Act was passed on 12 February 2015). The Explanatory Notes to the 2015 Act say (at para 91) that s 10 applies to all express and implied warranties, including the implied marine warranties in ss 39, 40 and 41 of the Marine Insurance Act 1906. Explanatory Notes do not form part of a statute, are not endorsed by Parliament and cannot be amended by it; in so far as they cast light on the objective setting or contextual scene of a statute and the mischief to which it is aimed, they are an admissible aid to construction: *Flora v Wakom (Heathrow) Ltd* [2006] EWCA Civ 1103, [2007] 1 WLR 482, paras 15–16 (Brooke LJ).
2 Insurance Act 2015, s 10(1).
3 The term 'attributable to' is not defined in the 2015 Act, and its use is likely to give rise to argument about the strength of the causal link required between the breach of warranty and the loss for these purposes.
4 Insurance Act 2015, s 10(2). Section 33 of the Marine Insurance Act 1906 is amended, and s 34 is repealed, to reflect the terms of s 10(2): see s 10(7).
5 The Explanatory Notes to the 2015 Act say (at para 89) that the 'attributable to something happening' wording in s 10(4) is intended to cater for the situation in which loss arises as a result of an event which

occurred during the period of suspension, but is not actually suffered until after the breach has been 'remedied'. For the status of Explanatory Notes, see note 1 above. See also note 3 above.

6 Insurance Act 2015, s 10(4).
7 Insurance Act 2015, s 10(3).
8 Insurance Act 2015, s 10(5)(a) and (6). The Explanatory Notes to the 2015 Act say (at para 90) that some warranties require something to be done by an ascertainable time and that, if a deadline is missed, the insured could never cease to be in breach because the critical time for compliance has passed, and that ss 10(5)(a) and 10(6) are intended to mean that this type of breach will be remedied if the warranty is ultimately complied with, albeit late. For the status of Explanatory Notes, see note 1 above.
9 Insurance Act 2015, s 10(5)(b).
10 Insurance Act 2015, s 11(4). See **PARA 3.10**.
11 Part 3 of the Insurance Act 2015, ss 9–11.
12 Insurance Act 2015, s 22(4).
13 A 'consumer insurance contract' has the same meaning as in the Consumer Insurance (Disclosure and Representations) Act 2012: Insurance Act 2015, s 1. 'Consumer insurance contract' in the 2012 Act means a contract of insurance between an individual who enters into the contract wholly or mainly for purposes unrelated to the individual's trade, business or profession, and a person who carries on the business of insurance and becomes a party to the contract of insurance by way of that business (whether or not in accordance with permission for the purposes of the Financial Services and Markets Act 2000): Consumer Insurance (Disclosure and Representations) Act 2012, s 1.
14 Insurance Act 2015, s 15(1). This also applies in relation to variations: s 15(2).
15 Insurance Act 2015, s 15(3).
16 A 'non-consumer insurance contract' means a contract of insurance that is not a consumer insurance contract: Insurance Act 2015, s 1. For the meaning of 'consumer insurance contract', see note 13 above.
17 Insurance Act 2015, ss 16(2) and 17(1). This applies to contracts and to variations: s 16(3).
18 Insurance Act 2015, ss 17(2) and (5).
19 Insurance Act 2015, s 17(3).
20 Insurance Act 2015, s 17(4).
21 Insurance Act 2015, s 16(4).

Innominate (or intermediate) terms

3.9 Breach of an innominate (or intermediate) term entitles the innocent party to treat the contract as repudiated if the consequences for him of the breach are sufficiently serious. Conflicting decisions of the Court of Appeal have suggested, and subsequently doubted, that there might, in contracts of insurance, be a variation on the traditional innominate term, breach of which may entitle the innocent party to reject an individual claim without the contract as a whole being repudiated. Until the first of these decisions, *Alfred McAlpine plc v BAI (Run off) Ltd*,[1] terms of insurance policies were generally held to be either conditions precedent (in the case of procedural conditions), warranties or ordinary terms (in the case of other terms of the policy), rather than innominate terms.

In *Alfred McAlpine plc v BAI (Run off) Ltd*,[2] the term under consideration was a notice provision. Having concluded that the notice provision was not a condition precedent, Waller LJ indicated[3] that he could see no reason why it should not be construed as an innominate term, so that the consequences of a breach may be so serious as to entitle the insurer to reject the claim albeit that the breach is not so serious as to amount to a repudiation of the whole contract.

Alfred McAlpine plc v BAI (Run off) Ltd[4] was applied by the Court of Appeal in *K/S Merc-Scandia XXXXII v Certain Lloyd's Underwriters, The Mercandian Continent*[5] and *Glencore International AG v Ryan, The Beursgracht*.[6]

The analysis adopted was then criticised by a majority of the Court of Appeal[7] in *Friends Provident Life & Pensions Ltd v Sirius International Insurance*.[8] In *Friends Provident v Sirius*, the majority of the Court of Appeal held that, as a matter of law, there was no such refinement to the category of innominate term in insurance contracts. Mance LJ said that the insurance policy under consideration was composite and that the premium was incapable of being severally allocated to any particular risk or claim, and concluded:[9]

> 'No authority was cited to us, apart from *BAI* and its successor cases, in which any court has suggested that a party to a contract may be relieved from a particular obligation under a composite contract such as the present, by reason of a serious breach with serious consequences relating to an ancillary obligation, absent some express or implied condition precedent or other provision to that effect. Either some conditional link can, as a matter of construction, be found between performance of the two obligations or it cannot. Where such a link cannot be found as a matter of contractual construction, I see no basis for a new doctrine of partial repudiatory breach to, in effect, introduce one.'

Following *Friends Provident Life & Pensions Ltd v Sirius International Insurance*,[10] it is doubtful whether, as a matter of law, there is any such variation on the innominate term as suggested in *BAI*. If such a variation does exist, the court will need to consider in each case whether the insured's breach of an innominate term and the consequences of the breach for insurers are sufficiently serious to justify the rejection of the claim.[11] This issue would be judged at the date of trial.[12]

1 [2000] 1 Lloyd's Rep 437, CA.
2 [2000] 1 Lloyd's Rep 437, CA.
3 At 444, para 32. This analysis was foreshadowed in a dictum (remark) of Hobhouse J in *Phoenix General Insurance Co of Greece SA v Halvanon Insurance Co Ltd* [1988] QB 216, 241.
4 [2000] 1 Lloyd's Rep 437, CA.
5 [2001] EWCA Civ 1275, [2001] 2 Lloyd's Rep 563, para 14; Carnwath J and Robert Walker LJ agreed.
6 [2001] EWCA Civ 2051, [2002] Lloyd's Rep IR 335.
7 Mance LJ and Sir William Aldous; the third member of the Court of Appeal was Waller LJ, who dissented on this issue.
8 [2005] EWCA Civ 601, [2005] Lloyd's Rep 517.
9 At 530, para 31.
10 [2005] EWCA Civ 601, [2005] Lloyd's Rep 517, paras 31–32 (Mance LJ).
11 *Friends Provident Life & Pensions Ltd v Sirius International Insurance* [2005] EWCA Civ 601, [2005] 2 Lloyd's Rep 517, para 31 (Mance LJ).
12 *K/S Merc-Scandia XXXXII v Certain Lloyd's Underwriters, The Mercandian Continent* [2001] EWCA Civ 1275, [2001] 2 Lloyd's Rep 563, para 16 (Longmore LJ).

'Terms not relevant to the actual loss': Insurance Act 2015

3.10 In relation to a contract entered into on or after 12 August 2016,[1] the Insurance Act 2015 makes provision for what it describes as 'terms not relevant to the actual loss'.[2] This is any term (express or implied) of a contract of insurance, other than a term defining the risk as a whole,[3] if compliance with it would tend to reduce the risk of one or more of the following: loss of a particular kind, loss at a particular location, and loss at a particular time.[4] If a loss occurs and a term with these characteristics has not been complied with, and if the insured shows[5] that the non-compliance with the term could not have increased the risk of loss which actually occurred in the circumstances in which it occurred, the insurer may not rely on the non-compliance to exclude, limit or discharge its liability under the contract for the loss.[6]

1 Insurance Act 2015, ss 11, 22(1) and (3), and 23(2) (the 2015 Act was passed on 12 February 2015).
2 See the heading to s 11 of the Insurance Act 2015.
3 The Explanatory Notes to the 2015 Act say (at para 94) that clauses which define the risk as a whole are expected to include, for example, a requirement that a property or vehicle is not to be used commercially. Explanatory Notes do not form part of a statute, are not endorsed by Parliament and cannot be amended by it; in so far as they cast light on the objective setting or contextual scene of a statute and the mischief to which it is aimed, they are an admissible aid to construction: *Flora v Wakom (Heathrow) Ltd* [2006] EWCA Civ 1103, [2007] 1 WLR 482, paras 15–16 (Brooke LJ).
4 Insurance Act 2015, s 11(1). In relation to a breach of a warranty (see **PARA 3.8**), this section may apply in addition to s 10: s 11(4). The Explanatory Notes to the 2015 Act say (at para 93) that the wording 'would tend to reduce the risk' of loss of a particular kind, or loss at a particular location or time is intended to enable an objective assessment of the 'purpose' of the provision, by considering what sorts of loss might be less likely to occur as a consequence of the term being complied with. For the status of Explanatory Notes, see note 3. If this was the intention, it would have been preferable to include in s 11(1) an express reference to the aim or purpose of the term. The wording adopted, 'would tend to reduce', seems more apt to denote the likely effect of compliance with the term, rather than (necessarily) the aim or purpose of the term, although the two may of course overlap.
5 This is the wording of s 11(3), which thereby expressly puts the burden of proof on this issue on the insured.
6 Insurance Act 2015, s 11(2) and (3). The Explanatory Notes to the 2015 Act say (at para 92) that in the event of non-compliance with a term to which s 11 applies, it is intended that the insurer should not be able to rely on that non-compliance to escape liability unless the non-compliance could potentially have had some bearing on the risk of the loss which actually occurred; and (at para 95) that ss 11(2) and 11(3) mean that the insurer cannot rely on that non-compliance to avoid or limit its liability for the loss, if the insured shows that the non-compliance could not have increased the risk of the loss which actually occurred in the circumstances in which it actually occurred. An example is given: where a property has been damaged by flooding, it is expected that an insured could show that a failure to use the required type of lock on a window could not have increased the risk of that loss, and in this case the insurer should pay out on the flood claim. The Explanatory Notes also say (at para 96) that a direct causal link between the breach and the ultimate loss is not required, ie the relevant test is not whether the non-compliance actually caused or contributed to the loss which has been suffered. For the status of Explanatory Notes, see note 3. The wording of s 11 is complicated and it seems inevitable that significant disputes will arise both as to its meaning and as to its application on the facts of individual cases.

CONSTRUCTION

3.11 The principles applicable to the construction of insurance contracts are considered in this section. Reference should also be made to the principles applicable to the construction of questions and answers contained in proposal forms, which are sometimes, but not always, contractual documents, depending on the terms of the contract, and which are considered separately in **CHAPTER 11**.

The contractual documents

3.12 Before construing a contract of insurance, the contractual documents must be identified. Prospectuses or other promotional materials by means of which the insured is induced to enter into contracts of insurance do not usually form part of the contract unless expressly incorporated by reference,[1] although there may be a finding of incorporation in an individual case.[2] Documents which are not incorporated may not be referred to in construing the contract, but may form the basis of a claim for rectification.[3] The proposal form forms part of the contract of insurance if it is incorporated by virtue of a clause, whether in the proposal form or in the policy, making it the basis of the contract (and therefore known as a 'basis clause').[4] In the absence of such a clause, the proposal form is not a contractual document, and its terms may not be considered in construing the policy.[5] Although a Lloyd's slip is a contractual document, it is generally superseded by the policy of insurance when the policy is issued.[6] Although probably not strictly inadmissible, a slip which has been superseded by a policy will be of no assistance to the court in construing the policy, as any differences from the slip are likely to be deliberate, and if the wording is identical, the slip adds nothing to the construction of the policy.[7] This is on the basis that the policy has been agreed by the parties,[8] and where this is not the case, reference may be made to the slip.[9] In *Standard Life Assurance Ltd v Oak Dedicated Ltd*,[10] the slip referred to wording 'as expiring' or to be agreed, and Tomlinson J referred to the slip as an aid to construction of the policy wording. In so doing, the judge said that, at the very least, reference to the slip was of some assistance as it demonstrated that the slip was thought to be consistent or capable of being read together with the expiring wording. The judge said that the critical words under consideration in that case ('and/or claimant') appeared in a position of prominence in the slip but were relegated to the schedule in the policy, and that it was counter-intuitive to regard words which appeared in the excess provision on the face of the slip as not being part of the substantive words descriptive of underwriters' obligations.[11]

Although the general position is that the policy wording supersedes the slip, this is not always the case, and if the court concludes that the parties did not intend the slip to be superseded, it will construe the slip and the policy together.[12]

1 *British Equitable Assurance Co Ltd v Baily* [1906] AC 35, 41, HL (Lord Lindley).
2 See *Sun Life Assurance Co of Canada v Jervis* [1943] 2 All ER 425, CA, in which the Court of Appeal held that an illustration formed part of the contract of insurance despite not being expressly incorporated by reference.
3 See **PARA 3.31**.
4 See **PARA 11.16**.
5 *Griffiths v Fleming* [1909] 1 KB 805, 817, CA (Farwell LJ).
6 *HIH Casualty and General Insurance Ltd v New Hampshire Insurance Co* [2001] EWCA Civ 735, [2001] 2 Lloyd's Rep 161, para 93 (Rix LJ).
7 *HIH Casualty and General Insurance Ltd v New Hampshire Insurance Co* [2001] EWCA Civ 735, [2001] 2 Lloyd's Rep 161, para 83 (Rix LJ). The earlier authorities suggested that the slip was inadmissible: see *Wimpey v Poole* [1984] 2 Lloyd's Rep 499, 513 (Webster J); *Youell v Bland Welch & Co Ltd* [1992] 2 Lloyd's Rep 127, CA, 133–134 (Staughton LJ), 141 (Beldam LJ).
8 See *Rust v Abbey Life Assurance Co Ltd* [1979] 2 Lloyd's Rep 334, 339, CA (Brandon LJ); *Yona International Ltd v La Réunion Française SA* [1996] 2 Lloyd's Rep 84, 110 (Moore-Bick J).
9 *New Hampshire Insurance Co v MGN Ltd* [1997] LRLR 24, 53–54, CA (Staughton LJ).
10 [2008] EWHC 222 (Comm), [2008] Lloyd's Rep IR 552.
11 At para 91.
12 *HIH Casualty and General Insurance Ltd v New Hampshire Insurance Co* [2001] EWCA Civ 735, [2001] 2 Lloyd's Rep 161, para 84 (Rix LJ).

Consensual nature of insurance contracts

3.13 A contract of insurance is an agreement between the parties, and in construing a contract of insurance, the court is ascertaining the parties' intentions. In principle, therefore, and subject to restrictions imposed by statute,[1] the parties are free to make any agreement they wish, provided that the outcome does not offend against either public policy or the fundamental nature of insurance, which is protection against chance events and not losses caused deliberately by the insured,[2] and provided that the language they use is sufficiently clear. In practice, this freedom is further restricted by the application of the principles of construction set out below, including the fundamental principle that the court is not ascertaining the parties' real or subjective intentions, but the intentions of reasonable persons in the position of the parties with the knowledge reasonably available to the parties at the time the contract of insurance was entered into.[3] Conversely, when construing a contract of insurance, the court is unlikely to be impressed by the argument that if the parties had intended a particular result, they could have used different, clearer words, because '[i]t is almost always possible to say after the event that the point could have been put beyond doubt, either way, by express words'.[4]

1 Eg the Consumer Insurance (Disclosure and Representations) Act 2012, the Insurance Act 2015 and the Consumer Rights Act 2015.
2 See **PARA 5.2**.
3 See **PARAS 3.15–3.16**.
4 *Dodson v Peter H Dodson Insurance Services* [2001] 1 Lloyd's Rep 520, CA, para 40 (Mance LJ); applied: *GE Frankona Reinsurance Ltd v CMM Trust No 1400, The Newfoundland Explorer* [2006] EWHC (Admiralty) 429, [2006] Lloyd's Rep IR 704, para 24(iii) (Gross J).

Natural or ordinary meaning

3.14 The ordinary rules of construction apply to contracts of insurance.[1] Insurance policy wordings are to be construed according to their natural or ordinary meaning[2] at the date the contract was entered into,[3] subject to any definitions contained in the policy.[4] In construing a policy of insurance, the whole document must be considered,[5] and every provision must be given effect to so far as possible; where two clauses overlap, the question is whether they can be read together without inconsistency, ie whether it can be said that there is multiplicity of language, rather than inconsistency.[6] The ordinary and natural meaning of words is not to be determined by considering the words in isolation, however clear the meaning appears, but by considering the words in context in the policy as a whole.[7] The context includes the nature of the insurance.[8]

There is no official source of the ordinary or natural meaning of a word or phrase. Although the courts will take notice of dictionary definitions, the words must also be placed in context;[9] and the ordinary or natural meaning is often a matter of first impression for the judge hearing the case.[10] In determining the natural or ordinary meaning of a clause in its context, it is unnecessary for the court to have recourse to any considerations of burden of proof.[11]

If the court is satisfied that the policy was drawn with sufficient precision, grammatical contrasts may be a guide to construction[12] However, the draftsmen of insurance documents are not equity draftsmen, and the courts will be slow to adopt any approach which assumes precision in drafting.[13] The courts recognise that surplusage, or redundant wording, is common in commercial policies of insurance,[14] and are therefore prepared to disregard such wording if it seems appropriate to do so in the course of the exercise of construction. However, a construction which avoids surplusage or treating words as redundant or irrelevant is likely to be preferred.[15] The court is reluctant to introduce words not used in the actual contractual provisions as part of the construction exercise, unless it is satisfied that the words selected by the parties are commercially nonsensical and it is clear that the parties intended some other purpose.[16]

1 *Smith v Accident Insurance Co* (1870) LR 5 Ex Ch 302, 307; *Jason v British Traders' Insurance Co Ltd* [1969] 1 Lloyd's Rep 281, 290 (Fisher J).
2 *Stanley v Western Insurance Co* (1868) LR 3 Exch 71 (a fire policy in respect of business premises excluded liability for loss or damage by explosion, except for loss or damage arising from explosion by gas; 'gas' was held to mean ordinary gas for heating or lighting, not a gas which was the by-product of a process of manufacture used by the insured); *Australian Agricultural Co v Saunders* (1875) LR 10 CP 668, 674 (Bramwell B); *Starfire Diamond Rings Ltd v Angel* [1962] 2 Lloyd's Rep 217, 219, CA (Lord Denning MR and Upjohn LJ, deprecating any attempt to define ordinary words in everyday use, such as 'left unattended'); *C F Turner v Manx Line Ltd* [1990] 1 Lloyd's Rep 137, 142, CA (Neill LJ).
3 *Bankers Insurance Co Ltd v South* [2003] EWHC 380 (QB), [2004] Lloyd's Rep IR 1.
4 *Jason v British Traders' Insurance Co Ltd* [1969] 1 Lloyd's Rep 281, 290 (Fisher J).
5 *Cornish v Accident Insurance Co* (1889) 23 QBD 453, 456, CA (Lindley LJ); *Hamlyn v Crown Accidental Insurance Co Ltd* [1893] 1 QB 750, 753–754, CA (Lopes LJ); *C F Turner v Manx Line Ltd* [1990] 1 Lloyd's Rep 137, 142, CA (Neill LJ); *Rodan International Ltd v Commercial Union Assurance Co plc* [1999] Lloyd's Rep IR 495, 497, CA (Hobhouse LJ); *Charter Reinsurance Co Ltd v Fagan* [1997] AC 313, 384, HL (Lord Mustill); *EL Trigger Litigation* [2012] UKSC 14, para 19 (Lord Mance); *Milton Furniture Ltd v Brit Insurance Ltd* [2015] EWCA Civ 671, [2016] Lloyd's Rep IR 192, para 32 (Gloster LJ).
6 *Milton Furniture Ltd v Brit Insurance Ltd* [2015] EWCA Civ 671, [2016] Lloyd's Rep IR 192, para 32 (Gloster LJ).
7 *Charter Reinsurance Co Ltd v Fagan* [1997] AC 313, 384, HL (Lord Mustill); *EL Trigger Litigation* [2012] UKSC 14, para 19 (Lord Mance). This is the first principle of construction: *Total Gas Marketing Ltd v Arco British Ltd* [1998] 2 Lloyd's Rep 209, 218, HL (Lord Steyn).
8 See, eg, *Wayne Tank and Pump Co Ltd v Employers Liability Assurance Corpn Ltd* [1974] QB 57, 75, CA (Roskill LJ) (public liability policy); *Horbury Building Systems Ltd v Hampden Insurance NV* [2004] EWCA Civ 418, [2007] Lloyd's Rep IR 237, para 25 (Keene LJ) (product liability policy); *Tesco Stores Ltd v Constable* [2008] EWCA Civ 362, [2008] Lloyd's Rep IR 636, para 14 (Tuckey LJ) (public liability policy); *Outokumpu Stainless Ltd v Axa Global Risks (UK) Ltd* [2007] EWHC 2555 (Comm), [2008] Lloyd's Rep IR 147, para 26 (Tomlinson J) (property cover subject to radioactive contamination extension); *Mopani Copper Mines plc v Millenium Underwriting Ltd* [2008] EWHC 1331 (Comm), [2009] Lloyd's Rep IR 158, paras 58–60 (Christopher Clarke J) (contractors' or engineers' all risks cover/operational or property insurance); *Employers' Liability Insurance Trigger Litigation* [2012] UKSC 14, [2012] Lloyd's Rep IR 371, para 48 (Lord Mance) (employers' liability and public liability policies); *Coven SpA v Hong Kong Chinese Insurance Co* [1999] Lloyd's Rep IR 565, 568–569, CA (Clarke LJ) (marine cargo policy); *Teal Assurance Co Ltd v W R Berkley Insurance (Europe) Ltd* [2013] UKSC 57, [2014] Lloyd's Rep IR 56, paras 14, 19 and 21 (Lord Mance) (liability insurance and reinsurance).
9 *Investors Compensation Scheme Ltd v West Bromwich Building Society* [1998] 1 WLR 896, 913, HL (Lord Hoffmann).
10 See *Young v Sun Alliance and London Insurance Ltd* [1977] 1 WLR 104, CA (meaning of 'flood' in householder's policy).
11 *Absalom v TCRU Ltd* [2005] EWCA Civ 1586, [2006] 2 Lloyd's Rep 129, para 10 (Longmore LJ).
12 See *L Schuler AG v Wickman Machine Tool Sales Ltd* [1974] AC 235, 249, HL (Lord Reid) (contract ill thought-out, and appropriate to take this into account in approaching construction); *Touche Ross & Co v Baker* [1992] 2 Lloyd's Rep 207, 213, HL (Lord Mustill) (insurance documents in London market rarely drawn with precision of language needed for grammatical contrasts to be reliable guide to intention).
13 *Arbuthnott v Fagan* [1996] LRLR 135, 142, CA (Hoffmann LJ); *New Hampshire Insurance Co v MGN Ltd* [1997] LRLR 24, 56, CA (Staughton LJ).
14 *Arbuthnott v Fagan* [1996] LRLR 135, 142, CA (Hoffmann LJ) (construction of Lloyd's standard agency agreement); *Kumar v AGF Insurance Ltd* [1999] 1 WLR 1747, 1756 (Thomas J): approved:

Genesis Housing Association Ltd v Liberty Syndicate Management Ltd [2013] EWCA Civ 1173, [2014] Lloyd's Rep IR 318, para 77 (Jackson LJ).

15 See eg *Pratt v Aigaion Insurance Co SA, The Resolute* [2008] EWCA Civ 1314, [2009] 1 Lloyd's Rep 225, para 24 (Sir Anthony Clarke MR); *A C Ward & Son Ltd v Catlin (Five) Ltd (No 2)* [2009] EWHC 3122 (Comm), paras 179–180 (Flaux J).

16 *Amlin Corporate Member Ltd v Oriental Assurance Corpn, The Princess of the Stars* [2014] EWCA Civ 1135, [2014] 2 Lloyd's Rep 561, paras 45 and 49 (Gloster LJ); Gloster LJ also said (at para 48) that, had the construction put forward by the claimant been the parties' intention, it would have been the easiest thing for the clause in question (a typhoon warranty) to have spelled this out.

Reasonable or commercial construction

3.15   The courts assume, in construing a contract, that the parties' intentions were reasonable, so that the more unreasonable a construction appears, the less likely it will be that it was what the parties intended.[1] Where the meaning of wording is ambiguous,[2] the court will prefer a sensible, business-like construction over an absurd or unreasonable construction.[3] There is no room for this approach where, although the meaning appears ambiguous on its face, the ambiguity is resolved by evidence as to the surrounding circumstances or factual matrix.[4] A reasonable construction may expand or modify the literal meaning of the policy wording.[5] If the meaning of the wording is clear and unambiguous, it will be applied, even if the outcome appears unreasonable[6] or hard on the insured.[7] There has been a shift from literal methods of interpretation of commercial contracts to a more commercial approach.[8] This is because a commercial construction is more likely to give effect to the intentions of the parties, and words are therefore interpreted in the way in which a reasonable commercial person would construe them.[9] Therefore 'if detailed semantic and syntactical analysis of a word in a commercial contract is going to lead to a conclusion that flouts business common sense, it must be made to yield to business common sense'.[10] In *Rainy Sky SA v Kookmin Bank*,[11] the Supreme Court said that where a term of a contract is open to more than one interpretation, it is generally appropriate to adopt the interpretation which is most consistent with business common sense;[12] that it is not necessary to conclude that a particular construction would produce an absurd or irrational result before having regard to the commercial purpose of the agreement;[13] and that if a clause is capable of two meanings, it is quite possible that neither meaning will flout common sense, but that, in such a case, it is much more appropriate to adopt the more, rather than the less, commercial construction.[14] However, this approach must be kept within limits as it is not the role of the court to substitute for the bargain made by the parties one which the court believes could have been better made[15] and there are dangers in judges deciding what the parties must have meant if they have not said what they meant for themselves.[16] This is particularly dangerous when the parties have selected from the shelf or the precedent book a clause which turns out to be unsuitable for its purpose, and the danger is then intensified if it is only one part of such a clause which is to be construed in accordance with 'business common sense'.[17] It clearly requires a strong case to persuade the court that something must have gone wrong with the language; and it is not unusual that an interpretation which does not strike one person as sufficiently irrational to justify a conclusion that there has been a linguistic mistake will seem commercially absurd to another.[18] All that is required is that it should be clear that something has gone wrong with the language and that it should be clear what a reasonable person would have understood the parties to have meant.[19] Commercial common sense is not to be invoked retrospectively, and is only relevant to the extent of how matters would or could have been perceived by the parties, or by reasonable persons in the position of the parties, as at the date that the contract was made.[20] It is right to have some regard to the broad nature of the policy, but the availability and cost of alternative types of cover are not relevant factors unless it can be shown that they were present to the minds of both parties at the time when the policy was renewed.[21]

So far as possible, consistently with the need to impose a reasonable construction on the wording, the same word will be given the same meaning wherever it appears in the policy.[22]

1 *L Schuler AG v Wickman Machine Tool Sales Ltd* [1974] AC 235, 251, HL (Lord Reid), 272 (Lord Kilbrandon).
2 Ambiguity means genuinely open to two possible constructions, and the fact that judges differ as to the correct construction of wording does not mean that it is necessarily ambiguous: *R v Personal Investment Authority Ombudsman Bureau, ex p Royal & Sun Alliance Life & Pensions Ltd* [2002] Lloyd's Rep IR 41, 43 (Langley J); *McGeown v Direct Travel Insurance* [2003] EWCA Civ 1606, [2004] Lloyd's Rep IR 599, para 13 (Auld LJ); *Re OT Computers Ltd (in administration)* [2004] EWCA Civ 653, [2004] Ch 317, para 39 (Longmore LJ) (statutory interpretation).
3 *Lion Mutual Marine Insurance Association Ltd v Tucker* (1883) 12 QBD 176, 190, CA (Brett MR); *London Guarantie Co v Fearnley* (1880) 5 App Cas 911, 916, HL (Lord Blackburn); *Hydarnes Steamship Co v Indemnity Mutual Marine Assurance Co* [1895] 1 QB 500, 504, CA (Lord Esher MR); *South British Fire and Marine Insurance Co of New Zealand v Da Costa* [1906] 1 KB 456, 461 (Bigham J); *National Protector Fire Insurance Co Ltd v Nivert* [1913] AC 507, 513, PC; *Prenn v Simmonds* [1971] 1 WLR 1381, 1389, HL (Lord Wilberforce); *L Schuler AG v Wickman Machine Tool Sales Ltd* [1974] AC 235, 255–256, HL (Lord Morris); *Schiffshypothekenbank Zu Luebeck AG v Compton, The Alexion Hope* [1988] 1 Lloyd's Rep 311, 313, CA (Lloyd LJ); *C F Turner v Manx Line Ltd* [1990] 1 Lloyd's Rep 137, CA, 142 (Neill LJ), 148–149 (Stuart-Smith LJ); *Yorkshire Water Services Ltd v Sun Alliance & London Insurance plc* [1997] 2 Lloyd's Rep 21, 28, CA (Stuart-Smith LJ); *Milton Furniture Ltd v Brit Insurance Ltd* [2015] EWCA Civ 671, [2016] Lloyd's Rep IR 192, paras 35–41 (Gloster LJ).
4 *Birrell v Dryer* (1884) 9 App Cas 345, 354–355, HL (Lord Watson); *McGeown v Direct Travel Insurance* [2003] EWCA Civ 1606, [2004] Lloyd's Rep IR 599, para 13 (Auld LJ).
5 *North British and Mercantile Insurance Co v London, Liverpool, and Globe Insurance Co* (1877) 5 Ch D 569, 576–577, Sir George Jessel MR) (situation which had arisen could not have been foreseen by framers of policy, and duty of court to adopt reasonable construction rather than that which, if not an absurd, would be a very unlikely construction); *Robinson Gold Mining Co v Alliance Insurance Co* [1902] 2 KB 489, CA (marine insurance policy form used for land transit insurance); *Home Insurance Co of New York v Victoria-Montreal Fire Insurance Co* [1907] AC 59, 64–65, PC (Lord MacNaghten) (reinsurance slip pasted onto printed form appropriate to insurance; all conditions except one held to be inapplicable to reinsurance; remaining condition held to be unreasonable in context of insurance, and therefore disregarded); *Re Coleman's Depositories Ltd* [1907] 2 KB 798, 807, CA (Fletcher Moulton LJ) ('immediate' notice of accident construed as meaning with all reasonable speed considering the circumstances of the case); *E Hulton & Co v Mountain* (1921) 8 Ll L Rep 249, 250, CA (Bankes LJ) (clause stating that no costs to be incurred without consent of underwriters construed to mean that consent should be applied for not at every stage of the proceedings, but at every important stage); *American Airlines Inc v Hope* [1974] 2 Lloyd's Rep 301, 305–306, HL (Lord Diplock) (obvious typographical error corrected by substitution of 'accidentally provoked' for 'accidentally unprovoked').
6 *L Schuler AG v Wickman Machine Tool Sales Ltd* [1974] AC 235, 251, HL, Lord Reid; *Rainy Sky SA v Kookmin Bank* [2011] UKSC 50, [2011] 1 WLR 2900, paras 23–24 (Lord Clarke); *Amlin Corporate Member Ltd v Oriental Assurance Corpn, The Princess of the Stars* [2014] EWCA Civ 1135, [2014] 2 Lloyd's Rep 561, para 44 (Gloster LJ).
7 *Re United London and Scottish Insurance Co Ltd* [1915] 2 Ch 167, 170, CA (Cozens-Hardy MR) (at first instance, a construction favourable to the insured was put on the condition in question by Astbury J).
8 *Sirius International Insurance Co (Publ) v FAI General Insurance Ltd* [2004] UKHL 54, [2004] 1 WLR 3251, para 19 (Lord Steyn); see also para 25 (Lord Steyn): rejection of Court of Appeal's interpretation as 'uncommercial and literalistic'.

9 *Mannai Investment Co Ltd v Eagle Star Life Assurance Co Ltd* [1997] AC 749, 771, HL (Lord Steyn), applied: *Sirius International Insurance Co (Publ) v FAI General Insurance Ltd* [2004] UKHL 54, [2004] 1 WLR 3251, paras 18–19 (Lord Steyn) and 34 (Lord Walker). In *Cook v Financial Insurance Co Ltd* [1998] 1 WLR 1765, 1768, HL, Lord Lloyd said that since the insured, who had applied for permanent health insurance cover, had the right to return the certificate of insurance within 14 days if not entirely satisfied with the protection afforded by the cover, the certificate must be construed in the sense in which it would have been reasonably understood by him as the consumer. In *Sea Glory Maritime Co v Al Sagr National Insurance Co, The MV Nancy* [2013] EWHC 2116 (Comm), [2014] 1 Lloyd's Rep 14, Blair J construed a warranty which provided 'Vessels ISM Compliant' as requiring documentary compliance with the International Safety Management (ISM) Code, on the basis that, if the warranty related to compliance with the Code as a matter of fact, even if limited to major non-conformities, that would be difficult to apply, difficult to evaluate, and would give rise to commercial uncertainty, and that that would not be what the parties intended (para 219).

10 *Antaios Compania Naviera SA v Salen Rederierna AB* [1985] AC 191, 201, HL (Lord Diplock), applied: *Sirius International Insurance Co (Publ) v FAI General Insurance Ltd* [2004] UKHL 54, [2004] 1 WLR 3251, para 19 (Lord Steyn); *Absalom v TCRU Ltd* [2005] EWCA Civ 1586, [2006] 2 Lloyd's Rep 129, para 7 (Longmore LJ); *Rainy Sky SA v Kookmin Bank* [2011] UKSC 50, [2011] 1 WLR 2900, paras 23–24 (Lord Clarke).

11 [2011] UKSC 50, [2011] 1 WLR 2900.

12 At para 30 (Lord Clarke); applied: *Employers' Liability Insurance Trigger Litigation* [2012] UKSC 14, [2012] Lloyd's Rep IR 371, para 26 (Lord Mance).

13 At para 43 (Lord Clarke).

14 At para 43 (Lord Clarke). In *Teal Assurance Co Ltd v W R Berkley Insurance (Europe) Ltd* [2013] UKSC 57, [2014] Lloyd's Rep IR 56, Lord Mance said (at paras 29–31) that he would have had no doubt about agreeing with Longmore LJ's view of commerciality (see [2011] EWCA Civ 1570, [2012] Lloyd's Rep IR 315, para 16), as confirming and reinforcing the conclusion which they had both reached, but that in his view it was unnecessary to do so as analysis of the terms and scheme of the relevant insurance policies provided the answer without more.

15 *Charter Reinsurance Co Ltd v Fagan* [1997] AC 313, 388, HL (Lord Mustill); *Arnold v Britton* [2015] UKSC 36, [2015] AC 1619, paras 19–20 (Lord Neuberger).

16 *Royal & Sun Alliance Insurance plc v Dornoch* [2005] EWCA Civ 238, [2005] Lloyd's Rep IR 544, para 16 (Longmore LJ).

17 *Royal & Sun Alliance Insurance plc v Dornoch* [2005] EWCA Civ 238, [2005] Lloyd's Rep IR 544, para 16 (Longmore LJ).

18 *Chartbrook Ltd v Persimmon Homes Ltd* [2009] UKHL 38, [2009] 1 AC 1101, para 15 (Lord Hoffmann).

19 *Chartbrook Ltd v Persimmon Homes Ltd* [2009] UKHL 38, [2009] 1 AC 1101, para 25 (Lord Hoffmann).

20 *Arnold v Britton* [2015] UKSC 36, [2015] AC 1619, para 19 (Lord Neuberger).

21 *James Budgett Sugars Ltd v Norwich Union Insurance* [2003] 1 Lloyd's Rep IR 110, para 26 (Moore-Bick J) (product liability insurance).

22 *North British and Mercantile Insurance Co v London, Liverpool, and Globe Insurance Co* (1877) 5 Ch D 569, 577 (Sir George Jessel MR) (word given different meaning in different parts of instruments to avoid unreasonable construction); *South Staffordshire Tramways Co Ltd v Sickness and Accident Assurance Association Ltd* [1891] 1 QB 402, 407, CA (Bowen LJ).

Extrinsic evidence including the 'factual matrix'

3.16   Where the parties have recorded their agreement in a written document, no evidence may be adduced to show what the parties meant, subjectively, by the words used, or to add to or vary the terms recorded in writing.[1] This principle, with all its variations, is known as the 'parol evidence rule', 'parol' meaning oral. Although still technically good law, it has largely been overtaken by a series of exceptions which allow extrinsic evidence to be admitted, and by the principle that the contract is not construed in a vacuum, but in the context of the surrounding circumstances as they were known to both parties, or as each might have expected the other to know.[2] The only remaining elements of the parol evidence rule of any real consequence are that evidence may not be adduced of negotiations, of the parties' subjective intentions or of their subsequent conduct, although such evidence may be admitted on a claim for rectification.[3] It is not a requirement for admissibility of extrinsic evidence that there should be any ambiguity on the face of the contract.[4]

There are various purposes for which it is now accepted that evidence may be admitted in connection with the construction of written agreements:

(1)   evidence of the 'surrounding circumstances' or 'factual matrix' against which the parties entered into the agreement is admissible in order to understand the intention of the parties;

(2)   to show that the written agreement does not contain all of the terms agreed between the parties, and to prove those terms;[5]

(3)   to identify the subject matter of the agreement;[6]

(4)   to prove a collateral contract;[7]

(5)   to show that particular words in the written agreement were used in an agreed sense;[8]

(6)   to show a subsequent waiver of the terms of the written agreement, or a subsequent new agreement covering the same subject matter;[9] or

(7)   to explain the meaning of technical words or phrases,[10] or expressions with a recognised meaning within a particular trade or business, such as shorthand expressions.[11]

Whichever ground is relied on by the party seeking to adduce the evidence, the proper course is to admit it *de bene esse* (which means on a provisional basis, pending the court's decision as to admissibility). This is because, if the court decides after considering the evidence that none of the exceptions applies, it must put the evidence out of its mind when construing the wording.[12]

It has long been established that the contract must not be construed in a vacuum, but in the light of the relevant circumstances, from the standpoint of reasonable persons in the position of the parties,[13] and evidence of the surrounding circumstances, or 'factual matrix', may therefore be required if these matters do not appear sufficiently from the terms of the contract itself.[14] This is particularly so where a court is asked to construe a novel type of insurance.[15] When seeking to discern the intention of the parties, the court is entitled to assume some knowledge of the law on their part.[16] Where the insurance is placed by a broker on behalf of the insured, the broker (as the insured's agent)[17] will be expected to be aware of the general significance of particular cover and this knowledge therefore forms part of the factual matrix.[18] The factual matrix may also include facts of which the court is prepared to take judicial notice.[19]

Evidence of negotiations is not admissible as an aid to construction of a written agreement;[20] nor is evidence of the parties' subjective intentions[21] or subsequent conduct.[22] In principle, no evidence may be adduced as to the negotiations themselves or as to the wording of earlier drafts of the contract,[23] although such evidence is admissible in support of a claim for rectification.[24] The authorities are divided as to whether the court may have regard to wording deleted from standard forms of wording, although the preponderance of authority is probably against admissibility.[25] In some cases, words deleted from a printed form have been used as an aid to construction without any discussion as to admissibility.[26] Sometimes, an agreement in its final form makes express reference to amendments or additions. In *Punjab National Bank v de Boinville*,[27] the parties to a concluded agreement, which was only partly a printed form, subsequently agreed in express terms that some words in it were to be replaced by others. The Court of Appeal decided that all aspects of the subsequent agreement could be considered in construing the contract, including the deletions. Similarly, in *Balfour v Beaumont*,[28] the information section of a policy drew attention to the fact that the line slip for the previous year had been amended, and the Court of Appeal considered that to this extent at least it must be permissible to consider the line slip for the previous year. Prior concluded contracts are admissible as an aid to construction, although they are unlikely to be of much assistance as the later contract replaces the earlier one and it is likely to be impossible to say that the parties have not wished to alter the terms of their earlier bargain; and where the later contract is identical to the earlier, its construction should be undertaken primarily by reference to its overall terms.[29] Where the court is construing a subsequent amendment to a concluded contract, the correct approach is to construe the contract in the light of the background knowledge reasonably available at the time when the amendment was agreed, which may include the knowledge that the new clause is to take the place of an existing clause.[30]

In practice, it may be difficult to draw the line between negotiations and surrounding circumstances. For example, the commercial purpose of a transaction, objectively ascertained, may be a surrounding fact, and this presupposes knowledge (and therefore evidence, which may be documentary or oral) of the genesis of the transaction, the background, the context, and the market in which the parties were operating.[31] The court is entitled to hear evidence of market practice falling short of trade usage or custom in order to assist it in a full understanding of the factual background to the proper construction of a written contract.[32] If there is a disagreement on what a market practice is, then the judge must decide whether a particular market practice exists of not; if it does, then it is again up to the judge to decide if it is useful background evidence against which to construe the contract in question.[33] Nevertheless, attempts to adduce a large volume of material under the head of surrounding circumstances are likely to be subjected to careful scrutiny by the trial judge, and the courts will not allow the parties to adduce material which is not clearly relevant.[34] Before taking extrinsic evidence into account, it is important to consider precisely why it is said to assist in deciding the meaning of what was subsequently agreed and to consider whether its relevance is sufficiently cogent to the determination of the joint intention of the parties to have regard to it.[35] Where the words used have an unambiguous and sensible meaning as a matter of ordinary language, it appears that the court is entitled to refuse to admit any evidence of the surrounding circumstances.[36] In approaching the construction of a commercial document such as an insurance or reinsurance slip to which there may be several parties who become bound by its terms on separate occasions and following separate negotiations, there is an added reason for caution before seeking to deduce an objective intention which could result in ascribing a meaning to the words used other than the meaning they would normally bear.[37]

In the case of compulsory professional indemnity insurance, the policy must be construed against the relevant regulatory background, and in particular the desire to protect clients;[38] where however compulsory professional indemnity policy wording is the result of negotiations between a regulator and the insurance industry, an aggregation clause has to be approached neutrally without any assumptions in favour of the insurers or the insured;[39] and where the origin of a clause has a published history, this is part of the 'matrix' against which the clause has to be construed and is a legitimate aid to construction.[40] Where there has been a change in the law, the law at the time the policy terms were agreed may form part of the background against which the policy is to be construed.[41] In the case of compulsory insurance, the statute which is the source of the obligation to insure forms part of the surrounding circumstances against which a policy is to be construed, with the result that expressions used in the statute will be given the same meaning in the policy unless it clearly states otherwise,[42] and the policy wording should, if possible, be read as providing the relevant cover required by statute: this is a powerful tool in the interpretation of such insurances.[43] Where a single risk is split into two risks which are then brokered side by side, information presented to underwriters in relation to the single risk in the previous year may form part of the factual matrix in relation to each of the risks, and information provided to underwriters in relation to one of the two new risks may form part of the factual matrix in relation to the other.[44]

1 *A & J Inglis v John Buttery & Co* (1878) 3 App Cas 552, HL, 558, 569 (Lord Hatherley), 571–572 (Lord O'Hagan), 577 (Lord Blackburn); *Reliance Marine Insurance Co v Duder* [1913] 1 KB 265, CA, 273 (Kennedy LJ), 278 (Buckley LJ); *Marine Insurance Co Ltd v Grimmer* (1944) 77 Ll L Rep 224, 234 (Atkinson J); *Prenn v Simmonds* [1971] 1 WLR 1381, 1384–1385, HL (Lord Wilberforce); *Absalom v TCRU Ltd* [2005] EWCA Civ 1586, [2006] 2 Lloyd's Rep 129, para 7 (Longmore LJ). The ascertainment of the parties' intentions is a question of law: *L Schuler AG v Wickman Machine Tool Sales Ltd* [1974] AC 235, 271, HL (Lord Kilbrandon).

2 See *Youell v Bland Welch & Co Ltd* [1992] 2 Lloyd's Rep 127, 133, CA (Staughton LJ); *Arbuthnott v Fagan* [1996] LRLR 135, 139, CA (Sir Thomas Bingham MR); *Absalom v TCRU Ltd* [2005] EWCA Civ 1586, [2006] 2 Lloyd's Rep 129, para 7 (Longmore LJ).

3 See **PARAS 3.28–3.35.**

4 *Arbuthnott v Fagan* [1996] LRLR 135, CA, 139 (Sir Thomas Bingham MR), 140–141 (Steyn LJ). Indeed, a court should be wary of starting its analysis by finding an ambiguity by reference to the words in question looked at on their own: *McGeown v Direct Travel Insurance* [2003] EWCA Civ 1606, [2004] Lloyd's Rep IR 599, para 13 (Auld LJ).

5 *Mercantile Bank of Sydney v Taylor* [1893] AC 317, 321, PC.

6 *L Schuler AG v Wickman Machine Tool Sales Ltd* [1974] AC 235, 261, HL (Lord Wilberforce).

7 See *De Lassalle v Guildford* [1901] 2 KB 215, CA (agreement between landlord and tenant collateral to lease).

8 *Youell v Bland Welch & Co Ltd* [1992] 2 Lloyd's Rep 127, 133, CA (Staughton LJ); *Chartbrook Ltd v Persimmon Homes Ltd* [2009] UKHL 38, [2009] 1 AC 1101, para 45 (Lord Hoffmann).

9 *James Miller & Partners Ltd v Whitworth Street Estates (Manchester) Ltd* [1970] AC 583, HL, 603 (Lord Reid), 614 (Lord Wilberforce); *L Schuler AG v Wickman Machine Tool Sales Ltd* [1974] AC 235, 260, HL (Lord Morris).

10 *A & J Inglis v John Buttery & Co* (1878) 3 App Cas 552, HL, 558 (Lord Hatherley); *Hart v Standard Marine Insurance Co Ltd* (1889) 22 QBD 499, CA, 502–503 (Bowen LJ); *L Schuler AG v Wickman Machine Tool Sales Ltd* [1974] AC 235, HL, 256 (Lord Morris), 261 (Lord Wilberforce); *Charter Reinsurance Co Ltd v Fagan* [1997] AC 313, 384, HL (Lord Mustill).

11 *Provincial Insurance Co Ltd v Morgan* [1933] AC 240, 250, HL (Lord Russell); *American Airlines Inc v Hope* [1974] 2 Lloyd's Rep 301, 305, HL (Lord Diplock) (meaning of 'as expiring' in aviation market at Lloyd's), applied: *Black King Shipping Corpn v Massie, The Litsion Pride* [1985] 1 Lloyd's Rep 437, 476 (Hirst J).

12 See *Partenreederei M/S Karen Oltmann v Scarsdale Shipping Co Ltd, The Karen Oltmann* [1976] 2 Lloyd's Rep 708, 712 (Kerr J) (disapproved on other grounds: *Chartbrook Ltd v Persimmon Homes Ltd* [2009] UKHL 38, [2009] 1 AC 1101).

13 *Hutton v Watling* [1948] Ch 398, 403, CA (Lord Greene MR); *Reardon Smith Line Ltd v Yngvar Hansen-Tangen* [1976] 1 WLR 989, 996, 997, HL (Lord Wilberforce); *Investors Compensation Scheme Ltd v West Bromwich Building Society* [1998] 1 WLR 896, 912, HL (Lord Hoffmann); *Bank of Credit and Commerce International SA v Ali* [2001] UKHL 8, [2002] 1 AC 251, paras 8 (Lord Bingham) and

39 (Lord Hoffmann); *Mannai Investment Co Ltd v Eagle Star Life Assurance Co Ltd* [1997] AC 749, 771, HL (Lord Steyn), applied: *Sirius International Insurance Co (Publ) v FAI General Insurance Ltd* [2004] UKHL 54, [2004] 1 WLR 3251, para 19 (Lord Steyn); *Absalom v TCRU Ltd* [2005] EWCA Civ 1586, [2006] 2 Lloyd's Rep 129, para 7 (Longmore LJ). In the commercial context, this means from the standpoint of reasonable commercial persons: *Mannai Investment Co Ltd v Eagle Star Life Assurance Co Ltd* [1997] AC 749, 771, HL (Lord Steyn); see also **PARA 3.15**.

14 *Prenn v Simmonds* [1971] 1 WLR 1381, 1383–1385, HL (Lord Wilberforce); *Reardon Smith Line Ltd v Yngvar Hansen-Tangen* [1976] 1 WLR 989, 995–997, HL (Lord Wilberforce); *Investors Compensation Scheme Ltd v West Bromwich Building Society* [1998] 1 WLR 896, 913, HL (Lord Hoffmann); *Arbuthnott v Fagan* [1996] LRLR 135, CA, 139 (Sir Thomas Bingham MR), 140–141 (Steyn LJ), 141 (Hoffmann LJ); *Absalom v TCRU Ltd* [2005] EWCA Civ 1586, [2006] 2 Lloyd's Rep 129, para 10 (Longmore LJ). Earlier authorities include: *A & J Inglis v John Buttery & Co* (1878) 3 App Cas 552, HL, 577–578 (Lord Blackburn) ('surrounding circumstances'); *Birrell v Dryer* (1884) 9 App Cas 345, HL; *Bank of New Zealand v Simpson* [1900] AC 182, 187, PC (applied: *Moss v Norwich and London Accident Insurance Association* (1922) 10 Ll L Rep 395, 396, CA (Bankes LJ)).

15 *HIH Casualty and General Insurance Ltd v New Hampshire Insurance Co* [2001] EWCA Civ 735, [2001] 2 Lloyd's Rep 161, paras 7–9 (Rix LJ).

16 *Horbury Building Systems Ltd v Hampden Insurance NV* [2004] EWCA Civ 418, [2007] Lloyd's Rep IR 237, para 27 (Keene LJ).

17 See **PARAS 16.2–16.6**.

18 *Dodson v Peter H Dodson Insurance Services* [2001] 1 Lloyd's Rep 520, CA, para 21 (Mance LJ).

19 *Birrell v Dryer* (1884) 9 App Cas 345, HL, 346–347 (Earl of Selbourne LC), 352 (Lord Blackburn): the geographical position and names of districts of a particular area.

20 *Prenn v Simmonds* [1971] 1 WLR 1381, HL; *Absalom v TCRU Ltd* [2005] EWCA Civ 1586, [2006] 2 Lloyd's Rep 129, para 7 (Longmore LJ); *Chartbrook Ltd v Persimmon Homes Ltd* [2009] UKHL 38, [2009] 1 AC 1101, paras 41 (Lord Hoffmann) and 69 (Lord Rodger).

21 *Deutsche Genossenschaftsbank v Burnhope* [1995] 1 WLR 1580, 1587, HL (Lord Steyn, dissenting); *Investors Compensation Scheme Ltd v West Bromwich Building Society* [1998] 1 WLR 896, 913, HL (Lord Hoffmann); *Absalom v TCRU Ltd* [2005] EWCA Civ 1586, [2006] 2 Lloyd's Rep 129, para 7 (Longmore LJ).

22 *James Miller & Partners Ltd v Whitworth Street Estates (Manchester) Ltd* [1970] AC 583, HL, 603 (Lord Reid), 606 (Lord Hodson), 611 (Viscount Dilhorne), 615 (Lord Wilberforce); *L Schuler AG v Wickman Machine Tool Sales Ltd* [1974] AC 235, HL. Where a contract is oral, or partly written and partly oral, evidence of subsequent conduct is admissible to determine its terms: *Maggs v Marsh* [2006] EWCA Civ 1058, [2006] BLR 395, paras 25–26 (Smith LJ).

23 *City and Westminster Properties (1934) Ltd v Mudd* [1959] Ch 129, 140–141 (Harman J) (evidence inadmissible to show wording included in earlier draft but subsequently excised).

24 *Investors Compensation Scheme Ltd v West Bromwich Building Society* [1998] 1 WLR 896, 913, HL (Lord Hoffmann); and see **PARA 3.29**.

25 Deleted words inadmissible as aid to construction: *A & J Inglis v John Buttery & Co* (1878) 3 App Cas 552, HL, 558, 569 (Lord Hatherley), 571–572 (Lord O'Hagan), 577 (Lord Blackburn); *M A Sassoon & Sons Ltd v International Banking Corpn* [1927] AC 711, 721, PC (Lord Sumner); *City and Westminster Properties (1934) Ltd v Mudd* [1959] Ch 129, 140–141 (Harman J); deleted words inadmissible as aid to construction: *Baumvoll Manufactur von Scheibler v Gilchrest & Co* [1892] 1 QB 253, CA, 256 (Lord Esher); *Louis Dreyfus & Cie v Parnaso Cia Naviera SA* [1959] 1 QB 498, 512–513, 515 (Diplock J) (permissible to consider deleted words in case of ambiguity). The authorities were comprehensively reviewed by Christopher Clarke J in *Mopani Copper Mines plc v Millenium Underwriting Ltd* [2008] EWHC 1331 (Comm), [2009] Lloyd's Rep IR 158, paras 100–123.

26 See *Caffin v Aldridge* [1895] 2 QB 648, 650, CA (Lord Esher MR, Lopes LJ); *London Transport Co Ltd v Trechmann Bros* [1904] 1 KB 635, 645, CA (Collins MR).

27 [1992] 1 WLR 1138, CA, 1148–1149 (Staughton LJ), 1155 (Dillon LJ).

28 [1984] 1 Lloyd's Rep 272, 275, CA.

29 *HIH Casualty and General Insurance Ltd v New Hampshire Insurance Co* [2001] EWCA Civ 735, [2001] 2 Lloyd's Rep 161, para 83 (Rix LJ).

30 *Portsmouth City Football Club Ltd v Sellar Properties (Portsmouth) Ltd* [2004] EWCA Civ 760, para 47 (Chadwick LJ).

31 *Prenn v Simmonds* [1971] 1 WLR 1381, 1385, HL (Lord Wilberforce); *Reardon Smith Line Ltd v Yngvar Hansen-Tangen* [1976] 1 WLR 989, 995–996, HL (Lord Wilberforce), applied: *Toomey v Eagle Star Insurance Co Ltd* [1994] 1 Lloyd's Rep 516, 519–520, CA (Hobhouse LJ). In *Heesens*

Yacht Builders BV v Cox Syndicate Management Ltd, The Red Sapphire [2006] EWCA Civ 384, [2006] 2 Lloyd's Rep 35, Rix LJ considered (para 40) that evidence that it was very difficult in the shipping insurance market to obtain risk guarantee cover separate from construction risk cover would be admissible, but was content to decide the construction issue on the basis of the language of the policy alone.

32 *Crema v Cenkos Securities plc* [2010] EWCA Civ 1444, [2011] 1 WLR 2066, para 43 (Aikens LJ); see also *Ted Baker plc v AXA Insurance UK plc* [2012] EWHC 1406 (Comm), [2013] Lloyd's Rep IR 174, paras 88 and 90 (Eder J) (point not considered: [2014] EWCA Civ 134).

33 *Crema v Cenkos Securities plc* [2010] EWCA Civ 1444, [2011] 1 WLR 2066, para 46 (Aikens LJ); see also *Ted Baker plc v AXA Insurance UK plc* [2012] EWHC 1406 (Comm), [2013] Lloyd's Rep IR 174, paras 88 and 90 (Eder J) (point not considered: [2014] EWCA Civ 134).

34 *NLA Group Ltd v Bowers* [1999] 1 Lloyd's Rep 109, 111–112 (Timothy Walker J). See also *Scottish Power v Britoil Exploration Ltd*, unreported, 18 November 1997 (Staughton LJ).

35 *The Tychy (No 2)* [2001] EWCA Civ 1198, [2001] 2 Lloyd's Rep 403, para 29 (Lord Phillips MR).

36 *National Bank of Sharjah v Dellborg*, (9 July 1997, unreported) CA (Saville LJ); applied: *NLA Group Ltd v Bowers* [1999] 1 Lloyd's Rep 109, 111–112 (Timothy Walker J).

37 *GE Reinsurance Corpn v New Hampshire Insurance Co* [2003] EWHC 302 (Comm), [2004] 1 Lloyd's Rep IR 404, para 42 (Langley J) (reinsurers scratched the reinsurance slip and endorsement at different times and one reinsurer saw none of the documents relied on by another reinsurer and the broker in their construction arguments).

38 *Kumar v AGF Insurance Ltd* [1999] 1 WLR 1747, 1752, 1754 (Thomas J) (solicitors). Similarly, in *J Rothschild Assurance plc v Collyear* [1999] Lloyd's Rep IR 6, Rix J construed professional indemnity policies against the background of the regulatory framework of the Financial Services Act 1986 as it applied to the sale of life assurance and pension policies.

39 *AIG Europe Ltd v OC320301 LLP (formerly The International Law Partnership LLP)* [2016] EWCA Civ 367, para 33(iii) (Longmore LJ): aggregation clause contained in all solicitors' indemnity policies pursuant to requirement in the Solicitors Act 1974 for compulsory liability for insurance and Minimum Terms and Conditions required to be incorporated into such policies: see para 2; in these circumstances it is not helpful to consider whether the approach should be from any particular perspective let alone whether the right perspective is that of the insured or that of the public who need the relevant advice or assistance and may be concerned that the solicitor should have adequate cover: see para 33(iii).

40 *AIG Europe Ltd v OC320301 LLP (formerly The International Law Partnership LLP)* [2016] EWCA Civ 367, para 30 (Longmore LJ) (history of origin of aggregation clause, including negotiations between commercial insurers and the Law Society following *Lloyds TSB General Insurance Holdings v Lloyds Bank Group Insurance Co Ltd* [2003] UKHL 48, [2003] Lloyd's Rep IR 623, published in Law Society Gazette).

41 *Kumar v AGF Insurance Ltd* [1999] 1 WLR 1747, 1755 (Thomas J).

42 *Laurence v Davies* [1972] 2 Lloyd's Rep 231, 233 (Dunn J) (definitions in the Road Traffic Act 1960 applied in construction of policy of motor vehicle insurance).

43 *Employers' Liability Insurance Trigger Litigation* [2012] UKSC 14, [2012] Lloyd's Rep IR 371, para 47 (Lord Mance).

44 *Encia Remediations Ltd v Canopius Managing Agents Ltd* [2007] EWHC 916 (Comm), [2008] Lloyd's Rep IR 79, para 183 (Cresswell J).

Previous judicial interpretation

3.17 Where the word or words to be construed have been the subject of previous long-standing judicial interpretation, the courts are understandably reluctant to depart from this meaning, and regard themselves as bound to follow earlier decisions unless there are compelling reasons not to do so.[1] Previous cases should not, however, be treated as authorities on a question of construction unless both the language and the circumstances are substantially identical.[2] Parties to a commercial contract are to be taken to have contracted against a background (or 'factual matrix')[3] which includes the previous decisions on the construction of similar contracts.[4] If as a result a phrase has connotations which a reasonably experienced layman might not appreciate or if the phrase leads to an inquiry which only a lawyer or a historian would be qualified to conduct, the concept of limiting this inquiry to background knowledge reasonably available to an insurance broker or to an insurer must necessarily fade into the background.[5] Where a contract uses wording similar to a statutory provision, its construction is at large and, taken out of its statutory context, there is no presumption that it should be construed in the same way as the statutory provision, unless there is some compelling reason for the two meanings to coincide.[6]

1 *Lawrence v Accidental Insurance Co* (1881) 7 QBD 216, 220, DC (Denman J); *Becker, Gray & Co v London Assurance Corpn* [1918] AC 101, 108, HL (Lord Dunedin); *Re Hooley Hill Rubber and Chemical Co Ltd* [1920] 1 KB 257, CA, 269–270 (Bankes LJ), 272 (Scrutton LJ); *Provincial Insurance Co Ltd v Morgan* [1933] AC 240, 246–247, HL (Lord Buckmaster); *Louden v British Merchants Insurance Co Ltd* [1961] 1 WLR 798, 801 (Lawton J); *L Schuler AG v Wickman Machine Tool Sales Ltd* [1974] AC 235, 255–256, HL (Lord Morris); *Toomey v Eagle Star Insurance Co Ltd* [1994] 1 Lloyd's Rep 516, 520, CA (Hobhouse LJ); *Sunport Shipping Ltd v Tryg-Baltica International (UK) Ltd (The Kleovoulos of Rhodes)* [2003] EWCA Civ 12, [2003] 1 Lloyd's Rep 138, paras 25–28 (Clarke LJ): applied: *Bedfordshire Police Authority v Constable* [2009] EWCA Civ 64, [2009] Lloyd's Rep IR 607, para 16 (Longmore LJ); *Ramco (UK) Ltd v International Insurance Co of Hannover Ltd* [2004] EWCA Civ 675, [2004] 2 Lloyd's Rep 595, para 32 (Waller LJ).

2 *Re Calf* [1920] 2 KB 366, 382, CA (Atkin LJ); *Welch v Royal Exchange Assurance* [1939] 1 KB 294, 311, CA (MacKinnon LJ); *L Schuler AG v Wickman Machine Tool Sales Ltd* [1974] AC 235, 256, HL (Lord Morris); *Morley v United Friendly Insurance plc* [1993] 1 WLR 996, CA, 1000 (Neill LJ) (decision of Scottish Court of Session as to meaning of exception clause in almost identical terms but where facts markedly different held to be of no assistance); *George Hunt Cranes Ltd v Scottish Boiler and General Insurance Co Ltd* [2001] EWCA Civ 1964, [2002] Lloyd's Rep IR 178, para 18 (Potter LJ).

3 See **PARA 3.16**.

4 *Toomey v Eagle Star Insurance Co Ltd* [1994] 1 Lloyd's Rep 516, 519–520, CA (Hobhouse LJ) (reinsurance contract); *MDIS Ltd v Swinbank* [1999] Lloyd's Rep IR 516, para 14 (Clarke LJ); *Dodson v Peter H Dodson Insurance Services* [2001] 1 Lloyd's Rep 520, CA, para 21 (Mance LJ); *Gan v Tai Ping (Nos 2 and 3)* [2001] EWCA Civ 1047, [2001] Lloyd's Rep IR 667, paras 22–24 (Mance LJ); *George Hunt Cranes Ltd v Scottish Boiler and General Insurance Co Ltd* [2001] EWCA Civ 1964, [2002] Lloyd's Rep IR 178, para 19 (Potter LJ); *Sunport Shipping Ltd v Tryg-Baltica International (UK) Ltd (The Kleovoulos of Rhodes)* [2003] EWCA Civ 12, [2003] 1 Lloyd's Rep 138, para 28 (Clarke LJ).

5 *Bedfordshire Police Authority v Constable* [2009] EWCA Civ 64, [2009] Lloyd's Rep IR 607, para 18 (Longmore LJ).

6 *Strive Shipping Corpn v Hellenic Mutual War Risks Association, The Grecia Express* [2002] 2 Lloyd's Rep 88, 160 (Colman J).

Exceptions or exclusions and limitations[1]

3.18 Exceptions or exclusions from cover, and limitations on the scope of cover, must be construed in a manner consistent with and not repugnant to the commercial purpose of the policy.[2] For example, there is a line of authority construing restrictively conditions in liability and property insurance which require the insured to take 'reasonable precautions' to prevent accidents or loss.[3] An exclusion should be construed in the context of the policy as a whole.[4] Exceptions will be given effect to only if they are plain and unambiguous.[5] In cases of ambiguity, the principle of construction *contra proferentem* applies, which will usually mean that the exceptions and limitations will be construed against the insurer and in favour of the insured.[6] In all risks cover, an exclusion from an exclusion results in there being cover for the relevant peril.[7]

The application of an exclusion in a contract entered into on or after 12 August 2016[8] may be affected by the provisions of the Insurance Act 2015 in relation to 'terms not relevant to the actual loss'.[9]

1 The burden of proof in relation to exceptions or exclusions from cover is considered at **PARA 5.1**.
2 *Morley v United Friendly Insurance plc* [1993] 1 WLR 996, CA, 1000 (Neill LJ), 1003 (Beldam LJ).
3 See **PARA 5.2**.
4 See eg *Handelsbanken Norwegian Branch of Svenska Handeslbanken AB (Publ) v Dandridge, The Aliza Glacial* [2002] EWCA Civ 577, [2002] 2 Lloyd's Rep 421, in which the requirement or imposition by the insurers of a warranty as to 'no illegal fishing' was regarded by Potter LJ (at para 34) as some indication of the parties' contemplation that fishing in breach of local laws or regulations would not otherwise be excluded from the scope of the policy by reason of the exception in respect of 'trading regulations'.
5 *Birrell v Dryer* (1884) 9 App Cas 345, HL, 354 (Lord Watson); *Royal & Sun Alliance Insurance plc v Dornoch* [2005] EWCA Civ 238, [2005] Lloyd's Rep IR 544, para 19 (Longmore LJ) (condition precedent to reinsurer's liability).
6 *Canelhas Comercio Importacao e Exportacao Ltd v Wooldridge* [2004] EWCA Civ 984, [2004] 1 Lloyd's Rep IR 915, para 13 (Mance LJ); *Tektrol Ltd v International Insurance Co of Hanover Ltd* [2005] EWCA Civ 845, [2005] 2 Lloyd's Rep 701, paras 7 and 8 (Buxton LJ) and 20 (Carnwath LJ). See further **PARA 3.19**.
7 See eg *Masefield AG v Amlin Corporate Member Ltd, The Bunga Melati Dua* [2011] EWCA Civ 24, [2011] 1 Lloyd's Rep 630, para 18 (Rix LJ): 'The policy was an all risks policy with a war exclusion clause which excluded "capture, seizure, arrest, restraint or detainment (piracy excepted)". So piracy was a peril insured against.'
8 Insurance Act 2015, ss 11, 22(1) and (3), and 23(2) (the 2015 Act was passed on 12 February 2015).
9 See **PARA 3.10**.

Construction *contra proferentem*

3.19 Where there is ambiguity[1] in the wording, which cannot be resolved by evidence as to the surrounding circumstances or factual matrix, provisions in policies of insurance are to be construed *contra proferentem* (which means, literally, that they are to be construed against the party putting them forward, who is sometimes referred to, particularly in the older cases, as the *proferens*). The expression has two meanings:

> There are two well established rules of construction, although one is perhaps more often relied on with success than the other. The first is that, in case of doubt, wording in a contract is to be construed against a party who seeks to rely on it in order to diminish or exclude his basic obligation. ... The second is that, again in case of doubt, wording is to be construed against the party who proposed it for inclusion in the contract: it was up to him to make it clear.[2]

The second meaning is more commonly applied.[3] Whichever meaning is adopted, the principle is not that, in case of ambiguity, contracts of insurance are to be construed against the insurer, and in favour of the insured, although it usually has this effect.[4] This means that where the policy is framed in accordance with a slip prepared by the insured's broker, it may be construed, in case of ambiguity, against the insured rather than against the insurer.[5] Although a party putting forward a wording usually does so with their own protection in mind, the second meaning has no application where the wording was put forward for the benefit of the other party, or of both parties, to the contract.[6] There is no reason to disapply the principle that resolves ambiguities in a particular exclusion clause by a narrow construction, merely because the same contract contains an exclusion clause limiting the extent of contractual warranties given by the other party: the same principle may be used where necessary to resolve ambiguities (if there are any) in either of them.[7]

The principle applies only where there is ambiguity in the wording which cannot be resolved by an application of ordinary principles of construction.[8] Difficulty of construction is not the same thing as ambiguity.[9] Accordingly, if the meaning of the wording is clear and unambiguous, it must be applied, even if the outcome appears hard on the insured.[10] Where there are two possible interpretations, only one of which makes any commercial sense, the principle is inapplicable.[11] The principle probably has no application where the wording under consideration is a standard wording, which should in principle receive a uniform construction whoever puts it forward.[12] If a wording has been the subject of previous long-standing judicial interpretation, this will generally be taken to have established the meaning so that there will be no ambiguity;[13] but if the court considers that there is ambiguity because it doubts the correctness of the earlier authority, or is able to distinguish it because of a material difference in wording, the *contra proferentem* principle may apply.[14] Where policy wording closely mirrors minimum terms and conditions prescribed by a regulatory authority, the *contra proferentem* principle of construction has no application.[15]

In cases to which Part 2 of the Consumer Rights Act 2015 applies,[16] insurers are under an obligation imposed to ensure that a written term in a consumer contract is transparent.[17] For these purposes, a term is transparent if it is expressed in plain and intelligible language and (in the case of a written term) is legible.[18] If a term in a consumer contract could have different meanings, the meaning that is most favourable to the consumer is to prevail.[19] This principle does not displace the normal exercise of construing the contract to determine its meaning, but applies only if, having construed in the normal way, ambiguity remains.[20] In the insurance context, this requirement is likely to have little impact, as this will usually be the result, in the case of ambiguity in the wording, of an application of the principle of construction *contra proferentem*.[21]

1 Ambiguity means genuinely open to two possible constructions, and the fact that judges differ as to the correct construction of wording does not mean that it is necessarily ambiguous: *R v Personal Investment Authority Ombudsman Bureau, ex p Royal & Sun Alliance Life & Pensions Ltd* [2002] Lloyd's Rep IR 41, 43 (Langley J); *McGeown v Direct Travel Insurance* [2003] EWCA Civ 1606, [2004] Lloyd's Rep IR 599, para 13 (Auld LJ); *Re OT Computers Ltd (in administration)* [2004] EWCA Civ 653, [2004] Ch 317, para 39 (Longmore LJ) (statutory interpretation). Ambiguity is not the same as lack of clarity: *R v Personal Investment Authority Ombudsman Bureau, ex p Royal & Sun Alliance Life & Pensions Ltd* [2002] Lloyd's Rep IR 41, 43 (Langley J); *McGeown v Direct Travel Insurance* [2003] EWCA Civ 1606, [2004] Lloyd's Rep IR 599, paras 20–21 (Auld LJ).
2 *Youell v Bland Welch & Co Ltd* [1992] 2 Lloyd's Rep 127, 134, CA (Staughton LJ), applied: *Zeus Tradition Marine Ltd v Bell, The Zeus V* [2000] 2 Lloyd's Rep 587, CA, para 30 (Potter LJ). For the construction of exclusions or exceptions from cover, see **PARA 3.18**; and for the burden of proof under an exclusion or exception, see **PARA 5.1**.
3 *Zeus Tradition Marine Ltd v Bell, The Zeus V* [2000] 2 Lloyd's Rep 587, CA, para 30 (Potter LJ). The second meaning was applied in *Birrell v Dryer* (1884) 9 App Cas 345, HL, 351–352 (Lord Blackburn), 354 (Lord Watson); both meanings, and the potential for conflict between the two meanings, were discussed by Staughton LJ in *Youell v Bland Welch & Co Ltd* [1992] 2 Lloyd's Rep 127, 134, CA.
4 *Zeus Tradition Marine Ltd v Bell, The Zeus V* [2000] 2 Lloyd's Rep 587, CA, para 30 (Potter LJ). The cases frequently describe the principle in a way which gives the impression: see *Smith v Accident Insurance Co* (1870) LR 5 Ex Ch 302, 307; *Cornish v Accident Insurance Co* (1889) 23 QBD 453, CA, 456 (Lindley LJ); *Etherington v Lancashire & Yorkshire Accident Insurance Co* [1909] 1 KB 591, 596, CA (Vaughan Williams LJ); *Re Bradley and Essex and Suffolk Accident Indemnity Society* [1912] 1 KB

415, 430, CA (Farwell LJ); *National Protector Fire Insurance Co Ltd v Nivert* [1913] AC 507, 513, PC; *Welch v Royal Exchange Assurance* [1939] 1 KB 294, CA (per MacKinnon LJ at 313, referring to 'the ancient principle that these provisions, inserted by [insurers] in limitation of their promise of indemnity, must be construed *contra proferentem*'); *Yorkshire Water Services Ltd v Sun Alliance & London Insurance plc* [1997] 2 Lloyd's Rep 21, 28, CA (Stuart-Smith LJ); *John A Pike (Butchers) Ltd v Independent Insurance Co Ltd* [1998] Lloyd's Rep IR 410, 418, CA (Evans LJ). This is probably a reflection of the fact that it is usually the insurer who puts forward the policy wording: see *Rowett, Leakey and Co v Scottish Provident Institution* [1927] 1 Ch 55, 72, CA (Sargant LJ).

5 *A/S Ocean v Black Sea and Baltic General Insurance Co Ltd* (1935) 51 Ll L Rep 305, CA, 307 (Greer LJ), 310 (Maugham LJ), applied: *Bartlett & Partners Ltd v Meller* [1961] 1 Lloyd's Rep 487, 493–494 (Sachs J), *Balfour v Beaumont* [1982] 2 Lloyd's Rep 493, 503 (Webster J) (point not considered on appeal: [1984] 1 Lloyd's Rep 272, CA); *Denby v English & Scottish Maritime Insurance Co Ltd*, [1998] Lloyd's Rep IR 343, CA (Hobhouse LJ) (this point not referred to in report of judgment at (1998) Times, 16 March); *New Hampshire Insurance Co v MGN Ltd* [1997] LRLR 24, 55, CA (Staughton LJ). In *T Dunn v W C Campbell* (1920) 4 Ll L Rep 36, CA, Bankes LJ considered that the principle of construction *contra proferentem* would entitle them to construe against the insurer wording used by the insured in the proposal form (at 39); although Donaldson J indicated, in *de Maurier (Jewels) Ltd v Bastion Insurance Co Ltd* [1967] 2 Lloyd's Rep 550, that, had there been any ambiguity, he would have applied *T Dunn v W C Campbell* and construed the broker's slip against the insurer (at 559–560), in *Jaglom v Excess Insurance Co Ltd* [1972] 2 QB 250, he referred to his earlier decision as authority for the proposition that:

> 'the *contra proferentem* rule of construction ... treats the slip as having been proffered by the assured ... in so far as he or his broker is the author of its wording or puts it forward' (at 258).

6 See *Birrell v Dryer* (1884) 9 App Cas 345, HL, 351–352 (Lord Blackburn), 354 (Lord Watson).

7 *Nobahar-Cookson v The Hut Group Ltd* [2016] EWCA Civ 128, para 20 (Briggs LJ).

8 *Birrell v Dryer* (1884) 9 App Cas 345, HL, 350 (Earl of Selbourne LC), 354–355 (Lord Watson); *Cornish v Accident Insurance Co* (1889) 23 QBD 453, 456, CA (Lindley LJ); *Etherington v Lancashire & Yorkshire Accident Insurance Co* [1909] 1 KB 591, CA; *Yorkshire Insurance Co Ltd v Campbell* [1917] AC 218, 223, PC (Lord Sumner); *London and Lancashire Fire Insurance Co Ltd v Bolands Ltd* [1924] AC 836, 848, HL (Lord Sumner); *Passmore v Vulcan Boiler & General Insurance Co Ltd* (1936) 54 Ll L Rep 92, 94 (du Parcq J); *R v Personal Investment Authority Ombudsman Bureau, ex p Royal & Sun Alliance Life & Pensions Ltd* [2002] Lloyd's Rep IR 41, 43 (Langley J); *McGeown v Direct Travel Insurance* [2003] EWCA Civ 1606, [2004] Lloyd's Rep IR 599, para 13 (Auld LJ); *Pratt v Aigaion Insurance Co SA, The Resolute* [2008] EWCA Civ 1314, [2009] 1 Lloyd's Rep 225, paras 14, 25 and 26 (Sir Anthony Clarke MR).

9 *Reilly v National Insurance and Guarantee Corpn Ltd* [2008] EWCA Civ 1460, [2009] Lloyd's Rep IR 488, para 10 (Moore-Bick LJ).

10 *Re United London and Scottish Insurance Co Ltd* [1915] 2 Ch 167, 170, CA (Cozens-Hardy MR).

11 *Gan v Tai Ping (Nos 2 and 3)* [2001] EWCA Civ 1047, [2001] Lloyd's Rep IR 667, para 21 (Mance LJ).

12 *Gan v Tai Ping (Nos 2 and 3)* [2001] EWCA Civ 1047, [2001] Lloyd's Rep IR 667, para 21 (Mance LJ).

13 *Dodson v Peter H Dodson Insurance Services* [2001] 1 Lloyd's Rep 520, CA, para 21 (Mance LJ).

14 *Dodson v Peter H Dodson Insurance Services* [2001] 1 Lloyd's Rep 520, CA, paras 41–42 (Mance LJ).

15 *Sutherland Professional Funding Ltd v Bakewells* [2011] EWHC 2658 (QB), para 77 (His Honour Judge Hegarty QC) (solicitors' indemnity insurance).

16 See **PARA 3.20**.

17 Section 68(1).

18 Section 64(3).

19 Section 69(1). This does not apply to the construction of a term in proceedings for an injunction (by a regulator) under paragraph 3 of Schedule 3: s 69(2).

20 *A J Building & Plastering Ltd v Turner* [2013] EWHC 484 (QB), [2013] Lloyd's Rep IR 629, paras 53–54 (HHJ Keyser QC).

21 See *A J Building & Plastering Ltd v Turner* [2013] EWHC 484 (QB), [2013] Lloyd's Rep IR 629, para 53 (HHJ Keyser QC); see also *Bache v Zurich Insurance plc* [2014] EWHC 2430 (TCC), [2014] Lloyd's Rep IR 663, para 23 (Akenhead J) (it is probably going to be an unusual case where a consumer contract will be construed differently from an ordinary contract, but presumably legislature had in mind that consumer contracts might be construed more adversely against the non-consumer party than might otherwise be the case).

Unfair terms in consumer contracts

3.20   Part 2 of the Consumer Rights Act 2015[1] applies to unfair terms in contracts[2] between traders and consumers.[3] Such contracts are referred to in Part 2 as 'consumer contracts'.[4] 'Trader' means a person acting for purposes relating to that person's trade, business, craft or profession, whether acting personally or through another person acting in the trader's name or on the trader's behalf[5], and would plainly include an insurer or insurance broker. 'Consumer' means an individual acting for purposes that are wholly or mainly outside that individual's trade, business, craft or profession.[6] A trader claiming that an individual was not acting for purposes wholly or mainly outside the individual's trade, business, craft or profession must prove it.[7] Part 2 of the Consumer Rights Act 2015 does not apply to a term of a contract to the extent that it reflects mandatory statutory or regulatory provisions, or the provisions or principles of international conventions to which the United Kingdom or the EU is a party.[8] If the law of a country or territory other than an EEA state is chosen by the parties to be applicable to a consumer contract, but the consumer contract has a close connection with the United Kingdom, Part 2 of the Consumer Rights Act 2015 applies despite that choice.[9] Section 62 of the Consumer Rights Act 2015 provides that a term is unfair if, 'contrary to the requirement of good faith', it causes a significant imbalance in the parties' rights and obligations under the contract to the detriment of the consumer,[10] and that whether a term is fair is to be determined taking into account the nature of the subject matter of the contract, and by reference to all the circumstances existing when the term was agreed and to all of the other terms of the contract or of any other contract on which it depends.[11] In determining whether a term is unfair:[12]

(1)   The test of 'significant imbalance' and 'good faith' merely defines in a general way the factors that render unfair a contractual term that has not been individually negotiated. A significant element of judgment is left to the national court, to exercise in the light of the circumstances of each case.

(2)   The question whether there is a 'significant imbalance' in the parties' rights depends mainly on whether the consumer is being deprived of an advantage which he would enjoy under national law in the absence of the contractual provision. In other words, this element of the test is concerned with provisions derogating from the legal position of the consumer under national law.

(3)   However, a provision derogating from the legal position of the consumer under national law will not necessarily be treated as unfair. The imbalance must arise 'contrary to the requirements of good faith'. That will depend on whether the seller or supplier, dealing fairly and equitably with the consumer, could reasonably assume that the consumer[13] would have agreed to such a term in individual contract negotiations.[14]

(4)   The national court is to take account of, among other things, the nature of the goods or services supplied under the contract. This includes the significance, purpose and practical effect of the term in question, and whether it is appropriate for securing the attainment of the objectives pursued by it in the member state concerned and does not go beyond what is necessary to achieve them. In the case of a provision whose operation is conditional upon the consumer's breach of another term of the contract, it is necessary to assess the importance of the latter term in the contractual relationship.

The requirement of good faith is one of fair and equitable dealing, taking into account the legitimate interests of the consumer; particular regard may be had to the strength of the bargaining position of the parties, whether the consumer had an inducement to agree to the term, and whether the services were supplied to the special order of the consumer.[15] This is not the English law concept of good faith, and it is not necessary to show lack of good faith in the sense in which English law understands the concept in order to succeed in a claim.[16]

In assessing the fairness of a term, the regulatory framework which determines how and in what circumstances it may be enforced is relevant.[17] Thus, in *Parker v National Farmers Union Mutual Insurance Society Ltd*,[18] Teare J said that a condition precedent which allowed an insurer to reject a claim for breach even if the insurer suffered no prejudice was not unfair once account was taken of ICOBS, because reliance upon a mere procedural transgression which did not prejudice an insurer in order to reject a claim would be unreasonable 'and therefore beyond the insurer's powers', and that the insurer could not claim to be entitled to exercise a right to reject a claim under a policy of insurance otherwise than in accordance with ICOBS.[19]

With the exception of the terms listed in Part 1 of Schedule 2 to the 2015 Act,[20] a term of a consumer contract may not be assessed for fairness under s 62 to the extent that it specifies the main subject matter of the contract, or the assessment is of the appropriateness of the price payable under the contract by comparison with the services supplied under it,[21] provided that it is transparent and prominent.[22] For these purposes, a term is transparent if it is expressed in plain and intelligible language and (in the case of a written term) is legible,[23] and is prominent if it is brought to the consumer's attention in such a way that an average consumer would be aware of the term.[24] In this context, 'average consumer' means a consumer who is reasonably well-informed, observant and circumspect.[25] The fact that there is a dispute between insurer and insured as to the meaning of a term in a contract of insurance does not mean that the language is not plain and intelligible.[26] An arbitration clause which has the effect of obliging an insured to engage in two sets of dispute resolution, one by arbitration and the other by litigation, because not all of the issues which the insured wishes to have resolved are within the scope of the arbitration agreement, may be held to cause a significant imbalance in the parties' rights and obligations under the contract of insurance to the detriment of the insured.[27]

Part 1 of Schedule 2 to the 2015 Act contains an indicative and non-exhaustive list of terms of consumer contracts that may be regarded as unfair for the purposes of Part 2 of the 2015 Act.[28] This includes terms which have the object or effect of irrevocably binding the consumer to terms with which the consumer has had no real opportunity of becoming acquainted before the conclusion of the contract.[29] This provision may be relevant where full policy terms and conditions are sent to the insured only after a contract of insurance has been entered into. Part 1 of Schedule 2 also includes terms which have the object or effect of excluding or hindering the consumer's right to take legal action or exercise any other legal remedy, in particular by requiring the consumer to take disputes exclusively to arbitration 'not covered by legal provisions', unduly restricting the evidence available to the consumer, or imposing on the consumer a burden of proof which, according to the applicable law, should lie with another party to the contract.[30] An exclusive jurisdiction clause may fall within the category of terms which have the object or effect of excluding or hindering the consumer's right to take legal action;[31] whether in any particular case such a clause is unfair is a fact-specific inquiry.[32]

A term which constitutes an arbitration agreement is unfair for the purposes of Part 2 of the Consumer Rights Act 2015 so far as it relates to a claim for a pecuniary remedy which does not exceed £5,000.[33] Part 1 of Schedule 2 does not create a rebuttable presumption that any term which falls within it is unfair, but constitutes guidelines as to the types of terms which the court may conclude, in the circumstances of a particular case, are unfair.[34] The preamble to the Directive on unfair terms in consumer contracts[35] makes express reference to contracts of insurance in this regard, indicating that the terms which clearly define or circumscribe the risk and the insurer's liability are not subject to an assessment of unfair character since these restrictions are taken into account in calculating the premium paid by the consumer.[36] In proceedings before a court which relate to a term of a consumer contract, the court must consider whether the term is fair even if none of the parties to the proceedings has raised the issue or indicated that it intends to raise it,[37] but only if the court considers that it has before it sufficient legal and factual material to enable it to consider the fairness of the term.[38]

Where a term of a consumer contract is not binding on the consumer as a result of Part 2 of the Consumer Rights Act 2015, the contract continues, so far as practicable, to have effect in every other respect.[39] In *Bankers Insurance Co Ltd v South*,[40] a term of a contract of travel insurance provided that the payment of claims was dependent on the insured (a) reporting to insurers in writing as soon as reasonably possible full details of any incidents which might result in a claim under the policy, and (b) forwarding to them immediately upon receipt every writ, summons, legal process or other communication in connection with the claim. Buckley J held that the introductory words rendered the obligations conditions precedent to the insurers' liability in respect of the claim, and that insurers were entitled to reject the claim even if they suffered no prejudice due to (in that case) late notification. The judge concluded as a result that the term was unfair as it caused a significant imbalance in the parties' obligations to the insured's detriment. He also held that it was not necessary to delete the clause entirely, as it was only the part of the clause which denied recovery whatever the consequences of the breach which was unfair and which was therefore not binding on the insured.[41] The judge found that the insurers had suffered prejudice by reason of the insured's failure to comply with the clauses, and concluded that insurers were entitled to rely on the conditions precedent in denying liability under the policy.[42] The difficulty with this approach is that the conditions precedent did not expressly state that they were to apply regardless of whether the insurer had suffered prejudice: this was simply their effect in English law. In adding the requirement of prejudice, the judge was not omitting part of the wording, but adding a proviso, and thereby rewriting the clause. This is not the correct approach: in Case C-618/10 *Banco Español de Crédito SA v Camino*,[43] the Court of Justice of the European Union held that it was not permissible for the national court to rewrite a term in this way, and that once a term had been held to be unfair and therefore not binding on the consumer, it could not be relied upon. There is in addition an obligation imposed on a trader under the 2015 Act to ensure that a written term in a consumer contract is transparent.[44] If a term in a consumer contract could have different meanings, the meaning that is most favourable to the consumer is to prevail.[45] This principle does not displace the normal exercise of construing the contract to determine its meaning, but applies only if, having construed in the normal way,[46] ambiguity remains.[47] In the insurance context, this requirement is likely to have little impact, as this will usually be the result, in the case of ambiguity in the wording, of an application of the principle of construction *contra proferentem*.[48]

1 The Consumer Rights Act 2015 revoked the Unfair Terms in Consumer Contracts Regulations 1999 (SI 1999/2083, as amended) with effect from 1 October 2015: Sch 4 to the 2015 Act, para 34. The 1999 Regulations, the Unfair Terms in Consumer Contracts Regulations 1994 (SI 1994/3159) which they revoked with effect from 1 October 1999, and the 2015 Act implemented Council Directive (EC) 93/13 on unfair terms in consumer contracts (OJ No L95, 21.4.93, p 29). Some decisions made under the 1994 or 1999 Regulations may remain relevant under the 2015 Act.

2 Part 2 of the Consumer Rights Act 2015 also applies to notices to the extent that they relate to rights or obligations as between a trader and a consumer, or purport to exclude or restrict a trader's liability to a consumer: s 61(4).

3 Section 61(1).

4 Sections 61(3) and 76(1).

5 Sections 2(2) and 76(2).

6 Sections 2(3) and 76(2). Whether an individual is a consumer for these purposes is fact-specific: see *AMT Futures Ltd v Marzillier* [2014] EWHC 1085 (Comm), [2014] 2 Lloyd's Rep 349, para 58 (Popplewell J). In *Standard Bank London Ltd v Apostolakis* [2000] CLC 933, a husband and wife who were, respectively, a civil engineer and a lawyer, were held to be acting for purposes outside their trade, business or profession, and therefore to be 'consumers' for the purposes of the Unfair Terms in Consumer Contracts Regulations 1994, when engaging for profit in foreign exchange transactions involving substantial sums of money (Longmore J, paras 13–22). In subsequent proceedings between the same parties (reported at [2001] Lloyd's Rep Bank 240), David Steel J said that the claimants were consumers even though the transactions they entered into were at the 'business' end of the scale, given their size (para 51). Longmore J's conclusion was doubted by Andrew Smith J in *Maple Leaf Macro Volatility Master Fund v Rouvroy* [2009] EWHC 257 (Comm), [2009] 1 Lloyd's Rep 475, at para 209. In Case C-269/95 *Benincasa v Dentalkit Srl* [1997] I-ECR 3767, the European Court of Justice was considering the definition of 'consumer' in article 13 of the Brussels Convention (a person acting 'for a purpose which can be regarded as being outside his trade or profession') and said, in relation to this wording, that 'only contracts concluded for the purpose of satisfying an individual's own needs in terms of private consumption come under the provisions designed to protect the consumer as the party deemed to be the weaker party economically' (para 17). In *AMT Futures Ltd v Marzillier* [2014] EWHC 1085 (Comm), [2014] 2 Lloyd's Rep 349, Popplewell J referred to *Benincasa v Dentalkit Srl* and said that it was not suggested that there was any relevant distinction, for the purposes of an application for a declaration that the court did not have jurisdiction, between the definition of consumer in the Brussels Convention and that under the Unfair Terms in Consumer Contracts Regulations 1999 (para 56).

7 Sections 2(4) and 76(3).

8 Section 73(1). In s 73(1), 'mandatory statutory or regulatory provisions' includes rules which, according to law, apply between the parties on the basis that no other arrangements have been established.

9 Section 74(1). For cases where the law applicable has not been chosen or the law of an EEA state is chosen, Regulation (EC) No 593/2008 of the European Parliament and of the Council of 17 June 2008 on the law applicable to contractual regulations (also known as 'Rome I') applies: s 74(2); and see PARA 15.6. For a list of states within the EEA (European Economic Area), see PARA 15.3, note 1.

10 Section 62(4). Under the 1999 Regulations, a term which had been individually negotiated was not unfair (see the former Regulation 5(1)). There is no equivalent provision in Part 2 of the 2015 Act.

11 Section 62(5).

12 *Cavendish Square Holding BV v El Makdessi* [2015] UKSC 67, [2015] 3 WLR 1373, [2016] 1 Lloyd's Rep 55, para 105 (Lords Neuberger and Sumption (Lord Carnwath agreeing)): applying Case C-415/11 *Aziz v Caixa d'Estalvis de Catalunya, Tarragona i Manresa* [2013] 3 CMLR 89 (in relation to the 1999 Regulations).

13 Or his lawyer; see *Director General of Fair Trading v First National Bank plc* [2001] UKHL 52, [2002] 1 AC, para 54 (Lord Millett) (a decision on the 1994 Regulations); and *Cavendish Square Holding BV v El Makdessi* [2015] UKSC 67, [2015] 3 WLR 1373, [2016] 1 Lloyd's Rep 55, paras 305 and 314 (Lord Toulson) (in relation to the 1999 Regulations).

14 Under the 1999 Regulations, a term which had been individually negotiated was not unfair (see the former Regulation 5(1)). There is no equivalent provision in Part 2 of the 2015 Act.

15 See the preamble to the Directive, Sixteenth Recital, and *Director General of Fair Trading v First National Bank plc* [2001] UKHL 52, [2002] 1 AC. This was a decision on the 1994 Regulations, which contained an additional schedule, omitted from the Consumer Rights Act 2015, which gave guidance as to the factors to which the court should have regard in making an assessment of good faith. As the provisions in the schedule were taken from the preamble to the Directive, and Part 2 of the 2015 Act must be interpreted in the light of the Directive, including, where appropriate, its preamble (see *R v Tymen* [1980] 3 CMLR 101, paras 28–29 (Watkins J) (interpretation of a European Community Regulation)), these remarks about the meaning of good faith are likely to remain relevant in relation to the 2015 Act.

16 *Zealander v Laing Homes Ltd* (2000) 2 TCLR 724, 727 (His Honour Judge Havery QC) (in relation to the Unfair Terms in Consumer Contracts Regulations 1994).

17 *Cavendish Square Holding BV v El Makdessi* [2015] UKSC 67, [2015] 3 WLR 1373, [2016] 1 Lloyd's Rep 55, para 111 (Lords Neuberger and Sumption (Lord Carnwath agreeing)) (in relation to the 1999 Regulations).

18 [2012] EWHC 2156 (Comm), [2013] Lloyd's Rep IR 253.

19 At paras 191 and 196–197 (in relation to the 1999 Regulations).

20 Section 64(6).

21 Section 64(1).

22 Section 64(2).

23 Section 64(3). A term is drafted in plain, intelligible language if it is not only grammatically intelligible to the consumer, but the contract also sets out transparently the specific functioning of the arrangements to which the relevant term refers and the relationship between those arrangements and the arrangements laid down in respect of other contractual terms, so that that consumer is in a position to evaluate, on the basis of precise, intelligible criteria, the economic consequences for him which derive from it: Case C-96/14 *Van Hove v CNP Assurances SA* [2016] Lloyd's Rep IR 61, CJEU, para 50.

24 Section 64(4).

25 Section 64(5).

26 *Bache v Zurich Insurance plc* [2014] EWHC 2430 (TCC), [2014] Lloyd's Rep IR 663, para 23 (Akenhead J).

27 *Zealander v Laing Homes Ltd* (2000) 2 TCLR 724, 725, 727–728 (His Honour Judge Havery QC) (in relation to the Unfair Terms in Consumer Contracts Regulations 1994).

28 Section 63(1).

29 Schedule 2, Part 1, para 10.

30 Schedule 2, Part 1, para 20. The meaning of the phrase 'not covered by legal provisions', which the 2015 Act has taken verbatim from the annex to the Directive, is obscure. In *Zealander v Laing Homes Ltd* (2000) 2 TCLR 724, His Honour Judge Havery QC declined (at 729) to give the words any meaning which would cut down the meaning of the other words in Schedule 2, para 1(q) of the Unfair Terms in Consumer Contracts Regulations 1999 (which was in substantially the same terms as Schedule 2, Part 1, para 20 of the Consumer Rights Act 2015); applied: *Mylcrist Builders Ltd v Buck* [2008] EWHC 2172 (TCC), para 54 (Ramsey J).

31 Joined Cases C-240/98 to C-244/98 *Océano Grupo Editorial SA v Murciano Quintero* [2000] ECR I-4941, ECJ, para 22, ECJ (clause conferred jurisdiction in respect of all disputes arising under contract on courts of specific area (Barcelona) in which seller or supplier had his principal place of business, and obliged consumer to submit to exclusive jurisdiction of court which might be long way from his domicile); applied: *AMT Futures Ltd v Marzillier* [2014] EWHC 1085 (Comm), [2014] 2 Lloyd's Rep 349, Popplewell J (paras 61–62). See also **PARA 15.9**.

32 *AMT Futures Ltd v Marzillier* [2014] EWHC 1085 (Comm), [2014] 2 Lloyd's Rep 349, Popplewell J (paras 61–62) (in relation to the 1999 Regulations).

33 Arbitration Act 1996, ss 89 and 91(1). For these purposes, Part 2 applies where the consumer is a legal person as it applies where the consumer is an individual: Arbitration Act 1996, s 90; and an arbitration agreement is any agreement to submit to arbitration present or future disputes or differences (whether or not contractual): s 89(1) of the Arbitration Act 1996. The relevant amount is specified by order: Arbitration Act 1996, s 91(2)–(4). The current order is the Unfair Arbitration Agreements (Specified Amount) Order 1999 (SI 1999/2167).

34 *Zealander v Laing Homes Ltd* (2000) 2 TCLR 724, 728, His Honour Judge Havery QC (referring to Schedule 3 to the 1994 Regulations).

35 Council Directive (EC) 93/13 on unfair terms in consumer contracts (OJ No L95, 21.4.93, p 29).
36 Preamble to the Directive, Seventeenth Recital. Part 2 of the 2015 Act must be interpreted in the light of the Directive, including, where appropriate, its preamble: see *R v Tymen* [1980] 3 CMLR 101, paras 28–29 (Watkins J) (interpretation of a European Community Regulation).
37 Section 71(1) and (2).
38 Section 71(3).
39 Section 67.
40 [2003] EWHC 380 (QB), [2004] 1 Lloyd's Rep IR 1 (Buckley J) (in relation to the Unfair Terms in Consumer Contracts Regulations 1994).
41 At paras 29–36.
42 At paras 37–41.
43 [2012] 3 CMLR 555.
44 Section 68(1). As to the meaning of 'transparent', see notes 23–24 and related text above.
45 Section 69(1). This does not apply to the construction of a term in proceedings for an injunction (by a regulator) under para 3 of Schedule 3: s 69(2).
46 See **PARAS 3.14–3.19**.
47 *A J Building & Plastering Ltd v Turner* [2013] EWHC 484 (QB), [2013] Lloyd's Rep IR 629, paras 53–54 (HHJ Keyser QC).
48 See *A J Building & Plastering Ltd v Turner* [2013] EWHC 484 (QB), [2013] Lloyd's Rep IR 629, para 53 (HHJ Keyser QC); see also *Bache v Zurich Insurance plc* [2014] EWHC 2430 (TCC), [2014] Lloyd's Rep IR 663, para 23 (Akenhead J) (it is probably going to be an unusual case where a consumer contract will be construed differently from an ordinary contract, but presumably legislature had in mind that consumer contracts might be construed more adversely against the non-consumer party than might otherwise be the case).

Words taking meaning from their neighbours (the *eiusdem generis* rule and the *noscitur a sociis* principle)

3.21 There is a principle of construction commonly referred to as the *eiusdem generis* rule, by the application of which the meaning of general words in a document may be narrowed if they are followed by specific descriptions of the subject matter to which they apply. The principle is based on the notion that all the words of an agreement should be given effect to, and that if the specific words are not read as narrowing the general words, they are mere surplusage, and therefore redundant. This principle has little application in the construction of commercial documents such as insurance policies, which are not drafted with the precision of equity draftsmen and often contain redundant words.[1] A related principle of construction, sometimes referred to by means of the Latin expression *noscitur a sociis*,[2] may be used in construing a policy of insurance where the meaning of one of a group of words is ambiguous. In such a case, the court will be inclined to read the word as having the meaning which renders it a member of the group. For example, in construing the word 'flood' in a householder's insurance policy in *Young v Sun Alliance and London Insurance Ltd*,[3] Shaw and Lawton LJJ were influenced by the juxtaposition of the words 'storm, tempest or flood', and concluded that 'flood' meant an ingress of water resulting from an unusual and sudden manifestation of a natural phenomenon, and not from seepage or trickling or dripping from a natural source of water.[4]

1 *Chandris v Isbrandtsen-Moller Co Inc* [1951] 1 KB 240, 245 (Devlin J). In *Melinda Holdings SA v Hellenic Mutual War Risks Association (Bermuda) Ltd, The Silva* [2011] 2 Lloyd's Rep 141, para 46(ii), Burton J applied the *eiusdem generis* principle in construing the third of three limbs of an exception clause.
2 This means literally 'it is known from its associates'.
3 [1977] 1 WLR 104, CA, 107 (Shaw LJ), 108 (Lawton LJ).

4 Similarly, in *Patrick v Royal London Mutual Insurance Society Ltd* [2006] EWCA Civ 421, [2006] 2 All ER (Comm) 344, Tuckey LJ said that in construing an exclusion of 'wilful, malicious or criminal acts' in a household and personal liability policy, 'malicious' and 'criminal' lent colour to 'wilful' so that in context a wilful act was an act which was blameworthy rather than merely deliberate or intentional (para 15); and in *Tektrol Ltd v International Insurance Co of Hanover Ltd* [2005] EWCA Civ 845, [2005] 2 Lloyd's Rep 701, Buxton LJ (at paras 11 and 12) construed 'malicious persons' in the phrase 'rioters strikers locked-out workers persons taking part in labour disturbances or civil commotion' as requiring malice targeted at the insured and therefore as excluding the author of a computer virus which had been released generally and happened by chance to damage the insured's computer system; and Sir Martin Nourse (at paras 28–29) construed 'loss' in the phrase 'other erasure loss distortion or corruption of information' as meaning loss by means of electronic interference and not loss by means of theft of computer hardware.

Special meanings of words

3.22 Where a word has a particular legal meaning, for example, a meaning derived from criminal law, it will usually be interpreted consistently with, or as including, that meaning.[1] However, the full technicalities of criminal law tend not to be applied by the civil courts in construing a policy of insurance.[2] Detailed analysis of the legal meaning of a concept such as 'robbery' or 'act of war' is inappropriate, and the proper approach is to interpret the wording in the context of the policy and through the eyes of an ordinary commercial man.[3]

Where words have acquired a particular meaning by usage in a trade or business which is distinct from their ordinary meaning, they must be construed according to the particular meaning.[4] Evidence is required to establish the meaning which is said to have become established by usage.[5]

1 *London and Lancashire Fire Insurance Co Ltd v Bolands Ltd* [1924] AC 836, HL, 843–844 (Viscount Finlay), 845 (Lord Atkinson), 847 (Lord Sumner) ('riot' construed in accordance with criminal law).
2 *Lake v Simmons* [1927] AC 487, HL, 503 (Viscount Haldane), 509–510 (Lord Sumner): criminal law of some assistance, but not determinative, when construing 'theft by customer'; *Nishina Trading Co Ltd v Chiyoda Fire and Marine Insurance Co Ltd* [1969] 2 QB 449, CA; in *Dobson v General Accident Fire and Life Assurance Corpn plc* [1990] 1 QB 274, CA, it was common ground between the parties that 'theft' in a householder's policy should be given its meaning under the Theft Act 1968, and the Court of Appeal proceeded on this basis: approved: *Deutsche Genossenschaftsbank v Burnhope* [1995] 1 WLR 1580, 1587, HL (Lord Steyn, dissenting) (bankers' policy).
3 *Canelhas Comercio Importacao e Exportacao Ltd v Wooldridge* [2004] EWCA Civ 984, [2004] 1 Lloyd's Rep IR 915, 918, para 11 (Mance LJ) ('robbery' in English law policy placed at Lloyd's through London brokers covering Brazilian insured against property and perils in Brazil); *IF P&C Insurance Ltd v Silversea Cruises Ltd* [2004] EWCA Civ 769, [2004] 1 Lloyd's Rep IR 696, paras 139–143 (Rix LJ) and 147–149 (Ward LJ) ('act of war' and 'armed conflict'). When seeking to discern the intention of the parties (see **PARA 3.16**), the court is entitled to assume some knowledge of the law on their part: *Horbury Building Systems Ltd v Hampden Insurance NV* [2004] EWCA Civ 418, [2007] Lloyd's Rep IR 237, para 27 (Keene LJ).
4 *Robertson v French* (1803) 4 East 130, 135–136 (Lord Ellenborough CJ); *Hart v Standard Marine Insurance Co Ltd* (1889) 22 QBD 499, CA, 500–501 (Lord Esher MR), 501–502 (Bowen LJ). The same principle applies where it can be shown that the parties intended to contract on the basis not of the ordinary meaning of a word or phrase, but on the basis of a special meaning: *Scragg v United Kingdom Temperance & General Provident Institution* [1976] 2 Lloyd's Rep 227 (Mocatta J) (special meaning in motor sport of phrase 'motor racing' known to both parties, and ordinary meaning rejected in favour of special meaning).
5 *Hart v Standard Marine Insurance Co Ltd* (1889) 22 QBD 499, CA, 501 (Lord Esher MR), 503 (Bowen and Fry LJJ); *NLA Group Ltd v Bowers* [1999] 1 Lloyd's Rep 109, 111 (Timothy Walker J); *Roar Marine Ltd v Bimeh Iran Insurance Co* [1998] 1 Lloyd's Rep 423, 429 (Mance J).

Level of premium as a guide to construction

3.23 Reference is sometimes made to the level of premium charged by underwriters as an indication of the scope of cover which they intended to offer.[1] Whether the level of premium is relevant has also been doubted.[2] On ordinary principles of construction,[3] the level of premium would only be relevant if both parties could reasonably be expected to know the usual premium charged for a particular type or level of cover, and evidence may therefore be required.[4] The fact that one party had a good negotiating position in the market is part of the 'factual matrix' which is potentially relevant to construction.[5]

1 See *Birrell v Dryer* (1884) 9 App Cas 345, HL, 349 (Earl of Selbourne LC); see also 351 (Lord Blackburn); *Youell v Bland Welch & Co Ltd* [1992] 2 Lloyd's Rep 127, CA, 133 (Staughton LJ), 139 (Beldam LJ); *Dornoch Ltd v Mauritius Union Assurance Co Ltd (No 2)* [2007] EWHC 155 (Comm), [2007] Lloyd's Rep IR 350, para 39 (David Steel J).
2 *Strong and Pearl v S Allison & Co Ltd* (1926) 25 Ll L Rep 504, 506–507 (Greer J); *Groupama Navigation et Transports v Catatumbo CA Seguros* [2000] 2 Lloyd's Rep 350, 355, CA (Mance LJ).
3 See **PARA 3.16**.
4 See eg *Flexsys America LP v XL Insurance Co Ltd* [2009] EWHC 1115 (Comm), [2010] Lloyd's Rep IR 132, in which Tomlinson J rejected a submission that it made no commercial sense for the insured to have a particular level of cover, saying the suggestion was meaningless without consideration of the cost of further cover and a balancing of that against the perception of the risk involved, an exercise which had not been attempted (at para 35).
5 *Absalom v TCRU Ltd* [2005] EWCA Civ 1586, [2006] 2 Lloyd's Rep 129, para 12 (Longmore LJ).

Standard wording supplemented by specific wording

3.24 Where a policy of insurance is made on the basis of standard wording, which has been supplemented by specific wording, the court will attempt to construe the policy as a whole.[1] In the older authorities, the distinction was between printed (ie standard) wording and written or typewritten (ie specific) wording. In the case of inconsistency between the two types of wording, the specific wording will prevail, on the basis that it is this wording which is more likely to reflect the true intentions of the parties.[2] If the standard wording is not reproduced but simply incorporated by reference, the court will be even more willing to give precedence to the specific wording.[3] Similarly, parts of the standard wording may simply be ignored, if they are clearly inapplicable to a contract of the type which the parties intended to enter into.[4] Where two clauses both form part of the standard terms of a policy, with the parties merely selecting which terms were going to apply, there is no special hierarchy conferring precedence on one clause rather than the other.[5]

1 *Joyce v Realm Marine Insurance Co* (1872) LR 7 QB 580, 583 (Blackburn J); *Farmers' Co-operative Ltd v National Benefit Assurance Co Ltd* (1922) 13 Ll L Rep 417 and 530, 532–533, CA (Atkin LJ); *General Accident Fire and Life Assurance Corpn Ltd v Midland Bank Ltd* [1940] 2 KB 388, 402, CA (Sir Wilfrid Greene MR); *Pratt v Aigaion Insurance Co SA, The Resolute* [2008] EWCA Civ 1314, [2009] 1 Lloyd's Rep 225, para 32 (Stanley Burnton J).
2 *Robertson v French* (1803) 4 East 130, 136 (Lord Ellenborough); *Joyce v Realm Marine Insurance Co* (1872) LR 7 QB 580, 583 (Blackburn J); *Glynn v Margetson & Co* [1893] AC 351, HL, 354–355 (Lord Herschell LC), 357–358 (Lord Halsbury); *Hydarnes Steamship Co v Indemnity Mutual Marine Assurance Co* [1895] 1 QB 500, 508, 509–510, CA (Rigby LJ); *Farmers' Co-operative Ltd v National Benefit Assurance Co Ltd* (1922) 13 Ll L Rep 417 and 530, 532–533, CA (Atkin LJ); *General Accident Fire and Life Assurance Corpn Ltd v Midland Bank Ltd* [1940] 2 KB 388, 402, CA (Sir Wilfrid Greene

MR); *Eagle Star Insurance Co Ltd v Cresswell* [2004] EWCA Civ 602, [2004] 1 Lloyd's Rep IR 537, paras 9 (Longmore LJ) and 68 (Chadwick LJ).

3 *Eurodale Manufacturing Ltd v Ecclesiastical Insurance Office plc* [2002] EWHC 697 (QB), para 19 (Andrew Smith J) (decision approved: [2003] EWCA Civ 203, [2003] Lloyd's Rep IR 444; point not considered on appeal).

4 *Dudgeon v Pembroke* (1877) 2 App Cas 284, 293, HL (Lord Penzance) (wording applicable to voyage policy ignored in construing time policy); *Hydarnes Steamship Co v Indemnity Mutual Marine Assurance Co* [1895] 1 QB 500, CA; *Western Assurance Co of Toronto v Poole* [1903] 1 KB 376, 389 (Bigham J); *South British Fire and Marine Insurance Co of New Zealand v Da Costa* [1906] 1 KB 456, 460 (Bigham J); *Home Insurance Co of New York v Victoria-Montreal Fire Insurance Co* [1907] AC 59, PC (reinsurance slip pasted onto printed form appropriate to insurance; conditions held inapplicable and disregarded); *Australian Widows' Fund Life Assurance Society Ltd v National Mutual Life Association of Australasia Ltd* [1914] AC 634, PC (clause incorporated by reference contradicted express terms of policy, and disregarded); *Yorkshire Insurance Co Ltd v Campbell* [1917] AC 218, 224, 225, PC (Lord Sumner).

5 *Milton Furniture Ltd v Brit Insurance Ltd* [2015] EWCA Civ 671, [2016] Lloyd's Rep IR 192, para 24 (Gloster LJ).

Significance of typeface and format

3.25   The use of different typefaces (fonts) in different parts of a document, and other aspects of its format such as lines separating sections of text, have no legal meaning and are of no significance in the construction of the document.[1] Similarly, there is no reason to disregard clauses printed in very small print unless the type is so small as to be illegible.[2]

1 *Yorkshire Insurance Co Ltd v Campbell* [1917] AC 218, 222, PC.
2 *D & J Koskas v Standard Marine Insurance Co Ltd* (1927) 27 Ll L Rep 59, CA, 61 (Bankes LJ), 62 (Scrutton LJ).

Conflicting provisions

3.26   As far as possible, the courts will construe apparently conflicting provisions in such a way as to give effect to both or all of them.[1] Where a policy contains a special clause and clauses of general application, such as claims conditions applying to a policy as a whole and a special clause applying only to one section of cover, the special clause takes precedence.[2] It has been suggested that where the terms of two documents conflict, the later document is to be regarded as more expressive of the final intention of the parties, and conflicting terms in the earlier document are disregarded.[3] Where a later contract is intended to be incorporated into an earlier contract, it is, prima facie at least, the later contract which may have to give way to the first in the event of inconsistency.[4]

1 See *Gale v Motor Union Insurance Co* [1928] 1 KB 359, 363–364 (Roche J) (later provision 'qualifies and explains' earlier provision); *HIH Casualty and General Insurance Ltd v New Hampshire Insurance Co* [2001] EWCA Civ 735, [2001] 2 Lloyd's Rep 161, para 83 (Rix LJ).
2 *National Farmers Union Mutual Insurance Society Ltd v HSBC Insurance (UK) Ltd* [2010] EWHC 773 (Comm), [2011] Lloyd's Rep IR 86, para 26 (Gavin Kealey QC, sitting as a Deputy High Court Judge).
3 *Kaufmann v British Surety Insurance Co Ltd* (1929) 33 Ll L Rep 315, 318 (Roche J) (schedule to policy later in time than proposal form, so terms of schedule take precedence over terms of proposal form), purporting to apply *Williams Bros v Agius Ltd* [1914] AC 510, 527, HL (Lord Atkinson) (where subject matter same and terms inconsistent, later contract supersedes or impliedly rescinds earlier contract);

HIH Casualty and General Insurance Ltd v New Hampshire Insurance Co [2001] EWCA Civ 735, [2001] 2 Lloyd's Rep 161, para 84 (Rix LJ).
4 *HIH Casualty and General Insurance Ltd v New Hampshire Insurance Co* [2001] EWCA Civ 735, [2001] 2 Lloyd's Rep 161, para 84 (Rix LJ).

Implied terms

3.27   Where a policy does not make provision by express terms for an eventuality which has arisen, the court will consider whether any term is to be implied into the policy to cover the situation. Before doing so, the court will construe the express terms of the policy, in the light of any admissible extrinsic evidence: only once the meaning of the relevant express terms has been established can the court proceed to determine whether a term should be implied.[1] A term will not be implied if it is inconsistent with an express term.[2] A term will be implied only if it is necessary for the business efficacy of the contract,[3] if it is so obvious that it goes without saying,[4] if it is implied by reason of trade usage or custom,[5] or if it is implied by law.[6]

The question whether a term is to be implied is to be judged at the date the contract is made.[7] If one approaches the question of implication of a term by reference to what the parties would have agreed, one is not strictly concerned with the hypothetical answer of the actual parties, but with that of notional reasonable people in the position of the parties at the time at which they were contracting.[8] As necessity is judged by reference to business efficacy, it may be that a more helpful way of putting this requirement is that a term can only be implied if, without the term, the contract would lack commercial or practical coherence.[9] Any term which it is sought to imply must be reasonable, although reasonableness is insufficient of itself to justify the implication of a term:[10] 'The touchstone is always *necessity* and not merely *reasonableness*'.[11]

Where insurers or reinsurers are given a contractual decision-making power, a term may be implied that the decision not be 'arbitrary, capricious or perverse' and that the decision-making process be lawful and rational.[12]

1 *Marks and Spencer plc v BNP Paribas Securities Service Trust Company (Jersey) Ltd* [2015] UKSC 72, para 28 (Lord Neuberger), disapproving Lord Hoffmann's remarks to this effect in *Attorney General of Belize v Belize Telecom Ltd* [2009] UKPC 10, [2009] 1 WLR 1988, paras 17–27.
2 *Re L Sutro & Co* [1917] 2 KB 348, CA, 357 (Swinfen Eady LJ), 363 (Scrutton LJ), 366 (Bray J); *Les Affréteurs Réunis SA v Leopold Walford (London) Ltd* [1919] AC 801, HL; *Euro-Diam Ltd v Bathurst* [1990] 1 QB 1, 41, CA (Kerr LJ); *Anders & Kern UK Ltd v CGU Insurance plc* [2007] EWCA Civ 1481, [2008] Lloyd's Rep IR 460, para 19 (Toulson LJ); *Marks and Spencer plc v BNP Paribas Securities Service Trust Company (Jersey) Ltd* [2015] UKSC 72, paras 28–31 (Lord Neuberger).
3 *The Moorcock* (1889) 14 PD 64, CA; see *Yorkshire Insurance Co Ltd v Nisbet Shipping Co Ltd* [1962] 2 QB 330, 340 (Diplock J); *Euro-Diam Ltd v Bathurst* [1990] 1 QB 1, 40–41, CA (Kerr LJ); *Anders & Kern UK Ltd v CGU Insurance plc* [2007] EWCA Civ 1481, [2008] Lloyd's Rep IR 460, para 19 (Toulson LJ); *Marks and Spencer plc v BNP Paribas Securities Service Trust Company (Jersey) Ltd* [2015] UKSC 72, paras 16–21 (Lord Neuberger).
4 *Shirlaw v Southern Foundries (1926) Ltd* [1939] 2 KB 206, 227, CA (MacKinnon LJ) (this is the 'officious bystander' test); *Marks and Spencer plc v BNP Paribas Securities Service Trust Company (Jersey) Ltd* [2015] UKSC 72, paras 16 and 21 (Lord Neuberger). The term must be both precise and obvious, and the more complicated the officious bystander's notional question, the less obvious the implication becomes: *Ashmore v Corpn of Lloyd's (No 2)* [1992] 2 Lloyd's Rep 620, 628 (Gatehouse J).
5 *Re L Sutro & Co* [1917] 2 KB 348, CA; *Les Affréteurs Réunis SA v Leopold Walford (London) Ltd* [1919] AC 801, HL. A term will be implied by reason of trade usage or custom only if it is notorious, certain and reasonable: *General Reinsurance Corpn v Fenna Patria* [1983] QB 856, 872, CA (Kerr LJ). It must also be regarded as binding by the commercial community, rather than as a matter of

grace or goodwill: *General Reinsurance Corpn v Fenna Patria* [1983] QB 856, CA, 871–872 (Kerr LJ), 874–875 (Slade LJ). The usage must be proved by evidence: *Les Affréteurs Réunis SA v Leopold Walford (London) Ltd* [1919] AC 801, HL; *General Reinsurance Corpn v Fenna Patria* [1983] QB 856, 873, CA (Kerr LJ). A failure to establish a trade practice in one set of proceedings does not prejudice other parties in subsequent proceedings: *Baker v Black Sea & Baltic General Insurance Co Ltd* [1998] 1 WLR 974, 984, HL (Lord Lloyd).

 6 *Liverpool City Council v Irwin* [1977] AC 239, HL; *Ashmore v Corporation of Lloyd's (No 2)* [1992] 2 Lloyd's Rep 620, 629–631 (Gatehouse J).

 7 *Marks and Spencer plc v BNP Paribas Securities Service Trust Company (Jersey) Ltd* [2015] UKSC 72, para 23 (Lord Neuberger).

 8 *Marks and Spencer plc v BNP Paribas Securities Service Trust Company (Jersey) Ltd* [2015] UKSC 72, para 21 (Lord Neuberger).

 9 *Marks and Spencer plc v BNP Paribas Securities Service Trust Company (Jersey) Ltd* [2015] UKSC 72, para 21 (Lord Neuberger).

10 *Comptoir Commercial Anversois v Power, Son and Co* [1920] 1 KB 868, 899–900, CA (Scrutton LJ); *Liverpool City Council v Irwin* [1977] AC 239, HL, 262 (Lord Salmon), 266 (Lord Edmund-Davies).

11 *Liverpool City Council v Irwin* [1977] AC 239, 266, HL (Lord Edmund-Davies) (emphasis as original); *Marks and Spencer plc v BNP Paribas Securities Service Trust Company (Jersey) Ltd* [2015] UKSC 72, para 21 (Lord Neuberger). It is questionable whether reasonableness and equitableness will usually, if ever, add anything: if a term satisfies other requirements, it is hard to think that it would not be reasonable and equitable: *Marks and Spencer plc v BNP Paribas Securities Service Trust Company (Jersey) Ltd* [2015] UKSC 72, para 21 (Lord Neuberger).

12 See further PARAS **5.4**, **8.9** and **14.4**.

RECTIFICATION

3.28   Rectification is technically a remedy. It is used to correct the written terms of contracts and other instruments, including policies of insurance. It is commonly granted where, as a result of a mistake in recording the terms of an agreement, a written document does not accurately reflect what was agreed orally by the parties or, where there is no prior oral agreement, the written document does not reflect the parties' common intention as to the content of the formal agreement. This is known as rectification on grounds of common or mutual mistake. In certain circumstances, rectification may also be granted to correct a unilateral mistake as to the terms of an agreement.

Common or mutual mistake

3.29   The notion that for rectification to be granted a prior agreement (albeit not necessarily legally enforceable)[1] was required[2] was finally laid to rest by the Court of Appeal in *Joscelyne v Nissen*.[3] What is required is a 'continuing common intention'[4] with regard to a particular provision or aspect of the agreement.[5] There must also be an 'outward expression of accord':[6] subjective intention alone, even if both parties happen to have the same intention, is not sufficient.[7] It is in the nature of the principles of rectification that, even where one contract is superseded by another contract, the later contract may still be rectified.[8]

The conditions which must be satisfied if rectification is to be granted on the grounds of common or mutual mistake may be summarised as follows:

'First, there must be a common intention in regard to the particular provisions of the agreement in question, together with some outward expression of accord.

Secondly, this common intention must continue up to the time of execution of the instrument. Thirdly, there must be clear evidence that the instrument as executed does not accurately represent the true agreement of the parties at the time of its execution. Fourthly, it must be shown that the instrument, if rectified as claimed, would accurately represent the true agreement of the parties at that time.'[9]

It is in the nature of the principles of rectification that, even where one contract is superseded by another contract, the later contract may still be rectified.[10]

It is not a bar to rectification that the mistake was made by the party seeking the remedy.[11] The expression 'mutual mistake' does not mean that both parties must be involved in the inaccurate recording of the terms of the agreement:[12]

'[Counsel for insurers] objects to the ordinary expression in reference to rectification of a document, and he says it is not a correct view to suggest that it is a mutual mistake that has to be established. I view that contention with considerable sympathy. It seems to me much more accurate to say that if you prove the parties have come to a definite parol agreement, and you then afterwards find in the document which was intended to carry out that definite agreement something other than that definite agreement has been inserted, then it is right to rectify that document in order that it may carry out the real agreement between the parties.'

It is not enough to show that the true agreement between the parties is not recorded in the policy or other document which it is sought to rectify: rectification will not be ordered unless there is proof to the required standard[13] of the terms of the agreement which was in fact reached.[14] It is not necessary that the precise form of words to be used should have been agreed.[15] It is in principle possible to have a prior consensus as a result of a discussion in general terms as to the extent of the insurance cover to be provided, rather than by specific discussion of the terms of particular clauses.[16]

Rectification will not be granted where the parties would have made provision in their agreement had they known certain facts, but did not in fact do so, as that would mean the court going further than correcting the written expression of terms agreed between the parties, and rewriting the agreement itself.[17]

1 See *United States of America v Motor Trucks Ltd* [1924] AC 196, PC.
2 See *Mackenzie v Coulson* (1869) LR 8 Eq 368, 375 (Sir W M James V-C); *United States of America v Motor Trucks Ltd* [1924] AC 196, 200–201, PC (Lord Birkenhead); *Frederick E Rose (London) Ltd v William H Pim Junior & Co Ltd* [1953] 2 QB 450, CA, 457 (Singleton LJ) and 461–462 (Denning LJ).
3 [1970] 2 QB 86. See also *Crane v Hegeman-Harris Co Inc* [1971] 1 WLR 1390 (Note) (Simonds J) (the report of Simonds J's judgment at [1939] 1 All ER 662 is incomplete and should not be relied on: *Prenn v Simmonds* [1971] 1 WLR 1381, 1389, HL (Lord Wilberforce)); affirmed: [1939] 4 All ER 68, CA; *Shipley v Bradford Corpn* [1936] Ch 375, 396–397 (Clauson J).
4 *Crane v Hegeman-Harris Co Inc* [1971] 1 WLR 1390 (Note), 1391 (Simonds J); affirmed: [1939] 4 All ER 68, CA; *Earl v Hector Whaling Ltd* [1961] 1 Lloyd's Rep 459, CA; *Kiriacoulis Lines SA v Compagnie d'Assurances Maritime Aériennes et Terrestres (The Demetra K)* [2002] EWCA Civ 1070, [2002] 2 Lloyd's Rep 581, 585, para 23 (Lord Phillips MR). The intention must continue until the moment the written agreement is executed: *Crane v Hegeman-Harris Co Inc* [1971] 1 WLR 1390 (Note), 1391 (Simonds J); affirmed: [1939] 4 All ER 68, CA; *Joscelyne v Nissen* [1970] 2 QB 86, CA.
5 *Earl v Hector Whaling Ltd* [1961] 1 Lloyd's Rep 459, 470, CA (Harman LJ).

6 *Joscelyne v Nissen* [1970] 2 QB 86, 98, CA (Russell LJ); *Kiriacoulis Lines SA v Compagnie d'Assurances Maritime Aériennes et Terrestres (The Demetra K)* [2002] EWCA Civ 1070, [2002] 2 Lloyd's Rep 581, para 22 (Lord Phillips MR); *Chartbrook Ltd v Persimmon Homes Ltd* [2009] UKHL 38, [2009] 1 AC 1101, paras 60 (Lord Hoffmann) and 100 (Baroness Hale).
7 *Frederick E Rose (London) Ltd v William H Pim Junior & Co Ltd* [1953] 2 QB 450, CA; *Earl v Hector Whaling Ltd* [1961] 1 Lloyd's Rep 459, CA; *Joscelyne v Nissen* [1970] 2 QB 86, CA; *Kiriacoulis Lines SA v Compagnie d'Assurances Maritime Aériennes et Terrestres (The Demetra K)* [2002] EWCA Civ 1070, [2002] 2 Lloyd's Rep 581, 590, para 55 (Lord Phillips MR); applied: *IF P&C Insurance Ltd v Silversea Cruises Ltd* [2004] EWCA Civ 769, [2004] 1 Lloyd's Rep IR 696, para 89 (Rix LJ).
8 *Dunlop Haywards (DHL) Ltd v Erinaceous Insurance Services Ltd* [2009] EWCA Civ 354, [2009] Lloyd's Rep IR 464.
9 *AGIP SpA v Navigazione Alta Italia SpA, The Nai Genova* [1984] 1 Lloyd's Rep 353, 359, CA (Slade LJ); applied: *Encia Remediations Ltd v Canopius Managing Agents Ltd* [2007] EWHC 916 (Comm), [2008] Lloyd's Rep IR 79, para 196 (Cresswell J); see also *Chartbrook Ltd v Persimmon Homes Ltd* [2009] UKHL 38, [2009] 1 AC 1101, para 48 (Lord Hoffmann).
10 *Dunlop Haywards (DHL) Ltd v Erinaceous Insurance Services Ltd* [2009] EWCA Civ 354, [2009] Lloyd's Rep IR 464, para 70 (Rix LJ).
11 *Fowler v Scottish Equitable Life Insurance Society* (1858) 28 LJ Ch 225, 229 (Stuart V-C); *Alliance Aeroplane Co Ltd v Union Insurance Society of Canton Ltd* (1920) 5 Ll L Rep 406, 407 (Bray J), in which insurers succeeded in having a policy rectified by reference to the slip where a mistake was made by their clerk in copying the slip into their books in preparation for the drawing up of the policy.
12 *A Gagnière & Co Ltd v Eastern Co of Warehouses Insurance and Transport of Goods with Advances Ltd* (1921) 8 Ll L Rep 365, 366, CA (Bankes LJ).
13 See **PARA 3.32**.
14 *A Gagnière & Co Ltd v Eastern Co of Warehouses Insurance and Transport of Goods with Advances Ltd* (1921) 8 Ll L Rep 365; *Crane v Hegeman-Harris Co Inc* [1971] WLR 1390 (Note), 1391 (Simonds J); affirmed: [1939] 4 All ER 68, CA; *Frederick E Rose (London) Ltd v William H Pim Junior & Co Ltd* [1953] 2 QB 450, 457, CA (Singleton LJ).
15 *Crane v Hegeman-Harris Co Inc* [1971] 1 WLR 1390 (Note), 1399 (Simonds J); affirmed: [1939] 4 All ER 68, CA.
16 *Kiriacoulis Lines SA v Compagnie d'Assurances Maritime Aériennes et Terrestres (The Demetra K)* [2002] EWCA Civ 1070, [2002] 2 Lloyd's Rep 581, 586, para 32 (Lord Phillips MR); applied: *Equity Syndicate Management Ltd v GlaxoSmithKline plc* [2015] EWHC 2163 (Comm), [2016] Lloyd's Rep IR 155, para 27 (Males J).
17 *Pasquali & Co v Traders' & General Insurance Association* (1921) 9 Ll L Rep 514, 515 (Rowlatt J); *American Airlines Inc v Hope* [1974] 2 Lloyd's Rep 301, 307, HL (Lord Diplock); see also *Etablissements Levy v Adderley Navigation Co Panama SA, The Olympic Pride* [1980] 2 Lloyd's Rep 67, 72–73 (Mustill J); and the well-known remark of Sir W M James V-C in *Mackenzie v Coulson* (1869) LR 8 Eq 368, 375: 'Courts of Equity do not rectify contracts; they may and do rectify instruments purporting to have been made in pursuance of the terms of contracts.' (Insofar as this suggests that a prior concluded agreement is necessary for rectification, it no longer represents the law.)

Unilateral mistake

3.30 Rectification may be ordered, in the absence of a prior oral agreement or continuing common intention, where one party believes a particular term to be included in the written instrument and the other party executes the instrument with an omission or a variation in that term in circumstances where this will benefit him, and in the knowledge that the first party believes the term to be included.[1] Alternatively, a term may be included (rather than omitted) by mistake.[2] This is known as a unilateral mistake. Actual knowledge is usually required,[3] although there may be rare cases where something less than actual knowledge will suffice.[4] The conduct of the defendant must be such as to make it inequitable that he should be allowed to object to the rectification of the document. Although some cases suggest that sharp practice is required,[5] it appears that something less than sharp practice may suffice.[6]

1 *A Roberts & Co Ltd v Leicestershire County Council* [1961] Ch 555, 570 (Pennycuick J); *Thomas Bates & Son Ltd v Wyndham's (Lingerie) Ltd* [1981] 1 WLR 505, 515–516, CA (Buckley LJ).
2 *Thomas Bates & Son Ltd v Wyndham's (Lingerie) Ltd* [1981] 1 WLR 505, 516, CA (Buckley LJ).
3 *AGIP SpA v Navigazione Alta Italia SpA, The Nai Genova and Nai Superba* [1984] 1 Lloyd's Rep 353, 361–362, CA (Slade LJ).
4 *Commission for the New Towns v Cooper (GB) Ltd* [1995] 2 All ER 929, 946, CA:

> '... were it necessary to do so in this case, I would hold that where A intends B to be mistaken as to the construction of the agreement, so conducts himself that he diverts B's attention from discovering the mistake by making false and misleading statements, and B in fact makes the very mistake that A intends, then notwithstanding that A does not actually know, but merely suspects that B is mistaken, and it cannot be shown that the mistake was induced by any misrepresentation, rectification may be granted' (Stuart-Smith LJ).

5 *Riverlate Properties Ltd v Paul* [1975] Ch 133, 140, CA (Russell LJ); *Etablissements Levy v Adderley Navigation Co Panama SA, The Olympic Pride* [1980] 2 Lloyd's Rep 67, 72 (Mustill J).
6 *A Roberts & Co Ltd v Leicestershire County Council* [1961] Ch 555, 570 (Pennycuick J); *Thomas Bates & Son Ltd v Wyndham's (Lingerie) Ltd* [1981] 1 WLR 505, CA.

Type of evidence required for rectification

3.31   There is no limit on the type of evidence which may be relied upon in support of a claim for rectification of a policy document. It is common for reference to be made to a document preceding the policy, such as a proposal form[1] or an illustration provided with it,[2] a slip,[3] a cover note[4] or other relevant document.[5] Rectification of a Lloyd's slip may be sought on the basis of a prior consensus, but not on the basis that a binding contract comes into existence at any stage before the slip is initialled, as that would be contrary to market belief and practice.[6] In a case in which the prior consensus was based wholly or in part on oral exchanges or conduct, the evidence of a party as to what terms he understood to have been agreed may be significant.[7] Evidence of subsequent conduct may also have some evidential value.[8] This is not to say that subsequent conduct may create a common intention where none existed at the time when the contract was concluded, but that evidence of what the parties said and did subsequently may cast light on what they intended at the time.[9] Other types of evidence may be relied upon: for example, reference might be made to the premium charged by underwriters, or the loss ratios provided on renewal, as an indication of the intended scope of cover.[10]

1 *Griffiths v Fleming* [1909] 1 KB 805, 817–818, CA (Farwell LJ); *Stanton & Stanton Ltd v Starr* (1920) Ll L Rep 259; *Sun Life Assurance Co of Canada v Jervis* [1943] 2 All ER 425, CA.
2 *Sun Life Assurance Co of Canada v Jervis* [1943] 2 All ER 425, CA.
3 *Rogers v Whittaker* [1917] 1 KB 942, 945 (Sankey J): the slip contained the words 'conditions as before', and the evidence on behalf of underwriters was that this was intended to mean that the conditions were to be the same as in the previous year's policy, to which reference was accordingly made to ascertain the conditions; *Alliance Aeroplane Co Ltd v Union Insurance Society of Canton Ltd* (1920) 5 Ll L Rep 406; *Eagle, Star & British Dominions Insurance Co Ltd v A V Reiner* (1927) 27 Ll L Rep 173. Rectification may be ordered whether the slip is a binding contract of insurance, as is the case with a Lloyd's slip (see *Youell v Bland Welch & Co Ltd* [1992] 2 Lloyd's Rep 127, 141, CA (Beldam LJ)), or simply a memorandum of the agreement to be concluded later by signing the policy (see *Alliance Aeroplane Co Ltd v Union Insurance Society of Canton Ltd* (1920) 5 Ll L Rep 406).
4 *A Gagnière & Co Ltd v Eastern Co of Warehouses Insurance and Transport of Goods with Advances Ltd* (1921) 8 Ll L Rep 365, 367 (Bankes LJ).
5 For example, a prospectus published by the insurer: *British Equitable Assurance Co Ltd v Baily* [1906] AC 35, 41, HL (Lord Lindley).

6 See *Pindos Shipping Corpn v Raven, The Mata Hari* [1983] 2 Lloyd's Rep 449, 453 (Bingham J) (marine insurance).
7 *Chartbrook Ltd v Persimmon Homes Ltd* [2009] UKHL 38, [2009] 1 AC 1101, paras 64–65 (Lord Hoffmann).
8 *Chartbrook Ltd v Persimmon Homes Ltd* [2009] UKHL 38, [2009] 1 AC 1101, para 65 (Lord Hoffmann).
9 *Equity Syndicate Management Ltd v GlaxoSmithKline plc* [2015] EWHC 2163 (Comm), [2016] Lloyd's Rep IR 155, para 26 (Males J).
10 *Equity Syndicate Management Ltd v GlaxoSmithKline plc* [2015] EWHC 2163 (Comm), [2016] Lloyd's Rep IR 155, paras 36–37, 42 and 45 (Males J) (premium charged and paid as fixed sum per vehicle within scheme and loss ratios based on claims on those vehicles).

Standard of proof

3.32   The courts have used various expressions to describe the standard of proof required for rectification, including 'clear evidence',[1] proof 'beyond doubt',[2] 'convincing proof',[3] 'proof beyond all reasonable doubt',[4] 'convincing evidence',[5] 'very clear and convincing evidence',[6] 'a high degree of conviction',[7] and 'the Court must be "sure" of the mistake'.[8] Proof on a bare balance of probabilities is therefore unlikely to be sufficient.[9] Whichever expression is used, it is clear that a party seeking to persuade a court to grant rectification of a written agreement takes on a heavy burden:[10]

> 'It is obvious that when parties put their hands to an agreement, it will take convincing evidence to show that the agreement does not contain their intended bargain. For in such a case there must be enough weight in the evidence to outweigh the inherent possibility that they meant what they wrote. It is a question of fact and degree what evidence is needed to overcome that inherent probability, and to establish that, contrary to it, the parties did not mean what they wrote. Such evidence would normally have to be very strong. It cannot be regarded as sufficient merely because it would, on a balance of probabilities, establish an oral agreement. It must be strong enough to overcome the fact that the parties signed a different agreement.'

The standard of proof required before the court will rectify a written instrument will nevertheless vary depending upon the particular facts of the case before it.[11] The standard is the same for unilateral mistake as for mutual mistake.[12]

1 *A Gagnière & Co Ltd v Eastern Co of Warehouses Insurance and Transport of Goods with Advances Ltd* (1921) 8 Ll L Rep 365, 367, CA (Bankes LJ).
2 *A Gagnière & Co Ltd v Eastern Co of Warehouses Insurance and Transport of Goods with Advances Ltd* (1921) 8 Ll L Rep 365, 366–367, CA (Bankes LJ).
3 *Crane v Hegeman-Harris Co Inc* [1971] 1 WLR 1390 (Note), 1391 (Simonds J); affirmed: [1939] 4 All ER 68, CA; *Joscelyne v Nissen* [1970] 2 QB 86, CA.
4 *Crane v Hegeman-Harris Co Inc* [1971] WLR 1390 (Note), 1391 (Simonds J); affirmed: [1939] 4 All ER 68, CA; *A Roberts & Co Ltd v Leicestershire County Council* [1961] Ch 555, 570–571 (Pennycuick J). The Court of Appeal in *Joscelyne v Nissen* [1970] 2 QB 86, 98 expressly preferred 'convincing proof' to 'beyond all reasonable doubt', which it regarded as having been imported from the criminal law, and to 'irrefragable', which it regarded as old-fashioned.
5 *Kiriacoulis Lines SA v Compagnie d'Assurances Maritime Aériennes et Terrestres (The Demetra K)* [2002] EWCA Civ 1070, [2002] 2 Lloyd's Rep 581, 585, para 24 (Lord Phillips MR).
6 *Earl v Hector Whaling Ltd* [1961] 1 Lloyd's Rep 459, 468–469, CA (Holroyd Pearce LJ).

7 *Etablissements Levy v Adderley Navigation Co Panama SA, The Olympic Pride* [1980] 2 Lloyd's Rep 67, 73 (Mustill J).

8 *Etablissements Levy v Adderley Navigation Co Panama SA, The Olympic Pride* [1980] 2 Lloyd's Rep 67, 73 (Mustill J).

9 See *Pindos Shipping Corpn v Raven, The Mata Hari* [1983] 2 Lloyd's Rep 449, 452 (Bingham J):

> 'Were it essential to my decision, I should be seriously concerned as to whether this marginal preference for the owners' version of the facts was sufficient to discharge the heavy onus that lies on a claimant for rectification seeking to prove a continuing common intention of the parties.'

10 *Earl v Hector Whaling Ltd* [1961] 1 Lloyd's Rep 459, 468, CA (Holroyd Pearce LJ). See also *Etablissements Levy v Adderley Navigation Co Panama SA, The Olympic Pride* [1980] 2 Lloyd's Rep 67:

> 'The Court requires the mistake to be proved with a high degree of conviction before granting relief. There are sound policy reasons for this. The Court is reluctant to allow a party of full capacity who has signed a document with opportunity of inspection, to say afterwards that it is not what he meant. Otherwise, certainty and ready enforceability would be hindered by constant attempts to cloud the issue by reference to pre-contractual negotiations. These considerations apply with particular force in the field of commerce, where certainty is so important' (per Mustill J at 73);

> and see *Thomas Bates & Son Ltd v Wyndham's (Lingerie) Ltd* [1981] 1 WLR 505, 521, CA (Brightman LJ).

11 See *Earl v Hector Whaling Ltd* [1961] 1 Lloyd's Rep 459, 470, CA: 'It is perfectly plain on the facts of this case that the learned Judge was right in demanding an unusually high degree of proof on the counterclaim for rectification' (Davies LJ); see also *Thomas Bates & Son Ltd v Wyndham's (Lingerie) Ltd* [1981] 1 WLR 505, 514, CA (Buckley LJ); and *Joscelyne v Nissen* [1970] 2 QB 86, 98, CA: 'the requisite accord and continuance of accord of intention may be the more difficult to establish if a complete antecedent concluded contract be not shown' (Russell LJ).

12 *Thomas Bates & Son Ltd v Wyndham's (Lingerie) Ltd* [1981] 1 WLR 505, 521, CA (Brightman LJ).

Relevance of broker's intention

3.33 Where the insured employs a broker and authorises him to negotiate cover on his behalf with insurers, it is suggested that it is the intentions of the broker which are relevant, rather than (or, depending on the facts, in addition to) those of the insured. However, this analysis is contrary to *Stanton & Stanton Ltd v Starr*,[1] a decision of Bailhache J. The insured's broker agreed with a Lloyd's broker to exclude cover for the insured's own premises, contrary to the proposal form completed by the insured and without their knowledge. The slip initialled by underwriters contained the exclusion, but when the policy was drawn up it omitted the exclusion. Underwriters signed the policy without comparing it to the slip. In the course of the argument,[2] Bailhache J is recorded as having said that there was no mutual mistake if one disregarded the intermediaries, and refused rectification on the grounds that there was no mutual mistake, as the insured intended to contract on the basis of the cover set out in the policy document. It is suggested that this case was wrongly decided. The first broker had authority to bind the insured, and agreed with the Lloyd's broker that cover for the insured's own premises could be excluded; there was a mutual mistake when the policy was drawn up and included such cover, and rectification should have been ordered by reference to the slip. The insured's remedy in such circumstances would then have been against the broker. Although there seems to be no other authority directly in point, this analysis is consistent with *Fowler v Scottish Equitable Life Insurance Society*,[3] in which the ground on which rectification was refused was that the insurer's agent, with whom the terms were agreed, did not have authority to bind the insurer.

1 (1920) 3 Ll L Rep 259.
2 At 261.
3 (1858) 28 LJ Ch 225.

Timing

3.34 Rectification may be sought at any stage until all sums due under a policy have been paid by insurers.[1] It is common for rectification to be sought after a loss has been suffered,[2] as it is often only at that stage that the parties apply their minds to the wording of the policy and its effects. In general terms, however, the longer a party waits before seeking rectification, the harder it will be to persuade the court to grant the remedy.

1 Rectification will not be granted of an agreement which has been performed: *Caird v Moss* (1886) 33 Ch D 22, CA; *Crane v Hegeman-Harris Co Inc* [1971] 1 WLR 1390 (Note), 1400 (Simonds J); affirmed: [1939] 4 All ER 68, CA.
2 See *Eagle, Star & British Dominions Insurance Co Ltd v A V Reiner* (1927) 27 Ll L Rep 173: a loss was suffered, and the reinsurer successfully sought rectification of the policy by way of a defence to the claim.

Construction and rectification

3.35 Rectification is often sought in the alternative where the primary claim is for a declaration as to the true construction of a policy. This may have the effect of allowing evidence to be adduced at trial in relation to rectification which would not have been admissible even as part of the 'factual matrix' had the only subject matter of the action been the construction of the policy.[1]

1 See *Prenn v Simmonds* [1971] 1 WLR 1381, 1383, HL (Lord Wilberforce). This complicates the judge's task because, after hearing all the evidence, he has to put that part of the evidence which is admissible only in relation to rectification out of his mind in order to consider the construction issue; but this is usually the only convenient course: see the comments of Clauson J in *Shipley UDC v Bradford Corpn* [1936] Ch 375 (at 390).

Chapter 4

Causation of loss

GENERAL PRINCIPLES OF CAUSATION

4.1   In every policy of insurance, the insurer agrees to indemnify the insured against identified perils.[1] The degree of connection which is required between the insured peril and the loss for the insurer to be liable to the insured may be agreed expressly between the parties.[2] In the absence of such agreement, the court will construe the policy on the basis that the parties intended that the doctrine of proximate cause should apply.[3] This means that only losses proximately (and not remotely) caused by an insured peril are recoverable.[4]

Questions of causation are questions of mixed fact and law.[5]

1 See further **PARA 5.2**.
2 See, eg, the wordings considered at **PARAS 4.5–4.8**.
3 See *Reischer v Borwick* [1894] 2 QB 548, 550, CA (Lindley LJ); *Coxe v Employers' Liability Assurance Corpn Ltd* [1916] 2 KB 629; *Becker, Gray & Co v London Assurance Corpn* [1918] AC 101, 112, HL (Lord Sumner); *Lloyds TSB General Insurance Holdings v Lloyds Bank Group Insurance Co Ltd* [2001] EWCA Civ 1643, [2002] Lloyd's Rep IR 113, para 42 (Potter LJ); point not considered on appeal: [2003] UKHL 48, [2003] Lloyd's Rep IR 623. In marine insurance, the doctrine is set out in s 55 of the Marine Insurance Act 1906.
4 See *Marsden v City and County Assurance Co* (1865) LR 1 CP 232; *Dudgeon v Pembroke* (1877) 2 App Cas 284, HL.
5 *Shell International Petroleum Co Ltd v Gibbs* [1983] 1 Lloyd's Rep 342, 350, HL; see also *Brown v GIO Insurance Ltd* [1998] Lloyd's Rep IR 201, 208, CA (Chadwick LJ). In *Global Process Systems Inc v Syarikat Takaful Malaysia Berhad, The Cendor Mopu* [2011] UKSC 5, [2011] 1 Lloyd's Rep 560, Lord Saville said (at para 46) that the identification of the proximate cause of the loss is a question of fact, to be decided on common sense principles. See further **PARA 4.2**.

IDENTIFYING THE PROXIMATE CAUSE IN A SEQUENCE OF EVENTS

4.2   Although it is often the last event to occur which is the proximate cause of loss, this is not always the case. The notion that it was the last event which was always the proximate cause was laid to rest by the House of Lords in *Leyland Shipping Co Ltd v Norwich Union Fire Insurance Society Ltd*.[1] In that decision, and since, the courts have used a variety of expressions to describe what it is the court is looking for when trying to identify the proximate cause. These include: immediate cause;[2] direct cause;[3] *causa causans*;[4] efficient cause;[5] dominant (or predominant) cause;[6] effective cause;[7] and real cause.[8] Where, in particular cases, the facts are similar to those of previous cases, the courts are reluctant to introduce uncertainty by departing from those decisions.[9] Otherwise, the previous cases offer little guidance as to which of a succession of causes is the proximate cause. No assistance is gained in difficult cases from the use of the 'but for' test, which simply identifies those events with causative potency, including both proximate and remote causes.[10] In these circumstances, the identification of the proximate cause by the court is largely a matter of impression, or 'common sense'.[11] There is high authority for the proposition that the real or dominant cause is to be ascertained by applying the common sense of a business or (in the context of marine insurance) seafaring man or 'hypothetical oracle'.[12]

The issue is sometimes said to be whether the last event in time is an intervening cause, which therefore qualifies as the proximate cause, or whether the last event is simply a natural consequence of an earlier event, which is the true proximate cause of the loss.[13] This is simply another way of asking whether it is the last event, or some earlier event, which is the effective or dominant cause. In *Leyland Shipping Co Ltd v Norwich Union Fire Insurance Society Ltd*,[14] a ship was torpedoed by a submarine. She reached harbour with the aid of tugs, but became grounded and sank two days later when her back broke due to the ebb and flow of the tide. The House of Lords held that the proximate cause of the loss of the ship was the torpedoing (excepted peril) and that the grounding, which was a peril of the sea (insured peril), was not an intervening cause, so that underwriters were not liable. Neither event would have led to the sinking of the ship without the other, and here also, it is difficult to escape from the conclusion that, in such circumstances, determining which of two potential events is the proximate cause is largely a matter of impression. This conclusion is supported by the language used in the speeches in the House of Lords: 'What was the cause of her becoming a total wreck there? In my opinion, in substance, it was the injury by the torpedo';[15] 'What was the cause of the loss of the ship? I do not think the ordinary man would have any difficulty in answering she was lost because she was torpedoed'.[16]

The following summaries of some of the leading cases may be of assistance in identifying the proximate cause in similar cases:

(1)   in *Marsden v City and County Assurance Co*,[17] a fire at a shop attracted a crowd, and the crowd broke a window at the insured's premises next door. The remote cause of the breakage of the window was the fire ('but for' the fire, the window would not have been broken), and the proximate or immediate cause was held to be the action of the crowd;

(2)   in *Taylor v Dunbar*,[18] bad weather delayed a journey by sea, and a cargo of meat was ruined by the delay. The delay was held to be the proximate cause, and the bad weather the remote cause. The policy provided cover against bad weather but not delay, and the insurer was not liable for the loss of the meat;

(3)   in *Dudgeon v Pembroke*,[19] a ship was lost due to bad weather, but would not have been lost had it been seaworthy. The policy provided cover in respect of perils of the sea. The bad weather was held to be the proximate cause, and the condition of the ship the remote cause, with the result that the insurer was liable;

(4)   in *Winspear v Accident Insurance Co*,[20] the insured suffered an epileptic fit (excepted peril) while fording a river, and as a result fell into the river and was accidentally drowned (insured peril). The court held that the drowning was

the proximate cause of death, and the fit a remote cause. As it construed the policy as requiring epilepsy to be the proximate cause in order to fall within the exception, the insured's widow recovered;

(5)　in *Lawrence v Accidental Insurance Co*,[21] the insured suffered a fit and fell off a platform at Waterloo station, and was run over and killed by a train. The Divisional Court considered *Winspear v Accident Insurance Co*, and again concluded that the fit was the remote cause, and the impact with the train was the proximate cause of death. It construed the policy as requiring the fit to be the proximate cause in order to fall within the exception, so that the insurers were liable;

(6)　in *Mardorf v Accident Insurance Co*,[22] the insured scratched his leg when removing his socks, and within weeks died from the resulting septicaemia. The court held that the insured's death was caused 'directly and solely' by an insured peril ('personal injury caused by external and accidental violence');

(7)　in *Etherington v Lancashire and Yorkshire Accident Insurance Co*,[23] the insured died of pneumonia after falling from a horse while hunting and becoming very wet. The Court of Appeal found that the effect of the shock and the wetting was to lower the insured's vitality, of which the pneumonia was a direct and natural consequence. The accident was therefore the 'direct or proximate cause' of the insured's death, as required by the policy;

(8)　in *Fidelity and Casualty Co of New York v Mitchell*,[24] the insured sprained his wrist after a fall, which activated a latent tuberculous tendency. The policy insured against accidental bodily injury, and provided that the insurer would pay the insured $75 per week 'so long as he lives and suffers the ... disability'. It was argued by underwriters that there were two causes of the injury, the fall and the latent tuberculosis. The Privy Council rejected this argument and held[25] that the accident had had two effects – the sprain and the inducement of the tuberculous condition, and that 'while they are both ingredients of the disabled condition, there has been and is, on the true construction of the policy, only one cause, namely, the accident';

(9)　in *British and Foreign Marine Insurance Co Ltd v Sanday*,[26] two British vessels deviated to British ports after the declaration of war made continuation of their voyages to Germany illegal, and the cargo owners claimed for a constructive total loss. The House of Lords held that the proximate cause of the loss was the declaration of war, which was an insured peril;

(10)　in *Becker, Gray & Co v London Assurance Corpn*,[27] a German vessel was put into a neutral port to avoid capture after the outbreak of war, the voyage was abandoned, and the British cargo owners gave notice of abandonment and claimed as for a total loss. The House of Lords held that the declaration of war did not render the voyage illegal as the vessel was not British, and that, accordingly, the loss was caused not by the declaration of war (an insured peril), but by the voluntary act of the captain in deciding to put it into a neutral port to avoid the risk of capture;

(11)　in *W & J Lane v Spratt*,[28] a lorry-load of bacon was stolen by a driver whose references had not been checked by his employer. The failure to take up the references was held to be the proximate cause of the loss, rather than the theft by the driver.

1 [1918] AC 350, HL; see *Global Process Systems Inc v Syarikat Takaful Malaysia Berhad, The Cendor Mopu* [2011] UKSC 5, [2011] 1 Lloyd's Rep 560, paras 19 (Lord Saville) and 49 (Lord Mance).

2 *Coxe v Employers' Liability Assurance Corpn Ltd* [1916] 2 KB 629, 633 (Scrutton J); *Becker, Gray & Co v London Assurance Corpn* [1918] AC 101, 114, HL (Lord Sumner).

3 *Becker, Gray & Co v London Assurance Corpn* [1918] AC 101, 114, HL (Lord Sumner).

4 *Becker, Gray & Co v London Assurance Corpn* [1918] AC 101, 114, HL (Lord Sumner).

5 *Leyland Shipping Co Ltd v Norwich Union Fire Insurance Society Ltd* [1918] AC 350, 369, HL (Lord Shaw).

6 *Leyland Shipping Co Ltd v Norwich Union Fire Insurance Society Ltd* [1918] AC 350, 363, HL (Lord Dunedin); *Yorkshire Dale Steamship Co Ltd v Minister of War Transport* [1942] AC 691, 698, HL (Viscount Simon); *T M Noten BV v Harding* [1990] 2 Lloyd's Rep 283, 286–287, CA (Bingham LJ); *Global Process Systems Inc v Syarikat Takaful Malaysia Berhad, The Cendor Mopu* [2011] UKSC 5, [2011] 1 Lloyd's Rep 560, paras 79 (Lord Mance) and 95 (Lord Collins).

7 *Leyland Shipping Co Ltd v Norwich Union Fire Insurance Society Ltd* [1918] AC 350, 370, HL (Lord Shaw); *Yorkshire Dale Steamship Co Ltd v Minister of War Transport* [1942] AC 691, 698, HL (Viscount Simon).

8 *T M Noten BV v Harding* [1990] 2 Lloyd's Rep 283, 286–287, CA (Bingham LJ); *Global Process Systems Inc v Syarikat Takaful Malaysia Berhad, The Cendor Mopu* [2011] UKSC 5, [2011] 1 Lloyd's Rep 560, paras 79 (Lord Mance) and 95 (Lord Collins).

9 See *Becker, Gray & Co v London Assurance Corpn* [1918] AC 101, 108, HL (Lord Dunedin).

10 See *Marsden v City and County Assurance Co* (1865) LR 1 CP 232.

11 See *Yorkshire Dale Steamship Co Ltd v Minister of War Transport* [1942] AC 691, 702, HL (Lord Macmillan); *Athel Line Ltd v Liverpool & London War Risks Insurance Association Ltd* [1946] KB 117, 122, CA (Lord Greene MR); *Gray v Barr* [1971] 2 QB 554, 567, CA (Lord Denning MR); *W & J Lane v Spratt* [1970] 2 QB 480, 495 (Roskill J).

12 *T M Noten BV v Harding* [1990] 2 Lloyd's Rep 283, 286–287, CA (Bingham LJ); approved: *Global Process Systems Inc v Syarikat Takaful Malaysia Berhad, The Cendor Mopu* [2011] UKSC 5, [2011] 1 Lloyd's Rep 560, paras 79 (Lord Mance) and 116 (Lord Clarke).

13 *Leyland Shipping Co Ltd v Norwich Union Fire Insurance Society Ltd* [1918] AC 350, HL; *P Samuel & Co v Dumas* [1924] AC 431, HL; *Boiler Inspection and Insurance Co of Canada v Sherwin-Williams Co of Canada Ltd* [1951] AC 319, PC.

14 [1918] AC 350, HL.

15 At 355 (Lord Finlay LC).

16 At 362 (Lord Dunedin).

17 (1865) LR 1 CP 232.

18 (1869) LR 4 CP 206.

19 (1877) 2 App Cas 284, HL; see also *Global Process Systems Inc v Syarikat Takaful Malaysia Berhad, The Cendor Mopu* [2011] UKSC 5, [2011] 1 Lloyd's Rep 560.

20 (1880) 6 QBD 42, CA.

21 (1881) 7 QBD 216.

22 [1903] 1 KB 584.

23 [1909] 1 KB 591, CA.

24 [1917] AC 592, PC.

25 At 597. See also **para 4.6**.

26 [1916] 1 AC 650, HL.

27 [1918] AC 101, HL.

28 [1970] 2 QB 480.

CONCURRENT CAUSES

4.3   A loss may have two proximate causes.[1] Thus, the court may conclude that:[2]

'... there [is] not one dominant cause, but two causes which were equal or nearly equal in their efficiency in bringing about the damage.'

The Court of Appeal said in *Wayne Tank and Pump Co Ltd v Employers' Liability Assurance Corpn Ltd* that:[3]

> '... unless one cause is clearly more decisive than the other, it should be accepted that there are two causes of the loss and no attempt should be made to give one of them the quality of dominance.'

Where there are two causes of loss, one of which is within the policy and the other of which is neither within the policy nor the subject of an exception,[4] the insurer will be liable.[5] Where there are two causes of loss, one within the policy and the other excepted, whether the insurer will be liable depends upon whether the insured peril would have caused the loss without the excepted peril. If so, the insurer will be liable for damage which the insured can establish was caused by the insured peril, and damage caused by the excepted peril will not be covered.[6] The burden of proving that the loss falls within the policy is on the insured, and therefore where the insured cannot establish which of the perils (the insured or the excepted peril) caused the loss, there will be no cover.[7] Where there are two proximate causes, neither of which would have caused loss without the other, the insurer is entitled to rely upon the exception.[8] The two causes do not have to be exactly co-extensive in time: a later cause may join with a previous and continuing cause so as to become concurrent.[9]

Loss by a combination of concurrent causes must be distinguished from loss by a single cause which may be properly described as amounting to a number of perils or (in a liability policy) as giving rise to a number of causes of action, one or more of which may be outside the terms of the policy, but one of which is plainly within its terms. In such a case, the insured is entitled to an indemnity.[10]

1 *Reischer v Borwick* [1894] 2 QB 548, CA; *Board of Trade v Hain Steamship Co Ltd* [1929] AC 534, 539, HL (Lord Buckmaster); *Wayne Tank and Pump Co Ltd v Employers' Liability Assurance Corpn Ltd* [1974] QB 57, CA; *J J Lloyd Instruments Ltd v Northern Star Insurance Co Ltd, The Miss Jay Jay* [1987] 1 Lloyd's Rep 32, CA; *Capel-Cure Myers Capital Management Ltd v McCarthy* [1995] LRLR 498, 503 (Potter J); *Kuwait Airways Corpn SAK v Kuwait Insurance Co SA* [1999] 1 Lloyd's Rep 803, 815, HL (Lord Hobhouse); *Midland Mainline Ltd v Eagle Star Insurance Co Ltd* [2004] EWCA Civ 1042, [2004] 2 Lloyd's Rep 604, 606, paras 8 and 12 (Sir Martin Nourse). In *West Wake Price & Co v Ching* [1957] 1 WLR 45, 49–50, Devlin J referred to *Reischer v Borwick* [1894] 2 QB 548, CA, and said that he would like to find a way of avoiding the making of minute distinctions between two causes 'of approximately equal efficacy'; but that if the price that had to be paid for the solution was the interposition of a category labelled 'cause of equal efficacy' between 'the cause' and 'a cause', the price might be too high.

2 *Wayne Tank and Pump Co Ltd v Employers' Liability Assurance Corpn Ltd* [1974] QB 57, 67, CA (Lord Denning MR). See also *J J Lloyd Instruments Ltd v Northern Star Insurance Co Ltd, The Miss Jay Jay* [1987] 1 Lloyd's Rep 32, 40, CA: 'On a common sense view of the facts both these two causes were, in my opinion, equal, or at least nearly equal, in their efficiency in bringing about the damage' (Slade LJ). The illogicality of refusing to accept that there might be two proximate causes of loss is illustrated by the example given by Cairns LJ in argument in *Wayne Tank and Pump Co Ltd v Employers' Liability Assurance Corpn Ltd* [1974] QB 57, 61, CA: Roskill LJ asked whether it was possible to have two proximate causes, and Cairns LJ said: 'Two drivers driving at the same speed may arrive at cross roads at the same time'.

3 *Wayne Tank and Pump Co Ltd v Employers' Liability Assurance Corpn Ltd* [1974] QB 57, 69, CA (Cairns LJ).

4 Loss which is 'warranted free' (in marine insurance) is the same as loss which is the subject of an exception (in non-marine insurance); the difference is simply terminology: *Wayne Tank and Pump Co Ltd v Employers' Liability Assurance Corpn Ltd* [1974] QB 57, CA (at 67, 69 and 75).

5 *P Samuel & Co v Dumas* [1924] AC 431, 468, HL; *J J Lloyd Instruments Ltd v Northern Star Insurance Co Ltd, The Miss Jay Jay* [1987] 1 Lloyd's Rep 32, CA; *Capel-Cure Myers Capital Management*

> *Ltd v McCarthy* [1995] LRLR 498, 503 (Potter J); *Global Process Systems Inc v Syarikat Takaful Malaysia Berhad, The Cendor Mopu* [2011] UKSC 5, [2011] 1 Lloyd's Rep 560, para 77 (Lord Mance); *International Energy Group Ltd v Zurich Insurance plc* [2015] UKSC 33, [2016] AC 509, para 73 (Lord Mance, with whom Lords Clarke, Carnwath and Hodge agreed).

> **6** See *Stanley v Western Insurance Co* (1868) LR 3 Exch 71; applied: *Re Hooley Hill Rubber and Chemical Co Ltd* [1920] 1 KB 257, CA.

> **7** See *Stanley v Western Insurance Co* (1868) LR 3 Exch 71; applied: *Re Hooley Hill Rubber and Chemical Co Ltd* [1920] 1 KB 257, CA. The burden of proof may be displaced by agreement: see **PARA 5.1**.

> **8** See *P Samuel & Co v Dumas* [1924] AC 431, 467, HL; *Board of Trade v Hain Steamship Co Ltd* [1929] AC 534, 541–542, HL (Lord Sumner); *Wayne Tank and Pump Co Ltd v Employers' Liability Assurance Corpn Ltd* [1974] QB 57, CA; *J J Lloyd Instruments Ltd v Northern Star Insurance Co Ltd, The Miss Jay Jay* [1987] 1 Lloyd's Rep 32, CA; *Handelsbanken Norwegian Branch of Svenska Handelsbanken AB (Publ) v Dandridge (The Aliza Glacial)* [2002] EWCA Civ 577, [2002] Lloyd's Rep 421, paras 47–48 (Potter LJ); *Kiriacoulis Lines SA v Compagnie d'Assurances Maritime Aériennes et Terrestres (The Demetra K)* [2002] EWCA Civ 1070, [2002] 2 Lloyd's Rep 581, para 18 (Lord Phillips MR); applied: *IF P&C Insurance Ltd v Silversea Cruises Ltd* [2004] EWCA Civ 769, [2004] 1 Lloyd's Rep IR 696, paras 99 and 102 (Rix LJ); see also *Global Process Systems Inc v Syarikat Takaful Malaysia Berhad, The Cendor Mopu* [2011] UKSC 5, [2011] 1 Lloyd's Rep 560, paras 22 (Lord Saville), 88 (Lord Mance), 96 (Lord Collins) and 99, 134 and 137 (Lord Clarke).

> **9** *Handelsbanken Norwegian Branch of Svenska Handelsbanken AB (Publ) v Dandridge (The Aliza Glacial)* [2002] EWCA Civ 577, [2002] Lloyd's Rep 421, paras 47–48 (Potter LJ).

> **10** *Capel-Cure Myers Capital Management Ltd v McCarthy* [1995] LRLR 498, 503 (Potter J).

WORDINGS DENOTING PROXIMATE CAUSE

4.4   In construing a policy of insurance in accordance with the intention of the parties, the court will assume that the parties intended the doctrine of proximate cause to apply, and clear words will be required to displace this assumption.[1] Any wording used to denote causation will, unless clearly qualified in some way, be construed as meaning proximately caused. Thus, the wordings 'caused by', 'arising from',[2] and 'resulting from'[3] denote proximate cause. Similarly, 'originating in' fire means proximately caused by fire.[4] The words 'traceable to' have been held to be too vague to extend the concept of proximate cause.[5]

> **1** *Coxe v Employers' Liability Assurance Corp Ltd* [1916] 2 KB 629, 633 (Scrutton J); *Lloyds TSB General Insurance Holdings v Lloyds Bank Group Insurance Co Ltd* [2001] EWCA Civ 1643, [2002] Lloyd's Rep IR 113, para 42 (Potter LJ); point not considered on appeal: [2003] UKHL 48, [2003] Lloyd's Rep IR 623. See also **PARA 6.9**.

> **2** *Coxe v Employers' Liability Assurance Corpn Ltd* [1916] 2 KB 629, 634 (Scrutton J). There have been suggestions in more recent cases that 'arising from' or 'arising out of' may denote a weaker causal connection than proximate cause: see *Kajima UK Engineering Ltd v The Underwriter Insurance Co Ltd* [2008] EWHC 83 (TCC), [2008] Lloyd's Rep IR 391, para 97 (Akenhead J); *Beazley Underwriting Ltd v The Travelers Companies Incorporated* [2011] EWHC 1520 (Comm), [2012] Lloyd's Rep IR 78, paras 120–128 (Christopher Clarke J); *British Waterways v Royal & Sun Alliance Insurance plc* [2012] EWHC 460 (Comm), [2012] Lloyd's Rep IR 562, paras 42–45 (Burton J). In *ARC Capital Partners Ltd v Brit Syndicates Ltd* [2016] EWHC 141 (Comm), paras 27 and 32–43, Cooke J construed the words 'arising from' in the phrase 'arising from or in any way involving' as denoting proximate cause, and 'in any way involving' as denoting an indirect causal connection.

> **3** *Lloyds TSB General Insurance Holdings v Lloyds Bank Group Insurance Co Ltd* [2001] EWCA Civ 1643, [2002] Lloyd's Rep IR 113, para 42 (Potter LJ); point not considered on appeal: [2003] UKHL 48, [2003] Lloyd's Rep IR 623.

> **4** See *Marsden v City and County Assurance Co* (1865) LR 1 CP 232.

> **5** *Coxe v Employers' Liability Assurance Corpn Ltd* [1916] 2 KB 629.

'DIRECTLY OR INDIRECTLY'

4.5   A policy may provide cover against loss caused 'directly or indirectly' by an insured peril. More commonly, this wording is used in connection with an exception. For example, in *Coxe v Employers' Liability Assurance Corpn Ltd*,[1] a policy of insurance provided cover against death caused accidentally by violence due to any external and visible means, but the policy was subject to the condition that it did not insure against death 'directly or indirectly caused by, arising from, or traceable to ... war'. The insured was a military officer who, in the course of military duty during the 1914–18 war, was walking beside railway tracks in order to visit guards and sentries posted at various points along the line, when he was accidentally killed by a train. Scrutton J construed the phrase 'directly or indirectly' as meaning that:[2]

> 'a more remote link in the chain of causation is contemplated than the proximate and immediate cause.'

Scrutton J held that the arbitrator's decision that the insured's death was indirectly caused by the war was a finding of fact which was open to him to make, because the insured's military duties had placed him in a position of particular danger, and he was killed as a result of exposure to that danger.

In *Spinney's (1948) Ltd v Royal Insurance Co Ltd*,[3] the policy contained an exception in the following terms:

> 'This insurance does not cover any loss or damage occasioned by or through or in consequence directly or indirectly of any of the following occurrences: (a) ... civil war; (b) ... civil commotion ...'[4]

Mustill J held that it was clear that the draftsman had intended to ensure that the doctrine of proximate cause did not apply, but that there must be some limit on the application of the clause:[5]

> 'for the chain of causation recedes infinitely into the past. The draftsman must have intended to stop somewhere: and that place must be the point at which an event ceases to be a cause of the loss, and becomes merely an item of history. The draftsman has not explained how that point is to be identified, nor indeed do I believe that words can be found to do so. It is, eventually, a matter of instinct – but an instinct guided by the fact that this is a policy which (unlike others in which similar clauses can be found) expressly insures against violent acts. In essence, the task is to assess whether the particular act of violence simply takes place against the background of a "warlike" state of affairs, or whether it has itself (even if in a rather remote way) a warlike aspect of its own.'

1 [1916] 2 KB 629.
2 At 634.
3 [1980] 1 Lloyd's Rep 406.
4 At 407.
5 [1980] 1 Lloyd's Rep 406, 441–442; applied in *Oei v Foster* [1982] 2 Lloyd's Rep 170 (Glidewell J).

'INDEPENDENT', 'EXCLUSIVE' OR 'SOLE' CAUSE

4.6 Where the policy requires that an insured peril be the 'independent', 'sole' or 'exclusive' cause of loss, or any combination of these, an insurer will not be liable if an insured peril caused loss concurrently with an uninsured peril, whether or not the uninsured peril was the subject of an exception.[1] In *Jason v British Traders' Insurance Co Ltd*,[2] an accident policy provided cover if the insured should 'sustain in any accident bodily injury resulting in and being – independently of all other causes – the exclusive direct and immediate cause of the ... injury or disablement'. Fisher J found that the insured would have had a coronary thrombosis three years later even if the accident had not occurred, and held that there were two causes of bodily injury (the coronary thrombosis), the accident and pre-existing arterial disease, and that this defeated the insured's claim.[3] In *Fidelity and Casualty Co of New York v Mitchell*,[4] the insured sprained his wrist after a fall, which activated a latent tuberculous tendency which would have remained harmless had it not been for the accident. The policy insured against bodily injury sustained through accidental means and resulting 'directly, independently and exclusively of all other causes' in total disablement from performing the duties of his occupation. The insurers argued that there were two causes of the injury, the fall and the latent tuberculosis. The Privy Council rejected this argument and held that there was one cause, the accident, which had two effects: the sprain, and the inducement of the tuberculous condition. The insurers were therefore liable to pay the insured the sum of $75 per week while the injury subsisted, even though it would have healed within six months after an ordinary sprain, but appeared unlikely ever to heal due to the tuberculous condition. In *Jason v British Traders' Insurance Co Ltd* there were found to be two proximate causes of the bodily injury (the coronary thrombosis), the pre-existing arterial disease and the accident, whereas in *Fidelity and Casualty Co of New York v Mitchell* the tuberculosis would have remained harmless had it not been for the accident and was therefore not a proximate cause of the disablement.

1 *Jason v British Traders' Insurance Co Ltd* [1969] 1 Lloyd's Rep 281.
2 [1969] 1 Lloyd's Rep 281.
3 In *Jason v British Traders' Insurance Co Ltd* [1969] 1 Lloyd's Rep 281, there was also an exclusion clause which provided that: 'No benefit shall be payable under the Policy in respect of Death, Injury or Disablement directly or indirectly caused by or arising or resulting from or traceable to ... Any physical defect or infirmity which existed prior to an accident', and Fisher J said that even if it had otherwise been within the insuring clause, the exclusion clause would have defeated the insured's claim in any event (290–291); approved: *Blackburn Rovers Football and Athletic Club plc v Avon Insurance plc* [2005] EWCA Civ 423, [2005] Lloyd's Rep IR 447, para 13 (Lord Phillips MR). In *Blackburn Rovers Football and Athletic Club plc v Avon Insurance plc* [2005] EWCA Civ 423, [2005] Lloyd's Rep IR 447, the policy excluded 'death or disablement directly or indirectly resulting or consequent upon' arthritic or other degenerative conditions, and the Court of Appeal held (Lord Phillips MR, at para 18) that disablement could not be said to be 'attributable, either directly or indirectly' to a pre-existing condition unless, at the least, the condition is a *causa sine qua non* (see **PARA 4.9**) of the disablement; therefore, if the accident would have disabled the player regardless of the pre-existing condition, and conversely, the player would not have been disabled had he not suffered the accident, the exclusion would not apply.
4 [1917] AC 592, PC.

'IN RESPECT OF'

4.7 The words 'in respect of' in the insuring clause in a public or products liability policy have a limiting effect on the extent of the cover and do not merely identify the causal event.[1] These words mean 'for' and not merely 'caused by', 'consequential upon' or 'in connection with', so that the insured's liability must be for death or injury, that is to say the liability must be to the person who has been killed or injured; the liability must be for loss or damage to material property of the person whose property it is – liability for loss suffered by someone else as a consequence of such damage is not 'in respect of' it; and liability for any of these torts must be to the person who has the right to claim – liability for loss suffered by someone else as a consequence of the tort is not 'in respect of' it.[2]

1 *Horbury Building Systems Ltd v Hampden Insurance NV* [2004] EWCA Civ 418, [2007] Lloyd's Rep IR 237, paras 24-25 (Keane LJ) and 35 (Mance LJ) (product liability policy). See also **PARAS 17.17** and **17.25**.
2 *Tesco Stores Ltd v Constable* [2008] EWCA Civ 362, [2008] Lloyd's Rep IR 636, para 22 (Tuckey LJ) (public liability policy). See also **PARAS 17.17** and **17.25**.

'ON ACCOUNT OF'

4.8 'On account of' are words which are plainly intended to provide a causal link between the damages sought in a third party claim against the insured and property damage in a products liability policy.[1] The fact that a claim is for economic loss and not for damage to property does not dictate a wholly negative answer to the question whether the damages are sought 'on account of physical injury' to the damaged products when made and installed, and the words are sufficiently wide to encompass claims for the cost of repair or replacement of damaged products; however, as a matter of ordinary language claims by any party for damages for loss of business or profits said to have resulted from the physical damage cannot be said to be claims for damages 'on account of' physical injury to damaged products; the words require a more direct connection between the loss claimed and an actual physical injury.[2]

1 *Tioxide Europe Ltd v CGU International Insurance plc* [2004] EWHC 216 (Comm), [2005] Lloyd's Rep IR 114, para 44 (Langley J). See also **PARA 17.17**.
2 *Tioxide Europe Ltd v CGU International Insurance plc* [2004] EWHC 216 (Comm), [2005] Lloyd's Rep IR 114, para 51 (Langley J).

LATIN TERMINOLOGY

4.9 Even in 1918, the use of plain English was being advocated in place of the Latin terminology,[1] but some Latin phrases are still commonly used. The key Latin phrases are the following:

(1) *'causa proxima non remota spectatur'*, sometimes shortened to *'causa proxima'*: used to denote the doctrine of proximate cause;
(2) *'causa sine qua non'*: used to denote the remote cause; and

(3)   '*novus casus interveniens*' or '*novus actus interveniens*': used to denote an intervening cause which breaks the chain of causation.

1 *Becker, Gray & Co v London Assurance Corpn* [1918] AC 101, 114, HL (Lord Sumner).

OPPORTUNITY TO AVERT LOSS

4.10   The principle that only loss which is proximately caused by an insured peril is recoverable means that, in certain circumstances, loss which could have been avoided (whether averted completely or reduced) by the insured taking reasonable steps will not be recoverable.[1] This is because the proximate cause of such loss is not the insured peril but the insured's failure to take reasonable steps to avoid it:[2]

> '... if after the advent of the insured peril or where the advent of the insured peril was obviously imminent the insured or his agent failed to act to avert or to minimise loss in circumstances where any prudent uninsured would have done so, the chain of causation between the insured peril and the loss will be broken. Clearly, if the insured peril is not the proximate cause of the loss, the assured cannot recover.'

It seems that this will apply only in the rare case where the insured's failure to take reasonable steps is so significant as to be held to displace the prior insured peril as the cause of the loss and the negligence of the insured or his agents is not an insured peril.[3]

1 *National Oilwell (UK) Ltd v Davy Offshore Ltd* [1993] 2 Lloyd's Rep 582, 618; *Yorkshire Water Services Ltd v Sun Alliance & London Insurance plc* [1997] 2 Lloyd's Rep 21, 32, CA (Otton LJ); see also *Webster v General Accident Fire and Life Assurance Corpn Ltd* [1953] 1 QB 520, 532:

> 'An assured is not entitled to sit by and do nothing. Equally, he is not bound to launch into legal proceedings or if necessary carry them to the House of Lords. The test, as it seems to me, is whether, after all reasonable steps to recover a chattel have been taken by the assured, recovery is uncertain' (Parker J).

2 *National Oilwell (UK) Ltd v Davy Offshore Ltd* [1993] 2 Lloyd's Rep 582, 618 (Colman J).
3 *State of the Netherlands v Youell* [1998] 1 Lloyd's Rep 236, 244–245 CA (Phillips LJ); applied: *Handelsbanken Norwegian Branch of Svenska Handeslbanken AB (Publ) v Dandridge, The Aliza Glacial* [2002] EWCA Civ 577, [2002] 2 Lloyd's Rep 421, para 58 (Potter LJ) (s 78(4) Marine Insurance Act 1906 and contractual sue and labour provision) and *Masefield AG v Amlin Corporate Member Ltd, The Bunga Melati Dua* [2011] EWCA Civ 24, [2011] 1 Lloyd's Rep 630, para 76 (Rix LJ). None of these decisions considered *A P Stephen v Scottish Boatowners Mutual Insurance Association, The Talisman* [1989] 1 Lloyd's Rep 535, HL, which held (in the context of a contractual sue and labour provision) that the question was whether an ordinarily competent skipper, in the circumstances in which the insured was placed, would reasonably be expected to take certain steps (in that case, to close the seacocks and to issue a Mayday call); applied: *Melinda Holdings SA v Hellenic Mutual War Risks Association (Bermuda) Ltd, The Silva* [2011] 2 Lloyd's Rep 141, para 51 (Burton J) (contractual sue and labour provision). See also *Strive Shipping Corpn v Hellenic Mutual War Risks Association, The Grecia Express* [2002] EWHC 203 (Comm), [2002] 2 Lloyd's Rep 88, 160 (Colman J) (s 78(4) applies only where negligence is proximate cause and breaks chain of causation, but meaning of contractual provision is at large; construed as contractual obligation on insured to take reasonable steps to avert or minimise loss or damage that would or might otherwise be caused by insured peril); applied: *Melinda Holdings SA v Hellenic Mutual War Risks Association (Bermuda) Ltd, The Silva* [2011] 2 Lloyd's Rep 141, para 48 (Burton J); *Linelevel Ltd v Powszechny Zaklad Ubezpieczen SA, The Nore Challenger* [2005] EWHC 421 (Comm), [2005] 2 Lloyd's Rep 534, paras 80-83 (Cooke J) (insured was in breach of

s 78(4) duty and contractual sue and labour provision, but breach caused virtually no additional financial cost); *Clothing Management Technology Ltd v Beazley Solutions Ltd* [2012] EWHC 727 (QB), [2012] Lloyd's Rep IR 571, para 54 (HHJ Mackie QC) (no breach of s 78(4) where insured made reasonable and informed judgment in unusual circumstances: not routine insurance event where insured failed to take conventional and recognised steps to minimise loss).

NEGLIGENCE BY THE INSURED

4.11 Where negligence by the insured is an insured peril, or is excepted, the normal principles apply. Where negligence is neither an insured peril nor excepted, the insured is entitled to recover even if the proximate cause of the loss is an event brought about by the negligence of the insured.[1]

The courts have interpreted clauses imposing an obligation on the insured to take reasonable precautions to prevent loss as requiring that the insured should not merely be negligent, but must at least be reckless.[2]

1 *Trinder, Anderson & Co v Thames and Mersey Marine Insurance Co* [1898] 2 QB 114, CA; *A-G v Adelaide Steamship Co Ltd* [1923] AC 292, 308, HL (Lord Wrenbury); *Etherington v Lancashire and Yorkshire Accident Insurance Co* [1909] 1 KB 591, 599, CA (Kennedy LJ); *Board of Trade v Hain Steamship Co Ltd* [1929] AC 534, HL; *Harris v Poland* [1941] 1 KB 462; *Canada Rice Mills Ltd v Union Marine and General Insurance Co Ltd* [1941] AC 55, 69, PC; *Yorkshire Dale Steamship Co Ltd v Minister of War Transport* [1942] AC 691, 711, HL (Lord Wright); *Global Tankers Inc v Amercoat Europa NV* [1977] 1 Lloyd's Rep 61, 66 (Kerr J). See also **PARAS 4.3, 4.12** and **5.2**.
2 *Fraser v B N Furman (Productions) Ltd* [1967] 1 WLR 898, 906, CA (Diplock LJ; employers' liability insurance); *W & J Lane v Spratt* [1970] 2 QB 480 (Roskill J; property insurance); *Devco Holder Ltd v Legal & General Assurance Society Ltd* [1993] 2 Lloyd's Rep 567, CA (no indemnity for theft of valuable car while unattended and unlocked with keys in ignition); *Sofi v Prudential Assurance Co Ltd* [1993] 2 Lloyd's Rep 559, CA (indemnity for theft of valuable jewellery left out of sight in unattended car); *Hayward v Norwich Union Insurance Ltd* [2001] EWCA Civ 243, [2001] Lloyd's Rep IR 410 (no indemnity for theft of valuable car and contents while within sight and immobilised but unlocked with keys in ignition). See further **PARA 5.2**.

ATTEMPTS TO AVOID A PERIL

4.12 Once a peril has started to operate, loss due to an attempt to avoid the peril will be regarded as proximately caused by the peril, and is therefore recoverable.[1] There are conflicting dicta as to whether a peril which is imminent has started to operate, so that loss due to action taken to avoid the peril is recoverable.[2] Loss caused by action taken merely as a precaution to avoid a peril is not proximately caused by that peril.[3] Nor is loss proximately caused by a peril where that peril is shown not to have been operating; and a bona fide belief that a peril is operating is not sufficient even where the insured has no means of knowing at the time whether or not the peril is in fact operating.[4] In *Joseph Watson & Son Ltd v Firemen's Fund Insurance Co of San Francisco*,[5] goods were damaged by steam introduced into the hold, where the captain mistakenly believed there to be a fire. Rowlatt J held that insurers were not liable under the policy, on the following basis:[6]

> 'The underwriters insured against fire in fact, and if there had been a fire they would have had to pay. But why are they to pay if in fact there was no fire? They

did not insure against an error of judgment on the part of the captain in deciding whether there was a peril or not.'

1 *Stanley v Western Insurance Co* (1868) LR 3 Exch 71 (the examples given, obiter, are of items insured against fire being damaged when attempts are made to save them, such as by water from a fire extinguisher, or when they are thrown out of a window; it was assumed that the insured peril (fire) had begun to operate, but had not damaged the goods); *Etherington v Lancashire and Yorkshire Accident Insurance Co* [1909] 1 KB 591, 599, CA (Vaughan Williams LJ); *Kacianoff v China Traders Insurance Co Ltd* [1914] 3 KB 1121, 1128 (Lord Reading CJ); *Becker, Gray & Co v London Assurance Corpn* [1918] AC 101, HL.

2 See *The Knight of St Michael* [1898] P 30 (there was 'imminent danger of fire', but the fire had not started, and insurers were not liable); approved: *Symington & Co v Union Insurance Society of Canton Ltd* (1928) 31 Ll L Rep 179, CA; and contrast *Kacianoff v China Traders Insurance Co Ltd* [1914] 3 KB 1121, 1128 (Lord Reading CJ): the danger was present, and if nothing had been done spontaneous combustion and fire would have followed in the natural course; therefore the peril had begun to operate, and insurers were liable; *Linelevel Ltd v Powszechny Zaklad Ubezpieczen SA, The Nore Challenger* [2005] EWHC 421 (Comm), [2005] 2 Lloyd's Rep 534, para 85 (Cooke J): s 78(4) Marine Insurance Act 1906 and contractual sue and labour clause: trite law that duty to sue and labour operates when peril has arisen or is imminent – when vessel is 'in the grip of a peril'.

3 *Britain Steamship Co Ltd v R* [1921] 1 AC 99, 108 (Viscount Cave); *Becker, Gray & Co v London Assurance Corpn* [1918] AC 101, 108, HL (Lord Dunedin).

4 *Joseph Watson & Son Ltd v Firemen's Fund Insurance Co of San Francisco* [1922] 2 KB 355.

5 [1922] 2 KB 355.

6 At 359.

Chapter 5

Proof of loss

BURDEN OF PROOF

Scope of cover and exceptions or exclusions

5.1 In order to recover under a policy of insurance, the insured must prove such facts as bring him prima facie within the scope of the cover,[1] and the burden is then on the insurer to show, if he can, that an exception applies.[2] Where cover is qualified by an exception or exclusion which extends to its entire scope, the burden is on the insured to bring himself within the cover as qualified. It is a matter of construction of the policy whether the cover is subject to an exception, or is qualified in this way, and the precise wording is therefore of the utmost importance.[3] Where an exception is itself qualified by an exception, the burden is on the insured to prove that the second exception applies, thereby bringing the insured within the scope of cover.[4] A condition precedent to the liability of an insurer operates as an exemption to that prima facie liability,[5] and the burden of proving that the insured is in breach of a condition precedent is on the insurer.[6]

These general principles may be displaced by agreement between the parties, and the burden of proof of any particular fact, or of its non-existence, may be placed on either party in accordance with the agreement between them.[7] In *Spinney's (1948) Ltd v Royal Insurance Co Ltd*,[8] the policy contained a clause which purported to reverse the normal burden of proof in relation to the cause of the loss. The clause appeared after a series of exceptions in a policy condition:

> 'In any action ... where the [insurer] alleges that by reason of the provision of this Condition any loss or damage is not covered by this insurance, the burden of proving that such loss or damage is covered shall be upon the insured.'

Mustill J indicated that the clause should not be construed so as to make the policy unworkable, and concluded that a bare assertion by the insurer was not enough. The clause required the insurer to produce evidence from which it could reasonably be argued that a state of affairs existed or an event occurred falling within an exception, and that the excepted peril directly caused the loss; and that only if the insurer did so was the insured required to disprove it.[9] This construction differs from that of the Privy Council in *Levy v Assicurazioni Generali*,[10] which concluded that the insurers bore no burden of proof under the clause. In assessing the evidence, however, the Privy Council was not satisfied with a bare allegation by the insurers,[11] so that in the result the two approaches were not dissimilar. Similarly, in the case of a condition precedent to the insurer's liability, clear words will be required to displace the presumption that the burden is on the insurer to show that the condition precedent has been breached.[12] The courts are reluctant to decide cases on the basis of the incidence of the burden of proof, but there are cases in which, owing to the unsatisfactory state of the evidence or otherwise, this is the only just course.[13] If the court takes the view, having considered the evidence, that it is unlikely that the loss was caused by an insured peril, it should reject the evidence even if no evidence has been adduced of any, more likely, cause of loss.[14] As a matter of common sense, it will usually be safe for a judge to conclude, where there are two competing theories before him, either of which is improbable, that having rejected one it is logical to accept the other as being the cause on the balance of probabilities;[15] of course, the judge has to be satisfied that the second theory is, on the balance of probabilities, correct.[16] A policy may make express provision for circumstances in which it is not possible to ascertain the cause of a loss.[17]

1 Unless the policy provides otherwise, what the insured has to show is that a loss has occurred which was proximately caused by an insured peril: see **PARAS 4.1** and **4.2.**

2 *Munro, Brice & Co v War Risks Association Ltd* [1918] 2 KB 78 (Bailhache J) (decision overruled on an inference of fact: *Munro, Brice & Co v Marten* [1920] 3 KB 94, CA); *Gaunt v British and Foreign Insurance Co Ltd* [1920] 1 KB 903, CA (decision affirmed by the House of Lords without reference to this point: [1921] 2 AC 4); *Boggan v Motor Union Insurance Co* (1923) 16 Ll L Rep 64, 65, HL (Lord Birkenhead); *Greaves v Drysdale* (1936) 55 Ll L Rep 95, 97, CA (Greer LJ); *Bond Air Services Ltd v Hill* [1955] 2 QB 417, 428 (Lord Goddard CJ); *Ted Baker plc v AXA Insurance UK plc (No 2)* [2014] EWHC 3548 (Comm), [2015] Lloyd's Rep IR 325, paras 137 and 153 (Eder J). *Hurst v Evans* [1917] 1 KB 352, in which Lush J held that the onus was on the insured to prove that the loss did not fall within either of the exceptions to the policy, was considered by Bailhache J in *Munro, Brice & Co v War Risks Association Ltd* [1918] 2 KB 78, 87–88, and not followed. A clause which requires the insured to prove his loss does not require him to prove that his loss is not within an excluded category of loss: *All Leisure Holidays Ltd v Europaische Reiseversicherung AG* [2011] EWHC 2629 (Comm), [2012] Lloyd's Rep IR 193, para 28 (Teare J). For the principles applicable to the construction of exclusions or exceptions, see **PARA 3.18.**

3 *Munro, Brice & Co v War Risks Association Ltd* [1918] 2 KB 78 (Bailhache J) (decision overruled on an inference of fact: *Munro, Brice & Co v Marten* [1920] 3 KB 94, CA); and see also *National Farmers Union Mutual Insurance Society Ltd v HSBC Insurance (UK) Ltd* [2010] EWHC 773 (Comm), [2011] Lloyd's Rep IR 86, para 20 (Gavin Kealey QC, sitting as a Deputy High Court Judge) (an extension of cover which was granted subject to a proviso ('What is not covered') was construed as a qualified extension of cover); *Ted Baker plc v AXA Insurance UK plc (No 2)* [2014] EWHC 3548 (Comm), [2015] Lloyd's Rep IR 325, para 153 (Eder J) (excess not properly to be characterised as an exclusion, but as defining cover provided, so that insured only entitled to recover losses caused by an insured peril which exceeded stipulated excess (of £5,000) each and every loss, and burden on insured to show on balance of probability that claimed losses exceeded £5,000 each and every loss).

4 *Rowett, Leakey and Co v Scottish Provident Institution* [1927] 1 Ch 55, CA.

5 *Royal & Sun Alliance Insurance plc v Dornoch* [2005] EWCA Civ 238, [2005] Lloyd's Rep IR 544, para 19 (Longmore LJ); applied: *Beazley Underwriting Ltd v Al Ahleia Insurance Co* [2013] EWHC, 677 (Comm), [2013] Lloyd's Rep IR 561, para 90 (Eder J).

6 *Bond Air Services Ltd v Hill* [1955] 2 QB 417, 427–428 (Lord Goddard CJ); *Sofi v Prudential Assurance Co Ltd* [1993] 2 Lloyd's Rep 559, 564, CA (Lloyd LJ); *Royal & Sun Alliance Insurance plc v Dornoch* [2005] EWCA Civ 238, [2005] Lloyd's Rep IR 544, para 19 (Longmore LJ).

7 *Levy v Assicurazioni Generali* [1940] AC 791, PC (exception); *Bond Air Services Ltd v Hill* [1955] 2 QB 417, 428 (Lord Goddard CJ). See also *Sofi v Prudential Assurance Co Ltd* [1993] 2 Lloyd's Rep 559, 564, CA (Lloyd LJ) (nothing in language of wording of condition precedent to shift ordinary burden of proof of breach).

8 [1980] 1 Lloyd's Rep 406.

9 At 427.

10 [1940] AC 791, PC.

11 At 800–801.

12 *Bond Air Services Ltd v Hill* [1955] 2 QB 417, 428 (Lord Goddard CJ).

13 *Rhesa Shipping Co SA v Edmunds (The Popi M)* [1985] 1 WLR 948, 955–956, HL (Lord Brandon).
14 *Rhesa Shipping Co SA v Edmunds (The Popi M)* [1985] 1 WLR 948, 951, HL (Lord Brandon).
15 *Ide v ATB Sales Ltd* [2008] EWCA Civ 424, [2009] RTR 8, para 6 (Thomas LJ); applied: *ACE European Group Ltd v Chartis Insurance UK Ltd* [2013] EWCA Civ 224, [2013] Lloyd's Rep IR 485, para 35 (Longmore LJ).
16 *ACE European Group Ltd v Chartis Insurance UK Ltd* [2013] EWCA Civ 224, [2013] Lloyd's Rep IR 485, para 35 (Longmore LJ).
17 See eg the 50/50 clauses considered in *European Group Ltd v Chartis Insurance UK Ltd* [2012] EWHC 1245 (Comm), [2012] 2 Lloyd's Rep 117, para 82 (Popplewell J) (decision affirmed on appeal under name *ACE European Group Ltd v Chartis Insurance UK Ltd* [2013] EWCA Civ 224, [2013] Lloyd's Rep IR 485).

Insured perils

5.2   The essence of any insuring or indemnity clause is that the insured must prove a loss.[1] The onus to show that the loss was due to an insured peril is on the insured.[2] What the insured has to show in order to succeed in his claim on a policy depends on the nature of the insured peril. In *Holmes v Payne*,[3] an insured necklace which was believed lost, and in respect of which a settlement agreement had been entered into, was subsequently found in an article of the insured's clothing within her house, and Roche J made the following remarks in relation to the meaning of 'loss' in property insurance:[4]

'Uncertainty as to recovery of the thing insured is, in my opinion, in non-marine matters the main consideration on the question of loss. In this connection it is, of course, true that a thing may be mislaid and yet not lost, but, in my opinion, if a thing has been mislaid and is missing or has disappeared and a reasonable time has elapsed to allow of diligent search and of recovery and such diligent search has been made and has been fruitless, then the thing may properly be said to be lost. The recovery of the thing is at least uncertain and, I should say, unlikely. … Subsequent discovery or recovery of the thing assured is, of course, of itself no disproof of the loss.'

Similarly, in order to establish a loss under a policy of motor insurance, an insured does not have to prove that the vehicle is in all circumstances irrecoverable, simply that its recovery remains uncertain after the insured has taken all reasonable steps to recover it.[5] In the case of a liability policy, the insured suffers a loss when it is found liable to a third party.[6]

On a claim under a fire policy, the burden is on the insured to show that the loss was caused by fire. If he discharges his burden, the onus is then on the insurers to show, if they so allege, that the fire was caused or connived at by the insured.[7] This is so even where the facts are peculiarly within the knowledge of the insured.[8] In any case, if the insurer succeeds in showing that the peril insured against was caused deliberately and fraudulently or connived at by the insured, the insured will not recover under the policy. This is a matter of construction of the policy,[9] and overlaps with the well-known principle of insurance law that no man can recover for a loss which he himself has deliberately and fraudulently caused, which is itself an extension of the general principle that no man can take advantage of his own wrong (in Latin, *ex turpi causa non oritur actio*).[10]

Where loss is due to the insured's negligence, he will be entitled to recover unless loss caused by negligence is excepted from cover.[11] Where a policy insures against liability for bodily injury 'caused by accidents', an act which is merely negligent is 'caused by accident' and within the scope of cover, whereas an act which is intended to cause injury is not; between these two extremes, whether injury caused by an act which is deliberate and intentional is 'caused by accident' will depend on the facts of the case including the state of mind of the insured.[12] Where a policy insuring against liability for accidental damage to property excludes losses 'arising from any wilful, malicious or criminal acts', a 'wilful' act is an act which is either deliberate and intended to cause damage of the kind in question, or reckless, meaning that the act is done in the knowledge that it might cause the damage or not caring whether or not it might.[13] The courts have interpreted clauses in employer's liability and property policies which impose an obligation on the insured to take reasonable precautions to prevent loss as requiring that the insured should not merely be negligent, but must at least be reckless, because it is improbable that the parties intended to negate a core part of the insurance cover.[14] In this context, recklessness means deliberately courting a danger, the existence of which the insured recognises, by refraining from taking any measures to avert it or by taking measures which he himself knows are inadequate.[15] The recklessness must be that of the insured and not his sub-contractors or employees.[16] For these purposes, where the insured is a company, the recklessness must be committed by people of such seniority within the insured company that their recklessness will be attributed to the insured itself.[17] In motor insurance, reasonable precautions clauses which impose a positive obligation to maintain a vehicle in good repair have been interpreted as requiring that the insured should not be negligent, on the basis that this is not repugnant to the commercial object of the contract because the insurer is not covering and does not intend to cover the insured for liability arising out of negligent maintenance of the vehicle, but there is cover for liability arising out of the negligent uses of a vehicle which is properly maintained.[18]

The onus of proof is different under a marine policy, as cover against 'perils of the sea' connotes accidental or fortuitous loss, and the burden is therefore on the insured to prove that the cause of the loss was accidental in order to come within the cover.[19] There is therefore no obligation on underwriters to suggest and to seek to prove some other cause of loss, against which the ship was not insured, and if they choose to do so, there is no obligation on them to prove, even on a balance of probabilities, the truth of their alternative case.[20] The marine insurance authorities on this issue therefore have no application in the non-marine context.

Where cover is 'all risks', the insured must show that the loss was due to an accident or fortuitous occurrence or casualty in order to recover,[21] but need not prove the precise nature of the accident.[22] Thus, loss which is inevitable due to ordinary wear and tear or depreciation, or which is caused by voluntary conduct (including wilful misconduct) on the part of the insured, is not within the scope of 'all risks' cover.[23] Conversion of the insured's goods is within the scope of such cover.[24]

1 *West Wake Price & Co v Ching* [1957] 1 WLR 45, 49 (Devlin J).
2 *Becker, Gray & Co v London Assurance Corpn* [1918] AC 101, 108, HL (Lord Dunedin); see also *Ted Baker plc v AXA Insurance UK plc (No 2)* [2014] EWHC 3548 (Comm), [2015] Lloyd's Rep IR 325, para 137 (Eder J).
3 [1930] 2 KB 301, 310 (Roche J).
4 At 310.

5 *Webster v General Accident Fire and Life Assurance Corpn Ltd* [1953] 1 QB 520, 531–532 (Parker J).

6 See eg *West Wake Price & Co v Ching* [1957] 1 WLR 45, 49 (Devlin J).

7 *Slattery v Mance* [1962] 1 QB 676. If the insurers do not plead a positive case as to the cause of loss, they are entitled to test in cross-examination the insured's evidence as to cause of loss, but may not cross-examine on the basis of any alternative possible cause of loss: *Regina Fur Co Ltd v Bossom* [1958] 2 Lloyd's Rep 425, 428, CA (Lord Evershed MR).

8 *Slattery v Mance* [1962] 1 QB 676 (a case of fire at sea).

9 *Beresford v Royal Insurance Co Ltd* [1938] AC 586, 594–595, HL (Lord Atkin); *Charlton v Fisher* [2001] EWCA Civ 112, [2002] QB 578, para 51 (Rix LJ).

10 *Beresford v Royal Insurance Co Ltd* [1938] AC 586, 596–599, HL (Lord Atkin); *Slattery v Mance* [1962] 1 QB 676, 681 (Salmon J), applied: *Schiffshypothekenbank Zu Luebeck AG v Compton, The Alexion Hope* [1987] 1 Lloyd's Rep 60, 67 (Staughton J); [1988] 1 Lloyd's Rep 311, 316–318, CA (Lloyd LJ); *Gray v Barr* [1971] 2 QB 554, CA (insured threatened victim with loaded shotgun; insured deliberately fired one shot into the ceiling and during struggle which ensued a second shot was fired involuntarily which killed the victim; held that on these facts public policy would prevent enforcement of a policy of insurance against liability for bodily injury); *Charlton v Fisher* [2001] EWCA Civ 112, [2002] QB 578, para 31 (Laws LJ). Public policy is not static: *Gray v Barr* [1971] 2 QB 554, 581–582, CA (Salmon LJ).

11 See **PARA 4.11**.

12 *Gray v Barr* [1971] 2 QB 554, CA (see note 10 above); *Charlton v Fisher* [2001] EWCA Civ 112, [2002] QB 578, paras 58–60 (Rix LJ). Although public policy and construction of 'caused by accident' or 'accident' in policy wording may lead to the same conclusion, they are separate grounds for rejecting a claim and are considered separately: see, eg, *Gray v Barr* [1971] 2 QB 554, CA; *Charlton v Fisher* [2001] EWCA Civ 112, [2002] QB 578. Additional considerations arise in relation to compulsory motor insurance: see *Charlton v Fisher* [2001] EWCA Civ 112, [2002] QB 578; *Bristol Alliance Limited Partnership v Williams* [2011] EWHC 1657 (QB). Whether liability for injuries caused deliberately by an employee of the insured is within the scope of cover depends on whether the acts of the employee are to be attributed to the insured; this is a question of construction of the policy: *Hawley v Luminar Leisure Ltd* [2006] EWCA Civ 18, [2006] Lloyd's Rep IR 307, para 107 (Hallett LJ); *KR v Royal and Sun Alliance plc* [2006] EWCA Civ 1454, [2007] Lloyd's Rep IR 368, paras 60–61 and 63–65 (Scott Baker LJ).

13 *Patrick v Royal London Mutual Insurance Society Ltd* [2006] EWCA Civ 421, [2007] Lloyd's Rep IR 85, paras 15–16 (Tuckey LJ) (household and personal liability policy). Where an insured seeks to recover under a policy of insurance for the consequences of his own act in setting a fire, he will need to prove, on the balance of probabilities, that he was insane, within the meaning of the M'Naghten rules, at the time of the fire; the nature and extent of this test should not be underestimated: the insured must show that he 'was labouring under such a defect of reason, from disease of the mind, as not to know the nature and quality of the act he was doing; or, if he did know it, that he did not know he was doing what was wrong': *Porter v Zurich Insurance Co* [2009] EWHC 376 (QB), [2010] Lloyd's Rep IR 373, paras 17 and 18 (Coulson J).

14 *Fraser v B N Furman (Productions) Ltd* [1967] 1 WLR 898, 906, CA (Diplock LJ; employers' liability insurance); *W & J Lane v Spratt* [1970] 2 QB 480 (Roskill J; property insurance); *Devco Holder Ltd v Legal & General Assurance Society Ltd* [1993] 2 Lloyd's Rep 567, CA (property insurance; no indemnity for theft of valuable car while unattended and unlocked with keys in ignition); *Sofi v Prudential Assurance Co Ltd* [1993] 2 Lloyd's Rep 559, CA (property insurance; indemnity for theft of valuable jewellery left out of sight in unattended car); *Hayward v Norwich Union Insurance Ltd* [2001] EWCA Civ 243, [2001] Lloyd's Rep IR 410 (property insurance; no indemnity for theft of valuable car and contents while within sight and immobilised but unlocked with keys in ignition); *Paine v Catlins* [2004] EWHC 3054 (TCC), [2005] Lloyd's Rep IR 665 (HHJ Peter Coulson QC; condition in fire policy requiring the taking of reasonable precautions including as to maintenance of property insured); *The Board of Trustees of the Tate Gallery v Duffy Construction Ltd (No 2)* [2007] EWHC 912 (TCC), [2008] Lloyd's Rep IR 159 (Jackson J; general condition in combined contract works and third party liability insurance requiring insured to take reasonable precautions to prevent loss or damage).

15 *Fraser v B N Furman (Productions) Ltd* [1967] 1 WLR 898, 905–906, CA (Diplock LJ).

16 *The Board of Trustees of the Tate Gallery v Duffy Construction Ltd (No 2)* [2007] EWHC 912 (TCC), [2008] Lloyd's Rep IR 159, para 26 (Jackson J). In *The Board of Trustees of the Tate Gallery v Duffy Construction Ltd (No 2)* [2007] EWHC 912 (TCC), [2008] Lloyd's Rep IR 159, a general condition requiring the insured to 'take and cause to be taken' reasonable precautions to prevent loss was interpreted as applying only to the insured; Jackson J said (at para 29) that if the insurers intended substantially to cut down the cover which the insured was reasonably expecting to receive, it behoved them to do so expressly and with clarity, and they had failed to do so.

17 *The Board of Trustees of the Tate Gallery v Duffy Construction Ltd (No 2)* [2007] EWHC 912 (TCC), [2008] Lloyd's Rep IR 159, para 31 (Jackson J).
18 *Amey Properties Ltd v Cornhill Insurance plc* [1996] LRLR 259, 264 (Tucker J).
19 *Slattery v Mance* [1962] 1 QB 676; *Rhesa Shipping Co SA v Edmunds (The Popi M)* [1985] 1 WLR 948, HL.
20 *Rhesa Shipping Co SA v Edmunds (The Popi M)* [1985] 1 WLR 948, HL.
21 *British and Foreign Marine Insurance Co Ltd v Gaunt* [1921] 2 AC 41, HL; *Regina Fur Co Ltd v Bossom* [1958] 2 Lloyd's Rep 425, CA.
22 *British and Foreign Marine Insurance Co Ltd v Gaunt* [1921] 2 AC 41, HL.
23 *British and Foreign Marine Insurance Co Ltd v Gaunt* [1921] 2 AC 41, HL; *J J Lloyd Instruments Ltd v Northern Star Insurance Co Ltd, The Miss Jay Jay* [1987] 1 Lloyd's Rep 32, CA; *Ikerigi Compania Naviera SA v Palmer, The Wondrous* [1991] 1 Lloyd's Rep 400, 416 (Hobhouse J) (point not considered on appeal: [1992] 2 Lloyd's Rep 566).
24 *London and Provincial Leather Processes Ltd v Hudson* [1939] 2 KB 724.

STANDARD OF PROOF

5.3   The civil standard of proof is the balance of probabilities: that is, proof that the fact in issue more probably occurred than not.[1] This is a lower standard of proof than in a criminal prosecution, in which proof is required 'beyond reasonable doubt', or, to use an alternative formulation, the tribunal of fact must be 'sure'.[2] This is so even in a civil case in which allegations of dishonest or otherwise criminal conduct are made.[3] In *Hornal v Neuberger Products Ltd*, Lord Denning MR suggested that, although the criminal standard does not apply in such cases, a more rigorous standard is applied than in an ordinary civil case:[4]

> 'The more serious the allegation the higher the degree of probability that is required: but it need not, in a civil case, reach the very high standard required by the criminal law'.

More recently, there has been a move away from the notion of a flexible standard of proof. Instead, the inherent probability or improbability of an event is taken into account, to whatever extent is appropriate, when weighing the probabilities and deciding whether, on balance, the event occurred.[5] There is only one civil standard of proof, and only one rule of law, namely that the occurrence of the fact in issue must be proved to have been more probable than not; common sense, not law, requires that in deciding this question, regard should be had, to whatever extent appropriate, to inherent probabilities.[6] The more improbable the event, such as that a particular person or persons would be guilty of dishonest or criminal conduct, the stronger the evidence must be that it did occur before, on the balance of probability, its occurrence will be established.[7] In practice, the result is likely to be the same.[8]

1 *Re B (children) (care proceedings: standard of proof)* [2008] UKHL 35, [2009] 1 AC 11, para 13 (Lord Hoffmann).
2 See also **PARA 3.32**.
3 *Hornal v Neuberger Products Ltd* [1957] 1 QB 247, CA.
4 At 258. This issue may, however, be no more than semantic: *National Justice Compania Naviera SA v Prudential Assurance Co Ltd, The Ikarian Reefer* [1995] 1 Lloyd's Rep 455, 459, CA (Stuart-Smith LJ).
5 *Re H (minors) (sexual abuse: standard of proof)* [1996] AC 563, 586–587, HL (Lord Nicholls); *Re B (children) (care proceedings: standard of proof)* [2008] UKHL 35, [2009] 1 AC 11, paras 15 (Lord Hoffmann).

6 *Re B (children) (care proceedings: standard of proof)* [2008] UKHL 35, [2009] 1 AC 11, paras 13 and 15 (Lord Hoffmann) and 70 (Baroness Hale).

7 *Anonima Petroli Italiana SpA v Marlucidez Armadora SA, The Filiatra Legacy* [1991] 2 Lloyd's Rep 337, 365–366, CA (Mustill LJ); applied: *National Justice Compania Naviera SA v Prudential Assurance Co Ltd, The Ikarian Reefer* [1995] 1 Lloyd's Rep 455, 459, CA (Stuart-Smith LJ); *Re H (minors) (sexual abuse: standard of proof)* [1996] AC 563, 586–587, HL (Lord Nicholls). *Re B (children) (care proceedings: standard of proof)* [2008] UKHL 35, [2009] 1 AC 11, paras 15 (Lord Hoffmann) and 70 (Baroness Hale).

8 *Anonima Petroli Italiana SpA v Marlucidez Armadora SA, The Filiatra Legacy* [1991] 2 Lloyd's Rep 337, 365–366, CA (Mustill LJ); *Re H (minors) (sexual abuse: standard of proof)* [1996] AC 563, 586–587, HL (Lord Nicholls); *Strive Shipping Corpn v Hellenic Mutual War Risks Association, The Grecia Express* [2002] 2 Lloyd's Rep 88, 97–100 (Colman J).

PROOF 'SATISFACTORY TO' INSURER

5.4 In *Napier v UNUM Ltd*,[1] Tuckey J considered a provision in a permanent health insurance policy which provided that insurers would pay 'on proof satisfactory to [them]' of the insured's entitlement to benefits under the policy. The judge construed the provision as imposing an obligation on the insured to provide such evidence to support his claim as the insurers might reasonably require. As the insured had provided such evidence, it was for the court, and not insurers, to evaluate the evidence provided by the insured and that obtained by insurers, in deciding whether insurers were obliged to make a payment under the policy. In coming to this conclusion, the judge rejected both the insured's argument that a term was to be implied that the insurers would act reasonably (meaning that they would be satisfied with such proof as would satisfy reasonable men), and the insurers' argument that their decision to reject the claim was not susceptible to legal challenge except on grounds of lack of good faith.[2] In *Braganza v BP Shipping Ltd*,[3] the Supreme Court considered contractual terms in which one party to a contract is given the power to exercise a discretion, or to form an opinion as to relevant facts. The Supreme Court held that the court will imply a term that the decision must not be 'arbitrary, capricious or perverse',[4] and that the decision-making process must be lawful and rational in the public law sense, meaning that the decision-maker must exclude extraneous considerations and take into account those considerations which are obviously relevant to the decision in question, in accordance with its contractual purpose;[5] and that whatever term may be implied will depend on the terms and the context of the particular contract involved.[6] The scope for scrutiny by the court differs according to the nature of the decision: the courts are in a much better position to review the good faith and rationality of the decision-making process where the issue is whether or not a state of fact existed, rather than a bona fide and rational exercise of a discretion.[7] The reasoning in *Napier v UNUM Ltd*, although expressly limited to proof or evidence, amounted in substance to a refusal to accept insurers' rejection of the claim based on their evaluation of the evidence, and although *Napier v UNUM* was not considered in *Braganza*, it is difficult to see how its reasoning can survive the reasoning of the Supreme Court. The relationship between insurer and insured, and the nature of the contract of insurance in question, may however be relevant to the degree of scrutiny which the court will consider appropriate pursuant to the implied term,[8] so that the court might, for example, subject to a more intense scrutiny a decision made by insurers under a consumer insurance policy than under a reinsurance contract.

A clause which requires an insured to prove his loss to the reasonable satisfaction of insurers does not implicitly require the insured to complete any particular claim form.[9]

1 [1996] 2 Lloyd's Rep 550.
2 At 552–554.
3 [2015] UKSC 17, [2015] 1 WLR 1661.
4 Paragraphs 18–23 and 42 (Lady Hale, approving: *CVG Siderurgicia del Orinoco SA v London Steamship Owners' Mutual Insurance Association Ltd, The Vainqueur José* [1979] 1 Lloyd's Rep 557 and *Gan v Tai Ping (Nos 2 and 3)* [2001] EWCA Civ 1047, [2002] Lloyd's Rep IR 667), 52 (Lord Hodge) and 104 and 106 (Lord Neuberger). See also, to similar effect although not considered by the Supreme Court: *West of England Shipowners Mutual Insurance Association (Luxembourg) v Cristal Ltd, The Glacier Bay* [1996] 1 Lloyd's Rep 370, CA and *Brown v GIO Insurance Ltd* [1998] Lloyd's Rep IR 201, CA; and see **PARA 14.4**.
5 Paragraphs 28–29 (Lady Hale), 53 (Lord Hodge) and 103 (Lord Neuberger).
6 Paragraphs 18 and 31 (Lady Hale).
7 *Braganza v BP Shipping Ltd* [2015] UKSC 17, [2015] 1 WLR 1661, paras 56–57 (Lord Hodge), comparing a decision as to the cause of death, which was a finding of fact, with the assessment of whether an employee was entitled to a discretionary bonus, which was an exercise that involved a qualitative judgement of the employee's performance.
8 See, by analogy, *Braganza v BP Shipping Ltd* [2015] UKSC 17, [2015] 1 WLR 1661, para 55 (Lord Hodge): 'The personal relationship which employment involves may justify a more intense scrutiny of the employer's decision-making process than would be appropriate in some commercial contracts'; he distinguished this from the implied term of trust and confidence in a contract of employment, on which he said he did not rely in reaching his decision (see para 61). Lord Neuberger said that he found it difficult to accept that trust and confidence would require more than what in a normal commercial context would be expected, and appeared to reject any suggestion that the approach to be adopted should differ according to whether the contract was one of employment as opposed to a commercial contract (see para 104).
9 *All Leisure Holidays Ltd v Europaische Reiseversicherung AG* [2011] EWHC 2629 (Comm), [2012] Lloyd's Rep IR 193, paras 27–28 (Teare J).

Chapter 6

Measurement of loss

INDEMNITY AND CONTINGENCY INSURANCE

6.1   Policies of indemnity insurance may be valued or unvalued (or open). The principles applicable to each are discussed below. The amount payable under a policy of contingency insurance (including life, accident and permanent health insurance) on the happening of an insured event is specified in the policy.

TOTAL LOSS

6.2   There are in marine insurance doctrines of actual and constructive total loss.[1] The doctrine of constructive total loss in marine insurance has meant that the test for an actual total loss has always been applied with the utmost rigour: for an insured has always had the option of claiming for a constructive total loss.[2] Outside marine insurance, the doctrine of total loss may be found to be more flexible; thus a motor car may be treated as a total loss when it is not worth repairing.[3]

1 See Marine Insurance Act 1906, ss 56–61.
2 *Masefield AG v Amlin Corporate Member Ltd, The Bunga Melati Dua* [2011] EWCA Civ 24, [2011] 1 Lloyd's Rep 630, para 16 (Rix LJ).
3 *Masefield AG v Amlin Corporate Member Ltd, The Bunga Melati Dua* [2011] EWCA Civ 24, [2011] 1 Lloyd's Rep 630, para 16 (Rix LJ).

VALUED AND UNVALUED POLICIES

6.3   If the insurance policy is a valued policy, the amount recoverable by the insured on a total loss is the agreed value as stated in the policy.[1] The fundamental principle of indemnity insurance is that the insured, in the case of a loss within the terms of the policy, should be fully indemnified, but should never be more than fully indemnified.[2] Although valued policies arguably offend against this principle, in that they may allow an insured to recover more than he has lost, they are treated by the courts as contracts of indemnity on the basis that the insured is entitled to be indemnified against the relevant loss, but the parties have agreed in advance the amount of such loss.[3] Consequently, under a valued policy, the insured may recover more (or indeed less) than his actual loss without offending against the indemnity principle.[4]

It is a question of construction whether a policy is a valued policy. The term 'sum insured' will normally indicate the amount for which the subject matter is insured and will not be read as an agreed value.[5] Valued policies are common in the context of marine insurance, whereas it is unusual for a non-marine policy to be construed as a valued policy.[6] In *Leppard v Excess Insurance Co Ltd*,[7] the Court of Appeal rejected a submission that a fire policy was a valued policy, holding that, on its true construction, the policy was 'an ordinary indemnity-only contract'[8] under which the insured was entitled to recover his actual loss. The reference in the policy to the cost of replacement represented not an agreed amount payable on a total loss, but rather the maximum amount for which the insurer might be liable. In *Elcock v Thomson*,[9] on the other hand, a fire policy on a mansion expressly provided that the value of the mansion was agreed at £100,000, and was held to be a valued policy.

Rather than stating a specific agreed figure, a policy may state an agreed basis of assessment of the loss. Though perhaps not strictly a valued policy, such a policy will operate in a similar way to a valued policy, with the agreed basis of assessment displacing any other way of assessing the insured's actual loss.[10]

In the case of a partial loss, the court will assess the actual value before and after the loss, and calculate the amount of depreciation as a fraction of the actual value. It will then apply this fraction to the value as stated in the policy.[11] As a matter of principle, it would seem that insurers ought not to be entitled, where the policy is a valued policy, to limit their liability to the cost of reinstatement (whether or not the property is reinstated).[12]

Where a policy is an unvalued policy, the insured is entitled to recover an indemnity in respect of his actual loss,[13] subject to the application of the limit of indemnity, the excess or deductible, any aggregation wording and any provision for reinstatement of the policy limits, and the application of the principles of average and under-insurance.[14] What amounts to actual loss may be governed by the policy wording, and the policy may provide for the method of assessment of the loss, for example, by providing that the insured is entitled to the cost of reinstatement if the property insured is in fact reinstated.[15] Once the insured has shown on a balance of probabilities that the loss was caused by an insured peril, the court will generally assess damages as best it can by reference to the materials available to it; the balance of probability test is not an appropriate yardstick to measure loss, and lack of precision as to the amount of quantum is not a bar to recovery.[16]

1 *Irving v Manning* (1847) 1 HL Cas 287, HL; see also s 27(2) of the Marine Insurance Act 1906: 'A valued policy is a policy which specifies the agreed value of the subject-matter insured'.
2 *Castellain v Preston* (1883) 11 QBD 380, 386, CA (Brett LJ).
3 *Irving v Manning* (1847) 1 HL Cas 287, HL; *Lucena v Craufurd* (1806) 2 Bos & PNR 269, 322 (Lord Eldon); *Maurice v Goldsbrough Mort & Co Ltd* [1939] AC 452, PC; *Leppard v Excess Insurance Co Ltd* [1979] 1 WLR 512, 519, CA (Megaw LJ).
4 *Maurice v Goldsbrough Mort & Co Ltd* [1939] AC 452, 466–467, PC.
5 *Kyzuna Investments Ltd v Ocean Marine Mutual Insurance Association (Europe)* [2000] 1 Lloyd's Rep 505, 509 (Thomas J).
6 See *Quoram AS v Schramm* [2002] 1 Lloyd's Rep 249, 260 (Thomas J) (fine art policy not a valued policy); *Clothing Management Technology Ltd v Beazley Solutions Ltd* [2012] EWHC 727 (QB), [2012] Lloyd's Rep IR 571, para 60 (HHJ Mackie QC) (rare for marine insurance policy to be unvalued).
7 [1979] 1 WLR 512, CA.
8 Geoffrey Lane LJ, at 520–521.
9 [1949] 2 KB 755.
10 *Maurice v Goldsbrough Mort & Co Ltd* [1939] AC 452, 462, PC; *Leppard v Excess Insurance Co Ltd* [1979] 1 WLR 512, 519, CA (Megaw LJ).

11 *Elcock v Thomson* [1949] 2 KB 755 (fire).
12 In *Elcock v Thomson* [1949] 2 KB 755, Morris J's provisional view (at 764) was that insurers could limit their liability to the cost of reinstatement where the policy was a valued policy, but it was unnecessary for him to express a final view, and he did not do so.
13 Section 28 of the Marine Insurance Act 1906 provides: 'An unvalued policy is a policy which does not specify the value of the subject-matter insured, but, subject to the limit of the sum insured, leaves the insurable value to be subsequently ascertained …'.
14 See **PARA 6.10**.
15 See **PARA 6.5**.
16 *Ted Baker plc v AXA Insurance UK plc (No 2)* [2014] EWHC 3548 (Comm), [2015] Lloyd's Rep IR 325, para 140 (Eder J).

Assessment of actual loss

6.4   Where the insurance is on property, and does not provide for the method of assessment of loss, one or other of the following measures may be applied: diminution in value as a result of the insured event, or cost of repair. There is no agreement as to which is the primary measure, and much depends on the facts of the case, the aim being to adopt the approach which most nearly puts the insured in the position he would have been in had the insured event not occurred.[1] Expert assistance is often required, whichever measure is preferred. Diminution in value is usually assessed as at the date of loss.[2] It may be different in the case of cost of repair, however: if the cost of repair has increased since the loss, the court may award the cost at the date of trial, in order to indemnify the insured against his actual loss.[3] Evidence of the price paid by the insured is a factor to be taken into account in assessing the market value immediately before the insured event, but is not conclusive, as the insured may have paid more (or indeed less) than the market value, market values may have fluctuated by more or less than the rate of inflation since the property was purchased, and the condition of the property may have changed since it was purchased. If the value of the subject matter has increased during the policy period, the insured may be entitled to an indemnity based on the increased value, subject to the policy limits.[4] Where there is more than one market, the value is assessed by reference to the market actually used or, if none is used, the value is assessed by reference to the highest of the markets.[5]

It may be difficult to assess the open market value of some types of property, such as old or unusual buildings. Where the court concludes that the insured is not entitled to the cost of reinstatement, it may adopt an alternative method of assessing the insured's loss, such as to award damages based on the cost of erecting a new building which will meet the purpose for which the old building was, or could have been, used.[6]

1 In *Pleasurama Ltd v Sun Alliance and London Insurance Ltd* [1979] 1 Lloyd's Rep 389, 393 (bingo hall damaged by fire), Parker J considered cost of repair to be the primary measure, whereas in *Quoram AS v Schramm* [2002] 1 Lloyd's Rep 249, 265 (Degas painting damaged by fire), Thomas J preferred diminution in value.
2 *Edney v De Rougemont* (1927) 28 Ll L Rep 215; *Richard Aubrey Film Productions Ltd v Graham* [1960] 2 Lloyd's Rep 101 (cost of reshooting greater than market value of lost negative of feature film); *Reynolds v Phoenix Assurance Co Ltd* [1978] 2 Lloyd's Rep 440; *Leppard v Excess Insurance Co Ltd* [1979] 1 WLR 512, CA; *McClean Enterprises Ltd v Ecclesiastical Insurance Office plc* [1986] 2 Lloyd's Rep 416; *Quoram AS v Schramm* [2002] 1 Lloyd's Rep 249.
3 See *Reynolds v Phoenix Assurance Co Ltd* [1978] 2 Lloyd's Rep 440, 462–463 (Forbes J). In *Tonkin v UK Insurance Ltd* [2006] EWHC 1120 (TCC), [2007] Lloyd's Rep IR 283, HHJ Peter Coulson QC

declined to assess reinstatement costs at the date of trial rather than the date of loss on the grounds that the latter was the correct date, and that any increase in costs due to delay in payment by insurers could be compensated for only by an award of interest (paras 21–26). Although damages for breach of contract are normally assessed at the date of breach, this approach may be departed from if necessary to do justice in a particular case: see, eg, *Agnew v Johnson* [1980] AC 367, HL (sale of land). This should not be confused with the principle that damages are not available for consequential loss caused by insurers' delay in paying a claim: see **PARA 6.6**.

4 *Re Wilson and Scottish Insurance Corpn Ltd* [1920] 2 Ch 28.

5 *Quoram AS v Schramm* [2002] 1 Lloyd's Rep 249, 265 (Thomas J) (auction and private dealers' markets for fine art).

6 *Reynolds v Phoenix Assurance Co Ltd* [1978] 2 Lloyd's Rep 440, 447–448 (Forbes J).

Reinstatement or replacement of damaged or destroyed property

6.5 A clause commonly found in fire policies, which on the face of it appears to give the insurer an option where property is damaged or destroyed as to whether to pay the value of property destroyed or the amount of the damage, or alternatively to reinstate or replace the property, has been construed[1] as entitling the insured to the cost of reinstatement if he can prove that he intends to reinstate the property (or, perhaps, that at the date of the fire he so intended, but was prevented from so doing by the insurers' refusal to indemnify against the cost of reinstatement).[2] The clause is as follows:

> 'In the event of destruction or damage to the property or any part of such property described in the schedule to this section by the perils specified hereafter the Company will pay to the Insured the value of the property at the time of the happening of its destruction or the amount of such damage or at its option reinstate or replace such property or any part thereof. Provided that the liability of the Company under this section shall in no case exceed in respect of each item the sum expressed in the schedule to be insured thereon or in the whole the total sum insured hereby ...'

In construing the clause as having the meaning set out above, both Forbes J in *Reynolds v Phoenix Assurance Co Ltd*[3] and Staughton J in *McClLlean Enterprises Ltd v Ecclesiastical Insurance Office plc*[4] were strongly influenced by the fact that the property was insured for its reinstatement value, rather than its replacement value. In *Pleasurama Ltd v Sun Alliance and London Insurance Ltd*,[5] Parker J construed a similar clause, in the light of the policy terms and conditions as a whole, to mean that the primary measure of damage under the policy was the cost of reinstatement, even where the insured did not intend to reinstate the property.

In *Reynolds v Phoenix Assurance Co Ltd*, Forbes J considered it to be a question of fact and degree whether the insured was entitled to the reinstatement value of the property in order to be properly indemnified. He rejected a submission that the test he should apply was whether a commercial concern, using its own money, would reinstate, and instead considered whether the insured genuinely intended to reinstate the property, for a reason that would appeal to an ordinary man in their position (ie for reasons which were not absurd or eccentric) if they recovered an indemnity from insurers. Applying this formulation, Forbes J awarded damages for the cost of reinstatement. In *McClean Enterprises Ltd v Ecclesiastical Insurance Office plc*, Staughton J held that the insured, who had sold the property between the date of the fire and the trial, had never intended to reinstate the premises, which he had already decided to sell at the date of the fire, and awarded only damages for reduction in open market value.

In *Pleasurama Ltd v Sun Alliance and London Insurance Ltd*, the cost of reinstatement measure was held to entitle the insured to recover an amount in respect of professional fees (provided for in the policy in relation to reinstatement), even though such fees would not be incurred in fact because the insured did not intend to reinstate the property. However, the insured was held not to be entitled to recover an amount in respect of the additional cost of complying with public authorities' requirements because the policy provided expressly that such additional costs were recoverable only if in fact incurred. In practice, the *Pleasurama* construction is likely to be the exception, and the *Reynolds* and *McClean Enterprises* construction likely to be the rule, as the courts will be reluctant to construe a policy so as to entitle the insured to have his actual loss assessed by reference to the cost of reinstatement even where he does not intend to reinstate his damaged property.

Where a policy gives insurers the option of replacement or reinstatement of property, or of paying the value of the property or the amount of the damage, they are entitled to insist on replacement or reinstatement.[6] If however replacement or reinstatement is not possible, it is a matter of construction of the policy whether insurers are obliged to pay the value of the property or the amount of the damage, or are discharged altogether.[7] In the case of goods such as plant and machinery, the right of insurers to exercise the option to replace or reinstate the property is not affected by the mere fact of the building in which it is located having been destroyed or of the insured's right to occupy the building having been determined: the insurer must do what is reasonable in the circumstances, and there is no reason why the insurers should not reinstate or replace the goods in another location within a reasonable distance where the insured may be willing to receive them.[8]

Where the insured has a contractual right under the policy to reinstatement, rather than at insurers' option, the only question is whether it genuinely intends to reinstate the property, and no question of 'eccentricity' arises.[9] A requirement in the policy that the insured reinstate the property 'with reasonable despatch otherwise no payment' cannot be read to arise until the insurer has confirmed that it will indemnify the insured, nor will there be an absence of reasonable despatch before the insurer's obligation is accepted or established.[10] This applies whether or not the insured can afford to pay for the reinstatement without the benefit of the indemnity.[11] In these circumstances, the court may grant a declaration that the insured is entitled to be indemnified for the cost of reinstatement.[12]

The insured has a number of options in relation to a claim for reinstatement:

(1) the insured may decide to reinstate the property to a lay-out and condition that, as closely as possible, mirrors what was there before;

(2) the insured may decide to reinstate the building generally but at the same time to take advantage of its destruction to make certain minor changes so as to improve what was there before. If the insured takes this option, then he or she needs to make it plain to the insurer at the outset that the scheme will include some elements of improvement. If the improvements are relatively minor, the insurer may be prepared to bear the cost of them; otherwise, they will be at the expense of the insured;

(3)   the insured may take advantage of the destruction of the property to make significant changes, at his own expense, to improve what was there before.[13]

Where option (2) or (3) is pursued, it is important that there is a priced bill of quantities or detailed specification, which is the subject of a priced breakdown by those tendering for the construction contract, so that the parties can identify what elements of the work are to be paid for by the insurer and what elements by the insured.[14]

1 *Reynolds v Phoenix Assurance Co Ltd* [1978] 2 Lloyd's Rep 440, 450–453 (Forbes J) (maltings badly damaged by fire); *McClean Enterprises Ltd v Ecclesiastical Insurance Office plc* [1986] 2 Lloyd's Rep 416, 424–427 (Staughton J) (hotel badly damaged by fire).
2 *McClean Enterprises Ltd v Ecclesiastical Insurance Office plc* [1986] 2 Lloyd's Rep 416, 426 (Staughton J).
3 [1978] 2 Lloyd's Rep 440.
4 *McClean Enterprises Ltd v Ecclesiastical Insurance Office plc* [1986] 2 Lloyd's Rep 416.
5 [1979] 1 Lloyd's Rep 389 (bingo hall badly damaged by fire).
6 *Anderson v The Commercial Union Assurance Co* (1885) 55 LJQB 146, CA.
7 *Anderson v The Commercial Union Assurance Co* (1885) 55 LJQB 146, CA, 150 (Bowen LJ).
8 *Anderson v The Commercial Union Assurance Co* (1885) 55 LJQB 146, CA, 148 (Lord Esher MR), 148–149 (Cotton LJ) and 149–150 (Bowen LJ).
9 *Western Trading Ltd v Great Lakes Reinsurance (UK) Ltd* [2015] EWHC 103 (QB), [2015] Lloyd's Rep IR 561, para 146 (HHJ Mackie QC).
10 *Western Trading Ltd v Great Lakes Reinsurance (UK) Ltd* [2015] EWHC 103 (QB), [2015] Lloyd's Rep IR 561, paras 127–129 (HHJ Mackie QC).
11 *Western Trading Ltd v Great Lakes Reinsurance (UK) Ltd* [2015] EWHC 103 (QB), [2015] Lloyd's Rep IR 561, paras 127–129 (HHJ Mackie QC).
12 *Western Trading Ltd v Great Lakes Reinsurance (UK) Ltd* [2015] EWHC 103 (QB), [2015] Lloyd's Rep IR 561, paras 130 and 148–149 (HHJ Mackie QC).
13 *Tonkin v UK Insurance Ltd* [2006] EWHC 1120 (TCC), [2007] Lloyd's Rep IR 283, paras 150–156 (HHJ Peter Coulson QC); applied: *Western Trading Ltd v Great Lakes Reinsurance (UK) Ltd* [2015] EWHC 103 (QB), [2015] Lloyd's Rep IR 561, paras 142–144 (HHJ Mackie QC).
14 *Tonkin v UK Insurance Ltd* [2006] EWHC 1120 (TCC), [2007] Lloyd's Rep IR 283, paras 152–156 (HHJ Peter Coulson QC). In *Western Trading Ltd v Great Lakes Reinsurance (UK) Ltd* [2015] EWHC 103 (QB), [2015] Lloyd's Rep IR 561, HHJ Mackie QC said (at para 141) that this approach would require a reinstatement plan to be devised, with the assistance of professional experts, and that issues about the detail could be resolved by agreement, informal or formal ADR (alternative dispute resolution), or if necessary by the court.

CONSEQUENTIAL LOSS

6.6   It is a matter of construction whether a policy covers consequential loss and, if so, what type of consequential loss.[1] An ordinary marine insurance policy does not cover loss of time or the wages and maintenance of the crew.[2] Similarly, a policy described as an insurance on goods does not cover loss of profits unless expressly stated,[3] and a policy against loss does not, in the absence of express terms, cover consequential loss.[4] Save insofar as a cause of action is available for breach of ICOBS,[5] delay in accepting a claim or in making a payment which leads to loss of profits or other business losses, such as hire charges, or interest charges on borrowings, does not give rise to a cause of action in damages, although the court may award interest on any damages awarded in respect of the claim to an indemnity.[6] It was acknowledged in *Sprung v Royal Insurance (UK) Ltd*,[7] that there may be an exception where the purpose of the policy is to provide for immediate repair of damaged plant and equipment,[8] as is the case with business interruption insurance.

In *Pride Valley Foods Ltd v Independent Insurance Co Ltd*,[9] the Court of Appeal gave the insured leave to appeal against the striking out of its claim for damages consequential on the insurer's failure to accept liability and indemnify it under a business interruption insurance policy.[10] By contrast, in *Mandrake Holdings Ltd v Countrywide Assured Group plc*[11] it was common ground between the parties, and the Court of Appeal accepted, that the Court of Appeal was bound by the decision in *Sprung v Royal Insurance (UK) Ltd* and that therefore the issue was open to appeal only at the level of the House of Lords.

ICOBS provides that an insurer must handle claims promptly and fairly, provide reasonable guidance to help a policyholder make a claim and appropriate information on its progress, not unreasonably reject a claim (including by terminating or avoiding a policy), and settle claims promptly once settlement terms are agreed.[12] Breach of ICOBS is actionable at the suit of a 'private person'.[13]

As far as damages for hardship, inconvenience or mental distress for breach of the insurer's obligations under a policy of insurance are concerned (as opposed to an indemnity under a policy which expressly provides such cover), the usual principle applies, which is that such damages are only recoverable in contract where the contract which has been broken was itself a contract to provide peace of mind or freedom from distress.[14] Accordingly, such damages will rarely be awarded, and never where the claimant is not an individual but a company.[15]

1 See *Shelbourne & Co v Law Investment and Insurance Corpn Ltd* [1898] 2 QB 626 (river insurance policy held to cover damage to barges but not loss of profits and crew wages while barges being repaired).

2 *Shelbourne & Co v Law Investment and Insurance Corpn Ltd* [1898] 2 QB 626.

3 *Maurice v Goldsbrough Mort & Co Ltd* [1939] AC 452, PC (wool).

4 *England v Guardian Insurance Ltd* [2000] Lloyd's Rep IR 404, para 73 (HHJ Thornton QC); *Mitsui Sumitomo Insurance Co (Europe) Ltd v The Mayor's Office for Policing and Crime* [2013] EWHC 2734, [2014] Lloyd's Rep IR 20, para 120 (Flaux J).

5 See below.

6 *Ramwade Ltd v W J Emson & Co Ltd* [1987] RTR 72, CA (damages for broker's negligence in failing to arrange comprehensive policy assessed by reference to what insured could have recovered from insurers if policy had been in place; see **PARA 16.34**); *Ventouris v Mountain, The Italia Express (No 2)* [1992] 2 Lloyd's Rep 281; *Sprung v Royal Insurance (UK) Ltd* [1999] Lloyd's Rep IR 111, CA; *Insurance Corpn of the Channel Islands Ltd v McHugh* [1997] LRLR 94, 136–137 (Mance J); *Tonkin v UK Insurance Ltd* [2006] EWHC 1120 (TCC), [2007] Lloyd's Rep IR 283, paras 34–41 (HHJ Peter Coulson QC). See also *McClean Enterprises Ltd v Ecclesiastical Insurance Office plc* [1986] 2 Lloyd's Rep 416, 427–428 (Staughton J) (insurer investigated claim and declined to pay on grounds of fraud; insured succeeded at trial; interest awarded from date on which insurer began to investigate claim). Although the Court of Appeal and Supreme Court recently confirmed (in *The Alexandros T* [2013] UKSC 70, [2014] 1 Lloyd's Rep 223, para 6 (Lord Clarke), approving: [2012] EWCA Civ 1714, [2013] 1 Lloyd's Rep 217, para 1 (Longmore LJ)) that damages are not recoverable for late payment under a policy of insurance at common law, the issue was not considered in any detail as the proceedings were about jurisdiction, and the law in this area cannot be regarded as settled, particularly following the decision of the House of Lords in *Sempra Metals Ltd v Inland Revenue Commissioners* [2007] UKHL 34, [2008] 1 AC 561, which decided that the loss suffered as a result of the late payment of money is recoverable at common law, subject to the ordinary rules of remoteness which apply to all claims of damages; there is also a statutory right to damages for late payment of insurance claims in the Enterprise Bill: see further **PARA 8.3**.

7 [1999] Lloyd's Rep IR 111, CA.

8 At 119 (Beldam LJ).

9 [1999] Lloyd's Rep IR 120, CA. *Sprung v Royal Insurance (UK) Ltd* was reported only after a delay of three years (the date of the decision was 14 June 1996). Similarly, although the date of the decision in *Pride Valley Foods Ltd v Independent Insurance Co Ltd* was 27 February 1997, it was only reported (together with *Sprung v Royal Insurance (UK) Ltd*) in 1999.

10 It appears that the appeal in *Pride Valley Foods Ltd v Independent Insurance Co Ltd* was not heard.
11 [2005] EWCA Civ 840.
12 ICOBS 8.1.1R.
13 See PARA 8.2.
14 *Ventouris v Mountain, The Italia Express (No 2)* [1992] 2 Lloyd's Rep 281, 293 (Hirst J); *England v Guardian Insurance Ltd* [2000] Lloyd's Rep IR 404, para 74 (His Honour Judge Thornton QC); *Pine v DAS Legal Expenses Insurance Co Ltd* [2011] EWHC 658 (QB), [2012] Lloyd's Rep IR 346, paras 45–46 (His Honour Richard Seymour QC, sitting as a Judge of the High Court).
15 *Ventouris v Mountain, The Italia Express (No 2)* [1992] 2 Lloyd's Rep 281, 293 (Hirst J); *Pine v DAS Legal Expenses Insurance Co Ltd* [2011] EWHC 658 (QB), paras 45–46 (His Honour Richard Seymour QC, sitting as a Judge of the High Court).

BETTERMENT AND GIVING CREDIT FOR COLLATERAL BENEFITS

6.7   In a property policy, the principle of betterment requires that, unless the insurance expressly provides that it is on a 'new for old' basis, an allowance be made, in assessing the sum to be paid to the insured, for the fact that he is receiving something new in place of something old. The principle has been described as 'too well established in the law of insurance to be departed from at this stage even though it may sometimes work hardship on the assured'.[1] The hardship derives from the fact that the deduction for betterment may mean that the insured is deprived of the subject matter of the insurance because he cannot afford to replace it new and cannot obtain a secondhand replacement, or is effectively obliged to replace a secondhand article with a new one against his will. The doctrine applies whether the basis of payment is cost of reinstatement or replacement value.[2]

It seems that, in the absence of express wording, the insured is under no obligation to give credit where, as a result of an insured loss, it is able to avoid expenditure which it would otherwise have incurred, such as loss of hire due to a vessel being in dry dock at a later period for scheduled works.[3]

1 *Reynolds v Phoenix Assurance Co Ltd* [1978] 2 Lloyd's Rep 440, 453 (Forbes J).
2 *Reynolds v Phoenix Assurance Co Ltd* [1978] 2 Lloyd's Rep 440, 453–454 (Forbes J); *Pleasurama Ltd v Sun Alliance and London Insurance Ltd* [1979] 1 Lloyd's Rep 389, 393 (Parker J).
3 See *Sealion Shipping Ltd v Valiant Insurance Co ('The Toisa Pisces')* [2012] EWCA Civ 1625, [2013] 1 Lloyd's Rep 108, para 32 (Gross LJ) (loss of hire policy).

EXCESS CLAUSES AND DEDUCTIBLES

6.8   Most indemnity insurance policies contain a clause, usually known as an excess clause or deductible, which provides that the insured will bear the first element of any loss.[1] The excess is usually expressed as a fixed sum, although it can be a percentage, and a single policy may contain more than one excess provision, each applicable in respect of a different insured peril or element of cover.

Where there are successive losses under a single policy, it is a matter of construction whether the excess applies to each loss, or is payable only once. The excess clause usually indicates to what it is to apply; for example, it may apply to 'each and every' loss or claim,[2] and loss or claim may be defined in the policy. The policy may allow for the aggregation of claims or losses for the purposes of the application of the excess or deductible, in which case the excess or deductible will apply only once in relation to the aggregated claims or losses.[3]

1 For the allocation of recoveries as between the insured and insurer where the insured bears part of the loss, see **PARA 12.11**.
2 See further **PARA 6.9**. As to the meaning of 'claim' in a liability policy, see **PARA 7.8**.
3 See further **PARA 6.9**.

AGGREGATION

6.9 A clause which enables two or more separate losses covered by a policy to be treated as a single loss for deductible or other purposes when they are linked by a unifying factor of some kind is known as an aggregation clause.[1] The underlying concept of aggregation is that of a '*single unifying* event'.[2] In the absence of any such provision, the policy will respond to each peril up to the limit of liability.[3] An aggregation clause has to be approached neutrally without any assumptions in favour of the insurers or the insured.[4] An aggregation clause may apply for the benefit of both parties to the contract: it may be advantageous to the insurer because he can rely upon the relevant limit of his liability in relation to the aggregation of the relevant losses, and it may be advantageous to the insured because the retention/excess also falls to be applied to the aggregate of the claims not to the individual claims.[5]

Each case depends on its own terms and circumstances,[6] but certain wordings have come before the courts and have acquired established meanings. When those or similar wordings are used, the parties will be assumed to have intended the same or a similar meaning.[7] Where the origin of a clause has a published history, this is part of the 'matrix' against which the clause has to be construed and is a legitimate aid to construction.[8]

After 40 people were injured when a tram overturned at the end of the nineteenth century, and the incident was held to have given rise to a multiplicity of 'accidents' within the meaning of an accident policy taken out by the tram company,[9] insurers began to limit their liability in third party liability policies by reference to 'occurrences'.[10] In *Allen v London Guarantee and Accident Co Ltd*,[11] in which two men were injured by a cart belonging to the insured, this was held to be effective to limit insurers' liability, as the court held that although there were two 'accidents', there was only one 'occurrence'.[12] 'Occurrence' therefore has a wider meaning, and, when used to limit insurers' liability, is more restrictive than 'accident'.[13] Two separate acts of negligence by a solicitor in relation to the same matter are separate 'occurrences' for the purposes of a professional negligence policy in which the limit of indemnity was '(a) in respect of any one claim or number of claims arising out of the same occurrence the sum of £3,000; (b) in respect of all claims under this policy the sum of £15,000'.[14] Similarly, the underwriting of each of 32 insurance policies by a single underwriter in *Caudle v Sharp*[15] was a separate 'occurrence', and the underwriting of all 32 policies was a 'series of occurrences', but the underwriter's failure to conduct the necessary research and investigation into the problems of asbestosis before underwriting the policies was not an 'event', so that the losses under the policies, or the underwriting of the policies, were not to be regarded as 'a series of losses and/or occurrences ... arising out of one event'. The matter must be scrutinised from the point of view of an informed observer placed in the position of the insured.[16] In assessing the degree of unity regard may be had to such factors as cause, locality and time and the intentions of the human agents.[17]

'Originating cause' is wider than 'event': in *Axa Reinsurance (UK) plc v Field*,[18] the House of Lords held that an 'event'[19] is something which happens at a particular time, at a particular place, in a particular way, whereas a 'cause' is much less constricted: it can be a continuing state of affairs, or the absence of something happening. Further, the adjective 'originating' opens up the widest possible search for a unifying factor in the history of the losses which it is sought to aggregate.[20] Where therefore parties do not use the wording of originating or original cause, but use alternative wording such as 'related series of acts or omissions', a single underlying cause or common origin will not be sufficient to trigger the application of the clause.[21] For there to be a 'series of losses and/or occurrences ... arising out of one event', the event must be a 'relevant' event, which means the series was linked by a common factor which can be described as an event and which was not too remote from them.[22] To form part of a 'series' there must be some connecting factor which links occurrences which would otherwise be separate; they must be 'of a sufficiently similar kind' or must be 'sufficiently related'.[23] The word 'series' itself usually implies some connection between the events or concepts which constitute the series.[24] As used in the phrase 'in a series of related ... transactions', it is even more obvious that there has to be a connection since the transactions have to be 'related' and that can only mean related to one another.[25] When one speaks of events being 'related' or forming a 'series', the nature of the unifying factor or factors which makes them related or a series may be expressed or implied in a sentence in which the words are used: it may sometimes be necessary to imply a unifying factor from the general context, but the express language may make such an implication unnecessary or impermissible.[26] Where wording refers to 'a series of ... claims' which 'result from any single act or omission (or related series of acts or omissions)', the only unifying factor provided by the clause itself for describing the acts or omissions in the parenthesis as 'related' and a 'series' is that they 'result' in a series of claims; in other words, the unifying element is a common causal relationship.[27] When construing the words 'a series of related matters or transactions', it is necessary to imply the unifying factor from the general context, because the express language ('a related ... transaction') is both itself imprecise and deliberately avoids the available wide formulations;[28] there must be some restriction on the concept of relatedness and the most satisfactory approach is that the relation must be an intrinsic relationship not a remote or extrinsic one; this means that there must be a relationship of some kind between the transactions relied on rather than a relationship with some outside connecting factor, even if that extrinsic relationship is common to the transactions.[29]

An excess provision which is expressed to be 'per claimant' does not permit the aggregation of related claims made by separate claimants.[30] In the context of an aggregation clause, the words 'arising out of' or 'arising from' may denote a causal link which is wider or looser than that of proximate cause.[31] Some degree of remoteness, or lack of remoteness, is implied in the context of an aggregation clause, but the test is less stringent than the normal insurance requirement of direct and proximate cause.[32] The causative link inherent in the words 'arising from', when coupled with the expression 'one event', should be regarded as a relatively strong and significant link.[33] 'In connection with' is extremely broad and indicates that it is not even necessary to show a direct causal relationship between the claims and the state of affairs identified, and that some form of connection between the claims and the unifying factor is all that is required.[34]

In *Mabey & Johnson Ltd v Ecclesiastical Insurance Office plc*,[35] the policy included a limit of cover ('each and every claim'), but did not contain an aggregation clause, and the court rejected the insurers' contention that such a clause was to be implied on the basis of obviousness or of market custom and practice.[36]

Before construing and applying any aggregation provision, it is necessary to decide the number of relevant claims or losses. For example, in the context of a claims made policy, the correct approach is to begin by asking how many claims were made, and if the answer is that there were more than one, to ask whether an entitlement arises to aggregate them under any of the provisions of the insurance or reinsurance.[37] The answer to the question very much depends on the facts;[38] the policy wording may also be relevant, particularly if it includes a definition of the relevant term.[39] In a claims made policy, although the formulation of the claim by the third party is a good starting point for determining whether there is one claim or more than one claim, it is the underlying facts which are determinative, and even multiple sets of legal proceedings against the insured may in substance be a single claim.[40] In the case of a goods in transit policy, where the cover is against physical loss or damage to goods, the fact that a failure to redeliver a missing quantity of goods may give rise to a single cause of action in conversion (if the claimant chooses to pursue a claim in that way) does not mean that there has been only one loss within the meaning of the policy.[41] A single course of conduct repeated at frequent intervals over a period of time may not be a single overall loss, but several takings and several losses.[42] The fact that individual misappropriations result in a progressive reduction in the subject-matter insured is apt to disguise the real nature of the business.[43] In *Glencore International AG v Alpina Insurance Co Ltd*,[44] Moore-Bick J gave the following examples:[45]

> 'This is a policy against physical loss and damage to goods, so in the ordinary way a loss within the meaning of the policy occurs whenever the goods insured are damaged, destroyed or lost to the insured. Thus, several unrelated fires affecting goods in storage would give rise to several losses, as would several unrelated thefts. The position may be more complicated if several losses are related – as, for example, where an arsonist sets fire to two adjacent tanks in the course of a single attack – and no doubt a certain amount of common sense has to be applied when deciding how many losses have occurred in any given case. Thus, if thieves enter a warehouse containing bagged goods which they remove using a number of different vehicles, pausing from time to time to bring up a new vehicle, it is difficult to see how that could be regarded as more than one loss. … In both these examples the unifying factor is that the loss occurred on one occasion in the course of a single enterprise. However, the fact that similar goods are stolen on several occasions from the same location by the same person using the same method does not in my view entitle the insurers to treat them all as a single loss under this policy.'

1 *Lloyds TSB General Insurance Holdings v Lloyds Bank Group Insurance Co Ltd* [2003] UKHL 48, [2003] Lloyd's Rep IR 623, paras 14–15 (Lord Hoffmann).

2 *Scott v Copenhagen Reinsurance Co (UK) Ltd* [2003] EWCA Civ 688, [2003] Lloyd's Rep IR 696, para 61 (Rix LJ); emphasis as original.

3 This common law principle is reflected in s 77(1) of the Marine Insurance Act 1906, which provides:

'Unless the policy otherwise provides, and subject to the provisions of this Act, the insurer is liable for successive losses, even though the total amount of such losses may exceed the sum insured.'

4 *AIG Europe Ltd v OC320301 LLP (formerly The International Law Partnership LLP)* [2016] EWCA Civ 367, para 33(iii) (Longmore LJ): aggregation clause contained in all solicitors' indemnity policies pursuant to the requirement in the Solicitors Act 1974 for compulsory liability for insurance and Minimum Terms and Conditions required to be incorporated into such policies: see para 2; in these circumstances it is not helpful to consider whether the approach should be from any particular perspective let alone whether the right perspective is that of the insured or that of the public who need the relevant advice or assistance and may be concerned that the solicitor should have adequate cover: see para 33(iii).

5 *Municipal Mutual Insurance Ltd v Sea Insurance Co Ltd* [1998] Lloyd's Rep IR 421, 434, CA (Hobhouse LJ).

6 *Mann v Lexington Insurance Co* [2001] 1 Lloyd's Rep 1, CA, para 15 (Waller LJ).

7 See for example *Lloyds TSB General Insurance Holdings v Lloyds Bank Group Insurance Co Ltd* [2003] UKHL 48, [2003] Lloyd's Rep IR 623, para 51 (Lord Hobhouse):

'The parties could, if they had so chosen, have used a clause such as that found in the *Axa [v Field]* and *Municipal [Mutual Insurance Ltd v Sea Insurance Co Ltd]* cases. They chose not to and, no doubt, the cost of obtaining insurance cover was reduced as a result. Their choice should be respected'.

8 *AIG Europe Ltd v OC320301 LLP (formerly The International Law Partnership LLP)* [2016] EWCA Civ 367, para 30 (Longmore LJ) (history of origin of aggregation clause, including negotiations between commercial insurers and the Law Society following *Lloyds TSB General Insurance Holdings v Lloyds Bank Group Insurance Co Ltd* [2003] UKHL 48, [2003] Lloyd's Rep IR 623, published in Law Society Gazette). See further **PARAS 3.15–3.16**.

9 *South Staffordshire Tramways Co Ltd v Sickness and Accident Assurance Association Ltd* [1891] 1 QB 402, CA.

10 *Forney v Dominion Insurance Co Ltd* [1969] 1 WLR 928, 934 (Donaldson J).

11 (1912) 28 TLR 254.

12 It may also embrace a plurality of 'losses': *Kuwait Airways Corpn v Kuwait Insurance Co SAK* [1996] 1 Lloyd's Rep 664, 686, Rix J (point not considered on appeal: [1997] 2 Lloyd's Rep 687, CA, [1999] 1 Lloyd's Rep 803, HL).

13 See also *Kuwait Airways Corpn v Kuwait Insurance Co SAK* [1996] 1 Lloyd's Rep 664, in which, in the context of a policy of insurance against war risks, Rix J held that a broad interpretation of 'any one occurrence, any one location' as applied to the maximum ground limit was appropriate, and that the occurrence was the successful invasion of Kuwait incorporating the capture of the airport and with it the insured's aircraft on the ground; but that in any event, at its narrowest, the occurrence was the capture of the insured's fleet at Kuwait airport, and on either view those matters were appropriately described as 'one occurrence' (point not considered on appeal: [1997] 2 Lloyd's Rep 687, CA, [1999] 1 Lloyd's Rep 803, HL). In *Mann v Lexington Insurance Co* [2001] 1 Lloyd's Rep 1, CA, Waller LJ said (at paras 44–45) that, even assuming a factor such as central orchestration of the riots by the government, damage by rioters over a period of two days to a number of stores owned by the insured lacked the necessary unity of time and place and could not constitute an 'occurrence' within the meaning of the retrocession contract.

14 *Forney v Dominion Insurance Co Ltd* [1969] 1 WLR 928.

15 *Caudle v Sharp* [1995] LRLR 433, CA.

16 *Kuwait Airways Corpn v Kuwait Insurance Co SAK* [1996] 1 Lloyd's Rep 664, 686, Rix J (point not considered on appeal: [1997] 2 Lloyd's Rep 687, CA, [1999] 1 Lloyd's Rep 803, HL); applied: *Aioi Nissay Dowa Insurance Co Ltd v Heraldglen Ltd* [2013] EWHC 154 (Comm), [2013] Lloyd's Rep IR 281, paras 30–32 (Field J); *Forney v Dominion Insurance Co Ltd* [1969] 1 WLR 928, 934 (Donaldson J) (giving a series of examples in the context of claims against architects).

17 *Kuwait Airways Corpn v Kuwait Insurance Co SAK* [1996] 1 Lloyd's Rep 664, 686, Rix J (point not considered on appeal: [1997] 2 Lloyd's Rep 687, CA, [1999] 1 Lloyd's Rep 803, HL).

18 [1996] 1 WLR 1026, 1035, HL (Lord Mustill).

19 In the context of the contracts of reinsurance under consideration in *American Centennial Insurance Co v Insco Ltd* [1996] LRLR 407, Moore-Bick J accepted that the words 'event' and 'occurrence' had similar meanings, although an 'event' might embrace something other than a physical occurrence, so that the collapse of a financial institution could naturally be described as an 'event' (at 413). Similarly,

in *Kuwait Airways Corpn v Kuwait Insurance Co SAK* [1996] 1 Lloyd's Rep 664, Rix J held that the meaning of an 'occurrence' was similar to that of an 'event' or happening, unless the contractual context required some distinction to be made (at 686). In *Brown v GIO Insurance Ltd* [1998] Lloyd's Rep IR 201, CA, 204 (Waller LJ), 210 (Chadwick LJ), the Court of Appeal said that the decision of the House of Lords in *Axa Reinsurance (UK) plc v Field* went no further than saying that an originating cause is not necessarily an event, and whether or not that was the case would depend on the particular facts under consideration.

20 *Axa Reinsurance (UK) plc v Field* [1996] 1 WLR 1026, 1035, HL (Lord Mustill); applied: *Municipal Mutual Insurance Ltd v Sea Insurance Co Ltd* [1998] Lloyd's Rep IR 421, 434, CA (Hobhouse LJ) ('in respect of or arising out of all occurrences of a series consequent on or attributable to one source or original cause').

21 *Lloyds TSB General Insurance Holdings v Lloyds Bank Group Insurance Co Ltd* [2003] UKHL 48, [2003] Lloyd's Rep IR 623, para 51 (Lord Hobhouse):

'The parties could, if they had so chosen, have used a clause such as that found in the *Axa [v Field]* and *Municipal [Mutual Insurance Ltd v Sea Insurance Co Ltd]* cases. They chose not to and, no doubt, the cost of obtaining insurance cover was reduced as a result. Their choice should be respected';

applied: *AIG Europe Ltd v OC320301 LLP (formerly The International Law Partnership LLP)* [2016] EWCA Civ 367, para 25 (Longmore LJ) ('similar acts or omissions in a series of related matters or transactions').

22 *Caudle v Sharp* [1995] LRLR 433, 440, CA (Evans LJ).

23 *Countrywide Assured Group plc v Marshall* [2002] EWHC 2082 (Comm), [2003] Lloyd's Rep IR 195, para 14 (Morison J) ('all occurrences of a series consequent upon or attributable to one source or original cause'), referring to *The Distillers Company Bio-Chemicals (Australia) Pty Ltd v Ajax (Insurance) Co Ltd* (1974) 130 CLR 1, a decision of the High Court of Australia in relation to a similarly-worded clause. Stephen J said at 21 (paras 26–27 of his judgment):

'The meaning of "series" in the proviso is, I think, that of a number of events of a sufficiently similar kind following one another in temporal succession. … Since any number of distinct events will, unless by coincidence they occur simultaneously, necessarily occur in a temporal sequence, the only remaining attribute of the concept of a "series" to be satisfied is that the events should be, in a sufficient degree, similar in nature. The characteristic of the similarity of events which may form a series I take from those dictionary meanings of series which refer to the concept of being "of one kind" or of having some "characteristic in common" – Shorter Oxford English Dictionary …'

In *AIG Europe Ltd v OC320301 LLP (formerly The International Law Partnership LLP)* [2015] EWHC 2398 (Comm), [2016] Lloyd's Rep IR 147, Teare J declined to follow *Countrywide Assured Group plc v Marshall [2002] EWHC 2082 (Comm), [2003] Lloyd's Rep IR 195* or to apply the reasoning of *The Distillers Company Bio-Chemicals (Australia) Pty Ltd v Ajax (Insurance) Co Ltd (1974) 130 CLR 1*. Neither of these cases was considered on appeal: [2016] EWCA Civ 367. The clause under consideration in *AIG Europe Ltd v OC320301 LLP* was 'similar acts or omissions in a series of related matters or transactions'; the Court of Appeal observed that the conclusion it had reached as to the construction of the wording 'in a related series of matters or transactions' (as requiring an intrinsic relationship between the matters or transactions) might possibly have some influence on how one should look at 'similar acts or omissions': see para 32 (Longmore LJ; declining to affirm the first instance decision on this point ([2015] EWHC 2398 (Comm), [2016] Lloyd's Rep IR 147, paras 28–31 (Teare J)) and preferring to leave the point open for decision by the judge hearing the re-trial).

24 *AIG Europe Ltd v OC320301 LLP (formerly The International Law Partnership LLP)* [2016] EWCA Civ 367, para 17 (Longmore LJ), adding (at para 17) that the word is derived from the Latin 'serere' which means to connect, and illustrating the point with a quotation from Jane Austen.

25 *AIG Europe Ltd v OC320301 LLP (formerly The International Law Partnership LLP)* [2016] EWCA Civ 36Z7, para 18 (Longmore LJ).

26 *Lloyds TSB General Insurance Holdings v Lloyds Bank Group Insurance Co Ltd* [2003] UKHL 48, [2003] Lloyd's Rep IR 623, para 26 (Lord Hoffmann); applied: *AIG Europe Ltd v OC320301 LLP (formerly The International Law Partnership LLP)* [2016] EWCA Civ 367, para 26 (Longmore LJ).

27 *Lloyds TSB General Insurance Holdings v Lloyds Bank Group Insurance Co Ltd* [2003] UKHL 48, [2003] Lloyd's Rep IR 623, para 27 (Lord Hoffmann: the common causal relationship is downstream of the acts and omissions within the parenthesis, which means that the acts or events form a related

series if they together resulted in each of the claims); considered: *AIG Europe Ltd v OC320301 LLP (formerly The International Law Partnership LLP)* [2016] EWCA Civ 367, para 27 (Longmore LJ).

28 *AIG Europe Ltd v OC320301 LLP (formerly The International Law Partnership LLP)* [2016] EWCA Civ 367, para 26 (Longmore LJ).

29 *AIG Europe Ltd v OC320301 LLP (formerly The International Law Partnership LLP)* [2016] EWCA Civ 367, paras 19, 30 and 33(i) (Longmore LJ); thus, transactions which all take place with reference to one large area of land in a particular country might be related transactions if they refer to or (perhaps) envisage one another, but if the relevant transaction is the payment of money out of an escrow account which should not have been paid out of that account, the fact of geography is too remote; what will be intrinsic will depend on the circumstances of that payment: para 19 (Longmore LJ). It is not necessary that the transactions be dependent on each other in order for them to be related: para 20 (Longmore LJ).

30 *Standard Life Assurance Ltd v Oak Dedicated Ltd* [2008] EWHC 222 (Comm), [2008] Lloyd's Rep IR 552, para 100 (Tomlinson J).

31 *Caudle v Sharp* [1995] LRLR 433, 439, CA (Evans LJ); *Scott v Copenhagen Reinsurance Co (UK) Ltd* [2003] EWCA Civ 688, [2003] Lloyd's Rep IR 696, paras 61 and 63 (Rix LJ).

32 *Caudle v Sharp* [1995] LRLR 433, 440, CA (Evans LJ).

33 *Scott v Copenhagen Reinsurance Co (UK) Ltd* [2003] EWCA Civ 688, [2003] Lloyd's Rep IR 696, paras 65 (Rix LJ) and 90 (Schiemann LJ).

34 *Standard Life Assurance Ltd v ACE European Group* [2012] EWHC 104 (Comm), [2012] Lloyd's Rep IR 655, para 262 (Eder J) (point not considered on appeal: *ACE European Group v Standard Life Assurance Ltd* [2012] EWCA Civ 1713, [2013] Lloyd's Rep IR 415).

35 [2001] Lloyd's Rep IR 369.

36 At paras 14–17 (Morison J).

37 *American Centennial Insurance Co v Insco Ltd* [1996] LRLR 407, 412 (Moore-Bick J).

38 *Thorman v New Hampshire Insurance Co (UK) Ltd* [1988] 1 Lloyd's Rep 7, 11–12, CA (Sir John Donaldson MR).

39 In *Mitsubishi Electric UK Ltd v Royal London Insurance (UK) Ltd* [1994] 2 Lloyd's Rep 249, CA, 94 toilet cubicles were constructed off site using defective cementitious board and lifted into position by crane; the deductible of '[t]he first £250,000 of each and every loss in respect of any component part' was held to apply once, rather than 94 times, on the basis that there was a single, albeit composite, claim or head of loss rather than multiple claims (see 252–253 (Sir Thomas Bingham MR)).

40 *Haydon v Lo & Lo* [1997] 1 WLR 198, 206, PC (Lord Lloyd), applying *West Wake Price & Co v Ching* [1957] 1 WLR 45 (see **PARA 7.8**); *Citibank NA v Excess Insurance Co Ltd* [1999] 1 Lloyd's Rep 122, 127–128 (Thomas J); *Mabey & Johnson Ltd v Ecclesiastical Insurance Office plc (No 2)* [2003] EWHC 1523 (Comm), [2004] Lloyd's Rep IR 10, para 12 (Morison J). See also **PARA 8.12.**

41 *Glencore International AG v Alpina Insurance Co Ltd* [2003] EWHC 2792 (Comm), [2004] 1 Lloyd's Rep 111, para 304 (Moore-Bick LJ).

42 *Pennsylvania Company for Insurances on Lives and Granting Annuities v Mumford* [1920] 2 KB 537, CA (limit of liability applied 'in respect of any one loss'; held that no cover under policy, but would have been 41 losses where 41 thefts of securities by single employee over several years, all disguised in same way, all discovered at the same time); *Equitable Trust Company of New York v Whittaker* (1923) 17 Ll L Rep 153, 155 (Greer J) (insurance against losses by taking false documents; policy excess applied 'in respect of each and every loss' (154); once a month, pursuant to an original contract to advance monies on valid documents, forged documents were presented and monies advanced; and a separate loss occurred on each occasion); *Philadelphia National Bank v Price* (1938) 60 Ll L Rep 257, CA, 265–266 (Sir Wilfred Greene MR), 268 (MacKinnon LJ) (insurance against losses by having made advances against false documents; policy excess applied to 'each and every loss or occurrence'; each production of documents led to a separate advance, which proved irrecoverable, and a separate loss was sustained on each occasion; at 265, Sir Wilfrid Greene MR distinguished a situation in which, by means of a forged document, the bank were persuaded to grant an ordinary running overdraft up to a particular amount; he said that it would be difficult to say in that case that each cheque which the customer drew on the account ought to be viewed as a separate advance and that the bank's inability to recover it had led to a separate loss, and that the loss would be the loss due to the giving of the overdraft on the faith of the forged document); *Glencore International AG v Alpina Insurance Co Ltd* [2003] EWHC 2792 (Comm), [2004] 1 Lloyd's Rep 111, para 299 (Moore-Bick LJ) (limit of indemnity applied 'any one loss'; misappropriation of various quantities and grades of oil belonging to insured over a period of many months, mainly by drawing without authority on stocks held to the order of the insured held to be one loss); *Dornoch Ltd v Mauritius Union Assurance Co Ltd (No 2)* [2007] EWHC 155 (Comm), [2007] Lloyd's Rep IR 350, paras 33–34 (David Steel J) (excess reinsurance provided

cover for 'any one loss' in excess of primary policy deductible which applied 'each and every loss'; various defalcations by fraudulent bank employee; held that no cover under policy, but that transfers or procurement of transfers, each a separate conscious act, separated by days or months or years and perpetrated against one or other of a range of different accounts in favour of a range of different counterparties would each undoubtedly have been an individual loss which could have been subject of separate claim under a policy providing cover for losses of this nature).

43 *Philadelphia National Bank v Price* (1938) 60 Ll L Rep 257, CA, 268 (MacKinnon LJ); *Glencore International AG v Alpina Insurance Co Ltd* [2003] EWHC 2792 (Comm), [2004] 1 Lloyd's Rep 111, para 299 (Moore-Bick LJ).
44 [2003] EWHC 2792 (Comm), [2004] 1 Lloyd's Rep 111.
45 At paras 292–293.

AVERAGE AND UNDER-INSURANCE

6.10   Where property is insured on the basis of a declaration of value by the insured, and the declaration understates the true value, the insurer may be entitled on a loss (if he does not avoid the contract on the ground of misrepresentation or non-disclosure[1] or decline to pay a claim on the basis of breach of warranty)[2] to treat the insured as though he were his own insurer in respect of the difference,[3] and pay subject to average. Payment subject to average means payment of the proportion of the loss which the declared value bears to the true value. Thus, if a building is worth £100,000 but its value is declared as £50,000, and damage is done which reduces its value by £25,000, the insured would be entitled to 25 per cent of the declared value, ie £12,500. In non-marine insurance,[4] average applies only if there is an express clause to that effect.[5] Fire and theft policies, and 'all risks' policies on commercial properties, almost invariably include such a clause, commonly known as a pro rata condition of average or, sometimes, a co-insurance clause. The principles of average and under-insurance have no application in liability insurance.[6]

1 See **CHAPTER 11**, Insurers' defences.
2 See **CHAPTER 3**, The contract of insurance.
3 See *British & Foreign Insurance Co Ltd v Wilson Shipping Co Ltd* [1921] 1 AC 188, 214, 215, HL (Lord Sumner).
4 Average is applied to marine insurance by s 81 of the Marine Insurance Act 1906, which provides: 'Where the assured is insured for an amount less than the insurable value or, in the case of a valued policy, for an amount less than the policy valuation, he is deemed to be his own insurer in respect of the uninsured balance'.
5 In *Carreras Ltd v Cunard Steamship Co Ltd* [1918] 1 KB 118, Bailhache J was prepared to imply a pro rata condition of average into a contract for warehousing goods at a weekly rental to include fire insurance. His reasoning (at 122–123), that such clauses were almost universally found in fire insurance policies, would tend to suggest the opposite conclusion in the case of a fire policy which did not contain such a clause.
6 *ACE European Group v Standard Life Assurance Ltd* [2012] EWCA Civ 1713, [2013] Lloyd's Rep IR 415, paras 44–45 (Tomlinson LJ). See also **PARA 8.11**.

SALVAGE

6.11   The doctrine of salvage applies to all indemnity insurance, including non-marine insurance.[1] It requires the insured, if the insurer has paid on a total loss basis, both to cede his rights in, and to assist the insurer in attempting to obtain something of value from, the subject matter of the insurance.[2] The theoretical basis of the doctrine is that, without it, the insured may recover more than a full indemnity.[3]

However, the insured may recover more than a full indemnity if underwriters expressly disclaim their right to take over the insured's interests, and the insured subsequently sells the insured property at a price which does not apparently reflect a discount to reflect the damage.[4] This does not offend against the indemnity principle because it is as a result of underwriters' express choice that the insured potentially receives more than a full indemnity.[5] Blackburn J, in *Rankin v Potter*,[6] considered that salvage was an application of general principles of equity, although, by analogy with the doctrine of subrogation, there would appear to be a competing theoretical basis for the doctrine: the implication of a term.[7] Whatever its theoretical basis, the doctrine may be modified or supplanted by express provisions in the policy.

1 Marine insurance has developed detailed rules governing the operation of the doctrine of salvage, which have no application to non-marine insurance.
2 *Dane v Mortgage Insurance Corpn Ltd* [1894] 1 QB 54, 61 (Lord Esher MR).
3 *Dane v Mortgage Insurance Corpn Ltd* [1894] 1 QB 54, 61 (Lord Esher MR).
4 *The WD Fairway (No 3)* [2009] EWHC 1782 (Admlty), [2009] 2 Lloyd's Rep 420, para 16 (Tomlinson J).
5 *The WD Fairway (No 3)* [2009] EWHC 1782 (Admlty), [2009] 2 Lloyd's Rep 420, para 16 (Tomlinson J).
6 (1873) LR 6 HL 83, 118, HL.
7 See **CHAPTER 12**, Subrogation.

LIMITED INTEREST IN PROPERTY

6.12   An insured with a limited interest in property is entitled to recover in respect of his own interest in the property in the case of a loss. In the case of bailees and some others in analogous positions, a commercial or mercantile 'trust' is held to have arisen which entitles the insured, where he has insured the whole property, to recover in respect of the entire loss, subject to an obligation to account in respect of the surplus to others interested in the property.[1]

1 See **PARA 2.10**.

MITIGATION OF LOSS

6.13   Policies frequently contain an express term imposing a duty on the insured to make reasonable efforts to prevent or minimise loss which might otherwise fall to the insurers. In *Yorkshire Water Services Ltd v Sun Alliance & London Insurance plc*,[1] an argument that, in the absence of any express term, such a term should be implied was emphatically rejected by the Court of Appeal on the grounds that although the implication of such a term might be reasonable, it was neither necessary for business efficacy nor obvious. Even without an express term, however, there is what may loosely be described as a duty to mitigate loss, as loss which could have been avoided (whether completely or in part) by the insured taking reasonable steps to do so is not recoverable. This is because the proximate cause of such loss is not the insured peril but the insured's failure to take reasonable steps to avoid it.[2] On this basis, the cost of taking reasonable preventative steps must fall to the insured. Where there is an express obligation to minimise loss, it is a matter of construction whether the cost of taking the necessary steps falls on the insurer or on the insured.[3]

A policy of liability insurance may provide an indemnity in respect of costs and expenses reasonably or necessarily incurred by the insured in avoiding a loss which would otherwise be the subject of indemnity under the policy, sometimes referred to as mitigation costs.[4] If as a matter of construction of the policy wording, such costs and expenses fall within the scope of the policy, they are not subject to apportionment simply because they are also incurred for another incidental objective such as the protection of the insured's reputation.[5]

1 [1997] 2 Lloyd's Rep 21, CA.
2 *National Oilwell (UK) Ltd v Davy Offshore Ltd* [1993] 2 Lloyd's Rep 582, 618 (Colman J); *Yorkshire Water Services Ltd v Sun Alliance & London Insurance plc* [1997] 2 Lloyd's Rep 21, 32, CA (Otton LJ). See **CHAPTER 4**, Causation of loss.
3 *Yorkshire Water Services Ltd v Sun Alliance & London Insurance plc* [1997] 2 Lloyd's Rep 21, CA; considered: *The Netherlands Insurance Co Est 1845 Ltd v Karl Ljungberg & Co AB* [1986] 2 Lloyd's Rep 19, PC.
4 See eg *ACE European Group v Standard Life Assurance Ltd* [2012] EWCA Civ 1713, [2013] Lloyd's Rep IR 415; *Teal Assurance Co Ltd v W R Berkley Insurance (Europe) Ltd* [2013] UKSC 57, [2014] Lloyd's Rep IR 56.
5 *ACE European Group v Standard Life Assurance Ltd* [2012] EWCA Civ 1713, [2013] Lloyd's Rep IR 415, paras 22 and 25 (Tomlinson LJ).

Chapter 7

Presentation of claims

7.1 Policy terms requiring the insurers to be notified within a particular period, or in a particular manner, of a loss or a claim, or of circumstances likely to give rise to a loss or a claim, are found, with variations in wording, in all modern policies of insurance. Since at least the middle of the nineteenth century, the courts have accepted that such clauses serve legitimate aims, in particular, by allowing early investigation of accidents and claims, which enables the insurer to avoid the additional expense he would incur if he had to investigate the circumstances long after the event, allowing him an opportunity to minimise loss and, where appropriate, enabling him to perform his role as *dominus litis* (which means the person in control of the litigation).[1] A similarly difficult factual investigation would have to be conducted, long after the event, to ascertain the loss caused to insurers by breach of a notification provision, and to avoid these difficulties and protect their position in circumstances where, although they had suffered prejudice, they would be unable to prove their loss, insurers often attempt to confer on such provisions the status of condition precedent.[2]

1 See *Mason v Harvey* (1853) 8 Ex Ch 819; *Re Coleman's Depositories* [1907] 2 KB 798, 807, CA (Fletcher Moulton LJ); *Re Bradley and Essex and Suffolk Accident Indemnity Society* [1912] 1 KB 415, CA, 426 (Fletcher Moulton LJ) and 431 (Farwell LJ); *Pioneer Concrete (UK) Ltd v National Employers Mutual General Insurance Association Ltd* [1985] 1 Lloyd's Rep 274, 278 (Bingham J); *George Hunt Cranes Ltd v Scottish Boiler and General Insurance Co Ltd* [2001] EWCA Civ 1964, [2002] Lloyd's Rep IR 178, para 14 (Potter LJ); *Aspen Insurance UK Ltd v Pectel Ltd* [2008] EWHC 2804, [2009] Lloyd's Rep IR, paras 64–66 (Teare J).
2 See *London Guarantie Co v Fearnley* (1880) 5 App Cas 911, HL, 916, 917 (Lord Blackburn); *Re Bradley and Essex and Suffolk Accident Indemnity Society* [1912] 1 KB 415, 427, CA (Fletcher Moulton LJ, dissenting).

ICOBS

7.2 The Insurance Conduct of Business Sourcebook ('ICOBS') provides that an insurer must not unreasonably reject a claim (including by terminating or avoiding a policy),[1] and that a rejection of a consumer policyholder's claim is unreasonable, except where there is evidence of fraud, except in certain circumstances including breach of condition where the circumstances of the claim are connected with the breach.[2] If a failure to comply with a condition precedent has not caused prejudice to the insurer, it is suggested that ICOBS would require the insurer not to reject the claim on this basis alone, as it would be unreasonable to reject the claim for failure to comply with the condition precedent, and the circumstances of the claim would not be connected with the breach of the condition. Breach of ICOBS is actionable at the suit of a 'private person',[3] and the loss caused by the breach in these circumstances would generally be the value of the claim.

1 ICOBS 8.1.1R.
2 ICOBS 8.1.2R.
3 See **PARA 8.2**.

BURDEN OF PROOF

7.3 Procedural conditions operate as exceptions to cover,[1] and the onus of proving breach of a procedural condition is on the insurer, whether or not the provision is a condition precedent.[2] This applies equally to provisions in policies requiring notification and, accordingly, the burden of proof is on the insurer.[3]

1 *Pioneer Concrete (UK) Ltd v National Employers Mutual General Insurance Association Ltd* [1985] 1 Lloyd's Rep 274, 278 (Bingham J).
2 *Bond Air Services Ltd v Hill* [1955] 2 QB 417, 427–428 (Lord Goddard CJ); *Sofi v Prudential Assurance Co Ltd* [1993] 2 Lloyd's Rep 559, 564, CA (Lloyd LJ). See further **PARA 5.1**. Potter LJ's remark in *Virk v Gan Life Holdings plc* [2000] Lloyd's Rep IR 159, CA (at para 12) that if a procedural condition is a condition precedent, the onus of proving breach is on the insured, does not represent the law.
3 See *Baltic Insurance Association of London Ltd v Cambrian Coaching & Goods Transport Ltd* (1926) 25 Ll L Rep 195, 197 (MacKinnon J); *Pioneer Concrete (UK) Ltd v National Employers Mutual General Insurance Association Ltd* [1985] 1 Lloyd's Rep 274, 278 (Bingham J).

CONSTRUCTION OF PROCEDURAL CONDITIONS INCLUDING NOTIFICATION CLAUSES

Conditions precedent

Construction

7.4 The normal principles of construction apply in respect of procedural conditions including notification clauses,[1] and whether or not a provision requiring notification is a condition precedent to payment under a policy of insurance is 'a question of pure construction'.[2]

Where certain terms in a policy are expressed to be conditions precedent, and the notification provision is not, the court is likely to conclude that the notification provision is not a condition precedent.[3] Where a policy states that the liability of insurers shall be conditional on the insured observing the terms and conditions of the policy, the commercial purpose underlying an obligation to notify an occurrence which may give rise to indemnify under the policy, namely to enable insurers to investigate a potential claim at the earliest opportunity, justifies compliance being a condition precedent to liability in respect of that claim.[4] The commercial purpose underlying an obligation to forward or notify to insurers immediately on receipt any letter, claim, writ, summons or process which may form the subject of indemnity under the policy is different, though related.[5]

Although the courts are wary of placing undue reliance on authorities in which similar but not identically-worded clauses have been construed, earlier decisions may be of assistance as regards the approach to be taken where similar clauses have been considered, both because the draftsman of a later clause who adopts wording which has previously been construed by the courts will be assumed to have had that construction in mind, and because they may indicate that a clause is of a type, the nature of which would permit it to be deemed a condition precedent.[6]

The essence of a 'claims made' policy is that it provides cover for claims first brought against the insured during the policy year; such policies commonly also extend cover to claims first brought against the insured after the policy year provided such claims arise out of circumstances previously notified to insurers of which the insured became aware during the policy year.[7] In *HLB Kidsons v Lloyd's Underwriters subscribing to policy 621/PKID00101*,[8] the clause by which this extension of cover was granted provided as follows:[9]

> 'The Assured shall give to the Underwriters notice in writing as soon as practicable of any circumstance of which they shall become aware during the period specified in the Schedule which may give rise to a loss or claim against them. Such notice having been given any loss or claim to which that circumstance has given rise which is subsequently made after the expiration of the period specified in the Schedule shall be deemed for the purpose of this Insurance to have been made during the subsistence hereof.'

This language reflects the functional and purposive basis of the insurance as a whole by making the extension or deeming of cover depend on the giving of the notice defined in the clause's first sentence, and that is a paradigm example of a condition precedent; without the notice, there is no extension of cover.[10] This was so notwithstanding that the provision requiring notification of a claim stated expressly that the notification of a claim to the insurer was a condition precedent.[11]

The question of compliance with a policy condition, and of whether that condition is a condition precedent to insurers' liability for a claim, may in an appropriate case be determined as a preliminary issue.[12]

1 See **PARA 3.5**.
2 *Stoneham v Ocean, Railway, and General Accident Insurance Co* (1887) 19 QBD 237, 240 (Mathew J). In *Hassett v Legal & General Assurance Society Ltd* (1939) 63 Ll L Rep 278, at 281, Atkinson J construed a notification provision construed as a condition precedent simply on the basis of the importance of the term to insurers and in the absence of express wording. This is not the modern approach: see *Virk v Gan Life Holdings plc* [2000] Lloyd's Rep IR 159, paras 14–15, CA (Potter LJ); *George Hunt Cranes Ltd v Scottish Boiler and General Insurance Co Ltd* [2001] EWCA Civ 1964, [2002] Lloyd's Rep IR 178, para 11 (Potter LJ); and see **PARA 3.5**.
3 See *Stoneham v Ocean, Railway, and General Accident Insurance Co* (1887) 19 QBD 237, 240 (Mathew J) and 241 (Cave J); *Re Coleman's Depositories* [1907] 2 KB 798, CA. Contrast an obligation notify circumstances, which is an extension or deeming of cover: see the discussion of *HLB Kidsons v Lloyd's Underwriters subscribing to policy 621/PKID00101* [2008] EWCA Civ 1206, [2009] 1 Lloyd's Rep 8 below.
4 *Aspen Insurance UK Ltd v Pectel Ltd* [2008] EWHC 2804, [2009] Lloyd's Rep IR, paras 64–66 (Teare J).
5 *Aspen Insurance UK Ltd v Pectel Ltd* [2008] EWHC 2804, [2009] Lloyd's Rep IR, para 71 (Teare J).
6 See the remarks of Potter LJ in *George Hunt Cranes Ltd v Scottish Boiler and General Insurance Co Ltd* [2001] EWCA Civ 1964, [2002] Lloyd's Rep IR 178 (at paras 18–19), about a clause requiring the insured to provide information within a reasonable time, a predecessor of which had been construed by the Court of Appeal to be a condition precedent in *Welch v Royal Exchange Assurance* [1939] 1 KB 294.
7 *HLB Kidsons v Lloyd's Underwriters subscribing to policy 621/PKID00101* [2008] EWCA Civ 1206, [2009] 1 Lloyd's Rep 8, para 4 (Rix LJ). See further **PARA 7.9**.

8 [2008] EWCA Civ 1206, [2009] 1 Lloyd's Rep 8.
9 *HLB Kidsons v Lloyd's Underwriters subscribing to policy 621/PKID00101* [2008] EWCA Civ 1206, [2009] 1 Lloyd's Rep 8, para 4 (Rix LJ).
10 *HLB Kidsons v Lloyd's Underwriters subscribing to policy 621/PKID00101* [2008] EWCA Civ 1206, [2009] 1 Lloyd's Rep 8, para 114 (Rix LJ).
11 *HLB Kidsons v Lloyd's Underwriters subscribing to policy 621/PKID00101* [2008] EWCA Civ 1206, [2009] 1 Lloyd's Rep 8, para 114 (Rix LJ). That provision needed to state expressly that the notification of a claim to the insurer was a condition precedent since the insuring clause was written in terms of what the insured had received ('claims made' against him) and not in terms of the claims passed on to underwriters within the policy year: *HLB Kidsons v Lloyd's Underwriters subscribing to policy 621/PKID00101* [2008] EWCA Civ 1206, [2009] 1 Lloyd's Rep 8, para 114 (Rix LJ).
12 See eg *Aspen Insurance UK Ltd v Pectel Ltd* [2008] EWHC 2804, [2009] Lloyd's Rep IR, para 5 (Teare J).

Prejudice

7.5 An insurer may refuse an indemnity in reliance on a condition precedent without showing that it has suffered any prejudice as a result of the breach[1]. The fact that insurers' reliance upon breach of the condition precedent may be completely devoid of merit is, therefore, irrelevant.[2] Prejudice may however be relevant to a consideration of what is a 'reasonable time' for the provision of information where the requirement to provide information within a 'reasonable time' is a condition precedent to the insurer's liability: in this context there is no absolute principle which includes or excludes as relevant to the question what is a 'reasonable time' for the provision of information the fact of whether, as things turn out, insurers were prejudiced; each case turns on its own facts, but there is no determinative principle that a duty on the insured to provide relevant information within a reasonable time will not be broken if, in the end, it turns out that there is no prejudice to insurers.[3]

Additional considerations arise under ICOBS where the insured is a consumer policyholder,[4] and where the contract of insurance is one to which Part 2 of the Consumer Act 2015 applies.[5]

1 See, for example, *Pioneer Concrete (UK) Ltd v National Employers Mutual General Insurance Association Ltd* [1985] 1 Lloyd's Rep 274, 281 (Bingham J); approved: *Motor and General Insurance Co Ltd v Pavy* [1994] 1 WLR 462, 469, PC; *Virk v Gan Life Holdings plc* [2000] Lloyd's Rep IR 159, para 13 (Potter LJ), CA; *HLB Kidsons v Lloyd's Underwriters subscribing to policy 621/PKID00101* [2008] EWCA Civ 1206, [2009] 1 Lloyd's Rep 8, para 116 (Rix LJ). Authorities which are (or appear to be) to the contrary do not represent the law: these include the wider basis on which Lord Denning MR put his decision (Danckwerts LJ agreeing) in *Barrett Bros (Taxis) Ltd v Davies* [1966] 1 WLR 1334, CA (at 1340) (contrast Lord Denning MR's judgment in *Farrell v Federated Employers Insurance Ltd* [1970] 1 WLR 1400, CA, at 1406, where he appears to accept that no prejudice is required), and the remark of Mocatta J in *CVG Siderurgicia Del Orinoco SA v London Steamship Owners' Mutual Insurance Association Ltd, The Vainqueur José* [1979] 1 Lloyd's Rep 557 that it was 'probably the law' that some prejudice was required before insurers could refuse an indemnity in reliance on a condition precedent as to notice (at 566–567).
2 See eg *Widefree Ltd v Brit Insurance Ltd* [2009] EWHC 3671 (QB), [2011] Lloyd's Rep IR 63, para 96 (Peter Leaver QC, sitting as a Deputy High Court Judge).
3 *Shinedean Ltd v Alldown Demolition (London) Ltd* [2006] EWCA Civ 939, [2006] 1 WLR 2696, paras 22 (May LJ) and 28 (Sir Anthony Clarke MR).
4 See PARAS 3.5 and 8.2.
5 See PARA 3.20.

INNOMINATE OR INTERMEDIATE TERMS

7.6 In *Alfred McAlpine plc v BAI (Run-Off) Ltd*,[1] Waller LJ construed a notice provision as an innominate term 'where the consequences of a breach may be so serious as to entitle [the insurer] to reject the claim albeit that the breach is not so serious as to amount to a repudiation of the whole contract'.[2]

Following *Friends Provident Life & Pensions Ltd v Sirius International Insurance*,[3] it is doubtful whether, as a matter of law, there is any such variation on the classic innominate term as suggested in *BAI*.[4] If the refinement to the innominate term introduced by *Alfred McAlpine plc v BAI (Run-Off) Ltd*[5] survives the decision of the Court of Appeal in *Friends Provident Life & Pensions Ltd v Sirius International Insurance*,[6] the availability of the *BAI* innominate term as a matter of construction might disincline a court from treating a procedural condition, such as a notification clause, as a condition precedent.[7] If such a variation does exist, the court will need to consider in each case whether the insured's breach of an innominate term and the consequences of the breach for insurers are sufficiently serious to justify the rejection of the claim.[8] This issue would be judged at the date of trial.[9]

1 [2000] 1 Lloyd's Rep 437, CA.
2 At para 32. See further PARAS **3.4** and **3.9**.
3 [2005] EWCA Civ 601, [2005] Lloyd's Rep 517, paras 31–32 (Mance LJ).
4 See further PARA **3.9**.
5 [2000] 1 Lloyd's Rep 437, CA.
6 [2005] EWCA Civ 601, [2005] 2 Lloyd's Rep 517.
7 *Friends Provident Life & Pensions Ltd v Sirius International Insurance* [2005] EWCA Civ 601, [2005] 2 Lloyd's Rep 517, para 27 (Mance LJ).
8 *Friends Provident Life & Pensions Ltd v Sirius International Insurance* [2005] EWCA Civ 601, [2005] 2 Lloyd's Rep 517, para 31 (Mance LJ).
9 *K/S Merc-Scandia XXXXII v Certain Lloyd's Underwriters, The Mercandian Continent* [2001] EWCA Civ 1275, [2001] 2 Lloyd's Rep 563, para 16 (Longmore LJ).

DAMAGES FOR BREACH OF A PROCEDURAL CONDITION

7.7 In order to obtain damages for breach of a procedural condition, the insurer has to show what it would have done had the insured complied with the condition, and the prejudice which it has suffered as a result.[1] The correct basis for the assessment of damages may be as damages for loss of a chance.[2]

1 *Porter v Zurich Insurance Co* [2009] EWHC 376 (QB), [2010] Lloyd's Rep IR 373, paras 127 and 131–142 (Coulson J) (breach of a claims co-operation clause); *Milton Keynes Borough Council v Nulty* [2011] EWHC 2847 (TCC), [2012] Lloyd's Rep IR 453, paras 247–268 (Edwards-Stuart J); point not considered on appeal: [2013] EWCA Civ 15, [2013] Lloyd's Rep IR 243 (breach of a notification clause).
2 *Friends Provident Life & Pensions Ltd v Sirius International Insurance* [2005] EWCA Civ 601, [2005] 2 Lloyd's Rep 517, paras 32–33 (Mance LJ); *Milton Keynes Borough Council v Nulty* [2011] EWHC 2847 (TCC), [2012] Lloyd's Rep IR 453, paras 269–272 (Edwards-Stuart J); point not considered on appeal: [2013] EWCA Civ 15, [2013] Lloyd's Rep IR 243. In *Milton Keynes Borough Council v Nulty*, the indemnity was reduced by 15% to reflect the judge's finding that putting a value on the loss was fraught with difficulty, and that he had no hesitation in rejecting the insurer's argument that it should be assessed at 100%, or even 50%, but that he did not think that it was so nebulous as to be intangible, so that it could be put at nothing (paras 273–274); and that

there was no logical way of arriving at an appropriate percentage, and he had to do it largely as a matter of impression, looking at the circumstances of the case as a whole (para 274). The insurer would not have been able to show, as a matter of probability, that the outcome of the litigation would have been different if the circumstances had been promptly notified by the insured, and had that been the correct basis for assessing damages, the insurer's claim would have failed (para 269). The judge indicated that if the insured's liability exceeded the limit of indemnity, the reduction of 15% should be applied to the limit of indemnity of £2million, thereby reducing it to £1.7million (para 275).

WHAT MUST BE NOTIFIED

Accident, loss, damage, claim or occurrence

7.8 What must be notified depends on the construction of the clause requiring notification, and any relevant policy definitions. There is not usually much difficulty about determining whether an accident, loss or damage has occurred. 'Claim', however, is more complex: it may mean a claim made by a third party against the insured, or a claim by the insured under the policy. In liability insurance, 'claim' usually has the former meaning, although it may be used in both senses in different places in a single policy. More precisely, in the former sense, and in the absence of any contrary definition in the policy,[1] it means 'the occurrence of a state of facts which justifies a claim on underwriters';[2] or 'the assertion by a third party against the insured of a right to some relief'.[3] In *West Wake Price & Co v Ching*,[4] Devlin J said in relation to the use of the word 'claim' in a 'QC clause' in an accountants' indemnity policy:[5]

> 'If the word is to be used with any precision, it must be defined in relation to the object claimed. The grounds for the claim or the causes of action which support it can give it colour and character, but cannot give it its entity. If you say of a claim against a defendant that it is for £100, you have said all that is necessary to identify it as a claim; but if you say of it that it is for fraud or negligence, you have not distinguished it from a charge or allegation. In particular, if you identify a claim as something that has to be paid (and that is how it is referred to in the QC clause), it must be something that is capable of separate payment: you cannot pay a cause of action. It follows, I think, that if there is only one object claimed by one person, then there is only one claim, however many may be the grounds or the causes of action which can be raised in support of it: likewise, where several claims are each dependent on the same cause of action (as, for example, where one cause of action leads to alternative claims for an injunction, damages or an account or other different forms of relief), there remains only one cause of action, however many claims it may give rise to.'

The obvious commercial purpose of a provision requiring the insured to give written notice of 'any accident or claim or proceedings' is to enable the insurer to perform his role as *dominus litis* and to investigate accidents and claims at the earliest possible opportunity, and this phrase was accordingly construed conjunctively by Bingham J in *Pioneer Concrete (UK) Ltd v National Employers Mutual General Insurance Association Ltd*.[6]

In the context of a workers' compensation policy covering a motor vehicle plant, notice of 'an occurrence' requires notice to be given of a matter where it is 'known to the employers ... to be serious and it is known to the employers that the man is incapacitated temporarily and thereafter, from time to time, from doing his full work'.[7] Whether it requires 'notice of every trivial little matter which arises in the works' was expressly left open.[8] 'Knowledge' is (or can be) an elusive concept because in any given case a party to a contract may have difficulty showing what another party 'knows', and it would therefore be better if 'knowledge' were not used as the trigger for any requirement of notification to a liability insurer or reinsurer.[9]

A claim is not made until it is communicated to the insured, and a writ which is issued but not served on the insured does not constitute a 'claim' for the purposes of a notification clause in a liability policy.[10]

Even if there is no claim, either as a matter of law or within the meaning of the policy, the same facts may constitute a notifiable circumstance or intention to make a claim.[11]

1 In *ARC Capital Partners Ltd v Brit Syndicates Ltd* [2016] EWHC 141 (Comm), a professional indemnity insurance policy defined 'claim' as meaning, so far as relevant, 'a written demand for monetary damages or non-pecuniary relief'. The insured received a letter from solicitors which said that it was their view that their client had a strong claim against the insured for recovery of a payment the client had made, and all related losses, costs and interest, and that while the primary purpose of the letter was to agree a process for recovery of those sums from another party, they fully reserved their client's rights against the insured, and asked the insured to meet up front the costs of recovering the payment from the other party. Cooke J held (at para 54) that the letter did not constitute a demand, but was expressly a letter in which rights were reserved; and that the suggestion that the insured meet upfront the costs of the recovery strategy was not in itself a claim either: it was not a written demand for monetary damages or non-pecuniary relief.
2 *Australia and New Zealand Bank Ltd v Colonial and Eagle Wharves Ltd* [1960] 2 Lloyd's Rep 241, 255 (McNair J); considered: *Haydon v Lo & Lo* [1997] 1 WLR 198, PC.
3 *Thorman v New Hampshire Insurance Co (UK) Ltd* [1988] 1 Lloyd's Rep 7, 11, CA (Sir John Donaldson MR).
4 [1957] 1 WLR 45.
5 At 57; applied: *Haydon v Lo & Lo* [1997] 1 WLR 198, 206, PC (Lord Lloyd); see also PARA **6.9**.
6 [1985] 1 Lloyd's Rep 274.
7 *General Motors Ltd v Crowder* (1931) 40 Ll L Rep 87, 89 (Hawke J).
8 *General Motors Ltd v Crowder* (1931) 40 Ll L Rep 87, 89 (Hawke J).
9 *Royal & Sun Alliance Insurance plc v Dornoch* [2005] EWCA Civ 238, [2005] Lloyd's Rep IR 544, para 30 (Longmore LJ).
10 *Robert Irving & Burns v Stone* [1998] Lloyd's Rep IR 258, CA.
11 See PARA **7.9**.

Circumstances or intention to make a claim

7.9 Professional indemnity insurance policies, and other liability policies which provide cover on a claims made basis, typically include provisions which require or permit notification of circumstances or occurrences which may or are likely to give rise to a claim. In *HLB Kidsons v Lloyd's Underwriters subscribing to policy 621/PKID00101*,[1] Toulson LJ described the operation of such provisions as follows:[2]

'It is common for a proposal form for professional indemnity insurance to ask the proposer to state whether he is aware, after inquiry, of any circumstances which may or perhaps "are likely to" give rise to a claim against the would-be insured and, if so, to provide details. Even if such a question is not asked, information about potential claims (unless trivial or their likelihood can be dismissed as remote) is likely to be material to the prospective insurer and therefore disclosable in any event. The prospective insurer is then likely to exclude cover in respect of any claims which may arise from circumstances disclosed to him prior to the policy being agreed.

In order to secure protection for the insured against such claims it is also standard for professional indemnity policies, which basically provide cover against the risk of claims being made against the insured during the policy year, to contain a provision enabling the risk of a later claim to attach to the policy where it arises from circumstances of which the insured becomes aware and gives notice to the insurer. It is not merely the insured's awareness of the circumstances, but his giving of notice of them to the insurer, which causes the risk to attach to the policy.

These two features of professional indemnity insurance fit together. Their essence is simple and well understood by the market, but they can give rise to a variety of problems, especially when there is a change of insurer between different years.'

Thus, where a circumstance is notified to a policy, a subsequent claim arising out of that circumstance, whenever it is made, is deemed to have been made during the currency of the policy, and attaches to it.[3]

Depending on its wording, a policy may exclude liability not only in respect of claims arising from circumstances or occurrences notified to any earlier policy, but also in respect of claims which arise from circumstances or occurrences which the insured knew might give rise to claims, whether or not notified to an earlier policy year.[4] Whereas exclusions from cover identify claims that will not, during the future currency of the policy, be entertained, notice provisions come into operation with the execution of the policy and look to the future in the sense that they apply as events unfold.[5] For this reason, a notice provision which requires the insured to notify insurers of 'any occurrence of which they may become aware which may subsequently give rise to a claim' requires that the insured inform the insurers of events that happen as the policy term proceeds, and not of any previous event of which they are already aware at the execution of the policy.[6] The two questions which will typically arise, for instance in relation to the intimation of a possible complaint, will be whether such circumstances have come to the attention of the insured (during the policy period) so that he can be said to be aware of them, and whether such circumstances are such that they fall within the relevant wording, such as that they 'may give rise to a loss or claim' against him.[7] The question whether a circumstance may give rise to a claim is not a matter of simple knowledge, a question of fact of which a person may or may not be 'aware'; rather, it involves a degree of crystal ball-gazing, an estimation of the likelihood of a claim.[8] An occurrence 'likely to give rise to a claim' has been held by the Court of Appeal to mean at least a 50 per cent chance of a claim.[9] The likelihood of a claim being made falls to be assessed at the time of the relevant 'occurrence', which means that the fact that a claim is subsequently made has no bearing on the question of whether a claim was 'likely' at the time of the occurrence.[10] The test 'which may give rise to a claim' is 'a weak one'.[11] It is doubtful whether an insured's own concern, without more, that he may have made a mistake is a relevant circumstance which can entitle him to give notice of circumstances, thus extending his claims made policy into future years; otherwise, every insured could extend his policy indefinitely simply by a notification based on his own lack of confidence.[12] What is required is the existence of a substratum of underlying external fact, over and above the insured's mere concerns.[13] Thus, in the case of an insured architect:[14]

'A typical example would be a belated realization, based upon a study of professional journals, that perhaps he had specified inadequate foundations for a building which he had designed and which had already been erected.'

A policy may also require notification of receipt of notice of an intention to make a claim; if it does so, the policy will provide, as with notification of a circumstance, that the intended claim whenever subsequently made will be deemed to have been made during the currency of the policy.[15]

1 [2008] EWCA Civ 1206, [2009] 1 Lloyd's Rep 8.
2 At paras 131–133.
3 *Thorman v New Hampshire Insurance Co (UK) Ltd* [1988] 1 Lloyd's Rep 7, 9–10, CA (Sir John Donaldson MR). See also **PARA 7.18**.
4 See *National Employers Mutual General Insurance Association Ltd v Haydon* [1980] 2 Lloyd's Rep 149, 153, CA (Stephenson LJ).
5 *Tilley & Noad v Dominion Insurance Co Ltd* [1987] 2 EGLR 34, 37 (Mervyn Davies J).
6 *Tilley & Noad v Dominion Insurance Co Ltd* [1987] 2 EGLR 34, 37 (Mervyn Davies J).
7 *HLB Kidsons v Lloyd's Underwriters subscribing to policy 621/PKID00101* [2008] EWCA Civ 1206, [2009] 1 Lloyd's Rep 8, para 72 (Rix LJ).
8 *HLB Kidsons v Lloyd's Underwriters subscribing to policy 621/PKID00101* [2008] EWCA Civ 1206, [2009] 1 Lloyd's Rep 8, para 138 (Toulson LJ). Toulson LJ also suggested (at para 142) that the right general approach to a provision which entitled the insured to give notification of a circumstance which may give rise to a claim, and thereby cause the risk to attach to that policy, was to treat the right as subject to an implicit requirement that the circumstance may reasonably be regarded in itself as a matter which may give rise to a claim; and that the right general approach to a policy clause which went further and imposed a duty on the insured to give such a notification was to treat it as implicitly limited, not only by the requirement that the circumstance may reasonably be regarded as a matter which may give rise to a claim, but to a circumstance which either the insured notified or which any reasonable person in his position would recognise as a matter which may give rise to a claim and therefor requiring notification to the insurer.
9 *Layher Ltd v Lowe* [2000] Lloyd's Rep IR 510, CA; *Jacobs v Coster* [2000] Lloyd's Rep IR 506, CA.
10 *Layher Ltd v Lowe* [2000] Lloyd's Rep IR 510, CA; *Jacobs v Coster* [2000] Lloyd's Rep IR 506, CA. Contrast *J Rothschild Assurance plc v Collyear* [1999] Lloyd's Rep IR 6, in which Rix J held (at 23) that it was legitimate to test a notification (of 'circumstances which may give rise to a claim') against what happened in due course.
11 *J Rothschild Assurance plc v Collyear* [1999] Lloyd's Rep IR 6, 22 (Rix J). In *HLB Kidsons v Lloyd's Underwriters subscribing to policy 621/PKID00101* [2007] EWHC 1951 (Comm), [2008] Lloyd's Rep IR 237, at para 73, Gloster J said of this test: 'All that need exist is a state of affairs from which the prospects of a claim (whether good or bad) or loss emerging in the future are "real" as opposed to false, fanciful or imaginary' (point not considered on appeal: [2008] EWCA Civ 1206, [2009] 1 Lloyd's Rep 8); applied: *Aspen Insurance UK Ltd v Pectel Ltd* [2008] EWHC 2804, [2009] Lloyd's Rep IR, para 9 (Teare J).
12 *HLB Kidsons v Lloyd's Underwriters subscribing to policy 621/PKID00101* [2008] EWCA Civ 1206, [2009] 1 Lloyd's Rep 8, para 73 (Rix LJ).
13 *HLB Kidsons v Lloyd's Underwriters subscribing to policy 621/PKID00101* [2008] EWCA Civ 1206, [2009] 1 Lloyd's Rep 8, para 74 (Rix LJ).
14 *Thorman v New Hampshire Insurance Co (UK) Ltd* [1988] 1 Lloyd's Rep 7, 10, CA (Sir John Donaldson MR); applied: *HLB Kidsons v Lloyd's Underwriters subscribing to policy 621/PKID00101* [2008] EWCA Civ 1206, [2009] 1 Lloyd's Rep 8, para 74 (Rix LJ).
15 *Thorman v New Hampshire Insurance Co (UK) Ltd* [1988] 1 Lloyd's Rep 7, 9–10, CA (Sir John Donaldson MR).

Block, blanket or 'laundry list' notifications

7.10   Notifications are sometimes made to professional indemnity policies where no particular transaction or possible claimant has been identified, but something has happened to give rise to a concern on the part of the insured which may affect a large number of transactions or claimants.[1] A list or schedule of possibly relevant transactions or claimants may be appended to the notification, and these notifications are sometimes referred to as block, blanket or laundry list notifications. Notifications of this nature are not invalid simply because no particular transaction or possible claimant has been identified when the notification is made.[2] The separate question of whether any claim which is subsequently made arose out of the notified circumstances depends on the nature of the claim made and cannot be determined in advance, and declaratory relief is therefore unlikely to be appropriate.[3]

1 See eg *J Rothschild Assurance plc v Collyear* [1999] Lloyd's Rep IR 6 (blanket notification under financial advisers' professional indemnity policy of 2,500 pensions transactions in which insured had been involved and which fell within scope of regulator's review); *McManus v European Risk Insurance Co* [2013] EWHC 18 (Ch), [2013] Lloyd's Rep IR 533 (blanket notification under solicitors' professional indemnity policy of estimated 5,000 conveyancing transactions in which insured's predecessor firms had acted).
2 *J Rothschild Assurance plc v Collyear* [1999] Lloyd's Rep IR 6, 17, 22–23 (Rix J); *McManus v European Risk Insurance Co* [2013] EWHC 18 (Ch), [2013] Lloyd's Rep IR 533, paras 43–45 (Ms Vivien Rose, sitting as a Deputy High Court Judge): point not considered on appeal: [2013] EWCA Civ 1545, [2014] Lloyd's Rep IR 169; in both cases, the test of materiality for notification of circumstances was that they 'may' give rise to a claim.
3 *McManus v European Risk Insurance Co* [2013] EWHC 18 (Ch), [2013] Lloyd's Rep IR 533, paras 45–62 (Ms Vivien Rose, sitting as a Deputy High Court Judge, refusing to grant declaration as to validity of circumstances notified); decision upheld on appeal: [2013] EWCA Civ 1545, [2014] Lloyd's Rep IR 169, paras 34–38 (Davis LJ). See also PARA **7.18**.

WHO MUST GIVE NOTICE

7.11   Where a policy provides expressly that notice is to be given by 'the insured', notice given by an agent of the insured constitutes notice by the insured.[1] By a majority, the Court of Appeal in *Barrett Bros (Taxis) Ltd v Davies*[2] held that insurers are not entitled to insist on notification by the insured where they have received 'reliable information' from another source (in that case, the police). In the *Barrett Bros* case, a motorcyclist notified insurers that he had been involved in an accident with a taxi driver, but failed to forward to them immediately, as required by a condition precedent in the policy, a notice of prosecution and summons he subsequently received. The police wrote to the insurers, who then wrote to the insured asking him why he had not forwarded the documents to them. The Court of Appeal held that the failure to forward the documents did not entitle insurers to refuse to indemnify the driver. Lord Denning MR said:

> 'Seeing that they had received the information from the police, it would be a futile thing to require the motor-cyclist himself to give them the self-same information. The law never compels a person to do that which is useless and unnecessary.'[3]

In *The Vainqueur José*,[4] Mocatta J held that, as a matter of construction of the rules of a P & I club, notification of a claim had to be given by the insured or his agent, and could not be given by third parties or anyone who had an interest in so doing.[5] The evidence before Mocatta J established that the mere fact of an incident or accident that might give rise or did give rise to a claim against a third party against the insured did not entail, of necessity, that there would be a claim to indemnity by the insured against the defendants. Insureds often meet claims from their own resources; common reasons include the maintaining of good business relations with third parties, and a desire to avoid an increase in the premium or the imposition of an increased excess on renewal. In *Barrett Bros*, the insured had already notified the insurer of the accident, and the insurer had obtained from a reliable third party source exactly that which the policy subsequently required the insured to provide, which was the notice of prosecution and the summons. In *The Vainqueur José*, by contrast, it was only the insured who could provide the information which the policy required, which was the initial notification that a claim might be made, as it was only the insured who was entitled to decide whether or not to make a claim. On this basis, the two decisions are consistent with one another.[6]

1 *Davies v National Fire and Marine Insurance Co of New Zealand* [1891] AC 485, PC (loss, by fire, of a factory and its contents; notice was in fact given by a partner on behalf of the insured firm, and Lord Hobhouse indicated that the Privy Council considered that this amounted to notice by the insured, and that even if it did not, it was notice by an agent on behalf of the insured, which was sufficient).
2 [1966] 1 WLR 1334.
3 [1966] 1 WLR 1334, 1339. Danckwerts LJ agreed; Salmon LJ dissented but agreed that insurers had waived the right to demand the documents which contained the information.
4 *CVG Siderurgicia Del Orinoco SA v London Steamship Owners' Mutual Insurance Association Ltd, The Vainqueur José* [1979] 1 Lloyd's Rep 557.
5 In construing the rules in this manner, Mocatta J took into account the fact that the period within which notice had to be given was 12 months, which would be long enough to avoid difficulties in most situations, including death or insolvency of an insured.
6 See also *Tioxide Europe Ltd v CGU International plc* [2005] EWCA Civ 928, [2006] Lloyd's Rep IR 31, paras 18–20 (Tuckey LJ) (only the insured could validly exercise a loss notification option which provided further protection to the insured in a case in which a claim had been made).

THE PARTY WHO MUST BE GIVEN NOTICE

7.12 Where a term requires that insurers be notified of relevant matters, notification to an insurance broker is not sufficient unless, unusually, the broker is the agent of the insurer rather than the insured.[1] Further, notification to an agent of the insurer will suffice only if the agent is an agent to receive notice of claims and not, for example, merely a representative nominated to give advice and assistance in particular situations.[2]

1 See *Brook v Trafalgar Insurance Co Ltd* (1946) 79 Ll L Rep 365, 368, CA (Scott LJ); and see further PARAS 16.2–16.6.
2 See *CVG Siderurgicia Del Orinoco SA v London Steamship Owners' Mutual Insurance Association Ltd, The Vainqueur José* [1979] 1 Lloyd's Rep 557.

MEANING OF 'NOTICE' OR 'NOTIFICATION'

7.13 It seems there is no authority on the meaning of 'notice' or 'notification' in the insurance context. General contract law defines notice or notification in terms of the knowledge which is the subject of the notice or notification actually being received by the receiving party, and not in terms of the notifying party taking reasonable steps to impart the knowledge, for example, by putting a letter in the post, if the letter does not reach its destination. The position was described by Lawton LJ in *Holwell Securities v Hughes*, in the context of an option to purchase property which was to be exercised 'by notice in writing to' the owner, in these terms:

> 'Should any inference be drawn from the use of the word "notice"? In my judgment, yes. Its derivation is from the Latin word for knowing. A notice is a means of making something known. The Shorter Oxford English Dictionary gives as the primary meanings of the word: "Intimation, information, intelligence, warning, ... Formal intimation or warning of something." If a notice is to be of any value it must be an intimation to someone. A notice which cannot impinge on anyone's mind is not functioning as such.'[1]

Where notice is given in writing, it is unclear whether mere receipt of the notice by insurers is sufficient, or whether the contents of the notice must come to their attention within the time specified for the giving of notice. In *The Brimnes*,[2] which concerned a notice given by telex at 5.45pm but not read by the recipient until the following morning, Megaw LJ said:[3]

> '... if a notice arrives at the address of the person to be notified, at such a time and by such a means of communication that it would in the normal course of business come to the attention of that person on its arrival, that person cannot rely on some failure of himself or his servants to act in a normal businesslike manner in respect of taking cognisance of the communication so as to postpone the effective time of the notice until some later time when it in fact came to his attention.'

Cairns LJ was less sure that this principle could be relied upon where, as had happened in *The Brimnes*, notice had been sent just before the end of the last possible day, but was not seen until the following day. However, he was satisfied (as was Edmund Davies LJ) that notice had been validly given because, on the evidence, the notice should in the normal course of events have come to the attention of an employee of the recipient on the day on which it was sent, and that it did not do so was due to neglect of duty.[4]

Where a notification provision obliges the insured to provide certain information to insurers, the clause may be satisfied by the provision of the information, whatever the purpose for which, from the subjective viewpoint of the insured, the information is provided. Where, therefore, an insured provides information to its insurers about 'circumstances which might give rise to a claim' in the context of renewal of cover with those insurers for the following policy year, the information is capable of constituting notice to insurers under the current policy of the 'circumstances' described;[5] whether or not it does so will depend on the context in which it is provided.[6]

If the policy stipulates that notice must be given in writing, it is suggested that any form of writing, including email, is sufficient; and that if the policy does not stipulate that notice must be given in writing, any form of notice will suffice.

1 *Holwell Securities v Hughes* [1974] 1 WLR 155, 160, CA (Lawton LJ).
2 [1975] QB 929, CA.
3 At 966–967.

4 [1975] QB 929, 969–970, CA.
5 *Friends Provident Life & Pensions Ltd v Sirius International Insurance* [2005] EWCA Civ 601, [2005] Lloyd's Rep 517, paras 16–17 (Mance LJ); *HLB Kidsons v Lloyd's Underwriters subscribing to policy 621/PKID00101* [2008] EWCA Civ 1206, [2009] 1 Lloyd's Rep 8, para 18 (Rix LJ).
6 *HLB Kidsons v Lloyd's Underwriters subscribing to policy 621/PKID00101* [2008] EWCA Civ 1206, [2009] 1 Lloyd's Rep 8, para 18 (Rix LJ).

EXPRESSIONS AS TO TIME

'Immediate' or 'immediately'

7.14   'Immediate' has been construed to mean 'with all reasonable speed considering the circumstances of the case'.[1] In a case concerning a policy which provided that 'Notice shall be given in writing to the Association immediately on the occurrence of any accident or loss', the court held that it was appropriate to take into account, when considering the immediacy or otherwise of the notice which had been given, of when the accident in question came to the attention of the insured, and concluded that notice given immediately upon the insured receiving a letter from the third party informing it of the accident in which its driver had been involved was sufficient, notwithstanding the fact that the driver of the insured's vehicle knew of the accident from the instant it occurred, and another employee of the insured knew of it shortly afterwards.[2] Failure to forward a writ until eight weeks after receipt, during which period judgment was entered, was held to be a breach of a condition requiring that notice be given 'immediately on receipt'.[3] A provision requiring 'immediate' notice by an employer of any accident to an employee was breached where the employer learnt of the accident a week after it had occurred, but failed to notify the insurer until about six weeks later, after the employee had given written notice that he intended to claim compensation for his injuries.[4]

1 *Re Coleman's Depositories* [1907] 2 KB 798, 807, CA (Fletcher Moulton LJ); applied: *Aspen Insurance UK Ltd v Pectel Ltd* [2008] EWHC 2804, [2009] Lloyd's Rep IR, para 9 (Teare J).
2 *Baltic Insurance Association of London Ltd v Cambrian Coaching & Goods Transport Ltd* (1926) 25 Ll L Rep 195.
3 *Farrell v Federated Employers Insurance Ltd* [1970] 1 WLR 1400, CA.
4 *Re an Arbitration between Williams and Thomas and The Lancashire and Yorkshire Accident Insurance Co* (1902) 19 TLR 82.

'As soon as possible'

7.15   In *Verelst's Administratrix v Motor Union Insurance Co Ltd*,[1] Roche J held that a requirement that notice be given 'as soon as possible' meant as soon as possible in the circumstances which prevailed and applied to the person under the obligation to give notice, rather than as soon as anyone in the abstract could give notice.[2] The judge held that, as all existing circumstances must be taken into account, he could take into account the fact that although news of the death of the insured had reached the insured's administratrix within a month, the administratrix was unaware of the existence of the insurance policy until a year later, but had notified the insurer of the death within a short period of discovering the existence of the policy.[3] In

Maccaferri Ltd v Zurich Insurance plc,[4] a public and product liability insurance policy provided that the insured should give notice to the insurer 'as soon as possible after the occurrence of any event likely to give rise to a claim with full particulars thereof'.[5] Knowles J rejected the insurer's argument that the use of the words 'as soon as possible' indicated that the obligation to notify arose when an insured could with reasonable diligence discover that an event was likely to give rise to a claim, and held that the words referred simply to the promptness with which the notice in writing was to be given if there had been an event likely to give rise to a claim,[6] so that there was no requirement that a policyholder conduct a continuing or 'rolling assessment' of claim likelihood.[7]

1 [1925] 2 KB 137.
2 At 142–143.
3 At 143.
4 [2015] EWHC 1708 (Comm), [2015] Lloyd's Rep IR 594 (subject to appeal).
5 See para 4.
6 At paras 8–9.
7 At para 11.

SPECIFIC PERIODS

7.16 Terms requiring notification within a period as short as 48 hours have been construed as conditions precedent and upheld by the courts.[1] A provision requiring notice of any accident within seven days was upheld as a condition precedent in a case where the accident had caused the death of the policyholder 15 days later.[2] In *Diab v Regent Insurance Co Ltd*,[3] Lord Scott appeared to suggest that failure to comply with a condition precedent which required the insured to provide information about the claim 'within 15 days after the loss or damage, or such further time as the [insurer] may in writing allow'[4] might not entitle the insurer to reject the claim if the information were provided within a short time of expiry of that period.[5] Lord Scott also suggested[6] that equitable principles as to strict compliance with time periods (stipulations as to time not being deemed to be of the essence of the contract unless they would be so in equity) might have a role to play in the context of a failure to comply in due time with a condition precedent.

1 See *Roche v Roberts* (1921) 9 Ll L Rep 59 (death of a pedigree greyhound).
2 *Cawley v National Employers' Accident and General Assurance Association* (1885) 1 TLR 255.
3 [2006] UKPC 29, [2007] 1 WLR 797, [2006] Lloyd's Rep IR 779.
4 See para 13.
5 At para 14.
6 At paras 15–16. Further, in *Firma C-Trade SA v Newcastle P & I Association, The Fanti and the Padre Island (No 2)* [1991] 2 AC 1, HL, Lord Jauncey said, in construing a 'pay to be paid' clause (at 42): 'Although equity may distinguish between what is a matter of substance and what is a matter of form, as, for example, in the case of a time stipulated for performance, a contract will be construed alike both in equity and at law'.

Impossibility

7.17 When the courts are persuaded that compliance with a notice provision would have been impossible, they will not enforce it strictly.[1] Such cases are likely to be rare. In *T H Adamson & Sons v Liverpool & London & Globe Insurance Co Ltd*,[2] a policy covering an employer against theft from it by its own employees contained a provision that:

> 'The company shall be under no liability hereunder in respect of any loss which has not been notified to the company within fourteen days of its occurrence.'

The provision was held to preclude recovery even in circumstances where the insured had not discovered the loss within 14 days.[3] Lord Goddard CJ was influenced by the purpose of the clause, which he held to be to ensure that the employer was diligent in attempting to detect fraud by its employees.[4]

1 *Verelst's Administratrix v Motor Union Insurance Co Ltd* [1925] 2 KB 137, 143 (in the context of a requirement of 'immediate' notice); *Home Insurance Co of New York v Victoria-Montreal Fire Insurance Co* [1907] AC 59, PC (reinsurance slip pasted onto printed form appropriate to insurance; clause prescribing actions brought after expiration of one year held to be unreasonable and disregarded, as it was only possible for reinsured to comply if direct loss ascertained between parties over whom he had no control).
2 [1953] 2 Lloyd's Rep 355.
3 At 359 (Lord Goddard CJ).
4 At 359.

SCOPE OF NOTIFICATION OF CIRCUMSTANCES

7.18 Where notification is of circumstances which may or are likely to give rise to a claim in the context of a claims made policy, the question of whether a subsequent claim arises out of those circumstances so as to be within the scope of the notification can give rise to difficult issues of construction. The notification is construed in context and objectively.[1] In *Kajima UK Engineering Ltd v The Underwriter Insurance Co Ltd*, Akenhead J held that notification of circumstances by the insured construction contractors in respect of a design and build project related to:[2]

'(a) Water had been ponding on the walkways. It was believed to have occurred because the pods were settling and moving excessively.
(b)   This settlement and excessive movement was thought to be causing, actually or potentially, adjoining roofing balconies and walkways to distort by way of differential settlement. It was also believed that the service connections were under risk from that movement. There was associated with that movement potential internal damage and possible tenant risk, danger or inconvenience.'

Therefore the essential circumstances notified were settlement or movement of the accommodation 'pods' and distortion of adjoining balconies, walkways and roofing, and the actual and potential consequences of these circumstances were covered by the notification.[3] The notification was not effective in relation to any other matters, loss or damage save and to the extent that the other matters, defects or damage caused or related or contributed to the circumstances which were notified or were caused by the notified circumstances.[4] In general terms, the notification would cover: (i) the defects which caused (ii) the symptoms of; or (iii) the consequences of, the circumstances which were notified.[5] The fact that, subsequently and over a period of years, a number of other defects emerged of more or less seriousness did not enable the notified circumstances to be expanded; the notified circumstances could not be expanded by the later discovery of unrelated defects or damage which were not the subject matter of the notification, including those which had been discovered coincidentally in the course of investigating the notified circumstances;[6] it was insufficient that there was a historical 'continuum' of investigation which coincidentally revealed a number of defects or deficiencies which had or might have had nothing to do with the notified circumstances.[7] Even if the investigation referred to in the notification had revealed within the insurance period damage, defects and deficiencies which were not related to the notified circumstances, the original notification would not be wide enough to cover such laterally or coincidentally discovered matters.[8] Further notifications would therefore be required as the insured became aware of further circumstances which might give rise to a claim.[9] To the extent that the notified settlement, movement or distortion was not attributable to, or did not give rise to, any of the later discovered defects or damage, there would be no claim.[10] The position may however be different where the notification, properly construed, is not limited but is of a 'hornets' nest' or 'can of worms' set of circumstances, in which a general problem is known or believed to exist at the time of the notification.[11]

1 *Kajima UK Engineering Ltd v The Underwriter Insurance Co Ltd* [2008] EWHC 83 (TCC), [2008] Lloyd's Rep IR 391, para 104 (Akenhead J).
2 At para 104.
3 *Kajima UK Engineering Ltd v The Underwriter Insurance Co Ltd* [2008] EWHC 83 (TCC), [2008] Lloyd's Rep IR 391, para 104 (Akenhead J).
4 *Kajima UK Engineering Ltd v The Underwriter Insurance Co Ltd* [2008] EWHC 83 (TCC), [2008] Lloyd's Rep IR 391, para 111(b) (Akenhead J).
5 *Kajima UK Engineering Ltd v The Underwriter Insurance Co Ltd* [2008] EWHC 83 (TCC), [2008] Lloyd's Rep IR 391, para 111(c) (Akenhead J).
6 *Kajima UK Engineering Ltd v The Underwriter Insurance Co Ltd* [2008] EWHC 83 (TCC), [2008] Lloyd's Rep IR 391, para 108 (Akenhead J).
7 *Kajima UK Engineering Ltd v The Underwriter Insurance Co Ltd* [2008] EWHC 83 (TCC), [2008] Lloyd's Rep IR 391, para 111(d) (Akenhead J).
8 *Kajima UK Engineering Ltd v The Underwriter Insurance Co Ltd* [2008] EWHC 83 (TCC), [2008] Lloyd's Rep IR 391, para 111(e) (Akenhead J).
9 *Kajima UK Engineering Ltd v The Underwriter Insurance Co Ltd* [2008] EWHC 83 (TCC), [2008] Lloyd's Rep IR 391, para 111(e) (Akenhead J).
10 *Kajima UK Engineering Ltd v The Underwriter Insurance Co Ltd* [2008] EWHC 83 (TCC), [2008] Lloyd's Rep IR 391, para 111(g) (Akenhead J).
11 *Kajima UK Engineering Ltd v The Underwriter Insurance Co Ltd* [2008] EWHC 83 (TCC), [2008] Lloyd's Rep IR 391, para 104–105 (Akenhead J).

NO NOTIFICATION REQUIREMENT

7.19 In the unusual situation that there is no express provision in the policy requiring notice of a claim to be given within a specified time, a term may be implied requiring that notice be given within a reasonable time.[1]

Where a loss occurs before the insured has received a copy of the policy terms and conditions,[2] it is a question of construction whether a notification requirement contained in the policy forms part of the contract of insurance and is binding on the insured. In *Re Coleman's Depositories*,[3] the Court of Appeal held that a requirement that notice of accidents be given within a certain time was not binding on the insured in these circumstances. A cover note which had been issued to the insured made no mention of any requirements as to notification of accidents. The Unfair Terms in Consumer Contracts Regulations may also apply, if the insured is a natural person who is a consumer, as the non-exhaustive list of terms which may be regarded as unfair appended to the Regulations includes terms which have the object or effect of irrevocably binding the consumer to terms with which he had no real opportunity of becoming acquainted before the conclusion of the contract.[4]

1 *Hadenfayre Ltd v British National Insurance Society Ltd* [1984] 2 Lloyd's Rep 393, 402 (Lloyd J).
2 See further **PARA 3.3**.
3 [1907] 2 KB 798, CA. See also the discussion of the case in the judgment of Lord Greene MR in *Austin v Zurich General Accident and Liability Insurance Co Ltd* [1945] KB 250, 256–257, CA.
4 Paragraph 1(i) of Sch 2 to the Unfair Terms in Consumer Contracts Regulations 1999; see further **PARA 3.20**.

DELIVERY OF PARTICULARS OF LOSS AND DAMAGE OR OF CLAIM

7.20 Conditions requiring that the insured give notice of an insured event are often accompanied by conditions which require the insured, within a specified time, to deliver particulars of loss and damage, or to deliver a claim in a prescribed form.[1] Compliance with such conditions is commonly expressed to be a condition precedent to liability. Although the effect of such a clause is a question of construction in each case, the courts have been willing to construe such clauses as conditions precedent.[2] In the absence of a term in the policy that imposes any general duty of co-operation upon the insured, such a term might be implied, but not so as to make it a condition precedent.[3] A clause which requires an insured to prove his loss to the reasonable satisfaction of insurers does not implicitly require the insured to complete any particular claim form.[4]

In *Cox v Orion Insurance Co Ltd*,[5] a car driver's motor insurance policy contained the following condition: 'The insured ... shall give notice in writing to the company ... of any accident loss and damage and shall deliver ... detailed particulars in writing ...'. The insured notified the insurers in writing that an accident had taken place, and stated that damage to the vehicle had been sustained in a collision while the vehicle was being driven without his permission. It subsequently transpired that the account which the driver had given was false, and he was convicted of various road traffic offences as the driver in connection with the collision. The Court of Appeal held that the driver was in breach of the condition as to notice, which was a condition precedent, on the grounds that he had not given detailed particulars of the accident, loss or damage as required by the condition, but had instead given particulars of an entirely different accident. An obligation to provide full particulars means the best particulars the insured can reasonably give, and it is a question of fact whether the particulars given are sufficient.[6]

1 See also **PARA 9.13**.
2 See *Hiddle v National Fire and Marine Insurance Co of New Zealand* [1896] AC 372, PC; *Colonial Fire and General Insurance Co Ltd v Chung* (13 December 2000, unreported) PC (condition concluded with the words: 'No claim under this policy shall be payable unless the terms of this condition have been complied with'); *Ted Baker plc v AXA Insurance UK plc (No 2)* [2014] EWHC 3548 (Comm), [2015] Lloyd's Rep IR 325, para 108 (Eder J). See also **PARA 3.5**.
3 *Milton Keynes Borough Council v Nulty* [2011] EWHC 2847 (TCC), [2012] Lloyd's Rep IR 453, para 239 (Edwards-Stuart J); point not considered on appeal: [2013] EWCA Civ 15, [2013] Lloyd's Rep IR 243.
4 *All Leisure Holidays Ltd v Europaische Reiseversicherung AG* [2011] EWHC 2629 (Comm), [2012] Lloyd's Rep IR 193, paras 27–28 (Teare J).

5 [1982] RTR 1, CA.
6 *Ted Baker plc v AXA Insurance UK plc (No 2)* [2014] EWHC 3548 (Comm), [2015] Lloyd's Rep IR 325, para 103 (Eder J).

STATUS OF PROCEDURAL CONDITIONS FOLLOWING REPUDIATION OF LIABILITY

7.21   The insurer is entitled to rely in the alternative on a failure to comply with a procedural condition, such as a notification clause, and other grounds for rejecting a claim, such as that the claim does not fall within the scope of the policy or that the insurer is entitled to avoid the policy for non-disclosure by the insured.[1] Where insurers repudiate liability and refuse to have anything to do with the settlement of a claim or the defence of an action, whether they are entitled to rely upon subsequent (as opposed to accrued) non-compliance by the insured with a notification clause or other procedural condition when seeking to defend an action by the insured for an indemnity under the policy depends on the circumstances,[2] including whether insurers are estopped from requiring compliance with those conditions.[3] In practice, an insurer who denies liability and thereafter refuses to have anything to do with the claim on that account precludes co-operation by his very refusal; contrariwise an insurer can maintain a contention that he has already been discharged from liability whilst actively co-operating with the adjustment and settlement of the claim without prejudice to that contention (which may be wrong).[4]

1 *Bolton Metropolitan Borough Council v Municipal Mutual Insurance Ltd* [2006] EWCA Civ 50, [2006] 1 WLR 1492, 1506–1507, paras 31–34 (Longmore LJ); *Super Chem Products Ltd v American Life and General Insurance Co Ltd* [2004] UKPC 2, [2004] Lloyd's Rep IR 446, paras 12–13 (Lord Steyn) (laying to rest the so-called 'Jureidini defence', based on *Jureidini v National British and Irish Millers Insurance Co Ltd* [1915] AC 499, HL). See further **PARA 11.63**.
2 *Re Coleman's Depositories* [1907] 2 KB 798, 805–806, CA (Vaughan Williams LJ) (no obligation to comply with condition as to forwarding notice of claim after the insurer had repudiated); *Diab v Regent Insurance Co Ltd* [2006] UKPC 29, [2007] 1 WLR 797, [2006] Lloyd's Rep IR 779. In *Diab v Regent Insurance Co Ltd* [2006] UKPC 29, [2007] 1 WLR 797, [2006] Lloyd's Rep IR 779, paras 21–22, Lord Scott said that the correctness of Vaughan Williams LJ's dictum in *Re Coleman's Depositories* depended upon the circumstances in which the repudiation of liability by the insurers had taken place and the nature of the repudiation. Lord Scott placed reliance (at para 23) on the affirmation in a fire insurance context by the Privy Council in *Super Chem Products Ltd v American Life and General Insurance Co Ltd* [2004] UKPC 2, [2004] Lloyd's Rep IR 446, para 12 (Lord Steyn) that despite a repudiatory breach of contract, obligations under the contract survive until the breach is accepted by the innocent party as terminating the contract (applied: *Lexington Insurance Co v Multinacional de Seguros SA* [2008] EWHC 1170 (Com), [2009] Lloyd's Rep IR 1, para 70 (Christopher Clarke J)). However, Lord Scott appears not to have taken into account para 31 of Lord Steyn's speech in the *Super Chem* case in which he expressly declined to consider whether, after repudiation, an insured could be required to provide continued performance of a primary obligation to provide documentation and information in relation to claims, saying that the question did not arise on the facts of that case. See also **PARA 9.13**.
3 See **PARA 7.22**.
4 *Lexington Insurance Co v Multinacional de Seguros SA* [2008] EWHC 1170 (Comm), [2009] Lloyd's Rep IR 1, paras 71–74 (Christopher Clarke J).

WAIVER AND ESTOPPEL[1]

7.22 An insurer may be estopped from relying on an insured's failure to comply with a procedural condition precedent such as a requirement as to notice.[2] An estoppel will arise in circumstances where it can be said that the handling of a claim by an insurer is an unequivocal representation that the insurer accepts liability and/ or will not rely on breach of some condition precedent as affording a defence, and there has been such detrimental reliance by the insured as would make it inequitable for the insurer to go back on his representation.[3] Once insurers become aware that an insured has failed to comply with a requirement as to notification, they may refuse to indemnify, or they may accept a liability to indemnify, or they may delay their decision. Mere lapse of time will not lose insurers the right ultimately to decide to refuse to indemnify; the right will be lost only if the insured is prejudiced by the delay, or if third party rights intervene, or if the delay is so long that the court feels able to say that the delay in itself is of such a length as to be evidence that the insurers had in truth decided to accept liability.[4] Where the circumstances are equivocal, such as where an insurer is waiting for further information about an occurrence in answer to its own questions, there is no need for a reservation of rights.[5] This is because what a reservation of rights does is expressly preserve a situation where otherwise it might be held that something unequivocal had occurred.[6] Nonetheless, a reservation of rights may be both practical and wise.[7]

An estoppel may also arise by conduct. In *Yorkshire Insurance Co Ltd v Craine*,[8] the insured was unable to comply with a condition requiring him to deliver particulars of loss within a specified period because the insurer had exercised its right to go into possession of the insured's premises. The Privy Council held that the insurer was estopped by its conduct in going into possession from relying on the insured's failure to deliver the particulars within the time specified.[9]

Insofar as an insurer owes a relevant duty of good faith, it does not extend to any general duty to warn an insured that it needs to comply with policy terms.[10]

1 See further **para 11.63**.
2 *Kosmar Villa Holidays plc v Trustees of Syndicate 1243* [2008] EWCA Civ 147, [2008] Lloyd's Rep IR 489. In the *Kosmar Villa Holidays* case, Rix LJ said (para 54) that in *Barrett Bros (Taxis) Ltd v Davies* [1966] 1 WLR 1334, 1339, [1966] 2 Lloyd's Rep 1, 5, CA, Lord Denning MR described a waiver using the classic terms of promissory estoppel. It may be that references to waiver in some of the earlier cases, such as *Webster v General Accident Fire and Life Assurance Corpn Ltd* [1953] 1 QB 520, 532 (Parker J) and *Barrett Bros (Taxis) Ltd v Davies* [1966] 1 WLR 1334, CA, should properly be construed as references to waiver by estoppel (see further **para 11.63**). In *Diab v Regent Insurance Co Ltd* [2006] UKPC 29, [2007] 1 WLR 797, [2006] Lloyd's Rep IR 779, Lord Scott considered that waiver might be available in addition to estoppel (paras 24–26) in relation to the insurer's right to insist on compliance by the insured with a procedural condition precedent; following the *Kosmar Villa Holidays* case, this does not represent the law.
3 *Kosmar Villa Holidays plc v Trustees of Syndicate 1243* [2008] EWCA Civ 147, [2008] Lloyd's Rep IR 489. See also **para 11.63**.
4 *Allen v Robles* [1969] 1 WLR 1193, 1196, CA; see also *Kosmar Villa Holidays plc v Trustees of Syndicate 1243* [2008] EWCA Civ 147, [2008] Lloyd's Rep IR 489, para 80 (Rix LJ).
5 *Kosmar Villa Holidays plc v Trustees of Syndicate 1243* [2008] EWCA Civ 147, [2008] Lloyd's Rep IR 489, para 80 (Rix LJ).

6 *Kosmar Villa Holidays plc v Trustees of Syndicate 1243* [2008] EWCA Civ 147, [2008] Lloyd's Rep IR 489, para 80 (Rix LJ).

7 *Kosmar Villa Holidays plc v Trustees of Syndicate 1243* [2008] EWCA Civ 147, [2008] Lloyd's Rep IR 489, para 80 (Rix LJ). However, it would not be good practice for insurers to rush to repudiate a claim for late notification, or even to destabilise their relationship with their insured by immediately reserving their position, at a time when they were in any event asking pertinent questions about a claim arising out of an occurrence about which they had long been ignorant in the absence of prompt notification: *Kosmar Villa Holidays plc v Trustees of Syndicate 1243* [2008] EWCA Civ 147, [2008] Lloyd's Rep IR 489, para 82 (Rix LJ).

8 [1922] 2 AC 541, PC.

9 At 553. See also *Kosmar Villa Holidays plc v Trustees of Syndicate 1243* [2008] EWCA Civ 147, [2008] Lloyd's Rep IR 489, para 78 (Rix LJ) (applying *McCormick v National Motor & Accident Insurance Union Ltd* (1934) 49 Ll L Rep 361, CA, in which insurers continued to defend a claim at trial while making enquiries and were held not to be estopped from avoiding a policy of motor insurance, and *Soole v Royal Insurance Co Ltd* [1971] 2 Lloyd's Rep 332, in which insurers' assumption of control of defence of proceedings against the insured was held to be equivocal).

10 *Ted Baker plc v AXA Insurance UK plc (No 2)* [2014] EWHC 3548 (Comm), [2015] Lloyd's Rep IR 325, para 126 (Eder J).

DOUBLE INSURANCE

7.23 It sometimes happens that an insured has, perhaps without realising it, more than one policy of insurance covering the same risk. In such a situation, if he claims under one policy only, he may discover subsequently that the policy contains a rateable proportion clause which limits the insurer's obligation to indemnify him to the amount which the insurer would have had to pay had the liability been shared between all the relevant insurers. If the insured has failed to comply with the notice requirements under the other policies, those insurers will be entitled to repudiate the claim.[1]

1 See further **CHAPTER 13**, Double insurance and contribution.

Chapter 8

Claims handling

INTRODUCTION

8.1   Simple insurance claims are usually handled by the insurer's claims staff. For larger or more complicated claims, the insurer will usually use the services of a loss adjuster. In a high-value claim, the insured may also engage a loss adjuster to assist him in negotiations with the insurer. This chapter considers some of the issues that arise in connection with claims handling. Reference should also be made to **CHAPTER 9**, Insurance litigation.

REGULATORY OBLIGATIONS (ICOBS AND COBS)

8.2   Insurance underwriting and broking are regulated activities under the Financial Services and Markets Act 2000,[1] which insurers and brokers require permission to carry out, pursuant to Part IV of the Financial Services and Markets Act 2000. Once they have obtained a Part IV permission, they are authorised persons for the purposes of the 2000 Act.[2] Section 138D of the 2000 Act provides that contravention by an authorised person of a rule made by the Financial Conduct Authority ('the FCA') under the 2000 Act[3] is actionable at the suit of a 'private person' who suffers a loss as a result of the contravention, subject to the defences and other incidents applying to actions for breach of statutory duty.[4] In order to recover damages under s 138D, a claimant is required to establish that loss has been suffered as a result of a breach of duty.[5] Such a claim is subject to the same underlying principles relating to causation, foreseeability and remoteness of damage as may apply in contract or tort, but the principles may operate in different ways, as the purpose of a statutory rule may be more focussed than the general law of tort or contract.[6] 'Private person' includes any individual, unless he suffers the loss in question in the course of carrying on any regulated activity, and any person who is not an individual, unless he suffers the loss in question in the course of carrying on business of any kind, but does not include a government, a local authority (in the United Kingdom or elsewhere) or an international organisation.[7] The rules made by the FCA under the 2000 Act include those contained in the Insurance: Conduct of Business Sourcebook ('ICOBS') and the Conduct of Business Sourcebook ('COBS'). ICOBS applies to an insurer when effecting and carrying out non-investment insurance contracts,[8] and to an insurance intermediary (broker) when it carries on insurance mediation activities in relation to a non-investment insurance contract.[9] COBS applies to insurers in respect of claims handling under long-term care insurance contracts.[10] The obligations imposed by ICOBS and COBS in relation to claims handling are considered below.

1 Financial Services and Markets Act 2000, s 22(1) and Sch 2; Financial Services and Markets Act 2000 (Regulated Activities) Order 2001 (SI 2001/544), as amended.
2 See s 31 of the 2000 Act.
3 Pursuant to its rule-making powers: see ss 138 and 153 of the 2000 Act, and para 13 of Sch 17. 'Rule' means a rule made by the Financial Services Authority under the 2000 Act: s 417. The FSA may also give guidance, and the FSA Handbook indicates which provisions are binding rules (marked 'R'), and which are non-binding guidance (marked 'G'). A consolidated version of the rules and guidance is contained in the FSA Handbook (which includes ICOBS and COBS): see the FSA website at www.fsa.gov.uk.
4 Section 138D of the 2000 Act. With effect from 1 April 2013, s 138D of the 2000 Act was substituted for s 150. The sections are in essentially the same terms. Section 150 refers to rules made by the Financial Services Authority, and s 138D to rules made by the FCA. The cause of action under s 150 'can perhaps be described as an express cause of action for breach of statutory duty': *Green v Royal Bank of Scotland plc* [2013] EWCA Civ 1197, [2014] PNLR 6, para 28 (Tomlinson LJ).
5 *Zaki v Credit Suisse (UK) Ltd* [2011] EWHC 2422 (Comm), para 134 (Teare J).
6 *Rubenstein v HSBC Bank plc* [2012] EWCA Civ 1184, [2013] PNLR 9, paras 45–46 (Rix LJ).
7 Financial Services and Markets Act 2000 (Rights of Action) Regulations 2001 (SI 2001/2256), reg 3(1). The exception in the Regulations in respect of corporate entities 'carrying on business of any kind' should be given a wide interpretation: *Titan Steel Wheels Ltd v Royal Bank of Scotland plc* [2010] EWHC 211 (Comm), [2010] 2 Lloyd's Rep 92, paras 48 and 70 (David Steel J); applied: *Camerata Property Inc v Credit Suisse Securities (Europe) Ltd* [2012] EWHC 7 (Comm), [2012] PNLR 15, paras 89–98 (Flaux J); *Bailey v Barclays Bank plc* [2014] EWHC 2882 (QB), paras 37–44 (HHJ Keyser QC) (subject to appeal); *Thornbridge Ltd v Barclays Bank plc* [2015] EWHC 3430 (QB), paras 138–141 (HHJ Moulder). Corporate entities who sustain losses as a result of the purchase of financial products will usually be in business of some kind and will not therefore be 'private persons' pursuant to the Regulations; charities and similar bodies are the more obvious exceptions: *Titan Steel Wheels Ltd v Royal Bank of Scotland plc* [2010] EWHC 211 (Comm), [2010] 2 Lloyd's Rep 92, para 70 (David Steel J).
8 ICOBS 1.1.1(2)R; this 'general application rule' is subject to a series of exceptions including contracts of reinsurance (ICOBS 1, Annex 1, Part 2, para 1.1G). 'Non-investment insurance contract' means a contract of insurance which is a general insurance contract or a pure protection contract but which is not a long-term care insurance contract: see the FSA Handbook (Glossary Definition).
9 ICOBS 1.1.1(1)R; this 'general application rule' is subject to a series of exceptions, including reinsurance broking (ICOBS 1, Annex 1, Part 2, para 1.1G) and insurance broking activities in relation to large risks located outside the European Economic Area or for a commercial customer, within the EEA (ICOBS 1, Annex 1, Part 2, para 2.1G). 'Non-investment insurance contract' means a contract of insurance which is a general insurance contract or a pure protection contract but which is not a long-term care insurance contract: see the FSA Handbook (Glossary Definition).
10 COBS 17.1.1–3R. For the meaning of 'long-term care insurance contract' see the FSA Handbook (Glossary Definition).

SPEED AND EFFICIENCY IN HANDLING CLAIMS AND DAMAGES FOR LATE PAYMENT

8.3 In *Insurance Corpn of the Channel Islands Ltd v McHugh*,[1] Mance J rejected a submission on behalf of the insured that a term was to be implied into two policies of insurance (against material damage and business interruption) that the insurers would act with reasonable speed and efficiency in relation to the negotiation, assessment and payment of claims. The judge held that such a term was not obvious or necessary for business efficacy, in part because insurers are liable to the insured in damages from the date of loss, so that the implied term contended for would impose on them an obligation to assess, negotiate and pay damages for which they were liable already.[2] Further, the term was inconsistent with the express terms of the policies.

ICOBS provides that an insurer must handle claims promptly and fairly; provide reasonable guidance to help a policyholder make a claim and appropriate information on its progress; not unreasonably reject a claim (including by terminating or avoiding a policy); and settle claims promptly once settlement terms are agreed.[3] COBS makes similar provision in relation to claims handling for long-term care insurance contracts.[4] Breach of ICOBS and COBS is actionable at the suit of 'private persons'.[5]

With effect from 4 May 2017, an amendment to the Insurance Act 2015 will introduce an implied term in relation to late payment of insurance claims.[6] The term will be implied only into contracts of insurance entered into on or after 4 May 2017, and variations to such contracts.[7] It will be an implied term of every contract of insurance that if the insured makes a claim under the contract, the insurer must pay any sums due in respect of the claim within a reasonable time.[8] 'Reasonable time' includes a reasonable time to investigate and assess the claim,[9] and what is reasonable will depend on all the relevant circumstances, but the following are examples of things which may need to be taken into account:[10] the type of insurance,[11] the size and complexity of the claim,[12] compliance with any relevant statutory or regulatory rules or guidance,[13] and factors outside the insurer's control.[14] Further, if the insurer shows that there were reasonable grounds for disputing the claim (whether as to the amount of any sum payable, or as to whether anything at all is payable), the insurer does not breach the implied term merely by failing to pay the claim (or the affected part of it) while the dispute is continuing, but the conduct of the insurer in handling the claim may be a relevant factor in deciding whether that term was breached and, if so, when.[15] Remedies (for example, damages) available for breach of the implied term are in addition to and distinct from any right to enforce payment of the sums due (ie are in addition to the right of indemnity under the policy), and any right to interest on those sums (whether under the contract, under another enactment, at the court's discretion or otherwise).[16]

The term may not be contracted out of in relation to consumer insurance or non-consumer insurance where the breach of the term is deliberate or reckless.[17] A breach of the implied term is deliberate or reckless for these purposes if the insure knew that it was in breach or did not care whether or not it was in breach.[18] The term may otherwise be contracted out of in non-consumer insurance if the transparency requirements of the Insurance Act 2015[19] are satisfied.[20] These provisions do not apply in relation to a contract for the settlement of a claim arising under an insurance contract.[21]

An amendment to the Limitation Act 1980 (described in a heading as 'Additional time limit for actions for damages for late payment of insurance claims') provides that an action in respect of breach of the implied term may not be brought after the expiration of one year from the date on which the insurer has paid all the sums due in respect of the claim,[22] and that any payment which extinguishes an insurer's liability to pay such a sum is to be treated for these purposes as payment of that sum.[23]

1 [1997] LRLR 94, 136–137.
2 See further **PARA 6.6**.
3 ICOBS 8.1.1R. See also ICOBS 8.2 in relation to claims handling by motor vehicle liability insurers and ICOBS 8.4 in relation to employers' liability insurance.
4 COBS 17.1.1R–17.1.3R.
5 See **PARA 8.2**.
6 See the Enterprise Act 2016, Part 5 (Late Payment of Insurance Claims), ss 28–30 and 44(3). Section 44(3) provides that ss 28–30 come into force at the end of the period of one year beginning with the day on

which the Enterprise Act 2016 was passed. The 2016 Act was passed on 4 May 2016. Section 44(3) also provides that s 23(2) of the Insurance Act 2015 (which provides for the coming into force of provisions of that Act) does not apply to the provisions inserted by the Enterprise Act 2016.

7 Enterprise Act 2016, s 28(2), inserting a new s 22(3A) into the Insurance Act 2015.

8 Enterprise Act 2016, s 28(1), inserting a new s 13A(1) into the Insurance Act 2015.

9 Enterprise Act 2016, s 28(1), inserting a new s 13A(2) into the Insurance Act 2015. The Explanatory Notes to the Enterprise Act 2016 say (at para 269) that whether the insurer had reasonable grounds is intended to be judged objectively. Explanatory Notes do not form part of a statute, are not endorsed by Parliament and cannot be amended by it; in so far as they cast light on the objective setting or contextual scene of a statute and the mischief to which it is aimed, they are an admissible aid to construction: *Flora v Wakom (Heathrow) Ltd* [2006] EWCA Civ 1103, [2007] 1 WLR 482, paras 15–16 (Brooke LJ).

10 Enterprise Act 2016, s 28(1), inserting a new s 13A(3) into the Insurance Act 2015.

11 The Explanatory Notes to the Enterprise Act 2016 say (at para 266) that the type of insurance involved may be relevant because, for example, claims under business interruption policies usually take longer to value than claims for property damage. For the status of Explanatory Notes, see note 8 above.

12 The Explanatory Notes to the Enterprise Act 2016 say (at para 266) that in terms of size and complexity, larger more complicated claims will usually take longer to assess than straightforward claims; and that a claim may be complicated by its location, for example: if an insured peril occurs abroad, it is possible that investigation will be more difficult. For the status of Explanatory Notes, see note 8 above.

13 The Explanatory Notes to the Enterprise Act 2016 say (at para 267) that the reference to relevant statutory or regulatory rules or guidance might include, for example, rule 8 of ICOBS on claims handling, and para 27 of Sch 1 to the Consumer Protection from Unfair Trading Regulations 2008 (SI 2008/1277) relating to commercial practices which are in all circumstances considered unfair. For the status of Explanatory Notes, see note 8 above.

14 The Explanatory Notes to the Enterprise Act 2016 (at para 268) give the following as examples of factors beyond the insurer's control that might delay payment: investigations may be held up because the policyholder or a third party fails to provide relevant information in a timely manner; an insurer's decision may also be dependent on the actions of another insurer, which may arise as a result of the interaction between business interruption and property insurance, or in the subscription market where a follower may be dependent on the lead insurer. For the status of Explanatory Notes, see note 8 above.

15 Enterprise Act 2016, s 28(1), inserting a new s 13A(4) into the Insurance Act 2015. The Explanatory Notes to the Enterprise Act 2016 say (at para 270) that an insurer who has a reasonable basis for disputing a claim or at least conducting further investigations may nevertheless be found to be in breach of the implied term if, for example, it conducts its investigation unreasonably slowly, or is slow to change its position when further information confirming the validity of the claim comes to light. For the status of Explanatory Notes, see note 8 above. Attempts to introduce into the House of Lords a right to allow insurers to rely on legal advice about a dispute in this context without waiving privilege in that advice were unsuccessful. It seems likely that insurers and their legal advisers will start to record the facts on which a decision to dispute a claim is based separately from any legal advice received, but that there will nonetheless be disputes about waiver of privilege in individual cases.

16 Enterprise Act 2016, s 28(1), inserting a new s 13A(5) into the Insurance Act 2015.

17 Enterprise Act 2016, s 29(1), inserting a new s 16A(1)–(2) and (5) into the Insurance Act 2015.

18 Enterprise Act 2016, s 29(1), inserting a new s 16A(3) and (5) into the Insurance Act 2015. The same terms are used in relation to the duty of fair presentation: see PARA **11.39**.

19 See PARA **3.8**.

20 Enterprise Act 2016, s 29(1), inserting a new s 16A(4) into the Insurance Act 2015. Where insurers are entitled to contract out of the implied term, they may elect to impose a limit on their liability for damages for late payment rather than contracting out entirely. It is suggested that contracting out entirely is more likely in relation to mutual insurance or reinsurance (in the latter case, assuming that the 2015 Act applies to reinsurance; this seems likely, although there is no express provision to this effect).

21 Enterprise Act 2016, s 29(1), inserting a new s 16A(6) into the Insurance Act 2015.

22 Enterprise Act 2016, s 30, inserting a new s 5A(1) into the Limitation Act 1980.

23 Enterprise Act 2016, s 30, inserting a new s 5A(2) into the Limitation Act 1980. The Explanatory Notes to the Enterprise Act 2016 say (at para 281) that this payment may be, for example, a payment in accordance with a court or arbitral award, or an amount agreed by the insurer and insured in a binding settlement agreement. The Explanatory Notes also say (at para 281) that late payment action will be barred by the expiry of whichever period ends soonest: the one-year period after payment of all sums due in respect of the insurance claim, or the usual limitation period (contained in s 5 of the Limitation Act 1980: time limit for actions founded on simple contract) of six years from the date of breach of

the implied term as to payment within a reasonable time. For the six-year time limit for claims for an indemnity under the contract of insurance, see PARA **11.60**. For the status of Explanatory Notes, see note 8 above.

RESERVATION OF RIGHTS BY INSURER

8.4 An assertion by an insurer that it is entitled to avoid a policy of insurance for misrepresentation or non-disclosure, or that it is entitled to rely upon breach of a procedural condition in repudiating liability for a claim, is often met by an assertion by the insured that the insurer has waived its right to avoid, or has affirmed the policy; or that the insurer is estopped from relying on a policy condition or from denying that the policy operates as contended by the insured.[1] Where the circumstances are equivocal, such as where an insurer is waiting for further information about an occurrence in answer to its own questions, there is no need for a reservation of rights.[2] This is because what a reservation of rights does is expressly preserve a situation where otherwise it might be held that something unequivocal had occurred.[3] Nonetheless, a reservation of rights may be both practical and wise.[4] Accordingly, if insurers wish to reserve their rights to refuse an indemnity, it is prudent for them to do so expressly, and to repeat the reservation in all communications with the insured.[5]

A reservation of rights is an 'obstacle to finding an unequivocal communication of a decision to affirm the policy'.[6] Insurers' rights may be reserved without the phrase 'reservation of rights' being used, provided that insurers make clear that they might not be providing cover.[7] The use by a loss adjuster of the phrase 'without prejudice', when involved in discussions with the insured in the course of factual investigations on behalf of the insurer, but before any dispute may be said to have arisen between insured and insurer, will not be effective to protect those discussions from disclosure and admissibility in evidence; It may, however, amount to an effective reservation of rights on behalf of the insurers.[8]

1 See PARA **11.63**.
2 *Kosmar Villa Holidays plc v Trustees of Syndicate 1243* [2008] EWCA Civ 147, [2008] Lloyd's Rep IR 489, para 80 (Rix LJ).
3 *Kosmar Villa Holidays plc v Trustees of Syndicate 1243* [2008] EWCA Civ 147, [2008] Lloyd's Rep IR 489, para 80 (Rix LJ). In *Involnert Management Inc v Aprilgrange Ltd* [2015] EWHC 2225 (Comm), [2015] 2 Lloyd's Rep 289, Leggatt J said in the context of avoidance and waiver by election (at para 179) that a reservation of rights is an 'obstacle to finding an unequivocal communication of a decision to affirm the policy'.
4 *Kosmar Villa Holidays plc v Trustees of Syndicate 1243* [2008] EWCA Civ 147, [2008] Lloyd's Rep IR 489, para 80 (Rix LJ). However, it would not be good practice for insurers to rush to repudiate a claim for late notification, or even to destabilise their relationship with their insured by immediately reserving their position, at a time when they were in any event asking pertinent questions about a claim arising out of an occurrence about which they had long been ignorant in the absence of prompt notification: *Kosmar Villa Holidays plc v Trustees of Syndicate 1243* [2008] EWCA Civ 147, [2008] Lloyd's Rep IR 489, para 82 (Rix LJ).
5 See further PARAS **7.22** and **11.63**.
6 *Involnert Management Inc v Aprilgrange Ltd* [2015] EWHC 2225 (Comm), [2015] 2 Lloyd's Rep 289, para 179 (Leggatt J).
7 *Brit UW Ltd v F & B Trenchless Solutions Ltd* [2015] EWHC 2237 (Comm), [2016] Lloyd's Rep IR 69, paras 174–180 (Carr J).
8 *Victor Melik & Co Ltd v Norwich Union Fire Insurance Society Ltd* [1980] 1 Lloyd's Rep 523, 525 (Woolf J).

HUMAN RIGHTS ACT 1998

8.5 Article 8 of the European Convention on Human Rights provides that everyone has the right to respect for his private and family life, his home and his correspondence,[1] and that there shall be no interference by a public authority with the exercise of this right, except such as in accordance with the law and is necessary in a democratic society.[2] The protection provided by art 8 extends to business, as well as residential, premises, and to all types of correspondence.[3] Insurers are not public authorities for the purposes of the European Convention on Human Rights or the Human Rights Act 1998, neither of which therefore imposes any obligations on them. Insurers, therefore, need not be concerned directly about possible breaches of art 8 when investigating claims. However, in certain circumstances the United Kingdom has 'positive obligations' under art 8, which give rise to a duty to prevent interference by others (private parties) in an individual's art 8 rights. The courts of England and Wales are themselves 'public authorities' under the 1998 Act,[4] and must therefore act in a way which is compatible with the Convention.[5]

The use of a private investigator by insurers to carry out surveillance of a claimant in a personal injury action, or an insured under an accident policy, is commonplace, and may give rise to issues concerning the admissibility in court proceedings of the evidence obtained by the investigator. In *Arnott v United Kingdom*,[6] the applicants complained to the European Court of Human Rights that over a period of three years and on about 25 occasions, they had been the subject of surveillance, by mistake, by a private investigator working for an insurance company. The insurer was attempting to prove fraud by a claimant in ongoing proceedings (with whom the applicants had no connection), and the private investigator followed the wrong couple. In these circumstances, it would be difficult to justify the interference with the applicants' art 8 rights, and the *Arnott* case was settled by the government. In *Jones v University of Warwick*,[7] an investigator, engaged by an insurer, obtained video film of the claimant, for use in defending an action for damages for personal injuries brought by the claimant against the insured. The investigator obtained access to the claimant's home by posing as a market researcher, and the claimant had no idea that she was being filmed. The Court of Appeal held that the insurers had been responsible for the trespass involved in entering the claimant's house and infringing her privacy, and appears to have assumed that this amounted to a breach of art 8(1) by the investigator (and therefore by the insurers, as the investigator's principals), but that if, in the exercise of its discretion, they decided that it was necessary to admit the evidence in order to deal with the case justly, the breach would be justified under art 8(2).[8] Accordingly, the fact that the evidence had been obtained in breach of art 8(1) was a circumstance which should be weighed in the balance in the exercise of the court's discretion as to whether to admit the evidence obtained on that occasion.[9] The Court of Appeal recognised that the significance of the evidence would vary, as would the gravity of the breach of art 8, according to the facts of each case, and decided that, on the facts of the case before it, the evidence should be admitted, but that the insurers should be penalised in costs to reflect the court's disapproval of their conduct.

1 Article 8, para 1.
2 Article 8, para 2, which contains an exhaustive list of factors against which the necessity of an interference with an art 8 right may be judged, such as the prevention of disorder or crime, or the protection of the rights and freedoms of others.

3 *Niemietz v Germany*, Series A no 251-B, (1992) 16 EHRR 97.
4 Section 6(3)(a).
5 *Venables v News Group Newpapers Ltd* [2001] Fam 430, paras 24–27 (Dame Elizabeth Butler-Sloss P).
6 No 44866/98, Dec 3.10.2000.
7 [2003] EWCA Civ 151, [2003] 1 WLR 954.
8 It is suggested that the correct analysis would be that the United Kingdom was in breach of its positive obligation to prevent interference with the claimant's rights under art 8, and that the court was therefore obliged to conduct a balancing exercise between the defendant's right to a fair trial under art 6, which would be supported by the admission of the evidence, and the claimant's right to respect for her home and private life under art 8, which would be supported by the exclusion of the evidence.
9 Video evidence will usually be admitted in a personal injury case: see *Rall v Hume* [2001] EWCA Civ 146, [2001] 3 All ER 248.

COSTS OF INVESTIGATING FRAUDULENT CLAIMS

8.6   Where proceedings have been issued, the costs incurred in investigating a fraudulent claim may be recoverable as legal costs.[1] Alternatively, damages for the tort of deceit may be awarded.[2] The measure of damages would be the costs incurred by the insurer less the amount of the claim and any costs which would have been incurred but for the deceit, without any deduction for contributory negligence or a failure to mitigate.[3]

1 *London Assurance v Clare* (1937) 57 Ll L Rep 254, 270 (Goddard J) (rejecting the insurers' argument that a term should be implied that claims would be made honestly, and that they were entitled to damages for breach of such a term); *Owners of the Ship 'Ariela' v Owners and/or Demise Charterers of the Dredger 'Kamal XXVI' and the Barge 'Kamal XXIV'* [2009] EWHC 3256 (Comm), [2010] 2 Lloyd's Rep 247, para 30 (Burton J) (costs on the indemnity basis).
2 *Owners of the Ship 'Ariela' v Owners and/or Demise Charterers of the Dredger 'Kamal XXVI' and the Barge 'Kamal XXIV'* [2009] EWHC 3256 (Comm), [2010] 2 Lloyd's Rep 247, paras 34–36 (Burton J); see also *London Assurance v Clare* (1937) 57 Ll L Rep 254, 270 (Goddard J) ('It is put, not as damages for fraud, for which I think there might be something to be said, but it is put as damages for breach of contract').
3 *Owners of the Ship 'Ariela' v Owners and/or Demise Charterers of the Dredger 'Kamal XXVI' and the Barge 'Kamal XXIV'* [2009] EWHC 3256 (Comm), [2010] 2 Lloyd's Rep 247, paras 36–39 (Burton J).

REJECTION OF A CLAIM

8.7   Insurers may decide, after investigating a claim, to reject it. The grounds on which they may do so are considered in **CHAPTER 11**, Insurers' defences.

INTERIM PAYMENTS

8.8   In the absence of any provision in the policy, there is no right to interim payments prior to settlement of the claim,[1] although insurers often make interim payments on a voluntary basis. In some circumstances, failing to make interim payments might breach ICOBS.[2] An agreement to make an interim payment entered into after the loss has been suffered may be enforceable if consideration is provided and the parties intend it to be contractually binding, although this will not usually be the case.[3] Where an interim payment is made, and it is subsequently established that the insured is not entitled to an indemnity, the insurer is entitled to recover the interim payment from the insured, whether or not the payment was expressly stated to be 'on account'.[4]

1 *Anderson v Commercial Union Assurance Co* 1998 SLT 826 (Court of Session): no basis for implying term obliging insurers to make interim payments.
2 See **PARA 8.2–8.3**.
3 In *Insurance Corpn of the Channel Islands v Royal Hotel Ltd* [1998] Lloyd's Rep IR 151, Mance J held that insurers were in breach of an agreement to make an interim payment of £1m. Insurers did not suggest that there was no contractual intent or consideration (at 150).
4 *Attaleia Marine Co Ltd v Bimeh Iran (Iran Insurance Co), The Zeus* [1993] 2 Lloyd's Rep 497, 501 (Phillips J). See also **PARA 8.15**.

REQUIREMENT FOR INSURER'S CONSENT

8.9   Where the policy provides that the insurer's consent must be sought before specified action is taken by the insured – for example, before costs are incurred or a claim by a third party is settled – the insurer is under an obligation to respond promptly to a request from the insured that he consider the question and decide whether he will consent.[1] A breach of this obligation does not sound in damages,[2] but entitles the insured to proceed as if he were uninsured and carry out the repairs or settle the claim, and disqualifies the insurer from relying on a breach of the consent provision.[3] The clause may provide expressly that insurers must not withhold their consent unreasonably, but if it does not, it appears that a term to this effect will be implied,[4] unless the policy contains some other mechanism for determining whether costs should be incurred, such as a 'QC' clause.[5] Where the obligation is to seek the insurer's consent as to the incurring of costs, consent must be sought at every important stage of the proceedings, so that if consent is given to defend the proceedings, and an appeal is necessary thereafter, consent should be sought anew in relation to the appeal.[6] Where consent is required before costs are incurred, the insured is entitled to be paid the costs 'from time to time' on an interim basis without awaiting the outcome of the proceedings.[7] Where there is no provision requiring the insurer's consent, the insured is under no obligation to obtain the insurer's consent to repairs or a settlement with a third party, but would be prudent to attempt to do so, in order to avoid there being any issue between the insured and the insurer as to whether the insured is entitled to be indemnified.[8]

1 *Sprung v Royal Insurance (UK) Ltd* [1999] Lloyd's Rep IR 111, CA.
2 Except, possibly, where the purpose of the policy is to provide for the immediate repair of damaged plant and equipment, as in the case of a business interruption policy: *Sprung v Royal Insurance (UK) Ltd* [1999] Lloyd's Rep IR 111, 119, CA (Beldam LJ). See further **PARA 6.6**.
3 *Sprung v Royal Insurance (UK) Ltd* [1999] Lloyd's Rep IR 111, CA. In *Capel-Cure Myers Capital Management Ltd v McCarthy* [1995] LRLR 498, insurers indicated that the insured should act as a prudent uninsured and instruct solicitors to act for them while the insurers considered issues of policy coverage, and were held to have waived compliance with the requirement that the insurers' consent be sought before costs were incurred.
4 *E Hulton & Co v Mountain* (1921) 8 Ll L Rep 249, CA: insurers acted unreasonably in failing to consent to the defence of libel proceedings where the insured was a newspaper proprietor who wished to defend the proceedings on the grounds of justification, when a settlement would have been much less expensive; *Capel-Cure Myers Capital Management Ltd v McCarthy* [1995] LRLR 498, 503–504 (Potter J). Colman J refused to imply such a term, and indicated his disagreement with Potter J's approach, in *Thornton Springer v NEM Insurance Co Ltd* [2000] Lloyd's Rep IR 590, [2000] 2 All ER 489,

paras 89–94; it is suggested that Colman J's reasoning is inconsistent with the approach of the Supreme Court in *Braganza v BP Shipping Ltd* [2015] UKSC 17, [2015] 1 WLR 1661, to contractual terms in which one party to a contract is given the power to exercise a discretion: see **PARA 5.4**.

5 *Thornton Springer v NEM Insurance Co Ltd* [2000] Lloyd's Rep IR 590, [2000] 2 All ER 489, paras 89–94 (Colman J).

6 *E Hulton & Co v Mountain* (1921) 8 Ll L Rep 249, CA, where the clause provided as follows: 'no costs shall be incurred without the consent of the underwriters'.

7 *Capel-Cure Myers Capital Management Ltd v McCarthy* [1995] LRLR 498, 503–504 (Potter J); applied: *Thornton Springer v NEM Insurance Co Ltd* [2000] Lloyd's Rep IR 590, [2000] 2 All ER 489, para 47 (Colman J).

8 See *Adcock v Co-operative Insurance Society Ltd* [2000] Lloyd's Rep IR 657, CA, where the insured recovered only part of the cost of reinstatement works to his house after a fire.

CLAIMS CO-OPERATION AND CLAIMS CONTROL CLAUSES

8.10 Claims co-operation and claims control clauses are considered at **PARA 9.13**.

COSTS OF DEFENDING CLAIMS

8.11 Liability policies typically provide cover in respect of both legal liability for any claim or claims which may be brought against the insured and the cost of defending such claims.[1] An indemnity in respect of 'loss arising from any claim or claims' is wide enough to include a liability to a third party in costs as well as damages.[2] The insuring clause in such a policy is engaged only where the insured's legal liability to a third party is established,[3] in the absence of clear wording displacing this basic principle of liability insurance.[4] Whether the costs clause in a policy of liability insurance applies to the insured's costs of successfully defending a claim, which accordingly does not result in liability under the policy, within the meaning of the insuring clause, depends on its wording. If insurers' liability for costs is stated to be in respect of a claim for damages within the meaning of the insuring clause, no costs are payable unless liability is established.[5] In *Thornton Springer v NEM Insurance Co Ltd*,[6] the costs clause was in respect of 'any claim ... which falls to be dealt with under this certificate', and was held to include the costs of a successful defence of a claim, as well as those of an unsuccessful defence, provided that in substance it was capable of falling within the scope of the indemnity under the insuring clauses.[7] A very clear provision would be required in order for there to be an entitlement to defence costs where the potential liability is not within the scope of the policy.[8] Where the policy provides that the cover would include 'defence costs resulting from a claim against an insured', such a claim is one in respect of liabilities which are covered under the policy.[9]

Further, if insurers' liability for costs is stated to be in respect of a claim for damages within the meaning of the insuring clause, the insured is entitled to any item of cost which is wholly and exclusively related to the defence of the claim; any item of cost which is in no way related to the defence of the claim is not covered by the policy; and so far as any defence costs are concerned which are reasonably related to the defence of the claim but do not exclusively do so, they are covered by the policy even though they also relate to the defence of some other party who is not insured[10] or to some other claim which is not within the insuring clause.[11]

1 See also **PARA 9.13**.
2 *Forney v Dominion Insurance Co Ltd* [1969] 1 WLR 928, 934–935 (Donaldson J).
3 *West Wake Price & Co v Ching* [1957] 1 WLR 45; approved: *Bradley v Eagle Star Insurance Co Ltd* [1989] AC 957, 964–966, HL (Lord Brandon); *Thornton Springer v NEM Insurance Co Ltd* [2000] Lloyd's Rep IR 590, [2000] 2 All ER 489; *AstraZeneca Insurance Co Ltd v XL Insurance Ltd* [2013] EWCA Civ 1660, [2014] Lloyd's Rep IR 509, paras 16–17 and 23 (Christopher Clarke LJ).
4 See *AstraZeneca Insurance Co Ltd v XL Insurance Ltd* [2013] EWCA Civ 1660, [2014] Lloyd's Rep IR 509, para 19 (Christopher Clarke LJ).
5 *Thornton Springer v NEM Insurance Co Ltd* [2000] Lloyd's Rep IR 590, [2000] 2 All ER 489, para 47 (Colman J); *AstraZeneca Insurance Co Ltd v XL Insurance Ltd* [2013] EWCA Civ 1660, [2014] Lloyd's Rep IR 509, paras 76–81 (Christopher Clarke LJ).
6 [2000] Lloyd's Rep IR 590, [2000] 2 All ER 489.
7 At paras 47–49 (Colman J).
8 *Rathbone Brothers plc v Novae Corporate Underwriting Ltd* [2014] EWCA Civ 1464, [2015] Lloyd's Rep IR 95, para 63 (Elias LJ).
9 *Rathbone Brothers plc v Novae Corporate Underwriting Ltd* [2014] EWCA Civ 1464, [2015] Lloyd's Rep IR 95, para 64 (Elias LJ).
10 *New Zealand Forest Products Ltd v New Zealand Insurance Co Ltd* [1997] 1 WLR 1237, 1242–1243, 1246, PC; *John Wyeth & Brothers Ltd v Cigna Insurance Company of Europe SA/NV* [2001] EWCA Civ 175, [2001] Lloyd's Rep IR 420, para 50 (Waller LJ); *International Energy Group Ltd v Zurich Insurance plc* [2015] UKSC 33, [2016] AC 509, paras 38 (Lord Mance, with whom Lords Clarke, Carnwath and Hodge agreed) and 176 (Lord Sumption, with whom Lords Neuberger and Reed agreed).
11 *Capel-Cure Myers Capital Management Ltd v McCarthy* [1995] LRLR 498, 504–505 (Potter J); *Thornton Springer v NEM Insurance Co Ltd* [2000] Lloyd's Rep IR 590, [2000] 2 All ER 489, para 50 (Colman J); *John Wyeth & Brothers Ltd v Cigna Insurance Company of Europe SA/NV* [2001] EWCA Civ 175, [2001] Lloyd's Rep IR 420, paras 53–56 (Waller LJ); see also the discussion of these cases in *ACE European Group v Standard Life Assurance Ltd* [2012] EWCA Civ 1713, [2013] Lloyd's Rep IR 415, para 24 (Tomlinson LJ).

INDEMNITY UNDER LIABILITY POLICY FOLLOWING JUDGMENT, AWARD OR SETTLEMENT BETWEEN INSURED AND THIRD PARTY

8.12 In order to recover under a policy of liability insurance, the insured must establish both a loss and a liability.[1] The former will be established by a judgment or arbitration award against him or by a settlement, but the latter may not.[2] The law is, in summary, as follows:[3]

'(1) The insured must establish that it has suffered a loss which is covered by one of the perils insured against.[4]

(2) That may be done by showing a judgment or an arbitration award against the insured or an agreement to pay.

(3) The loss must be within the scope of the cover provided by the policy.

(4) As a matter of practicality, the judgment, award, or agreement may settle the question as to whether the loss is covered by the policy because the insurers will accept it as showing a basis of liability which is within the scope of the cover.

(5) But neither the judgment nor the agreement are determinative of whether or not the loss is covered by the policy (assuming that the insurer is not a party to either and that there is no agreement by the insurer to be bound).

(6) It is, therefore, open to the insurers to dispute that the insured was in fact liable, or that it was liable on the basis specified in the judgment; or to show that the true basis of his liability fell within an exception.

(7) Thus, an insured against whom a claim is made in negligence, which is the subject of a judgment, may find that his insurer seeks to show that in reality the claim was for fraud or for something else which was not covered, or excluded by, the policy.[5]

(8) Similarly, an insured who is held liable in fraud (which the policy does not cover) may be able to establish, in a dispute with his insurers, that, whatever the judge found, he was not in fact fraudulent, but only negligent and that he was entitled to cover under the policy on that account.'

It seems therefore that a global settlement between an insured and a third party which does not specifically identify the cost to the insured of discharging the insured liability, or which does not contain an admission of liability or is made with an express non-admission or a denial of liability, is no bar to a claim by an insured under a liability policy, as it remains open to the insured to prove the fact and extent of its liability to the third party for the purposes of a claim against insurers.[6]

1 *AstraZeneca Insurance Co Ltd v XL Insurance Ltd* [2013] EWCA Civ 1660, [2014] Lloyd's Rep IR 509, para 23 (Christopher Clarke LJ).

2 *Post Office v Norwich Union Fire Insurance Society Ltd* [1967] 2 QB 363, CA; *Bradley v Eagle Star Insurance Co Ltd* [1989] AC 957, HL; *AstraZeneca Insurance Co Ltd v XL Insurance Ltd* [2013] EWCA Civ 1660, [2014] Lloyd's Rep IR 509, para 23 (Christopher Clarke LJ).

3 At para 49; approved: *AstraZeneca Insurance Co Ltd v XL Insurance Ltd* [2013] EWCA Civ 1660, [2014] Lloyd's Rep IR 509, para 23 (Christopher Clarke LJ). In *London Borough of Redbridge v Municipal Mutual Insurance Ltd* [2001] Lloyd's Rep IR 545, Tomlinson J held that the insured's liability to third parties was established by a series of binding determinations made by Pensions Ombudsman; this must now be regarded as wrongly decided.

4 The judge cited the following authorities for this proposition: *West Wake Price & Co v Ching* [1957] 1 WLR 45; *Post Office v Norwich Union Fire Insurance Society Ltd* [1967] 2 QB 363, CA; *Bradley v Eagle Star Insurance Co Ltd* [1989] AC 957, HL; *Horbury Building Systems Ltd v Hampden Insurance NV* [2004] EWCA Civ 418, [2007] Lloyd's Rep IR 237, 245.

5 The judge cited '*MDIS Ltd v Swinbank*' as authority for this proposition; he had previously referred to the case at both first instance and Court of Appeal level: *McDonnell Information Systems Ltd v Swinbank* [1999] Lloyd's Rep IR 98 (Mance J) and *MDIS Ltd v Swinbank* [1999] Lloyd's Rep IR 516, CA.

6 See *Structural Polymer Systems Ltd v Brown* [2000] Lloyd's Rep IR 64; *Omega Proteins Ltd v Aspen Insurance UK Ltd* [2010] EWHC 2280 (Comm), [2011] Lloyd's Rep IR 183; *Enterprise Oil Ltd v Strand Insurance Co Ltd* [2006] EWHC 58 (Comm), [2006] 1 Lloyd's Rep 500, paras 163–169 (Aikens J); see also *Peninsular & Oriental Steam Navigation Co v Youell* [1997] 2 Lloyd's Rep 136, 141, CA (Potter LJ) ('It seems to me ... that all that it was necessary for P&O [the insured] to demonstrate was a liability in damages to the passengers compensated. If such liability existed, the form and nature of the compromise designed to avoid and/or satisfy claims in respect of such liability should not be determinative of the question whether or not there was a claim under the policy'). Following the approval by the Court of Appeal in *AstraZeneca Insurance Co Ltd v XL Insurance Ltd* [2013] EWCA Civ 1660, [2014] Lloyd's Rep IR 509, para 23 (Christopher Clarke LJ), of the summary of the law in *Omega Proteins Ltd v Aspen Insurance UK Ltd* [2010] EWHC 2280 (Comm), [2011] Lloyd's Rep IR 183, para 49 (Christopher Clarke J) (see note 5 and related text above), Colman J's controversial decision in *Lumbermens Mutual Casualty Co v Bovis Lend Lease Ltd* [2004] EWHC 2197 (Comm), [2005] 1 Lloyd's Rep 494 (that a global settlement which did not specifically identify the cost to the insured of discharging the insured liability barred a claim by an insured under a liability policy) must now be regarded as wrongly decided.

PRIVILEGE

8.13 Loss adjusters frequently advise insurers on legal issues, such as whether the loss or damage falls within the terms of the policy of insurance, and on factual issues which may become the subject of legal proceedings, such as whether there has been underinsurance, or whether the amount being claimed is exaggerated. Where the dominant purpose of a loss adjuster's report is to enable the insurers to ascertain the facts in order to come to a decision as to whether or not they should repudiate liability, the report is not privileged, even if a secondary purpose of obtaining the report was to enable the insurers to take advice from solicitors on the facts in the event of their deciding to repudiate.[1] If, however, it is clear when the report is commissioned that repudiation is likely, and that if insurers were to repudiate, litigation would follow, the report will be regarded as having been obtained for the dominant purpose of obtaining legal advice and will therefore be privileged.[2] Insurers and loss adjusters need to bear in mind, when issuing, and acting on, instructions to investigate claims, the fact that a loss adjuster's report is not automatically privileged.

Legal advice given by claims consultants is not protected by legal advice privilege, even where those giving the advice happen to be qualified solicitors or barristers, unless the claims consultants were retained as solicitors or barristers.[3]

Where solicitors are instructed by insurers on behalf of themselves and their insured to defend a claim brought against the insured, there is a waiver of privilege implicit in the joint retainer which extends to all communications made by the insured to the solicitors until such time as an actual conflict of interest emerges.[4]

1 *Victor Melik & Co Ltd v Norwich Union Fire Insurance Society Ltd* [1980] 1 Lloyd's Rep 523, 524–525 (Woolf J).
2 *Re Highgrade Traders Ltd* [1984] BCLC 151, 173–174, CA (Oliver LJ) (insurers suspicious about the cause of a fire instructed a loss adjuster to investigate; *Victor Melik & Co Ltd v Norwich Union Fire Insurance Society Ltd* was not cited); see also *Axa Seguros SA de CV v Allianz Insurance plc* [2011] EWHC 268 (Comm), [2011] Lloyd's Rep IR 544, para 49 (Christopher Clarke J) (finding of duality of purpose in relation to reports from civil engineers obtained on reinsurers' behalf by loss adjusters following a claim).
3 *Walter Lilly & Co Ltd v Mackay* [2012] EWHC 649 (TCC), paras 15–18 (Akenhead J).
4 *TSB Bank Ltd v Robert Irving & Burns* [1999] Lloyd's Rep IR 528, [2000] 2 All ER 826, CA. See further **PARA 9.33**.

AGREEMENTS WITH THIRD PARTIES FOR REPAIR OR REINSTATEMENT

8.14 The insurer often arranges the repair or reinstatement of the insured's property. In *Godfrey Davis Ltd v Culling*,[1] which concerned the obligation to pay for repairs to the insured's car following an accident, the Court of Appeal discussed three possible analyses of the obligation: first, the insured may enter into a contract with the repairer, and claim an indemnity from the insurer; second, the insurer may enter into a contract with the repairer; and, third, the insurer may enter into a contract with the repairer as an agent for the insured. The correct analysis in any particular case depends on an application of the ordinary principles of the law of agency to the facts and to the documents, including the terms of the policy and of any agreement entered into with the repairer,[2] and that standard claims control and co-operation clauses in the policy of insurance, entitling the insurer to undertake claims and defences, and to bind the insured in the settlement of claims by third parties, have no bearing on the issue.[3] In *Charnock v Liverpool Corpn*,[4] the Court of Appeal indicated that in many cases the correct inference on the facts might be a fourth variation, that the insured entered into the contract with the repairer on the basis that the insurer would pay. In a case where the insured has to bear part of the cost of repair in the form of an excess, the correct analysis may be that there are two contracts to pay for the repairs, one with the insured for the amount of the excess, and the other with the insurer for the balance.[5] In most cases, the analysis will be of academic interest only because the insurer will pay for the repairs directly or will reimburse the insured only after a receipted invoice has been produced. In some cases, however, if one of the parties has become insolvent or the insured is dissatisfied with the repairs, the analysis will be of importance.[6] In *Charnock v Liverpool Corpn*,[7] the Court of Appeal held that there were two contracts: first, between the repairer and the insured, which included an obligation to carry out the repairs carefully and skilfully, and with reasonable expedition; and, secondly, between the repairer and the insurer, to pay for the repairs. In *Brown & Davis Ltd v Galbraith*,[8] Sachs LJ preferred to describe this as a tripartite agreement, rather than two separate contracts, while acknowledging that in most cases the terminology would make no difference to the result. Whether the insured undertakes a subsidiary obligation to pay for the repairs, should the insurer fail to pay for any reason, depends on the facts of the case. In *Brown & Davis Ltd v Galbraith*,[9] the Court of Appeal rejected an argument that a term to this effect should be implied on the grounds of the business efficacy of the transaction. As Longmore LJ observed (without deciding the issue) in *Bee v Jenson (No 2)*,[10] *Charnock v Liverpool Corpn* and *Brown & Davis Ltd v Galbraith* are not easily reconcilable, and in neither case was the Court of Appeal referred to *Adams v London Improved Motor Coach Builders Ltd*[11] where it was held in terms that a claimant whose claim was being supported and paid for by a trade union was nevertheless liable to the solicitor instructed by the union for that solicitor's costs.

1 [1962] 2 Lloyd's Rep 349, CA.
2 *Godfrey Davis Ltd v Culling* [1962] 2 Lloyd's Rep 349, CA, 352 (Ormerod LJ), 353 (Upjohn LJ); *Cooter & Green Ltd v Tyrell* [1962] 2 Lloyd's Rep 377, CA; *Charnock v Liverpool Corpn* [1968] 1 WLR 1498, CA; *Brown & Davis Ltd v Galbraith* [1972] 1 WLR 997, 1004, CA (Cairns LJ). In *Brown & Davis Ltd v Galbraith* [1972] 1 WLR 997, CA, Sachs LJ said (at 1008–1009) that the suggestion of agency for the owner on the part of the insurer had been 'exploded' in the three earlier Court of Appeal authorities.
3 *Godfrey Davis Ltd v Culling* [1962] 2 Lloyd's Rep 349, CA, 354 (Upjohn LJ).
4 [1968] 1 WLR 1498, 1505, CA (Salmon LJ).
5 *Godfrey Davis Ltd v Culling* [1962] 2 Lloyd's Rep 349, CA, 354 (Upjohn LJ).
6 See eg *A J Building & Plastering Ltd v Turner* [2013] EWHC 484 (QB), [2013] Lloyd's Rep IR 629 (insurer paid contractor; contractor became insolvent before paying sub-contractor).
7 [1968] 1 WLR 1498, 1505, CA, 1502–1503 (Harman LJ), 1505 (Salmon LJ).
8 [1972] 1 WLR 997, 1007, CA (Sachs LJ).
9 [1972] 1 WLR 997, CA.
10 [2007] EWCA Civ 923, [2008] Lloyd's Rep IR 221, para 14.
11 [1921] 1 KB 495, CA.

RECOVERY OF PAYMENTS MADE TO SETTLE CLAIMS

8.15   An insurer may settle a claim under a policy of insurance by making a payment to the insured.[1] Where the claim is more complex, or where a claim is settled following a dispute regarding the parties' rights and obligations under the policy, a compromise agreement may be entered into.

After a payment has been made by an insurer, facts may come to light which show that the insurer was under no obligation to make the payment. It has long been established that payments made by insurers on the basis of a mistake of fact are recoverable.[2] Recent decisions have established that no distinction is to be drawn in the law of restitution or unjust enrichment between mistakes of law and of fact[3] and that these principles also apply where the parties have entered into a contract (rather than simply making a payment) in reliance on mistake of law or fact.[4]

Where therefore a payment is made by an insurer to an insured as a result of a fundamental or basic mistake, whether of fact or law, it is in principle recoverable,[5] subject to the insured establishing a defence such as change of position in good faith.[6] In order for a payment by an insurer to be recoverable on the basis that it was paid by mistake:[7]

'It is, however, essential that the mistake relied on should be of such a nature that it can be properly described as a mistake in respect of the underlying assumption of the contract or transaction or as being fundamental or basic. Whether the mistake does satisfy this description may often be a matter of great difficulty.'

Whether a mistake is fundamental is a question of fact; lack of insurable interest is likely to be sufficient,[8] as is a mistaken belief that loss was caused by an insured peril.[9]

Where a compromise agreement has been entered into it is unclear whether the proper test to apply is whether the mistake in question renders the contract 'impossible of performance' (the expression used by Lord Phillips MR in *Great Peace Shipping*),[10] or whether the mistake must render the subject matter of the contract essentially and radically different from the subject matter which the parties believed to exist;[11] the two approaches may amount to the same thing;[12] and it is normally not easy to say precisely why a difference is or is not 'radical and essential'.[13] The insurer will not be entitled to recover the payment on the basis of a mistake of fact or law if at the time the compromise was agreed there was doubt as to the parties' rights and obligations, so that the agreement represented a 'give-and-take' compromise of doubtful rights.[14] It is unclear whether this is a defence to an otherwise valid claim for unjust enrichment[15] or whether there is no mistake sufficient to justify recovery of the payment – perhaps because where the law is in doubt each party is deemed to have accepted the risk that he might be mistaken about the law[16] or because a state of doubt is different from that of mistake.[17]

The limitation period for recovery of a payment made under a mistake of law is six years from the date on which the party seeking the return of the payment discovered the mistake or could with reasonable diligence have discovered it.[18]

It appears that an insurer is in principle entitled to recover a payment made in reliance on a misrepresentation by the insured,[19] and, following the developments in relation to mistake of law referred to above, that this is so whether the misrepresentation is of fact or of law.[20] However, the courts are likely to be reluctant to allow restitution on the basis of a representation of law made by one party to another in the context of a negotiation in good faith as this would stultify genuine negotiations.[21] This could be achieved by a variety of means, including applying in this context the principle that a representation of law is not actionable if the parties have equal means of knowing what the law is;[22] finding that the party to whom the representation was made did not rely on it in settling the claim;[23] or characterising a representation of law made in this context as a representation of opinion, as these are deemed by s 20(5) of the Marine Insurance Act 1906 to be true if made in good faith.[24] Where a compromise agreement is entered into, it is suggested that the principles set out above in relation to mistake will apply, and that the opportunities for challenge on the basis of misrepresentation will be limited.

The subsequent discovery by a party that a statement which he had thought genuine but mistaken was in fact fraudulent might be sufficient for rescission of a settlement agreement, but where a party believes that statements made in a claim are fraudulent and nonetheless elects to enter into a settlement, that party was not induced by the fraudulent statements to enter into the settlement and is not entitled to set the agreement aside simply because better evidence of fraud subsequently comes to light.[25]

1 See **PARA 8.14**.
2 *Piper v Royal Exchange Assurance* (1932) 44 Ll L R 103, 117 (Roche J); *Norwich Union Fire Insurance Society Ltd v William H Price Ltd* [1934] AC 455, PC.
3 *Kleinwort Benson Ltd v Lincoln City Council* [1999] 2 AC 349, HL.
4 *Brennan v Bolt Burdon* [2004] EWCA Civ 1017, [2005] QB 303, para 10 (Maurice Kay LJ).
5 *Norwich Union Fire Insurance Society Ltd v William H Price Ltd* [1934] AC 455, 462–463, PC (Lord Wright).
6 *Lipkin Gorman v Karpnale* [1991] 2 AC 548, HL.
7 *Norwich Union Fire Insurance Society Ltd v William H Price Ltd* [1934] AC 455, 462–463, PC (Lord Wright).
8 See, eg, *Piper v Royal Exchange Assurance* (1932) 44 Ll L R 103, 117 (Roche J): insured had no insurable interest in ship during voyage on which damage sustained.
9 See, eg, *Norwich Union Fire Insurance Society Ltd v William H Price Ltd* [1934] AC 455, PC: insurer paid claim in respect of damage caused to cargo of lemons by an insured peril; the lemons were later discovered to have been sold not because of damage by an insured peril but because they were ripening, which was not an insured peril; *Attaleia Marine Co Ltd v Bimeh Iran (Iran Insurance Co), The Zeus* [1993] 2 Lloyd's Rep 497, 501 (Phillips J). In *Holmes v Payne* [1930] 2 KB 301, an insured necklace which was believed lost was subsequently found, in an article of the insured's clothing within her house, after a settlement agreement had been entered into; Roche J held (at 309) that there was no mistake sufficient to invalidate the agreement: both the insured and the insurer (who had investigated the loss) thought that in all probability the loss occurred outside the house, but the inference was not very certain nor was it the basis of the agreement.
10 *Great Peace Shipping Ltd v Tsavliris Salvage (International) Ltd* [2002] EWCA Civ 1407, [2003] QB 679, para 162.
11 *Kyle Bay Ltd v Underwriters Subscribing to Policy no 019057/08/01* [2007] EWCA Civ 57, [2007] Lloyd's Rep IR 460, paras 21–26 (Neuberger LJ).
12 *Kyle Bay Ltd v Underwriters Subscribing to Policy no 019057/08/01* [2007] EWCA Civ 57, [2007] Lloyd's Rep IR 460, para 25 (Neuberger LJ).
13 *Kyle Bay Ltd v Underwriters Subscribing to Policy no 019057/08/01* [2007] EWCA Civ 57, [2007] Lloyd's Rep IR 460, para 27 (Neuberger LJ).
14 *Huddersfield Banking Co Ltd v Henry Lister & Son Ltd* [1895] 2 Ch 273, CA; applied: *Brennan v Bolt Burdon* [2004] EWCA Civ 1017, [2005] 1 QB 303; *Deutsche Morgan Grenfell Group plc v IRC* [2006] UKHL 49, [2007] 1 AC 558, para 27 (Lord Hoffmann). It is suggested that the majority judgments in *Magee v Pennine Insurance Co Ltd* [1969] 2 QB 507, CA, which apply *Solle v Butcher* [1950] 1 KB 671, CA, are no longer good law following the decision of the Court of Appeal in *Great*

Peace Shipping Ltd v Tsavliris Salvage (International) Ltd [2002] EWCA Civ 1407, [2003] QB 679. In *Brennan v Bolt Burdon* [2004] EWCA Civ 1017, [2005] 1 QB 303, Maurice Kay LJ (para 22) and Bodey J (para 44) distinguished the situation where the compromise is agreed in ignorance of significant facts and the law which would be applicable to them, as in *Bank of Credit and Commerce International SA v Ali* [2001] UKHL 8, [2002] 1 AC 251.

15 See *Kleinwort Benson Ltd v Lincoln City Council* [1999] 2 AC 349, HL, 382 (Lord Goff) and 412–415 (Lord Hope). The conceptual difficulties in relation to compromise agreements arise largely from the declaratory nature of the common law, by virtue of which the courts do not change the law, but merely declare what it always has been. This means that if a judicial decision changes the law, in legal terms this amounts to a declaration that the law when the parties entered into the compromise was not what they thought it was. Therefore, if the change is sufficiently great to be characterised as basic or fundamental (typically, moneys which were due under the 'old' law are not due under the 'new' law), the parties contracted, and the money was paid, on the basis of a fundamental mistake of law, and following the removal of the distinction between restitution of moneys paid on the basis of mistakes of fact and law, the payment ought to be recoverable on normal principles. These issues are discussed in detail in *Brennan v Bolt Burdon* [2005] 1 QB 303, CA; see also *Kleinwort Benson Ltd v Lincoln City Council* [1999] 2 AC 349, HL.

16 See *Deutsche Morgan Grenfell Group plc v IRC* [2006] UKHL 49, [2007] 1 AC 558, para 27 (Lord Hoffmann).

17 See *Kleinwort Benson Ltd v Lincoln City Council* [1999] 2 AC 349, 410, HL (Lord Hope); *Brennan v Bolt Burdon* [2004] EWCA Civ 1017, [2005] 1 QB 303, para 19 (Maurice Kay LJ).

18 *Kleinwort Benson Ltd v Lincoln City Council* [1999] 2 AC 349, HL; *Deutsche Morgan Grenfell Group plc v IRC* [2006] UKHL 49, [2007] 1 AC 558.

19 *Kyle Bay Ltd v Underwriters Subscribing to Policy no 019057/08/01* [2007] EWCA Civ 57, [2007] Lloyd's Rep IR 460, paras 29–43 (Neuberger LJ).

20 *Pankhania v London Borough of Hackney* [2002] EWHC 2441 (Ch), paras 47–57 (Rex Todd QC); *Brennan v Bolt Burdon* [2004] EWCA Civ 1017, [2005] 1 QB 303, para 10 (Maurice Kay LJ); *Mainstream Properties Ltd v Young* [2005] EWCA Civ 861, [2005] IRLR 964, para 84 (Arden LJ); *Kyle Bay Ltd v Underwriters Subscribing to Policy no 019057/08/01* [2006] EWHC 607 (Comm), [2006] Lloyd's Rep IR 718, paras 46–47 and 52–54 (Jonathan Hirst QC) (not considered on appeal: [2007] EWCA Civ 57, [2007] Lloyd's Rep IR 460).

21 See, eg, *Kyle Bay Ltd v Underwriters Subscribing to Policy no 019057/08/01* [2006] EWHC 607 (Comm), [2006] Lloyd's Rep IR 718, para 47 (Jonathan Hirst QC) (not considered on appeal: [2007] EWCA Civ 57, [2007] Lloyd's Rep IR 460).

22 *West London Commercial Bank Ltd v Kitson* (1884) 13 QBD 360, 363, CA (Bowen LJ) (the position is probably different if the representation is made fraudulently: Bowen LJ at 362–363); and see *Kyle Bay Ltd v Underwriters Subscribing to Policy no 019057/08/01* [2007] EWCA Civ 57, [2007] Lloyd's Rep IR 460, para 35 (Neuberger LJ).

23 See, eg, *Kyle Bay Ltd v Underwriters Subscribing to Policy no 019057/08/01* [2007] EWCA Civ 57, [2007] Lloyd's Rep IR 460, paras 38–43 (Neuberger LJ); see also note 25 below and related text.

24 See, eg, *Kyle Bay Ltd v Underwriters Subscribing to Policy no 019057/08/01* [2006] EWHC 607 (Comm), [2006] Lloyd's Rep IR 718, paras 52–54 (Jonathan Hirst QC) (referring to s 20(5)), [2007] EWCA Civ 57, [2007] Lloyd's Rep IR 460, paras 33–34 (Neuberger LJ) (not referring to s 20(5); statements or assertions made in negotiations are contentions, not representations). See also **PARA 11.22**.

25 *Hayward v Zurich Insurance Co plc* [2015] EWCA Civ 327, [2015] Lloyd's Rep IR 585, paragraphs 23–25 (Underhill LJ) and 30–31 (Briggs LJ) (in July 2015 the Supreme Court granted permission to appeal). The settlement agreement was embodied in a Tomlin order, and in an earlier appeal in the same proceedings, the Court of Appeal held that the principles of res judicata or abuse of process were not a bar to an application to set aside the settlement agreement or for damages for the tort of deceit: see *Zurich Insurance Co plc v Hayward* [2011] EWCA Civ 641, [2011] CP Rep 39.

Chapter 9

Insurance litigation

9.1   Insurance litigation is governed by the Civil Procedure Rules ('CPR'), modified to some extent for actions in the Commercial Court by CPR Part 58, Practice Direction 58 and the *Admiralty and Commercial Courts Guide*, and modified (but to a lesser extent) for actions in the Mercantile Courts by CPR Part 59, Practice Direction 59 and the *Mercantile Court Guide*. This chapter focuses on areas of particular practical relevance to those involved in insurance litigation.

THE PRE-ACTION PROTOCOLS

9.2   There is no specific pre-action protocol governing claims against insurers, which are therefore governed by the Practice Direction (Pre-Action Conduct and Protocols). Before commencing proceedings, the court will expect the parties to have exchanged sufficient information to understand each other's position, make decisions about how to proceed, try to settle the issues without proceedings, consider a form of alternative dispute resolution to assist with settlement, support the efficient management of those proceedings, and reduce the costs of resolving the dispute.[1] Bearing in mind that compliance should be proportionate, this will usually include the claimant writing to the defendant with concise details of the claim, the defendant responding within a reasonable time, including whether the claim is accepted and, if it is not accepted, the reasons why, together with an explanation as to which facts and parts of the claim are disputed and whether the defendant is making a counterclaim as well as providing details of any counterclaim, and the parties disclosing key documents relevant to the issues in dispute.[2] There is also provision for expert evidence to be obtained.[3]

Claims against insurance brokers are governed by the Professional Negligence Pre-Action Protocol. The Protocol provides for a preliminary notice of claim, which should include a request that the professional inform his professional indemnity insurers, if any, immediately; an acknowledgement by the professional; a detailed letter of claim, and letters of acknowledgement, response or settlement (or both), together with the exchange of essential documents.[4] The Protocol also provides for alternative dispute resolution to be considered, and, if required, for expert evidence to be obtained.[5]

The court will expect the parties to have complied with the Practice Direction (Pre-Action Conduct and Protocols) or Professional Negligence Pre-Action Protocol.[6] Sanctions for non-compliance include ordering that the party at fault pays costs, or pays costs on an indemnity basis; depriving the party at fault of interest to which it would otherwise have been entitled; or ordering the party at fault to pay interest at a higher rate than would otherwise have been awarded.[7] In deciding what order (if any) to make about costs, the court must have regard to all the circumstances, including the conduct of the parties, which includes conduct before, as well as during, the proceedings, and in particular the extent to which the parties followed the Practice Direction (Pre-Action Conduct and Protocols) or the Professional Negligence Pre-Action Protocol.[8]

The Practice Direction (Pre-Action Conduct and Protocols) and Professional Negligence Pre-Action Protocol do not alter the statutory time limits for commencing court proceedings.[9]

1 CPR Practice Direction (Pre-Action Conduct and Protocols), para 3.
2 CPR Practice Direction (Pre-Action Conduct and Protocols), para 6.
3 CPR Practice Direction (Pre-Action Conduct and Protocols), para 7.
4 Professional Negligence Pre-Action Protocol, paras 5–10.
5 Professional Negligence Pre-Action Protocol, paras 11–12.
6 CPR Practice Direction (Pre-Action Conduct and Protocols), paras 1–2.
7 CPR Practice Direction (Pre-Action Conduct and Protocols), para 16.
8 CPR r 44.2(5)(a); see also CPR Practice Direction (Pre-Action Conduct), para 16.
9 CPR Practice Direction (Pre-Action Conduct and Protocols), para 17; Professional Negligence Pre-Action Protocol, para 4.

IDENTIFYING THE APPROPRIATE COURT

9.3 If the dispute has not been settled by the conclusion of the pre-action protocol stage, the next issue which needs to be addressed is where to start proceedings. Any claim relating to insurance or reinsurance is a 'commercial claim'.[1] Lower value insurance claims are likely to be suitable to be tried in the Mercantile Courts of the Queen's Bench Division[2] rather than in the Commercial Court. If an action which is started in the Commercial Court is suitable for transfer to the London Mercantile Court or one of the Mercantile Courts outside London, either party may apply to the Commercial Judge for transfer prior to the Case Management Conference ('CMC') or, if no such application is made, the Commercial Judge will usually consider this with the parties at the CMC.[3] He will expect the parties to have considered this issue prior to the CMC.[4] Among the factors which are relevant are the size and complexity of the claim, the location of the parties and their legal advisers and the convenience of the witnesses.[5] The London Mercantile Court is established in the Commercial Court.[6] Outside London, Mercantile Courts are established in the district registries of the Queen's Bench Division (High Court) in Birmingham, Bristol, Cardiff, Chester, Leeds, Liverpool, Manchester, Mold and Newcastle upon Tyne.[7] Certain cases may be suitable for trial in more than one court.[8] Claims which give rise to insurance issues but in which other issues predominate may be more appropriately tried elsewhere in the High Court (either in the Queen's Bench Division or the Chancery Division), or in another specialist list such as the Technology and Construction Court, in relation to which other practice directions and guides may apply.

1 CPR Pt 58, r 58.1(2)(e) and 58.4(1). See also para B13.5 and Appendix 19 of the *Admiralty and Commercial Courts Guide*.

2 Proceedings may not be started in the High Court unless the value of the claim is more than £100,000: CPR Practice Direction 7, para 2.1. There is no formal upper limit for Mercantile Court cases. Insurance claims may be started in a Mercantile Court because they relate to 'a commercial or business matter in a broad sense' (CPR Pt 59, r 59.1(2)(a)), are not required to proceed in the Chancery Division or in another specialist list (CPR Pt 59, r 59.1(2)(b)), and are likely to 'benefit from the expertise of a Mercantile Judge' (para 2.1 of CPR Practice Direction 59).
3 Paragraph B13.5 and Appendix 19 of the *Admiralty and Commercial Courts Guide*.
4 Appendix 19 of the *Admiralty and Commercial Courts Guide*, para 1.
5 Paragraph B13.5 of the *Admiralty and Commercial Courts Guide* and Appendix 19, para 1.
6 CPR Practice Direction 59, para 1.2(2).
7 CPR Practice Direction 59, para 1.2(1).
8 For example, an insurance broker's negligence claim where the parties, their legal advisers and most of the witnesses were based in London might, depending on its size and complexity, be suitable for trial in the Queen's Bench Division, the Commercial Court or the London Mercantile Court.

REPRESENTATIVE ACTIONS

9.4   Where more than one person has the same interest in a claim, the claim may be begun, or the court may order that the claim be continued, by or against one or more of the persons who have the same interest as representatives of any other persons who have that interest.[1] Thus, where an action is brought against a single Lloyd's underwriter in a non-representative capacity, the court may order that the action should continue against him in a representative capacity or may order that the correct defendants be added or substituted.[2] The usual wording for the claim form and statements of case is: 'AB for and on behalf of itself and those listed in the appendix [to the claim form]' or 'AB (sued on [his][her] own behalf and on behalf of all members in [year] of Lloyd's Syndicates [numbers])'. Where the positions of various underwriters, and therefore their interests, are different, a single underwriter should not be made a representative party,[3] and the court may make an order that an underwriter who has been made a representative party should cease to be so.[4] Unless the court otherwise directs, any judgment or order given in a claim in which a party is acting as a representative is binding on all persons represented in the claim, but the permission of the court is required before it may be enforced by or against a person who is not a party to the claim.[5]

1 CPR Pt 19, r 19.6(1). For the procedure following the addition or substitution of a new defendant, see CPR Practice Direction 19, paras 3.1–3.3.
2 See *Bank of America National Trust and Savings Association v Taylor* [1992] 1 Lloyd's Rep 484 (decided under the former RSC Ord 15, r 12).
3 *Arash Shipping Enterprises Co Ltd v Groupama Transport* [2011] EWCA Civ 620, [2012] Lloyd's Rep IR 40, paras 27–28 (Stanley Burnton LJ) and 54 (Tomlinson LJ).
4 *Arash Shipping Enterprises Co Ltd v Groupama Transport* [2011] EWCA Civ 620, [2012] Lloyd's Rep IR 40, paras 27–28 (Stanley Burnton LJ) and 54 (Tomlinson LJ).
5 CPR Pt 19, r 19.6(4).

AFTER THE EVENT (ATE) LEGAL EXPENSES INSURANCE AND SECURITY FOR COSTS

9.5   An after the event (ATE) policy of legal expenses insurance may be avoided after trial for non-disclosure or misrepresentation based on facts as found at trial, and thereby in practice deny a successful defendant its costs against an impecunious claimant.[1] For this reason, the courts have been reluctant to accept that an ATE policy provides adequate security for costs,[2] at least in the absence of appropriate anti-avoidance provisions.[3] The ATE market is now more mature and the funding of litigation by ATE policies is a central feature of the ability of parties to gain access to justice; and the court's starting position should be that a properly drafted ATE policy provided by a substantial and reputable insurer is a reliable source of litigation funding.[4] An ATE policy may be sufficient security for costs; the question is not whether the assurance provided by an ATE policy is better security than cash or its equivalent, but whether there is reason to believe that the claimant will be unable to pay the defendant's costs despite the existence of the ATE policy.[5] Alternatively, the court may accept that a deed of indemnity executed by the claimant's ATE insurers in favour of the defendants provides adequate security for the defendant's costs.[6]

1 *Persimmon Homes Ltd v Great Lakes Reinsurance (UK) Ltd* [2010] EWHC 1705, [2011] Lloyd's Rep IR 101; *Nasser v United Bank of Kuwait* [2001] EWCA Civ 556, [2002] 1 WLR 1868, para 60 (Mance LJ); *Al-Koronky v Time-Life Entertainment Group Ltd* [2006] EWCA Civ 1123, para 36 (Sedley LJ).
2 *Nasser v United Bank of Kuwait* [2001] EWCA Civ 556, [2002] 1 WLR 1868, para 60 (Mance LJ); *Al-Koronky v Time-Life Entertainment Group Ltd* [2006] EWCA Civ 1123, paras 33–37 (Sedley LJ); *Belco Trading Co v Kondo* [2008] EWCA Civ 2005; *Michael Phillips Associates Ltd v Riklin* [2010] EWHC 834 (TCC), [2010] Lloyd's Rep IR 479, para 18 (Akenhead J).
3 *Nasser v United Bank of Kuwait* [2001] EWCA Civ 556, [2002] 1 WLR 1868, para 60 (Mance LJ); *Geophysical Service Centre Co v Dowell Schlumberger (ME) Inc* [2013] EWHC 147 (TCC), 147 Con LR 240; *Harlequin Property (SVG) Ltd v Wilkins Kennedy* [2015] EWHC 1122 (TCC), [2016] Lloyd's Rep IR 53.
4 *Geophysical Service Centre Co v Dowell Schlumberger (ME) Inc* [2013] EWHC 147 (TCC), 147 Con LR 240, para 15 (Stuart-Smith J).
5 *Geophysical Service Centre Co v Dowell Schlumberger (ME) Inc* [2013] EWHC 147 (TCC), 147 Con LR 240, para 20 (Stuart-Smith J).
6 See *Versloot Dredging BV v HDI Gerling Industrie Vesicherung AG* [2013] EWHC 658 (Comm) (incorrectly named 'Verslot' Dredging BV in the judgment).

HUMAN RIGHTS ACT 1998

9.6 Article 6 of the European Convention on Human Rights guarantees the right to a fair trial. In cases in which 'civil rights and obligations' or criminal charges[1] are being determined, the right to a fair trial includes a right of access to court, a right to a fair hearing, a right to a public hearing, a right to a hearing within a reasonable time, and a right to a hearing by an independent and impartial tribunal.[2] The protection of the Convention[3] (and the Human Rights Act 1998)[4], including art 6, is available to corporate bodies as well as to individuals. What follows is a brief account of the case law, with particular emphasis on those aspects most likely to be of relevance to insurance litigation.

1 Determination of a 'criminal charge' attracts the guarantees of paras (2) and (3) of art 6, which have no application in cases involving the determination of 'civil rights', in addition to the guarantees of art 6(1). In doubtful cases, reference should be made to the case law of the Strasbourg institutions and the developing jurisprudence of the English courts. For example, the European Court of Human Rights has held that proceedings under the Company Directors Disqualification Act 1986 determine 'civil rights' within the meaning of art 6(1), rather than a 'criminal charge': see *DC, HS and AD v United Kingdom*, No 39031/97, [2000] BCC 710 (the applicants were directors of a company which had traded as a members' agent at Lloyd's).
2 Article 6(1).
3 See *Air Canada v United Kingdom*, Series A, No 316, (1995) 20 EHRR 150.
4 See *Mousaka Inc v Golden Seagull Maritime Inc* [2002] 1 WLR 395, 397, [2001] 2 Lloyd's Rep 657, 658, para 1 (David Steel J).

Freezing injunctions and search orders

9.7 Applications for freezing injunctions and search orders are unlikely to be held to fall within art 6 because there is no determination of the applicant's civil rights or obligations, a necessary precondition for the application of the article.[1]

1 See *Ewing v United Kingdom*, No 14720/89, Comm Dec 6.5.89. Ewing concerned an application for a Mareva injunction, but the reasoning applies with equal force to applications for freezing injunctions and search orders under the Civil Procedure Rules. In principle, the grant and execution of a search order does not breach art 8 of the Convention, although shortcomings in the procedure followed in a particular case might give rise to a violation: see *Chappell v United Kingdom*, Series A No 152-A, (1989) 12 EHRR 1 (decided in relation to the grant and execution of an Anton Piller order under the procedure which applied prior to the introduction of the Civil Procedure Rules).

Right of access to court

9.8 The right of access to court is not expressly set out in art 6 but has long[1] been considered to be inherent in the notion of a right to a fair trial. As one might expect, this does not mean that arbitration agreements are unenforceable: provided they are consensual, such agreements are compatible with the right of access to court.[2] In addition, arbitral tribunals need not comply with art 6, although it may be that art 6 requires a degree of review by the domestic courts,[3] as provided by the Arbitration Act 1996.[4] Similarly, exclusive jurisdiction clauses are compatible with the right of access to court, and the Commercial Court has shown a willingness to enforce such clauses by means of injunctive relief.[5]

1 Since the judgment of the European Court of Human Rights in *Golder v United Kingdom*, Series A, No 18, (1975) 1 EHRR 524.
2 See *Nordström-Janzon v Netherlands*, No 28101/95, Comm Dec 27.11.1996.
3 See *Nordstrom-Janzon v Netherlands*, No 28101/95, Comm Dec 27.11.1996.
4 See further PARAS **9.9** and **10.11**.
5 *O T Africa Line Ltd v Hijazy, The Kribi* [2001] 1 Lloyd's Rep 76, 86–87 (Aikens J).

Right to a fair hearing

9.9 Article 6 guarantees the right to a fair hearing.[1] This has a number of constituent parts, including the requirement that litigants be allowed to participate effectively in proceedings, the principle that each litigant should be given the same opportunity to present his case,[2] and the requirement that proceedings be adversarial in nature. The right to a fair hearing will often require the giving of reasons for a decision, particularly where the losing party has a right of appeal.[3] In refusing permission to appeal to the High Court from an arbitration award on a point of law under s 69 of the Arbitration Act 1996, an indication by a first instance judge as to which of the statutory criteria the applicant has failed to fulfil will usually be sufficient to comply with art 6, and full reasons need not be given.[4] Where however the judge rejects an application for leave made on grounds that the decision of the arbitral tribunal was 'obviously wrong' or, in addition to being a question of general public importance, was 'at least open to serious doubt',[5] further brief reasons may be necessary.[6] Although only the court at first instance, and not the Court of Appeal, may grant leave to appeal from a decision of the first instance court granting or refusing leave to appeal under s 67 of the Arbitration Act 1996,[7] or under s 69 of the Arbitration Act 1996,[8] the Court of Appeal retains a residual jurisdiction to enquire into unfairness in the process of a refusal of leave.[9] The test is whether the judge's refusal of leave to appeal amounted to such unfairness in the process as to amount to a breach of art 6.[10] The fact that the decision is vested in the judge who has himself decided whether the point argued is right or wrong is proportionate and compatible with art 6.[11] The European Commission on Human Rights has approved the practice of the House of Lords[12] and Privy Council[13] of dismissing petitions for leave to appeal without giving reasons.

1 The second and third paragraphs of art 6 have no direct application in civil cases, although to some degree they represent aspects of the right to a fair trial guaranteed by the first paragraph.
2 Often referred to as the principle of 'equality of arms'. This does not extend to the provision of legal aid to fund the instruction of leading counsel simply because a privately paying party has such representation: *R v Liverpool Crown Court, ex p Shields* [2001] EWHC Admin 90, [2001] UKHHR 610 (co-defendant to serious criminal charges, whom it was clear would be mounting a 'cut-throat' defence, had retained junior and leading counsel).
3 See *North Range Shipping Ltd v Seatrans Shipping Corpn* [2002] EWCA Civ 405, [2002] 1 WLR 2397, [2002] 2 Lloyd's Rep 1. It is not a requirement of art 6 that a right of appeal be provided: see *Tolstoy Miloslavsky v United Kingdom* (1995) 20 EHRR 442, 475 (para 59); but art 6 is engaged where a state grants a right of appeal but seeks to restrict that right: *Republic of Kasakhstan v Istil Group Ltd* [2007] EWCA Civ 471, [2007] 2 Lloyd's Rep 548, para 21 (Longmore LJ).
4 *North Range Shipping Ltd v Seatrans Shipping Corpn* [2002] 1 WLR 2397, [2002] 2 Lloyd's Rep 1, CA, para 27 (Tuckey LJ). See further **PARA 10.11**.
5 See s 69(3)(c)(i) and (ii), Arbitration Act 1996.
6 *North Range Shipping Ltd v Seatrans Shipping Corpn* [2002] 1 WLR 2397, [2002] 2 Lloyd's Rep 1, CA, para 27 (Tuckey LJ). The Court of Appeal has discouraged in fairly strong terms the making of 'nitpicking' points about whether the same is said in a judge's subsequent written reasons as in an earlier oral judgment: *Republic of Kasakhstan v Istil Group Ltd* [2007] EWCA Civ 471, [2007] 2 Lloyd's Rep 548, para 31 (Longmore LJ).
7 Arbitration Act 1996, ss 67(4) and 105.
8 Sections 69(6) and 105, Arbitration Act 1996; *Henry Boot Construction (UK) Ltd v Malmaison Hotel (Manchester) Ltd* [2001] QB 388, CA; *Athletic Union of Constantinople v National Basketball Association (No 2)* [2002] EWCA Civ 830, [2002] 1 WLR 2863, 2868, para 12 (Lord Phillips MR).
9 *North Range Shipping Ltd v Seatrans Shipping Corpn* [2002] 1 WLR 2397, [2002] 2 Lloyd's Rep 1, CA, para 1 (Tuckey LJ); *CGU International plc v AstraZeneca Insurance Co Ltd* [2006] EWCA Civ 1340, [2007] 1 Lloyd's Rep 142; *Republic of Kasakhstan v Istil Group Ltd* [2007] EWCA Civ 471, [2007] 2 Lloyd's Rep 548, para 27 (Longmore LJ).
10 *CGU International plc v AstraZeneca Insurance Co Ltd* [2006] EWCA Civ 1340, [2007] 1 Lloyd's Rep 142, para 98 (Rix LJ); *Republic of Kasakhstan v Istil Group Ltd* [2007] EWCA Civ 471, [2007] 2 Lloyd's Rep 548, para 27 (Longmore LJ).
11 *Republic of Kasakhstan v Istil Group Ltd* [2007] EWCA Civ 471, [2007] 2 Lloyd's Rep 548, paras 26 and 27 (Longmore LJ), 35 (Toulson LJ) and 37 (Arden LJ).
12 *Comninos v United Kingdom* (1996) 23 EHRR CD 165.
13 *Webb v United Kingdom* (1997) 24 EHRR CD 73.

Right to a public hearing

9.10   The right to a public hearing is qualified by reference to an exhaustive list of factors set out in art 6. These include the interests of national security, or where the protection of the private life of the parties so requires, or where publicity would prejudice the interests of justice. The right to a public hearing under art 6 arguably does not extend to interim applications.[1]

1 *X v United Kingdom* (1970) 30 EHRR CD 70. Hearings in chambers are, unless otherwise ordered, open to the public, and such access as is practical should be granted: *Hodgson v Imperial Tobacco Ltd* [1998] 1 WLR 1056, CA.

Right to a hearing within a reasonable time

9.11   The right to a hearing within a reasonable time applies in civil proceedings just as it does in criminal proceedings. Time starts to run when proceedings are commenced, and ends at the conclusion of any appeal. This means that time taken to prepare and deliver a judgment, after the conclusion of a hearing, falls within the relevant period. Litigants are understandably reluctant to invoke art 6 when they consider that they have been waiting too long for a judgment and a joint approach by all parties may be advisable.

Right to a hearing by an independent and impartial tribunal

9.12   Independence and impartiality are separate, although overlapping, concepts. To determine whether a body is 'independent', it is necessary to consider various factors, including the manner of appointment of its members and their term of office, the existence of guarantees against outside pressure, and whether the body presents an appearance of independence.[1] The concept of impartiality has two aspects: the tribunal must be subjectively free of personal prejudice or bias; and it must be impartial from an objective viewpoint, which means that it must offer sufficient guarantees to exclude any legitimate doubt.[2] This is the test which now applies in England, displacing the common law test.[3]

1 See *Campbell and Fell v United Kingdom*, Series A, No 80, para 78, (1984) 7 EHRR 165.
2 See *Pullar v United Kingdom*, (1996) 22 EHRR 391, Reports 1996-III, para 30.
3 *Director General of Fair Trading v Proprietary Association of Great Britain* [2001] 1 WLR 700, CA; *Porter v Magill* [2001] UKHL 67, [2002] 2 AC 357. (For the common law test, see *R v Gough* [1993] AC 646, HL and *R v Bow Street Metropolitan Stipendiary Magistrate, ex p Pinochet* [2000] 1 AC 119, HL.)

CLAIMS CO-OPERATION AND CLAIMS CONTROL CLAUSES

9.13   Policies commonly contain provisions allowing insurers to control proceedings brought by or against the insured in relation to the subject matter of the insurance, and imposing on the insured an obligation to co-operate with the insurer in relation to such proceedings and in relation to any claims or circumstances which precede them.[1] Such provisions are known as claims co-operation and claims control clauses. The following are examples of typical wordings:

> 'The company ... shall be entitled if it so desires to take over and conduct in the name of the insured the defence or settlement of any claim or to prosecute in the

name of the insured for its own benefit any claim for indemnity or damages or otherwise, and shall have full discretion in the conduct of any proceedings or in the settlement of any claim and the insured shall give all such information and assistance as the company may require'[2]

and:

'The company shall be entitled ... to undertake in the name of, and on behalf of, the Insured the absolute conduct, control and settlement of any proceedings, and at any time to take proceedings at its own expense and for its own benefit, but in the name of the Insured, to recover compensation or secure indemnity from the Third Party in respect of anything covered by this policy.'[3]

Clauses of this nature reflect the common interest of insurers and the insured in ensuring, for example, that any judgment against the insured should be for as small a sum as possible. The insurer's interest stems from its obligation to provide an indemnity; the insured's interest derives from one or more factors, including his obligation to pay an excess pursuant to the policy terms, his obligation to satisfy any claim in excess of the policy limits, his obligation to satisfy the judgment should the insurers become insolvent, and in many cases, including most obviously professional indemnity insurance, his interest in defending his reputation. The presence of a claims control clause in a policy may, if it extends to rights of recovery against third parties, entitle insurers to take over the recovery of claims against third parties at a time when, because they have not yet indemnified the insured, they are not yet entitled to exercise rights of subrogation.[4] In *Horwood v Land of Leather Ltd*,[5] a clause headed 'control of claims' provided as follows:[6]

'The Insured shall not, except at his own cost, take any steps to compromise or settle any claim or admit liability without specific instructions in writing from the Insurer nor give any information or assistance to any person claiming against him, but the Insurer shall for so long as they shall so desire have the absolute conduct and control of all proceedings (including arbitrations) in respect of any claims for which the Insurer may be liable under this policy, and may use the name of the Insured to enforce for the benefit of the Insurer any order made for costs or otherwise or to make or defend any claim for indemnity or damages against any third party or for any other purpose connected with this policy.'

Teare J held the words 'all proceedings ... in respect of any claims for which the Insurer may be liable' were capable of including not only claims against the insured but also recourse actions by the insured against those responsible for causing the insured to be liable in respect of a claim, and that that was clear from the express permission given to the insurer to use the name of the insured not only to defend any claim but also to make any claim for indemnity or damages against any third party,[7] and that the prohibitions on the insured, which were part and parcel of the mechanism by which the insurer had control of 'all proceedings', extended to both claims against the insured and to claims by the insured.[8]

Claims control clauses entitle insurers, by implication if not expressly, to nominate solicitors to act for the insured, to decide upon the tactics to pursue in the conduct of the action,[9] and to enter into a settlement on behalf of the insured,[10] whether before or after proceedings are issued.[11] The rights and obligations of insurers and the insured will always depend on the construction of the clause in question. A claims control clause usually has the effect of limiting the insured's rights, for example, by entitling insurers to deal with the financial risk to which they are exposed by virtue of the proceedings as economically for themselves as they can. However, insurers' rights are subject to implied limitations, even where the clause is very widely worded – purporting, for example, to give insurers the right to 'absolute conduct and control' of proceedings against the insured. Thus, when exercising the rights under a claims control clause, insurers must not act arbitrarily, but must act reasonably in the interests of both themselves and the insured, and in good faith.[12] If they fail to do so, insurers may be ordered to pay the costs of proceedings as a non-party pursuant to s 51 of the Senior Courts Act 1981.[13]

Where a clause imposes an obligation on an insured to provide information and documents requested by the insurer, any request for documents must be relevant to the claim being made by the insured[14] or, presumably, to circumstances notified pursuant to the insured's obligations under the policy. Where there is an obligation to provide all such proofs and information relating to the claim as may be 'reasonably required' by insurers, the question is what information may be reasonably required by insurers in the particular circumstances of the case.[15] Generally speaking, it may be perfectly reasonable for insurers to reserve their position pending receipt of further documents or information, and a requirement by insurers that the insured should deliver such documents or information may be entirely reasonable because a review of such documents or information by insurers is necessary in order to decide, for example, whether cover exists or not.[16]

A sub-clause will be construed in the context of the claims control clause as a whole, and this may mean that apparently general words are construed more restrictively: thus, a provision in a reinsurance contract that: 'No settlement and/or compromise shall be made and no liability admitted without the prior approval of Reinsurers' was construed as being limited to settlements in respect of the share of the claimant reinsurers, not the share of another reinsurer who had settled with the defendant insureds, nor the defendant insureds' retained share.[17] A reference in such a sub-clause to settlement (or compromise) 'and' admission of liability is likely to be held to be disjunctive, so that the sub-clause is triggered if there is *either* a settlement or an admission of liability.[18] 'Settlement' in this context is likely to mean a legally binding settlement, whether or not it is expressed to be 'without prejudice to liability', at least where those words are intended simply to make plain that the parties are agreeing to a settlement without admitting any underlying liability, or to mean the actual transfer of consideration of some kind (whether money or otherwise) including what are sometimes described as 'ex gratia payments'.[19] In order to fall within the scope of such a sub-clause, an admission of liability must be communicated in clear and unequivocal terms by one party to the other; an admission of liability for part of the claim is sufficient.[20] In this context, the word 'admitted' imports the acceptance of the validity of a previous liability; this means that an offer to settle or pay certain money is not, of itself, an admission of liability.[21]

In *Groom v Crocker*,[22] a motor insurance policy contained a claims control clause in the following terms:

'The [insurer] shall, if and so long as it so desires, have absolute conduct and control of all or any proceedings against the insured (including arbitration and negotiations).'

The insurers instructed the solicitors on the record for the insured, who were nominated and paid by them, to admit negligence in circumstances where the risk of a finding of negligence against the insured at trial was remote. Their motive in making the admission was to obtain a benefit wholly extraneous to the proceedings in which the insured was involved (by virtue of a 'knock for knock' agreement which they had entered into with another insurer, in relation to the proceedings involving the insured and an unconnected action, because they took the view that dealing with both actions in this way would save them a significant sum of money). The Court of Appeal held that the claims control clause in the policy did not entitle the insurers to instruct the solicitors to make an admission for this reason. As a result, the solicitors were held to be in breach of duty to the insured.[23]

A claims control clause in a liability policy may provide that, in the event of the insurers requiring a claim to be contested by the insured, the insurers will pay defence costs. If insurers decide not to contest a claim on the grounds that the insured will be found liable for a sum in excess of the limit of indemnity, and the insured is found to be liable for a sum within the limit of indemnity, the insured may be entitled to damages for repudiation of the claims control clause.[24] The measure of damages will be the amount of costs which the insurers would have incurred, or authorised the insured to incur, had they not wrongfully repudiated the claims control clause.[25]

Although the solicitor is on the record as acting for the insured, and not the insurer,[26] the insured is not entitled to interfere with the conduct of the proceedings by the insurer by requiring the solicitor to act according to his instructions.[27] If the insured insists on a course of action with which the insurer disagrees, the insurer is entitled to refuse to conduct the proceedings, and to leave the insured to do so, at the risk of failing to recover his costs under the policy if the insurer's approach is subsequently held to have been correct.[28] This issue (and the issue of whether the insured was entitled to be indemnified by the insurer in respect of any judgment against him in the proceedings, or any settlement he might enter into) would then need to be resolved by proceedings between the insurer and the insured, in the absence of any dispute resolution mechanism in the policy of insurance. These would usually be separate proceedings, although in an appropriate case the court might give leave for the insurer to be joined to the proceedings in the main action pursuant to CPR 19.2(2).[29]

Issues often arise as to whether claims co-operation or claims control clauses are conditions precedent to the liability of the insurer.[30] This is a matter of construction of the policy wording.[31] Where such a clause is a condition precedent to the liability of the insurer, it operates as an exception to the insurer's prima facie liability,[32] and should be construed as such.[33]

1 See also **PARA 12.8**.
2 Taken from *Beacon Insurance Co Ltd v Langdale* (1939) 65 Ll L Rep 57, [1939] 4 All ER 204, CA.
3 Taken from *Kitchen Design and Advice Ltd v Lea Valley Water Co* [1989] 2 Lloyd's Rep 221.
4 See *Formica Ltd v Export Credits Guarantee Department* [1995] 1 Lloyd's Rep 692, 702 (Colman J); see also **PARA 12.8**.
5 [2010] EWHC 546 (Comm), [2010] Lloyd's Rep IR 453.
6 At para 2.
7 At para 46.

8 At paras 46–55.
9 *Groom v Crocker* [1939] 1 KB 194, CA.
10 *Beacon Insurance Co Ltd v Langdale* (1939) 65 Ll L Rep 57, [1939] 4 All ER 204, CA.
11 *Kitchen Design and Advice Ltd v Lea Valley Water Co* [1989] 2 Lloyd's Rep 221, 224–225: Phillips J held that it was implicit in the claims control clause (the wording of which is set out above) that insurers had authority to settle a claim not only once proceedings had been commenced, but also to settle a claim prior to and without the issue of proceedings.
12 *Groom v Crocker* [1939] 1 KB 194, CA; *Beacon Insurance Co Ltd v Langdale* (1939) 65 Ll L Rep 57, [1939] 4 All ER 204, CA; *Cox v Bankside Members Agency Ltd* [1995] 2 Lloyd's Rep 437, 462, CA (Sir Thomas Bingham MR); *K/S Merc-Scandia XXXXII v Certain Lloyd's Underwriters* [2001] EWCA Civ 1275, [2001] 2 Lloyd's Rep 563, 572, para 22(7) (Longmore LJ); see also *Gan Insurance Co Ltd v Tai Ping Insurance Co Ltd (Nos 2 and 3)* [2001] EWCA 1047, [2002] Lloyd's Rep IR 667, CA, paras 51–54 and 67–68 (Mance LJ) (reinsurance) and PARAS **14.3–14.4**.
13 See PARA **9.46**.
14 *Parker v National Farmers Union Mutual Insurance Society Ltd* [2012] EWHC 2156 (Comm), [2013] Lloyd's Rep IR 253, para 189 (Teare J) (the clause provided: 'If anything happens which might result in a claim, you must do the following: … provide all the written details and documents that we ask for.').
15 *Ted Baker plc v AXA Insurance UK plc (No 2)* [2014] EWHC 3548 (Comm), [2015] Lloyd's Rep IR 325, para 108 (Eder J).
16 *Ted Baker plc v AXA Insurance UK plc (No 2)* [2014] EWHC 3548 (Comm), [2015] Lloyd's Rep IR 325, para 108 (Eder J) (on facts of that case, not reasonable for insurers to require delivery of certain categories of documents, having regard in particular to time and expense that would have to be incurred by insured in complying with requirement, unless and until insurers confirmed that 'employee theft' was an insured peril (without which there was no cover for claim); but management accounts should have been provided: paras 107 and 108).
17 *Beazley Underwriting Ltd v Al Ahleia Insurance Co* [2013] EWHC 677 (Comm), [2013] Lloyd's Rep IR 561, paras 86–87 (Eder J).
18 *Gan Insurance Co Ltd v Tai Ping Insurance Co Ltd (Nos 2 and 3)* [2001] EWCA 1047, [2002] Lloyd's Rep IR 667, CA, paras 17–20 (Mance LJ), 80 (Latham LJ) and 83–84 (Sir Christopher Staughton) (reinsurance); *Beazley Underwriting Ltd v Al Ahleia Insurance Co* [2013] EWHC 677 (Comm), [2013] Lloyd's Rep IR 561, para 91 (Eder J) (reinsurance).
19 *Beazley Underwriting Ltd v Al Ahleia Insurance Co* [2013] EWHC, 677 (Comm), [2013] Lloyd's Rep IR 561, para 90 (Eder J) (reinsurance).
20 *Beazley Underwriting Ltd v Al Ahleia Insurance Co* [2013] EWHC 677 (Comm), [2013] Lloyd's Rep IR 561, para 92 (Eder J) (reinsurance).
21 *Beazley Underwriting Ltd v Al Ahleia Insurance Co* [2013] EWHC 677 (Comm), [2013] Lloyd's Rep IR 561, para 93 (Eder J) (reinsurance).
22 [1939] 1 KB 194, CA.
23 The insured was awarded nominal damages only, as the insurers had satisfied the judgment entered against him, although he recovered substantial damages for libel from the solicitors.
24 *Forney v Dominion Insurance Co Ltd* [1969] 1 WLR 928, 936 (Donaldson J).
25 *Forney v Dominion Insurance Co Ltd* [1969] 1 WLR 928, 936 (Donaldson J).
26 Although the solicitors are on the record as acting for the party to the proceedings, who is the insured, Longmore LJ's suggestion in *K/S Merc-Scandia XXXXII v Certain Lloyd's Underwriters, The Mercandian Continent* [2001] EWCA Civ 1275, [2001] 2 Lloyd's Rep 563, para 2, that it is only the insured, and not the insurer, who is the solicitors' client, appears to overlook the fact that where solicitors are appointed pursuant to a claims control clause in a liability policy, the solicitors are typically retained by the insurer to act jointly for it and for the insured: see *TSB Bank Ltd v Robert Irving & Burns* [1999] Lloyd's Rep IR 528, [2000] 2 All ER 826, CA.
27 *Groom v Crocker* [1939] 1 KB 194, 202–203, CA (Lord Greene MR).
28 *Groom v Crocker* [1939] 1 KB 194, 227–228, CA (MacKinnon LJ).
29 See PARA **9.47**.
30 See, eg, *Hassett v Legal & General Assurance Society Ltd* (1939) 63 Ll L Rep 278, 281 (Atkinson J) (clause held to be condition precedent); *Virk v Gan Life Holdings plc* [2000] Lloyd's Rep IR 159, para 12, CA (Potter LJ).
31 See PARA **3.5**; see also PARAS **14.3–14.4**.
32 *Royal & Sun Alliance Insurance plc v Dornoch* [2005] EWCA Civ 238, [2005] Lloyd's Rep IR 544, para 19 (Longmore LJ) (reinsurance); applied: *Beazley Underwriting Ltd v Al Ahleia Insurance Co* [2013] EWHC, 677 (Comm), [2013] Lloyd's Rep IR 561, para 90 (Eder J) (reinsurance).
33 See PARA **3.18**.

DISCLOSURE

General principles

9.14 The rules governing disclosure and inspection of documents are set out in Part 31 of the Civil Procedure Rules and the corresponding practice direction. *The Commercial Court Guide* contains additional provisions governing disclosure in actions proceeding in the Commercial Court.[1]

At the first case management conference, the court will normally consider whether to order disclosure. The normal order is for standard disclosure,[2] which requires a party to make a reasonable search for[3] and disclose only the documents on which he relies, and the documents which adversely affect his own case, adversely affect another party's case, or support another party's case.[4] Parties should also attempt to reach agreement in relation to the disclosure of electronic documents in a proportionate and cost-effective manner.[5] Documents may be withheld from disclosure[6] or, if disclosed, from inspection,[7] for reasons of proportionality. A party's duty to disclose documents is limited to documents which are or have been in his control, which means a document which is or was in his physical possession, a document of which he has or has had a right to possession, or a document of which he has or has had a right to inspect or take copies.[8] Once litigation is begun it seems that the duty of good faith under s 17 of the Marine Insurance Act 1906 is superseded or exhausted by the rules of litigation, and that it is the procedural rules which govern the extent of the disclosure which should be given in the litigation, not s 17 as such, although s 17 may influence the court in the exercise of its discretion.[9]

1 Section E.
2 Practice Direction 31, para 1.1.
3 CPR Pt 31, r 31.7(1).
4 CPR Pt 31, r 31.6.
5 CPR Pt 31, r 31.2A; Practice Direction 31B – Disclosure of Electronic Documents.
6 CPR Pt 31, r 31.7.
7 CPR Pt 31, r 31.3(2).
8 CPR Pt 31, r 31.8.
9 *Manifest Shipping Co Ltd v Uni-Polaris Insurance Co Ltd, The Star Sea* [2001] UKHL 1, [2003] AC 469, paras 73–77 (Lord Hobhouse), para 110 (Lord Scott) (preferring to leave the decision for a case where the point was critical to the result); *K/S Merc-Scandia XXXXII v Certain Lloyd's Underwriters Subscribing to Lloyd's Policy No 25T 105487, The Mercandian Continent* [2001] EWCA Civ 1275, [2001] 2 Lloyd's Rep 563, para 22 (Longmore LJ); *Agapitos v Agnew, The Aegeon* [2002] EWCA Civ 247, [2003] QB 556, paras 50–51 (Mance LJ). See also **PARA 11.49**.

Disclosure of insurance policy or information

9.15 The court has no jurisdiction pursuant to CPR Part 31 to require disclosure of a party's liability insurance position.[1] There is, further, no power to order disclosure pursuant to CPR Part 18.[2] The courts have however used their case management powers to order parties to disclose an insurance policy or information in relation to insurance in group litigation where the existence or amount of the insurance may determine the ability of a party to fund, and therefore to continue to participate in, the litigation,[3] but establishing in advance how much money is available from an insurer is not a matter of case management.[4]

1 *West London Pipeline and Storage Ltd v Total UK Ltd* [2008] EWHC 1296 (Comm), [2008] Lloyd's Rep IR 688, para 21 (David Steel J).
2 *West London Pipeline and Storage Ltd v Total UK Ltd* [2008] EWHC 1296 (Comm), [2008] Lloyd's Rep IR 688, paras 22–24 (David Steel J); applied: *XYZ v Various Companies (The PIP Breast Implant Litigation)* [2013] EWHC 3643 (QB), [2014] Lloyd's Rep IR 431, paras 20–29 (Thirlwall J). David Steel J declined to follow the decision of Irwin J in *Harcourt v F E F Griffin* [2007] EWHC 1500 (QB), [2008] Lloyd's Rep IR 386 in which disclosure of a policy of liability insurance had been ordered pursuant to Part 18. It is suggested that the reasoning of David Steel J (which included consideration of an unreported decision of the Court of Appeal in *Cox v Bankside Members Agency Ltd* of 29 November 1994) is correct.
3 *Barr v Biffa Waste Services Ltd* [2009] EWHC 1033 (TCC), [2010] Lloyd's Rep IR 428, paras 72–76 (Coulson J) (claimant ordered to disclose after the event (ATE) legal expenses insurance policy); *XYZ v Various Companies (The PIP Breast Implant Litigation)* [2013] EWHC 3643 (QB), [2014] Lloyd's Rep IR 431, paras 34–36 (Thirlwall J) (liability insurance: defendant ordered pursuant to CPR 3.1(2)(m) to provide witness statement setting out whether it had insurance adequate to fund its participation in the litigation to the completion of trial and conclusion of any appeal).
4 *XYZ v Various Companies (The PIP Breast Implant Litigation)* [2013] EWHC 3643 (QB), [2014] Lloyd's Rep IR 431, para 35 (Thirlwall J) (refusing make any order pursuant to CPR 31.3.1(2)(m) which required defendant to say whether it had sufficient insurance to meet any order for damages or for costs); *XYZ v Various* [2014] EWHC 4056 (QB), para 31 (Thirlwall J).

Insurance brokers

9.16   Where an insured employs an insurance broker, the broker will normally be the agent of the insured,[1] and the insured will therefore have within its control, and be obliged to disclose if they otherwise fall within the scope of standard disclosure, those documents in the broker's placing file, which by reason of the contract of agency he is entitled to require the broker to deliver up.[2] In practice, brokers commonly disclose the entire contents of their files for the purposes of litigation relating to a policy, although it is doubtful whether they are under an obligation to do so.[3] In *Formica Ltd v Secretary of State acting by the Exports Credit Guarantee Department*,[4] Colman J held that in the absence of an express or implied term giving the client a greater entitlement, the distinction is between documents, the creation of which is one of the functions for which the broker was employed, such as those which record the terms of the insurance contract or are communications with insurers, which are within the client's control; and documents which are the means by which the broker discharges his functions, such as internal memoranda or rough notes of telephone conversations, which are not.

This decision may be contrasted with the decision of Clauson J in relation to solicitors' papers in *Re Crocker*,[5] in which he held that a client was entitled to inspect and take copies of all papers relating to the proceedings which the solicitors had conducted on his behalf. In *Re Crocker*, the solicitors were nominated and paid by the client's motor insurers to act in proceedings arising out of a road traffic accident. An application for delivery up by the solicitors of all papers belonging to the client was not pursued, and Clauson J indicated that he might have felt some difficulty in allowing the papers to go out of the solicitors' control without hearing from the insurers on this point. Colman J based his decision in *Formica Ltd v Secretary of State acting by the Exports Credit Guarantee Department* squarely on the absence of an express or implied term, and this may explain the differing outcomes in the two cases as, having found that the solicitors, though nominated and paid for by insurers, were acting for the client pursuant to a contractual retainer, Clauson J considered it obvious that the client was entitled to inspect and take copies of the solicitors' papers.

In addition, there may be other documents on the broker's placing file which are not within the insured's control. This is the case, notably, with loss adjusters' reports which result from the practice at Lloyd's of brokers instructing claims assessors on behalf of underwriters. This practice is a breach of the broker's fiduciary obligations to the insured, as the broker thereby puts himself in a position where his duty and his interest may conflict, but, despite adverse judicial comment, the practice continues.[6] The conflict of interest does not entitle the insured either to possession of the reports or to take copies of them, and the insured is therefore under no obligation to disclose them.[7]

In the Lloyd's market, a term is implied in the insurance contracts between underwriters and insureds to this effect: that placing and claims documents which have been previously shown to underwriters, and premium accounting documents which are necessary to the operation of the contract, where retained by the insureds' Lloyd's brokers, should be available to underwriters in case of reasonable necessity.[8] Availability includes the right to take copies, and the costs of inspection and copying fall to be met by the underwriters who make the request.[9] Reasonable necessity may arise because copies of documents have not been retained by underwriters, because they have been lost, or (in the case of premium accounting documents) because underwriters have never had copies.[10] There is no obligation to provide underwriters with documents they already have, or which the brokers have not retained.[11] In the absence of bad faith, underwriters' motivation for seeking inspection is irrelevant.[12] In the period prior to the Terms of Business Agreement 2001, a contract was implied by reason of necessity directly between brokers and underwriters in the Lloyd's market which obliged brokers to perform the duty undertaken by their principals, the insureds, to make available documents necessary for the effective performance of the insurance contracts.[13]

1 See PARA 16.2.
2 *Formica Ltd v Secretary of State acting by the Exports Credit Guarantee Department* [1995] 1 Lloyd's Rep 692, 702–703 (Colman J).
3 Since the amendment, on the introduction of the Civil Procedure Rules, of s 34 of the Senior Courts Act 1981 and s 53 of the County Courts Act 1984, it has been possible to make an application for disclosure under CPR r 31.17 against brokers who are not parties to the proceedings. The principles which are summarised here remain relevant because they define the limits of the insured's obligation to call for and disclose the contents of the broker's files within the context of standard disclosure.
4 [1995] 1 Lloyd's Rep 692, 702–703.
5 [1936] Ch 696; approved by Scott LJ in *Groom v Crocker* [1939] 1 KB 194, 218, CA.
6 *North and South Trust Co v Berkeley* [1971] 1 WLR 470 (Donaldson J), approved by the Privy Council in *Kelly v Cooper* [1993] AC 205; *Callaghan and Hedges v Thompson* [2000] Lloyd's Rep IR, 132 125 (David Steel J).
7 *North and South Trust Co v Berkeley* [1971] 1 WLR 470 (Donaldson J), approved by the Privy Council in *Kelly v Cooper* [1993] AC 205. The insured may be entitled to damages for breach of fiduciary duty: see PARA 16.40.
8 *Goshawk Ltd v Tyser & Co Ltd* [2006] EWCA Civ 54, [2006] 1 Lloyd's Rep 566, para 58 (Rix LJ).
9 *Goshawk Ltd v Tyser & Co Ltd* [2006] EWCA Civ 54, [2006] 1 Lloyd's Rep 566, para 58 (Rix LJ).
10 *Goshawk Ltd v Tyser & Co Ltd* [2006] EWCA Civ 54, [2006] 1 Lloyd's Rep 566, para 57 (Rix LJ).
11 *Goshawk Ltd v Tyser & Co Ltd* [2006] EWCA Civ 54, [2006] 1 Lloyd's Rep 566, para 57 (Rix LJ).
12 *Goshawk Ltd v Tyser & Co Ltd* [2006] EWCA Civ 54, [2006] 1 Lloyd's Rep 566, para 59 (Rix LJ).
13 *Goshawk Ltd v Tyser & Co Ltd* [2006] EWCA Civ 54, [2006] 1 Lloyd's Rep 566, paras 64 and 66 (Rix LJ). The regulatory requirement that Lloyd's brokers enter into terms of business agreements with managing agents which provide for inspection by underwriters of accounting records, placing and claims documentation in the possession of brokers was removed in the Lloyd's market reforms in 2009.

The mechanics of disclosure

9.17 Disclosure is by list of documents, verified by a disclosure statement.[1] This is a statement setting out the extent of the search which has been made to locate documents which the disclosing party is required to disclose, certifying that the maker understands the duty to disclose documents and that to the best of his knowledge he has carried out that duty.[2] An insurer may sign a disclosure statement on behalf of a party where the insurer has a financial interest in the result of proceedings brought wholly or partially by or against that party.[3] However, care should always be taken to ensure that the person signing the disclosure statement is in a position to make the statements which it contains. In some cases, a party's legal representative may not be an appropriate person to sign the disclosure statement. The Commercial Court will normally regard as an appropriate person to sign a disclosure statement any person who is in a position responsibly and authoritatively to search for the documents required to be disclosed by that party and to make the statements contained in the disclosure statement.[4] A party may not rely on any document which he fails to disclose, or in respect of which he fails to permit inspection, unless the court gives permission.[5]

A party need not disclose more than one copy of a document.[6] However, a copy of a document that contains a modification, obliteration or other marking or feature on which a party intends to rely, or which adversely affects his own case or another party's case, is treated as a separate document.[7] In this way it will be necessary, where copies in both forms exist, to disclose not only the slip prepared by Lloyd's brokers, but also the copy (or copies) of the slip which has been scratched (signed and stamped) by underwriters.

If the physical structure of a file may be of evidential value, as may, for example, be the case with a placing file, the solicitors for the party making disclosure should make one complete copy of the file in the form in which they received it before any documents are removed, for example, for reasons of privilege, for the purpose of giving disclosure or inspection.[8]

1 CPR r 31.10.
2 CPR r 31.10(6).
3 CPR r 31.10(9) and Practice Direction 31A, para 4.7.
4 Admiralty and Commercial Courts Guide, para E3.8.
5 CPR r 31.21.
6 CPR r 31.9(1).
7 CPR r 31.9(2).
8 The Admiralty and Commercial Courts Guide makes specific provision to this effect at para E3.3, but it is suggested that the principle is of general application.

Continuing duty of disclosure

9.18 The duty of disclosure continues until the proceedings are concluded, and if documents come to a party's notice at any time during the proceedings, he must immediately notify every other party.[1] The Practice Direction provides that this should be done by way of a supplemental list of documents,[2] but the parties to whom disclosure is made may be prepared to accept disclosure by way of letter, in order to save costs.

1 CPR r 31.11 and Practice Direction 31A, para 3.3.
2 Practice Direction 31A, para 3.3.

Specific disclosure

9.19   A party who believes that the disclosure of documents given by a disclosing party is inadequate may make an application for an order for specific disclosure.[1] An order for specific disclosure is an order that a party must do one or more of the following things: disclose documents or classes of documents specified in the order; carry out a search to the extent stated in the order; and disclose any documents located as a result of that search.[2]

1 Practice Direction 31A, para 5.1.
2 CPR r 31.12(2).

Documents mentioned in statements of case, etc

9.20   A party may also inspect[1] a document 'mentioned' in a statement of case, a witness statement, a witness summary or an affidavit,[2] and may apply for an order for inspection of any document mentioned in an expert's report which has not already been disclosed.[3] The document in question does not have to be relied on, or referred to in any particular way or for any particular purpose, in order to be 'mentioned' for these purposes.[4]

1 Notice must be given by the inspecting party and inspection must be permitted by the disclosing party not more than 7 days after date of receipt of the notice: CPR r 31.15(a) and (b). Copies must be provided within 7 days of a request being made if an undertaking is given to pay reasonable copying charges: CPR r 31.15(c).
2 CPR r 31.14(1). See eg *Barr v Biffa Waste Services Ltd* [2009] EWHC 1033 (TCC), [2010] Lloyd's Rep IR 428, paras 33–36, in which Coulson J ordered disclosure pursuant to CPR 31.14 of an after the event (ATE) legal expenses insurance policy which was mentioned in a witness statement made in support of an application for a group litigation order.
3 CPR r 31.14(2).
4 *Rubin v Expandable Ltd* [2008] EWCA Civ 59, [2008] 1 WLR 1099, para 24 (Rix LJ). Mention of a document does not entail an automatic and absolute waiver of privilege: *Rubin v Expandable Ltd* [2008] EWCA Civ 59, [2008] 1 WLR 1099, para 37 (Rix LJ).

Privilege and disclosure

9.21   Privilege[1] does not relieve a party of the obligation to make disclosure,[2] but protects a document from inspection.[3] If privilege is to be asserted, this must be done in the list of documents in which the document is disclosed.[4] Where a party inadvertently allows a privileged document to be inspected, the party who has inspected the document may use it or its contents only with the permission of the court.[5]

Where part only of a document is privileged, a party giving disclosure may cover up that part of the document when making disclosure, even when both parts of the document deal with the same subject matter.[6] This is not to be confused with the position where the document as a whole is privileged, in which case a waiver of privilege in relation to part of the document waives privilege in relation to the whole.[7] The same principle applied under the old rules, where the test for disclosure was relevance, in relation to irrelevant parts of otherwise relevant documents; indeed, even if relevant and irrelevant material was contained in the same sentence, it was permissible to blank out the irrelevant material, if this could be done without destroying the sense of the rest or making it misleading.[8] The test is no longer relevance. In principle, however, there would seem to be no objection to a party blanking out those parts of a document which are not required to be disclosed pursuant to the definition of standard disclosure. This technique is likely to be of particular use where, for example, a single entry on a bank statement is relied on, and the other entries have no connection with the subject matter of the proceedings, or where a document which is required to be disclosed contains elements of confidential business information unconnected with the proceedings.

1 See **PARA 9.25**.
2 Except where disclosure would damage the public interest: CPR r 31.19(1).
3 CPR r 31.19(3).
4 CPR r 31.19(4). The list should be in practice form N265: CPR Practice Direction 31A, para 3.1; or, in the Commercial Court, in Form N265(CC): Admiralty and Commercial Courts Guide, para E3.9.
5 CPR r 31.20. See **PARA 9.31**, note 14.
6 *GE Capital Corporate Finance Group Ltd v Bankers Trust Co* [1995] 1 WLR 172, CA.
7 See **PARA 9.33**.
8 *GE Capital Corporate Finance Group Ltd v Bankers Trust Co* [1995] 1 WLR 172, CA.

Pre-action disclosure

9.22   The court may order disclosure before proceedings have been started.[1] CPR r 31.16 applies where an application is made to the court under any Act of Parliament for disclosure before proceedings have started.[2] Rule 31.16(3) provides that the court may make an order for pre-action disclosure only where:

(a)   the respondent is likely to be a party to subsequent proceedings;
(b)   the applicant is also likely to be a party to those proceedings;
(c)   if proceedings had started, the respondent's duty by way of standard disclosure would extend to the documents or classes of documents of which the applicant seeks disclosure; and
(d)   disclosure before proceedings have started is desirable in order to:
   (i)   dispose fairly of the anticipated proceedings;
   (ii)   assist the dispute to be resolved without proceedings; or
   (iii)   save costs.

A person is 'likely to be a party to subsequent proceedings' within the meaning of CPR r 31.16(3)(a) or (b) if he 'may well'[3] be a party to proceedings if those proceedings are subsequently issued. The extent of standard disclosure cannot easily be discerned without clarity as to the issues which would arise once pleadings in the prospective litigation had been formulated, so that the court must be clear what the issues in the litigation are likely to be, both in terms of the case the claimant is likely to be making, and what defence is likely to be run.[4] Sub-rule (3)(d) imposes a two-part test, the first jurisdictional ('only where') and the second discretionary ('desirable').[5] This means that once the court is satisfied that it has jurisdiction to order pre-action disclosure on the basis of one of the criteria set out in sub-rule (d) (i) to (iii),[6] it must go on to consider whether to exercise its discretion in favour of making such an order, although in the case of sub-rule (3)(d), the questions of principle and of detail may merge into one another, and it may be difficult to keep the two stages of the process separate.[7]

1 Senior Courts Act 1981, s 33 (as amended); County Courts Act 1984, s 52 (as amended); CPR r 31.16. Before amendment, the statutory provisions were limited in scope to actions for damages for personal injuries but are now of general application.
2 CPR r 31.16(1).
3 *Black v Sumitomo Corpn* [2001] EWCA Civ 1819, [2002] 1 WLR 1562, paras 70–73 (Rix LJ) (a decision in relation to s 33(2) of the Senior Courts Act 1981, as amended); *Three Rivers District Council v Bank of England (No 4)* [2002] EWCA Civ 1182, [2003] 1 WLR 210, 224–226, CA, paras 30–33.
4 *Black v Sumitomo Corpn* [2001] EWCA Civ 1819, [2002] 1 WLR 1562, para 76 (Rix LJ). If possible, a draft pleading should be prepared and annexed to the application (para 91) (Rix LJ), but the fact that the applicant is not able to do this is not necessarily fatal and to the contrary will often be a proper context for addressing the provisions of CPR 31.16: *XL London Market Ltd v Zenith Syndicate Management Ltd* [2004] EWHC 1181 (Comm), para 24 (Langley J) (order for disclosure made pursuant to CPR 31.16: potential action for breach of term in run-off agreement imposing obligation to exercise reasonable care in running off business; the applicants did not know what had gone wrong, were not able to make specific allegations of negligence and had not determined to sue come what may, but the facts called for an explanation, which had not been forthcoming).
5 *Black v Sumitomo Corpn* [2001] EWCA Civ 1819, [2002] 1 WLR 1562, para 79 (Rix LJ).
6 *Black v Sumitomo Corpn* [2001] EWCA Civ 1819, [2002] 1 WLR 1562, para 81 (Rix LJ).
7 *Black v Sumitomo Corpn* [2001] EWCA Civ 1819, [2002] 1 WLR 1562, paras 81–85 (Rix LJ); *First Gulf Bank v Wachovia Bank National Association* [2005] EWHC 2827 (Comm), para 22 (Christopher Clarke J).

Disclosure against a non-party

9.23   The court also has power to order disclosure against a person who is not a party to the proceedings where the documents of which disclosure is sought satisfy the following threshold condition: they are likely to support the case of the applicant or adversely affect the case of one of the other parties to the proceedings, and disclosure is necessary in order to dispose fairly of the claim or to save costs.[1] 'Likely' in this context means 'may well'.[2] An order may be made in respect of a class of documents, rather than individual documents, but only if the court is satisfied that all documents within the class satisfy the threshold condition.[3] Moreover, the threshold condition cannot be circumvented by an order which imposes on the non-party the task of identifying those documents within a composite class which do, and those which do not, meet the condition.[4] There is no obligation on a non-party to serve evidence in response to an application for disclosure, or to attend a hearing; it may simply adopt a neutral stance, neither consenting to the application nor opposing it, and leave it to the court to decide what to do. If the non-party is neutral as to whether or not a disclosure order is made against it, this will often be the most cost-effective approach.

1 Senior Courts Act 1981, s 34 (as amended); County Courts Act 1984, s 53 (as amended); CPR r 31.17.
2 *Three Rivers District Council v Bank of England (No 4)* [2002] EWCA Civ 1182, [2003] 1 WLR 210, paras 30–33.
3 *American Home Products Corpn v Novartis Pharmaceuticals UK Ltd (No 2)* [2001] EWCA Civ 165, [2001] FSR 784.
4 *Three Rivers District Council v Bank of England (No 4)* [2002] EWCA Civ 1182, [2003] 1 WLR 210, para 36, approving *Wakefield v Outhwaite* [1990] 2 Lloyd's Rep 157, 163–164 (Potter J) (a decision concerning a subpoena *duces tecum*).

Restriction on use of documents disclosed

9.24   As a general rule, a party to whom a document has been disclosed may use the document only for the purpose of the proceedings in which it is disclosed.[1] Where copies of third-party documents are produced by a client, legal advisers should be alert to the possibility that they were obtained in previous proceedings, and make enquiries as to their source. If the documents were obtained in previous proceedings, and were not read to or by the court, or referred to, at a hearing held in public,[2] the party wishing to use them should, before doing so, apply to the court for permission to do so[3] or seek the agreement of the party who disclosed the document and, if different, its owner.[4]

1 CPR r 31.22(1).
2 CPR r 31.22(1)(a).
3 CPR r 31.22(1)(b).
4 CPR r 31.22(1)(c).

LEGAL PROFESSIONAL PRIVILEGE

General principles

9.25   There are two distinct classes of legal professional privilege. The first, commonly known as 'legal advice privilege', extends to all communications between the client and his legal adviser for the dominant purpose of obtaining legal advice.[1] It exists whether litigation is anticipated or not.[2] The second ('litigation privilege') attaches only to communications which come into existence with the dominant purpose of being used in existing or contemplated litigation.[3]

In *Waugh v British Railways Board*,[4] the plaintiff's husband was employed by the defendant and was fatally injured in a collision between locomotives. A report was prepared by the defendant, partly for safety purposes and partly for obtaining legal advice in anticipation of legal proceedings. The House of Lords held that the latter purpose had to be the 'dominant' purpose in order for the claim to privilege to succeed. It rejected both a more stringent 'sole purpose' test, and a test which would have allowed a claim to privilege where there were two purposes of equal rank, accordingly to which the defendant's claim would have succeeded. It also indicated that the fact that the report stated on its face that it had finally to be sent to the defendant's solicitor for the purpose of enabling him to advise the defendant could not be conclusive as to the dominant purpose for which it was prepared. At the time the document is created, litigation must be reasonably in prospect and not a mere possibility, but it is not necessary to show that there was more than a 50 per cent chance of litigation.[5] Protection may be claimed for documents which come into existence at any time after the date on which litigation is first anticipated, whatever the date on which solicitors are first instructed.[6] Where an insurer instructs lawyers for the purpose of investigating and advising on a casualty, that meets the dominant purpose test, for the purpose of investigation is inseparable from the purpose of the advice.[7]

Communications passing between a solicitor and a prospective client with a view to the client retaining the solicitor are privileged from disclosure, even if the solicitor does not accept the retainer.[8] Documents prepared by the client in relation to an intended action, whether at the request of the solicitor or not, and whether ultimately laid before the solicitor or not, are privileged if prepared with a bona fide intention of being laid before him for the purpose of taking his advice.[9]

The functions of solicitors are not limited to the provision of legal advice;[10] in relation to legal advice privilege what matters is whether the advice has 'a relevant legal context'.[11] Whether documents passing between a solicitor and client are privileged or not depends on whether they are part of that necessary exchange of information of which the object is the giving of legal advice as and when appropriate, and it is not necessary to consider each individual document and determine whether it was created for the purpose of giving or receiving legal advice.[12] The 'dominant purpose' test applies not only to litigation privilege, but also to legal advice privilege, so the question is whether the dominant purpose of creating the document was the giving or receiving of legal advice.[13]

1 This formulation is taken from the judgment of Lord Denning MR in *Buttes Oil Co v Hammer (No 3)* [1981] QB 223, 243, CA, with the addition of the adjective 'dominant' in the light of the decision of the Court of Appeal in *Three Rivers District Council v Bank of England (No 5)* [2003] EWCA Civ 474, [2003] QB 1556 (see further note 4 below and related text). *Minter v Priest* [1930] AC 558, HL appears to suggest that all communications between a client and solicitor which are fairly referable to the relationship of solicitor and client are privileged. It is suggested that Lord Denning MR's formulation, which includes the additional qualification that the communications must be for the purpose of obtaining legal advice, is obviously to be preferred. See also **PARA 8.13**.
2 *Buttes Oil Co v Hammer (No 3)* [1981] QB 223, CA.
3 *Buttes Oil Co v Hammer (No 3)* [1981] QB 223, CA; *Three Rivers District Council v Bank of England (No 5)* [2003] EWCA Civ 474, [2003] QB 1556, para 1 (Longmore LJ). See also **PARA 8.13**. Litigation includes alternative dispute resolution, such as mediation: *Buttes Oil Co v Hammer (No 3)* [1981] QB 223, 246, CA (Lord Denning MR). It is unclear whether it extends to adjudication proceedings: *Walter Lilly & Co Ltd v Mackay* [2012] EWHC 649 (TCC), para 20 (Akenhead J).
4 [1980] AC 521, HL.
5 *Axa Seguros SA de CV v Allianz Insurance plc* [2011] EWHC 268 (Comm), [2011] Lloyd's Rep IR 544, para 13 (Christopher Clarke J). This is an objective question, and evidence as to the actual perception of the insurer or reinsurer or his lawyers at the time is neither conclusive nor irrelevant, but is some guide as to whether there was a reasonable prospect of litigation: *Axa Seguros SA de CV v Allianz Insurance plc* [2011] EWHC 268 (Comm), [2011] Lloyd's Rep IR 544, paras 14 and 47 (Christopher Clarke J).
6 *Buttes Oil Co v Hammer (No 3)* [1981] QB 223, 244, CA (Lord Denning MR).
7 *Hellenic Mutual War Risks Association (Bermuda) Ltd v Harrison, The Sagheera* [1997] 1 Lloyd's Rep 160, 168 (Rix J); approved: *Westminster International BV v Dornoch* [2009] EWCA Civ 1323, para 32 (Etherton LJ).
8 *Minter v Priest* [1930] AC 558, HL.
9 *The Southwark and Vauxhall Water Co v Quick* (1878) 3 QBD 315, CA.
10 In *Three Rivers District Council v Bank of England (No 6)* [2004] UKHL 48, [2005] 1 AC 610, Lord Rodger said (at para 58) that Taylor LJ's remarks in *Balabel v Air India* [1988] Ch 317, CA, 331–332, that the range of solicitors' activities at the time the earlier cases were decided was more restrictive than in recent times, were 'at best, an over-simplification'; in contrast, Lord Carswell (at paras 111–113) appeared to endorse Taylor LJ's remarks.
11 *Three Rivers District Council v Bank of England (No 6)* [2004] UKHL 48, [2005] 1 AC 610, paras 38 (Lord Scott) and 114 (Lord Carswell), adopting the phraseology of Taylor LJ in *Balabel v Air India* [1988] Ch 317, CA, 330. Lord Rodger preferred (para 58) to ask whether the lawyers were being asked qua (in their capacity as) lawyers to provide legal advice; it is suggested that this is simply a different way of asking the same question. Lady Hale (para 61) and Lord Brown (para 122) agreed with both formulations. See also **PARA 8.13**.
12 *Balabel v Air India* [1988] Ch 317, CA, 332 (Taylor LJ), adding that documents which are so minor as not to be privileged are likely to be irrelevant and therefore not subject to production in any event.

13 *Hellenic Mutual War Risks Association (Bermuda) Ltd v Harrison, The Sagheera* [1997] 1 Lloyd's Rep 160, 168–169 (Rix J); *Three Rivers District Council v Bank of England (No 5)* [2003] EWCA Civ 474, [2003] QB 1556 (doubting (at para 28) Rix J's reformulation of the question by reference to the dominant purpose of the retainer; see similarly *United States of America v Philip Morris Inc* [2004] EWCA Civ 330, para 79 (Brooke LJ)).

Letters of notification

9.26 In *Guinness Peat Properties Ltd v Fitzroy Robinson Partnership*,[1] a firm of architects sent a letter of notification via its insurance brokers to its liability insurers, before proceedings had begun, informing the insurers, in accordance with the policy terms and conditions, that a claim had been made against them. The Court of Appeal applied an objective test of intention in deciding that the dominant purpose of the insurers in requiring notice to be given to them was to produce a letter of notification which would be used in order to obtain legal advice or to conduct or aid in the conduct of litigation which was at the time of its production in reasonable prospect;[2] and that the letter was accordingly privileged, even though the subjective intention of its author (the insured) was not to seek legal advice, and even though, in a small minority of straightforward and simple cases, legal advice was not in fact sought by insurers on receipt of a letter of notification. The application of an objective test means that letters of notification in respect of liability policies will be privileged except in the most unusual factual circumstances. This is obviously consistent with the realities of the situation: policy terms and conditions usually require notification not only of claims but of circumstances (or, less commonly, occurrences) which may or are likely to give rise to a claim, so that insurers can ensure that steps are taken to safeguard their interests at the earliest possible stage, and it would be impossible for there to be a frank exchange between insured and insurer in this situation were such communications not protected from production in any subsequent litigation. It is suggested that this reasoning does not apply to insurers requiring notice to be given by the insured of a claim under a policy of casualty insurance (for example, 'all risks', fire or property) and that, although it depends to some degree on the facts of each case, such letters are unlikely to be privileged.

1 [1987] 1 WLR 1027, CA.
2 *Guinness Peat Properties Ltd v Fitzroy Robinson Partnership* [1987] 1 WLR 1027, CA, 1037 (Slade LJ)

Internal documents reproducing privileged communications

9.27 Internal documents reproducing or otherwise revealing the content of privileged communications are also covered by privilege, whatever the purpose or motive (short of fraud) for which the document comes into existence.[1] This will include informing the decision takers within a client business of the advice which has been given, in order for a commercial decision to be taken.[2]

1 *Bank of Nova Scotia v Hellenic Mutual War Risks Association (Bermuda) Ltd, The Good Luck* [1992] 2 Lloyd's Rep 540 (Saville J); *Hellenic Mutual War Risks Association (Bermuda) Ltd v Harrison, The Sagheera* [1997] 1 Lloyd's Rep 160, 168–169 (Rix J).
2 *Bank of Nova Scotia v Hellenic Mutual War Risks Association (Bermuda) Ltd, The Good Luck* [1992] 2 Lloyd's Rep 540 (Saville J); *Hellenic Mutual War Risks Association (Bermuda) Ltd v Harrison, The Sagheera* [1997] 1 Lloyd's Rep 160, 168–169 (Rix J).

Foreign legal advisers

9.28   Communications with foreign legal advisers are also protected,[1] whether or not the advice is given in relation to a legal system in which the adviser is a qualified lawyer.[2]

1 *Great Atlantic Insurance Co v Home Insurance Co* [1981] 1 WLR 529, CA (US attorneys).
2 *International Business Machines Corpn v Phoenix International (Computers) Ltd* [1995] 1 All ER 413 (US attorney with an English law degree advising in relation to English law).

Burden of proof

9.29   The burden of proof is on the party refusing disclosure on grounds of privilege.[1]

1 *Waugh v British Railways Board* [1980] AC 521, HL, 541 (Lord Edmund-Davies); *Guinness Peat Properties Ltd v Fitzroy Robinson Partnership* [1987] 1 WLR 1027, CA, 1033 (Slade LJ).

Production of documents to the court

9.30   The court may determine a claim that a party has a right or duty to withhold inspection of a document or part of a document and, if it does so, it may require the person seeking to withhold disclosure or inspection to produce the document to the court, and it may invite any person, whether or not a party, to make representations.[1]

1 CPR 31.19(5)–(6).

'Common interest' privilege

9.31   Where parties have a common interest in litigation, they may be entitled to share privileged communications between themselves without losing the right to maintain the privilege against the rest of the world.[1] Examples include owners of adjoining houses who complain of a nuisance which affects them both equally, only one of whom brings proceedings; the author and the publisher of a book which is said to contain a libel or to be an infringement of copyright.[2] The recognition of common interest privilege reflects the utility in such circumstances of sharing information between the parties, including information collected for the purposes of the litigation and legal advice given by solicitors or counsel. The public policy considerations which underlie common interest privilege apply with equal force whether the privilege is litigation privilege or legal advice privilege, and common interest privilege may validly be asserted in either case.[3]

In order for parties to assert common interest privilege, what is required is that the nature of their mutual interest in the context of their relationship is such that the party to whom the documents are passed receives them subject to a duty of confidence.[4] The very fact of the provision of privileged information may be some evidence of the existence of the requisite relationship, although it will self-evidently not be sufficient in and of itself; however, receipt of privileged information pursuant to a contractual entitlement in the context of a transaction in which both parties have an interest (or were considering an interest) is likely to be sufficient.[5] In relation to insurers and reinsurers, a contractual right to the provision of privileged information is likely to be sufficient for there to be an entitlement to common interest privilege, whether it is contained in a 'follow settlements' clause, or a provision governing the manner in which litigation is to be conducted, or some other contractual provision.[6] In *Svenska Handelsbanken v Sun Alliance and London Insurance plc*,[7] there was no specific contractual provision because no policies were brought into existence, and the reinsurance contracts rested on slips, but the insurers had felt obliged to communicate to reinsurers the legal advice they had received, and had done so. Rix J held that this was sufficient for there to be common interest privilege in the legal advice.

Although there will often be a right to obtain disclosure of confidential documents between parties entitled to assert common interest privilege against a third party, this is not a precondition to the existence of the privilege.[8] Indeed, if one considers the examples given by Lord Denning MR in *Buttes Oil Co v Hammer (No 3)*[9] of parties entitled to assert common interest privilege in advice communicated by one to the other, there could be no suggestion, unless the parties had entered into an agreement to this effect, that one houseowner could compel the other to communicate the advice which the other had obtained, or that the publisher of a book could compel the author to do so. In the absence of a specific contractual entitlement to communication of privileged documents, what is required is evidence that the information was obtained by one party in the furtherance of a joint interest, and in that sense on behalf of the party seeking disclosure, even where the interests of the two parties were potentially (though not actually) in conflict at the time the information was obtained.[10] A follow settlements clause has been held to be sufficient for these purposes, so that reinsurers will be entitled to production of privileged documents brought into being for the purposes of handling the original claim.[11] However, reinsurers will not be permitted, in proceedings against insurers in which they are denying the validity of the reinsurance contract after a purported avoidance, to rely upon the follow settlements clause in the contract as entitling them to production of those documents.[12]

1 *Buttes Oil Co v Hammer (No 3)* [1981] QB 223, CA. Litigation in this context includes alternative dispute resolution, such as mediation: at 246 (Lord Denning MR).
2 The examples are taken from *Buttes Oil Co v Hammer (No 3)* [1981] QB 223, 243, CA (Lord Denning MR).
3 *Svenska Handelsbanken v Sun Alliance and London Insurance plc* [1995] 2 Lloyd's Rep 84, 88 (Rix J).
4 *Formica Ltd v Secretary of State acting by the Export Credits Guarantee Department* [1995] 1 Lloyd's Rep 692, 699 (Colman J).
5 *Formica Ltd v Secretary of State acting by the Export Credits Guarantee Department* [1995] 1 Lloyd's Rep 692, 699–700 (Colman J).
6 *Svenska Handelsbanken v Sun Alliance and London Insurance plc* [1995] 2 Lloyd's Rep 84, 87 (Rix J); *Commercial Union Insurance Co plc v Mander* [1996] 2 Lloyd's Rep 640.
7 [1995] 2 Lloyd's Rep 84, 87 (Rix J).
8 *Commercial Union Insurance Co plc v Mander* [1996] 2 Lloyd's Rep 640, 644–645 (Moore-Bick J).
9 [1981] QB 223, 243, CA.
10 *Commercial Union Insurance Co plc v Mander* [1996] 2 Lloyd's Rep 640, 645–646 (Moore-Bick J).
11 *Commercial Union Insurance Co plc v Mander* [1996] 2 Lloyd's Rep 640, 647 (Moore-Bick J).
12 *Commercial Union Insurance Co plc v Mander* [1996] 2 Lloyd's Rep 640, 648 (Moore-Bick J).

Copies and privilege

9.32 If an original document is privileged (as having come into existence with the dominant purpose of being used in the anticipated litigation), so also is any copy made by the solicitor.[1] If the original is not privileged, a copy of it is also not privileged, even though it was made by a solicitor for the purpose of the litigation.[2] There is an exception in relation to documents not already in the possession of a party but obtained for the purpose of the litigation and which might reveal the solicitor's view as to the merits of the client's case, or give a clue as to the advice which he had given the client: such documents are privileged.[3]

A copy of a privileged document is admissible in evidence, even if obtained by improper or even criminal means,[4] but the court may, on the application of the owner of the privileged original, prevent the holder of the copy from making use of it, by means of an action for delivery up and to restrain the holder from publishing or copying it.[5]

1 *Buttes Oil Co v Hammer (No 3)* [1981] QB 223, CA.
2 *Buttes Oil Co v Hammer (No 3)* [1981] QB 223, CA; *Dubai Bank Ltd v Galadari* [1990] Ch 98, CA; *Ventouris v Mountain* [1991] 1 WLR 607, CA, 619 (Bingham LJ).
3 *Lyell v Kennedy (No 3)* (1884) 27 Ch D 1, CA; *Dubai Bank Ltd v Galadari* [1990] Ch 98, CA; *Ventouris v Mountain* [1991] 1 WLR 607, CA, 615 (Bingham LJ).
4 *Calcraft v Guest* [1898] 1 QB 759, CA.
5 *Ashburton v Pape* [1913] 2 Ch 469, CA.

Waiver of privilege

9.33 It is often said that the privilege in a document is that of the client, and that only the client, and not his legal representative, can waive that privilege. This is true, but potentially misleading. A solicitor or barrister has ostensible authority to bind his client in any matter which arises in, or is incidental to, litigation, including the waiver of privilege on his behalf.[1] This explains how it is that privilege is sometimes waived by legal representatives by mistake.[2] However, where the interests of the client and the legal representative conflict, as, for example, on an application for wasted costs against the legal representatives, the latter cannot waive privilege on behalf of the client, in the exercise of the authority given to him by the client as his legal representative.[3]

Waiver of privilege in respect of part of a document waives privilege as to the whole,[4] unless it can be said that a single document deals with entirely different subject matters or different incidents and could be divided into two separate documents each dealing with a separate subject matter and each of which is complete.[5] If part of a privileged document is read by counsel in opening the case, or put to a witness in cross-examination, the opposing party is entitled to production of the whole of the privileged document,[6] and the court has no discretion not to order production.[7] However, if a client consents to disclosure of a privileged document for an expressly limited purpose, those limits will be respected, and the privilege will not be waived generally or lost altogether.[8]

Privilege does not cease on the conclusion of litigation, or of the matter in respect of which the advice was sought:

> '... as a general rule, one may say once privileged always privileged. I do not mean to say that privilege cannot be waived, but that the mere fact that documents used in a previous litigation are held and have not been destroyed does not amount to a waiver of the privilege.'[9]

Ordinarily, a party may inspect any document mentioned in a statement of case, witness statement, witness summary or affidavit.[10] Mention of a document does not entail an automatic and absolute waiver of privilege.[11] To say no more than 'I am acting on the advice of my solicitors and counsel' will not ordinarily justify further disclosure of the advice or of the circumstances in which any new witness statement came to be drafted.[12] The same principle seems likely to apply both in relation to witness statements and to affidavits.[13] Where a party inadvertently allows a privileged document to be inspected, the party who has inspected the document may use it or its contents only with the permission of the court.[14]

Where solicitors are instructed by insurers on behalf of themselves and their insured to defend a claim brought against the insured or to bring proceedings funded by a policy of legal expenses insurance, insurers and insured are entitled to assert privilege against third parties,[15] but there is a waiver of privilege as between insurers and the insured implicit in the joint retainer.[16] This is in addition to any entitlement to information which insurers have under the policy.[17] The waiver extends to all communications made by the insured to the solicitors until such time as an actual conflict of interest emerges, it being inherent in the original joint retainer that there is a potential conflict of interest.[18] If, after notification of an actual conflict of interest, the insured elects not to instruct separate solicitors, the waiver also extends to all communications made by the insured to the solicitors after such notification and the lapse of such further time as the insured reasonably requires in order to decide whether to instruct separate solicitors.[19] After the waiver has ceased, the insurer remains entitled to the provision of information obtained by the solicitors while the waiver subsisted, even if that information was not previously communicated to it.[20] In *TSB Bank Ltd v Robert Irving & Burns*,[21] the insurer argued that it was too late to assert privilege once the relevant information (answers given by an insured in conference) had been passed onto it by solicitors. The judge at first instance rejected this argument, striking out those paragraphs of the insurer's defence which made use of the relevant information, and accepting undertakings restraining use of the information by insurers.[22] The point was not pursued in the Court of Appeal, and it is suggested that the fact that the information has been communicated to insurers is not a bar to the court granting appropriate relief,[23] according to the usual equitable principles.

1 *Great Atlantic Insurance Co v Home Insurance Co* [1981] 1 WLR 529, CA.
2 See *Burnell v British Transport Commission* [1956] 1 QB 187, CA; *Great Atlantic Insurance Co v Home Insurance Co* [1981] 1 WLR 529, CA.
3 *Ridehalgh v Horsefield* [1994] Ch 205, 236–237, CA.
4 *Burnell v British Transport Commission* [1956] 1 QB 187, CA.
5 *Great Atlantic Insurance Co v Home Insurance Co* [1981] 1 WLR 529, CA.
6 *Burnell v British Transport Commission* [1956] 1 QB 187, CA (cross-examination); *Great Atlantic Insurance Co v Home Insurance Co* [1981] 1 WLR 529, CA (opening).
7 *Great Atlantic Insurance Co v Home Insurance Co* [1981] 1 WLR 529, CA.
8 *B v Auckland District Law Society* [2003] UKPC 38, [2003] 2 AC 736, 762, para 71 (Lord Millett).
9 *Calcraft v Guest* [1898] 1 QB 759, 761–762, CA (Lindley MR).
10 CPR r 31.14.
11 *Rubin v Expandable Ltd* [2008] EWCA Civ 59, [2008] 1 WLR 1099, para 37 (Rix LJ). See **PARA 9.20**.
12 *Re D (A Child)* [2011] EWCA Civ 684, [2011] 4 All ER 434, para 24 (Ward LJ). In any event, documents which merely contained advice as to the legal merits, as opposed to the factual basis on which the advice was tendered, were irrelevant and therefore not subject to disclosure under the old rules: *Svenska Handelsbanken v Sun Alliance and London Insurance plc* [1995] 2 Lloyd's Rep 84, 85 (Rix J); it is suggested that, similarly, they would not fall within the definition of standard disclosure under CPR r 31.6, and would not be subject to disclosure.

13 The same principle applied in relation to affidavits under the old rules: *Infields Ltd v P Rosen & Son* [1938] 3 All ER 591, 597, CA (Lord Greene MR).
14 CPR r 31.20. The court is exercising an equitable jurisdiction under r 31.20, so there are no rigid rules, but relief is likely to be granted where an inspecting party is seeking to take advantage of an error by the disclosing party which would have been obvious to a reasonable solicitor: see *Guinness Peat Properties Ltd v Fitzroy Robinson Partnership* [1987] 1 WLR 1027, CA; applied: *Pizzey v Ford Motor Co Ltd* [1994] PIQR P15, CA; *International Business Machines Corpn v Phoenix International (Computers) Ltd* [1995] 1 All ER 413; *Rawlinson & Hunter Trustees SA v Director of the Serious Fraud Office (No 2)* [2014] EWCA Civ 1129, [2015] 1 WLR 797, paras 9–11 (Moore-Bick LJ) and 49–52 (Longmore LJ) (saying that he regretted that the Court was bound by previous authorities, and that he would prefer a simpler approach: that where a privileged document was inadvertently disclosed, it should be returned). See also the warning given by Brightman LJ in *Buttes Oil Co v Hammer (No 3)* [1981] QB 223, 268, CA, that if the party making reference to the document in the pleading were to 'sit on the fence' until trial began, they would do so at their own risk.
15 *Hellenic Mutual War Risks Association (Bermuda) Ltd v Harrison, The Sagheera* [1997] 1 Lloyd's Rep 160, 165–166 (Rix J); *Winterthur Swiss Insurance Co v AG (Manchester) Ltd* [2006] EWHC 839 (Comm), para 113 (Aikens J).
16 *TSB Bank Ltd v Robert Irving & Burns* [1999] Lloyd's Rep IR 528, [2000] 2 All ER 826, CA.
17 See *Brown v Guardian Royal Exchange Assurance plc* [1994] 2 Lloyd's Rep 325, CA.
18 *TSB Bank Ltd v Robert Irving & Burns* [1999] Lloyd's Rep IR 528, [2000] 2 All ER 826, CA.
19 *TSB Bank Ltd v Robert Irving & Burns* [1999] Lloyd's Rep IR 528, [2000] 2 All ER 826, CA.
20 *TSB Bank Ltd v Robert Irving & Burns* [1999] Lloyd's Rep IR 528, [2000] 2 All ER 826, CA. Depending on the terms of the policy of insurance (or other agreement between insurer and insured) the purposes for which the information provided may be used may include the bringing of proceedings against a third party: *Winterthur Swiss Insurance Co v AG (Manchester) Ltd* [2006] EWHC 839 (Comm), para 116 (Aikens J) (subrogation clause in policy of after the event (ATE) legal expenses insurance sufficiently wide to allow access to and use of documents subject to common interest privilege in recovery action). If the insurer assigns its rights under a policy of insurance, the assignee is entitled to assert any legal professional privilege that was available to the insurer and is therefore entitled to documents which were subject to common interest privilege between insurer and insured: *Winterthur Swiss Insurance Co v AG (Manchester) Ltd* [2006] EWHC 839 (Comm), para 130 (Aikens J).
21 [1999] Lloyd's Rep IR 528, [2000] 2 All ER 826, CA.
22 The judgment appears only in the report at [1999] Lloyd's Rep IR 528.
23 Compare the position where a privileged document has been disclosed and inspected, in circumstances where it should have been obvious to the inspecting party that the document was privileged, and relief may nevertheless be granted: see note 14 above.

Fraud

9.34 Legal professional privilege does not attach to communications between lawyer and client if the purpose of the client (or where the client is being used by a third party as a mechanism for achieving a fraud, the purpose of that third party)[1] in seeking advice is to further or facilitate crime or fraud.[2] This is known as 'the fraud exception'.[3] The fraud exception applies to both legal advice privilege and litigation privilege.[4] This does not mean that any party against whom fraud is alleged cannot assert privilege: it is only in exceptional cases, in which there is strong prima facie evidence of fraud, that this will be the case.[5] Further, if all one has is a disputed version of events, it will be difficult to say that there is even a prima facie case of fraud, and particularly where the disputed version of events is the very same issue that is to be tried in the proceedings; and it may be unfair in the ordinary run of cases to order inspection merely because communications with a party's solicitors are untrue and would, if acted upon, lead to the commission of the crime of perjury; if however the evidence of crime or fraud is freestanding and independent and particularly if its evaluation does not require any judgment to be reached in relation to the issues to be tried, it may be perfectly possible, even on a prima facie case basis, to decide whether the fraud exception applies.[6]

1 *R v Central Criminal Court, ex parte Francis* [1989] 1 AC 346, HL; *The Owners and/or Demise Charterers of the Dredger 'Kamal XXVI' and the Barge 'Kamal XXIV' v The Owners of the Ship 'Ariela'* [2010] EWHC 2531 (Comm), [2011] 1 Lloyd's Rep 291, para 32 (Burton J).
2 *R v Cox and Railton* (1884) 14 QBD 153; *O'Rourke v Darbishire* [1920] AC 581, HL, 604 (Viscount Finlay), 613 (Lord Sumner), 621–623 (Lord Parmoor), 632–633 (Lord Wrenbury); *Kuwait Airways Corpn v Iraqi Airways Co (No 6)* [2005] EWCA Civ 286, [2005] 1 WLR 2734, para 42 (Longmore LJ).
3 *Kuwait Airways Corpn v Iraqi Airways Co (No 6)* [2005] EWCA Civ 286, [2005] 1 WLR 2734, para 21 (Longmore LJ).
4 *Kuwait Airways Corpn v Iraqi Airways Co (No 6)* [2005] EWCA Civ 286, [2005] 1 WLR 2734.
5 *O'Rourke v Darbishire* [1920] AC 581, HL, 604 (Viscount Finlay), 613 (Lord Sumner), 621–623 (Lord Parmoor), 632–633 (Lord Wrenbury); *Buttes Oil Co v Hammer (No 3)* [1981] QB 223, CA; *Kuwait Airways Corpn v Iraqi Airways Co (No 6)* [2005] EWCA Civ 286, [2005] 1 WLR 2734, paras 36–37 and 42 (Longmore LJ).
6 *O'Rourke v Darbishire* [1920] AC 581, 632–633, HL (Lord Wrenbury); *Kuwait Airways Corpn v Iraqi Airways Co (No 6)* [2005] EWCA Civ 286, [2005] 1 WLR 2734, paras 36–37 and 42 (Longmore LJ). This is similar to the position in relation to the fraud exception to 'without prejudice' privilege: see **PARA 9.38**, note 5.

'WITHOUT PREJUDICE' COMMUNICATIONS

The general rule

9.35   Offers to settle are sometimes made on an 'open' basis, which means that they can be referred to without restriction in legal proceedings. More usually, however, parties to litigation, or between whom a dispute has arisen, negotiate on a 'without prejudice' basis, either in writing or orally. It has long been established that such communications are not admissible in evidence, even as to costs at the conclusion of litigation.[1] The rule is based partly on public policy, and partly on implied agreement.[2] The public policy considerations were summarised by Oliver LJ in *Cutts v Head*:[3]

> 'That the rule rests, at least in part, upon public policy is clear from many authorities, and the convenient starting point of the inquiry is the nature of the underlying policy. It is that parties should be encouraged so far as possible to settle their disputes without resort to litigation and should not be discouraged by the knowledge that anything that is said in the course of such negotiations (and that includes, of course, as much the failure to reply to an offer as an actual reply) may be used to their prejudice in the course of the proceedings. They should ... be encouraged fully and frankly to put their cards on the table ... The public policy justification, in truth, essentially rests on the desirability of preventing statements or offers made in the course of negotiations for settlement being brought before the court of trial as admissions on the question of liability.'

In *Rush & Tompkins v Greater London Council*,[4] the House of Lords decided that, in addition to being inadmissible in evidence, without prejudice communications are privileged from disclosure.[5]

The protection given to 'without prejudice' communications covers all genuine negotiations,[6] and extends to all documents forming part of the negotiations, whether or not they are documents making offers, including the initial offer letter.[7] Although it is normal practice to mark communications 'without prejudice', if it is clear from the surrounding circumstances that the parties were seeking to compromise an action, evidence of the content of those negotiations will, as a general rule, not be admissible at trial and cannot be used to establish an admission or partial admission.[8] Conversely, marking a letter 'without prejudice' does not make it privileged if it does not form part of negotiations to settle a dispute, and the court can examine documentation which is said to be 'without prejudice' in order to determine its true nature.[9]

1 See *Walker v Wilsher* (1889) 23 QBD 335, CA; applied: *Reed Executive plc v Reed Business Information Ltd* [2004] EWCA Civ 887, [2004] 1 WLR 3026, para 34 (Jacob LJ). This means that where the parties hold discussions on a 'without prejudice' (rather than 'without prejudice save as to costs') basis about whether to mediate, the court when it comes to the question of costs may not be able to decide whether one side or the other was unreasonable in refusing mediation: *Reed Executive plc v Reed Business Information Ltd* [2004] EWCA Civ 887, [2004] 1 WLR 3026, para 34 (Jacob LJ).
2 See *Cutts v Head* [1984] Ch 290, CA.
3 [1984] Ch 290, 306, CA; this passage was cited with approval by Lord Griffiths in *Rush & Tompkins Ltd v Greater London Council* [1989] AC 1280, 1299, HL.
4 [1989] AC 1280, HL.
5 At 1304–1305 (Lord Griffiths).
6 *Rush & Tompkins v Greater London Council* [1989] AC 1280, HL.
7 *South Shropshire District Council v Amos* [1986] 1 WLR 1271, CA.
8 *Rush & Tompkins v Greater London Council* [1989] AC 1280, 1299–1300, HL (Lord Griffiths).
9 *South Shropshire District Council v Amos* [1986] 1 WLR 1271, CA. See also **PARA 8.4**.

'Without prejudice save as to costs'

9.36 The implied agreement which arises out of marking communications 'without prejudice' is that they will not be referred to at all in the litigation, even in relation to costs.[1] Where communications are marked 'without prejudice save as to costs', the implied agreement is to the effect that although the communications remain inadmissible as to the merits, they are admissible on questions of costs, in all cases where the issue is more than a simple money claim so that a payment into court is not an appropriate way of proceeding.[2] In *Cutts v Head*, the Court of Appeal decided, having heard submissions establishing a practice amongst the legal profession of making offers 'without prejudice save as to costs', that the implied agreement arising out of the use of the words 'without prejudice' was altered if the offer contained a reservation in these terms.[3] In addition, Oliver LJ indicated that in his view the public policy considerations did not prevent such an implied agreement, and in fact favoured it, as it was likely to encourage, rather than to discourage, settlement if parties knew that 'without prejudice' correspondence could be shown to the court in relation to costs, but only after the merits had been decided.[4] In *Unilever plc v Procter & Gamble Co*,[5] Robert Walker LJ said that there seemed to be no reason why, in principle, parties to without prejudice negotiations should not expressly or impliedly agree to vary the application of the public policy rule in other respects, either by extending or by limiting its reach.[6]

1 *Cutts v Head* [1984] Ch 290, 307, CA (Oliver LJ).
2 *Cutts v Head* [1984] Ch 290, CA, approved in *Rush & Tompkins v Greater London Council* [1989] AC 1280, HL. See also **PARA 9.35**, note 1.
3 [1984] Ch 290, 310, 316, CA.
4 At 307–308.
5 [2000] 1 WLR 2436, CA.
6 At 2445.

Subsequent litigation and other parties to the same litigation

9.37   The 'without prejudice' rule extends to any subsequent litigation connected with the same subject matter, so that admissions made in a genuine attempt to reach a settlement in the earlier litigation are inadmissible.[1] Similarly, admissions made to reach settlement with a different party in the same litigation are also inadmissible whether or not settlement was reached with that party.[2]

1 *Rush & Tompkins v Greater London Council* [1989] AC 1280, 1301, HL (Lord Griffiths).
2 *Rush & Tompkins v Greater London Council* [1989] AC 1280, 1301, HL (Lord Griffiths).

Exceptions to the 'without prejudice' rule

9.38   There are certain situations in which the court will allow reference to 'without prejudice' communications. These include the eight situations set out by Robert Walker LJ in *Unilever plc v Procter & Gamble Co*,[1] and two additions by the Supreme Court in *Oceanbulk Shipping and Trading SA v TMT Asia Ltd*:[2]

(1)   where the issue is whether 'without prejudice' communications have resulted in a concluded compromise agreement;[3]
(2)   in order to show that an agreement apparently concluded between the parties during the negotiations should be set aside on the ground of misrepresentation, fraud or undue influence;
(3)   even if there is no concluded compromise, where a clear statement is made by one party to negotiations and on which the other party is intended to act and does in fact act, the statement may be admissible as giving rise to an estoppel;[4]
(4)   apart from any concluded contract or estoppel, where the exclusion of the evidence as to what one party said or wrote in 'without prejudice' communications would act as a cloak for perjury, blackmail or other 'unambiguous impropriety';[5]
(5)   in order to explain delay or apparent acquiescence (for instance, on an application to strike out proceedings for want of prosecution);
(6)   in an action for negligence against solicitors, to show whether the claimant had acted reasonably to mitigate his loss in his conduct and conclusion of negotiations for the compromise of proceedings;[6]
(7)   where the offer is expressly made 'without prejudice except as to costs';[7] or
(8)   in specific circumstances limited to matrimonial cases;
(9)   in order to show that a settlement agreement should be rectified;[8]
(10)   as an aid to construction of an agreement which results from without prejudice negotiations, as part of the factual matrix or surrounding circumstances.[9]

In addition, the protection afforded to 'without prejudice' communications may be lost. If they are referred to at trial by one party, the other party may then deploy them freely. If they are referred to by one party on an interim application, the usual rule is that they may not be referred to by the other party at trial before a different judge.[10] However, if 'without prejudice' communications are referred to by one party on an interim application in order to advance its case on the merits, that party loses the right it would otherwise have had to object to the admissibility at trial of any admissions made in the course of the same 'without prejudice' communications.[11]

1 [2000] 1 WLR 2436, 2444–2445, CA; approved: *Bradford & Bingley plc v Rashid* [2006] UKHL 37, [2006] 1 WLR 2066, paras 18 (Lord Hoffmann), 63 (Lord Brown) and 88 (Lord Mance); *Oceanbulk Shipping and Trading SA v TMT Asia Ltd* [2010] UKSC 44, [2011] 1 AC 662, para 32 (Lord Clarke).

2 [2010] UKSC 44, [2011] 1 AC 662.

3 See also *Muller v Linsley & Mortimer* [1996] PNLR 74, CA; *Bradford & Bingley plc v Rashid* [2006] UKHL 37, [2006] 1 WLR 2066, paras 66–67 (Lord Brown).

4 See, eg, *Fortisbank SA v Trenwick International Ltd* [2005] EWHC 399 (Comm), [2005] Lloyd's Rep IR 464, 472, para 37 (Gloster J) (reference made to 'without prejudice' correspondence in support of (unsuccessful) allegation of estoppel).

5 The test is 'unambiguous impropriety' and a serious and substantial risk of perjury is not sufficient: *Berry Trade Ltd v Moussavi* [2003] EWCA Civ 715, para 48 (Peter Gibson LJ). Inconsistency between an admission made in 'without prejudice' negotiations and a pleaded case or stated position is not sufficient to lose the admitting party the protection of the privilege; what is required is abuse of the privilege, for example by using a privileged occasion to make a threat in the nature of blackmail (such as a threat of future perjury): *Savings & Investment Bank Ltd v Fincken* [2003] EWCA Civ 1630, [2004] 1 WLR 667, para 57 (Rix LJ); approved: *Bradford & Bingley plc v Rashid* [2006] UKHL 37, [2006] 1 WLR 2066, para 65 (Lord Brown). This is similar to the position in relation to the fraud exception to legal advice and litigation privilege: see **PARA 9.34**. The fact that the party alleged to have made the admission does not challenge the evidence of the admission is not a critical factor: *Savings & Investment Bank Ltd v Fincken* [2003] EWCA Civ 1630, [2004] 1 WLR 667, para 56 (Rix LJ). See also *Re Daintrey, ex p Holt* [1893] 2 QB 116 (a 'without prejudice' letter containing a statement amounting to an act of bankruptcy was held to be admissible in bankruptcy proceedings to prove that the statement was made); *Bradford & Bingley plc v Rashid* [2006] UKHL 37, [2006] 1 WLR 2066 ('without prejudice' rule has no application to apparently open communications designed only to discuss repayment of an admitted liability rather than to negotiation and compromise a disputed liability: paras 1 (Lord Hoffmann), 37 (Lord Walker), 73 (Lord Brown) and 83 (Lord Mance)).

6 *Muller v Linsley & Mortimer* [1996] PNLR 74, CA.

7 See **PARA 9.36**.

8 *Oceanbulk Shipping and Trading SA v TMT Asia Ltd* [2010] UKSC 44, [2011] 1 AC 662, para 33 (Lord Clarke).

9 *Oceanbulk Shipping and Trading SA v TMT Asia Ltd* [2010] UKSC 44, [2011] 1 AC 662.

10 *Family Housing Association (Manchester) Ltd v Michael Hyde and Partners* [1993] 1 WLR 354, CA (application to strike out claim for want of prosecution).

11 *Family Housing Association (Manchester) Ltd v Michael Hyde and Partners* [1993] 1 WLR 354, CA; *Somatra Ltd v Sinclair Roche & Temperley* [2000] 1 WLR 2453, CA ('without prejudice' discussions covertly recorded with audio and video equipment).

EVIDENCE FOR TRIAL

Witnesses of fact

9.39   The formal requirements for witness statements are set out in Practice Direction 32. The Commercial Court Guide also emphasises certain points. These include two in particular which are often overlooked: the witness statement should be in the witness's own words;[1] and the statement should not contain lengthy quotations from documents.[2] Witness statements stand as evidence-in-chief unless the trial judge orders that the witness should give some or all of his evidence-in-chief orally, before he is cross-examined.[3] Permission is required for a witness to amplify the evidence in his witness statement or to give evidence in relation to new matters which have arisen since the witness statement was served, and will be given only if the court considers that there is good reason not to confine the evidence of the witness to the contents of his witness statement.[4] Where a witness proposes materially to add to, alter, correct or retract what is said in his first statement, a supplemental statement (for which permission is required) should normally be served.[5] A party who has decided not to call, to give oral evidence at trial, a witness whose statement has been served but wishes to rely upon the evidence must put the statement in as hearsay evidence unless the court otherwise orders.[6] If he does not put the statement in as hearsay evidence, any other party may do so.[7]

1 Paragraph H1.1(i).
2 Paragraph H1.1(iii).
3 CPR r 32.5(2); Commercial Court Guide, para H1.6.
4 CPR r 32.5(3)– (4).
5 Commercial Court Guide, para H1.7(b).
6 CPR r 32.5(1); Commercial Court Guide, para H1.8(a).
7 CPR r 32.5(5); Commercial Court Guide, para H1.8(b).

Expert evidence

9.40   The Civil Procedure Rules make detailed provision for the instruction of expert witnesses, including single joint experts in appropriate cases, and production of expert reports.[1] It is unusual for a single joint expert to be instructed to give evidence as to underwriting or broking practice in the Commercial Court; indeed, the Commercial Court Guide acknowledges that in many cases in the Commercial Court, the use of single joint experts is not appropriate.[2]

1 CPR Pt 35 and Practice Direction 35. Reference should also be made to the *Guidance for the Instruction of Experts in Civil Claims 2014*.
2 Paragraph H2.2.

REMEDIES

Damages not debt

9.41   A claim under a policy of insurance is a claim for damages, not a claim in debt.[1]

The principles applicable to measurement of loss in claims against insurers are considered in **CHAPTER 6**.

1 See *Grant v Royal Exchange Assurance Co* (1816) 5 M&S 438 (marine policy: claim was for unliquidated damages); *Luckie v Bushby* (1853) 13 CB 864 (policy on goods: claim was for unliquidated damages); *Irving v Manning* (1847) 1 HLC 287, HL (valued policy on a ship: claim was for liquidated damages); *Chandris v Argo Insurance Co Ltd* [1963] 2 Lloyd's Rep 65, 74 (Megaw J); *Firma C-Trade SA v Newcastle P & I Association, The Padre Island (No 2)* [1991] 2 AC 1, 35–36, HL (Lord Goff); *I M Properties plc v Cape & Dalgleish* [1999] QB 297, 304, CA (Waller LJ). See also **PARA 11.60**.

Declarations

9.42   Proceedings are sometimes brought in insurance cases for a declaration,[1] for example, by insurers seeking a declaration that they have validly avoided a policy of insurance, or that the insured is not entitled to an indemnity in respect of a particular claim; and by insureds seeking a declaration that a policy has not been validly avoided, or that insurers are obliged to indemnify them in respect of a particular claim. Save perhaps in exceptional circumstances, a reinsurer may not seek a declaration in respect of the rights of the insured and insurers under the underlying contract of insurance.[2]

Particular issues arise in the context of liability insurance, in which the right to indemnity arises only when the insured's liability to the third party claimant has been ascertained, whether by judgment, award or agreement.[3] The court has jurisdiction to grant declarations as to the extent to which valid and applicable cover exists under such a policy in proceedings brought by the insured against the insurer before the insured's liability to the third party claimant has been fully determined.[4] Whether it will do so is ultimately a matter of practicality and convenience.[5] The court may also grant a negative declaration (that is, a declaration that the claimant is not liable to the defendant, in which the usual roles of claimant and defendant are reversed) in favour of an insured who brings an action at the instigation of his liability insurers,[6] although such a course in personal injury actions is and should be unusual.[7] The role of the court is to resolve actual not hypothetical issues and where no proceedings have been issued in relation to the third party claim, the court may be reluctant to entertain proceedings for a declaration which may ultimately be unnecessary.[8] Other factors which the court is likely to take into account include whether the parties have admitted or agreed the facts on the basis of which the court is asked to adjudicate, the extent to which any assumptions on the basis of which it is asked to adjudicate may prove to be artificial and inaccurate, and whether, after an unfavourable adjudication on one set of assumptions, a party might advance another factual or expert case in order to avoid or circumvent the outcome of the initial adjudication.[9] The court is not necessarily bound by or anchored to the precise words of the relief as set out in the claim form or particulars of claim, and if any part of such wording is objectionable, it is always open to the court to modify it and to make one or more declarations in a form as may be just and appropriate.[10] If proceedings for a declaration have been determined at first instance, the appellate court is unlikely to invoke the hypothetical or otherwise unsatisfactory nature of the proceedings as grounds for refusing to hear an appeal.[11]

Where an insurer claims a declaration that it is not liable under a policy and the insured counterclaims that it is entitled to be indemnified for its losses, both parties are substantial claimants founding their claims on the same body of facts so that if the claim fails the counterclaim will succeed, and in these circumstances an order for security for costs may be made in favour of the insurer in respect of the full amount of their costs of the counterclaim, and not the amount by which the insurer's costs are likely to be increased by the counterclaim over what they would otherwise be.[12]

1 CPR r 40.20 provides: 'The court may make binding declarations whether or not any other remedy is claimed.'
2 *Meadows Indemnity Co Ltd v The Insurance Corporation of Ireland plc* [1989] 2 Lloyd's Rep 298, CA, 305 (Neill LJ) and 309 (May LJ) (in relation to RSC Ord 15, r 16); considered: *Raiffeisen Zentralbank Österreich AG v Five Star Trading LLC* [2001] EWCA Civ 68, [2001] QB 825, para 87 (Mance LJ). Although matters have moved on since *Meadows*, and the modern approach is that the grant of relief is discretionary and therefore not subject to rigid rules, a person not a party to a contract generally has no locus (standing), save perhaps in exceptional circumstances, to obtain a declaration in respect of rights of other parties to that particular contract at least where the contracting parties themselves are not in dispute as to their respective rights and obligations: *Federal-Mogul Asbestos Personal Injury Trust v Federal-Mogul Ltd* [2014] EWHC 2002 (Comm), [2014] Lloyd's Rep IR 671, paras 93-94 (Eder J).

3 *West Wake Price & Co v Ching* [1957] 1 WLR 45, 49 (Devlin J); *Post Office v Norwich Union Fire Insurance Society Ltd* [1967] 2 QB 363, CA, 374–375 (Lord Denning MR), 376 (Harman LJ), 377–378 (Salmon LJ); *Bradley v Eagle Star Insurance Co Ltd* [1989] AC 957, 966, HL (Lord Brandon); *Horbury Building Systems Ltd v Hampden Insurance NV* [2004] EWCA Civ 418, [2007] Lloyd's Rep IR 237, para 30 (Mance LJ).

4 *Carpenter v Ebblewhite* [1939] 1 KB 347, CA, 357–358 (Greer LJ) and 363 (MacKinnon LJ) (third party claimant joined insurer as co-defendant in action against insured; claim for a declaration premature because no dispute had yet arisen between third party claimant and insurer); *Post Office v Norwich Union Fire Insurance Society Ltd* [1967] 2 QB 363, 374, CA (Lord Denning MR); *Brice v J H Wackerbarth (Australasia) Pty Ltd* [1974] 2 Lloyd's Rep 274, 276, CA (Lord Denning MR); *Firma C-Trade SA v Newcastle P & I Association, The Fanti and the Padre Island (No 2)* [1989] 1 Lloyd's Rep 239, CA, 258 (Stuart-Smith LJ: insured can obtain a declaration of entitlement to indemnity before payment under 'pay to be paid' clause; point not considered on appeal: [1991] 2 AC 1, HL); *Horbury Building Systems Ltd v Hampden Insurance NV* [2004] EWCA Civ 418, [2007] Lloyd's Rep IR 237, para 30 (Mance LJ); *William McIlroy (Swindon) Ltd v Quinn Insurance Ltd* [2011] EWCA Civ 825, paras 19 (Sir Henry Brooke) and 28–30 and 47 (Rix LJ).

5 *Horbury Building Systems Ltd v Hampden Insurance NV* [2004] EWCA Civ 418, [2007] Lloyd's Rep IR 237, para 30 (Mance LJ).

6 *Toropdar v D* [2009] EWHC 567 (QB), [2010] Lloyd's Rep IR 358, paras 85–91 (Christopher Clarke J).

7 *Toropdar v D* [2009] EWHC 567 (QB), [2010] Lloyd's Rep IR 358, para 101 (Christopher Clarke J).

8 *E I Du Pont de Nemours & Co v Agnew* [1987] 2 Lloyd's Rep 585, 595, CA (Bingham LJ); *Horbury Building Systems Ltd v Hampden Insurance NV* [2004] EWCA Civ 418, [2007] Lloyd's Rep IR 237, paras 13 (Keene LJ) and 29–34 (Mance LJ). The fact that an issue may be of general importance to the insurance market is likely to make the court more cautious about deciding it in circumstances where a decision is not required in order to determine the rights of the parties to the proceedings: *Arash Shipping Enterprises Co Ltd v Groupama Transport* [2011] EWCA Civ 620, [2012] Lloyd's Rep IR 40, paras 45–48 (Stanley Burnton LJ) and 61–64 (Tomlinson LJ). In *Arash Shipping*, additional factors tending towards caution were that the issue was as to the effect of legislation which created a criminal offence (Council Regulation (EU) No 961/2010 imposing economic sanctions on Iranian persons and entities), the case had come before the court on an expedited basis with the need for an immediate decision and the time available did not permit full and considered argument, and neither the Court of Appeal nor the Supreme Court was the court of final decision in relation to the correct interpretation of the legislative provision, which was the European Court of Justice (paras 47–50 (Stanley Burnton LJ) and 63–64 (Tomlinson LJ)). Tomlinson LJ did however think it appropriate to give an indication of his preliminary views on the issue (para 64).

9 *Horbury Building Systems Ltd v Hampden Insurance NV* [2004] EWCA Civ 418, [2007] Lloyd's Rep IR 237, paras 29–34 (Mance LJ); *Aspen Insurance UK Ltd v Adana Construction Ltd* [2015] EWCA Civ 176, [2015] Lloyd's Rep IR 511, paras 24–26 (Christopher Clarke LJ) and 75 (Gloster LJ).

10 *Federal-Mogul Asbestos Personal Injury Trust v Federal-Mogul Ltd* [2014] EWHC 2002 (Comm), [2014] Lloyd's Rep IR 671, para 84 (Eder J).

11 *Horbury Building Systems Ltd v Hampden Insurance NV* [2004] EWCA Civ 418, [2007] Lloyd's Rep IR 237, paras 13 (Keene LJ) and 34 (Mance LJ).

12 *Jones v Environcom Ltd* [2009] EWHC 16 (Comm), [2010] Lloyd's Rep IR 190, paras 26–27 (Gloster J).

Rectification

9.43   Rectification is, technically, an equitable remedy. The principles applicable to rectification are considered at **PARAS 3.28–3.35**.

Claims against insurance brokers

9.44   The principles governing the award of damages in proceedings against insurance brokers are considered at **PARAS 16.33–16.44**.

INTEREST[1]

9.45 The court has a discretion to award simple interest on damages for all or any of the period between the date on which the cause of action arose, and the date on which judgment was given, or the sum was paid, if before judgment.[2] There is no power to award interest in respect of sums paid in respect of damages before proceedings are issued.[3] After judgment and until payment, the party in whose favour the judgment was awarded is entitled to interest under the Judgments Act 1838. An award of interest is almost invariably made, with the judge exercising his discretion as to the rate and the period for which interest is awarded. In *Birkett v Hayes*,[4] Eveleigh LJ summarised the position in this way:

> 'In awarding interest the judge is exercising a discretion. In the great majority of cases the plaintiff could have proceeded with greater dispatch; and yet it may well be wrong to deprive him of interest particularly as the defendant will have had the use of the money. I therefore think that we should approach this matter on the basis that the court should arrive at a final figure which will be fair, generally speaking, to both parties.'

Following the decision of the House of Lords in *Sempra Metals Ltd v Inland Revenue Commissioners*,[5] the loss suffered as a result of the late payment of money is recoverable at common law, subject to the ordinary rules of remoteness which apply to all claims of damages. A claimant must plead and prove his actual interest losses if he wishes to recover compound interest on this basis.[6] Where interest is claimed by an assignee by reference to loss of return on investments, the losses which an assignee is entitled to recover are the insured's losses, and are to be assessed by reference to the returns which the insured would have achieved if there had been no assignment.[7] It is not legitimate to avoid the statutory limitation on the basis on which interest can be awarded under the Senior Courts Act 1981 (ie simple not compound interest) by claiming interest under the statute at a higher rate than would otherwise be appropriate.[8]

The award of interest will generally run from the accrual of the cause of action,[9] which means, in the case of a policy of insurance, from the date of loss.[10] Where a claim is made under a policy of insurance which is not straightforward, insurers will need to investigate the claim, whether as to liability or quantum, or both, before making payment to the insured, and this has sometimes been reflected by awarding interest from a date later than the date of loss.[11]

Occasionally, the court will decide not to award interest. For example, in *Reynolds v Phoenix Assurance Co Ltd*,[12] Forbes J awarded damages to the insured based on the cost of reinstatement of a building after a fire. There was evidence before him that the cost of reinstating the building at the date of trial was 15 per cent higher than it had been at the date of the fire, whereas simple interest at prevailing rates for the same period (three years and nine months) would have amounted to an additional 34 per cent. Forbes J awarded the increased cost of reinstatement without interest, on the basis that this was sufficient to put the insured in the position they would have been in had the insurer not refused to pay under the policy.

Insurers who have indemnified an insured are entitled to bring a recovery action in its name not only to recover the loss but also interest, and the fact that they have paid off the insured is *res inter alios acta* as far as the defendant to the recovery action is concerned (which means it is no business of his, and that interest is awarded on the same basis as it would have been if the insurer had not indemnified the insured).[13] As between the insurer and the insured, a term is implied into the contract of insurance allowing the insured to retain interest accruing prior to the date of settlement by the insurers, and entitling the insurers to interest thereafter.[14]

Delay resulting from failure by the claimant to prosecute the claim may lead to a reduction in the period during which interest is payable,[15] or a reduction in the rate of interest awarded,[16] although this will depend on the circumstances: the court may take the view that no reduction is appropriate as the paying party has had the benefit of the money for the whole of the period, including the period of delay.[17] The delay must be exceptional and inexcusable, having made allowance for the fact that delays and lulls do occur in litigation.[18]

Historically the Commercial Court generally awarded interest at base rate plus one per cent under s 35A of the Senior Courts Act 1981 unless that was shown to be unfair to one party or the other or to be otherwise inappropriate, but in the light of recent interest rate developments there is no presumption that base rate plus one per cent is the appropriate measure of a commercial rate of interest.[19] At the present time, a commercial rate of interest is generally taken in the Commercial Court to be 2% above base rate.[20] The rate which is generally applied may be displaced by evidence as to the rate at which claimants with the general attributes of the actual claimant in the case (though not with any special or particular attribute) could borrow funds during the relevant period.[21] The Commercial Court practice is likely to be followed in commercial cases in other courts.[22]

The devaluation of the currency of an indemnity or damages ordered to be paid pursuant to a judgment is unlikely to affect the rate of interest awarded in a purely domestic case which does not raise issues of comparative currency values.[23] Although detailed investigation of a claimant's tax position is unlikely to be appropriate, the court will not award interest for loss of use of money if it appears that the effect of taxation would have been such that the claimant is unlikely to have suffered the loss in question.[24]

1 See also PARAS **6.6** and **16.45**.
2 Section 35A of the Senior Courts Act 1981; s 69 of the County Courts Act 1984; *Adcock v Co-operative Insurance Society Ltd* [2000] Lloyd's Rep IR 657, 661, CA (Waller LJ). Section 35A of the Senior Courts Act and s 69 of the County Courts Act 1984 are in virtually identical terms, and decisions in relation to one may usually be applied to the other.
3 *I M Properties plc v Cape & Dalgleish* [1999] QB 297, CA, distinguishing *Westdeutsche Landesbank Girozentrale v Islington London Borough Council* [1996] AC 669, HL.
4 [1982] 1 WLR 816, 824, CA. Although *Birkett v Hayes* was a personal injury case, it is suggested that Eveleigh LJ's dictum represents the approach generally taken to the discretion to award interest on damages.
5 [2007] UKHL 34, [2008] 1 AC 561.
6 *Sempra Metals Ltd v Inland Revenue Commissioners* [2007] UKHL 34, [2008] 1 AC 561. In *Equitas Ltd v Walsham Brothers & Co Ltd* [2013] EWHC 3264 (Comm), [2014] Lloyd's Rep IR 398, Males J said (at para 118) that *Sempra Metals* was a case where, despite what was actually said about the need to plead and prove a loss, the damages actually awarded were determined by taking a conventional rate and awarding compound interest; and (at para 123(v)) that it was both principled and predictable, as well as being in accordance with what was actually awarded in *Sempra Metals*, to conclude that, at least in a typical commercial case, the normal and conventional measure of damages for breach of an obligation to remit funds consists of compound interest at a conventional rate.

7 *Equitas Ltd v Walsham Brothers & Co Ltd* [2013] EWHC 3264 (Comm), [2014] Lloyd's Rep IR 398, paras 132–133 (Males J).

8 *Thai Airways International Public Company Ltd v KI Holdings Co Ltd* [2015] EWHC 1476 (Comm), para 23 (Leggatt J).

9 *BP Exploration (Libya) Ltd v Hunt (No 2)* [1979] 1 WLR 783, 846 (Robert Goff J).

10 *Quorum v Schramm (No 2)* [2002] 2 Lloyd's Rep 72, paras 3–6 (Thomas J); as to accrual of the cause of action, see further **PARA 11.60**.

11 See *Quorum v Schramm (No 2)* [2002] 2 Lloyd's Rep 72, para 7 (Thomas J), and the cases referred to there; *Synergy Health (UK) Ltd v CGU Insurance plc* [2010] EWHC 2583 (Comm), [2011] Lloyd's Rep IR 500, para 263 (Flaux J).

12 [1978] 2 Lloyd's Rep 440.

13 *H Cousins & Co Ltd v D & C Carriers Ltd* [1971] 2 QB 230, CA, distinguishing *Harbutt's Plasticine Ltd v Wayne Tank and Pump Co Ltd* [1970] 1 QB 447, CA. See further **CHAPTER 12**, Subrogation.

14 *H Cousins & Co Ltd v D & C Carriers Ltd* [1971] 2 QB 230, CA.

15 See *Metal Box Co Ltd v Currys Ltd* [1988] 1 WLR 175; *Adcock v Co-operative Insurance Society Ltd* [2000] Lloyd's Rep IR 657, CA.

16 See *Derby Resources AG v Blue Corinth Marine Co Ltd (No 2), The Athenian Harmony* [1998] 2 Lloyd's Rep 425 (Colman J).

17 See *Berger and Light Diffusers Pty Ltd v Pollock* [1973] 2 Lloyd's Rep 442, 466 (Kerr J).

18 *Challinor v Juliet Bellis & Co* [2013] EWHC 620 (Ch), para 48 (Hildyard J); applied: *Hackney Empire Ltd v Aviva Insurance UK Ltd (No 2)* [2013] EWHC 2212 (TCC), 149 Con LR 213, paras 19 and 28 (Edwards-Stuart J).

19 *Admiralty and Commercial Courts Guide* (9th edition, 2011), para J14.

20 *Involnert Management Inc v Aprilgrange Ltd* [2015] EWHC 2834 (Comm), para 9 (Leggatt J).

21 *Shearson Lehman Hutton Inc v Maclaine Watson & Co Ltd (No 2)* [1990] 3 All ER 723, 732–734, [1990] 1 Lloyd's Rep 441, 451–453 (Webster J); *Baker v Black Sea and Baltic General Insurance Co Ltd* [1996] LRLR 353, CA (point not considered on appeal: [1998] 1 WLR 974, HL); *Jaura v Ahmed* [2002] EWCA Civ 210; *West v Ian Finlay and Associates* [2014] EWCA Civ 316, [2014] BLR 324, paras 70–82 (Gloster LJ). See also note 7 above.

22 *Adcock v Co-operative Insurance Society Ltd* [2000] Lloyd's Rep IR 657, 662, CA (Waller LJ); and see *Reinhard v Ondra LLP* [2015] EWHC 2943 (Ch); *Challinor v Juliet Bellis & Co* [2013] EWHC 620 (Ch), paras 13–46 (Hildyard J) (rate of interest not considered on appeal: [2015] EWCA Civ 59); *Persimmon Homes (South Coast) Ltd v Hall Aggregates (South Coast) Ltd* [2012] EWHC 2429 (TCC), paras 10–17 (Ramsey J); *West v Ian Finlay and Associates* [2014] EWCA Civ 316, [2014] BLR 324, paras 70–82 (Gloster LJ) (appeal from TCC).

23 *Berger and Light Diffusers Pty Ltd v Pollock* [1973] 2 Lloyd's Rep 442, 466 (Kerr J) (devaluation of sterling in 1967).

24 *Deeny v Gooda Walker Ltd (No 4)* [1995] STC 696 (Phillips J).

COSTS AGAINST NON-PARTIES

9.46 The main principles governing awards of costs in civil proceedings are contained in s 51 of the Senior Courts Act 1981, which applies to proceedings in the High Court and the county courts, and to the Civil Division of the Court of Appeal, in Parts 43 to 48 of the Civil Procedure Rules and the accompanying Practice Directions, and in related case law.

Of particular importance in the context of insurance is the extent to which insurers who fund proceedings may, if their insured is unsuccessful in the proceedings, be ordered to pay the costs of the successful party.[1] Where an insurer is pursuing a recovery action by way of subrogation, the issue is less likely to arise, as the insurer is obliged to indemnify the insured against the costs of the proceedings, including any costs ordered to be paid by the insured to the successful party.[2] The jurisdiction of the High Court and county courts to order a non-party to pay costs is based on s 51(3) of the Senior Courts Act 1981,[3] which provides:

'The court shall have full power to determine by whom and to what extent the costs are to be paid.'

Although wording in materially identical terms first appeared in s 5 of the Supreme Court of Judicature Act 1890, early decisions of the Court of Appeal had limited its application to parties to proceedings,[4] and it was not until the decision of the House of Lords in *Aiden Shipping Co Ltd v Interbulk Ltd*[5] in 1986 that it was established that the jurisdiction to award costs pursuant to s 51 included jurisdiction to award costs against non-parties.

The jurisdiction is limited to costs incurred in the proceedings before the court, and does not extend to costs incurred in earlier actions between the same parties.[6] A party wishing to make an application for costs pursuant to s 51(3) should make an application to add the insurer as a party to the proceedings for the purposes of costs only.[7] The insurer must then be given a reasonable opportunity to attend a hearing at which the matter may be considered.[8] The making of an order for costs against a party does not preclude the making of an order for costs against a non-party under s 51(3), although the successful party will only be entitled to recover in all up to the total of their (assessed) costs.[9]

It is only in exceptional cases that the court will make an order for the payment of costs by a person who is not a party to proceedings.[10] The circumstances in which the funding of litigation by insurers may be considered exceptional so as to warrant an award of costs pursuant to s 51(3) are as follows. Where the limit of indemnity is insufficient to cover the costs of the successful party, and insurers take a decision to defend proceedings, fund the defence of the claim, control and conduct the case on behalf of the insured, fight the claim exclusively or predominantly in their own commercial interests, and the defence fails in its entirety, an order for costs against the insurers is likely to be made under s 51(3).[11] This is on the basis that such circumstances, although commonplace in the context of insurance, are exceptional when viewed against the background of the entire range of litigation, so that the key requirement for an order pursuant to s 51(3) is satisfied.[12] In *Cormack v Excess Insurance Co Ltd*,[13] Auld LJ accepted a submission that where these circumstances were present, although the insurer was not formally a party to the proceedings, it was the insurer and not the insured who was, for all practical purposes, the defendant to the proceedings. This will be the case, for example, where the only interest being pursued is the insurers' wish to limit their liability to meet the claim under the Third Party (Rights Against Insurers) Act 1930.[14] Where, by way of contrast, the proceedings have been defended sensibly and reasonably for the benefit of both the defendants and the insurers, the court may take the view that the case is not exceptional and decline to order the insurers to pay costs.[15] It may be desirable, given the importance in determining whether an order should be made pursuant to s 51(3) of the issue as to whether the proceedings are being defended solely for the benefit of the insurer, or for the benefit of both insured and insurer, that where a solicitor is appointed by insurers to defend a claim where the indemnity is limited, the terms of the solicitor's retainer be clearly established and recorded, and the involvement of the insurers and the insured in the decision-making be contemporaneously recorded.[16] Where it appears that insurers have acted in breach of the contract of insurance in allowing their own interests to predominate over those of the insured, the court is likely to conclude that the case is an exceptional one warranting an order for costs under s 51(3).[17] The same principles apply in relation to legal expenses insurance.[18] Where litigation is funded by insurers pursuant to a before the event legal expenses insurance policy which provides for the payment of the insured's costs and of any costs which the insured may be ordered to pay to the other party, and the limit of indemnity is exhausted, the mere fact that the insurer has funded the insured's legal expenses under a policy of insurance, up to the limit of cover under that policy, is not sufficient to justify an order under s 51(3) that the insurer pay the successful party's costs in excess of the limit of indemnity.[19] Similarly, where litigation is funded by an after the event legal expenses policy, the mere fact that insurers subsequently avoid the policy and refuse to indemnify the insured in respect of the other party's costs is not sufficient to justify an order under s 51(3).[20] It appears that an order may be made under s 51(3) if the insurer's conduct has been a cause of the successful party incurring the costs it seeks to recover, and that the test is not whether, but for the exceptional circumstances justifying the s 51(3) order, the costs sought would have been incurred.[21] Where underwriters have funded a fraudulent subrogated claim, it is at least arguable that the issue as to whether they could and should have discovered the fraud, and if so when, is as much of an issue on the question of whether it is just and equitable to order them to pay costs under s 51 as the counter-balancing issue that the underwriters themselves have also been the victims of fraud and have paid out monies that they will have great difficulty in, if not impossibility of, recovering from the insured.[22]

An order may be made against insurers whether they fund the claimant or the defendant to proceedings,[23] although the court will bear in mind that the public policy reasons for making s 51(3) orders against non-parties may not be so strong in the case of insured defendants as it is for insured claimants, as a claimant can choose whether to sue, the cause of action, the amount to claim and when to sue, whereas the defendant has no choice in those matters.[24] The insurer is under no duty to disclose the limit of indemnity to the other party, and failure to do so is not a factor which the court may take into account in deciding whether or not to make an order under s 51(3).[25]

Where insurers who have funded litigation are subject to a contractual obligation to the insured to indemnify him against his liability to pay the costs of the successful party, the court is likely to make an order under s 51(3) that the insurer pay those costs directly to the unsuccessful party.[26] This may save time and costs in short-circuiting the Third Parties (Rights Against Insurers) Act 1930,[27] although where the applicant's only right is under the 1930 Act and the right is not clear, a summary process under s 51(3) is not appropriate.[28] Where litigation is funded by insurers who have provided cover against liability which is not subject to any relevant limit, but the insurers are not under any contractual obligation to the insured to indemnify him against his liability to pay the costs of the successful party, the court may nevertheless make an order under s 51(3).[29]

Where an application is made for an order under s 51(3), the procedure for the determination of costs is a summary procedure, not necessarily subject to all the rules that would apply in an action.[30] Where there has been a trial, findings of fact made at trial are admissible and the application should be heard by the trial judge.[31] The application should be dealt with as speedily and inexpensively as possible, consistently with fairness to both sides;[32] depending on the extent to which relevant findings of fact have already been made at trial, disclosure, witness statements and oral evidence may be required.[33]

1 For the insured's entitlement to an indemnity in respect of the costs of defending liability proceedings, see **PARA 8.11**.

2 See **PARA 12.3**.

3 Sub-section (3) was substituted by s 4 of the Courts and Legal Services Act 1990. No alteration was made to the wording of sub-s (3), which had previously formed part of sub-s (1).

4 See *Aiden Shipping Co Ltd v Interbulk Ltd* [1986] AC 965, HL.

5 [1986] AC 965, HL.

6 *Zanussi v Anglo Venezuelan Real Estate and Agricultural Development Ltd* (1996) Times, 17 April, CA.

7 CPR 48.2(1)(a). The application to join the insurer to the proceedings is made pursuant to CPR Part 19. For the procedure where the non-party is domiciled outside the jurisdiction, see *National Justice Compania Naviera SA v Prudential Assurance Co Ltd (No 2)* [2000] 1 WLR 603, CA. An application may be made under s 51(3) even after a final order has been made between the parties and sealed: *Dymocks Franchise Systems (NSW) Pty Ltd v Todd* [2004] UKPC 39, [2004] 1 WLR 2807, para 17 (Lord Brown).

8 CPR 48.2(1)(b). See also *Murphy v Young & Co's Brewery* [1997] 1 WLR 1591, 1598, CA (Phillips LJ) (necessary for the insurer to be brought before the court so that it may make representations and, where necessary, adduce evidence).

9 *Dymocks Franchise Systems (NSW) Pty Ltd v Todd* [2004] UKPC 39, [2004] 1 WLR 2807, para 17 (Lord Brown).

10 *Aiden Shipping Co Ltd v Interbulk Ltd* [1986] AC 965, 980, HL (Lord Goff); *Symphony Group plc v Hodgson* [1994] QB 179, 192–193, CA (Balcombe LJ); *Cormack v Excess Insurance Co Ltd* [2002] Lloyd's Rep IR 398, CA.

11 *T G A Chapman Ltd v Christopher* [1998] 1 WLR 12, CA; *Pendennis Shipyard Ltd v Magrathea (Pendennis) Ltd* [1998] 1 Lloyd's Rep 315, 320 (His Honour Judge Raymond Jack QC); *Cormack v Excess Insurance Co Ltd* [2002] Lloyd's Rep IR 398, CA (circumstances in which conduct of defence predominantly, although not exclusively, in insurer's interests may be sufficient).

12 *T G A Chapman Ltd v Christopher* [1998] 1 WLR 12, 20, CA; *Citibank NA v Excess Insurance Co Ltd* [1999] Lloyd's Rep IR 122, 131 (Thomas J).

13 *Cormack v Excess Insurance Co Ltd* [2002] Lloyd's Rep IR 398, 405, CA.

14 *Plymouth & South West Co-operative Society v Architecture, Structure & Management Ltd* [2006] WEHC 3252 (TCC), [2007] Lloyd's Rep IR 596, para 27 (HHJ Anthony Thornton QC).

15 See *Gloucestershire Health Authority v M A Torpy and Partners Ltd* [1999] Lloyd's Rep IR 203, 207 (His Honour Judge Bowsher QC). This was a case of professional indemnity insurance, which will typically involve proceedings being defended for the benefit of both the defendant and the insurers, as the defendant professional has an interest in defending his name. In some cases, he may also bear a large uninsured excess. In *Plymouth & South West Co-operative Society v Architecture, Structure & Management Ltd* [2006] WEHC 3252 (TCC), [2007] Lloyd's Rep IR 596, HHJ Anthony Thornton QC took into account, in making a s 51 costs order against professional indemnity insurers, the fact that the defendant architects' practice had no continuing professional reputation to preserve, as it had ceased trading and had lost its entire workforce before the claim had started, and that although the architect and quantity surveyor involved in the claim had taken on new roles elsewhere, there was no evidence that enabled the court to conclude that their professional reputation in their new roles and firms was being preserved by the defence of the claim (para 26).

16 See *Citibank NA v Excess Insurance Co Ltd* [1999] Lloyd's Rep IR 122, 136 (Thomas J).

17 *Cormack v Excess Insurance Co Ltd* [2002] Lloyd's Rep IR 398, 405–406, CA (Auld LJ). In *Palmer v Palmer* [2008] EWCA Civ 46, [2008] Lloyd's Rep IR 535, in which a s 51 order was upheld on appeal, Rimer LJ said that rejection of a settlement offer within the limit of liability made no commercial sense

from the point of view of the insured, which was a limited liability company for which failure at trial would be terminal, and could only benefit the products liability insurer (paras 17, 31 and 33).

18 See *Worsley v Tambrands Ltd* [2002] Lloyd's Rep IR 382 (before the event ('BTE') legal expenses insurance); *Herridge v Parker* [2014] Lloyd's Rep IR 177 (after the event ('ATE') legal expenses insurance).

19 *Murphy v Young & Co's Brewery* [1997] 1 WLR 1591, CA. In *Arkin v Borchard Lines Ltd (Nos 2 and 3)* [2005] EWCA Civ 655, [2005] 1 WLR 3055, the Court of Appeal said (at para 41) that a 'professional funder' who finances part of a claimant's costs of litigation should be potentially liable under s 51(3) for the costs of the opposing party to the extent of the funding provided. The 'professional funder' was a claims company which funded the costs of expert evidence in return for a proportion of any damages recovered, although the reference (at para 31) to insurers suggested that the expression might extend to insurers. The fact that in a successful case an ATE insurer recovers the premium does not mean that an ATE insurer is to be treated as a professional funder with an agreed stake in the recoveries within the meaning of *Arkin v Borchard Lines Ltd*: the insurer does not 'fund' the claim except in so far as it pays the insured's disbursements, and does not recover a share in the proceeds, but a fixed premium, which may be subject to assessment by the court: *Herridge v Parker* [2014] Lloyd's Rep IR 177, para 89(5) (Mr Recorder Thom QC).

20 *Herridge v Parker* [2014] Lloyd's Rep IR 177, paras 89 and 94 (Mr Recorder Thom QC). It is suggested that the same principle would apply whatever the legal basis on which insurers were entitled to refuse an indemnity.

21 *Bristol and West plc v Bhadresa (No 2)* [1999] 1 Lloyd's Rep IR 138, 146 (Lightman J); *Globe Equities Ltd v Globe Legal Services Ltd* [1999] BLR 232, 240–241, CA, para 28 (Morritt LJ); *Worsley v Tambrands Ltd* [2002] Lloyd's Rep IR 382, 391–392 (His Honour Judge Hegarty QC); *Cormack v Excess Insurance Co Ltd* [2002] Lloyd's Rep IR 398, 406–407, CA (Auld LJ); *Dymocks Franchise Systems (NSW) Pty Ltd v Todd* [2004] UKPC 39, [2004] 1 WLR 2807, para 20 (Lord Brown); *Goodwood Recoveries Ltd v Breen* [2005] EWCA Civ 414, [2006] 1 WLR 2723, paras 61, 62 and 64 (Rix LJ). The insurer may be ordered to pay the costs of part of the hearing only: see *Citibank NA v Excess Insurance Co Ltd* [1999] Lloyd's Rep IR 122, 131 (Thomas J) (insurer ordered to pay costs of hearing on quantum).

22 *The Owners and/or Demise Charterers of the Dredger 'Kamal XXVI' and the Barge 'Kamal XXIV' v The Owners of the Ship 'Ariela'* [2010] EWHC 2531 (Comm), [2011] 1 Lloyd's Rep 291, para 22 (Burton J).

23 *T G A Chapman Ltd v Christopher* [1998] 1 WLR 12, 23, CA (Phillips LJ).

24 *Gloucestershire Health Authority v M A Torpy and Partners Ltd* [1999] Lloyd's Rep IR 203, 205 (His Honour Judge Bowsher QC); *Cormack v Excess Insurance Co Ltd* [2002] Lloyd's Rep IR 398, 403, CA (Auld LJ).

25 *Cormack v Excess Insurance Co Ltd* [2002] Lloyd's Rep IR 398, 406, CA (Auld LJ). For disclosure of a party's insurance position, see **PARAS 2.23, 2.33** and **9.14**.

26 *Murphy v Young & Co's Brewery* [1997] 1 WLR 1591, 1601, CA (Phillips LJ).

27 *Murphy v Young & Co's Brewery* [1997] 1 WLR 1591, 1601, CA (Phillips LJ).

28 See *Tharros Shipping Co Ltd v Bias Shipping Ltd (No 3)* [1995] 1 Lloyd's Rep 541, 555–556 (Rix J), [1997] 1 Lloyd's Rep 246, 251, CA (Phillips LJ); *Monkton Court Ltd v Perry Prowse (Insurance Services) Ltd* [2002] Lloyd's Rep IR 408, 412 (His Honour Judge Raymond Jack QC). Where the policy limits are not exhausted, an order under s 51(3) will usually be unnecessary because the insurer will simply satisfy the costs order made against the insured: *Cormack v Excess Insurance Co Ltd* [2002] Lloyd's Rep IR 398, 400, CA (Auld LJ).

29 *Murphy v Young & Co's Brewery* [1997] 1 WLR 1591, 1601, CA (Phillips LJ).

30 *Symphony Group plc v Hodgson* [1994] QB 179, 193, CA (Balcombe LJ).

31 *Symphony Group plc v Hodgson* [1994] QB 179, 193, CA (Balcombe LJ); applied: *The Owners and/or Demise Charterers of the Dredger 'Kamal XXVI' and the Barge 'Kamal XXIV' v The Owners of the Ship 'Ariela'* [2010] EWHC 2531 (Comm), [2011] 1 Lloyd's Rep 291, para 2 (Burton J).

32 *The Owners and/or Demise Charterers of the Dredger 'Kamal XXVI' and the Barge 'Kamal XXIV' v The Owners of the Ship 'Ariela'* [2010] EWHC 2531 (Comm), [2011] 1 Lloyd's Rep 291, paras 4–5 (Burton J).

33 See eg *The Owners and/or Demise Charterers of the Dredger 'Kamal XXVI' and the Barge 'Kamal XXIV' v The Owners of the Ship 'Ariela'* [2010] EWHC 2531 (Comm), [2011] 1 Lloyd's Rep 291 (disclosure); *Herridge v Parker* [2014] Lloyd's Rep IR 177 (disclosure, witness statements and oral evidence).

JOINDER OF INSURER OR BROKER TO PROCEEDINGS INVOLVING INSURED

9.47   An application may be made for a liability insurer to be joined to proceedings brought by a third party against an insured, or for an insurer to be joined to proceedings brought by an insured against its broker. Similarly, an application may be made to join a broker to proceedings brought by an insured against the insurer. Typically, an application is made under the Brussels Regulation[1] or where the insurer has rejected a claim.

The application is made under CPR 19.2(2) which provides:

> 'The court may order a person to be added as a new party if –
> (a)   it is desirable to add the new party so that the court can resolve all the matters in dispute in the proceedings; or
> (b)   there is an issue involving the new party and an existing party which is connected to the matters in dispute in the proceedings, and it is desirable to add the new party so that the court can resolve that issue.'

Whether the court will permit the insurer to be joined is therefore a matter of discretion. The issue typically arises in various situations. An insured may wish to have the issue of whether the policy responds resolved at the same time as its liability to the third party claimant.[2] Alternatively, in an action for negligence brought by an insured against an insurance broker following repudiation of liability by the insurer, the broker may wish to argue that the insurer is liable under the policy, and either the insured or the broker may then apply to join the insurer for these purposes.[3] Whether the court will grant the application to join the insurer will depend on factors such as whether the issue is suitable for resolution in that particular court, or whether it is more suitable for resolution in another court, such as the Commercial Court or a Mercantile Court; and whether there are substantial issues of fact common to the third party's claim against the insured and to the insured's claim for an indemnity under the policy which it would be convenient to have resolved in an action in which the insurer was a party. An application is unlikely to be granted if its purpose is to establish in advance of liability being determined how much money is available from liability insurers.[4]

An application for joinder may also be made by the insurer if it has repudiated liability under the policy and wishes to defend the proceedings against the insured on the merits without the insured[5] being able to argue that it has affirmed the policy of insurance by undertaking the insured's defence of the proceedings. In *Wood v Perfection Travel Ltd*,[6] the Court of Appeal said that they doubted whether the exercise of the right to take over the conduct of the action would constitute an affirmation of the contract of insurance, but said that if it would they could see no reason why the insurers should be put on the horns of that dilemma rather than being permitted to join the action as a defendant; and said that, on the contrary, justice required that the insurers should be permitted to take that course which would enable them to challenge both their insured's liability to the third party claimant and their own liability to the insured. An application for joinder is likely to be made where an insurer has repudiated liability and there is reason to believe that the insured will not conduct an adequate defence of the proceedings (for example, if it is insolvent or, although solvent, does not have sufficient funds to conduct its own defence). Whether the application will succeed is likely to depend on whether the court considers that justice requires that the insurer be permitted to defend the proceedings against the insured on the merits; and if it does, even an application made after judgment in default has been entered against the insured may succeed.[7]

In *Chubb Insurance Co of Europe SA v Davies*,[8] the third party claimant had obtained judgment against the insured, execution of which was stayed pending an appeal. This meant that the third party claimant could not petition to have the insured made bankrupt. While the appeal was pending, the insurer brought proceedings seeking a declaration that it was not liable to the insured under the policy of insurance, and applied for summary judgment. Although the insured was solvent, it was clear that if the appeal failed it would be hopelessly insolvent whether or not the insurance policy responded to the claim. The third party claimant applied to be joined to the proceedings between the insurer and the insured. Langley J granted the application on the grounds that it was the third party claimant, and not the insured, that was the real target of the insurer's application.[9] In so doing he rejected the insurer's submission that as the third party claimant had no subsisting cause of action against the insured, it should not be permitted to be joined to the insurer's action against the insured, pointing to the fact that the insurer was itself seeking prospective relief in the form of a declaration.[10]

1 See **PARA 15.9**.
2 See eg **PARA 2.24**.
3 In *Dunlop Haywards (DHL) Ltd v Erinaceous Insurance Services Ltd* [2009] EWCA Civ 354, [2009] Lloyd's Rep IR 464, the broker applied successfully for excess insurers to be joined pursuant to CPR 19.2(2) in circumstances in which it was arguing that, as a matter of construction, the excess policies responded, and that, in the alternative, the policies should be rectified. Rix LJ concluded (at para 89) that it was desirable for the excess insurers to be joined so that the issues of rectification and construction could be fully litigated between all the parties concerned in them, and so that all the parties could be bound.
4 See eg *XYZ v Various* [2014] EWHC 4056 (QB), para 31 (Thirlwall J).
5 Or, if liability is established and the insured becomes insolvent, the third party, in the exercise of its rights under the Third Parties (Rights Against Insurers) Act 1930 or 2010: see **PARAS 2.25** and **2.34**.
6 [1996] LRLR 233, 237, CA (Hirst LJ).
7 Compare *Rees v Mabco (102) Ltd* (1998) Times, 16 December, CA, in which an application to be joined and to set aside judgment in default was refused, and *Humber Work Boats Ltd v Owners of The Selby Paradigm* [2004] 2 Lloyd's Rep 714, in which the insurers' application to be joined and to set aside judgment in default was granted. In the former, but not the latter, the insurer was held to have 'nailed its colours' to the mast of repudiation of liability under the policy.
8 [2004] EWHC 2138, [2005] Lloyd's Rep IR 1.
9 [2004] EWHC 2138, [2005] Lloyd's Rep IR 1, paras 18–19.
10 [2004] EWHC 2138, [2005] Lloyd's Rep IR 1, paras 18–19; applied: *XYZ v Various* [2014] EWHC 4056 (QB), para 22 (Thirlwall J).

Chapter 10

Alternatives to litigation

10.1   The purpose of this chapter is to give a brief outline of the main alternatives to litigation available to those involved in insurance disputes. These are arbitration and mediation, and complaints to the Financial Ombudsman Service.

ALTERNATIVE DISPUTE RESOLUTION

10.2   The term alternative dispute resolution may be used to denote any dispute resolution procedure except litigation, or the more informal dispute resolution procedures, to the exclusion of not only litigation but also arbitration. This section sets out the key features of arbitration and mediation. Alternative dispute resolution may take place before proceedings are issued in court, or be used during the proceedings. In the Commercial Court, the parties may be invited to consider whether their dispute, or particular issues in it, could be resolved through alternative dispute resolution (including mediation and early neutral evaluation),[1] and the judges will readily stay cases, particularly at an early stage, in order to allow alternative dispute procedures to be followed. 'Early neutral evaluation' is offered by the Commercial Court in appropriate cases, and where the parties agree.[2] This is a 'without prejudice', non-binding evaluation by a judge of the Commercial Court, of the dispute as a whole or of particular issues. If the proceedings continue after the evaluation, the judge who conducted the evaluation will take no further part in the case unless the parties agree otherwise.

1 See the *Admiralty and Commercial Courts Guide*, Section G1, and the Case Management Information Sheet (Appendix 6 to the Guide) which the parties are required to complete before the first Case Management Conference.
2 See, generally, the *Admiralty and Commercial Courts Guide*, Section G2, and the Note to Appendix 7 to the Guide (the Draft ADR Order).

Arbitration

10.3   The key features of arbitration are that it is consensual (in that it is based on agreement between the parties, although that agreement may have been entered into long before any dispute arose), that it takes place in private, and that the outcome is binding on the parties. Arbitration in England and Wales is subject to the provisions of the Arbitration Act 1996, which also gives the court certain powers in relation to arbitrations taking place outside England and Wales, such as staying legal proceedings or securing the attendance of witnesses.[1]

1 Section 2, Arbitration Act 1996.

Confidentiality

10.4 Where an application in connection with an arbitration agreement is made to the court, the arbitration claim form may only be inspected with the permission of the court.[1] There is an obligation, implied by law and arising out of the nature of arbitration, on both parties not to disclose or use for any other purpose any documents prepared for and used in the arbitration, or disclosed or produced in the course of the arbitration, or transcripts or notes of the evidence in the arbitration or the award, and not to disclose in any way what evidence has been given by any witness in the arbitration.[2] This is in reality a substantive rule of arbitration law reached through the device of an implied term.[3] The limits of the obligation are still in the process of development on a case by case basis; on the authorities as they now stand, the principal cases in which disclosure will be permissible are: where there is consent, express or implied; where there is an order, or leave of the court (but that does not mean that the court has a general discretion to lift the obligation of confidentiality); where it is reasonably necessary for the protection of the legitimate interests of an arbitrating party; and where the interests of justice require disclosure, and also (perhaps) where the public interest requires disclosure.[4]

1 Practice Direction 62, para 5.1.
2 *Emmott v Michael Wilson & Partners Ltd* [2008] EWCA Civ 184, [2008] 1 Lloyd's Rep 616, para 105 (Lawrence Collins LJ).
3 *Emmott v Michael Wilson & Partners Ltd* [2008] EWCA Civ 184, [2008] 1 Lloyd's Rep 616, paras 84 and 106 (Lawrence Collins LJ).
4 *Emmott v Michael Wilson & Partners Ltd* [2008] EWCA Civ 184, [2008] 1 Lloyd's Rep 616, paras 84 and 106 (Lawrence Collins LJ).

Arbitration agreements

10.5 An arbitration agreement is an agreement to submit to arbitration in present or future disputes,[1] and an arbitration clause may be validly incorporated by reference.[2] Arbitration agreements are separable, which means that, unless otherwise agreed by the parties, an arbitration agreement which forms or was intended to form part of another agreement is not invalid, non-existent or ineffective simply because that other agreement is invalid, or did not come into existence, or has become ineffective.[3] Unless otherwise agreed by the parties, the arbitral tribunal may rule on its own substantive jurisdiction, including as to whether there is a valid arbitration agreement.[4] In certain limited circumstances, an application may also be made to the court to determine questions as to the substantive jurisdiction of the tribunal.[5]

1 Section 6(1), Arbitration Act 1996.
2 Section 6(2), Arbitration Act 1996.
3 Section 7, Arbitration Act 1996.
4 Section 30(1), Arbitration Act 1996.
5 Section 32, Arbitration Act 1996.

Stay of legal proceedings

10.6 A party to an arbitration agreement against whom legal proceedings are brought (whether by way of claim or counterclaim) in respect of a matter which under the agreement is to be referred to arbitration may (on notice to the other parties to the proceedings) apply to the court in which the proceedings have been brought to stay the proceedings so far as they concern that matter.[1] An application for a stay may be made even though the matter is to be referred to arbitration only after the exhaustion of other dispute resolution procedures.[2] The court will grant a stay unless satisfied that the arbitration agreement is null and void, inoperative, or incapable of being performed,[3] or, in the case of a domestic arbitration agreement, also on the alternative grounds that there are other sufficient grounds for not requiring the parties to abide by the arbitration agreement.[4] These conditions are exhaustive, and the court does not have jurisdiction to give summary judgment on a claim made by one party to an agreement which contains an arbitration clause if the other party does not admit or pay the claim, as this is sufficient to constitute a 'dispute' under s 9 of the 1996 Act.[5] If the court refuses to stay the legal proceedings, any provision that an award is a condition precedent to the bringing of legal proceedings in respect of any matter is of no effect in relation to those proceedings.[6]

1 Section 9(1), Arbitration Act 1996.
2 Section 9(2), Arbitration Act 1996.
3 Section 9(4), Arbitration Act 1996.
4 Section 86, Arbitration Act 1996. A domestic arbitration agreement means an arbitration agreement to which none of the parties is an individual who is a national of, or habitually resident in, a state other than the United Kingdom, or a body corporate which is incorporated in, or whose central control and management is exercised in, a state other than the United Kingdom, and under which the seat of the arbitration (if the seat has been designated or determined) is in the United Kingdom: s 85(2), Arbitration Act 1996.
5 *Halki Shipping Corpn v Sopex Oils Ltd* [1998] 1 WLR 726, CA.
6 Section 9(5), Arbitration Act 1996.

Procedural and evidential matters

10.7   The arbitral tribunal is under a general duty to act fairly and impartially as between the parties, giving each party a reasonable opportunity of putting his case and dealing with that of his opponent, and to adopt procedures suitable to the circumstances of the particular case, avoiding unnecessary delay or expense, so as to provide a fair means for the resolution of the matters falling to be determined.[1] The tribunal must comply with this duty in conducting the arbitral proceedings, in its decisions on matters of procedure and evidence, and in the exercise of all other powers conferred on it.[2] Subject to this general duty, it is for the tribunal to decide all procedural and evidential matters, subject to the right of the parties to agree any matter.[3] For example, it is for the tribunal to decide whether, and if so what form of, written statements of claim and defence are to be used, when these should be supplied, and the extent to which such statements can be later amended; whether any, and if so which, documents or classes of documents should be disclosed between and produced by the parties and at what stage; whether to apply strict rules of evidence; and whether and to what extent there should be oral or written evidence or submissions.[4] If the tribunal gives permission or the parties agree, a party to arbitral proceedings may use the same court procedures as are available in relation to legal proceedings to secure the attendance before the tribunal of any witness who is in the United Kingdom in order to give oral testimony or to produce documents or other material evidence.[5] Unless otherwise agreed by the parties, a party to arbitral proceedings may be represented in the proceedings by a lawyer or other person chosen by him.[6]

1 Section 33(1), Arbitration Act 1996.
2 Section 33(2), Arbitration Act 1996.
3 Section 34(1), Arbitration Act 1996; see also s 4 and Sch 1.
4 Section 34(2), Arbitration Act 1996.
5 Section 43, Arbitration Act 1996. The procedure is set out at paras 7.1 to 7.3 of Practice Direction 62, and CPR Part 34.
6 Section 36, Arbitration Act 1996.

Interim injunctions

10.8　Unless otherwise agreed by the parties, the court has, for the purposes of and in relation to arbitral proceedings, the same power to grant an interim injunction as it has for the purposes of and in relation to legal proceedings,[1] although the court's power to grant an interim injunction pursuant to s 44(2)(e) of the Arbitration Act 1996 may be exercised only in cases of urgency[2] and where the tribunal cannot give the appropriate remedy at the time in question,[3] and is restricted[4] to the preservation of evidence or assets.[5]

1 Section 44(1) and (2)(e), Arbitration Act 1996.
2 Section 44(4), Arbitration Act 1996.
3 Section 44(5), Arbitration Act 1996.
4 By s 44(3), Arbitration Act 1996.
5 *Cetelem SA v Roust Holdings Ltd* [2005] EWCA Civ 618, [2005] 1 WLR 3555, overruling *Hiscox Underwriting Ltd v Dickson Manchester & Co Ltd* [2004] EWHC 479 (Comm), [2004] 2 Lloyd's Rep 438, paras 36–39 (Cooke J). There is a tension, as yet unresolved by the courts, between the apparently wide powers conferred on the court by s 37 of the Senior Courts Act 1981 and the much narrower powers conferred on the court by s 44 of the Arbitration Act 1996: *Cetelem SA v Roust Holdings Ltd* [2005] EWCA Civ 618, [2005] 1 WLR 3555, para 74 (Clarke LJ).

Determination of preliminary point of law

10.9　Unless otherwise agreed by the parties,[1] the court may on the application of a party to arbitral proceedings (on notice to the other parties) determine any question of law arising in the course of the proceedings which the court is satisfied substantially affects the rights of one or more of the parties.[2] The permission of the tribunal is required for such an application unless all parties agree, and in addition the court must be satisfied that the application was made without delay and that the determination of the question is likely to produce substantial savings in costs.[3]

1 In the case of a domestic arbitration agreement, any agreement to exclude the jurisdiction of the court in relation to the determination of preliminary points of law is not effective unless entered into after the commencement of the arbitral proceedings in which the question arises or the award is made: s 87(1)(a), Arbitration Act 1996.
2 Section 45(1), Arbitration Act 1996.
3 Section 45(2), Arbitration Act 1996.

Enforcement of award

10.10　An award made by the tribunal pursuant to an arbitration agreement may, by leave of the court, be enforced in the same manner as a judgment or order of the court to the same effect; and where leave is given, judgment may be entered in terms of the award.[1] Leave to enforce an award will not be given where the person against whom it is sought to be enforced shows that the tribunal lacked substantive jurisdiction to make the award.[2] The Arbitration Act 1996 also makes provision for recognition and enforcement of certain foreign arbitration awards.[3]

1 Section 66, Arbitration Act 1996. This is not confined to enforcement by one of the normal forms of execution of a judgment which are provided under the Civil Procedure Rules, but may include other means of giving judicial force to the award on the same footing as a judgment; a court may therefore give leave for judgment to be entered in the terms of a declaratory award, thereby enabling the enforcement of the award through the doctrine of res judicata: *West Tankers Inc v Allianz SpA, The Front Comor* [2012] EWCA Civ 27, 1 [2012] Lloyd's Rep 398, paras 35–38 (Toulson LJ).
2 Sections 66(3) and 67, Arbitration Act 1996. A jurisdictional challenge under s 67 involves a rehearing, not merely a review: *Dallah Real Estate and Tourism Holding Co v Ministry of Religious Affairs of the Government of Pakistan* [2010] UKSC 46, [2011] 1 AC 763, paras 26 (Lord Mance) and 96 (Lord Collins). The evidence which may be adduced is not limited to the evidence which was before the arbitrators but is subject to the control of the court: *Central Trading & Exports Ltd v Fioralba Shipping Co, The Kalisti* [2014] EWHC 2397 (Comm), [2014] 2 Lloyd's Rep 449, paras 30-33 (Males J). The right to raise a jurisdictional challenge may be lost: Arbitration Act 1996, s 73.
3 Part III (ss 99–104).

Appeal on point of law

10.11   Unless otherwise agreed by the parties, a party to arbitral proceedings may, on notice to the other parties and to the tribunal, appeal to the court on a question of law arising out of an award made in the proceedings.[1] For these purposes, an agreement to dispense with reasons for the tribunal's award is an agreement to exclude the court's jurisdiction to hear an appeal on a question of law.[2] An appeal may be brought only with the agreement of all the other parties to the proceedings,[3] or with leave of the court.[4] The requirements which must be satisfied for leave to appeal to be given are that the determination of the question will substantially affect the rights of one or more of the parties, that the question is one which the tribunal was asked to determine, that on the basis of the findings of fact in the award the decision of the tribunal on the question is obviously wrong, or the question is one of general public importance and the decision of the tribunal is at least open to serious doubt, and that, despite the agreement of the parties to resolve the matter by arbitration, it is just and proper in all the circumstances for the court to determine the question.[5] In refusing permission to appeal to the High Court from an arbitration award on a point of law, an indication by a first instance judge as to which of the statutory criteria the applicant has failed to fulfil will usually be sufficient to comply with art 6 of the European Convention on Human Rights, and full reasons need not be given.[6] Where however the judge rejects an application for leave made on grounds that the decision of the arbitral tribunal was 'obviously wrong' or, in addition to being a question of general public importance, was 'at least open to serious doubt',[7] further brief reasons may be necessary.[8] An application for leave to appeal will be determined without a hearing unless it appears to the court that a hearing is required.[9] Although only the court at first instance, and not the Court of Appeal, may grant leave to appeal from a decision of the first instance court granting or refusing leave to appeal under s 69 of the Arbitration Act 1996,[10] the Court of Appeal retains a residual jurisdiction to enquire into unfairness in the process of a refusal of leave under s 69(8) of the Arbitration Act 1996.[11] The test is whether the judge's refusal of leave to appeal amounted to such unfairness in the process as to amount to a breach of art 6.[12] The fact that the decision is vested in the judge who has himself decided whether the point argued is right or wrong is proportionate and compatible with art 6.[13]

1 Arbitration Act 1996, s 69(1).
2 Arbitration Act 1996, s 69(1).
3 In the case of a domestic arbitration agreement, any agreement to exclude the jurisdiction of the court in relation to the determination of preliminary points of law is not effective unless entered into after the commencement of the arbitral proceedings in which the question arises or the award is made: Arbitration Act 1996, s 87(1)(b).
4 Arbitration Act 1996, s 69(2).
5 Arbitration Act 1996, s 69(3). A decision is 'obviously wrong' if the error is one which can be grasped simply by a perusal, that is, a study, of the award itself; the memorable phrase 'a major intellectual aberration' is a useful way of bringing to mind that the error must be an obvious one: *HMV UK v Propinvest Friar Limited Partnership* [2011] EWCA Civ 1708, [2012] 1 Lloyd's Rep 416, paras 7–8 (Arden LJ) and 42 (Longmore LJ).
6 *North Range Shipping Ltd v Seatrans Shipping Corpn* [2002] EWCA Civ 405, [2002] 1 WLR 2397, para 27 (Tuckey LJ).
7 See Arbitration Act 1996, s 69(3)(c)(i) and (ii).
8 *North Range Shipping Ltd v Seatrans Shipping Corpn* [2002] EWCA Civ 405, [2002] 1 WLR 2397, para 27 (Tuckey LJ).
9 Arbitration Act 1996, s 69(5). This procedure is compatible with art 6: *HMV UK v Propinvest Friar Limited Partnership* [2011] EWCA Civ 1708, [2012] 1 Lloyd's Rep 416, para 39 (Arden LJ) and 44 (Longmore LJ).
10 Arbitration Act 1996, ss 69(6) and 105; *Henry Boot Construction (UK) Ltd v Malmaison Hotel (Manchester) Ltd* [2001] QB 388, CA; *Athletic Union of Constantinople v National Basketball Association (No 2)* [2002] EWCA Civ 830, [2002] 1 WLR 2863, para 12 (Lord Phillips MR).
11 *North Range Shipping Ltd v Seatrans Shipping Corpn* [2002] EWCA Civ 405, [2002] 1 WLR 2397, para 1 (Tuckey LJ); *CGU International plc v AstraZeneca Insurance Co Ltd* [2006] EWCA Civ 1340, [2007] 1 Lloyd's Rep 142.
12 *CGU International plc v AstraZeneca Insurance Co Ltd* [2006] EWCA Civ 1340, [2007] 1 Lloyd's Rep 142, para 98 (Rix LJ). Potential examples are a decision made by a judge without hearing any argument or thinking that he is making it in one case but actually making it in another because he has muddled two separate cases in his mind; the jurisdiction has never been invoked successfully: see *Michael Wilson & Partners Ltd v Emmott* [2015] EWCA Civ 1285, para 3 (Moore-Bick LJ).
13 *Republic of Kazakhstan v Istil Group Ltd* [2007] EWCA Civ 471, [2007] 2 Lloyd's Rep 548, paras 26 and 27 (Longmore LJ), 35 (Toulson LJ) and 37 (Arden LJ) (in relation to an application for leave under s 67(4)).

Arbitration proceedings

10.12   Applications to the court under the Arbitration Act 1996 are begun by issuing an arbitration claim form in accordance with the CPR Part 8 procedure, unless the application is for a stay of legal proceedings, which is made by application notice to the court dealing with those proceedings.[1] An arbitration claim form may be issued out of various courts, including the Commercial Court and district registries of the High Court where a mercantile court is established.[2] Cases may be transferred out of the Commercial Court,[3] and special provision is made for transfer between the Commercial Court and the London Mercantile Court.[4] Specific provision is made for the procedure to be followed in arbitration proceedings in CPR Part 62 and the accompanying Practice Direction.

1 The High Court and County Courts (Allocation of Arbitration Proceedings) Order 1996 (SI 1996/3215), art 3 (which provides that proceedings under s 9 of the 1996 Act are to be commenced in the court in which the legal proceedings are pending), and CPR 62.3(1) and (2). The arbitration claim form must be substantially in the form set out in Appendix A to the Practice Direction (Arbitration): see para 2.2 of the Practice Direction.

2 Practice Direction (Arbitration), para 2.3.
3 Art 6 of the High Court and County Courts (Allocation of Arbitration Proceedings) Order 1996 (SI 1996/3215) provides that the 1996 Order does not prevent the judge in charge of the commercial list from transferring proceedings under the Arbitration Act 1996 to another list, court or division of the High Court to which he has power to transfer proceedings.
4 The High Court and County Courts (Allocation of Arbitration Proceedings) Order 1996 (SI 1996/3215), art 4, as amended. The 1996 Order refers to the Central London County Court Mercantile List, which has been replaced by the London Mercantile Court. The criteria to be applied by the relevant court in determining whether a case should be transferred are set out at art 5(4) of the 1996 Order. Where the financial substance of the dispute exceeds £200,000, the proceedings must be taken in the High Court unless they do not raise questions of general importance to persons who are not parties: art 5(4) of the 1996 Order.

Human Rights Act 1998

10.13   The right of access to court is not expressly set out in art 6 but is inherent in the notion of a right to a fair trial.[1] Where parties have voluntarily or freely entered into an arbitration agreement they are to be treated as waiving their rights under art 6.[2] In addition, arbitral tribunals need not comply with art 6, although it may be that art 6 requires a degree of review by the domestic courts,[3] as provided by the Arbitration Act 1996.[4]

1 *Golder v United Kingdom*, judgment of 21 February 1975, Series A, No 18, ECtHR; 1 EHRR 524.
2 *Stretford v Football Association Ltd* [2007] EWCA Civ 238, [2007] 2 Lloyd's Rep 31, para 45 (Sir Anthony Clarke MR).
3 See *Nordström-Janzon v Netherlands*, No 28101/95, Comm Dec 27.11.1996.
4 *Stretford v Football Association Ltd* [2007] EWCA Civ 238, [2007] 2 Lloyd's Rep 31, para 65 (Sir Anthony Clarke MR). See further PARAS **9.9** and **10.11**.

Unfair terms in consumer contracts

10.14   Part 2 of the Consumer Rights Act 2015 applies to unfair terms in contracts between traders and consumers.[1] An arbitration clause which has the effect of obliging an insured to engage in two sets of dispute resolution, one by arbitration and the other by litigation, because not all of the issues which the insured wishes to have resolved are within the scope of the arbitration agreement, may be held to be unfair within the meaning of the 2015 Act.[2] Part 1 of Schedule 2 to the 2015 Act contains an indicative and non-exhaustive list of terms of consumer contracts which may be regarded as unfair for the purposes of Part 2 of the 2015 Act. This includes terms which have the object or effect of excluding or hindering the consumer's right to take legal action or exercise any other legal remedy, in particular by requiring the consumer to take disputes exclusively to arbitration 'not covered by legal provisions'.[3] In addition, a term which constitutes an arbitration agreement is unfair for the purposes of the Regulations so far as it relates to a claim for a pecuniary remedy which does not exceed £5,000.[4]

1 The Consumer Rights Act 2015 revoked the Unfair Terms in Consumer Contracts Regulations 1999 (SI 1999/2083, as amended) with effect from 1 October 2015: Sch 4 to the 2015 Act, para 34. Both the 1999 Regulations, the Unfair Terms in Consumer Contracts Regulations 1994 (SI 1994/3159) which they revoked with effect from 1 October 1999, and the Act implemented Council Directive (EC) 93/13 on unfair terms in consumer contracts (OJ No L95, 21.4.93, p 29). See further PARA **3.20**.

2 *Zealander v Laing Homes Ltd* (2000) 2 TCLR 724, 725, 727–728 (His Honour Judge Havery QC) (in relation to the Unfair Terms in Consumer Contracts Regulations 1994); and see **PARA 3.20**.
3 Schedule 2, Part 1, para 20. The meaning of the phrase 'not covered by legal provisions', which the Regulations have taken verbatim from the annex to the Directive, is obscure. In *Zealander v Laing Homes Ltd* (2000) 2 TCLR 724, His Honour Judge Havery QC declined (at 729) to give the words any meaning which would cut down the meaning of the other words in Schedule 1, para 1(q) of the Unfair Terms in Consumer Contracts Regulations 1999 (which was in substantially the same terms as Schedule 2, Part 1, para 20 of the Consumer Rights Act 2015); applied: *Mylcrist Builders Ltd v Buck* [2008] EWHC 2172 (TCC), para 54 (Ramsey J).
4 Arbitration Act 1996, ss 89 and 91(1). For these purposes, Part 2 applies where the consumer is a legal person as it applies where the consumer is an individual: Arbitration Act 1996, s 90; and an arbitration agreement is any agreement to submit to arbitration present or future disputes or differences (whether or not contractual): s 89(1) of the Arbitration Act 1996. The relevant amount is specified by order: Arbitration Act 1996, s 91(2)–(4). The current order is The Unfair Arbitration Agreements (Specified Amount) Order 1999 (SI 1999/2167).

Mediation

10.15 Mediation is a consensual process in which a neutral third party becomes involved in the parties' negotiations, and which takes place in private. Unlike arbitration, a mediator has no power to make a decision which binds the parties, and there is no statutory scheme governing mediation in England and Wales. This means that there is no prescribed framework for mediations, and a variety of procedures may be adopted by the mediator in agreement with the parties. In commercial mediations, it is usual for the parties to enter into a mediation agreement in advance of the mediation. Matters dealt with in such an agreement might include the duration of the mediation, costs, confidentiality, whether the mediation is to be conducted on a 'without prejudice' basis, and the use which may be made outside the mediation of any documents disclosed. In a commercial mediation, the mediator will usually ask the parties to prepare and exchange a position statement in advance of the mediation. The mediator may bring the parties together at the beginning of the mediation, after which they will go into separate rooms while he moves between them; or there may be no direct contact between the parties at all. Where no agreement is reached during the mediation itself, the mediator may continue to be involved in negotiations, sometimes sporadically over a period of days, or the parties may conclude the negotiations directly, on the basis of progress made towards settlement during the mediation.

The court may take into account, when awarding or assessing costs under CPR Part 44, an unreasonable refusal by a party to enter into mediation.[1]

1 See *Halsey v Milton Keynes General NHS Trust* [2004] EWCA Civ 576, [2004] 1 WLR 3002; *Reed Executive plc v Reed Business Information Ltd* [2004] EWCA Civ 887, [2004] 1 WLR 3026, paras 34 and 40–47 (Jacob LJ).

FINANCIAL OMBUDSMAN SERVICE

10.16 This section considers the Financial Ombudsman Service ('FOS'). The FOS replaced eight previous schemes, including the Insurance Ombudsman Bureau.

Statutory basis and powers

10.17   The FOS is an independent dispute resolution service set up pursuant to the Financial Services and Markets Act 2000.[1] The scheme is governed by detailed rules made by the Financial Conduct Authority or its predecessor the Financial Services Authority (the 'FCA')[2] and the FOS.[3] The role of the FOS is to resolve disputes 'quickly and with minimum formality';[4] it has no disciplinary or regulatory powers.

The ombudsman determines complaints by reference to what is, in his opinion, fair and reasonable in all the circumstances of the case.[5] In considering what is fair and reasonable in all the circumstances of the case, the ombudsman takes into account relevant law and regulations, regulators' rules, guidance and standards, codes of practice and, where appropriate, what he considers to have been good industry practice at the relevant time.[6] If the ombudsman's opinion as to what is fair and reasonable in all the circumstances of the case is perverse or irrational, that opinion, and any determination made pursuant to it, is liable to be set aside on conventional judicial review grounds.[7] This complies with art 6 and art 1 of protocol 1.[8]

Where a complaint is determined in favour of the complainant, the ombudsman's determination may include one or more of the following: a money award, interest award or costs award against the respondent, or a direction to the respondent.[9] A money award may be such amount as the ombudsman considers to be fair compensation for one or more of the following: financial loss (including consequential or prospective loss), pain and suffering, damage to reputation, or distress or inconvenience, whether or not a court would award compensation.[10] An interest award may provide for the amount payable under the money award to bear interest at a rate and as from a date specified in the award.[11] The maximum money award which the ombudsman may make is £150,000, excluding any interest, costs and interest on costs.[12] Whether a determination is a money award or a direction depends on the substance of the decision and not on the form in which it is expressed, and if the determination requires the payment of money to the complainant or for his benefit it is a money award.[13] The ombudsman does not have power to make a direction that would require a firm to make a payment that exceeds the statutory cap on money awards.[14] However, if the ombudsman considers that an amount more than the maximum is required as fair compensation, he may in addition recommend that the respondent pay the complainant the balance.[15] The doctrine of res judicata applies to awards by the ombudsman, which means that a complainant who has accepted an award may not raise the same claim in court proceedings in order to obtain a higher level of compensation.[16] It does not matter whether the award was for the maximum sum that can be awarded or for a lesser amount.[17] Compliance with a valid direction is enforceable by an injunction.[18]

1 See Pt XVI, The Ombudsman Scheme (ss 225 to 234), and Sch 17 to the 2000 Act. The body corporate set up to administer the scheme is the Financial Ombudsman Service Ltd.
2 Pursuant to its rule-making powers: see ss 138 and 153 of the 2000 Act, and para 13 of Sch 17. The FCA and FOS may also give guidance (see s 157 of the 2000 Act and para 8 of Sch 17), and the FCA Handbook indicates which provisions are binding rules (marked 'R'), and which are non-binding guidance (marked 'G'). A consolidated version of the rules and guidance is contained in the FCA Handbook (in the section 'Dispute Resolution: Complaints' (DISP)), which is on the FCA website.
3 See s 225 and paras 14 and 18 of Sch 17 to the 2000 Act.
4 Section 225(1) of the 2000 Act.
5 Section 228(2) of the 2000 Act; FCA Handbook, DISP 3.6.1R.

6 FCA Handbook, DISP 3.6.4R. The FOS publishes anonymised decisions and information about its approach to complaints on its website.

7 *R (IFG Financial Services Ltd) v Financial Ombudsman Ltd* [2005] EWHC 1153, [2006] 1 BCLC 534, para 13 (Stanley Burnton J); *R (Heather Moor & Edgecomb) v FOS* [2008] EWCA Civ 642, [2008] 1 All ER 328.

8 *R (Heather Moor & Edgecomb) v FOS* [2008] EWCA Civ 642, [2008] 1 All ER 328; *Heather Moor & Edgecomb Ltd v United Kingdom* (2011) 53 EHRR SE144, ECtHR.

9 Section 229 of the 2000 Act; FCA Handbook, DISP 3.7.1R.

10 FCA Handbook, DISP 3.7.2R.

11 FCA Handbook, DISP 3.7.8R.

12 FCA Handbook, DISP 3.7.4R and 3.7.5G.

13 *Bunney v Burns Anderson plc* [2007] EWHC 1240 (Ch), [2008] Lloyd's Rep IR 198, para 68 (Lewison J).

14 *Bunney v Burns Anderson plc* [2007] EWHC 1240 (Ch), [2008] Lloyd's Rep IR 198, para 68 (Lewison J).

15 Section 229(5) of the 2000 Act; FCA Handbook, DISP 3.7.6G.

16 *Clark v In Focus Asset Management and Tax Solutions Ltd* [2014] EWCA Civ 118, [2014] 1 WLR 2502, paras 121 (Arden LJ), 124 (Black LJ) and 125 (Davis LJ). The Court of Appeal left open the question whether the doctrine of *Henderson v Henderson* (1843) 3 Hare 100 could be applied, in legal proceedings brought subsequent to a prior complaint to the ombudsman, on an application by the adviser to stay the legal proceedings on the footing that such claim could and should have been raised in the ombudsman proceedings, even if it had not been: see paras 90 (Arden LJ) and 129–130 (Davis LJ) (although Arden LJ appears to have assumed, in the example she gave at para 80, that the doctrine would apply).

17 *Clark v In Focus Asset Management and Tax Solutions Ltd* [2014] EWCA Civ 118, [2014] 1 WLR 2502, para 123 (Arden LJ).

18 Section 229(9)(a) of the 2000 Act; *Bunney v Burns Anderson plc* [2007] EWHC 1240 (Ch), [2008] Lloyd's Rep IR 198, para 76 (Lewison J). It is open to a respondent to raise in the injunctive proceedings the question whether the ombudsman had formal jurisdiction to make the determinations that he purported to make, and the respondent is not confined to judicial review: *Bunney v Burns Anderson plc* [2007] EWHC 1240 (Ch), [2008] Lloyd's Rep IR 198, para 53 (Lewison J) (declining to indicate a view as to whether other grounds on which judicial review might be sought (eg bias, irrationality etc) could be raised in the injunctive proceedings, or only by way of a claim for judicial review).

Jurisdiction to consider complaints

10.18 Insurance underwriting and broking are regulated activities under the Financial Services and Markets Act 2000,[1] which insurers and brokers require permission to carry out, pursuant to Part IV of the Financial Services and Markets Act 2000. Once they have obtained a Part IV permission, they are authorised persons for the purposes of the 2000 Act.[2] Detailed rules on the FOS's jurisdiction are made by the FCA[3] and are set out in the FCA Handbook.[4] A decision of the FOS as to its own jurisdiction is reviewable by the court.[5] The FOS is the primary fact finder and its fact finding is reviewable by the court only on traditional grounds.[6] The FOS must direct itself correctly on the law, as to the meaning of words and phrases, and as to the defining characteristics which must be present for a phrase to apply.[7] Further, the FOS's assessment of the way in which the law, correctly understood, applies to the facts will be regarded by the court as at least persuasive, but if the court is persuaded that on the facts found by the FOS, the correctly understood law had been applied wrongly, the court must rule that the FOS had no jurisdiction.[8] The question is not whether the decision of the FOS was reasonable: the reviewing court will have to be satisfied that the FOS as the body experienced in dealing with these issues was wrong in its jurisdictional decision before overturning it, and will give due weight to that decision, but if the decision was wrong but reasonable, the FOS will not have jurisdiction.[9]

A complaint may be dealt with by the FOS only if it is brought by a consumer, a micro enterprise, and small charities and trusts.[10] Eligibility to make a complaint is determined by reference to the complainant's status at the time the complaint is made.[11]

1 Financial Services and Markets Act 2000, s 22(1) and Sch 2; Financial Services and Markets Act 2000 (Regulated Activities) Order 2001 (SI 2001/544), as amended.
2 See s 31 of the Financial Services and Markets Act 2000.
3 See s 226 of the Financial Services and Markets Act 2000.
4 FCA Handbook, DISP 2: Jurisdiction of the Financial Ombudsman Service. The ombudsman's jurisdiction includes a 'compulsory jurisdiction' and a 'voluntary jurisdiction': see ss 226 and 227 of the 2000 Act.
5 See eg *R (Chancery (UK) LLP) v The Financial Ombudsman Service Ltd and Sir Ian Robinson* [2015] EWHC 407 (Admin).
6 *R (Chancery (UK) LLP) v The Financial Ombudsman Service Ltd and Sir Ian Robinson* [2015] EWHC 407 (Admin), para 70 (Ouseley J) (appeal pending).
7 *R (Chancery (UK) LLP) v The Financial Ombudsman Service Ltd and Sir Ian Robinson* [2015] EWHC 407 (Admin), para 71 (appeal pending).
8 *R (Chancery (UK) LLP) v The Financial Ombudsman Service Ltd and Sir Ian Robinson* [2015] EWHC 407 (Admin), para 71 (appeal pending).
9 *R (Chancery (UK) LLP) v The Financial Ombudsman Service Ltd and Sir Ian Robinson* [2015] EWHC 407 (Admin), para 72 (appeal pending).
10 Sections 226 and 227 of the 2000 Act and FCA Handbook, DISP 2.7.1R–2.7.3R. A 'consumer' for these purposes is 'any natural person acting for purposes outside his trade, business or profession': FCA Handbook Glossary. An individual making a claim for an indemnity under a directors' and officers' insurance policy in respect of his liability to a third party by virtue of his acting in the capacity of director or official or employee is not acting for purposes outside his trade, business, or profession and is not a 'consumer' for these purposes; accordingly, the FOS does not have jurisdiction to hear his complaint: *R (Bluefin Insurance Services Ltd) v Financial Ombudsman Service Ltd* [2014] EWHC 3413 (Admin), [2015] Lloyd's Rep IR 457, paras 116–125 (Wilkie J). A micro enterprise is an enterprise which employs fewer than 10 persons and has a turnover or annual balance sheet that does not exceed €2million. Charities and trusts which are eligible complainants are: a charity with an annual income of less than £1m, or a trust with a net asset value of less than £1m. There are additional rules and guidance setting out who may make a complaint: FCA Handbook, DISP 2.7.6–2.7.10.
11 *R (Bluefin Insurance Services Ltd) v Financial Ombudsman Service Ltd* [2014] EWHC 3413 (Admin), [2015] Lloyd's Rep IR 457, paras 81–84 (Wilkie J); see also FCA Handbook, DISP 2.7.3.

Procedure

10.19 As authorised persons, insurers and brokers are subject to detailed rules and guidance in relation to the prompt and fair treatment of complaints.[1]

The ombudsman can only consider a complaint if the respondent has already sent the complainant its final response, or eight weeks have elapsed since the respondent received the complaint.[2] Unless a respondent insurer or broker has already had eight weeks to consider the complaint or has issued a final response, the ombudsman will refer the complaint to the respondent.[3] The FOS cannot consider a complaint if the complainant refers it to the FOS:

(1) more than six months after the date on which the respondent sent the complainant its final response or redress determination;[4] or

(2) more than six years after the event complained of, or, if later, more than three years from the date on which the complainant became aware, or ought reasonably to have become aware, that he had cause for complaint;[5]

unless the complainant referred the complaint to the respondent or to the FOS within that period and has a written acknowledgment or some other record of the complaint having been received.[6]

The ombudsman may consider complaints outside these time limits when, in his view, the failure to comply with the time limits was as a result of exceptional circumstances or where the respondent does not object.[7] Complaints to the FOS should be made using the complaint form on the FOS website.

A complaint may be dismissed without consideration of its merits on various grounds,[8] including that the ombudsman considers that:

(1)   the complainant has not suffered, or is unlikely to suffer, financial loss, material distress or material inconvenience;[9]
(2)   the complaint is frivolous or vexatious;[10]
(3)   the complaint clearly does not have any reasonable prospect of success;[11]
(4)   the insurer or broker has already made an offer of compensation which is fair and reasonable in relation to the circumstances alleged by the complainant and which is still open for acceptance;[12]
(5)   the insurer or broker has reviewed the subject matter of the complaint in accordance with the regulatory standards for the review of such transactions prevailing at the time of the review or any formal regulatory requirement, standard or guidance published by the FCA or other regulator in respect of that type of complaint, including, if appropriate, making an offer of redress to the complainant, unless he considers that they did not address the particular circumstances of the case;[13]
(6)   the matter has previously been considered or excluded under the FOS or a former scheme (unless material new evidence likely to affect the outcome has subsequently become available);[14]
(7)   the matter has been dealt with, or is being dealt with, by a comparable independent complaints scheme or dispute resolution process;[15]
(8)   the subject matter of the complaint has been the subject of court proceedings where there has been a decision on the merits,[16] or is the subject of current court proceedings, unless proceedings are stayed in order that the matter may be considered by the FOS;[17]
(9)   it would be more suitable for the matter to be dealt with by a court, arbitration or another complaints scheme;[18] or
(10) there are other compelling reasons why it is inappropriate for the complaint to be dealt with by the FOS.[19]

The FOS may, with the complainant's consent, cease to consider its merits so that it may be referred to a court to consider as a test case, if he considers that the complaint raises an important or novel point of law which has important consequences and would more suitably be dealt with by a court as a test case, provided that certain requirements are satisfied.[20]

Where the ombudsman considers that the complaint may be one which should be dismissed without consideration of its merits, he will give the complainant an opportunity to make representations before he makes his decision.[21] If he then decides that the complaint should be dismissed, he will give reasons to the complainant for that decision and inform the insurer or broker respondent.[22]

The ombudsman will attempt to resolve complaints at the earliest possible stage and by whatever means appear to him to be most appropriate, including mediation or investigation.[23] If the ombudsman decides that an investigation is necessary, he will ensure both parties have been given an opportunity of making representations, send the parties a provisional assessment, setting out his reasons and a time limit within which either party must respond, and if either party indicates disagreement with the provisional assessment within the time limit prescribed, proceed to determination.[24] The ombudsman may give directions as to the issues on which evidence is required, the extent to which evidence should be oral or written, and the way in which evidence should be presented.[25] He may exclude evidence that would be admissible in a court, or include evidence which would not be admissible, and, where he considers it appropriate, may accept information in confidence, so that only an edited version, or summary or description, is disclosed to the other party.[26]

If the ombudsman considers that a complaint can be fairly determined without convening a hearing, he will determine the complaint. If not, he will invite the parties to take part in a hearing. A hearing may be held by any means which the ombudsman considers appropriate in the circumstances, including by telephone.[27] In deciding whether there should be a hearing and, if so, whether it should be in public or in private, the ombudsman will have regard to the provisions of the European Convention on Human Rights.[28] A public hearing in judicial review proceedings is available to any complainant or respondent who considers that the ombudsman has made an unlawful decision, and the lack of any right to a public hearing does not breach art 6.[29]

When a complaint has been determined, the ombudsman will give both parties a signed written statement of the determination, stating the reasons for it.[30] The statement will invite the complainant to notify the ombudsman in writing, before the date specified in the statement, whether he accepts or rejects the determination.[31] If the complainant notifies the ombudsman that he accepts the determination within the time limit set, it is final and binding on both parties.[32] If the complainant does not notify the ombudsman by the specified date that he accepts the determination, the complainant will be treated as having rejected the determination, and neither party will be bound by it,[33] although, if the complainant has not notified the ombudsman of the rejection of the determination, the ombudsman may allow the complainant to accept the determination after the specified date in exceptional circumstances.[34] The ombudsman will notify the respondent of the outcome.[35]

1 FCA Handbook, DISP 1: Treating complainants fairly.
2 FCA Handbook, DISP 2.8.1R.
3 FCA Handbook, DISP 3.2.2R.
4 FCA Handbook, DISP 2.8.2R(1).
5 FCA Handbook, DISP 2.8.2R(2).
6 FCA Handbook, DISP 2.8.2R. The question whether a complaint is brought within six months as required by the rules or not is primarily a decision for the FOS, subject only to review by the court on usual judicial review grounds: *R (Bankole) v Financial Ombudsman Service* [2012] EWHC 3555 (Admin), para 20 (Sales J).
7 FSA Handbook, DISP 2.8.2R(3).
8 FCA Handbook, DISP 3.3.4.
9 FCA Handbook, DISP 3.3.4R(1).
10 FCA Handbook, DISP 3.3.4R(2).
11 FCA Handbook, DISP 3.3.4R(3).
12 FCA Handbook, DISP 3.3.4R(4).

13 FCA Handbook, DISP 3.3.4R(5).
14 FCA Handbook, DISP 3.3.4R(6).
15 FCA Handbook, DISP 3.3.4R(7).
16 FCA Handbook, DISP 3.3.4R(8).
17 FCA Handbook, DISP 3.3.4R(9).
18 FCA Handbook, DISP 3.3.4R(10).
19 FCA Handbook, DISP 3.3.4R(17).
20 FCA Handbook, DISP 3.4.2R. Factors which the ombudsman may take into account in considering whether to cease to consider a complaint on this basis are set out at 3.4.3G.
21 FCA Handbook, DISP 3.3.1R.
22 FCA Handbook, DISP 3.3.2R.
23 FCA Handbook, DISP 3.5.1R.
24 FCA Handbook, DISP 3.5.4R. The provisional assessment is made by one of the adjudicators employed by the FOS rather than by an ombudsman.
25 FCA Handbook, DISP 3.5.8R.
26 FCA Handbook, DISP 3.5.9R.
27 FCA Handbook, DISP 3.5.5R.
28 FCA Handbook, DISP 3.5.7G.
29 *R (Heather Moor & Edgecomb) v FOS* [2008] EWCA Civ 642; *Heather Moor & Edgecomb Ltd v United Kingdom* (application no 1550/09), decision dated 14 June 2011, ECtHR.
30 Section 228(4)(a) and (b) of the Financial Services and Markets Act 2000; FCA Handbook, DISP 3.6.6R(1).
31 Section 228(4)(c) of the Financial Services and Markets Act 2000; FCA Handbook, DISP 3.6.6R(2).
32 Section 228(5) of the Financial Services and Markets Act 2000; FCA Handbook, DISP 3.6.6R(3).
33 Section 228(6) of the Financial Services and Markets Act 2000; FCA Handbook, DISP 3.6.6R(4).
34 Section 228(6A) of the Financial Services and Markets Act 2000; FCA Handbook, DISP 3.6.6(4A).
35 Section 228(6) of the Financial Services and Markets Act 2000; FCA Handbook, DISP 3.6.6R(5).

Chapter 11

Insurers' defences

INTRODUCTION

11.1   When an insured brings an action under a policy of insurance, the main defences which may be available to insurers in any particular case are the following: that the insured is in breach of a condition precedent as to liability; that the insured is in breach of a warranty in the policy; that the policy has been avoided or the insured is entitled to only a proportionate remedy for non-disclosure or misrepresentation in the making of the contract; that the insurer is entitled to reject the claim as fraudulent, including the use of a fraudulent device in relation to an otherwise genuine claim; and that the action has been brought outside contractual or statutory time limits. These defences, along with some others which are less common but which are adopted from time to time, are considered in this chapter. Waiver, affirmation and estoppel are often invoked in response, and these are also considered.

BREACH OF CONDITION PRECEDENT AS TO LIABILITY

11.2   Insurance cases share with general commercial law the use of the term 'condition precedent' for a clause which must be fulfilled by the insured before the insurer may be liable on a policy. In determining whether a clause is a condition precedent, the ordinary principles of construction of contracts apply, and the court will consider the wider context and commercial purpose of the condition, whatever its label. The crucial question, to be determined by construing the terms of the particular contract, is whether the parties intended that the insurer's duty to perform its obligations under the policy was to be dependent on the prior fulfilment by the insured of the specified condition. If so, the clause is a condition precedent. Breach of a condition precedent entitles the insurer to refuse payment even though he may have suffered no prejudice from the breach. Conditions precedent in policies of insurance are usually procedural conditions, such as notice provisions and claims co-operation clauses. This is because breach of a procedural condition may have significant adverse consequences for insurers, making it more difficult for them to investigate a claim or defend third party proceedings; and because these consequences are in themselves likely to make it difficult for insurers to prove the loss which they have suffered as a result of the insured's breach.[1]

1 See further **PARA 3.5** and **CHAPTER 7**, Presentation of claims.

BREACH OF WARRANTY

11.3 Policy terms which are not conditions precedent to insurers' liability[1] are traditionally divided into three categories:[2]

(1)   'warranties';
(2)   'innominate' or 'intermediate' terms; and
(3)   all other terms: these 'ordinary' terms are, confusingly, called 'warranties' in ordinary contract law; they have no special name in insurance law.

The consequences of breach of a warranty depend on whether the contract was entered into before, or on or after, 12 August 2016.[3] In contracts entered into prior to 12 August 2016 and variations to such contracts, the answers given by the insured to questions in a proposal form are often converted into warranties by a clause which either stipulates expressly that the insured warrants the truth of the answers, or provides that the answers are to be the basis of the contract between the parties.[4] Such clauses are known as 'basis' clauses. For contracts entered into on or after 12 August 2016 and variations to such contracts, contractual clauses are no longer capable of converting pre-contractual representations into warranties.[5]

1   See PARA 3.5.
2   See PARAS 3.4 and 3.7–3.9.
3   See PARA 3.7.
4   See PARA 11.16.
5   Insurance Act 2015, ss 9 and 22(2)–(3).

DUTY OF UTMOST GOOD FAITH

11.4   Contracts of insurance belong to a small group of contracts known as contracts of utmost good faith, often referred to as contracts *'uberrimae fidei'*. The facts material to the bargain to be struck are within the knowledge of one of the parties only (in the case of insurance, the person proposing the risk), and a duty of utmost good faith is accordingly imposed on that party. The key characteristic of a contract of utmost good faith, which distinguishes it from contracts of other types, is that mere non-disclosure of material circumstances (as opposed to misrepresentation) is sufficient grounds for avoidance of the contract. In a contract of insurance, the circumstances material to the risk are usually wholly within the knowledge of the insured, and the insurer decides whether to accept the risk, and at what premium and on what other terms, on the basis of the insured's presentation of the risk. Although the duty of utmost good faith is a mutual duty owed by insurer and insured to one another,[1] the original remedy of avoidance of the contract of insurance, rather than damages, meant that it was difficult to envisage a situation in which the insured would want to rely upon it.[2]

Both the content of the duty of good faith and the consequences of breach depend on whether the contract or any variation of it was entered into before, or on or after, 12 August 2016[3] or, in the case of consumer insurance, before, or on or after, 6 April 2013.[4]

The duty of utmost good faith is described in s 17 of the Marine Insurance Act 1906. This is one of a group of sections which were a partial codification of the common law, and which are treated by the courts as applying in disputes concerning non-marine insurance even though they apply directly only to marine insurance.[5] As a result, it is a convenient statement of the principle. Section 17 provides as follows (the words in square brackets are repealed by the Insurance Act 2015[6]):

'17 Insurance is uberrimae fidei

A contract of insurance is a contract based on the utmost good faith[, and, if the utmost good faith be not observed by either party, the contract may be avoided by the other party].'

Sections 18 to 20 of the Marine Insurance Act 1906 are concerned with non-disclosure and misrepresentation in the negotiation of a contract of insurance. These are specific aspects of the general principle of utmost good faith.[7]

Despite its position in the Marine Insurance Act 1906 at the beginning of a group of sections dealing with pre-contractual negotiations, s 17 is a broad provision, on the face of it unlimited in scope, which has been construed as applying both to pre-contractual negotiations and after the contract of insurance has been entered into.[8] In relation to pre-contractual negotiations, the duty of utmost good faith applies in the form of the doctrines of non-disclosure and misrepresentation, each of which has its own detailed rules.[9] After the underwriter has assessed the risk and the contract has been entered into, the core element of the duty of utmost good faith which remains is one of honesty in the presentation of a claim.[10] There are, however, certain other circumstances in which the duty of good faith may arise. These include the following (the summary is taken from the judgment of Longmore LJ in *K/S Merc-Scandia XXXXII v Certain Lloyd's Underwriters Subscribing to Lloyd's Policy No 25T 105487, The Mercandian Continent*):[11]

(1) variations to the risk: breach of the duty of good faith entitles the insurer to avoid the variation, but not the original policy;
(2) renewals: breach of the duty of good faith does not entitle the insurer to avoid the existing policy; this is just the normal pre-contractual duty of good faith, operating between parties to an existing contract of insurance;
(3) 'held covered' cases;
(4) request by insurer for information during the currency of the policy: if the insurer has a right to information by virtue of an express or implied term, there may be a duty of good faith in the giving of such information. The right to information is typically a feature of liability policies, including reinsurance contracts. This appears to be an example of a contractual duty of good faith, as distinct from the duty of good faith which arises by operation of law. Breach may give rise to a claim in damages, according to ordinary principles of construction, but does not give rise to a right to avoid the policy; and
(5) defence of a claim by insurers under a liability policy. If insurers decide to take over the insured's defence of a claim under a liability policy, the insured and insurer are required to act in good faith towards each other.

The existence of a right to cancel a policy does not give rise to a continuing duty of good faith, or duty of disclosure, during the currency of the policy.[12] Further, once parties to a contract of insurance become involved in litigation, it seems that the duty of good faith ceases to apply, and their obligations to one another are governed by the Civil Procedure Rules.[13]

Insofar as an insurer owes a relevant duty of good faith, it does not extend to any general duty to warn an insured that it needs to comply with policy terms.[14] It has been suggested, but not decided, that the duty of utmost good faith might itself restrict insurers' right to avoid for non-disclosure[15] or to refuse an extension of time for compliance with a condition precedent.[16]

For contracts entered into from 12 August 2016 onwards, and variations agreed after that date to contracts entered into at any time, ss 18 to 20 of the Marine Insurance Act 1906 are omitted and replaced by a statutory 'duty of fair presentation', any rule of law to the same effect ss 18 to 20 is abolished,[17] and any rule of law permitting a party to a contract of insurance to avoid the contract on the ground that the utmost good faith has not been observed by the other party is abolished.[18] Further, any rule of law to the effect that a contract of insurance is a contract based on the utmost good faith is modified to the extent required by the Insurance Act 2015 and the Consumer Insurance (Disclosure and Representations) Act 2012;[19] accordingly, the application of s 17 of the Marine Insurance Act 1906 is subject to the provisions of those Acts.[20]

1 *Manifest Shipping Co Ltd v Uni-Polaris Insurance Co Ltd, The Star Sea* [2001] UKHL 1, [2003] AC 469, para 47 (Lord Hobhouse).

2 The example given by Lord Mansfield in *Carter v Boehm* (1766) 3 Burr 1905, 1909, is of the insurer who privately knows at the time of entering into a contract of marine insurance that the ship has already arrived. In *Diab v Regent Insurance Co Ltd* [2006] UKPC 29, [2007] 1 WLR 797, the Privy Council rejected the insured's argument that the insurer was in breach of the post-contractual duty of good faith by failing to warn him when discussing a potential claim that time was about to run out for compliance with a condition precedent in respect of the claim (para 28).

3 Insurance Act 2015, ss 2–8, 22(1) and (3), and 23(2) (the Insurance Act 2015 was passed on 12 February 2015).

4 See **PARAS 11.40–11.47**. In addition, ICOBS provides that an insurer must not unreasonably reject a claim (including by terminating or avoiding a policy), and that a rejection of a consumer policyholder's claim is unreasonable, except where there is evidence of fraud, if it is, in relation to contracts entered into or variations agreed on or before 5 April 2013, for non-disclosure of a fact material to the risk which the policyholder could not reasonably be expected to have disclosed, or non-negligent misrepresentation of a fact material to the risk, or breach of warranty or condition unless the circumstances of the claim are connected to the breach, or if it is, in relation to contracts entered into or variations agreed on or after 6 April 2013, for misrepresentation by a customer and the misrepresentation is not a 'qualifying misrepresentation' as defined in ICOBS 8.1.3R (ICOBS 8.1.1R–ICOBS 8.1.2R). For the meaning of 'evidence of fraud', see **PARA 11.49**. Breach of ICOBS is actionable at the suit of a 'private person': see **PARA 8.2**.

5 *Pan Atlantic Insurance Co Ltd v Pine Top Insurance Co Ltd* [1995] 1 AC 501, 518, 541, [1994] 2 Lloyd's Rep 427, 432, 447, HL (Lord Mustill); *PCW Syndicates v PCW Reinsurers* [1996] 1 WLR 1136, 1140, CA (Staughton LJ); *HIH Casualty and General Insurance Ltd v Chase Manhattan Bank* [2003] UKHL 6, [2003] 2 Lloyd's Rep 61, para 42 (Lord Hoffmann). The group includes ss 17 to 20 of the Marine Insurance Act 1906.

6 Section 14(3)(a).

7 *Société Anonyme d'Intermédiaires Luxembourgeois v Farex Gie* [1995] LRLR 116, 142, CA (Dillon LJ); *PCW Syndicates v PCW Reinsurers* [1996] 1 WLR 1136, 1145, CA (Staughton LJ). An insured acting with the utmost good faith may nevertheless be deemed, by virtue of the provisions of s 17, to be guilty of non-disclosure (and therefore, technically, in breach of the duty of utmost good faith).

8 *Manifest Shipping Co Ltd v Uni-Polaris Insurance Co Ltd, The Star Sea* [2001] UKHL 1, [2003] AC 469; *Agapitos v Agnew, The Aegeon* [2002] EWCA Civ 247, [2003] QB 556, para 13 (Mance LJ).

9 See further **PARAS 11.5–11.34**.

10 *Manifest Shipping Co Ltd v Uni-Polaris Insurance Co Ltd, The Star Sea* [2001] UKHL 1, [2003] AC 469,; *K/S Merc-Scandia XXXXII v Certain Lloyd's Underwriters Subscribing to Lloyd's Policy No 25T*

105487, The Mercandian Continent [2001] EWCA Civ 1275, [2001] 2 Lloyd's Rep 563, 571, para 22 (Longmore LJ). This aspect is considered at **PARAS 11.49–11.53**.

11 [2001] EWCA Civ 1275, [2001] 2 Lloyd's Rep 563, CA, para 22.

12 *New Hampshire Insurance Co v MGN Ltd* [1997] LRLR 24, 59–62, CA (Staughton LJ); *Manifest Shipping Co Ltd v Uni-Polaris Insurance Co Ltd, The Star Sea* [2001] UKHL 1, [2003] AC 469, para 56 (Lord Hobhouse); *K/S Merc-Scandia XXXXII v Certain Lloyd's Underwriters Subscribing to Lloyd's Policy No 25T 105487, The Mercandian Continent* [2001] EWCA Civ 1275, [2001] 2 Lloyd's Rep 563, paras 21 and 22 (Longmore LJ). In his speech in *Manifest Shipping Co Ltd v Uni-Polaris Insurance Co Ltd, The Star Sea* [2001] UKHL 1, [2003] AC 469, Lord Hobhouse (at para 71) disapproved the use of the decision of Hirst J in *Black King Shipping Corpn v Massie, The Litsion Pride* [1985] 1 Lloyd's Rep 437 to support a general view of the post-contractual duty of good faith (and see *New Hampshire Insurance Co v MGN Ltd* [1997] LRLR 24, 59–62, CA (Staughton LJ).

13 *Manifest Shipping Co Ltd v Uni-Polaris Insurance Co Ltd, The Star Sea* [2001] UKHL 1, [2003] AC 469, paras 73–77 (Lord Hobhouse) and 110 (Lord Scott) (preferring to leave the decision for a case where the point was critical to the result); *K/S Merc-Scandia XXXXII v Certain Lloyd's Underwriters Subscribing to Lloyd's Policy No 25T 105487, The Mercandian Continent* [2001] EWCA Civ 1275, [2001] 2 Lloyd's Rep 563, para 22 (Longmore LJ); *Agapitos v Agnew, The Aegeon* [2002] EWCA Civ 247, [2003] QB 556, para 52 (Mance LJ).

14 *Ted Baker plc v AXA Insurance UK plc (No 2)* [2014] EWHC 3548 (Comm), [2015] Lloyd's Rep IR 325, para 126 (Eder J).

15 *Drake Insurance plc v Provident Insurance plc* [2003] EWCA Civ 1834, [2004] 1 Lloyd's Rep 268, paras 79–93 (Rix LJ), 143–145 (Clarke LJ) and 165–178 (Pill LJ).

16 *Diab v Regent Insurance Co Ltd* [2006] UKPC 29, [2007] 1 WLR 797, para 28 (Lord Scott).

17 Insurance Act 2015, ss 2–8, 21(1)–(3) and 22(1) and (3).

18 Insurance Act 2015, s 14(1).

19 Insurance Act 2015, s 14(2).

20 Insurance Act 2015, s 14(3). The Explanatory Notes to the 2015 Act say (at para 116) that the intention of s 14 is that good faith will remain an interpretative principle, with s 17 of the 1906 Act and the common law continuing to provide that insurance contracts are contracts of good faith. Explanatory Notes do not form part of a statute, are not endorsed by Parliament and cannot be amended by it; in so far as they cast light on the objective setting or contextual scene of a statute and the mischief to which it is aimed, they are an admissible aid to construction: *Flora v Wakom (Heathrow) Ltd* [2006] EWCA Civ 1103, [2007] 1 WLR 482, paras 15–16 (Brooke LJ).

DUTY OF UTMOST GOOD FAITH IN THE PRESENTATION OF THE RISK: NON-DISCLOSURE AND MISREPRESENTATION: PRE-CONSUMER INSURANCE (DISCLOSURE AND REPRESENTATIONS) ACT 2012 AND PRE-INSURANCE ACT 2015

11.5   The duty of utmost good faith in the presentation of the risk has undergone significant statutory reform in recent years. Contracts entered into before the new statutory provisions come into force remain subject to the old law, which is set out here. This is the law as it applies to contracts of consumer insurance entered into, and variations agreed, before 6 April 2013[1] and contracts of non-consumer insurance entered into, and variations agreed, before 12 August 2016.[2] In addition, the duty of fair presentation under the Insurance Act 2015 retains or adapts many of the features of the law as it has been developed by the courts over many years, and this is therefore likely to remain relevant to cases decided under the 2015 Act.

As we have seen, the inequalities of knowledge between insured and underwriter led, in insurance law, to the creation of a special duty to make accurate disclosure of sufficient facts to restore the balance and remedy the injustice of holding the underwriter to what is, essentially, a speculative agreement which he would otherwise be unable fairly to assess.[3] Although non-disclosure was, in the earliest cases, referred to as 'concealment', even an innocent non-disclosure has always been sufficient for avoidance, provided the other necessary requirements are met. The same is true of misrepresentations.

The basic principles governing non-disclosure and misrepresentation in insurance contracts are set out in ss 17 to 20 of the Marine Insurance Act 1906. These sections were a partial codification of the common law, and are applied by the courts in disputes concerning non-marine insurance, even though they do not apply directly outside the marine insurance sphere.[4] Non-disclosure and misrepresentation are separate but substantially overlapping doctrines, and many of the applicable legal principles are common to both. This is unsurprising given that in most situations it would be possible to convert a failure to disclose into an implied representation that the information put forward gave a true and fair picture of the risk. For example, if the question, 'Have you ever sustained a loss?' were answered, 'Yes, last March, £150' when the insured had sustained two other losses, this would be, simultaneously, a failure to disclose the two other losses and an implied misrepresentation that the insured had suffered only one loss of £150 the previous March.[5] Indeed, a plea of non-disclosure is almost invariably supported by an alternative plea of misrepresentation of this nature.[6] What follows applies equally to both non-disclosure and misrepresentation, unless otherwise stated. The duty to make disclosure arises only in relation to contracts of insurance, and not contracts for insurance,[7] including binding authorities,[8] which are not contracts *uberrimae fidei* and are not governed by ss 17 to 20 of the Marine Insurance Act 1906.

1 Consumer Insurance (Disclosure and Representations) Act 2012, s 12(4) (the 2012 Act came into force on 6 April 2013). For the 2012 Act, see **PARAS 11.40–11.47**.
2 Insurance Act 2015, ss 2–8, 22(1) and (3), and 23(2) (the 2015 Act was passed on 12 February 2015). For the 2015 Act, see **PARAS 11.35–11.39**.
3 See *Carter v Boehm* (1766) 3 Burr 1905, 1909 (Lord Mansfield); *Greenhill v Federal Insurance Co Ltd* [1927] 1 KB 65, 76–77, CA (Scrutton LJ); and see, generally, the extensive discussion of the historical development of the duty of disclosure in the speech of Lord Mustill in *Pan Atlantic Insurance Co Ltd v Pine Top Insurance Co Ltd* [1995] 1 AC 501, [1994] 2 Lloyd's Rep 427, HL.
4 See **PARA 11.4**, note 10.
5 The question and answer are taken from *Krantz v Allan* (1921) 9 Ll L Rep 410.
6 See *HIH Casualty and General Insurance Ltd v Chase Manhattan Bank* [2003] UKHL 6, [2003] 2 Lloyd's Rep 16, paras 21 (Lord Bingham) and 71 (Lord Hoffmann).
7 *HIH Casualty and General Insurance Ltd v Chase Manhattan Bank* [2001] 1 Lloyd's Rep 30; affd: [2001] EWCA Civ 1250, [2001] 2 Lloyd's Rep 483, (point not considered on appeal: [2003] UKHL 6, [2003] 2 Lloyd's Rep 61).
8 *John W Pryke v Gibbs Hartley Cooper Ltd* [1991] 1 Lloyd's Rep 602, 616 (Waller J).

Materiality and inducement

11.6 The insured is under an obligation to disclose to the insurer circumstances material to the risk which he wishes to insure. In order to avoid a policy for non-disclosure or misrepresentation, the insurer must show not only that the non-disclosure or misrepresentation was material, which is an objective test, but that it induced him to enter into the contract, either at all or on the terms on which it was made. Materiality and inducement are judged at the time of placement of the risk.[1] The requirement of materiality is contained in s 18(1) of the Marine Insurance Act 1906. The requirement for inducement, which does not appear in the sub-section, was established only as a result of the decision of the House of Lords in *Pan Atlantic Insurance Co Ltd v Pine Top Insurance Co Ltd*.[2] Section 18(1) provides as follows:

> 'Subject to the provisions of this section, the assured must disclose to the insurer, before the contract is concluded, every material circumstance which is known to the assured, and the assured is deemed to know every circumstance which, in the ordinary course of business, ought to be known by him. If the assured fails to make such disclosure, the insurer may avoid the contract.'

The same test of materiality applies in relation to non-disclosure and to misrepresentation, and is conveniently stated in s 18(2) of the Marine Insurance Act, which provides:[3]

> 'Every circumstance is material which would influence the judgment of a prudent insurer in fixing the premium, or in determining whether he will take the risk.'

Section 18(2) is subject to s 18(3), which sets out a series of circumstances which need not be disclosed, in the absence of inquiry from the insurer. These include any circumstance which diminishes the risk, any circumstance which is known or presumed to be known to the insurer,[4] any circumstance as to which information is waived by the insurer,[5] and any circumstance which it is superfluous to disclose by reason of any express or implied warranty.[6] The obligation to disclose material facts or circumstances includes intelligence received or known to the insured which raises doubts as to the risk, but does not extend to mere speculation or rumour.[7]

Whether a non-disclosure or misrepresentation is material is a question of fact.[8] The concept of the hypothetical prudent insurer employed in ss 18(2) and 20(2) makes it clear that the test of materiality is an objective one.[9] The rationale for the principle was explained by Bayley J in *Lindenau v Desborough*:[10]

> '... the proper question is, whether any particular circumstance was in fact material? and not whether the party believed it to be so. The contrary doctrine would lead to frequent suppression of information, and it would often be extremely difficult to shew that the party neglecting to give the information thought it material. But if it be held that all material facts must be disclosed, it will be the interest of the assured to make a full and fair disclosure of all the information within their reach.'

It may be that some characteristics of the particular insurer should however be taken into account in order to identify what the reasonably prudent insurer would regard as material;[11] for example, in the case of a proposed motor insurance, it might be appropriate to ask what the reasonably prudent motor insurer would regard as material;[12] and in the case of an insurer whose underwriting criteria in relation to both acceptability of a proposal and the rating of the premium were formulated in advance and applied by a broker pursuant to a binding authority by means of a rigid 'points' system,[13] it might be relevant to ask whether a fact such as a speeding conviction would be material to the reasonably prudent insurer with a 'points' system of underwriting.[14] The characteristics to be imputed to a prudent insurer are in substance a matter for the courts to decide.[15] The materiality of an individual fact must be considered in the light of those other facts which are, and those which are not, disclosed to underwriters.[16] There is room for a test of proportionality, having regard to the nature of the risk and the moral hazard under consideration; there may be things which are too old, or insufficiently serious to require disclosure.[17]

There is a line of cases in which it is said (often obliquely) that the test of materiality is whether a reasonable man with the insured's knowledge would have recognised that the knowledge was material.[18] This is not the test: if it were, the hypothetical prudent underwriter would not be relevant, and expert underwriting evidence as to materiality would not be admissible.[19] This is clear not only from the wording of ss 18(2) and 20(2) of the Marine Insurance Act 1906, but also from another line of cases in which the issue has been considered expressly, culminating in the decision of the House of Lords in *Pan Atlantic Insurance Co Ltd v Pine Top Insurance Co Ltd.*[20]

In *Pan Atlantic Insurance Co Ltd v Pine Top Insurance Co Ltd,*[21] the House of Lords, by a bare majority, rejected the so-called 'decisive influence' construction of ss 18(2) and 20(2), holding that it was not necessary to show that full and accurate disclosure would have led the prudent underwriter to a different decision on accepting or rating the risk, but that circumstances were material if they would have been taken into account by the underwriter when assessing the risk which he was consenting to assume. In addition, and unanimously, their Lordships decided that, in order to entitle an insurer to avoid a policy for material non-disclosure or misrepresentation, it was necessary to show (the burden of proof being on the insurer) that the non-disclosure or misrepresentation had induced the making of the policy, either at all or on the terms on which it was made (the so-called 'actual inducement' test), and that this requirement should be implied into the Act despite being absent from its wording. In so doing, their Lordships rejected the argument that the establishment of a material non-disclosure or misrepresentation was sufficient to enable the underwriter to avoid the policy, and in this respect overruled the decision of the Court of Appeal in *Container Transport International Inc v Oceanus Mutual Underwriting Association (Bermuda) Ltd* ('the *CTI* case').[22] The decision in the *CTI* case was much criticised, not least because without any requirement for inducement:[23]

> '... one could in theory reach the absurd position where the Court might be satisfied that the insurer in question would, in fact, not have been so influenced but that other prudent insurers would have been. It would then be a very odd result if the defendant insurer could nevertheless avoid the policy.'

The meaning of 'inducement' in this context is the same as in the general law of contract,[24] and applies equally to misrepresentation and to non-disclosure.[25] The misrepresentation or non-disclosure need not be the sole cause of the underwriter acting as he did: the fact that it was a cause is sufficient to constitute inducement, and whether or not this was so is a question of fact.[26]

It appears that a misrepresentation by a broker to the leading underwriter which entitles him to avoid his contract with the insured does not automatically entitle the following market to avoid.[27] This is consistent with the requirement of actual inducement of the underwriter and, at least in the case of non-disclosure, would allow the insured to argue that an underwriter who had been content to rely solely on the leading underwriter's assessment of the risk had waived the insured's duty of disclosure. This raises the interesting prospect of the following market attempting to establish that they were induced to enter into their respective contracts with the insurer by a material (and partially implied) representation that the leading underwriter had accepted the risk, on the terms set out in the slip, and after a fair presentation of the risk.[28]

1 *Brotherton v Aseguradora Colseguros SA* [2003] EWCA Civ 705, [2003] Lloyd's Rep IR 746, para 15 (Mance LJ) and para 39 (Buxton LJ).
2 [1995] 1 AC 501, [1994] 2 Lloyd's Rep 427, HL.
3 Section 18(2) applies in relation to non-disclosure. Misrepresentation by an assured or his agent is dealt with in similar terms in s 20(2).
4 See further **PARA 11.8**.
5 See further **PARA 11.14**.
6 See further **PARA 11.8**.
7 *Carter v Boehm* (1766) 3 Burr 1905, 1917–1918 (Lord Mansfield); *Decorum Investments Ltd v Atkin, The Elena G* [2001] 2 Lloyd's Rep 378, para 27 (Steel J); *Brotherton v Aseguradora Colseguros SA* [2003] EWCA Civ 705, [2003] Lloyd's Rep IR 746, paras 28 (Mance LJ) and 39 (Buxton LJ).
8 Sections 18(4) and 20(7) of the Marine Insurance Act 1906. See also **PARA 11.19**.
9 See also *Anglo-African Merchants Ltd v Bayley* [1970] 1 QB 311, 319 (Megaw J); *Lambert v Co-operative Insurance Society Ltd* [1975] 2 Lloyd's Rep 485, CA, followed in *Woolcott v Sun Alliance and London Insurance Ltd* [1978] 1 WLR 493, 498 (Caulfield J) (retrial ordered on other grounds [1979] 1 Lloyd's Rep 231, CA); *St Paul Fire & Marine Insurance Co (UK) Ltd v McConnell Dowell Constructors Ltd* [1995] 2 Lloyd's Rep 116, 122, CA (Evans LJ: the 'prudent insurer' is 'no more than the anthropomorphic conception of the standards of professional underwriting which the Court finds it appropriate to uphold').
10 (1828) 8 B & C 586, 592.
11 *Drake Insurance plc v Provident Insurance plc* [2003] EWCA Civ 1834, [2004] 1 Lloyd's Rep 268, paras 140 and 142 (Clarke LJ); *Norwich Union Insurance Ltd v Meisels* [2006] EWHC 2811, [2007] 1 Lloyd's Rep IR 69, para 25 (Tugendhat J).
12 *Drake Insurance plc v Provident Insurance plc* [2003] EWCA Civ 1834, [2004] 1 Lloyd's Rep 268, paras 140 and 142 (Clarke LJ).
13 *Drake Insurance plc v Provident Insurance plc* [2003] EWCA Civ 1834, [2004] 1 Lloyd's Rep 268, para 3 (Rix LJ).
14 *Drake Insurance plc v Provident Insurance plc* [2003] EWCA Civ 1834, [2004] 1 Lloyd's Rep 268, paras 141–142 (Clarke LJ).
15 *Norwich Union Insurance Ltd v Meisels* [2006] EWHC 2811, [2007] 1 Lloyd's Rep IR 69, para 25 (Tugendhat J).
16 *Inversiones Manria SA v Sphere Drake Insurance Co plc, The Dora* [1989] 1 Lloyd's Rep 69, 89 (Phillips J).
17 *Norwich Union Insurance Ltd v Meisels* [2006] EWHC 2811, [2007] 1 Lloyd's Rep IR 69, para 25 (Tugendhat J).
18 These include *Joel v Law Union and Crown Insurance Co Ltd* [1908] 2 KB 863, 884, CA (Fletcher Moulton LJ); *Roselodge Ltd v Castle* [1966] 2 Lloyd's Rep 113, 129–131 (McNair J). In *Horne v Poland* [1922] 2 KB 364, Lush J stated (at 366–367) that the requirement is to disclose facts within the insured's knowledge, or which would be within the knowledge of an ordinary reasonable person, if they would naturally influence a reasonable underwriter; but he also referred (at 367) to the requirement to disclose what a reasonable man would disclose. See also *Anglo-African Merchants Ltd v Bayley* [1970] 1 QB 311, in which Megaw J skirted round the issue (at 319). In *North Star Shipping Ltd v Sphere Drake Insurance plc* [2006] EWCA Civ 378, [2006] 2 Lloyd's Rep 183, Longmore LJ suggested (at para 53) that it might be time to change the law at least to the extent that an insured's disclosure obligation should be to disclose matters which the insured knows are relevant to the insurer's decision to accept the risk or which a reasonable insured could be expected to know are relevant to that decision. See also **PARAS 8.7** and **11.40–11.47**.
19 *Lambert v Co operative Insurance Society Ltd* [1975] 2 Lloyd's Rep 485, 492, CA (Cairns LJ).
20 [1995] 1 AC 501, [1994] 2 Lloyd's Rep 427, HL. The cases include: *Ionides v Pender* (1874) LR 9 QB 531; *Re Yager and Guardian Assurance Co* (1912) 108 LT 38, 44 (Channell J); *Mutual Life Ins Co of New York v Ontario Metal Products Co Ltd* [1925] AC 344, 350–351, PC, applied: *Zurich General Accident and Liability Insurance Co Ltd v Morrison* [1942] 2 KB 53, CA (a decision concerning the wording of s 10(5) of the Road Traffic Act 1934, which is essentially in the same terms as s 18(2) of the Marine Insurance Act 1906); *Lambert v Co-operative Insurance Society Ltd* [1975] 2 Lloyd's Rep 485, CA.

21 [1995] 1 AC 501, [1994] 2 Lloyd's Rep 427, HL; see, also, *St Paul Fire & Marine Insurance Co (UK) Ltd v McConnell Dowell Constructors Ltd* [1995] 2 Lloyd's Rep 116, 122–124, CA (Evans LJ).

22 [1984] 1 Lloyd's Rep 476, CA.

23 *Berger and Light Diffusers Pty Ltd v Pollock* [1973] 2 Lloyd's Rep 442, 463 (Kerr J). This neat encapsulation of the problem with the decision in the *CTI* case in fact pre-dated that decision by about ten years. As a member of the Court of Appeal in the *CTI* case, Kerr J was subsequently persuaded to change his mind. At the same time as partially overruling the *CTI* case, the House of Lords expressly approved *Berger and Light Diffusers Pty Ltd v Pollock* [1973] 2 Lloyd's Rep 442.

24 *Pan Atlantic Insurance Co Ltd v Pine Top Insurance Co Ltd* [1995] 1 AC 501, 550, [1994] 2 Lloyd's Rep 427, 452, HL (Lord Mustill); *St Paul Fire & Marine Insurance Co (UK) Ltd v McConnell Dowell Constructors Ltd* [1995] 2 Lloyd's Rep 116, 124, CA (Evans LJ).

25 *Pan Atlantic Insurance Co Ltd v Pine Top Insurance Co Ltd* [1995] 1 AC 501, 549–550, [1994] 2 Lloyd's Rep 427, 452, HL (Lord Mustill).

26 *Edgington v Fitzmaurice* (1885) 29 Ch D 459, 481, CA (Cotton LJ); *JEB Fasteners Ltd v Marks Bloom & Co* [1983] 1 All ER 583, CA; *St Paul Fire & Marine Insurance Co (UK) Ltd v McConnell Dowell Constructors Ltd* [1995] 2 Lloyd's Rep 116, 124, CA (Evans LJ); *Avon Insurance plc v Swire Fraser Ltd* [2000] Lloyd's Rep IR 535, 540 (Rix J) (the misrepresentation or non-disclosure must be 'a real and substantial part' of what induced the insurer to enter into the contract); *Assicurazioni Generali SpA v Arab Insurance Group* [2002] EWCA Civ 1642, [2003] Lloyd's Rep IR 131, 148, paras 59 and 62 (Clarke LJ), 175, para 215 (Ward LJ).

27 *General Accident Fire and Life Assurance Corpn v Tanter, The Zephyr* [1985] 2 Lloyd's Rep 529, 539, CA (Mustill LJ).

28 In *Brotherton v Aseguradora Colseguros SA* [2003] EWHC 1741 (Comm), [2003] 1 Lloyd's Rep IR 762, Morison J held (at para 44) that the following market wrote the risk partly on the basis that there had been a fair presentation to the lead underwriter, and that if the lead underwriter was entitled to avoid the policy, so was the following market.

Proof of materiality and inducement

11.7   The burden of proof in relation to both materiality and inducement is on the insurer seeking to avoid the policy.[1] In determining, in any given case, whether the insurer is entitled to avoid the policy on grounds of non-disclosure or misrepresentation, it will normally be necessary for expert evidence to be called in order to establish materiality, on the basis of the hypothetical prudent underwriter of s 18(2) of the 1906 Act, and for the actual underwriter to give evidence as to whether the non-disclosure or misrepresentation, if found to be material, did in fact induce him to enter into the policy.[2] Although a question of fact as opposed to law,[3] the question whether a particular circumstance is material requires the court to make a value judgment; in deciding whether a circumstance would affect the thinking of a prudent insurer, evidence of how reputable insurers experienced in the relevant class of business exercise their underwriting judgment, and what matters do in fact influence such judgment, is generally helpful and important to ensure that the court's findings are grounded in commercial reality, but such evidence cannot be conclusive of what the notional prudent insurer would regard as material.[4] It should always be borne in mind that the usefulness of the evidence may be undermined if the expert gives his view on the basis of unreliable assumptions of fact.[5] In a clear case, no evidence will be necessary to discharge the burden of proving materiality.[6]

Once materiality has been shown, the test of inducement is not a heavy one;[7] there is no presumption that the insurer was induced to enter into the contract by the material misrepresentation or non-disclosure, but the facts may be such that it is to be inferred that the particular insurer was so induced even in the absence of evidence from him.[8] Conversely, the court may reject evidence given by the particular underwriter that he was induced by the material non-disclosure or misrepresentation to enter into the policy on the terms on which he did.[9] In *North Star Shipping Ltd v Sphere Drake Insurance plc*,[10] Colman J said:[11]

> 'In evaluating the underwriters' evidence it is important to keep firmly in mind that all their evidence is necessarily hypothetical and that hypothetical evidence by its very nature lends itself to exaggeration and embellishment in the interests of the party on whose behalf it is given. It is very easy for an underwriter to convince himself that he would have declined a risk or imposed special terms if given certain information. For this reason, such evidence has to be rigorously tested by reference to logical self-consistency, and to such independent evidence as may be available.'

Avoidance is a drastic remedy, and where the alleged non-disclosure or misrepresentation is innocent, or at least not dishonest, it may be that the court will place more emphasis on the burden of proof of inducement which lies on the insurer.[12]

The hypothetical full disclosure which is under consideration is such disclosure as would ordinarily be made on a fair presentation of the risk.[13] It seems that this may include consideration of additional undisclosed facts which are not in themselves material but without which disclosure of the material facts would have been meaningless and inaccurate.[14] Where diffuse matters can be said to be material facts, it is unrealistic to evaluate the issue of inducement except on the hypothesis of the disclosure of all the facts found to be material facts as distinct from isolated material matters.[15]

Where the underwriter uses set underwriting guidelines, a rigid 'points' system or a computer program which automatically rejects certain risks, evidence of the basis on which the system operates may be sufficient to establish inducement.[16] If a material fact, had it been known to the insurer prior to the conclusion of the policy, would have led to an increase in the premium, inducement is established even if the amount of the increase is uncertain.[17]

In order to determine whether the making of a misrepresentation induced the insurer to enter into a contract, the critical counterfactual question to ask is in principle whether the insurer would still have contracted on the same terms if the representation had not been made; the question of what the insurer would have done if told the truth can only be relevant insofar as the answer bears on this critical question,[18] or insofar as the insured was under a duty to disclose the true facts.[19]

Where the underwriter relies on expert opinion in deciding whether to accept a risk in a specialist field – for example, from doctors in respect of life insurance – evidence from experts in the same discipline may be admissible at trial on the issue of materiality,[20] although it should be noted that in an Australian case in 1985 the Privy Council criticised the trial judge (after he had ruled, for reasons which are not relevant here, that the expert underwriting evidence was inadmissible) for proceeding to determine the issue of materiality solely by reference to the views of expert veterinary surgeons.[21]

Insurers can readily request that any oral statement on which they have relied be put in writing, and for this reason are likely to face difficulties in discharging the burden of proof when relying on an alleged oral misrepresentation which is not recorded on the slip, or in an endorsement, or in a contemporary scratched document.[22]

11.7 Insurers' defences

1 *Corcos v De Rougemont* (1925) 23 Ll L Rep 164, 167–168 (McCardie J) (materiality); *Drake Insurance plc v Provident Insurance plc* [2003] EWCA Civ 1834, [2004] 1 Lloyd's Rep 268, para 64 (Rix LJ) (inducement).

2 *Pan Atlantic Insurance Co Ltd v Pine Top Insurance Co Ltd* [1995] 1 AC 501, 571, [1994] 2 Lloyd's Rep 427, 466, HL (Lord Lloyd); *Roselodge Ltd v Castle* [1966] 2 Lloyd's Rep 113, 129–131 (McNair J).

3 Marine Insurance Act 1906, ss 18(4) and 20(7); *Involnert Management Inc v Aprilgrange Ltd* [2015] EWHC 2225 (Comm), [2015] 2 Lloyd's Rep 289, para 97 (Leggatt J).

4 *Involnert Management Inc v Aprilgrange Ltd* [2015] EWHC 2225 (Comm), [2015] 2 Lloyd's Rep 289, para 98 (Leggatt J).

5 See *Decorum Investments Ltd v Atkin, The Elena G* [2001] 2 Lloyd's Rep 378, para 109, 393 (Steel J).

6 *Glicksman v Lancashire and General Assurance Co Ltd* [1927] AC 139, 143, HL (Viscount Dunedin); *Taylor v Eagle Star Insurance Co Ltd* (1940) 67 Ll L Rep 136 (Macnaghten J); *Mundi v Lincoln Assurance Ltd* [2005] EWHC 2678 (Ch), [2006] 1 Lloyd's Rep IR 353, para 62 (Lindsay J); *Bonner v Cox* [2005] EWCA Civ 1512, [2006] 2 Lloyd's Rep 152, 162, para 38 (Waller LJ); *A C Ward & Son Ltd v Catlin (Five) Ltd (No 2)* [2009] EWHC 3122 (Comm), [2010] Lloyd's Rep IR 695, para 218 (Flaux J); *Synergy Health (UK) Ltd v CGU Insurance plc* [2010] EWHC 2583 (Comm), [2011] Lloyd's Rep IR 500, para 152 (Flaux J); *Brit UW Ltd v F & B Trenchless Solutions Ltd* [2015] EWHC 2237 (Comm), [2016] Lloyd's Rep IR 69, paras 102, 108 and 139 (Carr J).

7 *WISE (Underwriting Agency) Ltd v Grupo Nacional Provincial SA* [2004] EWCA Civ 962, [2004] 2 Lloyd's Rep 483, para 99 (Rix LJ).

8 *Pan Atlantic Insurance Co Ltd v Pine Top Insurance Co Ltd* [1995] 1 AC 501, 551, [1994] 2 Lloyd's Rep 427, 453, HL (Lord Mustill); *St Paul Fire & Marine Insurance Co (UK) Ltd v McConnell Dowell Constructors Ltd* [1995] 2 Lloyd's Rep 116, 127, CA (Evans LJ); *Marc Rich & Co AG v Portman* [1996] 1 Lloyd's Rep 430, 441–442 (Longmore J) (point not expressly considered by the Court of Appeal in their finding on inducement: [1997] 1 Lloyd's Rep 225, 234–235 (Leggatt LJ)); *Assicurazioni Generali SpA v Arab Insurance Group* [2002] EWCA Civ 1642, [2003] Lloyd's Rep IR 131, 149, para 62 (Clarke LJ); *Bonner v Cox* [2005] EWCA Civ 1512, [2006] 2 Lloyd's Rep 152, 162, para 40 (Waller LJ). There is no room for the drawing of inferences in a case where the actual underwriter gives evidence: *Sea Glory Maritime Co v Al Sagr National Insurance Co, The MV Nancy* [2013] EWHC 2116 (Comm), [2014] 1 Lloyd's Rep 14, para 116 (Blair J).

9 See eg *Sugar Hut Group Ltd v Great Lakes Reinsurance (UK) plc* [2010] EWHC 2636 (Comm), [2011] Lloyd's Rep IR 198, para 27 (Burton J) (underwriter's evidence accepted); *A C Ward & Son Ltd v Catlin (Five) Ltd (No 2)* [2009] EWHC 3122 (Comm), [2010] Lloyd's Rep IR 695, paras 225–226 and 232 (Flaux J) (underwriter's evidence accepted); *Synergy Health (UK) Ltd v CGU Insurance plc* [2010] EWHC 2583 (Comm), [2011] Lloyd's Rep IR 500, paras 185–186 (Flaux J) (underwriter's evidence rejected); *Involnert Management Inc v Aprilgrange Ltd* [2015] EWHC 2225 (Comm), [2015] 2 Lloyd's Rep 289, paras 218–220 (Leggatt J) (underwriter's evidence rejected); *Axa Versicherung AG v Arab Insurance Group (BSC)* [2015] EWHC 1939, [2016] Lloyd's Rep IR 1, paras 120–121 and 179 (Males J) (underwriter's evidence rejected).

10 [2005] EWHC 665 (Comm), [2005] 2 Lloyd's Rep 76.

11 At para 254 (point not considered on appeal: [2006] EWCA Civ 378, [2006] 2 Lloyd's Rep 183).

12 *Kausar v Eagle Star Insurance Co Ltd* [2000] Lloyd's Rep IR 154, CA, 157 (Staughton LJ); applied: *Axa Versicherung AG v Arab Insurance Group (BSC)* [2015] EWHC 1939, [2016] Lloyd's Rep IR 1, paras 121–122 and 179 (Males J) and *Brit UW Ltd v F & B Trenchless Solutions Ltd* [2015] EWHC 2237 (Comm), [2016] Lloyd's Rep IR 69, para 118 (Carr J).

13 *Synergy Health (UK) Ltd v CGU Insurance plc* [2010] EWHC 2583 (Comm), [2011] Lloyd's Rep IR 500, para 187 (Flaux J).

14 *Sea Glory Maritime Co v Al Sagr National Insurance Co, The MV Nancy* [2013] EWHC 2116 (Comm), [2014] 1 Lloyd's Rep 14, para 162–166 (Blair J) (this is not disclosure of other matters, in addition to material ones: if insured had disclosed PSC (Port State Control) detentions of vessel for stated deficiencies, would have been meaningless and inaccurate simply to disclose fact of detentions without saying what was done about them); see also *Drake Insurance plc v Provident Insurance plc* [2003] EWCA Civ 1834, [2004] 1 Lloyd's Rep 268, paras 74–75 (Rix LJ), 138 (Clarke LJ) and 162–163 (Pill LJ: disagreeing, and taking the view that it was the information which was with the insurer which was relevant, not the true position).

15 *North Star Shipping Ltd v Sphere Drake Insurance plc* [2005] EWHC 665 (Comm), [2005] 2 Lloyd's Rep 76, para 255 (Colman J) (point not considered on appeal: [2006] EWCA Civ 378, [2006] 2 Lloyd's Rep 183); *Joseph Fielding Properties (Blackpool) Ltd v Aviva Insurance Ltd* [2010] EWHC 2192 (QB), [2011] Lloyd's Rep IR 238, paras 144 and 150 (HHJ Waksman QC).

16 See *Hazel v Whitlam* [2004] EWCA Civ 1600, [2005] 1 Lloyd's Rep IR 168, paras 15–19 (Scott Baker LJ) and 34 (May LJ): inducement found on the basis of evidence regarding the computer program which had been used to consider and rate the risk; *Drake Insurance plc v Provident Insurance plc* [2003] EWCA Civ 1834, [2004] 1 Lloyd's Rep 268: a rigid 'points' system was used and in which the facts were more complicated; and *Mundi v Lincoln Assurance Ltd* [2005] EWHC 2678 (Ch), [2006] 1 Lloyd's Rep IR 353, para 69 (Lindsay J): inducement found on the basis of evidence regarding the insurer's guidelines and practices without evidence from the actual underwriter concerned with acceptance and assessment of the risk.

17 *New Hampshire Insurance Co v Oil Refineries Ltd* [2002] 2 Lloyd's Rep 462, paras 45–46 (HHJ Chambers QC); applied: *Brit UW Ltd v F & B Trenchless Solutions Ltd* [2015] EWHC 2237 (Comm), [2016] Lloyd's Rep IR 69, para 114 (Carr J).

18 *Involnert Management Inc v Aprilgrange Ltd* [2015] EWHC 2225 (Comm), [2015] 2 Lloyd's Rep 289, paras 211–212 (Leggatt J).

19 *Involnert Management Inc v Aprilgrange Ltd* [2015] EWHC 2225 (Comm), [2015] 2 Lloyd's Rep 289, paras 213–217 (Leggatt J). It is suggested that situations in which a misrepresentation is material, but the insured was not under concomitant a duty to disclose the true facts, are likely to be rare.

20 *Yorke v Yorkshire Insurance Co* [1918] 1 KB 662; see also *Mutual Life Ins Co of New York v Ontario Metal Products Co Ltd* [1925] AC 344, PC, in which the Privy Council admitted the evidence of the insurers' medical examiner on the basis that he was the person by whom they would be guided in accepting or declining risks.

21 *Eagle Star Insurance Co Ltd v National Westminster Finance Australia Ltd* (1985) 58 ALR 165, 172, PC.

22 *Re Universal Non-Tariff Fire Insurance Co* (1875) LR 19 Eq 485, 499–500 (Sir R Malins V-C); *Sirius International Insurance Corpn v Oriental Assurance Corpn* [1999] Lloyd's Rep IR 343, 354 (Longmore J).

Circumstances which need not be disclosed

11.8   In the absence of inquiry by the insurer, the insured need not disclose any circumstance which diminishes the risk,[1] any circumstance which is known or presumed to be known to the insurer,[2] any circumstance as to which information is waived by the insurer,[3] or any circumstance which it is superfluous to disclose by reason of any express or implied warranty.[4]

Knowledge for the purposes of s 18(3)(b) is actual knowledge,[5] which includes circumstances of which the insurer was wilfully blind, but does not extend to those in respect of which he merely had means of discovering the truth.[6] The insurer is presumed to know matters of common notoriety or knowledge, and matters which an insurer in the ordinary course of his business, as such, ought to know.[7] The insurer is therefore deemed to know the risks which are an ordinary attribute of the class of business in question.[8] The fact that a matter has appeared in the Lloyd's List does not in itself mean that it is something which an insurer, in the ordinary course of his business, ought to know.[9] Electronic databases should not be treated as equivalent to information in hard copy such as newpapers: the underwriter does not have to carry the information in an electronic database in his head, and online information is available to be called up when required.[10] However, the fact that information is available to an underwriter online does not necessarily give rise to a presumption of knowledge.[11]

In the case of superfluity pursuant to s 18(3)(d), disclosure is only excused where the insurers have the full protection of the warranty; in other words, material facts do not have to be disclosed if those facts will amount to a breach of warranty enabling the insurers to avoid liability.[12] If a draft warranty as to a third party approval is deleted shortly before a policy is issued because it has been fulfilled, s 18(3)(d) does not apply,[13] but the insurer may be held to have waived any further disclosure by the insured in relation to the subject-matter of the draft warranty.[14]

1 Section 18(3)(a) of the Marine Insurance Act 1906.
2 Section 18(3)(b) of the Marine Insurance Act 1906.
3 Section 18(3)(c) of the Marine Insurance Act 1906. See **PARA 11.14**.
4 Section 18(3)(d) of the Marine Insurance Act 1906.
5 *Bates v Hewitt* (1867) LR 2 QB 595.
6 *Bates v Hewitt* (1867) LR 2 QB 595; *Morrison v Universal Marine Insurance Co* (1872) LR 8 Exch 40 (material fact appeared in Lloyd's List, to which underwriters subscribed; broker not relieved of obligation to make disclosure unless underwriters actually aware of fact); *Container Transport International Inc v Oceanus Mutual Underwriting Association (Bermuda) Ltd* [1984] 1 Lloyd's Rep 476, CA, 497 (Kerr LJ), 529 (Stephenson LJ: 'an underwriter is not a detective'); *Newbury International Ltd v Reliance National Insurance Co (UK) Ltd* [1994] 1 Lloyd's Rep 83, 90 (Hobhouse J); *Winter v Irish Life Assurance plc* [1995] 2 Lloyd's Rep 274, 280–281 (Sir Peter Webster).
7 Section 18(3)(b) of the Marine Insurance Act 1906.
8 *Bates v Hewitt* (1867) LR 2 QB 595, 610–611 (Shee J); *Hales v Reliance Fire & Accident Insurance Corpn Ltd* [1960] 2 Lloyd's Rep 391 (presence on newsagent's premises of small quantity of fireworks around bonfire night).
9 *Morrison v Universal Marine Insurance Co* (1872) LR 8 Exch 40.
10 *Sea Glory Maritime Co v Al Sagr National Insurance Co, The MV Nancy* [2013] EWHC 2116 (Comm), [2014] 1 Lloyd's Rep 14, paras 173–174 (Blair J).
11 *Sea Glory Maritime Co v Al Sagr National Insurance Co, The MV Nancy* [2013] EWHC 2116 (Comm), [2014] 1 Lloyd's Rep 14, paras 175–178 (Blair J).
12 *Synergy Health (UK) Ltd v CGU Insurance plc* [2010] EWHC 2583 (Comm), [2011] Lloyd's Rep IR 500, para 184 (Flaux J); *Garnat Trading & Shipping (Singapore) Pte Ltd v Baominh Insurance Corporation* [2010] EWHC 2578 (Comm), [2011] 1 Lloyd's Rep 589, para 153 (Christopher Clarke J); point not considered on appeal: [2011] EWCA Civ 773, [2011] 2 Lloyd's Rep 492. See also *Inversiones Manria SA v Sphere Drake Insurance Co plc, The Dora* [1989] 1 Lloyd's Rep 69, 91–92 (Phillips J); *J Kirkaldy & Sons Ltd v Walker* [1999] Lloyd's Rep IR 410, 423 (Longmore J); *O'Kane v Jones, The Martin P* [2003] EWHC 3470 (Comm), [2004] 1 Lloyd's Rep 389, para 240 (Deputy High Court Judge Richard Siberry QC); *International Management Group (UK) Ltd v Simmonds* [2003] EWHC 177 (Comm), [2004] Lloyd's Rep IR 247, para 126 (Cooke J).
13 *Garnat Trading & Shipping (Singapore) Pte Ltd v Baominh Insurance Corporation* [2010] EWHC 2578 (Comm), [2011] 1 Lloyd's Rep 589, para 153 (Christopher Clarke J: 'The section does not apply to draft warranties which are not incorporated in the policy'); point not considered on appeal: [2011] EWCA Civ 773, [2011] 2 Lloyd's Rep 492.
14 *Garnat Trading & Shipping (Singapore) Pte Ltd v Baominh Insurance Corporation* [2010] EWHC 2578 (Comm), [2011] 1 Lloyd's Rep 589, paras 153–155 (Christopher Clarke J); point not considered on appeal: [2011] EWCA Civ 773, [2011] 2 Lloyd's Rep 492.

Knowledge of the insured and his agents

11.9 The insured's duty to disclose material circumstances extends to four categories of knowledge:

(1) the insured's actual knowledge;
(2) knowledge which the insured is deemed to have for these purposes, pursuant to s 18(1) of the Marine Insurance Act 1906;
(3) knowledge of those concerned in the insured's business, which is imputed to the insured according to ordinary agency principles; and
(4) knowledge of the insured's agent to insure (in other words, his broker), which must be disclosed pursuant to s 19 of the Marine Insurance Act 1906.

Insured's actual knowledge

11.10   Where the insured is a natural person, actual knowledge means that which is known to him personally.[1] For these purposes, an insured has knowledge if he deliberately shuts his eyes to the truth (this is 'Nelsonian blindness' – the deliberate putting of the telescope to the blind eye).[2] In *Horne v Poland*,[3] Lush J adopted a slightly different formulation, saying that the insured was under a duty to disclose material facts which were within his knowledge, 'or would be within the knowledge of an ordinary reasonable person'.[4]

1 *PCW Syndicates v PCW Reinsurers* [1996] 1 WLR 1136, 1142, CA (Staughton LJ); *Economides v Commercial Assurance Co plc* [1998] QB 587, 601, CA (Simon Brown LJ).
2 *Economides v Commercial Assurance Co plc* [1998] QB 587, 602, CA (Simon Brown LJ).
3 [1922] 2 KB 364.
4 At 367 (in a passage summarising the effect of Fletcher Moulton LJ's judgment in *Joel v Law Union and Crown Insurance Co* [1908] 2 KB 863, CA).

Insured's deemed knowledge

11.11   Where the insured is a natural person, he must disclose that which is known to him personally,[1] together with the knowledge which, in the ordinary course of business, ought to be known by him.[2] Where the insured is effecting insurance solely in his private capacity, therefore, the only knowledge which he must disclose is that which is known to him personally.[3] The suggestion in the judgment of Fletcher Moulton LJ in *Joel v Law Union and Crown Insurance Co*,[4] that '[t]he duty is a duty to disclose, and you cannot disclose what you do not know',[5] is therefore accurate only in relation to the insured acting in a private capacity.

Whether a circumstance is one which, in the ordinary course of business, ought to be known by the insured, can only be determined by considering the ordinary course of business in which the insured is involved.[6] Further, whether a circumstance is one which, in the ordinary course of business, ought to be known by the insured, depends on whether an honest and competent agent would communicate it to the insured in the ordinary course of business.[7] In *London General Insurance Co v General Marine Underwriters' Association*,[8] a lack of efficiency or organisation within the insured's business meant that the employees of the insured, which was an insurer seeking to place reinsurance of a particular risk, had failed to consult the casualty slips which had been delivered to the office, and were not aware that it had suffered a partial loss in respect of the risk. The Court of Appeal held that the loss ought to have been known to the company, in the ordinary course of business, and it was therefore deemed to know of the loss. As the company had not disclosed the loss, the reinsurer was entitled to avoid the reinsurance.

The insured is under no duty to disclose the fact that its agents are defrauding it, either because that is not something which is communicated in the ordinary course of business, or because if an agent is acting in fraud of his principal, the knowledge of an agent is not imputed to the principal, by way of exception to the normal rule.[9] In *PCW Syndicates v PCW Reinsurers*, Staughton LJ preferred to rest his decision on this issue on the wording of s 18 of the Marine Insurance Act 1906, and it is suggested that this is consistent with the approach of ss 18 and 19 of that Act, which do not import from the law of agency the concept of imputation of knowledge, but instead adopt a freestanding concept of deemed knowledge in defined circumstances. Whether the insured is under any duty to disclose to the insured the fact that its agents, although not acting fraudulently, are acting in breach of duty, was expressly left open by the Court of Appeal in *Kingscroft Insurance Co Ltd v Nissan Fire & Marine Insurance Co Ltd*,[10] Colman J having held at first instance that the insured was under no such duty because, due to the nature of the information, it could not be inferred that the agent would disclose it to his principal in the ordinary course of business.[11]

1 *PCW Syndicates v PCW Reinsurers* [1996] 1 WLR 1136, 1142, CA (Staughton LJ); *Economides v Commercial Assurance Co plc* [1998] QB 587, 601, CA (Simon Brown LJ).
2 Section 18 of the Marine Insurance Act 1906, which may be taken as stating the law in relation to all types of 40 insurance: see **PARA 11.5**.
3 *Economides v Commercial Assurance Co plc* [1998] QB 587, 601, CA (Simon Brown LJ). See also **PARAS 11.40–11.47**.
4 [1908] 2 KB 863, CA.
5 At 884.
6 *Sea Glory Maritime Co v Al Sagr National Insurance Co, The MV Nancy* [2013] EWHC 2116 (Comm), [2014] 1 Lloyd's Rep 14, para 307 (Blair J) (in that case, the business of shipowning and managers).
7 *PCW Syndicates v PCW Reinsurers* [1996] 1 WLR 1136, 1143, CA (Staughton LJ). For the position of members of underwriting syndicates at Lloyd's, who may have no knowledge of the syndicate's business, see Staughton LJ's remarks at 1143.
8 [1921] 1 KB 104, CA.
9 *Re Hampshire Land Co* [1896] 2 Ch 743; *Newsholme Bros v Road Transport and General Insurance Co Ltd* [1929] 2 KB 356, 375–376, CA (Scrutton LJ); *Société Anonyme d'Intermédiaires Luxembourgeois v Farex Gie* [1995] LRLR 116, 143, CA (Dillon LJ); *PCW Syndicates v PCW Reinsurers* [1996] 1 WLR 1136, 1143–1144, CA (Staughton LJ).
10 [1999] Lloyd's Rep IR 371, CA.
11 See, similarly, *Arab Bank plc v Zurich Insurance Co* [1999] 1 Lloyd's Rep 262, 282–283 (Rix J); see also *Group Josi Re v Walbrook Insurance Co Ltd* [1996] 1 Lloyd's Rep 345, 366–367, CA (Saville LJ).

Knowledge imputed to the insured of those concerned in his business

11.12 Where the insured is a legal person, such as a limited company, it can know nothing directly, and can only know anything through its employees or agents. The extent of knowledge of a company for any given purpose can only be determined by reference to the rule of law – in this case, s 18 of the Marine Insurance Act 1906 – which makes the enquiry necessary.[1] For the purposes of s 18, therefore, knowledge held by employees whose business it is to arrange insurance for the company is relevant.[2]

1 *Meridian Global Funds Management Asia Ltd v Securities Commission* [1995] 2 AC 500, 507, PC (Lord Hoffmann); *PCW Syndicates v PCW Reinsurers* [1996] 1 WLR 1136, 1142, CA (Staughton LJ).
2 *PCW Syndicates v PCW Reinsurers* [1996] 1 WLR 1136, 1142, CA (Staughton LJ), leaving open the question of whether the knowledge of other employees might also be relevant for this purpose.

Knowledge of 'agent to insure'/broker

11.13 Where insurance is effected for the insured by an 'agent to insure', the agent must disclose to the insurer not only every material circumstance which the insured would be bound to disclose to the insurer if he effected the insurance directly according to the principles set out above (unless the information comes to the agent too late to be disclosed),[1] but also every material circumstance which is known to the agent.[2] Failure by the broker to disclose all material circumstances in accordance with s 19 entitles the insurer to avoid the policy.[3] For the purposes of s 19, the agent's knowledge includes both actual knowledge and deemed knowledge, an agent to insure being deemed to know every circumstance which, in the ordinary course of business, ought to be known by him or ought to have been communicated to him.[4] The broker is under no duty to disclose, pursuant to s 19, any circumstances which the insured himself is under no duty to disclose pursuant to s 18.[5] The effect of s 19 is not to impute the agent's knowledge to the insured: the section imposes a freestanding duty on the agent to disclose material facts which are within the agent's knowledge, breach of which entitles the insurer to avoid the policy.[6]

An 'agent to insure' within the meaning of s 19 is the broker who places the insurance with the insurers, and makes the contract, and does not include any intermediate broker.[7] But if intermediaries have information which in the ordinary course of business ought to be known or communicated to the agent to insure, or which the agent to insure ought to know, s 19 imposes a duty on the agent to insure to disclose that information.[8] The wording of s 19 is without limitation, and appears to require disclosure of all material circumstances known to the broker, whether his knowledge was acquired in his capacity as broker for the insured or otherwise.[9] If material facts are known to a broker but not communicated to the insured, the broker is under a duty, pursuant to s 19, to disclose those facts to the insurer if the broker places the risk on behalf of the insured; but as the broker is an 'agent to insure' and not an 'agent to know', the insured is not deemed to know of those facts, and if he subsequently changes brokers and the same risk is then placed with insurers, he is under no duty to disclose those facts to insurers.[10] However, if the insured's broker has knowledge of material facts but, having commenced negotiations with insurers, fails to disclose the facts to the insurers and then ceases to act, and the insured itself adopts and concludes the negotiations with the insurers, the insurers are entitled to avoid the policy for non-disclosure of the material facts.[11] Section 19 does not impose a duty on the broker to disclose to the insurer the fact that he is acting in fraud of his principal.[12]

Where the broker is the insurer's agent, rather than the insured's, the broker's knowledge of material facts will be imputed to the insurer, and the insurer will not be able to rely, as against the insured, upon any failure by the broker to disclose this information.[13] The insurer will not be entitled to avoid the policy on the grounds of misrepresentation by its own agent.[14] A condition which provides that any omission or misrepresentation of material fact in the proposal form renders the policy void, even if known to an agent of the company, is enforceable if it is expressed in clear terms.[15]

A misrepresentation made by an agent of the insured to the insurer will entitle the insurers to avoid the policy as if the misrepresentation had been made by the insured directly.[16] In *Sharp v Sphere Drake Insurance plc, The Moonacre*,[17] the brokers forged the client's signature on the proposal form and the court held that this entitled the insurer to avoid the policy for non-disclosure of material facts and misrepresentation. In *Woolcott v Excess Insurance Co Ltd*,[18] the broker held a binding authority[19] and was for this reason held to be the agent of the insurer (it being also conceded). As a result, the insurer was not entitled to avoid the policy on grounds of material non-disclosure (of the insured's criminal record) but was entitled to an indemnity from the broker, who was held to have known of the criminal record and failed to disclose it to the insurer.

1 Section 19(b) of the Marine Insurance Act 1906, which may be taken as stating the law in relation to all types of insurance. See further **PARA 11.5**.
2 Section 19 of the Marine Insurance Act 1906. 'Agent to insure' is the phrase used in the section.
3 *Blackburn, Low & Co v Haslam* (1888) 21 QBD 144 (breach of agent's duty to disclose at common law, which was subsequently codified in s 19 of the Marine Insurance Act 1906).
4 Section 19(a) of the Marine Insurance Act 1906. See the discussion of these concepts in relation to s 18(1) of the Marine Insurance Act 1906 at **PARA 11.11**.
5 *Société Anonyme d'Intermédiaires Luxembourgeois v Farex Gie* [1995] LRLR 116, 157 (Saville LJ), CA; see also *HIH Casualty and General Insurance Ltd v Chase Manhattan Bank* [2003] UKHL 6, [2003] 2 Lloyd's Rep 61, paras 7–8 (Lord Bingham), 50–55 (Lord Hoffmann) and 93 (Lord Hobhouse) (clause in contract of insurance construed not as waiving disclosure of information as to material circumstances, but as relieving the insured of any personal duty to make disclosure). The circumstances which the insured is under no duty to disclose are set out at **PARA 11.8**.
6 *Blackburn, Low & Co v Vigors* (1887) 12 App Cas 531, HL (reinsurance, but principle equally applicable to insurance: see, eg, at 540 (Lord Watson)); *Société Anonyme d'Intermédiaires Luxembourgeois v Farex Gie* [1995] LRLR 116, 142, CA (Dillon LJ); *PCW Syndicates v PCW Reinsurers* [1996] 1 WLR 1136, 1145, CA (Staughton LJ).
7 *PCW Syndicates v PCW Reinsurers* [1996] 1 WLR 1136, 1148 (Rose LJ), 1149–1151 (Saville LJ), CA.
8 *PCW Syndicates v PCW Reinsurers* [1996] 1 WLR 1136, 1150–1151, CA (Saville LJ); *Group Josi Re v Walbrook Insurance Co Ltd* [1996] 1 Lloyd's Rep 345, CA, 361, 365–367 (Saville LJ).
9 The following favour a wide interpretation of the duty of disclosure: *Thames and Mersey Marine Insurance Co Ltd v Gunford Ship Co Ltd* [1911] AC 529, HL (agent insured ship on behalf of owner of the ship, and insured on his own behalf moneys due to him from the ship; held that s 19 required disclosure of agent's own policies to insurers of the ship); dicta in *El Ajou v Dollar Land Holdings plc* [1994] 2 All ER 685, 702, CA (Hoffmann LJ); *Société Anonyme d'Intermédiaires Luxembourgeois v Farex Gie* [1995] LRLR 116, 143 (Dillon LJ), 149 (Hoffmann LJ), CA; there are dicta in favour of restricting s 19 to knowledge acquired by the agent in his capacity as agent: *PCW Syndicates v PCW Reinsurers* [1996] 1 WLR 1136, 1146–1147 (Staughton LJ), 1148 (Rose LJ), CA.
10 *Blackburn, Low & Co v Vigors* (1887) 12 App Cas 531, HL (reinsurance, but principle equally applicable to insurance: see, eg, at 540 (Lord Watson)); *Société Anonyme d'Intermédiaires Luxembourgeois v Farex Gie* [1995] LRLR 116, 142, CA (Dillon LJ).
11 *Blackburn, Low & Co v Haslam* (1888) 21 QBD 144.
12 *PCW Syndicates v PCW Reinsurers* [1996] 1 WLR 1136, 1145–1147 (Staughton LJ), 1148 (Rose LJ), CA.
13 See, for example, *Woolcott v Excess Insurance Co Ltd* [1979] 2 Lloyd's Rep 210 (Cantley J): the insurer was held to be entitled to an indemnity from the broker for failing to disclose to the insurer the insured's criminal record, of which it was aware.
14 *Re Universal Non-Tariff Fire Insurance Co* (1875) LR 19 Eq 485: agent solicited business on behalf of insurer, inspected insured's property and reported to insurer, who sought unsuccessfully to avoid on basis of alleged misrepresentation in description of construction of roof of part of property.
15 *Broad & Montague Ltd v South East Lancashire Insurance Co Ltd* (1931) 40 Ll L Rep 328, 330 (Rowlatt J).
16 Section 20(1) of the Marine Insurance Act 1906 (which applies to all types of insurance: see **PARA 11.5**). See *Anderson v Pacific Fire and Marine Insurance Co* (1872) LR 7 CP 65; *Allen v Universal Automobile Insurance Co Ltd* (1933) 45 Ll L Rep 55, 58 (Wright J).
17 [1992] 2 Lloyd's Rep 501 (Mr A D Colman QC, sitting as a Deputy Judge of the High Court).
18 [1979] 2 Lloyd's Rep 210 (Cantley J).
19 The holder of a binding authority is authorised to bind insurance for the insurer's account, and initial documents of insurance and endorsements, in accordance with a written agreement.

Fair presentation of risk

11.14   In order to discharge the duty to make disclosure of material facts, the insured must make a fair presentation of those facts to the underwriter.[1] In some markets and types of insurance, proposal forms containing a series of standard questions are used for this purpose.[2] In others, including Lloyd's, the risk is placed by the broker on the basis of information provided to the underwriter in a face-to-face meeting. In *Greenhill v Federal Insurance Co Ltd*,[3] Scrutton LJ gave the following description of the placement of a risk in these circumstances:[4]

> 'I have always understood the proper line that an underwriter should take, except in matters that he is bound to know, is absolutely to abstain from asking any questions, and to leave the insured to fulfil his duty of good faith, and make full disclosure of all material facts, without being asked.'

To consider whether there has been a fair presentation of the risk it is necessary to look at the whole picture presented to underwriters and to compare that with the picture as the insured or the insured's agents knew it to be.[5] A fair presentation of the facts in summary form is sufficient to discharge the duty to make disclosure.[6] Section 18(3) (c) of the Marine Insurance Act 1906 provides that, in the absence of inquiry, any circumstance as to which information is waived by the insurer need not be disclosed.[7] The insurer does not waive disclosure of material information by asking no questions at all, or by asking questions about other matters.[8] In order to establish a waiver, an insurer must have received information such as would put an ordinary careful insurer on inquiry, and nevertheless failed to inquire.[9] For example, if an underwriter is told that the insured intends to ship a cargo of goods of a type unfamiliar to him, and does not ask what they are, he will be held to have waived disclosure of the ordinary qualities of such goods.[10] In the normal case, an underwriter on the London market dealing with a London broker should be able to accept at face value a description of the goods to be insured.[11]

Only once there has been a fair presentation of the material facts is the onus on the underwriter to make inquiries if he wishes to have more information.[12] The duty is not discharged if a material fact is not drawn to the underwriter's attention, but could have been extracted by the underwriter from the information to which he had access or which was cursorily shown to him.[13] A presentation is not fair if unusual facts are not disclosed.[14] An insured's loss experience is always special to the insured, and a presentation is not fair if it does not disclose material losses.[15]

The test of materiality assumes a hypothetical prudent underwriter, and, in some fields, a specialist underwriter may be assumed to know already many of the facts material to a risk.[16] In these circumstances, the duty to make disclosure of material facts is limited to facts special to the risk.[17] It follows that an insured will not be held to have failed to make adequate disclosure simply because the particular underwriter was inexperienced, incompetent or careless.[18] Similarly, if a broker is presenting data to the underwriter, he is under no obligation to disclose his own calculations based on that data, as the underwriter is in as good a position as he is to perform the calculations.[19] In all cases, it is for the underwriter to exercise his judgment of the risk, both as to whether to accept it, and how to rate it: it is no part of the duty of the broker (or the insured) to tell the underwriter how to exercise his judgment.[20] Nevertheless, in assessing the evidence, the court may regard a gross error of judgment by an underwriter as an indication that the risk was not presented fairly.[21]

1 *Container Transport International Inc v Oceanus Mutual Underwriting Association (Bermuda) Ltd* [1984] 1 Lloyd's Rep 476, 497, CA (Kerr LJ).
2 Proposal forms are considered at **PARA 11.15**.

3 [1927] 1 KB 65, CA.

4 At 86; approved: *Marc Rich & Co AG v Portman* [1997] 1 Lloyd's Rep 225, 232, CA (Leggatt LJ).

5 *Inversiones Manria SA v Sphere Drake Insurance Co plc, The Dora* [1989] 1 Lloyd's Rep 69, 89 (Phillips J).

6 *Asfar & Co v Blundell* [1896] 1 QB 123, 129, CA (Lord Esher MR); *Container Transport International Inc v Oceanus Mutual Underwriting Association (Bermuda) Ltd* [1984] 1 Lloyd's Rep 476, 497, CA (Kerr LJ); *Newbury International Ltd v Reliance National Insurance Co (UK) Ltd* [1994] 1 Lloyd's Rep 83, 90 (Hobhouse J).

7 In addition to waiving disclosure on placement of the risk, there may be waiver by the insurer of non-disclosure subsequently discovered: see **PARA 11.63**.

8 *Greenhill v Federal Insurance Co Ltd* [1927] 1 KB 65, CA; *March Cabaret Club & Casino Ltd v London Assurance Ltd* [1975] 1 Lloyd's Rep 169, 176 (May J) (which concerned questions on a proposal form; this issue is considered at **PARA 11.15**).

9 *Greenhill v Federal Insurance Co Ltd* [1927] 1 KB 65, 89, CA (Sargant LJ); *Anglo-African Merchants Ltd v Bayley* [1970] 1 QB 311, 320 (Megaw J); *Container Transport International Inc v Oceanus Mutual Underwriting Association (Bermuda) Ltd* [1984] 1 Lloyd's Rep 476, 511–512 (Parker LJ), 529–530 (Stephenson LJ), CA; *Marc Rich & Co AG v Portman* [1997] 1 Lloyd's Rep 225, 234, CA (Leggatt LJ); *WISE (Underwriting Agency) Ltd v Grupo Nacional Provincial SA* [2004] EWCA Civ 962, [2004] Lloyd's Rep 483, paras 108–111 (Longmore LJ).

10 *Greenhill v Federal Insurance Co Ltd* [1927] 1 KB 65, 73 (Lord Hanworth MR), 85 (Scrutton LJ), CA; *Marc Rich & Co AG v Portman* [1997] 1 Lloyd's Rep 225, 231–232, CA (Leggatt LJ).

11 *WISE (Underwriting Agency) Ltd v Grupo Nacional Provincial SA* [2004] EWCA Civ 962, [2004] Lloyd's Rep 483, paras 116 (Longmore LJ) and 132 (Peter Gibson LJ).

12 *Container Transport International Inc v Oceanus Mutual Underwriting Association (Bermuda) Ltd* [1984] 1 Lloyd's Rep 476, 497, CA (Kerr LJ); *Newbury International Ltd v Reliance National Insurance Co (UK) Ltd* [1994] 1 Lloyd's Rep 83, 90 (Hobhouse J); *Hill v Citadel Insurance Co Ltd* [1997] LRLR 167, 171, CA (Saville LJ); *WISE (Underwriting Agency) Ltd v Grupo Nacional Provincial SA* [2004] EWCA Civ 962, [2004] Lloyd's Rep 483, paras 111 (Longmore LJ) and 130 (Peter Gibson LJ).

13 *Container Transport International Inc v Oceanus Mutual Underwriting Association (Bermuda) Ltd* [1984] 1 Lloyd's Rep 476, 497, CA (Kerr LJ).

14 *Container Transport International Inc v Oceanus Mutual Underwriting Association (Bermuda) Ltd* [1984] 1 Lloyd's Rep 476, 529, CA (Stephenson LJ); *Marc Rich & Co AG v Portman* [1997] 1 Lloyd's Rep 225, 234, CA (Leggatt LJ); see also *Asfar & Co v Blundell* [1896] 1 QB 123, 133, CA (Kay LJ).

15 *Marc Rich & Co AG v Portman* [1997] 1 Lloyd's Rep 225, 232, 234, CA (Leggatt LJ).

16 See **PARA 11.8**.

17 *Newbury International Ltd v Reliance National Insurance Co (UK) Ltd* [1994] 1 Lloyd's Rep 83, 86 (Hobhouse J).

18 *Simner v New India Assurance Co Ltd* [1995] LRLR 240, 250–251 (His Honour Judge Anthony Diamond QC); see also *Ted Baker plc v AXA Insurance UK plc* [2012] EWHC 1406 (Comm), [2013] Lloyd's Rep IR 174, paras 126 and 127 (Eder J; not persuaded that any reliance by underwriter on alleged misrepresentation was reasonable) (point not considered: [2014] EWCA Civ 134).

19 *Aiken v Steward Wrightson Members Agency Ltd* [1995] 2 Lloyd's Rep 618, 648 (Potter J) (reinsurance; the report at [1995] 1 WLR 1281 does not include section J of the judgment, in which the relevant remarks appear).

20 *Newbury International Ltd v Reliance National Insurance Co (UK) Ltd* [1994] 1 Lloyd's Rep 83, 86 (Hobhouse J); *Decorum Investments Ltd v Atkin, The Elena G* [2001] 2 Lloyd's Rep 378, para 25, 382 (Steel J).

21 See *Newbury International Ltd v Reliance National Insurance Co (UK) Ltd* [1994] 1 Lloyd's Rep 83, 88 (Hobhouse J).

Proposal forms and declarations of facts

11.15 In many types of insurance, insurers require the completion of a proposal form, which contains a series of standard questions, before they will accept a risk. The proposer is under an obligation to disclose material facts whether or not there is a proposal form.[1] There is a presumption that matters dealt with in a proposal form are material.[2]

Instead of asking the insured to complete a proposal form, the insurer may ask the insured to sign a declaration or statement of facts, or may inform the insured that the contract is written on the basis that a series of assumptions set out in a statement of facts are true. There is an analogy between insurers asking the insured to make a declaration of facts and requiring the completion of a proposal form,[3] and the cases dealing with proposal forms provide guidance as to how the question of construction, and of waiver, should be approached in the context of a declaration of facts.[4]

The courts apply the same principles of construction whether or not the proposal form is a contractual document.[5] In construing a question in a proposal form, and considering whether the answer given was true, the proposal form must be considered as a whole.[6] If there is any ambiguity in the questions, they will be construed against the insurer, as he drafted them, in accordance with the general principle of construction *contra proferentem*.[7] This is sometimes put another way: where there is ambiguity in the question, the answer must be considered in the light of a 'fair and reasonable construction' of the question,[8] or the construction which an ordinary reasonable man on the street would put on the question.[9] The insured's subjective understanding of the question is not relevant.[10]

These points may be illustrated by examples from decided cases. In *Connecticut Mutual Life Insurance Co of Hertford v Moore*,[11] a proposal form included the following question: 'Have you had any other illness, local disease, or personal injury? and if so, of what nature, how long since, and what effect upon general health?' The deceased insured had answered 'No', and a condition in the policy warranted the truth of the answers given by the insured in the proposal form. Sir Robert P Collier, in giving the judgment of their Lordships, said:[12]

> '... this is a question of a somewhat embarrassing character, and one which the company could hardly have expected to be answered with strict and literal truth. They could not reasonably expect a man of mature age to recollect and disclose every illness, however slight, or every personal injury, consisting of a contusion, or a cut, or a blow, which he might have suffered in the course of his life. It is manifest that this question must be read with some limitation and qualification to render it reasonable ...'

Similarly, in *Dent v Blackmore*,[13] McCardie J indicated that, in answering the question, 'Have you previously held a motor insurance policy; if so, please state the name of the insurance company?', it was not necessary for the proposer to mention 'an insurance policy of a generation ago which can have no bearing at all upon the position at the present time'. As the proposer had omitted to mention a policy which he had held only two or three years earlier, the judge held that the answer to the question was untrue, and that as the proposal was the basis of the policy, the insurer was entitled to avoid the policy.

In *Austin v Zurich General Accident and Liability Insurance Co Ltd*,[14] Tucker J construed a question in a proposal form for motor insurance which asked whether the insured suffered from defective vision, as meaning defects in vision which in some degree affected the competence of the insured as a driver and had not been corrected by glasses or other means. In *Holt's Motors Ltd v South-East Lancashire Insurance Co Ltd*,[15] Scrutton LJ held that the question, 'Has any company or underwriter declined to insure?' clearly required disclosure of the fact that a previous insurer had intimated to the insured that they did not invite renewal, owing to the claims experience. Scrutton LJ's remarks were obiter, as there was a further example of an unambiguous refusal to insure which had also not been disclosed. Greer LJ expressly declined to comment on the first issue, regarding it as a more difficult question.

The inclusion of specific questions in a proposal form may be construed as a waiver by the insurer of the duty to make disclosure of similar information which is not made the subject of a question.[16] For example, if the insured is asked whether he has suffered any loss by theft within the past three years, the insurer is likely to be held to have waived disclosure of any loss by theft occurring before that time, even if such a loss would otherwise be material. The question is whether a reasonable man reading the proposal form would be justified in thinking that the insurer had restricted his right to receive all material information and consented to the omission of the particular information in issue,[17] and the approach is the same whether the insured is a consumer or a business.[18] The inclusion of questions on particular subjects does not constitute a waiver by the insurer of material circumstances in relation to other subjects,[19] but in any event, proposal forms usually contain a general question which asks the insured to disclose any material facts not disclosed elsewhere on the form.[20] The courts apply the same principles of construction to questions of this nature as they do to any other question on the proposal form, and will reject any construction which does not appear reasonable. Unless the general question is worded clearly, it may be construed narrowly as applying only to the questions and answers elsewhere on the proposal form, and not to any matters going beyond their reach.[21]

An unanswered question, or an obviously incomplete answer to a question, may be construed as putting the insurer on inquiry.[22] If, however, the omission to deal with the question or part of it carries with it the clear inference that the proposer intends the answer, or that part of it, to be negative, insurers are not put on inquiry.[23] Here, also, any doubt will be resolved in favour of the insured.[24] Similarly, where an apparently complete answer is given to a question, it will be construed as such. For example, in *Hales v Reliance Fire & Accident Insurance Corpn Ltd*,[25] the proposer answered 'Lighter fuel', to the question 'Are any inflammable oils or goods used or kept on the premises?' The answer was construed by McNair J as meaning that the proposer kept no inflammable oils or goods at the premises except lighter fuel. To this limited extent, *Hales v Reliance* is still good law. However, in another important respect it has been overruled by the Court of Appeal in *Hussain v Brown*.[26] In reaching his conclusion in *Hales v Reliance*, McNair J approved a passage from *MacGillivray on Insurance Law* to the effect that, in fire and burglary insurance, warranties as to the nature of the premises and precautions taken against loss will prima facie be read as applicable to the whole duration of the policy, and held that the warranty as to the keeping of inflammable oils or goods at the premises continued during the currency of the risk. In *Hussain v Brown*,[27] the Court of Appeal held that there is no special principle of insurance law requiring answers in proposal forms to be read, prima facie or otherwise, as importing promises to the future, and that whether they do or not depends on ordinary rules of construction. To this extent, *Hales v Reliance* was held to have been wrongly decided. This is consistent with the general approach to the construction of proposal forms in cases of ambiguity.

Here, again, the position may be affected by a general question in the proposal form seeking disclosure of any material facts not mentioned elsewhere on the form. Where the proposal form includes such a general question, this will be effective to catch matters which the insured might otherwise be entitled to say he was not required to disclose by reason of an ambiguity in one of the specific questions.[28]

Finally, if an insured signs a proposal form before the answers to some of the questions are inserted, he will be taken to have adopted any answers subsequently inserted by his agent.[29]

In any event, deemed knowledge in relation to the risks ordinarily inherent in a particular class of business will not excuse an incorrect answer to a specific question. In *Hales v Reliance*,[30] the proposer was a newsagent whose premises were damaged by a fire caused by the combustion of fireworks which he was offering for sale. As we have seen, he had answered 'Lighter fuel' to the question 'Are any inflammable oils or goods used or kept on the premises?' The answer was construed as meaning that the proposer kept no inflammable oils or goods at the premises except lighter fuel, which was incorrect, as a small quantity of fireworks were usually kept on the premises around Guy Fawkes Day.[31] The fact that an insurer writing this class of business would be deemed to know that a newsagent would be likely to have fireworks on the premises at that time of year was held to be of no relevance to the question of the accuracy of the answer given to the question. As there was a basis clause, the insurer was entitled to repudiate liability under the policy.[32]

It seems that a renewal does not incorporate automatically and implicitly all questions asked in the proposal form or a request for updates on all answers given in the proposal form.[33] It is suggested that whether a misrepresentation made at the time of proposal of the risk or a previous renewal is impliedly repeated on renewal depends on all the circumstances.[34]

1 *Woolcott v Sun Alliance and London Insurance Ltd* [1978] 1 WLR 493.
2 *Mutual Life Ins Co of New York v Ontario Metal Products Co Ltd* [1925] AC 344, 351, PC; *March Cabaret Club & Casino Ltd v London Assurance Ltd* [1975] 1 Lloyd's Rep 169, 176 (May J).
3 *Synergy Health (UK) Ltd v CGU Insurance plc* [2010] EWHC 2583 (Comm), [2011] Lloyd's Rep IR 500, para 165 (Flaux J).
4 *Synergy Health (UK) Ltd v CGU Insurance plc* [2010] EWHC 2583 (Comm), [2011] Lloyd's Rep IR 500, para 165 (Flaux J) (which considered only waiver; it is suggested that the analogy is also apt in relation to the question of construction).
5 The principles discussed here apply specifically to the construction of proposal forms, whether or not the proposal form is a contractual document (see further **PARA 11.16**). The general principles of construction of contracts of insurance are also relevant if the proposal form is a contractual document: see **PARAS 3.11–3.27**.
6 *Glicksman v Lancashire and General Assurance Co Ltd* [1925] 2 KB 593, CA (basis clause), affirmed: [1927] AC 139, HL.
7 *Anderson v Fitzgerald* (1853) 4 HL Cas 484, HL, 498 (Parke B), 507 (Lord St Leonards); *Thomson v Weems* (1884) 9 App Cas 671, 687, HL (Lord Watson); *Condogianis v Guardian Assurance Co Ltd* [1921] 2 AC 125, 130, PC; *Roberts v Plaisted* [1989] 2 Lloyd's Rep 341, 346, CA (Purchas LJ: no ambiguity so no need to construe *contra proferentem*); *Doheny v New India Assurance Co Ltd* [2004] EWCA Civ 1705, [2005] Lloyd's Rep IR 251, para 28 (Staughton LJ: no ambiguity so no need to construe *contra proferentem*); *R & R Developments Ltd v AXA Insurance UK plc* [2009] EWHC 2429 (Ch), [2010] Lloyd's Rep IR 521, para 26 (Nicholas Strauss QC, sitting as a Deputy High Court Judge); *Involnert Management Inc v Aprilgrange Ltd* [2015] EWHC 2225 (Comm), [2015] 2 Lloyd's Rep 289, para 194 (Leggatt J). See further **PARA 3.19**.

8 *Condogianis v Guardian Assurance Co Ltd* [1921] 2 AC 125, 130, PC (basis clause); *Corcos v De Rougemont* (1925) 23 Ll L Rep 164, 166 (McCardie J); *Winter v Irish Life Assurance plc* [1995] 2 Lloyd's Rep 274, 279 (Sir Peter Webster) ('fair'); *Hair v Prudential Assurance Co Ltd* [1983] 2 Lloyd's Rep 667, 672–673 (Woolf J) ('reasonable').

9 *Revell v London General Insurance Co Ltd* (1934) 50 Ll L Rep 114; *Taylor v Eagle Star Insurance Co Ltd* (1940) 67 Ll L Rep 136; *Roberts v Avon Insurance Co Ltd* [1956] 2 Lloyd's Rep 240.

10 *R & R Developments Ltd v AXA Insurance UK plc* [2009] EWHC 2429 (Ch), [2010] Lloyd's Rep IR 521, paras 11–26 (Nicholas Strauss QC, sitting as a Deputy High Court Judge); applied: *Involnert Management Inc v Aprilgrange Ltd* [2015] EWHC 2225 (Comm), [2015] 2 Lloyd's Rep 289, para 193 (Leggatt J).

11 (1881) LR 6 HL 644, PC.

12 At 648.

13 (1927) 29 Ll L Rep 9, 11 (McCardie J).

14 (1944) 77 Ll L Rep 409, 415–416, approved by the Court of Appeal: [1945] KB 250.

15 (1930) 37 Ll L Rep 1, 4, CA.

16 *Joel v Law Union and Crown Insurance Co* [1908] 2 KB 863, 878, CA (Vaughan Williams LJ); *Newsholme Bros v Road Transport and General Insurance Co Ltd* [1929] 2 KB 356, 363, CA (Scrutton LJ); *Schoolman v Hall* [1951] 1 Lloyd's Rep 139, 143, CA (Asquith LJ); *Roberts v Plaisted* [1989] 2 Lloyd's Rep 341, 347–348, CA (Purchas LJ).

17 *Doheny v New India Assurance Co Ltd* [2004] EWCA Civ 1705, [2005] Lloyd's Rep IR 251, paras 17–19 (Longmore LJ) and 37 (Potter LJ).

18 *Doheny v New India Assurance Co Ltd* [2004] EWCA Civ 1705, [2005] Lloyd's Rep IR 251, para 20 (Longmore LJ).

19 *Austin v Zurich General Accident and Liability Insurance Co Ltd* (1944) 77 Ll L R 409, 416 (Tucker J) (issue not considered on appeal: [1945] KB 250, CA); *Zurich General Accident and Liability Insurance Co Ltd v Morrison* [1942] 2 KB 53, CA, approved: *Container Transport International Inc v Oceanus Mutual Underwriting Association (Bermuda) Ltd* [1984] 1 Lloyd's Rep 476, 529, CA (Stephenson LJ); *Schoolman v Hall* [1951] 1 Lloyd's Rep 139, CA, 142 (Cohen LJ), 143 (Asquith LJ); *March Cabaret Club & Casino Ltd v London Assurance Ltd* [1975] 1 Lloyd's Rep 169, 176 (May J).

20 *Lindenau v Desborough* (1828) 8 B & C 586, 591–592 (Lord Tenterden CJ), 593 (Littledale J); *Doheny v New India Assurance Co Ltd* [2004] EWCA Civ 1705, [2005] Lloyd's Rep IR 251, paras 37–38 (Potter LJ).

21 See *Hair v Prudential Assurance Co Ltd* [1983] 2 Lloyd's Rep 667, 673 (Woolf J).

22 *Roberts v Avon Insurance Co Ltd* [1956] 2 Lloyd's Rep 240, 249 (Barry J).

23 *Roberts v Avon Insurance Co Ltd* [1956] 2 Lloyd's Rep 240, 249 (Barry J).

24 *Roberts v Avon Insurance Co Ltd* [1956] 2 Lloyd's Rep 240, 247 (Barry J).

25 [1960] 2 Lloyd's Rep 391.

26 [1996] 1 Lloyd's Rep 627, CA.

27 [1996] 1 Lloyd's Rep 627, CA.

28 *Cleland v London General Insurance Co Ltd* (1935) 51 Ll L Rep 156, CA.

29 *Biggar v Rock Life Assurance Co* [1902] 1 KB 516, 524 (Wright J); *Winter v Irish Life Assurance plc* [1995] 2 Lloyd's Rep 274, 278 (Sir Peter Webster). Note the curious case of *Pearl Life Assurance Co v Johnson* [1909] 2 KB 288, in which the Divisional Court decided that, the proposal having been made without the claimant's knowledge or authority, the insurer could not rely on misrepresentations in the proposal as grounds for avoidance. The factual background to the claimant's involvement (if any) in procuring the issue of the policy is not fully explored in the judgment.

30 [1960] 2 Lloyd's Rep 391.

31 The construction was disapproved in *Hussain v Brown*: see above.

32 See **PARA 11.16**.

33 *Drake Insurance plc v Provident Insurance plc* [2003] EWCA Civ 1834, [2004] 1 Lloyd's Rep 268, para 68 (Rix LJ).

34 In *Sharp v Sphere Drake Insurance plc, The Moonacre* [1992] 2 Lloyd's Rep 501, brokers forged their client's signature to a proposal form, and Mr A D Colman QC, sitting as a Deputy Judge of the High Court, held (at 521–522) that as no subsequent proposal was tendered on renewal, there was continuing reliance by underwriters on the proposal and a continuing duty to disclose any material facts and to correct any misrepresentation included on it. In *Magee v Pennine Insurance Co Ltd* [1969] 2 QB 507, CA, Winn LJ, dissenting, said (at 517) that he was not aware of any authority for the proposition that a warranty given at the inception of a contract of insurance by the terms of the proposal form and its acceptance by the insurers is to be implied indefinitely into renewals of the first contract of insurance which is made of which that warranty is an express term as a condition precedent to liability, and that in every case it must depend on the length of time elapsed, the probability of changes of circumstances, the practicability of adjusting some ages by the addition of a year or more perhaps, and many other considerations, such, for example, as the improbability that the proposer who has called himself the holder of a provisional licence will continue to be either a holder of a provisional licence or a holder of any licence at all indefinitely. See also PARA **11.21**.

'Basis clauses'

11.16   In non-consumer insurance contracts entered into prior to 12 August 2016 and variations to such contracts,[1] where an express clause makes the insured's answers to questions in a proposal form the basis of the contract (commonly known as a 'basis clause'),[2] or if the insured warrants that the answers are true,[3] or both,[4] an inaccurate answer has the effect that the insurance cover never attaches under the contract,[5] however immaterial the answers might otherwise be, without those answers having induced the insurer to enter into the contract,[6] and without there being any connection between the breach of warranty and the loss.[7] The result is the same if the truth of the statements in the proposal form is made a condition precedent to the insurer's liability to make any payments under the policy.[8] Lord Watson said in *Thomson v Weems*:[9]

> 'When the truth of a particular statement has been the subject of warranty, no question can arise as to its materiality or immateriality to the risk, it being the very purpose of the warranty to exclude all controversy upon that point.'

A declaration that the answers given in the proposal form is true is not sufficient to make those answers the basis of the contract.[10] If the insurer wishes to make the answers the basis of the contract, this must be stipulated expressly,[11] either in the proposal form or in the policy. A basis clause is equally effective whether it appears in the proposal form[12] or in the policy,[13] or in both.[14] The same is true of a provision restricting the insurer's right to avoid to cases of wilful misrepresentation.[15]

It is sometimes said that a warranty as to the truth of particular statements demonstrates that the parties consider those matters to be material,[16] although whether or not this is so is of no practical importance.[17] Once the statement is part of the contract, all that matters is whether or not, as a matter of fact, it is true; its materiality or otherwise is irrelevant.

In *Joel v Law Union and Crown Insurance Co*,[18] the Court of Appeal construed a series of questions, the answers to which were declared to be true, as requiring honest answers, but not answers which were warranted to be true. Vaughan Williams LJ's reasoning was as follows:[19]

> '... on their face the questions are questions the answers to which no person would warrant. The questions are such that no one but a medical man could answer with an approach to certainty. They are questions to which it would be unreasonable to expect warranted answers. Honest answers were the most any one could expect.'

In *Condogianis v Guardian Assurance Co Ltd*,[20] the Privy Council rejected an argument[21] that an express condition entitling insurers to avoid for material misrepresentation or non-disclosure was to be construed as reintroducing a requirement of materiality even in respect of matters warranted by the insured to be true pursuant to a basis clause. A similar argument was rejected by the House of Lords in *Dawsons Ltd v Bonnin*.[22] In addition, the inclusion of a basis clause does not relieve the insured of his duty of disclosure in relation to material circumstances which are not the subject of questions in the proposal form.[23]

It is unclear whether s 20(5) of the Marine Insurance Act 1906, which provides that a representation as to a matter of expectation or belief is true if made in good faith, and which has been held to be subjective, requiring only honesty and not requiring reasonable grounds for the belief,[24] applies to representations which are warranted to be true and made the basis of the contract. In *Economides v Commercial Assurance Co plc*,[25] there was a basis clause in the proposal form, but the Court of Appeal did not expressly consider its effect. Further, s 20(5) is concerned with misrepresentations which are material, and it would therefore be surprising if it applied to representations warranted to be true and made the basis of the contract, in relation to which considerations of materiality do not arise.

The Consumer Insurance (Disclosure and Representations) Act 2012 provides that representations made by a consumer in connection with a proposed consumer insurance contract, or in connection with a proposed variation to a consumer insurance contract are not capable of being converted into a warranty by means of any provision of the consumer insurance contract (or of the terms of the variation), or of any other contract (and whether by declaring the representation to form the basis of the contract or otherwise).[26]

For non-consumer insurance contracts entered into on or after 12 August 2016 and variations to such contracts, contractual clauses are no longer capable of converting pre-contractual representations into warranties.[27]

The effect of a breach of warranty may be modified by ICOBS.[28]

1 Insurance Act 2015, ss 9 and 22(3).
2 *Dawsons Ltd v Bonnin* [1922] 2 AC 413, HL.
3 *Thomson v Weems* (1884) 9 App Cas 671, HL.
4 *Provincial Insurance Co Ltd v Morgan* [1933] AC 240, HL.
5 *Brit Syndicates Ltd v Italaudit SpA* [2008] UKHL 18, [2008] Lloyd's Rep IR 601, para 24 (Lord Mance).
6 *Winter v Irish Life Assurance plc* [1995] 2 Lloyd's Rep 274, 285 (Sir Peter Webster).
7 See *Hussain v Brown* [1996] 1 Lloyd's Rep 627, 630, CA (Saville LJ).
8 See *Allen v Universal Automobile Insurance Co Ltd* (1933) 45 Ll L Rep 55.
9 (1884) 9 App Cas 671, 689, HL.
10 The reverse is not true: a declaration of truth is not required in addition to a basis clause (see *Dawsons Ltd v Bonnin* [1922] 2 AC 413, HL).
11 *Joel v Law Union and Crown Insurance Co* [1908] 2 KB 863, 874, 886, 894, CA.
12 *Genesis Housing Association Ltd v Liberty Syndicate Management Ltd* [2013] EWCA Civ 1173, [2014] Lloyd's Rep IR 318, para 57 (Jackson LJ); the question of whether the statements in the proposal form were absorbed into the contract of insurance or constituted collateral warranties was expressly left open: see para 63.
13 See *Connecticut Mutual Life Insurance Co of Hertford v Moore* (1881) LR 6 HL 644, PC.
14 See *Thomson v Weems* (1884) 9 App Cas 671, HL.
15 *Hemmings v Sceptre Life Association Ltd* [1905] 1 Ch 365, 369 (Kekewich J).
16 See *Anderson v Fitzgerald* (1853) 4 HL Cas 484, HL, 503 (Lord Cranworth LC); *London Assurance v Mansel* (1879) 11 Ch D 363, 371 (Sir George Jessel MR); *Yorkshire Insurance Co Ltd v Campbell* [1917] AC 218, 225, PC (Lord Sumner); *Dawsons Ltd v Bonnin* [1922] 2 AC 413, 434 (Viscount Cave), 437 (Lord Wrenbury), HL; *Glicksman v Lancashire and General Assurance Co Ltd* [1927] AC 139, 144, HL (Viscount Dunedin).

17 See *Newcastle Fire Insurance Co v Macmorran & Co* (1815) 3 Dow 255, 262–263 (Lord Eldon).
18 [1908] 2 KB 863, CA.
19 At 874.
20 [1921] 2 AC 125, PC.
21 At 130.
22 [1922] 2 AC 413.
23 *Schoolman v Hall* [1951] 1 Lloyd's Rep 139, CA, 142–143 (Cohen LJ), 143 (Asquith LJ).
24 *Economides v Commercial Assurance Co plc* [1998] QB 587, CA.
25 [1998] QB 587, CA.
26 Section 6. See further PARAS **11.40–11.47**.
27 Insurance Act 2015, ss 9 and 22(2)–(3). Section 16(1) of the Insurance Act 2015 provides that a term of a non-consumer insurance contract, or of any other contract, which would put the insured in a worse position as respects representations to which s 9 applies than the insured would be in by virtue of that section is to that extent of no effect. This means that it is not possible to contract out of the statutory prohibition on basis clauses in non-consumer insurance contracts in s 9. Section 9 applies only to non-consumer insurance contracts because basis clauses were prohibited in consumer insurance contracts by the Consumer Insurance (Disclosure and Representations) Act 2012: see note 25 and related text.
28 See PARAS **8.2** and **11.4**.

Statutory limitations on the obligation to disclose material facts

11.17 The obligation to disclose material facts is affected by statute in some areas. The most important is the Rehabilitation of Offenders Act 1974. Criminal convictions are not required to be disclosed, even if material, if they are 'spent' convictions within the meaning of s 1 of the Act.[1] In civil proceedings, evidence as to spent conviction is not admissible, unless the court is satisfied that justice cannot be done without admitting the evidence, and questioning about a spent conviction is not permitted.[2] A rehabilitated person is entitled to treat a question about convictions as not relating to spent convictions.[3] Forbes J suggested, obiter, in *Reynolds v Phoenix Assurance Co Ltd*,[4] that if an insurer would regard a conviction as a material fact, it ought to have been disclosed and therefore justice could almost never be done (the test for admissibility of evidence under the Act) unless evidence as to the conviction were admitted. It is suggested that this pays insufficient regard to the purpose of the Act, and to the wording of s 4(1), which states that an offender whose conviction is spent 'shall be treated for all purposes in law' as a person without such a conviction and that, in the ordinary case, a person with a spent conviction is entitled not to disclose it even if it might otherwise be considered material. If, before a conviction becomes 'spent' within the meaning of the Act, an insured fails to disclose the conviction in circumstances where he is under a duty to do so, that non-disclosure may be a material fact in the context of a subsequent proposal.[5] In these circumstances, the fact that the conviction has become 'spent' within the meaning of the Act such that the insured is no longer under a duty to disclose the conviction itself does not relieve the insured of the duty to disclose his earlier failure to disclose the conviction before it became spent.[6]

A conviction becomes spent after a certain period, depending on the length and type of sentence imposed. A conviction resulting in a sentence of imprisonment of more than six months but no more than 30 months becomes spent after ten years; a sentence of six months or less after seven years.[7] A conviction resulting in a fine becomes spent after five years.[8] These periods are reduced by half where the offender was under the age of 18 at the date of conviction,[9] and specific provision is made for certain sentences confined to young offenders.[10] Convictions resulting in sentences of imprisonment of more than 30 months, including life imprisonment and detention during Her Majesty's pleasure, are expressly excluded from the ambit of the Act.[11]

The proposer's nationality was in the past sometimes held to be a material fact which ought to have been disclosed.[12] An insurer who avoided a policy for failure to disclose the insured's nationality, or his colour, race, ethnic or national origins, would now be liable for race discrimination pursuant to the Race Relations Act 1976.[13]

1 Section 4 of the Rehabilitation of Offenders Act 1974.
2 Sections 4(1) and 7(3) of the 1974 Act.
3 Section 4(2) of the 1974 Act.
4 [1978] 2 Lloyd's Rep 440, 461.
5 *Joseph Fielding Properties (Blackpool) Ltd v Aviva Insurance Ltd* [2010] EWHC 2192 (QB), [2011] Lloyd's Rep IR 238, paras 220–222 (HHJ Waksman QC).
6 *Joseph Fielding Properties (Blackpool) Ltd v Aviva Insurance Ltd* [2010] EWHC 2192 (QB), [2011] Lloyd's Rep IR 238, paras 220–222 (HHJ Waksman QC).
7 Section 5(2)(a) of the 1974 Act.
8 Section 5(2)(a) of the 1974 Act.
9 Section 5(2)(a) of the 1974 Act.
10 Section 5(2)(b) of the 1974 Act.
11 Section 5(1) of the 1974 Act.
12 See *Horne v Poland* [1922] 2 KB 364.
13 Sections 1, 3 and 20 of the Race Relations Act 1976, as amended.

Change in circumstances

11.18   The duty to disclose material facts continues until the contract is concluded (becomes binding).[1] A representation may be withdrawn or corrected before the contract is concluded,[2] and it is at the date the contract is concluded that the truth of a representation is to be assessed.[3] Thus, if a pre-contractual representation as to a material fact is true when it is made, but circumstances subsequently change so as to render it untrue, a failure to correct it before the contract is concluded will entitle the insurer to avoid the policy,[4] the failure to correct the representation constituting both non-disclosure (of the changed circumstances) and misrepresentation (the original representation being now untrue). The existence of a right to cancel a policy does not give rise to a continuing duty of good faith, or duty of disclosure, during the currency of the policy.[5]

In *Kausar v Eagle Star Insurance Co Ltd*,[6] the policy included a condition which provided:

> 'You must tell us of any change of circumstances after the start of the insurance which increases the risk of injury or damage. You will not be insured under the policy until we have agreed in writing to accept the increased risk.'

The Court of Appeal construed this condition as meaning that without the further agreement of the insurer, there would be no cover where the circumstances had so changed that it could properly be said by the insurers that the new situation was something which, on the true construction of the policy, they had not agreed to cover; and that the mere fact that the chances of an insured peril operating increase during the period of the cover would not, save possibly in the most extreme of circumstances, enable the insurer properly to say this, since the insurance bargain is one where, in return for the premium, they take upon themselves the risk that an insured peril will operate.[7] This is also the position at common law in the absence of any such policy term or condition.[8]

1 *Re Yager and Guardian Assurance Co* (1912) 108 LT 38, 44 (Channell J); *Looker v Law Union and Rock Insurance Co Ltd* [1928] 1 KB 554, 559–560 (Acton J); *Hadenfayre Ltd v British National Insurance Society Ltd* [1984] 2 Lloyd's Rep 393, 398 (Lloyd J); *Newbury International Ltd v Reliance National Insurance Co (UK) Ltd* [1994] 1 Lloyd's Rep 83, 85 (Hobhouse J). The time at which the contract becomes binding is considered at **PARA 3.3**.

2 Section 20(6) of the Marine Insurance Act 1906. Section 20 applies outside the scope of marine insurance, to other types of insurance: *Avon Insurance plc v Swire Fraser Ltd* [2000] Lloyd's Rep IR 535, 540 (Rix J); and see **PARA 11.5**.

3 *Canning v Farquhar* (1886) 16 QBD 727, CA; *Looker v Law Union and Rock Insurance Co Ltd* [1928] 1 KB 554 (obiter, as the policy made express provision for change in the proposer's health before payment of the first premium); *Newbury International Ltd v Reliance National Insurance Co (UK) Ltd* [1994] 1 Lloyd's Rep 83, 85 (Hobhouse J).

4 *Canning v Farquhar* (1886) 16 QBD 727, CA; *Looker v Law Union and Rock Insurance Co Ltd* [1928] 1 KB 554 (obiter, as the policy made express provision for change in the proposer's health before payment of the first premium).

5 *New Hampshire Insurance Co v MGN Ltd* [1997] LRLR 24, 59–62, CA (Staughton LJ); *Manifest Shipping Co Ltd v Uni-Polaris Insurance Co Ltd, The Star Sea* [2001] UKHL 1, [2003] AC 469, [2001] 1 Lloyd's Rep 389, para 56 (Lord Hobhouse); *K/S Merc-Scandia XXXXII v Certain Lloyd's Underwriters Subscribing to Lloyd's Policy No 25T 105487, The Mercandian Continent* [2001] EWCA Civ 1275, [2001] 2 Lloyd's Rep 563, 570–571, paras 21 and 22 (Longmore LJ). In his speech in *Manifest Shipping Co Ltd v Uni-Polaris Insurance Co Ltd, The Star Sea* [2001] UKHL 1, [2003] AC 469, [2001] 1 Lloyd's Rep 389, Lord Hobhouse (at para 71) disapproved the use of the decision of Hirst J in *Black King Shipping Corpn v Massie, The Litsion Pride* [1985] 1 Lloyd's Rep 437 to support a general view of the post-contractual duty of good faith (see, similarly, the judgment of Staughton LJ in *New Hampshire Insurance Co v MGN Ltd* [1997] LRLR 24, CA, at 59–62). See also **PARA** 11.4.

6 [2000] Lloyd's Rep IR 154, CA.

7 At 156–157 (Saville LJ) and 158 (Staughton LJ). A similar approach has been adopted in other cases in relation to differently worded clauses of this nature: see *Exchange Theatre Ltd v Iron Trades Mutual Insurance Co Ltd* [1984] 1 Lloyd's Rep 149, CA, 152 (Eveleigh LJ) (policy condition providing: 'This policy shall be avoided with respect to any item thereof in regard to which there be any alteration after the commencement of this policy ... whereby the risk of destruction or damage is increased ... unless such alteration be admitted by memorandum signed by or on behalf of the insurers'); *Ansari v New India Assurance Ltd* [2009] EWCA Civ 93, [2009] Lloyd's Rep IR 562, paras 41-45 (Moore-Bick LJ) (policy condition headed 'Changes in Facts' providing: 'This insurance shall cease to be in force if there is any material alteration to the Premises or Business or any material change in the facts stated in the Proposal Form or other facts supplied to the Insurer unless the Insurer agrees in writing to continue the Insurance').

8 *Law Guarantee Trust and Accident Society v Munich Re-insurance Co* [1912] 1 Ch 138, 153–154 (Warrington J); *Kausar v Eagle Star Insurance Co Ltd* [2000] Lloyd's Rep IR 154, CA, 156–157 (Saville LJ); *Swiss Reinsurance Co v United India Insurance Co Ltd* [2005] EWHC 237 (Comm), [2005] Lloyd's Rep IR 341, para 32 (Morison J).

Examples of circumstances generally accepted to be material

11.19   Whether any particular circumstance, which is not disclosed, is material or not is, in each case, a question of fact.[1] For these purposes, a 'circumstance' includes any communication made to, or information received by, the insured.[2] As materiality is a question of fact, past cases have no status as precedents on the question of materiality and their only relevance is in providing a 'sanity test' or reasonableness check on the conclusions reached by the court on the evidence in a particular case.[3] It may be useful, however, to know that there are certain circumstances which are generally understood by insurers and by the courts to be material, and to know which these are. They include the following, although this list is not exhaustive:

(1) Previous claims under a theft,[4] home contents,[5] motor[6] or fire insurance policy. In relation to theft, the fact that a loss has been suffered, and a claim made, is likely to remain material even if the property is later recovered.[7]

(2) Refusal of the risk by other insurers is not material in marine insurance,[8] but refusal of the risk or imposition of special conditions is frequently held to be material in non-marine insurance. Refusal of the risk was considered to be clearly material (obiter, due to the presence of a basis clause) by Sir George Jessel MR in *London Assurance v Mansel*[9] (life assurance). The Master of the Rolls commented:

> 'I should say, no human being acquainted with the practice of companies or of insurance societies or underwriters could doubt for a moment that is a fact of great materiality, a fact upon which the offices place great reliance. They always want to know what other offices have done with respect to the lives.'

Similarly, failure to disclose the refusal of a proposal on one previous occasion was held to be material in *Glicksman v Lancashire and General Assurance Co Ltd*.[10] In both of these cases, the insurer had sought details of previous refusals in the proposal form.[11] In *Glasgow Assurance Corpn Ltd v Symondson & Co*,[12] however, which concerned the reinsurance of marine risks at Lloyd's, Scrutton J took a restricted view of materiality, saying that it was limited to the subject matter, the ship, and the perils to which the ship is exposed, and rejected the argument that the fact that the risk had been previously refused by six other underwriters was a material fact which ought to have been disclosed.

(3) Refusal by a previous insurer to increase the insured value under the policy.[13]

(4) Criminal convictions may be material, depending on the nature and seriousness of the offence, and how recently it was committed.[14] The obligation to disclose material convictions may be affected by the Rehabilitation of Offenders Act 1974.[15] Criminal convictions are one aspect of 'moral hazard', which is the term used to denote the increased risk of it being made to appear, falsely, that loss or damage has occurred falling within the scope of the policy, either by loss or damage being deliberately caused by the insured, or by means of a fictitious or exaggerated claim.[16]

(5) Excessive valuation or over-insurance of the subject matter insured.[17] Blackburn J, delivering the judgment of the court in *Ionides v Pender*, which concerned the excessive valuation of a ship's cargo and profits on charter, explained the rationale for holding an excessive valuation to be material:[18]

> 'It is to be observed that the excessive valuation not only may lead to a suspicion of foul play, but that it has a direct tendency to make the assured less careful in selecting the ship and captain, and to diminish the efforts which in the case of disaster he ought to make to diminish the loss as far as possible ...'

The burden of showing that the valuation was excessive, thereby changing the character of the risk from an ordinary business risk to a speculative risk (described by a witness in a case which reached the House of Lords in 1911, as insurance 'for loss and not against loss'),[19] is on the insurer.[20]

(6)   A recent allegation of serious dishonesty, the truth or falsity of which has yet to be determined, even if it is quite unconnected with insurance or the risk being insured.[21]

1 Marine Insurance Act 1906, s 18(4). Section 18 applies to all types of insurance: see **PARA 11.5**.

2 Marine Insurance Act 1906, s 18(5). Section 18 applies to all types of insurance: see **PARA 11.5**.

3 *Involnert Management Inc v Aprilgrange Ltd* [2015] EWHC 2225 (Comm), [2015] 2 Lloyd's Rep 289, para 97 (Leggatt J).

4 *Rozanes v Bowen* (1928) 32 Ll L Rep 98, 102, CA (Scrutton LJ); cf *Roberts v Avon Insurance Co Ltd* [1956] 2 Lloyd's Rep 240 (Barry J noted, at 242, that although it was common knowledge that insurers express considerable interest in a proposer's past history of losses or claims, no evidence had been adduced as to materiality in that case).

5 *Lyons v J W Bentley Ltd* (1944) 77 Ll L Rep 335.

6 *Dent v Blackmore* (1927) 29 Ll L Rep 9, 12 (McCardie J).

7 *Morser v Eagle, Star & British Dominions Insurance Co Ltd* (1931) 40 Ll L Rep 254 (Lord Hewart CJ, sitting with a jury).

8 See *Glicksman v Lancashire and General Assurance Co Ltd* [1925] 2 KB 593, CA, affirmed: [1927] AC 139, HL.

9 *London Assurance v Mansel* (1879) 11 Ch D 363, 370–372 (Sir George Jessel MR).

10 [1925] 2 KB 593, CA (obiter, due to the presence of a basis clause).

11 Similarly, in *Holt's Motors Ltd v South-East Lancashire Insurance Co Ltd* (1930) 37 Ll L Rep 1, 2–3, CA (Scrutton LJ).

12 (1911)104 LT 254, 257; see also *Rozanes v Bowen* (1928) 32 Ll L Rep 98, 102, CA, in which Scrutton LJ indicated that he maintained the view that he had expressed in *Glasgow Assurance Corpn v Symondson & Co* ('the fact that somebody else wants a particular rate for a particular risk or will not insure a particular risk at a particular rate is not a material fact in the policy'), but did not rest his decision on those grounds as he had not heard counsel for the underwriters on the point.

13 *Eagle Star Insurance Co Ltd v National Westminster Finance Australia Ltd* (1985) 58 ALR 165, 172, PC (unvalued policy; it is suggested that the same would apply, but with greater force, in relation to a valued policy).

14 In *Woolcott v Sun Alliance and London Insurance Ltd* [1978] 1 WLR 493, Caulfield J accepted the evidence of underwriting witnesses that a conviction as serious as robbery affects the moral hazard which insurers have to assess, and was therefore material. The offence had been committed 12 years before the proposal of the risk. A retrial was subsequently ordered on other grounds: [1979] 1 Lloyd's Rep 231, CA. In *McCormick v National Motor & Accident Insurance Union Ltd* (1934) 49 Ll L Rep 361, 363–364, CA, which concerned motor vehicle insurance, Scrutton LJ regarded the previous convictions of the insured for motoring offences as obviously material.

15 See **PARA 11.17**.

16 *Pan Atlantic Insurance Co Ltd v Pine Top Insurance Co Ltd* [1995] 1 AC 501, [1994] 2 Lloyd's Rep 427, HL, 534, 538, 442, 445 (Lord Mustill), 561, 562, 459, 460 (Lord Lloyd), *PCW Syndicates v PCW Reinsurers* [1996] 1 WLR 1136, 1138, CA (Staughton LJ); *Insurance Corpn of the Channel Islands v Royal Hotel Ltd* [1998] Lloyd's Rep IR 151, 156 (Mance J). It is on this basis that the fact that an insured is in financial difficulties may be material.

17 *Ionides v Pender* (1874) LR 9 QB 531; *Thames and Mersey Marine Insurance Co Ltd v Gunford Ship Co Ltd* [1911] AC 529, HL; *Mathie v Argonaut Marine Insurance Co Ltd* (1925) 21 Ll L Rep 145, HL (applying *Iones v Pender*); *Berger and Light Diffusers Pty Ltd v Pollock* [1973] 2 Lloyd's Rep 442 (Kerr J) (approving, obiter, *Ionides v Pender*).

18 At 538–539.

19 *Thames and Mersey Marine Insurance Co Ltd v Gunford Ship Co Ltd* [1911] AC 529, 545, HL (Lord Shaw).

20 *Mathie v Argonaut Marine Insurance Co Ltd* (1925) 21 Ll L Rep 145, 146, HL (Lord Buckmaster).

21 *North Star Shipping Ltd v Sphere Drake Insurance plc* [2006] EWCA Civ 378, [2006] 2 Lloyd's Rep 183, paras 19, 35 and 42–43 (Waller LJ).

Misrepresentation

11.20 Misrepresentation raises some issues distinct from non-disclosure, mainly as to the actionability of certain types of misrepresentation, and these are considered in this section. The general law in relation to misrepresentation applies in relation to contracts of insurance. Under the general law, damages may be available for misrepresentation. Although this is in principle the case in the context of contracts of insurance, in practice the remedy for misrepresentation will be the same as for non-disclosure, namely avoidance of the contract of insurance with retrospective effect.[1] The Consumer Insurance (Disclosure and Representations) Act 2012 makes significant changes to the law of non-disclosure and misrepresentation in relation to policies of insurance where the insured is a consumer.[2]

1 Section 20(1) provides that every material representation made by the insured or his agent to the insurer during the negotiations for the contract, and before the contract is concluded, must be true; and that if it is untrue, the insurer may avoid the contract. Section 20 applies outside the scope of marine insurance, to other types of insurance: *Avon Insurance plc v Swire Fraser Ltd* [2000] Lloyd's Rep IR 535, 540 (Rix J); and see PARA **11.5**.
2 See PARAS **11.40–11.47**.

Statements of fact and statements of expectation or belief

11.21 Every material representation of fact, or of expectation or belief, made by the insured or his agent to the insurer during the negotiations for the contract of insurance, and before the contract is concluded, must be true, or the insurer may avoid the contract.[1] A representation made before negotiations for renewal have begun is not made during the negotiations for the contract of insurance.[2] A representation made during the negotiations for the previous year's contract of insurance may be impliedly repeated on renewal.[3] Whether that is so depends on the nature of the representation, including whether it relates to a matter which is prone to variation.[4] Where a misrepresentation is made to insurers before negotiations for the renewal of a contract of insurance have begun, about a matter which is material to the risk and to its renewal, then if it is not subsequently corrected at renewal, the misrepresentation may be implicitly repeated at renewal.[5]

The existence of a warranty can limit the duty of disclosure owed by an insured and for similar reasons can render a representation immaterial.[6] This will be the case if there are no circumstances in which any inaccuracy in the representation could increase the risk but in which the insurer would not be fully protected by the warranty.[7]

A representation of fact is true if it is substantially correct, which means that the difference between what is represented and what is actually correct would not be considered material by a prudent insurer.[8] A representation of expectation or belief is true if it is made in good faith.[9]

1 Section 20(1) of the Marine Insurance Act 1906.
2 *Synergy Health (UK) Ltd v CGU Insurance plc* [2010] EWHC 2583 (Comm), [2011] Lloyd's Rep IR 500, para 158 (Flaux J).
3 *Glencore International AG v Alpina Insurance Co Ltd* [2003] EWHC 2792, [2004] 1 Lloyd's Rep 111, para 69 (Moore-Bick J); *Sharp v Sphere Drake Insurance plc, The Moonacre* [1992] 2 Lloyd's Rep 501, 521–522 (Mr A D Colman QC, sitting as a Deputy Judge of the High Court) (brokers forged

client's signature to proposal form; no subsequent proposal tendered on renewal so continuing reliance by underwriters on proposal and continuing duty to correct any misrepresentation included on it; also continuing duty to disclose any material facts omitted from it).

4 *Glencore International AG v Alpina Insurance Co Ltd* [2003] EWHC 2792, [2004] 1 Lloyd's Rep 111, para 69 (Moore-Bick J); *Limit No 2 Ltd v Axa Versicherung AG* [2008] EWCA Civ 1231, [2009] Lloyd's Rep IR 396, paras 25–26 (Longmore LJ).

5 *Synergy Health (UK) Ltd v CGU Insurance plc* [2010] EWHC 2583 (Comm), [2011] Lloyd's Rep IR 500, para 161 (Flaux J).

6 *De Maurier (Jewels) Ltd v Bastion Insurance Co Ltd* [1967] 2 Lloyd's Rep 550, 557 (Donaldson J), referring, in relation to non-disclosure, to s 18(3)(d) of the Marine Insurance Act 1906: as to which, see **PARA 11.8**.

7 *De Maurier (Jewels) Ltd v Bastion Insurance Co Ltd* [1967] 2 Lloyd's Rep 550, 557 (Donaldson J).

8 Section 20(4) of the Marine Insurance Act 1906. Section 20 applies outside the scope of marine insurance, to other types of insurance: *Avon Insurance plc v Swire Fraser Ltd* [2000] Lloyd's Rep IR 535, 540 (Rix J); and see **PARA 11.5**.

9 Section 20(5) of the Marine Insurance Act 1906. Section 20 applies outside the scope of marine insurance, to other types of insurance: *Avon Insurance plc v Swire Fraser Ltd* [2000] Lloyd's Rep IR 535, 540 (Rix J); and see **PARA 11.5**.

Statements of opinion

11.22   Statements of opinion do not give rise to a right to avoid a contract, unless made fraudulently.[1] It should be noted, however, that the making of any statement of opinion constitutes an implied representation of fact – that the person making the statement holds that opinion – and that it may have further representations of fact inherent in it.[2] Whether this is so depends upon the facts of the transaction in which the parties are involved, their respective knowledge, their relative positions, the words of representation used, and the actual condition of the subject matter spoken of.[3] In *Bisset v Wilkinson*,[4] a vendor of land had made a representation as to the carrying capacity of the land for sheep. In deciding that the representation was a statement of opinion, the Privy Council took into account the fact that, as both parties were aware, no one, including the vendor of the land, had carried on sheep farming on the unit of land in question.

There is a line of authority which is commonly put forward as supporting the proposition that a statement of opinion or belief may be construed as amounting to a representation that the speaker has reasonable grounds for his opinion or belief so that, if the speaker does not have reasonable grounds for the opinion or belief, the statement constitutes a misrepresentation. Thus, in *Ionides v Pacific Fire and Marine Insurance Co*,[5] the insured's clerk was asked by the underwriter whether goods were to be shipped on a particular vessel (the 'Socrates'), and the clerk answered, honestly, 'I think so'. The clerk had made a mistake about the identity of the ship, and the goods were in fact shipped on a much older vessel with a similar name (the 'Socrate'). The clerk's response was construed as a representation that the vessel was the 'Socrates', but the court relied, in the alternative, on the fact that the insured (through his clerk) did not have reasonable grounds for believing that the ship was the 'Socrates'. Similarly, in *Smith v Land and House Property Corpn*,[6] Bowen LJ said:

> '... a statement of opinion by one who knows the facts best involves very often a statement of a material fact, for he impliedly states that he knows facts which justify his opinion.'

However, in *Economides v Commercial Assurance Co plc*,[7] the Court of Appeal held that in making a statement of belief as to the total value of items insured under a household contents policy, the insured is only under a duty of honesty, not a duty of care, and that, provided the insured has some basis for his statement of belief and makes it in good faith, the statement is deemed, pursuant to s 20(5) of the Marine Insurance Act 1906, to be honest. Objectively, reasonable grounds for the belief are therefore not required and there is no room for the implication of a representation that the insured had reasonable grounds for his belief.

It is crucial, therefore, to determine whether a representation is merely of expectation or belief or is on analysis an assertion of a specific fact.[8] In *Rendall v Combined Insurance Co of America*[9], Cresswell J held[10] that an estimate of the next year's travel exposure in terms of number of days' travel did not constitute an assertion of specific fact that the estimate had been based on historical information and experience, but was as to a matter of expectation or belief made in good faith and deemed by s 20(5) to be true, and that there was no scope for inquiry as to whether there were objectively reasonable grounds for the representation or belief. In *Kamidian v Holt*[11], Tomlinson J said,[12] in determining that the representation made by the insured was not simply one of honest belief as to the provenance of an antique clock but was that there was general belief as to that provenance in the art world, that the context was very different from that of household contents insurance such as was under discussion in *Economides v Commercial Assurance Co plc*, where the applicant for insurance was asked on the proposal form to declare that the statements and particulars given on the proposal form were to the best of his 'knowledge and belief, true and complete', and that in the context of specialised fine art insurance sought by professional exhibition organisers on behalf of collectors and dealers lending pieces for the purpose of showing at an exhibition, it would be a wholly uncommercial and unlikely approach for underwriters to agree an insured value on the basis of belief for which there might be no reasonable grounds.[13]

1 *Bisset v Wilkinson* [1927] AC 177, 181–182, PC; *Irish National Insurance Co Ltd v Oman Insurance Co Ltd* [1983] 2 Lloyd's Rep 453, 462 (Leggatt J); s 20(3) of the Marine Insurance Act 1906 (which confines the application of s 20 (including the remedy of avoidance for misrepresentation) to representations as to matters of fact, or as to matters of expectation or belief). Section 20 applies outside the scope of marine insurance, to other types of insurance: *Economides v Commercial Assurance Co plc* [1998] QB 587, 598, CA (Simon Brown LJ); *Avon Insurance plc v Swire Fraser Ltd* [2000] Lloyd's Rep IR 535, 540 (Rix J); and see PARA 11.5.

2 *Bisset v Wilkinson* [1927] AC 177, 182, 184, PC; *Irish National Insurance Co Ltd v Oman Insurance Co Ltd* [1983] 2 Lloyd's Rep 453, 462 (Leggatt J) (statement of opinion contained no representation except honest belief); *Synergy Health (UK) Ltd v CGU Insurance plc* [2010] EWHC 2583 (Comm), [2011] Lloyd's Rep IR 500, para 157 (Flaux J) (it was impossible on 28 December, only two working days before the end of December, to construe the statement that '[t]his will be completed by end December' as no more than a statement of future intention: necessarily implicit in the statement was a representation that the work was in fact underway and was about to be completed).

3 *Bisset v Wilkinson* [1927] AC 177, 182, PC.

4 [1927] AC 177, PC.

5 (1871) LR 6 QB 674, 683–684. Other cases include *Irish National Insurance Co Ltd v Oman Insurance Co Ltd* [1983] 2 Lloyd's Rep 453, 461, 462 (Leggatt J); *Highland Insurance Co v Continental Insurance (Note)* [1987] 1 Lloyd's Rep 109, 112–113 (Steyn J) (considered in *Economides v Commercial Assurance Co plc* [1998] QB 587, CA and held to have been wrongly decided); *Bank Leumi Le Israel BM v British National Insurance Co Ltd* [1988] 1 Lloyd's Rep 71, 75 (Saville J); *Sirius International Insurance Corpn v Oriental Assurance Corpn* [1999] Lloyd's Rep IR 343, 351 (Longmore J).

6 (1884) 28 Ch D 7, 15, applied in *Brown v Raphael* [1958] Ch 636, CA.

7 [1998] QB 587, CA.

8 *Economides v Commercial Assurance Co plc* [1998] QB 587, 599, CA (Simon Brown LJ).
9 [2005] EWHC 678 (Comm), [2006] Lloyd's Rep IR 732.
10 At para 103.
11 [2008] EWHC 1483 (Comm), [2009] Lloyd's Rep IR 242.
12 At para 90.
13 See also *Zeller v British Caymanian Insurance Co Ltd* [2008] UKPC 4, [2008] Lloyd's Rep IR 545, in which the insured was asked to complete a health questionnaire truthfully to the best of his knowledge and belief, and Lord Bingham said (at para 18) that the judge was right to regard the real question as being whether the insured, if he honestly believed he was answering the questions in a health questionnaire truthfully, was guilty of non-disclosure.

Misrepresentation Act 1967

11.23 Section 2(1) of the Misrepresentation Act 1967 establishes a statutory right to damages for negligent misrepresentation. It is a defence to a claim under s 2(1) for the representor to prove that he had reasonable grounds to believe, and did believe up until the contract was made, that the facts represented were true. This is a reversal of the common law burden of proof for negligent misstatement. Section 2(1) has been construed as applying only to representations of fact[1], although in *Sumitomo Bank Ltd v Banque Bruxelles Lambert SA*,[2] Langley J took the view that the section could operate where a representation of opinion carried with it an implied representation that the representor had reasonable grounds for his belief, as this was a representation of fact. The operation of the sub-section would be limited in these circumstances, however, because in order to show that the statement of opinion amounted to a misrepresentation, the representee would have to show that the opinion was not based on reasonable grounds; and there would therefore be no room for the operation of the reverse burden of proof.[3] Following the decision of the Court of Appeal in *Economides v Commercial Assurance Co plc*,[4] it would appear that these issues are of no practical importance in the context of insurance policies, as the result of *Economides* is that a statement of opinion is not a misrepresentation even if it carries with it an implication of reasonable grounds where there were none; and there is, accordingly, no room for s 2(1) to operate.[5]

The courts are prepared to classify a statement as one of fact even it if involves an element of opinion. In *Thomson v Weems*, the House of Lords had to consider whether the insured had given a true answer to the question, '(1) Are you temperate in your habits? (2) and have you always been strictly so?'. The answer given was '(1) Temperate. (2) Yes.' The House of Lords held that in answering the question, the insured had made a statement of fact, not of opinion, that the answer was untrue as a matter of fact, and that the insurer was entitled to avoid the policy. Similarly, in *Yorke v Yorkshire Insurance Co*,[6] the insured answered 'None of any consequence' to the question 'What illnesses have you suffered?'. McCardie J applied *Thomson v Weems*, and held that the jury were justified, on the facts, in finding the answer to constitute a breach of the warranty of truth in the policy. In reaching this conclusion, McCardie J said:[7]

> 'A question may be a question of fact although the element of opinion is involved therein.'

Indeed, consistently with this approach, McCardie J admitted expert medical evidence on the question of whether an illness suffered by the insured should be regarded as one of consequence.[8]

1 *Lancaster City Council v Unique Group Ltd* (15 December 1995, unreported) (Jonathan Parker J).
2 [1997] 1 Lloyd's Rep 487.
3 *Sumitomo Bank Ltd v Banque Bruxelles Lambert SA* [1997] 1 Lloyd's Rep 487, 515 (Langley J).
4 [1998] QB 587, CA; see **PARA 11.22**.
5 In *HIH Casualty and General Insurance Ltd v Chase Manhattan Bank* [2003] UKHL 6, [2003] 2 Lloyd's Rep 61, para 5, Lord Bingham made reference to an insurer's right to damages for non-disclosure or misrepresentation pursuant to s 2(1) of the Misrepresentation Act 1967. However, this was by way of background only, and the impact of s 20 of the Marine Insurance Act 1906 was not considered. See also *Argo Systems FZE v Liberty Insurance (Pte), The Copa Casino* [2011] EWHC 301 (Comm), [2011] 2 Lloyd's Rep 61, paras 41–45 (HHJ Mackie QC) (point not considered on appeal: *Liberty Insurance Pte Ltd v Argo Systems FZE, The Copa Casino* [2011] EWCA Civ 1572, [2012] 1 Lloyd's Rep 129).
6 [1918] 1 KB 662.
7 At 669.
8 At 669–670.

Statements of intention

11.24 A false statement of intention constitutes a misrepresentation of fact. As Bowen LJ said in his celebrated dictum in *Edgington v Fitzmaurice*:[1]

'There must be a misstatement of an existing fact: but the state of a man's mind is as much a fact as the state of his digestion. It is true that it is very difficult to prove what the state of a man's mind at a particular time is, but if it can be ascertained it is as much a fact as anything else. A misrepresentation as to the state of a man's mind is, therefore, a misstatement of fact.'

In *Limit No 2 Ltd v Axa Versicherung AG*,[2] Longmore LJ said,[3] before referring to Bowen LJ's dictum:

'Once it has been decided that the fax cover sheet did contain a representation that the Syndicates intended to write construction business with the stated deductibles, this ground [of appeal] is not seriously arguable. It is not a statement of opinion or belief; nor is it framed as a statement of expectation. The words "would not normally write construction unless . . . " mean that the Syndicates will normally write (namely intend normally to write) with the stated deductibles. That statement of intention is a representation of existing fact.'

Similarly, in *Synergy Health (UK) Ltd v CGU Insurance plc*,[4] Flaux J said[5] that it was impossible on 28 December, when only two working days remained before the end of December, to construe a statement in relation to the installation of an intruder alarm that '[t]his will be completed by end December' as no more than a statement of future intention, and that necessarily implicit in the statement was a representation that the relevant work was in fact underway and was about to be completed.

In *Dawsons Ltd v Bonnin*,[6] a statement was made in a proposal form that the address at which a lorry would usually be garaged was 46 Cadogan Street, Glasgow. In fact, the lorry was usually garaged at the insured's garage at Dovehill Farm, Newlands, on the outskirts of Glasgow. As there was no accommodation for lorries at 46 Cadogan Street, the insurer had no difficulty in showing that the statement, although a statement of intention, was untrue.

1 (1885) 29 Ch D 459, 483, CA.
2 [2008] EWCA Civ 1231, [2009] Lloyd's Rep IR 396.
3 At para 17.

4 [2010] EWHC 2583 (Comm), [2011] Lloyd's Rep IR 500.
5 At para 157.
6 [1922] 2 AC 413, HL.

Representation of law

11.25   It is appears that, following the developments in relation to mistake of law,[1] an insurer is in principle entitled to avoid a contract of insurance for misrepresentation whether the misrepresentation is of fact or of law. However, it is suggested that the court will be slow to find a misrepresentation of law to be material, as in most cases both parties will have equal means of knowing what the law is;[2] alternatively, the court may characterise a representation of law made in this context as a representation of opinion, which is deemed by s 20(5) of the Marine Insurance Act 1906 to be true provided that it is made in good faith.[3]

1 See **PARA 8.15**.
2 This was the basis for the old rule that a representation of law was not actionable: see *West London Commercial Bank Ltd v Kitson* (1884) 13 QBD 360, 363, CA (Bowen LJ) (the position is probably different if the representation is made fraudulently: Bowen LJ at 362–363); and see *Kyle Bay Ltd v Underwriters Subscribing to Policy no 019057/08/01* [2007] EWCA Civ 57, [2007] Lloyd's Rep IR 460, para 35 (Neuberger LJ). A representation as to private rights has always been actionable, albeit by characterising it as a representation of fact: see, eg, *West London Commercial Bank Ltd v Kitson* (1884) 13 QBD 360, CA, which concerned a representation as to the powers of a company to accept bills, which depended on private Acts of Parliament. In *Soole v Royal Insurance Co Ltd* [1971] 2 Lloyd's Rep 332, Shaw J said (at 340), in support of his conclusion that a representation as to the construction of the policy was not a representation of fact in the circumstances of that case, that the insured himself was always aware of the facts on which the construction of the policy depended.
3 See, eg, *Kyle Bay Ltd v Underwriters Subscribing to Policy no 019057/08/01* [2006] EWHC 607 (Comm), [2006] Lloyd's Rep IR 718, paras 52–54 (Jonathan Hirst QC) (referring to s 20(5)), [2007] EWCA Civ 57, [2007] Lloyd's Rep IR 460, paras 33–34 (Neuberger LJ) (not referring to s 20(5); statements or assertions made in negotiations are contentions, not representations). See also **PARA 11.22**.

Representation implied by conduct

11.26   A representation may be implied by conduct. For example, in *West London Commercial Bank v Kitson*,[1] the acceptance of a bill was construed as an implied representation by the defendants, who were directors of the company, that the company had power to accept the bill, and that the directors were authorised by the company to accept the bill.

1 (1884) 13 QBD 360, CA.

Fraudulent misrepresentation

11.27   Before the enactment of the Marine Insurance Act 1906, a fraudulent misrepresentation inducing a contract gave rise to a right to avoid without proof of materiality, whereas an innocent misrepresentation did not.[1] Fraud in this context means the making of a false representation knowing it to be false, or without belief in its truth, or recklessly, not caring whether it is true or false.[2] A false statement is not made fraudulently if the maker honestly believes it to be true, even if the statement is made carelessly and without reasonable grounds for the belief.[3] The important distinction in insurance contracts is therefore between fraudulent misrepresentations, on the one hand, and negligent and innocent misrepresentations, on the other. Proof of fraud only relieves the insurer of the need to show materiality, and he must still prove inducement.[4] If the false representation did not induce him to enter into the contract, the insurer will not be entitled to avoid. If, as will usually be the case, the aim of the false statement was to induce the insurer to enter into the contract, it is unlikely to be difficult to prove inducement even if, strictly speaking, the statement was not material. In any event, where the false statement was material, the insurer may decide to adduce evidence of materiality in order to support his case on inducement.

1 *Pan Atlantic Insurance Co Ltd v Pine Top Insurance Co Ltd* [1995] 1 AC 501, 532–533, [1994] 2 Lloyd's Rep 427, 441–442, HL (Lord Mustill); considered: *Agapitos v Agnew, The Aegeon* [2002] EWCA Civ 247, [2003] QB 556, para 36 (Mance LJ).
2 *Derry v Peek* (1889) 14 App Cas 337, HL.
3 *Derry v Peek* (1889) 14 App Cas 337, HL.
4 *MacLeay v Tait* [1906] AC 24, HL (proof of inducement required in an action for damages for deceit).

Creating false impression

11.28 Intentionally creating a false impression constitutes fraudulent misrepresentation, even if the impression is created by means of a number of statements, each of which, taken individually, is true.[1] Similarly, if a false impression is created by giving an incomplete answer to a question, or by providing information which does not answer the question, the accuracy of the information in fact provided will not prevent a finding of misrepresentation or non-disclosure.[2] For example, in *Condogianis v Guardian Assurance Co Ltd*,[3] the proposal form asked, 'Has proponent ever been a claimant on a fire insurance company in respect of the property now proposed, or any other property? If so, state when and name of company.' The insured answered, 'Yes. 1917, "Ocean".' The answer, taken very literally, was true, but the insured omitted a further relevant claim against another company in 1912. The Privy Council held that the obvious intention of the question, and its plain meaning, was to elicit the insured's insurance record. The insured's answer was untrue, and the insurer was entitled to avoid the policy. *Condogianis v Guardian Assurance Co Ltd* was followed by Bray J in *Krantz v Allan*,[4] in which the question, 'Have you ever sustained a loss? If so, please give short particulars', was answered, 'Yes, last March, £150', despite there having been two earlier losses which ought to have been disclosed.

1 *Aaron's Reefs Ltd v Twiss* [1896] AC 273, 281, HL (Lord Halsbury LC).
2 *London Assurance v Mansel* (1879) 11 Ch D 363, 370 (Sir George Jessel MR) (the statement was subject to a basis clause, but the principle is the same); *Condogianis v Guardian Assurance Co Ltd* [1921] 2 AC 125, 131, PC.
3 [1921] 2 AC 125, 131, PC.
4 (1921) 9 Ll L Rep 410.

Proof of non-disclosure or misrepresentation

11.29 The onus of proving non-disclosure[1] or misrepresentation,[2] including in relation to an answer given by the insured to a question in a proposal form,[3] is on the insurer. In addition to direct documentary evidence and oral testimony, the court may take account of the rate of premium charged by the underwriter, and of any increase or reduction in the ordinary rate for the risk consistent with material facts having been concealed or misrepresented.[4]

1 *Joel v Law Union and Crown Insurance Co* [1908] 2 KB 863, 880, 892, 897, CA; *Greenhill v Federal Insurance Co Ltd* [1927] 1 KB 65, 68, CA (Lord Hanworth MR); *Strive Shipping Corpn v Hellenic Mutual War Risks Association, The Grecia Express* [2002] EWHC 203 (Comm), [2002] 2 Lloyd's Rep 88, 97–100 (Colman J).
2 *Davies v National Fire and Marine Insurance Co of New Zealand* [1891] AC 485, 489–490, PC; *Goldstein v Salvation Army Assurance Society* [1917] 2 KB 291, 294 (Rowlatt J).
3 *Thomson v Weems* (1884) 9 App Cas 671, 684, HL (Lord Blackburn); *Austin v Zurich General Accident and Liability Insurance Co Ltd* (1944) 77 Ll L Rep 409, 416 (Tucker J) (issue not considered on appeal: [1945] KB 250, CA).
4 See *Greenhill v Federal Insurance Co Ltd* [1927] 1 KB 65, 78–79, CA (Scrutton LJ).

Impact of non-disclosure or misrepresentation on joint and composite insurance

11.30   Where insurance is composite rather than joint,[1] misrepresentation or non-disclosure, or fraud,[2] by one of the insureds will not entitle the insurer to avoid or forfeit the policy as against the others.[3] Conversely, affirmation of the policy in respect of one insured does not constitute affirmation of the policy in respect of another.[4]

1 See **PARA 2.3**.
2 For the impact of fraud by one insured, see further **PARA 11.52**.
3 *General Accident Fire and Life Assurance Corpn Ltd v Midland Bank Ltd* [1940] 2 KB 388, 404–406, CA (Sir Wilfred Greene MR); *Woolcott v Sun Alliance and London Insurance Ltd* [1978] 1 WLR 493, 496–497 (Caulfield J) (interests of mortgagor and mortgagee not joint; retrial ordered by Court of Appeal on other grounds: [1979] 1 Lloyd's Rep 231, CA); *New Hampshire Insurance Co v MGN Ltd* [1997] LRLR 24, 56–58, CA (Staughton LJ).
4 *Black King Shipping Corpn v Massie, The Litsion Pride* [1985] 1 Lloyd's Rep 437, 516–517 (Hirst J).

Remedy for breach of duty of utmost good faith, including non-disclosure or misrepresentation: pre-Consumer Insurance (Disclosure and Representations) Act 2012 and pre-Insurance Act 2015

11.31   The duty of utmost good faith in the presentation of the risk has undergone significant statutory reform in recent years. Contracts entered into before the new statutory provisions come into force remain subject to the old law, which is set out here.[1]

After two recent cases in the House of Lords, *Banque Financière de la Cité SA v Westgate Insurance Co Ltd*[2] and *Manifest Shipping Co Ltd v Uni-Polaris Insurance Co Ltd, The Star Sea*,[3] it is now beyond doubt that the duty of utmost good faith arises from a principle of law, and not from an implied term of the contract of insurance, and that, accordingly, breach of the duty of utmost good faith gives rise to a right to avoid the contract, but not to any right to damages,[4] except in the case of a misrepresentation,[5] where damages are theoretically available. This is so whether the breach of duty occurs before or after the contract has been concluded,[6] with one potential difference: where breach of the duty occurs before conclusion of the contract, in the form of misrepresentation or non-disclosure, the avoidance has retrospective effect.[7] The remedy for non-disclosure or misrepresentation also differs, therefore, in important respects from the remedy for breach of warranty, which automatically discharges the insurer for the future.[8]

The duty of utmost good faith is a mutual duty owed by insurer and insured to one another,[9] and continues to be mutual in character after the contract has been entered into. However, the right to avoid the contract is, in practical terms, likely to be of value only to the insurer, allowing him to escape retrospectively from a liability to indemnify which he has previously undertaken. The circumstances in which the insured would want to avoid an otherwise valid policy of insurance for breach by the insurer of the duty of utmost good faith in the context of pre-contractual negotiations are likely to be rare, and rarer still after a contract has been entered into.

Avoidance is not automatic. If circumstances give rise to a right to avoid the policy, the policy is voidable unless and until the party entitled to avoid elects to do so,[10] unless the right is lost by affirmation, waiver or estoppel.[11] A policy is avoided by act of the insurer, operating independently of the court. The court's role is not to permit, or to refuse to permit, avoidance,[12] but is to ascertain whether the policy has been validly avoided. Avoidance of the policy does not destroy clauses intended to operate in the case of a dispute between the parties, such as jurisdiction[13] and arbitration[14] clauses.

The policy may provide expressly for the consequences of a breach of the duty of utmost good faith.[15] This is common in relation to fraudulent or exaggerated claims, although such clauses typically restate the common law position. Professional indemnity policies sometimes contain restrictions on the insurer's common law remedies in respect of non-disclosure and misrepresentation, or breach of warranty. A policy may, for example, exclude the insurer's right to avoid in respect of innocent non-disclosure.[16]

If there is a breach of the good faith obligation in relation to an amendment to an existing contract of insurance, the insurer's remedy is to avoid the amendment but not the whole contract.[17]

1 See **PARA 11.5**.
2 [1991] 2 AC 249, HL, affirming the decision of the Court of Appeal at [1990] 1 QB 665, CA.
3 [2001] UKHL 1, [2003] AC 469, [2001] 1 Lloyd's Rep 389.
4 *Banque Financière de la Cité SA v Westgate Insurance Co Ltd* [1990] 1 QB 665, 777–781, CA (Slade LJ), affirmed by the House of Lords at [1991] 2 AC 249, 280 (Lord Templeman), 281 (Lord Jauncey); *Manifest Shipping Co Ltd v Uni-Polaris Insurance Co Ltd, The Star Sea* [2001] UKHL 1, [2003] AC 469, [2001] 1 Lloyd's Rep 389, para 46 (Lord Hobhouse); *HIH Casualty and General Insurance Ltd v Chase Manhattan Bank* [2003] UKHL 6, [2003] 2 Lloyd's Rep IR 61, 253, para 75 (Lord Hoffmann). A contractual duty of good faith may nevertheless arise: see, for example, the obligation to provide information to insurers during the currency of the policy, *K/S Merc-Scandia XXXXII v Certain Lloyd's Underwriters Subscribing to Lloyd's Policy No 25T 105487, The Mercandian Continent* [2001] EWCA Civ 1275, [2001] 2 Lloyd's Rep 563, CA, para 40, 576 (Longmore LJ).
5 *Banque Financière de la Cité SA v Westgate Insurance Co Ltd* [1990] 1 QB 665, 777–781 and 788, CA (Slade LJ), affirmed by the House of Lords at [1991] 2 AC 249, 280 (Lord Templeman), 281 (Lord Jauncey); *HIH Casualty and General Insurance Ltd v Chase Manhattan Bank* [2003] UKHL 6, [2003] 2 Lloyd's Rep 61, para 75 (Lord Hoffmann); and see **PARA 11.32**.
6 *Manifest Shipping Co Ltd v Uni-Polaris Insurance Co Ltd, The Star Sea* [2001] UKHL 1, [2003] AC 469, [2001] 1 Lloyd's Rep 389. As to when the contract is concluded, see **PARA 3.3**.

7 *Cornhill Insurance Co Ltd v Assenheim* (1937) 58 Ll L Rep 27, 31 (MacKinnon J); *Manifest Shipping Co Ltd v Uni-Polaris Insurance Co Ltd, The Star Sea* [2001] UKHL 1, [2003] AC 469, [2001] 1 Lloyd's Rep 389, para 51 (Lord Hobhouse). See further **PARA 11.49**.

8 *HIH Casualty and General Insurance Ltd v New Hampshire Insurance Co* [2001] EWCA Civ 735, [2001] 2 Lloyd's Rep 161, 185, para 124 (Rix LJ); and see **PARA 3.7**.

9 *Manifest Shipping Co Ltd v Uni-Polaris Insurance Co Ltd, The Star Sea* [2001] UKHL 1, [2003] AC 469, [2001] 1 Lloyd's Rep 389, para 47 (Lord Hobhouse).

10 *Mackender, Hill and White v Feldia AG* [1966] 2 Lloyd's Rep 449, 455, CA (Lord Denning MR).

11 See **PARA 11.63**.

12 *Brotherton v Aseguradora Colseguros SA* [2003] EWCA Civ 705, [2003] Lloyd's Rep IR 746, paras 26–27 (Mance LJ), disapproving *Strive Shipping Corpn v Hellenic Mutual War Risks Association, The Grecia Express* [2002] 2 Lloyd's Rep 88, 132–133 (Colman J).

13 *Mackender, Hill and White v Feldia AG* [1966] 2 Lloyd's Rep 449, CA.

14 Section 7 of the Arbitration Act 1996.

15 See *Tilley & Noad v Dominion Insurance Co Ltd* [1987] 2 EGLR 34 (surveyors and valuers' professional indemnity policy); *James v CGU Insurance plc* [2002] Lloyd's Rep IR 206, para 106 (Moore-Bick J) (clause in the general conditions in a combined policy, in which different types of cover were dealt with in separate sections, held to entitle the insurers to avoid the policy as a whole for material non-disclosure in relation to any one section).

16 See *Arab Bank plc v Zurich Insurance Co* [1999] 1 Lloyd's Rep 262, 269 (surveyors and valuers' professional indemnity policy).

17 *Limit No 2 Ltd v Axa Versicherung AG* [2008] EWCA Civ 1231, [2009] Lloyd's Rep IR 396, para 20 (Longmore LJ).

Misrepresentation Act 1967, s 2(2)

11.32 Section 2(2) of the Misrepresentation Act 1967 provides that the court may, where a contract has been validly avoided, declare it to be subsisting and award damages instead, if it considers that it would be equitable to do so. Once a court has decided that a contract of insurance has been validly avoided on grounds of material misrepresentation, it is difficult to envisage circumstances in which it would be equitable to declare it subsisting and award damages instead, not least because to award damages at a level lower than the value of the insured's claim under the contract would be clearly inequitable. Section 2(2) appears unlikely to have any role to play in insurance cases.[1]

1 See *Highlands Insurance v Continental Insurance (Note)* [1987] 1 Lloyd's Rep 109, 118 (Steyn J) (referring to commercial insurance cases).

Restoring the status quo (restitutio in integrum)

11.33 It is a general principle of the law of contract that a party seeking avoidance (or rescission) of a contract for misrepresentation must be in a position to restore the status quo. This is sometimes described, particularly in the older cases, as *restitutio in integrum* – meaning returning the parties to the contract to the positions they were in before the contract was entered into.[1]

In insurance contracts, the insurer must return the premium;[2] if the insured disputes the validity of the avoidance, he will usually refuse to accept the return of the premium, pending the outcome of legal proceedings. Where a previous claim has been paid, the insurer is entitled to repayment by the insured[3] and will usually request repayment at the same time as tendering the premium. Similarly, where an interim payment was made, and it is subsequently established that, for any reason, the insured is not entitled to an indemnity, the insurer is entitled to recover the payment from the insured, whether or not it was expressly stated to be 'on account'.[4] If the insurer's right to avoid is confirmed in legal proceedings, the court will order the insurer to return the premium.[5] Where the policy has been avoided on grounds of fraudulent non-disclosure or misrepresentation, it appears that the insurer is entitled to retain the premium. In *Rivaz v Gerussi Bros & Co*,[6] Brett LJ said:[7]

> 'Here it was not only a concealment, but a fraudulent concealment, for the matter concealed was kept back from the knowledge of the underwriters in order that the assured might thereby derive an advantage. Being therefore fraudulent, it seems to me there should be no return of premium ...'

This question was not raised in argument, and was not referred to by the other members of the Court of Appeal. At the conclusion of the report of *Dent v Blackmore*,[8] after McCardie J had given judgment in favour of insurers, whom he found had been entitled to avoid the policy, counsel for the proposer sought the return of the premium. This was resisted by counsel for the insurers on the grounds that the judge had found that the proposer had made statements knowing them to be untrue, and was therefore not entitled to the return of the premium. McCardie J refused to consider the question, saying that it did not arise. This is, however, the position in relation to marine insurance, pursuant to s 84(3)(a) of the Marine Insurance Act 1906, and it is suggested that this also represents the position at common law.[9]

1 *First National Reinsurance Co v Greenfield* [1921] 2 KB 260, 267 (Lush J).
2 *Cornhill Insurance Co Ltd v Assenheim* (1937) 58 Ll L Rep 27, 31 (MacKinnon J).
3 *Cornhill Insurance Co Ltd v Assenheim* (1937) 58 Ll L Rep 27, 31 (MacKinnon J); *Marc Rich & Co AG v Portman* [1996] 1 Lloyd's Rep 430, 448 (Longmore J) (the point was conceded, and a declaration made).
4 *Attaleia Marine Co Ltd v Bimeh Iran (Iran Insurance Co), The Zeus* [1993] 2 Lloyd's Rep 497, 501 (Phillips J).
5 *Cornhill Insurance Co Ltd v Assenheim* (1937) 58 Ll L Rep 27, 31 (MacKinnon J); *Eagle Star Insurance Co Ltd v National Westminster Finance Australia Ltd* (1985) 58 ALR 165, 173, PC.
6 (1880) 6 QBD 222, CA.
7 At 229–230.
8 (1927) 29 Ll L Rep 9, 12.
9 Section 84(3)(a) was referred to by Lord Hoffmann in *HIH Casualty and General Insurance Ltd v Chase Manhattan Bank* [2003] UKHL 6, [2003] 2 Lloyd's Rep IR 61, which concerned non-marine insurance, but the issue of return of premium and applicability of s 84(3)(a) in a non-marine case was not expressly considered (para 73). If insurers are not obliged to return the premium in cases of avoidance for fraud, this represents a departure from the general law, according to which the return of moneys paid is a condition of rescission even of a contract voidable on grounds of fraud: *Sheffield Nickel and Silver Plating Co Ltd v Unwin* (1877) 2 QBD 214, 223 (Lush J, delivering the judgment of the court). In relation to contracts of consumer insurance entered into, or variations agreed, from 6 April 2013, s 84 of the Marine Insurance Act 1906 is to be read subject to the provisions of Sch 1 to the Consumer Insurance (Disclosure and Representations) Act 2011: the 2012 Act, ss 4, 12(4), and Sch 1, para 17 (the 2012 Act came into force on 6 April 2013). In relation to contracts of non-consumer insurance entered into, or variations agreed, from 12 August 2016, s 84 of the Marine Insurance Act 1906 is to be read subject to the provisions of Sch 1 to the Insurance Act 2015: the 2015 Act, ss 2–8, 22(1) and (3), 23(2), and Sch 1, para 12 (the Insurance Act 2015 was passed on 12 February 2015).

Agreement to restrict or exclude duty of utmost good faith

11.34   The parties may, by agreement, exclude, restrict or otherwise define the insured's duty of disclosure[1] and that of his agent,[2] and exclude or limit the insured's liability for misrepresentations.[3] It is against public policy for an insured to exclude liability for his own fraud.[4] Whether an insured may exclude liability for his agent's fraud, if sufficiently clear words are used, remains undecided.[5]

1 See *Sumitomo Bank Ltd v Banque Bruxelles Lambert SA* [1997] 1 Lloyd's Rep 487, 495 (Langley J) (limits of duty of disclosure defined); *HIH Casualty and General Insurance Ltd v Chase Manhattan Bank* [2003] UKHL 6, [2003] 2 Lloyd's Rep 61 (duty of disclosure excluded).
2 *HIH Casualty and General Insurance Ltd v Chase Manhattan Bank* [2003] UKHL 6, [2003] 2 Lloyd's Rep IR 61.
3 *HIH Casualty and General Insurance Ltd v Chase Manhattan Bank* [2003] UKHL 6, [2003] 2 Lloyd's Rep 61.
4 See *HIH Casualty and General Insurance Ltd v Chase Manhattan Bank* [2003] UKHL 6, [2003] 2 Lloyd's Rep 61, paras 14–17 (Lord Bingham), 76–82 (Lord Hoffmann), 96–98 (Lord Hobhouse) and 118–127 (Lord Scott).
5 See *HIH Casualty and General Insurance Ltd v Chase Manhattan Bank* [2003] UKHL 6, [2003] 2 Lloyd's Rep 61, paras 14–17 (Lord Bingham), 76–82 (Lord Hoffmann), 96–98 (Lord Hobhouse) and 118–127 (Lord Scott).

DUTY OF FAIR PRESENTATION: INSURANCE ACT 2015

11.35   A new 'duty of fair presentation' applies in relation to non-consumer insurance contracts[1] entered into on or after 12 August 2016 and variations agreed after that date to non-consumer insurance contracts entered into at any time.[2]

Unless the contrary intention appears, where the provisions of the Insurance Act 2015 in relation to the duty of fair presentation refer to something done by or in relation to the insurer or the insured,[3] those references include it being done by or in relation to that person's agent.[4]

The parties may contract out of the duty of fair presentation, but only if certain requirements are fulfilled. A term in relation to the duty of fair presentation which would put the insured in a worse position than under the Insurance Act 2015 is known as a 'disadvantageous term' and is to no effect unless the transparency requirements in the 2015 Act are complied with.[5] This means that the insurer must take sufficient steps to draw the disadvantageous term to the insured's attention before the contract is entered into or variation agreed (unless the insured or its agent had actual knowledge of the disadvantageous term at that stage),[6] and that the disadvantageous term must be clear and unambiguous as to its effect.[7] In determining whether these requirements have been met, the characteristics of insured persons of the kind in question, and the circumstances of the transaction, are to be taken into account.[8]

1 A 'non-consumer insurance contract' means a contract of insurance that is not a consumer insurance contract; and a 'consumer insurance contract' has the same meaning as in the Consumer Insurance (Disclosure and Representations) Act 2012: Insurance Act 2015, s 1. 'Consumer insurance contract' in the 2012 Act means a contract of insurance between an individual who enters into the contract wholly or mainly for purposes unrelated to the individual's trade, business or profession, and a person who carries on the business of insurance and becomes a party to the contract of insurance by way of that business (whether or not in accordance with permission for the purposes of the Financial Services and Markets Act 2000): Consumer Insurance (Disclosure and Representations) Act 2012, s 1.

2 Insurance Act 2015, ss 2–8, 22(1) and (3), and 23(2) (the Insurance Act 2015 was passed on 12 February 2015). The position in relation to warranties is different: the provisions of the Insurance Act 2015 apply to contracts of insurance entered into before 12 August 2016, and variations to such contracts: see **PARA 3.6**.
3 Part 2 of the Insurance Act 2015, ss 2–8.
4 Insurance Act 2015, s 22(4).
5 Insurance Act 2015, ss 16(2) and 17(1). This applies to contracts and to variations: s 16(3).
6 Insurance Act 2015, ss 17(2) and (5).
7 Insurance Act 2015, s 17(3).
8 Insurance Act 2015, s 17(4).

The duty of fair presentation

11.36   Before a non-consumer insurance contract is entered into, the insured must make to the insurer a fair presentation of the risk.[1] This duty is known as 'the duty of fair presentation'.[2] A fair presentation need not be contained in only one document or oral presentation.[3]

A fair presentation of the risk is one which makes disclosure of every material circumstance which the insured knows or ought to know[4] or, failing that, disclosure which gives the insurer sufficient information to put a prudent insurer on notice that it needs to make further enquiries for the purpose of revealing those material circumstances,[5] which makes that disclosure in a manner which would be reasonably clear and accessible to a prudent insurer,[6] and in which every material representation as to a matter of fact is substantially correct, and every material representation as to a matter of expectation or belief is made in good faith.[7]

The term 'circumstance' includes any communication made to, or information received by, the insured.[8] A circumstance or representation is material if it would influence the judgment of a prudent insurer in determining whether to take the risk and, if so, on what terms.[9] Examples of things which may be material circumstances are special or unusual facts relating to the risk,[10] any particular concerns which led the insured to seek insurance cover for the risk,[11] and anything which those concerned with the class of insurance and field of activity in question would generally understand as being something that should be dealt with in a fair presentation of risks of the type in question.[12]

A material representation is substantially correct if a prudent insurer would not consider the difference between what is represented and what is actually correct to be material.[13] A representation may be withdrawn or corrected before the contract of insurance is entered into.[14]

In the absence of enquiry, the duty of fair presentation does not require the insured to disclose a circumstance if it diminishes the risk,[15] the insurer knows it,[16] ought to know it[17] or is presumed to know it,[18] or it is something as to which the insurer waives information.[19] These concepts are considered further below.

Unless the contrary intention appears, references to something being done by or in relation to the insurer or the insured in the context of the duty of fair presentation includes its being done by or in relation to that person's agent.[20]

The insurer has a remedy against the insured for a breach of the duty of fair presentation only if the insurer shows that, but for the breach, the insurer would not have entered into the contract of insurance at all, or would have done so only on different terms.[21]

1 Insurance Act 2015, ss 2(1) and 3(1). 'Insured' means the party to a contract of insurance who is the insured under the contract, or would be if the contract were entered into, and 'insurer' means the party to a contract of insurance who is the insurer under the contract, or would be if the contract were entered into: Insurance Act 2015, s 1. The Explanatory Notes to the Insurance Act 2015 say (at para 42) that in some situations one party may enter into a contract on behalf of others, and that who is the 'insured' in such cases is, and will continue to be, determined by reference to the particular contract. Explanatory Notes do not form part of a statute, are not endorsed by Parliament and cannot be amended by it; in so far as they cast light on the objective setting or contextual scene of a statute and the mischief to which it is aimed, they are an admissible aid to construction: *Flora v Wakom (Heathrow) Ltd* [2006] EWCA Civ 1103, [2007] 1 WLR 482, paras 15–16 (Brooke LJ).
2 Insurance Act 2015, s 2(2).
3 Insurance Act 2015, s 7(1). The Explanatory Notes to the 2015 Act say (at para 72) that the Act is intended to recognise that the insurer may need to ask questions about the information in the initial presentation in order to draw out the information it requires to make the underwriting decision, and that all information which has been provided to the insurer by the time the contract is entered into will therefore form part of the presentation to be assessed. For the status of Explanatory Notes, see note 1 above.
4 Insurance Act 2015, ss 3(3)(a) and 4(a).
5 Insurance Act 2015, ss 3(3)(a) and 4(b).
6 Insurance Act 2015, s 3(3)(b). The Explanatory Notes to the 2015 Act say (at para 46) that this provision is intended to target, at one end of the scale, 'data dumps', where the insurer is presented with an overwhelming amount of undigested information, and that, at the other end, it is not expected that this requirement would be satisfied by an overly brief or cryptic presentation. For the status of Explanatory Notes, see note 1 above.
7 Insurance Act 2015, s 3(3)(c).
8 Insurance Act 2015, s 7(2). The Explanatory Notes to the 2015 Act say (at para 73) that s 7(2) repeats the terms of s 18(5) of the Marine Insurance Act 1906 in order to make clear that the term 'circumstance' is used in the same way in both pieces of legislation. For the status of Explanatory Notes, see note 1 above.
9 Insurance Act 2015, s 7(3). The Explanatory Notes to the 2015 Act say (at para 74) that s 7(3), which contains a definition of material circumstance and material representation, terms used in s 3, is based on ss 18(2) and 20(2) of the 1906 Act, and that the term 'prudent insurer' is also taken from the 1906 Act. For the status of Explanatory Notes, see note 1 above. In fact, 'circumstance' is defined in s 7(2), and 'representation' is not defined in the 2015 Act; what s 7(3) does is define 'material', by reference to the concept of 'prudent insurer' which appears in s 18(2) (disclosure) and 20(2) (representations) of the 1906 Act; s 7(3) states that a material circumstance or representation is one which would influence the judgment of a prudent insurer in determining whether to take the risk and, if so, on what terms, and thereby updates the statutory wording. The wording of ss 18(2) and 20(2) of the 1906 Act is narrower than that of s 7(3) as it refers to 'fixing the premium, or determining whether he will take the risk', but it has been given a broader application in the case-law: see **PARA 11.6**. The retention of the concept of the 'prudent insurer' in s 7(3) means that the test for materiality remains defined by reference to the hypothetical prudent insurer rather than by what a reasonable insured would have recognised as material (see **PARA 11.6**), and will normally require expert evidence at trial (see **PARA 11.7**).
10 Insurance Act 2015, s 7(4)(a).
11 Insurance Act 2015, s 7(4)(b).
12 Insurance Act 2015, s 7(4)(c).
13 Insurance Act 2015, s 7(5).
14 Insurance Act 2015, s 7(6).
15 Insurance Act 2015, s 3(5)(a).
16 Insurance Act 2015, s 3(5)(b).
17 Insurance Act 2015, s 3(5)(c).
18 Insurance Act 2015, s 3(5)(d).
19 Insurance Act 2015, s 3(5)(e).
20 Insurance Act 2015, s 22(4).
21 See **PARA 11.39**.

The knowledge of the insured

11.37 The Insurance Act 2015 sets out the categories of individual[1] whose knowledge will be directly attributed to the insured, and the type of knowledge which is relevant.

For the purposes of the insured's duty to disclose every material circumstance which he knows or ought to know, an insured who is an individual knows only what is known to the individual and what is known to one or more individuals who are responsible for the insured's insurance;[2] and an insured who is not an individual knows only what is known to one or more of the individuals who are part of the insured's senior management, or responsible for the insured's insurance,[3] subject in each case to the operation of any rule of law according to which knowledge of a fraud perpetrated by one of these individuals on the insured is not to be attributed to the insured.[4]

An insured is not taken to know confidential information known to an individual responsible for the insured's insurance if the individual is, or is an employee of, the insured's agent, and the information was acquired by the insured's agent or by an employee of that agent through a business relationship with a person who is not connected with the contract of insurance.[5] For these purposes, the persons connected with a contract of insurance are the insured and any other persons for whom cover is provided by the contract, and if the contract re-insures risks covered by another contract, the persons who are connected (in the same sense) with that other contract.[6] An 'employee', in relation to the insured's agent, includes any individual working for the agent, whatever the capacity in which the individual acts.[7] An individual is responsible for the insured's insurance if the individual participates on behalf of the insured in the process of procuring the insured's insurance, whether the individual does so as the insured's employee or agent, as an employee of the insured's agent or in any other capacity.[8] 'Senior management' means those individuals who play significant roles in the making of decisions about how the insured's activities are to be managed or organised.[9]

Whether an individual or not, an insured ought to know what should reasonably have been revealed by a reasonable search of information available to the insured (whether the search is conducted by making enquiries or by any other means).[10] For these purposes, 'information' includes information held within the insured's organisation or by any other person, such as the insured's agent or a person for whom cover is provided by the contract of insurance.[11] This is potentially a wide category: for example, a policy of liability insurance may provide cover to employees, partners, directors and consultants of the insured, and also to former employees, partners, directors and former consultants.

The practical effect of imputing to an insured the knowledge which would reasonably have been revealed by a reasonable search of information available to the insured is to impose an obligation on the insured to conduct a reasonable search. This is an important element of the duty of fair presentation under the 2015 Act, and it is suggested that there is significant scope for argument about what is required, both as to matters of general principle, and as to matters of fact in any particular case.

References to an individual's knowledge include not only actual knowledge, but also matters which the individual suspected, and of which the individual would have had knowledge but for deliberately refraining from confirming them or enquiring about them.[12]

1 'Individual' is the term used in the 2015 Act. It is not defined, but it is clear from the context that it denotes a natural person, ie a human being, as opposed to legal person such as a company.
2 Insurance Act 2015, ss 3(4)(a) and 4(1)–(2). The Explanatory Notes to the 2015 Act say (at para 52) that the categories of 'senior management' and persons 'responsible for the insured's insurance' reflect important decisions on the common law rules of attribution in the insurance context, but that the intended effect of the phrase 'knows only' is that the common law on attribution of knowledge to the insured is replaced by the terms of the Act. Explanatory Notes do not form part of a statute, are not endorsed by Parliament and cannot be amended by it; in so far as they cast light on the objective setting or contextual scene of a statute and the mischief to which it is aimed, they are an admissible aid to construction: *Flora v Wakom (Heathrow) Ltd* [2006] EWCA Civ 1103, [2007] 1 WLR 482, paras 15–16 (Brooke LJ).
3 Insurance Act 2015, ss 3(4)(a), 4(1) and (3). In evidence to The Special Public Bill Committee of the House of Lords on 9 December 2014, Lord Mance said that these provisions omitted the third common law category of imputed knowledge, which was the knowledge of an agent responsible for managing the insured activity or property (see *Proudfoot v Montefiore* (1867) LR 2 QB 511), and arguably reversed that line of authority; he said that the reasonable search provision was presumably intended to cater for that, and that reasonable search was very sensible if you do not expect to have information already, but where you have an agent whose duty is to pass you information and who is charged with responsibility for the subject matter of the insurance, you would, on the face of it, have no duty to search or inquire.
4 Insurance Act 2015, ss 4(2)(b), 4(3) and 6(2). The Explanatory Notes to the 2015 Act say (at para 70) that s 6(2) is intended to capture a common law exception to the general rules of attribution, known as the *Hampshire Land* principle, which broadly means that a company or other principal is not fixed with knowledge of a fraud practised against it by its agent or officer. For the status of Explanatory Notes, see note 1. Section 6(2) sensibly does not attempt to codify the *Hampshire Land* principle (which takes its name from *Re Hampshire Land Company* [1896] 2 Ch 743), thereby allowing for future developments in the common law to apply in relation to the 2015 Act.
5 Insurance Act 2015, s 4(4). The Explanatory Notes to the 2015 Act say (at para 59) that this provision is expected to be particularly relevant to the insured's broker who is likely to hold confidential information on behalf of many unconnected clients. For the status of Explanatory Notes, see note 2 above.
6 Insurance Act 2015, s 4(5).
7 Insurance Act 2015, s 8(a).
8 Insurance Act 2015, s 8(b). The Explanatory Notes to the 2015 Act say (at para 53) that 'responsible for the insured's insurance' is expected to catch, for example, the insured's risk manager if they have one, and any employee who assists in the collection of data or negotiates the terms of the insurance; and that it may also include an individual acting as the insured's broker. For the status of Explanatory Notes, see note 2 above.
9 Insurance Act 2015, s 8(c). The Explanatory Notes to the 2015 Act say (at para 54) that 'senior management' captures those individuals who play significant roles in the making of decisions about how the insured's activities are to be managed or organised, and that, in a corporate context, this is likely to include members of the board of directors but may extend beyond this, depending on the structure and management arrangements of the insured. For the status of Explanatory Notes, see note 2 above. (The Explanatory Notes on the Insurance Bill as introduced in the House of Lords on 17 July 2014 said (at paragraph 54) that 'senior management' was intended to include (and be more or less limited to) board members or their equivalent in a non-corporate organisation. In evidence to The Special Public Bill Committee of the House of Lords on 9 December 2014, Lord Mance said that there had been a number of contradictory statements about the meaning of the relevant provision; he criticised the Law Commissions' July 2014 Report (Law Com No 353; Cm 8898; see paras 8.58–8.59) for quoting a very old case, *Gibson v Barton* (1875) LR 10 QB 329, which was on a particular statutory provision that would suggest, if read literally, that the only senior management outside the board would be someone entrusted with the whole management of the company; that this seemed to be completely inapposite and contrary to the language of the Act; and that modern authorities such as *Meridian Global Funds Management Asia Ltd v Securities Commission* [1995] 2 AC 500, PC, looked at the matter of who was the senior management in a much more context-specific way. He said that it seemed to him that the statutory wording was perfectly acceptable, and that what had gone wrong was a lot of encrustation in the form of the Law Commissions' Report and the Explanatory Notes (ie the July 2014 version).)

10 Insurance Act 2015, s 4(6). The Explanatory Notes to the 2015 Act say (at para 55) that the knowledge of those individuals who do not fall within the category of senior management, yet who perform management roles or otherwise possess relevant information or knowledge about the risk to be insured, may be captured by the 'reasonable search'. For the status of Explanatory Notes, see note 2 above. In evidence to The Special Public Bill Committee of the House of Lords on 9 December 2014, Lord Mance said that what ought reasonably to be revealed by a reasonable search was not beyond argument, and that if you asked someone who ought to tell you but he failed to do so, he supposed that that was something that ought reasonably to have been revealed by your inquiry; but that it was not quite so obvious what the position would be if the inquiry was made of some third party who was not under a duty to tell you.

11 Insurance Act 2015, s 4(7).

12 Insurance Act 2015, s 6(1). The Explanatory Notes to the 2015 Act say (at para 69) that what an individual knows includes not only what it actually knows but also 'blind eye' knowledge, as the courts have consistently interpreted knowledge to include cases where someone has deliberately failed to make an enquiry in case it results in the confirmation of a suspicion, and refer to *Manifest Shipping Co Ltd v Uni-Polaris Insurance Co Ltd* [2001] UKHL 1, [2003] 1 AC 469. For the status of Explanatory Notes, see note 2 above. In fact, the discussion of 'blind eye' knowledge in *Manifest Shipping* concerned the meaning of a ship being sent to sea in an unseaworthy state 'with the privity of the assured' in s 39(5) of the 1906 Act, not the knowledge required in the context of the duty of good faith under ss 17 to 20 of the Marine Insurance Act 1906; however, it is likely that the same approach to 'blind eye' knowledge would be applied in the context of the duty of good faith under the 1906 Act. Section 6(1) codifies the meaning of 'blind eye' knowledge, rather than making provision for the common law to apply (the approach taken in relation to *Hampshire Land* principle in s 6(2): see note 4 above); it is suggested that this is likely to give rise to arguments about whether, and to what extent, developments in the case-law in other contexts are relevant to the construction and application of s 6(1).

The knowledge of the insurer

11.38 The Insurance Act 2015 sets out the categories of individual[1] whose knowledge will be directly attributed to the insurer, and the type of knowledge which is relevant.

An insurer knows a circumstance, and the insured is therefore not required to disclose it, only if it is known to one or more of the individuals who participate on behalf of the insurer in the decision whether to take the risk, and if so on what terms, whether the individual does so as the insurer's employee or agent, as an employee of the insurer's agent, or in any other capacity,[2] subject in each case to the operation of any rule of law according to which knowledge of a fraud perpetrated by one of these individuals on the insured is not to be attributed to the insured.[3]

An insurer ought to know a circumstance, and the insured is therefore not required to disclose it, only if any employee or agent of the insurer knows it, and ought reasonably to have passed on the relevant information to an individual who participates on behalf of the insurer in the decision to take the risk, and if so on what terms, whether the individual does so as the insurer's employee or agent, as an employee of the insurer's agent, or in any other capacity; or if the relevant information is held by the insurer and is readily available to such an individual;[4] subject in each case to the operation of any rule of law according to which knowledge of a fraud perpetrated by one of these individuals on the insured is not to be attributed to the insured.[5]

An insurer is presumed to know, and the insured is therefore not required to disclose, things which are common knowledge,[6] and things which an insurer offering insurance of the class in question to insureds in the field of activity in question would reasonably be expected to know in the ordinary course of business.[7]

References to an individual's knowledge include not only actual knowledge, but also matters which the individual suspected, and of which the individual would have had knowledge but for deliberately refraining from confirming them or enquiring about them.[8]

1 'Individual' is the term used in the 2015 Act. It is not defined, but it is clear from the context that it denotes a natural person, ie a human being, as opposed to legal person such as a company.
2 Insurance Act 2015, ss 3(5)(b) and 5(1).
3 Insurance Act 2015, ss 5(1) and 6(2). The Explanatory Notes to the 2015 Act say (at para 70) that s 6(2) is intended to capture a common law exception to the general rules of attribution, known as the *Hampshire Land* principle, which broadly means that a company or other principal is not fixed with knowledge of a fraud practised against it by its agent or officer. Explanatory Notes do not form part of a statute, are not endorsed by Parliament and cannot be amended by it; in so far as they cast light on the objective setting or contextual scene of a statute and the mischief to which it is aimed, they are an admissible aid to construction: *Flora v Wakom (Heathrow) Ltd* [2006] EWCA Civ 1103, [2007] 1 WLR 482, paras 15–16 (Brooke LJ). Section 6(2) sensibly does not attempt to codify the *Hampshire Land* principle (which takes its name from *Re Hampshire Land Company* [1896] 2 Ch 743), thereby allowing for future developments in the common law to apply in relation to the 2015 Act.
4 Insurance Act 2015, ss 3(5)(c) and 5(2).
5 Insurance Act 2015, ss 5(1) and 6(2). See further note 1 above.
6 Insurance Act 2015, ss 3(5)(d) and 5(3)(a). The Explanatory Notes to the 2015 Act say (at para 66) that the reference to 'common knowledge' in section 5(3)(a) replicates the language of the 1906 Act, but that the reference to 'common notoriety' has not been retained because the meaning of that phrase appears to have changed since 1906, from being 'well known' to now suggesting an element of infamy. The intention therefore appears to be to retain the meaning of the equivalent provision in s 18(3)(b) of the 1906 Act, which provides that the insurer is presumed to know, and the insured need not disclose, 'matters of common notoriety or knowledge'. For the status of Explanatory Notes, see note 3 above.
7 Insurance Act 2015, ss 3(5)(d) and 5(3)(b). The Explanatory Notes to the 2015 Act say (at para 67) that s 5(3)(b) is intended to be a modernisation of s 18(3)(b) of the 1906 Act, which refers to 'matters which an insurer in the ordinary course of his business, as such, ought to know'; that many underwriters work by class of business (such as property or professional indemnity insurance) rather than by industry sector (such as oil and gas); and that an insurer ought to have some insight into the industry for which it is providing insurance, but this insight may reasonably be limited to matters relevant to the type of insurance provided. For the status of Explanatory Notes, see note 3 above.
8 Insurance Act 2015, s 6(1). The Explanatory Notes to the 2015 Act say (at para 69) that what an individual knows includes not only what it actually knows but also 'blind eye' knowledge, as the courts have consistently interpreted knowledge to include cases where someone has deliberately failed to make an enquiry in case it results in the confirmation of a suspicion, and refer to *Manifest Shipping Co Ltd v Uni-Polaris Insurance Co Ltd* [2001] UKHL 1, [2003] 1 AC 469. For the status of Explanatory Notes, see note 3.In fact, the discussion of 'blind eye' knowledge in *Manifest Shipping* concerned the meaning of a ship being sent to sea in an unseaworthy state 'with the privity of the assured' in s 39(5) of the 1906 Act, but it is correct that 'blind eye' knowledge has been held to amount to knowledge for the purposes of s 18 of the 1906 Act: see para **PARA 11.10**. Section 6(1) codifies the concept of 'blind eye' knowledge (a different approach is taken in s 6(2) in relation to *Hampshire Land* principle: see note 3 above), and it is suggested that this is likely to give rise to arguments about whether, and to what extent, developments in the case-law in relation to 'blind eye' knowledge in other contexts are relevant to the construction and application of s 6(1).

Remedies for breach

11.39   The insurer has a remedy against the insured for a breach of the duty of fair presentation only if the insurer shows that, but for the breach, the insurer would not have entered into the contract of insurance at all,[1] or would have done so only on different terms.[2]

A breach for which the insurer has a remedy against the insured is a 'qualifying breach',[3] and is either deliberate or reckless,[4] or neither deliberate nor reckless.[5]

A qualifying breach is deliberate or reckless if the insured knew that it was in breach of the duty of fair presentation, or did not care whether it was in breach of that duty.[6] It is for the insurer to show that a qualifying breach was deliberate or reckless.[7]

If a qualifying breach was deliberate or reckless, the insurer may avoid the contract and refuse all claims, and need not return any of the premiums paid.[8]

If a qualifying breach was neither deliberate nor reckless, the remedy depends on what the insurer would have done in the absence of that breach.[9] If the insurer would not have entered into the contract on any terms, the insurer may avoid the contract and refuse all claims, but must return the premiums paid.[10] If the insurer would have entered into the contract, but on different terms (other than terms relating to the premium), the contract is to be treated as if it had been entered into on those different terms if the insurer so requires.[11] In addition, if the insurer would have entered into the contract (whether the terms relating to matters other than the premium would have been the same or different), but would have charged a higher premium, the insurer may reduce proportionately the amount to be paid on a claim.[12] This means that the insurer need pay on the claim only X% of what it would otherwise have been under an obligation to pay under the terms of the contract (or, if applicable, under the different terms on which it would have entered into the contract), where 'X' is the premium actually charged divided by the higher premium and multiplied by 100.[13]

Similar provisions apply in relation to qualifying breaches of the duty of fair presentation in relation to variations to non-consumer insurance contracts.[14]

1 Insurance Act 2015, s 8(1)(a). In order for the insurer to be entitled to avoid the policy for non-disclosure or misrepresentation under ss 18 or 20 of the Marine Insurance Act 1906, he has to show not only material non-disclosure or misrepresentation, ie a non-disclosure or misrepresentation which would influence the judgment of a prudent insurer in deciding whether to take the risk or, if he does, on what terms, but also that the actual underwriter was 'induced' by the non-disclosure or misrepresentation to do so: see **PARA 11.6**. The Explanatory Notes to the 2015 Act say (at para 77) that s 8(1) reflects the current law on inducement as developed following the decision in *Pan Atlantic Insurance Co Ltd v Pine Top Insurance Co Ltd* [1995] 1 AC 501, HL: see **PARA 11.6**. Explanatory Notes do not form part of a statute, are not endorsed by Parliament and cannot be amended by it; in so far as they cast light on the objective setting or contextual scene of a statute and the mischief to which it is aimed, they are an admissible aid to construction: *Flora v Wakom (Heathrow) Ltd* [2006] EWCA Civ 1103, [2007] 1 WLR 482, paras 15–16 (Brooke LJ). If the intention of s 8(1) was to reflect the current law on inducement, this may not have been achieved, as the law on inducement is the same as in the general law of contract and the non-disclosure or misrepresentation under ss 18 and 20 of the 1906 Act must be 'a real and substantial part' of what induced the insurer to enter into the contract (see **PARA 11.6**), and it is suggested that the express adoption in the statutory wording of the 'but for' test of causation may lead to a different result in some cases. Further, introducing a statutory test for inducement rather than defining the concept by reference to the general law of contract, which would have allowed the law to continue to develop in line with the common law (the approach adopted in relation to the *Hampshire Land* principle: see **PARA 11.38**, note 3) has the effect of isolating the law on inducement in insurance contracts and potentially restricts or distorts its development.
2 Insurance Act 2015, s 8(1)(b). See further note 1 above.
3 Insurance Act 2015, s 8(3).
4 Insurance Act 2015, s 8(4)(a). The Explanatory Notes to the 2015 Act say (at para 80) that an insured will have acted deliberately if it knew that it did not make a fair presentation, and that an insured will have acted recklessly if it 'did not care' whether or not it was in breach of the duty, but that this is intended to indicate a greater degree of culpability than acting 'carelessly'; and that 'deliberate or reckless' will include fraudulent behaviour. For the status of Explanatory Notes, see note 1 above. Although the approach taken in the Explanatory Notes in attributing part of the statutory wording to 'deliberate' and part to 'reckless' breaches is logical, it goes beyond the wording of the 2015 Act: this does not define each term separately, as there is a single remedy for both.

5 Insurance Act 2015, s 8(4)(b). The Explanatory Notes to the 2015 Act say (at para 81) that breaches do not have to be careless or deliberate/reckless in order to be actionable: 'innocent' breaches of the duty will also give an insurer a remedy if the insurer can show inducement; and that this reflects the current law for non-consumer insurance. For the status of Explanatory Notes, see note 1 above.
6 Insurance Act 2015, s 8(5). The same terms are used in the Enterprise Bill in relation to the proposed implied term in relation to late payment of insurance claims: see **PARA 8.3**.
7 Insurance Act 2015, s 8(6).
8 Insurance Act 2015, Sch 1, para 2.
9 See Insurance Act 2015, Sch 1, paras 3–6.
10 Insurance Act 2015, Sch 1, paras 3 and 4.
11 Insurance Act 2015, Sch 1, paras 3 and 5. The Explanatory Notes to the 2015 Act say (at para 157) that if the insurer would have included an exemption clause or imposed an excess, the claim would be treated as if the contract included that exemption clause or excess, and (at para 159) that if the insurer would have entered into the contract on different terms and would have charged a higher premium, those alternative terms may be applied to the contract and, in addition, the claim may be reduced proportionately. For the status of Explanatory Notes, see note 1 above.
12 Insurance Act 2015, Sch 1, paras 3 and 6(1). The Explanatory Notes to the 2015 Act say (at para 159) that if the insurer would have entered into the contract on different terms and would have charged a higher premium, those alternative terms may be applied to the contract and, in addition, the claim may be reduced proportionately. For the status of Explanatory Notes, see note 1 above.
13 Insurance Act 2015, Sch 1, paras 3 and 6(2).
14 Insurance Act 2015, Sch 1, Part 2.

CONSUMER INSURANCE (DISCLOSURE AND REPRESENTATIONS) ACT 2012

11.40 In December 2009, the Law Commission published a Report on Consumer Insurance Law: Pre-Contract Disclosure and Misrepresentation.[1] The Consumer Insurance (Disclosure and Representations) Act 2012 is based on that Report and makes significant changes to the law of non-disclosure and misrepresentation in connection with consumer insurance contracts.

1 Law Com No 319, Cm 7758.

Application and commencement

11.41 The Consumer Insurance (Disclosure and Representations) Act 2012 defines a consumer as an individual who enters into a consumer insurance contract, or proposes to do so, and defines insurer as the person who is, or would become, the other party to a consumer insurance contract.[1] A consumer insurance contract is a contract of insurance between an individual who enters into the contract wholly or mainly for purposes unrelated to the individual's trade, business or profession, and a person who carries on the business of insurance and becomes a party to the contract of insurance by way of that business (whether or not in accordance with permission for the purposes of the Financial Services and Markets Act 2000).[2]

The 2012 Act applies in modified form to group insurance[3] and in relation to insurance on the life of another.[4]

Section 1 (the definitions of consumer insurance contract, consumer and insurer) and the commencement provisions came into force on 8 March 2012, the day on which the Act was passed, but otherwise the Act came into force on 6 April 2013.[5]

The Act applies only in relation to consumer insurance contracts entered into, and variations to consumer contracts agreed, after the Act comes into force.[6]

1 Section 1.
2 Section 1.
3 Section 7 and Sch 1, paras 13–16.
4 Section 8.
5 Section 12(2); Consumer Insurance (Disclosure and Representations) Act 2012 (Commencement) Order 2013 (SI 2013/450).
6 Section 12(4). Special provision is made in relation to group insurance: s 12(4).

Modification of duty of good faith: the duty to take reasonable care

11.42 The Consumer Insurance (Disclosure and Representations) Act 2012 provides that it is the duty of the consumer to take reasonable care not to make a misrepresentation to the insurer before a consumer insurance contract is entered into or varied.[1] This duty replaces any duty relating to disclosure or representations by a consumer to an insurer which existed in the same circumstances before the Act applied.[2] Accordingly, any rule of law to the effect that a consumer insurance contract is one of the utmost good faith is modified to the extent required by the provisions of the Act,[3] and the application of s 17 of the Marine Insurance Act 1906 in relation to a contract of marine insurance which is a consumer insurance contract is subject to the provisions of the Act.[4] Any rule of law to the same effect as ss 18 to 20 of the Marine Insurance Act 1906 is abolished in relation to consumer insurance contracts, and those sections are amended to give effect to the Act.[5]

A failure by the consumer to comply with the insurer's request to confirm or amend particulars previously given is capable of being a misrepresentation for the purposes of the Act.[6]

1 Section 2(1) and (2).
2 Section 2(4).
3 Section 2(5)(a). In relation to consumer insurance contracts entered into on or after 12 August 2016, and variations agreed on or after that date to contracts entered into at any time, s 2(5)(a) is omitted from the 2012 Act, and replaced by a provision to equivalent effect in the Insurance Act 2015 which also applies to non-consumer insurance contracts: Insurance Act 2015, ss 14(2) and (4), 22(1) and (3), and 23(2).
4 Section 2(5)(b). In relation to consumer insurance contracts entered into on or after 12 August 2016, s 2(5)(b) is omitted from the 2012 Act, and replaced by a provision to equivalent effect in the Insurance Act 2015 which also applies to non-consumer insurance contracts: Insurance Act 2015, ss 14(3)–(4), 22(1) and (3), and 23(2).
5 Section 11(1). In relation to consumer insurance contracts entered into on or after 12 August 2016, s 11(1) is omitted from the 2012 Act, and replaced by a provision to equivalent effect in the Insurance Act 2015 which also applies to non-consumer insurance contracts: Insurance Act 2015, ss 21(2)–(3) and (6), 22(1) and (3) and 23(2).
6 Section 2(3).

Determining whether the consumer has taken reasonable care

11.43 Whether or not a consumer has taken reasonable care not to make a misrepresentation is to be determined in the light of all the relevant circumstances.[1] The following are examples of things which may need to be taken into account in making such a determination: the type of consumer insurance contract in question, and its target market; any relevant explanatory material or publicity produced or authorised by the insurer, how clear, and how specific, the insurer's questions were; in the case of a failure to respond to the insurer's questions in connection with the renewal or variation of a consumer insurance contract, how clearly the insurer communicated the importance of answering those questions (or the possible consequences of failing to do so); whether or not an agent was acting for the consumer.[2]

The standard of care is that of a reasonable consumer, but this is subject to the following:[3] if the insurer was, or ought to have been, aware of any particular characteristics or circumstances of the actual consumer, those are to be taken into account;[4] and a misrepresentation made dishonestly is always to be taken as showing lack of reasonable care.[5]

1 Consumer Insurance (Disclosure and Representations) Act 2012, s 3(1).
2 Section 3(2); see **PARA 11.46**.
3 Section 3(3).
4 Section 3(4).
5 Section 3(5).

Actionable misrepresentations

11.44   A misrepresentation for which the insurer has a remedy against the consumer is referred to in the Consumer Insurance (Disclosure and Representations) Act 2012 as a qualifying misrepresentation.[1] For the purposes of the Act, a qualifying (ie actionable) misrepresentation is either deliberate or reckless,[2] or careless.[3]

A qualifying misrepresentation is deliberate or reckless if the consumer knew that it was untrue or misleading, or did not care whether or not it was untrue or misleading, and knew that the matter to which the misrepresentation related was relevant to the insurer, or did not care whether or not it was relevant to the insurer.[4] It is for the insurer to show that a qualifying misrepresentation was deliberate or reckless,[5] but it is to be presumed, unless the contrary is shown, that the consumer had the knowledge of a reasonable consumer, and that the consumer knew that a matter about which the insurer asked a clear and specific question was relevant to the insurer.[6]

A qualifying misrepresentation is careless if it is not deliberate or reckless.[7]

1 Section 4(2).
2 Section 5(1)(a).
3 Section 5(1)(b).
4 Section 5(2).
5 Section 5(4).
6 Section 5(5).
7 Section 5(3).

Remedies

11.45 If a qualifying misrepresentation was deliberate or reckless, the insurer may avoid the contract and refuse all claims, and need not return any of the premiums paid, except to the extent (if any) that it would be unfair to the consumer to retain them.[1]

If a qualifying misrepresentation was careless, the insurer's remedies are based on what it would have done if the consumer had complied with the duty to take reasonable care not to make a misrepresentation to the insurer.[2] If the insurer would not have entered into the consumer insurance contract on any terms, the insurer may avoid the contract and refuse all claims, but must return the premiums paid.[3] If the insurer would have entered into the consumer insurance contract, but on different terms (excluding terms relating to the premium), the contract is to be treated as if it had been entered into on those different terms if the insurer so requires.[4] In addition, if the insurer would have entered into the consumer insurance contract (whether the terms relating to matters other than the premium would have been the same or different), but would have charged a higher premium, the insurer may reduce proportionately the amount to be paid on a claim.[5] This means that the insurer need pay on the claim only X% of what it would otherwise have been under an obligation to pay under the terms of the contract (or, if applicable, under the different terms on which it would have entered into the contract), where 'X' is the premium actually charged divided by the higher premium and multiplied by 100.[6]

If the qualifying misrepresentation was careless but does not relate to any outstanding claim, the insurer's remedies are based on what it would have done if the consumer had complied with the duty to take reasonable care not to make a misrepresentation to the insurer.[7] If the insurer would not have entered into the consumer insurance contract on any terms, the insurer may avoid the contract, but must return the premiums paid;[8] and if the insurer would have entered into the consumer insurance contract, but on different terms (excluding terms relating to the premium), the contract is to be treated as if it had been entered into on those different terms if the insurer so requires.[9] In both circumstances, the insurer may either give notice to that effect to the consumer, or may alternatively terminate the contract by giving reasonable notice to the consumer.[10] If the insurer gives notice to the consumer that the contract is to be treated as if it had been entered into on the different terms, the consumer may terminate the contract by giving reasonable notice to the insurer.[11] If either party terminate the contract pursuant to these provisions, the insurer must refund any premiums paid for the terminated cover in respect of the balance of the contract term.[12] Such termination does not affect the treatment of any claim arising under the contract in the period before termination.[13] These provisions do not affect any contractual right to terminate the contract.[14]

If the subject-matter of a variation can reasonably be treated separately from the subject-matter of the rest of the contract, these provisions apply (with any necessary modifications) in relation to the variation as it applies in relation to a contract.[15] Otherwise, the provisions apply (with any necessary modifications) as if the qualifying misrepresentation had been made in relation to the whole contract (for this purpose treated as including the variation) rather than merely in relation to the variation.[16]

Representations made by a consumer in connection with a proposed consumer insurance contract, or in connection with a proposed variation to a consumer insurance contract are not capable of being converted into a warranty by means of any provision of the consumer insurance contract (or of the terms of the variation), or of any other contract (and whether by declaring the representation to form the basis of the contract or otherwise).[17]

1 Consumer Insurance (Disclosure and Representations) Act 2012, s 4(3) and Sch 1, para 2.
2 Section 4(3) and Sch 1 para 4.
3 Section 4(3) and Sch 1, para 5.
4 Section 4(3) and Sch 1, para 6.
5 Section 4(3) and Sch 1, para 7.
6 Section 4(3) and Sch 1, para 8.
7 Section 4(3) and Sch 1, paras 4 and 9(2).
8 Section 4(3) and Sch 1, paras 5 and 9(2).
9 Section 4(3) and Sch 1, paras 6 and 9(2).
10 Section 4(3) and Sch 1, para 9(4). The insurer may not terminate a contract under this provision if it is wholly or mainly one of life insurance: Sch 1, para 9(5).
11 Section 4(3) and Sch 1, para 9(6).
12 Section 4(3) and Sch 1, para 9(7).
13 Section 4(3) and Sch 1, para 9(8).
14 Section 4(3) and Sch 1 para 9(9).
15 Section 4(3) and Sch 1, para 11.
16 Section 4(3) and Sch 1, para 12.
17 Section 6.

Rules for determining status of agents

11.46   One of the circumstances to be taken into account in determining whether or not a consumer has taken reasonable care not to make a misrepresentation is whether or not an agent was acting for the consumer.[1] The Consumer Insurance (Disclosure and Representations) Act 2012 sets out rules for determining, for these purposes only, whether an agent through whom a consumer insurance contract is effected is acting as the agent of the consumer or of the insurer.[2] These are as follows.

The agent is to be taken as the insurer's agent in each of the following cases: when the agent does something in the agent's capacity as the appointed representative of the insurer for the purposes of the Financial Services and Markets Act 2000 (see s 39 of that Act); when the agent collects information from the consumer, if the insurer had given the agent express authority to do so as the insurer's agent; when the agent enters into the contract as the insurer's agent, if the insurer had given the agent express authority to do so.[3]

In any other case, it is to be presumed that the agent is acting as the consumer's agent unless, in the light of all the relevant circumstances, it appears that the agent is acting as the insurer's agent.[4]

The 2012 Act sets out some factors which may be relevant, as follows.[5] Examples of factors which may tend to confirm that the agent is acting for the consumer are: the agent undertakes to give impartial advice to the consumer; the agent undertakes to conduct a fair analysis of the market; the consumer pays the agent a fee.[6] Examples of factors which may tend to show that the agent is acting for the insurer are: the agent places insurance of the type in question with only one of the insurers who provide insurance of that type; the agent is under a contractual obligation which has the effect of restricting the number of insurers with whom the agent places insurance of the type in question; the insurer provides insurance of the type in question through only a small proportion of the agents who deal in that type of insurance; the insurer permits the agent to use the insurer's name in providing the agent's services; the insurance in question is marketed under the name of the agent; the insurer asks the agent to solicit the consumer's custom.[7]

Nothing in the Act affects the circumstances in which a person is bound by the acts or omissions of that person's agent.[8]

1 Section 3(2).
2 Section 9 and Sch 2.
3 Section 9 and Sch 2, para 2.
4 Section 9 and Sch 2, para 3(1).
5 Section 9 and Sch, 2 para 3(2).
6 Section 9 and Sch 2, para 3(3).
7 Section 9 and Sch 2, para 3(4).
8 Section 12(5).

Avoidance or contracting out provisions

11.47   A term of a consumer contract, or of any other contract, which would put the consumer in a worse position, as respects disclosure and representations by the consumer to the insurer before the contract is entered into or varied, and any remedies for qualifying misrepresentations, than the consumer would be in by virtue of the provisions of the 2012 Act is of no effect.[1] This does not apply in relation to a contract for the settlement of a claim arising under a consumer insurance contract.[2]

1 Consumer Insurance (Disclosure and Representations) Act 2012, s 10(1) and (2).
2 Section 10(3).

FRAUDULENT CLAIMS AND FRAUDULENT DEVICES

11.48   The law which applies in relation to fraudulent claims depends on whether the contract of insurance under which the claim is made was entered into before, or on or after, 12 August 2016.[1]

1 Insurance Act 2015, ss 12, 22(1) and (3), and 23(2) (the Insurance Act 2015 was passed on 12 February 2015). See PARAS **11.49–11.54**.

Fraudulent claims and fraudulent devices: pre-Insurance Act 2015

11.49   This paragraph sets out the law as it applies to claims made under contracts of insurance entered into before 12 August 2016 and variations to such contracts.[1]

An insurer is not liable for a fraudulent or exaggerated claim, including any lesser claim which could have been honestly made.[2] This result is not dependent upon the inclusion of a term having that effect, although insurance contracts commonly contain such provisions, but is the consequence of a rule of law, the purpose of which is to deter both wholly fraudulent and simply exaggerated claims:[3]

> 'The logic is simple. The fraudulent insured must not be allowed to think: if the fraud is successful, then I will gain; if it is unsuccessful, I will lose nothing.'[4]

As a result, Part 2 of the Consumer Rights Act 2015 (unfair terms) has no application.[5] Further, the restrictions imposed by ICOBS on insurers' right to reject a claim by a consumer policyholder in certain circumstances do not apply where is 'evidence of fraud',[6] which includes both a fraudulent claim and fraud used in making or pursuing a claim (ie a fraudulent device).[7]

The parties may, notwithstanding that the obligation is not based on an implied term but on a rule of law, make express provision for the consequences of making a fraudulent claim, which may stop short of avoidance.[8] The fraudulent claim rule has no application after the commencement of litigation, when it is superseded or exhausted by the rules of litigation.[9]

Although the rule of law which defeats a fraudulent claim under a policy of insurance is linked to the observation of the duty of utmost good faith,[10] the authorities in relation to fraudulent claims have traditionally not used the language of avoidance, but have instead spoken of the insured 'forfeiting' his rights under the policy. For example, in *Britton v Royal Insurance Co*,[11] Willes J directed the jury in the following terms:

> 'The law upon such a case is in accordance with justice and also with sound policy. The law is, that a person who has made such a fraudulent claim could not be permitted to recover at all. The contract of insurance is one of perfect good faith on both sides, and it is most important that such good faith should be maintained. It is the common practice to insert in fire policies conditions that they shall be void in the event of a fraudulent claim; and there was such a condition in the present case. Such a condition is only in accord with legal principle and sound policy. It would be most dangerous to permit parties to practise such frauds, and then, notwithstanding their falsehood and fraud, to recover the real value of the goods consumed. And if there is wilful falsehood and fraud in the claim, the insured forfeits all claim whatever upon the policy.'

In *Manifest Shipping Co Ltd v Uni-Polaris Insurance Co Ltd, The Star Sea*,[12] the House of Lords indicated that there is a clear distinction to be made between the pre-contract duty of disclosure and any duty of disclosure which may exist after the contract has been made, and said that it was not right to reason from the existence of an extensive duty pre-contract positively to disclose all material facts to the conclusion that post-contract there is a similarly extensive obligation to disclose all facts which the insurer has an interest in knowing and which might affect his conduct, and that to do so would bestow a disproportionate benefit on the insurer.[13]

The scope and effect of the common law rule relating to fraudulent insurance claims, and its relationship with s 17 and the right to avoid for breach of the pre-contractual duty of disclosure, was considered further by the Court of Appeal in *Agapitos v Agnew, The Aegeon*.[14] The insured had not made a fraudulent claim, but the insurer contended that he had made use of a 'fraudulent device' in support of an otherwise genuine claim. Mance LJ referred to the 'present imperfect state of the law, fettered as it is by section 17', and attempted to summarise his conclusions in what he called a 'tentative view of an acceptable solution', as follows:[15]

'(a) To recognise that the fraudulent claim rule applies as much to the fraudulent maintenance of an initially honest claim as to a claim which the insured knows from the outset to be exaggerated.[16]

(b) To treat the use of a fraudulent device as a sub-species of making a fraudulent claim – at least as regards forfeiture of the claim itself in relation to which the fraudulent device or means is used ...

(c) To treat as relevant for this purpose any lie, directly related to the claim to which the fraudulent device relates, which is intended to improve the insured's prospects of obtaining a settlement or winning the case, and which would, if believed, tend, objectively, prior to any final determination at trial of the parties' rights, to yield a not insignificant[17] improvement in the insured's prospects – whether they be prospects of obtaining a settlement, or a better settlement, or of winning at trial.

(d) To treat the common law rules governing the making of a fraudulent claim (including the use of fraudulent device) as falling outside the scope of s 17 ... On this basis no question of avoidance ab initio would arise.'[18]

Although this passage was obiter (not necessary to the decision and therefore not strictly binding), the principles were applied by the Court of Appeal,[19] by the Privy Council[20] and by judges at first instance.[21] Subject to requiring a 'significant improvement', rather than a 'not insignificant improvement' in the insured's prospects,[22] the principles set out by Mance LJ have since been formally approved by the Court of Appeal in *Versloot Dredging BV v HDI Gerling Industrie Versicherung AG*.[23] The Court of Appeal also held that application of the forfeiture rule to fraudulent devices was a proportionate means of securing the aim of deterring fraud in insurance claims and was therefore compatible with art 1 of protocol 1.[24]

The effect of a fraudulent claim is retrospectively to remove or bar the insured's pre-existing cause of action.[25] It may be that, as no question arises of making a claim under a liability policy until the liability of the insured is established, whether by agreement, judgment or arbitration award, nothing done before the insured's liability is established is capable of constituting the making of a fraudulent claim;[26] alternatively, there may be a distinction between the making of a claim and the accrual of a cause of action against professional indemnity insurers,[27] in which case fraud at an earlier stage, for example in providing information to insurers to assist in the defence of a claim, might bar the insured's right to indemnity under the policy.

The rule enables recovery from a fraudulent insured of all sums paid out in ignorance of the fraud subsequent to its commission, including any sums relating to genuine loss in respect of which the insured was entitled to indemnity apart from the effect of the fraud.[28] The insured may thus not only be exposed to lack of cover in respect of genuine uninsured loss which would, but for his fraud, have been insured, but also to having to repay any sum received by way of indemnity in respect of such loss before the fraud is discovered, including payments on account or interim payments.[29] The presentation of a dishonest or fraudulent claim constitutes a breach of duty that entitles the insurer to repudiate any liability for the claim and, prospectively at least, to avoid any liability under the policy.[30] However, unlike avoidance for breach of the pre-contractual duty of disclosure, the common law rule relating to fraudulent claims has no retrospective effect on prior, separate claims which have already been settled under the same policy before any fraud occurs.[31] The extent of the prospective release of the insurer from liability at common law, including the position in relation to separate claims which are still unpaid at the time of the fraud, is unclear.[32] Where one claim gives rise to two heads of loss, fraud within one head of loss taints the claim as a whole.[33] The insured cannot, by subsequently attempting to retract the fraudulent element of a claim, avoid the consequences of having advanced a fraudulent claim.[34] Where a claim is compromised by a written agreement by insurers as to payment, the rule ceases to apply.[35]

1 Insurance Act 2015, ss 12, 22(1) and (3), and 23(2) (the Insurance Act 2015 was passed on 12 February 2015).

2 *Britton v Royal Insurance Co* (1866) 4 F & F 905; *Manifest Shipping Co Ltd v Uni-Polaris Insurance Co Ltd, The Star Sea* [2001] UKHL 1, [2003] AC 469, [2001] 1 Lloyd's Rep 389, paras 61–64, HL (Lord Hobhouse).

3 *Britton v Royal Insurance Co* (1866) 4 F & F 905; *Manifest Shipping Co Ltd v Uni-Polaris Insurance Co Ltd, The Star Sea* [2001] UKHL 1, [2003] AC 469, [2001] 1 Lloyd's Rep 389, paras 61–72, HL (Lord Hobhouse); and see *Banque Financière de la Cité SA v Westgate Insurance Co Ltd* [1990] 1 QB 665, 777–781, CA (Slade LJ), affirmed by the House of Lords at [1991] 2 AC 249, 280 (Lord Templeman), 281 (Lord Jauncey). The judgments in *Orakpo v Barclays Insurance Services Ltd* [1995] LRLR 443, CA adopted a contractual analysis (implying a term into the policy, there being, unusually, no express term) rather than an analysis based on a rule of law and therefore cannot be treated as fully authoritative: *Manifest Shipping Co Ltd v Uni-Polaris Insurance Co Ltd, The Star Sea* [2001] UKHL 1, [2003] AC 469, [2001] 1 Lloyd's Rep 389, HL, para 66 (Lord Hobhouse).

4 *Manifest Shipping Co Ltd v Uni-Polaris Insurance Co Ltd, The Star Sea* [2001] UKHL 1, [2003] AC 469, [2001] 1 Lloyd's Rep 389, HL, para 62 (Lord Hobhouse).

5 *Direct Line Insurance v Khan* [2001] EWCA Civ 1794, [2002] Lloyd's Rep IR 364, CA (in relation to the Unfair Terms in Consumer Contracts Regulations 1994); see also *Direct Line Insurance plc v Fox* [2009] EWHC 386 (QB), [2010] Lloyd's Rep IR 324, paras 50–53 (HHJ Richard Seymour QC) (in relation to the Unfair Terms in Consumer Contracts Regulations 1999). For Part 2 of the Consumer Rights Act 2015, see **PARA 3.20**.

6 ICOBS 8.1.2R. See further **PARA 11.4**.

7 *Bate v Aviva Insurance UK Ltd* [2014] EWCA Civ 334, [2014] Lloyd's Rep IR 527, para 49 (Tomlinson LJ) (in relation to ICOB 7.3.6, since replaced by ICOBS 8.1).

8 *K/S Merc-Scandia XXXXII v Certain Lloyd's Underwriters Subscribing to Lloyd's Policy No 25T 105487, The Mercandian Continent* [2001] EWCA Civ 1275, [2001] 2 Lloyd's Rep 563, 568, para 11 (Longmore LJ).

9 *Agapitos v Agnew, The Aegeon* [2002] EWCA Civ 247, [2003] QB 556, [2002] 2 Lloyd's Rep 42, paras 51–53 (Mance LJ).

10 *Manifest Shipping Co Ltd v Uni-Polaris Insurance Co Ltd, The Star Sea* [2001] UKHL 1, [2003] AC 469, [2001] 1 Lloyd's Rep 389, paras 61–64 (Lord Hobhouse).

11 (1866) 4 F & F 905.

12 [2001] UKHL 1, [2003] AC 469, [2001] 1 Lloyd's Rep 389.

13 *Manifest Shipping Co Ltd v Uni-Polaris Insurance Co Ltd, The Star Sea* [2001] UKHL 1, [2003] AC 469, [2001] 1 Lloyd's Rep 389, para 57 (Lord Hobhouse).

14 [2002] EWCA Civ 247, [2003] QB 556, [2002] 2 Lloyd's Rep 42.

15 At para 45.

16 Mance LJ gave the example of an insured who thought at the time of his initial claim that he had lost property in a theft, but then discovered it in a drawer, and continued to maintain both the genuine and the now knowingly false part of his claim (para 15).

17 See further below.

18 This issue was considered but not decided in *Manifest Shipping Co Ltd v Uni-Polaris Insurance Co Ltd, The Star Sea* [2001] UKHL 1, [2003] AC 469, [2001] 1 Lloyd's Rep 389.

19 *Axa General Insurance Ltd v Gottlieb* [2005] EWCA Civ 112, [2005] Lloyd's Rep IR 369.

20 *Stemson v AMP General Insurance (NZ) Ltd* [2006] UKPC 30, [2006] Lloyd's Rep IR 852, paras 30–36 (Lord Mance).

21 See eg *Eagle Star Insurance Co Ltd v Games Video Co (GVC) SA, The Game Boy* [2004] EWHC 15 (Comm), [2004] 1 Lloyd's Rep 238 (claim forfeit for use of fraudulent devices); *Danepoint Ltd v Underwriting Insurance Ltd* [2005] EWHC 2318 (TCC), [2006] Lloyd's Rep IR 429 (interim payment in respect of one head of loss forfeit for fraud in respect of different head of loss arising out of same claim for indemnity in respect of fire); *Sharon's Bakery (Europe) Ltd v Axa Insurance UK plc* [2011]

EWHC 210 (Comm), [2012] Lloyd's Rep IR 164 (claim forfeit for use of fraudulent device (false invoice submitted in support of claim)).

22 At paras 165–166 (Christopher Clarke LJ) and 168 (Vos LJ, agreeing) (appeal heard by the Supreme Court in March 2016; decision pending). This part of the decision is not part of the ratio (not necessary for the decision on the facts of the case, and therefore not binding); Sir Timothy Lloyd preferred (at 169) to express no view on this point.

23 [2014] EWCA Civ 1349, [2015] QB 608, paras 165–166 (Christopher Clarke LJ) (appeal heard by the Supreme Court in March 2016; decision pending).

24 At paras 154–155 (Christopher Clarke LJ) (appeal heard by the Supreme Court in March 2016; decision pending). This issue was not considered in *The Aegeon*.

25 *Axa General Insurance Ltd v Gottlieb* [2005] EWCA Civ 112, [2005] Lloyd's Rep IR 369, para 26 (Mance LJ).

26 *K/S Merc-Scandia XXXXII v Certain Lloyd's Underwriters Subscribing to Lloyd's Policy No 25T 105487, The Mercandian Continent* [2001] EWCA Civ 1275, [2001] 2 Lloyd's Rep 563, 568, para 10 (Longmore LJ).

27 *Axa General Insurance Ltd v Gottlieb* [2005] EWCA Civ 112, [2005] Lloyd's Rep IR 369, para 23 (Mance LJ).

28 *Axa General Insurance Ltd v Gottlieb* [2005] EWCA Civ 112, [2005] Lloyd's Rep IR 369, para 24 (Mance LJ), applying: *Direct Line Insurance v Khan* [2001] EWCA Civ 1794, [2002] Lloyd's Rep IR 364, CA.

29 *Axa General Insurance Ltd v Gottlieb* [2005] EWCA Civ 112, [2005] Lloyd's Rep IR 369, paras 26–27 and 32 (Mance LJ). This is a special rule confined to insurance claims and has no application in relation to claims in tort: *Churchill Car Insurance v Kelly* [2007] EWHC 18 (QB), para 15 (Gibb J).

30 *Manifest Shipping Co Ltd v Uni-Polaris Insurance Co Ltd, The Star Sea* [2001] UKHL 1, [2003] AC 469, [2001] 1 Lloyd's Rep 389, para 110 (Lord Scott).

31 *Axa General Insurance Ltd v Gottlieb* [2005] EWCA Civ 112, [2005] Lloyd's Rep IR 369, para 22 (Mance LJ).

32 *Agapitos v Agnew, The Aegeon* [2002] EWCA Civ 247, [2003] QB 556, [2002] 2 Lloyd's Rep 42, para 21 (Mance LJ); *Axa General Insurance Ltd v Gottlieb* [2005] EWCA Civ 112, [2005] Lloyd's Rep IR 369, para 22 (Mance LJ).

33 *Danepoint Ltd v Underwriting Insurance Ltd* [2005] EWHC 2318 (TCC), [2006] Lloyd's Rep IR 429, para 146 (His Honour Judge Peter Coulson QC) (property damage and loss of rent following a fire).

34 *Direct Line Insurance plc v Fox* [2009] EWHC 386 (QB), [2010] Lloyd's Rep IR 324, para 43 (HHJ Richard Seymour QC).

35 *Direct Line Insurance plc v Fox* [2009] EWHC 386 (QB), [2010] Lloyd's Rep IR 324, para 36 (HHJ Richard Seymour QC) (dishonest submission of false invoice in support of claim for payment of balance due under written agreement did not result in insured forfeiting whole claim). Settlement by the lead underwriter was held, at least arguably, not to prevent an underwriter who was otherwise bound by a follow clause from defending a claim on the grounds that the insured deployed a fraudulent device after the settlement was agreed and that this resulted in the claim being forfeit: *PT Buana Samudra Pratama v Marine Mutual Association (NZ) Ltd, The Buana Dua* [2011] EWHC 2413 (Comm), [2012] Lloyd's Rep IR 52, para 49 (Teare J).

Dishonesty required

11.50 Fraud, or breach of the duty of good faith, means dishonesty.[1] For these purposes, deliberate falsehood is not necessary, but recklessness as to the truth of a claim is sufficient.[2] Lord Herschell described the relevant principles in *Derry v Peek*:[3]

'First, in order to sustain an action of deceit, there must be proof of fraud, and nothing short of that will suffice. Secondly, fraud is proved when it is shewn that a false representation has been made (1) knowingly, or (2) without belief in its truth, or (3) recklessly, careless whether it be true or false. Although I have treated the second and third as distinct cases, I think the third is but an instance of the second, for one who makes a statement under such circumstances can have no real belief in the truth of what he states. To prevent a false statement being fraudulent, there must, I think, always be an honest belief in its truth. And this probably covers the whole ground, for one who knowingly alleges that which is false, has obviously no such honest belief. Thirdly, if fraud be proved, the motive of the person guilty of it is immaterial. It matters not that there was no intention to cheat or injure the person to whom the statement was made.'

1 *Manifest Shipping Co Ltd v Uni-Polaris Insurance Co Ltd, The Star Sea* [2001] UKHL 1, [2001] 1 Lloyd's Rep 389, 411 and 413, paras 102 and 111 (Lord Scott).
2 *Derry v Peek* (1889) 14 App Cas 337, HL, 350 (Lord Bramwell), 374 (Lord Herschell); *Lek v Mathews* (1927) 29 Ll L Rep 141, 145, HL (Viscount Sumner) (in which there was a special clause avoiding the policy if the insured made a 'false claim'); *AIC Ltd v ITS Testing Services (UK) Ltd, The Kriti Palm* [2006] EWCA Civ 1601, [2007] 1 Lloyd's Rep 555, paras 251–258 (Rix LJ) and 398–399 (Buxton LJ); *Aviva Insurance Ltd v Brown* [2011] EWHC 362 (QB), [2012] Lloyd's Rep IR 211, paras 61–70 (Eder J). In *Aviva Insurance Ltd v Brown* [2011] EWHC 362 (QB), [2012] Lloyd's Rep IR 211, Eder J doubted (at para 67) whether the 'combined test' of dishonesty enunciated in *Twinsectra Ltd v Yardley* [2002] UKHL 12, [2002] 2 AC 164, HL applied in relation to a fraudulent claim or fraudulent device.
3 (1889) 14 App Cas 337, 374, HL.

Fraud element de minimis

11.51 Where an insured has fraudulently exaggerated an otherwise valid claim, the insurer is entitled to reject the whole of the claim unless the fraudulent element is 'so unsubstantial as to make the maxim de minimis applicable'.[1] In seeking to apply this principle in *Galloway v Guardian Royal Exchange (UK) Ltd*, Lord Woolf MR expressed the view that the test was whether the fraud was material, and concluded that a fraudulent claim for a computer which added £2,000 to an otherwise honest claim for £16,000, amounting to about ten per cent of the whole, satisfied the test, so that the insured's entire claim failed. Millett LJ agreed in the result, but for different reasons:[2]

'Assuming (without deciding) that a policy of insurance is avoided only by a claim which is "substantially fraudulent" or "fraudulent to a substantial degree",[3] I reject the submission that this is to be tested by reference to the proportion of the entire claim which is represented by the fraudulent claim. That would lead to the absurd conclusion that the greater the genuine loss, the larger the fraudulent claim which may be made at the same time without penalty. In my judgment, the size of the genuine claim is irrelevant. In my view, the right approach ... is to consider the fraudulent claim as if it were the only claim and then to consider whether, taken in isolation, the making of that claim by the insured is sufficiently serious to justify stigmatising it as a breach of his duty of good faith so as to avoid the policy.'

As Mummery LJ agreed with both judgments, there is an element of uncertainty as to the test to be applied. The phrase used by Mance LJ in *Agapitos v Agnew, The Aegeon*[4] in the related context of the degree of improvement of the insured's prospects of success in relation to its claim was 'not insignificant'.[5] It is likely that, whichever test is applied, it will largely be a matter of impression for the trial judge, taking into account all the circumstances, whether or not the fraudulent element of claim is sufficient to justify the rejection of the claim in its entirety.[6]

1 *Lek v Mathews* (1927) 29 Ll L Rep 141, 145, HL (Viscount Sumner) (special clause avoiding the policy if the insured made a 'false claim').
2 At 214.

3 The insured in *Galloway v Guardian Royal Exchange (UK) Ltd* having placed reliance on the use of these or similar phrases in the judgments of Hoffmann LJ and Sir Roger Parker in *Orakpo v Barclays Insurance Services* [1995] LRLR 443, CA: see the judgment of Lord Woolf MR at 213.

4 [2002] EWCA Civ 247, [2003] QB 556, [2002] 2 Lloyd's Rep 42.

5 See **PARA 11.49**; see also *Aviva Insurance Ltd v Brown* [2011] EWHC 362 (QB), [2012] Lloyd's Rep IR 211, para 77 (Eder J).

6 In *Aviva Insurance Ltd v Brown* [2011] EWHC 362 (QB), [2012] Lloyd's Rep IR 211, Eder J rejected an argument that the court was required to carry out 'some kind of value judgment with regard to the seriousness of the breach' (para 77). The judge held that the whole of the claim was forfeited, including two substantial payments already made by the insurer, on the basis that one of the 21 allegations of fraud made by the insurer was made out, and that that allegation was regarded by the insured and was in fact a substantial and material part of the insured's claim; the initial claim was for subsidence, and the fraud was in connection with a claim for alternative accommodation which was not in the event pursued by the insured. See, further, the discussion in the judgment of Staughton LJ (dissenting on the fraudulent claim issue) in *Orakpo v Barclays Insurance Services* [1995] LRLR 443, 450, CA.

Impact of fraud on joint and composite insurance

11.52 Where insurance is composite rather than joint,[1] misrepresentation or non-disclosure, or fraud, by one of the insureds will not entitle the insurer to avoid or forfeit the policy as against the others.[2] Conversely, affirmation of the policy in respect of one insured does not constitute affirmation of the policy in respect of another.[3] This is illustrated by *P Samuel & Co v Dumas*,[4] in which the interests of a shipowner and mortgagee were insured under a single policy. The mortgagee was held not to be affected by the owner's fraud in scuttling the ship and, although the language of the distinction between 'joint' and 'composite' interests had yet to be developed, the analysis is in fact that of joint and composite interests.[5] Viscount Cave described the relevant principle as follows:[6]

> 'It may well be that, when two persons are jointly insured and their interests are inseparably connected so that a loss or gain necessarily affects them both, the misconduct of one is sufficient to contaminate the whole insurance: Phillips on Marine Insurance, vol. I., § 235. But in this case there is no difficulty in separating the interest of the mortgagee from that of the owner; and if the mortgagee should recover on the policy, the owner will not be advantaged, as the insurers will be subrogated as against him to the rights of the mortgagee.'

Similarly, Lord Sumner distinguished between the interests of the owner and the mortgagee, saying:[7]

> 'Of course, it is true that [the insured] cannot take advantage of his own wrong ... This, however, seems to me to be obviously a case of personal disability, which cannot affect persons, who are neither parties to the dolus nor stand in the guilty person's shoes. Fraud is not something absolute, existing in vacuo; it is a fraud upon some one. A man who tries to cheat his underwriters fails if they find him out, but how does his wrong against them invest them with new rights against innocent strangers to it?'

By means of a subrogated claim, an insurer may recover from a fraudulent insured the amount of an indemnity paid to an innocent insured.[8] In the special situation of a composite policy in which the interests of the co-insureds are pervasive, as in a contractors' all risks policy, fraud by one insured severs the unity of interest, so that the innocent insureds are not affected by the fraud.[9]

In many cases, there will be no need to embark on an analysis of the interests of the co-insureds, because an application of agency principles will provide a short answer to the question of whether fraud by one affects another. In *Direct Line Insurance v Khan*,[10] the Court of Appeal held that a fraudulent claim had been made on behalf of both policyholders, and that, accordingly, in making the fraudulent claim, the fraudulent policyholder had been acting as agent of the innocent insured within the scope of his actual or apparent authority. Consequently, the innocent insured was bound by the consequences of those fraudulent actions.

Where fraud has been committed by the assignor of a policy, the assignee can be on no better footing than the assignor and will therefore be affected by the fraud.[11]

1 See **PARA 2.3**.
2 *General Accident Fire and Life Assurance Corpn Ltd v Midland Bank Ltd* [1940] 2 KB 388, 404–406, CA (Sir Wilfred Greene MR); *Woolcott v Sun Alliance and London Insurance Ltd* [1978] 1 WLR 493, 496–497 (Caulfield J) (interests of mortgagor and mortgagee not joint; retrial ordered by Court of Appeal on other grounds: [1979] 1 Lloyd's Rep 231, CA); *New Hampshire Insurance Co v MGN Ltd* [1997] LRLR 24, 56–58, CA (Staughton LJ).
3 *Black King Shipping Corpn v Massie, The Litsion Pride* [1985] 1 Lloyd's Rep 437, 516–517 (Hirst J).
4 [1924] AC 431, HL.
5 *Netherlands v Youell* [1997] 2 Lloyd's Rep 440, 447 (Rix J).
6 At 445–446.
7 At 469.
8 *P Samuel & Co v Dumas* [1924] AC 431, 445–446, HL (Viscount Cave): see text to note 5 above; *Parker v National Farmers Union Mutual Insurance Society Ltd* [2012] EWHC 2156 (Comm), [2013] Lloyd's Rep IR 253, para 203 (Teare J).
9 *Netherlands v Youell* [1997] 2 Lloyd's Rep 440, 450–451 (Rix J).
10 [2001] EWCA Civ 1794, [2002] Lloyd's Rep IR 364, CA.
11 *Re Carr and Sun Fire Insurance Co* (1897) 13 TLR 186, CA; *P Samuel & Co v Dumas* [1924] AC 431, HL; *Patel v Windsor Life Assurance Co Ltd* [2008] EWHC 76 (Comm), [2008] Lloyd's Rep IR 359, para 94 (Teare J).

Recovery of costs of investigating fraudulent claim

11.53 Where proceedings have been issued, the costs incurred in investigating a fraudulent claim may be recoverable as legal costs.[1] Alternatively, damages for the tort of deceit may be awarded.[2] The measure of damages would be the costs incurred by the insurer less the amount of the claim and any costs which would have been incurred but for the deceit, without any deduction for contributory negligence or a failure to mitigate.[3]

1 *London Assurance v Clare* (1937) 57 Ll L Rep 254, 270 (Goddard J) (rejecting the insurers' argument that a term should be implied that claims would be made honestly, and that they were entitled to damages for breach of such a term); *Owners of the Ship 'Ariela' v Owners and/or Demise Charterers of the Dredger 'Kamal XXVI' and the Barge 'Kamal XXIV'* [2009] EWHC 3256 (Comm), [2010] 2 Lloyd's Rep 247, para 30 (Burton J) (costs on the indemnity basis).
2 *Owners of the Ship 'Ariela' v Owners and/or Demise Charterers of the Dredger 'Kamal XXVI' and the Barge 'Kamal XXIV'* [2009] EWHC 3256 (Comm), [2010] 2 Lloyd's Rep 247, paras 34–36 (Burton J); see also *London Assurance v Clare* (1937) 57 Ll L Rep 254, 270 (Goddard J) ('It is put, not as damages

for fraud, for which I think there might be something to be said, but it is put as damages for breach of contract').

3 *Owners of the Ship 'Ariela' v Owners and/or Demise Charterers of the Dredger 'Kamal XXVI' and the Barge 'Kamal XXIV'* [2009] EWHC 3256 (Comm), [2010] 2 Lloyd's Rep 247, paras 36–39 (Burton J).

Fraudulent claims and fraudulent devices: Insurance Act 2015

11.54   This paragraph sets out the law as it applies to claims made under contracts of insurance entered into before 12 August 2016 and variations to such contracts.[1] If the insured makes a fraudulent claim under a contract of insurance, the insurer is not liable to pay the claim, the insurer may recover from the insured any sums paid by the insurer to the insured in respect of the claim, and, in addition, the insurer may by notice to the insured treat the contract as having been terminated with effect from the time of the fraudulent act.[2] If the insurer does treat the contract as having been terminated, it may refuse all liability to the insured under the contract in respect of a relevant event giving rise to the insurer's liability under the contract which occurs after the time of the fraudulent act, including, for example, the occurrence of a loss, the making of a claim, or the notification of a potential claim, depending on how the contract is written, and the insurer need not return any of the premiums paid under the contract.[3] Treating a contract as having been terminated does not affect the rights and obligations of the parties to the contract with respect to any event giving rise to the insurer's liability under the contract which occurs before the time of the fraudulent act.[4]

'Fraudulent claim' is not defined in the Insurance Act 2015; nor does the Act state whether, or to what extent, the use of a fraudulent device in relation to an otherwise honest claim[5] means that a claim is a fraudulent claim to which its provisions apply.[6]

Unless the contrary intention appears, where the provisions of the Insurance Act 2015 in relation to fraudulent claims refer to something done by or in relation to the insurer or the insured,[7] those references include it being done by or in relation to that person's agent.[8]

Where a contract of insurance is entered into by one person and provides cover for one or more other persons who are not parties to it (ie group insurance), and a fraudulent claim is made under the contract by or on behalf of one of those non-parties, the insurer's rights in relation to fraudulent claims apply in relation to the claim as if the cover provided for the claimant were provided under an individual insurance contract between the insurer and the claimant as the insured, and accordingly, the insurer's rights are exercisable only in relation to the person making the fraudulent claim, and the exercise of any of those rights does not affect the cover provided under the contract for anyone else.[9] The restrictions on contracting out of certain provisions in the Insurance Act 2015 in consumer and non-consumer contracts of insurance[10] apply to terms relating to fraudulent claims in a group insurance contract.[11] These provisions do not apply in relation to a contract for the settlement of a claim.[12]

1 Insurance Act 2015, ss 12, 22(1) and (3), and 23(2) (the Insurance Act 2015 was passed on 12 February 2015).
2 Insurance Act 2015, s 12(1). The Explanatory Notes to the 2015 Act say (at para 102) that the 'fraudulent act' is intended to be the behaviour that makes a claim fraudulent, such as the addition to a genuine

claim of fraudulent element, for example, adding an additional, fabricated, head of loss. Explanatory Notes do not form part of a statute, are not endorsed by Parliament and cannot be amended by it; in so far as they cast light on the objective setting or contextual scene of a statute and the mischief to which it is aimed, they are an admissible aid to construction: *Flora v Wakom (Heathrow) Ltd* [2006] EWCA Civ 1103, [2007] 1 WLR 482, paras 15–16 (Brooke LJ).

3 Insurance Act 2015, s 12(2) and (4).

4 Insurance Act 2015, s 12(3)–(4).

5 See **PARA 11.49**.

6 The meaning of 'fraudulent claim' was deliberately left by the Law Commissions to be determined by the courts in all the circumstances of any particular case: see the Law Commissions' July 2014 Report (Law Com No 353; Cm 8898), para 22.6. It is however clear from paragraphs 22.22–22.24 of the Report that the Law Commissions considered that the use of a fraudulent device was in principle capable of amounting to a 'fraudulent claim' within the meaning of s 12. The Explanatory Notes to the 2015 Act do not address this issue; they say (at para 99) that s 12 does not define 'fraud' or 'fraudulent claim' and that the remedies will apply once fraud has been determined in accordance with common law principles, and refers by way of example to the text for fraud in *Derry v Peek* (1889) 14 App Cas 337, HL (see **PARA 11.50**). For the status of Explanatory Notes, see note 2 above. In evidence to The Special Public Bill Committee of the House of Lords on 3 December 2014, Lord Justice Longmore said that fraudulent devices were not exactly claims, and that it did not seem that the relevant clause in the Insurance Bill was intended to deal with fraudulent devices unless the courts could be a little more sensible than they had been, and adapt the word 'claim' to include devices, which he thought might happen if the clause were to be enacted in its then form (which it was). In evidence to The Special Public Bill Committee of the House of Lords on 9 December 2014, Lord Mance said that he would not express a view as to whether the relevant clause in the Insurance Bill covered fraudulent devices, as some had assumed, and that, whichever way was intended, it might have been better if it had been made clear.

7 Part 5 of the Insurance Act 2015, ss 12–13.

8 Insurance Act 2015, s 22(4).

9 Insurance Act 2015, s 13(1)–(3). The 'insured' is defined by s 1 of the Insurance Act 2015 to mean the party to a contract who is the insured under the contract; this definition is modified by s 13(3) to allow for the application of s 12 to group insurance, including in relation to the recovery of sums paid and of premium (see s 13(3)(a) and (d)). The Explanatory Notes to the 2015 Act say (at para 106) that group schemes are an important form of insurance, many are set up by employers to provide protection insurance for their employees and the policyholder is typically the employer, who arranges the scheme directly with the insurer, while the group members (typically employees) have no specific status; and that, as they are not policyholders, if a group member makes a fraudulent claim, the insurer's remedies are uncertain; and (at para 107) that s 13 is intended to give the insurer a remedy against a fraudulent group member, while protecting the other members who are covered by the insurance. The Explanatory Notes also say (at para 108) that the effect of s 13(1) is that s 13 may cover not only the typical employment scheme, but many other types of arrangement including block building policies taken out by landlords for tenants, and potentially insurance arranged by one company for a group of companies, if the contract is so structured; and that it is possible for group insurance to cover only one member, where (for example) a freeholder takes out insurance for a single leaseholder. For the status of Explanatory Notes, see note 2 above.

10 See **PARA 3.8**.

11 Insurance Act 2015, s 18(1)–(4). This also applies in relation to variations: s 18(5).

12 Insurance Act 2015, s 18(6).

LACK OF INSURABLE INTEREST

11.55 In order to be entitled to enforce a policy of insurance, a person must have an insurable interest in the subject matter of the insurance.[1] Although, strictly, a positive plea by a claimant of insurable interest is required,[2] claimants tend not to plead insurable interest unless the facts are very unusual, and insurers are slow to raise lack of insurable interest as a defence. Although the court might take the point of its own motion in an extreme case, it is unlikely to do so if insurers do not take the point. The subject or terms of the policy may be so specific as to force a court to hold that the policy has failed to cover the insurable interest, but it will be reluctant so to hold,[3] and if underwriters make a contract in deliberate terms which covers their assured in respect of a specific situation, it is likely to hesitate before accepting a defence of lack of insurable interest.[4]

In the case of a claim based on the principle in *Hepburn v A Tomlinson (Hauliers) Ltd*,[5] the burden is on the insurer to show that the insured did not intend to insure on behalf of the third party. In marine insurance, where the insured has no insurable interest, he is entitled, pursuant to s 84(3)(c) of the Marine Insurance Act 1906, to the return of the premium, unless the policy is held to have been effected by way of gaming or wagering. It is suggested that the position at common law should be the same.

1 See **PARAS** 2.4–2.11.
2 See *Macaura v Northern Assurance Co Ltd* [1925] AC 619, 632, HL (Lord Sumner).
3 *Stock v Inglis* (1884) 12 QBD 564, 571, CA (Brett MR); *Feasey v Sun Life Assurance Corpn of Canada* [2003] EWCA Civ 885, [2003] 1 Lloyd's Rep IR 637, paras 92 (Waller LJ), 116–117 (Dyson LJ) and 140–142 (Ward LJ).
4 *Cepheus Shipping Corpn v Guardian Royal Exchange Assurance plc, The Capricorn* [1995] 1 Lloyd's Rep 622, 641 (Mance J).
5 *Hepburn v A Tomlinson (Hauliers) Ltd* [1966] AC 451, 481–482, HL (Lord Pearce). See further **PARAS** 2.8 and 2.10.

SUPERVENING ILLEGALITY AND FRUSTRATION

11.56   A contract of insurance may be discharged by supervening illegality or frustration.[1] Where performance of part only of a contract of insurance has become unlawful, there is no reason for the legal part of the contract which is performable not to remain in force.[2]

1 *Islamic Republic of Iran Shipping Lines v Steamship Mutual Underwriting Association (Bermuda) Ltd* [2010] EWHC 2661 (Comm) (Beatson J held that measures taken by HM Treasury pursuant to powers conferred by the Counter-Terrorism Act 2008 permitted a P&I Club to continue to provide the insured with insurance cover in respect of certain risks, and that the contract was not frustrated).
2 *Islamic Republic of Iran Shipping Lines v Steamship Mutual Underwriting Association (Bermuda) Ltd* [2010] EWHC 2661 (Comm), para 126 (Beatson J).

LIMITATION OF ACTIONS

11.57   The limitation of actions is entirely statutory. Statutes of limitation are regarded as beneficial enactments and are construed liberally.[1] The underlying policy to which they give effect is that a defendant should be spared the injustice of having to face a stale claim.[2] Limitations on the time in which an insured may bring proceedings against an insurer[3] in relation to a policy of insurance derive from two sources: statute; and the contract between the insurer and the insured. There are surprisingly few authorities regarding limitation of actions, perhaps because once a claim has been made and rejected, the issues between the underwriter and the insured have crystallised. A decision is usually taken at that stage, which tends to be well before the expiry of the limitation period, as to whether proceedings will be brought.

1 *Cave v Robinson Jarvis & Rolf* [2002] UKHL 18, [2003] 1 AC 384, para 5 (Lord Millett).
2 *Cave v Robinson Jarvis & Rolf* [2002] UKHL 18, [2003] 1 AC 384, para 6 (Lord Millett).

3 Limitation of actions in relation to contracts of reinsurance is considered at PARA **14.5**, and in relation to claims against insurance brokers at PARAS **16.29–16.32**.

Contractual limitations on the right of action

11.58   The contract of insurance may reduce[1] or enlarge[2] the period within which an action may be brought by the insured. It is a question of construction of the policy whether procedural conditions which are conditions precedent to the insurer's liability have the effect of delaying the accrual of the insured's cause of action.[3] In *William McIlroy (Swindon) Ltd v Quinn Insurance Ltd*,[4] a clause in a liability policy provided that any dispute between the insured and the insurer concerning the insurer's liability in respect of a claim or the amount to be paid must be referred to an arbitrator within nine months of the dispute arising, and that if the dispute was not referred to arbitration within the nine month period, the claim would be deemed to have been abandoned and would not be recoverable thereafter. The Court of Appeal held that in the context of a liability policy, no dispute could arise, and the nine month period could not start to run, until the existence and amount of insured's liability to third party claimant had been established.[5] However, as the insurer had refused to pay the claim at an earlier stage, the Court of Appeal said that if for any reason the insured had wanted to challenge the insurer's purported repudiation of the policy, they could have issued court proceedings seeking a declaration as to the ongoing validity of the policy at any time within six years of the date of the purported repudiation, because such a dispute would not have triggered the contractual limitation provision.[6] In the absence of clear words, the court is likely to construe procedural conditions which must be fulfilled by the insured before payment becomes due not as delaying the accrual of the cause of action, but as providing insurers with a defence to a claim if they are not fulfilled.[7]

1 *William McIlroy (Swindon) Ltd v Quinn Insurance Ltd* [2011] EWCA Civ 825.
2 See *Chandris v Argo Insurance Co Ltd* [1963] 2 Lloyd's Rep 65, at 74 and 80 (the contract may provide that the cause of action accrues only on the happening of a specific event); *Virk v Gan Life Holdings plc* [2000] Lloyd's Rep IR 159, 162, CA.
3 See eg *Callaghan v Dominion Insurance Co Ltd* [1997] 2 Lloyd's Rep 541 (fire insurance; start of limitation period not postponed by conditions precedent to insurer's liability under policy); *Virk v Gan Life Holdings plc* [2000] Lloyd's Rep IR 159, CA (critical illness insurance payable 30 days after confirmed diagnosis provided insured then alive; start of limitation period postponed); *Universities Superannuation Scheme Ltd v Royal Insurance (UK) Ltd*, [2000] Lloyd's Rep IR 524 (Langley J) (employee fidelity policy covering fraudulent acts if discovered within 24 months; limitation period started at date of loss, not date of discovery of loss).
4 [2011] EWCA Civ 825.
5 At paras 12–13 (Sir Henry Brooke) and 28–37 (Rix LJ) (distinguishing *Walker v Pennine Insurance Co Ltd* [1980] 2 Lloyd's Rep 156, CA: see paras 14–17 (Sir Henry Brooke) and 39–45 (Rix LJ)). See also PARA **9.42**.
6 At paras 19 (Sir Henry Brooke), 37 and 47 (Rix LJ). See also PARA **9.42**.
7 *Callaghan v Dominion Insurance Co Ltd* [1997] 2 Lloyd's Rep 541, 546 (Webster J) (fire insurance; start of limitation period not postponed by conditions precedent to insurer's liability under policy), *Teal Assurance Co Ltd v W R Berkley Insurance (Europe) Ltd* [2013] UKSC 57, [2014] Lloyd's Rep IR 56, para 22 (Lord Mance); see also *Teal Assurance Co Ltd v W R Berkley Insurance (Europe) Ltd* [2011] EWCA Civ 1570, paras 14–15 (Longmore LJ, referring to *Coburn v Colledge* [1897] 1 QB 702, CA) and 22 (Tomlinson LJ).

Cause of action[1]

11.59 An action on a policy of insurance is an action on a simple contract,[2] and the limitation period is six years.[3]

1 'A cause of action is simply a factual situation the existence of which entitles one person to obtain from the court a remedy against another person': *Letang v Cooper* [1965] 1 QB 232, 242–243 (Diplock LJ).
2 *Chandris v Argo Insurance Co Ltd* [1963] 2 Lloyd's Rep 65, 73 (Megaw J).
3 'An action founded on simple contract shall not be brought after the expiration of six years from the date on which the cause of action accrued': Limitation Act 1980, s 5. This is so even where the insured does not become aware of the loss until a later date, unless s 32 of the Limitation Act applies (see **PARA 16.31**): *Cartledge v E Jopling & Sons Ltd* [1963] AC 758; *Pirelli General Cable Works Ltd v Oscar Faber & Partners* [1983] 2 AC 1.

Accrual of cause of action

11.60 A contract of indemnity insurance is an agreement by an insurer to confer on an insured a contractual right to indemnity which on the face of it comes into existence immediately when loss is suffered by the happening of an event insured against.[1]

In *Firma C-Trade SA v Newcastle P & I Association, The Padre Island (No 2),*[2] Lord Goff considered the date of accrual of a cause of action in a case concerning the construction of 'pay to be paid' provisions and the Third Party (Rights Against Insurers) Act 1930, and said:[3]

> 'I accept that ... a contract of indemnity gives rise to an action for unliquidated damages, arising from the failure of the indemnifier to prevent the indemnified person from suffering damage, for example, by having to pay a third party. I also accept that ... the cause of action does not (unless the contract provides otherwise) arise unless the indemnified person can show actual loss ... This is, as I understand it, because a promise of indemnity is simply a promise to hold the indemnified person harmless against a specified loss or expense. On this basis, no debt can arise before the loss is suffered or the expense incurred; however, once the loss is suffered or the expense incurred, the indemnifier is in breach of contract for having failed to hold the indemnified person harmless against the relevant loss or expense.'

For the purposes of determining the date at which an insured's cause of action accrued, there is in general a distinction to be drawn between policies of liability insurance on the one hand and all other types of insurance on the other.[4] The cause of action does not accrue under a liability policy until the existence and the amount of the liability of the insured to relevant third parties has been established, whether by judgment or by an arbitration award or by agreement.[5] In respect of other types of insurance policy, including property, life, marine and other forms of insurance, the law has long been that, because an insurance policy is to be construed as insurance against the occurrence of an insured event, the occurrence of that event is treated as equivalent to a breach of contract by an insurer.[6] Accordingly, in the absence of policy terms affecting the matter,[7] the limitation period begins to run as soon as the insured event occurs, even though no claim has been made.[8] Thus, in relation to particular types of indemnity insurance, the cause of action will generally accrue as follows. In marine insurance, it accrues on the date of the casualty, even though terms of the policy for the very nature of the loss may require a particular method of computation or process of quantification of loss before payment is due.[9] In property insurance, the cause of action accrues on the occurrence of the peril.[10] In life insurance the cause of action accrues on the death of the assured.[11] Where a policy provides an indemnity for the incurring of ascertained expenses, such as mitigation costs in an engineering liability policy, the cause of action accrues as and when quantified expenditure is incurred.[12]

1 *Virk v Gan Life Holdings plc* [2000] Lloyd's Rep IR 159, CA, para 9 (Potter LJ); *Quorum v Schramm (No 2)* [2002] 2 Lloyd's Rep 72, para 6 (Thomas J).

2 [1991] 2 AC 1.

3 At 35–36. Lord Goff's remarks were equally applicable both to liability insurance and to other types of insurance: see *Ventouris v Mountain, The Italia Express (No 2)* [1992] 2 Lloyd's Rep 281, 291–292 (Hirst J).

4 *Virk v Gan Life Holdings plc* [2000] Lloyd's Rep IR 159, CA, para 9 (Potter LJ).

5 *Post Office v Norwich Union Fire Insurance Society Ltd* [1967] 2 QB 363, CA, 373–374 (Lord Denning MR), 376 (Harman LJ) and 377–378 (Salmon LJ); *Bradley v Eagle Star Ins Co Ltd* [1989] AC 957, HL; *Virk v Gan Life Holdings plc* [2000] Lloyd's Rep IR 159, CA, para 9 (Potter LJ); *William McIlroy (Swindon) Ltd v Quinn Insurance Ltd* [2011] EWCA Civ 825, paras 12 (Sir Henry Brooke) and 46 (Rix LJ) (distinguishing *Walker v Pennine Insurance Co Ltd* [1980] 2 Lloyd's Rep 156, CA: see paras 14–17 (Sir Henry Brooke) and 39–45 (Rix LJ)); *Teal Assurance Co Ltd v W R Berkley Insurance (Europe) Ltd* [2013] UKSC 57, [2014] Lloyd's Rep IR 56, paras 13–15, 17 and 19 (Lord Mance).

6 *Virk v Gan Life Holdings plc* [2000] Lloyd's Rep IR 159, CA, para 10 (Potter LJ). See also *Grant v Royal Exchange Assurance Co* (1816) 5 M&S 438 (marine policy: claim was for unliquidated damages); *Luckie v Bushby* (1853) 13 CB 864 (policy on goods: claim was for unliquidated damages); *Irving v Manning* (1847) 1 HLC 287, HL (valued policy on a ship: claim was for liquidated damages); *William Pickersgill & Sons Ltd v London and Provincial Marine and General Insurance Co Ltd* [1912] 3 KB 614 at 622 ('a policy of insurance is only a promise of indemnity giving a right of action for unliquidated damages in case of non-payment'); *F & K Jabbour v Custodian of Israeli Absentee Property* [1954] 1 WLR 139, 143–144 (Pearson J) (the claim is for unliquidated damages, but the word 'damages' is used in a somewhat unusual sense: the right to indemnity arises, not by reason of any wrongful act or omission of the insurer (who did not promise that the loss would not happen or that he would prevent it) but only under his promise to indemnify the insured in the event of a loss).

7 *Virk v Gan Life Holdings plc* [2000] Lloyd's Rep IR 159, CA, para 10 (Potter LJ). See **PARA 11.58**.

8 *Virk v Gan Life Holdings plc* [2000] Lloyd's Rep IR 159, CA, para 10 (Potter LJ).

9 *Chandris v Argo Insurance Co Ltd* [1963] 2 Lloyd's Rep 65; approved: *Castle Insurance Co Ltd v Hong Kong Islands Shipping Co Ltd* [1984] AC 226, 237–238, PC (Lord Diplock); *Bank of America National Trust and Savings Association v Chrismas, The Kyriaki* [1993] 1 Lloyd's Rep 137 (in marine insurance, the cause of action in a constructive total loss case arises at the date of casualty because the notice of abandonment is not an essential ingredient of the cause of action but a notification of an election between two alternative quanta of damage); *Virk v Gan Life Holdings plc* [2000] Lloyd's Rep IR 159, CA, para 10 (Potter LJ) (the Lloyd's Rep IR report refers in error to 'qualification' rather than 'quantification' of loss).

10 *Callaghan v Dominion Insurance Co Ltd* [1997] 2 Lloyd's Rep 541 (fire insurance: time runs from date of loss, not from date of avoidance of policy); *Virk v Gan Life Holdings plc* [2000] Lloyd's Rep IR 159, CA, para 10 (Potter LJ).

11 *Virk v Gan Life Holdings plc* [2000] Lloyd's Rep IR 159, CA, para 10 (Potter LJ).

12 *Teal Assurance Co Ltd v W R Berkley Insurance (Europe) Ltd* [2013] UKSC 57, [2014] Lloyd's Rep IR 56, paras 18–19 (Lord Mance).

Computing the statutory limitation period

11.61 In computing the period within which the action should be brought, the day on which the cause of action accrues is to be excluded;[1] and where a claim form cannot be issued on what would otherwise be the last day of the limitation period because the court office is not open, that period is extended to the first day on which the office is open.[2]

1 *Marren v Dawson Bentley & Co Ltd* [1961] 2 QB 135 (a case concerning s 2(1) of the Limitation Act 1939), approved in *Pritam Kaur v S Russel & Sons Ltd* [1973] QB 336, CA. Thus, if a cause of action accrues on 3 October 2012, an action will be in time if a claim form is issued on 3 October 2018.
2 *Pritam Kaur v S Russel & Sons Ltd* [1973] QB 336, CA.

Limitation and estoppel

11.62   Insurers may be prevented from relying upon a limitation defence by the operation of an estoppel. The conditions which must be fulfilled in order for an estoppel to arise are fairly stringent. Ward LJ (with whom Thorpe and Keene LJJ agreed) summarised the relevant principles in *Seechurn v Ace Insurance SA-NV:*[1]

'(i)   Is there a clear, unequivocal, unambiguous and unconditional promise by the insurers that they will not raise the defence that the action is statute barred. The focus has to be on whether or not they were giving up that right.

(ii)   The promise must be construed objectively, not subjectively. The question is whether the correspondence can reasonably be understood to contain that particular promise. It does not matter what [the insured] thought it meant nor does it matter what a layman might have thought ... unless, of course, that layman is a passenger on the Clapham omnibus.

(iii)   The third question is whether [the insured] relying on the promise, altered his position to his detriment or whether it would be inequitable or unconscionable not to hold the insurers to their promise.'

The mere fact that a party has continued to negotiate with the other party about the claim after the limitation period had expired, without anything being agreed about what happens if the negotiations break down, cannot give rise to a waiver or estoppel.[2] In *Seechurn v Ace Insurance SA-NV*, insurers had repeatedly indicated to the insured, both before and after expiry of the limitation period, that they would not reconsider his claim of permanent disablement under a health insurance policy unless he agreed to submit to a further medical examination. Ward LJ considered the correspondence in detail in determining the first question (whether there was a clear, unequivocal promise or representation, or common assumption, that the insurers would forego their right to plead the limitation defence) in favour of insurers. Ward LJ indicated that:[3]

'To say that the door was open to further negotiations or even to point out that the proceedings could be stayed pending medical examination, did not in my judgment, carry any implication that the limitation defence would not be taken. As Lord Steyn observed in *Republic of India*,[4] there was no duty on the defendant's solicitor to warn of this impending fall of the guillotine. Furthermore, as the authorities make clear, silence or inaction are of their nature equivocal.'

In relation to detriment, Ward LJ indicated that he was content to approach the case on the basis that detriment was not always required, provided that the court was satisfied that it would nevertheless be inequitable for the promisor to go back on its promise. In relation to events prior to expiry of the limitation period, Ward LJ stated that if the necessary representation had been established, he would have had no difficulty in accepting that it was intended to be acted upon, and was relied upon, with the result that the insured suffered the detriment of losing his right to approach the judgment seat; it would then have been inequitable and unconscionable for the insurer to plead the time bar.[5]

Ward LJ considered that the position was different after expiry of the limitation period because even if the insured had established representation and reliance, he could not alter his position to his detriment as the claim was statute-barred, and his position could not be any worse.[6] A claimant whose claim was already time-barred at the time the necessary representation was made might nevertheless suffer a detriment (using the term in a non-technical sense) in terms of the costs of bringing legal proceedings in which the insurer, contrary to the representation, pleaded a limitation defence. Ward LJ was aware of the distinction between these two types of detriment – that which would flow from the denial of the assumption upon which the insured had relied, and the lesser detriment which he had already suffered by relying upon the assumption[7] – and his decision that requisite detriment was not present on the facts of the case demonstrates that it is the first (broader) type of detriment that is required to found an estoppel (in the absence of any other factor rendering it unconscionable for the insurer to go back on its representation). The reason for this is that the effect of an estoppel is to prevent the promisor from denying the truth of the relevant representation or assumption, so that a finding of estoppel on the basis of a narrower detriment would lead to a windfall for the promisee, who would receive a benefit based on the representation or assumption, and which would therefore be out of proportion to the detriment suffered.

1 [2002] EWCA Civ 67, [2002] 2 Lloyd's Rep 390, 397, para 26; applied: *Super Chem Products Ltd v American Life and General Insurance Co Ltd* [2004] UKPC 2, [2004] Lloyd's Rep IR 446, 454, para 23 (Lord Steyn). For an example of an estoppel arising in the context of a claim by an employee against his employers under the Workmen's Compensation Act 1897, see *Wright v John Bagnall & Sons Ltd* [1900] QB 240, CA, in which the time limit for submitting a claim expired while the parties were negotiating; as there was evidence of an agreement that compensation was to be paid, the only question left open being that of amount, the employers were held to be debarred from raising the point that the statutory limitation period applied.
2 *Super Chem Products Ltd v American Life and General Insurance Co Ltd* [2004] UKPC 2, [2004] Lloyd's Rep IR 446, para 23 (Lord Steyn); *Hillingdon Borough Council v ARC Ltd (No 2)* [2000] 3 EGLR 97, CA (a decision about estoppel and limitation in a non-insurance context); see also PARA **11.63**.
3 At 401, para 54, in relation to events before expiry of the limitation period. Ward LJ made a finding in similar terms in relation to the events after expiry of the limitation period (at 401, paras 57 and 58).
4 *Republic of India v India Steamship Co (No 2)* [1998] AC 878, HL. See further PARA **11.63**.
5 At para 56.
6 At para 59.
7 At para 25. In making the distinction, Ward LJ referred to the judgment of Mason CJ in the High Court of Australia in *Commonwealth of Australia v Verwayen* (1990) 170 CLR 394. In *Verwayen*, the representation that limitation would not be pleaded was made after the expiry of the limitation period, but the court held that, in starting the proceedings, the insured had not relied on the representation.

WAIVER, AFFIRMATION AND ESTOPPEL

11.63 An assertion by an insurer that it is entitled to avoid a policy of insurance for misrepresentation or non-disclosure, or that it is entitled to rely upon breach of a procedural condition in repudiating liability for a claim, is often met by an assertion by the insured that the insurer has waived its right to avoid, or has affirmed the policy; or that the insurer is estopped from relying on a policy condition or from denying that the policy operates as contended by the insured. It is important to distinguish between waiver (or affirmation) ('waiver by election')[1] and estoppel ('waiver by estoppel')[2], because although there are similarities in their operation and effect, there are also important differences, and the two concepts are not interchangeable.[3]

Both doctrines require that the person who is alleged to have 'waived' the relevant contractual right has made an unequivocal representation, by words or conduct, that he does not, in future, intend to enforce that legal right which he has against the other party to the contract; however, in the case of estoppel, it also has to be demonstrated that the other party relied upon that unequivocal representation in such a way that it would render it inequitable for the representor to go back on his representation.[4]

For there to be a waiver by one party to a contract, there is no requirement of acting on it by, or detriment to, the other party; what is required is that there should be alternative courses of action which are inconsistent or, as it is sometimes said, mutually exclusive.[5] In the insurance context, there are various situations in which waiver typically arises. The insurer may waive disclosure of information when the risk is placed.[6] In addition, the insurer may discover at a later date that the insured failed to comply with his duty of disclosure, or made a misrepresentation, when the risk was placed, but may elect to waive his right to avoid the policy.[7] Where there is a breach of warranty there is no scope for waiver because the insurer is automatically discharged from liability upon breach and therefore has no choice to make.[8] Similarly, a waiver has no application, in the context of a merely procedural condition precedent, to the conduct of a claim on behalf of an insured by an insurer.[9] The exercise of a right under a policy to conduct an insured's defence may however be unequivocally inconsistent with a right to avoid the policy.[10] Denying liability on coverage grounds does not of itself give rise to a waiver of the right to deny liability for late notification, or vice versa, as both courses lead to a denial of liability and are not inconsistent or mutually exclusive.[11] Similarly, an insurer is entitled to resist a claim on alternative bases, one of which involves an allegation of fraud and the other breaches of policy conditions.[12]

Waiver requires knowledge by the insurer of the facts giving rise to the right to avoid or treat the contract of insurance as discharged for breach of warranty,[13] and of his right to do so;[14] and an unequivocal representation (viewed objectively by a reasonable person in the position of the insured)[15] that he has decided not to do so.[16] Where an insurer has knowledge of the facts giving rise to the right to avoid, knowledge of the right to avoid will usually be inferred.[17] Where the insurer has been represented by solicitors and counsel whose conduct is relied upon as amounting to an election, it is normally to be inferred that such conduct has been specifically authorised by the insurer and has been the subject of legal advice, although the inference may be rebutted by evidence if the insurer is prepared to waive privilege.[18] Constructive knowledge is not sufficient, but a deliberate decision, for tactical reasons, not to acquire definite knowledge of a matter which he believes it likely he could confirm will be treated as knowledge of that matter.[19] Knowledge of an agent or employee is imputed to the insurer for these purposes only if the agent or employee is authorised to decide what course to take with reference to the information received.[20] Knowledge on the part of an agent of the insurer authorised to enter into contracts and to collect premiums was held, in *Ayrey v British Legal and Provident Assurance Co Ltd*, to constitute knowledge of the insurer for the purposes of affirmation of an existing contract even though that agent did not have authority to vary the contract;

the specific issue of authority to decide what course to take with reference to the information received was not considered.[21] An effective election requires that it be communicated to the opponent party.[22] A document which does not at the time lead the opponent party to believe that a choice has been made is at the very least unlikely to be, objectively viewed, sufficiently clear and unequivocal to constitute an election and is in any event ineffective because it does not cause the opponent party to understand that a choice has been made.[23]

Waiver does not merely suspend the insurer's right to avoid in relation to the particular non-disclosure, but extinguishes it: once made, the election is final.[24] It does not, however, prevent the insurer from exercising any further right to avoid which may subsequently arise, even on similar facts.[25] An insurer may decide not to avoid a policy initially, but reasonably wish to do so when additional non-disclosure comes to light; in order to be entitled to avoid, the new non-disclosure must make a material difference to the reasonable insurer's decision whether to affirm or to avoid the policy.[26] The insurer is entitled to a reasonable time to evaluate information, make appropriate inquiries, and reach a decision.[27] Unlike equitable estoppel, there is no requirement of reliance by the insured such as would make it inequitable for the insurer to go back on its election.[28] Delay alone cannot constitute affirmation.[29] However, where the insurer delays beyond the time reasonably required to make appropriate inquiries and decide whether to affirm or avoid, and the insured relies to his detriment on the insurer's failure to avoid, the insurer may be estopped from relying on his right to avoid.[30] Even a fraudulent non-disclosure may be waived.[31] In *Morrison v Universal Marine Insurance Co*,[32] the court held that if underwriters became aware of a non-disclosure of a material fact after signing a slip but before issuing a policy, the subsequent issue of the policy constituted an election to affirm the policy. If insurers require more time to investigate and make a decision, they should expressly reserve their rights before taking any positive step in relation to the policy; if they fail to do so, they may be held to have affirmed it.[33] Examples of conduct which, when not accompanied by an effective reservation of rights,[34] has been held to be sufficient to constitute affirmation of a policy include: allowing further performance by an arbitrator whose decision will give rise to enforceable rights and duties between the insurer and the insured in connection with the policy;[35] issuing a policy;[36] extending the policy period on payment of an additional premium;[37] accepting an instalment of premium;[38] approving security measures to protect the subject matter of the policy;[39] exercising a contractual right to inspect documents;[40] and payment under the policy.[41] A simple failure to return the premium after the policy has been avoided is not a representation sufficient to constitute affirmation;[42] nor is the authorisation of a payment on an expressly 'without prejudice' basis.[43]

Promissory estoppel requires a 'clear and unambiguous',[44] or 'unequivocal'[45] representation by the insurer that he will not insist on his legal rights against the insured, and such reliance by the insured as will render it inequitable for the insurer to go back upon his representation.[46] Although the insurer does not have to have knowledge of the legal right upon which he will not insist, unless the representation carries with it some apparent awareness of rights it goes nowhere: the insured will not understand the representation to mean that the insurer is not going to insist upon his rights because he has said or done nothing to suggest that he has any.[47] Thus, an insurer who is unaware that he has rights is unlikely to make a representation which carries with it some apparent awareness that he has rights; and conversely an insured who is not aware that the insurer has a particular right is unlikely to understand the representation to mean that the insurer is not going to insist on that right or abandon any rights he might have unless he expressly says so.[48] In relation to a breach of warranty, an estoppel involves a clear and unequivocal representation that the insurer will not stand on its right to treat the cover as having been discharged, on which the insured has relied in circumstances in which it would be inequitable to allow the insurer to resile from its representation.[49] Similarly, an estoppel will arise in circumstances where it can be said that the handling of a claim by an insurer is an unequivocal representation that the insurer accepts liability and/or will not rely on breach of some condition precedent as affording a defence, and there has been such detrimental reliance by the insured as would make it inequitable for the insurer to go back on his representation.[50] The assumption of control of the defence of proceedings brought against the insured[51] and the continuation of a defence at trial while insurers made enquiries about new information which came to light shortly before and during the trial[52] have been held to be equivocal and therefore not to give rise to an estoppel. Mere silence and inaction are of their nature equivocal.[53] The reliance must be positive in the sense that the insured must show that it attached significance to the representation alleged and acted on it.[54] The effect of the estoppel may be a temporary suspension of the insurer's rights, or it may be permanent, depending upon the terms of the representation and the circumstances of the insured's reliance.[55]

Given a right to claim under a contract of insurance, which is an independent and pre-existing cause of action, it seems that an estoppel may prevent insurers from denying that particular facts lie within the scope of the contract, notwithstanding that a claim may succeed which would otherwise fail for being outside it; and that the fact that there is an independent and pre-existing cause of action means that this does not offend against the principle that an estoppel is essentially defensive in nature (a shield rather than a sword).[56] Although, depending on the circumstances, a representation as to the construction of the contract may be treated as a representation of law rather than of fact,[57] this distinction is unlikely to be of importance in practice, as the principle that a representation of law cannot give rise to an estoppel[58] is unlikely to survive the recent developments in relation to mistake of law.[59] A representation of law is in future likely to be held to be capable of giving rise to an estoppel, but the circumstances in which such an estoppel are found are in practice likely to be limited on the grounds that both parties have equal means of knowing what the law is.[60]

Estoppel by convention arises where the parties to a transaction have proceeded on the basis of an underlying assumption of fact or law (including as to the true construction of an agreement), due either to mistake or misrepresentation, and it would be unjust or unconscionable to allow one of them to go back on that assumption.[61] Mere silence, inactivity or failure to take a point cannot be enough to found an estoppel by convention.[62] It is not enough that each of the two parties acts on an assumption not communicated to the other, but a concluded agreement is not required.[63] The borderline between estoppel by convention and the requirement that, to be enforceable, a contractual variation must be supported by consideration has not yet been fully explored,[64] although the key appears to lie in the development of the concept of unconscionability in these circumstances.

If the insured intends to rely on a waiver by the insurer, or to allege an estoppel, it should be pleaded and properly particularised.[65]

1 The principles of affirmation, or waiver, or election, are also known as waiver by election: *Insurance Corpn of the Channel Islands Ltd v McHugh* [1997] LRLR 94, 126 (Mance J); *HIH Casualty and General Insurance Ltd v Axa Corporate Solutions* [2002] EWCA Civ 1253, [2003] Lloyd's Rep IR 1, para 7 (Tuckey LJ); see also *Kosmar Villa Holidays plc v Trustees of Syndicate 1243* [2008] EWCA Civ 147, [2008] Lloyd's Rep IR 489, paras 36–38 (Rix LJ).

2 The doctrine of promissory estoppel is also known as waiver by estoppel: *HIH Casualty and General Insurance Ltd v Axa Corporate Solutions* [2002] EWCA Civ 1253, [2003] Lloyd's Rep IR 1, para 7 (Tuckey LJ) (which concerned an alleged waiver by estoppel of the insured's breach of warranty); see also *Kosmar Villa Holidays plc v Trustees of Syndicate 1243* [2008] EWCA Civ 147, [2008] Lloyd's Rep IR 489, paras 36–38 (Rix LJ).

3 In *Kosmar Villa Holidays plc v Trustees of Syndicate 1243* [2008] EWCA Civ 147, [2008] Lloyd's Rep IR 489, para 54, Rix LJ said that in *Barrett Bros (Taxis) Ltd v Davies* [1966] 1 WLR 1334, 1339, [1966] 2 Lloyd's Rep 1, 5, CA, Lord Denning MR described a waiver using the classic terms of promissory estoppel. It may be that references to waiver in some of the earlier cases, such as *Webster v General Accident Fire and Life Assurance Corpn Ltd* [1953] 1 QB 520, 532 (Parker J) and *Barrett Bros (Taxis) Ltd v Davies* [1966] 1 WLR 1334, CA, should properly be construed as references to waiver by estoppel.

4 *Liberty Insurance Pte Ltd v Argo Systems FZE, The Copa Casino* [2011] EWCA Civ 1572, [2012] 1 Lloyd's Rep 129, para 39 (Aikens LJ).

5 *Motor Oil Hellas (Corinth) Refineries SA v Shipping Corpn of India, The Kanchenjunga* [1990] 1 Lloyd's Rep 391, 398, HL (Lord Goff); applied: *Bolton Metropolitan Borough Council v Municipal Mutual Insurance Ltd* [2006] EWCA Civ 50, [2006] 1 WLR 1492, para 31 (Longmore LJ); *Kosmar Villa Holidays plc v Trustees of Syndicate 1243* [2008] EWCA Civ 147, [2008] Lloyd's Rep IR 489, paras 36–38 (Rix LJ).

6 See **PARA 11.14**.

7 See **PARA 11.31**.

8 *HIH Casualty and General Insurance Ltd v Axa Corporate Solutions* [2002] EWCA Civ 1253, [2003] Lloyd's Rep IR 1, para 7 (Tuckey LJ). In this context, the doctrine of estoppel applies: see below. For breach of warranty, see **PARA 3.7**.

9 *Kosmar Villa Holidays plc v Trustees of Syndicate 1243* [2008] EWCA Civ 147, [2008] Lloyd's Rep IR 489, para 70 (Rix LJ). In this context, the doctrine of estoppel applies: see below.

10 *Kosmar Villa Holidays plc v Trustees of Syndicate 1243* [2008] EWCA Civ 147, [2008] Lloyd's Rep IR 489, para 69 (Rix LJ).

11 *Bolton Metropolitan Borough Council v Municipal Mutual Insurance Ltd* [2006] EWCA Civ 50, [2006] 1 WLR 1492, para 32 (Longmore LJ). As to whether insurers are entitled, following a repudiation of liability, to rely upon subsequent (as opposed to accrued) non-compliance by the insured with a procedural condition, see **PARA 7.21**.

12 *Super Chem Products Ltd v American Life and General Insurance Co Ltd* [2004] UKPC 2, [2004] Lloyd's Rep IR 446, para 13 (Lord Steyn) (laying to rest the so-called 'Jureidini defence', based on *Jureidini v National British and Irish Millers Insurance Co Ltd* [1915] AC 499, HL).

13 *Motor Oil Hellas (Corinth) Refineries SA v Shipping Corpn of India, The Kanchenjunga* [1990] 1 Lloyd's Rep 391, 398–399, HL (Lord Goff).

14 *McCormick v National Motor & Accident Insurance Union Ltd* (1934) 49 Ll L Rep 361, CA; *Peyman v Lanjani* [1985] Ch 457, CA; *Simner v New India Assurance Co Ltd* [1995] LRLR 240, 258 (His Honour Judge Diamond QC); *Insurance Corpn of the Channel Islands v Royal Hotel Ltd* [1998] Lloyd's Rep IR 151, 161 (Mance J); *Callaghan and Hedges v Thompson* [2000] Lloyd's Rep IR 125, 133 (David Steel J).

15 *Insurance Corpn of the Channel Islands v Royal Hotel Ltd* [1998] Lloyd's Rep IR 151, 163 (Mance J); Mance J also said (at 163) that a reasonable person in the position of the insured is treated as having a general understanding of the possibility of choice between affirmation and objection, and adverted to the difficulties to which this formulation might be said to give rise in a borderline case (which the case before him was not), as the reasonable insured would be required to be aware what matters were material to a prudent underwriter, or what matters had induced the actual underwriter.

16 *Motor Oil Hellas (Corinth) Refineries SA v Shipping Corpn of India, The Kanchenjunga* [1990] 1 Lloyd's Rep 391, 399, HL (Lord Goff), applied: *Insurance Corpn of the Channel Islands Ltd v McHugh* [1997] LRLR 94, 126 (Mance J); *Involnert Management Inc v Aprilgrange Ltd* [2015] EWHC 2225 (Comm), [2015] 2 Lloyd's Rep 289, para 161 (Leggatt J).

17 *Simner v New India Assurance Co Ltd* [1995] LRLR 240, 258 (His Honour Judge Diamond QC), in which it was not disputed that the underwriter had knowledge of an insurer's right to avoid a contract of insurance on grounds of non-disclosure or misrepresentation.

18 *Moore Large & Co Ltd v Hermes Credit & Guarantee plc* [2003] EWHC 26 (Comm), [2003] Lloyd's Rep IR 315, 335–336, paras 100–101 (Colman J); *Involnert Management Inc v Aprilgrange Ltd* [2015] EWHC 2225 (Comm), [2015] 2 Lloyd's Rep 289, para 160 (Leggatt J).

19 *McCormick v National Motor & Accident Insurance Union Ltd* (1934) 49 Ll L Rep 361, 365, CA (Scrutton LJ: being put on inquiry is not sufficient), applied: *Container Transport International Inc v Oceanus Mutual Underwriting Association (Bermuda) Ltd* [1984] 1 Lloyd's Rep 476, 498, CA (Kerr LJ); *Insurance Corpn of the Channel Islands v Royal Hotel Ltd* [1998] Lloyd's Rep IR 151, 161–162, 172 (Mance J), indicating that whether the insurer has sufficient knowledge for these purposes is a 'jury question' incapable of precise analysis.

20 *Evans v Employers' Mutual Insurance Association Ltd* [1936] 1 KB 505, CA, applied: *Malhi v Abbey Life Assurance Co Ltd* [1996] LRLR 237, CA; *Brook v Trafalgar Insurance Co Ltd* (1946) 79 Ll L Rep 365, CA. In *Haydenfayre Ltd v British National Insurance Society Ltd* [1984] 2 Lloyd's Rep 393, Lloyd J held (at 400–401) that a person answering the phone and accepting a telephone message on behalf of the underwriters had ostensible authority to do so, and that this was sufficient to constitute knowledge of the contents of the message on behalf of the underwriters themselves.

21 *Ayrey v British Legal and Provident Assurance Co Ltd* [1918] 1 KB 136.

22 *Callaghan and Hedges v Thompson* [2000] Lloyd's Rep IR 125, 134 (David Steel J); *The WD Fairway (No 3)* [2009] EWHC 1782 (Admlty), [2009] 2 Lloyd's Rep 420, para 19 (Tomlinson J).

23 *The WD Fairway (No 3)* [2009] EWHC 1782 (Admlty), [2009] 2 Lloyd's Rep 420, para 19 (Tomlinson J).

24 *Motor Oil Hellas (Corinth) Refineries SA v Shipping Corpn of India, The Kanchenjunga* [1990] 1 Lloyd's Rep 391, 399, HL (Lord Goff); applied: *Insurance Corpn of the Channel Islands Ltd v McHugh* [1997] LRLR 94, 126 (Mance J).

25 *Insurance Corpn of the Channel Islands Ltd v McHugh* [1997] LRLR 94, 127 (Mance J).

26 *Spriggs v Wessington Court School Ltd* [2004] EWHC 1432 (QB), [2005] Lloyds Rep IR 474, para 77 (Burton J); applied: *Involnert Management Inc v Aprilgrange Ltd* [2015] EWHC 2225 (Comm), [2015] 2 Lloyd's Rep 289, para 169 (Leggatt J).

27 *Morrison v Universal Marine Insurance Co* (1872) LR 8 Exch 40, 55–56 (Bramwell B); *McCormick v National Motor & Accident Insurance Union Ltd* (1934) 49 Ll L Rep 361, CA, applied: *Insurance Corpn of the Channel Islands Ltd v McHugh* [1997] LRLR 94, 127, 132 (Mance J); *Allen v Robles* [1969] 1 WLR 1193, CA; *Sea Glory Maritime Co v Al Sagr National Insurance Co, The MV Nancy* [2013] EWHC 2116 (Comm), [2014] 1 Lloyd's Rep 14, para 126 (Blair J) (no affirmation where insurer avoided six days after sending email stating that cover was in place, as this was reasonable period of time to conduct its enquiries).

28 *Peyman v Lanjani* [1985] Ch 457, 500, CA (May LJ); *Motor Oil Hellas (Corinth) Refineries SA v Shipping Corpn of India, The Kanchenjunga* [1990] 1 Lloyd's Rep 391, 399, HL (Lord Goff), applied: *Insurance Corpn of the Channel Islands Ltd v McHugh* [1997] LRLR 94, 126 (Mance J).

29 *Allen v Robles* [1969] 1 WLR 1193, CA.

30 *Allen v Robles* [1969] 1 WLR 1193, 1196–1197, CA (Fenton Atkinson LJ) (reversing the decision of Mocatta J at first instance that insurers had affirmed the contract by reason of delay beyond a reasonable time, in circumstances where there was no detrimental reliance by the insured); *Peyman v Lanjani* [1985] Ch 457, CA; *Callaghan and Hedges v Thompson* [2000] Lloyd's Rep IR 125, 134 (David Steel J).

31 *Morrison v Universal Marine Insurance Co* (1872) LR 8 Exch 40, 55–56 (Bramwell B); *Black King Shipping Corpn v Massie, The Litsion Pride* [1985] 1 Lloyd's Rep 437, 516–517 (Hirst J); *Insurance Corpn of the Channel Islands Ltd v McHugh* [1997] LRLR 94, 127 (Mance J).

32 (1872) LR 8 Exch 40.

33 *Morrison v Universal Marine Insurance Co* (1872) LR 8 Exch 40, 57 (Bramwell B) (issue of policy without protest); *Svenska Handelsbanken v Sun Alliance and London Insurance plc* [1996] 1 Lloyd's Rep 519, 569 (Rix J).

34 A reservation' of rights is an 'obstacle to finding an unequivocal communication of a decision to affirm the policy': *Involnert Management Inc v Aprilgrange Ltd* [2015] EWHC 2225 (Comm), [2015] 2 Lloyd's Rep 289, para 179 (Leggatt J). See further **PARA 8.4**.

35 *Insurance Corpn of the Channel Islands v Royal Hotel Ltd* [1998] Lloyd's Rep IR 151, 173 (Mance J).

36 *Morrison v Universal Marine Insurance Co* (1872) LR 8 Exch 40 (insurers became aware of non-disclosure between signing slip and issuing policy); *Haydenfayre Ltd v British National Insurance Society Ltd* [1984] 2 Lloyd's Rep 393, 400 (Lloyd J).

37 *Scottish Coal Co Ltd v Royal & Sun Alliance Insurance plc* [2008] EWHC 880 (Comm), [2008] Lloyd's Rep IR 718, para 94 (David Steel J).

38 *Hemmings v Sceptre Life Association Ltd* [1905] 1 Ch 365; *Ayrey v British Legal and Provident Assurance Co Ltd* [1918] 1 KB 136; *Haydenfayre Ltd v British National Insurance Society Ltd* [1984] 2 Lloyd's Rep 393, 400 (Lloyd J); *Black King Shipping Corpn v Massie, The Litsion Pride* [1985] 1 Lloyd's Rep 437, 516–517 (Hirst J).

39 *De Maurier (Jewels) Ltd v Bastion Insurance Co Ltd* [1967] 2 Lloyd's Rep 550, 559 (Donaldson J).

40 *Iron Trades Mutual Insurance Co Ltd v Companhia de Seguros Imperio* (1992) 1 Re LR 213, 223–224 (Hobhouse J); applied: *Involnert Management Inc v Aprilgrange Ltd* [2015] EWHC 2225 (Comm), [2015] 2 Lloyd's Rep 289, para 169 (Leggatt J). In *Involnert Management Inc v Aprilgrange Ltd* [2015] EWHC 2225 (Comm), [2015] 2 Lloyd's Rep 289, Leggatt J rejected Colman J's analysis in *Strive Shipping Corpn v Hellenic Mutual War Risks Association, The Grecia Express* [2002] 2 Lloyd's Rep 88, 162–163, that, in the context of avoidance and affirmation, a right to inspect documents is an ancillary provision akin to an arbitration clause, reliance on which is incapable of telling the other party anything about the future performance of the primary provisions of the contract. Leggatt J said (at paras 177–178) that the function of a clause entitling a party to inspect documents might support an inference that it was intended to remain binding even after the parties had been discharged from further performance of their substantive obligations by the termination of the contract, but that it would be another and a far stronger thing to infer that such a clause was intended to constitute an independent contract between the parties which would remain in existence even if the contract of which it formed part was retroactively avoided; and that, in the case of arbitration clauses, there were powerful reasons for giving effect to the parties' choice of a tribunal to resolve all their disputes, including disputes about whether the contract exists, and that there were no comparable reasons which applied to a contractual right to inspect documents. It is suggested that Leggatt J's analysis is correct.

41 *Svenska Handelsbanken v Sun Alliance and London Insurance plc* [1996] 1 Lloyd's Rep 519, 569 (Rix J); applying *Barber v Imperio Reinsurance Co (UK) Ltd*, CA, 15 July 1993 (unreported).

42 *March Cabaret Club & Casino Ltd v London Assurance Ltd* [1975] 1 Lloyd's Rep 169, 178 (May J).

43 *Callaghan and Hedges v Thompson* [2000] Lloyd's Rep IR 125, 133 (David Steel J).

44 *Low v Bouverie* [1891] 3 Ch 82, CA; *Woodhouse A C Israel Cocoa Ltd SA v Nigerian Produce Marketing Co Ltd* [1972] AC 741, HL.

45 *Motor Oil Hellas (Corinth) Refineries SA v Shipping Corpn of India, The Kanchenjunga* [1990] 1 Lloyd's Rep 391, 399, HL (Lord Goff), applied: *Insurance Corpn of the Channel Islands Ltd v McHugh* [1997] LRLR 94, 126 (Mance J).

46 *Motor Oil Hellas (Corinth) Refineries SA v Shipping Corpn of India, The Kanchenjunga* [1990] 1 Lloyd's Rep 391, 399, HL (Lord Goff), applied: *Insurance Corpn of the Channel Islands Ltd v McHugh* [1997] LRLR 94, 126 (Mance J).

47 *Motor Oil Hellas (Corinth) Refineries SA v Shipping Corpn of India, The Kanchenjunga* [1990] 1 Lloyd's Rep 391, 399, HL (Lord Goff), applied: *HIH Casualty and General Insurance Ltd v Axa Corporate Solutions* [2002] EWCA Civ 1253, [2003] Lloyd's Rep IR 1, paras 9 and 21 (Tuckey LJ).

48 *HIH Casualty and General Insurance Ltd v Axa Corporate Solutions* [2002] EWCA Civ 1253, [2003] Lloyd's Rep IR 1, para 22 (Tuckey LJ).

49 *HIH Casualty and General Insurance Ltd v Axa Corporate Solutions* [2002] EWCA Civ 1253, [2003] Lloyd's Rep IR 1, para 7 (Tuckey LJ).

50 *Kosmar Villa Holidays plc v Trustees of Syndicate 1243* [2008] EWCA Civ 147, [2008] Lloyd's Rep IR 489.

51 *Soole v Royal Insurance Co Ltd* [1971] 2 Lloyd's Rep 332; approved in *Kosmar Villa Holidays plc v Trustees of Syndicate 1243* [2008] EWCA Civ 147, [2008] Lloyd's Rep IR 489, paras 48–50 and 78 (Rix LJ).

52 *McCormick v National Motor & Accident Insurance Union Ltd* (1934) 49 Ll L Rep 361, CA; see also *Kosmar Villa Holidays plc v Trustees of Syndicate 1243* [2008] EWCA Civ 147, [2008] Lloyd's Rep IR 489, para 78 (Rix LJ).

53 *Allied Marine Transport Ltd v Vale do Rio Doce Navegacao SA, The Leonidas D* [1985] 1 WLR 925, 937 and 941, [1985] 2 Lloyd's Rep 18, 25 and 28, CA (Robert Goff LJ); applied: *Seechurn v Ace Insurance SA-NV* [2002] EWCA Civ 67, [2002] 2 Lloyd's Rep 390, para 20 (Ward LJ); *Fortisbank SA v Trenwick International Ltd* [2005] EWHC 399 (Comm), [2005] Lloyd's Rep IR 464, para 30 (Gloster J); *Liberty Insurance Pte Ltd v Argo Systems FZE, The Copa Casino* [2011] EWCA Civ 1572, [2012] 1 Lloyd's Rep 129, para 46 (Aikens LJ).

54 *HIH Casualty and General Insurance Ltd v Axa Corporate Solutions* [2002] EWCA Civ 1253, [2003] Lloyd's Rep IR 1, para 29 (Tuckey LJ).

55 *Motor Oil Hellas (Corinth) Refineries SA v Shipping Corpn of India, The Kanchenjunga* [1990] 1 Lloyd's Rep 391, 399, HL (Lord Goff), applied: *Insurance Corpn of the Channel Islands Ltd v McHugh* [1997] LRLR 94, 126 (Mance J).

56 *Hiscox v Outhwaite (No 3)* [1991] 2 Lloyd's Rep 524, 534–535 (Evans J).
57 *Soole v Royal Insurance Co Ltd* [1971] 2 Lloyd's Rep 332, 340 (Shaw J); approved in *Kosmar Villa Holidays plc v Trustees of Syndicate 1243* [2008] EWCA Civ 147, [2008] Lloyd's Rep IR 489, paras 48–50 and 78 (Rix LJ) but not on this point.
58 See eg *Soole v Royal Insurance Co Ltd* [1971] 2 Lloyd's Rep 332, 339, 340 (Shaw J).
59 See **PARA 8.15**.
60 See further **PARA 11.25**, note 2. In *Soole v Royal Insurance Co Ltd* [1971] 2 Lloyd's Rep 332, Shaw J said (at 340), in support of his conclusion that a representation as to the construction of the policy was not a representation of fact in the circumstances of that case, that the insured himself was always aware of the facts on which the construction of the policy depended.
61 *Amalgamated Investment & Property Co Ltd v Texas Commerce International Bank Ltd* [1982] QB 84, CA; *Norwegian American Cruises A/S v Paul Mundy Ltd, The Vistafjord* [1988] 2 Lloyd's Rep 343, CA; *Republic of India v India Steamship Co Ltd (No 2)* [1998] AC 878, 913, HL (Lord Steyn); *Johnson v Gore Wood & Co* [2002] 2 AC 1, HL, 33 (Lord Bingham), 38–41 (Lord Goff); *HIH Casualty and General Insurance Ltd v Axa Corporate Solutions* [2002] EWCA Civ 1253, [2003] Lloyd's Rep IR 1, 8–9, paras 30–32 (Tuckey LJ).
62 *HIH Casualty and General Insurance Ltd v Axa Corporate Solutions* [2002] EWCA Civ 1253, [2003] Lloyd's Rep IR 1, para 29 (Tuckey LJ); applied: *Fortisbank SA v Trenwick International Ltd* [2005] EWHC 399 (Comm), [2005] Lloyd's Rep IR 464, 473, para 43 (Gloster J).
63 *Republic of India v India Steamship Co Ltd (No 2)* [1998] AC 878, 913, HL (Lord Steyn). The assumption must be communicated between the parties, and it is the shared assumption which is apparent objectively from the parties' communications which is relevant, not their subjective intentions, although the two will usually coincide: *The WD Fairway (No 3)* [2009] EWHC 1782 (Admlty), [2009] 2 Lloyd's Rep 420, para 22 (Tomlinson J).
64 *Johnson v Gore Wood & Co* [2002] 2 AC 1, 38–41, HL (Lord Goff).
65 *Brook v Trafalgar Insurance Co Ltd* (1946) 79 Ll L Rep 365, CA, 367 (Scott LJ), 368 (Tucker LJ) (waiver).

Chapter 12

Subrogation

INTRODUCTION

12.1   In insurance law, the doctrine of subrogation allows an insurer, once he has indemnified his insured, to benefit from all the rights of the insured, in relation to the loss to which the policy responds, and by the exercise of which the loss could be, or has been, diminished.[1]

The doctrine of subrogation has its genesis in the fundamental principle that a contract of insurance is a contract of indemnity: once the insured has been fully indemnified by the insurer, the doctrine of subrogation is available to ensure that he is never more than fully indemnified.[2] It applies only in relation to contracts of indemnity,[3] such as property or third party liability insurance, and has no application in relation to contingency insurance (life, personal accident and similar policies).[4] Subrogation, in relation to contracts of insurance, rests on two fundamental and interdependent principles: first, that it is no defence to a claim by an insured under a policy of insurance that the insured has a cause of action against a third party in respect of the same loss;[5] and, second, that it is no defence to a claim by the insured against a third party that the insured has a right to an indemnity under a policy of insurance in respect of the same loss.[6]

1 *Castellain v Preston* (1883) 11 QBD 380, CA.
2 *Castellain v Preston* (1883) 11 QBD 380, 386, CA (Brett LJ).
3 See *Re Miller, Gibb & Co Ltd* [1957] 1 WLR 703, 707–708, 711 (Wynn-Parry J).
4 *Arab Bank plc v John D Wood Commercial Ltd* [2000] 1 WLR 857, CA, paras 94–95 (Mance LJ) (distinguishing *Parry v Cleaver* [1970] AC 1, HL, on this basis).
5 *Collingridge v Royal Exchange Assurance Corpn* (1877) 3 QBD 173.
6 *Bradburn v Great Western Railway Co* (1874) LR 10 Ex Ch 1; *The Yasin* [1979] 2 Lloyd's Rep 45 (Lloyd J); *Arab Bank plc v John D Wood Commercial Ltd* [2000] 1 WLR 857, CA.

NATURE OF THE DOCTRINE

12.2   Subrogation is not an exclusively equitable doctrine. It was applied by the common law courts in insurance cases long before the fusion of law and equity, although the common law courts sometimes needed the assistance of the courts of equity in order to give full effect to the doctrine, for example, by compelling an insured to allow his name to be used by the insurer for the purposes of a recovery action.[1] The approach taken by the courts in recent decades in deciding important questions in relation to subrogation in insurance cases has been influenced by the extent to which, during different periods, subrogation was treated as a creature of the common law, based on implied terms, or of equity.[2] The House of Lords in *Lord Napier and Ettrick v Hunter*[3] resurrected equity's role in subrogation in the context of contracts of indemnity,[4] alongside the common law approach to subrogation as arising out of implied terms. This represents a significant step away from the approach of Lord Diplock, which was to emphasise the development of the doctrine of subrogation at common law and to downplay the intervention of equity.[5] The current position is that the common law approach based on implied terms has been confined to subrogation in the context of contracts of indemnity, and that subrogation, in the sense of an equitable remedy to reverse or prevent unjust enrichment which is not based on agreement or common intention of the party enriched and the party deprived, is treated as a distinct doctrine.[6] As a result, authorities in relation to the creation and exercise of rights of subrogation in other areas of the law may be of limited relevance in insurance cases.

1 *Yorkshire Insurance Co Ltd v Nisbet Shipping Co Ltd* [1962] 2 QB 330, 339 (Diplock J); *Morris v Ford Motor Co Ltd* [1973] QB 792, 800, CA (Lord Denning MR).
2 Notably, in *Re Miller, Gibb & Co Ltd* [1957] 1 WLR 703 (Wynn-Parry J); *Yorkshire Insurance Co Ltd v Nisbet Shipping Co Ltd* [1962] 2 QB 330 (Diplock J); *Morris v Ford Motor Co Ltd* [1973] QB 792, CA; *Hobbs v Marlowe* [1978] AC 16, 39, HL (Lord Diplock); *Orakpo v Manson Investments Ltd* [1977] 1 WLR 347, CA; affirmed [1978] AC 95, HL; *Lord Napier and Ettrick v Hunter* [1993] AC 713, HL; *Banque Financière de la Cité v Parc (Battersea) Ltd* [1999] AC 221, HL.
3 [1993] AC 713, HL.
4 See **PARA 12.11**.
5 See *Yorkshire Insurance Co Ltd v Nisbet Shipping Co Ltd* [1962] 2 QB 330 (Diplock J) and *Hobbs v Marlowe* [1978] AC 16, 39, HL (Lord Diplock).
6 *Banque Financière de la Cité v Parc (Battersea) Ltd* [1999] 1 AC 221, 231–232, HL (Lord Hoffmann).

ENTITLEMENT TO EXERCISE SUBROGATED RIGHTS

12.3   The insurer is not subrogated to a right of action until it has paid the sum insured.[1] In an appropriate case, the court may make a declaration as to the insurer's entitlement to be subrogated before the insurer has paid the sum insured.[2]

Once the insurer has fully indemnified the insured, it is entitled to bring a recovery action in the name of the insured[3] as *dominus litis* (which means the person in control of the litigation), provided that it indemnifies the insured against costs.[4] Further, in order for insurers to be entitled to exercise subrogation rights, the payment must be made pursuant to a valid contract of indemnity.[5] No right of subrogation arises on payment pursuant to a wager or honour policy.[6] However, in the case of an ordinary policy, it is sufficient that insurers have acted in good faith in settling a claim by an insured.[7] In these circumstances, a third party against whom a recovery action is brought cannot escape liability by calling into question the insurers' liability to the insured.[8] As Lord Hobhouse pointed out in delivering the judgment of the Privy Council in *King v Victoria Insurance Co Ltd*,[9] if this were the law, insurers would never be able to settle a claim under a policy which they had any grounds to dispute, without risking becoming involved in that same dispute with a third party when they sought to exercise rights of subrogation.

If the insured has more than one claim arising out of the same facts under a single policy, such as a claim to be indemnified in respect of damage to his own motor vehicle and a claim to be indemnified for his liability for damage to a third party's liability, the insurer is entitled to exercise subrogation rights only after it has indemnified the insured in relation to all the claims.[10]

In *Commercial Union Assurance Co v Lister*,[11] the court indicated that, in bringing proceedings to recover damages in respect of both insured and uninsured losses, the insured would owe the insurer a duty in equity to protect his interests. This analysis must now be viewed in the context of the debate about whether subrogation in contracts of indemnity is equitable or contractual. If the duty arises by virtue of a term implied into the contract, damages would be available for breach. A further possibility is that the duty is a post-contractual manifestation of the mutual duty of utmost good faith between insurer and insured. If so, damages would not be available for breach.[12] In the absence of an express provision in the policy, where there is an excess provision in the policy, the insured would be entitled to insist on his position as *dominus litis* even if the insurer had paid its maximum liability under the policy, as the excess would constitute an uninsured loss in these circumstances. This is unlikely to be of practical importance in most cases, as modern policies invariably include clauses entitling insurers to take control of proceedings; and where they do not, insurers usually obtain a letter of subrogation, on payment of the loss, expressly assigning to them the insured's rights of recovery against third parties.[13]

Although the right of subrogation cannot be exercised until payment, it is a contingent right which vests when the policy is entered into, and which the insured cannot restrict by entering into a subsequent contract of insurance with another insurer on the same subject matter.[14] It seems that the insurer's right of subrogation crystallises at the date of payment to the insured, and does not extend to subsequently-acquired rights.[15] The insurer's interest in the insured's cause of action is not a proprietary interest.[16]

1 *Castellain v Preston* (1883) 11 QBD 380, 388, CA (Brett LJ); *John Edwards & Co v Motor Union Insurance Co Ltd* [1922] 2 KB 249; *Page v Scottish Insurance Corpn Ltd* (1929) 33 Ll L Rep 134, CA; *Scottish Union & National Insurance Co v Davis* [1970] 1 Lloyd's Rep 1, CA.

2 *Parker v National Farmers Union Mutual Insurance Society Ltd* [2012] EWHC 2156 (Comm), [2013] Lloyd's Rep IR 253, para 203 (Teare J). By means of a subrogated claim, an insurer may recover from a fraudulent insured the amount of an indemnity paid to an innocent insured: see *Parker v National Farmers Union Mutual Insurance Society Ltd* [2012] EWHC 2156 (Comm), [2013] Lloyd's Rep IR 253, para 203 (Teare J); and see **PARA 11.52**.

3 *Simpson v Thomson* (1877) 3 App Cas 279, 284, HL (Lord Cairns LC).

4 *John Edwards & Co v Motor Union Insurance Co Ltd* [1922] 2 KB 249, 254 (McCardie J); *Morris v Ford Motor Co Ltd* [1973] QB 792, 801, CA (Lord Denning MR); *Netherlands Insurance Co Est 1845 Ltd v Karl Ljungberg & Co AB* [1986] 2 Lloyd's Rep 19, 22, PC (Lord Goff); *Cox v Bankside Members Agency Ltd* [1995] 2 Lloyd's Rep 437, 463, CA (Lord Bingham MR).

5 *John Edwards & Co v Motor Union Insurance Co Ltd* [1922] 2 KB 249, 254–255 (McCardie J).

6 *John Edwards & Co v Motor Union Insurance Co Ltd* [1922] 2 KB 249.

7 *King v Victoria Insurance Co Ltd* [1896] AC 250, PC, considered in *John Edwards & Co v Motor Union Insurance Co Ltd* [1922] 2 KB 249, 256 (McCardie J).

8 *King v Victoria Insurance Co Ltd* [1896] AC 250, PC.

9 [1896] AC 250, PC.

10 *Page v Scottish Insurance Corpn Ltd* (1929) 33 Ll L Rep 134, CA.

11 (18/4) 9 Ch App 483, CA.

12 See further **PARA 11.31**.

13 *Banque Financière de la Cité v Parc (Battersea) Ltd* [1999] 1 AC 221, 231, HL (Lord Hoffmann).

14 *Boag v Standard Marine Insurance Co Ltd* [1937] 2 KB 113, CA.

15 See *The WD Fairway (No 3)* [2009] EWHC 1782 (Admlty), [2009] 2 Lloyd's Rep 420, para 16, in which Tomlinson J said that in *Castellain v Preston* (1883) 11 QBD 380 the right to enforce the sale of the fire-damaged property was a right which subsisted at the date of the fire, and that the case did not decide that if, subsequent to being indemnified for fire damage, an owner of insured property managed

to sell it at a price which did not apparently reflect a discount to reflect the damage, the owner must account to the insurer for a sum equal to the insurance recovery.
16 *Re Ballast plc, St Paul Travelers Insurance Co Ltd v Dargan* [2006] EWHC 3189 (Ch), [2007] Lloyd's Rep IR 742, paras 90–109 (Lawrence Collins J).

Implied waiver of subrogated rights

12.4   Rights of subrogation do not arise against the insured himself,[1] or against a co-insured in the case of joint insurance, where the interests of the insureds are so inseparably connected that they are to be considered as one insured.[2] Where a bailee is insured against liability to the bailor, and the bailor is insured under the same insurance, the insurer cannot exercise a right of subrogation against the bailee.[3] Similarly, the insurer will not be permitted to exercise a right of subrogation in the case of co-insurance of property even where the interests of the insureds are not joint, provided that those interests are pervasive and relate to the whole of the property.[4] There may also be an implied waiver of subrogation rights where one party to a commercial relationship is required to pay premiums for an insurance against loss or damage to the property insured, and loss occurs as a result of a breach of contract or negligent conduct by the party who pays the premium.[5] Outside these contexts, implied waiver of rights of subrogation is rare; however, whether there is a waiver will depend on the circumstances of each individual case, and the principles set out below may apply by analogy.

Earlier dicta (judicial remarks) suggested that this resulted from an application of the rules against circuity of actions[6] and the implication of a term in the policy preventing the insurer from bringing an action against a co-insured in respect of liability for loss and damage caused by a peril insured for his benefit, thus providing the co-insured with a defence to any subrogated action brought by the insurer.[7] However, more recent dicta suggest that it results from the intentions of the contracting parties: express provisions in the contract between the co-insureds relating to insurance may, when viewed in conjunction with other terms of the contract, demonstrate an intention that matters are to be settled between co-insureds 'not on the basis of liability and litigation, but on the basis of an insurance funded solution',[8] and therefore to relieve the co-insureds from liabilities to which they would otherwise be subject;[9] alternatively, in the absence of any express term, the court may be prepared to imply a term to this effect into the contract between the parties.[10]

There may similarly be a waiver of subrogation rights, either expressly or impliedly, where one party to a commercial relationship is required to pay premiums for an insurance against loss or damage to the property insured.[11] In *Gard Marine & Energy Ltd v China National Chartering Co Ltd, The Ocean Victory*,[12] the Court of Appeal said that the prima facie position where a contract required a party to that contract to insure should be that the parties had agreed to look to the insurers for indemnification rather than to each other, and that that would be all the more so if it was agreed that the insurance was to be in joint names for the parties' joint interest or if there were other relevant circumstances, as in *Rathbone Brothers plc v Novae Corporate Underwriting Ltd*,[13] where the underlying contract consisted of an employer's indemnity granted to an employee.[14]

The issue may always arise in any event, were an insurance company to fail, as to who bears that ultimate risk: if upon their contract's true construction the regime for joint names insurance has supplanted and excluded any liability on the part of the contractor to compensate or indemnify the employer, then the risk will fall on the employer; but if however the true construction is that the contractor's liability is supplanted only to the extent of a recovery obtained from the insurer, then the risk of the insurer's insolvency would appear to fall back on the contractor.[15] The contract cannot however be construed by reference to the possibility of insurers becoming insolvent or refusing to pay, as the contract has to be construed at the time when it is made and neither party contemplates insolvency or refusal to pay.[16] Losses caused by wilful misconduct or fraud by a co-insured are not covered under the policy and the rule therefore does not apply in respect of a subrogated claim brought by insurers against one insured in respect of losses arising out of that insured's wilful misconduct or fraud for which the insurer has indemnified a co-insured.[17]

The circumstances in which, in the absence of an express term in a contract of *insurance* waiving the insurer's right to subrogation, such a term may be implied into that contract are not settled, although the balance of authority is in favour of such a term being implied only in exceptional circumstances. In *Tyco Fire & Integrated Solutions (UK) Ltd v Rolls-Royce Motor Cars Ltd*,[18] Rix LJ said that where the underlying contract envisaged that one co-assured may be liable to another for negligence even within the sphere of the cover provided by the policy, he was inclined to think that there was nothing in the doctrine of subrogation to prevent the insurer suing in the name of the relevant co-insured to recover the insurance proceeds which the insurer has paid in the absence of any express ouster of the right of subrogation, either generally or at least in cases where the joint names insurance was really a bundle of composite insurance policies which insure each insured for his respective interest.[19] Such a term was however implied by Elias and Sharp LJJ in *Rathbone Brothers plc v Novae Corporate Underwriting Ltd*,[20] notwithstanding an express term in the policy confirming insurers' general right of subrogation, on the basis that it could not have been the intention of the parties that the insurers should be able to enforce a contractual indemnity against a co-insured where the co-insured was indemnifying the very same risk as the insurers.[21] Beatson LJ disagreed with the majority on this point, saying that, in practice, in all but an exceptional case only an express waiver of the right of subrogation would suffice.[22] He preferred to proceed on the basis of the construction of the underlying contract as having the effect that there was no claim to which the insurer's right to subrogation could attach, and also said that in these circumstances it did not appear necessary to imply additional provisions into the insurance policy itself.[23] Subsequently, in *Gard Marine & Energy Ltd v China National Chartering Co Ltd, The Ocean Victory*,[24] Longmore LJ, giving the judgment of the Court of Appeal, said that it was now clear that the question whether the parties had agreed on an insurance solution without any rights of subrogation ultimately depended on the contract of the parties rather than on the terms of the insurance policy made pursuant to that contract.[25]

1 *Simpson v Thomson* (1877) 3 App Cas 279, HL (collision between two ships belonging to the same owner).
2 *Petrofina (UK) Ltd v Magnaload Ltd* [1984] QB 127, 139–140 (Lloyd J). See **PARA 11.52**.
3 *Talbot Underwriting Ltd v Nausch, Hogan & Murray Inc (The Jascon 5)* [2006] EWCA Civ 889, [2006] 2 Lloyd's Rep 195, para 51 (Moore-Bick LJ); see also *HSBC Rail (UK) Ltd v Network Rail*

Infrastructure Ltd [2005] EWCA Civ 1437, [2006] 1 Lloyd's Rep 358, paras 34–38 (Longmore LJ). The suggestions in *The 'Yasin'* [1979] 2 Lloyd's Rep 45, 54–55 (Lloyd J) and *Petrofina (UK) Ltd v Magnaload Ltd* [1984] QB 127, 139–140 (Lloyd J) that the rule might be based on the rules about circuity of actions were doubted in *Co-operative Retail Services Ltd v Taylor Young Ltd* [2002] UKHL 17, [2002] 1 WLR 1419, para 65 (Lord Hope).

4 *Petrofina (UK) Ltd v Magnaload Ltd* [1984] QB 127, 139–140 (Lloyd J); *Co-operative Retail Services Ltd v Taylor Young Ltd* [2002] UKHL 17, [2002] 1 WLR 1419, paras 61–65 (Lord Hope). See also PARA **2.10**.

5 *Gard Marine & Energy Ltd v China National Chartering Co Ltd, The Ocean Victory* [2015] EWCA Civ 16, [2015] 1 Lloyd's Rep 381, para 74 (Longmore LJ). The fact that a borrower has been required to pay the premium is not a basis for implying a waiver of subrogation rights into either the policy or the underlying loan agreement where a policy protects a lender against the borrower's default: it is difficult to conceive of a policy payable on the eventuality of non-payment enuring to the benefit of the non-payer; and implying a term into the contract of borrowing would involve releasing the borrower from part of his indebtedness if he failed to pay whether or not he had the ability to do so: see *Woolwich Building Society v Brown* [1996] CLC 625, 627–629 (mortgage indemnity guarantee insurance); approved: *Banfield v Leeds Building Society*, CA, unreported, 19 December 2007, paragraphs 46 and 48 (Lawrence Collins LJ).

6 *The 'Yasin'* [1979] 2 Lloyd's Rep 45, 54–55 (Lloyd J); *Petrofina (UK) Ltd v Magnaload Ltd* [1984] QB 127, 139–140 (Lloyd J); *National Oilwell (UK) Ltd v Davy Offshore Ltd* [1993] 2 Lloyd's Rep 582, 612–615 (Colman J).

7 *National Oilwell (UK) Ltd v Davy Offshore Ltd* [1993] 2 Lloyd's Rep 582, 612–615 (Colman J).

8 *Tyco Fire & Integrated Solutions (UK) Ltd v Rolls-Royce Motor Cars Ltd* [2008] EWCA Civ 286, [2008] Lloyd's Rep IR 617, para 78 (Rix LJ); *Gard Marine & Energy Ltd v China National Chartering Co Ltd, The Ocean Victory* [2015] EWCA Civ 16, [2015] 1 Lloyd's Rep 381, para 89 (Longmore LJ) (the right construction of the clause was 'an insurance funded result', or, to use another phrase, the clause provided 'a code for what is to happen').

9 *Co-operative Retail Services Ltd v Taylor Young Ltd* [2002] UKHL 17, [2002] 1 WLR 1419, paras 61–65 (Lord Hope). See also PARA **2.10**.

10 *Hopewell Project Management Ltd v Ewbank Preece Ltd* [1998] 1 Lloyd's Rep 448, 458 (Mr Recorder Jackson QC, obiter: it would be nonsensical if co-insureds under a contractors' all risks policy could make claims against one another in respect of damage to the contract works; such a result could not have been intended by the parties and the judge would if necessary have implied a term to that effect on the grounds of obviousness), approved: *Co-operative Retail Services Ltd v Taylor Young Ltd* [2002] UKHL 17, [2002] QB 1419, para 65 (Lord Hope). See also PARA **2.10**.

11 *Gard Marine & Energy Ltd v China National Chartering Co Ltd, The Ocean Victory* [2015] EWCA Civ 16, [2015] 1 Lloyd's Rep 381.

12 [2015] EWCA Civ 16, [2015] 1 Lloyd's Rep 381.

13 [2014] EWCA Civ 1464, [2015] Lloyd's Rep IR 95.

14 At para 83. In the employment context, see also *Morris v Ford Motor Co Ltd* [1973] QB 792, CA (waiver of subrogation implied by Lord Denning MR and James LJ on the grounds that a subrogated claim would be likely to result in industrial action; it is suggested that Stamp LJ's dissenting judgment is persuasive and to be preferred).

15 *Tyco Fire & Integrated Solutions (UK) Ltd v Rolls-Royce Motor Cars Ltd* [2008] EWCA Civ 286, [2008] Lloyd's Rep IR 617, para 79 (Rix LJ).

16 *Gard Marine & Energy Ltd v China National Chartering Co Ltd, The Ocean Victory* [2015] EWCA Civ 16, [2015] 1 Lloyd's Rep 381, para 91 (Longmore LJ).

17 *National Oilwell (UK) Ltd v Davy Offshore Ltd* [1993] 2 Lloyd's Rep 582, 614–616 (Colman J); *Netherlands v Youell* [1997] 2 Lloyd's Rep 440, 450–451 (Rix J).

18 [2008] EWCA Civ 286, [2008] Lloyd's Rep IR 617.

19 At para 77.

20 [2014] EWCA Civ 1464, [2015] Lloyd's Rep IR 95.

21 At paras 83–86 (Elias LJ) and 123–124 (Sharp LJ). Elias and Sharp LJJ each relied on Lord Hoffmann's remarks in *Attorney General of Belize v Belize Telecom Ltd* [2009] UKPC 10, [2009] 1 WLR 1988 as the basis for implication of a term; this approach is no longer valid following the decision of the Supreme Court in *Marks and Spencer plc v BNP Paribas Securities Services Trust Company (Jersey) Ltd* [2015] UKSC 72, para 31 (Lord Neuberger), but the analysis of Elias and Sharp LJJ is not unsound for that reason, as their reasoning would have allowed them to imply a term on the basis of obviousness or necessity for business efficacy.

22 At paras 117–119.
23 At para 121.
24 [2015] EWCA Civ 16, [2015] 1 Lloyd's Rep 381.
25 At paras 78–79. Longmore LJ referred (at para 83) to *Rathbone Brothers plc v Novae Corporate Underwriting Ltd* but not on this point.

Express waiver of subrogated rights

12.5   The parties may agree expressly to limit the insurer's rights of subrogation by including a waiver of subrogation clause in the policy wording. An insured might negotiate to have such a clause included in order to protect a subsidiary or affiliated company,[1] or to avoid a potentially damaging claim against an important client. A waiver of subrogation rights may also be agreed after a loss, for example as part of a settlement between insurer and insured.

1 See *The Surf City* [1995] 2 Lloyd's Rep 242.

EXERCISE OF RIGHTS OF SUBROGATION

Defining the subrogated right

12.6   The insurer is entitled to the benefit of all the rights of the insured, in relation to the loss to which the policy responds, by the exercise of which the loss could be, or has been, diminished.[1] Any limitation or restriction to which the insured would have been subject in exercising his rights applies equally to the exercise of the rights by the insurer, who simply 'steps into the shoes' of the insured.[2] The insured may have ceased to exist, in which case, in the absence of an assignment,[3] no action may be brought in its name.[4] Alternatively, the insured may have agreed with a third party, either before or after a loss is suffered, to limit his right of recourse against that party. If so, the insurer's right will be similarly limited, even though the insurer is not aware of the agreement until after the loss has been suffered. The insured is not entitled to enter into any agreement with a third party which prejudices the rights which the insurer may otherwise exercise by way of subrogation.[5] In the absence of an express term which has this effect, a term will be implied that the insured will act reasonably and in good faith with due regard to the insurer's interests and rights of subrogation under the policy; the implied term arises because the insurer has a right to be subrogated to the rights of the insured when he indemnifies him pursuant to the policy of insurance, and if he the insured acts without regard to that contingent right he may harm the value of that right to the insurer.[6] The most obvious harm occurs where the insured settles a claim he may have against a third party for an indemnity and so deprives the insurer of its benefit in whole or in part; but harm may be caused to the insurer's rights of subrogation where the claim against the third party is not lost or reduced in value by settlement, as where, for example, the documents necessary to establish the claim are destroyed.[7] The insurer's remedy in this situation is against its own insured rather than against the third party: if the insured entered into the agreement before proposal of the risk, the insurer may be entitled to avoid the policy on grounds of non-disclosure;[8] otherwise, it will be entitled to damages for breach of contract.[9] Whether a letter of subrogation is a contract for good consideration, for breach of which the insurer would be entitled to damages, will depend on the circumstances.[10] The third party is not entitled to rely on the subrogated nature of the claim, for example by arguing that any profit made by the insurer in relation to arrangements made by it under the policy to hire a replacement vehicle for the insured following a road traffic accident should be deducted from the cost of hire recoverable by the insured from the third party,[11] or that what the insurer could obtain on the open market by way of a 'reasonable repair charge' is relevant in determining the insured's loss.[12] Similarly, it is not permissible for the court to have regard to the fact that a claimant is insured (and has been fully indemnified) in considering the question whether it was reasonable for the claimant (or his insurers) to instruct solicitors on terms which included a success fee.[13]

1 *Castellain v Preston* (1883) 11 QBD 380, 388, CA (Brett LJ).
2 See *Mark Rowlands Ltd v Berni Inns Ltd* [1986] QB 211, 229–232, CA (Kerr LJ), in which a landlord was held not to be entitled under the terms of a lease to bring proceedings against a tenant for negligence in causing a fire, and there was therefore no cause of action to which the landlord's insurer could be subrogated.
3 *Re Ballast plc, St Paul Travelers Insurance Co Ltd v Dargan* [2006] EWHC 3189 (Ch), [2007] Lloyd's Rep IR 742, para 100 (Lawrence Collins J).
4 *M H Smith (Plant Hire) Ltd v D L Mainwaring (t/a Inshore)* [1986] 2 Lloyd's Rep 244, CA; *Re Ballast plc, St Paul Travelers Insurance Co Ltd v Dargan* [2006] EWHC 3189 (Ch), [2007] Lloyd's Rep IR 742, para 100 (Lawrence Collins J). In *M H Smith (Plant Hire) Ltd v D L Mainwaring (t/a Inshore)* [1986] 2 Lloyd's Rep 244, CA, an action was commenced after the insured, which was a limited company, had been wound up. The action was struck out and the solicitors were ordered to pay the costs. As the Court of Appeal indicated, if the solicitors had realised before starting proceedings that the insured had been wound up, an application could have been made to restore it to the register.
5 *Dufourcet & Co v Bishop* (1886) 18 QBD 373, 378–379 (Denman J).
6 *Horwood v Land of Leather* [2010] EWHC 546 (Comm), [2010] Lloyd's Rep IR 453, paras 58 and 67 (Teare J).
7 *Horwood v Land of Leather* [2010] EWHC 546 (Comm), [2010] Lloyd's Rep IR 453, para 67 (Teare J).
8 See *Tate & Sons v Hyslop* (1885) 15 QBD 368, CA (agreement entered into before proposal of risk).
9 *West of England Fire Insurance Co v Isaacs* [1897] 1 QB 226, CA; *Phoenix Assurance Co v Spooner* [1905] 2 KB 753; *Boag v Standard Marine Insurance Co Ltd* [1937] 2 KB 113, CA; *Re Ballast plc, St Paul Travelers Insurance Co Ltd v Dargan* [2006] EWHC 3189 (Ch), [2007] Lloyd's Rep IR 742, para 104 (Lawrence Collins J); *Horwood v Land of Leather* [2010] EWHC 546 (Comm), [2010] Lloyd's Rep IR 453, para 64 (Teare J).
10 The issue was mentioned, but not decided, in *Boag v Standard Marine Insurance Co Ltd* [1937] 2 KB 113, 129, CA (Scott LJ).
11 *Bee v Jenson (No 2)* [2007] EWCA Civ 923, [2008] Lloyd's Rep IR 221; applied: *Coles v Hetherton* [2013] EWCA Civ 1704, [2014] Lloyd's Rep IR 367, para 36 (Aikens LJ).
12 *Coles v Hetherton* [2013] EWCA Civ 1704, [2014] Lloyd's Rep IR 367, paras 34–37 (Aikens LJ).
13 *Sousa v Waltham Forest London Borough Council* [2011] EWCA Civ 194, [2011] 1 WLR 2197, paras 2 and 39 (Ward LJ) and 45-47 (Moore–Bick LJ).

Disclosure

12.7 The obligations as to disclosure and inspection of documents contained in the Civil Procedure Rules (CPR)[1] are imposed on the parties to proceedings. As insurers exercising rights of subrogation bring proceedings in the name of the insured, it is the insured who is the party on the record, and, as a matter of principle, it is the insured on whom the obligation to make disclosure rests. This was the approach taken under the old rules, and it would be surprising if a different result were reached under the Civil Procedure Rules. In *Wilson v Raffalovich*,[2] the Court of Appeal decided that in a recovery action brought by the insurer in the name of the insured, it is the party on the record (ie, the insured) who is required to comply with the rules. The court rejected a submission that the insurers were the 'real' plaintiffs,[3] as the insured had received a full indemnity and had no interest in its outcome, and insisted on full compliance with the insured's disclosure obligations. Jessel MR said:[4]

'As long as these plaintiffs are the plaintiffs on the record, they must be taken to be the parties conducting the litigation, and they must conduct it according to the rules of English jurisprudence and obey the orders of the English Court in which the action is brought.'

Conversely, as the insurers are not the party on the record, they are not subject to any disclosure obligations in relation to documents of their own, such as a report into the circumstances of an accident.[5] If known to exist, such a report might be obtained from insurers by means of an application for disclosure against a non-party under CPR r 31.17.[6]

1 CPR Pt 31.
2 (1881) 7 QBD 553, CA.
3 At 557.
4 At 557–558.
5 *James Nelson & Sons Ltd v Nelson Line (Liverpool) Ltd* [1906] 2 KB 217, CA.
6 See PARA **9.23**.

Funding and control of subrogated actions

12.8 If the insurer has a right to be subrogated to the insured's rights, the insured is obliged to provide all necessary assistance to the insurer, including lending its name to a recovery action brought against a third party.[1] If the insured refuses to authorise a recovery action, the insurer must either bring an action against the insured to compel him to authorise the insurer to proceed in the name of the insured against the third party, or bring an action against both the insured and the third party, in which (1) he claims an order that the insured authorise him to proceed against the third party in the name of the insured, and (2) he seeks to proceed, so authorised, against the third party.[2] In the absence of an assignment, the insurer is not entitled to bring the action in his own name.[3] Alternatively, if the insured brings a recovery action in its own name against a third party, the insurer can recover from him at common law, in an action for money had and received, any moneys recovered by the insured above those required for a full indemnity.[4] In these circumstances, before accounting to the insurer for the sums recovered, the insured is entitled to those costs which may be reasonably and properly attributable to the recovery of the money in question.[5] If an action brought by the insured is only partly covered by insurance, there is no rule of law as to the bearing of costs, and in the absence of any express agreement between insurer and insured, the court is likely to infer from the circumstances an agreement between insurer and insured to bear the costs in proportion to their respective interests in the litigation.[6]

In the absence of a subrogation agreement such as an appropriately worded claims control clause,[7] it appears that if the insured is not fully indemnified by the insurer, the doctrine of subrogation entitles him to bring recovery proceedings in his own name and remain *dominus litis* (the person in control of the litigation).[8] In *Morley v Moore*,[9] the insurer had indemnified the insured in respect of his insured losses and the insured brought proceedings against a third party for both his insured losses and his excess under the policy, which represented his uninsured loss. The insurer had entered into a 'knock-for-knock' agreement with the third party's insurer, and informed the insured that they did not wish him to seek to recover the insured element of his losses. The Court of Appeal rejected the argument by the third party (the defendant to the action) that the effect of the payment of an indemnity by the insurer was to prevent the insured from suing for the insured losses.[10] *Morley v Moore* is therefore authority for the proposition that, where the insured has a claim for uninsured losses against a third party, the insurer has no right under the doctrine of subrogation to prevent the insured from including in that claim losses for which the insurer has indemnified him. In *Hobbs v Marlowe*,[11] the House of Lords declined to decide whether this part of the decision in *Morley v Moore* was correct, on the grounds that all standard forms of motor insurance policies (including that before the House of Lords in *Hobbs v Marlowe*) contained express provisions giving to the insurers the right to institute, conduct and settle legal proceedings in the name of the insured, so the rights of the insurer were unlikely to depend upon the application of the doctrine of subrogation alone but to involve consideration of express clauses in insurance policies.[12]

In *Lord Napier and Ettrick v Hunter*,[13] the House of Lords implied that if the insured wishes to bring proceedings, he is entitled to do so as *dominus litis*. Lord Templeman said that an insured who has been indemnified, in whole or in part, retains the right to enforce any cause of action against the party who occasioned the loss, but the insurer becomes subrogated to the right of the insured to sue and recover damages, and therefore has an interest in the right of action possessed by the insured, as soon as the loss is suffered.[14] The action, if brought by the insured, would be an action for the benefit of the insured and the insurer. The insurer would be entitled to bring an action in the name of the insured if the insured refused to pursue the action.[15] Lord Jauncey said that if an insured suffers an insured loss and an uninsured loss, full indemnification of the former subrogates the insurers irrespective of the fact that the insured has not yet recovered the uninsured loss.[16] Whether these remarks were directed at the issue of who would have control of proceedings against a third party, rather than at the issue of the order of entitlement as between insurer and insured to any recoveries obtained in those proceedings, is unclear. The entitlement to bring and control the proceedings was not in issue in *Lord Napier and Ettrick v Hunter*, which was solely concerned with the allocation of recoveries after the event.

1 *Dufourcet & Co v Bishop* (1886) 18 QBD 373, 379 (Denman J); *Yorkshire Insurance Co Ltd v Nisbet Shipping Co Ltd* [1962] 2 QB 330, 341 (Diplock J).
2 *Esso Petroleum Co Ltd v Hall Russell & Co Ltd* [1989] AC 643, 663, HL (Lord Goff); *Re Ballast plc, St Paul Travelers Insurance Co Ltd v Dargan* [2006] EWHC 3189 (Ch), [2007] Lloyd's Rep IR 742, para 92 (Lawrence Collins J).
3 *Esso Petroleum Co Ltd v Hall Russell & Co Ltd* [1989] AC 643, 663, HL (Lord Goff).
4 *Yorkshire Insurance Co Ltd v Nisbet Shipping Co Ltd* [1962] 2 QB 330, 341–342 (Diplock J). See also **PARA 12.11**.
5 *Assicurazioni Generali de Trieste v Empress Assurance Co Ltd* [1907] 2 KB 814.
6 See *Duus Brown & Co v Binning* (1906) 11 Com Cas 190, 194–195 (Walton J) (insurers would have been entitled to 184/220 of the damages had the recovery action succeeded, and were ordered to pay 184/220 of the costs); applied: *England v Guardian Insurance Ltd* [2000] Lloyd's Rep IR 404, paras 82 and 87 (HHJ Thornton QC).
7 See **PARA 9.13**.
8 *Commercial Union Assurance Co v Lister* (1874) 9 Ch App 483, CA; *Morley v Moore* [1936] 2 KB 359, CA; *Re Ballast plc, St Paul Travelers Insurance Co Ltd v Dargan* [2006] EWHC 3189 (Ch),

[2007] Lloyd's Rep IR 742, paras 102–103 (Lawrence Collins J). The question was expressly left open by the Court of Appeal in *Page v Scottish Insurance Corpn Ltd* (1929) 33 Ll L Rep 134, 138 (Scrutton LJ), before being considered by the Court of Appeal in *Morley v Moore* [1936] 2 KB 359.

9 [1936] 2 KB 359, CA.
10 The Court of Appeal was openly hostile to the idea that a 'knock-for-knock' agreement entered into between insurers for their own purposes might prejudice the insured's rights.
11 [1978] AC 16, HL.
12 At 37–38 (Lord Diplock). See **PARA 9.13**.
13 [1993] AC 713, HL.
14 The insurer's interest in the insured's cause of action is not a proprietary interest: *Re Ballast plc, St Paul Travelers Insurance Co Ltd v Dargan* [2006] EWHC 3189 (Ch), [2007] Lloyd's Rep IR 742, paras 90–109 (Lawrence Collins J).
15 At 731–732.
16 At 747.

Release and settlement

12.9 There may be a clause in the policy of insurance entitling the insurer to control the proceedings and enter into a settlement with third parties, or the insurer and insured may have entered into such an agreement on payment by the insurer of the insured's losses under the policy. Where there is no such agreement, and the insured has exercised his right to bring and control proceedings, he retains the right to release the defendant and to settle any proceedings. It is suggested that the insurer would be entitled to damages for breach of contract if its interests were prejudiced in these circumstances.[1]

1 This is the position where the insured enters into an agreement with a third party which prejudices the rights which the insurer may otherwise exercise by way of subrogation (see **PARA 12.6**), and it is suggested that the remedy must be the same whether the agreement is entered into before or after the commencement of litigation.

Interest[1]

12.10 Insurers who have indemnified an insured are entitled to bring a recovery action in its name not only to recover the loss but also interest, and the fact that they have paid off the insured is *res inter alios acta* as far as the defendant to the recovery action is concerned (which means it is no business of his, and that interest is awarded on the same basis as it would have been if the insurer had not indemnified the insured).[2] Conversely, if the insured has not had to borrow, it is irrelevant that insurers may have had to do so: subrogated insurers cannot be in a better position to recover than the nominal claimant.[3] As between the insurers and the insured, a term is implied into the contract of insurance allowing the insured to retain interest accruing prior to the date of settlement by the insurers, and entitling the insurers to interest thereafter.[4]

1 See **PARA 9.45**.
2 *H Cousins & Co Ltd v D & C Carriers Ltd* [1971] 2 QB 230, CA, distinguishing *Harbutt's Plasticine Ltd v Wayne Tank and Pump Co Ltd* [1970] 1 QB 447, CA.
3 *Pattni v First Leicester Buses Ltd* [2011] EWCA Civ 1384, [2012] Lloyd's Rep IR 577 para 68 (Aikens LJ).
4 *H Cousins & Co Ltd v D & C Carriers Ltd* [1971] 2 QB 230, CA.

Allocation of recoveries

12.11   There are two particular areas of interest in relation to the allocation of insurance recoveries. The first is the allocation of recoveries as between different layers of insurance cover in relation to the same risk where the recoveries are insufficient to allow all losses to be recouped. The law in this respect was authoritatively stated by the House of Lords in *Lord Napier and Ettrick v Hunter*[1] as follows. Where there are layers of insurance, including a self-insured excess, recoveries are allocated to the insurers, to the extent of the indemnity they have paid out, from the top layer downwards. This is because the insurer on the top layer agreed to indemnify the insured only after the lower layers had been exhausted, and so on; and the insured agreed to bear the first layer of the loss, represented by the self-insured excess. In *Lord Napier and Ettrick v Hunter*, the example was given of an underwriting Name at Lloyd's who has suffered a loss of £160,000, and who is insured with a limit of indemnity of £100,000 in excess of the policy excess of £25,000. After the stop loss insurer had paid the name £100,000, the Name recovered £130,000, and an issue arose as to the allocation of that sum as between the insured and the insurer. At first instance, Saville J decided that the hypothetical Name would be entitled to be fully indemnified for his loss of £160,000 before paying any part of the recoveries to the insurer. The Name had received £100,000 from insurers and £130,000 from the third party, so £230,000 in all, of which he would be entitled to retain £160,000. The insurer would therefore be entitled to recover £70,000 from the Name. The Court of Appeal and the House of Lords both disagreed with this analysis. Lord Templeman said that,[2] if there had been three separate insurances for each layer (in excess of £125,000; £100,000 excess of £25,000; and up to £25,000), the third insurer would be first to be subrogated because he only agreed to pay if the first two insurances did not cover the total loss. He would therefore be entitled to recover the £35,000 he had paid to the Name. The second insurer would be entitled to be subrogated second because he only agreed to pay if the first insurance cover proved insufficient; accordingly, he would be entitled to recover £95,000, as that would exhaust the £130,000 recovered from the third party. There would be nothing to recoup to the second insurer, the balance of £5,000 out of the £100,000 he had paid under his policy, and nothing left by way of subrogation for the first insurer in respect of the first £25,000 which he agreed to bear. Lord Templeman held that the position was no different simply because the Name had agreed to act as his own insurer in respect of the first and third layers in the example, and that the insured was not entitled to be indemnified against a loss which he had agreed to bear. He was entitled to recoup his losses in excess of £125,000 out of the £130,000 (the first £35,000, as in the example of the three insurances), but not the £25,000 excess, as he had agreed to bear the first £25,000 of the loss, and therefore to recoup these losses last.

The second area of interest is the allocation of recoveries which exceed the insured's loss. This is a situation likely to occur only rarely. Where an insurer pays for the total loss of the subject matter insured and an action is brought against a third party in which more than the amount paid by the insurer is recovered, it is the insured who is entitled to thè surplus, whether the action is brought before or after payment by the insurer and whether the action is brought by the insured or by the insurer in the insured's name.[3] In *Lord Napier and Ettrick v Hunter*, Lord Templeman's reasoning was as follows:[4]

'In my opinion promises implied in a contract of insurance with regard to rights of action vested in the insured person for the recovery of an insured loss from a third party responsible for the loss confer on the insurer an equitable interest in those rights of action to the extent necessary to recoup the insurer who has indemnified the insured person against the insured loss.'

The insurer holds the surplus recoveries on trust for the insured.[5]

1 [1993] AC 713, HL.
2 At 729–731.
3 *Glen Line v Attorney General* (1930) 36 Com Cas 1, 13–14, HL (Lord Atkin); *Yorkshire Insurance Co Ltd v Nisbet Shipping Co Ltd* [1962] 2 QB 330 (Diplock J); *Lord Napier and Ettrick v Hunter* [1993] AC 713, HL.
4 [1993] AC 713, 736, HL.
5 *Lonrho Exports Ltd v Export Credit Guarantee Department* [1999] Ch 158, 181–182, [1996] 2 Lloyd's Rep 649, 661 (Lightman J).

Enforcement of insurer's right of recovery against insured

12.12   The insured holds the recovery on trust for the insurer,[1] and the insurer has a personal right of action at law to recover the amount received by the insured as money had and received to the use of the insurer.[2] The equitable interest in the insured's rights of action, identified by the House of Lords in *Lord Napier and Ettrick v Hunter*[3] provides the insurer with protection against the bankruptcy or insolvency of the insured.[4] The insurer can give notice of his equitable interest to the third party against whom the insured has a right of action, and his interest will be protected by the court, if necessary by the grant of injunctive relief.[5] If the third party agrees or is ordered to pay damages to the insured, he should either pay the damages into court or decline to pay without the consent of both the insured and the insurer.[6]

1 *Bee v Jenson (No 2)* [2007] EWCA Civ 923, [2008] Lloyd's Rep IR 221, para 9 (Longmore LJ).
2 *Yorkshire Insurance Co Ltd v Nisbet Shipping Co Ltd* [1962] 2 QB 330 (Diplock J); *Lord Napier and Ettrick v Hunter* [1993] AC 713, HL.
3 See **PARA 12.11**.
4 *Lord Napier and Ettrick v Hunter* [1993] AC 713, 737, IIL (Lord Templeman).
5 *Lord Napier and Ettrick v Hunter* [1993] AC 713, 738–739, HL (Lord Templeman).
6 *Lord Napier and Ettrick v Hunter* [1993] AC 713, 738, HL (Lord Templeman).

Definition of recoveries

12.13   The doctrine of subrogation has its roots in the principle that an insured should be indemnified in respect of his loss, but should never receive more than a full indemnity, because that would convert a contract of indemnity into a wager. In determining whether a payment made to the insured is to be taken into account in determining whether he has received a full indemnity, the crucial question is whether the payment reduces or diminishes the loss in respect of which an indemnity is provided pursuant to the policy of insurance.[1] This is usually a straightforward question. Particular problems have arisen, however, in relation to gifts.

The basic principle is uncontroversial: the doctrine of subrogation does not extend to gifts made to the insured by a third party. It is well established that insurers are not entitled to the benefit of such gifts and, accordingly, that allowing the insured to retain gifts made in connection with a loss covered by an insurance policy does not offend against the principle that the insured should receive a full indemnity but no more.[2] In principle, a gift reduces the insured's loss in just the same way as damages for breach of contract or tort obtained pursuant to a recovery action, and the true reason for excepting gifts is not that they do not reduce the loss, but that it would be repugnant to allow a wrongdoer to take advantage of a third party's benevolence, and might discourage such acts of benevolence.

The difficulty has arisen in connection with determining which voluntary payments by third parties are gifts, and which are not. An obvious approach to the problem of identifying gifts would be to allow an insurer to have a sum brought into account in diminution of the loss only if it were the product of a right existing in the insured at the time of the loss.[3] However, this approach would be inconsistent with the decision in *Randal v Cockran*,[4] in which insurers were held to be subrogated to prizes granted by the King to compensate the insureds, as British subjects, for losses which they had suffered at the hands of the Spanish.

In *Burnand v Rodocanachi*, the principle that a gift is not to be taken to reduce the insured's loss was conceded, and the argument concerned whether the money paid to the insured pursuant to a US Act of Congress was to be taken to reduce the insured's loss or was to be treated as if it were a simple gift. The Act was passed subsequent to the loss, and so the claim to compensation was not a right existing in the insured at the time of the loss. The Act declared expressly that no payments were to be made on account of loss which was covered by insurance, and that underwriters were not to receive any benefit from funds distributed under the Act. Lord Blackburn stated that the question was whether the party paying the money to the insured did so for the purpose of repaying or reducing the loss against which the insurance company had indemnified him.[5] As it did not, the insurer was not entitled to take the benefit of the payment. In *Colonia Versicherung AG v Amoco Oil Co*,[6] the Court of Appeal considered *Burnand v Rodocanachi*, and identified the crucial question to be whether the party making the payment intended to benefit the insured to the exclusion of the insurer.[7] This formulation appears to presuppose knowledge of the doctrine of subrogation, and to that extent is probably only applicable in a commercial context, where borderline cases are most likely to arise.[8] Outside the commercial sphere, a donor may intend to benefit the insured and have no intention either way in relation to the insurer, but there is arguably a presumption in these circumstances that the intention would not be to benefit the insurer.

1 *Burnand v Rodocanachi* (1882) 7 App Cas 333, 339, HL (Lord Blackburn).
2 *Burnand v Rodocanachi* (1882) 7 App Cas 333, HL; *Colonia Versicherung AG v Amoco Oil Co* [1997] 1 Lloyd's Rep 261, 270, CA (Hirst LJ).
3 *Castellain v Preston* (1883) 11 QBD 380, 395, CA (Cotton LJ).
4 (1748) 1 Ves Sen 98. The entire case report is only one paragraph long. If there was any discussion of the fact that the prizes were gifts, it does not appear in the report.
5 (1882) 7 App Cas 333, 341, HL.
6 [1997] 1 Lloyd's Rep 261, CA.
7 At 270 (Hirst LJ).
8 See *Merrett v Capitol Indemnity Corpn* [1991] 1 Lloyd's Rep 169 (payment made by brokers to the reinsured for the purpose of retaining the reinsured's goodwill, and therefore to benefit the reinsured and

not for the benefit of the reinsurer); approved: *Talbot Underwriting Ltd v Nausch, Hogan & Murray Inc (The Jascon 5)* [2006] EWCA Civ 889, [2006] 2 Lloyd's Rep 195, paras 64 and 66 (Moore-Bick LJ).

SUBROGATION AND CONTRIBUTION

12.14   The insured may have a contractual right of both indemnity and insurance in respect of the same loss. Whether insurers are entitled to bring a subrogated recovery action to enforce the insured's contractual right of indemnity against the other contracting party, or whether the claim is one for contribution between two parties liable to indemnify the insured, depends on the construction of the agreement containing the contractual indemnity.[1] In *Caledonia North Sea Ltd v British Telecommunications plc*,[2] the House of Lords held that the contract between the parties and the commercial scheme of which it was part made it plain that the primary liability was to fall on the contractor, so that the insurer was entitled to be subrogated to the insured's contractual right of indemnity.

1 *Caledonia North Sea Ltd v British Telecommunications plc* [2002] UKHL 4, [2002] 1 Lloyd's Rep 553, approving *North British and Mercantile Insurance Co v London, Liverpool and Globe Insurance Co* (1877) 5 Ch D 569, CA.
2 [2002] UKHL 4, [2002] 1 Lloyd's Rep 553.

SUBROGATION AND S 14A OF THE LIMITATION ACT 1980

12.15   Section 14A of the Limitation Act 1980 applies to actions for negligence where facts relevant to the cause of action are not known at the date of accrual, and extends the limitation period to three years from the earliest date on which the claimant or any person in whom the cause of the action was vested before him first had both the knowledge required for bringing an action in damages in respect of the relevant damage and a right to bring such an action.[1] In the context of a subrogated claim, the person whose knowledge is relevant for these proposals, referred to s 14A as 'the plaintiff', has been construed as 'meaning/extending to a plaintiff whether suing in his own name or the name of another by way of subrogation'.[2] It would appear, from the inclusion of the phrase 'extending to', that in an appropriate case the knowledge of both insurer and insured might be taken into account for the purposes of s 14A. This construction appears to be based on the notion that it is the insurer who is the 'real' claimant, and sits uneasily with the principle that it is the insured, as the party on the record, on whom the obligation to make disclosure rests.[3] In *Graham v Entec Europe Ltd*,[4] the knowledge of a loss adjuster appointed by insurers to investigate the insured's claim was held to be attributable to insurers, and was thereby held to constitute knowledge of the claimant ('plaintiff') for the purposes of s 14A(5) of the 1980 Act.

1 See **PARA 16.31**.
2 *Graham v Entec Europe Ltd* [2003] EWCA Civ 1177, [2004] Lloyd's Rep IR 660, para 37 (Potter LJ).
3 See **PARA 12.7**.
4 [2003] EWCA Civ 1177, [2004] Lloyd's Rep IR 660, para 38 (Potter LJ).

Chapter 13

Double insurance and contribution

DOUBLE INSURANCE

13.1   It sometimes happens that more than one indemnity policy covers the same subject matter, the same interest, and the same peril or risk.[1] This is known as double insurance. Double insurance usually results from an overlap of cover between two policies, each designed primarily to cover a different interest: for example, the insured may have a household insurance policy with an extension to cover certain items of personal property outside the home, and a motor insurance policy under which those items are also covered when in the vehicle. The indemnity principle requires that the insured should not recover more than the amount of his loss, and he cannot therefore recover the full amount of his loss from both insurers.[2] He may, however, in the absence of any provision to the contrary in the policy, recover the whole of his loss from either insurer, rather than claiming a proportion of the loss from each. If he does so, the insurer who has indemnified the insured is entitled to contribution from the other insurer. This is an equitable principle, the operation of which is commonly modified by standard provisions in insurance contracts,[3] and by agreements between insurers.[4] Special principles apply to contribution in employer's liability insurance in respect of diseases within what is known as the '*Fairchild* enclave', including mesothelioma.[5]

1 If there is any doubt as to whether there is double insurance, the doubt is usually resolved in favour of the insured: see *Australian Agricultural Co v Saunders* (1875) LR 10 CP 668; *Portavon Cinema Co Ltd v Price* (1939) 65 Ll L Rep 161, [1939] 4 All ER 601.
2 See *Bovis Construction Ltd v Commercial Union Assurance Co plc* [2001] 1 Lloyd's Rep 416, paras 10–11 (David Steel J).
3 For example, non-contribution or rateable proportion clauses (see **PARAS 13.3–13.5**), or clauses which provide that the insurance is to respond only when the limit of indemnity under the other insurance is reached.
4 Such agreements do not give rise to legally enforceable obligations: *Drake Insurance plc v Provident Insurance plc* [2003] EWCA Civ 1834, [2004] 1 Lloyd's Rep 268, para 40 (Rix LJ).
5 See **PARA 13.14**.

INTEREST AND INSURED MUST BE SAME UNDER EACH POLICY

13.2   Contribution applies only in respect of insurance by the same person in respect of the same rights, and does not apply where different persons insure different rights.[1]

It does not apply therefore in respect of bailee and owner of goods,[2] mortgagor and mortgagee,[3] or successive mortgagees.[4]

In *North British and Mercantile Insurance Co v London, Liverpool and Globe Insurance Co*,[5] a firm of wharfingers, Barnett & Co, insured grain, some of which they owned, and for some of which, although it was owned by others, they were responsible. The policy contained the following condition:

> 'if at the time of any loss or damage by fire happening to any property hereby insured, there be any other subsisting insurance or insurances, whether effected by the insured or by any other person, covering the same property, the company shall not be liable to pay or contribute more than its rateable proportion of such loss or damage.'

A fire destroyed a quantity of the grain, some of which belonged to Rodocanachi & Co. Rodocanachi & Co had also taken out merchants' policies on the grain, which included a similar condition to that contained in the wharfingers' policy. The Court of Appeal held that there could be no contribution between the two insurers, as the right to contribution arose only where the same person insured the same interest with more than one insurer.[6] The condition applied only where a right to contribution arose.[7] The decision is important both because it established the basis for a right of contribution between insurers, and because many modern policies contain a similar condition.

In *National Farmers Union Mutual Insurance Society Ltd v HSBC Insurance Ltd*,[8] a house was badly damaged by fire between exchange and completion. The sellers of a house were covered under a policy of buildings insurance issued by HSBC (the HSBC policy) which included an extension of cover which applied until completion of the sale in favour of 'anyone buying your home'. The extension was subject to a proviso that there was no cover 'if the buildings are insured under any other insurance'. The buyers took out buildings insurance with NFU (the NFU policy) which contained no provision excluding coverage in the event that the buyers were otherwise insured in respect of the same risk. The judge held that the grant of buildings cover by HSBC to buyers of its insured's home was directly qualified by the proviso: the one could not properly be separated from the other and any buyer had to take the grant as it found it, viz as a qualified extension of cover.[9] As the buyers had taken out cover covering the same risks as those in the HSBC policy with another insurer, the HSBC policy did not provide an indemnity to the buyers in respect of the fire and damage to the property.[10]

1 *North British and Mercantile Insurance Co v London, Liverpool and Globe Insurance Co* (1877) 5 Ch D 569, 583, CA (Mellish LJ).
2 *North British and Mercantile Insurance Co v London, Liverpool and Globe Insurance Co* (1877) 5 Ch D 569, CA.
3 *North British and Mercantile Insurance Co v London, Liverpool and Globe Insurance Co* (1877) 5 Ch D 569, CA (see, eg, 583 (Mellish LJ)).
4 *North British and Mercantile Insurance Co v London, Liverpool and Globe Insurance Co* (1877) 5 Ch D 569, 577, CA (Jessel MR, judgment approved by the Court of Appeal at 580–588).
5 (1877) 5 Ch D 569, CA. The case is also known as the King and Queen Granaries case, after the granaries in Rotherhithe in which the grain was stored.
6 At 581 (James LJ).
7 At 582 (James LJ).
8 [2010] EWHC 773 (Comm), [2011] Lloyd's Rep IR 86.

9 At para 20 (Gavin Kealey QC, sitting as a Deputy High Court Judge).
10 At para 23 (Gavin Kealey QC, sitting as a Deputy High Court Judge).

NON-CONTRIBUTION AND EXCESS INSURANCE CLAUSES

13.3 At one time, motor insurance policies commonly included a clause designed, in a case of double insurance, to relieve the insurer of his equitable obligation to contribute. Such clauses are sometimes referred to as 'non-contribution clauses'. As a matter of principle, non-contribution clauses are effective.[1] However, where two or more policies each contain such a clause, the courts have rejected as absurd any construction relieving both insurers of their liability to the insured, and leaving the insured without insurance. They have, instead, treated the clauses as cancelling each other out, with liability being shared equally between the two insurers. In *Gale v Motor Union Insurance Co*,[2] the driver of a motor car was involved in an accident. He was insured in respect of third party damage by two policies, one in his own name and one in the name of the owner of the vehicle. Each policy contained clauses which provided that if the risk was covered by another policy, the insurers would not be liable, and that where two policies covering the risk were in existence, the insurers should pay a rateable proportion of any loss. Roche J construed the clauses as meaning, first, that if there were another policy which would provide a full indemnity, insurers would not be liable; and second, that a partial indemnity would be provided in a case of double insurance. Where, therefore, each policy included such clauses, the provision as to rateable contribution qualified and explained the preceding clause negativing liability, and each insurer was obliged to pay a rateable proportion, agreed to be half, of the loss. In *Weddell v Road Transport and General Insurance Co Ltd*,[3] the driver was insured under two polices, each of which contained a clause which provided that if the risk was covered by another policy, the insurers would not be liable. One policy also contained a rateable proportion clause, but the other did not. Rowlatt J held that the reasonable construction of each clause was to exclude from the category of 'other existing insurance' any cover which was expressed to be cancelled by such co-existence, so that both insurers were liable, subject to any rateable proportion clause. *Weddell v Road Transport and General Insurance Co Ltd*[4] was followed by Tucker J in *Austin v Zurich General Accident and Liability Insurance Co Ltd*.[5] In *Austin's* case, the driver was insured under two motor insurance policies, each of which contained a clause which provided that if the risk was covered by another policy, the insurers would not be liable. One policy contained a rateable proportion clause in the standard form (the Zurich policy). The other contained a clause which provided that, where there was another 'subsisting' insurance, the insurer would not be liable to pay or contribute towards the injury, loss or damage, 'except in excess of the sum or sums actually recovered or recoverable under such other indemnity or insurance' (the Bell policy). Tucker J rejected an argument that *Weddell's* case was distinguishable and held, without further analysis, that each insurer was (as in *Weddell's* case) liable to indemnify the insured to the extent of 50% of his loss. The correctness of this conclusion was doubted by Gavin Kealey QC (sitting as a Deputy High Court Judge) in *National Farmers Union Mutual Insurance Society Ltd v HSBC Insurance Ltd*[6]. The judge said that he was uncertain as to how one could equate the rateable proportion clause in the Zurich policy with the excess provision in the Bell policy in order to come to the result that each of Bell and Zurich agreed to pay its insured, if that insured was equivalently covered by another insurer, 50 per cent of the insured loss, and suggested that the correct outcome in *Austin's* case would have been that the Zurich policy was liable to indemnify the driver to the extent of its limits without contribution from the Bell policy, above which the Bell policy provided excess cover.[7]

In *National Farmers Union Mutual Insurance Society Ltd v HSBC Insurance Ltd*,[8] the HSBC policy included an 'other insurance' clause in the following terms: 'We will not pay any claim if any loss, damage or liability covered under this insurance is also covered wholly or in part under any other insurance except in respect of any excess beyond the amount which would have been covered under such other insurance had this insurance not been effected'.[9] This clause applied to all sections of the HSBC policy including buildings insurance. The judge held that, as a matter of construction, the qualification provision in HSBC's buildings insurance section was a special clause applying specifically to qualify any potential extension of the insurance granted by HSBC to its insured so as to cover a buyer of the insured's home and that, as a matter of construction, this special clause took precedence over the general provisions in the policy including the 'other insurance' clause.[10]

1 See *Legal and General Assurance Society Ltd v Drake Insurance Co Ltd* [1992] QB 887, 893, CA (Lloyd LJ).
2 [1928] 1 KB 359.
3 [1932] 2 KB 563; approved (obiter, ie not necessary for the judge's conclusion in the case and therefore not binding as a matter of precedent): *National Employers' Mutual General Insurance Association Ltd* [1980] 2 Lloyd's Rep 149, CA; applied (obiter): *Structural Polymer Systems Ltd v Brown* [2000] Lloyd's Rep IR 64, 75 (Moore-Bick J).
4 [1932] 2 KB 563.
5 (1944) 77 Ll L Rep 409; approved: [1945] KB 250, CA.
6 [2010] EWHC 773 (Comm), [2011] Lloyd's Rep IR 86.
7 At para 46. This was obiter, ie not necessary for the judge's conclusion in the case and therefore not binding as a matter of precedent); although there was no cross-appeal by Zurich in *Austin*'s case requiring the Court of Appeal to consider the double insurance aspects of Tucker J's judgment, that judgment was nonetheless expressly approved by MacKinnon LJ in the Court of Appeal: [1945] KB 250, 258: 'The judgment of Tucker J seems to me to be a masterly and admirable one in which no error can be found.'
8 [2010] EWHC 773 (Comm), [2011] Lloyd's Rep IR 86; see **PARA 13.2**.
9 At para 25.
10 At para 26 (Gavin Kealey QC, sitting as a Deputy High Court Judge).

CONTRIBUTION WHERE ONE INSURER ENTITLED TO REPUDIATE LIABILITY

13.4 In *Weddell v Road Transport and General Insurance Co Ltd*,[1] it was argued that a policy which did not respond to the claim, because of failure to comply with a condition as to the giving of notice of an accident, did not amount to 'other existing insurance' for the purposes of a rateable proportion clause. Rowlatt J rejected the argument as 'too obviously unsound as to require further notice', and said, without giving any reasons, that the relevant time for considering the position was before the time for giving notice had expired. In *Jenkins v Deane*,[2] Goddard J took the opposite view, holding that a policy which had been repudiated was not 'subsisting' within the meaning of the rateable proportion clause, the burden of proving that the policy had not been repudiated being on the insurer seeking to apply the clause. As the insurer was, on the evidence available, unable to prove that the policy had not been repudiated, it was liable for the whole loss as against the plaintiff, subject to its right of contribution against the other insurer. In neither of these cases was a claim being made for contribution, and they are, in strict terms, binding only on the issue of construction of non-contribution clauses.[3] However, in *Austin v Zurich General Accident and Liability Insurance Co Ltd*,[4] a claim for contribution between insurers was brought, incorrectly, in the name of the insured. The Court of Appeal held that Zurich were entitled to repudiate liability because the driver, Austin, who was insured to drive the car by Zurich not by his own policy with them but by virtue of an extension to the owner's policy, had failed to notify Zurich of an impending prosecution in accordance with the conditions of the owner's policy. The Court of Appeal's analysis was that Austin could not take the benefit of the policy without complying with its conditions.[5]

In *Monksfield v Vehicle and General Insurance Co Ltd*,[6] another case of double motor vehicle insurance, the first insurer paid the whole of a third party accident claim, and sought contribution from the second insurer. Each of the policies contained a condition which relieved the insurer from liability if the insured was entitled to an indemnity under any other policy of insurance. The insured had failed to comply with the conditions as to notice in the policy issued by the second insurer, who would therefore have been entitled to repudiate if the claim had been brought by the insured. The court held that the second insurer was entitled to rely on the conditions in its policy, and was therefore not liable for contribution. Although *Monksfield v Vehicle and General Insurance Co Ltd* was overruled by a majority decision of the Court of Appeal in *Legal and General Assurance Society Ltd v Drake Insurance Co Ltd*,[7] it was approved shortly afterwards by the Privy Council in *Eagle Star Insurance Co Ltd v Provincial Insurance plc*.[8] The approach taken by the majority in *Legal and General Assurance Society Ltd v Drake Insurance Co Ltd* was that it was at the date of loss that the question of double insurance should be assessed, so that if the insurer was 'potentially liable' at that date (would be liable if the insured complied with the policy conditions, in circumstances in which the insured was still able to do so), there was double insurance. If, however, the insurer was already entitled to repudiate as at the date of loss, for example, by reason of misrepresentation or non-disclosure, even if he had not done so (or even, it would seem, if he was not aware that he was entitled to do so), there was no double insurance.[9] In *Eagle Star Insurance Co Ltd v Provincial Insurance plc*, the Privy Council was considering the position as between two motor insurers where both insurers were required by statute to indemnify a third party. The Privy Council held that the respective liabilities of the insurers should be decided according to their respective contractual liabilities to the person insured, rather than their respective statutory liabilities, and that no arbitrary cut-off date for considering the contractual liabilities, such as the date of loss, should be imposed simply for the purposes of contribution. It is suggested that the approach of the Privy Council should be preferred as it respects the contractual position as between the insured and each insurer.[10] The apparent unfairness of an insurer being unable to claim contribution due to the failure of an insured to comply with contractual conditions is mitigated by the fact that, in the normal course of events, neither insurer knows of the other's existence until after the loss has occurred, so that each is expecting to bear the whole of any loss; and that the same insurer is entitled to rely on similar failures to comply with contractual conditions in respect of other claims.

1 [1932] 2 KB 563.
2 (1933) 47 LL L Rep 342, 346.
3 See *Eagle Star Insurance Co Ltd v Provincial Insurance plc* [1994] 1 AC 130, 141, PC, approving the dissenting judgment of Ralph Gibson LJ in *Legal and General Assurance Society Ltd v Drake Insurance Co Ltd* [1992] QB 887, 902–904, CA.
4 [1945] KB 250, CA.
5 At 255 (Lord Greene MR) (approved by Lord Denning MR and applied in the context of the Third Parties (Rights Against Insurers) Act 1930: *Farrell v Federated Employers Insurance Association Ltd* [1970] 1 WLR 1400, 1406, CA).
6 [1971] 1 Lloyd's Rep 139.
7 [1992] QB 887.
8 [1994] 1 AC 130.
9 At 892–893 (Lloyd LJ).
10 In *Bolton Metropolitan Borough Council v Municipal Mutual Insurance Ltd* [2006] EWCA Civ 50, [2006] 1 WLR 1492, paras 36–38, Longmore LJ said, without deciding the issue, that he preferred the reasoning of the Privy Council.

RATEABLE PROPORTION CLAUSES

13.5 Policies often contain a clause which provides that, where there is double insurance, the insurer will not be liable for more than its rateable proportion of the loss. The intended effect of such a clause is to seek to supersede the doctrine of equitable contribution by limiting the primary liability of each insurer to the rateable proportion which the doctrine would otherwise achieve.[1] 'Rateable proportion' means that proportion which would ultimately be borne by any one insurer if the insured were entitled to claim, and had claimed, from him alone, and the insurer had then exercised his right to claim equitable contribution from any other insurers.[2] Although rateable proportion clauses do not oblige the insured to claim from each insurer, it will be necessary for the insured to do so if he is to obtain a full indemnity. Instead of the insured being able to claim the whole of his loss from one insurer, the insured has to claim a proportion of the loss from each insurer, both relieving the insurer of the administrative burden of claiming from the co-insurers,[3] and transferring from the insurers and onto the insured the risk of insolvency of any of the co-insurers. Where each of two policies of insurance contains a rateable proportion clause and one insurer rejects the insured's claim, the other insurer will not be regarded as a volunteer if it pays the whole claim, provided that it does so under reserve or protest to the first insurer; and if it thereafter succeeds in establishing that the first insurer was liable to the insured, it will be entitled to recover from the first insurer the proportion of the claim which the first insurer was liable to pay to the insured pursuant to the rateable proportion clause.[4] Where there are multiple insureds, it is a matter of construction whether a rateable proportion clause will apply where there is other insurance effected by any one of the insureds, or only where the other insurance is effected by all of them.[5]

1 *Drake Insurance plc v Provident Insurance plc* [2003] EWCA Civ 1834, [2004] 1 Lloyd's Rep 268, para 32 (Rix LJ).
2 *Commercial Union Assurance Co Ltd v Hayden* [1977] 1 Lloyd's Rep 1, 3 (Donaldson J).
3 This was the purpose behind the introduction of such clauses: *North British and Mercantile Insurance Co v London, Liverpool and Globe Insurance Co* (1877) 5 Ch D 569, 588, CA (Baggallay JA).

4 *Drake Insurance plc v Provident Insurance plc* [2003] EWCA Civ 1834, [2004] 1 Lloyd's Rep 268, paras 124–127 (Rix LJ), 158 (Clarke LJ) and 188 (Pill LJ).
5 See *General Accident Fire and Life Assurance Corpn Ltd v Midland Bank Ltd* [1940] 2 KB 388, 409, CA (Sir Wilfred Greene MR).

CALCULATION OF CONTRIBUTION

13.6 Historically, the calculation of contribution between insurers has been the subject of agreement, either on a case-by-case basis, or pursuant to market agreements. As a result, there is very little case law available for guidance in difficult or controversial cases.

The two leading methods for calculating contribution are the 'maximum liability' method and the 'independent liability' method. Under the maximum liability method, contribution is calculated in proportion to the limits of the respective policies, so that where one policy has a limit of liability which is twice that of the other, that insurer will contribute twice as much as the other (two-thirds of the total). Under the independent liability method, contribution is calculated in accordance with the respective liabilities of each insurer had each been the sole insurer, so that where the claim is within the limit of liability of both policies, liability is shared equally between the insurers.

The leading authority on the method of calculation of contribution is the decision of the Court of Appeal in *Commercial Union Assurance Co Ltd v Hayden*,[1] a case of contribution between public liability insurers.[2] The insured effected two public liability policies, one with the claimant insurer with a limit of £100,000 for any one accident, and the other with the defendant insurer with a sum insured of £10,000. An accident occurred at the insured's premises, and a claim arising out of the accident was settled in the sum of approximately £4,425. The question was, the Court of Appeal said, one of construction of the policies, the language of which was equally capable of bearing the maximum liability or independent liability construction. This being so, the Court of Appeal preferred the independent liability method, as being more realistic in its results and therefore more likely to be intended by reasonable business men. In reaching this conclusion, the Court of Appeal took into account the fact that the obvious purpose of having a limit of liability under an insurance policy was not to adjust liability between insurers in a case of double insurance, but to protect the insurer from the effect of large claims, and that there would be situations in which it would be difficult to apply the maximum liability method, for example, where one policy had no limit on liability, or where one policy had a limit for 'any one accident' and the other for 'any one accident or series of accidents arising out of any one event'. An application of the independent liability method resulted in the insurers sharing the liability equally. If the claim had exceeded the lower of the two limits of liability, the claim would have been shared equally up to the lower limit, and that part of the claim above the limit would have been borne by the insurer who had accepted the higher limit.[3]

1 [1977] 1 Lloyd's Rep 1, CA.
2 See also *American Surety Co of New York v Wrightson* (1910) 16 Com Cas 37 (liability insurance).
3 At 16–17 (Lawton LJ).

CLAUSES REQUIRING DISCLOSURE OF 'OTHER INSURANCE'

13.7 Policies sometimes contain a condition requiring disclosure of other insurance, whether pre-existing or subsequent, and provide that if disclosure is not made, no claim will be paid. The courts have mitigated the rigours of such conditions by construing them strictly against insurers, and striving to reach a reasonable construction, having regard to the business nature of insurance transactions.[1] In *Australian Agricultural Co v Saunders*,[2] a consignment of wool was insured under a goods policy and also under a marine policy. The wool was damaged by fire while in the stevedores' warehouse. The marine policy was held not to cover the wool in the stevedores' warehouse, and there was therefore no double insurance. The decision is of interest for the construction placed on the following provision in the goods policy:

> 'No claim shall be recoverable if the property insured be previously or subsequently insured elsewhere, unless the particulars of such insurance be notified to the company in writing.'

The court held that the provision applied only to insurances specifically covering the same risk (in respect of which it would have been effective), and did not apply where there was merely a possibility of an accidental overlap between some portion of the risk covered by each policy.[3] Similarly, where a policy has been delivered, but is not effective until the first premium is paid, and no premium is paid, the policy is not an insurance which needs to be disclosed pursuant to a condition of this type.[4] Further, a requirement that other insurance be disclosed does not require disclosure of the identity of the insurer; nor is there any need to disclose the fact that the policies originally disclosed have been substituted.[5]

1 See *National Protector Fire Insurance Co Ltd v Nivert* [1913] AC 507, 513, PC (Lord Atkinson).
2 (1875) LR 10 CP 668.
3 In *National Employers' Mutual General Insurance Association Ltd v Hayden* [1979] 2 Lloyd's Rep 235, Lloyd J distinguished *Australian Agricultural Co v Saunders* and held that, in deciding whether there was double insurance, once an overlap was found to exist, the extent of the overlap in relation to the cover as a whole provided by either policy was irrelevant (at 239; this point was not considered on appeal: [1980] 2 Lloyd's Rep 149, CA).
4 *Equitable Fire and Accident Office Ltd v Ching Wo Hong* [1907] AC 96, PC.
5 *National Protector Fire Insurance Co Ltd v Nivert* [1913] AC 507, PC.

PROHIBITION OF OTHER INSURANCES

13.8 In *General Insurance Co of Trieste Ltd (Assicurazioni Generali) v Cory*,[1] a policy was taken out by a ship owner to cover the probable deficiency on a policy underwritten by a group of underwriters whose insolvency, or probable insolvency, was known. The court held that, to the extent that any of the underwriters proved not to be insolvent, this amounted to double insurance and would be recoverable by means of contribution between insurers, and on this basis did not breach a warranty that, of the £12,000 declared value of the steamship, £2,400 would remain uninsured.

1 [1897] 1 QB 335.

VOLUNTARY PAYMENTS

13.9 There is no right of contribution in respect of payments made voluntarily by insurers.[1] The right to contribution arises whether the obligation to make the payment is contractual only, or is supplemented by statute,[2] but where a statute permits the insurer making the payment to recover from the insured any amount paid in excess of its contractual entitlement, the insurer will not be entitled to contribution from any other insurer in respect of the overpayment.[3] Where each of two policies of insurance contains a rateable proportion clause and one insurer rejects the insured's claim, the other insurer will not be regarded as a volunteer if it pays the whole claim, provided that it does so under reserve or protest to the first insurer; and if it thereafter succeeds in establishing that the first insurer was liable to the insured, it will be entitled to recover from the first insurer the proportion of the claim which the first insurer was liable to pay to the insured pursuant to the rateable proportion clause.[4]

1 *Eagle Star Insurance Co Ltd v Provincial Insurance plc* [1994] 1 AC 130, PC; *Bovis Construction Ltd v Commercial Union Assurance Co plc* [2001] 1 Lloyd's Rep 416 (David Steel J).
2 See *Eagle Star Insurance Co Ltd v Provincial Insurance plc* [1994] 1 AC 130, PC.
3 *Legal and General Assurance Society Ltd v Drake Insurance Co Ltd* [1992] QB 887, CA: the statutory provision in question was s 151 of the Road Traffic Act 1988.
4 *Drake Insurance plc v Provident Insurance plc* [2003] EWCA Civ 1834, [2004] 1 Lloyd's Rep 268, paras 124–127 (Rix LJ), 158 (Clarke LJ) and 188 (Pill LJ).

CIVIL LIABILITY (CONTRIBUTION) ACT 1978

13.10 An alternative possible avenue of recourse against a 'double insurer' in respect of policy liabilities based on breach of an obligation assumed on or after 1 January 1979 is the Civil Liability (Contribution) Act 1978.[1] The argument would be that both insurers are liable for 'the same damage' within the meaning of s 1(1) of the Act.[2] If insurance contract liabilities are viewed as sounding in damages, it appears somewhat surprising if the Act could operate as an alternative statutory remedy with different effect in a case of true double insurance.[3]

An insurer's obligation to indemnify its insured in respect of damage caused by a third party does not render it liable 'in respect of the same damage' as that third party for the purposes of s 1(1) of the Civil Liability (Contribution) Act 1978.[4] The third party is therefore not entitled to contribution from the insurer under the Act.

1 *International Energy Group Ltd v Zurich Insurance plc* [2015] UKSC 33, [2016] AC 509, paras 64 (Lord Mance, with whom Lords Clarke, Carnwath and Hodge agreed). Lord Sumption said at para 181 (Lords Neuberger and Reed agreeing) that he thought it clear that there was a statutory right of contribution under the 1978 Act and could see no principled reason for questioning it.
2 *International Energy Group Ltd v Zurich Insurance plc* [2015] UKSC 33, [2016] AC 509, para 64 (Lord Mance).
3 *International Energy Group Ltd v Zurich Insurance plc* [2015] UKSC 33, [2016] AC 509, para 64 (Lord Mance).
4 *Royal Brompton Hospital NHS Trust v Hammond* [2002] UKHL 14, [2002] 1 WLR 1397, para 34 (Lord Steyn), approving *Bovis Construction Ltd v Commercial Union Assurance Co plc* [2001] 1 Lloyd's Rep 416, para 28 (David Steel J).

CONTRIBUTION AND AVERAGE

13.11 In property insurance, a pro rata condition of average or co-insurance clause brings contribution into operation between insured and insurer. The effect of such a condition is to make the insured his own insurer to the extent that he has under-declared the value of the property insured.[1]

1 See further **PARA 6.10**.

PARTIES TO A CLAIM FOR CONTRIBUTION

13.12 A claim for contribution is an action between insurers, and should be brought in the name of the insurer rather than the insured.[1]

1 *Austin v Zurich General Accident and Liability Insurance Co Ltd* [1945] KB 250, 258, CA (MacKinnon LJ and Uthwatt J).

CONTRIBUTION AND SUBROGATION

13.13 Where an insured, in addition to his rights under a policy of insurance, also has a contractual right to an indemnity in respect of the same loss or damage, it is a matter of construction whether the contractual obligation to indemnify is the primary or secondary liability. If it is the primary liability, the party indemnifying the insured pursuant to the contract will not be entitled to seek contribution from the insurer; and if the insurer makes payment to the insured, he will be entitled to be subrogated to the insured's rights against the party who has agreed to indemnify the insured.[1] In *Caledonia North Sea Ltd v British Telecommunications plc*,[2] the House of Lords held that the contract between the parties and the commercial scheme of which it was part made it plain that the primary liability was to fall on the contractor, so that the insurer was entitled to be subrogated to the insured's contractual right of indemnity. In *Rathbone Brothers plc v Novae Corporate Underwriting Ltd*,[3] a policy of professional indemnity insurance provided that 'Insurance provided by this policy applies excess over insurance and indemnification available from any other source', and the insured company had provided an indemnity to a consultant who was a former employee, and who was a co-insured under the policy. The Court of Appeal held that it would require very clear language to treat the indemnity granted by the insured company as the primary source of cover ahead of the insurance for which the insured company had paid, and the policy provision was construed as applying to non-insurance indemnification from an external source only.[4]

1 *Caledonia North Sea Ltd v British Telecommunications plc* [2002] UKHL 4, [2002] 1 Lloyd's Rep 553, approving *North British and Mercantile Insurance Co v London, Liverpool and Globe Insurance Co* (1877) 5 Ch D 569, CA.
2 [2002] UKHL 4, [2002] 1 Lloyd's Rep 553.
3 [2014] EWCA Civ 1464, [2015] Lloyd's Rep IR 95.
4 At paras 55–57 (Elias LJ).

EMPLOYER'S LIABILITY INSURANCE AND THE 'FAIRCHILD ENCLAVE'

13.14 Special principles apply to contribution in employer's liability insurance in respect of cases within what is known as the '*Fairchild* enclave', including mesothelioma.[1] Cases within the *Fairchild* enclave are those to which the special rule of causation established in *Fairchild v Glenhaven Funeral Services Ltd*[2] applies. The rule was developed by the courts to do justice to the victims of wrongful exposure to asbestos fibres who have contracted mesothelioma as a result.[3] For cases within the *Fairchild* enclave, an employer's liability insurer is entitled not only to recover contribution from any other insurer but also to look to the employer to make a contribution based on the proportionate part of the overall risk in respect of which it did not recover contribution from any other insurer.[4] Whether the insurer's right of contribution against the insured constitutes a full or partial answer to a victim's policy claim based on a transfer under the Third Parties (Rights Against Insurers) Act 1930 is a question of great potential importance, which is as yet undecided.[5] There is conflicting authority as to whether, where an insurer has a right of set-off, the right is excluded by the 1930 Act.[6] Any right of set-off arising from the special right of contribution in employer's liability insurance in cases within the *Fairchild* enclave is best analysed as arising from circumstances outside the insurance policy, and on that basis as not capable of giving rise to a set-off at all.[7] There is a strongly arguable case for treating the language of s 1(1) of the Act as entitling the third party to recover against the insurer in such a case, leaving the insurer to enforce any claim for contribution which it may have against anyone separately and, in the ordinary course, subsequently.[8]

1 See *International Energy Group Ltd v Zurich Insurance plc* [2015] UKSC 33, [2016] AC 509. The '*Fairchild* enclave' denotes cases to which the special rule of causation established in *Fairchild v Glenhaven Funeral Services Ltd* [2002] UKHL 22, [2003] 1 AC 32 applies; the rule was developed by the courts to do justice to the victims of wrongful exposure to asbestos fibres who have contracted mesothelioma as a result: see *International Energy Group Ltd v Zurich Insurance plc* [2015] UKSC 33, [2016] AC 509, para 102 (Lord Hodge).
2 [2002] UKHL 22, [2003] 1 AC 32.
3 See *International Energy Group Ltd v Zurich Insurance plc* [2015] UKSC 33, [2016] AC 509, para 102 (Lord Hodge).
4 *International Energy Group Ltd v Zurich Insurance plc* [2015] UKSC 33, [2016] AC 509, para 78 (Lord Mance, with whom Lords Clarke, Carnwath and Hodge agreed). Lord Sumption (with whom Lords Neuberger and Reed agreed), arrived at the same result by a different route: that the loss must be prorated between every policy year during which the employer exposed the victim to asbestos, and that the liability of the employer to the victim is apportioned to the insurer according to the proportion which its period on risk bears to the whole period during which that employer has tortiously exposed the victim to asbestos (paras 160 and 163).
5 *International Energy Group Ltd v Zurich Insurance plc* [2015] UKSC 33, [2016] AC 509, para 85 (Lord Mance, with whom Lords Clarke, Carnwath and Hodge agreed). Lord Mance said that this raised questions of great complexity, which it was unnecessary to answer on that appeal, but about which he wished to make some observations.
6 *International Energy Group Ltd v Zurich Insurance plc* [2015] UKSC 33, [2016] AC 509, para 92 (Lord Mance, with whom Lords Clarke, Carnwath and Hodge agreed), referring to *Murray v Legal and General Assurance Society Ltd* [1970] 2 QB 495, 503 (Cumming-Bruce J: insurer's right to recovery of unpaid premiums not set off against claim for indemnity by third party claimant) and *Cox v Bankside Members Agency Ltd* [1995] 2 Lloyd's Rep 437, 451 (Phillips J: obligation of insured to reimburse defence costs funded by underwriters within the excess subject to set off against claim for indemnity (point not considered on appeal: *Cox v Bankside Members Agency Ltd* [1995] 2 Lloyd's Rep 437, CA)).

7 *International Energy Group Ltd v Zurich Insurance plc* [2015] UKSC 33, [2016] AC 509, para 92 (Lord Mance, with whom Lords Clarke, Carnwath and Hodge agreed); this was an observation: see note 5 above.

8 *International Energy Group Ltd v Zurich Insurance plc* [2015] UKSC 33, [2016] AC 509, para 93 (Lord Mance, with whom Lords Clarke, Carnwath and Hodge agreed). Lord Mance's references to the Third Parties (Rights Against Insurers) Act 2010 in his observations suggest that his view would have been the same in relation to the 2010 Act.

Chapter 14

Reinsurance

14.1 Before any steps are taken by or on behalf of an insurer in relation to an insurance claim, the terms of any contract of reinsurance which may respond to the claim should be considered. This is because contracts of reinsurance often include provisions linking the settlement of claims under the contract of insurance to the insurer's right of recovery under the reinsurance. These are, typically, 'follow the settlements' clauses, claims co-operation and claims control clauses, or a combination of the two. Consideration should also be given to the time period within which a claim must be brought under the contract of reinsurance. Finally, the existence and terms of a policy of reinsurance may on occasion be admissible evidence, as part of the 'factual matrix', in relation to the construction of the policy of insurance. This chapter provides an outline of these key reinsurance law concepts.[1]

1 For a comprehensive account of the law of reinsurance, reference should be made to the specialist works. These include Butler and Merkin's *Reinsurance Law*; Edelman & Burns, *The Law of Reinsurance* (2nd edn, 2013); and O'Neill and Woloniecki, *The Law of Reinsurance* (4th edn, 2015).

'FOLLOW THE SETTLEMENTS' CLAUSES

14.2 In order to recover from the reinsurer under a contract of reinsurance, subject to any provision to the contrary the insurer must prove the loss in the same manner as the original insured must prove it against the insurer, and the reinsurer can raise all the defences which were open to the insurer against the original insured; and this is so whether or not the insurer has paid the insured, and whether or not the insurers were themselves reinsurers.[1] In *Hill v Mercantile and General Reinsurance Co plc*,[2] Lord Mustill said that the construction of 'follow the settlements' and similar clauses in contracts of reinsurance does not involve questions of deep principle, and that there were only two rules, both obvious: the first was that the reinsurer cannot be held liable unless the loss falls within the cover of the policy reinsured and within the cover created by the reinsurance; and the second was that the parties are free to agree on ways of proving that these requirements are satisfied.[3] Beyond this, Lord Mustill said, all the problems came from the efforts of those in the market to strike a workable balance between conflicting practical demands and then to express the balance in words.[4]

These efforts began in the nineteenth century. Early decisions established that a clause requiring reinsurers 'to pay as may be paid thereon' did not prevent reinsurers from requiring insurers to prove that they were liable to the insured, but simply prevented them from challenging the quantum of a proper and businesslike settlement arrived at honestly.[5] Provisions requiring a reinsurer 'to pay as may be paid thereon and to follow the settlements' made by the insurer with its insured bind the reinsurer to any compromise of the question of liability made by the insurer provided that the compromise was a proper and businesslike settlement arrived at honestly, so that it is not a defence for the reinsurer to show that the insurer was not legally liable to the insured.[6] The effect of a clause simply binding reinsurers to 'follow the settlements' of the insurers is that the reinsurers agree to indemnify insurers in the event that they settle a claim by the insured, ie when they dispose, or bind themselves to dispose, of a claim, whether by reason of admission or compromise, provided that the claim so recognised by them falls within the risks covered by the policy of reinsurance as a matter of law, and provided also that in settling the claim the insurers have acted honestly and have taken all proper and businesslike steps in making the settlement.[7] The first of these provisos does not require that insurers show that the claim they have settled in fact fell within the risks covered by the reinsurance, but requires them to show that the basis on which they settled it was one which fell within the terms of the reinsurance as a matter of law.[8] The second proviso does not impose an obligation to take care to ascertain the loss, but the less onerous obligation to take proper steps to have it ascertained.[9] It appears that the burden of proof in relation to the second proviso is on the reinsurer, who must show that the insurer has not acted honestly or has not taken all proper and businesslike steps in making the settlement,[10] and that a term is to be implied by law or by market custom or practice entitling the reinsurers to information and documents reasonably required by them to enable them to satisfy themselves that facts existed such as to entitle the insurer to rely upon the cover.[11]

A clause which provides that compromises reached by the insurer are 'unconditionally binding' on the reinsurer has the same effect as a standard 'follow settlements' provision.[12] The effect of the addition of the words 'liable or not liable' is to clarify rather than to qualify or limit the obligations of an insurer under an ordinary 'follow settlements' clause.[13] Similarly, in construing a contract of reinsurance 'as original' which contained a 'follow the settlements' provision which binds reinsurers 'to pay as may be paid thereon and to follow without question the settlements of the Reassured except *ex-gratia* and/or without prejudice settlements', the Court of Appeal held that the addition of the words 'without question' did not qualify or limit the obligations of the insurer under an ordinary follow the settlements clause.[14] The effect of the clause was therefore that the reinsurer could not require the insurer to prove that the insured's claim was in fact covered by the original policy, but required him to show that the basis on which he settled it was one which fell within the terms of the reinsurance as a matter of law or arguably did so.[15] The addition of the words 'excluding without prejudice and ex-gratia settlements' cuts down the ambit of the follow the settlements clause[16] so where a settlement is made with no admission of the existence of any liability by the insurer under the terms and conditions of the original policy to indemnify the insured (a 'without prejudice' settlement) or where there is a payment of money by the insurer to the assured where there was no liability under the policy to indemnify the insured (an 'ex-gratia' settlement), the insured must prove that there was, in fact, a liability under the original policy.[17] The effect of the clause appears to be, in practical terms, that the reinsurer is required to follow the insurer's settlements only where, properly construed, they include an admission of liability.

Although the use of a clause which has a recognised meaning is likely to be respected,[18] a clause which departs from the recognised wordings will be construed according to normal principles of construction and without reference to authority.[19]

In *Hill v Mercantile and General Reinsurance Co plc*[20] the contract of reinsurance contained the following term:[21]

'All loss settlements by the reassured including compromise settlements and the establishment of funds for the settlement of losses shall be binding upon the reinsurers, providing such settlements are within the terms and conditions of the original policies and/or contracts ... and within the terms and conditions of this reinsurance.'

The House of Lords held that the clause drew a distinction between the facts which generated claims under the contracts of insurance and reinsurance and the legal extent of the respective covers: the purpose of the distinction being to ensure that the reinsurer's original assessment and rating of the risks assumed was not falsified by a settlement which, even if soundly based on the facts, transferred into the inward or outward policies, or both, risks which properly lay outside them.[22]

1 *London County Commercial Reinsurance Office Ltd* [1922] Ch 67, 80 (P O Lawrence J); approved: *Toomey v Eagle Star Insurance Co Ltd* [1994] 1 Lloyd's Rep 516, 523, CA (Hobhouse LJ). It is debatable whether this principle applies where an insurer has exercised a discretion in good faith and not irrationally, when he could also have exercised it the other way: *AstraZeneca Insurance Co Ltd v XL Insurance Ltd* [2013] EWCA Civ 1660, [2014] Lloyd's Rep IR 509, paras 67 and 71 (Christopher Clarke LJ).
2 [1996] 1 WLR 1239, HL.
3 At 1251.
4 At 1251.
5 *Western Insurance Co of Toronto v Poole* [1903] 1 KB 376, 386 (Bigham J). Conversely, the clause did not require insurers to have paid the insured in order to be entitled to an indemnity from reinsurers: *Re Eddystone Marine Insurance Co* [1892] 2 Ch 423. Similarly, the word 'actually' in an ultimate net loss clause ('ultimate net loss' being defined as 'the sum actually paid by the reinsured in settlement of losses or liability after making deductions for all recoveries', etc) does not restrict the reinsurer's liability to the amount by which the insurer's liability for the loss had been discharged, but simply serves to emphasise that the loss for which the reinsurer is to be liable is net. *Charter Reinsurance Co Ltd v Fagan* [1997] 1 AC 313, 394, HL (Lord Hoffmann).
6 *Excess Insurance Co Ltd v Mathews* (1925) 23 Ll L R 71, 76 (Branson J) (clause requiring the reinsurer 'to pay as may be paid thereon and to follow their settlements' (at 75)). Although this decision was doubted by Scrutton LJ in *Sir William Garthwaite (Insurance) Ltd v Port of Manchester Insurance Co Ltd* (1930) 37 Ll L R 194, 195, CA, it is correct: see *The Insurance Co of Africa v Scor (UK) Reinsurance Co Ltd* [1985] 1 Lloyd's Rep 312, 330, CA (Robert Goff LJ).
7 *The Insurance Co of Africa v Scor (UK) Reinsurance Co Ltd* [1985] 1 Lloyd's Rep 312, 330, CA (Robert Goff LJ). For the inter-relationship between 'follow the settlements' and claims co-operation or control clauses, see **PARA 14.4**.
8 *Wasa International Insurance Co v Lexington Insurance Co* [2009] UKHL 40, [2010] 1 AC 180, paras 35–36 (Lord Mance); *Assicurazioni Generali SpA v CGU International Insurance plc* [2004] EWCA Civ 429, [2004] Lloyd's Rep IR 457, 464, paras 16–17 (Tuckey LJ), approving: *Hiscox v Outhwaite (No 3)* [1991] 2 Lloyd's Rep 524, 530 (Evans J). In *Assicurazioni Generali SpA v CGU International Insurance plc* [2004] EWCA Civ 429, [2004] Lloyd's Rep IR 457, Tuckey LJ said (at para 17) that the insurer remained obliged to show that the basis on which the claim had been settled was 'one which fell within the terms of the reinsurance as a matter of law or arguably did so'; in *Wasa International Insurance Co v Lexington Insurance Co* [2009] UKHL 40, [2010] 1 AC 180, Lord Mance said (at para 36) that the last three words ('arguably did so') must be read in the context of that case, where the insurance and reinsurance incorporated materially identical terms with materially identical effect (and the issue was whether and on what basis the facts fell within such terms), and that it was less obvious that they could apply in a case like *Wasa v Lexington* where the like terms in the insurance and reinsurance had different effects due to the application of different governing laws.
9 *Charman v Guardian Royal Exchange Assurance plc* [1992] 2 Lloyd's Rep 607, 612–614 (Webster J). In the absence of evidence of market practice to different effect, the insurer is to be identified with the conduct of his loss adjusters and other agents he employs for the purpose of making the settlement, so

that the insurer does not comply with his businesslike obligation if, in a businesslike way, he appoints a competent loss adjuster who then acts in an unbusinesslike or careless way: *Charman v Guardian Royal Exchange Assurance plc* [1992] 2 Lloyd's Rep 607, 612 (Webster J). In *Tokio Marine Europe Insurance Ltd v Novae Corporate Underwriting Ltd (No 2)* [2014] EWHC 2105 (Comm), [2014] Lloyd's Rep IR 638, Field J accepted a submission that an allegation that a reinsured did not act in a proper and businesslike manner in settling a claim was tantamount to an allegation of professional negligence (paras 29 and 32).

10 *Charman v Guardian Royal Exchange Assurance plc* [1992] 2 Lloyd's Rep 607, 614 (Webster J); *Tokio Marine Europe Insurance Ltd v Novae Corporate Underwriting Ltd (No 2)* [2014] EWHC 2105 (Comm), [2014] Lloyd's Rep IR 638, paras 29 and 32 (Field J).

11 *Hiscox v Outhwaite (No 3)* [1991] 2 Lloyd's Rep 524, 529–530 (Evans J); approved: *Assicurazioni Generali SpA v CGU International Insurance plc* [2004] EWCA Civ 429, [2004] Lloyd's Rep IR 457, para 20 (Tuckey LJ).

12 *Charman v Guardian Royal Exchange Assurance plc* [1992] 2 Lloyd's Rep 607, 611 (Webster J).

13 *Charman v Guardian Royal Exchange Assurance plc* [1992] 2 Lloyd's Rep 607, 612 (Webster J); approved: *Assicurazioni Generali SpA v CGU International Insurance plc* [2004] EWCA Civ 429, [2004] Lloyd's Rep IR 457, para 20 (Tuckey LJ).

14 *Assicurazioni Generali SpA v CGU International Insurance plc* [2004] EWCA Civ 429, [2004] Lloyd's Rep IR 457, paras 19 and 20 (Tuckey LJ).

15 *Assicurazioni Generali SpA v CGU International Insurance plc* [2004] EWCA Civ 429, [2004] Lloyd's Rep IR 457, para 17 (Tuckey LJ). The Court of Appeal expressly declined to comment on the hypothetical examples given by the judge at first instance: para 18 (Tuckey LJ).

16 *Faraday Capital Ltd v Copenhagen Reinsurance Co Ltd* [2006] EWHC 1474 (Comm), [2007] Lloyd's Rep IR 23, para 44 (Aikens J).

17 *Faraday Capital Ltd v Copenhagen Reinsurance Co Ltd* [2006] EWHC 1474 (Comm), [2007] Lloyd's Rep IR 23, paras 46 and 47 (Aikens J).

18 *Tokio Marine Europe Insurance Ltd v Novae Corporate Underwriting Ltd* [2013] EWHC 3362 (Comm), [2014] Lloyd's Rep IR 490, paras 118–119 (Hamblen J). See also **PARA 3.17**.

19 *Hill v Mercantile and General Reinsurance Co plc* [1996] 1 WLR 1239, 1251–1252, HL (Lord Mustill).

20 [1996] 1 WLR 1239, HL.

21 At 1242.

22 At 1252–1253 (Lord Mustill). Where there is a single contract of reinsurance, the inward policy is the original contract of insurance and the outward policy is the contract of reinsurance. The terminology is usually reserved for situations in which there are chains of contracts of reinsurance, in which it is necessary to differentiate between two policies of reinsurance, one of which (the outward policy) is higher up the chain than the other (the inward policy).

CLAIMS CO-OPERATION AND CLAIMS CONTROL CLAUSES

14.3 Contracts of reinsurance often require the insurer to co-operate with the reinsurer in relation to claims and to obtain the reinsurer's consent to any settlement.[1] In the absence of any such provision, the reinsurer is not entitled to be actually involved in or consulted about the steps taken to settle the claim or the amount at which it should be settled.[2]

In *The Insurance Co of Africa v Scor (UK) Reinsurance Co Ltd*[3] a contract of reinsurance contained both a 'follow the fortunes' clause and a claims co-operation clause which provided as follows:[4]

'It is a condition precedent to liability under this Insurance that all claims be notified immediately to the Underwriters subscribing to this Policy and the Reassured hereby undertake in arriving at the settlement of any claim, that they will co-operate with the Reassured Underwriters and that no settlement shall be made without the approval of the Underwriters subscribing to this Policy.'

The Court of Appeal construed the claims co-operation clause as falling into two parts: the first part, concerned with notification of claims, was a condition precedent to the reinsurers' liability; the second part, concerned with co-operation with reinsurers, and not making settlement without their approval, was not a condition precedent but a twofold undertaking.[5]

In *Gan v Tai Ping (Nos 2 and 3)*[6] a reinsurance agreement contained both a follow the fortunes clause and a claims co-operation clause in the following terms:[7]

'Notwithstanding anything contained in the reinsurance agreement and/or policy wording to the contrary, it is a condition precedent to any liability under this policy that

(a)   The reinsured shall, upon knowledge of any circumstances which may give rise to a claim against them, advise the reinsurers immediately, and in any event not later than 30 days.

(b)   The reinsured shall co-operate with reinsurers and/or their appointed representatives subscribing to this policy in the investigation and assessment of any loss and/or circumstances giving rise to a loss.

(c)   No settlement and/or compromise shall be made and liability admitted without the prior approval of insurers. All other terms and conditions of this policy remain unchanged.'

The Court of Appeal said that it was apparent that the draftsman had separated out the three parts of the clause considered in *The Insurance Co of Africa v Scor (UK) Reinsurance Co Ltd* and had determined to make each into a condition precedent.[8] The Court of Appeal held that all three sub-clauses were capable of being conditions precedent, and construed them as such.[9] In relation to sub-clause (b), the fact that there could be major or minor failures to co-operate was held to be relevant only to the scope of the sub-clause, and not to whether it was a condition precedent to liability.[10]

In *Eagle Star Insurance Co Ltd v Cresswell*[11] policies of reinsurance included a clause in the following terms:[12]

'The company agree

(a)   To notify all claims or occurrences likely to involve the underwriters within seven days from the time that such claims or occurrences become known to them.

(b)   The underwriters hereon shall control the negotiations and settlements of any claims under this policy. In this event the underwriters hereon will not be liable to pay any claim not controlled as set out above.

'Omission however by the company to notify any claim or occurrence which at the outset did not appear to be serious but which at a later date threatened to involve the company shall not prejudice their right of recovery hereunder.'

Although the clause was headed 'Claims co-operation clause' it was clear from its wording that it was in fact a claims control clause.[13] The Court of Appeal held that it was not essential that the very words 'condition precedent' be used to achieve the result that reinsurers would not be liable unless a certain event happened, and that other words could be used, if they were clear; that the words used were clear; and that compliance with the clause was a condition precedent to reinsurers' liability.[14]

1 See also **PARA 9.13**.
2 *Charman v Guardian Royal Exchange Assurance plc* [1992] 2 Lloyd's Rep 607, 614 (Webster J).
3 [1985] 1 Lloyd's Rep 312, CA.
4 At 330.
5 At 330 (Robert Goff LJ). For conditions precedent generally see **PARA 3.5**. As to the construction of the second part in a policy which also contains a follow the settlements clause, see **PARA 14.4**.
6 [2001] EWCA Civ 1047, [2002] Lloyd's Rep IR 667.
7 At para 3.
8 At para 24 (Mance LJ).
9 At para 26 (Mance LJ); Latham LJ and Sir Christopher Staughton agreed on this issue. As to the effect of sub-clause (c), see **PARA 14.4**.
10 At para 26 (Mance LJ); Latham LJ and Sir Christopher Staughton agreed on this issue.
11 [2004] EWCA Civ 602, [2004] 1 Lloyd's Rep IR 537.
12 At para 1.
13 At para 1.
14 At paras 20 (Longmore LJ), 41 and 53 (Rix LJ). As to the effect of the follow the settlements clause, see **PARA 14.4**.

POLICIES CONTAINING BOTH 'FOLLOW THE SETTLEMENTS' AND CLAIMS CO-OPERATION AND CONTROL CLAUSES

14.4 The contract of reinsurance at issue in *The Insurance Co of Africa v Scor (UK) Reinsurance Co Ltd*[1] contained both a 'follow the settlements' clause and a claims co-operation clause.[2] The Court of Appeal held that the second part of the claims co-operation clause, which was concerned with co-operation with reinsurers, and not making settlement without their approval, was not a condition precedent but a twofold undertaking.[3] It held, further,[4] that the undertaking by the insurers not to make a settlement without the approval of reinsurers must have been intended to circumscribe the power of insurers to make settlements binding upon reinsurers, so that reinsurers would only be bound to follow a settlement when it had received their approval; that, in other words, the follow settlements clause must be construed in its context in the policy, containing as it did a claims co-operation clause in that particular form, as only requiring reinsurers to follow settlements which were authorised by the policy, ie those which had received their approval.[5] In this situation, insurers could either settle with the insured and attempt to prove that they were liable to the insured under the policy, or they could defend the insured's claim, on the basis that they might defeat it or, if they did not, they would be in a better position to establish their claim against reinsurers.[6] This effectively emasculated the follow settlements clause, but must have been what the parties intended by agreeing to a policy which included both a follow settlements clause and the claims co-operation clause.[7] The Court of Appeal also held that there was no basis for the implication of a term that if reinsurers declined to give their approval to a settlement of the insured's claim on a certain basis they agreed that they would indemnify the insurers against such loss and expense as they incurred in consequence, which they might not otherwise have suffered.[8]

In *Gan v Tai Ping (Nos 2 and 3)*[9] the Court of Appeal construed a sub-clause (sub-clause (c)) in a reinsurance agreement which provided: 'No settlement and/or compromise shall be made and liability admitted without the prior approval of Reinsurers'.[10] The Court of Appeal held that the sub-clause was a condition precedent to reinsurers' liability,[11] and that it was to be construed disjunctively, so that it applied in relation to settlements or compromises and to admissions of liability, not simply to settlements or compromises in which insurers' liability was admitted.[12] The contract of reinsurance also contained a full reinsurance clause which included a follow the settlements clause as follows: 'Being a Reinsurance of and warranted same gross rate, terms and conditions and to follow the settlements of the Company …'.[13] The Court of Appeal concluded that the meaning of sub-clause (c) was so clearly expressed ('the words really brook no doubt'[14]) that it was not possible to cut down the scope of its application by limiting it to situations in which insurers sought to rely on the follow the settlements provision.[15] The effect of sub-clause (c) was to remove the first option identified by the Court of Appeal in the *Scor* case, that the insurers could settle with the insured and attempt to prove that they were liable to the insured under the policy, as any settlement with the insured without reinsurers' approval would be a breach of the condition precedent, with the result that reinsurers would not be liable for the claim.

In these circumstances, the Court of Appeal considered whether there were any restrictions on the reinsurers' right to withhold their approval of the settlement. The preliminary issue asked whether a term was to be implied into the reinsurance agreement that reinsurers may not withhold approval of a settlement unless there are reasonable grounds for withholding approval.[16] The Court of Appeal, differing from Longmore J at first instance, unanimously rejected the implication of the term formulated in the preliminary issues and, by a majority, decided that a more limited qualification on reinsurers' right to withhold approval of settlements was to be implied.

The majority (Mance and Latham LJJ) held that although the right to withhold approval was that of the reinsurer, who was entitled to impose his own judgment and policy on matters such as whether the particular claim was one that should be strictly proved by the original insured or the level of appropriate settlement, a term was implied into the reinsurance agreement by reason of necessity for business efficacy that any withholding of approval by reinsurers should take place in good faith after consideration of and on the basis of the facts giving rise to the particular claim and not with reference to considerations wholly extraneous to the subject matter of the particular reinsurance.[17] Mance LJ indicated that the implied qualification on the exercise of reinsurers' right to withhold approval did not arise from any principles or considerations special to the law of insurance but was an implication arising from the nature and purpose of the relevant contractual provisions; it was not therefore an inadmissible extension of the duty of good faith in insurance law.[18] This is consistent with the approach taken by the Supreme Court in *Braganza v BP Shipping Ltd*,[19] in which Mance LJ's remarks were considered with approval in the context of the exercise of contractual powers without any reference to the special nature of the duty of good faith in insurance contracts.[20] Mance LJ's analysis therefore seems to be correct, and Rix LJ's subsequently expressed view that the implication of the term may not depend only on necessity for business efficacy but may be inherent as a matter of law in the very essence of the reinsurers' mutual obligation of good faith[21] is likely to be of little significance in practice.

Mance LJ indicated provisionally that the following were examples of circumstances in which reinsurers' refusal of approval might be considered to be for reasons extraneous to the claim and prejudice insurers: a refusal not for any reason connected with the merits of the claim but as part of an attempt to influence an insurer's attitude in relation to a matter arising under another quite separate reinsurance or to harm an insurer as a competitor in respect of another business or in the eyes of a local regulator; or a reinsurer withholding approval because it had decided, for reasons unrelated to a particular claim, that it wished as reinsurer to prolong payment of any claims for as long as possible, however obvious that it might be that they would have to be met in full and should as claims be settled on the best terms possible.[22]

Similarly, in *Eagle Star Insurance Co Ltd v Cresswell*,[23] the Court of Appeal construed policies of reinsurance which contained a claims control clause, which it held to be a condition precedent to reinsurers' liability,[24] a clause which provided that no settlement of a loss by agreement shall be effected by the insurers for a sum in excess of the deductible without the consent of the underwriters,[25] and a follow the settlements clause in the standard form.[26] Having construed the claims control clause as a condition precedent to reinsurers' liability, the Court of Appeal concluded (each by slightly different reasoning) that the claims control clause excluded reinsurers' liability for any claim the settlement of which they had not controlled.

1 [1985] 1 Lloyd's Rep 312, CA.

2 See **PARA 14.3.**

3 *The Insurance Co of Africa v Scor (UK) Reinsurance Co Ltd* [1985] 1 Lloyd's Rep 312, 330, CA (Robert Goff LJ).

4 By a majority (Robert Goff and Fox LJJ); Stephenson LJ dissented.

5 *The Insurance Co of Africa v Scor (UK) Reinsurance Co Ltd* [1985] 1 Lloyd's Rep 312, CA, 331 (Robert Goff LJ) and 334 (Fox LJ).

6 *The Insurance Co of Africa v Scor (UK) Reinsurance Co Ltd* [1985] 1 Lloyd's Rep 312, 332, CA (Robert Goff LJ).

7 *The Insurance Co of Africa v Scor (UK) Reinsurance Co Ltd* [1985] 1 Lloyd's Rep 312, 331, CA (Robert Goff LJ). Robert Goff LJ added that reinsurers could presumably waive the requirement for approval if they wished (at 331).

8 *The Insurance Co of Africa v Scor (UK) Reinsurance Co Ltd* [1985] 1 Lloyd's Rep 312, CA, 332–333 (Robert Goff LJ), 335 (Fox LJ). An attempt to imply a term by law into a contract of proportional reinsurance that the costs of defending claims be shared was rejected by the House of Lords in *Baker v Black Sea & Baltic General Insurance Co Ltd* [1998] 1 WLR 974, 979–982 (Lord Lloyd). The House of Lords remitted to the Commercial Court the issue of implication of such a term by reason of trade practice and usage (984–985; Lord Lloyd).

9 [2001] EWCA Civ 1047, [2002] Lloyd's Rep IR 667.

10 At para 3. The entire clause is set out at **PARA 14.3.**

11 At para 26 (Mance LJ); Latham LJ and Sir Christopher Staughton agreed on this issue.

12 At paras 24 (Mance LJ), 80 (Latham LJ) and 83–84 (Sir Christopher Staughton).

13 At para 3.

14 At para 29 (Mance LJ).

15 At paras 29 (Mance LJ), 81 (Latham LJ) and 87 (Sir Christopher Staughton).

16 At para 4.

17 At paras 67, 76 and 77 (Mance LJ) and 81 (Latham LJ); Sir Christopher Staughton dissented on this issue, saying (at paras 97–98) that the implication of the term implied by Mance and Latham LJJ was neither necessary for business efficacy nor would the parties have regarded it as so obvious that it goes without saying, and declining to express a view on the implication of any other hypothetical term which had not been pleaded. Mance LJ's remarks at para 67 were approved by the Supreme Court in *Braganza v BP Shipping Ltd* [2015] UKSC 17, [2015] 1 WLR 1661, paras 28–29 (Baroness Hale) (adding that, if it is part of a rational decision-making process to exclude extraneous considerations, it is also part of a rational decision-making process to take into account those considerations which are obviously relevant to the decision in question; in most situations, this is likely to add little to Mance LJ's reference to taking the decision after consideration of and on the basis of the facts giving rise to the particular claim).

18 At para 68 (Mance LJ).

19 [2015] UKSC 17, [2015] 1 WLR 1661.

20 See eg para 28 (Baroness Hale).

21 See *Eagle Star Insurance Co Ltd v Cresswell* [2004] EWCA Civ 602, [2004] 1 Lloyd's Rep IR 537, para 54. Rix LJ was commenting on the implied term found by Mance and Latham LJJ in *Gan v Tai Ping (Nos 2 and 3)*.

22 At para 68 (Mance LJ).

23 [2004] EWCA Civ 602, [2004] 1 Lloyd's Rep IR 537.

24 See **PARA 14.3**.

25 [2004] EWCA Civ 602, [2004] 1 Lloyd's Rep IR 537, paras 7–9. The reinsurers were proportionately liable for sums greater than the deductible: para 9.

26 Lloyd's standard J1 form: 'Being a reinsurance of and warranted same gross rate, terms and conditions as and to follow the settlements of the company': at para 2.

LIMITATION OF ACTIONS

14.5   In the absence of any agreement displacing the statutory limitation period, the limitation period applicable to a claim under a contract of reinsurance is six years.[1]

A contract of reinsurance being a contract of indemnity for the losses of the reinsured, unless the contract of reinsurance provides otherwise, the reinsurer's liability to indemnify the reinsured arises on the date on which the reinsured sustained a loss, which is the date on which his liability to his underlying insured is ascertained, whether by agreement, arbitration award or judgment.[2] The amount then ascertained to be due from the reinsured is the measure of the reinsurer's obligation of indemnity.[3] In the absence of special clauses, the accrual of the cause of action is not postponed until the rendering of an account[4] or payment by the reinsured.[5] In the case of quota share reinsurance, it may be the ascertainment and quantification of the reinsured's liability to the next reinsurer in the chain which triggers the running of time as opposed to the ascertainment of liability at the bottom of the chain with the original insured.[6] This is likely to be the case if the quota share agreement provides that premium and losses payable are to be set off periodically, as the true construction of an agreement in such terms is likely to be that it is only when the mutual liabilities are set off, in accordance with the agreement, that a cause of action accrues.[7]

1 *Nissan Fire & Marine v Malaysia British* (8 July 1996, unreported, Waller J), p 3 of transcript; see also **PARA 11.59**.

2 *Baker v Black Sea and Baltic General Insurance Co Ltd* [1995] Lloyd's Rep IR 261, 286 (Potter J) (proportional facultative obligatory reinsurance); *Halvanon Insurance Co Ltd v Companhia de Seguros do Estado de Sao Paulo* [1995] Lloyd's Rep IR 303, CA, 306 (Steyn LJ); *Gan v Tai Ping (Nos 2 and 3)* [2001] EWCA Civ 1047, [2002] Lloyd's Rep IR 667, paras 39–41 (Mance LJ: a proposition that insurers' rights against reinsurers arise at the earlier stage of any original loss would create very great potential difficulties in the operation of reinsurances and in matters of limitation).

3 *Baker v Black Sea and Baltic General Insurance Co Ltd* [1995] Lloyd's Rep IR 261, 286 (Potter J).

4 *Baker v Black Sea and Baltic General Insurance Co Ltd* [1995] Lloyd's Rep IR 261, 286 (Potter J) (proportional facultative obligatory reinsurance); *Halvanon Insurance Co Ltd v Companhia de Seguros do Estado de Sao Paulo* [1995] Lloyd's Rep IR 303, 306, CA (Steyn LJ). An argument a term should be implied that the cause of action accrued on the rendering of accounts, or failure to render accounts, was rejected in *Halvanon Insurance Co Ltd v Companhia de Seguros do Estado de Sao Paulo* [1995] Lloyd's Rep IR 303, CA on the grounds that it was not necessary because the contract of reinsurance was perfectly workable without it (at 306, Steyn LJ).

5 *North Atlantic Insurance Co Ltd v Bishopsgate Insurance Ltd* [1998] 1 Lloyd's Rep 459, 462 (Timothy Walker J).

6 *Nissan Fire & Marine v Malaysia British* (8 July 1996, unreported, Waller J), pp 8–9 of transcript; *Charter Reinsurance Co Ltd v Fagan* [1997] 1 AC 313, 385, HL (Lord Steyn: not the place to discuss the question, perhaps not yet finally resolved, whether there can be cases where a contract of reinsurance is an insurance of the reinsurer's liability under the inward policy or whether it is always an insurance on the original subject matter, the liability of the reinsured serving merely to give him an insurable interest); *Agnew v Länsforsäkringsbolagens AB* [2001] 1 AC 223, 237, HL (Lord Woolf).

7 *Nissan Fire & Marine v Malaysia British* (8 July 1996, unreported, Waller J), pp 8–9 of transcript.

CONSTRUCTION OF POLICY OF INSURANCE IN LIGHT OF REINSURANCE

14.6   Where the same wording is used in policies of insurance and reinsurance, the court may infer that the parties intended the wording to have the same meaning in both policies.[1] Whether the wording of the policy of reinsurance is part of the 'factual matrix' and is therefore admissible evidence in relation to the construction of a policy of insurance will depend, in accordance with normal principles, on whether the insured was or could reasonably be expected to be aware of the existence and wording of the policy of reinsurance.[2]

In the case of a proportional facultative reinsurance contract, the reinsurer takes a proportional share of the premium and bears the risk of the same share of any losses; consequently, the starting point is that normally reinsurance of that kind is back-to-back with the insurance, and that the reinsurer and the original insurer enter into a bargain that if the insurer is liable under the insurance contract, the reinsurer will be liable to pay the proportion which it has agreed to reinsure.[3] Where the insurance and reinsurance policies are subject to different governing laws, the construction of the insurance contract is unaffected, but the question arises of the extent to which the coverage under a proportional facultative reinsurance contract is, or should be construed as being, co-extensive with the coverage under the insurance contract.[4]

1 See *Axa Reinsurance (UK) plc v Field* [1996] 1 WLR 1026, 1035–1056, HL (Lord Mustill) (insured did not use the same wording in relation to the measure of loss in its inward and outward reinsurance contracts and thereby accepted the possibility that the outcomes might be different; and the only safe course was to construe the words actually used).

2 See **PARA 3.16.**

3 *Wasa International Insurance Co v Lexington Insurance Co* [2009] UKHL 40, [2010] 1 AC 180, para 55 (Lord Collins).

4 See *Forsikringsaktieselskapet Vesta v Butcher* [1989] AC 852, HL; *Groupama Navigation et Transports v Catatumbo CA Seguros* [2000] 2 Lloyd's Rep 350, CA; *Wasa International Insurance Co v Lexington Insurance Co* [2009] UKHL 40, [2010] 1 AC 180.

Chapter 15

Conflict of laws

15.1 A contract of insurance may have a connection with more than one country. This gives rise to issues about the substantive law (for example, whether it is the law of England and Wales which applies to a contract of insurance, or the law of another country, whether within or outside the European Union), and about which courts have jurisdiction to hear the proceedings, including any applications for interim relief. These subjects are considered below.

APPLICABLE LAW

Introduction

15.2 Different regimes determine the applicable law depending on whether the contract of insurance was entered into before 17 December 2009, in relation to which there are two separate regimes according to where the risks covered are situated, or from that date onwards, in relation to which a single unified regime applies.

Contracts entered into before 17 December 2009

15.3 Two different regimes determine the applicable law of contracts of insurance entered into before 17 December 2009 according to where the risks which they cover are situated. The applicable law of contracts of insurance which cover risks situated in an EEA state[1] is governed by the Financial Services and Markets Act 2000 (Law Applicable to Contracts of Insurance) Regulations 2001.[2] The applicable law of contracts of insurance which cover risks situated outside the European Economic Community ('EEC')[3] is governed by the Rome Convention, which has the force of law in England and Wales pursuant to the Contracts (Applicable Law) Act 1990.[4] It is unclear which regime applies to a contract of insurance which covers a single risk or two risks situated in an EEA state and a non-EEA state.[5] In some cases, it will not be necessary to determine which scheme applies, as the concepts of choice and closest connection are the same under both regimes.[6] Each regime is considered below.

1 The states within the European Economic Area are Austria, Belgium, Bulgaria, Croatia, Cyprus, the Czech Republic, Denmark, Germany, Estonia, Finland, France, Greece, Hungary, Iceland, Ireland, Italy, Latvia, Liechtenstein, Lithuania, Luxembourg, Malta, the Netherlands, Norway, Poland, Portugal, Romania, Slovenia, Slovakia, Spain, Sweden and the United Kingdom (ie the member states of the European Union together with Iceland, Liechtenstein and Norway).
2 See **PARA 15.4**.

3 The member states of the European Economic Community are: Austria, Belgium, Bulgaria, Croatia, Cyprus, the Czech Republic, Denmark, Germany, Estonia, Finland, France, Greece, Hungary, Ireland, Italy, Latvia, Lithuania, Luxembourg, Malta, the Netherlands, Poland, Portugal, Romania, Slovenia, Slovakia, Spain, Sweden and the United Kingdom (ie the member states of the European Union).

4 See PARA **15.5**.

5 *American Motorists Insurance Co v Cellstar Corpn* [2003] EWCA Civ 206, [2003] Lloyd's Rep IR 295, paras 23–30 (Mance LJ). Although the rules for ascertaining a governing law set out in art 7 of the second general insurance Directive were never intended to apply to, for example, a United States insurer which is not established and providing services in a member state of the European Union, but which underwrites in the United States a policy covering a risk relating to a United Kingdom establishment of its policyholder, it remains possible (although it could perhaps seem surprising) that the United Kingdom legislature went further and determined upon a wider scheme, aimed at defining the governing law of all policies, wherever and by whomsoever issued, which could be said to relate to an establishment of the policyholder in any member state of the European Union: *American Motorists Insurance Co v Cellstar Corpn* [2003] EWCA Civ 206, [2003] Lloyd's Rep IR 295, paras 29–30 (Mance LJ).

6 *American Motorists Insurance Co v Cellstar Corpn* [2003] EWCA Civ 206, [2003] Lloyd's Rep IR 295, para 19 (Mance LJ); *Travelers Casualty and Surety Co of Canada v Sun Life Assurance Co of Canada (UK) Ltd* [2006] EWHC 2716 (Comm), paras 19–20 (Christopher Clarke J).

Risks situated in an EEA state – contracts entered into before 17 December 2009

15.4   The applicable law of contracts of general insurance[1] entered into before 17 December 2009[2] which cover risks situated in an EEA state[3] is governed by the Financial Services and Markets Act 2000 (Law Applicable to Contracts of Insurance) Regulations 2001 ('the 2001 Regulations').[4] There are many similarities between the drafting of the Rome Convention and the 2001 Regulations and it is unrealistic not to take into account that the former influenced the latter; and it is therefore helpful and appropriate to approach the consideration of the 2001 Regulations having informed oneself of the scheme of the Rome Convention.[5] Similarly, although the Guiliano-Lagarde report, which the courts are expressly permitted to consider in ascertaining the meaning or effect of any provision of the Rome Convention,[6] has no direct weight in this context, it is likely in practice to assist in both contexts.[7] It is clear from the recitals to the second general insurance Directive that one of its purposes is to protect the interests of policyholders, which underlies and informs the understanding of the drafting of its provisions.[8] Similarly it is always important to have in mind that the provisions are intended to have a uniform international application.[9]

Unlike the Rome Convention, the 2001 Regulations and the second general insurance Directive contain no statement that the applicable law is to be the law chosen by the parties.[10] Rather, there are provisions which state what law shall be the applicable law subject to limited rights of the parties to agree that a different law shall apply.[11] Thus the 2001 Regulations subordinate and restrict the power of the parties to choose.[12] The policy of the Directive is that the location of the insured should be the primary consideration.[13] If the policyholder resides[14] in the EEA state in which the risk is situated,[15] the applicable law is the law of that EEA state unless the parties, being permitted to do so, choose another law; the situations in which and extent to which they are permitted to do so is as follows:[16]

(1)   the parties to the contract may choose the law of another country if such a choice is permitted under the law of the EEA state in which the risk is situated;

(2)   if the risks covered by the contract are limited to events occurring in one EEA
state other than the EEA state in which the risk is situated, the parties may
choose the law of the former EEA state as the applicable law; and

(3)   if the risk covered by the contract is a large risk,[17] the parties may choose any
law as the applicable law.

If the policyholder does not reside in the EEA state in which the risk is situated, the
parties may choose another law, as follows:[18]

(1)   the parties to the contract may choose as the applicable law the law of the
EEA state in which the risk is situated or the law of the country in which the
policyholder resides;

(2)   if either of those EEA states grants greater freedom of choice of the applicable
law, the parties to the contract may take advantage of that freedom;

(3)   if the risks covered by the contract are limited to events occurring in one EEA
state other than the EEA state in which the risk is situated, the parties may
choose the law of the former EEA state as the applicable law;

(4)   if the risk covered by the contract is a large risk,[19] the parties may choose any
law as the applicable law.

If the policyholder carries on a business (including a trade or profession) and the
contract covers two or more risks relating to that business which are situated in
different EEA states:[20]

(1)   the freedom of the parties to choose the applicable law extends to the law of any
of those EEA states and of the country in which the policyholder resides, and,
if any of those EEA states grants greater freedom of choice of the applicable
law, the parties to the contract may take advantage of that freedom;

(2)   if the risks covered by the contract are limited to events occurring in one EEA
state other than the EEA state in which the risk is situated, the parties may
choose the law of the former EEA state as the applicable law, and, if any of
those EEA states grants greater freedom of choice of the applicable law, the
parties to the contract may take advantage of that freedom;

(3)   if the risk covered by the contract is a large risk,[21] the parties may choose any
law as the applicable law.

Subject to the provisions summarised above, the Contracts (Applicable Law)
Act 1990 is to be treated as applying to a contract of general insurance for the
purposes of determining the applicable law.[22] In determining what freedom of choice
the parties have under the law of a part of the United Kingdom, the 1990 Act is to be
treated as applying to the contract.[23]

Where the provisions summarised above allow the parties to the contract to choose the
applicable law and if no choice has been made, or no choice has been made which is
expressed or demonstrated with reasonable certainty by the terms of the contract or the
circumstances of the case, the applicable law is the law of the country, from amongst
the permitted choices, which is most closely connected with the contract; however,
where a severable part of the contract has a closer connection with another country
whose law may be chosen, the law applicable to that part is, by way of exception, the
law of that country.[24] For these purposes, the contract is rebuttably presumed to be most
closely connected with the EEA state in which the risk is situated.[25]

Consistent with the policy of the Directive, reproduced in the 2001 Regulations, in considering the 'closest connection' test the court must look for links with the subject-matter and performance of the contract of insurance and their connection with a particular country, such as the location of the subject-matter of the risk and the place of performance of the contract by the payment of premiums and payment of claims.[26] References to the currency of payment or to provisions of domestic law do not relate to the location of the performance of the contract or to the location of either of the performing parties and are therefore not relevant; nor are the fact that a world-wide programme of insurance was negotiated in a particular country.[27]

The mandatory rules of the law of England and Wales, or, if the parties to the contract choose the applicable law and if all the other elements relevant to the situation at the time when the parties make their choice are connected with one EEA state only, the mandatory rules of that EEA state, continue to apply irrespective of the parties' choice of applicable law.[28] Where the risk to which the contract relates is covered by Community co-insurance, references above to 'the parties' do not include co-insurers other than the leading insurer.[29]

The applicable law of contracts of long-term insurance[30] is governed by the Financial Services and Markets Act 2000 (Law Applicable to Contracts of Insurance) Regulations 2001 if, where the policyholder is an individual, he resides in an EEA state, and otherwise if the establishment of the policyholder to which the contract relates is situated in an EEA state.[31] The applicable law is the law of the EEA state of the commitment[32] unless, if such a choice is permitted under the law of that EEA state, the parties choose the law of another country.[33] If the policyholder is an individual and resides in one EEA state but is a national or citizen of another, the parties to the contract may choose the law of the EEA state of which he is a national or citizen as the applicable law.[34] The mandatory rules of the law of England and Wales continue to apply.[35]

Subject to the provisions summarised above, the Contracts (Applicable Law) Act 1990 is to be treated as applying to a contract of long-term insurance for the purposes of determining the applicable law.[36] In determining what freedom of choice the parties have under the law of a part of the United Kingdom, the 1990 Act is to be treated as applying to the contract.[37]

1 'Contract of general insurance' means any contract falling within Part I of Sch 1 to the Financial Services and Markets Act 2000 (Regulated Activities) Order 2001 (SI 2001/544), para 3(1): reg 2(1) of the Financial Services and Markets Act 2000 (Law Applicable to Contracts of Insurance) Regulations 2001 (SI 2001/2635). This includes property and liability insurance, business interruption and legal expenses insurance, and accident and sickness insurance other than permanent health insurance (this includes, essentially, policies providing for payment of a lump-sum or relatively short-term benefits). Specific provision is made in respect of the application of the 2001 Regulations to contracts of insurance entered into by friendly societies: see reg 3(2). The 2001 Regulations do not apply to reinsurance: reg 3(1).
2 The Financial Services and Markets Act 2000 (Law Applicable to Contracts of Insurance) Regulations 2001, reg 3(1A).
3 It is unclear which regime applies to contracts of insurance which cover risks situated within the EEA but outside the EEC (ie in Iceland, Liechtenstein and Norway, which are within the EEA but not within the EEC). This is because the rules of the Rome Convention (which has the force of law within England and Wales pursuant to the Contracts (Applicable Law) Act 1990) apply to contractual obligations in any situation involving a choice between the laws of different countries (art 1(1)) but do not apply to contracts of insurance which cover risks situated in the territories of the member states of the EEC (art 1(3)) and that in order to determine whether a risk is situated in these territories, the court shall apply its internal law. The 1990 Act provides that the internal law for the purposes of art 1(3)

is the provisions of the regulations for the time being in force under s 424(3) of the Financial Services and Markets Act 2000 (s 2(1A) of the 1990 Act), ie the Financial Services and Markets Act 2000 (Law Applicable to Contracts of Insurance) Regulations 2001. The rules of the Rome Convention would appear therefore to apply to contracts of insurance which cover risks situated outside the EEC but within the EEA. However, the 2001 Regulations also appear to apply to these contracts, at least so far as general insurance is concerned: the 2001 Regulations apply to contracts of general insurance (see note 1 above) which cover risks situated in an EEA state (reg 4(1)) and to contracts of long-term insurance (see note 30 below) if, where the policyholder is an individual, he resides in an EEA state, and otherwise if the establishment of the policyholder to which the contract relates is situated in an EEA state (art 8(1)).

4 The Financial Services and Markets Act 2000 (Law Applicable to Contracts of Insurance) Regulations 2001, reg 4(1). Where an EEA state (including the United Kingdom) includes several territorial units, each of which has its own laws concerning contractual obligations, each unit is to be considered as a separate state for the purposes of identifying the applicable law under the 2001 Regulations: reg 2(4). The 2001 Regulations are in similar terms to the earlier scheme under s 94B and Sch 3A of the Insurance Companies Act 1982 (now repealed, and replaced by the 2001 Regulations). Like s 94B and Sch 3A of the 1982 Act, the 2001 Regulations implement the first to third general insurance Directives (Council Directives 73/239/EEC of 24 July 1973, 88/357/EEC of 22 June 1988 and 92/49/EEC of 18 June 1992; these are often referred to as the first to third 'non-life' directives) and the first to third life insurance Directives (Council Directives 79/267/EEC of 5 March 1979, 90/619/EEC of 8 November 1990 and 92/96/EEC of 10 November 1992; these are often referred to as the first to third 'life' directives).

5 *Crédit Lyonnais v New Hampshire Insurance Co* [1997] 2 Lloyd's Rep 1, 5, CA (Hobhouse LJ), considering Sch 3A of the 1982 Act and referring to art 7 of Council Directive 88/357/EEC of 22 June 1988 (the second non-life directive), which is now implemented by Regulation 4 of the 2001 Regulations. Domestic legislation which implements a Directive is to be interpreted purposively so as to give effect to the Directive: see, eg, *Litster v Forth Dry Dock and Engineering Co Ltd* [1990] 1 AC 546, HL.

6 See s 3(3)(a) of the 1990 Act; for the report, see OJ C282/1, 31.10.80.

7 *American Motorists Insurance Co v Cellstar Corpn* [2003] EWCA Civ 206, [2003] Lloyd's Rep IR 295, para 19 (Mance LJ) (in relation to Sch 3A of the Insurance Companies Act 1982; see note 4 above).

8 *Crédit Lyonnais v New Hampshire Insurance Co* [1997] 2 Lloyd's Rep 1, 5, CA (Hobhouse LJ) (in relation to Sch 3A of the Insurance Companies Act 1982; see note 4 above).

9 *Crédit Lyonnais v New Hampshire Insurance Co* [1997] 2 Lloyd's Rep 1, 5, CA (Hobhouse LJ) (in relation to Sch 3A of the Insurance Companies Act 1982; see note 4 above).

10 *Crédit Lyonnais v New Hampshire Insurance Co* [1997] 2 Lloyd's Rep 1, 6, CA (Hobhouse LJ) (in relation to Sch 3A of the Insurance Companies Act 1982; see note 4 above).

11 *Crédit Lyonnais v New Hampshire Insurance Co* [1997] 2 Lloyd's Rep 1, 6, CA (Hobhouse LJ) (in relation to Sch 3A of the Insurance Companies Act 1982; see note 4 above).

12 *Crédit Lyonnais v New Hampshire Insurance Co* [1997] 2 Lloyd's Rep 1, 6, CA (Hobhouse LJ) (in relation to Sch 3A of the Insurance Companies Act 1982; see note4 above).

13 *Crédit Lyonnais v New Hampshire Insurance Co* [1997] 2 Lloyd's Rep 1, 6, CA (Hobhouse LJ) (in relation to Sch 3A of the Insurance Companies Act 1982; see note 4 above).

14 The country in which a person resides is, if he is an individual, the country in which he has his habitual residence, and in any other case, the country in which he has his central administration: reg 2(3).

15 The EEA state where the risk covered by a contract of insurance is situated is, if the contract relates to buildings or to buildings and their contents (in so far as the contents are covered by the same contract of insurance), the EEA state in which the property is situated; if the contract relates to vehicles of any type, the EEA state of registration; if the contract covers travel or holidays risks and has a duration of four months or less, the EEA state in which the policyholder entered into the contract; in any other case, if the policyholder is an individual, the EEA state in which he resides on the date the contract is entered into, and otherwise, the EEA state in which the establishment of the policyholder to which the contract relates is situated on that date: reg 2(2). 'Establishment' means a head office, an agency or branch, or any permanent presence in an EEA state, which need not take the form of a branch or agency and which may consist of an office managed by employees or by a person who is independent but has permanent authority to act, as if he were an agency: reg 2(1).

16 The Financial Services and Markets Act 2000 (Law Applicable to Contracts of Insurance) Regulations 2001, reg 4(2), (6) and (7).

17 As defined in Article 5(d) of the First Council Directive 73/239/EEC of 24 July 1973 on non-life insurance. Broadly, 'large risks' are: railway rolling stock, aircraft (including liability), ships (including liability), goods in transit, commercial risks in relation to credit and suretyship, and contracts of insurance covering land vehicles (other than railway rolling stock), fire and natural forces, other damage to property and general liability issued to commercial policyholders who exceed at least two of the following three criteria: (1) balance sheet total of €6.2m; (2) net turnover of €12.8m; and (3) average number of employees during the financial year of 250.

18 The Financial Services and Markets Act 2000 (Law Applicable to Contracts of Insurance) Regulations 2001, reg 4(3) and (5)–(7).

19 See note 17 above.

20 The Financial Services and Markets Act 2000 (Law Applicable to Contracts of Insurance) Regulations 2001, reg 4(4)–(7).

21 See note 17 above.

22 The Financial Services and Markets Act 2000 (Law Applicable to Contracts of Insurance) Regulations 2001, reg 7(1).

23 The Financial Services and Markets Act 2000 (Law Applicable to Contracts of Insurance) Regulations 2001, reg 7(3).

24 The Financial Services and Markets Act 2000 (Law Applicable to Contracts of Insurance) Regulations 2001, regs 4(8) and 6(1).

25 The Financial Services and Markets Act 2000 (Law Applicable to Contracts of Insurance) Regulations 2001, reg 4(9). The presumption may be rebutted only by relevant material, and in the absence of such material it may not simply be treated as inapplicable or disregarded: *Crédit Lyonnais v New Hampshire Insurance Co* [1997] 2 Lloyd's Rep 1, 7, CA (Hobhouse LJ) (in relation to Sch 3A of the Insurance Companies Act 1982; see note 4 above).

26 *Crédit Lyonnais v New Hampshire Insurance Co* [1997] 2 Lloyd's Rep 1, 6, CA (Hobhouse LJ) (in relation to Sch 3A of the Insurance Companies Act 1982; see note 4 above); however, in *American Motorists Insurance Co v Cellstar Corpn* [2003] EWCA Civ 206, [2003] Lloyd's Rep IR 295, the circumstances and manner in which the policy was effected, and the fact that it was a group policy, were held decisively to outweigh the presumption (Mance LJ, para 49) (also in relation to Sch 3A of the Insurance Companies Act 1982; see note 4 above).

27 *Crédit Lyonnais v New Hampshire Insurance Co* [1997] 2 Lloyd's Rep 1, 6–7, CA (Hobhouse LJ) (in relation to Sch 3A of the Insurance Companies Act 1982; see note 4 above). These factors were however taken into account in relation to this question, without any reference to *Crédit Lyonnais v New Hampshire Insurance Co*, in *Travelers Casualty and Surety Co of Canada v Sun Life Assurance Co of Canada (UK) Ltd* [2006] EWHC 2716 (Comm), para 26 (Christopher Clarke J) (in relation to Sch 3A of the Insurance Companies Act 1982; see note 4 above).

28 The Financial Services and Markets Act 2000 (Law Applicable to Contracts of Insurance) Regulations 2001, reg 5. In determining whether the mandatory rules of another EEA state should be applied where the parties have chosen the law of a part of the United Kingdom as the applicable law, the Contracts (Applicable Law) Act 1990 is to be treated as applying to the contract: the 2001 Regulations, reg 7(2).

29 Within the meaning of Council Directive 78/473/EEC on the co-ordination of laws, regulations and administrative provisions relating to Community co-insurance: The Financial Services and Markets Act 2000 (Law Applicable to Contracts of Insurance) Regulations 2001, reg 6(2).

30 'Contract of long-term insurance' means any contract falling within Part II of Sch 1 to the Financial Services and Markets Act 2000 (Regulated Activities) Order 2001, art 3(1): The Financial Services and Markets Act 2000 (Law Applicable to Contracts of Insurance) Regulations 2001, reg 2(1). This includes life insurance and permanent health insurance. Specific provision is made in respect of the application of the Financial Services and Markets Act 2000 (Law Applicable to Contracts of Insurance) Regulations 2001 to contracts of insurance entered into by friendly societies: see reg 3(2).

31 The Financial Services and Markets Act 2000 (Law Applicable to Contracts of Insurance) Regulations 2001, reg 8(1).

32 'EEA state of the commitment' means, in relation to a contract of long-term insurance entered into on a date, if the policyholder is an individual, the EEA state in which he resides on that date; and otherwise, the EEA state in which the establishment of the policyholder to which the contract relates is situated on that date: 2001 Regulations, reg 2(1).

33 The Financial Services and Markets Act 2000 (Law Applicable to Contracts of Insurance) Regulations 2001, reg 8(2).

34 The Financial Services and Markets Act 2000 (Law Applicable to Contracts of Insurance) Regulations 2001, reg 8(3).
35 The Financial Services and Markets Act 2000 (Law Applicable to Contracts of Insurance) Regulations 2001, reg 9.
36 The Financial Services and Markets Act 2000 (Law Applicable to Contracts of Insurance) Regulations 2001, reg 10(1). For example, in relation to matters such as validity of contracts and incapacity of contracting parties: see arts 8, 9 and 11 of the Rome Convention.
37 The Financial Services and Markets Act 2000 (Law Applicable to Contracts of Insurance) Regulations 2001, reg 10(2).

Risks situated outside the EEC – contracts entered into before 17 December 2009

15.5   The applicable law of contracts of insurance entered into before 17 December 2009 which cover risks situated outside the European Economic Community[1] is determined by the Rome Convention,[2] which pursuant to the Contracts (Applicable Law) Act 1990 has the force of law in England and Wales and in the case of conflicts between the laws of different parts of the United Kingdom.[3] The contract, or any part of it, is governed by the law chosen by the parties.[4] The choice must be express or demonstrated with reasonable certainty by the terms of the contract or the circumstances of the case.[5] The applicable law specified by the Rome Convention may be the law of any country, including countries outside the European Union.[6] The factors which the court is likely to take into account in determining whether the parties' choice has been demonstrated with reasonable certainty by the terms of the contract or the circumstances of the case include the location of the insured (or parent company or principal insured in the case of a composite policy), the location of the insurers, the location of the brokers, the location where the contract of insurance was negotiated, the use (or otherwise) of a standard form such as a Lloyd's policy, references to time zones, the place of payment of premium and management of claims, the currency of payment, references to a particular newspaper to determine the exchange rate, the language and spelling of the contract of insurance, the governing law of other layers of insurance, and references to domestic law.[7]

The court is unlikely to be persuaded that the parties intended that different aspects of a composite policy of insurance providing cover in respect of several insureds in different countries should be subject to different applicable laws.[8] The parties may at any time agree to subject the contract to a law other than that which previously governed it.[9] The fact that the parties have chosen a foreign law, does not, where all the other elements relevant to the situation at the time of the choice are connected with one country only, prejudice the application of mandatory rules of the law of that country.[10] If the law applicable to the contract is not chosen by the parties or demonstrated with reasonable certainty by the terms of the contract or the circumstances of the case, the contract, or any severable part of it, is governed by the law of the country with which it is most closely connected.[11] Although the report on the Rome Convention by Professors Giuliano and Lagarde states that the court is not permitted to infer a choice of law which the parties might have made where they had no clear intention of making a choice,[12] the court is nevertheless likely to take into account the same factors both in identifying the country with which a contract of insurance is most closely connected and in determining whether the parties have demonstrated a choice of law with reasonably certainty.[13] Unless it appears from the circumstances as a whole that the contract is more closely connected with another country, there is a presumption that the contract is most closely connected with the country where the party who is to effect the performance which is characteristic of the contract has, at the time of conclusion of the contract, his habitual residence or its central administration.[14] The performance characteristic of a contract of insurance is effected by the insurer.[15] However, if the contract is entered into in the course of that party's trade or profession, there is a presumption that the contract is most closely connected with the country in which the principal place of business is situated or, where under the terms of the contract the performance is to be effected through a place of business other than the principal place of business, the country in which that other place of business is situated.[16]

The Rome Convention also makes provision in relation to other matters such as validity of contracts and incapacity of contracting parties, assignment and subrogation.[17] The Rome Convention does not apply to arbitration agreements and agreements on the choice of court.[18]

The report on the Rome Convention by Professors Giuliano and Lagarde may be considered in ascertaining the meaning or effect of any provision of the Convention.[19]

1 For the position in relation to Iceland, Liechtenstein and Norway, which are within the EEA but outside the European Union, see **PARA 15.4**, note 2.
2 The Rome Convention is contained in Sch 1 to the Contracts (Applicable Law) Act 1990.
3 Contracts (Applicable) Law Act 1990, s 2(1); there is an exception in relation to arts 7(1) and 10(1)(e) of the Rome Convention, which do not have the force of law in England and Wales: s 2(2) of the 1990 Act. The 1990 Act applies in relation to contracts entered into from 1 April 1991: see s 7 of the 1990 Act and art 17 of the Rome Convention (the governing law of contracts entered into before 1 April 1991 is determined according to common law principles, which are not considered in this chapter). Different rules apply in relation to reinsurance: Rome Convention, arts 1(3) and (4).
4 Article 3(1) of the Rome Convention. The applicable law of the contract includes any presumptions of law or rules determining the burden of proof which are contained in the law of contract: art 14(1) of the Rome Convention. The freedom of the parties to choose the applicable law is restricted where the insured is a consumer (ie where the insurance is for a purpose which can be regarded as being outside his trade or profession) and will usually be the law of the country in which the insured has his habitual residence: art 5 of the Rome Convention.
5 Article 3(1) of the Rome Convention.
6 Article 2 of the Rome Convention.
7 *American Motorists Insurance Co v Cellstar Corpn* [2003] EWCA Civ 206, [2003] Lloyd's Rep IR 295, paras 44–48 (Mance LJ); *Travelers Casualty and Surety Co of Canada v Sun Life Assurance Co of Canada (UK) Ltd* [2006] EWHC 2716 (Comm), para 23 (Christopher Clarke J).
8 *American Motorists Insurance Co v Cellstar Corpn* [2003] EWCA Civ 206, [2003] Lloyd's Rep IR 295, para 21 (Mance LJ); *Travelers Casualty and Surety Co of Canada v Sun Life Assurance Co of Canada (UK) Ltd* [2006] EWHC 2716 (Comm), para 22 (Christopher Clarke J).
9 Article 3(2) of the Rome Convention.
10 Article 3(3) of the Rome Convention. See also art 7 which makes further provision for the application of mandatory rules of law.
11 Article 4(1) of the Rome Convention.
12 See para 3 of the discussion of art 3 of the Rome Convention in the Giuliano-Lagarde report (the report is at OJ C282/1, 31.10.80).
13 See, eg, *Travelers Casualty and Surety Co of Canada v Sun Life Assurance Co of Canada (UK) Ltd* [2006] EWHC 2716 (Comm), para 26 (Christopher Clarke J).
14 Article 4(2) and (5) of the Rome Convention.

15 *Crédit Lyonnais v New Hampshire Insurance Co* [1997] 2 Lloyd's Rep 1, 6, CA (Hobhouse LJ); *American Motorists Insurance Co v Cellstar Corpn* [2003] EWCA Civ 206, [2003] Lloyd's Rep IR 295, para 50 (Mance LJ); para 3 of the discussion of art 4 of the Rome Convention in the Giuliano-Lagarde report (for the report, see OJ C282/1, 31.10.80).
16 Article 4(2) and (5) of the Rome Convention.
17 Articles 8, 9 and 11–13 of the Rome Convention.
18 Article 1(2)(d) of the Rome Convention.
19 Section 3(3)(a) of the 1990 Act; for the report, see OJ C282/1, 31.10.80.

Contracts entered into on or after 17 December 2009 (the 'Rome I' Regulation)

15.6 The applicable law of contracts of insurance entered into after 17 December 2009 is determined by Regulation 593/2008, known as the 'Rome I' Regulation.[1]

Contracts of insurance covering large risks[2] are governed by the law chosen by the parties in accordance with Article 3 of the Rome I Regulation.[3] The choice must be express or demonstrated with reasonable certainty by the terms of the contract or the circumstances of the case.[4] The parties may select the law applicable to the whole or to part only of the contract.[5] To the extent that the applicable law has not been chosen by the parties, the insurance contract is governed by the law of the country where the insurer has his habitual residence, unless it is clear from all the circumstances of the case that the contract is manifestly more closely connected with another country, in which case the law of that country applies.[6]

In the case of all other contracts of insurance, only the following laws may be chosen by the parties in accordance with Article 3 of the Rome I Regulation: the law of any member state where the risk is situated at the time of conclusion of the contract;[7] the law of the country where the policy holder has his habitual residence;[8] in the case of life insurance, the law of the member state of which the policy holder is a national;[9] for insurance contracts covering risks limited to events occurring in one member state other than the member state where the risk is situated, the law of that member state;[10] where the policy holder pursues a commercial or industrial activity or a liberal profession and the insurance contract covers two or more risks which relate to those activities and are situated in different member states, the law of any of the member states concerned or the law of the country of habitual residence of the policyholder.[11] To the extent that the law applicable has not been chosen by the parties in accordance with these provisions, such a contract is governed by the law of the member state in which the risk is situated at the time of conclusion of the contract.[12]

The following additional rules apply to insurance contracts covering risks for which a member state imposes an obligation to take out insurance: the insurance contract will not satisfy the obligation to take out insurance unless it complies with the specific provisions relating to that insurance laid down by the member state in which the risk is situated and the law of the member state imposing the obligation to take out insurance contradicts each other, the latter prevails;[13] and a member state may lay down that the insurance contract shall be governed by the law of the member state that imposes the obligation to take out insurance.[14]

The country in which the risk is situated for these purposes is determined as follows.[15] Where the insurance relates either to buildings, or to buildings and their contents covered by the same insurance policy, the country in which the risk is situated is the member state in which the property is situated.[16] Where the insurance relates to vehicles of any type, the country in which the risk is situated is the member state of registration.[17] Where the policy is of a duration of four months or less covering travel or holiday risks, the country in which the risk is situated is the member state where the policy holder took out the policy.[18] In all other non-life insurance cases, the country in which the risk is situated is the member state where the policy holder concerned has his habitual residence or, if the policy holder is a legal person, the member state where the latter's establishment, to which the risk relates, is situated.[19] In the case of life insurance, the member state is the member state where the policy holder has his or her habitual residence or, if the policy holder is a legal person, the member state where the latter's establishment, to which the contract relates, is situated.[20]

1 Regulation 593/2008 of the European Parliament and of the Council of 17 June 2008 on the law applicable to contractual obligations (Rome I), OJ L177/6, 4.7.08, as corrected (Corrigendum, OJ L309/87, 24.11.09).
2 As defined in Article 5(d) of the First Council Directive 73/239/EEC of 24 July 1973 on non-life insurance. Broadly, 'large risks' are: railway rolling stock, aircraft (including liability), ships (including liability), goods in transit, commercial risks in relation to credit and suretyship, and contracts of insurance covering land vehicles (other than railway rolling stock), fire and natural forces, other damage to property and general liability issued to commercial policyholders who exceed at least two of the following three criteria: (1) balance sheet total of €6.2m, (2) net turnover of €12.8m, and (3) average number of employees during the financial year of 250.
3 Article 7(2) of Rome I Regulation.
4 Article 3(1) of Rome I Regulation.
5 Article 3(1) of Rome I Regulation.
6 Article 7(2) of Rome I Regulation.
7 Article 7(3)(a) of Rome I Regulation; where the law of that member state grants greater freedom of choice of the law applicable to the insurance contract, the parties may take advantage of that freedom: Article 7(3), second sub-paragraph, Rome I Regulation.
8 Article 7(3)(b) of Rome I Regulation; where the law of that member state grants greater freedom of choice of the law applicable to the insurance contract, the parties may take advantage of that freedom: Article 7(3), second sub-paragraph, Rome I Regulation.
9 Article 7(3)(c) of Rome I Regulation.
10 Article 7(3)(d) of Rome I Regulation.
11 Article 7(3)(e) of Rome I Regulation; where the law of those member states grant greater freedom of choice of the law applicable to the insurance contract, the parties may take advantage of that freedom: Article 7(3), second sub-paragraph, Rome I Regulation.
12 Article 7(3), third sub-paragraph, Rome I Regulation.
13 Article 4(a) of Rome I Regulation.
14 Article 4(b) of Rome I Regulation; this is by way of derogation from Article 7(2) and (3): Article 4(b) of Rome I Regulation.
15 Article 7(6) of Rome I Regulation, which provides that the country in which the risk is determined is determined in accordance with Article 2(d) of the second non-life insurance Directive 88/357/EEC of 22 June 1988, and in the case of life insurance, the country in which the risk is situated is the country of the commitment within the meaning of Article 1(1)(g) of life insurance Directive 2002/83/EC.
16 Article 7(6) of Rome I Regulation and Article 2(d) of the second non-life insurance Directive 88/357/EEC of 22 June 1988.
17 Article 7(6) of Rome I Regulation and Article 2(d) of the second non-life insurance Directive 88/357/EEC of 22 June 1988.
18 Article 7(6) of Rome I Regulation and Article 2(d) of the second non-life insurance Directive 88/357/EEC of 22 June 1988.
19 Article 7(6) of Rome I Regulation and Article 2(d) of the second non-life insurance Directive 88/357/EEC of 22 June 1988.
20 Article 7(6) of Rome I Regulation and Article 1(1)(g) of life insurance Directive 2002/83/EC of 19 December 2002.

JURISDICTION UNDER REGULATION 1215/2012 (THE 'BRUSSELS I' REGULATION)

Introduction

15.7 Common rules govern jurisdiction in relation to the member states of the European Economic Area, with the exception of Denmark.[1] Regulation 1215/2012, known as the 'Brussels I' Regulation, provides for persons domiciled in a member state to be sued in the courts of that member state, subject to specific provisions for jurisdiction in certain areas including matters relating to insurance.[2] '[M]atters relating to insurance' within the meaning of art 10 of the Brussels I Regulation and to which the provisions of arts 10 to 16 of the Brussels I Regulation apply is broad enough to embrace allegations of insurance fraud and claims to be entitled to avoid a contract of insurance.[3] These provisions are a self-contained and exclusive code governing insurance and other provisions of the Brussels I Regulation therefore do not apply in this area.[4] In determining whether the Brussels I Regulation applies, the test is whether the claimant is able to establish a 'good arguable case', meaning a serious issue to be tried.[5]

Different rules apply according to whether proceedings are brought by or against an insurer, where the defendant enters an appearance, and in relation to related actions. Each of these situations is considered below.

1 Regulation 1215/2012 of 12 December 2012 (the 'Brussels I' Regulation) applies to legal proceedings instituted, authentic instruments formally drawn up or registered, and court settlements approved or concluded, on or after 10 January 2015: Brussels I Regulation, art 66(1). Council Regulation 44/2001/EC of 22 December 2000 is revoked by the Brussels I Regulation but continues to apply to judgments given in legal proceedings instituted, authentic instruments formally drawn up or registered, and court settlements approved or concluded, before 10 January 2015: Brussels I Regulation, arts 66(2) and 80. Regulation 44/2001 replaced, for the member states of the European Union with the exception of Denmark, the Brussels and Lugano Conventions with effect from 1 March 2002 (Regulation 44/2001, art 76). Denmark is not a party to the Brussels I Regulation. A revised Lugano Convention remains in force between Denmark and the other member states of the European Union, together with those members of the European Free Trade Association which are parties to it (Iceland, Norway and Switzerland). Jurisdiction is allocated within the constituent parts of the United Kingdom pursuant to a modified version of the Brussels Convention: Civil Jurisdiction and Judgments Act 1982: ss 16 and 17 and Sch 4.
2 For these purposes, 'insurance' does not include reinsurance: *Agnew v Länsförsäkringsbolagens AB* [2001] 1 AC 223, HL.
3 *Jordan Grand Prix Ltd v Baltic Insurance Group* [1999] 2 AC 127, 132, HL (Lord Steyn) (in relation to the equivalent provisions of the Brussels Convention).
4 *Jordan Grand Prix Ltd v Baltic Insurance Group* [1999] 2 AC 127, 133–134, HL (Lord Steyn) (in relation to the equivalent provisions of the Brussels Convention).
5 *New England Reinsurance Corpn v Messoghios Insurance Co SA* [1992] 2 Lloyd's Rep 251, CA, 252–253 (Leggatt LJ), 256 (Balcombe LJ) and 257 (Dillon LJ) (in relation to the Brussels Convention).

Proceedings brought by an insurer

15.8 An insured domiciled[1] in a member state must be sued in that member state[2] unless he is joined to an action brought by an injured party directly against an insurer,[3] he is sued pursuant to the terms of a jurisdiction agreement,[4] he enters an appearance,[5] or the provisions of the Brussels I Regulation in relation to related actions apply.[6] An insurer, whether or not it is domiciled in a member state,[7] may bring proceedings only in the courts of the member state in which the defendant is domiciled, irrespective of whether he is the policyholder, the insured or a beneficiary.[8]

1 In order to determine whether a party is domiciled in the member state whose courts are seised of a matter, the court shall apply its internal law: Brussels I Regulation, art 62(1). If a party is not domiciled in the member state whose courts are seised of the matter, then, in order to determine whether the party is domiciled in another member state, the court shall apply the law of that member state: Brussels I Regulation, art 62(2). For the purposes of Brussels I Regulation, a company or other legal person or association of natural or legal persons is domiciled at the place where it has its statutory seat, central administration or principal place of business: Brussels I Regulation, art 63(1). For the purposes of the United Kingdom, 'statutory seat' means the registered office or, where there is no such office anywhere, the place of incorporation or, where there is no such place anywhere, the place under the law of which the formation took place: Brussels I Regulation, art 63(2).
2 Brussels I Regulation, arts 4, 5(1) and 10–16; see further **PARA 15.9**.
3 Brussels I Regulation, art 13(2) and (3); see further **PARA 15.9**.
4 Brussels I Regulation, arts 15 and 16; see further **PARA 15.9**.
5 See **PARA 15.10**.
6 See **PARA 15.11**.
7 *Jordan Grand Prix Ltd v Baltic Insurance Group* [1999] 2 AC 127, 133–134, HL (Lord Steyn) (in relation to the equivalent provisions of the Brussels Convention).
8 Brussels I Regulation, art 14(1). This does not prevent insurer from bringing a counterclaim in the court in which the original claim is pending: art 14(2). Article 14(2) does not permit a counterclaim against parties other than the original claimant: *Jordan Grand Prix Ltd v Baltic Insurance Group* [1999] 2 AC 127, 134–135, HL (Lord Steyn) (in relation to the equivalent provision of the Brussels Convention).

Proceedings brought against an insurer

15.9   An insurer domiciled in a member state may be sued:

(1)   in the courts of the member state where he is domiciled;
(2)   in another member state, in the case of actions brought by the policyholder, the insured or a beneficiary, in the courts for the place where the claimant is domiciled; or
(3)   if he is a co-insurer, in the courts of a member state in which proceedings are brought against the leading insurer.[1]

An insurer who is not domiciled in a member state but has a branch, agency or other establishment in one of the member states shall, in disputes arising out of the operations of the branch, agency or establishment, be deemed to be domiciled in that member state.[2]

In respect of liability insurance or insurance of immovable property, the insurer may in addition be sued in the courts for the place where the harmful event occurred.[3] The same applies if movable and immovable property are covered by the same insurance policy and both are adversely affected by the same contingency.[4]

In respect of liability insurance, the insurer may also, if the law of the court permits it, be joined in proceedings which the injured party has brought against the insured.[5]

If the law permits the bringing of a direct action against the insurer, the principles set out above in relation to jurisdiction apply,[6] and if the law provides that the policyholder or the insured may be joined as a party to the action, the same court shall have jurisdiction over them.[7] This means that the injured party may bring an action directly against the insurer before the courts for the place in a member state where that injured party is domiciled, provided that a direct action is permitted and the insurer is domiciled in a member state.[8] That is so irrespective of whether the national law of the claimant's domicile classifies a direct claim by an injured party against an alleged tortfeasor's liability insurer as an action in tort or as an action relating to insurance,[9] and irrespective of whether there is a policy dispute.[10] Whether a direct action is permitted is determined by the law of the court to be seised including its private international law rules.[11] Although the issue has not yet been decided, it seems that an insurer cannot force an insured tortfeasor to be sued by the injured party in the court of the latter's domicile by the simple expedient of consenting to the jurisdiction of that court, in circumstances where it would not otherwise have jurisdiction over the insured tortfeasor,[12] and that in principle the insured should be entitled to mount an independent challenge to the existence of the court's jurisdiction over the insurer, since the existence of such jurisdiction is a pre-condition to the exercise of jurisdiction over himself.[13] This makes it necessary to identify the system of law by reference to which the existence of a direct right of action against a liability insurer is to be determined.[14] The provisions governing jurisdiction in matters relating to insurance may be departed from only by an agreement:[15]

(1)   which is entered into after the dispute has arisen;[16]
(2)   which allows the policyholder, the insured or a beneficiary to bring proceedings in courts other than those indicated in these provisions;[17]
(3)   which is concluded between a policyholder and an insurer, both of whom are at the time of conclusion of the contract domiciled or habitually resident in the same member state, and which has the effect of conferring jurisdiction on the courts of that state even if the harmful event were to occur abroad, provided that such an agreement is not contrary to the law of that state;[18]
(4)   which is concluded with a policyholder who is not domiciled in a member state, except in so far as the insurance is compulsory or relates to immovable property in a member state;[19] or
(5)   which relates to a contract of insurance in so far as it covers large risks[20] or certain commercial risks relating to shipping, aviation, installations situated offshore or on the high seas or transport of goods.[21]

Where the English court has jurisdiction pursuant to the Brussels I Regulation and no other member state is concerned, the Regulation precludes the English court from declining the jurisdiction conferred on it on the ground that a court of a non-member state would be a more appropriate forum for the trial of the action even if the jurisdiction of no other member state is in issue or the proceedings have no connecting factors to any other member state.[22] There are conflicting decisions at first instance as to whether the English courts are required to accept jurisdiction in circumstances where, if the Brussels I Regulation were applied reflexively, the court would decline jurisdiction on the basis of *lis alibi pendens* or of an exclusive jurisdiction clause in favour of the courts of a non-member state.[23]

---

1 Brussels I Regulation, art 11(1). The rules of special jurisdiction in matters relating to insurance do not apply to disputes between a reinsurer and a reinsured in connection with a reinsurance contract: C-412/98 *Group Josi Reinsurance Co SA v Universal General Insurance Co* [2000] ECR I-5925, ECJ, para 73; or to actions between insurers, whether in their own right: Case C-77/04 *Groupement d'Intérêt Economique Réunion Européenne v Zurich España* [2006] Lloyd's Rep IR 215, ECJ, paras 16–20; *Youell v La Réunion Aerienne* [2009] EWCA Civ 175, [2009] 1 Lloyd's Rep 586, paras 18–20 (Lawrence Collins LJ) (both cases decided in relation to the equivalent provisions of the Brussels Convention); or as assignees: C-89/91 *Shearson Lehmann Hutton Inc v TVB* [1993] ECR I-139, ECJ; *Youell v La Réunion Aerienne* [2009] EWCA Civ 175, [2009] 1 Lloyd's Rep 586, paras 18–20 (Lawrence Collins LJ) (both cases decided in relation to the equivalent provisions of the Brussels Convention).

2 Brussels I Regulation, art 11(2).

3 Brussels I Regulation, art 12.

4 Brussels I Regulation, art 12.

5 Brussels I Regulation, art 13(1).

6 Brussels I Regulation, art 13(2).The rules of special jurisdiction in matters relating to insurance are fully applicable where, under the law of a contracting state, the policy holder, the insured or the beneficiary of an insurance contract has the option to approach directly any reinsurer of the insurer in order to assert his rights under the contract as against that reinsurer, for example in the case of the bankruptcy or liquidation of the insurer: C-412/98 *Group Josi Reinsurance Co SA v Universal General Insurance Co* [2000] ECR I-5925, ECJ, para 75 (in relation to the equivalent provisions of the Brussels Convention).

7 Brussels I Regulation, art 13(3). The purpose of art 13(3) is to ensure that issues common to both the insured and insurer are decided in the same proceedings where it is necessary to do so to avoid the risk of irreconcilable judgments: *Maher v Groupama Grand Est* [2009] EWCA Civ 1191, [2010] 1 WLR 1564, para 21 (Moore-Bick LJ); *Mapfre Mutualidad Compania de Seguros y Reaseguros SA v Keefe* [2015] EWCA Civ 598, [2016] Lloyd's Rep IR 94, para 82 (Moore-Bick LJ).

8 Case C-463/06 *FBTO Schadeverzekeringen NV v Odenbreit* [2008] Lloyd's Rep IR 354, ECJ, para 31; *Mapfre Mutualidad Compania de Seguros y Reaseguros SA v Keefe* [2015] EWCA Civ 598, [2016] Lloyd's Rep IR 94, paras 25–28 (Gloster LJ) and 74–75 (Moore-Bick LJ).

9 *Mapfre Mutualidad Compania de Seguros y Reaseguros SA v Keefe* [2015] EWCA Civ 598, [2016] Lloyd's Rep IR 94, paras 25–28 (Gloster LJ), 60 (Black LJ) and 74–75 (Moore-Bick LJ). See further note 14.

10 *Mapfre Mutualidad Compania de Seguros y Reaseguros SA v Keefe* [2015] EWCA Civ 598, [2016] Lloyd's Rep IR 94, para 47 (Gloster LJ), 60 (Black LJ) and 82 (Moore-Bick LJ).

11 *Mapfre Mutualidad Compania de Seguros y Reaseguros SA v Keefe* [2015] EWCA Civ 598, [2016] Lloyd's Rep IR 94, paras 35–37 (Gloster LJ).

12 *Mapfre Mutualidad Compania de Seguros y Reaseguros SA v Keefe* [2015] EWCA Civ 598, [2016] Lloyd's Rep IR 94, paras 38 (Gloster LJ) and 79 (Moore-Bick LJ).

13 *Mapfre Mutualidad Compania de Seguros y Reaseguros SA v Keefe* [2015] EWCA Civ 598, [2016] Lloyd's Rep IR 94, para 79 (Moore-Bick LJ).

14 *Mapfre Mutualidad Compania de Seguros y Reaseguros SA v Keefe* [2015] EWCA Civ 598, [2016] Lloyd's Rep IR 94, para 80 (Moore-Bick LJ). It was not necessary to decide whether the national law of the claimant's domicile classified a direct claim by an injured party against an alleged tortfeasor's liability insurer as an action in tort or as an action relating to insurance since the proper law of the contract of insurance was Spanish law and the accident occurred in Spain, but Moore-Bick LJ said that, contrary to the view he expressed in passing in *Maher v Groupama Grand Est* [2009] EWCA Civ 1191, [2010] 1 WLR 1564 (at para 11), he thought the existence of a direct right of action against the insurer would generally fall to be determined by reference to the law of the place where the wrongful act of the insured occurred: see paras 80–81.

15 Article 25 of Brussels I Regulation contains additional formal requirements which were applied by the Court of Appeal in the insurance context in *New Hampshire Insurance Co v Strabag Bau AG* [1992] 1 Lloyd's Rep 361, 371–372, CA (Lloyd LJ) (in relation to the equivalent provision of the Brussels Convention). The Court of Appeal did not discuss whether (adopting the numbering of Brussels I Regulation) art 15 applied instead of, or in addition to, art 25. Applying the requirements of art 25 in the insurance context is arguably inconsistent with *Jordan Grand Prix Ltd v Baltic Insurance Group* [1999] 2 AC 127, in which the House of Lords decided that the provisions governing jurisdiction in matters relating to insurance are a self-contained and exclusive code and that other provisions of Brussels I Regulation therefore do not apply in this area (Lord Steyn at 133–134); however, art 25 contains formal requirements in relation to jurisdiction agreements (which can be satisfied in various ways including that the agreement is in writing or evidenced in writing) which are not repeated in art 15, and it is suggested that to apply art 25 would be more consistent with the purpose of the special jurisdiction in matters relating to insurance which is to protect the insured: see *Jordan Grand Prix Ltd v Baltic Insurance Group* [1999] 2 AC 127, 134, HL (Lord Steyn).

16 Brussels I Regulation, art 15(1).

17 Brussels I Regulation, art 15(2). In *Sherdley v Nordea Life and Pension SA* [2012] EWCA Civ 88, [2012] Lloyd's Rep IR 437, there were three potential exclusive jurisdiction clauses, and Rix LJ concluded (at para 66) that none of the exclusive jurisdiction clauses canvassed in the proceedings could survive art 15(2). See also **PARA 3.20** (unfair terms in consumer contracts), notes 31–32 and related text.

18 Brussels I Regulation, art 15(3).

19 Brussels I Regulation, art 15(4).

20 As defined in Article 5(d) of the First Council Directive 73/239/EEC of 24 July 1973 on non-life insurance. Broadly, 'large risks' are: railway rolling stock, aircraft (including liability), ships (including liability), goods in transit, commercial risks in relation to credit and suretyship, and contracts of insurance covering land vehicles (other than railway rolling stock), fire and natural forces, other damage to property and general liability issued to commercial policyholders who exceed at least two of the following three criteria: (1) balance sheet total of €6.2m, (2) net turnover of €12.8m, and (3) average number of employees during the financial year of 250.

21 Brussels I Regulation, arts 15(5) and 16.

22 Case C-281/02 *Owusu v Jackson* [2005] QB 801, ECJ (in relation to mandatory jurisdiction under the Brussels Convention), effectively overruling *Re Harrods (Buenos Aires) Ltd* [1992] Ch 72, CA (which held that the English court retained a discretion to refuse jurisdiction on the grounds of *forum non conveniens* (ie that the courts of a non-member state were the appropriate forum)).

23 See eg (all decisions under Brussels I Regulation): *Catalyst Investment Group Ltd v Lewinsohn* [2009] EWHC 1964 (Ch), [2010] Ch 218 (jurisdiction accepted); *Ferexpo AG v Gilson Investments Ltd* [2012] EWHC 721 (Comm), [2012] 1 Lloyd's Rep 588 (jurisdiction declined); *Plaza BV v Law Debenture Trust Corp plc* [2015] EWHC 43 (Ch) (jurisdiction declined).

Entering an appearance

15.10   Apart from jurisdiction derived from other provisions of the Brussels I Regulation, if in a matter relating to insurance a defendant enters an appearance before a court of a member state other than to contest the jurisdiction, that court has jurisdiction.[1]

1 Brussels I Regulation, arts 24 and 26.

Related actions *(lis pendens)*

15.11   Irrespective of the domicile of the parties,[1] where proceedings involving the same cause of action and between the same parties are brought in the courts of different member states, any court other than the court first seised is required to stay its proceedings of its own motion until such time as the jurisdiction of the court first seised is established.[2] Where the jurisdiction of the court first seised is established, any court other than the court first seised is required to decline jurisdiction in favour of that court.[3] Where actions come within the exclusive jurisdiction of several courts, any court other than the court first seised is required to decline jurisdiction in favour of that court.[4]

Where related actions are pending in the courts of different member states, any court other than the court first seised may stay its proceedings.[5] Where the actions are pending at first instance, any court other than the court first seised may also, on the application of one of the parties, decline jurisdiction if the court first seised has jurisdiction over the actions in question and its law permits the consolidation thereof.[6] For these purposes, actions are deemed to be related where they are so closely connected that it is expedient to hear and determine them together to avoid the risk of irreconcilable judgments resulting from separate proceedings.[7]

Without prejudice to the provisions in relation to entering an appearance,[8] where a court of a member state is seised pursuant to an exclusive jurisdiction clause which complies with the relevant formal requirements,[9] any court of another member state is required to stay the proceedings until such time as the court seised on the basis of the agreement declares that it has no jurisdiction under the agreement.[10]

For these purposes, a court is deemed to be seised at the time when the document instituting the proceedings or an equivalent document is lodged with the court, provided that the plaintiff has not subsequently failed to take the steps he was required to take to have service effected on the defendant, or if the document has to be served before being lodged with the court, at the time when it is received by the authority responsible for service, provided that the plaintiff has not subsequently failed to take the steps he was required to take to have the document lodged with the court.[11]

1 *Overseas Union Insurance Ltd v New Hampshire Insurance Co* [1992] QB 434, ECJ, para 18 (in relation to the equivalent provision of the Brussels Convention).
2 Brussels I Regulation, art 29(1). See further *The Alexandros T* [2013] UKSC 70, [2014] Lloyd's Rep 223.
3 Brussels I Regulation, art 29(3).
4 Brussels I Regulation, art 31(1).
5 Brussels I Regulation, art 30(1). See further *The Alexandros T* [2013] UKSC 70, [2014] Lloyd's Rep 223.
6 Brussels I Regulation, art 30(2).
7 Brussels I Regulation, art 30(3).
8 Brussels I Regulation, art 26.
9 Brussels I Regulation, art 25.
10 Brussels I Regulation, art 31(2). See further *The Alexandros T* [2013] UKSC 70, [2014] Lloyd's Rep 223.
11 Brussels I Regulation, art 32.

Provisional and protective measures

15.12 Application may be made to the courts of a member state for such provisional, including protective, measures as may be available under the law of that state, even if, under Regulation 1215/2012, the courts of another member state have jurisdiction as to the substance of the matter.[1]

1 Regulation 1215/2012, art 31.

JURISDICTION WHERE BRUSSELS I REGULATION DOES NOT APPLY

15.13 In the absence of a jurisdiction agreement, if the defendant does not enter an appearance before a court of a member state and is not domiciled in a member state, the jurisdiction of the courts of each member state in relation to contracts of insurance is determined by the law of that member state.[1] In order to be effective as a matter of English law, a jurisdiction agreement must be express; it will not be implied.[2] A jurisdiction clause which provides: 'This insurance shall be subject to the exclusive jurisdiction of the English courts ...' is not limited to the contract or policy of insurance, but goes beyond the purely contractual to include, for example, a freestanding tort said to arise in respect of any of the parties to the insurance as against another or a claim for unjust enrichment in respect of a mistaken payout.[3] The effect of such a clause may be to prevent a party from bringing a claim which it would have been able to bring in an alternative jurisdiction.[4]

In the absence of a jurisdiction agreement and where jurisdiction is not determined by the Brussels I Regulation, jurisdiction is determined by the common law principles known by the Latin tag *forum non conveniens* and restated by the House of Lords in *Spiliada Maritime Corpn v Cansulex Ltd*.[5] The basic principle is that English proceedings will only be stayed on the ground of *forum non conveniens* where the court is satisfied that there is some other available forum, having competent jurisdiction, which is clearly or distinctly the appropriate forum for the trial of the action, ie in which the case may be tried more suitably for the interests of all the parties and the ends of justice.[6] In general the burden of proof rests on the defendant to persuade the court to exercise its discretion to grant a stay, but each party will seek to establish the existence of certain matters which will assist him in persuading the court to exercise its discretion in his favour, and in respect of any such matter the evidential burden will rest on the party who asserts its existence; further, if the court is satisfied that there is another available forum which is prima facie the appropriate forum for the trial of the action, the burden will then shift to the claimant to show that there are special circumstances by reason of which justice requires that the trial should nevertheless take place in England and Wales.[7] There is no presumption at common law, rebuttable or otherwise, that because English proceedings were started before proceedings in another jurisdiction, the English proceedings should be allowed to continue.[8]

The court is seeking to identify the forum with which the action has the most real and substantial connection.[9] It is connecting factors in this sense for which the court must first look, and these will include not only factors affecting convenience or expense (such as availability of witnesses), but also other factors such as the law governing the relevant transaction and the places where the parties respectively reside or carry on business.[10] If the court concludes at that stage that there is no other available forum which is clearly more appropriate for the trial of the action, it will ordinarily refuse a stay; indeed, it is difficult to imagine circumstances in which a stay might be granted.[11] If however the court concludes at that stage that there is some other available forum which prima facie is clearly more appropriate for the trial of the action, it will ordinarily grant a stay unless there are circumstances by reason of which justice requires that a stay should nevertheless not be granted.[12] An application for a stay of English proceedings brought by the party who started those proceedings will only be granted in special or rare circumstances.[13]

1 Brussels I Regulation (Regulation 1215/2012), arts 4(1) and 22–24.
2 *New Hampshire Insurance Co v Strabag Bau AG* [1992] 1 Lloyd's Rep 361, 371–372, CA (Lloyd LJ).
3 *Beazley v Horizon Offshore Contractors Inc* [2004] EWHC 2555 (Comm), [2005] Lloyd's Rep IR 231, para 22 (His Honour Judge Chambers QC).
4 *Beazley v Horizon Offshore Contractors Inc* [2004] EWHC 2555 (Comm), [2005] Lloyd's Rep IR 231, paras 22–23 and 46 (His Honour Judge Chambers QC).
5 [1987] AC 460. See also **PARA 15.9**, note 15. There are three requirements for service of proceedings outside the jurisdiction: a jurisdictional gateway (contained in CPR 6.36 and paragraph 3.1 of Practice Direction 6B), a merits requirement (formally, 'a good arguable case', although in practice the test is higher and can be formulated by asking 'who has the better of the argument') and a *forum conveniens* requirement: see *Faraday Reinsurance Co Ltd v Howden North America Inc* [2011] EWHC 2837 (Comm), [2012] Lloyd's Rep. IR 631, paras 44–48 (Beatson J) (point not considered on appeal: [2012] EWCA Civ 980, [2012] Lloyd's Rep. IR 631).

6 *Spiliada Maritime Corpn v Cansulex Ltd* [1987] AC 460, 476–477, HL (Lord Goff).

7 *Spiliada Maritime Corpn v Cansulex Ltd* [1987] AC 460, 476, HL (Lord Goff).

8 *Travelers Casualty and Surety Co of Europe Ltd v Sun Life Assurance Co of Canada (UK) Ltd* [2004] EWHC 1704 (Comm), [2004] Lloyd's Rep IR 846, para 99 (Jonathan Hirst QC, sitting as a Deputy Judge of the High Court). A claim in respect of a contract of insurance may be started by either party, as the insurer may claim negative declaratory relief, reversing the normal roles of claimant and defendant: *Travelers Casualty and Surety Co of Europe Ltd v Sun Life Assurance Co of Canada (UK) Ltd* [2004] EWHC 1704 (Comm), [2004] Lloyd's Rep IR 846, para 100 (Jonathan Hirst QC, sitting as a Deputy Judge of the High Court).

9 *Spiliada Maritime Corpn v Cansulex Ltd* [1987] AC 460, 477–478, HL (Lord Goff).

10 *Spiliada Maritime Corpn v Cansulex Ltd* [1987] AC 460, 477–478, HL (Lord Goff).

11 *Spiliada Maritime Corpn v Cansulex Ltd* [1987] AC 460, 478, HL (Lord Goff).

12 *Spiliada Maritime Corpn v Cansulex Ltd* [1987] AC 460, 478, HL (Lord Goff); *Connelly v RTZ Corpn plc* [1998] AC 854, HL; *Lubbe v Cape plc* [2000] 1 WLR 1545, HL.

13 *Insurance Co of the State of Pennsylvania v Equitas Insurance Ltd* [2013] EWHC 3713 (Comm), [2013] Lloyd's Rep IR 195, paras 30–35 (Field J) (stay refused).

Chapter 16

Claims against insurance brokers

INTRODUCTION

16.1 Insurance brokers are specialist intermediaries who arrange insurance and offer advice to clients. An insurance broker is usually the agent of the insured. The identity of the party for whom the broker is acting has important practical consequences in relation to disclosure of material facts and provision of other information, such as in relation to notification of claims, to the insurer.

Insurance brokers typically owe their clients duties in both contract and tort, and fiduciary duties. They are also carrying on a 'regulated activity' pursuant to the Financial Services and Markets Act 2000, and may be liable to a client in damages for breach of statutory duty.[1] In certain, limited, circumstances they may owe duties to third parties, including insurers.

1 See PARA **16.9**.

IDENTIFYING THE PRINCIPAL

16.2 There is a common misapprehension that an insurance broker is the agent of the insurer rather than of the insured. In fact, this depends on the type of broker (Lloyd's or non-Lloyd's), and on the surrounding circumstances, but for most functions typically performed by insurance brokers, the broker is almost invariably the agent of the insured. This has important consequences, which are considered below.

Lloyd's brokers

16.3 A Lloyd's broker is a broker authorised to transact business at Lloyd's. The criteria for authorisation have recently been relaxed, but it is suggested that this has no impact on the established principle that Lloyd's brokers are always the agent of the insured, not of the underwriter.[1] This follows from the nature of the Lloyd's market, in which a broker does not know, when he sets out to place a risk, which (if any) of the underwriters at Lloyd's will accept it.[2] There is a limited exception to the general position, which is that, in principle at least, a Lloyd's broker may become the agent of the underwriter in relation to certain acts after inception of cover. The broker will, however, remain the agent of the insured for all other purposes.[3]

1 See *Newsholme Bros v Road Transport and General Insurance Co Ltd* [1929] 2 KB 356, 362, CA (Scrutton LJ); *General Accident Fire and Life Assurance Corpn v Tanter, The Zephyr* [1984] 1 Lloyd's Rep 58, 80 (Hobhouse J); *Eagle Star Insurance Co Ltd v National Westminster Finance Australia Ltd* (1985) 58 ALR 165, 171, PC; *Pryke v Gibbs Hartley Cooper Ltd* [1991] 1 Lloyd's Rep 602, 614 (Waller J). It is however unclear whether it is the insured or the underwriter who is liable to pay the broker: *Carvill America Inc v Camperdown UK Ltd* [2005] EWCA Civ 645, [2005] 2 Lloyd's Rep 457, para 32 (Clarke LJ).
2 See *Rozanes v Bowen* (1928) 32 Ll L Rep 98, 103, CA (Scrutton LJ).
3 See *North and South Trust Co v Berkeley* [1971] 1 WLR 470 (Donaldson J), considering the practice of Lloyd's brokers instructing claims assessors on behalf of underwriters. The practice is a breach of the broker's duty to the insured, which sounds in damages: *North and South Trust Co v Berkeley* [1971] 1 WLR 470 (Donaldson J), approved by the Privy Council in *Kelly v Cooper* [1993] AC 205; *Callaghan and Hedges v Thompson* [2000] Lloyd's Rep IR 125, 132 (David Steel J).

Other brokers

16.4 The usual position in relation to a non-Lloyd's broker (such as a high-street insurance broker) is that the broker is the agent of the insured.[1] This is so in relation to both the placing of insurance and the handling of claims,[2] and even where (as is usually the case) the broker is paid a commission on the premium by the insurer, rather than being paid directly by the insured.[3] In relation to the issue of cover notes, however, the position is different: the broker has implied authority to issue on behalf of the insurer, or enter into as agent for the insurer, contracts of interim insurance, which are normally recorded in cover notes, although an oral agreement (typically, by telephone) is sufficient even without the issue of a cover note.[4] Similarly, where a broker is retained by an insurer to generate business, the broker will usually be the agent of the insurer, but even here there are exceptions, most notably where the broker assists the insured in completing a proposal form.[5]

It is necessary to consider the facts of each case to determine whether a broker is the agent of the insurer or the insured. The decided cases offer little guidance as to the factors which should be taken into account. In *Newsholme Brothers v Road Transport and General Insurance Co Ltd*,[6] Scrutton LJ noted the conflict in the cases between a desire to hold the insurer, who employs an agent to bring him business, liable for anything that the agent does in procuring business, and the contention that a man who signs a promise that certain written statements are true and the basis of his contract, which statements, if he read before signing, he would know to be untrue, cannot claim to vary his contract by omitting that promise and misstatement. Scrutton LJ was clearly unimpressed by the attempt on the part of the insured to distance himself from the untrue answers which had been given on his behalf, and held the broker to be the agent of the insured.[7] In *London Borough of Bromley v Ellis*,[8] the broker was held to be the agent of the insurer, but at the same time to owe the insured a duty of care in negligence; the decision contains no analysis of the agency issue and it is suggested that, in so far as it decided that the broker was the agent of the insurer, it was wrongly decided.

In *Woolcott v Excess Insurance Co Ltd*,[9] the broker held a binding authority[10] and was for this reason held (it being also conceded) to be the agent of the insurer. However, in *Vesta v Butcher*[11] and *Callaghan and Hedges v Thompson*,[12] brokers were held to be the agent of the insured[13] despite the existence of a binding authority. The acceptance by a broker of instructions to act as agent of the insurer even in breach of its duties to the insured does not terminate its relationship with the insured, although it may expose the broker to the risk of a claim for injunctive relief or damages,[14] and where a broker holds a binding authority, he may at one and the same time be the agent of the insured for some purposes and the agent of the insurer for others.[15] It is suggested that the same analysis applies where the broker issues a cover note to the insured.[16]

1 *Anglo-African Merchants Ltd v Bayley* [1970] 1 QB 311, 322–324 (Megaw J); see also *North and South Trust Co v Berkeley* [1971] 1 WLR 470 (Donaldson J); *McNealy v The Pennine Insurance Co Ltd* [1978] 2 Lloyd's Rep 18, CA; *Winter v Irish Life Assurance plc* [1995] 2 Lloyd's Rep 274, 282 (Sir Peter Webster); *Searle v A R Hales & Co Ltd* [1996] LRLR 68, 71 (Mr Adrian Whitfield QC).

2 *Anglo-African Merchants Ltd v Bayley* [1970] 1 QB 311, 322–324 (Megaw J); see also *North and South Trust Co v Berkeley* [1971] 1 WLR 470 (Donaldson J); *Callaghan and Hedges v Thompson* [2000] Lloyd's Rep IR 125 (David Steel J).

3 *Brook v Trafalgar Ins Co Ltd* (1946) 79 Ll L Rep 365, CA; *Searle v A R Hales & Co Ltd* [1996] LRLR 68, 71 (Mr Adrian Whitfield QC).

4 *Stockton v Mason* [1978] 2 Lloyd's Rep 430, CA; *Searle v A R Hales & Co Ltd* [1996] LRLR 68, 71 (Mr Adrian Whitfield QC). The broker's implied authority does not extend to entering into the complete policy of insurance which is substituted for the interim or temporary policy evidenced by the cover note: *Stockton v Mason* [1978] 2 Lloyd's Rep 430, 431, CA (Lord Diplock). This is the modern position: in *Newsholme Brothers v Road Transport and General Insurance Co Ltd* [1929] 2 KB 356, 377, CA, Greer LJ stated that, in the absence of express authority, an agent to procure signed proposal forms was not authorised to give cover notes or enter into any policy of insurance.

5 *Rozanes v Bowen* (1928) 32 Ll L Rep 98, CA, 101 (Scrutton LJ); *Newsholme Bros v Road Transport and General Insurance Co Ltd* [1929] 2 KB 356, 362–363, CA (Scrutton LJ).

6 [1929] 2 KB 356, 362–363, CA (Scrutton LJ).

7 At 364–365, 369.

8 [1971] 1 Lloyd's Rep 97, CA.

9 [1979] 2 Lloyd's Rep 210 (Cantley J).

10 The holder of a binding authority is authorised to bind insurance for the insurer's account, and initial documents of insurance and endorsements, in accordance with a written agreement.

11 [1986] 2 Lloyd's Rep 179, [1986] 2 All ER 488 (Hobhouse J). The finding on this issue was not considered on appeal: [1989] AC 852, CA and HL.

12 [2000] Lloyd's Rep IR 125, 132 (David Steel J).

13 *Vesta v Butcher* concerned reinsurance, and the broker was held to be the agent of the reinsured.

14 See **PARAS 16.10** and **16.40**.

15 *Drake Insurance plc v Provident Insurance plc* [2003] EWCA Civ 1834, [2004] 1 Lloyd's Rep 268, para 62 (Rix LJ), in which the broker had authority to rate each proposal for motor insurance and to determine the premium on the basis of the insurer's underwriting criteria.

16 As to cover notes, see **PARAS 1.10** and **3.2**.

Sub-agency between producing and placing broker

16.5 A sub-agency relationship often arises where a producing broker employs a specialist broker, such as a Lloyd's broker, to place insurance for a client. The producing broker will normally be taken to have contracted on the basis of an implied promise that the work required to carry out the client's instructions will be done carefully by whomever the broker gets to do it, whether that person is its own employee or a subcontractor.[1] In such a case, the responsibility assumed by the broker which gives rise to a concurrent liability in tort will generally be co-extensive with what has been contractually agreed.[2] If however what the producing broker agreed was not to arrange insurance for its client, but to get another broker to do so, the duty of the producing broker, both in contract and in tort, would be limited to taking care to choose a competent sub-broker and giving appropriate instructions to the sub-broker.[3] There is, in normal circumstances, no privity of contract between the client (the insured) and the sub-agent.[4] Whether the sub-agent owes the insured a duty of care in tort to avoid economic loss will depend on the application of ordinary principles;[5] this question can give rise to considerable difficulty.[6] In the slightly more complex situation of an umbrella agreement, which enables the directors, partners or employees of the non-Lloyd's broker to transact business at Lloyd's using the Lloyd's broker's slips, the non-Lloyd's broker is the agent of the insured in exercising these functions.[7] Where there is a chain of insurance intermediaries between the insurer and the customer, ICOBS applies only to the insurance intermediary in contact with the customer.[8]

1 *Involnert Management Inc v Aprilgrange Ltd* [2015] EWHC 2225 (Comm), [2015] 2 Lloyd's Rep 289, para 280 (Leggatt J).
2 *Involnert Management Inc v Aprilgrange Ltd* [2015] EWHC 2225 (Comm), [2015] 2 Lloyd's Rep 289, para 280 (Leggatt J).
3 *Involnert Management Inc v Aprilgrange Ltd* [2015] EWHC 2225 (Comm), [2015] 2 Lloyd's Rep 289, para 280 (Leggatt J).
4 *Prentis Donegan & Partners Ltd v Leeds & Leeds Co Inc* [1998] 2 Lloyd's Rep 326 (Rix J); *Pangood Ltd v Barclay Brown & Co Ltd* [1999] Lloyd's Rep IR 405, CA.
5 See *Pangood Ltd v Barclay Brown & Co Ltd* [1999] Lloyd's Rep IR 405, CA (no general duty of care owed by sub-agent to insured); *European International Reinsurance Co Ltd v Curzon Insurance Ltd* [2003] EWCA Civ 1074, [2003] Lloyd's Rep IR 793, paras 28–29 (Longmore LJ) (it must be at least arguable that someone who holds himself out as 'A Lloyd's Broker' assumes a personal responsibility to the person seeking to use his broking services; he may at the same time say that he is the agent of another broker or broking company but that does not, of itself and without question, negate any liability on his part; indeed, it is surprising that brokers would wish to argue that they could at one and the same time call themselves 'A Lloyd's Broker' and yet say that in presenting a reinsurance slip in their own name even to the non-Lloyds' market, they are not accepting any responsibility at all in relation to disclosure towards the company who is the reinsured pursuant to that slip); see also *Fisk v Brian Thornhill & Son* [2007] EWCA Civ 152, [2007] Lloyd's Rep IR 699 (no dispute on appeal that sub-broker owed duty of care to broker and to insured; liability and costs of main action apportioned between broker and sub-broker); *Involnert Management Inc v Aprilgrange Ltd* [2015] EWHC 2225 (Comm), [2015] 2 Lloyd's Rep 289, paras 290–291 (Leggatt J) (no duty of care owed by sub-agent to insured where insured did not rely on placing broker's expertise, but relied solely on producing broker).
6 *Involnert Management Inc v Aprilgrange Ltd* [2015] EWHC 2225 (Comm), [2015] 2 Lloyd's Rep 289, para 284 (Leggatt J).
7 *Callaghan and Hedges v Thompson* [2000] Lloyd's Rep IR 125, 132 (David Steel J).
8 ICOBS 1.1.2, Part 2, 4.1R; see also **PARA 16.9**.

THE IMPORTANCE OF IDENTIFYING THE PRINCIPAL

16.6   The issue of whether the broker is the agent of the insured or of the insurer is of central importance in many insurance disputes, and will often be determinative of the insurer's liability to the insured. This is because, where the broker is the insured's agent, the broker's knowledge of material facts will not be imputed to the insurer, and the insurer will be entitled to rely, as against the insured, upon any failure by the broker to disclose this information.[1]

Brokers acting for an insured are typically remunerated by way of commission agreed with the insurer rather than by fees received directly from the insured. In *Absalom v TCRU Ltd*,[2] Longmore LJ said:[3]

'It is a curiosity of the law relating to insurance and reinsurance brokers that such brokers procure their remuneration by negotiation with the insurers or reinsurers and not by arrangements with their own principals who are the insured or the reinsured. In the first instance, at any rate, the insured or reinsured will usually not be told and will not know what part of the insurance premium will be collected by the broker by way of commission. All that the insured or reinsured will know is the amount of premium which he has to pay which will be inclusive of the brokers' remuneration, see *Great Western Insurance Co v Cunliffe* (1874) LR 9 Ch App 525. The premium will normally be paid by the insured or reinsured to the broker who will then normally pass the premium to the insurer or reinsurer after deducting his commission.'

The fact that the broker agrees his level of remuneration with the insurer and not the insured is not therefore an indication that the insurer is the broker's principal.

Section 19 of the Marine Insurance Act 1906 requires disclosure by the broker of all material circumstances known to him, whether his knowledge was acquired in his capacity as broker for the assured or otherwise.[4] Failure by the broker to disclose all material circumstances in accordance with s 19 entitles the insurer to avoid the policy.[5] If material facts are known to a broker but not communicated to the insured, the broker is under a duty, pursuant to s 19, to disclose those facts to the insurer if the broker places the risk on behalf of the insured. As the broker is an 'agent to insure' and not an 'agent to know', the insured is not deemed to know those facts, and if he subsequently changes brokers and the same risk is then placed with insurers he is under no duty to disclose those facts to insurers.[6] However, if the insured's broker has knowledge of material facts but, having commenced negotiations with insurers, fails to disclose the facts to the insurers and then ceases to act, and the insured adopts and concludes the negotiations with the insurers directly, the insurers are entitled to avoid the policy for non-disclosure of the material facts.[7]

Where the broker is the insurer's agent, the broker's knowledge of material facts may be imputed to the insurer, with the result that the insurer will not be able to rely, as against the insured, upon any failure by the broker to disclose this information.[8] Where the insurer's agent completes a proposal form on behalf of the insured, he is for these purposes the agent of the insured, and as a result any knowledge he gains in performing this duty is not imputed to the insurer.[9] But knowledge of the falsity of the answers given by the insured would not be imputed in any event: if the insurer's agent is unaware that the insured's answers are untrue, there is no knowledge to be imputed to the insurer;[10] and if the insurer's agent knows that the answers are untrue, he is committing a fraud on his principal, and his knowledge is not imputed to the insurer, who is entitled to avoid the policy.[11] The insurer will not be entitled to avoid the policy on the grounds of non-fraudulent misrepresentation by its own agent,[12] unless there is a provision making the inaccurate statement the basis of the contract.[13]

A condition which provides that any omission of, or misrepresentation of, material fact in the proposal form renders the policy void, even if known to an agent of the company, is enforceable if it is expressed in clear terms.[14]

1 See **PARAS 11.5–11.34** and **16.19**. The Consumer Insurance (Disclosure and Representations) Act 2012 includes detailed rules for determining whether an agent was acting as the agent of the consumer or of the insurer: s 9 and Sch 2. The 2012 Act also provides that nothing in the Act affects the circumstances in which a person is bound by the acts or omissions of that person's agent: s 12(5).
2 [2005] EWCA Civ 1586, [2006] 2 Lloyd's Rep 129.

3 At para 6; see, similarly, *HIH Casualty and General Insurance Ltd v JLT Risk Solutions Ltd* [2007] EWCA Civ 710, [2007] 2 Lloyd's Rep 278, para 60 (Auld LJ).

4 *Société Anonyme d'Intermédiaires Luxembourgeois v Farex Gie* [1995] LRLR 116, CA, 143 (Dillon LJ), 149 (Hoffmann LJ).

5 *Blackburn, Low & Co v Haslam* (1888) 21 QBD 144 (breach of agent's duty to disclose at common law, which was subsequently codified in s 19 of the Marine Insurance Act 1906).

6 *Blackburn, Low & Co v Vigors* (1887) 12 App Cas 531, HL (reinsurance, but principle equally applicable to insurance: at 540 (Lord Watson)); *Société Anonyme d'Intermédiaires Luxembourgeois v Farex Gie* [1995] LRLR 116, 142, CA (Dillon LJ).

7 *Blackburn, Low & Co v Haslam* (1888) 21 QBD 144.

8 See, for example, *Woolcott v Excess Insurance Co Ltd* [1979] 2 Lloyd's Rep 210 (Cantley J) (the insurer was held to be entitled to an indemnity from the broker for failing to disclose to the insurer the insured's criminal record, of which it was aware).

9 *Newsholme Bros v Road Transport and General Insurance Co Ltd* [1929] 2 KB 356, CA, 364, 369, 375–376 (Scrutton LJ), 382 (Greer LJ).

10 *Newsholme Bros v Road Transport and General Insurance Co Ltd* [1929] 2 KB 356, 375–376, CA (Scrutton LJ).

11 *Re Hampshire Land Co* [1896] 2 Ch 743, 749–750 (Vaughan Williams J); *Biggar v Rock Life Assurance Co* [1902] 1 KB 516, 524 (Wright J); *Newsholme Bros v Road Transport and General Insurance Co Ltd* [1929] 2 KB 356, 375–376, CA (Scrutton LJ); *Dunn v Ocean Accident & Guarantee Corpn Ltd* (1933) 47 Ll L Rep 129, CA; *Société Anonyme d'Intermédiaires Luxembourgeois v Farex Gie* [1995] LRLR 116, 143, CA (Dillon LJ).

12 *Re Universal Non-Tariff Fire Insurance Co* (1875) LR 19 Eq 485 (agent solicited business on behalf of insurer, inspected insured's property and reported to insurer, who sought unsuccessfully to avoid on basis of alleged misrepresentation in description of construction of roof of part of property).

13 *Newsholme Bros v Road Transport and General Insurance Co Ltd* [1929] 2 KB 356, 364, 374, 376, CA (Scrutton LJ).

14 *Broad & Montague Ltd v South East Lancashire Insurance Co Ltd* (1931) 40 Ll L Rep 328, 330 (Rowlatt J).

DUTIES TO CLIENT

16.7 The relationship between insurance broker and client is normally contractual. There may be a written retainer, although this is frequently not the case. Brokers are normally paid by means of commission on the sale of an insurance product, which is paid by the insurer, rather than by any direct payment by the client to the broker.[1] In addition to express terms, the contract will commonly include implied terms, notably the implied term that the broker will exercise reasonable skill and care in acting on behalf of the client. Such a term is implied at common law[2] and pursuant to statute.[3]

In addition to the duties arising pursuant to his contractual retainer, the broker owes a duty of care in tort to exercise reasonable skill and care in acting on behalf of the client.[4] Individual brokers may also owe a client a duty of care in tort.[5]

In selling or giving advice in relation to buying policies of insurance, a broker is carrying on a 'regulated activity' pursuant to the Financial Services and Markets Act 2000 and regulations made thereunder,[6] and may be liable to a client in damages for breach of statutory duty.[7]

The broker also owes fiduciary duties to the client.[8]

A broker must not seek to exclude or restrict, or to rely on any exclusion or restriction of, any duty or liability it may have to a customer or other policyholder unless it is reasonable for it to do so and the duty or liability arises other than under the regulatory system.[9]

1 See **PARA 16.6**.
2 *Youell v Bland Welch & Co Ltd, The Superhulls Cover Case (No 2)* [1990] 2 Lloyd's Rep 431, 458 (Phillips J).
3 Supply of Goods and Services Act 1982, s 13. The statute adds nothing to the implication of a term at common law and is typically not pleaded.
4 *Henderson v Merrett Syndicates Ltd* [1995] 2 AC 145, HL; see also *Midland Bank Trust Co Ltd v Hett, Stubbs and Kemp* [1979] Ch 384.
5 See **PARA 16.8**.
6 See the Financial Services and Markets Act 2000, s 22 and Sch 2 and the Financial Services and Markets Act 2000 (Regulated Activities) Order 2001 (SI 2001/544), as amended.
7 See **PARA 16.9**.
8 See **PARA 16.10**.
9 ICOBS 2.5.1. See also **PARA 16.9**.

Duties owed by individual brokers in tort

16.8   Actions are usually brought not against individual brokers but against their employers, who are responsible for the actions of their employees on the basis of the ordinary principles of vicarious liability.[1] However, there may be cases in which it is preferable or necessary to bring proceedings against an individual broker; for example, where that person has changed employment during the relevant period and it is unclear in relation to some of the broker's actions which of the employers is responsible. Individuals usually rely upon their employer's professional indemnity insurance, which may not provide cover should an action be brought directly against the individual broker.[2]

Whether an individual broker owes a tortious duty of care to the client will depend upon the circumstances, and in particular on what he is employed to do. The question is whether the individual may fairly be said to have voluntarily assumed the duties of the broker towards the client.[3] Although the usual assumption will be that a director or employee of a company does not himself voluntarily assume responsibility on his own behalf but on behalf of his employer,[4] if an individual broker is entrusted with the whole, or nearly the whole, of the task which his employer has undertaken, he may owe the client a duty of care.[5]

Where the individual broker owes a duty of care to the client, the individual broker and the employer may both be held to be liable, and the client may therefore seek to enforce the judgment against either or both until he has recovered the full amount.[6]

1 See *Clerk & Lindsell on Torts* (21st edn, 2014), paras 6–28 to 6–58. In addition, an authorised person is responsible for the acts and omissions of its appointed representatives in carrying on business for which the authorised person has accepted responsibility: s 39(3) of the 2000 Act. In determining whether an authorised person has complied with a provision contained in or made under the 2000 Act, anything which an appointed representative has done or omitted as respects business for which the authorised person has accepted responsibility is to be treated as having been done or omitted by the authorised person: s 39(4) of the 2000 Act.
2 Individual brokers would be well advised to consider whether their employer's professional indemnity insurance would cover them should an action be brought against them directly; see, in the context of surveyors' negligence, *Merrett v Babb* [2001] EWCA Civ 214, [2001] QB 1174, para 19 (May LJ).
3 *European International Reinsurance Co Ltd v Curzon Insurance Ltd* [2003] EWCA Civ 1074, [2003] Lloyd's Rep IR 793, para 25 (Longmore LJ).
4 *Williams v Natural Life Health Foods Ltd* [1998] 1 WLR 830, HL; *European International Reinsurance Co Ltd v Curzon Insurance Ltd* [2003] EWCA Civ 1074, [2003] Lloyd's Rep IR 793, para 24 (Longmore LJ).

5 *Punjab National Bank v De Boinville* [1992] 1 WLR 1138, 1154, CA (Staughton LJ); in *European International Reinsurance Co Ltd v Curzon Insurance Ltd* [2003] EWCA Civ 1074, [2003] Lloyd's Rep IR 793, Longmore LJ said (para 25) that the decision of the Court of Appeal in *Punjab National Bank v De Boinville* was not necessarily inconsistent with *Williams v Natural Life Health Foods Ltd* [1998] 1 WLR 830, HL. The contractual relationship is between the client and the broker's employer.
6 In normal circumstances, the employer's professional indemnity insurers would satisfy the judgment, but there might be circumstances in which this would not happen; for example, if either the employer or the insurer were insolvent.

Breach of statutory duty (ICOBS and COBS)

16.9 A breach of ICOBS or COBS may expose a broker to liability for breach of statutory duty.[1] In many cases, there will be an overlap between the broker's duties at common law, whether contractual, tortuous or fiduciary, and the obligations imposed by ICOBS and COBS. Indeed, in the advisory context,[2] the regulatory background provides guidance as to the professional standards to be expected of insurance brokers.[3] The regulatory background includes ICOBS and COBS, and their predecessors ICOB and COB.[4]

1 See **PARA 8.2**.
2 See *Green v Royal Bank of Scotland plc* [2013] EWCA Civ 1197, [2014] PNLR 6, paras 17–18 and 23 (Tomlinson LJ), in which the Court of Appeal said that this did not apply where a firm was simply giving information about and selling a product (in that case, an interest rate swap), and was not giving advice.
3 See eg *Dunlop Haywards (DHL) Ltd v Barbon Insurance Group Ltd* [2009] EWHC 2900 (Comm), [2010] Lloyd's Rep IR 149, paras 159–167 (Hamblen J).
4 See *Dunlop Haywards (DHL) Ltd v Barbon Insurance Group Ltd* [2009] EWHC 2900 (Comm), [2010] Lloyd's Rep IR 149, paras 160–167 (Hamblen J) (referring to the Codes of Conduct issued by the General Insurance Standards Council (GISC) and ICOB). ICOB replaced the GISC Codes of Conduct with effect from 14 January 2005, and ICOBS replaced ICOB with effect from 6 January 2008.

Fiduciary duties

16.10 An insurance broker undertakes to act for his client in circumstances which give rise to a relationship of trust and confidence. He is therefore a fiduciary, and owes a duty of loyalty to the client. This means that he must act in good faith; he must not make a profit out of his trust; he must not place himself in a position where his duty and his interest may conflict; and he may not act for his own benefit or for the benefit of a third party without the informed consent of the client. The practice of Lloyd's brokers instructing claims assessors on behalf of underwriters is a breach of the broker's fiduciary obligations to the insured, as the broker thereby puts himself in a position where his duty and his interest may conflict.[1]

Moreover:[2]

'The role of an insurance broker is notoriously anomalous for its inherent scope for engendering conflict of interest in the otherwise relatively tidy legal world of agency. In its simplest form, the negotiation of insurance, the broker acts as agent for the insured, but normally receives his remuneration from the insurer in the form of commission; he may, in certain circumstances, act for both. Where there is reinsurance of an insured risk, the same broker may act on behalf of the insured in placing the insurance and on behalf of the insurer in placing the reinsurance.'

There is a fundamental difference between breach of fiduciary obligation and simple incompetence, in that breach of fiduciary obligation connotes disloyalty or infidelity.[3] For this reason, where a claim is made for breach of a tortious duty of care, a claim for breach of fiduciary duty based on the same facts should not be pleaded as an alternative.[4]

1 *North and South Trust Co v Berkeley* [1971] 1 WLR 470 (Donaldson J), approved by the Privy Council in *Kelly v Cooper* [1993] AC 205; *Callaghan and Hedges v Thompson* [2000] Lloyd's Rep IR 125, 132 (David Steel J). See also PARA **16.23** in relation to claims handling carried out by brokers on behalf of insurers. The breach sounds in damages: see PARA **16.40**.
2 *HIH Casualty and General Insurance Ltd v JLT Risk Solutions Ltd* [2007] EWCA Civ 710, [2007] 2 Lloyd's Rep 278, para 60 (Auld LJ).
3 *Bristol and West Building Society v Mothew* [1998] 9 Ch 1, 18, CA (Millett LJ).
4 See Lord Browne-Wilkinson's analysis of the relationship between fiduciary duties and tortious duties of care in *Henderson v Merrett Syndicates Ltd* [1995] 2 AC 145, 204–206, HL. His Lordship described the putting forward of such an alternative claim by the Names as 'misconceived' (at 205).

DUTIES TO INSURER

16.11   In the absence of an express agreement between a broker and an insurer, the broker will typically be the agent of, and owe contractual and tortious duties to, the insured, and not the insurer.[1] The broker may nevertheless be under an obligation to the insurer in certain circumstances. For example, it seems that a Lloyd's broker owes a duty to exercise reasonable care when giving a signing-down indication to an insurer.[2] It is a vexed question whether the duty is contractual or tortious. It was held by Hobhouse J to be tortious at first instance in *General Accident Fire and Life Assurance Corpn v Tanter, The Zephyr*.[3] On appeal, Mustill LJ preferred to analyse the obligation as contractual, while acknowledging that it might be tortious.[4] In *Pryke v Gibbs Hartley Cooper Ltd*,[5] Waller J rejected the argument that a broker owed a contractual duty to the insurer, holding that brokerage was paid for the introduction of business, not for the service of administering the contract, but that a tortious duty of care might be owed in certain circumstances, for example, where the broker, not being under any duty to the insurer to supply information to it, nevertheless supplied the information. The duty would then be to exercise reasonable care in supplying the information.

1 See PARAS **16.2–16.4**.
2 *General Accident Fire and Life Assurance Corpn v Tanter, The Zephyr* [1984] 1 Lloyd's Rep 58 (Hobhouse J); [1985] 2 Lloyd's Rep 529, CA. Signing down is the process whereby each line written by underwriters is proportionally reduced, after the broker has finished taking his slip round the market, so as to ensure that the subscriptions add up to 100 per cent and no more. A signing-down indication is a statement by the broker to the underwriter as to the percentage of the written line which he believes the underwriter will actually have to bear when the process of signing down is completed.
3 *General Accident Fire and Life Assurance Corpn v Tanter, The Zephyr* [1984] 1 Lloyd's Rep 58 (Hobhouse J).
4 *General Accident Fire and Life Assurance Corpn v Tanter, The Zephyr* [1985] 2 Lloyd's Rep 529, CA (obiter; and note that Mustill LJ's reasoning in relation to the duty of care in tort should now be read in the light of the acceptance of the House of Lords in *Henderson v Merrett Syndicates Ltd* [1995] 2 AC 145 and *White v Jones* [1995] 2 AC 207 that liability may arise in tort in certain circumstances for economic loss caused by negligent omissions).
5 [1991] 1 Lloyd's Rep 602.

DUTIES TO OTHER THIRD PARTIES

16.12   Brokers may, in certain limited circumstances, owe a tortious duty of care to parties other than the insurer and the client. In *Punjab National Bank v De Boinville*,[1] the brokers knew that it was intended that the plaintiff bank would take an assignment of the policy which it was arranging on behalf of its client, and that the bank was actively participating in giving instructions for the insurance. The Court of Appeal followed *Caparo Industries plc v Dickman*[2] in seeking to develop novel categories of the duty of care in negligence incrementally and by analogy with established categories, and held that it was a justifiable increment to extend to the bank in these circumstances the category of persons to whom an insurance broker owes a duty of care in tort. The Court of Appeal emphasised the bank's involvement in the giving of instructions for the insurance, and indicated that to hold that a substantial creditor of an insurance broker's client was necessarily owed a duty of care in tort might well be more than a justifiable increment. This result is consistent with the earlier decision of Evans J in *Macmillan v A W Knott Becker Scott Ltd*.[3] Evans J rejected arguments by the clients of Knott Becker Scott, insurance brokers who had gone into insolvent liquidation without valid E & O (errors and omissions) cover, that a duty of care was owed directly to them in tort by Nelson Hurst & Marsh, the brokers who had placed the E & O cover on behalf of Knott Becker Scott, and who were said to have been negligent.

Similarly, in *Verderame v Commercial Union Assurance Co plc*,[4] a broker had arranged insurance on the stock of a company in the name of Mr Verderame, one of the directors and shareholders of the company. The stock was stolen, and the insurers repudiated liability on the grounds that Mr Verderame had no insurable interest in the stock. Mr Verderame claimed an indemnity against the insurers in the proceedings, but that claim had not yet been determined. Claims were brought against the brokers by the company and by Mr and Mrs Verderame. The claims alleged that the brokers were the agents of the company, but also owed Mr and Mrs Verderame a duty of care in tort in arranging the insurance. An application by the brokers to strike out Mr and Mrs Verderame's claim succeeded. The Court of Appeal held that if the claim against the insurers succeeded, there would be no loss of indemnity, and that if it were unsuccessful, it would be because Mr Verderame did not have an insurable interest in the stock, and accordingly it would be the company which had lost the right to an indemnity and not Mr or Mrs Verderame. Significantly, the Court of Appeal also held that the broker did not owe Mr and Mrs Verderame a duty of care in tort in effecting the insurance to prevent them from suffering the kind of damage alleged in their pleadings (loss of salary as directors of the company, the company having gone into liquidation; anxiety, depression and inconvenience; and the costs of the proceedings against the insurers).

In *Gorham v British Telecommunications plc*,[5] an insurance company which, in advising the deceased about his pension and life cover, knew that he intended to make provision for his dependants in the event of his death, was held to owe the dependants a duty of care. It is suggested that the reasoning is equally applicable where advice is given by a broker, rather than by the insurance company directly, in relation to the purchase of life insurance or pension products.

1 [1992] 1 WLR 1138, 1153–1154, CA.
2 [1990] 2 AC 605, HL.

3 [1990] 1 Lloyd's Rep 98 (Evans J).
4 [1992] BCLC 793, CA.
5 [2000] 1 WLR 2129, CA, applying *White v Jones* [1995] 2 AC 207, HL.

STANDARD OF SKILL AND CARE REQUIRED

16.13   An insurance broker is under a duty to exercise reasonable skill and care, which means the skill and care to be expected of a reasonably competent insurance broker.[1] The standard of skill and care to be expected of a broker depends on the market in which the broker operates. Thus, it is appropriate to require that a non-specialist marine broker should bear no greater skill than that which would be expected from a reasonably skilled non-specialist broker, which means, in the case of the insurance of a motor yacht, the standard of a broker who has such general knowledge of the yacht insurance market and the cover available in it as to be able to advise his client on all matters on which a lay client would in the ordinary course of events predictably need advice, in particular in the course of the selection of cover and the completion of the proposal.[2] This is not the same thing as saying that the standard is that of a marine broker substantially inexperienced in the insurance of large yachts.[3]

The regulatory background provides guidance as to the professional standards to be expected of insurance brokers, and the exercise of the duty to exercise reasonable care and skill will ordinarily include compliance with the rules of the relevant regulator, such as ICOBS.[4] The general duties of insurance brokers have been considered by the courts in many cases and, to a substantial extent, have become a matter of law.[5] There is thus a danger that the evidence of an insurance broker called as an expert witness will involve expressing opinions about the broker's understanding of the law.[6] It should not be assumed that in every case where an allegation of negligence is made against an insurance broker, expert evidence is reasonably required to resolve the proceedings; and where expert evidence is required, careful thought always needs to be given to its legitimate and useful scope.[7] In some instances, the absence of any supporting expert evidence may undermine allegations made by a claimant about the scope of the duty owed by a broker; but the mere fact that an allegation of negligence is not supported by the opinion of a broking expert that the relevant act or omission fell below the standard of a competent and careful insurance broker is not a deficiency in a claimant's case.[8]

Rattee J considered the admissibility of expert evidence as to the practice of insurance brokers in *O'Brien v Hughes-Gibb and Co Ltd*.[9] The judge was critical of the expert evidence which had been called, saying that a significant amount consisted of inadmissible statements by Lloyd's underwriters and brokers as to what, in their view, the defendant brokers should have done in discharging their duties to the client. He referred to the judgment of Oliver J in *Midland Bank Trust Co Ltd v Hett, Stubbs & Kemp*, and said:[10]

'As Mr Justice Oliver said,[11] expert evidence is admissible on the question of the duty of a professional person to the extent that it shows "… some practice in a particular profession, some accepted standard of conduct which is laid down by a professional institute or sanctioned by common usage".'

In rare cases the court may decide that the practice of insurance brokers represents a standard which is lower[12] or higher than that imposed by the law. In *United Mills*

Agencies Ltd v Harvey, Bray & Co,[13] McNair J held that it was the practice of insurance brokers generally to notify the client as soon as possible when cover has been placed, and that that was good business and prudent office management, but that it was not part of the duty owed by the broker to the client in the sense that a failure to notify would involve the broker in legal liability.

Similarly, Oliver J's classic description, in *Midland Bank Trust Co Ltd v Hett, Stubbs & Kemp*,[14] of solicitors' duties, is applicable by analogy to insurance brokers:

> 'Now no doubt the duties owed by a solicitor to his client are high, in the sense that he holds himself out as practising a highly skilled and exacting profession, but I think that the court must beware of imposing upon solicitors – or upon professional men in other spheres – duties which go beyond the scope of what they are requested to undertake to do. It may be that a particularly meticulous and conscientious practitioner would, in his client's general interests, take it upon himself to pursue a line of inquiry beyond the strict limits comprehended by his instructions. But that is not the test. The test is what the reasonably competent practitioner would do having regard to the standards normally adopted in his profession ...'

1 *Chapman v Walton* (1833) 10 Bing 57, 63 (Lord Tindal CJ); *Sharp v Sphere Drake Insurance plc, The Moonacre* [1992] 2 Lloyd's Rep 501, 523 (Mr A D Colman QC, sitting as a Deputy Judge of the High Court).
2 *Sharp v Sphere Drake Insurance plc, The Moonacre* [1992] 2 Lloyd's Rep 501, 523 (Mr A D Colman QC, sitting as a Deputy Judge of the High Court); applying *Duchess of Argyll v Beuselinck* [1972] 2 Lloyd's Rep 172, 183 (Megarry J).
3 *Sharp v Sphere Drake Insurance plc, The Moonacre* [1992] 2 Lloyd's Rep 501, 523 (Mr A D Colman QC, sitting as a Deputy Judge of the High Court).
4 See eg *Dunlop Haywards (DHL) Ltd v Barbon Insurance Group Ltd* [2009] EWHC 2900 (Comm), [2010] Lloyd's Rep IR 149, paras 159–169 (Hamblen J); *Green v Royal Bank of Scotland plc* [2013] EWCA Civ 1197, [2014] PNLR 6, para 18 (Tomlinson LJ) (Conduct of Business rules (COB): interest rate swap).
5 *Involnert Management Inc v Aprilgrange Ltd* [2015] EWHC 2225 (Comm), [2015] 2 Lloyd's Rep 289, para 294 (Leggatt J).
6 *Involnert Management Inc v Aprilgrange Ltd* [2015] EWHC 2225 (Comm), [2015] 2 Lloyd's Rep 289, para 294 (Leggatt J).
7 *Involnert Management Inc v Aprilgrange Ltd* [2015] EWHC 2225 (Comm), [2015] 2 Lloyd's Rep 289, para 297 (Leggatt J).
8 *Involnert Management Inc v Aprilgrange Ltd* [2015] EWHC 2225 (Comm), [2015] 2 Lloyd's Rep 289, para 297 (Leggatt J).
9 [1995] LRLR 80.
10 At 96–97.
11 At 402.
12 See *Edward Wong Finance Co Ltd v Johnson Stokes & Master* [1984] AC 296, PC (solicitors followed conveyancing practice established in Hong Kong but were held to be negligent as the practice involved foreseeable risks).
13 [1951] 2 Lloyd's Rep 631, 644.
14 [1979] Ch 384, 402–403.

BREACH OF DUTY

16.14 A broker owes his client concurrent duties in contract and in tort to use reasonable skill and care when acting on the client's behalf.[1] In the absence of any agreement to the contrary, the duties are not absolute.[2] The general duty to exercise reasonable skill and care encompasses a wide range of more specific duties, depending on the factual circumstances, but includes the following:[3]

'… (i) He must ascertain his client's needs by instruction or otherwise. (ii) He must use reasonable skill and care to procure the cover which his client has asked for, either expressly or by necessary implication. (iii) If he cannot obtain what is required, he must report in what respects he has failed and seek his client's alternative instructions.'

Similarly:[4]

'(1)   It is the duty of a broker to identify and advise the client about the type and scope of cover which the client needs and, in doing so, to match as precisely as possible the risk exposures which have been identified within the client's business with the coverage available.

(2)   Having identified what cover the client needs, it is the broker's duty to arrange insurance cover which clearly meets those requirements. …

(3)   If the cover which is needed by the client is not available, the broker must take care to ensure that the precise nature of what is and is not covered is made entirely clear to the client.

(4)   In relation to the preparation of the policy, the broker must be careful to ensure that the policy language clearly encompasses the needs of the client.

(5)   The duties of the broker on the renewal of an existing policy are no different from on the initial placement, and at each renewal the broker must ensure that the cover arranged clearly meets the client's needs in the most appropriate manner.'

In addition, a broker may be liable to certain clients for breach of statutory duty if he breaches ICOBS or COBS.[5]

Aspects of the general duty of care, and obligations imposed by ICOBS and COBS, are considered further below.

1   See *Vesta v Butcher* [1986] 2 Lloyd's Rep 179, [1986] 2 All ER 488 (Hobhouse J), [1989] AC 852, CA and HL; *Youell v Bland Welch & Co Ltd, The Superhulls Cover Case (No 2)* [1990] 2 Lloyd's Rep 431, 458–459 (Phillips J); *Punjab National Bank v De Boinville* [1992] 1 WLR 1138, 1154, CA.
2   *Youell v Bland Welch & Co Ltd, The Superhulls Cover Case (No 2)* [1990] 2 Lloyd's Rep 431, 458 (Phillips J). In *Hood v West End Motor Car Packing Co* [1917] 2 KB 38, CA, the broker was held to have agreed expressly to procure insurance.
3   *Youell v Bland Welch & Co Ltd, The Superhulls Cover Case (No 2)* [1990] 2 Lloyd's Rep 431, 458 (Phillips J; reinsurance), applied in *Sharp v Sphere Drake Insurance plc, The Moonacre* [1992] 2 Lloyd's Rep 501, 523 (Mr A D Colman QC, sitting as a Deputy Judge of the High Court) and in *O'Brien v Hughes-Gibb and Co Ltd* [1995] LRLR 80, 98 (Rattee J).
4   *Standard Life Assurance Ltd v Oak Dedicated Ltd* [2008] EWHC 222 (Comm), [2008] Lloyd's Rep IR 552, para 102 (Tomlinson J, describing these as 'uncontroversial propositions' emerging from a report on London market practice).
5   See PARA **16.9**.

Failure to effect insurance

16.15   A broker is under a duty to use reasonable skill and care to procure insurance.[1] Where insurance is not available, the broker will not be liable for failing to procure it,[2] but may be liable for failing to keep the client informed if he does not report the failure to the client and, if necessary, seek further instructions.[3] Where there is an issue as to whether or not the broker has effected insurance, the issue of negligence is likely to be straightforward once the insurance position has been established. Indeed, if the court finds that there is no cover in place, the broker may concede that it has been negligent,[4] and defend the proceedings on the basis of any available arguments concerning causation and loss and damage.

1 See the authorities referred to in **PARA 16.14**, note 3, and *Eagle Star Insurance Co Ltd v National Westminster Finance Australia Ltd* (1985) 58 ALR 165, 174, PC. A broker may, of course, agree expressly that he will procure insurance, as was held to be the case in *Hood v West End Motor Car Packing Co* [1917] 2 KB 38, CA, but this is unusual, and in the absence of any such agreement, the duty will be to use reasonable skill and care to procure insurance.
2 See, eg, *Waterkeyn v Eagle, Star & British Dominions Insurance Co Ltd* (1920) 5 Ll L Rep 42 (insurance not available on terms specified by client).
3 *Eagle Star Insurance Co Ltd v National Westminster Finance Australia Ltd* (1985) 58 ALR 165, 174, PC.
4 See, eg, *Seavision Investment SA v Evennett, The Tiburon* [1990] 2 Lloyd's Rep 418; *Mander v Commercial Union Assurance Co plc* [1998] Lloyd's Rep IR 93, 145.

Failure to effect insurance which meets client's requirements

16.16   A broker owes his client a duty to take reasonable steps to obtain a policy which clearly meets his needs and is suitable for the client.[1] As with a failure to effect insurance at all, the issue of negligence may be relatively straightforward once the insurance position has been established, but this may not be so: for instance, where there are factual issues as to the instructions given by the client, and any advice given by the broker in connection with the instructions, a finding of negligence will not automatically follow from a finding that the cover does not meet the client's requirements.[2] Where insurance which met the client's requirements would not have been available, the broker will not be liable for failing to procure such cover, but may be liable for failing to keep the client informed.[3] An insurance broker who is instructed to obtain insurance cover against the death of a racehorse is not negligent if he obtains such cover but does not obtain wider cover, even if that wider cover would have been available in the market for no additional cost, unless it is established that there is a market practice of obtaining that wider cover.[4]

An aspect of the duty to take reasonable steps to obtain a policy which clearly meets the client's needs and is suitable for the client is that the client should not be exposed to unnecessary risk of legal disputes with the insurer.[5] In securing insurance cover appropriate to a client's requirements:[6]

> '... it is not the function of an insurance broker to take a view on undetermined points of law. The protection to be afforded to the client should, if reasonably possible, be such that the client does not become involved in legal disputes at all. As in the case of a solicitor the insurance broker should protect his client from unnecessary risks including the risk of litigation.'

Further:[7]

> '... it is the duty of a broker to obtain, so far as is possible, insurance coverage which clearly meets his client's requirements. Coverage is only clear in so far as it leaves no room for significant debate. The coverage will be unclear, and the broker in breach of duty, if the form thereof exposes the client insured to an

unnecessary risk of litigation. Of course the risk of litigation can never be wholly avoided and the broker is not in breach of duty in consequence alone of insurers putting forward a spurious construction of the cover.'

ICOBS requires a broker to take reasonable care to ensure the suitability of its advice for any customer who is entitled to rely upon its judgment;[8] and to take reasonable steps to ensure a customer is given appropriate information about a policy in good time and in a comprehensible form so that the customer can make an informed decision about the arrangements proposed.[9] This applies both before and after conclusion of the contract of insurance, and so includes matters such as mid-term changes and renewals, and also applies to the price of the policy.[10] The level of information required will vary according to matters such as the knowledge, experience and ability of a typical customer for the policy; the policy terms, including its main benefits, exclusions, limitations, conditions and its duration; the policy's overall complexity; whether the policy is bought in connection with other goods and services; distance communication information requirements; and whether the same information has been provided to the customer previously and, if so, when.[11]

1 *Ground Gilbey Ltd v Jardine Lloyd Thompson UK Ltd* [2011] EWHC 124 (Comm), [2012] Lloyd's Rep IR 12, para 73 (Blair J).
2 See *Chapman v Walton* (1833) 10 Bing 57 (issue as to meaning of client's instructions); *Youell v Bland Welch & Co Ltd, The Superhulls Cover Case (No 2)* [1990] 2 Lloyd's Rep 431 (reinsurance).
3 See **PARA 16.20**.
4 *O'Brien v Hughes-Gibb and Co Ltd* [1995] LRLR 80 (Rattee J).
5 *Ground Gilbey Ltd v Jardine Lloyd Thompson UK Ltd* [2011] EWHC 124 (Comm), [2012] Lloyd's Rep IR 12, para 73 (Blair J).
6 *First International Commercial Bank plc v Barnet Devanney (Harrow) Ltd* [1999] Lloyd's Rep IR 459, 467–468, CA (Morritt LJ); see, similarly, *Dodson v Peter H Dodson Insurance Services* [2001] 1 WLR 1012, CA, para 21 (Mance LJ): 'there may be something to be said for the view that, even if the broker's advice … proves under this judgment to have been correct, nonetheless it should not have been given in apparently unqualified terms, or without confirming the existence of cover with insurers, so as to avoid any arguments'.
7 *Standard Life Assurance Ltd v Oak Dedicated Ltd* [2008] EWHC 222 (Comm), [2008] Lloyd's Rep IR 552, para 102 (Tomlinson J); *Ground Gilbey Ltd v Jardine Lloyd Thompson UK Ltd* [2011] EWHC 124 (Comm), [2012] Lloyd's Rep IR 12, para 103 (Blair J). In *Talbot Underwriting Ltd v Nausch, Hogan & Murray Inc, The Jascon 5* [2005] EWHC 2359 (Comm), [2006] 2 Lloyd's Rep 195, Cooke J said (at para 104) that '… the duty of a broker is, so far as possible, to obtain insurance coverage which clearly and indisputably meets its clients' requirements' (issue not considered on appeal: [2006] EWCA Civ 889, [2006] 2 Lloyd's Rep 195).
8 ICOBS 5.3.1R.
9 ICOBS 6.1.5R.
10 ICOBS 6.1.6G.
11 ICOBS 6.1.7G.

Failure to effect insurance on terms specified by client

16.17   Where insurance is not available on terms specified by the client, the broker will not be liable for failing to procure it.[1] He may, however, be liable if he effects insurance on terms other than those specified by the client, those being all that is available, and fails to inform the client of what he has done;[2] or if he does not effect any insurance and fails to keep the client informed.[3] In these circumstances the broker would, it is suggested, at least be liable for nominal damages for breach of contract even if the client was unable to prove any loss. However, this was not the result in *Waterkeyn v Eagle, Star & British Dominions Insurance Co Ltd*,[4] in which Greer J held that the broker had done all he could, and did not consider whether he had advised the client adequately or at all about the insurance which he had procured. It had been argued for the client that the broker had told him wrongly that the insurance which had been procured was not materially different from that which he had specified. If a broker relies on his own interpretation of the policy wording, and his interpretation turns out to be mistaken, he will be liable for failing to procure insurance on the terms specified by the client.[5] Similarly, the broker may be liable for failing to procure insurance on the terms specified by the client if he misconstrues the client's instructions where a reasonably competent insurance broker would have correctly understood the instructions.[6] Again, if the instructions are ambiguous, or would appear so to a reasonably competent broker, the broker may be liable if he fails to seek clarification from the client.

1 *Waterkeyn v Eagle, Star & British Dominions Insurance Co Ltd* (1920) 5 Ll L Rep 42; *Eagle Star Insurance Co Ltd v National Westminster Finance Australia Ltd* (1985) 58 ALR 165, 174, PC.
2 *Youell v Bland Welch & Co Ltd, The Superhulls Cover Case (No 2)* [1990] 2 Lloyd's Rep 431, 445–446 (reinsurance).
3 *Eagle Star Insurance Co Ltd v National Westminster Finance Australia Ltd* (1985) 58 ALR 165, 174, PC.
4 (1920) 5 Ll L Rep 42.
5 See *National Insurance and Guarantee Corpn v Imperio Reinsurance Co (UK) Ltd* [1999] Lloyd's Rep IR 249, 258 (Colman J).
6 See *Chapman v Walton* (1833) 10 Bing 57 (Tindal CJ); *James Vale & Co v Van Oppen & Co Ltd* (1921) 6 Ll L Rep 167 (Roche J); and see also *Sharp v Sphere Drake Insurance plc, The Moonacre* [1992] 2 Lloyd's Rep 501, 524–525 (Mr A D Colman QC, sitting as a Deputy Judge of the High Court) (construction of documents relating to the placing of the risk).

Failure to act with reasonable speed

16.18 A broker may be liable for failure to act with reasonable speed.[1] What is reasonable speed will depend on the circumstances.[2] A failure to act at all after receiving instructions from the client will, of course, also be negligent. This was the basis of a finding of negligence in *Vesta v Butcher*,[3] which involved the placing of reinsurance, and in which the brokers forgot about a telephone call from insurers asking them to inform reinsurers that the insured had indicated that it could not comply with a warranty that a 24-hour watch be kept on its fish farm, and to seek the reinsurers' confirmation that this was acceptable to them.

1 See *Cock, Russell & Co v Bray, Gibb & Co Ltd* (1920) 3 Ll L Rep 71 (Bailhache J; broker not negligent).
2 See *Cock, Russell & Co v Bray, Gibb & Co Ltd* (1920) 3 Ll L Rep 71 (Bailhache J). In *Alexander Forbes Europe Ltd v SBJ Ltd* [2003] Lloyd's Rep IR 432, the combination of the end of the period of insurance and the impact of a limitation period on the proceedings meant that the claimant was obliged to allege that within a period of three working days the defendant insurance broker ought to have assessed the situation in relation to a potential notification, advised the claimant and then acted (paras 32 and 39). The judge (Mr David Mackie QC, sitting as a Deputy Judge of the High Court) accepted the impracticability in the real world of the claimant and the defendant insurance broker achieving much dialogue in this period but said that there would still have been time for a competent broker to assess the situation and advise and act promptly, although he appreciated that the opportunity would have been brief (para 39).
3 [1986] 2 Lloyd's Rep 179, [1986] 2 All ER 488 (Hobhouse J; finding on this issue not considered on appeal: [1989] AC 852, CA and HL).

Misrepresentation and failure to disclose material facts to insurer

16.19   It is common for brokers to complete proposal forms on behalf of clients, on the basis of answers given by clients to the questions in the form. The form is then signed by the client and may form the basis of the contract with the insurer.[1] A failure to complete a proposal form accurately, or an inaccurate presentation of the risk to the insurer, may allow the insurer to avoid the insurance policy for misrepresentation or non-disclosure,[2] or to repudiate liability on grounds of breach of warranty,[3] for which the broker may be held liable to the client.[4] Whether responsibility for the non-disclosure rests with the broker or the client will depend on the circumstances. A failure by a broker to disclose to the insurer material facts of which he has been made aware by his client will constitute a breach of duty to the client,[5] as will a misrepresentation as to the facts where the broker knows, or a reasonably competent broker would know, the true position.[6] A failure to obtain a proposal form before placing cover may also constitute a breach of duty.[7]

The broker must take reasonable care to elicit matters which ought to be disclosed but which the client might not think it necessary to mention, bearing in mind that the client may not realise without assistance that a particular matter is or is arguably material.[8] Whether a failure by the broker to ask questions of the client which would have elicited material information amounts to a breach of duty depends upon whether the questions are ones which a competent broker might have been expected to ask in the circumstances, and a broker will not be negligent if he fails to ask questions about the risk which he had no reason to ask or if he does ask appropriate questions and the insured does not disclose important information to the broker.[9] For example, in *McNealy v Pennine Insurance Co Ltd*,[10] the insured was a property repairer and part-time musician. The broker asked the insured his occupation, which was given as property repairer, and wrote it down on the proposal form for motor insurance, but failed to ask him whether the insured was involved in any of the excluded categories of occupation (he being aware of the excluded categories but having failed to communicate this to the insured). The insurer avoided the policy, and the Court of Appeal held that the broker had failed to exercise reasonable care in obtaining insurance cover for the insured.

The broker owes a duty to use reasonable care to ensure that the client's answers to factual questions are recorded accurately, but does not owe a duty to ensure that the answers are correct.[11] A reasonable broker is entitled to assume, in the absence of evidence to the contrary, that his commercial client is doing what he is telling the broker he is doing.[12] The authorities do not provide clear guidance as to the circumstances in which a broker is likely to be held liable in respect of inaccurate answers which the client has confirmed to be correct, whether by signing the form or otherwise. In *O'Connor v B D B Kirby & Co*,[13] the insurer repudiated liability on the basis of an inaccurate statement in a proposal form completed by the broker and signed by the client. The Court of Appeal held that the signature on the form by the client, after a request by the broker that he check the form, was a complete defence to an action for negligence against the broker.[14] Similarly, in *Gunns v Par Insurance Brokers*,[15] the client had given an inaccurate answer in response to a question from a proposal form read out to him by the brokers, and sought to rely on his dyslexia and occasional errors in answering the brokers' questions in imposing liability for the error on the brokers. Sir Michael Ogden said, in rejecting this argument:[16]

'The [client] was an experienced businessman who knew perfectly well that misrepresentation or non-disclosure could lead to claims being repudiated. His occasional errors in answering the questions, all of which (other than those of which only the [client] had knowledge) were picked up and dealt with during the meeting. Stupid, illiterate, senile people, and other such persons in similar categories may well call for a broker to take unusual precautions when proposal forms are filled in. In my view in this case there was no call for the [brokers] to do more than they did.'

However, in *Dunbar v A & B Painters Ltd*,[17] the current insurers were seeking a higher premium, but the broker stated on the proposal form to be sent to prospective new insurers that this was not the case. The broker succeeded in showing that the client had been aware of the answer given on the proposal form, and had also been aware that the answer was not correct, but the judge brushed this aside, saying that the client:

'… could not and would not have known the details at that stage and, in my judgment, his approach to [the question] was that it was really a matter peculiarly within the knowledge of [the broker] and they would know better than he what was the correct answer to put. To complete the picture, [the client] said that he would never knowingly have entered a false answer and I am satisfied that he was telling the truth about that.'

Dunbar v A & B Painters Ltd concerned employers' liability insurance, and a claim for damages for serious personal injuries by an employee against a firm of painters and decorators. Where the client is an expert in insurance matters, the position may be different. Thus, in *Commonwealth Insurance Co of Vancouver v Groupe Sprinks SA*,[18] where the client was an insurer seeking reinsurance, the judge indicated (obiter, the remark not being necessary to the decision in the case) that the broker would have had a defence to a claim for negligence by way of misrepresentation in circumstances where it had asked the client to confirm the accuracy of a statement before it was provided to reinsurers, and the client had done so. The broker's duties are likely to be reconsidered in the light of the modern practice which is for brokers to complete an electronic proposal form for signature by the client, who no longer has the option of reading the questions in his own time, perhaps at home, and completing the form himself. The enforceability of standard terms limiting the broker's liability for negligence or breach of contract in relation to the completion of proposal forms is also likely to be considered in this context.

More generally, a broker owes his client a duty to take reasonable care in the provision of information to the insurer.[19] In *Warren v Henry Sutton & Co*, a broker was held liable for making a misrepresentation to insurers that a driver who was being added to the insured's motor insurance policy had no convictions and had been involved in no accidents. A majority of the Court of Appeal distinguished a failure by the insured (on the broker's evidence) to disclose the additional driver's record, and the positive misrepresentation made by the broker to the insurer as to the driver's record. The judges in the majority did not go on to consider whether the insurer would have been entitled to repudiate liability in any event on the basis of the insured's failure to disclose the additional driver's record. Such an argument would, it is suggested, have had a good chance of succeeding. Indeed, Lord Denning MR dissented on the grounds that the insured's failure to disclose the additional driver's record to the broker was the cause of the broker's 'non-disclosure' (rather than misrepresentation) to the insurer.[20]

ICOBS provides that a broker should bear in mind the restriction on rejecting claims for non-disclosure,[21] and that ways of ensuring that a customer knows what he must disclose include explaining to a commercial customer the duty to disclose all circumstances material to a policy, what needs to be disclosed, and the consequences of any failure to make such a disclosure and ensuring that the customer is asked clear questions about any matter material to the insurer;[22] explaining to a consumer customer the responsibility of consumers to take reasonable care not to make a misrepresentation and the possible consequences if a consumer is careless in answering the insurer's questions, or if a consumer recklessly or deliberately makes a misrepresentation;[23] and asking the customer clear and specific questions about the information relevant to the policy being arranged or varied.[24]

1 See PARA **11.16**.
2 See PARAS **11.5–11.34**.
3 Where there is a basis clause: see PARA **11.16**.
4 See *Lyons v J W Bentley Ltd* (1944) 77 Ll L R 335 (broker found not liable on the facts).
5 See *Eagle Star Insurance Co Ltd v National Westminster Finance Australia Ltd* (1985) 58 ALR 165, 174, PC; *O & R Jewellers Ltd v Terry* [1999] Lloyd's Rep IR 436 (Sir Godfrey Le Quesne QC, sitting as a Deputy Judge of the High Court). It will also constitute a breach of s 19 of the Marine Insurance Act 1906: see PARA **16.6**.
6 *Eagle Star Insurance Co Ltd v National Westminster Finance Australia Ltd* (1985) 58 ALR 165, 174, PC.
7 *Fisk v Brian Thornhill & Son* [2007] EWCA Civ 152, [2007] Lloyd's Rep IR 699, para 38 (Sir Peter Gibson).
8 *Jones v Environcom Ltd* [2010] EWHC 759 (Comm), [2010] Lloyd's Rep IR 676, para 54 (David Steel J); issue not considered on appeal: [2011] EWCA Civ 1152, [2012] Lloyd's Rep IR 277; *Involnert Management Inc v Aprilgrange Ltd* [2015] EWHC 2225 (Comm), [2015] 2 Lloyd's Rep 289, para 321 (Leggatt J).
9 *Synergy Health (UK) Ltd v CGU Insurance plc* [2010] EWHC 2583 (Comm), [2011] Lloyd's Rep IR 500, para 206 (Flaux J).
10 [1978] 2 Lloyd's Rep 18, CA.
11 *O'Connor v B D B Kirby & Co* [1972] 1 QB 90, CA; *Gunns v Par Insurance Brokers* [1997] 1 Lloyd's Rep 173.
12 *Ground Gilbey Ltd v Jardine Lloyd Thompson UK Ltd* [2011] EWHC 124 (Comm), [2012] Lloyd's Rep IR 12, para 75 (Blair J).
13 [1972] 1 QB 90, CA.
14 The decision is considered and explained by Stuart-Smith LJ in *Kapur v J W Francis & Co* [2000] Lloyd's Rep IR 361, 367–368, CA.
15 [1997] 1 Lloyd's Rep 173.
16 At 177.
17 [1985] 2 Lloyd's Rep 616 (this point was not challenged on appeal: [1986] 2 Lloyd's Rep 38, CA).
18 [1983] 1 Lloyd's Rep 67 (Lloyd J).
19 See *Everett v Hogg, Robinson & Gardner Mountain (Insurance) Ltd* [1973] 2 Lloyd's Rep 217 (broker held liable for negligence for answering reinsurer's query without checking accuracy of information with underwriters); *Eagle Star Insurance Co Ltd v National Westminster Finance Australia Ltd* (1985) 58 ALR 165, 174, PC. The broker may also owe a duty in like terms to the insurer: see PARA **16.11**.
20 At 278–279.
21 The restriction is at ICOBS 8.1.1(3)R.
22 ICOBS 5.1.4(1)–(2)G.
23 ICOBS 5.1.4(3)G.
24 ICOBS 5.1.4(4)G.

Failure to keep client properly informed as to the existence or terms of cover

16.20   A broker is under a duty to provide the client with appropriate information about the existence or terms of cover. If the only insurance which the broker is able to obtain contains unusual, limiting or exempting provisions which, if they are not brought to the notice of the assured, may result in the policy not conforming to the client's requirements, the agent is under a duty to inform the client of those provisions and take reasonable steps to obtain alternative insurance, if any is available, or give the client appropriate advice to enable him to comply, so far as possible, with the policy requirements.[1]

In *Cherry Ltd v Allied Insurance Brokers Ltd*,[2] the client gave notice of termination of its brokers' retainer and asked the brokers to cancel all policies which had been obtained on their behalf, such cancellation to be effective from the date of termination of the brokers' retainer. Following termination of the retainer, the brokers informed the client that it would not be possible to cancel a policy covering loss of profit and other consequential loss caused by destruction of, or damage to, the client's premises, but that they would do whatever possible to cancel another of the client's policies. Two days later, the client cancelled the new policy which it had obtained in respect of loss of profit and other consequential loss, but did not inform the brokers that it had done so. Within a few days of cancellation, the insurer agreed after all to the cancellation of the original policy, with effect from the date of termination of the brokers' retainer. The brokers did not inform the client that the original policy had been cancelled, and the client was therefore left without insurance. A fire subsequently occurred at the client's premises, causing substantial consequential damage in respect of which the client had no available insurance, but which would have been covered by either the original or the replacement consequential loss policy. Cantley J held that in cancelling the replacement policy the client was simply doing what the brokers had advised it to do, and it was unaware of any need for urgency in informing the brokers that the replacement policy had been cancelled; accordingly, the brokers were negligent in not informing the client of the cancellation of the original policy, and there was no finding of contributory negligence against the client.

The broker is also under a duty to take reasonable steps to ensure that the client understands the basis on which the insurance is written, including, in property insurance, the existence and effect of any average clause and the consequences of under-insurance.[3] The duty does not extend to advising the client as to the value to be placed on the client's property.[4]

1 *Harvest Trucking Co Ltd v P B Davis Insurance Services* [1991] 2 Lloyd's Rep 638, 643 (His Honour Judge Diamond QC sitting as a judge of the High Court); *Youell v Bland Welch & Co Ltd, The Superhulls Cover Case (No 2)* [1990] 2 Lloyd's Rep 431, 446–447 (Phillips J: reinsurance is usually placed on terms 'as original' and if, unusually, cover is only available on a different basis, the broker is under a duty to inform the insurer that this is the basis on which cover has been obtained. The period of reinsurance also expired before the period of insurance expired, and the brokers were held to be negligent for allowing this to occur, and for failing to inform the insurers that it had occurred); *Fisk v Brian Thornhill & Son* [2007] EWCA Civ 152, [2007] Lloyd's Rep IR 699, paras 36–38 and 41–42) (Sir Peter Gibson: broker was in breach of his duty to insured in not making clear that a new policy with different insurers on different terms and conditions was being suggested by him, including a more onerous provision that any in the previous policy, and in giving a warranty (that the premises were of

standard construction) without the insured's authority); *Ground Gilbey Ltd v Jardine Lloyd Thompson UK Ltd* [2011] EWHC 124 (Comm), [2012] Lloyd's Rep IR 12, paras 73 and 78 (Blair J).
2 [1978] 1 Lloyd's Rep 274.
3 *J W Bollom & Co Ltd v Byas Moseley & Co Ltd* [2000] Lloyd's Rep IR 136, 146 (Moore-Bick J).
4 *J W Bollom & Co Ltd v Byas Moseley & Co Ltd* [2000] Lloyd's Rep IR 136, 146, 150 (Moore-Bick J).

Duty to advise

16.21 A broker is under a duty to give his client appropriate advice in relation to the placing of the risk. In many cases, this will include advising the client on the type of insurance best suited to his requirements,[1] on the selection of an appropriate insurer, and on whether facts of which he is made aware by the client are material and should be disclosed to the insurer.

The broker must also advise his client in relation to his duties of disclosure. In *Jones v Environcom Ltd*,[2] David Steel J summarised the broker's duties in this regard as follows:[3]

'In short, a broker:

(i)   must advise his client of the duty to disclose all material circumstances;
(ii)   must explain the consequences of failing to do so;
(iii)   must indicate the sort of matters which ought to be disclosed as being material (or at least arguably material);
(iv)   must take reasonable care to elicit matters which ought to be disclosed but which the client might not think it necessary to mention.

All this flows from the requirement that the broker should take reasonable steps to ensure that the proposed policy is suitable for the client's needs. By definition, a policy which is voidable for non-disclosure is not suitable.'

David Steel J also said that where a change in personnel led to a new person being responsible for insurance matters in the client's organisation, the broker must ensure that an appropriate understanding of questions of materiality was held by that person.[4] In *Synergy Health (UK) Ltd v CGU Insurance plc*,[5] Flaux J said it was not an immutable requirement that, in order to comply with their duty, brokers should have given the advice orally, and he said that whether it necessary to do so, and whether the failure to do so was a breach of duty, would depend upon the circumstances. The judge rejected the allegation of breach, on the grounds that there had been a long history of dealings with the client and a written document sent to the client which summarised the various insurance covers spelt out the duty of disclosure in clear terms; and that although the brokers were dealing with a new person responsible for insurance, that person was in fact well aware of the need to comply with the duty to make disclosure of all material facts and of the serious consequences of failing to do so.[6]

In *Osman v J Ralph Moss Ltd*,[7] the broker was criticised by the Court of Appeal for advising his client to insure with a company which was widely known in insurance circles to be in financial difficulties at that time. The insurer was compulsorily wound up shortly after the client had paid his premium, which was for third-party motor cover, and the Court of Appeal strongly criticised the broker for, in addition, not having taken reasonable steps to draw to the client's attention the fact that he was no longer covered by insurance and was therefore driving whilst uninsured.

If there is any doubt in the broker's mind as to the meaning of a question on the proposal form, it is his duty to ask the insurers what meaning they attach to the question.[8] Moreover, a broker is not entitled to rely upon his own assumption as to factual matters which are or may be material, but must seek confirmation from the client.[9]

Once cover is in place, a broker is expected to be familiar with its terms, and to take reasonable steps to ensure that the client understands the basis on which the insurance is written, including, in property insurance, the existence and effect of any average clause and the consequences of under-insurance.[10] In *Eurokey Recycling Ltd v Giles Insurance Brokers Ltd*,[11] Blair J held that the principles which applied to the broker's duties in respect of business interruption insurance included the following:[12]

'(1) Whilst a broker is not expected himself to calculate the business interruption sum insured or choose an indemnity period, both of which are matters for the commercial client, the broker must provide sufficient explanation to enable the client to do so. This will include an explanation of the method of calculating the sum insured, which will likely require an explanation of terms such as "estimated gross profits", "maximum indemnity period", and the considerations to take into account when choosing a maximum indemnity period.

(2) In order to do this, the broker will need to take reasonable steps to ascertain the nature of the client's business and its insurance needs …

(3) In Arbory Group Ltd v West Craven Insurance Services,13 Judge Grenfell pointed out14 that "Insurable 'Gross Profit' is a term of art which means something very different from what an experienced businessman might expect", adding that "a broker owes a duty to his client to ensure that he fully understands that term of art". I would respectfully put it slightly differently, and say that the duty is to take reasonable steps to ensure that the client fully understands the term.

(4) An insurance broker providing the type of service that Giles was providing in this case is neither required nor expected to conduct a detailed investigation into a client's business. However, and in so far as this was suggested, the broker's duty is not diminished because his firm may offer an enhanced service at additional cost… Regardless of the availability of additional services, the above duties apply to any broker who takes on business of this kind…

(5) The nature and scope of a broker's obligation to assess a commercial client's business interruption insurance needs will depend upon the particular circumstances of the case, including the client's sophistication, and the number of times the broker has met the client in the past … Contrary to the claimant's submission, the fact that ICOBS 6.1.5 to 6.5.7 does not make reference to a client's sophistication is not inconsistent with this, since the matters referred to in these rules are stated to be non-exclusive…

(6) In that regard, although business interruption insurance is for commercial clients, the level of client sophistication will clearly vary enormously.

It cannot be assumed that an SME (like the claimant in this case) will have any understanding of the nature of the insurance ...'

The broker must also give advice appropriate to the circumstances of which he is informed by his client. For example, in *Strong and Pearl v S Allison & Co Ltd*,[15] a boat was insured on a particular mooring, and the owners of the boat informed the broker that they intended to move the boat to a different mooring. The broker informed the insurers of the intended change of mooring but did not warn the client not to move the boat until the insurer's agreement had been secured. As a result the boat was not covered, and the broker was held to be liable for the loss of the boat due to an explosion on board.

Whether a duty to advise arises depends on the facts: for example, an instruction to transfer a risk from one set of business premises to another may not give rise to a general duty to advise the client. This was the situation in *Avondale Blouse Co Ltd v Williamson & Geo Town*.[16] The broker had informed the client that insurers had agreed to immediately provide cover against fire at the new premises, but that they would not agree to provide cover against burglary until a survey had been completed. Lynskey J found that the client's only instructions were to transfer the risk on the policy from the old premises to the new premises, that he was not asking for general advice and was not indicating to him that he was relying on him generally to see that the goods were covered under all circumstances. In the circumstances, the judge found that the broker had fulfilled his duty to the client, and rejected the argument that he was under an obligation to arrange for temporary or interim cover.[17] Similarly, a broker asked to obtain export insurance in respect of goods does not owe a duty to inquire whether the goods are covered while in the hands of packers or in store, as he is entitled to assume that the client has conducted his business prudently and covered his goods by the appropriate form of insurance.[18]

If the broker is asked to explain the terms of a policy to his client and does so, he must exercise reasonable care in giving the explanation.[19] The client may effectively be seeking advice from the broker which involves the broker in giving legal advice, for example, as to the construction of a policy. If the broker agrees to give such advice, he cannot rely upon his lack of legal expertise as a defence to a claim for negligence.[20] In relation to the construction of documents, the standard of skill and care is the same as with any other aspect of the broker's duties: the broker is not in breach of his duty of professional skill and care merely because he has given to a document relevant to the placing of the risk a meaning which on its proper construction the document does not bear; the question is whether a body of opinion in the profession would have come to the same conclusion.[21]

The fact that the broker's view as to the law is subsequently shown to have been correct is not sufficient to absolve him from breach of duty where, at the time the risk was placed, the law was uncertain. This is because, in securing insurance cover appropriate to a client's requirements:[22]

'... it is not the function of an insurance broker to take a view on undetermined points of law. The protection to be afforded to the client should, if reasonably possible, be such that the client does not become involved in legal disputes at all. As in the case of a solicitor the insurance broker should protect his client from unnecessary risks including the risk of litigation.'

In *Melik & Co v Norwich Union Fire Insurance Society Ltd*,[23] there was a problem with a burglar alarm at the insured's premises, and the plaintiffs asked the broker to confirm that they were still insured. The broker communicated with insurers, but essentially relied upon his own judgment in giving the confirmation sought. Woolf J indicated that if he had not held that the insurers were liable, he would have found the broker negligent, as he should have communicated with insurers more effectively than he did, and obtained the clear and positive answer which the insured required.[24]

In order to establish liability on the part of a broker for failure to give advice, the client must show that the broker was under a legal obligation to give advice on the matter in question; it is not enough that he would have volunteered the information if asked.[25]

ICOBS also imposes obligations on insurance intermediaries in relation to identifying client needs and advising, and the provision of product information.[26]

1 *Harvest Trucking Co Ltd v P B Davis Insurance Services* [1991] 2 Lloyd's Rep 638, 643 (His Honour Judge Diamond QC sitting as a judge of the High Court).
2 [2010] EWHC 759 (Comm), [2010] Lloyd's Rep IR 676; issue not considered on appeal: [2011] EWCA Civ 1152, [2012] Lloyd's Rep IR 277.
3 At para 54; issue not considered on appeal: [2011] EWCA Civ 1152.
4 At para 55; issue not considered on appeal: [2011] EWCA Civ 1152.
5 [2010] EWHC 2583 (Comm), [2011] Lloyd's Rep IR 500.
6 At paras 212–213 (Flaux J).
7 [1970] 1 Lloyd's Rep 313, CA. As the appeal was on quantum only, with no cross-appeal on liability, the criticisms of the broker's conduct are obiter.
8 *Sharp v Sphere Drake Insurance plc, The Moonacre* [1992] 2 Lloyd's Rep 501, 525 (Mr A D Colman QC, sitting as a Deputy Judge of the High Court).
9 *Sharp v Sphere Drake Insurance plc, The Moonacre* [1992] 2 Lloyd's Rep 501, 526 (Mr A D Colman QC, sitting as a Deputy Judge of the High Court).
10 *J W Bollom & Co Ltd v Byas Moseley & Co Ltd* [2000] Lloyd's Rep IR 136, 146 (Moore-Bick J). The duty does not extend to advising the client as to the value to be placed on the client's property: at 146, 150 (Moore-Bick J).
11 [2014] EWHC 2989 (Comm), [2015] Lloyd's Rep IR 225.
12 At para 86 (Blair J).
13 [2007] Lloyd's Rep IR 491.
14 At para 25.
15 (1926) 25 Ll L Rep 504.
16 (1948) 81 Ll L Rep 492.
17 At 498 (Lynskey J).
18 *United Mills Agencies Ltd v Harvey, Bray & Co* [1951] 2 Lloyd's Rep 631, 643 (McNair J).
19 *Harvest Trucking Co Ltd v P B Davis Insurance Services* [1991] 2 Lloyd's Rep 638, 643 (His Honour Judge Diamond QC sitting as a judge of the High Court).
20 *Sarginson Bros v Keith Moulton & Co Ltd* (1942) 73 Ll L Rep 104, 107 (Hallett J).
21 *Sharp v Sphere Drake Insurance plc, The Moonacre* [1992] 2 Lloyd's Rep 501, 524–525 (Mr A D Colman QC, sitting as a Deputy Judge of the High Court), applying *Chapman v Walton* (1833) 10 Bing 57 (Tindal CJ) and *James Vale & Co v Van Oppen & Co Ltd* (1921) 6 Ll L Rep 167 (Roche J). The *Moonacre* concerned the construction of documents relating to the placing of the risk; *Chapman v Walton* and *James Vale & Co v Van Oppen & Co Ltd* both concerned the meaning of the broker's instructions.
22 *First International Commercial Bank plc v Barnet Devanney (Harrow) Ltd* [1999] Lloyd's Rep IR 459, 467–468, CA (Morritt LJ); see, similarly, *Dodson v Peter H Dodson Insurance Services* [2001] 1 WLR 1012, CA, para 21 (Mance LJ): 'there may be something to be said for the view that, even if the broker's advice … proves under this judgment to have been correct, nonetheless it should not have been given in apparently unqualified terms, or without confirming the existence of cover with insurers, so as to avoid any arguments'. See also **PARA 16.16**.
23 [1980] 1 Lloyd's Rep 523.
24 At 534. See, similarly, *T O'Donoghue Ltd v Harding* [1988] 2 Lloyd's Rep 281, 291 (Otton J).

25 *Aneco Reinsurance Underwriting Ltd v Johnson & Higgins Ltd* [2001] UKHL 51, [2002] 1 Lloyd's Rep 157, 191, (para 66), HL (Lord Millett, dissenting).
26 See **PARA 16.16**.

Drafting documents

16.22 If a broker drafts insurance documents such as slips or policy wordings, he is bound to exercise reasonable skill and care so as to ensure that the documents give clear expression to the terms that have been agreed.[1]

1 *Youell v Bland Welch & Co Ltd (The 'Superhulls Cover' Case) (No 2)* [1990] 2 Lloyd's Rep 431, 446 (Phillips J).

Duties post-placement

16.23 Whether a broker owes a duty of care post-placement, and the scope of any such duty, depends on the circumstances.[1] Such a duty is likely to be held to arise if a client provides the broker with information in relation to a claim or a potential claim.[2] There is no rule of law which obliges a broker who has not been ask to assist the assured in dealing with a potential claim to volunteer advice on claim procedures.[3] If a duty of care is held to arise post-placement, a broker does not discharge his duties by simply passing the information on to the insurers: his duties go beyond those of a post box and are to get a grip on the proposed notification, to appraise it and to ensure that the information is relayed to the right place in the right form; the broker should have a strategy in place to ensure that when information is received from clients, he is alive to making notifications accurately and promptly.[4]

In *HIH Casualty and General Insurance Ltd v JLT Risk Solutions Ltd*,[5] the broker devised, structured and established a scheme of film finance insurance, acting together with insurer and reinsurers, in which the insurer was little more than a 'front' for the reinsurers who shouldered the bulk of the risk,[6] and Auld LJ said:[7]

> 'Where a broker has been at the centre of devising and structuring a risky scheme of that sort for insurers and reinsurers, as JLT was, it is plainly a strong candidate for post-placement monitoring obligations of the sort alleged here.'

The Court of Appeal concluded that there was a post-placement duty on the broker owed to the insurer; that it was to do more than act as 'a mere postbox'; and it had a duty of care, specific to that case, to have sought instructions or at least ensured that the insurer was sufficiently aware of the potential concern to assess what, if any, instructions to give.[8] Longmore LJ described the duty as follows:[9]

> '… an insurance broker who, after placing the risk, becomes aware of information which has a material and potentially deleterious effect on the insurance cover which he has placed is under an obligation to act in his client's best interest by drawing it to the attention of his client and obtain his instructions in relation to it.

> To the extent that JLT argued that their only duty with regard to post-placing information was to act as a postbox, merely passing on such information as and when they received it, the judge rightly rejected the argument … Indeed, as between

a lay client unversed in insurance matters and his insurance broker, I would think that the existence of such a duty should be comparatively uncontroversial.'

ICOBS provides, in relation to claims handling, that an insurance intermediary is expected to comply with the general law on the duties of an insurance intermediary.[10]

1 *HIH Casualty and General Insurance Ltd v JLT Risk Solutions Ltd* [2006] EWHC 485 (Comm), [2006] Lloyd's Rep IR 493, para 131 (Langley J) (decision upheld on appeal: [2007] EWCA Civ 710, [2007] 2 Lloyd's Rep 278); *Great North Eastern Railway Ltd v JLT Corporate Risks Ltd* [2006] EWHC 1478 (Comm), [2007] Lloyd's Rep IR 38, paras 24–33 (Cresswell J; brokers' application to strike out claim that they owed continuing duty of care post-placement to inform insured that instructions not carried out; application refused on grounds court should not decide issue without expert evidence).
2 See, eg, *Alexander Forbes Europe Ltd v SBJ Ltd* [2003] Lloyd's Rep IR 432 (professional indemnity insurance; the defendant brokers admitted that they owed a duty to pass on to the insurers notification of claims or circumstances within a reasonable time: para 33).
3 *Involnert Management Inc v Aprilgrange Ltd* [2015] EWHC 2225 (Comm), [2015] 2 Lloyd's Rep 289, para 324 (Leggatt J) (rejecting, in absence of expert evidence supporting the proposition that a broker has a duty as a matter of custom and practice to give such advice, allegation that broker negligently failed to advise client after loss as to requirements for making a claim, and in particular, of requirement to file sworn proof of loss within 90 days).
4 *Alexander Forbes Europe Ltd v SBJ Ltd* [2003] Lloyd's Rep IR 432, paras 36–37 (Mr David Mackie QC, sitting as a Deputy Judge of the High Court) (professional indemnity insurance; incorrect notification of potential claim to group rather than company policy). In *Eurokey Recycling Ltd v Giles Insurance Brokers Ltd* [2014] EWHC 2989 (Comm), [2015] Lloyd's Rep IR 225, at para 137, Blair J contrasted a broker's duty in circumstances such as these with the broker's obligation to pass the insured's accounts on to the credit provider in respect of the premium, saying that the broker 'was literally to act as a mere postbox' and was under no obligation to read the accounts.
5 [2007] EWCA Civ 710, [2007] 2 Lloyd's Rep 278.
6 At para 61.
7 At para 61.
8 At paras 67 (Auld LJ) and 116–117 (Longmore LJ).
9 At paras 116–117; applied: *Ground Gilbey Ltd v Jardine Lloyd Thompson UK Ltd* [2011] EWHC 124 (Comm), [2012] Lloyd's Rep IR 12, paras 73 and 78 (Blair J).
10 ICOBS 8.3.2G.

Failure to retain documents

16.24   Where an insurance broker holds documents belonging to his client, such as a policy, or documents belonging to the broker which may be required if a claim is made on the policy, he is under a duty to exercise reasonable skill and care in relation to the retention of those documents, and in particular owes the client a duty not to destroy the documents without obtaining the client's instructions.[1] If documents are lost through the broker's carelessness during the period in which a reasonable broker would have regarded a claim as possible, the broker will be liable for breach of his duty to take reasonable care to safeguard his client's documents[2]. But if documents are lost without any fault on the part of the broker – if, for example, they are destroyed in a fire – the broker will not be liable.[3]

ICOBS does not generally have detailed record-keeping requirements.[4]

1 *Johnston v Leslie & Godwin Financial Services Ltd* [1995] LRLR 472 (Clarke J), which concerned retrocessions entered into in 1956 in respect of long-tail business (asbestosis liabilities). The judge found that it was an ordinary incident of the duty of a Lloyd's broker to collect claims on behalf of his principal, and implied a term to that effect into the contract between the broker and the client. It is suggested that the principle is equally applicable to non-Lloyd's brokers, subject to expert evidence establishing a duty to retain particular classes of documents.

2 *Johnston v Leslie & Godwin Financial Services Ltd* [1995] LRLR 472 (Clarke J).
3 *Johnston v Leslie & Godwin Financial Services Ltd* [1995] LRLR 472 (Clarke J).
4 ICOBS 2.4.1G.

Duties in relation to renewal

16.25   An insurance broker is subject at renewal to the same duty as is imposed on a broker at an original placement namely a duty to take reasonable care to ensure that his client's insurance needs are clearly met.[1] The broker is under a duty to consider the terms of the insurance and their suitability each year.[2] This is particularly so where the insurance is markedly different from earlier years.[3] If a broker fails to appreciate that the insurance he has brokered does not fulfil the needs of his client when, had he looked at it with any care, that ought to have been apparent, it is no defence to say that he did not look at the terms of the previous insurance again because the wording did not change from the wording in previous years when he had also failed to spot the problem.[4] The broker is also under a duty to check and clarify with the insured prior to renewal any outstanding matters such as compliance with risk requirements following a survey by insurers.[5]

The obligations imposed by ICOBS on brokers in relation to the provision of appropriate information apply to renewals.[6]

1 *Beazley Underwriting Ltd v The Travelers Companies Inc* [2011] EWHC 1520 (Comm), [2012] Lloyd's Rep IR 78, para 135 (Christopher Clarke J).
2 *Beazley Underwriting Ltd v The Travelers Companies Inc* [2011] EWHC 1520 (Comm), [2012] Lloyd's Rep IR 78, para 136 (Christopher Clarke J).
3 *Beazley Underwriting Ltd v The Travelers Companies Inc* [2011] EWHC 1520 (Comm), [2012] Lloyd's Rep IR 78, para 136 (Christopher Clarke J) (the differences in that case were an excess point increased tenfold from £2.5 to £25million, an upper limit doubled from £52.5 to £100million, the structure changed from three layers to one, and the term increased from one year to three).
4 *Beazley Underwriting Ltd v The Travelers Companies Inc* [2011] EWHC 1520 (Comm), [2012] Lloyd's Rep IR 78, para 139 (Christopher Clarke J).
5 *Synergy Health (UK) Ltd v CGU Insurance plc* [2010] EWHC 2583 (Comm), [2011] Lloyd's Rep IR 500, paras 216–217 (Flaux J).
6 See **PARA 16.16**.

SPECIFIC DEFENCES

Ratification

16.26   A client may, in ratifying a contract entered into by the broker without authority, release the broker from claims for breach of duty. This will only be the case where the conduct by which the contract is ratified evidences an intention to be bound by it and, at the same time, amounts to a representation that the principal (the client) releases the agent from claims in respect of the contract.[1] This will rarely be the case in relation to brokers and policies of insurance.

Ratification has occasionally been relied upon as a defence in other circumstances. In *General Accident Fire & Life Assurance Corpn Ltd v J H Minet & Co Ltd*,[2] the Court of Appeal rejected an argument that receipt of a cover note setting out the terms of reinsurance cover constituted ratification by the client insurers of the broker's actions in obtaining cover on terms different from those which they had been instructed to obtain. The result might have been different, as it was in *Vesta v Butcher* and *Youell v Bland Welch* on similar facts, had the Court of Appeal been able to make a finding of contributory negligence against the client insurers.

1 See *National Insurance and Guarantee Corpn v Imperio Reinsurance Co (UK) Ltd* [1999] Lloyd's Rep IR 249, 260–261 (Colman J).
2 (1942) 74 Ll L Rep 1, CA.

Waiver

16.27 Waiver of breach of duty is occasionally pleaded as a defence by an insurance broker. Such a plea is unlikely to succeed except in very unusual circumstances, since a statement by a client to a broker that he is satisfied with the cover obtained by the broker will not amount to an unequivocal representation capable of founding a waiver, even where the client is an insurance industry professional:[1]

> 'A broker cannot be heard to assert a waiver merely because a client who has relied upon his services has mistakenly expressed his view that policy wording seems to be effective. That would involve a major dilution of his whole professional responsibility.'

1 *National Insurance and Guarantee Corpn v Imperio Reinsurance Co (UK) Ltd* [1999] Lloyd's Rep IR 249, 258–259 (Colman J). See also *Youell v Bland Welch & Co Ltd, The Superhulls Cover Case (No 2)* [1990] 2 Lloyd's Rep 431, 448–455 (Phillips J).

Estoppel

16.28 A defence based on estoppel, although theoretically possible, is in practice unlikely to succeed in an action brought by a client against a broker for breach of duty. This is because, in most cases, the professional relationship between the broker and the client (whether a lay client or an insurance professional) will be such that one of the essential ingredients of the defence will be absent: for example, an unequivocal representation that the client would not rely on his strict legal rights.[1] In addition, the ability to reduce the damages recoverable by the client to the extent which it considers just and equitable pursuant to s 1(1) of the Law Reform (Contributory Negligence) Act 1945 means that the court is unlikely to be faced with a situation in which it would be unconscionable to allow the client to rely on its legal rights (and thereby wholly to preclude the client from relying on those rights).[2]

1 See *National Insurance and Guarantee Corpn v Imperio Reinsurance Co (UK) Ltd* [1999] Lloyd's Rep IR 249, 259–260 (Colman J); *Youell v Bland Welch & Co Ltd, The Superhulls Cover Case (No 2)* [1990] 2 Lloyd's Rep 431, 448–452 (Phillips J).
2 See *National Insurance and Guarantee Corpn v Imperio Reinsurance Co (UK) Ltd* [1999] Lloyd's Rep IR 249, 260 (Colman J).

Limitation of actions

16.29 Claims against insurance brokers usually involve allegations of breach of a duty to exercise reasonable skill and care and are pleaded in the alternative in contract and in tort.[1] The primary limitation period in either case is six years, and starts to run when the cause of action accrues.[2] Where the claim is for breach of contract, the cause of action accrues when the breach occurs.[3] By contrast, the cause of action in negligence accrues only when damage is suffered.[4] This is because damage is an ingredient of the cause of action in negligence, and negligence which does not cause loss or damage is not actionable.[5] Further, to amount to actual damage for the purpose of constituting a tort, the loss sustained must be a loss falling within the measure of damage applicable to the wrong in question.[6] The effect of having different triggers for the accrual of the cause of action in contract and tort is that different limitation periods may apply to causes of action in contract and in tort arising out of the same facts.[7]

It is sometimes difficult to identify with precision the point at which damage has been suffered so that the cause of action in negligence accrues. In *Knapp v Ecclesiastical Insurance Group plc*,[8] allegations of negligence were made against an insurance broker who had obtained a fire policy on behalf of the claimants which was voidable at inception due to material non-disclosure. There was a serious fire at the claimants' property, and the policy was subsequently avoided. Hobhouse LJ described the court's task in determining when the cause of action accrued in tort as follows:[9]

> 'The inquiry which we have to undertake therefore is one which asks when the [broker's] negligence first became actionable. It was at that moment that the cause of action accrued. It is immaterial that at some later time the damage suffered by the [insured] became more serious or was capable of more precise quantification. Provided that some damage has been suffered by the [insured] as a result of the [broker's] negligence which was "real damage" (as distinct from purely minimal damage) or damage "beyond what can be regarded as negligible" that suffices for the accrual of the cause of action.'

Reference is often made to a passage from the judgment of Bingham LJ in *D W Moore & Co Ltd v Ferrier*[10] as a means of identifying whether the cause of action in tort had arisen at a particular date. After forming the view that the cause of action in tort had arisen at a particular date, Bingham LJ went on to test his conclusion by reference to whether more than nominal damages would have been recoverable at that date on a claim for breach of contract, saying:[11]

> 'If, in a contractual claim for negligence, the court would have awarded other than nominal damages, I do not see how it can be said that an action in tort based on the same negligence would have been bound to fail for want of any damage as an essential ingredient of the cause of action.'

In the context of the voidable fire policy, Hobhouse LJ's analysis of the date on which damage was suffered was that the cause of action accrued, and the clients suffered damage, once they had acted on the broker's advice to their detriment and failed to get that to which they were entitled, in this case a binding contract of indemnity from the insurance company. There was from this moment a risk of loss, and the fact that how serious the consequences of the negligence would be depended upon subsequent events and contingencies was relevant only to the quantification of the loss, not to whether or not they had suffered loss.[12] Similarly, Buxton LJ held that any period of time, however short, between the failure to warn the claimants on the inception of the policy and the putting right of the mistake would be a period during which the claimants had a voidable rather than a valid policy, and that that amounted to damage sufficient to found a cause of action in negligence.[13]

Prospective or contingent damage alone is not enough,[14] although the distinction between actual and prospective or contingent damage is not always easy to draw.[15] However, the fact that the full extent of the insured's losses might not have been clear until later does not delay the accrual of the cause of action.

The Court of Appeal has repeatedly emphasised the distinction between the accrual of a cause of action and the quantification of damage.[16] The quantification of damage based upon uncertain future events is a difficult and necessarily imprecise exercise of the kind that judges are often called upon to perform in other areas of the law.[17] In practice, however, it is rarely necessary for the court to attempt to quantify uncertain future events in brokers' negligence cases, as insureds do not typically issue proceedings until substantial damage (and not merely damage 'beyond what can be regarded as negligible') has been suffered, so that the task which the court has to perform is the retrospective identification of the date when proceedings could have been issued. As a result, in some cases the period for reflection and preparation available to an insured before issuing proceedings after suffering substantial damage may be far less than six years. Prudence obviously dictates that, wherever possible, proceedings should be issued within six years of the allegedly negligent act or omission. Where the issue of the date of accrual of the cause of action arises, it may be appropriate to ask the court to order that there be a trial of preliminary issues on limitation. The court will want to be sure that a trial of preliminary issues has a realistic prospect of reducing costs or shortening the proceedings, and, where there is a significant overlap with the factual issues which go to the substance of the case, may decline to make the order.

1 See **PARA 16.7**.
2 Section 2 of the Limitation Act 1980 (tort) provides: 'An action founded on tort shall not be brought after the expiration of six years from the date on which the cause of action accrued'. Section 5 of the Limitation Act 1980 (contract) provides: 'An action founded on simple contract shall not be brought after the expiration of six years from the date on which the cause of action accrued'.
3 See *Nykredit Mortgage Bank plc v Edward Erdman Group Ltd (No 2)* [1997] 1 WLR 1627, 1630, HL (Lord Nicholls).
4 See *Nykredit Mortgage Bank plc v Edward Erdman Group Ltd (No 2)* [1997] 1 WLR 1627, 1630, HL (Lord Nicholls).
5 *Knapp v Ecclesiastical Insurance Group plc* [1998] PNLR 172, 177, CA (Hobhouse LJ); *Law Society v Sephton & Co* [2006] UKHL 22, [2006] 2 AC 543, para 9 (Lord Hoffmann).
6 *Nykredit Mortgage Bank plc v Edward Erdman Group Ltd (No 2)* [1997] 1 WLR 1627, 1630, HL (Lord Nicholls).
7 See *Law Society v Sephton & Co* [2006] UKHL 22, [2006] 2 AC 543, para 80 (Lord Mance).
8 [1998] PNLR 172, CA; approved: *Law Society v Sephton & Co* [2006] UKHL 22, [2006] 2 AC 543. See also *Iron Trades Mutual Insurance Co Ltd v J K Buckenham Ltd* [1989] 2 Lloyd's Rep 85 and *Islander Trucking Ltd v Hogg, Robinson & Gardner Mountain (Marine) Ltd* [1990] 1 All ER 826, both cited with approval by Lord Nicholls in *Nykredit Mortgage Bank plc v Edward Erdman Group Ltd (No 2)* [1997] 1 WLR 1627, 1634, HL.
9 [1998] PNLR 172, 178, CA.
10 [1988] 1 WLR 267, CA.
11 *D W Moore & Co Ltd v Ferrier* [1988] 1 WLR 267, 280, CA, cited with approval by Lord Nicholls in *Nykredit Mortgage Bank plc v Edward Erdman Group Ltd (No 2)* [1997] 1 WLR 1627, 1632–1633, HL.
12 [1998] PNLR 172, 184, CA.
13 *Knapp v Ecclesiastical Insurance Group plc* [1998] PNLR 172, 190, CA.

14 *First National Commercial Bank plc v Humberts* [1995] 2 All ER 673, 680, CA (Neill LJ); *Law Society v Sephton & Co* [2006] UKHL 22, [2006] 2 AC 543.

15 See *Nykredit Mortgage Bank plc v Edward Erdman Group Ltd (No 2)* [1997] 1 WLR 1627, HL and *Law Society v Sephton & Co* [2006] UKHL 22, [2006] 2 AC 543.

16 *Forster v Outred & Co* [1982] 1 WLR 86, CA; *D W Moore & Co Ltd v Ferrier* [1988] 1 WLR 267, CA; *Bell v Peter Browne & Co* [1990] 2 QB 495, CA; *Knapp v Ecclesiastical Insurance Group plc* [1998] PNLR 172, CA; each of these decisions was approved in *Law Society v Sephton & Co* [2006] UKHL 22, [2006] 2 AC 543.

17 *D W Moore & Co Ltd v Ferrier* [1988] 1 WLR 267, 280, CA (Bingham LJ).

Breach of continuing duty of care

16.30   An insurance broker may be under a continuing duty to perform a particular function on behalf of a client.[1] Where the broker is under a continuing duty, a new cause of action arises each day the broker fails to carry out the function, and proceedings will be in time if they are issued within six years of the last day on which the function could have been carried out.

1 *Johnston v Leslie & Godwin Financial Services Ltd* [1995] LRLR 472 (Clarke J; retention of documentation in relation to contract of reinsurance); *HIH Casualty and General Insurance Ltd v JLT Risk Solutions Ltd* [2006] EWHC 485 (Comm), [2006] Lloyd's Rep IR 493, paras 132–133 (Langley J; brokers placed insurance and reinsurance; held to owe insurers a duty, notwithstanding lack of instructions from insurers, to read risk management reports carefully and if any of the information was or ought to have been thought to be a matter of at least potential concern on coverage issues, to alert both insurer and reinsurer to it); *Great North Eastern Railway Ltd v JLT Corporate Risks Ltd* [2006] EWHC 1478 (Comm), [2007] Lloyd's Rep IR 38, paras 24–33 (Cresswell J; brokers' application to strike out claim that they owed continuing duty of care to inform insured that instructions not carried out; application refused on grounds court should not decide issue without expert evidence). See also: *Midland Bank Trust Co Ltd v Hett, Stubbs & Kemp* [1979] Ch 384 (solicitors).

Extension of limitation period: ss 14A and 32 of the Limitation Act 1980

16.31   The Limitation Act 1980 contains various provisions which extend, suspend or postpone the commencement of the limitation period in prescribed circumstances. Section 14A of the Act[1] applies to actions for negligence[2] where facts relevant to the cause of action are not known at the date of accrual, and extends the limitation period to three years from the earliest date on which the claimant or any person in whom the cause of action was vested before him first had both the knowledge required for bringing an action for damages in respect of the relevant damage and a right to bring such an action.[3] The knowledge required is knowledge of the material facts about the damage in respect of which damages are claimed, the knowledge that the damage was attributable in whole or in part to the act or omission which is alleged to constitute negligence,[4] the identity of the defendant and, if it is alleged that the act or omission was that of a person other than the defendant, the identity of that person and the additional facts supporting the bringing of an action against the defendant.[5] The material facts about the damage are such facts about the damage as would lead a reasonable person who had suffered such damage to consider it sufficiently serious to justify his instituting proceedings for damages against a defendant who did not dispute liability and was able to satisfy a judgment.[6] Knowledge that any acts or omissions did or did not, as a matter of law, involve negligence is irrelevant.[7] For the purposes of s 14A, a person's knowledge includes knowledge which he might reasonably have been expected to acquire from facts observable or ascertainable by him, or from facts ascertainable by him with the help of appropriate expert advice which it is reasonable for him to seek, but he is not taken to have knowledge of a fact ascertainable only with the help of expert advice so long as he has taken all reasonable steps to obtain (and, where appropriate, act on) that advice.[8] Section 14A applies only to actions brought in tort, and not to actions for breach of a contractual duty to exercise reasonable skill and care.[9]

Section 32 of the Limitation Act 1980 provides for the postponement of the commencement of the limitation period in cases of fraud, deliberate concealment or mistake. Where an action is based upon the fraud of the defendant,[10] or any fact relevant to the claimant's right of action has been deliberately concealed from him by the defendant,[11] or the action is for relief from the consequences of a mistake,[12] the period of limitation[13] does not start to run until the claimant has discovered the fraud, concealment or mistake, or could with reasonable diligence have discovered it. Section 32(1)(b) applies both where concealment of relevant facts is contemporaneous with the accrual of the cause of action and where it occurs subsequently. In either case, deliberate concealment has the effect of excluding the ordinary time limits, and time begins to run (or, strictly, begins to run again, if it had already started to run before the concealment) on the discovery or imputed discovery of the relevant facts by the claimant.[14]

Section 32(1)(b) should be read with s 32(2), which provides that deliberate concealment of a breach of duty in circumstances in which it is unlikely to be discovered for some time amounts to deliberate concealment of the facts involved in that breach of duty.[15] The Court of Appeal decided in *Brocklesby v Armitage & Guest*[16] that it was sufficient to bring a case within s 32(2) that a professional adviser had intentionally given the advice in question and that (if negligent) it amounted to a breach of duty; it was not necessary that he should have appreciated that the advice was wrong or that he had been negligent. The effect of this interpretation of s 32(2) was to deprive professional advisers of any effective limitation defence in respect of negligence claims, and it was rejected by the House of Lords in *Cave v Robinson Jarvis & Rolf*.[17] As a result, where a defendant is ignorant of his own inadvertent breach of duty, his conduct does not fall within s 32(2), s 32(1)(b) does not apply, and the limitation period is not postponed.[18]

1 Section 14A was inserted by the Latent Damage Act 1986, s 1.
2 Other than actions in respect of personal injuries: ss 11 and 14A(1) of the 1980 Act.
3 Section 14A(5) of the 1980 Act.
4 Knowledge that the damage was attributable in whole or in part to the act or omission which is alleged to constitute negligence means that the act or omission of which the claimant must have knowledge must be that which is causally relevant for the purposes of an allegation of negligence, and the facts of which the claimant must have knowledge are those which can fairly be described as constituting the negligence of which the claimant complains: *Hallam-Eames v Merrett Syndicates Ltd* [2001] Lloyd's Rep PN 178, 181, CA (Hoffmann LJ); approved: *Haward v Fawcetts* [2006] UKHL 9, [2006] 1 WLR 682.
5 Section 14A(6) and (8) of the 1980 Act.
6 Section 14A(7) of the 1980 Act.
7 Section 14A(9) of the 1980 Act.
8 Section 14A(10) of the 1980 Act.
9 *Société Commerciale de Réassurances v ERAS (International) Ltd* [1992] 1 Lloyd's Rep 570, CA.
10 Section 32(1)(a) of the 1980 Act.

11 Section 32(1)(b) of the 1980 Act.
12 Section 32(1)(c) of the 1980 Act.
13 Section 14A of the 1980 Act does not apply to any action to which s 32(1)(b) applies, and accordingly the period of limitation referred to here is the period applicable under s 2 of the Act: see s 32(5).
14 *Sheldon v R H M Outhwaite (Underwriting Agencies) Ltd* [1996] AC 102, HL.
15 Section 32(2) of the 1980 Act.
16 [2002] 1 WLR 589 (solicitors' negligence), followed in *Liverpool Roman Catholic Archdiocese Trustees Inc v Goldberg* [2001] 1 All ER 182 (tax advice).
17 [2002] UKHL 18, [2003] 1 AC 384.
18 *Cave v Robinson Jarvis & Rolf* [2002] UKHL 18, [2003] 1 AC 384.

Computing the statutory limitation period

16.32 In computing the period within which the action should be brought, the day on which the cause of action accrues is to be excluded;[1] and where a claim form cannot be issued on what would otherwise be the last day of the limitation period because the court office is not open, that period is extended to the first day on which the office is open.[2]

1 *Marren v Dawson Bentley & Co Ltd* [1961] 2 QB 135 (a case concerning s 2(1) of the Limitation Act 1939), approved in *Pritam Kaur v S Russel & Sons Ltd* [1973] QB 336, CA. Thus, if a cause of action accrues on 3 October 2012, an action will be in time if a claim form is issued on 3 October 2018.
2 *Pritam Kaur v S Russel & Sons Ltd* [1973] QB 336, CA.

DAMAGES

General principle

16.33 The fundamental principle underlying the measure of damages is that the damages awarded to the claimant should put him in the same position as he would have been in had he not suffered the wrong for which he is being compensated.[1] Where damages are awarded for breach of the duty to exercise reasonable skill and care, the principles governing the measure of damage will be the same whether the duty is pleaded in contract or in tort,[2] and no distinction is made in the discussion below. In relation to breach of duty by an insurance broker, the courts have developed general principles which will apply in typical cases, although they remain subject to the application of the fundamental principle just referred to, and may lead to a different result in particular cases. It is important to bear in mind that only losses which fall within the scope of the duty owed by the broker, and are caused by his negligence, are recoverable.[3] The first step in any broker's negligence action is therefore to define the scope of the duty owed by the broker to the client:[4]

'It is never sufficient to ask simply whether A owes B a duty of care. It is always necessary to determine the scope of the duty by reference to the kind of damage from which A must take care to save B harmless.'

In *Jones v Environcom Ltd*,[5] David Steel J held that the client's case was that, had the broker not been negligent, it would have adopted fire precautions and the fire which was the subject of the claim would not have occurred. The judge said that it followed that even if, contrary to his earlier finding, cover would have been obtained by the client, it would not have been called upon as no loss by fire would have been sustained. He also said that the loss claimed was not of the kind or type for which the broker ought fairly to be taken to accept liability; or, taking the issue of remoteness by reference to more familiar lines, that he was not persuaded that the loss suffered was within the reasonable contemplation of the parties as likely to result from the breach of retainer. Putting it another way, he said that if no fire would have occurred, it followed that the loss sustained by the client was not caused by the broker: the fire and consequential loss was attributable to the client's failure to identify and enforce appropriate fire precautions by way of changes in the whole working process without which the process was effectively uninsurable.[6] On appeal, the Court of Appeal refused permission to amend the pleadings to advance the case that, had the broker not been negligent, the fire which was the subject of the claim would not have occurred, and that the fact that it did occur was due to and caused by and within the scope of the broker's duty to advise.[7]

The absence of written documents evidencing the broker's retainer often causes difficulty in defining the scope of the duty owed by the broker, and even where there is a written record of the retainer, the broker's role may develop over time, so that the documents no longer fairly reflect the tasks he has agreed to undertake. The burden of proving causation is on the client.[8] If the client succeeds in establishing breach of duty and causation, any damages awarded may also be reduced on the grounds of contributory negligence by the client; however, although contributory negligence is frequently pleaded, such pleas are rarely successful.

1 *Livingstone v Rawyards Coal Co* (1880) 5 App Cas 25, 39, HL (Lord Blackburn); *Dodd Properties v Canterbury City Council* [1980] 1 WLR 433, 451, CA (Megaw LJ); *County Personnel (Employment Agency) Ltd v Alan R Pulver & Co* [1987] 1 WLR 916, 925, CA (Bingham LJ).
2 *Swingcastle Ltd v Gibson* [1991] 2 AC 223, 238, HL (Lord Lowry). Lord Lowry noted that a different standard of remoteness may apply in contract and in tort, though the result may be the same. See also *Watts v Morrow* [1991] 1 WLR 1421, 1434–1436, CA (Ralph Gibson LJ).
3 *Caparo Industries plc v Dickman* [1990] 2 AC 605, HL; *South Australia Asset Management Corpn v York Montague Ltd* [1997] AC 191, HL; *Aneco Reinsurance Underwriting Ltd v Johnson & Higgins Ltd* [2001] UKHL 51, HL [2002] 1 Lloyd's Rep 157 (see further **PARA 16.37**). See also the discussion of the authorities of causation in the context of negligence advice in *Hagen v ICI Chemicals and Polymers Ltd* [2002] IRLR 31 (Elias J), at paras 105–132.
4 *Caparo Industries plc v Dickman* [1990] 2 AC 605, 627, HL (Lord Bridge). See, similarly, *South Australia Asset Management Corpn v York Montague Ltd* [1997] AC 191, 211, HL (Lord Hoffmann).
5 [2010] EWHC 759 (Comm), [2010] Lloyd's Rep IR 676.
6 At paras 106–109.
7 [2011] EWCA Civ 1152, [2012] Lloyd's Rep IR 277.
8 *Wilsher v Essex Area Health Authority* [1988] AC 1074, HL; *J W Bollom & Co Ltd v Byas Moseley & Co Ltd* [2000] Lloyd's Rep IR 136, 142 (Moore-Bick J).

Client left without cover or with inadequate cover

16.34   Where as a result of the broker's negligence the client is left without cover, the measure of damages is the amount which the client would have been entitled to be paid by the insurer by way of indemnity pursuant to the policy had the broker not been negligent.[1]

Where cover exists but, due to the broker's negligence, is inadequate, the measure of damages will generally be the amount which the client would have been entitled to be paid by way of indemnity less any indemnity in fact received. In either case, in order to recover damages, the insured must show that he would have been able to obtain a valid insurance policy if the broker had not been negligent. For example, in *McNealy v Pennine Insurance Co Ltd*,[2] the insurer avoided a motor insurance policy for failure to disclose that the insured was a part-time musician. The Court of Appeal held that if the broker had gone through the list of excluded occupations and asked the insured whether he was a part-time musician, in addition to asking him his occupation (which was that of property repairer), he would have disclosed that he played the guitar, and the insurer would not have accepted the risk. Motor insurance would have been available elsewhere, albeit at a higher premium.[3] In *Thomas Cheshire and Co v Vaughan Bros and Co*, the insurer avoided the client's PPI policy (policy payable 'without proof of interest', also known as an 'honour' policy) for non-disclosure and the client sued the broker for negligence, claiming damages assessed by reference to the value of the PPI policy, had it not been avoided. The Court of Appeal held that the client was not entitled to damages, on the grounds that the policy which the broker had been instructed to obtain, and had obtained, was a PPI policy, which was void under statute.[4]

Where the allegation against a broker is that he failed to obtain insurance cover, or to obtain insurance cover on the terms specified by the client, even where a breach of duty is shown, damages[5] will be awarded only where insurance of the type required by the client was available in the market at the relevant time.[6] The onus is on the client to show that it has suffered loss as a result of the broker's breach of duty. In order to do so, the client must show that it would have been able to obtain cover in the market. In practice, a client may succeed on this issue with little or no evidence. In *Mint Security Ltd v Blair*,[7] Staughton J was prepared to assume that had the broker discharged its duty, so that all material facts had been disclosed, cover would have been available, perhaps on slightly different terms or at a slightly increased premium.[8] Similarly, in *Mander v Commercial Assurance Co plc*, Rix J took the view that:[9]

'Prima facie, the loss of effective insurance gives rise to a claim against a negligent broker in the sum which the client would have recovered under the insurance, if it had been effective: it is therefore for the brokers to prove that the reinsurances could not have been obtained elsewhere, or only on less favourable terms etc.'

It would nevertheless be prudent for a claimant to plead that alternative cover would have been available in the market at the relevant time, and to plead the terms on which the cover would have been available, and to lead evidence on the issue if it is not admitted by the defendant broker. Similarly, if the defendant broker wishes to allege that the claimant has suffered no loss because cover would have been successfully resisted by underwriters on other grounds, this should also be pleaded.[10] Quantum will be governed by the terms and conditions, including as to the limit of indemnity and any applicable excess, of the policy (if any) which the court finds would have been available to the claimant.

Credit must also be given for the premium which would have been payable in order to secure the cover.[11] In some cases, had the broker not been negligent, cover would have been available but only on payment of an additional premium: for example, if insurers avoid as a result of material non-disclosure for which the broker is responsible, and full disclosure would have led to insurers demanding a higher premium to reflect the true risk.[12] The level of premium in such a case will be a matter for expert evidence, unless it can be agreed, although the brokers or their legal representatives might decide not to take the point as the cost of obtaining expert evidence on the issue would in many cases be disproportionate to the likely reduction in damages. Where the broker has been in breach of duty for a number of years before the loss occurs, resulting in a lower premium not just in the policy year in which the loss occurs but for several years before that date, the broker is entitled to credit only for the year in which the loss occurred, and in respect of which the claim is made, and not for previous years.[13]

Where the client has settled with the insurer, the broker may challenge the level of the settlement and argue that it was unreasonably low. In *Mander v Commercial Union Assurance Co plc*,[14] Rix J suggested that the burden of showing that the settlement was unreasonable was on the broker, because it was tantamount to saying that the client had failed to mitigate its loss. The judge said that the correct approach was to determine the reasonableness of the settlement by reference to the client's chances of success in the litigation which had been settled (presumably, by adopting a broad-brush approach), and not by re-litigating the underlying issues in the absence of one of the parties.

On the current state of the authorities, losses consequent upon lack of cover, or inadequate cover, are not recoverable.[15] In *Ramwade Ltd v W J Emson & Co Ltd*,[16] the client's lorry was written off in the course of a road accident. The lorry was insured against third-party risks only, and the defendant insurance brokers accepted that they had negligently failed to obtain a comprehensive policy of insurance. The plaintiff claimed damages in respect of not only the replacement value of the lorry, but also the cost of hiring replacement vehicles in the period between the accident and the date of judgment. The Court of Appeal held that the plaintiff was entitled to damages in an amount which would put them in the position they would have been but for the defendants' negligence; that if the defendants had not been negligent, the plaintiff would have recovered the value of the lorry from insurers under a comprehensive policy; that there would have been no cover for hire charges pending replacement; and that on this basis the replacement value of the lorry was recoverable, but hire charges were not.[17] In support of its conclusion, the Court of Appeal indicated that the incurring of hire charges did not flow from the failure to obtain a comprehensive policy, but from either:

(1)   the impecuniosity of the plaintiffs, which rendered them unable promptly to buy a replacement vehicle; if this were the cause, the hire charges were irrecoverable on the principles established in *The Liesbosch*;[18] or

(2)   the failure of the defendant insurance brokers promptly to pay that which comprehensive insurers would have paid had there been comprehensive insurance.

This amounted to a claim for damages for non-payment of damages, which is not a permissible claim: even though damages had not been quantified, a failure to meet the claim when made could give rise only to a claim for money plus interest from the date when it fell due until judgment, but not to a claim that the late payment resulted in further or other claims.[19] In *Alcoa Minerals of Jamaica Inc v Broderick*,[20] the Privy Council approved *Ramwade Ltd v W J Emson & Co Ltd*'s application of *The Liesbosch* on the grounds that in both cases there were two heads of damage

(damage to property and cost of hire), only the first of which was directly caused by the negligence for which the defendant was liable.[21]

It is suggested that *Ramwade v Emson* is potentially distinguishable where the purpose of the insurance is to protect the client's cashflow, as is the case, for example, with business interruption or permanent health insurance, as damage caused by lack of cashflow will have been in the reasonable contemplation of the parties.[22]

1 See *Cherry Ltd v Allied Insurance Brokers Ltd* [1978] 1 Lloyd's Rep 274, 280 (Cantley J); *Mint Security Ltd v Blair* [1982] 1 Lloyd's Rep 188; *Dunbar v A & B Painters Ltd* [1986] 2 Lloyd's Rep 38, 40, CA (May LJ); *Ramwade Ltd v W J Emson & Co Ltd* [1987] RTR 72, CA. The loss must be within the scope of the duty: see **PARA 16.33**.
2 [1978] 2 Lloyd's Rep 18, CA.
3 It would have been open to the broker to claim credit for the additional premium which the insured would have had to pay, but he did not do so.
4 Section 4(2)(b) of the Marine Insurance Act 1906. Policies payable 'without proof of interest' (also known as 'honour' policies) are void for lack of insurable interest, as to which, see **PARAS 2.4–2.10**.
5 Damage being an ingredient of the tort of negligence, the lack of available insurance is a defence to the charge of negligence if no other damage is proved; although damages will be awarded in contract for a technical breach of duty which has caused no loss, they will be nominal only.
6 *Aneco Reinsurance Underwriting Ltd v Johnson & Higgins Ltd* [2001] UKHL 51, [2002] 1 Lloyd's Rep 157, para 103 (Lord Millett, dissenting); and see *Avondale Blouse Co Ltd v Williamson & Geo Town* (1948) 81 Ll L Rep 492, 498 (Lynskey J).
7 [1982] 1 Lloyd's Rep 188.
8 At 201.
9 [1998] Lloyd's Rep IR 93, 146–147 (obiter, as the trial was on liability only).
10 *Alexander Forbes Europe Ltd v SBJ Ltd* [2003] Lloyd's Rep IR 432, para 44 (Mr David Mackie QC, sitting as a Deputy Judge of the High Court).
11 See *Sharp v Sphere Drake Insurance plc, The Moonacre* [1992] 2 Lloyd's Rep 501, 527 (Mr A D Colman QC, sitting as a Deputy Judge of the High Court); *George Barkes (London) Ltd v LFC (1988) Ltd* [2000] PNLR 21 (His Honour Judge Hallgarten QC, declining to follow, on the grounds that it was contrary to principle, the indication in the speech of Lord Roskill in the Privy Council in *Eagle Star Insurance Co Ltd v National Westminster Finance Australia Ltd* (1985) 58 ALR 165 (at 175) that the brokers were not entitled to credit for the premium recoverable by the insured from insurers; it is suggested that the approach of His Honour Judge Hallgarten QC is correct). Insurers are obliged to tender a return of premium on avoidance of the policy: see **PARA 11.33**.
12 See *J W Bollom & Co Ltd v Byas Moseley & Co Ltd* [2000] Lloyd's Rep IR 136 (Moore-Bick J).
13 *J W Bollom & Co Ltd v Byas Moseley & Co Ltd* [2000] Lloyd's Rep IR 136, 151 (Moore-Bick J).
14 [1998] Lloyd's Rep IR 93, 148–149 (Rix J; obiter, as the trial was on liability only).
15 *Ramwade Ltd v W J Emson & Co Ltd* [1987] RTR 72, CA, considered: *Alcoa Minerals of Jamaica Inc v Broderick* [2002] 1 AC 371, PC. The law in this area cannot be regarded as settled, particularly following the decision of the House of Lords in *Sempra Metals Ltd v Inland Revenue Commissioners* [2007] UKHL 34, [2008] 1 AC 561, which decided that the loss suffered as a result of the late payment of money is recoverable at common law, subject to the ordinary rules of remoteness which apply to all claims of damages.
16 [1987] RTR 72, CA.
17 At 75 (Parker LJ).
18 [1933] AC 449, HL.
19 As to circumstances in which insurers may now be liable to pay damages for late payment of a claim under an insurance policy, see **PARAS 6.6** and **8.2–8.3**.
20 [2002] 1 AC 371, PC.
21 See 379 and 382. The House of Lords has since held that the law has moved on since *The Liesbosch* was decided and that the correct test of remoteness today is whether the loss was reasonably foreseeable; that the wrongdoer must take his victim as he finds him; that this rule applies to the economic state of the victim in the same way as it applies to his physical and mental vulnerability; and that it requires the wrongdoer to bear the consequences if it was reasonably foreseeable that the injured party would have to borrow money or incur some other kind of expenditure to mitigate his damages: *Lagden v O'Connor* [2003] UKHL 64, [2004] 1 AC 1067, paras 8 (Lord Nicholls), 12 (Lord Slynn), 61 (Lord Hope) (Lords Scott and Walker dissenting).

22 See *Wellesley Partners LLP v Withers LLP* [2015] EWCA Civ 1146, paras 80 (Floyd LJ), 163 (Roth J) and 186 (Tomlinson LJ) (solicitors' negligence, applicable by analogy to insurance brokers: normal contractual measure of damages applies where solicitor negligently fails to follow his instructions: client should be restored to position he would have been in if instructions had been complied with, but is only liable for loss which could reasonably have been contemplated by the parties when the retainer came into existence).

Loss of a chance

16.35 An insurer may rely upon more than one basis for repudiating liability; for example, there may have been both a material non-disclosure in the proposal of the risk, and breach of condition through late notification after the loss has arisen. The broker may be responsible for one of the grounds for repudiation but not the other. In these circumstances, if the insurer repudiates liability on the basis only of the ground for which the broker is not responsible, the broker's negligence will have caused the client no loss. If, however, the insurer repudiates liability on the basis of the ground for which the broker is responsible, it is still open to the broker to seek to show that the insurer could and would have relied upon the second ground for repudiation had the first not been available to it.[1] The onus of proof seems to be on the broker on this issue.[2] In these circumstances, the approach that is taken is that of the Court of Appeal in *Allied Maples Group Ltd v Simmons & Simmons*.[3] The court will award damages on the basis of an assessment of the likelihood that the insurer would have repudiated, with a corresponding reduction in the damages to be awarded.[4] This was the approach taken by Kerr J in *Everett v Hogg, Robinson & Gardner Mountain (Insurance) Ltd*,[5] in which the brokers were found to have negligently provided inaccurate answers to reinsurers' questions on behalf of underwriters. The underwriters had failed to disclose the claims history, which Kerr J held to be a material non-disclosure, and the damages recovered by underwriters were reduced by 33 per cent to reflect the judge's assessment of the chances of the reinsurers repudiating liability on the basis of the non-disclosure of the claims history had they not repudiated on the grounds of the material non-disclosure by the brokers. This approach is consistent with the authorities on solicitors' negligence, in which the issue has received greater attention.[6] It is also consistent with the statement of general principle in Lord Diplock's speech in *Mallett v McMonagle* in the House of Lords:[7]

> 'The role of the court in making an assessment of damages which depends upon its view as to what will be and what would have been is to be contrasted with its ordinary function in civil actions of determining what was. In determining what did happen in the past a court decides on the balance of probabilities. Anything that is more probable than not it treats as certain. But in assessing damages which depend upon its view as to what will happen in the future or would have happened in the future if something had not happened in the past, the court must make an estimate as to what are the chances that a particular thing will or would have happened and reflect those chances, whether they are more or less than even, in the amount of damages which it awards.'

1 See *Fraser v B N Furman (Productions) Ltd* [1967] 1 WLR 898, 909–910, CA (Diplock LJ, obiter); see also *Ground Gilbey Ltd v Jardine Lloyd Thompson UK Ltd* [2011] EWHC 124 (Comm), [2012]

Lloyd's Rep IR 12, para 124 (Blair J) (loss of chance analysis not relevant where there are no alternative coverage issues which the insurer might have raised). In *Gunns v Par Insurance Brokers* [1997] 1 Lloyd's Rep 173, Sir Michael Ogden held that the client had breached a policy condition and would not have been entitled to damages even if he had held that they (and not the client) were responsible for material non-disclosure in the proposal form, on the basis of which the insurers had denied liability.

2 See *Everett v Hogg, Robinson & Gardner Mountain (Insurance) Ltd* [1973] 2 Lloyd's Rep 217, 223 (Kerr J, obiter, in the context of reinsurance); see also *O & R Jewellers Ltd v Terry* [1999] Lloyd's Rep IR 436, 449 (Sir Godfrey Le Quesne QC, sitting as a Deputy Judge of the High Court). See also *Fraser v B N Furman (Productions) Ltd* [1967] 1 WLR 898, 909, CA (Diplock LJ). In *Dunbar v A & B Painters Ltd* [1986] 2 Lloyd's Rep 38, CA, May LJ noted (at 41), without commenting on the burden of proof, that all of the evidence on this issue was called by the brokers. The question whether insurers would have taken an available point is to be answered on the assumption that they would have discovered the relevant facts: *O & R Jewellers Ltd v Terry* [1999] Lloyd's Rep IR 436, 449 (Sir Godfrey Le Quesne QC, sitting as a Deputy Judge of the High Court).

3 [1995] 1 WLR 1602, CA. Moore-Bick J would have taken this approach in *J W Bollom & Co Ltd v Byas Moseley & Co Ltd* [2000] Lloyd's Rep IR 136 had the issue arisen for decision (see 143).

4 *Dunbar v A & B Painters Ltd* [1986] 2 Lloyd's Rep 38, CA. In *Pryke v Gibbs Hartley Cooper Ltd* [1991] 1 Lloyd's Rep 602, insurers had been deprived by the broker's negligence of an opportunity to cancel a policy of insurance. Waller J held (at 620–621) that there was no contract, and that the broker owed the insurers a duty of care in tort; and that the measure of damages was the same in either case (loss of a chance):

> '"Loss of a chance" may in fact be the correct measure of damage even in a case where there is only ever one potential ground of avoidance, but if the broker is found liable, the "chance" will be assessed as 100 per cent with no reduction in the damages awarded, with the result that the analysis is likely to be of theoretical interest only';

and see *J W Bollom & Co Ltd v Byas Moseley & Co Ltd* [2000] Lloyd's Rep IR 136, 143 (Moore-Bick J). Similarly, in *Alexander Forbes Europe Ltd v SBJ Ltd* [2003] Lloyd's Rep IR 432, Mr David Mackie QC, sitting as a Deputy Judge of the High Court, said that it seemed to him more likely than not that but for the defendant broker's errors the insurers would have agreed to pay, and that the broker's submissions that the evidence revealed other grounds on which the insurers might have justified a refusal to pay did not begin to contravert what would be the usual course of events (para 47).

5 [1973] 2 Lloyd's Rep 217. See also *O & R Jewellers Ltd v Terry* [1999] Lloyd's Rep IR 436.

6 See *Kitchen v RAF Association* [1958] 1 WLR 563, CA (proceedings statute-barred); *Harrison v Bloom Camillin (No 2)* [2000] Lloyd's Rep PN 89 (writ served outside limitation period).

7 [1970] AC 166, at 176, considered in *Dunbar v A & B Painters Ltd* [1986] 2 Lloyd's Rep 38, CA. See also *Allied Maples Group Ltd v Simmons & Simmons* [1995] 1 WLR 1602, CA.

Client exposed to unnecessary risk of legal disputes with insurer

16.36 In *Talbot Underwriting Ltd v Nausch, Hogan & Murray Inc, The Jascon 5*[1], Cooke J said[2] that the duty of a broker was, so far as possible, to obtain insurance coverage which clearly and indisputably met its clients' requirements, and that:[3]

> 'Whether or not the argument advanced by the broker ... is ultimately found to be correct, the fact remains that, by not doing what a competent professional person would do to avoid such argument, cost and expense can be incurred. In those circumstances liability for loss and damage which flows from that negligence and is not too remote must be recoverable.'

1 [2005] EWHC 2359 (Comm), [2006] 2 Lloyd's Rep 195.
2 At para 104. See **PARA 16.16**.
3 At para 106 (issue not considered on appeal: [2006] EWCA Civ 889, [2006] 2 Lloyd's Rep 195).

Breach of duty to advise

16.37   Where the broker assumes a duty to advise the client, rather than to provide specific information,[1] the measure of loss will be the whole of the loss suffered by the client as a result of acting on the broker's advice.[2] This may result in recovery of far greater damages than if the broker's duty had been limited to obtaining insurance against a particular risk. In *Aneco Reinsurance Underwriting Ltd v Johnson & Higgins Ltd*,[3] the brokers were acting both for the insured, in seeking to place the risk, and for the insurer, in seeking to reinsure part of the risk. The insurer suffered a loss of $35m (US dollars) on the insurance, and the reinsurers successfully avoided the cover which the brokers had placed with them, on the grounds of non-disclosure. The reinsurance cover would have been worth $11m. The House of Lords held, on the facts of the case, that the brokers' duty was not confined to the obtaining of reinsurance protection for the insured, and informing it that it had done so, but that the brokers also owed a duty to inform the insurer whether or not reinsurance was available. If the brokers had discharged this duty, it would have been obvious to the insurer that the lack of availability of reinsurance was due to the current market assessment of the risks. Consequently, the brokers were liable for the full extent of the losses attributable to their breach of duty. The insurer would not have written the insurance if the brokers had not advised it that reinsurance was available, and it recovered the whole of its losses on the insurance, which amounted to $35m, rather than the $11m which it would have recovered had the reinsurance not been avoided for non-disclosure. Whether a broker has assumed a duty to provide specific information, or to advise more generally, may be a difficult question of fact, as the *Aneco* case itself demonstrates.

It is usual practice for brokers to advise clients that their insurance cover is about to expire. Whether a broker is under a legal obligation to do so will, it is suggested, depend on the circumstances, such as the length of the relationship between the parties, and in particular the terms of the broker's retainer.

1 As to the distinction between information and advice, see *South Australia Asset Management Corpn v York Montague Ltd* [1997] AC 191, HL, explained in *Aneco Reinsurance Underwriting Ltd v Johnson & Higgins Ltd* [2001] UKHL 51, [2002] 1 Lloyd's Rep 157, 190, para 62 (Lord Millett, dissenting).
2 *Aneco Reinsurance Underwriting Ltd v Johnson & Higgins Ltd* [2001] UKHL 51, [2002] 1 Lloyd's Rep 157.
3 [2001] UKHL 51, [2002] 1 Lloyd's Rep 157.

Contributory negligence

16.38   The court may reduce the damages recoverable by the client to the extent which it considers just and equitable, pursuant to s 1(1) of the Law Reform (Contributory Negligence) Act 1945. Allegations of contributory negligence are often made by brokers against clients; for example, on the basis of failure to examine policy documents. The allegation is usually framed with an allegation in the alternative that the loss was wholly caused by the client's actions.

It is now well established that the 1945 Act applies in relation to concurrent contractual and tortious duties owed by brokers to their clients.[1] As long as the cause of action could have been framed as a breach of duty of care in tort, any damages awarded can properly be reduced and apportioned in accordance with the 1945 Act.[2]

The test to be applied is whether the client has been 'guilty of "neglect of what would be prudent in respect of their own interests"'.[3]

In the context of a client and a professional adviser, this means that the client will not be found to be contributorily negligent unless he has failed to guard against a risk that was reasonably foreseeable, and that, in the context of the relationship between the client and the broker, the client will not be found to be contributorily negligent unless he ought reasonably to have foreseen that the broker might fail to carry out his responsibilities.[4] Even in cases where the professional's duty is to protect his client against the very damage that has occurred, there is no rule of law that contributory negligence is not available as a defence.[5] However, although it is frequently pleaded, contributory negligence is rarely established against lay clients in these circumstances.[6] *Sharp v Sphere Drake Insurance plc, The Moonacre*[7] is a good example of a typical plea of contributory negligence, and a typical reaction from the judge hearing the case. The broker argued that the client should have checked through the copy of the proposal form and policy which he was sent, that had he done so he should have realised that a question which asked whether the yacht which was the subject of the insurance was used as a houseboat had been wrongly answered in the negative, and so informed the broker, who would have corrected the error. It was argued that failing to check the proposal form and policy amounted to contributory negligence. Mr A D Colman QC, sitting as a Deputy Judge of the High Court, described this argument as 'entirely misconceived'. He said:[8]

> '[The broker] had specifically questioned [the client] about houseboat use in the course of the telephone conversation … [The client], as a layman, was clearly entitled to rely on [the broker's] skill and judgment as a professional broker in identifying what kind of information was required from [the client] in order to answer the question. Having given [the broker] precisely the information for which he was asked he was entitled to assume, when he subsequently received the proposal form and the policy that what he had told [the broker] was all that was needed to bring about effective cover. It was no part of his duty to second-guess his own professional adviser and there was thus no "fault" on his part. He had no share in the responsibility for the damage he sustained.'

Similarly, in *Arbory Group Ltd v West Craven Insurance Services*,[9] the judge rejected a plea of contributory negligence based on an argument that the insured was best placed to calculate the proper sum for which his company should be insured for business interruption insurance, and accordingly to know that the insured gross profit figure of £250,000 was too low.[10] The judge held that an essential prerequisite for the calculation and knowledge was an understanding of the concept of insured gross profit, that the insured did not have that understanding, and that the broker was in breach of duty for failing to explain that concept; and, further, that the figures which the insured gave to the broker should immediately have put an insurance broker holding himself out as a specialist commercial broker on enquiry because properly analysed they indicated a significantly higher insurable gross profit; that, at the very least the broker should have gone through the figures; and that, if he had done so, he would have advised that the insured gross profit was in the region of £1 million instead of £250,000.[11] Conversely, in *Eurokey Recycling Ltd v Giles Insurance Brokers Ltd*,[12] the insured provided inaccurate estimated turnover and stock and machinery figures to the broker, and the judge said that, had he found in favour of the insured, he would have assessed contributory negligence at 50 per cent.[13]

The courts are, on the whole, more willing to find contributory negligence in the context of reinsurance, where the client is a fellow insurance professional rather than a lay client. For example, in *Youell v Bland Welch & Co Ltd, The Superhulls Cover Case (No 2)*,[14] which involved reinsurance, Phillips J took into account, in finding contributory negligence on the part of the brokers' clients,[15] the fact that the clients were Lloyd's agents, and that their personnel were marine underwriters of great experience.[16] Similar considerations appear to have led to a finding of contributory negligence in *Vesta v Butcher*.[17] The insured received policy documentation containing a warranty that there would be a 24-hour watch over their fish farm. They immediately informed their insurers that they could not accept the clause. The insurers telephoned the brokers and informed them that a 24-hour watch could not be kept on the fish farm, and sought confirmation that this was acceptable to reinsurers. The brokers forgot about the telephone call. Several months later, there was a loss. Hobhouse J held that the clause was not applicable, but that if it had been, the brokers would have been negligent for failing to act on the request. He accepted an argument by the brokers that the insurers were contributorily negligent in failing to follow up the telephone call, and assessed the relative degree of blameworthiness as 75 per cent in relation to the insurers, and 25 per cent in relation to the brokers.[18]

1 *Vesta v Butcher* [1986] 2 Lloyd's Rep 179, [1986] 2 All ER 488 (Hobhouse J), [1989] AC 852, CA and HL; *Youell v Bland Welch & Co Ltd, The Superhulls Cover Case (No 2)* [1990] 2 Lloyd's Rep 431.
2 *Youell v Bland Welch & Co Ltd, The Superhulls Cover Case (No 2)* [1990] 2 Lloyd's Rep 431, 456 (Phillips J).
3 *Youell v Bland Welch & Co Ltd, The Superhulls Cover Case (No 2)* [1990] 2 Lloyd's Rep 431, 460, Phillips J (quoting with approval the dictum of Blackburn J in *Swan v North British Australasian Co* (1863) 2 H & C 175, at 182).
4 *J W Bollom & Co Ltd v Byas Moseley & Co Ltd* [2000] Lloyd's IR Rep 136, 152–153 (Moore-Bick J), applying *Barclays Bank plc v Fairclough Building Ltd* [1995] QB 214, CA (building maintenance contract).
5 *Sahib Foods Ltd v Paskin Kyriakides Sands* [2003] EWCA Civ 1832, [2004] PNLR 22, para 70; *Synergy Health (UK) Ltd v CGU Insurance plc* [2010] EWHC 2583 (Comm), [2011] Lloyd's Rep IR 500, para 235 (Flaux J) (insured failed to comply with risk requirement imposed by insurer following survey; broker found not to have been negligent, but judge would otherwise have made a deduction from the insured's damages of 90%).
6 See, eg, *British Citizens Assurance Co v L Woolland & Co* (1921) 8 Ll L Rep 89; *Mint Security Ltd v Blair* [1982] 1 Lloyd's Rep 188, 200 (Staughton J); *J W Bollom & Co Ltd v Byas Moseley & Co Ltd* [2000] Lloyd's Rep IR 136, 152–153 (Moore-Bick J). In *Synergy Health (UK) Ltd v CGU Insurance plc* [2010] EWHC 2583 (Comm), [2011] Lloyd's Rep IR 500, in which the insured failed to comply with a risk requirement imposed by the insurer following a survey, Flaux J said (at paras 236-238) that this was not a case in which the insured did not act because it assumed that the brokers had done their job properly, and that had he found the brokers negligent, he would have made a deduction from the insured's damages of 90%.
7 [1992] 2 Lloyd's Rep 501.
8 At 527.
9 [2007] Lloyd's Rep IR 491.
10 At para 79 (His Honour Judge Grenfell).
11 At para 80 (His Honour Judge Grenfell).
12 [2014] EWHC 2989 (Comm), [2015] Lloyd's Rep IR 225.
13 At para 157 (Blair J).
14 [1990] 2 Lloyd's Rep 431.
15 Responsibility was apportioned on the basis of 20 per cent (client) and 80 per cent (brokers).
16 At 460.
17 [1986] 2 Lloyd's Rep 179, [1986] 2 All ER 488 (Hobhouse J; finding on this issue not considered on appeal: [1989] AC 852, CA and HL). Allegations of contributory negligence against insurance

professionals are by no means always successful: see, eg, *Johnston v Leslie & Godwin Financial Services Ltd* [1995] LRLR 472 (Clarke J).

18 In the Court of Appeal, Sir Roger Ormrod expressed surprise at the apportionment, but declined to interfere with it: [1989] AC 852, CA and HL (at 879).

Damages for mental distress

16.39 Damages for mental distress are not recoverable in proceedings against insurance brokers for breach of duty, either in contract or in tort.[1] This is in accordance with the normal principle that damages for mental distress are recoverable only where the object of a contract between the parties is to provide peace of mind,[2] whereas the object of an insurance broker's retainer is to secure an obligation on the part of insurers to provide an indemnity on the occurrence of agreed contingencies.

1 *Verderame v Commercial Union Assurance Co plc* [1992] BCLC 793, 803, CA.
2 See *Hayes v Dodd* [1990] 2 All ER 815, CA; *Watts v Morrow* [1991] 1 WLR 1421, CA.

Conflicts of interest

16.40 Damages, or an account of profits, are recoverable where loss is suffered by the insured as a result of the broker's inability, due to a conflict of interest, fully to discharge his duty to his client.[1] The measure of damage may be the whole of the loss suffered, or it may be the loss of a chance, depending on the circumstances.[2]

1 *North and South Trust Co v Berkeley* [1971] 1 WLR 470, 484–486 (Donaldson J), approved by the Privy Council in *Kelly v Cooper* [1993] AC 205. See also *Callaghan and Hedges v Thompson* [2000] Lloyd's Rep IR 125, 132 (David Steel J); *Aneco Reinsurance Underwriting Ltd v Johnson & Higgins Ltd* [2001] UKHL 51, [2002] 1 Lloyd's Rep 157, 187, para 42 (Lord Steyn); *Hilton v Barker Booth and Eastwood* [2005] UKHL, [2005] 1 WLR 567, paras 44 and 46 (Lord Walker) (solicitors).
2 See *Allied Maples Group Ltd v Simmons & Simmons* [1995] 1 WLR 1602, CA; *Kelly v Cooper* [1993] AC 205, 216, PC.

Criminal convictions

16.41 Where the client is required by law to have insurance, and the broker's negligence leaves him uninsured, any fine which he is ordered to pay on conviction will be recoverable from the broker in civil proceedings, together with the costs of the criminal proceedings, on the grounds that the prosecution was a reasonably foreseeable consequence of the broker's negligence, and not too remote.[1] This is not contrary to public policy, provided that the offence does not require *mens rea*.[2]

1 See *Osman v J Ralph Moss Ltd* [1970] 1 Lloyd's Rep 313, CA (driving without insurance under the Road Traffic Acts).
2 See *Osman v J Ralph Moss Ltd* [1970] 1 Lloyd's Rep 313, CA.

Costs of civil proceedings brought by third parties

16.42 Where the broker's negligence has left the insured without liability insurance, and he is involved in an accident, the costs of any civil proceedings brought against the insured by third parties will also be recoverable, provided that it was reasonable for him to defend the proceedings.[1]

1 *Osman v J Ralph Moss Ltd* [1970] 1 Lloyd's Rep 313, CA.

Mitigation of damage

16.43   The ordinary principles of mitigation of damage apply in proceedings against insurance brokers. The test for failure to mitigate loss is much higher than that for contributory negligence.[1] While there is no invariable rule that a claimant does not have to embark on litigation as part of mitigating damage, this is in practice generally the case.[2] If the insured settles with insurers before suing the broker, the broker may put the reasonableness of the settlement in issue, which is tantamount to saying that the insured has failed to mitigate its loss.[3] The broker should not be prejudiced by the fact that the insured were keen to reach an early settlement; if, as a result, the insured proceeded on the basis of a 'spurious construction of the cover', that cannot be held against the broker.[4]

Where the client is unaware that the broker has committed a breach of duty, the principles which apply are not those of mitigation of damage, but of causation of loss.[5] If it is not reasonably foreseeable that the client will remain in ignorance of the breach and fail to react to it so as to avoid loss, the loss may be too remote. If the client negligently fails to discover the breach, so that he takes no steps to mitigate its effect, the normal consequences of negligence will follow, including, where appropriate, the application of the Law Reform (Contributory Negligence) Act 1945. An allegation of failure to mitigate damage should be pleaded.[6]

1 *HIH Casualty and General Insurance Ltd v JLT Risk Solutions Ltd* [2006] EWHC 485 (Comm), [2006] Lloyd's Rep IR 493, para 156 (Langley J) (point not considered on appeal: [2007] EWCA Civ 710, [2007] 2 Lloyd's Rep 278).
2 *Alexander Forbes Europe Ltd v SBJ Ltd* [2003] Lloyd's Rep IR 432, para 47 (Mr David Mackie QC, sitting as a Deputy Judge of the High Court).
3 *Mander v Commercial Union Assurance Co plc* [1998] Lloyd's Rep IR 93, 148–149 (Rix J); *Ground Gilbey Ltd v Jardine Lloyd Thompson UK Ltd* [2011] EWHC 124 (Comm), [2012] Lloyd's Rep IR 12, para 109 (Blair J).
4 *Ground Gilbey Ltd v Jardine Lloyd Thompson UK Ltd* [2011] EWHC 124 (Comm), [2012] Lloyd's Rep IR 12, para 103 (Blair J) (the phrase 'spurious construction of the cover' is taken from *Standard Life Assurance Ltd v Oak Dedicated Ltd* [2008] EWHC 222 (Comm), [2008] Lloyd's Rep IR 552, para 102 (Tomlinson J); see **PARA 16.16**).
5 *Youell v Bland Welch & Co Ltd, The Superhulls Cover Case (No 2)* [1990] 2 Lloyd's Rep 431, 461–462 (Phillips J).
6 *Alexander Forbes Europe Ltd v SBJ Ltd* [2003] Lloyd's Rep IR 432, para 44 (Mr David Mackie QC, sitting as a Deputy Judge of the High Court). Although the burden of proving failure to mitigate loss is on the defendant, CPR Practice Direction 16 provides at para 8.2(8) that any facts relating to mitigation of loss or damage must be specifically set out in the particulars of claim if relied on.

Other costs and expenses

16.44   It may be appropriate to make further deductions from the client's damages to reflect other costs and expenses which it would have incurred if the broker had performed its duties. For example, in *J W Bollom & Co Ltd v Byas Moseley & Co Ltd*,[1] the client's recovery from insurers was reduced as a result of the brokers' negligence, and the brokers were ordered to pay damages assessed by reference to the difference between the amount the client would have recovered had the brokers not been negligent, and what the client in fact recovered. As the client had paid its loss adjusters on a percentage basis, the loss adjusters' fees would have increased had it recovered the full amount of its loss from insurers rather than the lower amount for which it settled, and the brokers were given credit for this amount.

1 [2000] Lloyd's Rep IR 136, 151 (Moore-Bick J).

INTEREST

16.45   Interest is in the discretion of the court. Where, as a result of the broker's negligence, the insurer has declined liability for a claim, interest will typically run from the date on which, in the ordinary course of events, the claim would have been paid.[1]

1 See eg *George Barkes (London) Ltd v LFC (1988) Ltd* [2000] PNLR 21, 32 (His Honour Judge Hallgarten QC). See also **PARAS 9.45** and **16.34**.

WHETHER TO JOIN THE BROKER TO AN ACTION AGAINST THE INSURER

16.46   Where there is a dispute between his client and the insurer regarding coverage, the broker is frequently joined in the proceedings so that the court may consider not only whether the insurer was entitled to refuse to pay the claim, but also whether this state of affairs was caused by a breach of duty by the broker.[1] Although the interests of justice will often, probably in most cases, favour this approach, there are likely to be cases in which practical considerations consistent with the interests of justice will properly lead to a decision to take a different course.[2] A broker is not bound by a decision as to the construction of a policy of insurance in proceedings between client and insurer, and if further evidence is adduced in proceedings involving the broker, the court may reach a different conclusion.[3] It may nonetheless be an abuse of process for the insured to seek to re-litigate an issue as to policy construction or coverage, if there is no new evidence which casts doubt on the earlier decision.[4] This may be so even where an arbitration clause prevents all the issues involving the broker and insurer being resolved in a single set of proceedings.[5]

1 See **PARA 9.47**.
2 *Kennecott Utah Copper Corpn v Minet Ltd* [2003] EWCA Civ 905, [2003] Lloyd's Rep IR 503, paras 73–75 (Pill LJ), considering *Aneco Reinsurance (Underwriting) Ltd v Johnson & Higgins Ltd* [1998] 1 Lloyd's Rep 565, 567 (Cresswell J).
3 *HIH Casualty and General Insurance Ltd v JLT Risk Solutions Ltd* [2006] EWHC 485 (Comm), [2006] Lloyd's Rep IR 493, paras 9 and 162 (Langley J) (reaching the same conclusion in relation to construction as the Court of Appeal in *HIH Casualty and General Insurance Ltd v New Hampshire Insurance Co* [2001] EWCA Civ 735, [2001] 2 Lloyd's Rep 161). An application may be made to join the insurer or broker to the existing proceedings in order to avoid this possibility: see **PARA 9.47**.
4 *Arts & Antiques Ltd v Richards* [2013] EWHC 3361 (Comm), [2014] Lloyd's Rep IR 219, paras 43–47 (Hamblen J).
5 See *Arts & Antiques Ltd v Richards* [2013] EWHC 3361 (Comm), [2014] Lloyd's Rep IR 219, paras 23–24 (Hamblen J).

COSTS OF CIVIL PROCEEDINGS BROUGHT AGAINST BROKER AND INSURER

16.47   Civil proceedings are often brought against both insurer and broker due to doubt as to whether the insurer was liable in full or in part under the policy apparently obtained by the broker. In this situation, one of the defendants will typically be successful in its defence and the other will be found liable. In these circumstances, in determining who should pay the costs of the action, or of particular issues, the provisions of CPR 44.3 are the essential working tool.[1] If the broker is found to have negligently failed to obtain appropriate insurance, the claimant will normally recover against the broker not only the costs of the action against him, but also the costs of the action against the insurer.[2] In *Seavision Investment SA v Evennett, The Tiburon*,[3] the brokers accepted for the first time at the commencement of the hearing that if the underwriters were not liable, the brokers would be liable to compensate the client. In these circumstances, the client had no interest in the outcome of the case, as it was bound to succeed against one or other party, and its legal team withdrew, leaving it to the brokers to put forward (in the event, unsuccessfully) the case against the underwriters on its behalf. The judge ordered the brokers to pay the client's costs of the whole action, including the costs of the action against underwriters. The Court of Appeal held that the judge had been right to try to make an order for costs which would produce the same result as would have been produced had there been consecutive actions against first the underwriters and then the brokers.[4] If points taken by the insurer in its defence cause the claimant to join the broker, and the insurer takes the risk of pursuing those points to trial, and is unsuccessful, an application of the provisions of CPR 44.3 is likely to result in the insurer being ordered to pay a substantial proportion of the broker's costs in addition to the whole of the claimant's costs.[5]

1 *Groupama Insurance Co Ltd v Overseas Partners Re Ltd* [2003] EWCA Civ 1846, [2004] 1 All ER (Comm) 893, para 27 (Brooke LJ).
2 *Strong and Pearl v S Allison & Co Ltd* (1926) 25 Ll L Rep 504, 508 (Greer J); *Seavision Investment SA v Evennett, The Tiburon* [1992] 2 Lloyd's Rep 26, CA. These are pre-CPR authorities, but it is suggested that the provisions set out in CPR r 44.3 would normally lead to the same result.
3 [1990] 2 Lloyd's Rep 418.
4 *Seavision Investment SA v Evennett, The Tiburon* [1992] 2 Lloyd's Rep 26, 29, CA (Parker LJ).
5 See *Groupama Insurance Co Ltd v Overseas Partners Re Ltd* [2003] EWCA Civ 1846, [2004] 1 All ER (Comm) 893, paras 39–43 (Brooke LJ): unsuccessful reinsurer ordered to pay the claimant insurer's costs of the action, and to pay 90 per cent of the defendant broker's costs; reduction of 10 per cent to reflect the fact that the broker had departed from market practice when placing the reinsurance.

Chapter 17

Specific types of insurance

INTRODUCTION

17.1 This chapter covers some commonly arising issues in relation to the following types of insurance: accident insurance; business interruption insurance; contractors' all risks insurance; legal expenses insurance; permanent health insurance; product liability insurance; professional indemnity insurance; and public liability insurance.

The general principles discussed below can be displaced by express wording, but the type of insurance is always an important aid to construction,[1] so that the more unlikely it is that a particular type of policy would be expected to provide a particular type of cover, the clearer the wording will need to be before the court will construe it in that way.

1 See **PARA 3.14**.

ACCIDENT INSURANCE

Causation

17.2 Some of the cases in respect to causation of loss in relation to policies insuring against personal accidents are considered at **PARA 4.2**. Such policies often require that the insured peril be the 'independent', 'sole' or 'exclusive' cause of the loss, or sometimes all three in combination. This wording is considered at **PARA 4.6**.

The use of the words 'caused by accidental means' in a policy insuring against bodily injury are a clear indication that it is the cause of the injury to which the court must direct its attention.[1] An injury which is the natural and direct consequence of an act deliberately done by the insured is not caused by accident.[2] Where an insured embarks deliberately on a course of conduct which leads to some bodily injury one has to consider these questions: (a) Did the insured intend to inflict some bodily injury to himself? (b) Did the insured take a calculated risk that if he continued with that course of conduct he might sustain some bodily injury? (c) Was some bodily injury the natural and direct consequence of the course of conduct? (d) Did some fortuitous cause intervene?[3]

Where the insuring clause provides for cover where the insured sustains 'accidental bodily injury caused solely and directly by outward, violent and visible means', the words 'outward, violent and visible means' serve to expound the expression 'accidental bodily injury', and the wording should be construed as a whole, not broken into fragments.[4]

1 *Dhak v Insurance Co of North America (UK) Ltd* [1996] 1 WLR 936, 947, CA (Neill LJ).
2 *De Sousa v Home and Overseas Insurance Co Ltd* [1995] LRLR 453, 458-459, CA (Mustill LJ); *Dhak v Insurance Co of North America (UK) Ltd* [1996] 1 WLR 936, 948, CA (Neill LJ). See also **PARA 5.2**.
3 *Dhak v Insurance Co of North America (UK) Ltd* [1996] 1 WLR 936, 949-950, CA (Neill LJ). See also **PARA 5.2**.
4 *De Sousa v Home and Overseas Insurance Co Ltd* [1995] LRLR 453, 462, CA (Mustill LJ).

'Permanent total disablement', 'any occupation' and 'own occupation'

17.3 Accident policies typically provide an indemnity in an amount which is a sum fixed according to the nature of the bodily injury suffered by the insured. There is also usually an indemnity of a fixed sum payable in respect of 'permanent total disablement', or sometimes 'temporary total disablement'. This is usually defined by reference to the insured's ability to work or to follow or carry on an occupation. Cover may be provided in respect of the insured's inability to follow or carry on his or her 'own occupation', which is usually identified in the policy schedule, or in respect of the insured's inability to follow or carry on 'any occupation'. These and similar phrases have been considered by the courts on various occasions. The burden of proof on this issue is on the insured.[1] In *Hooper v The Accidental Death Insurance Co*,[2] the court held that, on a reasonable construction of the policy wording, a solicitor who sprained his ankle and was confined to his bedroom and an adjoining room on the first floor of his house but remained able to see his clerks, write letters and study law books was 'wholly' disabled from following his usual occupation. In *Pocock v Century Insurance Company Ltd*,[3] weekly benefit was payable to the insured for 'temporary total disablement from attending to business of any or every kind'. The insured's nominated business was that of a wholesale grocer, and he was in fact a jobbing buyer whose practice was to drive all over the country buying job lots of grocery. Mr Commissioner Molony QC said that a person could not be said to attend to business simply because he was capable of doing – perhaps rather badly – some minor part of the work involved in that or any other sort of business, and said that the conclusive example adverse to that argument was the business of selling matches at a street corner.[4] The judge said:

> 'The broad test that I think must be applied in order to understand the application of this clause is to ask oneself: Is a man fit to go to business? It does not mean that he has got to be fit to spend the whole day there; it does not mean that he has got to be fit to carry on all the activities which that business normally involves. The question is: Is he fit to attend there and play a worth-while part in the conduct of it?'[5]

In *Sargent v GRE (UK) Ltd*,[6] the Court of Appeal construed 'any occupation' in the context of the particular policy in question, which provided cover to members of the armed forces, as meaning any particular occupation or an occupation of whatever kind that the insured might happen to have been following at the date of his accident.[7] Leggatt LJ said that if that were wrong, the phrase would be completely ambiguous because, at one extreme it would be contended that the policy holder could not recover if he was physically able to sell matches though nothing else, while at the other, he could recover if he was not physically able to be a concert pianist, and the *contra proferentes* rule would apply and the insurers would still be liable.[8] Mummery LJ took into account, in construing the phrase 'any occupation', that the evident purpose of personal accident insurance against permanent disablement of a person who was not in the special position of a member of the armed forces (which was covered under a different provision in the policy) was to provide for the event that he was permanently disabled from attending to his occupation as at the time of his disabling injury and not just to provide for the more drastic and remote event that he would not be able to attend to any occupation of any kind ever again.[9] In *Walton v Airtours plc*,[10] the definition of incapacity in a permanent health insurance policy provided that the insured person should be 'totally unable by reason of injury or illness to follow the [insured's] own occupation and is not following any other' and that if incapacity should have persisted for 24 months it should be deemed to continue only if the insured was 'unable to follow any occupation'. The Court of Appeal said that 'to follow any occupation' naturally connoted to be engaged in regular work, not temporarily but for a substantial or indefinite period, that it also implied an element of continuity, and that, given that the purpose behind the relevant provision was to provide an entitlement to income to (in that case) an ex-employee who could not earn income by working, it made little commercial sense to treat the condition for the payment of benefit as not being satisfied if the person in question could only start a job for a few days but thereafter could not continue to earn income.[11] In *McGeown v Direct Travel Insurance*,[12] the phrase 'any paid work' in a policy of travel insurance which included accident cover was given a 'common sense meaning', namely 'any work that the insured had at the time of the accident or which is similar to it',[13] and provision in the same policy which provided cover for 'permanent disability which prevents [an insured] from doing all [his] usual activities' was construed as including 'all significant non-working activities of, say, a social, sporting, domestic or personal nature which, taken in the round, constitute so substantial an intrusion on his way of life as to compare with an inability to pursue his normal occupation, if he had one at the time of the accident, or one similar to it'.[14]

1 *Cathay Pacific Airways Ltd v Nation Life & General Assurance Co Ltd* [1966] 2 Lloyd's Rep 179, 188 (McNair J).
2 (1860) 5 H & N 546.
3 [1960] 2 Lloyd's Rep 150.
4 At 154.
5 At 154.
6 [2000] Lloyd's Rep IR 77, CA.
7 At 79 (Mummery LJ) and 79-80 (Leggatt LJ).
8 At 79-80. See also PARA **3.19**.
9 At 79.
10 [2002] EWCA Civ 1659, [2002] Lloyd's Rep IR 69.
11 At 72-73 (Peter Gibson LJ). See also *Jowitt v Pioneer Technology (UK) Ltd* [2003] EWCA Civ 411, [2003] ICR 1120, para 19 (Sedley LJ) (employee 'unable to work', in the context of the particular contract of employment, 'if there is no continuous remunerative full-time work which he can realistically be expected to do'); *Earl v Cantor Fitzgerald International* [2000] EWHC 555 (QB), para 33 (Moore-Bick J) (term incorporated into contract of employment; the expression 'totally unable … to follow his Occupation', taken by itself, naturally means that the employee is no longer capable of carrying out the duties which would enable him to be employed in his current position, whether full-time or part-time); and *Hopkins v UNUM Ltd* [2005] EWHC 1758 (QB), para 39 (Mr Nigel Wilkinson QC, sitting as a Deputy High Court Judge) (policy provided cover for the benefit of the partners from

time to time of a firm of solicitors who might become totally incapacitated through illness or injury from following their occupation; this meant asking the question whether the claimant was 'capable of making a worthwhile or substantial contribution to his role as a partner').

12 [2003] EWCA Civ 1606, [2004] Lloyd's Rep IR 599.

13 At para 19 (Auld LJ).

14 At para 20 (Auld LJ).

Pre-existing conditions

17.4 Pre-existing conditions are commonly the subject of exclusions in personal accident policies.[1]

1 See further **PARA 17.13**.

BUSINESS INTERRUPTION INSURANCE

17.5 Business interruption insurance provides an indemnity against losses consequential upon damage to property.[1] It is often written as part of a commercial combined policy which may include material damage, business interruption insurance and other covers such as public liability, employers' liability and goods in transit. If business interruption insurance is written separately from material damage cover, it will nonetheless cover losses consequential upon material damage to insured property, and recoverability under the policy will depend on the existence of valid material damage cover.[2] Progressive material damage over successive policy periods, for example due to subsidence, which causes business interruption, may give rise to claims under more than one policy.[3]

In *Coromin Ltd v AXA Re*,[4] a claim was made for business interruption in relation to a plant which was not in existence during the period of the policy but which was affected during the business interruption insurance indemnity period. The judge held that there was no requirement in the policy for 'business' to be insured as property, and that all that the reinsurance required was that insured property suffered damage which was covered for property damage and which they gave rise to business interruption of any kind; in those circumstances, a loss flowing from such interruption was itself covered, whether or not the business arose in relation to an asset which was insured under the property damage section of the policy.[5] The judge also rejected the reinsurers' argument that a term should be implied into the reinsurance limiting the word 'business' to 'business which was being carried on by the assured during the period of the policy'.[6]

In *Orient-Express Hotels Ltd v Assicurazioni Generali SA*,[7] a policy of business interruption insurance was construed as requiring a 'but for' test of causation, and therefore as indemnifying the insured in respect of losses on the basis of what would have happened but for the damage caused by two hurricanes, rather than on the basis of the loss in gross operating profit suffered as a result of the occurrence of the insured events (the hurricanes).[8] This was significant because not only was the hotel itself damaged by the hurricanes, but the city in which the hotel was situated was also shut down for a period, so that the loss would have occurred even if the hotel itself had suffered no damage.

The most common form of business interruption cover is written on the gross profits basis. Such a policy states a figure for gross annual profit. If that figure is less than the actual level of profit which has been lost, average is applied and the sum paid out is appropriately reduced; further, the sum paid out will never be based on a level of profit which exceeds the stated figure. In this form of cover, the annual premium is not subject to subsequent adjustment. Where a policy is declaration linked, the assured gives an estimate of gross annual profit and, in the event of a loss, the sum paid out is based on the actual profit subject to a maximum percentage uplift (or 'escalator'), typically 133.3 per cent, on the estimate, and average is not applied. The premium for declaration-linked cover is adjusted once the level of profit has been established.[9]

The difference between the two types of policy is important because the actual level of annual gross profit being (or which would have been) earned by the insured during the period of the interruption may be substantially more than the estimate. In the case of a policy on the gross profits basis, the sum payable under the policy is based on the estimated profit figure. On the other hand, in the case of a declaration-linked policy, the sum payable is based on the actual profit figure, subject to a maximum of the product of the estimated figure and the escalator recorded in the policy (for example 1.333), albeit that the premium is also retrospectively subject to increase as set out in the policy.[10]

In an appropriate case, the insured may necessarily and reasonably incur expenditure in avoiding or diminishing the reduction in turnover, which expenditure lasts beyond the indemnity period. A good example is the lease of a replacement building whilst repairs are undertaken to the insured's building, but the landlord will only grant a two-year lease, although the indemnity period is only 18 months. In principle, the costs incurred in leasing the building for two years should be recoverable, even though the reduction in turnover can only be recovered for 18 months.[11]

Depreciation is usually deducted over the projected life of machinery used in a business in order to reflect the expense of using and owning the machinery. As a matter of principle, and depending on the wording of the policy, depreciation not deducted as a consequence of the business interruption should be brought into account as a saving, reducing the amount of indemnity to which the insured is entitled under the policy.[12]

See also **PARAS 8.3** and **8.9**.

1 See eg *Loyaltrend Ltd v Creechurch Dedicated Ltd* [2010] EWHC 425 (Comm), [2010] Lloyd's Rep IR 466, paras 33-34 (HHJ Mackie QC); *Orient-Express Hotels Ltd v Assicurazioni Generali SA* [2010] EWHC 1186 (Comm), [2010] Lloyd's Rep IR 531, para 6 (Hamblen J).
2 See eg *Glengate-KG Properties Ltd v Norwich Union Fire Insurance Society Ltd* [1996] 1 Lloyd's Rep 614, CA.
3 *Loyaltrend Ltd v Creechurch Dedicated Ltd* [2010] EWHC 425 (Comm), [2010] Lloyd's Rep IR 466, para 34 (HHJ Mackie QC).
4 [2007] EWHC 2818 (Comm), [2008] Lloyd's Rep IR 467.
5 At para 98 (Cooke J).
6 At para 100 (Cooke J).
7 [2010] EWHC 1186 (Comm), [2010] Lloyd's Rep IR 531.
8 At paras 34-35 (Hamblen J).
9 This paragraph is based on paragraph 3 of the judgment of Neuberger LJ in *Kyle Bay Ltd v Underwriters Subscribing to Policy No 019057/08/01* [2007] EWCA Civ 57, Lloyd's Rep IR 460.

10 This paragraph is based on paragraph 4 of the judgment of Neuberger LJ in *Kyle Bay Ltd v Underwriters Subscribing to Policy No 019057/08/01* [2007] EWCA Civ 57, Lloyd's Rep IR 460.
11 *Synergy Health (UK) Ltd v CGU Insurance plc* [2010] EWHC 2583 (Comm), [2011] Lloyd's Rep IR 500, para 245 (Flaux J).
12 *Synergy Health (UK) Ltd v CGU Insurance plc* [2010] EWHC 2583 (Comm), [2011] Lloyd's Rep IR 500, paras 251-253 (Flaux J).

CONTRACTORS' ALL RISKS INSURANCE

17.6 The concepts of insurable interest and implied waiver of subrogation raise issues of particular importance and complexity in the context of contractors' all risks insurance. These are considered at **PARAS 2.10** and **12.4** respectively.

LEGAL EXPENSES INSURANCE

General

17.7 Policies of legal expenses insurance may be written before any insured event has taken place (known as before the event, or BTE, policies) or after an insured event has taken place (known as after the event, or ATE, policies). In addition, policies of liability insurance may include legal expenses insurance cover;[1] alternatively, such policies may include a claims control clause which allows the insurer to take control of proceedings brought against the insured and sometimes also to take control of proceedings brought by the insured to recover insured and uninsured losses.[2]

The right to indemnity in respect of legal costs under a policy of legal expenses insurance is that of the insured, and such a policy does not confer on a solicitor who has acted for the insured any right to be paid legal costs by the insurer.[3]

1 See **PARA 8.11**.
2 See **PARA 9.13**.
3 *PM Law Ltd v Motorplus Ltd* [2016] EWHC 193 (QB), paras 39–48 (Picken J) (action brought against legal expenses insurers by solicitor in respect of 3,000 claims struck out).

Insurance Companies (Legal Expenses Insurance) Regulations 1990

17.8 Subject to certain exceptions, including legal expenses cover provided within a policy of liability insurance,[1] both ATE and BTE cover is regulated by the Insurance Companies (Legal Expenses Insurance) Regulations 1990,[2] which implement the provisions of a European Union Directive on legal expenses insurance.[3]

The 1990 Regulations provide that where, under a legal expenses insurance policy, recourse is had to a lawyer (or other person having such qualifications as may be necessary) to defend, represent or serve the interests of the insured in any inquiry or proceedings, the insured shall be free to choose that lawyer (or other person).[4] In addition, the Regulations provide that the insured shall also be free to choose a lawyer (or qualified person) to serve his interests whenever a conflict of interests arises.[5]

The Regulations also provide that any dispute between the insurer and insured arising out of a legal expenses insurance policy may be referred to arbitration.[6]

In a series of recent decisions, the courts have begun to explore the extent of the freedom to choose a lawyer under the Directive and the 1990 Regulations. There is no doubt that this area of law will continue to develop. In *Case C-199/08 Eschig v UNIQA Sachversicherung AG*,[7] the Court of Justice of the European Union ('CJEU') decided that the legal expenses insurer was not permitted to reserve the right, where a large number of insureds suffered loss as a result of the same event (in that case, the insolvency of an investment services business), itself to select the legal representative of all the insureds concerned.[8] In *Case C-293 Stark v DAS Österreichische Allgemeine Rechtsschutzversicherung AG*,[9] the insured wished to instruct a lawyer whose location meant that, due to the Austrian rules on costs recoverable in legal proceedings, his fees would be higher than those of a lawyer practising within the area of the court which was hearing the proceedings. The CJEU held that freedom of choice within the meaning of art 4(1) of the Directive (which reg 6 of the 1990 Regulations implements) did not mean that member states were obliged to require insurers, in all circumstances, to cover in full the costs incurred in connection with the defence of an insured person, irrespective of the place where the lawyer was established in relation to the court which was hearing the proceedings:

> '... on condition that the freedom is not rendered meaningless. That would be the case if the restriction imposed on the payment of those costs were to render de facto impossible a reasonable choice of representative by the insured person.'[10]

The CJEU went on to say that it was for the national courts, if an action was brought before them in this regard, to determine whether or not there was any such restriction;[11] and that in order not to render meaningless the freedom of choice of lawyer, the restriction must relate only to the extent of the cover by the legal expenses insurer in respect of costs linked to the involvement of a legal representative, and the reimbursement actually provided by the insurer must be sufficient, which was a matter for the national court.[12] This principle has since been applied in the domestic context in *Brown-Quinn v Equity Syndicate Management Ltd*.[13] In that case, the insured wished to instruct a specialist employment solicitor who was not on the insurer's panel. The insurer conceded that the insured was entitled to instruct a non-panel solicitor but argued that the solicitor must agree to panel rates, which were much lower than the solicitor's normal rates. Burton J decided that the reasonableness of the rate, and therefore how much the insured was entitled to recover from the insurer, should be dealt with through an assessment under CPR Part 48 at the conclusion of the case.[14] Burton J also decided that the insured's freedom of choice under reg 6 is not limited to one selection or election at the outset, as there may be all kinds of scenarios in which it is appropriate and reasonable for a client to decide to change representative: the firm might cease to exist or might close its relevant department or make members of it redundant; there might be a substantial and reasonable disagreement between the client and the solicitor; or there might be a situation, as in one of the cases considered in *Brown-Quinn v Equity Syndicate Management Ltd*, in which the case-handler left the firm and the client wished that case-handler to carry on acting for him in a new firm.[15] This is potentially significant in cases in which an insured has no freedom to choose the lawyer initially instructed on his or her behalf under the legal expenses insurance policy, and in which such a freedom arises at a later stage.

In *Case C-442/12 Sneller v DAS Nederlandse Rechtsbijstand Verzekeringsmaatschappij NV*,[16] the policy provided that the insured was entitled to choose his own lawyer where the insurer decided that it was necessary to have recourse to a lawyer, and the insurer indicated that it was prepared to provide legal assistance to the insured only through one of its own employees, who was not a lawyer.[17] The CJEU held that the insured person's right to choose his lawyer could not be restricted to situations in which the insurer decided that recourse should be had to an external lawyer rather than an employee of the insurer's,[18] It added, however, that the various methods by which the insured person may exercise the right to choose his legal representative do not rule out the possibility that, in certain cases, limitations may be imposed on the costs to be borne by the insurer,[19] and the contracting parties remain free to agree cover for a higher level of legal assistance costs, possibly against payment of a higher premium by the insured person.[20]

There is a related and unresolved issue about the precise stage at which the freedom to choose a lawyer arises, and in particular whether the insured is entitled to choose a lawyer to conduct pre-action protocol correspondence, or to draft and issue proceedings on his or her behalf, or whether the freedom of choice arises only once proceedings are issued.[21] This question of when the right arises may present particular problems in England and Wales due to the significance in that legal system of pre-action conduct and its potential impact on the course of any proceedings which are issued. An issue of a different nature was considered in *Pine v DAS Legal Expenses Insurance Co Ltd*.[22] In that case, the court held that the insurer was not entitled to prevent the insured from exercising her freedom to choose a lawyer by instructing a barrister on a public access basis rather than, as the insurer wished, instructing the barrister through a solicitor.

In England and Wales, before the event (BTE) legal expenses insurance cover has historically been sold as an inexpensive add-on to home contents or motor vehicle insurance. Legal expenses insurers have expressed concern about the impact which increased freedom to choose a lawyer, and the consequent increase in cost to the insurer who will no longer benefit from the lower rates negotiated with its panel solicitors, may have on the level of premiums and the consequent affordability of such cover.[23]

1 Insurance Companies (Legal Expenses Insurance) Regulations 1990 (SI 1990/1159), reg 3(3).
2 SI 1990 No 1159, as amended.
3 Directive 2009/138/EC of 25 November 2009 on the taking-up and pursuit of the business of Insurance and Reinsurance (Solvency II) (recast), which repealed Council Directive 87/344/EEC of 22 June 1987 on the coordination of laws, regulations and administrative provisions relating to legal expenses insurance, OJ L185/77, 4.7.87 and recast it in substantially the same terms (see Arts 198–205).
4 Regulation 6(1); Council Directive 87/344/EEC of 22 June 1987 on the coordination of laws, regulations and administrative provisions relating to legal expenses insurance, OJ L185/77, 4.7.87, art 4(1)(a). The right must be expressly recognised in the policy: reg 6(3). Regulation 6 does not apply in certain circumstances in relation to road accident assistance: reg 7.
5 Regulation 6(2). The right must be expressly recognised in the policy: reg 6(3). Regulation 6 does not apply in certain circumstances in relation to road accident assistance: reg 7.
6 Regulation 8(1). The right must be expressly recognised in the policy: reg 8(2).
7 [2010] Lloyd's Rep IR 552.
8 Para 68. The decision was based on the interpretation of art 4(1)(a) of Council Directive 87/344/EEC of 22 June 1987 on the coordination of laws, regulations and administrative provisions relating to legal expenses insurance, OJ L185/77, 4.7.87.
9 [2011] ECR I-4713.
10 At para 33; applied: *Case C-442/12 Sneller v DAS Nederlandse Rechtsbijstand Verzekeringsmaatschappij NV* [2014] Lloyd's Rep IR 238, para 27.

11 At para 33; applied: *Case C-442/12 Sneller v DAS Nederlandse Rechtsbijstand Verzekeringsmaatschappij NV* [2014] Lloyd's Rep IR 238, para 27.

12 At para 36.

13 [2011] EWHC 2661 (Comm), [2013] 1 WLR 1740.

14 At para 23. This option would of course not be available in a non-costs jurisdiction such as the employment tribunals.

15 At paras 32-34.

16 [2014] Lloyd's Rep IR 238.

17 See paragraphs 11 and 19. The decision was based on the interpretation of art 4(1)(a) of Council Directive 87/344/EEC of 22 June 1987 on the coordination of laws, regulations and administrative provisions relating to legal expenses insurance, OJ L185/77, 4.7.87.

18 At paragraph 23.

19 At paragraph 26.

20 At paragraph 28. In *Case C-293 Stark v DAS Österreichische Allgemeine Rechtsschutzversicherung AG* [2011] ECR I-4713, the CJEU made a similar point when it noted (at para 34) that the national legislation did not exclude the freedom of contracting parties to agree that legal expenses insurance was also to cover the reimbursement of costs relating to the involvement of representatives who were not established at the place of the court having jurisdiction, possibly against payment of a higher premium by the insured person (see further notes 9 and 10 and related text above).

21 See *Sarwar v Alam* [2001] EWCA Civ 1401, [2002] 1 WLR 125, para 44 (Lord Phillips MR).

22 [2011] EWHC 658 (QB), [2012] Lloyd's Rep IR 346.

23 See eg 'The Review of Civil Litigation Costs: Final Report' by Lord Justice Jackson (December 2009), Chapter 8, paras 5.6 and 6.3.

Liability insurance policies which include legal expenses insurance cover

17.9 Liability insurance policies which include legal expenses cover are considered at **PARA 8.11**, and claims control clauses are considered at **PARA 9.13**. There is no statutory right to choose a lawyer where legal expenses cover is provided within a policy of liability insurance,[1] and policies do not usually allow the insured to do so.[2]

1 Insurance Companies (Legal Expenses Insurance) Regulations 1990, SI 1990/1159, reg 3(3); Council Directive 87/344/EEC of 22 June 1987 on the coordination of laws, regulations and administrative provisions relating to legal expenses insurance, OJ L185/77, 4.7.87, art 2(2).

2 See also **PARA 9.33**.

Costs orders against legal expenses insurers

17.10 Costs orders may in principle be made against legal expenses insurers under s 51 of the Senior Courts Act 1981, although this is unlikely unless the insurers are also liability insurers with interests of their own to protect in the proceedings.[1]

1 See **PARA 9.46**.

PERMANENT HEALTH INSURANCE

Incapacity, 'any occupation' and 'own occupation'

17.11 Permanent health insurance (or PHI) policies typically provide an indemnity in respect of the incapacity of the insured, which is usually defined by reference to the insured's ability to work or to follow or carry on an occupation.[1] Some permanent health insurance policies define incapacity by reference to the inability of the insured to perform a number of specified tasks or activities. The indemnity under a permanent health insurance policy, which is usually described as 'benefit', is payable for the duration of the incapacity, and may be a fixed amount which does not increase over time, or it may be index-linked in some way.

1 See PARA 17.3.

Proof 'satisfactory to' insurer

17.12 Permanent health insurance policies often provide that for benefit to be payable, the insurer must be 'satisfied' that the insured is incapacitated within the meaning of the policy. In *Napier v UNUM Ltd*,[1] Tuckey J considered a provision in a permanent health insurance policy which provided that insurers would pay 'on proof satisfactory to [them]' of the insured's entitlement to benefits under the policy. The judge construed the provision as imposing an obligation on the insured to provide such evidence to support his claim as the insurers might reasonably require. As the insured had provided such evidence, it was for the court, and not insurers, to evaluate the evidence provided by the insured and that obtained by insurers, in deciding whether insurers were obliged to make a payment under the policy. In coming to this conclusion, the judge rejected both the insured's argument that a term was to be implied that the insurers would act reasonably (meaning that they would be satisfied with such proof as would satisfy reasonable men), and the insurers' argument that their decision to reject the claim was not susceptible to legal challenge except on grounds of lack of good faith.[2] This decision must now be considered in the light of the decision of the Supreme Court in *Braganza v BP Shipping Ltd*.[3]

1 [1996] 2 Lloyd's Rep 550, 552–554.
2 At 552–554. In some contexts, a party to contract of insurance or reinsurance may validly be given a decision-making power in relation to rights arising under the contract; any such power is subject to an obligation to act reasonably and in good faith: see *Brown v GIO Insurance Ltd* [1998] Lloyd's Rep IR 201, CA.
3 [2015] UKSC 17, [2015] 1 WLR 1661. See PARA 5.4.

Pre-existing conditions

17.13 Pre-existing conditions are commonly the subject of exclusions in permanent health insurance policies.[1] In *Cook v Financial Insurance Co Ltd*,[1] the House of Lords considered an exclusion clause which provided that no benefit would be payable for disability resulting from any sickness, disease, condition or injury for which an insured person received advice, treatment or counselling from any registered practitioner during the 12 months preceding the commencement date. Before he entered into the policy, the insured, who was otherwise fit and well, had collapsed while on a training run and had consulted his doctor, who had not made a diagnosis but had referred him to a consultant. Immediately after the policy incepted, the consultant diagnosed angina. By a majority, their lordships decided that the clause did not apply where the insured had experienced symptoms of angina and had consulted a doctor, but the condition had not at that stage been diagnosed;[2] however, had the referring doctor suspected angina, the result might have been different.[3]

1 [1998] 1 WLR 1765, HL.
2 See 1770–1771 (Lord Lloyd; Lords Steyn and Hope agreed at 1772).
3 See 1770 (Lord Lloyd; Lords Steyn and Hope agreed at 1772).

Claim by employee under group policy

17.14   A policy of permanent health insurance may be taken out by an employer in respect of the incapacity of its employees. Whether an employee is entitled to claim benefits directly under such a policy from the insurer depends on the policy wording including, in the case of policies entered into from 11 May 2000, whether the application of the Contracts (Rights of Third Parties) Act 1999 is excluded.[1] In the absence of a right to claim directly, the employee may bring a claim against the insurer if the employer assigns the benefit of the claim to the employee.[2] Benefits under a policy of group permanent health insurance usually end if the employee ceases to be an employee.[3]

1 See **PARA 2.18**. In *Cathay Pacific Airways Ltd v Nation Life & General Assurance Co Ltd* [1966] 2 Lloyd's Rep 179, McNair J said (at 183) that the policy documents were not happily or consistently drafted, but that it was agreed before him that the employers might be taken to be the insured effecting the policy for the benefit of their pilot employees as the persons insured, and that, if the employers recovered any sum under the policy, they would hold it as trustees for the pilot whose alleged incapacity was the subject of the claim. In *Mulchrone v Swiss Life (UK) plc* [2005] EWHC 1808 (Comm), [2006] Lloyd's Rep IR 339, Gavin Kealey QC (sitting as a Deputy Judge of the High Court) said (at para 11) that the claimant, who was seeking to enforce rights pursuant to the 1999 Act, was not seeking to enforce any rights to benefit payments accruing to her under any substantive contract of insurance between her employer and the insurer on the basis that the employer entered into the insurance as her agent, or that the employer was a trustee for her of the promises made for her benefit by the insurer under the insurance (as to which, he said, the decisions in such cases as *Les Affréteurs Réunis SA v Leopold Walford (London) Ltd* [1919] AC 801, HL and *Nisshin Shipping Co Ltd v Cleaves & Co Ltd* [2003] EWHC 2602 (Comm), [2004] 1 Lloyd's Rep 38 might be of relevance), and thereby appeared to suggest that he thought that those might be alternative ways in which an employee could bring a claim under a group policy of permanent health insurance in circumstances where the 1999 Act did not apply because the policy was not entered into after 11 May 2000.
2 See **PARA 2.13**.
3 See eg *Bastick v Yamaichi International Europe Ltd*, CA, 15 January 1993, unreported. The ordinary consequence of long-term incapacity is to bring a contract of employment to an end by frustration, and a term which entitles an employee to payment of benefit during incapacity has the effect of keeping the contract in being for the sole purpose of providing an income for the incapacitated employee: *Jowitt v Pioneer Technology (UK) Ltd* [2003] EWCA Civ 411, [2003] ICR 1120, para 15 (Sedley LJ).

PRODUCT LIABILITY INSURANCE

General

17.15   For the purposes of a policy of product liability insurance, the meaning of a 'product' may elude precise definition, depending as it does on whether the item in question is what you would really and naturally describe as a product; without attempting a precise definition, a hallmark of a product in this context is that it is something which, at least originally, was a tangible and moveable item which can be transferred from one person to another, and not something which only came into existence to form part of the land on which it was created.[1] Where the definition of 'product' includes a product 'installed' by the insured, product liability cover does not extend to defective installation: if there is something wrong with the product, it is covered by the product liability section; if the product is fine but installed in the wrong way, there is no cover for product liability.[2]

Product liability insurance is designed to protect the insured against liability for physical damage to physical property and not to afford an indemnity by way of guarantee for the quality and fitness of the commodity supplied.[3] A product liability policy does not, without more, cover deterioration in the commodity supplied.[4] In order to establish cover in respect of the loss claimed, the insured must demonstrate some physical damage caused by the commodity for which purpose a defect or deterioration in the commodity is not itself sufficient: the loss claimed must be a loss resulting from physical loss or damage to physical property of another (or some personal injury).[5] The complexities inherent in this area are illustrated by the difference of opinion between two members of the Court of Appeal in *Rodan International Ltd v Commercial Union Assurance Co plc*[6] as to whether damage to washing powder was within the policy in circumstances in which a defect in the powder caused it to damage the cartons in which it was packed, which in turn brought about the damage to the powder. Hobhouse LJ considered that since the damage to the contents was caused by the damage to the container there was no need or justification to distinguish between the container and its contents, whereas Pill LJ considered that the further damage to the powder should be regarded as an inevitable consequence of its unmerchantability.[7]

1 *Aspen Insurance UK Ltd v Adana Construction Ltd* [2015] EWCA Civ 176, [2015] Lloyd's Rep IR 522, para 42 (Christopher Clarke LJ).
2 *Aspen Insurance UK Ltd v Adana Construction Ltd* [2015] EWCA Civ 176, [2015] Lloyd's Rep IR 522, para 48 (Christopher Clarke LJ) (combined product and public liability policy, with cover available for defective installation (workmanship) under the public liability section of the policy).
3 *Pilkington United Kingdom Ltd v CGU Insurance plc* [2004] EWCA Civ 23, [2004] Lloyd's Rep IR 891, para 53 (Potter LJ).
4 *Rodan International Ltd v Commercial Union Assurance Co plc* [1999] Lloyd's Rep IR 495, CA, 500 (Hobhouse LJ) and 501 (Pill LJ); *Pilkington United Kingdom Ltd v CGU Insurance plc* [2004] EWCA Civ 23, [2004] Lloyd's Rep IR 891, para 34 (Potter LJ).
5 *Pilkington United Kingdom Ltd v CGU Insurance plc* [2004] EWCA Civ 23, [2004] Lloyd's Rep IR 891, para 35 (Potter LJ).
6 [1999] Lloyd's Rep IR 495, CA.
7 At 500 (Hobhouse LJ) and 501 (Pill LJ).

'Damage'

17.16 Generally speaking, damage requires some altered state, the relevant alteration being harmful in the commercial context, and this plainly covers a situation where there is a poisoning or contaminating effect on the property of a third party as a result of the introduction or intermixture of the product supplied; however, it will not extend to a position where the commodity supplied is installed in or juxtaposed with the property of the third party in circumstances where it does no physical harm and the harmful effect of any later defect or deterioration is contained within it.[1] Difficulties of application of such a test may arise in cases where a product or commodity supplied is installed by attachment to other objects in a situation in which it remains separately identifiable but, by reason of physical changes or deterioration within it, it requires to be renewed or replaced; in such a case, resort is necessary to the usual canons of construction in order to resolve the difficulty.[2]

1 *Pilkington United Kingdom Ltd v CGU Insurance plc* [2004] EWCA Civ 23, [2004] Lloyd's Rep IR 891, para 51 (Potter LJ). In *Horner (t/a F & H Contractors) v Commercial Union Assurance Co plc*, CA (unreported, 18 May 1993), uneven application of fertilizer due to the malfunctioning of a mechanical spreader resulted in some potato plants producing more and larger potatoes, and other producing too few, with an overall reduction in yield of 20–30%; this was not loss or damage to material property but purely economic loss and was therefore outside the scope of the policy (public liability insurance).
2 *Pilkington United Kingdom Ltd v CGU Insurance plc* [2004] EWCA Civ 23, [2004] Lloyd's Rep IR 891, para 52 (Potter LJ).

'In respect of' and 'on account of'

17.17   The words 'in respect of' in the insuring clause have a limiting effect on the extent of the cover and do not merely identify the causal event.[1] These words mean 'for' and not merely 'caused by', 'consequential upon' or 'in connection with', so that the insured's liability must be for death or injury, that is to say the liability must be to the person who has been killed or injured; the liability must be for loss or damage to material property of the person whose property it is – liability for loss suffered by someone else as a consequence of such damage is not 'in respect of' it; and liability for any of these torts must be to the person who has the right to claim – liability for loss suffered by someone else as a consequence of the tort is not 'in respect of' it.[2] An insuring clause which provides an indemnity against legal liability 'in respect of' bodily injury or damage to property carries with it a requirement that the liability relate to the identified injury or physical damage, so that cover is confined to liability for physical consequences caused by the commodity or article supplied; the liability of the insured in damages will have to be expressed in terms of money but that liability must be in respect of the consequences of the physical loss or damage to physical property (or some personal injury).[3] Provided that the commodity or article supplied has caused a physical consequence, the compensation payable by the insured to the third party will include, and the liability of the insurer to indemnify the insured will extend to, the totality of the loss which the third party is entitled to recover from the insured by way of damages in respect of that physical consequence.[4] Thus, if a defective article supplied by the insured causes bodily injury to the third party disabling him or, for example, causes his premises to be destroyed by fire, the third party will be entitled to recover from the insured the full value of what he has lost which will, in these examples, include compensation for future loss of earnings: they are part of what the third party has lost as a consequence of the physical loss or injury and they are accordingly part of the liability of the insured in respect of that physical consequence.[5]

Product liability cover which provides an indemnity in respect of 'all sums which the Insured shall become legally liable to pay in respect of death, bodily injury, illness, loss or damage happening ... during the period of insurance and caused by goods (including containers) manufactured, sold, supplied, repaired, altered, serviced, installed or treated in the course of the Business ...', is intended to cover physical loss or damage caused by the goods, and does not extend to loss of profit on repeat orders.[6]

'On account of' are words which are plainly intended to provide a causal link between the damages sought in a third party claim against the insured and the property damage.[7] The fact that a claim is for economic loss and not for damage to property does not dictate a wholly negative answer to the question whether the damages are sought 'on account of physical injury' to the damaged products when made and installed, and the words are sufficiently wide to encompass claims for the cost of repair or replacement of damaged products; however, as a matter of ordinary language claims by any party for damages for loss of business or profits said to have resulted from the physical damage cannot be said to be claims for damages 'on account of' physical injury to damaged products; the words require a more direct connection between the loss claimed and an actual physical injury.[8]

Similarly, the subject matter of product liability cover and any exclusion clause is the liability of the insured to pay compensation to a third party, and a clause which excludes 'liability in respect of recalling removing repairing replacing reinstating or the cost of or reduction in value of any commodity article or thing supplied installed or erected by the Insured if such liability arises from any defect therein or the harmful nature or unsuitability thereof' applies to liability for expenditure incurred by the third party;[9] similarly, the expressions 'personal injury' and 'loss of or damage to property' in the insuring clause are likely to refer to injury to a third party or damage to property belonging to a third party rather than to the insured.[10]

1 *Horbury Building Systems Ltd v Hampden Insurance NV* [2004] EWCA Civ 418, [2007] Lloyd's Rep IR 237, paras 24–25 (Keane LJ) and 35 (Mance LJ).
2 *Tesco Stores Ltd v Constable* [2008] EWCA Civ 362, [2008] Lloyd's Rep IR 636, para 22 (Tuckey LJ) (public liability insurance).
3 *Rodan International Ltd v Commercial Union Assurance Co plc* [1999] Lloyd's Rep IR 495, 500 (Hobhouse LJ), CA.
4 *Rodan International Ltd v Commercial Union Assurance Co plc* [1999] Lloyd's Rep IR 495, 500 (Hobhouse LJ), CA.
5 *Rodan International Ltd v Commercial Union Assurance Co plc* [1999] Lloyd's Rep IR 495, 500 (Hobhouse LJ), CA.
6 *A S Screenprint Ltd v British Reserve Insurance Co Ltd* [1999] Lloyd's Rep IR 430, CA, 434 (Hobhouse LJ) and 435 (Beldam LJ).
7 *Tioxide Europe Ltd v CGU International Insurance plc* [2004] EWHC 216 (Comm), [2005] Lloyd's Rep IR 114, para 44 (Langley J).
8 *Tioxide Europe Ltd v CGU International Insurance plc* [2004] EWHC 216 (Comm), [2005] Lloyd's Rep IR 114, para 51 (Langley J).
9 *Rodan International Ltd v Commercial Union Assurance Co plc* [1999] Lloyd's Rep IR 495, 501 (Hobhouse LJ), CA.
10 *James Budgett Sugars Ltd v Norwich Union Insurance* [2003] Lloyd's Rep IR 110, para 30 (Moore-Bick J).

Failure to fulfil 'intended function'

17.18   Product liability policies typically exclude liability for failure by a product to fulfil its intended function. The 'intended function' of a product which is incorporated into a larger structure can only have been to perform to the requirements of the design referable to that item, and the failure of the structure as a whole does not justify the attribution of failure across the board to every item.[1]

1 *Aspen Insurance UK Ltd v Adana Construction Ltd* [2015] EWCA Civ 176, [2015] Lloyd's Rep IR 522, paras 53–57 and 59 (Christopher Clarke LJ) (reinforced steel dowels connecting a concrete crane base to piles below).

PROFESSIONAL INDEMNITY INSURANCE

General

17.19   The purpose of professional indemnity insurance is to provide cover in respect of claims made against an insured in his professional capacity, such as claims made by dissatisfied clients alleging breach of a contractual duty of care or of a similar tortious duty in negligence, and one would not normally expect such insurance to cover liabilities incurred in connection with a professional practice which are essentially of a business nature, such as rent.[1] In a solicitor's indemnity policy, the essential purpose of an exclusion in respect of any trading or personal debt of any insured, or of breach by any insured of the terms of any contract or arrangement for the supply to, or use by, any insured of goods or services in the course of the insured firm's practice, is to prevent insurers from being liable for what one might call liabilities of a solicitor in respect of those aspects of his practice which affect him or her personally as opposed to liabilities arising from his professional obligations to his or her clients.[2] Liability to a photocopier supplier, obligations to a company providing office cleaning services, and obligations under a lease or mortgage (or any guarantee thereof) of the solicitor's premises may be part of a solicitor's practice but are examples of the sort of personal obligations which are not intended to be covered.[3] These are to be distinguished from the obligations which are to be incurred in connection with the solicitor's duty to his clients, which are intended to be covered.[4] These include a loan made to cover disbursements in intended litigation, which is essentially part and parcel of the obligations assumed by a solicitor in respect of his professional duties to his client rather than obligations personal to the solicitor: a solicitor who negligently advises his client that a claim is likely to succeed and causes a client to incur disbursements which should not have been incurred will be liable to the client for disbursements needlessly incurred, and it should make no difference, from the point of view of the professional indemnity insurer, that the disbursement has been incurred before such advice is given or without such advice having been given at all.[5]

1 *Sutherland Professional Funding Ltd v Bakewells* [2011] EWHC 2658 (QB), paras 34 and 36 (His Honour Judge Hegarty QC) (solicitors' indemnity insurance).

2 *Impact Funding Solutions Ltd v Barrington Support Services Ltd* [2015] EWCA Civ 31, [2015] Lloyd's Rep IR 371, para 19 (Longmore LJ) (solicitors indemnity insurance; appeal to the Supreme Court due to be heard in June 2016).

3 *Impact Funding Solutions Ltd v Barrington Support Services Ltd* [2015] EWCA Civ 31, [2015] Lloyd's Rep IR 371, para 19 (Longmore LJ) (solicitors indemnity insurance; appeal to the Supreme Court due to be heard in June 2016).

4 *Impact Funding Solutions Ltd v Barrington Support Services Ltd* [2015] EWCA Civ 31, [2015] Lloyd's Rep IR 371, para 19 (Longmore LJ) (solicitors indemnity insurance; appeal to the Supreme Court due to be heard in June 2016).

5 *Impact Funding Solutions Ltd v Barrington Support Services Ltd* [2015] EWCA Civ 31, [2015] Lloyd's Rep IR 371, para 21 (Longmore LJ) (solicitors indemnity insurance; appeal to the Supreme Court due to be heard in June 2016). It is difficult to reconcile this with *Sutherland Professional Funding Ltd v Bakewells* [2011] EWHC 2658 (QB), paras 149–151 (His Honour Judge Hegarty QC); *Sutherland* was considered in the judgment at first instance in *Impact Funding* ([2013] EWHC 4005 (QB)) but not in the Court of Appeal.

'Claims made' policies

17.20 Modern professional indemnity insurance is usually written on a 'claims made' basis. The essence of a 'claims made' policy is that it provides cover for claims first brought against the insured during the policy year. Such policies also commonly extend cover to claims first brought against the insured after the policy year, provided that such claims arise out of circumstances previously notified to insurers of which the insured became aware during the policy year. Particular issues arising in relation to notification of claims and circumstances under professional indemnity policies and other liability policies written on a claims made basis are considered at **PARAS 7.4, 7.8, 7.9–7.10** and **7.18**.

Cover for costs

17.21 In common with other liability policies, professional indemnity insurance policies typically include cover for third party claimant's costs for which the insured is liable, and for the cost of defending third party claims. These issues are considered at **PARAS 8.11**.

Relevance of regulatory or statutory background to construction

17.22 In the case of compulsory professional indemnity insurance, the policy must be construed against the relevant regulatory background and in particular the desire to protect clients; further, the statute which is the source of the obligation to insure forms part of the surrounding circumstances (or 'factual matrix') against which a policy is to be construed, with the result that expressions used in the statute will be given the same meaning in the policy unless it clearly states otherwise, and the policy wording should, if possible, be read as providing the relevant cover required by statute: this is a powerful tool in the interpretation of such insurances.[1] In *Rathbone Brothers plc v Novae Corporate Underwriting Ltd*,[2] the judge held at first instance that the insurers should not be held to have any special knowledge of Jersey legislation, but the Court of Appeal said that the fact that the relevant Jersey Regulations defined an employee as someone employed either under a contract of service or a contract for services demonstrated that a wide concept of employee was used for regulatory purposes and also that it was a perfectly normal commercial use of the term.[3] Where policy wording closely mirrors minimum terms and conditions prescribed by a regulatory authority, the *contra proferentem* principle of construction has no application.[4]

1 See further **PARA 3.16**.
2 [2014] EWCA Civ 1464, [2015] Lloyd's Rep IR 95.
3 *Rathbone Brothers plc v Novae Corporate Underwriting Ltd* [2014] EWCA Civ 1464, [2015] Lloyd's Rep IR 95, paras 35–36 (Elias LJ).
4 *Sutherland Professional Funding Ltd v Bakewells* [2011] EWHC 2658 (QB), para 77 (His Honour Judge Hegarty QC) (solicitors' indemnity insurance). See further **PARA 3.19**.

'Employee'

17.23 It is a matter of construction of a professional indemnity policy which provides cover for 'employees' whether the policy is intending to reflect the common law concept, or whether it is adopting a more expansive definition.[1]

1 *Rathbone Brothers plc v Novae Corporate Underwriting Ltd* [2014] EWCA Civ 1464, [2015] Lloyd's Rep IR 95, paras 33–36 (Elias LJ) (language of clause, construed in context of commercial purpose of policy, apt to cover former employee when employed under consultancy agreement).

PUBLIC LIABILITY INSURANCE

General

17.24 A public liability policy provides cover against liability to the public at large. By contrast private liability arises from contracts entered into between individuals. Public liability in this sense arises in tort; it does not and cannot arise only in contract. As a general rule a claim in tort cannot be founded upon pure economic loss. The fact that a policy provides public liability insurance cover is important in determining the scope of the cover; such policies do not generally cover liability in contract for pure economic loss. It is a strong pointer to the meaning of the words used. Of course it is not conclusive: the wording may extend cover to third party claims in contract even for pure economic loss although one would expect it to say so clearly and for such insurance to be described as contract liability, financial or consequential loss cover.[1]

1 This paragraph is based on paragraph 14 of the judgment of Tuckey LJ in *Tesco Stores Ltd v Constable* [2008] EWCA Civ 362, [2008] Lloyd's Rep IR 636. See also *Wayne Tank and Pump Co Ltd v Employers Liability Assurance Corpn Ltd* [1974] QB 57, 75, CA (Roskill LJ); and *Bedfordshire Police Authority v Constable* [2009] EWCA Civ 64, [2009] Lloyd's Rep IR 607, para 19 (Longmore LJ) (not unreasonable to start with the premise that a public liability policy will give indemnity in respect of liability to the public at large). In *Horner (t/a F & H Contractors) v Commercial Union Assurance Co plc*, CA (unreported, 18 May 1993), uneven application of fertilizer due to the malfunctioning of a mechanical spreader resulted in some potato plants producing more and larger potatoes, and other producing too few, with an overall reduction in yield of 20–30%; this was not loss or damage to material property but purely economic loss and was therefore outside the scope of the public liability policy.

'In respect of'

17.25 The words 'in respect of' in the insuring clause in a public liability policy have a limiting effect on the extent of the cover and do not merely identify the causal event.[1] These words mean 'for' and not merely 'caused by', 'consequential upon' or 'in connection with', so that the insured's liability must be for death or injury, that is to say the liability must be to the person who has been killed or injured; the liability must be for loss or damage to material property of the person whose property it is – liability for loss suffered by someone else as a consequence of such damage is not 'in respect of' it; and liability for any of these torts must be to the person who has the right to claim – liability for loss suffered by someone else as a consequence of the tort is not 'in respect of' it.[2]

1 *Horbury Building Systems Ltd v Hampden Insurance NV* [2004] EWCA Civ 418, [2007] Lloyd's Rep IR 237, paras 24–25 (Keane LJ) and 35 (Mance LJ) (product liability insurance).
2 *Tesco Stores Ltd v Constable* [2008] EWCA Civ 362, [2008] Lloyd's Rep IR 636, para 22 (Tuckey LJ). See also **PARA 17.17**.

Index

Absurdity
  construction of contract, and, **3**.15, **13**.3
Access to court
  arbitration agreements, and, **9**.8
  exclusive jurisdiction clauses, and, **9**.8
  human rights, and, **9**.8
Accident
  causation of loss, and, **5**.2
Accident insurance
  'any occupation', **17**.3
  causation, **17**.2
  'own occupation', **17**.3
  permanent total disablement, **17**.3
  pre-existing conditions, **17**.4, **17**.13
Accrual of cause of action
  limitation of actions, and
    insurance brokers, claims against, **16**.29,
      16.30
    insurers, claims against, **8**.3, **11**.60
Affirmation
  notification of claims, and, **7**.22, **8**.4
  repudiation of liability and, **8**.7
  reservation of rights, and, **7**.22, **11**.63
Agent to insure
  see INSURANCE BROKERS
Aggregation
  excess clauses, and, **6**.9
  generally, **6**.9
'All risks' policy
  average, and, **6**.10
  burden of proof of loss, and, **5**.2
Alternative dispute resolution
  arbitration
    access to court, and, **10**.13
    agreements, **10**.5
    appeal on point of law, **10**.11
    applications to court, **10**.12
    arbitration clause
      conditions precedent, and, **3**.5
      unfair terms, and, **3**.20, **10**.14
    award, enforcement of, **10**.10
    confidentiality, **10**.4
    determination of preliminary point of law,
      10.9

Alternative dispute resolution – *contd*
  arbitration – *contd*
    enforcement of award, **10**.10
    evidence, **10**.7
    generally, **10**.3–**10**.4
    human rights, and, **10**.13
    interim injunctions, **10**.8
    nature, **10**.4
    preliminary point of law, determination
      of, **10**.9
    procedure, **10**.7
    stay of legal proceedings, **10**.6
    unfair terms, and, **10**.14
  early neutral evaluation, **10**.2
  Financial Ombudsman Service
    introduction, **10**.17
    judicial review, and, **10**.17
    jurisdiction, **10**.18
    procedure, **10**.19
  generally, **10**.2
  mediation, **10**.15
Appeal on point of law
  arbitration, and, **10**.11
Applicable law
  risks situated in EEA State, **15**.3, **15**.4
  risks situated outside EEC, **15**.3, **15**.5
Appropriate court
  insurance litigation, and, **9**.3
Arbitration
  access to court, and, **10**.13
  agreements, **10**.5
  appeal on point of law, **9**.9, **10**.11
  applications to court, **10**.12
  arbitration clause
    conditions precedents, and, **3**.4
    unfair terms, and, **3**.20, **10**.14
  award, enforcement of, **10**.10
  determination of preliminary point of
    law, **10**.9
  enforcement of award, **10**.10
  evidence, **10**.7
  generally, **10**.3–**10**.4
  human rights, and, **9**.9, **10**.13
  interim injunctions, **10**.8

Arbitration – *contd*
nature, **10**.4
preliminary point of law, determination
  of, **10**.9
procedure, **10**.7
stay of legal proceedings, **10**.6
unfair terms, and, **10**.14
Arbitration proceedings, **10**.12
'Arising from', 'arising out of'
aggregation clause, **6**.9
causation of loss, and, **4**.4
'As soon as possible'
notification of claims, and, **7**.15
Assessment of loss
see MEASUREMENT OF LOSS
Assignment
clause prohibiting assignment,
  effect of, **2**.14
disposal of subject matter, **2**.15
equitable, **2**.13
fraud by assignor, effect on
  assignee of, **2**.13
insurer
  consent of, **2**.13
  notice to, **2**.13
interest, **9**.45
legal, **2**.13
notice to insurers, **2**.13
policy, of, **2**.13
privilege, and, **9**.33
proceeds, of, **2**.13
prohibitive clause, **2**.14
timing, **2**.13
Assurance
terminology, **1**.4
Attempts to avoid a peril
causation of loss, and, **4**.12
Average
contribution, and, **13**.11
liability insurance, and, **6**.10
measurement of loss, and, **6**.10
payment subject to, **6**.10
pro rata condition of, **6**.10
Avert loss, opportunity to
causation of loss, and, **4**.10
Avoid a peril, attempts to
causation of loss, and, **4**.12
Avoidance of policy of insurance
agreement to exclude or restrict, **11**.31
arbitration clause, and, **11**.31
by insurer, validity of, **8**.7
court's role, **8**.7
damages, and, **11**.32
grounds for
  see GOOD FAITH, DUTY OF
jurisdiction clause, and, **11**.31
retrospective effect, **11**.31
restitutio in integrum, and, **11**.33
return of premium, and, **11**.33

Bailees
commercial 'trust', **2**.10
contribution claim, and, **13**.2
insurable interest, and, **2**.8, **2**.10
measurement of loss, and, **6**.12
mercantile 'trust', **2**.10
Bailors
insurable interest, and, **2**.8, **2**.10
Balance of probabilities
see STANDARD OF PROOF
'Basis' clauses
contractual documents, and, **3**.12
documentation, and, **1**.10
generally, **11**.16
Belief, statements of
misrepresentation, and, **11**.21
Beneficiary
insurable interest, and, **2**.8
Betterment
measurement of loss, and, **6**.7
Breach of condition precedent, **3**.5, **7**.4–**7**.5
Breach of continuing duty
claims against insurance brokers
  limitation periods, and, **16**.30
Breach of duty by insurance brokers
and see INSURANCE BROKERS
act with reasonable speed, to, **16**.18
advise, to, **16**.21
continuing duty, **16**.30
drafting documents, in, **16**.22
effect insurance, to, **16**.15–**16**.17
failure to disclose material facts to insurer,
  16.19
generally, **16**.14
keep client properly informed, to, **16**.20
misrepresentation to insurer, by, **16**.19
proposal form, completing, in, **16**.19
providing information to insurer, in, **16**.19
retain documents, to, **16**.24
Breach of duty of utmost good faith
see GOOD FAITH, DUTY OF
Breach of innominate or intermediate term,
  11.3
Breach of statutory duty
claims against insurance brokers,
  and, **16**.1
Breach of warranty,
generally, **11**.3
waiver, **11**.63
Brokers
see INSURANCE BROKERS
Brokers, claims against
see INSURANCE BROKERS, CLAIMS AGAINST
Building contracts
insurable interest, and, **2**.4, **2**.10
Burden of proof
agreement as to, **5**.1
'all risks' policy, and, **5**.2
breach of condition, **5**.1

Burden of proof – *contd*
causation, and, **4**.1
condition precedent, **5**.1, **7**.3
facts within knowledge of insured, **5**.2
fire insurance, and, **5**.2
exceptions, **5**.1
insured perils, **5**.2
legal professional privilege, and, **9**.29
loss, as to
exceptions, **5**.1
insured perils, **5**.2
scope of cover, **5**.1
marine insurance, and, **5**.2
misrepresentation and non-disclosure
generally, **11**.29
inducement, **11**.6–**11**.7
materiality, **11**.6–**11**.7
motor insurance, and, **5**.2
nature of insured peril, and, **5**.2
non-disclosure, **11**.29
notification of claims, and, **7**.3
privilege, **9**.29
procedural conditions, and, **7**.3
scope of cover, **5**.1
wording, importance of, **5**.1
Business interruption insurance
causation, **17**.5
delay in payment, and, **6**.6
depreciation savings, and, **17**.5
generally, **17**.5

Cancellation, right of
duty of disclosure, and, **11**.4
CAR insurance
see **CONTRACTORS' ALL RISKS INSURANCE**
Causa causans
causation of loss, and, **4**.2
Causa proxima
causation of loss, and, **4**.9
Causa sine qua non
causation of loss, and, **4**.9
Causation of loss
accident, and, **5**.2
'arising from', 'arising out of', **4**.4
attempts to avoid a peril, **4**.12
'but for' test, **4**.2
'caused by', **4**.4
'common sense', and, **4**.2
concurrent causes, **4**.3
deliberate act of insured, and, **5**.2
'directly' caused loss, **4**.5
dominant cause, **4**.2
effective cause, **4**.2
efficient cause, **4**.2
'exclusive' cause of loss, **4**.6
ex turpi causa non oritur actio,
and, **5**.2
general principles, **4**.1
immediate cause, and, **4**.2

Causation of loss – *contd*
'independent' cause of loss, **4**.6
'indirectly' caused loss, **4**.5
intentional act, and, **5**.2
negligence by insured, and, **4**.11, **5**.2
opportunity to avert loss, **4**.10
'originating in', **4**.4
predominant cause, **4**.2
proximate cause
expressions denoting, **4**.2
general principle, **4**.1–**4**.2
identifying, **4**.2
last event in time, and, **4**.2
previous decisions, relevance of, **4**.2
reasonable precautions to prevent loss, failure
to take, and, **4**.11, **5**.2
reckless act, and, **4**.11, **5**.2
'resulting from', **4**.4
sequence of events, and, **4**.2
'sole' cause of loss, **4**.6
sue and labour clause, and, **4**.10, **4**.12
terminology, meaning of Latin
causa causans, **4**.2
causa proxima non remota spectatur, **4**.9
causa sine qua non, **4**.9
novus actus interveniens, **4**.9
novus casus interveniens, **4**.9
'traceable to', **4**.4
wilful act, and, **5**.2
wordings denoting proximate cause, **4**.4
Cause of action
accrual of, claims against brokers,
16.29, **16**.30
accrual of, claims against insurers, **8**.3, **11**.59,
11.60
insurance brokers, claims against, **16**.29, **16**.30
insurers, claims against, **8**.3, **9**.41, **11**.59, **11**.60
'Caused by'
causation of loss, and, **4**.4
Certificate of insurance
function of, **1**.10
Change in circumstances
non-disclosure and misrepresentation, and,
11.18
Choses in action
assignment, and, **2**.13
Circumstances
notification, and, **7**.9, **7**.10, **7**.18
non-disclosure and misrepresentation, and
see **MISREPRESENTATION AND**
NON-DISCLOSURE
Claim
aggregation, and, **6**.9
meaning, **7**.8
Claimant's costs
Indemnity in respect of, **8**.11
Claims control clauses,
see **CLAIMS CO-OPERATION AND CLAIMS**
CONTROL CLAUSES

**Claims co-operation and claims
control clauses**
conditions precedent, and, **3**.5
generally, **9**.13
reinsurance, and, **14**.4
Claims handling
brokers, and, **16**.23
claims control clauses, **9**.13
claims co-operation clauses, **9**.13
COBS (Conduct of Business Sourcebook),
obligations imposed by, **8**.3
consent of insurer to action, **8**.9
defence costs, **8**.11
duty to act with reasonable speed and
efficiency, **8**.3
fraudulent claims
costs of investigating, recovery of, **8**.6
generally, **8**.1
human rights, and, **8**.5
ICOBS (Insurance Conduct of Business
Sourcebook), obligations imposed by,
8.3, **8**.7
interim payments, **8**.8
late payment, **8**.3
loss adjusters
disclosure, and, **8**.13, **9**.16
private life of insured, right to
respect for, **8**.5
privilege, and, **8**.13
privilege, **8**.13
reinstatement arrangements, **8**.14
repair arrangements, **8**.14
repudiation of liability, **8**.7
reservation of rights, **8**.4, **9**.13
settlement, recovery of payments after, **8**.15
solicitors
claims control clause, and, **9**.13
claims co-operation clause, and, **9**.13
conflicts of interest, **9**.13, **9**.33
disclosure, and, **9**.16
privilege, and, **9**.33
speed and efficiency, duty to act with, **8**.3
'Claims made' policy, 7.4, **17**.20
Claims notification
see NOTIFICATION OF CLAIMS
COBS
see CONDUCT OF BUSINESS SOURCEBOOK
Coinsurance clause
contribution, and, **13**.11
London insurance market, and, **1**.9
measurement of loss, and, **6**.10
Co-insured, claim against
see SUBROGATION, DOCTRINE OF
Collateral contracts
parol evidence rule, and, **3**.16
Commercial Court
Admiralty and Commercial Courts Guide, **9**.1
arbitration proceedings, **10**.12
expert evidence, **9**.40

Commercial Court – *contd*
interest, **9**.45
jurisdiction, **9**.3, **10**.12
Mercantile Court, transfer to, **9**.3
Commercial 'trust'
generally, **2**.10
insurable interest, and, **2**.10
measurement of loss, and, **6**.12
Commission
insurance brokers, and, **16**.4, **16**.6,
16.7, **16**.10
'Common interest' privilege
legal professional privilege, and, **9**.31
Company market, **1**.5, **1**.7
Composite policy of insurance
construction contracts, and, **2**.10
fraud of one policyholder, and, **11**.52
joint insurance, and, **2**.3
non-disclosure or representation, and **11**.30
Concurrent causes
causation of loss, and, **4**.3
Conditions, **3**.4
Conditions precedent
arbitration clause, and, **3**.5
breach, consequences of
generally, **3**.4–**3**.5
prejudice to insurer, and, **7**.5
burden of proof, **3**.5, **7**.3
classification of terms of contract, and, **3**.4
claims co-operation and control clauses,
14.3, **14**.4
construction of contract, and, **3**.5, **7**.4
equity, and, **7**.5
generally, **3**.4–**3**.5
good faith, duty of, and, **11**.4
Insurance Conduct of Business Sourcebook
(ICOBS), and, **3**.5, **7**.2, **7**.5
notification of claims, and
generally, **7**.4
prejudice to insurer, and, **7**.5
specified periods, **7**.16
prejudice to insurer, and, **7**.5
time for compliance, **7**.5
waiver, and, **3**.5
Conduct
misrepresentation by, **11**.26
Conduct of Business Sourcebook (COBS)
breach, effect of, **8**.2
claims handling, and, **8**.2
insurance brokers, and, **16**.9
Conflicting provisions
construction of contract, and, **3**.26
Conflict of laws
applicable law
risks situated in EEA State, **15**.2, **15**.3,
15.4, **15**.6
risks situated outside EEC, **15**.2, **15**.3,
15.5, **15**.6
Brussels I, **15**.7-**15**.12

Conflict of laws – *contd*
jurisdiction
Brussels Convention, **15**.7
Council Regulation 44/2001/EC, **15**.7–**15**.12
entering an appearance, **15**.10
lis pendens, **15**.11
proceedings brought against insurer, **15**.6
proceedings brought by insurer, **15**.8
provisional and protective measures, **15**.12
related actions, **15**.11
forum non conveniens, **15**.13
United Kingdom, constituent parts,
within, **15**.7
Rome I, **15**.6
Third Parties (Rights Against Insurers)
Act 1930, and, **2**.19
Third Parties (Rights Against Insurers)
Act 2010, and, **2**.39
Conflicts of interest
claims against insurance brokers, and, **16**.40
legal expenses insurance, and, **17**.8
privilege, and, **9**.33
solicitors, and, **9**.33
Consent of insurer
incurring of costs, as to
breach, consequences of, **8**.9
generally, **8**.9
no express requirement, where, **8**.9
unreasonably withheld, not to be
express term, where, **8**.9
implied term, **8**.9
Consent of reinsurer
settlement, as to **14**.3–**14**.4
Consequential loss
measurement of loss, and, **6**.6
Consignee of goods
insurable interest, and, **2**.9
Contracting out
Consumer Insurance (Disclosure and
Representations) Act 2012, **11**.47
Insurance Act 2015
basis clauses, and, **11**.16
duty of fair presentation, and, **11**.35
warranties, and, **3**.8
Construction contracts
insurable interest, and, **2**.4, **2**.10
Construction of contract of insurance
absurdity, and, **3**.15, **13**.3
ambiguity, and, **3**.15, **3**.16, **3**.18, **3**.19
commercial, **3**.15
commercial purpose, and, **3**.16, **3**.18
compulsory insurance, and, **3**.16
conditions precedent, and, **3**.4, **3**.5, **7**.3
conflicting provisions, **3**.26
contra proferentem rule, **3**.19
consistency, internal, and, **3**.15
definitions, relevance of, **3**.14
deletions, and, **3**.16
dictionary definitions, and, **3**.14

Construction of contract of insurance – *contd*
earlier contract, and, **3**.16
eiusdem generis rule, **3**.21
exceptions from cover, **3**.18
exclusions from cover, **3**.18
extrinsic evidence, admissibility of, **3**.16
factual matrix, **3**.16, **3**.17, **3**.23, **14**.6
fonts, and, **3**.25
format of document, **3**.25
grammatical contrasts, and, **3**.14
implied terms
generally, **3**.27
inconsistency with express term, **3**.27
necessary for business efficacy, **3**.27
obviousness, **3**.27
reasonableness, and, **3**.27
trade usage or custom, **3**.27
innominate terms, and, **3**.4, **3**.9, **7**.6
intention of parties, and, **3**.4, **3**.13, **3**.15, **3**.16
intermediate terms, and, **3**.4, **3**.9, **7**.6
introduction, **3**.11
legal concept, words denoting, **3**.22
level of premium, and, **3**.23
limitations on scope of cover, **3**.18
literal meaning, and, **3**.15
market practice, and, **3**.16
narrowing general words, **3**.21
natural or ordinary meaning, **3**.14
nature of insurance, and, **3**.14
negotiations, admissibility of evidence as to,
3.16
noscitur a sociis principle, **3**.14
notification clauses
conditions precedent, **7**.4
innominate or intermediate term, **7**.6
prejudice, and, **7**.5
parol evidence rule, **3**.16
premium level, **3**.23
previous contract, and, **3**.16
previous judicial interpretation, **3**.17, **3**.19
printed forms, and, **3**.24
procedural conditions
conditions precedent, **7**.4
innominate or intermediate term, **7**.6
prejudice, and, **7**.5
proposal forms, and, **3**.11
public policy, and, **5**.2
reasonableness of, **3**.15
rectification, and, **3**.35
redundant wording, and, **3**.16, **3**.21
regulatory background, and, **3**.16
reinsurance, and, **14**.6
relevant contractual documents, **3**.12
small print, **3**.25
special clause, precedence over general
clauses, **3**.26
special meanings, **3**.16, **3**.22
standard wording, and, **3**.19, **3**.24
statute, wording reflecting, **3**.16, **3**.17

Construction of contract of insurance – *contd*
  procedural conditions – *contd*
    subsequent conduct of parties, admissibility of
      evidence as to, **3**.16
    supplementary specific wording, **3**.24
    surplusage, and, **3**.14, **3**.21
    surrounding circumstances, **3**.15, **3**.16
    type of insurance, and, **3**.15, **3**.16
    typefaces, and, **3**.25
    unfair terms, **3**.20
    unreasonableness, and, **3**.15
    valued policies, and, **6**.3
    warranties, and, **3**.4, **3**.6
    words deleted from standard form, and, **3**.16
Construction of notification clause
  see NOTIFICATION OF CLAIMS
Consumers
  Consumer Insurance (Disclosure and
    Representations) Act 2012
    actionable misrepresentations, **11**.44
    agents, and, **11**.46
    application, **11**.41
    avoidance or contracting out provisions,
      11.47
    commencement, **11**.41
    consumer, definition, **11**.41
    deliberate misrepresentation, **11**.44, **11**.45
    duty of good faith, modification of, **11**.42
    duty to take reasonable care, **11**.42, **11**.43
    group insurance, **11**.41
    qualifying misrepresentation, **11**.44
    reckless misrepresentation, **11**.44, **11**.45
    remedies, **11**.45
  see also INSURANCE CONDUCT OF BUSINESS
    SOURCEBOOK (ICOBS) and UNFAIR
    TERMS IN CONSUMER CONTRACTS
Contingency insurance
  generally, **1**.3
  measurement of loss, and, **6**.1
Continuing common intention
  rectification, and, **3**.29
Continuing duty
  claims against insurance brokers, and, **16**.30
  disclosure, and, **9**.18
***Contra proferentem* rule**
  construction of contract, and, **3**.19
  proposal forms, construction of, and, **11**.15
Contract certainty, **1**.5
Contract for insurance
  duty of utmost good faith, and, **11**.5
Contract of insurance
  binding, date when becomes, **1**.9, **3**.3
  classification of terms
    categories, **3**.4
    conditions precedent, and, **3**.4–**3**.5
    generally, **3**.4–**3**.5
    importance of, **3**.4–**3**.5
    innominate or intermediate term, **3**.4, **3**.9
    warranty, **3**.4, **3**.6

Contract of insurance – *contd*
  COBS, requirements of
    see CONDUCT OF BUSINESS SOURCEBOOK
  concluded, date when, **1**.9, **3**.3
  conditions
    generally, **3**.4
  conditions precedent
    classification of terms, and, **3**.4
  generally, **3**.5
  construction
    see CONSTRUCTION OF CONTRACT OF
      INSURANCE
  Conduct of Business Sourcebook,
    requirements of
    see CONDUCT OF BUSINESS
      SOURCEBOOK
  date when becomes binding, **3**.3
  documents constituting, **3**.12
  duty of good faith, and
    see GOOD FAITH, DUTY OF
  ICOBS, requirements of
    see INSURANCE CONDUCT OF BUSINESS
      SOURCEBOOK
  inception of risk, **3**.3
  innominate term
    consequences of breach, **3**.9
    construction, and, **3**.4
    meaning, **3**.4
  Insurance Conduct of Business Sourcebook,
    requirements of
    see INSURANCE CONDUCT OF BUSINESS
      SOURCEBOOK
  intermediate term
    see innominate term
  rectification
    see RECTIFICATION OF CONTRACT
      OF INSURANCE
  terms not seen by insured, effect of, **3**.3, **7**.19
  terms of contract of insurance
    see TERMS OF CONTRACT OF INSURANCE
  warranties
    breach
      avoidance contrasted, **3**.7
      consequences, **3**.7–**3**.8
    generally, **3**.4, **3**.6–**3**.8
    terminology, **3**.4, **3**.6
Contract of utmost good faith
  and see GOOD FAITH, DUTY OF
  key characteristics, **11**.4
Contractors' all risks insurance, **17**.5
Contractual documents
  and see DOCUMENTATION, STATUS OF
  cover note, **1**.10
  policy, **1**.10, **3**.12
  promotional materials, **3**.12
  proposal form, **3**.12
  prospectus, **3**.12
  quotation, **1**.10
  slip, **1**.10, **3**.12

Contractual duties of insurance brokers
  client, to, **16**.1, **16**.7
  insurer, to, **16**.11
  third parties, to, **16**.12
Contribution
  agreements between insurers, and, **13**.1
  average, and, **13**.11
  calculation
    maximum liability method, **13**.6
    independent liability method, **13**.6
  co-insurance clause, and, **13**.11
  disclosure of 'other insurance', **13**.7
  exclusion, **13**.3
  employer's liability insurance, **13**.1, **13**.14
  Fairchild enclave, **13**.1, **13**.14
  interest and insured the same under
    each policy, **13**.2
  introduction, **13**.1
  non-contribution clauses, **13**.3
  one insurer entitled to repudiate, where, **13**.4
  parties to claim, **13**.12
  prohibition of other insurances, **13**.8
  rateable proportion, **13**.3, **13**.5
  requirements, **13**.2
  subrogation, and, **12**.14, **13**.13
  third parties, and, **13**.10
  voluntary payments, and, **13**.5, **13**.9
Contributory negligence
  claims against insurance brokers,
    and, **16**.38
Control of actions
  subrogation, and, **12**.8
Conversion of goods
  burden of proof of loss, and, **5**.2
Copies
  legal professional privilege, and, **9**.32
Correspondence
  right to respect for
    claims handling, and, **8**.5
Cost of repair
  measurement of loss, and, **6**.4
Costs
  claims against insurance brokers,
    and, **16**.47
  defence of claim under liability policy, and,
    8.11
  investigation of fraudulent claim, and, **8**.6,
    11.53
  mediation, and, **10**.15
  non-parties, and, **9**.46
  'without prejudice' communications,
    and, **9**.36
Costs of civil proceedings against insured
  claims against insurance brokers, and, **16**.42
Cover note
  effect of, **1**.10, **3**.2, **7**.19
  issued by broker, where, **1**.10, **3**.2, **16**.4
Cover, scope of
  burden of proof, and, **5**.1

Creating false impression
  misrepresentation, and, **11**.28
Creditor
  insurable interest, **2**.8
Criminal convictions
  duty to disclose, **11**.17, **11**.19
  materiality of, **11**.19
  Rehabilitation of Offenders Act 1974, **11**.17
  'spent' convictions, duty to disclose, **11**.17

Damages
  insurance brokers, claims against, and
    client left without cover, **16**.34
    conflicts of interest, **16**.40
    costs of civil proceedings, **16**.42
    expenses, **16**.44
    failure to advise, **16**.37
    fines and costs in criminal
      proceedings, **16**.41
    general principle, **16**.33
    interest, **16**.45
    loss of a chance, **16**.35
    mental distress, **16**.39
    mitigation, and, **16**.43
    reduction of, **16**.38
  insurers, claims against,
    delay, **6**.6, **8**.3, **9**.45
    generally, **9**.41
    hardship, **6**.6
    inconvenience, **6**.6
    mental stress, **6**.6
  misrepresentation, and, **11**.32
  negligent misrepresentation, and, **11**.23
De bene esse
  construction of contract, and, **3**.16
De minimis
  fraud in making of claim, and, **11**.51
  warranty, approach to compliance, **3**.6
Decision-making power, contractual
  exercise of, **5**.4
Deductibles
  measurement of loss, and, **6**.8
Deemed knowledge of insured
  duty to disclose, **11**.11
Defeasible interest in property
  insurable interest, and, **2**.9
Defence, costs of
  liability insurance, and, **8**.11
Defences by insurance brokers
  see INSURANCE BROKERS, CLAIMS AGAINST
Defences by insurers
  see INSURERS' DEFENCES
Delay
  interest, and, **9**.45
  insurers, claims against
    business interruption insurance, and, **6**.6
    consequential loss, and, **6**.6, **8**.3
    generally, **6**.6, **8**.3
    waiver, and, **11**.63

Delimiting warranty, 3.6

Delivery of particulars or claim
notification of claims, and, **7**.20

Determination of preliminary point of law
arbitration, and, **10**.9

Diminution in value
measurement of loss, and, **6**.4

Diminution in risk
duty to disclose, **11**.8

Directly, loss caused
causation of loss, and, **4**.5

Disclose material facts to insurer, breach of duty to
claims against insurance brokers, and, **16**.19
and see MISREPRESENTATION AND NON-DISCLOSURE

Disclosure
see MISREPRESENTATION AND NON-DISCLOSURE

Disclosure of documents
insurance litigation, and
continuing duty, **9**.18
documents mentioned in statements of case, **9**.20, **9**.33
general principles, **9**.14
insurance brokers, and, **9**.16
insurance policy, **9**.14
loss adjusters, and, **9**.16
non-party, **9**.23
pre-action, **9**.22
privilege, **9**.21
procedure, **9**.17
restriction on use of documents disclosed, **9**.24
solicitors, and, **9**.16
specific disclosure, **9**.19
subrogated action, **12**.7

Disclosure of insurance policy or information
legal expenses insurance, and, **9**.15
liability insurance, and, **9**.15
see also THIRD PARTIES (RIGHTS AGAINST INSURERS) ACT 1930 and THIRD PARTIES (RIGHTS AGAINST INSURERS) ACT 2010

Disclosure of 'other insurance'
contribution, and, **13**.7
double insurance, and, **13**.7

Disposal of subject matter insured
assignment of policies, and, **2**.12

Dishonesty
fraud in making of claim, and, **11**.50

Documentation
certificate of insurance, **1**.10
cover note, **1**.10, **3**.31
endorsements, **1**.10
extensions, **1**.10
key features document, **1**.10

Documentation – *contd*
policy of insurance, **1**.10, **3**.12
promotional material, **3**.12, **3**.31
proposal form, **1**.10, **3**.12, **3**.31
prospectus, **3**.12
quotation, **1**.10
schedule to policy of insurance, **1**.10
slip, **1**.10, **3**.12, **3**.31
standard terms and conditions, **1**.10
statement of demands and needs, **1**.10

Documents mentioned in statements of case
disclosure, and, **9**.20
privilege, waiver of, and, **9**.33

Dominant cause
causation of loss, and, **4**.2

Dominus litis
insured as, **12**.8
insurer as, **7**.1, **12**.3
notification of claims, and, **7**.1
subrogation, and, **12**.3, **12**.8

Double insurance
agreements between insurers, and, **13**.1
contribution
average, and, **13**.11
calculation
maximum liability method, **13**.6
independent liability method, **13**.6
co-insurance clause, and, **13**.11
exclusion, **13**.3
one insurer entitled to repudiate, where, **13**.4
parties to claim, **13**.12
rateable proportion, **13**.3, **13**.5
requirements, **13**.2
subrogation, and, **13**.13
third parties, and, **13**.10
voluntary payments, and, **13**.5, **13**.9
disclosure of 'other insurance', **13**.7
employer's liability insurance, **13**.1, **13**.14
equitable doctrine, **13**.1
Fairchild enclave, **13**.1, **13**.14
interest and insured the same under each policy, **13**.2
introduction, **13**.1
non-contribution clauses, **13**.3
notification of claims, and, **7**.23
'other insurance', obligation to disclose, **13**.7
prohibition of other insurances, **13**.8
rateable proportion clauses, **13**.3, **13**.5
same interest, same insured, **13**.2
third parties, and, **13**.10

Drafting documents, breach of duty in
claims against insurance brokers, and, **16**.22

Duties of insurance brokers
client, to
contract, in, **16**.1, **16**.7, **16**.13
fiduciary, **16**.10
standard of skill and care, **16**.13

Duties of insurance brokers – *contd*
  client, to – *contd*
    statutory duties, **16**.1
    tort, in, **16**.1, **16**.8, **16**.13
    insurer, to, **16**.11
    third parties, to, **16**.12
Duty of fair presentation
    (Insurance Act 2015)
  agents, and, **11**.36, **11**.38
  breach, **11**.39
  contracting out, **11**.35
  generally, **11**.4, **11**.35–**11**.39
  insured's knowledge, **11**.37
  insurer's knowledge, **11**.38
  reasonable search, and, **11**.37
  remedy for breach, **11**.39
  requirements, **11**.36
Duty of utmost good faith
  see **GOOD FAITH, DUTY OF**

Early neutral evaluation, **10**.2
Efficiency
  implied term that insurer to act with, **8**.3
Eiusdem generis **rule**
  construction of contract, and, **3**.21
Election, **11**.63
Endorsements to policy, **1**.10
Enforcement of award
  arbitration, and, **10**.10
Equitable principles
  contribution, and, **13**.1
  subrogation, and, **12**.2
Estoppel
  estoppel by convention, **11**.63
  insurance brokers, claims against, and, **16**.28
  insurers, claims against, and, **11**.63
  limitation of actions, and, **11**.62
  notification of claims, and, **7**.22
  promissory estoppel, **11**.63
  repudiation of liability and, **8**.7
  waiver by estoppel, **11**.63
European Convention on Human Rights
  see **HUMAN RIGHTS**
Evidence
  arbitration, and, **10**.7
  construction of contract of insurance,
    and, **3**.16
  expert evidence, **9**.40, **11**.6, **11**.7, **11**.36
  standard of skill and care, and, **16**.13
  underwriter, **11**.7
  witnesses of fact, **9**.39
Examination by court
  legal professional privilege, and, **9**.30
Exceptions to cover
  burden of proof, and, **5**.1
  concurrent causes, and, **4**.3
  construction of contract, and, **3**.18
  notification of claims, and, **7**.3
  trading or personal debt, **17**.19

Excess clause
  measurement of loss, and, **6**.8
Excessive valuation of subject matter
  non-disclosure and misrepresentation, and,
    11.19
Exclusions from cover
  see **EXCEPTIONS TO COVER**
'Exclusive' cause of loss
  causation of loss, and, **4**.6
Executors
  insurable interest, and, **2**.9
Expectation or belief, statements of
  misrepresentation, and, **11**.21
Expert evidence
  construction of contract, and, **3**.16,
    3.23, **3**.27
  evidence for trial, and, **9**.40
  hypothetical prudent insurer or underwriter,
    11.6, **11**.7, **11**.36
  insurance brokers, claims against, **16**.13
  materiality, as to, **11**.6–**11**.7
  measurement of loss, and, **6**.4
  statement of opinion, and, **11**.23
Express waiver
  subrogation, and, **12**.5
Extensions to policy, **1**.10
Extrinsic evidence, admissibility of
  construction of contract, and, **3**.16

Fact, statements of
  misrepresentation, and, **11**.21
Factual matrix
  construction of contract, and, **3**.16
Failure to act with reasonable speed
  insurance brokers, claims against, and,
    16.18
  insurers, claims against, and, **8**.3
Failure to advise client
  insurance brokers, claims against
    damages, **16**.37
    generally, **16**.21
Failure to disclose material facts to insurer
  claims against insurance brokers,
    and, **16**.19
Failure to effect insurance
  insurance brokers, claims against
    damages, **16**.34
    generally, **16**.15
    in accordance with client's requirements,
      16.16
    on terms specified by client, **16**.17
Failure to give appropriate advice
  insurance brokers, claims against
    damages, **16**.37
    generally, **16**.21
Failure to keep client properly informed
  claims against insurance brokers, and, **16**.20
Failure to retain documents
  claims against insurance brokers, and, **16**.24

Failure to take reasonable precautions, 3.18, 4.11, **5**.2

Fair hearing, right to
human rights, and, **9**.9

Fair presentation of risk (pre-Insurance Act 2015)
assumed knowledge of insurer, and, **11**.14
inexperienced, incompetent or careless underwriter, and, **11**.14
inquiry, putting insurer on, **11**.14
loss experience of insured, and, **11**.14
meeting with underwriter, at, **11**.14
proposal forms
generally, **11**.15
use of, **11**.14
specialist underwriter, and, **11**.14
summary of facts sufficient for, **11**.14
unusual facts, and, **11**.14
waiver by insurer, and, **11**.14

False impression, creation of
misrepresentation, and, **11**.28

Fiduciary duties
insurance brokers, and, **16**.10

Financial Conduct Authority, **1**.6, **1**.8, **8**.2, **10**.17–**10**.19

Financial Ombudsman Service
generally, **10**.16–**10**.17
judicial review, and, **10**.17
jurisdiction, **10**.18
procedure, **10**.19

Financial Services Authority
see Financial Conduct Authority

Fines and costs in criminal proceedings
insurance brokers, claims against, and, **16**.41

Fire insurance
average, and, **6**.10
indemnity insurance, and, **1**.4
reinstatement or replacement, and, **6**.5

Fires Prevention (Metropolis) Act 1774
operation, **2**.11
insurable interest, and, **2**.11

Following market
Leading underwriter, decisions of, and, **1**.9

Font
Construction of contract, and, **3**.25

Foreign law
relevance of, **1**.2

Foreign legal advisers
legal professional privilege, and, **9**.28

Format of document
construction of contract, and, **3**.25

Fraud
legal professional privilege, and, **9**.34

Fraudulent claims and fraudulent devices
consumer insurance, and, **11**.44, **11**.45
costs of investigating, recovery of, **8**.6
de minimis, where, **11**.51
deceit, damages for tort of, **8**.6
dishonesty, **11**.50

Fraudulent claims and fraudulent devices – *contd*
exaggerated claim, impact on remainder, **11**.49
fraudulent device, use of, **11**.49
generally, **11**.48, **11**.49–**11**.54
joint and composite insurance, **11**.52
Insurance Act 2015, **11**.48, **11**.54
liability insurance, and, **11**.49
non-party costs order, and, **9**.46
remedy
avoidance contrasted **11**.49
exaggerated claim, **11**.49
forfeiture of benefit under policy, **11**.49
generally, **11**.49
recovery of earlier payments, **11**.49
retrospective nature, **11**.49
unfair terms, and, **11**.49

Fraudulent devices
see Fraudulent claims and fraudulent devices

Fraudulent misrepresentation, **11**.27

Freezing injunctions
human rights, and, **9**.7

Frustration, **11**.56

Funding of actions
subrogation, and, **12**.8

Gambling
insurable interest, and, **2**.2–**2**.9

Gaming
see Gambling

General insurance
ABI Statement
notification of claims, **7**.1
proposal forms, **11**.16

Good faith, duty of
and see Duty of fair presentation
after conclusion of contract, **11**.4, **11**.18, **11**.49
after commencement of litigation, **9**.14
agreement to exclude or restrict, **11**.34
before conclusion of contract
see Misrepresentation and non-disclosure
breach, remedy for
avoidance, **11**.4, **11**.31
breach of warranty, remedy contrasted, **11**.31
contract provides for remedy, where, **11**.31
damages, **11**.31–**11**.32
general principles, **11**.31–**11**.33
interim payment, return of, **11**.33
repayment of premium, and, **11**.33
restitutio in integrum, and, **11**.33
retrospective effect, whether, **11**.31
return of premium, and, **11**.33
contract for insurance, and, **11**.5
contract of insurance, and, **11**.5

Good faith, duty of – *contd*
fraud in making of claim
see FRAUDULENT CLAIMS
generally, **11**.4, **11**.49
Insurance Conduct of Business Sourcebook
(ICOBS), **11**.4
misrepresentation
see MISREPRESENTATION AND
NON-DISCLOSURE
mutual character of duty, **11**.4
non-disclosure
see MISREPRESENTATION AND
NON-DISCLOSURE
proof, **11**.31
remedy
see breach, remedy for
right of cancellation, and, **11**.18
Group insurance
companies, **11**.54
consumer insurance, representation and
non-disclosure, **11**.41
contract for benefit of third parties,
2.18, **11**.54
employee's right to benefit under employer's
policy, **2**.18, **11**.54
fraudulent claims, **11**.54
landlord and tenant, **2**.18, **11**.54
Guarantee, contract of
insurance, contracts of, and, **1**.3

Handling of claims
see CLAIMS HANDLING
Hardship, damages for
consequential loss, and, **6**.6
Hearing within reasonable time
human rights, and, **9**.11
Hearsay evidence
evidence for trial, and, **9**.39
'Held covered' cases
duty of utmost good faith, and, **11**.4
Human rights
access to court, **9**.8
appeal on point of law, and, **10**.11
arbitration, and, **10**.13
claims handling, and, **8**.5
correspondence, respect for, **8**.5
fair hearing, **9**.9
Financial Ombudsman Service,
and, **10**.17, **10**.19
freezing injunctions, **9**.7
hearing within reasonable time, **9**.11
independent and impartial
tribunal, **9**.12
introduction, **9**.6
privacy, **8**.5
public hearing, **9**.10
search orders, **9**.7
Hypothetical prudent underwriter or insurer,
11.6–**11**.7, **11**.14, **11**.36

ICOBS
see INSURANCE CONDUCT OF BUSINESS
SOURCEBOOK
Illegality, **11**.48
Immediate cause
causation of loss, and, **4**.2
'Immediately'
notification of claims, and, **7**.14
Implied terms
consent, requirement for, **8**.9, **14**.4
decision-making power, exercise of, **5**.4, **8**.9
generally, **3**.27
inconsistency with express term, **3**.27
insurance brokers, and, **16**.7
necessary for business efficacy, **3**.27
obviousness, **3**.27
reasonable speed and efficiency, **8**.3
reasonableness, and, **3**.27
trade usage or custom, **3**.27
Implied waiver
subrogation, and, **12**.4
Impossibility
notification of claims, and, **7**.17
Imputed knowledge
insured's duty to disclose, **11**.12
Inception of risk, **3**.3
Inconvenience, damages for
consequential loss, and, **6**.6
Indemnity insurance
excess and deductibles, and, **6**.8
fundamental principle
double insurance, and, **13**.1
subrogation, and, **12**.1
generally, **1**.3
insurable interest, and, **2**.4–**2**.6
measurement of loss, and
see MEASUREMENT OF LOSS
salvage, and, **6**.11
Indemnity principle
double insurance, and, **13**.1
salvage, and, **6**.11
subrogation, and, **12**.1
Independent and impartial tribunal
human rights, and, **9**.12
'Independent' cause of loss
causation of loss, and, **4**.6
'Indirectly', loss caused
causation of loss, and, **4**.5
Inducement
burden of proof, **11**.6–**11**.7
date when assessed, **11**.6
duty of fair presentation, and, **11**.39
generally, **11**.6
Innominate term
consequences of breach, **3**.9
construction, and, **3**.4
insurers' defences, and, **11**.3
meaning, **3**.4
notification of claims, and, **7**.6

Insolvency of insurer
  several liability, and, **1**.9
Inspection of documents
  and see DISCLOSURE
  subrogation, and, **12**.7
Institute of London Underwriters, 1.7
Insurable interest
  beneficial interest, and, **2**.4
  commercial trust, **2**.10
  date when insurable interest required,
    2.5, **2**.6
  defeasible interest in property, **2**.9
    consignee of goods under bill of lading, **2**.9
    executor, **2**.9
  definition, **2**.4
  detriment, suffering of, and, **2**.4
  Fires Prevention (Metropolis) Act 1774, **2**.11
  formal requirements
    indemnity insurance, **2**.6
    life insurance **2**.5
  gambling, and, **2**.4
  indemnity insurance, **2**.5
  insurers' defences, and, **11**.47
  Law Commission proposals, **2**.4
  legal interest, and, **2**.4
  liability insurance, **2**.4, **2**.6
  life insurance, **2**.4, **2**.4
  limited interest in subject-matter of insurance
    bailor and bailee, **2**.8, **2**.10
    building contractors and sub-contractors,
      2.10
    commercial 'trust', **2**.10
    construction contract, **2**.10
    creditor, **2**.8
    landlord and tenant, **2**.8
    mercantile 'trust', **2**.10
    mortgagor and mortgagee, **2**.8, **2**.10
    occupants of building damaged or destroyed
      by fire, **2**.11
    shareholder, **2**.8
    trade union, members and employers, **2**.10
    trustee and beneficiary, **2**.8
    vendor and purchaser, **2**.8, **2**.15
  mercantile trust, **2**.10
  prejudice, suffering of, and, **2**.4
  property insurance, **2**.4, **2**.6, **2**.8–**2**.10
  purpose, **2**.5
Insurance
  meaning, **1**.1, **1**.3–**1**.4
Insurance brokers
  agency,
    see identifying the principal
  binding authority, acting under, **16**.4
  claims against
    see INSURANCE BROKERS, CLAIMS AGAINST
  commission, **16**.4, **16**.6, **16**.7, **16**.10
  Conduct of Business Sourcebook (COBS),
    and, **16**.9, **16**.14
  conflicts of interest, **16**.10, **16**.23, **16**.40

Insurance brokers – *contd*
  construction, and, **3**.16
  contractual duties
    client, to
      generally, **16**.1, **16**.7
      standard of skill and care, **16**.13
    insurer, to, **16**.11
    third parties, to, **16**.12
  coverholder, acting as, **16**.4
  cover note, issued by, **1**.10, **3**.2, **16**.4
  disclosure, and, **9**.16
  documents, retention of, **9**.16, **16**.24
  duties
    breach of, **16**.14–**16**.25
    client, to, **16**.7–**16**.10
    insurer, to, **16**.11
    third parties, to, **16**.12
  duties to client
    advise, to, **16**.21
    contract, in, **16**.1, **16**.7, **16**.13
    fiduciary, **16**.1,**16**.10
    post-placement, **16**.23
    renewal, on, **16**.25
    standard of skill and care, **16**.13
    statutory duties, **16**.1
    tort, in, **16**.1, **16**.8, **16**.13
  duty to advise, breach of
    damages, **16**.37
    generally, **16**.21
  fiduciary duties, **16**.1, **16**.7, **16**.10
  generally, **16**.1
  implied terms, **16**.7
  identifying the principal
    brokers outside Lloyd's, **16**.4
    consumer insurance, **11**.46
    cover note, and **3**.2, **16**.4
    generally, **16**.2
    'high street' brokers, **16**.4
    importance of, **16**.2, **16**.6
    Lloyd's brokers, **16**.3
    sub-agency between producing and placing
      broker, **16**.5
  individual broker, duty to client, **16**.8
  Insurance Conduct of Business
    Sourcebook (ICOBS), and,
      16.5, **16**.9, **16**.14, **16**.16, **16**.19,
      16.21, **16**.23–**16**.25
  regulation of, **16**.1, **16**.7
  Lloyd's brokers, **16**.3, **16**.5
  London market, and, **1**.8
  non-disclosure, and, **11**.13
  notification of claim, and, **7**.12, **16**.23
  rectification, broker's intention,
    and, **3**.33
  'regulated activities', **16**.7
  regulation of, **16**.1, **16**.9
  retainer
    consideration for, **16**.7
    generally, **16**.7

Insurance brokers – *contd*
standard of skill and care, **16**.13
sub-agency between producing and placing
broker, **16**.5
Terms of Business Agreement at
Lloyd's, **9**.16
tortious duties
client, to
individual broker, owed by, **16**.8
generally, **16**.1, **16**.8
standard of skill and care, **16**.13
individual broker, owed by, **16**.8
insurer, to, **16**.11
third parties, to, **16**.12
vicarious liability, **16**.8
Insurance brokers, claims against
and see **INSURANCE BROKERS**
action against insurer, joining broker
to, **16**.46
breach of continuing duty, **16**.30
breach of duty
act with reasonable speed, to, **16**.18
advise, to, **16**.21
drafting documents, in, **16**.22
effect insurance, to, **16**.15–**16**.17
failure to disclose material facts to insurer,
16.19
generally, **16**.14
keep client properly informed,
to, **16**.20
misrepresentation to insurer, by, **16**.19
post-placement, **16**.23
proposal form, completing, in, **16**.19
providing information to insurer,
in, **16**.19
renewal, on, **16**.25
retain documents, to, **16**.24
breach of statutory duty, **16**.7, **16**.9, **16**.14
conflicts of interest, **16**.40
contributory negligence, **16**.38, **16**.43
costs, **16**.47
damages
breach of duty to advise, **16**.37
client left with inadequate over, **16**.34
client left without cover, **16**.34
conflicts of interest, **16**.40
contributory negligence, **16**.38, **16**.43
costs of civil proceedings brought by third
parties, **16**.42
contributory negligence, **16**.38
criminal proceedings, **16**.41
exposure of client to risk of legal disputes
with insurer, **16**.36
general principle, **16**.30
giving credit for costs and expenses saved,
16.44
interest, **16**.45
late payment, for, **16**.34
loss of a chance, **16**.35

Insurance brokers, claims against – *contd*
damages – *contd*
mental distress, **16**.39
mitigation, and, **16**.43
reduction of, **16**.38
settlement with insurer, reasonableness of,
16.43
defences
estoppel, **16**.28
limitation of actions
breach of continuing duty of care, **16**.30
computing limitation period, **16**.32
extension of limitation period, **16**.31
generally, **16**.29
ratification, **16**.25
waiver, **16**.27
estoppel, **16**.28
expert evidence, **16**.13
failure to act with reasonable speed, **16**.18
failure to advise
damages, **16**.37
generally, **16**.21
failure to disclose material facts to insurer,
16.19
failure to effect insurance
damages, **16**.34
generally, **16**.15
in accordance with client's requirements,
16.16
on terms specified by client, **16**.17
failure to give appropriate advice
damages, **16**.37
generally, **16**.21
failure to keep client properly informed, **16**.20
failure to notify claim to insurer, **16**.23
failure to retain documents, **16**.24
fiduciary duty, breach of, **16**.7, **16**.10
identifying the principal
generally, **16**.2
importance of, **16**.6
Lloyd's brokers, **16**.3
brokers outside Lloyd's, **16**.4
interest, **16**.45
generally, **16**.1
limitation period
breach of continuing duty, and, **16**.30
calculation, **16**.32
extension, **16**.31
generally, **16**.29
loss of a chance, **16**.35
mental distress, **16**.39
misrepresentation to insurer, **16**.19
mitigation of damage, **16**.43
proposal forms, completing, and, **16**.19
ratification, **16**.25
standard of care and skill, **16**.13
sub-agency between producing and placing
broker, **16**.5
waiver, **16**.27

Insurance Conduct of Business Sourcebook (ICOBS)
breach, effect of, **3**.7, **8**.2–**8**.3
claims handling, and, **7**.2, **8**.2–**8**.3
condition precedent, and, **3**.5, **7**.2, **7**.5
delay by insurers, and, **6**.6
insurance brokers, and, **16**.5, **16**.9, **16**.14, **16**.16, **16**.19, **16**.21, **16**.23–**16**.25
key features document, **1**.10
procedural condition, and, **7**.2, **7**.5
statement of demands and needs, **1**.10
warranties, and, **3**.7
Insurance documentation
generally, **1**.10
Insurance litigation
appropriate court, **9**.3
claims control clauses, and, **9**.13
claims co-operation clauses, and, **9**.13
contribution, parties to claim, **13**.12
costs against non-parties, **9**.46
disclosure
continuing duty, **9**.18
documents mentioned in statements of case, **9**.20, **9**.33
general principles, **9**.14
insurance brokers, and, **9**.16
loss adjusters, and, **9**.16
non-party, **9**.23
pre-action, **9**.22
privilege, **9**.21
procedure, **9**.17
restriction on use of documents disclosed, **9**.24
solicitors, and, **9**.16
specific disclosure, **9**.19
subrogated action, **12**.7
evidence for trial
expert evidence, **9**.40
witnesses of fact, **9**.39
freezing injunctions, **9**.7
human rights, and
access to court, **9**.8
fair hearing, **9**.9
freezing injunctions, **9**.7
hearing within reasonable time, **9**.11
independent and impartial tribunal, **9**.12
introduction, **9**.6
public hearing, **9**.10
search orders, **9**.7
hypothetical issues, **9**.42
interest, **9**.45
introduction, **9**.1
legal professional privilege
burden of proof, **9**.29
'common interest' privilege, **9**.31
copies, and, **9**.32
examination of documents by court, **9**.30
foreign legal advisers, **9**.28

Insurance litigation – *contd*
legal professional privilege – *contd*
fraud, and, **9**.34
general principles, **9**.25
internal documents reproducing privileged communications, **9**.27
loss adjusters, and, **8**.13
loss of, **9**.33–**9**.34
notification letters, **9**.26
waiver, and, **9**.33
list of documents, **9**.17
non-party, costs against, **9**.46
non-party disclosure, **9**.23
pre-action disclosure, **9**.22
pre-action protocols, **9**.2
privilege
'common interest' privilege, **9**.31
disclosure, and, **9**.21
legal professional privilege, **9**.25–**9**.34
relevant court, **9**.3
remedies, **9**.41–**9**.44
representative actions, **9**.4
search orders, **9**.7
security for costs, **9**.5, **9**.42
subrogation
disclosure and, **12**.7
waiver, pleading, **11**.63
'without prejudice' communications
costs, and, **9**.36
exceptions to rule, **9**.38
general rule, **9**.35
subsequent litigation, **9**.37
Insured
and see **GROUP INSURANCE**
identifying, **2**.2
insolvency of
see **THIRD PARTIES, CLAIMS AGAINST INSURERS**
third party, right to indemnity or other benefit, **2**.10, **2**.18
undisclosed principal doctrine, and, **2**.2
Insured perils
burden of proof, and, **5**.2
causation, and, **4**.1
Insurer, insolvency of
several liability, and, **1**.9
Insurers' defences
affirmation, and, **11**.63
alternative, defences in the, **7**.21, **11**.63
breach of condition precedent, **11**.2
breach of duty of utmost good faith
agreement to exclude or restrict, **11**.34
generally, **11**.4
misrepresentation and non-disclosure, **11**.5–**11**.28
proof, **11**.31
remedy, **11**.31–**11**.34
breach of innominate or intermediate term, **11**.3

Insurers' defences – *contd*
  breach of warranty, **11**.3
  duty of fair presentation, **11**.35–**11**.39
  estoppel, and, **11**.63
  fraudulent claims and fraudulent devices
    see FRAUDULENT CLAIMS AND
      FRAUDULENT DEVICES
  frustration, **11**.56
  generally, **11**.1
  good faith, duty of, and, **11**.4
  illegality, **11**.56
  innominate or intermediate term,
    and, **11**.3
  lack of insurable interest, **11**.55
  limitation of actions
    accrual of cause of action, **8**.3, **11**.60
    cause of action, **11**.59
    claims against insurance brokers, and,
      breach of continuing duty, and, **16**.30
      calculation, **16**.32
      extension, **16**.31
      generally, **16**.31
    computation of period, **11**.61
    contractual limitation on right of action,
      11.58
    estoppel, and, **11**.62
    generally, **11**.57
    limitation period, **11**.59
    subrogated action,
      extension of limitation period,
        and, **12**.15
  misrepresentation and non-disclosure
    see MISREPRESENTATION AND
      NON-DISCLOSURE
  non-disclosure
    see MISREPRESENTATION AND
      NON-DISCLOSURE
  waiver, and, **11**.63
  warranties, and, **11**.3
Intention of parties
  construction, and, **3**.4, **3**.13, **3**.15, **3**.16
  rectification, and, **3**.28–**3**.29, **3**.33
Intention to make a claim
  notification of, **7**.9
Intention, statements of
  misrepresentation, and, **11**.24
Interest
  assignee, claim by, **9**.45
  delay, and, **9**.45
  generally, **9**.45
  insurance brokers, claims against,
    and, **16**.45
  insurers, claim against, **9**.45
  period, **9**.45
  rate, **9**.45
  subrogated action, and, **12**.10
Interests in property
  defeasible interest, **2**.9
  limited interest, **2**.8

Interim injunctions
  arbitration, and, **10**.8
Interim insurance, contract of
  see COVER NOTE
Interim payments
  claims handling, and, **8**.8
Intermediate term
  consequences of breach, **3**.9
  construction, and, **3**.4
  insurers' defences, and, **11**.3
  meaning, **3**.4
  notification of claims, and, **7**.6
**Internal documents reproducing privileged
  communications**
  legal professional privilege, and, **9**.27
**International Underwriting Association
  of London**, **1**.7
Investigation costs
  fraudulent claims, and, **8**.6, **11**.53
IUA, **1**.7

Joinder of broker
  proceedings involving insured, **9**.47, **16**.46
Joinder of insurer
  proceedings involving broker, **9**.47, **16**.46
  proceedings involving insured, **9**.13, **9**.47
Joint insurance
  co-insured, claim against
    see SUBROGATION, DOCTRINE OF
  composite insurance, and, **2**.3
  fraud of one policyholder, and, **11**.52
  rateable proportion clauses, and, **13**.5
Judicial interpretation
  construction of contract, and, **3**.17
Jurisdiction
  see COMMERCIAL COURT
  and see CONFLICT OF LAWS
  and see MERCANTILE COURT

**Keep client properly informed, breach
  of duty to**
  claims against insurance brokers,
    and, **16**.20
Key features document, **1**.10
Knowledge of agent to insure/broker
  duty to disclose, and, **11**.13
Knowledge of insured
  and see KNOWLEDGE OF AGENT TO
    INSURE/BROKER
  duty to disclose
    actual knowledge, **11**.10
    deemed knowledge, **11**.11
    generally, **11**.9
    imputed knowledge, **11**.12
Knowledge of insurer
  duty to disclose, and, **11**.8

Law Commission proposals
  Insurable interest, **2**.4

Lack of insurable interest
insurers' defences, and, **11**.55
Landlord and tenant
insurable interest, and, **2**.8
Lapse of time
claims handling, and, **8**.4
Late payment of claims
damages for, **8**.3
remedy for, **8**.3
Leading underwriter
following market, and, **1**.9
Legal advice privilege
and see LEGAL PROFESSIONAL PRIVILEGE
generally, **9**.25
Legal expenses insurance
Disclosure of insurance position,
and, **9**.15
freedom to choose a lawyer, and, **17**.8
generally, **17**.7
liability insurance, and, **17**.9
non-party costs orders, and, **9**.46, **17**.10
privilege, and, **9**.33
security for costs, and, **9**.5
statutory requirements, **17**.8
Legal professional privilege
burden of proof, **9**.29
'common interest' privilege, **9**.31, **9**.34
copies, **9**.32
court, production of documents to, **9**.30
foreign legal advisers, **9**.28
fraud, and, **9**.34
general principles, **9**.25
internal documents reproducing privileged
communications, **9**.27
legal advice privilege, **9**.25
legal expenses insurance, and, **9**.33
litigation privilege, **9**.25
loss adjusters, and, **8**.13
notification letters, **9**.26
waiver, and, **9**.33
Liability, basis of
London market, **1**.9
several liability, **1**.9
Liability insurance
average, and, **6**.10
cause of action, accrual of, **11**.60
'claim', meaning, **7**.8
cost of defending claim, **8**.11
declaration, action seeking, **9**.42
disclosure of insurance position, **9**.15
see also THIRD PARTIES (RIGHTS AGAINST
INSURERS) ACT 1930 *and* THIRD
PARTIES (RIGHTS AGAINST INSURERS)
ACT 2010
insurable interest, **2**.4, **2**.7
legal expenses insurance, and, **17**.9
limitation of actions, **11**.60
loss, and, **5**.2
reasonable precautions clause, and, **5**.2

Liability insurance – *contd*
settlement with third party, and, **8**.12
under-insurance, and, **6**.10
Life insurance
insurable interest, and
formal requirements, **2**.5
date when required, **2**.5
generally, **2**.5
recovery limited to insured's interest in life
insured, **2**.5
LIIBA, **1**.6, **1**.8
Limit of liability, **6**.9
Limitation of actions
accrual of cause of action, **8**.3, **11**.60
cause of action, **11**.59
claims against insurance brokers, and
breach of continuing duty, and, **16**.30
calculation, **16**.32
extension, **16**.31
generally, **16**.29
computation of period, **11**.61
contractual limitation on right of
action, **11**.58
estoppel, and, **11**.62
generally, **11**.57
late payment, remedy for, and, **8**.3
limitation period, **11**.59
reinsurance, and, **14**.5
subrogated action,
extension of limitation period,
and, **12**.15
Third Parties (Rights Against Insurers)
Act 1930, claims under, **2**.27
Third Parties (Rights Against Insurers)
Act 2010, claims under, **2**.38
Limitation on scope of contract
construction of contract, and, **3**.18
Limited interest in subject-matter
of insurance
composite insurance, **11**.52
insurable interest, and
bailor and bailee, **2**.8, **2**.10
building contractors and sub-contractors,
2.4, **2**.10
commercial trust, **2**.10
creditor, **2**.8
landlord and tenant, **2**.8
mercantile trust, **2**.10
mortgagor and mortgagee, **2**.8, **2**.10
occupants of building damaged or destroyed
by fire, **2**.11
shareholder, **2**.8
trade union, members and employers, **2**.10
trustee and beneficiary, **2**.8
vendor and purchaser, **2**.8, **2**.15
joint insurance, **11**.52
measurement of loss, and, **6**.12
List of documents
disclosure, and, **9**.17

Litigation
see INSURANCE LITIGATION
Litigation privilege
and see LEGAL PROFESSIONAL PRIVILEGE
generally, **9**.25
Lloyd's broker
functions of, **1**.6, **16**.3
regulation of, **1**.6
Lloyd's Market Association, **1**.6
Lloyd's of London
broker
functions of, **1**.6, **16**.3
Council, **1**.6
insurance market
operation of, **1**.6
regulation of, **1**.6
managing agent, **1**.6
members' agent, **1**.6
syndicate, **1**.6, **1**.9
Terms of Business Agreement, **9**.16
Lloyd's slip
contents, **1**.9
contractual status, **1**.10
generally, **3**.12
initialling, **1**.9, **3**.3
Market Reform Contract – lineslip, **1**.9
non-disclosure, and, **11**.18
placing of risk, and, **1**.9
policy wording, as aid to construction of, **3**.12
rectification, and, **3**.31
'scratching', **1**.9, **3**.3
signature, **3**.3
stamping, **1**.9, **3**.3
LMA, **1**.6
London & International Insurance Brokers'
Association, **1**.6, **1**.8
London insurance market
brokers, **1**.8
co-insurance clause, use of, **1**.9
company market, **1**.7
Institute of London Underwriters, **1**.7
International Underwriting Association of
London, **1**.7
introduction, **1**.5
IUA, **1**.7
liability, basis of, **1**.9
Lloyd's, **1**.6
placing the risk, **1**.9
slip, use of, **1**.9
Loss
causation of,
see CAUSATION OF LOSS
measurement of,
see MEASUREMENT OF LOSS
proof of,
see PROOF OF LOSS
Loss adjusters
claims handling, and, **8**.1
disclosure, and, **8**.13, **9**.16

Loss adjusters – *contd*
private life of insured, right to respect for, **8**.5
privilege, and, **8**.13
Loss of a chance
claims against insurance brokers, and, **16**.35

Marine insurance
breach of warranty, and, **3**.7
burden of proof, **5**.2
consequential loss, and, **6**.6
insured perils, and, **5**.2
valued policies, and, **6**.3
Marine Insurance Act 1906
application to non-marine insurance, **1**.1, **3**.3,
11.4, **11**.5
codification of common law principles, as, **1**.1,
3.3, **11**.4, **11**.5, **11**.49
Market Reform Contract – Lineslip, **1**.9
Market value
measurement of loss, and, **6**.4
Materiality
see MISREPRESENTATION AND
NON-DISCLOSURE
Measurement of loss
actual total loss, **6**.2
aggregation, **6**.9
agreed basis of assessment, **6**.3
assignment, and, **2**.13, **2**.15
average, **6**.10
betterment, **6**.7
co-insurance clause, **6**.10
collateral benefits, giving credit for, **6**.7
consequential loss
delay by insurers, **6**.6
generally, **6**.6
goods insurance, **6**.6
policy against loss, **6**.6
constructive total loss, **6**.2
damages, and, **9**.41
deductibles, **6**.8
duty to mitigate loss, **6**.13
excess clause, **6**.8
fundamental principle, **6**.3
generally, **6**.1
limited interest in property, **2**.15, **6**.12
limit of liability, **6**.9
mitigation of loss, **6**.13
'new for old' policies, **6**.7
open policies
see unvalued policies
salvage, **6**.11
sub-limits of liability, **6**.9
sum insured, **6**.9
total loss, **6**.2
under-insurance, **6**.10
unvalued policies
actual loss, assessment of
alternative methods, **6**.4
cost of repair, **6**.4

Measurement of loss – *contd*
  unvalued policies – *contd*
    actual loss, assessment of – *contd*
      diminution in value, **6**.4
      evidence, **6**.4
      fundamental principle, **6**.4
      market value
        assessment of, **6**.4
        increase during policy period, **6**.4
        more than one market, where, **6**.4
        policy limits, effect of, **6**.4
        price paid by insured, and, **6**.4
      method of assessment, **6**.3, **6**.4
      policy wording, effect of, **6**.3
    generally, **6**.3
    reinstatement or replacement, **6**.5
  valued policies, **6**.3
    indemnity principle, and, **6**.3
    generally, **6**.3
    partial loss, **6**.3
    reinstatement or replacement, cost of, and, **6**.3
Mediation, **10**.15
Mental distress, damages for
  insurance brokers, claims against, and, **16**.39
  insurers, claims against, and, **6**.6
Mercantile Court
  arbitration proceedings, **10**.12
  expert evidence, **9**.40
  guide to using, **9**.1
  jurisdiction, **9**.3
  transfer from Commercial Court, **9**.3
Mercantile 'trust'
  generally, **2**.10
  insurable interest, and, **2**.10
  measurement of loss, and, **6**.12
Misrepresentation and non-disclosure
  agreement to exclude or restrict duty of disclosure, **11**.34
  agreement to exclude or restrict liability for misrepresentation, **11**.34
  'basis clauses', **11**.3, **11**.16
  brokers, and, **11**.13, **16**.19
  burden of proof, **11**.29
  change in circumstances, **11**.18
  circumstances generally accepted to be material, **11**.19
  circumstances not requiring disclosure, **11**.8
  claims against insurance brokers, and, **16**.19
  conduct, **11**.26
  consumer insurance, and, **11**.40-**11**.47
    see also CONSUMER INSURANCE (DISCLOSURE AND REPRESENTATIONS)
  contract for insurance, and, **11**.5
  contract of insurance, and, **11**.5
  creating false impression, **11**.28
  criminal convictions, **11**.17, **11**.19
  declarations of facts, **11**.15
  duty of good faith, and, **11**.4
  evidence, and, **11**.29

Misrepresentation and non-disclosure – *contd*
  excessive valuation of subject matter, **11**.19
  fair presentation of facts, **11**.14
  fraudulent misrepresentation, **11**.27
  generally, **11**.20
  good faith, duty of, and, **11**.4
  inducement
    burden of proof, **11**.6–**11**.7
    date when assessed, **11**.6
    generally, **11**.6
  insurance brokers, and, **11**.13, **16**.10, **16**.19
  introduction, **11**.5
  knowledge of agent to insure, duty to disclose, **11**.13, **16**.10
  knowledge of broker, duty to disclose, **11**.13, **16**.10
  knowledge of insured, duty to disclose
    actual knowledge, **11**.10
    deemed knowledge, **11**.11
    generally, **11**.9
    imputed knowledge, **11**.12
    knowledge of broker/agent to insure, and, **11**.13, **16**.10
  knowledge of insurer,
    duty to disclose, and, **11**.8
  materiality
    burden of proof, **11**.6–**11**.7
    circumstances diminishing risk, and, **11**.8
    circumstances generally accepted to be material, **11**.19
    circumstances requiring disclosure, **11**.6
    criminal convictions, and, **11**.19
    date when assessed, **11**.6
    excessive valuation, and, **11**.19
    expert evidence, and, **11**.6
    fraudulent misrepresentation, and, **11**.27
    generally, **11**.6
    hypothetical prudent underwriter, and, **11**.6–**11**.7
    knowledge of insured, duty to disclose
      actual knowledge, **11**.10
      deemed knowledge, **11**.11
      generally, **11**.9
      imputed knowledge, **11**.12
      knowledge of broker/agent to insure, and, **11**.13
    objective test, **11**.6
    over-insurance, and, **11**.19
    previous claims, and, **11**.19
    previous refusal of risk, and, **11**.19
    previous refusal to increase insured value, and, **11**.9
    proposal form questions, and, **11**.15
    prudent underwriter, and, **11**.6–**11**.7
  misrepresentation, particular considerations, **11**.20–**11**.28
  moral hazard, **11**.19
  nationality, and, **11**.17
  negligent misstatement, **11**.23

Misrepresentation and non-disclosure – *contd*
  materiality – *contd*
    over-valuation of subject matter, **11**.19
    post-contract, **11**.18, **11**.49
    pre-contract, **11**.49
    previous claims, **11**.19
    previous refusal of the risk, **11**.19
    previous refusal to increase value insured, **11**.19
    proposal forms
      construction, **11**.15
      questions, presumption of materiality, **11**.15
      see also **Proposal forms**
    relationship between misrepresentation and
      non-disclosure, **11**.5, **11**.28
    remedy for
      agreement to exclude or restrict, **11**.34
      avoidance of contract, **11**.31
      damages, **11**.31–**11**.32
      generally, **11**.31
      joint or composite insurance,
        and, **11**.30
      restitutio in integrum, and, **11**.33
      stipulated in contract, where, **11**.31
    representation implied by conduct, **11**.26
    representation of law, **11**.25
    restitutio in integrum
      generally, **11**.33
      repayment of interim payment, **11**.33
      repayment of premium, **11**.33
      repayment of previous claim, **11**.33
    settlement payment, recovery of, and, **8**.15
    'spent' convictions, and, **11**.17
    statements of expectation or belief, **11**.21
    statements of fact, **11**.21
    statements of intention, **11**.24
    statements of opinion
      generally, **11**.22
      implied representation
        opinion honestly held, that, **11**.22
        reasonable grounds for opinion,
          that, **11**.23
    statutory limitations on disclosure, **11**.17
    superfluity of disclosure, **11**.8
Mistake
  as to terms, **3**.29
  mutual mistake, **3**.29
  rectification, and, **3**.29
  settlement payment, recovery of,
    and, **8**.15
  unilateral mistake, **3**.33
Mitigation of loss
  attempts to avoid a peril, **4**.12
  insurance brokers, claims against,
    and, **16**.43
  measurement of loss, and, **6**.13
  opportunity to avert loss, **4**.10
  sue and labour clause, **4**.10, **4**.12
Moral hazard
  material circumstances, and, **11**.19

Mortgagor and mortgagee
  contribution claim, and, **13**.2
  insurable interest, and, **2**.7
  joint or composite nature of insurance,
    2.3, **11**.30, **11**.52
Motor insurance
  insured perils, and, **5**.2
Mutual mistake
  rectification, and, **3**.26

'Names'
  Lloyd's, at, **1**.6
Narrowing general words
  construction of contract, and, **3**.21
Nationality
  non-disclosure and misrepresentation,
    and, **11**.17
Natural or ordinary meaning
  construction of contract, and, **3**.14
Negligence by insured
  causation of loss, and, **4**.11
  failure to take reasonable precautions,
    and, **3**.18, **4**.11, **5**.2
Negligent misstatement
  misrepresentation, and, **11**.23
Negotiations
  construction of contract, and, **3**.16
  'without prejudice' communications,
    and, **9**.35
'New for old' policies
  betterment, and, **6**.7
Non-binding evaluation
  alternative dispute resolution,
    and, **10**.2
Non-contribution clauses
  contribution, and, **13**.3
Non-disclosure
  see **Misrepresentation and**
    non-disclosure
Non-indemnity insurance
  generally, **1**.3
  measurement of loss, and, **6**.1
Non-parties
  costs, and, **9**.46
  disclosure, and, **9**.23
Notification of claims
  'accident', and, **7**.8
  affirmation by insurer, and, **8**.4
  'as soon as possible', **7**.15
  avoidance of policy by insurer, insured's
    obligations following, **8**.7
  blanket notification, **7**.10
  block notification, **7**.10
  breach of obligations by insured, and
    affirmation, **8**.4
    estoppel
      waiver, and, **7**.22
    reservation of rights, **8**.4
    waiver, **7**.22, **8**.4

Notification of claims – *contd*
burden of proof, **7**.3
'claim', and, **7**.8
claims handling, and, **8**.4
conditions precedent
blanket provision, effect of, **7**.4
purpose, **7**.4
construction of notification clauses
and see CONSTRUCTION OF CONTRACT
OF INSURANCE
conditions precedent, **3**.5, **7**.4
innominate or intermediate term, **7**.6
contents, **7**.8
delivery of particulars or claim,
3.5, **7**.20
double insurance, and, **7**.23
equity, and, **7**.5
estoppel, **7**.22
form of notice, **7**.13
'knowledge', and, **7**.8
'immediately', **7**.14
impossibility, and, **7**.17
generally, **7**.1
'laundry list' notification, **7**.10
legal professional privilege, and, **9**.26
'loss or damage', and, **7**.8
no express provision, where, **7**.19
notice
given by whom, **7**.11
given to whom, **7**.12
meaning, **7**.13
notification, meaning of, **7**.13
'occurrence', and, **7**.8
prejudice to insurer, and, **7**.5
privilege, and, **9**.26
purpose for which information
provided, and, **7**.12
repudiation of liability, and, **7**.21
reservation of rights by insurer, **8**.4, **9**.13
specific periods, **7**.5, **7**.16
time limits
'as soon as possible', **7**.15
'as soon as reasonably possible', **7**.1
equity, and, **7**.5
'immediately', **7**.14
impossibility, and, **7**.17
no express provision, where, **7**.19
specific periods, **7**.16
unfair terms, and, **3**.20, **7**.19
waiver, **7**.22, **8**.13
written notice, **7**.13
Novus actus interveniens
causation of loss, and, **4**.9

**Occupants of building damaged or destroyed
by fire**
insurable interest, **2**.11
Occurrence
notification, and, **7**.9

Offers to settle
'without prejudice' communications,
and, **9**.35
Onus of proof *see* BURDEN OF PROOF
Open market value
measurement of loss, and, **6**.4
Open policies
see MEASUREMENT OF LOSS
Opinion of insurer,
contractual terms, effect, **5**.4
Opinion, statements of
misrepresentation, and, **11**.22
Opportunity to avert loss
causation of loss, and, **4**.10
Ordinary meaning
construction of contract, and, **3**.14
'Originating in'
causation of loss, and, **4**.4
'Other insurance'
disclosure of, **13**.7
'Outward expression of accord'
rectification, and, **3**.29
Over-valuation of subject matter
non-disclosure and misrepresentation, and,
11.19

Parol evidence rule
construction of contract, and, **3**.16
**Particulars of loss and damage or of claim,
obligation to provide**, **7**.20
Pensions review
complaint to Financial Ombudsman Service,
and, **10**.19
notification clauses, and, **7**.10
Permanent health insurance
'any occupation', **17**.11
group policy, **17**.14
'incapacity', **17**.11
measurement of loss, and, **6**.1,
17.12
'own occupation', **17**.11
pre-existing conditions, **17**.4, **17**.13
proof of loss, and, **5**.4
Personal accident insurance
see ACCIDENT INSURANCE
Placing of risk
insurance brokers, duty to advise in
relation to, **16**.21
company market, in, **1**.9
following market, and, **1**.9
lead underwriter, and, **1**.9
Lloyd's, at, **1**.9
London market, in, **1**.9
'signing down', **1**.9
slip, contents of, **1**.9
Policy of insurance
claim under, defendant to, **2**.1
documents making up, **1**.10
Policy summary, **1**.10

Pre-action disclosure
insurance litigation, and, **9**.22
pre-action protocols, and, **9**.2
Pre-action protocols
insurance litigation, and, **9**.2
professional negligence, **9**.2
Predominant cause
causation of loss, and, **4**.2
Prejudice
notification of claims, and, **7**.5
Preliminary point of law, determination of
arbitration, and, **10**.9
Premium, level of
construction of contract, and, **3**.23
Premium, return of
avoidance, and, **11**.33
Presentation of claims
see NOTIFICATION OF CLAIMS
Previous claims
non-disclosure and misrepresentation, and,
11.19
Previous judicial interpretation
construction of contract, and, **3**.17
Printed forms
construction of contract, and, **3**.16, **3**.24
Prior agreement
generally, **3**.29
mode of proof, **3**.31
Private investigators
claims handling, and, **8**.5
private life of insured, right to respect
for, **8**.5
video evidence, admissibility of, **8**.5
Private life, right to respect for
claims handling, and, **8**.5
search order, application for, and, **9**.7
Privilege
claims consultants, and, **8**.13
claims handling, and, **8**.13
disclosure and inspection of documents, and,
9.21
legal professional privilege
burden of proof, **9**.29
'common interest' privilege, **9**.31
copies, **9**.32
examination by court, **9**.30
foreign legal advisers, **9**.28
fraud, and, **9**.34
general principles, **9**.25
internal documents reproducing privileged
communications, **9**.27
legal advice privilege, **9**.25
litigation privilege, **9**.25
notification letters, **9**.26
waiver, and, **9**.33
loss adjusters, and, **8**.13
Procedural conditions
breach, damages for, **7**.7
claim in prescribed form, requirement for, **7**.20

Procedural conditions – *contd*
insurer, duty of good faith owed by, **7**.22
particulars of loss and damage, requirement
for, **7**.20
repudiation of liability, and, **7**.21
waiver, affirmation and estoppel, **11**.63
and see NOTIFICATION OF CLAIMS
Product liability insurance
'damage', **17**.16
generally, **17**.15
'in respect of', **17**.17
'product', meaning, **17**.15
'on account of', **17**.17
scope of cover, **17**.17
Professional indemnity insurance
'claims made' basis, **17**.20
construction of contract, and, **3**.16, **17**.22
costs, cover for, **17**.21
generally, **17**.19
non-party costs order, and, **9**.46
trading or personal debt, exclusion, **17**.19
Promotional materials
contractual documents, and, **3**.12
rectification, and, **3**.31
Proof of loss
burden of proof
agreement as to, **5**.1
'all risks' policy, and, **5**.2
breach of condition, **5**.1
condition precedent, **5**.1, **7**.3
exceptions, **5**.1
facts within knowledge of insured, **5**.2
fire insurance, and, **5**.2
insured perils, **5**.2
legal professional privilege, and, **9**.29
loss, **5**.2
marine insurance, and, **5**.2
misrepresentation and non-disclosure,
11.29
motor insurance, and, **5**.2
nature of insured peril, and, **5**.2
non-disclosure, **11**.29
notification of claims, and, **7**.3
procedural conditions, and, **3**.5, **7**.3
scope of cover, **5**.1
wording, importance of, **5**.1
liability insurance, **5**.2
property insurance, **5**.2
'satisfactory to' insurer, **5**.4
standard of proof, **5**.3
balance of probabilities, **5**.3
civil standard, **5**.3
criminal conduct alleged in civil case, **5**.3
criminal standard contrasted, **5**.3
dishonesty, **5**.3
modern approach, **5**.3
Proof of non-disclosure and
misrepresentation
breach of duty of utmost good faith, and, **11**.29

Property insurance
average, and, **6**.10
cause of action, accrual of, **11**.60
insurance brokers
failure to keep client properly informed, and,
16.20
limitation of actions, **11**.60
loss, and, **5**.2
measurement of loss, and, **6**.4
reasonable precautions clause, and, **5**.2
Proposal forms
'basis clause', and, **3**.12, **11**.16
basis of contract, express clause making, **3**.12,
11.16
completed by insurance broker, where,
16.19
construction, principles of
ambiguity, **11**.15
contra proferentem rule, **11**.15
fair and reasonable construction, **11**.15
generally, **11**.15
incomplete answer, **11**.15
specific questions
deemed knowledge of insurer, and,
11.15
waiver, and, **11**.15
unanswered question, **11**.15
waiver, **11**.15
construction of contracts of insurance, and,
3.11, **3**.12, **11**.15
contractual status, **1**.10
generally, **11**.15
non-disclosure and misrepresentation, and,
11.15
London market, placing of risk contrasted, **1**.9
materiality
basis clause, and, **11**.16
questions, presumption of, **11**.15
warranty as to truth of answer, and, **11**.16
renewal, and, **11**.15
signature by insured before completion by
agent, **11**.15
truth of answers
statement as to, **11**.16
warranty as to, **11**.16
warranties, and, **11**.16
Prospectuses
contractual documents, and, **3**.12
Proximate cause
see CAUSATION OF LOSS
Public hearing, right to
human rights, and, **9**.10
Public liability insurance
generally, **17**.24
'in respect of', **17**.25
Public policy
liability insurance, and, **2**.7
Purchaser
insurable interest, **2**.8, **2**.15

'QC' clause
claims handling, and, **8**.9

Rateable proportion clauses
contribution, and, **13**.5
double insurance, and, **7**.23
Ratification
insurance brokers' defences, and, **16**.25
Reasonableness
construction of contract, and, **3**.15
Reasonable speed
failure to act with, insurance brokers, and,
16.18
implied term that insurer to act with, **8**.3
Recovery of payments
fraudulent claim, and, **11**.49
settlement of claim, after, **8**.15
Recoveries
allocation, **12**.11
definition, **12**.13
enforcement of insurer's rights against insured,
12.12
gifts, and, **12**.13
Rectification
broker's intention, and, **3**.33
common mistake, and, **3**.29
construction of contract, and, **3**.35
'continuing common intention', and, **3**.29
contractual documents, and, **3**.12
documentary evidence, and, **3**.12, **3**.31
evidence, and, **3**.31
generally, **3**.28
intention
broker, of, **3**.33
'continuing common intention', **3**.29
objective, **3**.29
subjective, **3**.29
mistake as to terms, and, **3**.29
mutual mistake, and, **3**.29
'outward expression of accord', **3**.29
prior oral agreement, **3**.28, **3**.29, **3**.31
remedy, status as, **3**.28, **9**.43
standard of proof, **3**.32
timing of claim for, **3**.34
unilateral mistake, and, **3**.33
without prejudice rule, and, **9**.38
Refusal of the risk
non-disclosure and misrepresentation, and,
11.19
'Regulated activities'
insurance brokers, and, **16**.1, **16**.7
Regulatory background
aggregation, and, **6**.9
construction, and, **3**.16
professional standards, and, **16**.13
Reinstatement
agreements with third parties, **8**.14
betterment, and, **6**.7
claims handling, and, **8**.14

Reinstatement – *contd*
  Fires Prevention (Metropolis) Act 1774, and,
    2.11
  unvalued policies, and, **6**.5
Reinsurance
  approval of settlement, right to withhold, **14**.4
  claims co-operation and claims control clauses,
    14.3, **14**.4
  'ex gratia settlements', **14**.2
  'follow the settlements' clauses, **14**.2, **14**.4
  limitation of actions, **14**.5
  'pay as may be paid thereon', **14**.2
  Scor case, **14**.3, **14**.4
  'unconditionally binding', settlements to be,
    14.2
  'without prejudice settlements', **14**.2
Related occurrences, events or claims
  aggregation, and, **6**.9
Release of defendant
  subrogation, and, **12**.9
Remedies
  damages, **9**.41
  debt, **9**.41
  declarations, **9**.42
  fraudulent claims
    avoidance contrasted **11**.49
    exaggerated claim, **11**.49
    forfeiture of benefit under policy, **11**.49
    generally, **11**.49
  good faith, breach of duty of
    avoidance, **11**.31
    breach of warranty, remedy contrasted, **11**.31
    contract provides for remedy, where, **11**.31
    damages, **11**.31–**11**.32
    general principles, **11**.31–**11**.33
    interim payment, return of, **11**.33
    repayment of premium, and, **11**.33
    restitutio in integrum, and, **11**.33
    retrospective effect, whether, **11**.31
    return of premium, and, **11**.33
  insurance brokers, claims against
    see DAMAGES
  insurance litigation, and, **9**.41
  late payment of claims, **8**.3
  misrepresentation and non-disclosure
    agreement to exclude or restrict, **11**.34
    avoidance of contract, **11**.31
    damages, **11**.31–**11**.32
    generally, **11**.31
    restitutio in integrum, and, **11**.33
    stipulated in contract, where, **11**.31
  rectification, **9**.43
Remote cause
  causation of loss, and, **4**.9
Renewal of policy
  duty of utmost good faith, and, **11**.4
Repair arrangements
  agreements with third parties, and, **8**.14
  claims handling, and, **8**.14

Repair cost
  measurement of loss, and, **6**.4
Representation of law
  misrepresentation, and, **11**.25
Representative actions
  litigation, and, **9**.4
Request for information by insurer
  claims co-operation clause, **9**.13
  duty of utmost good faith, and, **11**.4
Res inter alios acta
  assignment, and, **2**.13
Reservation of rights
  affirmation, and, **7**.22, **11**.63
  claims handling, and, **8**.4, **9**.13
  generally, **8**.4, **9**.13
  notification of claims, and, **7**.22
  waiver, and, **7**.22, **11**.63
Restitutio in integrum
  non-disclosure and misrepresentation, and,
    11.33
Restriction on use of disclosed
  documents
  disclosure, and, **9**.24
'Resulting from'
  causation of loss, and, **4**.4
Retain documents, breach of duty to
  claims against insurance brokers,
    and, **16**.24
Retainer
  insurance brokers, and, **16**.7

Salvage
  measurement of loss, and, **6**.11
'Satisfactory to' insurer
  proof of loss, **5**.4
Schedule to policy of insurance, 1.10
Scope of cover
  burden of proof, and, **5**.1
Search orders
  human rights, and, **9**.7
Sequence of events
  causation of loss, and, **4**.2
Series of events or claims
  aggregation, and, **6**.9
Settlement of actions
  and see CLAIMS CO-OPERATION AND
    CONTROL CLAUSES
  and see REINSURANCE
  liability insurance, and, **8**.12
  recovery of payments following,
    8.15
  subrogation, and, **12**.9
  third parties, and, **8**.12
Several liability
  London market, and, **1**.9
Shareholder
  insurable interest, and, **2**.8
Skill and care, standard of
  insurance brokers, and, **16**.13

Slip
contents, **1**.9
contractual status, **1**.10
generally, **3**.12
initialling, **1**.9, **3**.3
non-disclosure, and, **11**.18
rectification, and, **3**.31
'scratching', **1**.9, **3**.3
signature, **3**.3
stamping, **1**.9, **3**.3
'Sole' cause of loss
causation of loss, and, **4**.6
Solicitor
claims control clause, and, **9**.13
claims co-operation clause, and, **9**.13
conflicts of interest, **9**.13, **9**.33
disclosure, and, **9**.16
privilege, and, **9**.33
Special meanings of words
construction of contract, and, **3**.22
Specific disclosure
litigation, and, **9**.19
'Spent' convictions
non-disclosure and misrepresentation, and,
 11.17
Standard of proof
balance of probabilities, **5**.3
civil standard, **5**.3
criminal conduct alleged in civil
 case, **5**.3
criminal standard contrasted, **5**.3
dishonesty, **5**.3
modern approach, **5**.3
rectification, and, **3**.32
Standard wording
deletions, and, **3**.16
policy document, and, **1**.10
printed forms, **3**.16
specific wording, and, **3**.24
unfair terms, and, **3**.20
Statement of demands and needs, **1**.10
Statements of expectation or belief
misrepresentation, and, **11**.21
Statements of fact
misrepresentation, and, **11**.21
Statements of intention
misrepresentation, and, **11**.24
Statements of opinion
misrepresentation, and, **11**.22
Stay of legal proceedings
arbitration, and, **10**.6
Subject matter of agreement
parol evidence rule, and, **3**.16
Subrogation, doctrine of
claims control clause, and, **9**.13, **12**.3, **12**.8,
 12.9
co-insured, claim against, **12**.4
contractual or equitable, whether, **12**.2
contribution, and, **12**.14

Subrogation, doctrine of – *contd*
disclosure and inspection of documents, and,
 12.7
entitlement to exercise subrogated rights
 claims control clause, and, **9**.13
 date when arises, **9**.13, **12**.3
 dominus litis
  insured as, **12**.8
  insurer as, **12**.3
 generally, **12**.3
 payment of sum insured, and, **12**.3, **12**.8
 settlement, and, **12**.3
equitable or contractual, whether, **12**.2
exercise of rights
 action brought by insured, costs of, **12**.8
 action brought by insurer against insured,
  9.13, **12**.8
 agreement by insured with third party, and,
  12.6
 claims control clause, and, **9**.13
 control of action, **9**.13, **12**.8
 defining subrogated right, **12**.6
 disclosure and inspection
  of documents, **12**.7
 dominus litis
  insured as, **12**.8
  insurer as, **12**.3
 entitlement, **12**.3
 extension of limitation period,
  and, **12**.15
 funding of action, **12**.8
 interest, **12**.10
 letter of subrogation, and, **12**.6
 recoveries, **12**.11–**12**.13
 release of defendant, **12**.9
 settlement of action, **12**.9
express waiver of subrogated rights, **12**.5
fundamental principles, **12**.1–**12**.2
gifts, and, **12**.13
implied waiver of subrogated rights, **12**.4
insured's obligations, **12**.8
interest, **12**.10
introduction, **12**.1
letter of subrogation, and, **12**.6
nature, **12**.2
recoveries
 allocation, **12**.11
 definition, **12**.13
 enforcement of insurer's rights against
  insured, **12**.12
 gifts, and, **12**.13
settlement, and, **12**.3, **12**.9
subsequent policy, and, **12**.3
subsequently-acquired rights, and, **12**.3
Sue and labour clause, **4**.10, **4**.12
Supplementary specific wording
construction of contract, and, **3**.24
Surrounding circumstances
construction of contract, and, **3**.16, **6**.9

Syndicates
following market, **1**.9
lead underwriter, **1**.9
Lloyd's, at, **1**.6
placing of risk, **1**.9

Technical words or phrases
construction of contract, and, **3**.16, **3**.22
Tenant
fraudulent claims, **11**.54
insurable interest, and, **2**.8
Terms of contract of insurance
classification of
categories, **3**.4
conditions precedent, and, **3**.5
generally, **3**.4
importance of, **3**.4
innominate or intermediate term,
3.4, **3**.9
terms not relevant to the actual
loss, **3**.10
warranty, **3**.4, **3**.7
conditions
generally, **3**.4
conditions precedent
classification of terms, and, **3**.4
generally, **3**.5
construction
see **CONSTRUCTION OF CONTRACT OF
INSURANCE**
generally, **3**.4
innominate term
consequences of breach, **3**.9
construction, and, **3**.4
meaning, **3**.4
intermediate term
see intermediate term
terms not relevant to the actual loss, **3**.10
warranties
breach
avoidance contrasted, **3**.7
consequences of, **3**.7–**3**.8
generally, **3**.4, **3**.6
terminology, **3**.4, **3**.6
Third parties, claims against insurers
arbitration agreement, and, **2**.18, **2**.25, **2**.30
Contracts (Rights of Third Parties) Act 1999,
2.10, **2**.18
contribution, and, **13**.10
Fairchild enclave, and, **13**.14
insurable interest, and, **2**.10
generally, **2**.10, **2**.17–**2**.40
liability insurance
see **THIRD PARTIES (RIGHTS AGAINST
INSURERS) ACT 1930** and **THIRD
PARTIES (RIGHTS AGAINST INSURERS)
ACT 2010**
and see **2**.18
statutory schemes, **2**.40

**Third Parties (Rights Against Insurers)
Act 1930**, **2**.19–**2**.27
anti-avoidance provisions, **2**.22
arbitration agreement, and, **2**.25
conflict of laws, and, **2**.19
dissolved company, restoring to register, **2**.24
distribution of proceeds of policy, order of, **2**.25
events triggering transfer to third party of
insured's rights, **2**.19
excess, application of, **2**.25
Fairchild enclave, and, **13**.14
foreign company, **2**.19
information from insurer, third parties'
entitlement to, **2**.23
insurers' defences, preservation of, **2**.25
liability insurance, types to which 1930 Act
applies, **2**.21
limitation periods, **2**.27
limit of indemnity, application of, **2**.25
nature of rights transferred, **2**.20, **2**.25
'pay first' clauses, and, **2**.25
premium, liability for, **2**.25
procedure, **2**.24
statutory transfer to third party of insured's
rights
generally, **2**.24
impact on third party's rights against insured,
2.26
timing of proceedings by third party against
insurer, **2**.24
timing of transfer of insured's rights, **2**.24
**Third Parties (Rights Against Insurers) Act
2010**, **2**.28–**2**.39
anti-avoidance provisions, **2**.32
arbitration agreement, and, **2**.30
dissolved company, claim against, **2**.28, **2**.29
events triggering transfer to third party of
insured's rights, **2**.29
generally, **2**.28
information, third party's entitlement to, **2**.33
insurers' defences, preservation of, **2**.34
jurisdiction, **2**.39
liability insurance, types to which 2010 Act
applies, **2**.31
limitation periods, **2**.38
'pay first' clauses, and, **2**.34
procedure, **2**.30
'relevant persons', **2**.29
retention of rights
insured against insurer, **2**.26
third party against insured, **2**.35
right of action against insurer, third party's **2**.30
right of set-off against third party, insurer's **2**.37
territorial scope, **2**.39
transitional provisions, **2**.28
Timing of notification
'as soon as reasonably possible', **7**.1
'as soon as possible', **7**.15
'immediately', **7**.14

Timing of notification – *contd*
  impossibility, and, **7**.17
  no express provision, where, **7**.19
  specific periods, **7**.17
Trade union
  claim on behalf of member, property
    insurance, and **2**.10
  insurable interest, **2**.10
Trustee and beneficiary
  insurable interest, and, **2**.8
Typeface of document
  construction of contract, and, **3**.25

Uberrimae fidei
  see GOOD FAITH, DUTY OF
Under-insurance
  liability insurance, and, **6**.10
  measurement of loss, and, **6**.10
Unfair terms in consumer contracts
  arbitration, and, **3**.20, **10**.14
  construction of contract, and
    construction in favour of consumer
      principle of, **3**.20,
      contra proferentem construction,
        compared, **3**.19
    generally, **3**.20
  consumer, meaning, **3**.20
  finding that term unfair, effect of, **3**.20
  liability insurance, and, **6**.10
  notification of claims, and
    prejudice to insurer, and, **7**.5
    terms not seen by insured until after loss,
      7.19
  plain, intelligible language, **3**.20
  scope of Consumer Rights Act 2015, Part 2,
    3.20
  standard terms, and, **3**.20
  unfairness
    meaning, **3**.20
  remedy, **3**.20
Unifying event or factor
  aggregation, **6**.9
Unilateral mistake
  rectification, and, **3**.33
Union
  see TRADE UNION
Unvalued policies
  see MEASUREMENT OF LOSS
Usage of words
  construction of contract, and, **3**.23
Use of disclosed documents, **9**.24
Utmost good faith, duty of
  see GOOD FAITH, DUTY OF

Valued policies
  see MEASUREMENT OF LOSS
Variations to risk
  duty of utmost good faith,
    and, **11**.4

Vendor and purchaser
  insurable interest, **2**.8, **2**.15
Vicarious liability
  insurance brokers, and, **16**.8
Voluntary payments
  contribution, and, **13**.5, **13**.9
  subrogation, and, **12**.13

Waiver
  breach of duty by insurance brokers,
    and, **16**.27
  breach of warranty, **11**.63
  construction of contract, and, **3**.16
  delay, and, **11**.63
  effect, **11**.63
  estoppel, and, **11**.63
  failure to reserve rights, and, **7**.22, **11**.63
  insurance brokers' defences, and, **16**.27
  insurer legally represented, where, **11**.63
  knowledge of insurer, **11**.63
  legal professional privilege, and, **9**.33
  notification of claims, and, **7**.22
  privilege, and, **9**.33
  procedural condition, breach of, **8**.4
  proposal form, and, **11**.15
  reliance, **11**.63
  right to avoid, of, **11**.63
  subrogation, and, **12**.4–**12**.5
  timing of, **11**.63
  unequivocal representation, **11**.63
  waiver by election, **11**.63
  waiver by estoppel, **11**.63
Warranties
  'basis clause', and, **3**.7, **11**.16
  breach
    avoidance contrasted, **3**.7
    consequences, **3**.7–**3**.8
    contracting out, Insurance Act 2015,
      and, **3**.8
    Insurance Conduct of Business Sourcebook
      (ICOBS), and, **3**.7
    waiver, **11**.63
  Consumer Insurance (Disclosure and
    Representations) Act 2012, and, **3**.7
  construction, and, **3**.4, **3**.7
  delimiting, **3**.7
  de minimis approach to compliance, **3**.7
  generally, **3**.4, **3**.7
  proposal forms, and, **11**.16
  terminology in insurance law, **3**.4
  'warranted', alternative meaning of, **3**.6
'Without prejudice' communications
  basis of rule, **9**.35
  communications not marked 'without
    prejudice', **9**.35
  costs, and, **9**.36, **9**.38
  disclosure, and, **9**.35
  communications to which principle applies,
    8.4, **9**.35

'Without prejudice' communications – *contd*
  examination of communications by
    court, **9**.35, **9**.36
  exceptions to rule
    delay or acquiescence, to explain, **9**.38
    estoppel, **9**.38
    fraud, application to set aside compromise
      for, **9**.38
    issue as to whether compromise reached,
      where, **9**.38
    misrepresentation, application to set aside
      compromise for, **9**.38
    perjury, blackmail or other unambiguous
      impropriety, **9**.38
    solicitors' negligence, action for, **9**.38
    undue influence, application to set aside
      compromise for, **9**.38
    want of prosecution, use on application to
      strike out for, **9**.38
  express agreement, and, **9**.36
  general rule, **9**.35
  implied agreement, and, **9**.35, **9**.36
  initial offer letter protected, **9**.35
  loss of protection
    interim application, reference on, **9**.38
    trial, reference at, **9**.38
  other parties to same litigation, **9**.37
  public policy, and, **9**.35, **9**.36
  subsequent litigation, and, **9**.37
Witness statements
  evidence for trial, and, **9**.39
Witnesses of fact
  evidence for trial, and, **9**.39
Words and phrases
  'accident', 'accidental', **5**.2, **6**.9, **17**.2
  'all risks' policy, **5**.2, **6**.10
  'any occupation', **17**.3, **17**.11
  'arising from', **4**.4, **6**.9
  'arising out of', **4**.4, **6**.9
  'as soon as possible', **7**.15
  'as soon as reasonably possible', **7**.1
  'assurance', **1**.4
  causa causans, **4**.2
  causa proxima non remota spectatur, **4**.9
  causa sine qua non, **4**.9
  'cause', **6**.9
  'caused by', **4**.4
  'circumstances', **7**.9
  'claim', **7**.8
  'claims made' policy, **7**.8
  'clause', **3**.4
  'condition', **3**.4
  'condition precedent', **3**.5, **7**.4
  contra proferentem, contra proferentes, **3**.18,
    3.19
  'damage', **17**.6
  'directly' caused loss, **4**.5
  dominus litis, **7**.1

Words and phrases – *contd*
  'each and every claim', **6**.9
  eiusdem generis, **3**.21
  'employee', **17**.23
  'event', **6**.9
  'exclusive' cause of loss, **4**.6
  'ex gratia settlements', **14**.2
  ex turpi causa non oritur action, **5**.2
  'follow the settlements', **14**.2, **14**.4
  forum non conveniens, **15**.13
  'knowledge', **7**.8
  'immediately', **7**.14
  'in any way involving', **4**.4
  in connection with, **6**.9
  'in respect of', **4**.7, **17**.17, **17**.25
  'independent' cause of loss, **4**.6
  'indirectly' caused loss, **4**.5
  'insurance', **1**.4
  'intended function', **17**.18
  lis pendens, **15**.11
  'losses', **6**.9
  'new for old', **6**.7
  noscitur a sociis, **3**.21
  'notice', **7**.13
  'notification', **7**.13
  novus actus interveniens, **4**.9
  novus casus interveniens, **4**.9
  'occurrence', **6**.9, **7**.8, **7**.9
  'on account of', **4**.8, **17**.17
  'original cause', **6**.9
  'originating cause', **6**.9
  'originating in', **4**.4
  'outward, violent and visible
    means', **17**.2
  'own occupation', **17**.3, **17**.11
  'pay as may be paid thereon', **14**.2
  'permanent total disablement', **17**.3
  'product', **17**.15
  'proof satisfactory to' insurer, **5**.4
  'reasonable precautions', **3**.18, **4**.11, **5**.2
  'reasonable time', **3**.5
  'related', **6**.9
  'resulting from', **4**.4
  'series', **6**.9
  'signing down', **1**.9
  'similar', **6**.9
  'sole' cause of loss, **4**.6
  'temporary total disablement', **17**.3
  'traceable to', **4**.4
  uberrimae fidei', contracts of, **11**.4
  'unconditionally binding', **14**.2
  'warranted', **3**.6
  'warranty', **3**.4, **3**.6, **11**.3
  'wilful', **5**.2, **12**.4
  'without prejudice', **9**.35
  'without prejudice save as to
    costs', **9**.36
  'without prejudice settlements', **14**.2